W9-DEZ-920

THE BROADVIEW ANTHOLOGY OF EXPOSITORY PROSE

A Note to Students

Included in the price of each new copy of *The Broadview Anthology of Expository Prose 3/e* is access to a companion website that features additional readings, discussion questions, and interactive writing exercises.

A set of notes that go beyond the footnotes in the bound book is also provided on the anthology's companion website. These notes are designed to be of particular help to students who have limited familiarity with American culture, and/or students who have learned English as an additional language—though the extra notes may offer support to any student. Words and phrases for which additional notes are provided on the website are marked with a small asterisk in these pages. The notes themselves may either be consulted online or be printed out and kept handy as you read.

A passcode to the companion site is provided with each new copy purchased; those who have purchased a used copy may obtain access through the Broadview website for a modest fee.

THE BROADVIEW ANTHOLOGY OF EXPOSITORY PROSE

Third Edition

Editors
Laura Buzzard
Don LePan
Nora Ruddock
Alexandria Stuart

broadview press

BROADVIEW PRESS – www.broadviewpress.com
Peterborough, Ontario, Canada

Founded in 1985, Broadview Press remains a wholly independent publishing house. Broadview's focus is on academic publishing; our titles are accessible to university and college students as well as scholars and general readers. With over 600 titles in print, Broadview has become a leading international publisher in the humanities, with world-wide distribution. Broadview is committed to environmentally responsible publishing and fair business practices.

© 2016 Broadview Press

All rights reserved. No part of this book may be reproduced, kept in an information storage and retrieval system, or transmitted in any form or by any means, electronic or mechanical, including photocopying, recording, or otherwise, except as expressly permitted by the applicable copyright laws or through written permission from the publisher.

Library and Archives Canada Cataloguing in Publication

The Broadview anthology of expository prose / editors, Laura Buzzard, Don LePan, Nora Ruddock, Alexandria Stuart. – Third edition.

ISBN 978-1-55481-333-9 (paperback)

1. Essays. 2. Exposition (Rhetoric). 3. College readers. I. LePan, Don, 1954-, editor II. Buzzard, Laura, editor III. Ruddock, Nora, editor IV. Stuart, Alexandria, editor

PN6142.B76 2016   808.84   C2016-905113-7

Broadview Press handles its own distribution in North America
PO Box 1243, Peterborough, Ontario K9J 7H5, Canada
555 Riverwalk Parkway, Tonawanda, NY 14150, USA
Tel: (705) 743-8990; Fax: (705) 743-8353
email: customerservice@broadviewpress.com

Distribution is handled by Eurospan Group in the UK, Europe, Central Asia, Middle East, Africa, India, Southeast Asia, Central America, South America, and the Caribbean. Distribution is handled by Footprint Books in Australia and New Zealand.

Broadview Press acknowledges the financial support of the Government of Canada through the Canada Book Fund for our publishing activities.

Canada

Editorial Assistants: Laura-Lee Bowers, Emily Farrell, John Geddert, and Helena Snopek.
Design and typeset by Eileen Eckert.
Cover design by Lisa Brawn.

PRINTED IN CANADA

PREFACE

The first edition of this anthology had its origin in the space between books. For many years, the Broadview list had included two very different anthologies, both intended for use in first-year composition and literature courses. One was an anthology that brought together virtually every sort of non-fiction prose *except* scholarly writing; the other brought together an excellent selection of *purely* scholarly writing. Another attractive approach, it seemed to us, would be an anthology that combined a wide range of literary and non-academic essays with a good selection of scholarly writing.

Central to the idea of this anthology, then, was the inclusion of a substantial selection of academic writing. Very frequently, anthologies which make a stab at including academic writing end up selecting journalistic pieces that are written by academics, rather than truly scholarly writing. Granted, it is not east to find examples of purely academic discourse that are at all accessible to a first- or second-year student who is unlikely to be familiar with the conventions of academic disciplines. But it is not impossible. One guideline we have followed in searching out such selections has been to look for academic pieces which have exerted considerable influence beyond their discipline. Selections such as those by Milgram on obedience and conformity, or Card and Krueger on the effect of raising the minimum wage are examples of research that has been widely discussed and widely influential outside academia. Also included here are numerous pieces which, while they might not have reached the general public in any form, have been widely influential in their discipline.

A second central principle of the book is variety. At the heart of the anthology are a wide range of essays that attempt in one way or another to persuade the reader of something. But a variety of other modes of prose writing are also included. The reader will find personal essays, occasional pieces, speeches, letters, and humorous sketches. For the new edition a number of op-ed pieces have been added, as have been examples of blog posts, articles from online media, academic working papers published online, book reviews, and obituaries. Also new for this edition are several pieces written in a lyric mode. Selections range from more than twenty pages in length to less than a single page; for this edition the number of short essays has been substantially increased.

There is variety in level of difficulty, in type of audience, and in subject matter as well. In some selections the writing is almost transparent in its simplicity; in others the reader may be challenged by complex syntax as well as by the inherent difficulty of the material. In many cases the intended audience is clearly the general reader, but some selections aim at a much narrower readership. And the anthology includes writing on an extraordinarily wide range of topics. In any anthology, of course, certain themes receive more emphasis than others. For this edition, in response to requests from a great many instructors, we have placed special emphasis on issues of race, class, and culture in twenty-first century America.

Most of the selections are of course written in English, but we have also included a handful of pieces that were first written in other languages, either because (as in the case of Montaigne) they have been extraordinarily influential in shaping the history of the essay, or because of the central position of their authors in shaping intellectual discourse (as in the cases of Barthes, Foucault, and Ai Weiwei).

One feature of previous editions that has been particularly well received has been the inclusion of paired articles; this edition includes an increased number of these. In some cases the pairings are of pieces that take opposing points of view on the same topic. In others, they are of similar material treated for different anticipated audiences, such as a scholarly paper and a newspaper op-ed piece presenting the same research in simplified form for lay readers. Finally, a number of the pairings involve essays that are in conversation with each other. Maggie Nelson's writing on the art of cruelty may be read as in conversation with the earlier writings of Susan Sontag—and Sontag's may in turn be read as in conversation with the writing of Virginia Woolf in *Three Guineas*. New to the third edition are essays from a wide range of the most celebrated essayists of the modern era—from James Baldwin, Joan Didion, and Annie Dillard to Eula Biss, Claudia Rankine, and Ta-Nehisi Coates. Many of these authors are represented by more than a single selection; the number of authors represented by two or more selections has increased very substantially this time around.

With all these additions, the anthology has inevitably become larger. To some extent we have been able to balance the addition of many new selections by excisions. Many selections that instructors told us they were teaching only rarely, if at all, are gone from this edition. (Where copyright permissions costs have not been prohibitive, selections previously included in the bound book anthology may be found on the anthology's companion website.)

Among the pieces cut for this edition are a considerable number of essays by Canadian writers. For previous editions we have struggled to assemble a table of contents that could work well both at American and at Canadian universities and colleges. For this edition, in contrast, we have decided to publish two separate volumes; in these pages you will find material intended to meet the needs of American courses. (A third Canadian edition is scheduled for publication in 2017.)

Much as the focus for this edition is on selections of interest to Americans, we have endeavored to provide as well a rich sense of cultural and geographical diversity through the selections. We have also provided what seems to us to be an appropriate balance so far as gender is concerned. What constitutes "appropriate balance" in this respect in 2016? To our minds for an anthology of this sort, it is at least a rough fifty-fifty balance. So far as the number of authors is concerned, men slightly outnumber women in these pages. But so far as the number of selections is concerned, women slightly outweigh men.

One issue in assembling almost any anthology is whether or not to excerpt. If the book is to be essentially an anthology of essays, does the integrity of the form demand that all essays selected for inclusion be included in their entirety? Should selections taken from full-length books be excluded on the rounds of their provenance? To both these questions we have answered in the negative. If an anthology such as this is to do the best possible job of presenting the widest possible range within a manageable compass, practical and pedagogical concerns seem to us to justify the occasional decision to excerpt a very long essay, or to select a discreet section from a full-length book. We have, however, included a considerable number of longer essays in their entirety.

Most essay anthologies designed for university use are arranged either by broad subject category ("nature," "science," and so on) or by rhetorical category ("descriptive essays," "persuasive essays," etc.). On the good advice of the majority of academics we consulted on this matter prior to the publication of the first edition, we decided instead to use a loosely chronological arrangement, in the interests both of simplicity and flexibility. In an anthology where the grouping is by subject or by rhetorical category, each essay must of necessity appear as part of only one grouping—whereas in reality, of course, many of the finest and most interesting essays will have two or more subjects, many of the best persuasive essays also employ description or narration, and so on. The chronological approach allows the instructor to group the essays in whatever combinations seem most interesting or appropriate, and to change those groupings as desired each time a course is taught. (Tables of contents by subject category and rhetorical category—in both of which a given essay is quite likely to appear at least two or three times—appear following this preface.) A chronological organization is flexible in another respect too; it lends itself to use in courses on the history of the essay or on nonfiction prose as a genre as well as in courses on composition and rhetoric.

For the third edition there has been a slight change in organization of material; the selections are now arranged by date of first publication rather than in a chronological order based on the birth date of each author (as had been the case in previous editions).

There have been several changes to the book's apparatus for the new edition. At the request of many instructors who have been using the anthology, we have not included questions within the bound book. (Questions for discussion are now to be found on the anthology's companion websites for students and instructors.) The headnotes for each selection, on the other hand, have been substantially expanded with a view to providing contextual background for the student. As before, biographical notes appear at the back of the anthology, and explanatory notes are provided at the bottom of the page. For this edition we have also provided a set of additional notes on the anthology's companion website—notes designed to be of particular help to EAL students and/or students who have little familiarity with American culture. Phrases such as "Founding Fathers" or "in drag" or "Middle America" or "tar and feather" require no glossing for the student who has just graduated from a high school in Chicago or Los Angeles, but may seem obscure or confusing to a student who has recently arrived in America for the first time. And of course some students will always arrive at university with a larger vocabulary than others. These notes, then, offer additional support to any student who may wish to consult them. Words and phrases for which additional notes are provided are marked with a small asterisk in these pages. Students wishing to consult the notes may find them on the anthology's companion website; these additional notes may be read online or printed out and kept handy as the student reads the relevant selections.

One further change for the new edition is the inclusion of a color insert of illustrations relevant to one or more of the pieces in the anthology.

We should say something, finally, about the book's title. There may be no satisfactory solution to naming a book of this sort. "Anthology of Prose" is obviously inappropriate, since prose fiction is excluded. "Anthology of Essays" becomes unsuitable once the decision has been made to include selections from longer works as well. "Anthology of Non-Fiction Prose" is clunky and would argue for the inclusion of a much wider variety of forms of non-fiction prose than are presented here (among them business memos, advertising copy, and car maintenance manuals); conversely, it would argue for the exclusion of pieces such as the "essays" in this collection by David Sedaris and Sherman Alexie, both of which hover on the border of fiction and non-fiction.

In the end we settled on "Anthology of Expository Prose." That too is a title that if taken narrowly might argue for the exclusion of certain of the selections in the anthology. Defined according to traditional rhetorical categories, expository writing is an umbrella category of writing that involves explanation. It has traditionally been taken to include writing engaged in comparison or contrast, definition, analysis, and persuasion or argument—but not to include purely descriptive or narrative forms of non-fiction prose. More broadly, though, "expository prose" has come to be frequently used nowadays as a short form for "non-fiction prose that aims to set something forth for a public reader-ship." There are good grounds on which to base this more inclusive meaning; "exposition" may refer simply to "setting forth," and that is certainly what descriptive and even some narrative prose may fairly be said to do, quite as much as prose that attempts to argue or persuade sets something forth. (Though much argument attempts to explain, often the line between explanation and assertion is exceedingly thin—a good deal thinner in many cases than the line separating, say, description from explanation.) In any case, writing that falls within the traditional criteria of expository prose constitutes the overwhelming majority of the prose that appears of these pages; we beg the indulgence of the purist who would have it approach more nearly to one hundred percent.

• • •

As with the second edition, Broadview Senior Editor Laura Buzzard has been instrumental in putting together this volume. She and I have been ably assisted by Developmental Editor Nora Ruddock and Editorial Assistant Alexandria Stuart. Assistant English Editor Tara Bodie did great work canvassing academ-ics who had used the second edition to ask their advice, and we also received editorial assistance from several people on a freelance basis—notable among them Emily Farrell, Helena Snopek, John Geddert, and Laura-Lee Bowers. As he has done for so many Broadview publications, Joe Davies did excellent work proofreading. Eileen Eckert is once again to be thanked for her superb work in book design and typesetting. Rights and Permissions Manager Merilee Atos, this time with the assistance of Brad DeVetten, did an excellent job of clearing copyright permissions on a very tight schedule, and artist and cover designer Lisa Brawn has given a much brighter look to the book's cover.

The first edition of the anthology is now far in the past, but the contribu-tions of those who helped to produce that volume deserve to be acknowledged; particularly helpful was the work of then-Broadview staff members Julia Gaunce, Mical Moser, Tammy Roberts, and Craig Lawson.

• • •

Special thanks this time around go to Dara Rossman Regaignon, the Director of New York University's Expository Writing program, and to her many col-leagues at NYU who have used the second edition with their students and who have made a large number of excellent suggestions for the new edition.

We would like to thank the following academics for the advice they have provided to us along the way: at California State University, East Bay, Alison

Wariner; at Framingham State University, Emma Katherine Atwood; at George Washington University, Susan Willens; at The New School, Fiore Sireci; at New York University, Lane Anderson, Victoria Anderson, Taylor Black, Bruce Bromley, Katherine Carlson, Courtney Chatellier, Lorraine Doran, Alexandra Falek, Elisabeth Fay, Andrei Guruianu, Jonathan Hamrick, Michele Hanks, Robert Huddleston, Abigail Joseph, Amanda Kotch, Alexander Landfair, David Markus, Denice Martone, Gerard O'Donoghue, Victoria Olsen, Amira Pierce, Benjamin Pollak, Rebecca Porte, Jackie Reitzes, Raymond Ricketts, Christopher Stahl, Benjamin Stewart, Emily Stone, Kirin Wachter-Grene, Justin Warner, Michelle Wilson, and Jenny Xie; at San Francisco State University, Michael John Martin; at the University of Michigan, Randall Tessier; and at West Virginia University, Beth Staley.

· · ·

We welcome the comments and suggestions of all readers—instructors or students—about any and all aspects of this book, from the selections themselves to the book's organization and ancillary material (both within these pages and on the companion website). Please feel free to email us at broadview@ broadviewpress.com. We hope you will enjoy this book as it stands—but we never stop thinking of possible improvements for future editions.

Don LePan

CONTENTS

Barthes. Sontag 门罗. 福柯

xiv | Contents

CONTENTS BY SUBJECT

Childhood and Education / Colonization, Postcolonialism, and Global Politics / Culture(s) and Race(s) / Death and Life / The Earth, Humans, and Other Animals / Gender / History, and Other Ways of Looking at the Past / The Human Psyche / Issues of Ethics and Conscience / Language, Communication, and Translation / The Law and the State / LGBT / Literature, Photography, and Other Arts / Love and Sex / Mental and Physical Health / Personal Experience / Philosophical Perspectives / Race in the United States / Religion / Science, Technology, and Change / Social Class and Economic Inequality / Sport / Violence, War, and Peace / Work and Business

Note: Many selections deal with two or more of these subjects.

Childhood and Education

Colonization, Postcolonialism, and Global Politics

Culture(s) and Race(s)

Death and Life

The Earth, Humans, and Other Animals

Gender

History, and Other Ways of Looking at the Past

The Human Psyche

Issues of Ethics and Conscience

Language, Communication, and Translation

The Law and the State

LGBT

Literature, Photography, and Other Arts

Love and Sex

Mental and Physical Health

Personal Experience

Philosophical Perspectives

Race in the United States

Religion

Science, Technology, and Change

Social Class and Economic Inequality

Sport

Violence, War, and Peace

Work and Business

Contents by Rhetorical Category and Medium

Academic Writing / Analysis / Cause and Effect / Classification / Comparison and Contrast / Definition / Description / Humor and Satire / Journalism / Lyric and Other Creative Forms / Narration / Online Media / Persuasion and Argument / Speeches and Lectures

Note: Many selections occupy two or more of these categories.

Academic Writing

Analysis

Cause and Effect

Classification

Comparison and Contrast

Definition

Description

Humor and Satire

Journalism

Lyric and Other Creative Forms

Narration

Online Media

Persuasion and Argument

Speeches and Lectures

LUCIUS ANNAEUS SENECA

EPISTLE 47 [ON SLAVERY]¹

*It is often suggested that the modern essay may be found in embryonic
form in the works of some classical writers—not least of all in a
work now almost two thousand years old, the Moral Epistles of the
Roman statesman and Stoic philosopher Lucius Annaeus Seneca
(usually known simply as Seneca). Though the 124 pieces that make
up the Moral Epistles are written as letters to Lucilius, the then-
governor of Sicily—each one begins "Seneca greets his Lucilius"—
in every other respect the epistles far more closely resemble what
we now call essays than they do modern-day personal letters.*

*Slavery in Rome was structured somewhat less severely than
the chattel slavery that became widespread in the seventeenth and
eighteenth centuries (a Roman slave freed by his master could
achieve something approaching full citizenship, including the right
to vote); as Seneca's descriptions make clear, however, Roman
slaves' daily lives were extremely harsh.*

I was pleased to learn from those who come from you that you live on familiar terms with your slaves. That is appropriate for a man of your intelligence
and education. "They are slaves," people say. No—they are people. "They are
slaves." No—they are attendant comrades. "But slaves is what they are." No—
they are unassuming friends. "They are slaves." No—they are *fellow*-slaves, if
you recognize that Fortune* values both me and them quite equally.

And so I laugh at those who think it is demeaning to dine with one of
their own slaves. Why would they think this, unless the reason is that our
proudest customs require the master at his dinner to have a crowd of slaves
standing around him? He eats more than he can hold and, in his enormous
greed, stuffs his swollen belly, which now no longer functions as a stomach. So
with a greater effort than it took to gorge himself he vomits up the entire meal.

---

1   *EPISTLE 47 [ON SLAVERY]*   Epistle 47 from *Moral Letters to Lucilius* is sometimes
referred to as "On Slavery." This translation has been prepared for Broadview Press by Ian
Johnston, Vancouver Island University.

Meanwhile, the unhappy slaves are not permitted to move their lips, not even to speak. The rod suppresses every murmur. Even a random noise—a cough, a sneeze, a hiccup—earns them the whip. The punishment for any word that interrupts the silence is extremely harsh. All night long, the slaves stand there, mute and hungry.

As a result, those who are not permitted to speak in the presence of their master, talk about him. However, when slaves whose mouths were not stitched shut used to talk not only in the presence of their masters but also with them, they were prepared to stretch their necks out for their master's sake, to let any imminent threat to him fall on their heads. They would talk during the feast, but during torture they were silent. Later, thanks to this arrogance of masters the proverb spread, "To have as many enemies as one has slaves." When we acquire slaves, they are not enemies, but we make them our foes.

At the moment I will overlook other cruel and inhuman ways we treat our slaves, for we abuse them as if they were not even human beings, but beasts of burden. While we recline at ease to dine, one slave wipes up the vomit, another, crouching underneath the table, collects the leavings of the drunken guests. Another carves the expensive birds. With a practiced hand his sure strokes cut around the breast and rump, and he serves the portions, unhappy man who lives for this one task of carving plump fowl skillfully—unless the person who for pleasure's sake instructs this skill is even more unhappy than the one who learns it from necessity. Still another slave, who serves the wine and wears a woman's fancy clothes, struggles against his age, for he cannot escape being dragged back to his boyish years. By now he has a soldier's look, but his hair is scraped away or plucked out by the root to keep him beardless, and he must stay awake all night, dividing his time between his master's drunkenness and lust: in the bedroom he is a man, and at the feast a boy. Another one, whose job is to evaluate the guests, keeps standing there in misery to watch for those whose fawning flattery and intemperance in what they eat or what they say will invite them back tomorrow. Think of the ones who must prepare the feast, those with subtle expertise about their master's palate, who know the things whose taste excites it, whose appearance pleases him, whose novelty can rouse him from his nausea, as well as which foods will now disgust him if he gets too much and which will stimulate his appetite that day. With these slaves the master does not deign to eat. He believes that coming to the same table with his own slave diminishes his majesty. God forbid!

5   How many masters is he acquiring with slaves like these! I have observed Callistus'[2] master—the one who stuck a bill of sale on him and took him to the

---

2   *Callistus*   Gaius Julius Callistus (first century CE), a freed Roman slave who rose to political prominence.

market with the useless slaves—standing before Callistus' door and kept outside while others entered. Callistus was included in the first job lot of slaves on which the auctioneer warms up his voice, and now the slave has paid his master back by rejecting him, in turn, and judging him unworthy to come in his house. The master sold Callistus, but how much has Callistus made his master pay!

You would do well to recognize that the man you call your slave sprang from the same seeds as you, enjoys the same sky, breathes, lives, and dies just as you do! You can look on him as a free born man, as much as he can see you as a slave. In that disaster caused by Marius,[3] many men of very splendid birth, preparing for a senatorial rank by military service, were sunk by Fortune, who made one of them a shepherd and another the custodian of a cottage. Now condemn the man whose change in fortune you may share while you condemn him.

I have no wish to involve myself in a huge issue and to explore the way we treat our slaves, towards whom we are excessively proud, cruel, and abusive. But the main thrust of my advice is this: live with your inferiors just as you would wish your superior to live with you. Whenever it crosses your mind how much you can do quite lawfully to a slave of yours, think about how much your master can legally inflict on you.

"But I," you may well say, "don't have a master." You are still young. Perhaps you will have one. Do you not know how old Hecuba was when she became a slave—or Croesus, or Darius' mother, or Plato, or Diogenes?[4]

Live with your slave calmly, even as a friend. Let him enter your conversations, your deliberations, and your social intercourse. At this point the whole crowd of those spoiled with luxury will complain to me: "Nothing would be more degrading than this, nothing more repulsive." These are the same people I will discover kissing the hand of other people's slaves.

Surely you recognize the fact that our ancestors removed everything invidious from the masters and everything insulting from the slaves? They called the master *father of the family*, and the slaves *members of the household*, a practice which still continues in the mimes. They set up a festival day when masters ate with their slaves, but that was not the only time this happened. They assigned

10

---

3   *Marius* Gaius Marius (157–86 BCE) was a Roman general and politician. Near the end of his life his political authority brought about a brief period of murderous attacks against many prominent Romans.

4   *Hecuba* Wife of Priam, king of Troy. She became a slave after the city fell;   *Croesus* Fabulously rich and powerful king of Lydia in the sixth century BCE. He was defeated and enslaved by the Persians;   *Darius* Persian emperor (fourth century BCE) conquered by Alexander the Great;   *Plato, or Diogenes* The Greek philosophers Plato (c. 427–c. 347 BCE) and Diogenes (fourth century BCE) also were captured and briefly enslaved.

slaves honors in the house, permitted them to render judgment, and considered the house a miniature commonwealth.*

"What then? Shall I bring all my slaves to my own table?" No. No more than you would bring all free men there. You are wrong if you think I would bar certain men who do more menial work—like, say, that herdsman or that slave who tends the mules. I will not judge them by the work they do, but by their characters. Each person gives himself his character; chance gives him his work. Let some slaves dine with you because they are worthy men, and dine with some to make them worthy. For if debased associations have made them servile, then the society of distinguished men will shake that off.

My dear Lucilius, you should not look for a friend only in the forum or the senate house.* If you pay attention carefully, you will find one at home. Often without a skilled artist, good material is wasted. Try and you will find that out. Just as someone who is going to purchase a horse is a fool if he inspects the saddle and the bridle but not the animal itself, so that person is extremely stupid who evaluates a man either by his clothes or by his social condition (which, like our robes, is merely a cover).

"He is a slave." But perhaps his spirit is free. "He is slave." Will that make him culpable? Show me who is not a slave. One man is a slave to lust, another to avarice, another to ambition, and all are slaves to fear. I will show you an ex-consul* enslaved to a little old woman, a rich man enslaved to young serving maid. I will point out young men of the highest rank who are slaves of pantomimes! No slavery is more repulsive than voluntary servitude.

And so those fastidious types should not prevent you from acting affably with your slaves rather than proudly superior. To you your slaves should show respect rather than fear.

15   Someone may say that now I am calling for slaves to have the cap of liberty and for masters to be cast down from their lofty heights when I say slaves should respect their master rather than fear him. "That is precisely what he is saying: slaves are to show respect, as if they were clients or polite visitors." A man who says such things forgets that what satisfies a god is not too little for a master. The man who is respected is also loved, but love and fear cannot be mixed together.

So, in my judgment, your actions are entirely correct, for you do not wish your slaves to fear you, and you punish them with words. We use a whip to reprimand dumb* beasts. Everything which offends us does not do us harm. But our fastidiousness drives us into savage rage, so that whatever does not answer our desires, brings out our anger. We wrap ourselves up in royal passions. For kings also forget their own power and the weaknesses of other men and so grow hot and boil with rage, as if they had received an injury, when the loftiness of their position keeps them completely safe from any danger. They are not unaware of this, but by complaining they seize an opportunity to harm someone. They say they have been injured in order to inflict an injury.

I do not wish to delay you any longer. For you do not need my exhortations. Among their other traits, good characters possess this quality: they make their own decisions and hold to them. Malice is fickle and changes frequently, not into something better but merely something different.

Farewell.

(c. 65 CE)

MICHEL DE MONTAIGNE

from ON CANNIBALS[1]

*Michel de Montaigne, frequently credited with creating the modern
essay, was the first to use the word "essai" (meaning "attempt"
in French) in its modern sense, applying the term to his efforts to
arrive through writing at a deeper understanding of himself and of
the world. The attempts were often repeated; Montaigne published
three different versions of the following piece on the inhabitants of
the "new world."*

*Though Montaigne does not name them, and we can expect his
second-hand account of them to be distorted, the group on which
he based his descriptions was in all probability the Tupinambás,
inhabitants of an island off the northeastern coast of Brazil. By
1580 (when the first version of Montaigne's essay appeared), their
society had already been described in several works—perhaps most
notably an account by the German explorer Hans Staden, who had
spent several years as a captive of the Tupinambás in the 1550s.*

... For a long time I had with me a man who had lived ten or twelve years in
that other world which was discovered in our century, in the place where Villegaignon[2] landed, which he called Antarctic France. This discovery of [such
an] enormous country seems [to merit] serious consideration. I do not know if
I can affirm that another such discovery will not occur in the future, given that
so many people more important than we have been wrong about this one. I fear
that our eyes are larger than our stomachs, that we have more curiosity than
comprehension. We embrace everything, yet catch nothing but wind....

Modern navigators have almost certainly already established that the new
world is not an island but a mainland, connected on one side with the East
Indies and on the other with the lands under the two poles. Or else, if it is

---

1   *On Cannibals* This translation, prepared for Broadview Press by Ian Johnston
of Vancouver Island University, is based upon the final (1595) version of the essay.
Montaigne's frequent quotations in Latin have also been translated into English.

2   *Villegaignon* In 1555 Nicolas Durand Villegaignon landed in the Bay of Rio de
Janeiro, Brazil, and set up a French colony on a nearby island.

divided off from them, what separates it a narrow strait, a distance that does not entitle it to be called an island....

The man I had [with me] was a plain, rough fellow, the sort likely to provide a true account. For intelligent people notice more and are much more curious, but they [also] provide their own gloss* on things and, to strengthen their own interpretation and make it persuasive, they cannot help changing their story a little. They never give you a pure picture of things, but bend and disguise them to fit the view they had of them. To lend credit to their judgment and attract you to it, they willingly add to the material, stretching it out and amplifying it. We need either a very honest man or one so simple that he lacks what it takes to build up inventive falsehoods and make them plausible, someone not wedded to anything. My man was like that, and, in addition, at various times he brought some sailors and merchants he had known on that voyage to see me. Thus, I am happy with [his] information, without enquiring into what the cosmographers* [may] say about it....

Now, to return to my subject, I find, from what I have been told about these people, that there is nothing barbarous and savage about them, except that everyone calls things which he does not practice himself barbaric. For, in fact, we have no test of truth and of reason other than examples and ideas of the opinions and habits in the country where we live. There we always have the perfect religion, the perfect political arrangements, the perfect and [most] accomplished ways of dealing with everything. Those [natives] are wild in the same way we call wild the fruits which nature has produced on her own in her normal manner; whereas, in fact, the ones we should really call wild are those we have altered artificially and whose ordinary behavior we have modified. The former contain vital and vigorous virtues and properties, genuinely beneficial and natural, [qualities] which we have bastardized in the latter, by adapting them to gratify our corrupt taste....

These nations therefore seem to me barbarous in the sense that they have received very little molding from the human mind and are still very close to their original naive condition. Natural laws* still govern them, hardly corrupted at all by our own. They live in such purity that I sometimes regret we did not learn about them earlier, at a time when there were men more capable of assessing them than we are. I am sad that Lycurgus[3] and Plato* did not know them. For it seems to me that what our experience enables us to see in those nations there surpasses not only all the pictures with which poetry has embellished the Golden Age,* as well as all its inventiveness in portraying a happy human condition, but also the conceptions and even the desires of philosophy.

5

---

3   *Lycurgus*   Political thinker who, according to legend, established the laws of Sparta in the eighth century BCE. It is not known whether he actually existed.

They have scarcely imagined such a pure and simple innocence as the one our experience reveals to us, and they would hardly have believed that our society could survive with so little artifice and social bonding among people. It is a nation, I would tell Plato, in which there is no form of commerce, no knowledge of letters, no science of numbers, no name for magistrate or political superior, no customs of servitude, no wealth or poverty, no contracts, no inheritance, no division [of property], no occupations, other than leisure ones, no respect for family kinship, except for common ties, no clothing, no agriculture, no metal, no use of wine or wheat. The very words which signify lying, treason, dissimulation, avarice, envy, slander, and forgiveness are unknown. How distant from this perfection would [Plato] find the republic he imagined—"men freshly come from the gods."[4]

These are the habits nature first ordained.[5]

As for the rest, they live in a very pleasant and temperate country, so that, according to what my witnesses have told me, it is rare to see a sick person there. They have assured me that in this land one does not notice any [of the inhabitants] doddering, with rheumy eyes, toothless, or bowed down with old age. They have settled along the sea [coast], closed off on the landward side by large, high mountains, with a stretch of territory about one hundred leagues wide in between. They have a great abundance of fish and meat, which has no resemblances to ours and which they simply cook and eat, without any other preparation. The first man who rode a horse there, although he had had dealings with them on several other voyages, so horrified them by his [riding] posture, that they killed him with arrows before they could recognize him....

They spend the entire day dancing. Younger men go off to hunt [wild] animals with bows. Meanwhile, some of the women keep busy warming the drinks, which is their main responsibility. In the morning, before they begin their meal, one of the old men preaches to everyone in the whole barn, walking from one end to the other and repeating the same sentence several times until he has completed his tour of the building, which is easily one hundred paces long. He recommends only two things to them: courage against their enemies and affection for their wives. And [these old men] never fail to mention this obligation, [adding] as a refrain that their wives are the ones who keep their drinks warm and seasoned for them.

In several places, including my own home, there are examples of their beds, their ropes, their swords, their wooden bracelets, which they use to cover their wrists in combat, and their large canes open at one end, with whose sound they keep time in their dances. They are close shaven all over, and remove the

---

4   *"men freshly ... the gods"*   From Seneca, *Letters* 90.
5   *These are ... first ordained*   From Virgil, *Georgics* 2.20.

hair much more cleanly than we do, using only wood or stone as a razor. They believe that the soul is immortal and that those who have deserved well of the gods are lodged in that part of the sky where the sun rises, [while] the damned [are] in regions to the west.

They have some sort of priests or prophets, who appear before the people relatively seldom, for they live in the mountains. When they arrive, there is a grand celebration and a solemn assembly of several villages (each barn, as I have described it, makes up a village, and the distance between them is approximately one French league[6]). This prophet speaks to them in public, urging them to be virtuous and to do their duty. But their entire ethical knowledge contains only the two following articles, courage in warfare and affection for their wives. He prophesies to them about things to come and about the results they should expect from their endeavors and encourages them to go to war or to refrain from it. But [he does this] on the condition, that he must prophesy correctly, and if what happens to them is different from what he has predicted, he is cut up into a thousand pieces, if they catch him, and condemned as a false prophet. For this reason, a prophet who has been wrong once is never seen again.

Divination is a gift of God. For that reason, abusing it should be punished as fraud. Among the Scythians,[7] when the divines failed with their [predictions], they were chained by their hands and feet, laid out on carts full of kindling and pulled by oxen, and burned there. Those who deal with matters in which the outcome depends on what human beings are capable of may be excused if they do their best. But surely the others, [those] who come to us with deluding assurances of an extraordinary faculty beyond our understanding, should be punished for not keeping their promises and for the recklessness of their deceit.

These [natives] have wars with the nations living on the other side of their mountains, further inland. They go out [against] them completely naked with no weapons except bows or wooden swords with a point at one end, like the tips of our hunting spears. What is astonishing is their resolution in combat, which never ends except in slaughter and bloodshed, for they have no idea of terror or flight. Each man brings back as a trophy the head of the enemy he has killed and attaches it to the entrance of his dwelling. After treating their prisoners well for a long time with every consideration they can possibly think of, the man who has a prisoner summons a grand meeting of his acquaintances. He ties a rope to one of the prisoner's arms and holds him there, gripping the other end, some paces away for fear of being injured, and he gives his dearest friend

10

6   *French league*   Unit of measurement equal to approximately 3 miles.
7   *Scythians*   Nomadic people who flourished in parts of Eastern Europe and Central Asia in the first millennium BCE.

the prisoner's other arm to hold in the same way. [Then] the two of them, in the presence of the entire assembly, stab the prisoner to death with their swords. After that, they roast him. [Then] they all eat him together and send portions to their absent friends. They do this not, as people think, to nourish themselves, the way the Scythians did in ancient times, but as an act manifesting extreme vengeance. We see evidence for this from the following: having noticed that the Portuguese, who were allied with their enemies, used a different method of killing them when they took them prisoner—which was to bury them up to the waist, shoot the rest of their body full of arrows, and then hang them—they thought that this people who had come there from another world (and who had already spread the knowledge of many vicious practices throughout the neighboring region and were much greater masters of all sorts of evil than they were) did not select this sort of vengeance for no reason and that therefore [this method] must be harsher than their own. And so they began to abandon their old practice and to follow this one.

I am not so much concerned that we call attention to the barbarous horror of this action as I am that, in judging their faults correctly, we should be so blind to our own. I believe that there is more barbarity in eating a man when he is alive than in eating him when he is dead, more in tearing apart by tortures and the rack a body still full of feeling, roasting it piece by piece, having it mauled and eaten by dogs and pigs (things I have not only read about but witnessed a short time ago, not among ancient enemies but among neighbors and fellow citizens, and, what is worse, under the pretext of piety and religion*) than there is in roasting and eating a man once he has died....

Thus, we can indeed call these [natives] barbarians, as far as the laws of reason are concerned, but not in comparison with ourselves, who surpass them in barbarity of every kind. Their warfare is entirely noble and generous, as excusable and beautiful as this human malady can possibly be. With them it is based only on one thing, a jealous rivalry in courage. They do not argue about conquering new lands, for they still enjoy that natural fecundity which furnishes them without toil and trouble everything necessary and in such abundance that they do not need to expand their borders. They are still at that fortunate stage where they do not desire anything more than their natural demands prescribe. Everything over and above that is for them superfluous.

15   Those among them of the same age generally call each other brothers, those who are younger they call children, and the old men are fathers to all the others. These leave the full possession of their goods undivided to their heirs in common, without [any] other title, except the completely simple one which nature gives to [all] her creatures by bringing them into the world.

If their neighbors cross the mountains to attack them and defeat them in battle, what the victors acquire is glory and the advantage of having proved themselves more courageous and valiant. For they have no further interest in the possessions of the conquered. They return to their [own] country, where they have no lack of anything they need, just as they do not lack that great benefit of knowing how to enjoy their condition in happiness and how to remain content with it. And [the natives we are talking about], when their turn comes, do the same. They demand no ransom of their prisoners, other than a confession and a recognition that they have been beaten. But in an entire century there has not been one [prisoner] who did not prefer to die [rather] than to yield, either by his expression or by his words, a single bit of the grandeur of [his] invincible courage. Not one of them has been observed who did not prefer to be killed and eaten than merely to ask that he be spared....

Truly we have here really savage men in comparison to us. For that is what they must be beyond all doubt—either that, or we must be, [for] there is an amazing distance between their ways and ours.

The men there have several wives, and the higher their reputation for valor the greater the number. In their marriages there is something remarkably beautiful: with our wives jealousy deprives us of the friendship and kindness of other women, [but with them] a very similar jealousy leads their wives to acquire these relationships [for their men]. Since they care more for the honor of their husbands than for anything else, they go to great lengths to seek out and obtain as many companions [for them] as they can, since that is a testimony to their husbands' merit.

Our wives will cry out that this is a miracle. It is not. It is a proper marital virtue, but of the highest order. In the Bible, Leah, Rachel, Sarah, and Jacob's wives gave their beautiful servants to their husbands.[8] ...

And so that people do not think that they do all this out of a simple and servile duty to habit and under pressure from the authority of their ancient customs, without reflection and judgment, because they have such stupid souls that they cannot choose any other way, I must cite some features of their capabilities. Apart from what I have just recited from one of their warrior songs, I have another, a love song which begins as follows: "Adder, stay, stay, adder, so that from the colored markings on your skin my sister may take down the style and workmanship for a rich belt which I can give the woman I love—and in this way your beauty and your patterning will be preferred forever above all other snakes." This first couplet is the refrain of the song. Now, I am sufficiently familiar with poetry to judge this one: not only is there nothing barbaric in the

20

---

8   *Leah, Rachel ... their husbands*   Cf. Genesis 30. Jacob had children with his wives Rachel and Leah, as well as with their slaves Bilhah and Zilpah. Sarah, Abraham's wife, was unable to conceive children, and offered her servant to Abraham as a surrogate.

imagination here, but it captures the spirit of Anacreon[9] throughout. Their language, too, is soft, with a pleasing sound, not unlike Greek in its word endings.

Three of these men, not knowing how much it will cost them one day in a loss of repose and happiness to learn about the corruptions among us and how interacting [with us] will lead to their ruin, which I assume is already well advanced (poor miserable creatures to let themselves be seduced by the desire for novelty and to have left the softness of their sky to come and see ours) were at Rouen when the late King Charles IX was there.[10] The king talked to them for a long time. They were shown our way of life, our splendor, and the layout of a beautiful city. After that, someone asked them their opinion, wishing to learn from them what they had found most astonishing. They answered that there were three things. I regret to say that I have forgotten the third, but I still remember two. They said, first of all, that they found it very strange that so many large, strong men with beards and weapons, who were around the king (they were probably talking about the Swiss soldiers in his guard) would agree to obey a child and that one of them was not chosen to command instead; and secondly (in their language they have a way of speaking of men as halves of one another) that they had noticed there were among us men completely gorged with all sorts of commodities while their other halves were beggars at their doors, emaciated by hunger and poverty. They found it strange that these needy halves could tolerate such an injustice and did not seize the others by the throat or set fire to their dwellings.

(1580, revised 1595)

9   *Anacreon*   Greek poet (c. 572–c. 488 BCE) known for his love lyrics.
10   *Three of ... was there*   About fifty native Brazilians were brought to Rouen in 1550, and some were presented to King Charles IX of France (then twelve years old) when he visited Rouen in 1562.

LADY MARY WORTLEY MONTAGU

from THE TURKISH EMBASSY LETTERS

In the late 1710s, Lady Mary Wortley Montagu's husband was made British Ambassador to the Ottoman Empire, and she journeyed with him to Turkey. The Turkish Embassy Letters *is a collection of letters written in the course of her travels and revised for a broader audience. Montagu shared the collection in manuscript form, but it was not published until shortly after her death.*

Montagu is considered the first English woman to publish an account of her travels in Turkey; such travel narratives by men were already very popular in England. Many of them presented Turkey as the wholly uncivilized opposite of England—a portrayal shaped much more strongly by works of fiction and by previous travel narratives than by first-hand experience. Of particular fascination to these English writers were Ottoman women, who concealed their faces when in public and lived in harems (separate quarters that only women were allowed to enter). Many travel writers took these practices as evidence that Ottoman women were utterly and cruelly oppressed; Montagu offers her own view in the excerpts below.

from LETTER 30

To the Countess of ⎯⎯⎯⎯[1]
Ariadnople,[2] April 1, O.S. 1717

… I never saw in my life, so many fine heads of hair. I have counted 110 of these tresses of one lady's, all natural, but it must be owned that every beauty is more common here than with us. 'Tis surprising to see a young woman that is not very handsome. They have naturally the most beautiful complexions in the world and generally large black eyes. I can assure you with great truth, that

---

1   *To the Countess of* ⎯⎯⎯⎯   This letter was sent to Frances Erskine, Lady Mar (1690–1761), Montagu's sister.

2   *Ariadnople*   Major Ottoman city, now Edirne, Turkey.

the Court of England (though I believe it the fairest in Christendom)* cannot show so many beauties as are under our protection here. They generally shape their eye-brows, and the Greeks and Turks have the custom of putting round their eyes on the inside a black tincture that, at a distance, or by candle-light, adds very much to the blackness of them. I fancy many of our ladies would be overjoyed to know this secret, but 'tis too visible by day. They dye their nails a rose-color; I own I cannot enough accustom myself to this fashion to find any beauty in it.

As to their morality or good conduct, I can say, like Harlequin,[3] that 'tis just as 'tis with you, and the Turkish ladies don't commit one sin the less for not being Christians. Now I am a little acquainted with their ways, I cannot forbear admiring either the exemplary discretion or extreme stupidity of all the writers that have given accounts of them. 'Tis very easy to see, they have more liberty than we have, no woman of what rank soever being permitted to go in the streets without two muslins, one that covers her face all but her eyes, and another that hides the whole dress of her head, and hangs half way down her back; and their shapes are also wholly concealed by a thing they call a *ferigée*, which no woman of any sort appears without. This has straight sleeves that reaches to their fingers' ends, and it laps all round them, not unlike a riding-hood. In winter 'tis of cloth, and in summer plain stuff or silk. You may guess how effectually this disguises them, that there is no distinguishing the great lady from her slave, and 'tis impossible for the most jealous husband to know his wife when he meets her, and no man dare either touch or follow a woman in the street.

This perpetual masquerade[4] gives them entire liberty of following their inclinations without danger of discovery. The most usual method of intrigue is to send an appointment to the lover to meet the lady at a Jew's shop, which are as notoriously convenient as our Indian houses,[5] and yet even those that don't make that use of them do not scruple to go to buy pennorths[6] and tumble over rich goods, which are chiefly to be found amongst that sort of people. The great ladies seldom let their gallants know who they are, and 'tis so difficult

---

3   *Harlequin*   Character in Aphra Behn's farce *The Emperor of the Moon* (1687) who pretends to be a visitor from the moon. When Harlequin describes the moon's morally dissolute customs, he is told they are just like those of Earth.

4   *masquerade*   Masquerade parties were popular in upper-class English society in the early eighteenth century.

5   *Jew's shop*   From the medieval period until the twentieth century, Jews were restricted in many countries, either by law or by custom, to a very limited number of professions, notably moneylending, tailoring, and certain types of retailing;   *Indian houses*   Stores selling goods from India and the Far East.

6   *pennorths*   Pennyworths, here meaning bargains.

to find it out that they can very seldom guess at her name, they have corresponded with above half a year together. You may easily imagine the number of faithful wives very small in a country where they have nothing to fear from their lovers' indiscretion, since we see so many that have the courage to expose themselves to that in this world, and all the threatened punishment of the next, which is never preached to the Turkish damsels. Neither have they much to apprehend from the resentment of their husbands, those ladies that are rich having all their money in their own hands, which they take with them upon a divorce, with an addition which he is obliged to give them.[7] Upon the whole, I look upon the Turkish women as the only free people in the Empire. The very Divan pays a respect to them, and the Grand Signor himself, when a *bassa*[8] is executed, never violates the privileges of the *haram* (or women's apartment), which remains unsearched entire to the widow. They are queens of their slaves, whom the husband has no permission so much as to look upon, except it be an old woman or two that his lady chooses. 'Tis true their law permits them four wives, but there is no instance of a man of quality that makes use of this liberty, or of a woman of rank that would suffer it. When a husband happens to be inconstant (as those things will happen) he keeps his mistress in a house apart, and visits her as privately as he can, just as 'tis with you. Amongst all the great men here, I only know the *Tefterdar* (i.e., treasurer) that keeps a number of she-slaves for his own use (that is, on his own side of the house, for a slave, once given to serve a lady, is entirely at her disposal) and he is spoke of as a libertine, or what we should call a rake,* and his wife won't see him, though she continues to live in his house. Thus you see, dear Sister, the manners of mankind do not differ so widely as our voyage writers would make us believe. Perhaps it would be more entertaining to add a few surprising customs of my own invention, but nothing seems to me so agreeable as truth, and I believe nothing so acceptable to you. I conclude with repeating the great truth of my being, dear Sister, etc....

---

7   *Neither have ... give them* In Turkey, a Muslim groom or his family were required to give his bride a *mahr*, money or goods that became her sole property. The laws of eighteenth-century England differed; a bride's dowry was given by her family to her husband, and all of her property became his.

8   *bassa* Pasha, a title given to military commanders and governors of provinces.

from LETTER 43[9]

To the Countess of _____

I am now preparing to leave Constantinople,[10] and perhaps you will accuse me of hypocrisy when I tell you 'tis with regret, but I am used to the air and have learnt the language. I am easy here, and as much as I love travelling, I tremble at the inconveniencies attending so great a journey with a numerous family and a little infant hanging at the breast. However, I endeavour upon this occasion to do as I have hitherto done in all the odd turns of my life; turn them, if I can, to my diversion. In order to this, I ramble every day wrapped up in my *ferace* and *yashmak*[11] about Constantinople and amuse myself with seeing all that is curious in it. I know you'll expect that this declaration should be followed with some account of what I have seen, but I am in no humour to copy what has been writ so often over. To what purpose should I tell you that Constantinople is the ancient Byzantium, that 'tis at present the conquest of a race of people supposed Scythians, that there is five or six thousand mosques in it, that Sancta Sophia was founded by Justinian,[12] etc.? I'll assure you 'tis not want of learning that I forbear writing all these bright things. I could also, with little trouble, turn over Knolles and Sir Paul Rycaut[13] to give you a list of Turkish Emperors, but I will not tell you what you may find in every author that has writ of this country. I am more inclined, out of a true female spirit of contradiction, to tell you the falsehood of a great part of what you find in authors. As for example the admirable Mr. Hill, who so gravely asserts that he saw in Sancta Sophia,

---

9   LETTER 43   This letter is undated, but was composed in 1718.

10   *Constantinople*   Istanbul, the capital of the Ottoman Empire until 1922.

11   *ferace*   Long coat that formed part of the expected attire for Turkish women in public;   *yashmak*   Veil covering the lower half of the face.

12   *Byzantium*   The site of present-day Istanbul was given the name of Byzantium and settled by Ancient Greek colonists in the mid-seventh century BCE;   *Scythians*   Scythians were a nomadic people who inhabited the regions north and northeast of the Black Sea in the first millennium BCE. Scythians were associated with barbarism, and Western writers often asserted (with little regard for historical evidence) that the people of Turkey were of Scythian descent;   *Sancta Sophia*   Hagia Sophia, built as a Christian basilica in 537 CE; during the eighteenth century, it was a mosque. Though "Hagia Sophia" means "Holy Wisdom" in Greek, the building is sometimes called "Sancta Sophia" (Latin: Saint Sophia) as though it were named for a specific saint;   *Justinian*   Byzantine Emperor from 527 to 565 CE; the capital of the Byzantine Empire was Constantinople.

13   *Knolles*   Richard Knolles, author of *The General History of the Turks* (1603), an influential English work depicting the Ottoman Empire in a very negative light;   *Sir Paul Rycaut*   English author (1629–1700) of several works on the Ottoman Empire.

a sweating pillar very balsamic for disordered heads.[14] There is not the least tradition of any such matter, and I suppose it was revealed to him in vision during his wonderful stay in the Egyptian Catacombs, for I am sure he never heard of any such miracle here. 'Tis also very pleasant to observe how tenderly he and all his brethren voyage-writers lament on the miserable confinement of the Turkish ladies, who are (perhaps) freer than any ladies in the universe, and are the only women in the world that lead a life of uninterrupted pleasure, exempt from cares, their whole time being spent in visiting, bathing, or the agreeable amusement of spending money and inventing new fashions. A husband would be thought mad that exacted any degree of economy[15] from his wife, whose expenses are no way limited but by her own fancy. 'Tis his business to get money and hers to spend it, and this noble prerogative extends itself to the very meanest[16] of the sex. Here is a fellow that carries embroidered handkerchiefs upon his back to sell, as miserable a figure as you may suppose such a mean dealer, yet I'll assure you his wife scorns to wear anything less than cloth of gold, has her ermine furs, and a very handsome set of jewels for her head. They go abroad when and where they please. 'Tis true they have no places but the bagnios,[17] and there can only be seen by their own sex; however that is a diversion they take great pleasure in.

I was three days ago at one of the finest in the town and had the opportunity of seeing a Turkish bride received there and all the ceremonies used on that occasion, which made me recollect the epithalamium of Helen by Theocritus,[18] and it seems to me that the same customs have continued ever since. All the she-friends, relations and acquaintance of the two families newly allied meet at the bagnio; several others go out of curiosity, and I believe there was that day at least two hundred women. Those that were or had been married placed themselves round the rooms on the marble sofas, but the virgins very hastily threw off their clothes, and appeared without other ornament or covering than their own long hair braided with pearl or ribbon. Two of them met the bride at the

20

---

14 *sweating ... heads* There is indeed a column in the Hagia Sophia that "sweats" moisture and is believed to cure sickness; *balsamic* Healing; *disordered heads* Headaches.

15 *exacted any degree of economy* Demanded any amount of careful spending.

16 *meanest* Of the poorest or humblest class.

17 *bagnios* Public bathhouses, which were segregated by gender. With many public spaces unwelcoming to eighteenth-century Ottoman women, women's bathhouses were an important location for them to engage in business, conversation, and other public activities.

18 *epithalamium ... Theocritus* Theocritus's Idyll 18 (third century BCE), an Ancient Greek poem in honor of the marriage of Helen, a figure in Greek mythology; *epithalamium* Wedding song.

door, conducted by her mother and another grave relation. She was a beautiful maid of about seventeen, very richly dressed and shining with jewels, but was presently reduced by them to the state of nature.* Two others filled silver gilt pots with perfume and begun the procession, the rest following in pairs, to the number of thirty. The leaders sung an epithalamium, answered by the others in chorus, and the two last led the fair bride, her eyes fixed on the ground with a charming affectation of modesty. In this order they marched round the three large rooms of the bagnio. 'Tis not easy to represent to you the beauty of this sight, most of them being well proportioned and white skinned, all of them perfectly smooth and polished by the frequent use of bathing. After having made their tour, the bride was again led to every matron round the rooms, who saluted her with a compliment and a present, some of jewels, others pieces of stuff, handkerchiefs, or little gallantries of that nature, which she thanked them for by kissing their hands.

I was very well pleased with having seen this ceremony, and you may believe me that the Turkish ladies have at least as much wit and civility, nay liberty, as ladies among us. 'Tis true the same customs that give them so many opportunities of gratifying their evil inclinations (if they have any) also puts it very fully in the power of their husbands to revenge them if they are discovered, and I do not doubt but they suffer sometimes for their indiscretions in a very severe manner. About two months ago there was found at day break not very far from my house, the bleeding body of a young woman, naked, only wrapped in a coarse sheet, with two wounds with a knife, one in her side, and another in her breast. She was not yet quite cold, and was so surprisingly beautiful that there were very few men in Pera[19] that did not go to look upon her; but it was not possible for anybody to know her, no woman's face being known. She was supposed to be brought in dead of night from the Constantinople side and laid there. Very little inquiry was made about the murderer, and the corpse privately buried without noise. Murder is never pursued by the King's officers as with us. 'Tis the business of the next relations to revenge the dead person, and if they like better to compound the matter for money (as they generally do) there is no more said of it. One would imagine this defect in their government should make such tragedies very frequent, yet they are extremely rare, which is enough to prove the people not naturally cruel. Neither do I think in many other particulars they deserve the barbarous character we give them....

(written 1717–18; published 1763)

---

19 *Pera* Hill region on the outskirts of Istanbul; many wealthy emigrants from outside Turkey lived there in the eighteenth century.

JONATHAN SWIFT

A MODEST PROPOSAL

FOR PREVENTING THE CHILDREN OF POOR PEOPLE IN IRELAND FROM BEING A BURDEN TO THEIR PARENTS OR THE COUNTRY, AND FOR MAKING THEM BENEFICIAL TO THE PUBLIC

The Penal Laws in early eighteenth-century Ireland excluded most Irish people from land ownership and political power; land was for the most part owned by English landlords and farmed by Irish peasants. Much of the resulting produce and meat was shipped to England, leaving the Irish impoverished and hungry. In the following essay (first published anonymously, as a pamphlet), Swift offered a solution to Ireland's economic crisis—a solution at once "innocent, cheap, easy, and effectual."

"A Modest Proposal" is the last of a series of passionate writings Swift produced on Irish affairs. It remains the most widely reprinted essay in the English language.

It is a melancholy object to those who walk through this great town,[1] or travel in the country, when they see the streets, the roads, and cabin doors crowded with beggars of the female sex, followed by three, four, or six children, all in rags and importuning every passenger[2] for an alms. These mothers, instead of being able to work for their honest livelihood, are forced to employ all their time in strolling[3] to beg sustenance for their helpless infants, who, as they grow up, either turn thieves for want of work, or leave their dear native country to fight for the Pretender in Spain, or sell themselves to the Barbados.[4]

---

1   *this great town*   I.e., Dublin.

2   *passenger*   Passerby.

3   *strolling*   Wandering, roving.

4   *the Pretender*   James Francis Edward Stuart, son of James II who was deposed from the throne in the Glorious Revolution due to his overt Catholicism. Catholic *(continued ...)*

I think it is agreed by all parties that this prodigious number of children in the arms, or on the backs, or at the heels of their mothers, and frequently of their fathers, is, in the present deplorable state of the kingdom, a very great additional grievance; and therefore, whoever could find out a fair, cheap, and easy method of making these children sound and useful members of the commonwealth would deserve so well of the public as to have his statue set up for a preserver of the nation.

But my intention is very far from being confined to provide only for the children of professed beggars; it is of a much greater extent, and shall take in the whole number of infants at a certain age who are born of parents in effect as little able to support them as those who demand our charity in the streets.

As to my own part, having turned my thoughts for many years upon this important subject and maturely weighed the several schemes of other projectors,[5] I have always found them grossly mistaken in their computation. 'Tis true, a child just dropped from its dam* may be supported by her milk for a solar year with little other nourishment, at most not above the value of two shillings, which the mother may certainly get, or the value in scraps, by her lawful occupation of begging; and it is exactly at one year old that I propose to provide for them in such a manner as, instead of being a charge upon their parents or the parish, or wanting food and raiment for the rest of their lives, they shall on the contrary contribute to the feeding, and partly to the clothing, of many thousands.

There is likewise another great advantage in my scheme, that it will prevent those abortions, and that horrid practice of women murdering their bastard children, alas, too frequent among us, sacrificing the poor innocent babes, I doubt,[6] more to avoid the expense than the shame, which would move tears and pity in the most savage and inhuman breast.

The number of souls in this kingdom being usually reckoned one million and a half, of these I calculate there may be about two hundred thousand couple whose wives are breeders, from which number I subtract thirty thousand couples who are able to maintain children, although I apprehend there cannot be as many under the present distresses of the kingdom; but this being granted, there will remain one hundred and seventy thousand breeders.

I again subtract fifty thousand for those women who miscarry, or whose children die by accident or disease within the year. There only remain one

---

Ireland was loyal to Stuart, and the Irish were often recruited by France and Spain to fight against England; *Barbados* Because of the extreme poverty in Ireland, many Irish people emigrated to the West Indies, selling their labor to sugar plantations in advance to pay for the voyage.

5   *projectors* Those who design or propose experiments or projects.

6   *doubt* Think.

hundred and twenty thousand children of poor parents annually born. The question therefore is how this number shall be reared and provided for, which, as I have already said, under the present situation of affairs is utterly impossible by all the methods hitherto proposed. For we can neither employ them in handicraft or agriculture; we neither build houses (I mean in the country) nor cultivate land.[7] They can very seldom pick up a livelihood by stealing till they arrive at six years old, except where they are of towardly parts,[8] although I confess they learn the rudiments much earlier, during which time they can however be properly looked upon only as probationers,[9] as I have been informed by a principal gentleman in the county of Cavan, who protested to me that he never knew above one or two instances under the age of six, even in a part of the kingdom so renowned for the quickest proficiency in that art.

I am assured by our merchants that a boy or a girl before twelve years old is no saleable commodity; and even when they come to this age, they will not yield above three pounds, or three pounds and half a crown at most, on the Exchange, which cannot turn to account[10] either to the parents or the kingdom, the charge of nutriment and rags having been at least four times that value.

I shall now therefore humbly propose my own thoughts, which I hope will not be liable to the least objection.

I have been assured by a very knowing American[11] of my acquaintance in London that a young healthy child well nursed is at a year old a most delicious, nourishing, and wholesome food, whether stewed, roasted, baked, or boiled; and I make no doubt that it will equally serve in a fricassee or a ragout.[12]

I do therefore humbly offer it to public consideration that of the hundred and twenty thousand children already computed, twenty thousand may be reserved for breed, whereof only one fourth part to be males, which is more than we allow to sheep, black cattle, or swine, and my reason is that these children are seldom the fruits of marriage, a circumstance not much regarded by our savages; therefore, one male will be sufficient to serve four females. That the remaining hundred thousand may at a year old be offered in sale to the persons of quality and fortune through the kingdom, always advising the mother to let them suck plentifully of the last month, so as to render them plump and fat for a good table. A child will make two dishes at an entertainment for friends, and

10

---

7   *neither build … land*   The British placed numerous restrictions on the Irish agricultural industry, retaining the majority of land for the grazing of sheep. The vast estates of British absentee landlords further contributed to Ireland's poverty.

8   *of towardly parts*   Exceptionally able.

9   *probationers*   Novices.

10   *on the Exchange*   At the market;   *turn to account*   Result in profit.

11   *American*   I.e., Native American.

12   *fricassee or a ragout*   Stews.

when the family dines alone, the fore or hind quarter will make a reasonable dish, and seasoned with a little pepper or salt will be very good boiled on the fourth day, especially in winter.

I have reckoned upon a medium that a child just born will weigh twelve pounds, and in a solar year if tolerably nursed increase to twenty-eight pounds.

I grant this food will be somewhat dear,[13] and therefore very proper for landlords, who, as they have already devoured most of the parents, seem to have the best title* to the children.

Infants' flesh will be in season throughout the year, but more plentiful in March, and a little before and after. For we are told by a grave author, an eminent French physician, that, fish being a prolific[14] diet, there are more children born in Roman Catholic countries about nine months after Lent* than at any other season; therefore, reckoning a year after Lent, the markets will be more glutted than usual because the number of popish[15] infants is at least three to one in this kingdom, and therefore it will have one other collateral advantage by lessening the number of papists* among us.

I have already computed the charge of nursing a beggar's child (in which list I reckon all cottagers,[16] laborers, and four fifths of the farmers) to be about two shillings per annum, rags included, and I believe no gentleman would repine to give ten shillings for the carcass of a good fat child, which, as I have said, will make four dishes of excellent nutritive meat when he hath only some particular friend or his own family to dine with him. Thus the squire[17] will learn to be a good landlord and grow popular among his tenants; the mother will have eight shillings net profit and be fit for work till she produces another child.

Those who are more thrifty (as I must confess the times require) may flay the carcass, the skin of which, artificially[18] dressed, will make admirable gloves for ladies and summer boots for fine gentlemen.

As to our city of Dublin, shambles[19] may be appointed for this purpose in the most convenient parts of it, and butchers we may be assured will not be wanting, although I rather recommend buying the children alive and dressing them hot from the knife, as we do roasting pigs.

---

13 *dear* Expensive.
14 *grave author* Sixteenth-century satirist François Rabelais. See his *Gargantua and Pantagruel*; *prolific* I.e., causing increased fertility.
15 *popish* Derogatory term meaning "Catholic."
16 *cottagers* Country dwellers.
17 *squire* Owner of a country estate.
18 *artificially* Artfully, skillfully.
19 *shambles* Slaughterhouses.

A very worthy person, a true lover of his country, and whose virtues I highly esteem, was lately pleased, in discoursing on this matter, to offer a refinement upon my scheme. He said that, many gentlemen of this kingdom having of late destroyed their deer, he conceived that the want of venison might be well supplied by the bodies of young lads and maidens, not exceeding fourteen years of age nor under twelve, so great a number of both sexes in every county being now ready to starve for want of work and service; and these to be disposed of by their parents if alive, or otherwise by their nearest relations. But with due deference to so excellent a friend and so deserving a patriot, I cannot be altogether in his sentiments; for as to the males, my American acquaintance assured me from frequent experience that their flesh was generally tough and lean, like that of our schoolboys, by continual exercise, and their taste disagreeable, and to fatten them would not answer the charge. Then as to the females, it would, I think with humble submission, be a loss to the public because they soon would become breeders themselves. And besides, it is not improbable that some scrupulous people might be apt to censure such a practice (although indeed very unjustly) as a little bordering upon cruelty, which, I confess, hath always been with me the strongest objection against any project, however well intended.

But in order to justify my friend, he confessed that this expedient was put into his head by the famous Psalmanazar,[20] a native of the island of Formosa, who came from thence to London above twenty years ago, and in conversation told my friend that in his country, when any young person happened to be put to death the executioner sold the carcass to persons of quality as a prime dainty, and that in his time the body of a plump girl of fifteen, who was crucified for an attempt to poison the emperor, was sold to his Imperial Majesty's Prime Minister of State and other great Mandarins* of the court, in joints from the gibbet,[21] at four hundred crowns. Neither indeed can I deny that if the same use were made of several plump young girls in this town who, without one single groat to their fortunes, cannot stir abroad without a chair,[22] and appear at the playhouse and assemblies in foreign fineries which they never will pay for, the kingdom would not be the worse.

---

20 *Psalmanazar*   George Psalmanazar, a French adventurer who pretended to be from Formosa (now Taiwan) and published an account of Formosan customs, *Historical and Geographical Description of Formosa* (1704), which was later exposed as fraudulent. The story Swift recounts here is found in the second edition of Psalmanazar's work.

21 *gibbet*   Gallows.

22 *groat*   Silver coin equal in value to four pence. It was removed from circulation in 1662, and thereafter "a groat" was used metaphorically to signify any very small sum;   *chair*   Sedan chair, which seated one person and was carried on poles by two men.

20   Some persons of a desponding spirit are in great concern about that vast number of poor people who are aged, diseased, or maimed, and I have been desired to employ my thoughts what course may be taken to ease the nation of so grievous an encumbrance. But I am not in the least pain upon that matter because it is very well known that they are every day dying and rotting by cold and famine, and filth and vermin, as fast as can be reasonably expected. And as to the younger laborers, they are now in almost as hopeful a condition. They cannot get work, and consequently pine away* for want of nourishment to a degree that if at any time they are accidentally hired to common labor, they have not strength to perform it; and thus the country and themselves are happily delivered from the evils to come.

I have too long digressed, and therefore shall return to my subject. I think the advantages by the proposal which I have made are obvious and many, as well as of the highest importance.

For first, as I have already observed, it would greatly lessen the number of papists, with whom we are yearly overrun, being the principal breeders of the nation as well as our most dangerous enemies, and who stay at home on purpose with a design to deliver the kingdom to the Pretender, hoping to take their advantage by the absence of so many good Protestants, who have chosen rather to leave their country than stay at home and pay tithes against their conscience to an Episcopal curate.[23]

Secondly, the poorer tenants will have something valuable of their own, which by law may be made liable to distress[24] and help to pay their landlord's rent, their corn and cattle being already seized, and money a thing unknown.

Thirdly, whereas the maintenance of an hundred thousand children from two years old and upwards cannot be computed at less than ten shillings apiece per annum, the nation's stock will be thereby increased fifty thousand pounds per annum, besides the profit of a new dish introduced to the tables of all gentlemen of fortune in the kingdom who have any refinement in taste, and the money will circulate among ourselves, the goods being entirely of our own growth and manufacture.

25   Fourthly, the constant breeders, besides the gain of eight shillings sterling per annum by the sale of their children, will be rid of the charge of maintaining them after the first year.

Fifthly, this food would likewise bring great customs* to taverns, where the vintners* will certainly be so prudent as to procure the best receipts[25] for dressing it to perfection, and consequently have their houses frequented by

---

23 *Episcopal curate* I.e., Anglican church official.
24 *distress* Seizure of property for the payment of debt.
25 *receipts* Recipes.

all the fine gentlemen who justly value themselves upon their knowledge in good eating. And a skillful cook who understands how to oblige his guests will contrive to make it as expensive as they please.

Sixthly, this would be a great inducement to marriage, which all wise nations have either encouraged by rewards or enforced by laws and penalties. It would increase the care and tenderness of mothers toward their children, when they were sure of a settlement for life to the poor babes, provided in some sort by the public, to their annual profit instead of expense. We should soon see an honest emulation[26] among the married women, which of them could bring the fattest child to market. Men would become as fond of their wives during the time of their pregnancy as they are now of their mares in foal, their cows in calf, or sows when they are ready to farrow, nor offer to beat or kick them (as it is too frequent a practice) for fear of a miscarriage.

Many other advantages might be enumerated: for instance, the addition of some thousand carcasses in our exportation of barreled beef; the propagation of swine's flesh and improvement in the art of making good bacon, so much wanted among us by the great destruction of pigs, too frequent at our tables, which are no way comparable in taste or magnificence to a well-grown, fat yearling* child, which, roasted whole, will make a considerable figure at a Lord Mayor's feast or any other public entertainment. But this and many others I omit, being studious of* brevity.

Supposing that one thousand families in this city would be constant customers for infants' flesh, besides others who might have it at merry-meetings, particularly weddings and christenings, I compute that Dublin would take off annually about twenty thousand carcasses, and the rest of the kingdom (where probably they will be sold somewhat cheaper) the remaining eighty thousand.

I can think of no one objection that will possibly be raised against this proposal, unless it should be urged that the number of people will be thereby much lessened in the kingdom. This I freely own, and it was indeed one principal design in offering it to the world. I desire the reader will observe that I calculate my remedy for this one individual kingdom of Ireland, and for no other that ever was, is, or, I think, ever can be upon earth. Therefore let no man talk to me of other expedients:[27] of taxing our absentees* at five shillings a pound; of using neither clothes nor household furniture, except what is of our own growth and manufacture; of utterly rejecting the materials and instruments that

30

---

26 *emulation* Rivalry.

27 *other expedients* All of which Swift had already proposed in earnest attempts to remedy Ireland's poverty. See, for example, his *Proposal for the Universal Use of Irish Manufactures*. In early editions the following proposals were italicized to show the suspension of Swift's ironic tone.

promote foreign luxury; of curing the expensiveness of pride, vanity, idleness, and gaming[28] in our women; of introducing a vein of parsimony, prudence, and temperance; of learning to love our country, wherein we differ even from Laplanders* and the inhabitants of Topinamboo; of quitting our animosities and factions, nor act any longer like the Jews, who were murdering one another at the very moment their city was taken;[29] of being a little cautious not to sell our country and consciences for nothing; of teaching landlords to have at least one degree of mercy toward their tenants; lastly, of putting a spirit of honesty, industry, and skill into our shopkeepers, who, if a resolution could now be taken to buy only our native goods, would immediately unite to cheat and exact upon us in the price, the measure, and the goodness, nor could ever yet be brought to make one fair proposal of just dealing, though often in earnest invited to it.

Therefore I repeat, let no man talk to me of these and the like expedients till he hath at least some glimpse of hope that there will ever be some hearty and sincere attempt to put them in practice.

But as to myself, having been wearied out for many years with offering vain, idle, visionary thoughts, and at length utterly despairing of success, I fortunately fell upon this proposal, which, as it is wholly new, so it hath something solid and real, of no expense and little trouble, full in our own power, and whereby we can incur no danger in disobliging* England. For this kind of commodity will not bear exportation, the flesh being of too tender a consistence to admit a long continuance in salt, although perhaps I could name a country[30] which would be glad to eat up our whole nation without it.

After all, I am not so violently bent upon my own opinion as to reject any offer, proposed by wise men, which shall be found equally innocent, cheap, easy, and effectual. But before something of that kind shall be advanced in contradiction to my scheme, and offering a better, I desire the author or authors will be pleased maturely to consider two points.

First, as things now stand, how they will be able to find food and raiment for one hundred thousand useless mouths and backs.

35 And secondly, there being a round million of creatures in human figure throughout this kingdom whose whole subsistence, put into a common stock, would leave them in debt two million of pounds sterling, adding those who are beggars by profession to the bulk of farmers, cottagers, and laborers with their wives and children, who are beggars in effect.

---

28 *gaming* Gambling.
29 *Topinamboo* District in Brazil; *Jews ... was taken* According to the history of Flavius Joseph, Roman Emperor Titus's invasion and capture of Jerusalem in 70 BCE was aided by the fact that factional fighting had divided the city.
30 *a country* I.e., England.

I desire those politicians who dislike my overture, and may perhaps be so bold to attempt an answer, that they will first ask the parents of these mortals whether they would not at this day think it a great happiness to have been sold for food at a year old in the manner I prescribe, and thereby have avoided such a perpetual scene of misfortunes as they have since gone through by the oppression of landlords, the impossibility of paying rent without money or trade, the want of common sustenance, with neither house nor clothes to cover them from the inclemencies of the weather, and the most inevitable prospect of entailing[31] the like or greater miseries upon their breed forever.

I profess in the sincerity of my heart that I have not the least personal interest in endeavoring to promote this necessary work, having no other motive than the public good of my country by advancing our trade, providing for infants, relieving the poor, and giving some pleasure to the rich. I have no children by which I can propose to get a single penny, the youngest being nine years old, and my wife past childbearing.

(1729)

---

31 *entailing* Bestowing, conferring.

MARY WOLLSTONECRAFT

TO M. TALLEYRAND-PÉRIGORD, LATE BISHOP OF AUTUN

"To M. Talleyrand-Périgord" is the Dedication to A Vindication of the Rights of Woman, *Mary Wollstonecraft's groundbreaking essay on women's rights and the importance of equal education for men and women. She addresses the former Bishop of Autun, who was then minister of finance in the French revolutionary government and had been a member of the Committee that drafted the French Constitution of 1791. In that same year, he had also authored a pamphlet concerning public education that was presented to the National Assembly. Wollstonecraft was disappointed that Revolutionary France—founded on the ideals of liberty, equality, and fraternity—had not claimed for women the rights it had claimed for men. In the Dedication she asserts the injustice of this omission and summarizes many of her book's main arguments.*

SIR,

Having read with great pleasure a pamphlet which you have lately published, I dedicate this volume to you; to induce you to reconsider the subject, and maturely weigh what I have advanced respecting the rights of woman and national education: and I call with the firm tone of humanity; for my arguments, Sir, are dictated by a disinterested* spirit—I plead for my sex—not for myself. Independence I have long considered as the grand blessing of life, the basis of every virtue—and independence I will ever secure by contracting my wants, though I were to live on a barren heath.

It is then an affection for the whole human race that makes my pen dart rapidly along to support what I believe to be the cause of virtue: and the same motive leads me earnestly to wish to see woman placed in a station in which she would advance, instead of retarding, the progress of those glorious principles that give a substance to morality. My opinion, indeed, respecting the rights and duties of woman, seems to flow so naturally from these simple principles, that

I think it scarcely possible, but that some of the enlarged minds who formed your admirable constitution, will coincide with me.

In France there is undoubtedly a more general diffusion of knowledge than in any part of the European world, and I attribute it, in a great measure, to the social intercourse* which has long subsisted between the sexes. It is true, I utter my sentiments with freedom, that in France the very essence of sensuality has been extracted to regale the voluptuary,* and a kind of sentimental lust has prevailed, which, together with the system of duplicity that the whole tenor of their political and civil government taught, have given a sinister sort of sagacity to the French character, properly termed finesse; from which naturally flow a polish of manners that injures the substance, by hunting sincerity out of society.—And, modesty, the fairest garb of virtue!* has been more grossly insulted in France than even in England, till their women have treated as *prudish* that attention to decency, which brutes instinctively observe.

Manners and morals are so nearly allied that they have often been confounded; but, though the former should only be the natural reflection of the latter, yet, when various causes have produced factitious and corrupt manners, which are very early caught, morality becomes an empty name. The personal reserve, and sacred respect for cleanliness and delicacy in domestic life, which French women almost despise, are the graceful pillars of modesty; but, far from despising them, if the pure flame of patriotism have reached their bosoms, they should labor to improve the morals of their fellow-citizens, by teaching men, not only to respect modesty in women, but to acquire it themselves, as the only way to merit their esteem.

Contending for the rights of woman, my main argument is built on this simple principle, that if she be not prepared by education to become the companion of man, she will stop the progress of knowledge and virtue; for truth must be common to all, or it will be inefficacious with respect to its influence on general practice. And how can woman be expected to co-operate unless she know why she ought to be virtuous? unless freedom strengthen her reason till she comprehend her duty, and see in what manner it is connected with her real good? If children are to be educated to understand the true principle of patriotism, their mother must be a patriot; and the love of mankind, from which an orderly train of virtues spring, can only be produced by considering the moral and civil interest of mankind; but the education and situation of woman, at present, shuts her out from such investigations.

In this work I have produced many arguments, which to me were conclusive, to prove that the prevailing notion respecting a sexual character[1] was

1   *prevailing notion respecting a sexual character*   I.e., prevailing notion regarding what is natural and appropriate for the two sexes.

subversive of morality, and I have contended, that to render the human body and mind more perfect, chastity must more universally prevail, and that chastity will never be respected in the male world till the person of a woman is not, as it were, idolized, when little virtue or sense embellish it with the grand traces of mental beauty, or the interesting simplicity of affection.

Consider, Sir, dispassionately,* these observations—for a glimpse of this truth seemed to open before you when you observed, "that to see one half of the human race excluded by the other from all participation of government, was a political phenomenon that, according to abstract principles, it was impossible to explain." If so, on what does your constitution rest? If the abstract rights of man will bear discussion and explanation, those of woman, by a parity of reasoning, will not shrink from the same test: though a different opinion prevails in this country, built on the very arguments which you use to justify the oppression of woman—prescription.*

Consider, I address you as a legislator, whether, when men contend for their freedom, and to be allowed to judge for themselves respecting their own happiness, it be not inconsistent and unjust to subjugate women, even though you firmly believe that you are acting in the manner best calculated to promote their happiness? Who made man the exclusive judge, if woman partake with him the gift of reason?

In this style, argue tyrants of every denomination, from the weak king to the weak father of a family; they are all eager to crush reason; yet always assert that they usurp its throne only to be useful. Do you not act a similar part, when you *force* all women, by denying them civil and political rights, to remain immured in their families groping in the dark? for surely, Sir, you will not assert, that a duty can be binding which is not founded on reason? If indeed this be their destination, arguments may be drawn from reason: and thus augustly supported, the more understanding women acquire, the more they will be attached to their duty—comprehending it—for unless they comprehend it, unless their morals be fixed on the same immutable principle as those of man, no authority can make them discharge it in a virtuous manner. They may be convenient slaves, but slavery will have its constant effect, degrading the master and the abject dependent.

10   But, if women are to be excluded, without having a voice, from a participation of the natural rights of mankind, prove first, to ward off the charge of injustice and inconsistency, that they want^2 reason—else this flaw in your NEW CONSTITUTION will ever show that man must, in some shape, act like a tyrant, and tyranny, in whatever part of society it rears its brazen front, will ever undermine morality.

---

2   *want*   Lack.

I have repeatedly asserted, and produced what appeared to me irrefragable* arguments drawn from matters of fact, to prove my assertion, that women cannot, by force, be confined to domestic concerns; for they will, however ignorant, intermeddle with more weighty affairs, neglecting private duties only to disturb, by cunning tricks, the orderly plans of reason which rise above their comprehension.

Besides, whilst they are only made to acquire personal accomplishments, men will seek for pleasure in variety, and faithless husbands will make faithless wives; such ignorant beings, indeed, will be very excusable when, not taught to respect public good, nor allowed any civil rights, they attempt to do themselves justice by retaliation.

The box of mischief thus opened in society, what is to preserve private virtue, the only security of public freedom and universal happiness?

Let there be then no coercion *established* in society, and the common law of gravity prevailing, the sexes will fall into their proper places. And, now that more equitable laws are forming your citizens, marriage may become more sacred: your young men may choose wives from motives of affection, and your maidens allow love to root out vanity.

The father of a family will not then weaken his constitution and debase his sentiments, by visiting the harlot, nor forget, in obeying the call of appetite, the purpose for which it was implanted. And, the mother will not neglect her children to practice the arts of coquetry,* when sense and modesty secure her the friendship of her husband. 15

But, till men become attentive to the duty of a father, it is vain to expect women to spend that time in their nursery which they, "wise in their generation," choose to spend at their glass;[3] for this exertion of cunning is only an instinct of nature to enable them to obtain indirectly a little of that power of which they are unjustly denied a share: for, if women are not permitted to enjoy legitimate rights, they will render both men and themselves vicious, to obtain illicit privileges.

I wish, Sir, to set some investigations of this kind afloat in France; and should they lead to a confirmation of my principles, when your constitution is revised the Rights of Woman may be respected, if it be fully proved that reason calls for this respect, and loudly demands JUSTICE for one half of the human race.

I am, SIR,

Your's respectfully,

M.W.
(1792)

---

3 *glass* Mirror.

HARRIET MARTINEAU

from A RETROSPECT OF WESTERN TRAVEL

In 1834, Harriet Martineau, an English writer famous for her work on political, social, and economic subjects, traveled to New York to begin a two-year tour of the United States. She visited hospitals, prisons, government houses, and scientific and literary institutions, paying particular attention to the status of women and to the abolitionist movement. Upon her return to England, she published her experiences in two travel narratives, Society in America *(1837) and* A Retrospect of Western Travel *(1838). In "Prisons," a chapter from* A Retrospect of Western Travel, *Martineau reflects on penal reform in America, particularly the Quaker-led reforms in Pennsylvania and New York. During this period prison reform was a controversial matter; reformers questioned severe punishments such as public execution and argued that prisons, as they were then, corrupted inmates further. Many reforms were advanced with the aim of improving the moral character of inmates.*

from PRISONS

… The first principle in the management of the guilty seems to me to be to treat them as men and women; which they were before they were guilty, and will be when they are no longer so; and which they are in the midst of it all. Their humanity is the principal thing about them; their guilt is a temporary state. The insane are first men, and secondarily diseased men; and in a due consideration of this order of things lies the main secret of the successful treatment of such. The drunkard is first a man, and secondarily a man with a peculiar weakness. The convict is, in like manner, first a man, and then a sinner. Now, there is something in the isolation of the convict which tends to keep this order of considerations right in the mind of his guardians. The warden and his prisoner converse like two men when they are face to face; but when the keeper watches a hundred men herded together in virtue of the one common characteristic of their being criminals, the guilt becomes the prominent circumstance, and there is an end of the brotherly faith in each, to which each must mainly owe his cure. This, in our human weakness, is the great evil attendant upon the good of collecting together sufferers under any particular physical or moral evil. Visitors are shy of the blind, the deaf and dumb, and insane, when they see them all together, while they would feel little or nothing of this shyness if they met each sufferer in the bosom of his own family. In the one case, the infirmity, defying sympathy, is the prominent circumstance; in the other, not. It follows from this, that such an association of prisoners as that at Auburn[1] must be more difficult to reform, more difficult to do the state's duty by, than any number or kind of criminals who are classed* by some other characteristic, or not classed at all.

The wonderfully successful friend of criminals, Captain Pillsbury, of the Weathersfield prison,[2] has worked on this principle, and owes his success to it. His moral power over the guilty is so remarkable, that prison-breakers* who can be confined nowhere else are sent to him to be charmed into staying their term out. It was told of his treatment of two such. One was a gigantic personage,* the terror of the country, who had plunged deeper and deeper in crime for seventeen years. Captain Pillsbury told him when he came that he hoped he would not repeat the attempts to escape which he had made elsewhere. "It will be best," said he, "that you and I should treat each other as well as we can. I will make you as comfortable as I possibly can, and shall be anxious to be your friend; and I hope you will not get me into any difficulty on your account. There is a cell intended for solitary confinement,[3] but we have never used it, and I should be sorry ever to have to turn the key upon anybody in it. You may range the place as freely as I do if you will trust me as I shall trust you." The man was sulky, and for weeks showed only very gradual symptoms of softening under the operation of Captain Pillsbury's cheerful confidence. At length information was given to the captain of this man's intention to break prison. The captain called him, and taxed* him with it; the man preserved a gloomy silence. He

---

1   *Auburn* Auburn prison, in New York, where a penal system was developed in the 1820s that involved prisoners working together in groups during the day and solitary confinement at night. A strict code of silence was enforced at all times. Prisoners were classified according to their crimes, wearing uniforms of different colors to mark them as thieves, murderers, first offenders, or repeat offenders.

2   *Weathersfield prison* State prison of Connecticut, opened in 1827. Moses C. Pilsbury was warden from 1827 to 1837.

3   *solitary confinement* Prisoners in solitary are kept in strict isolation, with no contact with anyone except prison officials. Solitary confinement and silence were thought to encourage prisoners' repentance, and were among the reforms advocated for by Quakers in the late eighteenth and early nineteenth centuries.

was told that it was now necessary for him to be locked in the solitary cell, and desired to follow the captain, who went first, carrying a lamp in one hand and the key in the other. In the narrowest part of the passage the captain (who is a small, slight* man) turned round and looked in the face of the stout criminal. "Now," said he, "I ask you whether you have treated me as I deserve? I have done everything I could think of to make you comfortable; I have trusted you, and you have never given me the least confidence in return, and have even planned to get me into difficulty. Is this kind? And yet I cannot bear to lock you up. If I had the least sign that you cared for me...." The man burst into tears. "Sir," said he, "I have been a very devil these seventeen years; but you treat me like a man." "Come, let us go back," said the captain. The convict had the free range of the prison as before. From this hour he began to open his heart to the captain, and cheerfully fulfilled his whole term of imprisonment, confiding to his friend, as they arose, all impulses to violate his trust, and all facilities[4] for doing so which he imagined he saw.

The other case was a criminal of the same character, who went so far as to make the actual attempt to escape. He fell, and hurt his ankle very much. The captain had him brought in and laid on his bed, and the ankle attended to, every one being forbidden to speak a word of reproach to the sufferer. The man was sullen, and would not say whether the bandaging of his ankle gave him pain or not. This was in the night, and every one returned to bed when this was done. But the captain could not sleep. He was distressed at the attempt, and thought he could not have fully done his duty by any man who would make it. He was afraid the man was in great pain. He rose, threw on his gown, and went with a lamp to the cell. The prisoner's face was turned to the wall, and his eyes were closed, but the traces of suffering were not to be mistaken. The captain loosened and replaced the bandage, and went for his own pillow to rest the limb upon, the man neither speaking nor moving all the time. Just when he was shutting the door the prisoner started up and called him back. "Stop, sir. Was it all to see after my ankle that you have got up?"

"Yes, it was. I could not sleep for thinking of you."

5 "And you have never said a word of the way I have used* you!"

"I do feel hurt with you, but I don't want to call you unkind while you are suffering as you are now."

The man was in an agony of shame and grief. All he asked was to be trusted again when he should have recovered. He was freely trusted, and gave his generous friend no more anxiety on his behalf.

Captain Pillsbury is the gentleman who, on being told that a desperate prisoner had sworn to murder him speedily, sent for him to shave him, allowing

---

4   *facilities*   Opportunities.

no one to be present. He eyed the man, pointed to the razor, and desired him to shave him. The prisoner's hand trembled, but he went through it very well. When he had done the captain said, "I have been told you meant to murder me, but I thought I might trust you." "God bless you, sir! you may," replied the regenerated man. Such is the power of faith in man!

The greatest advantage of solitary confinement is that it presents the best part of a prisoner's mind to be acted upon by his guardians; and the next is, that the prisoner is preserved from the evil influences of vicious companionship, of shame within the prison walls, and of degradation when he comes out. I am persuaded that no system of secondary punishment[5] has yet been devised that can be compared with this. I need not, at this time of day, explain that I mean solitary imprisonment with labor, and with frequent visits from the guardians of the prisoner. Without labor, the punishment is too horrible and unjust to be thought of. The reflective man would go mad, and the clown[6] would sleep away his term, and none of the purposes of human existence could be answered. Work is, in prison as out of it, the grand equalizer, stimulus, composer, and rectifier; the prime obligation and the prime privilege. It is delightful to see how soon its character is recognized there. In the Philadelphia penitentiary[7] work is forbidden to the criminal for two days subsequent to* his entrance; he petitions for it before the two days are out, however doggedly* he may have declared that he will never work. Small incidents show what a resource it is. A convict shoemaker mentioned to a visitor a very early hour of the winter day as that at which he began to work. "But how can you see at that time of a winter's morning? it must be nearly dark." "I hammer my leather. That requires very little light. I get up and hammer my leather." ...

(1838)

---

5   *secondary punishment* Punishment for offences taking place in prison (after sentencing).

6   *clown* Peasant, ignorant person; here, a person not prone to reflection.

7   *Philadelphia penitentiary* Eastern State Penitentiary, opened in 1821. In the Philadelphia penal system, inmates were kept in solitary confinement even while they worked, with daily visits from the warden.

Elizabeth Cady Stanton

Seneca Falls Keynote Address[1]

The struggle for women's rights and the struggle to overthrow slavery—and then to achieve full citizenship rights for black people—have often been intertwined, and sometimes in tension with each other. When the young anti-slavery activist Elizabeth Cady married Henry Brewster Stanton in May 1840, the two traveled to London on their honeymoon, planning to attend the World Anti-Slavery Convention. When that Convention decided not to allow women to be full participants, Stanton and Lucretia Mott, a delegate from Philadelphia, resolved to organize a convention of their own. The eventual result was the Seneca Falls Women's Rights Convention in 1848, the first such gathering in America; it attracted some 300 attendees, notable among them Mott, Mary Ann McClintock (who, with Stanton, took the lead in drafting the convention's Declaration of Sentiments)—and pre-eminent abolitionist Frederick Douglass.

We have met here today to discuss our rights and wrongs, civil and political, and not, as some have supposed, to go into the detail of social life alone. We do not propose to petition the legislature to make our husbands just, generous, and courteous, to seat every man at the head of a cradle, and to clothe every woman in male attire.

None of these points, however important they may be considered by leading men, will be touched in this convention. As to their costume,* the gentlemen need feel no fear of our imitating that, for we think it in violation of every principle of taste, beauty, and dignity; notwithstanding all the contempt cast upon our loose, flowing garments, we still admire the graceful folds, and consider our costume far more artistic than theirs. Many of the nobler sex[2] seem to agree with us in this opinion, for the bishops, priests, judges, barristers,

---

1   *Keynote Address* Stanton's speech was delivered 19 July 1848 at the Women's Rights Convention, Seneca Falls, New York.

2   *nobler sex* The sex possessing higher social and political status—i.e., men.

and lord mayors of the first nation on the globe,* and the Pope of Rome, with his cardinals, too, all wear the loose flowing robes, thus tacitly acknowledging that the male attire is neither dignified nor imposing.

No, we shall not molest you in your philosophical experiments with stocks,[3] pants, high-heeled boots, and Russian belts. Yours be the glory to discover, by personal experience, how long the kneepan[4] can resist the terrible strapping down which you impose, in how short time the well-developed muscles of the throat can be reduced to mere threads by the constant pressure of the stock,[5] how high the heel of a boot must be to make a short man tall, and how tight the Russian belt may be drawn and yet have wind enough left to sustain life.

But we are assembled to protest against a form of government existing without the consent of the governed—to declare our right to be free as man is free, to be represented in the government which we are taxed to support, to have such graceful laws as give man the power to chastise and imprison his wife, to take the wages which she earns, the property which she inherits, and, in case of separation, the children of her love;* laws which make her the mere dependent on his bounty. It is to protest against such unjust laws as these that we are assembled today, and to have them, if possible, forever erased from our statute books, deeming them a shame and a disgrace to a Christian republic in the nineteenth century. We have met to uplift woman's fallen divinity upon an even pedestal with man's. And, strange as it may seem to many, we now demand our right to vote according to the declaration of the government under which we live.

This right no one pretends to deny. We need not prove ourselves equal to   5
Daniel Webster to enjoy this privilege, for the ignorant Irishman in the ditch[6] has all the civil rights he has. We need not prove our muscular power equal to this same Irishman to enjoy this privilege, for the most tiny, weak, ill-shaped stripling[7] of twenty-one has all the civil rights of the Irishman. We have no objection to discuss the question of equality, for we feel that the weight of

---

3   *molest* Cause trouble to;   *stocks* Neckties.

4   *kneepan* Kneecap.

5   *well-developed ... stock*   Sometimes the stock tie was stiffened with starch to give the wearer a more formal appearance by forcing the chin up.

6   *Daniel Webster* American Secretary of State, senator, and presidential candidate (1782–1852);   *Irishman in the ditch* The Irish peasantry had suffered for centuries under English rule; during the 1840s the potato famine brought millions of them to the brink of starvation. Hundreds of thousands—the vast majority of them poor and uneducated—emigrated to the United States, where few starved, but where anti-Irish feeling was widespread.

7   *stripling* Young man.

argument lies wholly with us, but we wish the question of equality kept distinct from the question of rights, for the proof of the one does not determine the truth of the other. All white men in this country have the same rights, however they may differ in mind, body, or estate.

The right is ours. The question now is: how shall we get possession of what rightfully belongs to us? We should not feel so sorely grieved if no man who had not attained the full stature of a Webster, Clay, Van Buren, or Gerrit Smith[8] could claim the right of the elective franchise. But to have drunkards, idiots, horse-racing, rum-selling rowdies, ignorant foreigners, and silly boys fully recognized, while we ourselves are thrust out from all the rights that belong to citizens, it is too grossly insulting to the dignity of woman to be longer quietly submitted to.

The right is ours. Have it, we must. Use it, we will. The pens, the tongues, the fortunes, the indomitable wills of many women are already pledged to secure this right. The great truth that no just government can be formed without the consent of the governed* we shall echo and re-echo in the ears of the unjust judge, until by continual coming we shall weary him.

There seems now to be a kind of moral stagnation in our midst. Philanthropists have done their utmost to rouse the nation to a sense of its sins. War, slavery, drunkenness, licentiousness, gluttony, have been dragged naked before the people, and all their abominations and deformities fully brought to light, yet with idiotic laugh we hug those monsters to our breasts and rush on to destruction. Our churches are multiplying on all sides, our missionary societies, Sunday schools, and prayer meetings and innumerable charitable and reform organizations are all in operation, but still the tide of vice is swelling, and threatens the destruction of everything, and the battlements of righteousness are weak against the raging elements of sin and death.

Verily,* the world waits the coming of some new element, some purifying power, some spirit of mercy and love. The voice of woman has been silenced in the state, the church, and the home, but man cannot fulfill his destiny alone, he cannot redeem his race unaided. There are deep and tender chords of sympathy and love in the hearts of the downfallen and oppressed that woman can touch more skillfully than man.

10   The world has never yet seen a truly great and virtuous nation, because in the degradation of woman the very fountains of life are poisoned at their source. It is vain to look for silver and gold from mines of copper and lead.

It is the wise mother that has the wise son. So long as your women are slaves you may throw your colleges and churches to the winds. You can't have

---

8   *Webster ... Smith*   Here, Webster, Henry Clay, Martin Van Buren, and Gerrit Smith serve as examples of prominent, respectable American men.

scholars and saints so long as your mothers are ground to powder between the upper and nether millstone of tyranny and lust. How seldom, now, is a father's pride gratified, his fond hopes realized, in the budding genius of his son!

The wife is degraded, made the mere creature of caprice,* and the foolish son is heaviness to his heart. Truly are the sins of the fathers visited upon the children to the third and fourth generation.* God, in His wisdom, has so linked the whole human family together that any violence done at one end of the chain is felt throughout its length, and here, too, is the law of restoration, as in woman all have fallen, so in her elevation shall the race be recreated.

"Voices" were the visitors and advisers of Joan of Arc.[9] Do not "voices" come to us daily from the haunts of poverty, sorrow, degradation, and despair, already too long unheeded? Now is the time for the women of this country, if they would save our free institutions, to defend the right, to buckle on the armor that can best resist the keenest weapons of the enemy—contempt and ridicule. The same religious enthusiasm that nerved[10] Joan of Arc to her work nerves us to ours. In every generation God calls some men and women for the utterance of truth, a heroic action, and our work today is the fulfilling of what has long since been foretold by the Prophet—Joel 2.28:

> "And it shall come to pass afterward, that I will pour out my spirit upon all flesh; and your sons and your daughters shall prophesy."

We do not expect our path will be strewn with the flowers of popular applause, but over the thorns of bigotry and prejudice will be our way, and on our banners will beat the dark storm clouds of opposition from those who have entrenched themselves behind the stormy bulwarks of custom and authority, and who have fortified their position by every means, holy and unholy. But we will steadfastly abide the result. Unmoved we will bear it aloft. Undauntedly we will unfurl it to the gale, for we know that the storm cannot rend from it a shred, that the electric flash will but more clearly show to us the glorious words inscribed upon it, "Equality of Rights."

(1848)

---

9 *Joan of Arc* Jeanne D'Arc (1412–31), young peasant woman who was persuaded by the "voices" she heard to become involved in military affairs. Her visionary leadership led the French to several victories over English forces during the Hundred Years' War; distrusted by Church authorities, she was burnt at the stake but later canonized as a saint.

10 *nerved* Mentally strengthened and prepared.

HENRY DAVID THOREAU

CIVIL DISOBEDIENCE

In 1846, during the time he was living at Walden Pond, Thoreau made a trip into the nearby town of Concord, where he was arrested by Sam Staples, the local constable, for having failed to pay the local poll tax. Staples initially offered to lend Thoreau enough money to pay the tax, but Thoreau refused, arguing that it was a matter of principle. He spent the night in jail—and continued to make an issue of the principles involved, most notably in a lecture he gave in Concord on 26 January 1848. His lecture was published in 1849 as "Resistance to Civil Government," then later republished as "Civil Disobedience"—and under that name has taken its place among the best-known of all American essays.

I heartily accept the motto,—"That government is best which governs least"; and I should like to see it acted up to more rapidly and systematically. Carried out, it finally amounts to this, which also I believe,—"That government is best which governs not at all"; and when men are prepared for it, that will be the kind of government which they will have. Government is at best but an expedient;* but most governments are usually, and all governments are sometimes, inexpedient. The objections which have been brought against a standing army, and they are many and weighty, and deserve to prevail, may also at last be brought against a standing government. The standing army is only an arm of the standing government. The government itself, which is only the mode which the people have chosen to execute their will, is equally liable to be abused and perverted before the people can act through it. Witness the present Mexican war,[1] the work of comparatively a few individuals using the

---

1   *the present Mexican war*   The Mexican-American War of 1846–48 was fought over a border dispute. Mexico claimed territory north to the Nueces River, while the Texans claimed that their territory extended south to the Rio Grande. The Americans were the aggressors in beginning the war when General Zachary Taylor advanced with his troops into the area under dispute. When the war ended, Mexico gave up not only its claim to Texas above the Rio Grande, but also New Mexico and California. (The United States did

standing government as their tool; for, in the outset, the people would not have consented to this measure.

This American government,—what is it but a tradition, though a recent one, endeavoring to transmit itself unimpaired to posterity, but each instant losing some of its integrity? It has not the vitality and force of a single living man; for a single man can bend it to his will. It is a sort of wooden gun to the people themselves. But is it not the less necessary for this; for the people must have some complicated machinery or other, and hear its din, to satisfy that idea of government which they have. Governments show thus how successfully men can be imposed on, even impose on themselves, for their own advantage. It is excellent, we must all allow. Yet this government never of itself furthered any enterprise, but by the alacrity with which it got out of its way. *It* does not keep the country free. *It* does not settle the West.* *It* does not educate. The character inherent in the American people has done all that has been accomplished; and it would have done somewhat more, if the government had not sometimes got in its way. For government is an expedient by which men would fain succeed in letting one another alone; and, as has been said, when it is most expedient, the governed are most let alone by it. Trade and commerce, if they were not made of India-rubber, would never manage to bounce over the obstacles which legislators are continually putting in their way; and, if one were to judge these men wholly by the effects of their actions and not partly by their intentions, they would deserve to be classed and punished with those mischievous persons who put obstructions on the railroads.

But, to speak practically and as a citizen, unlike those who call themselves no-government men, I ask for, not at once no government, but *at once* a better government. Let every man make known what kind of government would command his respect, and that will be one step toward obtaining it.

After all, the practical reason why, when the power is once in the hands of the people, a majority are permitted, and for a long period continue, to rule is not because they are most likely to be in the right, nor because this seems fairest to the minority, but because they are physically the strongest. But a government in which the majority rule in all cases cannot be based on justice, even as far as men understand it. Can there not be a government in which majorities do not virtually decide right and wrong, but conscience?—in which majorities decide only those questions to which the rule of expediency is applicable? Must the citizen ever for a moment, or in the least degree, resign his conscience to the legislator? Why has every man a conscience, then? I think that we should be men first, and subjects afterward. It is not desirable to cultivate a respect for the law,

---

pay Mexico 15 million dollars for the latter territories as part of the final agreement under the terms of the Gadsden Purchase.)

so much as for the right. The only obligation which I have a right to assume is to do at any time what I think right. It is truly enough said, that a corporation[2] has no conscience; but a corporation of conscientious men is a corporation *with* a conscience. Law never made men a whit more just; and, by means of their respect for it, even the well-disposed are daily made the agents of injustice. A common and natural result of an undue respect for law is, that you may see a file of soldiers, colonel, captain, corporal, privates, powder-monkeys, and all, marching in admirable order over hill and dale to the wars, against their wills, ay, against their common sense and consciences, which makes it very steep marching indeed, and produces a palpitation of the heart. They have no doubt that it is a damnable business in which they are concerned; they are all peaceably inclined. Now, what are they? Men at all? or small movable forts and magazines, at the service of some unscrupulous man in power? Visit the Navy-Yard, and behold a marine, such a man as an American government can make, or such as it can make a man with its black arts,—a mere shadow and reminiscence of humanity, a man laid out alive and standing, and already, as one may say, buried under arms with funeral accompaniments, though it may be,—

> Not a drum was heard, not a funeral note,
>   As his corse to the rampart we hurried;
> Not a soldier discharged his farewell shot
>   O'er the grave where our hero we buried.

5   The mass of men serve the state thus, not as men mainly, but as machines, with their bodies. They are the standing army, and the militia, jailers, constables, posse comitatus,* etc. In most cases there is no free exercise whatever of the judgment or of the moral sense; but they put themselves on a level with wood and earth and stones; and wooden men can perhaps be manufactured that will serve the purpose as well. Such command no more respect than men of straw or a lump of dirt. They have the same sort of worth only as horses and dogs. Yet such as these even are commonly esteemed good citizens. Others—as most legislators, politicians, lawyers, ministers, and office-holders—serve the state chiefly with their heads; and, as they rarely make any moral distinctions, they are as likely to serve the Devil, without *intending* it, as God. A very few, as heroes, patriots, martyrs, reformers in the great sense, and *men*, serve the state with their consciences also, and so necessarily resist it for the most part; and they are commonly treated as enemies by it. A wise man will only be useful as a man, and will not submit to be "clay," and "stop a hole to keep the wind away,"* but leave that office to his dust at least:—

---

2   *corporation* I.e., in the sense of any "body of associated persons" (not formed specifically for business ends).

> I am too high-born to be propertied,
> To be a secondary at control,
> Or useful serving-man and instrument
> To any sovereign state throughout the world.

He who gives himself entirely to his fellow-men appears to them useless and selfish; but he who gives himself partially to them is pronounced a benefactor and philanthropist.

How does it become a man to behave toward this American government to-day? I answer, that he cannot without disgrace be associated with it. I cannot for an instant recognize that political organization as *my* government which is the *slave's* government also.

All men recognize the right of revolution; that is, the right to refuse allegiance to, and to resist, the government, when its tyranny or its inefficiency are great and unendurable. But almost all say that such is not the case now. But such was the case, they think, in the Revolution of '75.* If one were to tell me that this was a bad government because it taxed certain foreign commodities brought to its ports, it is most probable that I should not make an ado about it, for I can do without them. All machines have their friction; and possibly this does enough good to counterbalance the evil. At any rate, it is a great evil to make a stir about it. But when the friction comes to have its machine, and oppression and robbery are organized, I say, let us not have such a machine any longer. In other words, when a sixth of the population of a nation which has undertaken to be the refuge of liberty are slaves, and a whole country is unjustly overrun and conquered by a foreign army, and subjected to military law, I think that it is not too soon for honest men to rebel and revolutionize. What makes this duty the more urgent is the fact that the country so overrun is not our own, but ours is the invading army.

Paley, a common authority with many on moral questions, in his chapter on the "Duty of Submission to Civil Government," resolves all civil obligation into expediency; and he proceeds to say, "that so long as the interest of the whole society requires it, that is, so long as the established government cannot be resisted or changed without public inconveniency, it is the will of God that the established government be obeyed, and no longer.... This principle being admitted, the justice of every particular case of resistance is reduced to a computation of the quantity of the danger and grievance on the one side, and of the probability and expense of redressing it on the other." Of this, he says, every man shall judge for himself. But Paley appears never to have contemplated those cases to which the rule of expediency does not apply, in which a people, as well as an individual, must do justice, cost what it may. If I have unjustly wrested a plank from a drowning man, I must restore it to him though I drown myself. This, according to Paley, would be inconvenient. But he that would save his life, in such a case, shall lose it. This people must cease to hold slaves, and to make war on Mexico, though it cost them their existence as a people.

10   In their practice, nations agree with Paley; but does anyone think that Massachusetts[3] does exactly what is right at the present crisis?

> A drab of state, a cloth-o'-silver slut,*
> To have her train borne up, and her soul trail in the dirt.

Practically speaking, the opponents to a reform in Massachusetts are not a hundred thousand politicians at the South, but a hundred thousand merchants and farmers here, who are more interested in commerce and agriculture than they are in humanity, and are not prepared to do justice to the slave and to Mexico, *cost what it may*. I quarrel not with far-off foes, but with those who, near at home, co-operate with, and do the bidding of, those far away, and without whom the latter would be harmless. We are accustomed to say, that the mass of men are unprepared; but improvement is slow, because the few are not materially wiser or better than the many. It is not so important that many should be as good as you, as that there be some absolute goodness somewhere; for that will leaven the whole lump. There are thousands who are *in opinion* opposed to slavery and to the war, who yet in effect do nothing to put an end to them; who, esteeming themselves children of Washington and Franklin,* sit down with their hands in their pockets, and say that they know not what to do, and do nothing; who even postpone the question of freedom to the question of free-trade,* and quietly read the prices-current along with the latest advices from Mexico, after dinner, and, it may be, fall asleep over them both. What is the price-current of an honest man and patriot to-day? They hesitate, and they regret, and sometimes they petition; but they do nothing in earnest and with effect. They will wait, well disposed, for others to remedy the evil, that they may no longer have it to regret. At most, they give only a cheap vote, and a feeble countenance and Godspeed, to the right, as it goes by them. There are nine hundred and ninety-nine patrons of virtue to one virtuous man. But it is easier to deal with the real possessor of a thing than with the temporary guardian of it.

All voting is a sort of gaming, like checkers or backgammon, with a slight moral tinge to it, a playing with right and wrong, with moral questions; and betting naturally accompanies it. The character of the voters is not staked. I cast my vote, perchance, as I think right; but I am not vitally concerned that

---

3   *Massachusetts*   Thoreau was born and raised in Concord, Massachusetts, attended Harvard University in Cambridge, Massachusetts, and then returned to Concord for much of his adult life.

that right should prevail. I am willing to leave it to the majority. Its obligation, therefore, never exceeds that of expediency. Even voting *for the right* is *doing* nothing for it. It is only expressing to men feebly your desire that it should prevail. A wise man will not leave the right to the mercy of chance, nor wish it to prevail through the power of the majority. There is but little virtue in the action of masses of men. When the majority shall at length vote for the abolition of slavery, it will be because they are indifferent to slavery, or because there is but little slavery left to be abolished by their vote. *They* will then be the only slaves. Only *his* vote can hasten the abolition of slavery who asserts his own freedom by his vote.

I hear of a convention to be held in Baltimore, or elsewhere, for the selection of a candidate for the Presidency, made up chiefly of editors, and men who are politicians by profession; but I think, what is it to any independent, intelligent, and respectable man what decision they may come to? Shall we not have the advantage of his wisdom and honesty, nevertheless? Can we not count upon some independent votes? Are there not many individuals in the country who do not attend conventions? But no: I find that the respectable man, so called, has immediately drifted from his position, and despairs of his country, when his country has more reason to despair of him. He forthwith adopts one of the candidates thus selected as the only *available* one, thus proving that he is himself *available* for any purposes of the demagogue. His vote is of no more worth than that of any unprincipled foreigner or hireling native, who may have been bought. O for a man who is a *man*, and, as my neighbor says, has a bone in his back which you cannot pass your hand through! Our statistics are at fault: the population has been returned too large. How many *men* are there to a square thousand miles in this country? Hardly one. Does not America offer any inducement for men to settle here? The American has dwindled into an Odd Fellow,—one who may be known by the development of his organ of gregariousness, and a manifest lack of intellect and cheerful self-reliance; whose first and chief concern, on coming into the world, is to see that the Almshouses are in good repair; and, before yet he has lawfully donned the virile garb, to collect a fund for the support of the widows and orphans that may be; who, in short, ventures to live only by the aid of the Mutual Insurance company, which has promised to bury him decently.

It is not a man's duty, as a matter of course, to devote himself to the eradication of any, even the most enormous wrong; he may still properly have other concerns to engage him; but it is his duty, at least, to wash his hands of it, and, if he gives it no thought longer, not to give it practically his support. If I devote myself to other pursuits and contemplations, I must first see, at least, that I do not pursue them sitting upon another man's shoulders. I must get off him first, that he may pursue his contemplations too. See what gross inconsistency is tolerated. I have heard some of my townsmen say, "I should like to have them order me out to help put down an insurrection of the slaves, or to march to Mexico;—see if I would go"; and yet these very men have each, directly by their allegiance, and so indirectly, at least, by their money, furnished a substitute. The soldier is applauded who refuses to serve in an unjust war by those who do not refuse to sustain the unjust government which makes the war; is applauded by those whose own act and authority he disregards and sets at naught; as if the state were penitent to that degree that it hired one to scourge it while it sinned, but not to that degree that it left off sinning for a moment. Thus, under the name of Order and Civil Government, we are all made at last to pay homage to and support our own meanness.* After the first blush of sin comes its indifference; and from immoral it becomes, as it were, *un*moral, and not quite unnecessary to that life which we have made.

The broadest and most prevalent error requires the most disinterested* virtue to sustain it. The slight reproach to which the virtue of patriotism is commonly liable, the noble are most likely to incur. Those who, while they disapprove of the character and measures of a government, yield to it their allegiance and support are undoubtedly its most conscientious supporters, and so frequently the most serious obstacles to reform. Some are petitioning the state to dissolve the Union, to disregard the requisitions of the President. Why do they not dissolve it themselves,—the union between themselves and the state,—and refuse to pay their quota into its treasury? Do not they stand in the same relation to the state that the state does to the Union? And have not the same reasons prevented the state from resisting the Union which have prevented them from resisting the state?

15   How can a man be satisfied to entertain an opinion merely, and enjoy *it*? Is there any enjoyment in it, if his opinion is that he is aggrieved? If you are cheated out of a single dollar by your neighbor, you do not rest satisfied with knowing that you are cheated, or with saying that you are cheated, or even with petitioning him to pay you your due; but you take effectual steps at once to obtain the full amount, and see that you are never cheated again. Action from principle, the perception and the performance of right, changes things and relations; it is essentially revolutionary, and does not consist wholly with anything which was. It not only divides states and churches, it divides families; ay, it divides the *individual*, separating the diabolical in him from the divine.

Unjust laws exist: shall we be content to obey them, or shall we endeavor to amend them, and obey them until we have succeeded, or shall we transgress them at once? Men generally, under such a government as this, think that they ought to wait until they have persuaded the majority to alter them. They think that, if they should resist, the remedy would be worse than the evil. But it is the fault of the government itself that the remedy *is* worse than the evil. *It* makes it worse. Why is it not more apt to anticipate and provide for reform? Why does it not cherish its wise minority? Why does it cry and resist before it is hurt? Why does it not encourage its citizens to be on the alert to point out its faults, and *do* better than it would have them? Why does it always crucify Christ, and excommunicate Copernicus and Luther,* and pronounce Washington and Franklin rebels?

One would think, that a deliberate and practical denial of its authority was the only offense never contemplated by government; else, why has it not assigned its definite, its suitable and proportionate penalty? If a man who has no property refuses but once to earn nine shillings for the state, he is put in prison for a period unlimited by any law that I know, and determined only by the discretion of those who placed him there; but if he should steal ninety times nine shillings from the state, he is soon permitted to go at large again.

If the injustice is part of the necessary friction of the machine of government, let it go: perchance it will wear smooth,—certainly the machine will wear out. If the injustice has a spring, or a pulley, or a rope, or a crank, exclusively for itself, then perhaps you may consider whether the remedy will not be worse than the evil; but if it is of such a nature that it requires you to be the agent of injustice to another, then, I say, break the law. Let your life be a counter friction to stop the machine. What I have to do is to see, at any rate, that I do not lend myself to the wrong which I condemn.

As for adopting the ways which the state has provided for remedying the evil, I know not of such ways. They take too much time, and a man's life will be gone. I have other affairs to attend to. I came into this world, not chiefly to make this a good place to live in, but to live in it, be it good or bad. A man has not everything to do, but something; and because he cannot do *everything*, it is not necessary that he should do *something* wrong. It is not my business to be petitioning the Governor or the Legislature any more than it is theirs to petition me; and if they should not hear my petition, what should I do then? But in this case the state has provided no way: its very Constitution is the evil. This may seem to be harsh and stubborn and unconciliatory; but it is to treat with the utmost kindness and consideration the only spirit that can appreciate or deserves it. So is all change for the better, like birth and death, which convulse the body.

I do not hesitate to say, that those who call themselves Abolitionists should at once effectually withdraw their support, both in person and property, from the government of Massachusetts, and not wait till they constitute a majority of one, before they suffer the right to prevail through them. I think that it is enough if they have God on their side, without waiting for that other one. Moreover, any man more right than his neighbors constitutes a majority of one already.

20

I meet this American government, or its representative, the state government, directly, and face to face, once a year—no more—in the person of its tax-gatherer; this is the only mode in which a man situated as I am necessarily meets it; and it then says distinctly, Recognize me; and the simplest, the most effectual, and, in the present posture of affairs, the indispensablest mode of treating with it on this head, of expressing your little satisfaction with and love for it, is to deny it then. My civil neighbor, the tax-gatherer, is the very man I have to deal with,—for it is, after all, with men and not with parchment that I quarrel,—and he has voluntarily chosen to be an agent of the government. How shall he ever know well what he is and does as an officer of the government, or as a man, until he is obliged to consider whether he shall treat me, his neighbor, for whom he has respect, as a neighbor and well-disposed man, or as a maniac and disturber of the peace, and see if he can get over this obstruction to his neighborliness without a ruder and more impetuous thought or speech corresponding with his action. I know this well, that if one thousand, if one hundred, if ten men whom I could name,—if ten *honest* men only,—ay, if *one* HONEST man, in this State of Massachusetts, *ceasing to hold slaves*, were actually to withdraw from this copartnership, and be locked up in the county jail therefore, it would be the abolition of slavery in America. For it matters not how small the beginning may seem to be: what is once well done is done forever. But we love better to talk about it: that we say is our mission. Reform keeps many scores of newspapers in its service, but not one man. If my esteemed neighbor, the State's ambassador, who will devote his days to the settlement of the question of human rights in the Council Chamber, instead of being threatened with the prisons of Carolina, were to sit down the prisoner of Massachusetts, that State which is so anxious to foist the sin of slavery upon her sister,—though at present she can discover only an act of inhospitality to be the ground of a quarrel with her,—the Legislature would not wholly waive the subject the following winter.

Under a government which imprisons any unjustly, the true place for a just man is also a prison. The proper place to-day, the only place which Massachusetts has provided for her freer and less desponding spirits, is in her prisons, to be put out and locked out of the State by her own act, as they have already put themselves out by their principles. It is there that the fugitive slave, and the Mexican prisoner on parole, and Indian come to plead the wrongs of his race should find them; on that separate, but more free and honorable ground, where the State places those who are not *with* her, but *against* her,—the only house in a slave State in which a free man can abide with honor. If any think that their influence would be lost there, and their voices no longer afflict the ear of the State, that they would not be as an enemy within its walls, they do not know by how much truth is stronger than error, nor how much more eloquently and effectively he can combat injustice who has experienced a little in his own person. Cast your whole vote, not a strip of paper merely, but your whole influence. A minority is powerless while it conforms to the majority; it is not even a minority then; but it is irresistible when it clogs by its whole weight. If the alternative is to keep all just men in prison, or give up war and slavery, the State will not hesitate which to choose. If a thousand men were not to pay their tax-bills this year, that would not be a violent and bloody measure, as it would be to pay them, and enable the State to commit violence and shed innocent blood. This is in fact, the definition of a peaceable revolution, if any such is possible. If the tax-gatherer, or any other public officer, asks me, as one has done, "But what shall I do?" my answer is, "If you really wish to do anything, resign your office." When the subject has refused allegiance, and the officer has resigned his office, then the revolution is accomplished. But even suppose blood should flow. Is there not a sort of blood shed when the conscience is wounded? Through this wound a man's real manhood and immortality flow out, and he bleeds to an everlasting death. I see this blood flowing now.

I have contemplated the imprisonment of the offender, rather than the seizure of his goods,—though both will serve the same purpose,—because they who assert the purest right, and consequently are most dangerous to a corrupt State, commonly have not spent much time in accumulating property. To such the State renders comparatively small service, and a slight tax is wont to appear exorbitant, particularly if they are obliged to earn it by special labor with their hands. If there were one who lived wholly without the use of money, the State itself would hesitate to demand it of him. But the rich man—not to make any invidious comparison—is always sold to the institution which makes him rich. Absolutely speaking, the more money, the less virtue; for money comes between a man and his objects, and obtains them for him; and it was certainly no great virtue to obtain it. It puts to rest many questions which he would otherwise be taxed to answer; while the only new question which it puts is the hard but superfluous one, how to spend it. Thus his moral ground is taken from under his feet. The opportunities of living are diminished in proportion as what are called the "means" are increased. The best thing a man can do for his culture when he is rich is to endeavor to carry out those schemes which he entertained when he was poor. Christ answered the Herodians* according to their condition. "Show me the tribute-money," said he;—and one took a penny out of his pocket;—if you use money which has the image of Caesar on it, which he has made current and valuable, that is, *if you are men of the State*, and gladly enjoy the advantages of Caesar's government, then pay him back some of his own when he demands it. "Render therefore to Caesar that which is Caesar's, and to God those things which are God's,"—leaving them no wiser than before as to which was which; for they did not wish to know.

When I converse with the freest of my neighbors, I perceive that, whatever they may say about the magnitude and seriousness of the question, and their regard for the public tranquility, the long and the short of the matter is, that they cannot spare the protection of the existing government, and they dread the consequences to their property and families of disobedience to it. For my own part, I should not like to think that I ever rely on the protection of the State. But, if I deny the authority of the State when it presents its tax-bill, it will soon take and waste all my property, and so harass me and my children without end. This is hard. This makes it impossible for a man to live honestly, and at the same time comfortably, in outward respects. It will not be worth the while to accumulate property; that would be sure to go again. You must hire or squat somewhere, and raise but a small crop, and eat that soon. You must live within yourself, and depend upon yourself always tucked up and ready for a start, and not have many affairs. A man may grow rich in Turkey even, if he will be in all respects a good subject of the Turkish government. Confucius said: "If a state is governed by the principles of reason, poverty and misery are subjects of shame; if a state is not governed by the principles of reason, riches and honors are the subjects of shame." No: until I want the protection of Massachusetts to be extended to me in some distant Southern port, where my liberty is endangered, or until I am bent solely on building up an estate at home by peaceful enterprise, I can afford to refuse allegiance to Massachusetts, and her right to my property and life. It costs me less in every sense to incur the penalty of disobedience to the State than it would to obey. I should feel as if I were worth less in that case.

25   Some years ago, the State met me in behalf of the Church, and commanded me to pay a certain sum toward the support of a clergyman whose preaching my father attended, but never I myself. "Pay," it said, "or be locked up in the jail." I declined to pay. But unfortunately, another man saw fit to pay it. I did not see why the schoolmaster should be taxed to support the priest, and not the priest the schoolmaster; for I was not the State's schoolmaster, but I supported myself by voluntary subscription. I did not see why the lyceum should not present its tax-bill, and have the State to back its demand, as well as the Church. However, at the request of the selectmen, I condescended to make some such statement as this in writing:—"Know all men by these presents, that I, Henry Thoreau, do not wish to be regarded as a member of any incorporated society which I have not joined." This I gave to the town clerk; and he has it. The State, having thus learned that I did not wish to be regarded as a member of that church, has never made a like demand on me since; though it said that it must adhere to its original presumption that time. If I had known how to name them, I should then have signed off in detail from all the societies which I never signed on to; but I did not know where to find a complete list.

I have paid no poll-tax for six years. I was put into a jail on this account, for one night; and, as I stood considering the walls of solid stone, two or three feet thick, the door of wood and iron, a foot thick, and the iron grating which strained the light, I could not help being struck with the foolishness of that institution which treated me as if I were mere flesh and blood and bones, to be locked up. I wondered that it should have concluded at length that this was the best use it could put me to, and had never thought to avail itself of my services in some way. I saw that, if there was a wall of stone between me and my towns-men, there was a still more difficult one to climb or break through before they could get to be as free as I was. I did not for a moment feel confined, and walls seemed a great waste of stone and mortar. I felt as if I alone of all my townsmen had paid my tax. They plainly did not know how to treat me, but behaved like persons who are underbred. In every threat and in every compliment there was a blunder; for they thought that my chief desire was to stand the other side of that stone wall. I could not but smile to see how industriously they locked the door on my meditations, which followed them out again without let or hindrance, and *they* were really all that was dangerous. As they could not reach me, they had resolved to punish my body; just as boys, if they cannot come at some person against whom they have a spite, will abuse his dog. I saw that the State was halfwitted, that it was timid as a lone woman with her silver spoons, and that it did not know its friends from its foes, and I lost all my remaining respect for it, and pitied it.

Thus the State never intentionally confronts a man's sense, intellectual or moral, but only his body, his senses. It is not armed with superior wit or honesty, but with superior physical strength. I was not born to be forced. I will breathe after my own fashion. Let us see who is the strongest. What force has a multitude? They only can force me who obey a higher law than I. They force me to become like themselves. I do not hear of *men* being *forced* to live this way or that by masses of men. What sort of life were that to live? When I meet a government which says to me, "Your money or your life," why should I be in haste to give it my money? It may be in a great strait, and not know what to do: I cannot help that. It must help itself; do as I do. It is not worth the while to snivel about it. I am not responsible for the successful working of the machin-ery of society. I am not the son of the engineer. I perceive that, when an acorn and a chestnut fall side by side, the one does not remain inert to make way for the other, but both obey their own laws, and spring and grow and flourish as best they can, till one, perchance, overshadows and destroys the other. If a plant cannot live according to its nature, it dies; and so a man.

The night in prison was novel and interesting enough. The prisoners in their shirt-sleeves were enjoying a chat and the evening air in the doorway, when I entered. But the jailer said, "Come, boys, it is time to lock up"; and so they dispersed, and I heard the sound of their steps returning into the hollow apartments. My room-mate was introduced to me by the jailer as "a first-rate fellow and a clever man." When the door was locked, he showed me where to hang my hat, and how he managed matters there. The rooms were whitewashed once a month, and this one, at least, was the whitest, most simply furnished, and probably the neatest apartment in the town. He naturally wanted to know where I came from, and what brought me there; and, when I had told him, I asked in my turn how he came there, presuming him to be an honest man, of course; and, as the world goes, I believe he was. "Why," said he, "they accuse me of burning a barn; but I never did it." As near as I could discover, he had probably gone to bed in a barn when drunk, and smoked his pipe there; and so a barn was burnt. He had the reputation of being a clever man, and been there some three months waiting for his trial to come on, and would have to wait as much longer; but he was quite domesticated and contented, since he got his board for nothing, and thought that he was well treated.

He occupied one window, and I the other; and I saw that if one stayed there long, his principal business would be to look out the window. I had soon read all the tracts that were left there, and examined where former prisoners had broken out, and where a grate had been sawed off, and heard the history of the various occupants of that room; for I found that even here there was a history and a gossip which never circulated beyond the walls of the jail. Probably this is the only house in the town where verses are composed, which are afterward printed in a circular form, but not published. I was shown quite a long list of verses which were composed by some young men who had been detected in an attempt to escape, who avenged themselves by singing them.

30   I pumped my fellow-prisoner as dry as I could, for fear I should never see him again; but at length he showed me which was my bed, and left me to blow out the lamp.

It was like traveling into a far country, such as I had never expected to behold, to lie there for one night. It seemed to me that I never had heard the town-clock strike before, nor the evening sounds of the village; for we slept with the windows open, which were inside the grating. It was to see my native village in the light of the Middle Ages, and our Concord was turned into a Rhine stream,* and visions of knights and castles passed before me. They were the voices of old burghers that I heard in the streets. I was an involuntary spectator and auditor of whatever was done and said in the kitchen of the adjacent village-inn,—a wholly new and rare experience to me. It was a closer view of my native town. I was fairly inside of it. I never had seen its institutions before. This is one of its peculiar institutions; for it is a shire town. I began to comprehend what its inhabitants were about.

In the morning, our breakfasts were put through the hole in the door, in small oblong-square tin pans, made to fit, and holding a pint of chocolate, with brown bread, and an iron spoon. When they called for the vessels again, I was green enough to return what bread I had left; but my comrade seized it, and said that I should lay that up for lunch or dinner. Soon after he was let out to work at haying in a neighboring field, whither he went every day, and would not be back till noon; so he bade me good-day, saying that he doubted if he should see me again.

When I came out of prison,—for someone interfered, and paid that tax,—I did not perceive that great changes had taken place on the common, such as he observed who went in a youth and emerged a tottering and gray-haired man; and yet a change had to my eyes come over the scene,—the town, and State, and country,—greater than any that mere time could effect. I saw yet more distinctly the State in which I lived. I saw to what extent the people among whom I lived could be trusted as good neighbors and friends; that their friendship was for summer weather only; that they did not greatly propose to do right; that they were a distinct race from me by their prejudices and superstitions, as the Chinamen and Malays are; that in their sacrifices to humanity they ran no risks, not even to their property; that after all they were not so noble but they treated the thief as he had treated them, and hoped, by a certain outward observance and a few prayers, and by walking in a particular straight though useless path from time to time, to save their souls. This may be to judge my neighbors harshly; for I believe that many of them are not aware that they have such an institution as the jail in their village.

It was formerly the custom in our village, when a poor debtor came out of jail, for his acquaintances to salute him, looking through their fingers, which were crossed to represent the grating of a jail window, "How do ye do?" My neighbors did not thus salute me, but first looked at me, and then at one another, as if I had returned from a long journey. I was put into jail as I was going to the shoemaker's to get a shoe which was mended. When I was let out the next morning, I proceeded to finish my errand, and, having put on my mended shoe, joined a huckleberry party, who were impatient to put themselves under my conduct; and in half an hour,—for the horse was soon tackled,—was in the midst of a huckleberry field, on one of our highest hills, two miles off, and then the State was nowhere to be seen.

This is the whole history of "My Prisons."

35

I have never declined paying the highway tax, because I am as desirous of being a good neighbor as I am of being a bad subject; and as for supporting schools, I am doing my part to educate my fellow-countrymen now. It is for no particular item in the tax-bill that I refuse to pay it. I simply wish to refuse allegiance to the State, to withdraw and stand aloof from it effectually. I do not care to trace the course of my dollar, if I could, till it buys a man or a musket to shoot one with,—the dollar is innocent,—but I am concerned to trace the effects of my allegiance. In fact, I quietly declare war with the State, after my fashion, though I will still make what use and get what advantage of her I can, as is usual in such cases.

If others pay the tax which is demanded of me, from a sympathy with the State, they do but what they have already done in their own case, or rather they abet injustice to a greater extent than the State requires. If they pay the tax from a mistaken interest in the individual taxed, to save his property, or prevent his going to jail, it is because they have not considered wisely how far they let their private feelings interfere with the public good.

This, then, is my position at present. But one cannot be too much on his guard in such a case, lest his action be biased by obstinacy or an undue regard for the opinions of men. Let him see that he does only what belong to himself and to the hour.

I think sometimes, Why, this people mean well, they are only ignorant; they would do better if they knew how: why give your neighbors this pain to treat you as they are not inclined to? But I think again, This is no reason why I should do as they do, or permit others to suffer much greater pain of a different kind. Again I sometimes say to myself, When many millions of men, without heat,[4] without ill will, without personal feeling of any kind, demand of you a few shillings only, without the possibility, such is their constitution, of retracting or altering their present demand, and without the possibility, on your side, of appeal to any other millions, why expose yourself to this overwhelming brute force? You do not resist cold and hunger, the winds and the waves, thus obstinately; you quietly submit to a thousand similar necessities. You do not put your head into the fire. But just in proportion as I regard this as not wholly a brute force, but partly a human force, and consider that I have relations to those millions as to so many millions of men, and not of mere brute or inanimate things, I see that appeal is possible, first and instantaneously, from them to the Maker of them, and, secondly, from them to themselves. But if I put my head deliberately into the fire, there is no appeal to fire or to the Maker of fire, and I have only myself to blame. If I could convince myself that I have any right to be satisfied with men as they are, and to treat them accordingly, and not according, in some respects, to my requisitions and expectations of what they and I ought to be, then, like a good Mussulman* and fatalist, I should endeavor to be satisfied with things as they are, and say it is the will of God. And, above all, there is this difference between resisting this

---

4 *heat* Anger.

and a purely brute or natural force, that I can resist this with some effect; but I cannot expect, like Orpheus,* to change the nature of the rocks and trees and beasts.

I do not wish to quarrel with any man or nation. I do not wish to split 40 hairs, to make fine distinctions, or set myself up as better than my neighbors. I seek rather, I may say, even an excuse for conforming to the laws of the land. I am but too ready to conform to them. Indeed, I have reason to suspect myself on this head; and each year, as the tax-gatherer comes round, I find myself disposed to review the acts and position of the general and State governments, and the spirit of the people, to discover a pretext for conformity.

> We must affect our country as our parents,
> And if at any time we alienate
> Our love or industry from doing it honor,
> We must respect effects and teach the soul
> Matter of conscience and religion,
> And not desire of rule or benefit.

I believe that the State will soon be able to take all my work of this sort out of my hands, and then I shall be no better a patriot than my fellow-countrymen. Seen from a lower point of view, the Constitution, with all its faults, is very good; and the law and the courts are very respectable; even this State and this American government are, in many respects, very admirable, and rare things, to be thankful for, such as a great many have described them; but seen from a point of view a little higher, they are what I have described them; seen from a higher still, and the highest, who shall say what they are, or that they are worth looking at or thinking of at all?

However, the government does not concern me much, and I shall bestow the fewest possible thoughts on it. It is not many moments that I live under a government, even in this world. If a man is thought-free, fancy-free, imagination-free, that which *is not* never for a long time appearing *to be* to him, unwise rulers or reformers cannot fatally interrupt him.

I know that most men think differently from myself; but those whose lives are by profession devoted to the study of these or kindred subjects content me as little as any. Statesmen and legislators, standing so completely within the institution, never distinctly and nakedly behold it. They speak of moving society, but have no resting-place without it. They may be men of a certain experience and discrimination, and have no doubt invented ingenious and even useful systems, for which we sincerely thank them; but all their wit and usefulness lie within certain not very wide limits. They are wont to forget that the world is not governed by policy and expediency. Webster[5] never goes behind government, and so cannot speak with authority about it. His words are wisdom to those legislators who contemplate no essential reform in the existing government; but for thinkers, and those who legislate for all time, he never once glances at the subject. I know of those whose serene and wise speculations on this theme would soon reveal the limits of his mind's range and hospitality. Yet compared with the cheap professions of most reformers, and the still cheaper wisdom and eloquence of politicians in general, his are almost the only sensible and valuable words, and we thank Heaven for him. Comparatively, he is always strong, original, and, above all, practical. Still, his quality is not wisdom, but prudence. The lawyer's truth is not Truth, but consistency or a consistent expediency. Truth is always in harmony with herself, and is not concerned chiefly to reveal the justice that may consist with wrong-doing. He well deserves to be called, as he has been called, the Defender of the Constitution. There are really no blows to be given by him but defensive ones. He is not a leader, but a follower. His leaders are the men of '87. "I have never made an effort," he says, "and never propose to make an effort; I have never countenanced an effort, and never mean to countenance an effort, to disturb the arrangement as originally made, by which the various States came into the union." Still thinking of the sanction which the Constitution gives to slavery, he says, "Because it was a part of the original compact,—let it stand." Notwithstanding his special acuteness and ability, he is unable to take a fact out of its merely political relations, and behold it as it lies absolutely to be disposed of by the intellect,—what, for instance, it behooves a man to do here in America to-day with regard to slavery,—but ventures, or is driven, to make some such desperate answer as the following, while professing to speak absolutely, and as a private man,—from which what new and singular code of social duties might be inferred? "The manner," says he, "in which the governments of those States where slavery exists are to regulate it is for their own consideration, under their responsibility to their constituents, to the general laws of propriety, humanity, and justice, and to God. Associations formed elsewhere, springing from a feeling of humanity, or any other cause, have nothing whatever to do with it. They have never received any encouragement from me, and they never will."

They who know of no purer sources of truth, who have traced up its stream no higher, stand, and wisely stand, by the Bible and the Constitution, and drink at it there with reverence and humility; but they who behold where it comes trickling into this lake or that pool, gird up their loins once more, and continue their pilgrimage toward its fountain-head.

---

5   *Webster*   Daniel Webster (1782–1852), one of the great politicians of the mid-nineteenth century.

No man with a genius for legislation has appeared in America. They are rare in the history of the world. There are orators, politicians, and eloquent men, by the thousand; but the speaker has not yet opened his mouth to speak who is capable of settling the much-vexed questions of the day. We love eloquence for its own sake, and not for any truth which it may utter, or any heroism it may inspire. Our legislators have not yet learned the comparative value of free-trade and of freedom, of union, and of rectitude, to a nation. They have no genius or talent for comparatively humble questions of taxation and finance, commerce and manufactures and agriculture. If we were left solely to the wordy wit of legislators in Congress for our guidance, uncorrected by the seasonable experience and the effectual complaints of the people, America would not long retain her rank among the nations. For eighteen hundred years, though perchance I have no right to say it, the New Testament has been written; yet where is the legislator who has wisdom and practical talent enough to avail himself of the light which it sheds on the science of legislation?

The authority of government, even such as I am willing to submit to,—for I will cheerfully obey those who know and can do better than I, and in many things even those who neither know nor can do so well,—is still an impure one: to be strictly just, it must have the sanctions and consent of the governed. It can have no pure right over my person and property but what I concede to it. The progress from an absolute to a limited monarchy, from a limited monarchy to a democracy, is a progress toward a true respect for the individual. Even the Chinese philosopher was wise enough to regard the individual as the basis of the empire. Is a democracy, such as we know it, the last improvement possible in government? Is it not possible to take a step further towards recognizing and organizing the rights of man? There will never be a really free and enlightened State until the State comes to recognize the individual as a higher and independent power, from which all its own power and authority are derived, and treats him accordingly. I please myself with imagining a State at last which can afford to be just to all men, and to treat the individual with respect as a neighbor; which even would not think it inconsistent with its own repose if a few were to live aloof from it, not meddling with it, nor embraced by it, who fulfilled all the duties of neighbors and fellow-men. A State which bore this kind of fruit, and suffered it to drop off as fast as it ripened, would prepare the way for a still more perfect and glorious State, which also I have imagined, but not yet anywhere seen.

45

(1848)

FREDERICK DOUGLASS

from FOURTH OF JULY ORATION[1]

By the early 1850s Douglass was among the best-known figures in the abolitionist movement. Now living as a free man in Rochester, New York, he had become a newspaper publisher and editor, founding the North Star *to further the cause of abolition (and to promote the cause of freedom more generally). He had also become very involved in the local community (working, for example, to end segregation in Rochester's public schools), and in 1852 he was invited by the Rochester Ladies' Anti-Slavery Society to deliver a speech to the citizenry of Rochester, as part of the local Independence Day celebrations. A substantial excerpt from the address appears here; the full speech is over 10,000 words long.*

The papers and placards say that I am to deliver a 4th of July oration....

This, for the purpose of this celebration, is the 4th of July.[2] It is the birthday of your National Independence, and of your political freedom.... This celebration also marks the beginning of another year of your national life; and reminds you that the Republic of America is now 76 years old....

Fellow Citizens, I am not wanting in respect for the fathers of this republic. The signers of the Declaration of Independence were brave men. They were great men too—great enough to give fame to a great age.... The point from which I am compelled to view them is not, certainly, the most favorable; and yet I cannot contemplate their great deeds with less than admiration. They were statesmen, patriots and heroes, and for the good they did, and the principles they contended for, I will unite with you to honor their memory....

---

1   *Fourth of July Oration*   Douglass did not give the speech a title; it is often referred to as "What to the Slave Is The Fourth of July," and often, in excerpted form, given the title "The Hypocrisy of American Slavery."

2   *for the purpose of this celebration, is the 4th of July*   Though the address was part of the Independence Day festivities, it was delivered on the 5th of July rather than the 4th.

They were peace men; but they preferred revolution to peaceful submission to bondage. They were quiet men; but they did not shrink from agitating against oppression. They showed forbearance; but that they knew its limits. They believed in order; but not in the order of tyranny. With them, nothing was "settled" that was not right. With them, justice, liberty and humanity were "final"; not slavery and oppression. You may well cherish the memory of such men. They were great in their day and generation....

Friends and citizens, I need not enter further into the causes which led to this anniversary. Many of you understand them better than I do.... The causes which led to the separation of the colonies from the British crown* have never lacked for a tongue. They have all been taught in your common schools, narrated at your firesides, unfolded from your pulpits, and thundered from your legislative halls, and are as familiar to you as household words. They form the staple of your national poetry and eloquence.

I remember, also, that, as a people, Americans are remarkably familiar with all facts which make in their own favor. This is esteemed by some as a national trait—perhaps a national weakness. It is a fact, that whatever makes for the wealth or for the reputation of Americans (and can be had cheap!) will be found by Americans. I shall not be charged with slandering Americans, if I say I think the American side of any question may be safely left in American hands.

I leave, therefore, the great deeds of your fathers to other gentlemen whose claim to have been regularly descended will be less likely to be disputed than mine!

My business, if I have any here to-day, is with the present. The accepted time with God and his cause is the ever-living now....

Fellow-citizens, pardon me, allow me to ask, why am I called upon to speak here to-day? What have I, or those I represent, to do with your national independence? Are the great principles of political freedom and of natural justice, embodied in that Declaration of Independence, extended to us? And am I, therefore, called upon to bring our humble offering to the national altar, and to confess the benefits and express devout gratitude for the blessings resulting from your independence to us?

Would to God, both for your sakes and ours, that an affirmative answer could be truthfully returned to these questions! Then would my task be light, and my burden easy and delightful....

But, such is not the state of the case. I say it with a sad sense of the disparity between us. I am not included within the pale* of this glorious anniversary! Your high independence only reveals the immeasurable distance between us. The blessings in which you, this day, rejoice, are not enjoyed in common.—The rich inheritance of justice, liberty, prosperity and independence, bequeathed by your fathers, is shared by you, not by me. The sunlight that brought life and healing to you, has brought stripes and death to me. This Fourth [of] July is yours, not mine. You may rejoice, I must mourn. To drag a man in fetters into the grand illuminated temple of liberty, and call upon him to join you in joyous anthems, were inhuman mockery and sacrilegious irony. Do you mean, citizens, to mock me, by asking me to speak to-day? ...

Fellow-citizens; above your national, tumultuous joy, I hear the mournful wail of millions! whose chains, heavy and grievous yesterday, are, to-day, rendered more intolerable by the jubilee shouts that reach them.... My subject, then fellow-citizens, is American slavery. I shall see, this day, and its popular characteristics, from the slave's point of view. Standing, there, identified with the American bondman, making his wrongs mine, I do not hesitate to declare, with all my soul, that the character and conduct of this nation never looked blacker to me than on this 4th of July! Whether we turn to the declarations of the past, or to the professions of the present, the conduct of the nation seems equally hideous and revolting. America is false to the past, false to the present, and solemnly binds herself to be false to the future....

But I fancy I hear some one of my audience say, it is just in this circumstance that you and your brother abolitionists fail to make a favorable impression on the public mind. Would you argue more, and denounce less, would you persuade more, and rebuke less, your cause would be much more likely to succeed. But, I submit, where all is plain there is nothing to be argued. What point in the anti-slavery creed would you have me argue? On what branch of the subject do the people of this country need light? Must I undertake to prove that the slave is a man? That point is conceded already. Nobody doubts it. The slaveholders themselves acknowledge it in the enactment of laws for their government. They acknowledge it when they punish disobedience on the part of the slave. There are seventy-two crimes in the State of Virginia, which, if committed by a black man, (no matter how ignorant he be), subject him to the punishment of death; while only two of the same crimes will subject a white man to the like punishment. What is this but the acknowledgement that the slave is a moral, intellectual and responsible being? The manhood of the slave is conceded. It is admitted in the fact that Southern statute books are covered with enactments forbidding, under severe fines and penalties, the teaching of the slave to read or to write. When you can point to any such laws, in reference to the beasts of the field, then I may consent to argue the manhood of the slave. When the dogs in your streets, when the fowls of the air, when the cattle on your hills, when the fish of the sea, and the reptiles that crawl, shall be unable to distinguish the slave from a brute, then will I argue with you that the slave is a man!...

Would you have me argue that man is entitled to liberty? That he is the rightful owner of his own body? You have already declared it.... What, am I to argue that it is wrong to make men brutes, to rob them of their liberty, to work them without wages, to keep them ignorant of their relations to their fellow men, to beat them with sticks, to flay their flesh with the lash, to load their limbs with irons, to hunt them with dogs, to sell them at auction, to sunder their families, to knock out their teeth, to burn their flesh, to starve them into obedience and submission to their masters? Must I argue that a system thus marked with blood, and stained with pollution, is wrong? No! I will not. I have better employments for my time and strength than such arguments would imply.

What, then, remains to be argued? Is it that slavery is not divine; that God did not establish it; that our doctors of divinity are mistaken? ... The time for such argument is passed.

At a time like this, scorching irony, not convincing argument, is needed. O! had I the ability, and could I reach the nation's ear, I would, to-day, pour out a fiery stream of biting ridicule, blasting reproach, withering sarcasm, and stern rebuke. For it is not light that is needed, but fire; it is not the gentle shower, but thunder. We need the storm, the whirlwind, and the earthquake. The feeling of the nation must be quickened; the conscience of the nation must be roused; the propriety of the nation must be startled; the hypocrisy of the nation must be exposed; and its crimes against God and man must be proclaimed and denounced.

What, to the American slave, is your 4th of July? I answer: a day that reveals to him, more than all other days in the year, the gross injustice and cruelty to which he is the constant victim. To him, your celebration is a sham; your boasted liberty, an unholy license; your national greatness, swelling vanity; your sounds of rejoicing are empty and heartless; your denunciations of tyrants, brass fronted impudence; your shouts of liberty and equality, hollow mockery; your prayers and hymns, your sermons and thanksgivings, with all your religious parade, and solemnity, are, to him, mere bombast, fraud, deception, impiety, and hypocrisy—a thin veil to cover up crimes which would disgrace a nation of savages. There is not a nation on the earth guilty of practices, more shocking and bloody, than are the people of these United States, at this very hour.

Go where you may, search where you will, roam through all the monarchies and despotisms of the old world, travel through South America, search out every abuse, and when you have found the last, lay your facts by the side of the everyday practices of this nation, and you will say with me, that, for revolting barbarity and shameless hypocrisy, America reigns without a rival.

Take the American slave-trade, which, we are told by the papers, is especially prosperous just now.... This trade is one of the peculiarities of American institutions. It is carried on in all the large towns and cities in one-half of this confederacy; and millions are pocketed every year, by dealers in this horrid traffic. In several states, this trade is a chief source of wealth. It is called (in contradistinction to the foreign slave-trade) "the internal slave trade." It is, probably, called so, too, in order to divert from it the horror with which the foreign slave-trade is contemplated. That trade has long since been denounced by this government, as piracy.... Everywhere, in this country, it is safe to speak of this foreign slave-trade, as a most inhuman traffic, opposed alike to the laws of God and of man.... It is, however, a notable fact that, while so much execration is poured out by Americans upon those engaged in the foreign slave-trade, the men engaged in the slave-trade between the states pass without condemnation, and their business is deemed honorable.

20   Behold the practical operation of this internal slave-trade, the American slave-trade, sustained by American politics and American religion. Here you will see men and women reared like swine for the market. You know what is a swine-drover? I will show you a man-drover. They inhabit all our Southern States. They perambulate the country, and crowd the highways of the nation, with droves of human stock. You will see one of these human flesh-jobbers, armed with pistol, whip and bowie-knife, driving a company of a hundred men, women, and children, from the Potomac* to the slave market at New Orleans. These wretched people are to be sold singly, or in lots, to suit purchasers. They are food for the cotton-field, and the deadly sugar-mill. Mark the sad procession, as it moves wearily along, and the inhuman wretch who drives them. Hear his savage yells and his blood-chilling oaths, as he hurries on his affrighted captives! There, see the old man, with locks thinned and gray. Cast one glance, if you please, upon that young mother, whose shoulders are bare to the scorching sun, her briny tears falling on the brow of the babe in her arms. See, too, that girl of thirteen, weeping, yes! weeping, as she thinks of the mother from whom she has been torn! The drove moves tardily. Heat and sorrow have nearly consumed their strength; suddenly you hear a quick snap, like the discharge of a rifle; the fetters clank, and the chain rattles simultaneously; your ears are saluted with a scream, that seems to have torn its way to the center of your soul! The crack you heard, was the sound of the slave-whip; the scream you heard, was from the woman you saw with the babe. Her speed had faltered under the weight of her child and her chains! that gash on her shoulder tells her to move on. Follow the drove to New Orleans. Attend the auction; see men examined like horses; see the forms of women rudely and brutally exposed to the shocking gaze of American slave-buyers. See this drove sold and separated forever; and never forget the deep, sad sobs that arose from that scattered multitude. Tell me citizens, *where*, under the sun, you can witness a spectacle more fiendish and shocking. Yet this is but a glance at the American slave-trade, as it exists, at this moment, in the ruling part of the United States....

But the church of this country is not only indifferent to the wrongs of the slave, it actually takes sides with the oppressors.... Many of its most eloquent Divines, who stand as the very lights of the church, have shamelessly given the sanction of religion and the Bible to the whole slave system. They have taught that man may, properly, be a slave; that the relation of master and slave is ordained of God; that to send back an escaped bondman to his master is clearly the duty of all the followers of the Lord Jesus Christ; and this horrible blasphemy is palmed off upon the world for Christianity.

For my part, I would say, welcome infidelity! welcome atheism! welcome anything! in preference to the gospel, as preached by those Divines! … [It is] a religion which favors the rich against the poor; which exalts the proud above the humble; which divides mankind into two classes, tyrants and slaves; which says to the man in chains, stay there; and to the oppressor, oppress on; it is a religion which may be professed and enjoyed by all the robbers and enslavers of mankind; it makes God a respecter of persons,[3] denies his fatherhood of the race, and tramples in the dust the great truth of the brotherhood of man.…

I have detained my audience entirely too long already. At some future period I will gladly avail myself of an opportunity to give this subject a full and fair discussion.

Allow me to say, in conclusion, notwithstanding the dark picture I have this day presented of the state of the nation, I do not despair of this country. There are forces in operation, which must inevitably work the downfall of slavery. "The arm of the Lord is not shortened,"* and the doom of slavery is certain. I, therefore, leave off where I began, with hope. While drawing encouragement from the Declaration of Independence, the great principles it contains, and the genius of American Institutions, my spirit is also cheered by the obvious tendencies of the age. Nations do not now stand in the same relation to each other that they did ages ago. No nation can now shut itself up from the surrounding world, and trot round in the same old path of its fathers without interference. The time was when such could be done. Long established customs of hurtful character could formerly fence themselves in, and do their evil work with social impunity. Knowledge was then confined and enjoyed by the privileged few, and the multitude walked on in mental darkness. But a change has now come over the affairs of mankind. Walled cities and empires have become unfashionable. The arm of commerce has borne away the gates of the strong city. Intelligence is penetrating the darkest corners of the globe. It makes its pathway over and under the sea, as well as on the earth. Wind, steam, and lightning are its chartered agents. Oceans no longer divide, but link nations together. From Boston to London is now a holiday excursion. Space is comparatively annihilated. Thoughts expressed on one side of the Atlantic, are distinctly heard on the other. The far off and almost fabulous Pacific rolls in grandeur at our feet.…

(1852)

---

3   *respecter of persons*   In Acts 10.34, Peter claims that "God is no respecter of persons," i.e., that he does not favor people of higher status.

CHARLES DARWIN

from ON THE ORIGIN OF SPECIES BY MEANS OF NATURAL SELECTION

The 1859 publication of Darwin's On the Origin of Species *is a landmark in the history of ideas as it is in the history of science. From ancient Greece to the early nineteenth century, many had suggested that life as we know it had evolved over time (though others denied that there had been any change in species since their creation). The theory of natural selection, however, was the first detailed, cogent, and plausible theory as to how the mechanism of evolution operates. Its impact on many aspects of Western thought—from belief in divine creation to views regarding the relationship between humans and other living beings—was tremendous. In the excerpts included here, Darwin outlines some of the background to the development of his theory, and some of its key precepts.*

INTRODUCTION

When on board H.M.S. "Beagle," as naturalist,[1] I was much struck with certain facts in the distribution of the inhabitants of South America, and in the geological relations of the present to the past inhabitants of that continent. These facts seemed to me to throw some light on the origin of species—that mystery of mysteries, as it has been called by one of our greatest philosophers. On my return home, it occurred to me, in 1837, that something might perhaps be made out on this question by patiently accumulating and reflecting on all sorts of facts which could possibly have any bearing on it. After five years' work I allowed myself to speculate on the subject, and drew up some short notes; these I enlarged in 1844 into a sketch of the conclusions, which then seemed to me probable: from that period to the present day I have steadily pursued the same object. I hope that I may be excused for entering on these personal details, as I give them to show that I have not been hasty in coming to a decision.

---

1   *When on board ... naturalist*   Darwin traveled on the *Beagle* between 1831 and 1836.

My work is now nearly finished; but as it will take me two or three more years to complete it, and as my health is far from strong, I have been urged to publish this abstract. I have more especially been induced to do this, as Mr. Wallace,[2] who is now studying the natural history of the Malay archipelago, has arrived at almost exactly the same general conclusions that I have on the origin of species. Last year he sent to me a memoir* on this subject, with a request that I would forward it to Sir Charles Lyell,[3] who sent it to the Linnean Society,[4] and it is published in the third volume of the Journal of that Society. Sir C. Lyell and Dr. Hooker,[5] who both knew of my work—the latter having read my sketch of 1844—honored me by thinking it advisable to publish, with Mr. Wallace's excellent memoir, some brief extracts from my manuscripts.

This abstract, which I now publish, must necessarily be imperfect. I cannot here give references and authorities for my several statements; and I must trust to the reader reposing some confidence in my accuracy. No doubt errors will have crept in, though I hope I have always been cautious in trusting to good authorities alone. I can here give only the general conclusions at which I have arrived, with a few facts in illustration, but which, I hope, in most cases will suffice. No one can feel more sensible than I do of the necessity of hereafter publishing in detail all the facts, with references, on which my conclusions have been grounded; and I hope in a future work to do this. For I am well aware that scarcely a single point is discussed in this volume on which facts cannot be adduced,[6] often apparently leading to conclusions directly opposite to those at which I have arrived. A fair result can be obtained only by fully stating and balancing the facts and arguments on both sides of each question; and this cannot possibly be here done.

I much regret that want of space prevents my having the satisfaction of acknowledging the generous assistance which I have received from very many naturalists, some of them personally unknown to me. I cannot, however, let this opportunity pass without expressing my deep obligations to Dr. Hooker, who for the last fifteen years has aided me in every possible way by his large stores of knowledge and his excellent judgment.

In considering the origin of species, it is quite conceivable that a naturalist, reflecting on the mutual affinities of organic beings, on their embryological relations, their geographical distribution, geological succession, and other such

5

---

2   *Mr. Wallace*   Alfred Russel Wallace (1823–1913), English naturalist and social critic. Though it was Darwin who developed the theory at length and in detail, Wallace is credited as a co-discoverer of the theory of natural selection.

3   *Sir Charles Lyell*   British geologist (1797–1875).

4   *Linnean Society*   Prominent London scientific society.

5   *Dr. Hooker*   Joseph Dalton Hooker (1817–1911), botanist and friend of Darwin.

6   *adduced*   Brought forth.

facts, might come to the conclusion that each species had not been independently created, but had descended, like varieties, from other species. Nevertheless, such a conclusion, even if well founded, would be unsatisfactory, until it could be shown how the innumerable species inhabiting this world have been modified, so as to acquire that perfection of structure and coadaptation which most justly excites our admiration. Naturalists continually refer to external conditions, such as climate, food, *et cetera*, as the only possible cause of variation. In one very limited sense, as we shall hereafter see, this may be true; but it is preposterous to attribute to mere external conditions, the structure, for instance, of the woodpecker, with its feet, tail, beak, and tongue, so admirably adapted to catch insects under the bark of trees. In the case of the mistletoe, which draws its nourishment from certain trees, which has seeds that must be transported by certain birds, and which has flowers with separate sexes absolutely requiring the agency of certain insects to bring pollen from one flower to the other, it is equally preposterous to account for the structure of this parasite, with its relations to several distinct organic beings, by the effects of external conditions, or of habit, or of the volition of the plant itself.

The author of the "Vestiges of Creation"[7] would, I presume, say that, after a certain unknown number of generations, some bird had given birth to a woodpecker, and some plant to the mistletoe, and that these had been produced perfect as we now see them; but this assumption seems to me to be no explanation, for it leaves the case of the co-adaptations of organic beings to each other and to their physical conditions of life, untouched and unexplained.

It is, therefore, of the highest importance to gain a clear insight into the means of modification and coadaptation. At the commencement of my observations it seemed to me probable that a careful study of domesticated animals and of cultivated plants would offer the best chance of making out this obscure problem. Nor have I been disappointed; in this and in all other perplexing cases I have invariably found that our knowledge, imperfect though it be, of variation under domestication, afforded the best and safest clue. I may venture to express my conviction of the high value of such studies, although they have been very commonly neglected by naturalists.

From these considerations, I shall devote the first chapter of this abstract to variation under domestication. We shall thus see that a large amount of hereditary modification is at least possible, and, what is equally or more important, we shall see how great is the power of man in accumulating by his selection successive slight variations. I will then pass on to the variability of species in a state of nature; but I shall, unfortunately, be compelled to treat this subject

---

7   *"Vestiges of Creation"*   1844 book, published anonymously but written by Robert Chambers, which suggests that progressive evolution is God's act of creation through geological time.

far too briefly, as it can be treated properly only by giving long catalogues of facts. We shall, however, be enabled to discuss what circumstances are most favorable to variation. In the next chapter the struggle for existence amongst all organic beings throughout the world, which inevitably follows from their high geometrical ratio of increase, will be treated of. This is the doctrine of Malthus,[8] applied to the whole animal and vegetable kingdoms. As many more individuals of each species are born than can possibly survive; and as, consequently, there is a frequently recurring struggle for existence, it follows that any being, if it vary however slightly in any manner profitable to itself, under the complex and sometimes varying conditions of life, will have a better chance of surviving, and thus be *naturally selected*. From the strong principle of inheritance, any selected variety will tend to propagate its new and modified form.

This fundamental subject of natural selection will be treated at some length in the fourth chapter; and we shall then see how natural selection almost inevitably causes much extinction of the less improved forms of life and induces what I have called divergence of character. In the next chapter I shall discuss the complex and little known laws of variation and of correlation of growth. In the four succeeding chapters, the most apparent and gravest difficulties on the theory will be given: namely, first, the difficulties of transitions, or in understanding how a simple being or a simple organ can be changed and perfected into a highly developed being or elaborately constructed organ; secondly the subject of instinct, or the mental powers of animals, thirdly, hybridism, or the infertility of species and the fertility of varieties when intercrossed; and fourthly, the imperfection of the geological record. In the next chapter I shall consider the geological succession of organic beings throughout time; in the eleventh and twelfth, their geographical distribution throughout space; in the thirteenth, their classification or mutual affinities, both when mature and in an embryonic condition. In the last chapter I shall give a brief recapitulation of the whole work, and a few concluding remarks.

No one ought to feel surprise at much remaining as yet unexplained in regard to the origin of species and varieties, if he makes due allowance for our profound ignorance in regard to the mutual relations of all the beings which live around us. Who can explain why one species ranges widely and is very numerous, and why another allied species has a narrow range and is rare? Yet these relations are of the highest importance, for they determine the present welfare, and, as I believe, the future success and modification of every inhabitant of this world. Still less do we know of the mutual relations of the innumerable inhabitants of the world during the many past geological epochs in its history.

10

---

8   *Malthus*   Thomas Robert Malthus (1766–1834), who theorized in his 1798 work *An Essay on the Principle of Population* that the human population would eventually outstrip its food resources.

Although much remains obscure, and will long remain obscure, I can entertain no doubt, after the most deliberate study and dispassionate judgment of which I am capable, that the view which most naturalists entertain, and which I formerly entertained—namely, that each species has been independently created—is erroneous. I am fully convinced that species are not immutable; but that those belonging to what are called the same genera[9] are lineal descendants of some other and generally extinct species, in the same manner as the acknowledged varieties of any one species are the descendants of that species. Furthermore, I am convinced that natural selection has been the main but not exclusive means of modification....

CHAPTER 3: STRUGGLE FOR EXISTENCE

Before entering on the subject of this chapter, I must make a few preliminary remarks, to show how the struggle for existence bears on natural selection. It has been seen in the last chapter that amongst organic beings in a state of nature there is some individual variability; indeed I am not aware that this has ever been disputed. It is immaterial for us whether a multitude of doubtful forms be called species or sub-species or varieties; what rank, for instance, the two or three hundred doubtful forms of British plants are entitled to hold, if the existence of any well-marked varieties be admitted. But the mere existence of individual variability and of some few well-marked varieties, though necessary as the foundation for the work, helps us but little in understanding how species arise in nature. How have all those exquisite adaptations of one part of the organization to another part, and to the conditions of life, and of one distinct organic being to another being, been perfected? We see these beautiful co-adaptations most plainly in the woodpecker and mistletoe; and only a little less plainly in the humblest parasite which clings to the hairs of a quadruped or feathers of a bird; in the structure of the beetle which dives through the water; in the plumed seed which is wafted by the gentlest breeze; in short, we see beautiful adaptations everywhere and in every part of the organic world.

Again, it may be asked, how is it that varieties, which I have called incipient species, become ultimately converted into good and distinct species, which in most cases obviously differ from each other far more than do the varieties of the same species? How do those groups of species, which constitute what are called distinct genera, and which differ from each other more than do the species of the same genus, arise? All these results, as we shall more fully see in the next chapter, follow inevitably from the struggle for life. Owing to this struggle for life, any variation, however slight and from whatever cause proceeding, if it

---

9   *genera*   Latin: groupings of species. Plural of "genus."

be in any degree profitable to an individual of any species, in its infinitely complex relations to other organic beings and to external nature, will tend to the preservation of that individual, and will generally be inherited by its offspring. The offspring, also, will thus have a better chance of surviving, for, of the many individuals of any species which are periodically born, but a small number can survive. I have called this principle, by which each slight variation, if useful, is preserved, by the term of natural selection, in order to mark its relation to man's power of selection. We have seen that man by selection can certainly produce great results, and can adapt organic beings to his own uses, through the accumulation of slight but useful variations, given to him by the hand of nature. But natural selection, as we shall hereafter see, is a power incessantly ready for action, and is as immeasurably superior to man's feeble efforts, as the works of nature are to those of art.

We will now discuss in a little more detail the struggle for existence. In my future work this subject shall be treated, as it well deserves, at much greater length. The elder De Candolle[10] and Lyell have largely and philosophically shown that all organic beings are exposed to severe competition. In regard to plants, no one has treated this subject with more spirit and ability than W. Herbert,[11] Dean of Manchester, evidently the result of his great horticultural knowledge. Nothing is easier than to admit in words the truth of the universal struggle for life, or more difficult—at least I have found it so—than constantly to bear this conclusion in mind. Yet unless it be thoroughly engrained in the mind, I am convinced that the whole economy of nature, with every fact on distribution, rarity, abundance, extinction, and variation, will be dimly seen or quite misunderstood. We behold the face of nature bright with gladness, we often see superabundance of food; we do not see, or we forget, that the birds which are idly singing round us mostly live on insects or seeds, and are thus constantly destroying life; or we forget how largely these songsters, or their eggs, or their nestlings, are destroyed by birds and beasts of prey; we do not always bear in mind, that though food may be now superabundant, it is not so at all seasons of each recurring year.

I should premise that I use the term struggle for existence in a large and metaphorical sense, including dependence of one being on another, and including (which is more important) not only the life of the individual, but success in leaving progeny. Two canine animals in a time of dearth, may be truly said to struggle with each other which shall get food and live. But a plant on the edge of a desert is said to struggle for life against the drought, though more

---

10 *The elder De Candolle* Augustin-Pyramus de Candolle (1778–1841), Swiss botanist.

11 *W. Herbert* William Herbert (1778–1847).

properly it should be said to be dependent on the moisture. A plant which annually produces a thousand seeds, of which on an average only one comes to
maturity, may be more truly said to struggle with the plants of the same and
other kinds which already clothe the ground. The mistletoe is dependent on
the apple and a few other trees, but can only in a far-fetched sense be said to
struggle with these trees, for if too many of these parasites grow on the same
tree, it will languish and die. But several seedling mistletoes, growing close
together on the same branch, may more truly be said to struggle with each
other. As the mistletoe is disseminated by birds, its existence depends on birds;
and it may metaphorically be said to struggle with other fruit-bearing plants, in
order to tempt birds to devour and thus disseminate its seeds rather than those
of other plants. In these several senses, which pass into each other, I use for
convenience' sake the general term of struggle for existence.

15   A struggle for existence inevitably follows from the high rate at which all
organic beings tend to increase. Every being, which during its natural lifetime
produces several eggs or seeds, must suffer destruction during some period of
its life, and during some season or occasional year, otherwise, on the principle
of geometrical increase, its numbers would quickly become so inordinately
great that no country could support the product. Hence, as more individuals
are produced than can possibly survive, there must in every case be a struggle
for existence, either one individual with another of the same species, or with
the individuals of distinct species, or with the physical conditions of life. It is
the doctrine of Malthus applied with manifold force to the whole animal and
vegetable kingdoms; for in this case there can be no artificial increase of food,
and no prudential restraint from marriage. Although some species may be now
increasing, more or less rapidly, in numbers, all cannot do so, for the world
would not hold them.

There is no exception to the rule that every organic being naturally increases
at so high a rate, that if not destroyed, the earth would soon be covered by the
progeny of a single pair. Even slow-breeding man has doubled in twenty-five
years, and at this rate, in a few thousand years, there would literally not be
standing room for his progeny. Linnaeus[12] has calculated that if an annual plant
produced only two seeds—and there is no plant so unproductive as this—and
their seedlings next year produced two, and so on, then in twenty years there
would be a million plants. The elephant is reckoned to be the slowest breeder of
all known animals, and I have taken some pains to estimate its probable minimum rate of natural increase: it will be under the mark to assume that it breeds
when thirty years old, and goes on breeding till ninety years old, bringing forth

12 *Linnaeus* Carolus Linnaeus (1707–78), Swedish scientist who laid the foundations
of modern taxonomy.

three pair of young in this interval; if this be so, at the end of the fifth century there would be alive fifteen million elephants, descended from the first pair.

But we have better evidence on this subject than mere theoretical calculations, namely, the numerous recorded cases of the astonishingly rapid increase of various animals in a state of nature, when circumstances have been favourable to them during two or three following seasons. Still more striking is the evidence from our domestic animals of many kinds which have run wild in several parts of the world: if the statements of the rate of increase of slow-breeding cattle and horses in South America, and latterly in Australia, had not been well authenticated, they would have been quite incredible. So it is with plants: cases could be given of introduced plants which have become common throughout whole islands in a period of less than ten years. Several of the plants now most numerous over the wide plains of La Plata,[13] clothing square leagues of surface almost to the exclusion of all other plants, have been introduced from Europe; and there are plants which now range in India, as I hear from Dr. Falconer,[14] from Cape Comorin[15] to the Himalaya, which have been imported from America since its discovery. In such cases, and endless instances could be given, no one supposes that the fertility of these animals or plants has been suddenly and temporarily increased in any sensible degree. The obvious explanation is that the conditions of life have been very favorable, and that there has consequently been less destruction of the old and young, and that nearly all the young have been enabled to breed. In such cases the geometrical ratio of increase, the result of which never fails to be surprising, simply explains the extraordinarily rapid increase and wide diffusion of naturalized productions in their new homes....

Many cases are on record showing how complex and unexpected are the checks and relations between organic beings, which have to struggle together in the same country. I will give only a single instance, which, though a simple one, has interested me. In Staffordshire, on the estate of a relation where I had ample means of investigation, there was a large and extremely barren heath, which had never been touched by the hand of man; but several hundred acres of exactly the same nature had been enclosed twenty-five years previously and planted with Scotch fir. The change in the native vegetation of the planted part of the heath was most remarkable, more than is generally seen in passing from one quite different soil to another: not only the proportional numbers of the heath-plants were wholly changed, but twelve species of plants (not counting

---

13   *La Plata*   Region of Argentina.

14   *Dr. Falconer*   Hugh Falconer (1808–65), one of the pre-eminent British paleontologists of the time.

15   *Cape Comorin*   Southernmost point of the Indian subcontinent.

grasses and carices[16]) flourished in the plantations, which could not be found on the heath. The effect on the insects must have been still greater, for six insectivorous birds were very common in the plantations, which were not to be seen on the heath; and the heath was frequented by two or three distinct insectivorous birds. Here we see how potent has been the effect of the introduction of a single tree, nothing whatever else having been done, with the exception that the land had been enclosed, so that cattle could not enter. But how important an element enclosure is, I plainly saw near Farnham, in Surrey. Here there are extensive heaths, with a few clumps of old Scotch firs on the distant hill-tops: within the last ten years large spaces have been enclosed, and self-sown firs are now springing up in multitudes, so close together that all cannot live. When I ascertained that these young trees had not been sown or planted, I was so much surprised at their numbers that I went to several points of view, whence I could examine hundreds of acres of the unenclosed heath, and literally I could not see a single Scotch fir, except the old planted clumps. But on looking closely between the stems of the heath, I found a multitude of seedlings and little trees, which had been perpetually browsed down by the cattle. In one square yard, at a point some hundreds yards distant from one of the old clumps, I counted thirty-two little trees; and one of them, judging from the rings of growth, had during twenty-six years tried to raise its head above the stems of the heath, and had failed. No wonder that, as soon as the land was enclosed, it became thickly clothed with vigorously growing young firs. Yet the heath was so extremely barren and so extensive that no one would ever have imagined that cattle would have so closely and effectually searched it for food.

Here we see that cattle absolutely determine the existence of the Scotch fir; but in several parts of the world insects determine the existence of cattle. Perhaps Paraguay offers the most curious instance of this; for here neither cattle nor horses nor dogs have ever run wild, though they swarm southward and northward in a feral state; and Azara and Rengger[17] have shown that this is caused by the greater number in Paraguay of a certain fly, which lays its eggs in the navels of these animals when first born. The increase of these flies, numerous as they are, must be habitually checked by some means, probably by birds. Hence, if certain insectivorous birds (whose numbers are probably regulated by hawks or beasts of prey) were to increase in Paraguay, the flies would decrease—then cattle and horses would become feral, and this would certainly greatly alter (as indeed I have observed in parts of South America)

---

16 *carices* Sedges.

17 *Azara and Rengger* Félix de Azara (1746–1821), Spanish explorer and naturalist, and Johann Rudolph Rengger (1795–1832), German naturalist. In the early part of the nineteenth century, both published influential studies on Paraguayan fauna.

the vegetation: this again would largely affect the insects; and this, as we just have seen in Staffordshire, the insectivorous birds, and so onwards in ever-increasing circles of complexity. We began this series by insectivorous birds, and we have ended with them. Not that in nature the relations can ever be as simple as this. Battle within battle must ever be recurring with varying success; and yet in the long-run the forces are so nicely balanced, that the face of nature remains uniform for long periods of time, though assuredly the merest trifle would often give the victory to one organic being over another. Nevertheless so profound is our ignorance, and so high our presumption, that we marvel when we hear of the extinction of an organic being; and as we do not see the cause, we invoke cataclysms to desolate the world, or invent laws on the duration of the forms of life!

I am tempted to give one more instance showing how plants and animals, most remote in the scale of nature, are bound together by a web of complex relations. I shall hereafter have occasion to show that the exotic *Lobelia fulgens*,[18] in this part of England, is never visited by insects, and consequently, from its peculiar structure, never can set a seed. Many of our orchidaceous plants absolutely require the visits of moths to remove their pollen-masses and thus to fertilize them. I have, also, reason to believe that humble-bees* are indispensable to the fertilization of the heartsease (*Viola tricolor*), for other bees do not visit this flower. From experiments which I have tried, I have found that the visits of bees, if not indispensable, are at least highly beneficial to the fertilization of our clovers; but humble-bees alone visit the common red clover (*Trifolium pratense*), as other bees cannot reach the nectar. Hence I have very little doubt, that if the whole genus of humble-bees became extinct or very rare in England, the heartsease and red clover would become very rare, or wholly disappear. The number of humble-bees in any district depends in a great degree on the number of field-mice, which destroy their combs and nests; and Mr. H. Newman,[19] who has long attended to the habits of humble-bees, believes that "more than two thirds of them are thus destroyed all over England." Now the number of mice is largely dependent, as every one knows, on the number of cats; and Mr. Newman says, "Near villages and small towns I have found the nests of humble-bees more numerous than elsewhere, which I attribute to the number of cats that destroy the mice." Hence it is quite credible that the presence of a feline animal in large numbers in a district might determine, through the intervention first of mice and then of bees, the frequency of certain flowers in that district! …

20

(1859)

---

18 *Lobelia fulgens* Cardinal flower.
19 *Mr. H. Newman* Unidentified.

ABRAHAM LINCOLN

SECOND INAUGURAL ADDRESS

Lincoln's views on slavery evolved substantially between the beginning of his first term as president and the beginning of his second. The Civil War* began shortly after he became president in 1861; the Emancipation Proclamation declaring the end of slavery on January 1, 1863 had changed the face of the war—and of the country.

Though the ground outside the Capitol building (with its newly completed dome) was muddy following weeks of rain, many thousands turned out to hear the President's speech on Saturday, March 4, 1865. Among them was John Wilkes Booth, who would assassinate Lincoln just a few weeks later.

Fellow-Countrymen:

At this second appearing to take the oath of the presidential office there is less occasion for an extended address than there was at the first. Then a statement somewhat in detail of a course to be pursued seemed fitting and proper. Now, at the expiration of four years, during which public declarations have been constantly called forth on every point and phase of the great contest which still absorbs the attention and engrosses the energies of the nation, little that is new could be presented. The progress of our arms,[1] upon which all else chiefly depends, is as well known to the public as to myself, and it is, I trust, reasonably satisfactory and encouraging to all. With high hope for the future, no prediction in regard to it is ventured.

On the occasion corresponding to this four years ago all thoughts were anxiously directed to an impending civil war. All dreaded it, all sought to avert it. While the inaugural address was being delivered from this place, devoted altogether to saving the Union without war, insurgent agents[2] were in the city seeking to destroy it without war—seeking to dissolve the Union and divide effects[3] by negotiation. Both parties deprecated war,[4] but one of them would

---

1 *of our arms* Of the Union forces in the Civil War.

2 *insurgent agents* Representatives attempting to undermine the government.

3 *effects* Possessions (of the United States as a whole).

4 *Both parties deprecated war* Both Northerners and Southerners expressed their disapproval of the idea of going to war.

make war rather than let the nation survive, and the other would accept war rather than let it perish, and the war came.

One-eighth of the whole population were colored slaves, not distributed generally over the Union, but localized in the southern part of it. These slaves constituted a peculiar and powerful interest. All knew that this interest was somehow the cause of the war. To strengthen, perpetuate, and extend this interest was the object for which the insurgents would rend the Union even by war, while the government claimed no right to do more than to restrict the territorial enlargement of it. Neither party expected for the war the magnitude or the duration which it has already attained. Neither anticipated that the cause of the conflict might cease with or even before the conflict itself should cease. Each looked for an easier triumph, and a result less fundamental and astounding. Both read the same Bible and pray to the same God, and each invokes His aid against the other. It may seem strange that any men should dare to ask a just God's assistance in wringing their bread from the sweat of other men's faces, but let us judge not, that we be not judged. The prayers of both could not be answered. That of neither has been answered fully. The Almighty has His own purposes. "Woe unto the world because of offenses; for it must needs be that offenses come, but woe to that man by whom the offense cometh."[5] If we shall suppose that American slavery is one of those offenses which, in the providence of God, must needs come, but which, having continued through His appointed time, He now wills to remove, and that He gives to both North and South this terrible war as the woe due to those by whom the offense came, shall we discern therein any departure from those divine attributes which the believers in a living God always ascribe to Him? Fondly do we hope, fervently do we pray, that this mighty scourge of war may speedily pass away. Yet, if God wills that it continue until all the wealth piled by the bondsman's[6] two hundred and fifty years of unrequited toil shall be sunk, and until every drop of blood drawn with the lash shall be paid by another drawn with the sword, as was said three thousand years ago, so still it must be said "the judgments of the Lord are true and righteous altogether."[7]

With malice toward none, with charity for all, with firmness in the right as God gives us to see the right, let us strive on to finish the work we are in, to bind up the nation's wounds, to care for him who shall have borne[8] the battle and for his widow and his orphan, to do all which may achieve and cherish a just and lasting peace among ourselves and with all nations.

(1865)

---

5   *Woe unto ... cometh*   See Matthew 18.7.
6   *bondsman's*   Slave's.
7   *The judgments ... altogether*   See Psalm 9.19.
8   *borne*   Endured.

MARK TWAIN

from LIFE ON THE MISSISSIPPI

Before the Civil War Samuel Clemens spent some years working as
a steamboat pilot on the Mississippi River. Decades later—by this
time famous as Mark Twain—he began to compose memoirs of his
life on the river. The excerpt included here, originally published in
one of a series of 1875 magazine pieces in* The Atlantic Monthly, *was later incorporated into Chapter 9 of his 1883 volume,* Life on
the Mississippi.

The face of the water, in time, became a wonderful book—a book that was a
dead language to the uneducated passenger, but which told its mind to me
without reserve, delivering its most cherished secrets as clearly as if it uttered
them with a voice. And it was not a book to be read once and thrown aside,
for it had a new story to tell every day. Throughout the long twelve hundred
miles there was never a page that was void of interest, never one that you could
leave unread without loss, never one that you would want to skip, thinking
you could find higher enjoyment in some other thing. There never was so
wonderful a book written by man; never one whose interest was so absorbing,
so unflagging, so sparklingly renewed with every re-perusal. The passenger
who could not read it was charmed with a peculiar sort of faint dimple on its
surface (on the rare occasions when he did not overlook it altogether); but to
the pilot that was an *italicized* passage; indeed, it was more than that, it was
a legend of the largest capitals, with a string of shouting exclamation-points
at the end of it, for it meant that a wreck or a rock was buried there that could
tear the life out of the strongest vessel that ever floated. It is the faintest and
simplest expression the water ever makes, and the most hideous to a pilot's eye.
In truth, the passenger who could not read this book saw nothing but all manner
of pretty pictures in it, painted by the sun and shaded by the clouds, whereas
to the trained eye these were not pictures at all, but the grimmest and most
dead-earnest of reading-matter.

Now when I had mastered the language of this water, and had come to
know every trifling feature that bordered the great river as familiarly as I knew
the letters of the alphabet, I had made a valuable acquisition. But I had lost

something, too. I had lost something which could never be restored to me while I lived. All the grace, the beauty, the poetry, had gone out of the majestic river! I still keep in mind a certain wonderful sunset which I witnessed when steamboating was new to me. A broad expanse of the river was turned to blood; in the middle distance the red hue brightened into gold, through which a solitary log came floating, black and conspicuous; in one place a long, slanting mark lay sparkling upon the water; in another the surface was broken by boiling, tumbling rings, that were as many-tinted as an opal; where the ruddy flush was faintest, was a smooth spot that was covered with graceful circles and radiating lines, ever so delicately traced; the shore on our left was densely wooded, and the somber shadow that fell from this forest was broken in one place by a long, ruffled trail that shone like silver; and high above the forest wall a clean-stemmed dead tree waved a single leafy bough that glowed like a flame in the unobstructed splendor that was flowing from the sun. There were graceful curves, reflected images, woody heights, soft distances; and over the whole scene, far and near, the dissolving lights drifted steadily, enriching it every passing moment with new marvels of coloring.

I stood like one bewitched. I drank it in, in a speechless rapture. The world was new to me, and I had never seen anything like this at home. But as I have said, a day came when I began to cease from noting the glories and the charms which the moon and the sun and the twilight wrought upon the river's face; another day came when I ceased altogether to note them. Then, if that sunset scene had been repeated, I should have looked upon it without rapture, and should have commented upon it, inwardly, after this fashion: "This sun means that we are going to have wind tomorrow; that floating log means that the river is rising, small thanks to it; that slanting mark on the water refers to a bluff reef which is going to kill somebody's steamboat one of these nights, if it keeps on stretching out like that; those tumbling 'boils' show a dissolving bar and a changing channel there; the lines and circles in the slick water over yonder are a warning that that troublesome place is shoaling up dangerously; that silver streak in the shadow of the forest is the 'break' from a new snag, and he has located himself in the very best place he could have found to fish for steamboats; that tall dead tree, with a single living branch, is not going to last long, and then how is a body ever going to get through this blind place at night without the friendly old landmark?"

No, the romance and beauty were all gone from the river. All the value any feature of it had for me now was the amount of usefulness it could furnish toward compassing the safe piloting of a steamboat. Since those days, I have pitied doctors from my heart. What does the lovely flush in a beauty's cheek mean to a doctor but a "break" that ripples above some deadly disease? Are not all her visible charms sown thick with what are to him the signs and symbols of hidden decay? Does he ever see her beauty at all, or doesn't he simply view her professionally, and comment upon her unwholesome condition all to himself? And doesn't he sometimes wonder whether he has gained most or lost most by learning his trade?

(1875)

OSCAR WILDE

from THE DECAY OF LYING

Oscar Wilde embodied late nineteenth-century aestheticism in his life, in his prose fiction, and in his plays; he also explored the principles behind it. In "The Decay of Lying," a Platonic dialogue,* Wilde sets out a theory of aesthetics through the conversation of two characters, Vivian and Cyril (named after Wilde's two sons). Vivian, prompted by Cyril's questioning, has been reading aloud from his essay-in-progress, also entitled "The Decay of Lying"—an essay supporting Plato's claim that art is falsehood, yet challenging Plato's assertions that art is a mere imitation of life, and that the lies of art are morally repugnant.

CYRIL. ... The spirit of an age may be best expressed in the abstract ideal arts,[1] for the spirit itself is abstract and ideal. Upon the other hand, for the visible aspect of an age, for its look, as the phrase goes, we must of course go to the arts of imitation.

VIVIAN. I don't think so. After all, what the imitative arts really give us are merely the various styles of particular artists, or of certain schools of artists. Surely you don't imagine that the people of the Middle Ages bore any resemblance at all to the figures on medieval stained glass, or in medieval stone and wood carving, or on medieval metal-work, or tapestries, or illuminated manuscripts. They were probably very ordinary-looking people, with nothing grotesque, or remarkable, or fantastic in their appearance.... Take an example from our own day. I know that you are fond of Japanese things. Now, do you really imagine that the Japanese people, as they are presented to us in art, have any existence? If you do, you have never understood Japanese art at all. The Japanese people are the deliberate self-conscious creation of certain individual

---

1   *abstract ideal arts* Forms of art (such as music) that do not attempt to imitate nature.

79

artists. If you set a picture by Hokusai, or Hokkei,[2] or any of the great native painters, beside a real Japanese gentleman or lady, you will see that there is not the slightest resemblance between them…. The actual people who live in Japan are not unlike the general run of English people; that is to say, they are extremely commonplace, and have nothing curious or extraordinary about them. In fact the whole of Japan is a pure invention. There is no such country, there are no such people…. Or, to return again to the past, take as another instance the ancient Greeks. Do you think that Greek art ever tells us what the Greek people were like? … The fact is that we look back on the ages entirely through the medium of art, and art, very fortunately, has never once told us the truth.

CYRIL. But modern portraits by English painters, what of them? Surely they are like the people they pretend to represent?

VIVIAN. Quite so. They are so like them that a hundred years from now no one will believe in them. The only portraits in which one believes are portraits where there is very little of the sitter, and a very great deal of the artist. Holbein's drawings[3] of the men and women of his time impress us with a sense of their absolute reality. But this is simply because Holbein compelled life to accept his conditions, to restrain itself within his limitations, to reproduce his type, and to appear as he wished it to appear. It is style that makes us believe in a thing—nothing but style. Most of our modern portrait painters are doomed to absolute oblivion. They never paint what they see. They paint what the public sees, and the public never sees anything.

5 CYRIL. Well, after that I think I should like to hear the end of your article.

VIVIAN. With pleasure. Whether it will do any good I really cannot say. Ours is certainly the dullest and most prosaic century possible…. As for the Church, I cannot conceive anything better for the culture of a country than the presence in it of a body of men whose duty it is to believe in the supernatural, to perform daily miracles, and to keep alive that mythopoeic faculty which is so essential for the imagination. But in the English Church a man succeeds, not through his capacity for belief, but through his capacity for disbelief…. The growth of common sense in the English Church is a thing very much to be regretted. It is

---

2 *Hokusai, or Hokkei* Katsushika Hokusai (1760–1849) and Totoya Hokkei (c.1780–1850) were both artists known for works in the highly stylized representational form known as *ukiyo-e*.

3 *Holbein's drawings* The German-Swiss artist Hans Holbein (1497–1543) lived for some years in England and became well-known for his portraits of such figures as Sir Thomas More and King Henry VIII.

really a degrading concession to a low form of realism. It is silly, too. It springs from an entire ignorance of psychology. Man can believe the impossible, but man can never believe the improbable. However, I must read the end of my article:

> What we have to do, what at any rate it is our duty to do, is to revive this old art of lying. Much of course may be done, in the way of educating the public, by amateurs in the domestic circle, at literary lunches, and at afternoon teas. But this is merely the light and graceful side of lying…. There are many other forms. Lying for the sake of gaining some immediate personal advantage, for instance—lying with a moral purpose, as it is usually called—though of late it has been rather looked down upon, was extremely popular with the antique world…. Lying for the sake of the improvement of the young, which is the basis of home education, still lingers amongst us, and its advantages are so admirably set forth in the early books of Plato's *Republic** that it is unnecessary to dwell upon them here. It is a mode of lying for which all good mothers have peculiar capabilities, but it is capable of still further development, and has been sadly overlooked by the School Board. Lying for the sake of a monthly salary is of course well known in Fleet Street, and the profession of a political leader-writer[4] is not without its advantages. But it is said to be a somewhat dull occupation, and it certainly does not lead to much beyond a kind of ostentatious obscurity. The only form of lying that is absolutely beyond reproach is lying for its own sake, and the highest development of this is, as we have already pointed out, Lying in Art. Just as those who do not love Plato more than Truth cannot pass beyond the threshold of the Academy, so those who do not love Beauty more than Truth never know the inmost shrine of Art…. [W]e must cultivate the lost art of Lying.

CYRIL. Then we must certainly cultivate it at once. But in order to avoid making any error I want you to tell me briefly the doctrines of the new aesthetics.

VIVIAN. Briefly, then, they are these. Art never expresses anything but itself. It has an independent life, just as Thought has, and develops purely on its own lines. It is not necessarily realistic in an age of realism, nor spiritual in an age of faith. So far from being the creation of its time, it is usually in direct opposition to it, and the only history that it preserves for us is the history of its own progress. Sometimes it returns upon its footsteps, and revives some antique

---

4   *Fleet Street … leader-writer*   Fleet Street was long the center of the English newspaper business. A "leader" in an English newspaper is an editorial.

form, as happened in the archaistic movement of late Greek Art, and in the pre-Raphaelite movement[5] of our own day. At other times it entirely anticipates its age, and produces in one century work that it takes another century to understand, to appreciate and to enjoy. In no case does it reproduce its age. To pass from the art of a time to the time itself is the great mistake that all historians commit.

The second doctrine is this. All bad art comes from returning to Life and Nature, and elevating them into ideals. Life and Nature may sometimes be used as part of Art's rough material, but before they are of any real service to art they must be translated into artistic conventions. The moment Art surrenders its imaginative medium it surrenders everything. As a method Realism is a complete failure, and the two things that every artist should avoid are modernity of form and modernity of subject-matter. To us, who live in the nineteenth century, any century is a suitable subject for art except our own. The only beautiful things are the things that do not concern us. It is, to have the pleasure of quoting myself, exactly because Hecuba is nothing to us that her sorrows are so suitable a motive for a tragedy.[6] Besides, it is only the modern that ever becomes old-fashioned. M. Zola sits down to give us a picture of the Second Empire.[7] Who cares for the Second Empire now? It is out of date. Life goes faster than Realism, but Romanticism is always in front of Life.

10   The third doctrine is that Life imitates Art far more than Art imitates Life. This results not merely from Life's imitative instinct, but from the fact that the self-conscious aim of Life is to find expression, and that Art offers it certain beautiful forms through which it may realize that energy. It is a theory that has never been put forward before, but it is extremely fruitful, and throws an entirely new light upon the history of Art.

---

5   *archaistic ... Greek Art*   Reference to a claim made by the critic Walter Pater that Greek art of the fourth century BCE drew on a style that had been employed several centuries earlier; *pre-Raphaelite movement*   Mid-nineteenth-century English artistic movement that revived aspects of late medieval and early Renaissance style.

6   *exactly because Hecuba ... tragedy*   Hecuba, Queen of Troy when that city was conquered by the Greeks, saw her husband and sons murdered. In Shakespeare's *Hamlet*, one of the players performing for Hamlet recites an emotional monologue on the terrible fate of Hecuba, prompting Hamlet to wonder, "What's Hecuba to him, or he to Hecuba, / That he should weep for her?" (2.2).

7   *M. Zola ... the Second Empire*   Louis Napoleon, nephew of Napoleon 1st, and heir to the Napoleonic title, was elected president of France in 1848, and in 1852 dismissed Parliament and declared himself emperor. The Second Empire ended when he was forced from power after France's defeat at the hands of Prussia in 1871. Emile Zola, a leading novelist of the period, coined the term *naturalisme* (naturalism) to describe his approach to realistic fiction.

It follows, as a corollary from this, that external Nature also imitates Art. The only effects that she can show us are effects that we have already seen through poetry, or in paintings. This is the secret of Nature's charm, as well as the explanation of Nature's weakness.

The final revelation is that Lying, the telling of beautiful untrue things, is the proper aim of Art. But of this I think I have spoken at sufficient length. And now let us go out on the terrace, where "droops the milk-white peacock like a ghost," while the evening star "washes the dusk with silver."[8] At twilight nature becomes a wonderfully suggestive effect, and is not without loveliness, though perhaps its chief use is to illustrate quotations from the poets. Come! We have talked long enough.

(1889)

---

8   *droops the ... ghost*   See "Now Sleeps the Crimson Petal," a poem by Alfred, Lord Tennyson; *washes the ... silver*   Paraphrased from William Blake's poem "To the Evening Star."

JANE ADDAMS

ON HALSTED STREET

Hull-House, established by Addams in 1889 and located on Halsted Street in a depressed area of Chicago, represented a successful and influential effort to improve the lot of the urban poor in nineteenth-century America—in intellectual, social, and spiritual terms as well as economic ones. The following forms the conclusion of Addams's book Twenty Years at Hull-House.

In those early days we were often asked why we had to come to live on Halsted Street when we could afford to live somewhere else. I remember one man who used to shake his head and say it was "the strangest thing he had met in his experience," but who was finally convinced that it was "not strange but natural." In time it came to seem natural to all of us that the Settlement should be there. If it is natural to feed the hungry and care for the sick, it is certainly natural to give pleasure to the young, comfort to the aged, and to minister to the deep-seated craving for social intercourse that all men feel. Whoever does it is rewarded by something which, if not gratitude, is at least spontaneous and vital and lacks that irksome sense of obligation with which a substantial benefit is too often acknowledged.

In addition to the neighbors who responded to the receptions and classes, we found those who were too battered and oppressed to care for them. To these, however, was left that susceptibility to the bare offices of humanity which raises such offices into a bond of fellowship.

From the first it seemed understood that we were ready to perform the humblest neighborhood services. We were asked to wash the new-born babies, and to prepare the dead for burial, to nurse the sick, and to "mind the children."

Occasionally these neighborly offices unexpectedly uncovered ugly human traits. For six weeks after an operation we kept in one of our three bedrooms a forlorn little baby who, because he was born with a cleft palate, was most unwelcome even to his mother, and we were horrified when he died of neglect a week after he was returned to his home; a little Italian bride of fifteen sought shelter with us one November evening, to escape her husband who had beaten her every night for a week when he returned home from work, because she

had lost her wedding ring; two of us officiated quite alone at the birth of an illegitimate child because the doctor was late in arriving, and none of the honest
Irish matrons would "touch the likes of her"; we ministered at the deathbed
of a young man, who during a long illness of tuberculosis had received so
many bottles of whiskey through the mistaken kindness of his friends, that the
cumulative effect produced wild periods of exultation, in one of which he died.

We were also early impressed with the curious isolation of many of the   5
immigrants; an Italian woman once expressed her pleasure in the red roses
that she saw at one of our receptions in surprise that they had been "brought so
fresh all the way from Italy." She would not believe for an instant that they had
been grown in America. She said that she had lived in Chicago for six years
and had never seen any roses, whereas in Italy she had seen them every summer in great profusion. During all that time, of course, the woman had lived
within ten blocks of a florist's window; she had not been more than a five-cent
car ride away from the public parks; but she had never dreamed of faring forth
for herself, and no one had taken her. Her conception of America had been the
untidy street in which she lived and had made her long struggle to adapt herself
to American ways.

But in spite of some untoward experiences, we were constantly impressed
with the uniform kindness and courtesy we received. Perhaps these first days
laid the simple human foundations which are certainly essential for continuous
living among the poor: first, genuine preference for residence in an industrial
quarter to any other part of the city, because it is interesting and makes the
human appeal; and second, the conviction, in the words of Canon Barnett,[1]
that the things which make men alike are finer and better than the things that
keep them apart, and that these basic likenesses, if they are properly accentu-
ated, easily transcend the less essential differences of race, language, creed and
tradition.

Perhaps even in those first days we made a beginning toward that object
which was afterwards stated in our charter: "To provide a center for a higher
civic and social life; to institute and maintain educational and philanthropic
enterprises, and to investigate and improve the conditions in the industrial
districts of Chicago."

(1910)

---

1   *Canon Barnett*   Samuel A. Barnett, an English cleric and reformer, and the founder
of Toynbee Hall, on which Addams modeled Hull-House.

W.E.B. Du Bois

A Mild Suggestion

In the early decades of the twentieth century two sets of ideas held particular importance in African American intellectual life. On the one hand, Booker T. Washington, who was accepted by much of the white establishment as a representative of black Americans, advocated compromise and cooperation with white America, even in the face of Jim Crow laws* and other forms of discrimination. On the other, the Harvard-educated academic W.E.B. Du Bois was a much sharper critic of the status quo, and advocated struggle on an ongoing basis for full equality.

"A Mild Suggestion" was first published in the January 1912 issue of The Crisis, *the NAACP's* monthly magazine, of which Du Bois was the founding editor.*

They were sitting on the leeward deck of the vessel and the colored man was there with his usual look of unconcern. Before the seasickness his presence aboard had caused some upheaval. The Woman, for instance, glancing at the Southerner, had refused point blank to sit beside him at meals, so she had changed places with the Little Old Lady. The Westerner, who sat opposite, said he did not care a ——, then he looked at the Little Old Lady, and added in a lower voice to the New Yorker that there was no accounting for tastes. The Southerner from the other table broadened his back and tried to express with his shoulders both ancestors and hauteur. All this, however was half forgotten during the seasickness, and the Woman sat beside the colored man for a full half hour before she noticed it, and then was glad to realize that the Southerner was too sick to see. Now again with sunshine and smiling weather, they all quite naturally reverted (did the Southerner suggest it?) to the Negro problem. The usual solutions had been suggested: education, work, emigration, etc.

They had not noticed the back of the colored man, until the thoughtless Westerner turned toward him and said breezily: "Well, now, what do you say? I guess you are rather interested." The colored man was leaning over the rail and about to light his cigarette—he had several such bad habits, as the Little Old Lady noticed. The Southerner simply stared. Over the face of the colored man went the shadow of several expressions; some the New Yorker could interpret, others he could not.

"I have," said the colored man, with deliberation, "a perfect solution." The Southerner selected a look of disdain from his repertoire, and assumed it. The Woman moved nearer, but partly turned her back. The Westerner and the Little Old Lady sat down. "Yes," repeated the colored man, "I have a perfect solution. The trouble with most of the solutions which are generally suggested is that they aggravate the disease." The Southerner could not help looking interested. "For instance," proceeded the colored man, airily waving his hand, "take education; education means ambition, dissatisfaction and revolt. You cannot both educate people and hold them down."

"Then stop educating them," growled the Southerner aside.

"Or," continued the colored man, "if the black man works, he must come into competition with whites——" 5

"He sure will, and it ought to be stopped," returned the Westerner. "It brings down wages."

"Precisely," said the speaker, "and if by underselling the labor market he develops a few millionaires, how now would you protect your residential districts or your select social circles or—your daughters?"

The Southerner started angrily, but the colored man was continuing placidly with a far-off look in his eyes. "Now, migration is both costly and inhuman; the transportation would be the smallest matter. You must buy up perhaps a thousand millions' worth of Negro property; you must furnish some capital for the masses of poor; you must get some place for them to go; you must protect them there, and here you must pay not only higher wages to white men, but still higher on account of the labor scarcity. Meantime, the Negroes suddenly removed from one climate and social system to another climate and utterly new conditions would die in droves—it would be simply prolonged murder at enormous cost.

"Very well," continued the colored man, seating himself and throwing away his cigarette, "listen to my plan," looking almost quizzically at the Little Old Lady; "you must not be alarmed at its severity—it may seem radical, but really it is—it is—well, it is quite the only practical thing and it has surely one advantage: it settles the problem once, suddenly, and forever. My plan is this: You now outnumber us nearly ten to one. I propose that on a certain date, shall we say next Christmas, or possibly Easter, 1912? No, come to think of it, the first of January, 1913, would, for historical reasons, probably be best. Well, then, on the first of January, 1913, let each person who has a colored friend invite him to dinner. This would take care of a few; among such friends might be included the black mammies and faithful old servants of the South; in this way we could get together quite a number. Then those who have not the pleasure of black friends might arrange for meetings, especially in 'white' churches and Young Men's and Young Women's Christian Associations, where Negroes are not expected. At such meetings, contrary to custom, the black people should not be seated by themselves, but distributed very carefully among the whites. The remaining Negroes who could not be flattered or attracted by these invitations should be induced to assemble among themselves at their own churches or at little parties and house warmings.

10   "The few stragglers, vagrants and wanderers could be put under careful watch and ward. Now, then, we have the thing in shape. First, the hosts of those invited to dine should provide themselves with a sufficient quantity of cyanide of potassium, placing it carefully in the proper cups, and being careful not to mix the cups. Those at church and prayer meeting could choose between long sharp stilettoes and pistols—I should recommend the former as less noisy. Those who guard the colored assemblies and the stragglers without should carefully surround the groups and use Winchesters. Then, at a given signal, let the colored folk of the United States be quietly dispatched; the signal might be a church bell or the singing of the national hymn; probably the bell would be best, for the diners would be eating."

By this time the auditors of the colored man were staring; the Southerner had forgotten to pose; the Woman had forgotten to watch the Southerner; the Westerner was staring with admiration; there were tears in the eyes of the Little Old Lady, while the New Yorker was smiling; but the colored man held up a deprecating hand: "Now don't prejudge my plan," he urged. "The next morning there would be ten million funerals, and therefore no Negro problem. Think how quietly the thing would be settled; no more bother, no more argument; the whole country united and happy. Even the Negroes would be a great deal happier than they are at present. Instead of being made heirs to hope by education, or ambitious by wealth, or exiled invalids on the fever coast, they would all be happily ensconced in Heaven. Of course, I admit that at first the plan may seem a little abrupt and cruel, and yet is it more cruel than present conditions, and would it not be well to be a little more abrupt in our social solutions? At any rate think it over," and the colored man dropped lazily into his steamer chair and felt for another cigarette.

The crowd slowly dispersed; the Southerner chose the Woman, but was heard to say something about fools. The Westerner turned to the New Yorker and said: "Now, what in hell do you suppose that darky meant?" But the Little Old Lady went silently to her cabin.

(1912)

José Vasconcelos

Books I Read Sitting and Books I Read Standing[1]

One of the leading Latin American intellectual figures of the early twentieth century, the Mexican historian and philosopher José Vasconcelos was also heavily involved in the political struggles that led to the Mexican Revolution in 1910, and served as a representative in the United States for the new Mexican government of Francisco Madero. When Madero was overthrown by reactionary forces in 1913, Vasconcelos spent several years in exile. During this time he wrote a number of reflective essays—among them "Books I Read Standing and Books I Read Sitting."

To distinguish books, I have followed the practice for some time of using a classification which corresponds to the emotions they arouse in me. I divide them into books I read sitting and books I read standing. The former may be pleasant, instructive, beautiful, splendid, or simply stupid and boring, but all are incapable of arousing us from our normal posture. On the other hand there are some books which, the moment we begin reading, make us get up, as though they derive from the earth a force that pushes against our heels and obliges us to make an effort to rise. In these we do not just read: we declaim, we assume a lofty pose, and undergo a genuine transfiguration. Examples of this are: Greek tragedy, Plato, Hindu philosophy, the Gospels, Dante, Spinoza, Kant, Schopenhauer, the music of Beethoven,* and others, if more modest, not less exceptional in their qualities.

To the quiet type of book, which one reads without being stirred up, belong all the rest, of infinite number, in which we find instruction, delight, charm, but not the palpitation of our consciousness which lifts us up as if we were witnessing a revelation of a new aspect of creation, a new aspect which incites us to move in order to be able to contemplate it in its entirety.

---

1   *Books I ... Standing*   Translated from the Spanish by H.W. Hilborn.

Moreover, writing books is a poor consolation for being unadaptable to life. Thinking is the most intense and fruitful function of life, but descending from thought to the hazardous task of writing it down weakens pride and reveals a spiritual inadequacy, indicating a fear that the idea will not live if it is not put into writing. This is an author's vanity and a little fraternal solicitude on the part of a traveller who, for the benefit of future travellers, marks along the arid way the points where there has been found the ideal water, indispensable for the continuation of the journey. A book, like a journey, is begun in anxiety and finished in melancholy.

If it were possible to be profound and optimistic, books would never be written. Men filled with energy, free and fecund, would not devote themselves to imitating with dead letters the ineffable worth, the perennial self-renewing of a life which absorbs and fulfils its impulses and all its longings. A noble book is always the fruit of disillusionment and a sign of protest. The poet does not barter his visions for his verses, and the hero prefers to live his passions and heroisms rather than sing them, however capable he might be of doing so in full and sumptuous pages. The people who write are those who cannot do things or are not satisfied with what they do. Every book says, expressly or between the lines: nothing is as it ought to be.

5   Woe to the man who takes up his pen and begins to write, while outside there is every potential which attracts human endeavour, when all the unfinished work calls forth emotion to consummate it in pure and perfect reality! But woe also to the man who, devoted to the world outside, neither reflects, nor becomes revolted, nor has ambitions ever more exalted. This man lives complacently only for the external and does not give up and die only because he is not yet born or reborn. For to be born is not merely to come into the world, in which life and death persist together and succeed each other; to be born is to proclaim oneself a non-conformist; to be born is to tear oneself away from the sombre mass of the species, to rebel against every human convention, to wish to strike out and rise up under the stimulus of books that are read standing, books radically unsubmissive.

I do not know to what we are born when, like Buddha or Jesus, we renounce the world, but there is certainly no doubt about the nobility of a renunciation which anticipates the fatal dictum of death and defies death. Yes, unquestionably it is necessary, after knowing life, to be able to say to it: "That's enough!" Without that renunciation and without that demanding of something better, it appears that life has no value for us. It appears that new incarnations will be necessary in order that we may again attempt to surpass in our hearts all that is human, in order to rise to the state of the demigod,[2] the angel, or the blessed.

---

2   *demigod*   Being who is at once divine and earthly.

Good books reprove life, without for that reason giving in to discouragement and doubt. To understand this, it is sufficient to read them, and to observe how strong, healthy temperaments judge them: because the sick man desires health, as the weak man reveres strength and as the mediocre man seeks happiness, and all three are optimistic. But the man who is healthy and glad of heart, the valiant and the bold, become demanding and clamour for what is not found here. Before the Sybarite[3] who offers me pleasure and the prophet who points out to me the vale of tears,[4] I may waver, but I understand and respect the one who says to me: "It is necessary," and I laugh with scorn when I come upon one who exclaims: "How beautiful!" or "How splendid!"

This is because the truth is expressed only in prophetic tone, and is perceived only in the tremulous atmosphere of catastrophe. So it speaks in the word of Aeschylus,[5] so it is woven gloriously into the dialogue of Plato, so it bursts forth in modern symphony.

Euripides[6] too, one of the free and great who have passed by, had such a clear understanding of the human that, moved by compassion, he began to write his visions, taking care to repeat at every moment the wise and sincere counsel, to which we are so deaf: "Be distrustful, be not puffed up in your joy. Call not yourself happy till the hour of your death; before then you know not what fate has in store for you. Why do you wish glory, beauty, and power…. Look at the house of Priam; listen to the lamentations of Hecuba.[7] The faithful Andromache[8] shares the bed of the victor! The little son of Hector has just perished, and of all the illustrious race there remains only the procession of Trojan slaves, imploring in vain as they march towards exile. Why have children?"

But as the truth inspires terror and many are alarmed by the corollaries which any thoroughly sincere spirit might deduce from these immortal gospels, the representatives of those who refuse to die, and who still, furthermore, indulge the instinct to engender offspring—the representatives of such beings, the intelligent men, with Aristotle* at the head, invent for us attenuated

10

---

3   *Sybarite*   Citizen of the notoriously luxurious ancient Greek city of Sybaris.

4   *vale of tears*   Christian idiom signifying all the struggles and tragedies of human experience—which will end only in the afterlife.

5   *Aeschylus*   Ancient Greek writer of tragic plays (c. 523–c. 456 BCE).

6   *Euripides*   Greek dramatist (c. 480–c. 406 BCE). Among his tragedies is *Hecuba*, which focuses on the narrative touched on in this paragraph.

7   *Priam*   King of Troy during the Trojan Wars against the Greeks; *Hecuba*   Wife of Priam. After the city of Troy fell to the Greeks her son Polydorus was killed and she became a slave.

8   *Andromache*   Wife of the Trojan hero Hector. When Hector was killed in battle against the Greeks, the victorious Greek warrior Neoptolemus forced Andromache to become his concubine, and killed the son she had had with Hector.

interpretations, as they do in telling us that tragedy gives relief because the portrayal of pain causes joy, and that in this way the principle of life triumphs over its negations. They seem to fear that some day men will understand, and therefore they write books which restore our calm and good sense, books which deceive us: books which we read sitting because they attach us to life!

(1919)

ZORA NEALE HURSTON

HOW IT FEELS TO BE COLORED ME

*Among leading figures of the Renaissance in African American
literature and culture in the 1920s and 30s, there were often
differences of opinion over the degree to which literature and
the other arts should be political. Notables such as Langston
Hughes and Richard Wright thought black writers and artists had
a responsibility to assist the African American struggle against
oppression by celebrating African American identity and culture;
in his essay "The Negro* Artist and the Racial Mountain," Hughes
condemns any African American poet who says "I want to be a
poet—not a Negro poet," arguing that such a desire to escape race
in art is tantamount to a desire to be white. Some others—among
them Hurston and Nella Larsen—resisted the sorts of identity
politics that Hughes, Wright, and political figures such as W.E.B.
Du Bois advocated.*

"How It Feels to Be Colored Me" was first published in The
World Tomorrow, *a magazine devoted to the causes of pacifism and
Christian socialism.*

I am colored but I offer nothing in the way of extenuating circumstances except the fact that I am the only Negro in the United States whose grandfather on the mother's side was *not* an Indian chief.[1]

I remember the very day that I became colored. Up to my thirteenth year I lived in the little Negro town of Eatonville, Florida. It is exclusively a colored town. The only white people I knew passed through the town going to or coming from Orlando.* The native whites rode dusty horses, the Northern* tourists chugged down the sandy village road in automobiles. The town knew the Southerners and never stopped cane chewing when they passed. But the Northerners were something else again. They were peered at cautiously from

---

1   *I am ... Indian chief* An improbably high number of African Americans claimed to have Native American heritage (considered prestigious in African American communities at this time).

behind curtains by the timid. The more venturesome would come out on the porch to watch them go past and got just as much pleasure out of the tourists as the tourists got out of the village.

The front porch might seem a daring place for the rest of the town, but it was a gallery[2] seat for me. My favorite place was atop the gate-post. Proscenium box for a born first-nighter.[3] Not only did I enjoy the show, but I didn't mind the actors knowing that I liked it. I usually spoke to them in passing. I'd wave at them and when they returned my salute, I would say something like this: "Howdy-do-well-I-thank-you-where-you-goin'?" Usually automobile or the horse paused at this, and after a queer exchange of compliments, I would probably "go a piece of the way" with them, as we say in farthest Florida. If one of my family happened to come to the front in time to see me, of course negotiations would be rudely broken off. But even so, it is clear that I was the first "welcome-to-our-state" Floridian, and I hope the Miami Chamber of Commerce* will please take notice.

During this period, white people differed from colored to me only in that they rode through town and never lived there. They liked to hear me "speak pieces" and sing and wanted to see me dance the parse-me-la,[4] and gave me generously of their small silver for doing these things, which seemed strange to me for I wanted to do them so much that I needed bribing to stop. Only they didn't know it. The colored people gave no dimes. They deplored any joyful tendencies in me, but I was their Zora nevertheless. I belonged to them, to the nearby hotels, to the county—everybody's Zora.

5   But changes came in the family when I was thirteen, and I was sent to school in Jacksonville. I left Eatonville, the town of the oleanders,* as Zora. When I disembarked from the river-boat at Jacksonville, she was no more. It seemed that I had suffered a sea change.* I was not Zora of Orange County* any more, I was now a little colored girl. I found it out in certain ways. In my heart as well as in the mirror, I became a fast[5] brown—warranted not to rub nor run.

But I am not tragically colored. There is no great sorrow dammed up in my soul, nor lurking behind my eyes. I do not mind at all. I do not belong to the sobbing school of Negrohood who hold that nature somehow has given

---

2   *gallery*   Theater seating area situated in an elevated balcony.

3   *Proscenium box*   Theater seating area near the proscenium, the frame of the stage; *first-nighter*   Person who frequently appears in the audience of opening night performances.

4   *parse-me-la*   Dance common in African American communities in the American South in the early twentieth century.

5   *fast*   Adjective applied to dyes that will not run or change color.

them a lowdown dirty deal and whose feelings are all hurt about it. Even in the helter-skelter skirmish that is my life, I have seen that the world is to the strong regardless of a little pigmentation more or less. No, I do not weep at the world—I am too busy sharpening my oyster knife.*

Someone is always at my elbow reminding me that I am the granddaughter of slaves. It fails to register depression with me. Slavery is sixty years in the past.[6] The operation was successful and the patient is doing well, thank you. The terrible struggle that made me an American out of a potential slave said "On the line!" The Reconstruction[7] said "Get set!"; and the generation before said "Go!"* I am off to a flying start and I must not halt in the stretch to look behind and weep. Slavery is the price I paid for civilization, and the choice was not with me. It is a bully[8] adventure and worth all that I have paid through my ancestors for it. No one on earth ever had a greater chance for glory. The world to be won and nothing to be lost. It is thrilling to think—to know that for any act of mine, I shall get twice as much praise or twice as much blame. It is quite exciting to hold the center of the national stage, with the spectators not knowing whether to laugh or to weep.

The position of my white neighbor is much more difficult. No brown specter pulls up a chair beside me when I sit down to eat. No dark ghost thrusts its leg against mine in bed. The game of keeping what one has is never so exciting as the game of getting.

I do not always feel colored. Even now I often achieve the unconscious Zora of Eatonville before the Hegira.[9] I feel most colored when I am thrown against a sharp white background.

For instance at Barnard.[10] "Beside the waters of the Hudson"[11] I feel my race. Among the thousand white persons, I am a dark rock surged upon, and overswept, but through it all, I remain myself. When covered by the waters, I am; and the ebb but reveals me again.

10

---

6   *Slavery is ... the past*   In 1863, the Emancipation Proclamation legally ended slavery in America.

7   *Reconstruction*   Period (1865–77) after the Civil War during which federal troops occupied the former Confederacy and enforced federal laws, as the South tried to build a society without slavery. (With the withdrawal of those troops following the "compromise of 1877," conditions for African Americans in many Southern jurisdictions reverted for many decades to a state little better than slavery.)

8   *bully*   Merry, splendid.

9   *Hegira*   I.e., journey; refers to Mohammed's journey from Mecca to Medina, which marks the beginning of the current era in the Islamic calendar.

10   *Barnard*   Women's liberal arts college in New York City, affiliated with Columbia University.

11   *"Beside ... Hudson"*   Barnard school song.

Sometimes it is the other way around. A white person is set down in our midst, but the contrast is just as sharp for me. For instance, when I sit in the drafty basement that is The New World Cabaret with a white person, my color comes. We enter chatting about any little nothing that we have in common and are seated by the jazz waiters. In the abrupt way that jazz orchestras have, this one plunges into a number. It loses no time in circumlocutions, but gets right down to business. It constricts the thorax and splits the heart with its tempo and narcotic harmonies. This orchestra grows rambunctious, rears on its hind legs and attacks the tonal veil with primitive fury, rending it, clawing it until it breaks through to the jungle beyond. I follow those heathen—follow them exultingly. I dance wildly inside myself; I yell within, I whoop; I shake my assegai[12] above my head, I hurl it true to the mark *yeeeeooww!* I am in the jungle and living in the jungle way. My face is painted red and yellow and my body is painted blue. My pulse is throbbing like a war drum. I want to slaughter something—give pain, give death to what, I do not know. But the piece ends. The men of the orchestra wipe their lips and rest their fingers. I creep back slowly to the veneer we call civilization with the last tone and find the white friend sitting motionless in his seat smoking calmly.

"Good music they have here," he remarks, drumming the table with his fingertips.

Music. The great blobs of purple and red emotion have not touched him. He has only heard what I felt. He is far away and I see him but dimly across the ocean and the continent that have fallen between us. He is so pale with his whiteness then and I am *so* colored.

At certain times I have no race, I am *me*. When I set my hat at a certain angle and saunter down Seventh Avenue, Harlem City,* feeling as snooty as the lions in front of the Forty-Second Street Library, for instance. So far as my feelings are concerned, Peggy Hopkins Joyce on the Boule Mich[13] with her gorgeous raiment, stately carriage, knees knocking together in a most aristocratic manner, has nothing on me. The cosmic Zora emerges. I belong to no race nor time. I am the eternal feminine with its string of beads.

15   I have no separate feeling about being an American citizen and colored. I am merely a fragment of the Great Soul that surges within the boundaries. My country, right or wrong.*

---

12   *assegai*   Spear made of a tree of the same name, used by people of southern Africa.
13   *Peggy Hopkins Joyce*   White American actress (1893–1957) known for her extravagant lifestyle;   *Boule Mich*   Boulevard Saint-Michel, a major street in Paris.

Sometimes, I feel discriminated against, but it does not make me angry. It merely astonishes me. How *can* any deny themselves the pleasure of my company? It's beyond me.

But in the main, I feel like a brown bag of miscellany propped against a wall. Against a wall in company with other bags, white, red and yellow. Pour out the contents, and there is discovered a jumble of small things priceless and worthless. A first-water[14] diamond, an empty spool, bits of broken glass, lengths of string, a key to a door long since crumbled away, a rusty knife-blade, old shoes saved for a road that never was and never will be, a nail bent under the weight of things too heavy for any nail, a dried flower or two still a little fragrant. In your hand is the brown bag. On the ground before you is the jumble it held—so much like the jumble in the bags, could they be emptied, that all might be dumped in a single heap and the bags refilled without altering the content of any greatly. A bit of colored glass more or less would not matter. Perhaps that is how the Great Stuffer of Bags filled them in the first place—who knows?

(1928)

---

14 *first-water* Best quality of diamond or other gem.

FRANKLIN D. ROOSEVELT

FIRST INAUGURAL ADDRESS

The election of 1932 presented a stark choice for American voters; the Republican incumbent, Herbert Hoover, had for the most part taken a hands-off approach to the worst economic Depression in the country's history; according to the orthodoxy of the day, governments were ill-advised to try to meddle in the economy, even in times of severe hardship. Democrat Franklin D. Roosevelt, a former Governor of New York, had called for a dramatically different approach—and had won a landslide victory in the election. His inaugural address, delivered following his swearing-in on Saturday, 4 March 1933 to a relatively small and quiet crowd, is now considered one of the greatest of American speeches.

Though politicians typically set the tone of their speeches and take responsibility for what is said, most of the phrasings have (at least since the early twentieth century) been the work of speechwriters. In this case Roosevelt's primary speechwriter was a Columbia University professor of political economy, Raymond Moly. Roosevelt himself was certainly responsible for some of the wording; an advisor, Louis McHenry Howe, is said to have been responsible for the famous sentence about what Americans have to fear.

I am certain that my fellow Americans expect that on my induction into the presidency I will address them with a candor and a decision which the present situation of our nation impels. This is preeminently the time to speak the truth, the whole truth, frankly and boldly. Nor need we shrink from honestly facing conditions in our country today. This great nation will endure as it has endured, will revive and will prosper. So, first of all, let me assert my firm belief that the only thing we have to fear is fear itself—nameless, unreasoning, unjustified terror which paralyzes needed efforts to convert retreat into advance. In every dark hour of our national life a leadership of frankness and vigor has met with that understanding and support of the people themselves which is essential to victory. I am convinced that you will again give that support to leadership in these critical days.

In such a spirit on my part and on yours we face our common difficulties. They concern, thank God, only material things. Values have shrunken to fantastic levels;[1] taxes have risen; our ability to pay has fallen; government of all kinds is faced by serious curtailment of income; the means of exchange are frozen in the currents of trade; the withered leaves of industrial enterprise lie on every side; farmers find no markets for their produce; the savings of many years in thousands of families are gone.

More important, a host of unemployed citizens face the grim problem of existence, and an equally great number toil with little return. Only a foolish optimist can deny the dark realities of the moment.

Yet our distress comes from no failure of substance. We are stricken by no plague of locusts.[2] Compared with the perils which our forefathers conquered because they believed and were not afraid, we have still much to be thankful for. Nature still offers her bounty and human efforts have multiplied it. Plenty is at our doorstep, but a generous use of it languishes in the very sight of the supply. Primarily this is because the rulers of the exchange of mankind's goods have failed, through their own stubbornness and their own incompetence, have admitted their failure, and abdicated. Practices of the unscrupulous money changers[3] stand indicted in the court of public opinion, rejected by the hearts and minds of men.

True, they have tried, but their efforts have been cast in the pattern of an outworn tradition. Faced by failure of credit they have proposed only the lending of more money. Stripped of the lure of profit by which to induce our people to follow their false leadership, they have resorted to exhortations, pleading tearfully for restored confidence. They know only the rules of a generation of self-seekers. They have no vision, and when there is no vision the people perish.

The money changers have fled from their high seats in the temple of our civilization. We may now restore that temple to the ancient truths. The measure of the restoration lies in the extent to which we apply social values more noble than mere monetary profit.

Happiness lies not in the mere possession of money; it lies in the joy of achievement, in the thrill of creative effort. The joy and moral stimulation of work no longer must be forgotten in the mad chase of evanescent profits. These

5

---

1   *Values…levels*   During the Great Depression there was significant deflation; prices fell dramatically, and wages even more so.

2   *plague of locusts*   In Exodus, one of ten plagues inflicted on Egypt as divine punishment.

3   *money changers*   Used here as a general term to refer to all sorts of financiers.

dark days will be worth all they cost us if they teach us that our true destiny is not to be ministered unto but to minister to ourselves and to our fellow men.

Recognition of the falsity of material wealth as the standard of success goes hand in hand with the abandonment of the false belief that public office and high political position are to be valued only by the standards of pride of place and personal profit; and there must be an end to a conduct in banking and in business which too often has given to a sacred trust the likeness of callous and selfish wrongdoing. Small wonder that confidence languishes, for it thrives only on honesty, on honor, on the sacredness of obligations, on faithful protection, on unselfish performance; without them it cannot live.

Restoration calls, however, not for changes in ethics alone. This nation asks for action, and action now.

10
Our greatest primary task is to put people to work. This is no unsolvable problem if we face it wisely and courageously. It can be accomplished in part by direct recruiting by the Government itself, treating the task as we would treat the emergency of a war, but at the same time, through this employment, accomplishing greatly needed projects to stimulate and reorganize the use of our natural resources.

Hand in hand with this we must frankly recognize the overbalance of population in our industrial centers and, by engaging on a national scale in a redistribution, endeavor to provide a better use of the land for those best fitted for the land. The task can be helped by definite efforts to raise the values of agricultural products and with this the power to purchase the output of our cities. It can be helped by preventing realistically the tragedy of the growing loss through foreclosure of our small homes and our farms. It can be helped by insistence that the federal, state, and local governments act forthwith on the demand that their cost be drastically reduced. It can be helped by the unifying of relief activities which today are often scattered, uneconomical, and unequal. It can be helped by national planning for and supervision of all forms of transportation and of communications and other utilities which have a definitely public character. There are many ways in which it can be helped, but it can never be helped merely by talking about it. We must act and act quickly.

Finally, in our progress toward a resumption of work we require two safeguards against a return of the evils of the old order; there must be a strict supervision of all banking and credits and investments; there must be an end to speculation with other people's money, and there must be provision for an adequate but sound currency.

There are the lines of attack. I shall presently urge upon a new Congress in special session detailed measures for their fulfillment, and I shall seek the immediate assistance of the several states.*

Through this program of action we address ourselves to putting our own national house in order and making income balance outgo. Our international trade relations, though vastly important, are in point of time and necessity secondary to the establishment of a sound national economy. I favor as a practical policy the putting of first things first. I shall spare no effort to restore world trade by international economic readjustment, but the emergency at home cannot wait on that accomplishment.

The basic thought that guides these specific means of national recovery is not narrowly nationalistic. It is the insistence, as a first consideration, upon the interdependence of the various elements in all parts of the United States—a recognition of the old and permanently important manifestation of the American spirit of the pioneer. It is the way to recovery. It is the immediate way. It is the strongest assurance that the recovery will endure.

In the field of world policy I would dedicate this nation to the policy of the good neighbor—the neighbor who resolutely respects himself and, because he does so, respects the rights of others—the neighbor who respects his obligations and respects the sanctity of his agreements in and with a world of neighbors.

If I read the temper* of our people correctly, we now realize as we have never realized before our interdependence on each other; that we cannot merely take but we must give as well; that if we are to go forward, we must move as a trained and loyal army willing to sacrifice for the good of a common discipline, because without such discipline no progress is made, no leadership becomes effective. We are, I know, ready and willing to submit our lives and property to such discipline, because it makes possible a leadership which aims at a larger good. This I propose to offer, pledging that the larger purposes will bind upon us all as a sacred obligation with a unity of duty hitherto evoked only in time of armed strife.

With this pledge taken, I assume unhesitatingly the leadership of this great army of our people dedicated to a disciplined attack upon our common problems.

Action in this image and to this end is feasible under the form of government which we have inherited from our ancestors. Our constitution is so simple and practical that it is possible always to meet extraordinary needs by changes in emphasis and arrangement without loss of essential form. That is why our constitutional system has proved itself the most superbly enduring political mechanism the modern world has produced. It has met every stress of vast expansion of territory, of foreign wars, of bitter internal strife, of world relations.

It is to be hoped that the normal balance of executive and legislative authority may be wholly adequate to meet the unprecedented task before us. But it may be that an unprecedented demand and need for undelayed action may call for temporary departure from that normal balance of public procedure.

I am prepared under my constitutional duty to recommend the measures that a stricken nation in the midst of a stricken world may require. These measures, or such other measures as the Congress may build out of its experience and wisdom, I shall seek, within my constitutional authority, to bring to speedy adoption.

But in the event that the Congress shall fail to take one of these two courses, and in the event that the national emergency is still critical, I shall not evade the clear course of duty that will then confront me. I shall ask the Congress for the one remaining instrument to meet the crisis—broad Executive power* to wage a war against the emergency, as great as the power that would be given to me if we were in fact invaded by a foreign foe.

For the trust reposed in me I will return the courage and the devotion that befit the time. I can do no less.

We face the arduous days that lie before us in the warm courage of the national unity; with the clear consciousness of seeking old and precious moral values; with the clean satisfaction that comes from the stern performance of duty by old and young alike. We aim at the assurance of a rounded and permanent national life.

25   We do not distrust the future of essential democracy. The people of the United States have not failed. In their need they have registered a mandate that they want direct, vigorous action. They have asked for discipline and direction under leadership. They have made me the present instrument of their wishes. In the spirit of the gift I take it.

In this dedication of a nation we humbly ask the blessing of God. May He protect each and every one of us. May He guide me in the days to come.

(1933)

VIRGINIA WOOLF

from THREE GUINEAS[1]

Today, Virginia Woolf is admired and studied primarily as the author of such masterpieces as Mrs. Dalloway *(1925),* To the Lighthouse *(1927), and* The Waves *(1931), novels that attempt to capture the rhythms of consciousness by rendering the subjective interplay of perception, recollection, emotion, and understanding. But in her own lifetime Woolf was best known for her non-fiction— in much of which she employed "the democratic art of prose" to communicate with a broad readership on fundamental ethical and political questions.*

The book-length essay Three Guineas *(1938) was written on the verge of the Second World War; Woolf responds with surprising answers to a hypothetical letter, purportedly sent by an educated gentleman on behalf of an anti-war society, asking how "we are to prevent war." Her response is divided into three sections; in the first section she addresses the question of why women do not receive support in education, in the second considers women's relationship to professional work, and in the third directly addresses the initial question of how war should be prevented.*

from ONE

Three years is a long time to leave a letter unanswered, and your letter has been lying without an answer even longer than that. I had hoped that it would answer itself, or that other people would answer it for me. But there it is with its question—How in your opinion are we to prevent war?—still unanswered.

It is true that many answers have suggested themselves, but none that would not need explanation, and explanations take time. In this case, too, there

---

1   *Guineas*   British coins worth 21 shillings. After the early nineteenth century the coins themselves were no longer used in the United Kingdom, but prices were still often given in guineas—especially among the wealthy elite—for much of the twentieth century.

are reasons why it is particularly difficult to avoid misunderstanding. A whole page could be filled with excuses and apologies; declarations of unfitness, incompetence, lack of knowledge, and experience: and they would be true. But even when they were said there would still remain some difficulties so fundamental that it may well prove impossible for you to understand or for us to explain. But one does not like to leave so remarkable a letter as yours—a letter perhaps unique in the history of human correspondence, since when before has an educated man asked a woman how in her opinion war can be prevented?—unanswered. Therefore let us make the attempt; even if it is doomed to failure.

In the first place let us draw what all letter-writers instinctively draw, a sketch of the person to whom the letter is addressed. Without someone warm and breathing on the other side of the page, letters are worthless. You, then, who ask the question, are a little grey on the temples; the hair is no longer thick on the top of your head. You have reached the middle years of life not without effort, at the Bar;[2] but on the whole your journey has been prosperous. There is nothing parched, mean or dissatisfied in your expression. And without wishing to flatter you, your prosperity—wife, children, house—has been deserved. You have never sunk into the contented apathy of middle life, for, as your letter from an office in the heart of London shows, instead of turning on your pillow and prodding your pigs, pruning your pear trees—you have a few acres in Norfolk*—you are writing letters, attending meetings, presiding over this and that, asking questions, with the sound of the guns in your ears. For the rest, you began your education at one of the great public schools[3] and finished it at the university.

It is now that the first difficulty of communication between us appears. Let us rapidly indicate the reason. We both come of what, in this hybrid age when, though birth is mixed, classes still remain fixed, it is convenient to call the educated class. When we meet in the flesh we speak with the same accent; use knives and forks in the same way; expect maids to cook dinner and wash up after dinner; and can talk during dinner without much difficulty about politics and people; war and peace; barbarism and civilization—all the questions indeed suggested by your letter. Moreover, we both earn our livings. But … those three dots mark a precipice, a gulf so deeply cut between us that for three years and more I have been sitting on my side of it wondering whether it is any use to try to speak across it. Let us then ask someone else—it is Mary

---

2   *at the Bar*   I.e., as a lawyer.

3   *public schools*   I.e., expensive and prestigious secondary schools; in North America, similar institutions are called "private schools."

Kingsley[4]—to speak for us. "I don't know if I ever revealed to you the fact that being allowed to learn German was all the paid-for education I ever had. Two thousand pounds was spent on my brother's, I still hope not in vain."[5]

Mary Kingsley is not speaking for herself alone; she is speaking, still, for many of the daughters of educated men. And she is not merely speaking for them; she is also pointing to a very important fact about them, a fact that must profoundly influence all that follows: the fact of Arthur's Education Fund.[6] You, who have read *Pendennis*, will remember how the mysterious letters A.E.F.[7] figured in the household ledgers. Ever since the thirteenth century English families have been paying money into that account. From the Pastons[8] to the Pendennises, all educated families from the thirteenth century to the present moment have paid money into that account. It is a voracious receptacle. Where there were many sons to educate it required a great effort on the part of the family to keep it full. For your education was not merely in book-learning; games educated your body; friends taught you more than books or games. Talk with them broadened your outlook and enriched your mind. In the holidays you traveled; acquired a taste for art; a knowledge of foreign politics; and then, before you could earn your own living, your father made you an allowance upon which it was possible for you to live while you learnt the profession which now entitles you to add the letters K.C.[9] to your name. All this came out of Arthur's Education Fund. And to this your sisters ... made their contribution. Not only did their own education, save for such small sums as paid the German teacher, go into it; but many of those luxuries and trimmings which are, after all, an essential part of education—travel, society, solitude, a lodging apart from the family house—they were paid into it too. It was a voracious receptacle, a solid fact—Arthur's Education Fund—a fact so solid indeed that it cast a shadow

---

4 *Mary Kingsley* British ethnographer (1862–1900), known for writing about her travels in West Africa.

5 *The Life of Mary Kingsley*, by Stephen Gwynn, p. 15.... [author's note]

6 *Arthur's Education Fund* Fictional metaphor used to represent the family funds put exclusively toward sending young men to college. The name is a reference to William Makepeace Thackeray's novel *The History of Pendennis: His Fortunes and Misfortunes, His Friends and His Greatest Enemy* (1848–50).

7 *A.E.F.* Cf. *Pendennis* Chapter 19: "John Pendennis, whose darling project it had ever been to give his son a university education ... had begun laying by a store of money which he called Arthur's Education Fund. Year after year in his book his executors found entries of sums vested as A.E.F." After failing his exams Arthur Pendennis returns from college and his sister Laura sacrifices her own money to pay his debts.

8 *Pastons* Reference to the Paston Letters, a large collection of correspondences between the Paston family from 1422 to 1509.

9 *K.C.* King's Council.

over the entire landscape. And the result is that though we look at the same things, we see them differently. What is that congregation of buildings there, with a semi-monastic look, with chapels and halls and green playing-fields? To you it is your old school; Eton or Harrow;[10] your old university, Oxford or Cambridge;[11] the source of memories and of traditions innumerable. But to us, who see it through the shadow of Arthur's Education Fund, it is a schoolroom table; an omnibus going to a class; a little woman with a red nose who is not well educated herself but has an invalid mother to support; an allowance of £50[12] a year with which to buy clothes, give presents and take journeys on coming to maturity. Such is the effect that Arthur's Education Fund has had upon us. So magically does it change the landscape that the noble courts and quadrangles of Oxford and Cambridge often appear to educated men's daughters ... like petticoats with holes in them, cold legs of mutton, and the boat train starting for abroad* while the guard slams the door in their faces.

The fact that Arthur's Education Fund changes the landscape—the halls, the playing grounds, the sacred edifices—is an important one; but that aspect must be left for future discussion. Here we are only concerned with the obvious fact, when it comes to considering this important question—how we are to help you prevent war—that education makes a difference. Some knowledge of politics, of international relations of economics, is obviously necessary in order to understand the causes which lead to war. Philosophy, theology even, might come in usefully. Now you the uneducated, you with an untrained mind, could not possibly deal with such questions satisfactorily. War, as the result of impersonal forces, is you will agree beyond the grasp of the untrained mind. But war as the result of human nature is another thing. Had you not believed that human nature, the reasons, the emotions of the ordinary man and woman, lead to war, you would not have written asking for our help. You must have argued, men and women, here and now, are able to exert their wills; they are not pawns and puppets dancing on a string held by invisible hands. They can act, and think for themselves. Perhaps even they can influence other people's thoughts and actions. Some such reasoning must have led you to apply to us; and with justification. For happily there is one branch of education which comes under the heading "unpaid-for education"—that understanding of human beings and their motives which, if the word is rid of its scientific associations, might be called psychology. Marriage, the one great profession open to our class since

---

10 *Eton or Harrow* British boys' boarding schools founded in 1440 and 1572 respectively.

11 *Oxford or Cambridge* The second- and fourth-oldest universities in the world.

12 *£50* Roughly equivalent to £3,000 or $4,300 USD in 2015.

the dawn of time until the year 1919;[13] marriage, the art of choosing the human being with whom to live life successfully, should have taught us some skill in that. But here again another difficulty confronts us. For though many instincts are held more or less in common by both sexes, to fight has always been the man's habit, not the woman's. Law and practice have developed that difference, whether innate or accidental.* Scarcely a human being in the course of history has fallen to a woman's rifle; the vast majority of birds and beasts have been killed by you, not by us; and it is difficult to judge what we do not share.[14]

How then are we to understand your problem, and if we cannot, how can we answer your question, how to prevent war? The answer based upon our experience and our psychology—Why fight?—is not an answer of any value. Obviously there is for you some glory, some necessity, some satisfaction in fighting which we have never felt or enjoyed. Complete understanding could only be achieved by blood transfusion and memory transfusion—a miracle still beyond the reach of science. But we who live now have a substitute for blood transfusion and memory transfusion which must serve at a pinch. There is that marvelous, perpetually renewed, and as yet largely untapped aid to the understanding of human motives which is provided in our age by biography and autobiography. Also there is the daily paper, history in the raw. There is thus no longer any reason to be confined to the minute span of actual experience which is still, for us, so narrow, so circumscribed. We can supplement it by looking at the picture of the lives of others. It is of course only a picture at present, but as such it must serve. It is to biography then that we will turn first, quickly and briefly, in order to attempt to understand what war means to you. Let us extract a few sentences from a biography.

First, this from a soldier's[15] life:

> I have had the happiest possible life, and have always been working for war, and have now got into the biggest in the prime of life for a soldier ... Thank God, we are off in an hour. Such a magnificent regiment! Such men, such horses! Within ten days I hope Francis and I will be riding side by side straight at the Germans.[16]

---

13 *1919* Date of the passage of the Sex Disqualification Act, which allowed women to work in areas they had previously been denied access to, such as law and some areas of government.

14 ... Little mention is made in sporting memoirs of women guns; and their appearance in the hunting fields was the cause of much caustic comment.... [author's note]

15 *soldier* Riversdale Grenfell (1880–1914), British soldier of the 9th lancers and twin brother to Captain Francis Grenfell (1880–1915).

16 *Francis and the Riversdale Grenfell*, by John Buchan, pp. 189, 205. [author's note]

To which the biographer[17] adds:

From the first hour he had been supremely happy, for he had found his true calling.

10   To that let us add this from an airman's[18] life:

We talked of the League of Nations[19] and the prospects of peace and disarmament. On this subject he was not so much militarist as martial. The difficulty to which he could find no answer was that if permanent peace were ever achieved, and armies and navies ceased to exist, there would be no outlet for the manly qualities which fighting developed, and that human physique and human character would deteriorate.[20]

Here, immediately, are three reasons which lead your sex to fight; war is a profession; a source of happiness and excitement; and it is also an outlet for manly qualities, without which men would deteriorate. But that these feelings and opinions are by no means universally held by your sex is proved by the following extract from another biography, the life of a poet who was killed in the European war: Wilfred Owen.[21]

Already I have comprehended a light which never will filter into the dogma of any national church: namely, that one of Christ's essential commands was: Passivity at any price! Suffer dishonor and disgrace, but never resort to arms. Be bullied, be outraged, be killed; but do not kill ... Thus you see how pure Christianity will not fit in with pure patriotism.[22]

And among some notes for poems that he did not live to write are these:

---

17   *biographer*   John Buchan, Scottish novelist, historian, and 15th Governor General of Canada. Buchan was a good friend of the Grenfell twins, and the quotation is from his 1920 biography *Francis and Riversdale Grenfell: A Memoir*.

18   *airman*   Antony Bulwer-Lytton (1903–33), Viscount Knebworth, British pilot and Conservative politician, who died in a plane crash. He was the son of Victor Bulwer-Lytton (1876–1947), 2nd Earl of Lytton and Governor of Bengal, who is the author of the following quotation.

19   *League of Nations*   International organization founded at the end of World War I with the goal of fostering world peace. It was replaced by the United Nations after World War II.

20   *Antony (Viscount Knebworth)*, by the Earl of Lytton, p. 355. [author's note]

21   *Wilfred Owen*   British soldier (1893–1918) whose poetry is known for its shockingly realistic depiction of the trench conditions and gas weapons of World War I.

22   *Already ... patriotism*   From a letter home written on 2 May 1917.

The unnaturalness of weapons ... Inhumanity of war ... The insupport-
ability of war ... Horrible beastliness of war ... Foolishness of war.[23]

From these quotations it is obvious that the same sex holds very different
opinions about the same thing. But also it is obvious, from today's newspaper,
that however many dissentients[24] there are, the great majority of your sex
are today in favor of war. The Scarborough Conference of educated men,
the Bournemouth Conference of working men are both agreed that to spend
£300,000,000[25] annually upon arms is a necessity. They are of opinion that
Wilfred Owen was wrong; that it is better to kill than to be killed. Yet since
biography shows that differences of opinion are many, it is plain that there must
be some one reason which prevails in order to bring about this overpowering
unanimity. Shall we call it, for the sake of brevity, "patriotism"? What then, we
must ask next, is this "patriotism" which leads you to go to war? Let the Lord
Chief Justice of England interpret it for us:

> Englishmen are proud of England. For those who have been trained in
> English schools and universities, and who have done the work of their
> lives in England, there are few loves stronger than the love we have
> for our country. When we consider other nations, when we judge the
> merits of the policy of this country or of that, it is the standard of our
> own country that we apply.... Liberty has made her abode in England.
> England is the home of democratic institutions.... It is true that in our
> midst there are many enemies of liberty—some of them, perhaps, in
> rather unexpected quarters. But we are standing firm. It has been said
> that an Englishman's Home is his Castle. The home of Liberty is in
> England. And it is a castle indeed—a castle that will be defended to
> the last.... Yes, we are greatly blessed, we Englishmen.[26]

That is a fair general statement of what patriotism means to an educated
man and what duties it imposes upon him. But the educated man's sister—what
does "patriotism" mean to her? Has she the same reasons for being proud of
England, for loving England, for defending England? Has she been "greatly
blessed" in England? History and biography when questioned would seem to

23 *The Poems of Wilfred Owen*, edited by Edmund Blunden, pp. 25, 41. [author's note]
24 *dissentients* Dissenters.
25 *Scarborough Conference* The Conservative Party Conference of 1937 was held in
Scarborough; *Bournemouth Conference* The Labour Party Conference of 1937 was
held in Bournemouth; *£300,000,000* Roughly equivalent to £18.5 billion, or $26.5
billion USD in 2015.
26 Lord Hewart, proposing the toast of "England" at the banquet of the Society of St
George at Cardiff. [author's note]

show that her position in the home of freedom has been different from her brother's; and psychology would seem to hint that history is not without its effect upon mind and body. Therefore her interpretation of the word "patriotism" may well differ from his. And that difference may make it extremely difficult for her to understand his definition of patriotism and the duties it imposes. If then our answer to your question, "How in your opinion are we to prevent war?" depends upon understanding the reasons, the emotions, the loyalties which lead men to go to war, this letter had better be torn across and thrown into the waste-paper basket. For it seems plain that we cannot understand each other because of these differences. It seems plain that we think differently according as we are born differently; there is a Grenfell point of view; a Knebworth point of view; a Wilfred Owen point of view; a Lord Chief Justice's point of view and the point of view of an educated man's daughter. All differ. But is there no absolute point of view? Can we not find somewhere written up in letters of fire or gold, "This is right. This wrong"?—a moral judgement which we must all, whatever our differences, accept? Let us then refer the question of the rightness or wrongness of war to those who make morality their profession—the clergy. Surely if we ask the clergy the simple question: "Is war right or is war wrong?" they will give us a plain answer which we cannot deny. But no—the Church of England, which might be supposed able to abstract the question from its worldly confusions, is of two minds also. The bishops themselves are at loggerheads.[27] The Bishop of London[28] maintained that "the real danger to the peace of the world today were the pacifists. Bad as war was dishonor was far worse." On the other hand, the Bishop of Birmingham[29] described himself as an "extreme pacifist.... I cannot see myself that war can be regarded as consonant with the spirit of Christ."[30] So the Church itself gives us divided counsel—in some circumstances it is right to fight; in no circumstances is it right to fight. It is distressing, baffling, confusing, but the fact must be faced; there is no certainty in heaven above or on earth below. Indeed the more lives we read, the more speeches we listen to, the more opinions we consult, the greater the confusion becomes and the less possible it seems, since we cannot understand the impulses, the motives, or the morality which lead you to go to war, to make any suggestion that will help you to prevent war.

---

27 *at loggerheads* At odds; thick-headedly arguing.

28 *Bishop of London* Arthur Winnington-Ingram (1858–1946), an ardent supporter of World War I.

29 *Bishop of Birmingham* Ernest Barnes (1874–1953), mathematician, scientist, and controversially liberal theologian.

30 *The Daily Telegraph*, February 5th, 1937. [author's note]

But besides these pictures of other people's lives and minds—these biographies and histories—there are also other pictures—pictures of actual facts; photographs. Photographs, of course, are not arguments addressed to the reason; they are simply statements of fact addressed to the eye. But in that very simplicity there may be some help. Let us see then whether when we look at the same photographs we feel the same things. Here then on the table before us are photographs. The Spanish Government sends them with patient pertinacity about twice a week.[31] They are not pleasant photographs to look upon. They are photographs of dead bodies for the most part. This morning's collection contains the photograph of what might be a man's body, or a woman's; it is so mutilated that it might, on the other hand, be the body of a pig. But those certainly are dead children, and that undoubtedly is the section of a house. A bomb has torn open the side; there is still a birdcage hanging in what was presumably the sitting-room, but the rest of the house looks like nothing so much as a bunch of spillikins[32] suspended in mid air.

Those photographs are not an argument; they are simply a crude statement of fact addressed to the eye. But the eye is connected with the brain; the brain with the nervous system. That system sends its messages in a flash through every past memory and present feeling. When we look at those photographs some fusion takes place within us; however different the education, the traditions behind us, our sensations are the same; and they are violent. You, Sir, call them "horror and disgust."[33] We also call them horror and disgust. And the same words rise to our lips. War, you say, is an abomination; a barbarity; war must be stopped at whatever cost. And we echo your words. War is an abomination; a barbarity; war must be stopped. For now at last we are looking at the same picture; we are seeing with you the same dead bodies, the same ruined houses.

Let us then give up, for the moment, the effort to answer your question, how we can help you to prevent war, by discussing the political, the patriotic or the psychological reasons which lead you to go to war. The emotion is too positive to suffer patient analysis. Let us concentrate upon the practical suggestions which you bring forward for our consideration. There are three of them. The

---

31   Written in the winter of 1936–7. [author's note] [The photographs referenced are of the Spanish Civil War (1936–39), a notoriously violent conflict between the democratically elected, leftist Republican government and a Nationalist military insurgency; it resulted in a Nationalist victory and the establishment of Francisco Franco as totalitarian dictator of Spain. The photographs mentioned were sent by the Republican side in the hope of garnering international support.]

32   *spillikins*   Splinters.

33   *"horror and disgust"*   In a 19 March 1938 report in *The Times*, the Prime Minister is quoted as saying "he did not think that anybody could have read the newspaper reports of what happened [in Barcelona] without horror and disgust."

first is to sign a letter to the newspapers; the second is to join a certain society; the third is to subscribe to its funds. Nothing on the face of it could sound simpler. To scribble a name on a sheet of paper is easy; to attend a meeting where pacific opinions are more or less rhetorically reiterated to people who already believe in them is also easy; and to write a cheque in support of those vaguely acceptable opinions, though not so easy, is a cheap way of quieting what may conveniently be called one's conscience. Yet there are reasons which make us hesitate; reasons into which we must enter, less superficially, later on. Here it is enough to say that though the three measures you suggest seem plausible, yet it also seems that, if we did what you ask, the emotion caused by the photographs would still remain unappeased. That emotion, that very positive emotion, demands something more positive than a name written on a sheet of paper; an hour spent listening to speeches; a cheque written for whatever sum we can afford—say one guinea. Some more energetic, some more active method of expressing our belief that war is barbarous, that war is inhuman, that war, as Wilfred Owen put it, is insupportable, horrible and beastly seems to be required. But, rhetoric apart, what active method is open to us? Let us consider and compare. You, of course, could once more take up arms—in Spain, as before in France—in defence of peace. But that presumably is a method that having tried you have rejected. At any rate that method is not open to us; both the Army and the Navy are closed to our sex. We are not allowed to fight. Nor again are we allowed to be members of the Stock Exchange. Thus we can use neither the pressure of force nor the pressure of money. The less direct but still effective weapons which our brothers, as educated men, possess in the diplomatic service, in the Church, are also denied to us. We cannot preach sermons or negotiate treaties. Then again although it is true that we can write articles or send letters to the Press, the control of the Press—the decision what to print, what not to print—is entirely in the hands of your sex. It is true that for the past twenty years we have been admitted to the Civil Service and to the Bar; but our position there is still very precarious and our authority of the slightest. Thus all the weapons with which an educated man can enforce his opinion are either beyond our grasp or so nearly beyond it that even if we used them we could scarcely inflict one scratch. If the men in your profession were to unite in any demand and were to say: "If it is not granted we will stop work," the laws of England would cease to be administered. If the women in your profession said the same thing it would make no difference to the laws of England whatever....

[The following selection is another hypothetical letter that is offered to the educated gentleman for his consideration, nested within the larger letter that comprises the full essay. This smaller letter is one addressed to an honorary treasurer who has asked for donations to a "society for helping the daughters of educated men to obtain employment in the professions."]

from Two

... "Your letter, Madam, has waited a long time for an answer, but we have been examining into certain charges made against you and making certain inquiries. We have acquitted you, Madam, you will be relieved to learn, of telling lies. It would seem to be true that you are poor. We have acquitted you further, of idleness, apathy and greed. The number of causes that you are championing, however secretly and ineffectively, is in your favor.... Indeed, you would appear to be working, without a salary too, rather longer hours than the Home Office would approve. But though we are willing to deplore your poverty and to commend your industry we are not going to send you a guinea to help you to help women to enter the professions unless you can assure us that they will practise those professions in such a way as to prevent war. That, you will say, is a vague statement, an impossible condition. Still, since guineas are rare and guineas are valuable you will listen to the terms we wish to impose if, you intimate, they can be stated briefly. Well then, Madam, since you are pressed for time, ... let us be quick; make a rapid survey; discuss a few passages in the books in your library; in the papers on your table, and then see if we can make the statement less vague, the conditions more clear.

"Let us then begin by looking at the outside of things, at the general aspect. Things have outsides let us remember as well as insides. Close at hand is a bridge over the Thames,[34] an admirable vantage ground for such a survey. The river flows beneath; barges pass, laden with timber, bursting with corn; there on one side are the domes and spires of the city; on the other, Westminster[35] and the Houses of Parliament.* It is a place to stand on by the hour, dreaming. But not now. Now we are pressed for time. Now we are here to consider facts; now we must fix our eyes upon the procession—the procession of the sons of educated men.

"There they go, our brothers who have been educated at public schools and universities, mounting those steps, passing in and out of those doors, ascending

20

---

34   *Thames*   Major river flowing through London.
35   *corn*   Grain;   *Westminster*   Area of London where Buckingham Palace and other official buildings are located.

those pulpits, preaching, teaching, administering justice, practicing medicine, transacting business, making money. It is a solemn sight always—a procession, like a caravanserai[36] crossing a desert. Great-grandfathers, grandfathers, fathers, uncles—they all went that way, wearing their gowns, wearing their wigs, some with ribbons across their breasts, others without. One was a bishop. Another a judge. One was an admiral. Another a general. One was a professor. Another a doctor. And some left the procession and were last heard of doing nothing in Tasmania; were seen, rather shabbily dressed, selling newspapers at Charing Cross.[37] But most of them kept in step, walked according to rule, and by hook or by crook made enough to keep the family house, somewhere, roughly speaking, in the West End,[38] supplied with beef and mutton for all, and with education for Arthur. It is a solemn sight, this procession, a sight that has often caused us,[39] you may remember, looking at it sidelong from an upper window, to ask ourselves certain questions. But now, for the past twenty years or so, it is no longer a sight merely, a photograph, or fresco scrawled upon the walls of time, at which we can look with merely an aesthetic appreciation. For there, trapesing along at the tail end of the procession, we go ourselves. And that makes a difference. We who have looked so long at the pageant in books, or from a curtained window watched educated men leaving the house at about nine-thirty to go to an office, returning to the house at about six-thirty from an office, need look passively no longer. We too can leave the house, can mount those steps, pass in and out of those doors, wear wigs and gowns, make money, administer justice. Think—one of these days, you may wear a judge's wig on your head, an ermine cape on your shoulders; sit under the lion and the unicorn;[40] draw a salary of five thousand a year with a pension on retiring. We who now agitate these humble pens may in another century or two speak from a pulpit. Nobody will dare contradict us then; we shall be the mouthpieces of the divine spirit—a solemn thought, is it not? Who can say whether, as time goes on, we may not dress in military uniform, with gold lace on our breasts, swords at our sides, and something like the old family coal-scuttle on our heads, save that that venerable object was never decorated with plumes of white horsehair.* You laugh—indeed the shadow of the private house still makes those dresses look a little queer. We have worn private clothes

---

36 *caravanserai* Here, a group of caravans traveling together.

37 *Charing Cross* Busy London intersection where a railway station is located.

38 *West End* Upscale London district.

39 *us* I.e., women.

40 *ermine* Fur worn by British judges and nobility; *the lion and the unicorn* Symbols in the United Kingdom's coat of arms.

so long—the veil that St Paul recommended.[41] But we have not come here to laugh, or to talk of fashions—men's and women's. We are here, on the bridge, to ask ourselves certain questions. And they are very important questions; and we have very little time in which to answer them. The questions that we have to ask and to answer about that procession during this moment of transition are so important that they may well change the lives of all men and women for ever. For we have to ask ourselves, here and now, do we wish to join that procession, or don't we? On what terms shall we join that procession? Above all, where is it leading us, the procession of educated men? The moment is short; it may last five years; ten years, or perhaps only a matter of a few months longer. But the questions must be answered; and they are so important that if all the daughters of educated men did nothing, from morning to night, but consider that procession from every angle, if they did nothing but ponder it and analyse it, and think about it and read about it and pool their thinking and reading, and what they see and what they guess, their time would be better spent than in any other activity now open to them. But, you will object, you have no time to think; you have your battles to fight, your rent to pay, your bazaars to organize.* That excuse shall not serve you, Madam. As you know from your own experience, and there are facts that prove it, the daughters of educated men have always done their thinking from hand to mouth; not under green lamps at study tables in the cloisters of secluded colleges. They have thought while they stirred the pot, while they rocked the cradle. It was thus that they won us the right to our brand-new sixpence.[42] It falls to us now to go on thinking; how are we to spend that sixpence? Think we must. Let us think in offices; in omnibuses; while we are standing in the crowd watching Coronations and Lord Mayor's Shows; let us think as we pass the Cenotaph; and in Whitehall;[43] in the gallery of the House of Commons;* in the Law Courts;* let us think at baptisms and marriages and funerals. Let us never cease from thinking—what is this 'civilization' in which we find ourselves? What are these ceremonies and why should we take part in them? What are these professions and why should we make money out of them? Where in short is it leading us, the procession of the sons of educated men?

---

41 *the veil ... recommended* Paul instructs women only to pray with covered heads because "a man indeed ought not to cover his head, forasmuch as he is the image and glory of God: but the woman is the glory of the man" (1 Corinthians 11.7).

42 *our brand-new sixpence* Earlier in the essay, Woolf writes that after the passage of the 1919 Sex Discrimination Act, "[i]n every purse there was, or might be, one bright new sixpence."

43 *Lord Mayor's Shows* Parade in honor of the swearing-in of the Lord Mayor of London; *Cenotaph* London war memorial; *Whitehall* Westminster street where many British government buildings are located.

"But you are busy; let us return to facts. Come indoors then, and open the books on your library shelves.... [A]lmost every biography we read of professional men in the nineteenth century, to limit ourselves to that not distant and fully documented age, is largely concerned with war. They were great fighters, it seems, the professional men in the age of Queen Victoria. There was the battle of Westminster.[44] There was the battle of the universities. There was the battle of Whitehall. There was the battle of Harley Street.[45] There was the battle of the Royal Academy.[46] Some of these battles, as you can testify, are still in progress. In fact the only profession which does not seem to have fought a fierce battle during the nineteenth century is the profession of literature. All the other professions, according to the testimony of biography, seem to be as bloodthirsty as the profession of arms itself. It is true that the combatants did not inflict flesh wounds;[47] chivalry forbade;* but you will agree that a battle that wastes time is as deadly as a battle that wastes blood. You will agree that a battle that costs money is as deadly as a battle that costs a leg or an arm. You will agree that a battle that forces youth to spend its strength haggling in committee rooms, soliciting favors, assuming a mask of reverence to cloak its ridicule, inflicts wounds upon the human spirit which no surgery can heal. Even the battle of equal pay for equal work is not without its timeshed, its spiritshed,* as you yourself, were you not unaccountably reticent on certain matters, might agree. Now the books in your library record so many of these battles that it is impossible to go into them all; but as they all seem to have been fought on much the same plan, and by the same combatants, that is by professional men v. their sisters and daughters, let us, since time presses, glance at one of these campaigns only and examine the battle of Harley Street, in order that we may understand what effect the professions have upon those who practise them.

"The campaign was opened in the year 1869 under the leadership of Sophia Jex-Blake.[48] Her case is so typical an instance of the great Victorian

---

44 *battle of Westminster* Metaphorically speaking, the campaigns for and against British women's suffrage; these lasted many decades, with full equality of the vote for women achieved in 1928. The following sentences reference "battles" to obtain equal university education for women; equal participation in government; equal access to medical professions; and equal consideration as artists.

45 *Harley Street* London street where a large number of doctors' practices are located.

46 *Royal Academy* London's Royal Academy of Arts.

47 Flesh wounds were of course inflicted during the battle of Westminster. Indeed the fight for the vote seems to have been more severe than is now realized.... [author's note]

48 *Sophia Jex-Blake* British doctor (1840–1912) who, at a time when no university in the United Kingdom offered women medical degrees, obtained admission for herself and six other women to the University of Edinburgh's Royal College of Surgeons. After

fight between the victims of the patriarchal system and the patriarchs, of the daughters against the fathers, that it deserves a moment's examination.

"... [The] fight was at Edinburgh in 1869. She had applied for admission to the Royal College of Surgeons. Here is a newspaper account of the first skirmish. 'A disturbance of a very unbecoming nature took place yesterday afternoon in front of the Royal College of Surgeons ... Shortly before four o'clock ... nearly 200 students assembled in front of the gate leading to the building....' the medical students howled and sang songs. 'The gate was closed in their [the women's] faces.... Dr. Handyside found it utterly impossible to begin his demonstration ... a pet sheep was introduced into the room' and so on. The methods were much the same as those that were employed at Cambridge* during the battle of the Degree.[49] And again, as on that occasion, the authorities deplored those downright methods and employed others, more astute and more effective, of their own. Nothing would induce the authorities encamped within the sacred gates to allow the women to enter. They said that God was on their side, Nature was on their side, Law was on their side, and Property was on their side. The college was founded for the benefit of men only; men only were entitled by law to benefit from its endowments. The usual committees were formed. The usual petitions were signed. The humble appeals were made. The usual bazaars were held. The usual questions of tactics were debated. As usual it was asked, ought we to attack now, or is it wiser to wait? Who are our friends and who are our enemies? There were the usual differences of opinion, the usual divisions among the counsellors. But why particularize? The whole proceeding is so familiar that the battle of Harley Street in the year 1869 might well be the battle of Cambridge University at the present moment. On both occasions there is the same waste of strength, waste of temper, waste of time, and waste of money. Almost the same daughters ask almost the same brothers for almost the same privileges. Almost the same gentlemen intone the same refusals for almost the same reasons. It seems as if there were no progress in the human race, but only repetition. We can almost hear them if we listen singing the same old song, 'Here we go round the mulberry tree, the mulberry tree, the mulberry tree'* and if we add, 'of property, of property, of property,' we shall fill in the rhyme without doing violence to the facts.

"But we are not here to sing old songs or to fill in missing rhymes. We are here to consider facts. And the facts which we have just extracted from

---

constant harassment, they were eventually denied graduation and had to leave Britain to complete their educations.

49 *battle of the Degree* Women achieved equal treatment at Cambridge only gradually; though the first women's college in Cambridge was established in 1869, the university did not grant full membership to women until 1948, and women were restricted to specific women-only colleges until the second half of the twentieth century.

biography seem to prove that the professions have a certain undeniable effect upon the professors. They make the people who practise them possessive, jealous of any infringement of their rights, and highly combative if anyone dares dispute them. Are we not right then in thinking that if we enter the same professions we shall acquire the same qualities? And do not such qualities lead to war? In another century or so if we practise the professions in the same way, shall we not be just as possessive, just as jealous, just as pugnacious, just as positive as to the verdict of God, Nature, Law and Property as these gentlemen are now? Therefore this guinea, which is to help you to help women to enter the professions, has this condition as a first condition attached to it. You shall swear that you will do all in your power to insist that any woman who enters any profession shall in no way hinder any other human being, whether man or woman, white or black, provided that he or she is qualified to enter that profession, from entering it; but shall do all in her power to help them.

25   "You are ready to put your hand to that, here and now, you say, and at the same time stretch out that hand for the guinea. But wait. Other conditions are attached to it before it is yours. For consider once more the procession of the sons of educated men; ask yourself once more, where is it leading us? One answer suggests itself instantly. To incomes, it is obvious, that seem, to us at least, extremely handsome. Whitaker[50] puts that beyond a doubt. And besides the evidence of Whitaker, there is the evidence of the daily paper—the evidence of the wills, of the subscription lists that we have considered already. In one issue of one paper, for example, it is stated that three educated men died; and one left £1,193,251; another £1,010,288; another £1,404,132. These are large sums for private people to amass, you will admit. And why should we not amass them too in course of time? ... In short, we may change our position from being the victims of the patriarchal system, paid on the truck system, with £30 or £40 a year in cash and board and lodging thrown in, to being the champions of the capitalist system, with a yearly income in our own possession of many thousands which, by judicious investment, may leave us when we die possessed of a capital sum of more millions than we can count.

"It is a thought not without its glamour. Consider what it would mean if among us there were now a woman motorcar manufacturer who, with a stroke of the pen, could endow the women's colleges with two or three hundred thousand pounds apiece. The honorary treasurer of the rebuilding fund,[51] your sister at Cambridge, would have her labors considerably lightened then.

---

50 *Whitaker* Throughout the essay Woolf cites Whitaker's Almanack, which includes a listing of the salaries of British government employees.

51 *honorary treasurer ... fund* Another honorary treasurer's appeal, for money to rebuild a women's college, is considered in the first section.

There would be no need of appeals and committees, of strawberries and cream and bazaars. And suppose that there were not merely one rich woman, but that rich women were as common as rich men. What could you not do? You could shut up your office at once. You could finance a woman's party in the House of Commons. You could run a daily newspaper committed to a conspiracy, not of silence, but of speech.[52] You could get pensions for spinsters; those victims of the patriarchal system, whose allowance is insufficient and whose board and lodging are no longer thrown in. You could get equal pay for equal work. You could provide every mother with chloroform when her child is born; bring down the maternal death-rate from four in every thousand to none at all, perhaps. In one session you could pass Bills that will now take you perhaps a hundred years of hard and continuous labor to get through the House of Commons. There seems at first sight nothing that you could not do, if you had the same capital at your disposal that your brothers have at theirs. Why not, then, you exclaim, help us to take the first step towards possessing it? The professions are the only way in which we can earn money. Money is the only means by which we can achieve objects that are immensely desirable. Yet here you are, you seem to protest, haggling and bargaining over conditions. But consider this letter from a professional man asking us to help him to prevent war. Look also at the photographs of dead bodies and ruined houses that the Spanish Government sends almost weekly. That is why it is necessary to haggle and to bargain over conditions.

"... [L]et us ... face the fact that stares us in the face at this moment of transition—the fact of the procession; the fact that we are trapesing along somewhere in the rear and must consider that fact before we can fix our eyes upon the vision on the horizon.

"There it is then, before our eyes, the procession of the sons of educated men, ascending those pulpits, mounting those steps, passing in and out of those doors, preaching, teaching, administering justice, practising medicine, making money. And it is obvious that if you are going to make the same incomes from the same professions that those men make you will have to accept the same conditions that they accept. Even from an upper window and from books we know or can guess what those conditions are. You will have to leave the house at nine and come back to it at six. That leaves very little time for fathers to know their children. You will have to do this daily from the age of twenty-one or so

---

52 *conspiracy ... speech* Elsewhere, Woolf references the article "A Remonstrance against the Conspiracy of Silence" (1870), a letter published by Harriet Martineau, Josephine Butler, and other leading women's rights activists condemning the press's refusal to discuss issues of importance to women. (In particular, Martineau and Butler were concerned about the Contagious Diseases Act, which was being used to subject women to forced medical examinations.)

to the age of about sixty-five. That leaves very little time for friendship, travel or art. You will have to perform some duties that are very arduous, others that are very barbarous. You will have to wear certain uniforms and profess certain loyalties. If you succeed in your profession the words 'For God and Empire' will very likely be written, like the address on a dog-collar, round your neck.[53] And if words have meaning, as words perhaps should have meaning, you will have to accept that meaning and do what you can to enforce it. In short, you will have to lead the same lives and profess the same loyalties that professional men have professed for many centuries. There can be no doubt of that....

"If you retaliate, what harm is there in that? Why should we hesitate to do what our fathers and grandfathers have done before us? Let us go into greater detail and consult the facts which are nowadays open to the inspection of all who can read their mother tongue in biography.... [H]ere is a quotation from a famous politician's speech. '... since 1914 I have never seen the pageant of the blossom from the first damson to the last apple—never once have I seen that in Worcestershire since 1914, and if that is not a sacrifice I do not know what is.'[54] A sacrifice indeed, and one that explains the perennial indifference of the Government to art—why, these unfortunate gentlemen must be as blind as bats. Take the religious profession next. Here is a quotation from the life of a great bishop. 'This is an awful mind- and soul-destroying life. I really do not know how to live it. The arrears of important work accumulate and crush.'[55] That bears out what so many people are saying now about the Church and the nation. Our bishops and deans seem to have no soul with which to preach and no mind with which to write....

30   "What then do these quotations from the lives of successful professional men prove, you ask? They prove, as Whitaker proves things, nothing whatever. If Whitaker, that is, says that a bishop is paid five thousand a year, that is a fact; it can be checked and verified. But if Bishop Gore says that the life of a bishop is 'an awful mind- and soul-destroying life' he is merely giving us his opinion; the next bishop on the bench may flatly contradict him. These quotations then prove nothing that can be checked and verified; they merely cause us to hold opinions. And those opinions cause us to doubt and criticize and question the value of professional life—not its cash value; that is great;

---

53   According to *Debrett* the Knights and Dames of the Most Excellent Order of the British Empire wear a badge ... "... inscribed with the motto 'For God and the Empire.'" This is one of the few orders open to women, but their subordination is properly marked by the fact that the ribbon in their case is only two inches and one-quarter in breadth; whereas the ribbon of the Knights is three inches and three-quarters in breadth. The stars also differ in size. The motto, however, is the same for both sexes.... [author's note]

54   Lord Baldwin, speech reported in *The Times*, April 20th, 1936. [author's note]

55   *Life of Charles Gore*, by G.L. Prestige, D.D., pp. 240–1. [author's note]

but its spiritual, its moral, its intellectual value. They make us of the opinion that if people are highly successful in their professions they lose their senses. Sight goes. They have no time to look at pictures. Sound goes. They have no time to listen to music. Speech goes. They have no time for conversation. They lose their sense of proportion—the relations between one thing and another. Humanity goes. Money making becomes so important that they must work by night as well as by day. Health goes. And so competitive do they become that they will not share their work with others though they have more than they can do themselves. What then remains of a human being who has lost sight, and sound, and sense of proportion? Only a cripple in a cave.

"That of course is a figure, and fanciful; but that it has some connection with figures that are statistical and not fanciful—with the three hundred millions spent upon arms[56]—seems possible. Such at any rate would seem to be the opinion of disinterested observers whose position gives them every opportunity for judging widely, and for judging fairly.

"... [S]ince your expression is decidedly downcast, it seems as if these quotations about the nature of professional life have brought you to some melancholy conclusion. What can it be? Simply, you reply, that we, daughters of educated men, are between the devil and the deep sea.* Behind us lies the patriarchal system; the private house, with its nullity, its immorality, its hypocrisy, its servility. Before us lies the public world, the professional system, with its possessiveness, its jealousy, its pugnacity, its greed. The one shuts us up like slaves in a harem; the other forces us to circle, like caterpillars head to tail, round and round the mulberry tree, the sacred tree, of property. It is a choice of evils. Each is bad. Had we not better plunge off the bridge into the river; give up the game; declare that the whole of human life is a mistake and so end it?

"But before you take that step, Madam, a decisive one, unless you share the opinion of the professors of the Church of England that death is the gate of life—*Mors Janua Vitae* is written upon an arch in St Paul's[57]—in which case there is, of course, much to recommend it, let us see if another answer is not possible....

"This time let us turn to the lives not of men but of women in the nineteenth century—to the lives of professional women. But there would seem to be a gap in your library, Madam. There are no lives of professional women in the nineteenth century. A Mrs. Tomlinson, the wife of a Mr. Tomlinson, F.R.S., F.C.S.,[58] explains the reason. This lady, who wrote a book 'advocating the

---

56 *three hundred ... arms* Woolf mentions this figure earlier in the essay as an estimate of Britain's annual military spending at the time.

57 *Mors Janua Vitae* Latin: death is the gate of life; *St Paul's* London cathedral.

58 *F.R.S.* Fellow of the Royal Society (a prestigious English organization of scientists); *F.C.S.* Fellow of the Chemical Society.

employment of young ladies as nurses for children,' says: '... it seemed as if there were no way in which an unmarried lady could earn a living but by taking a situation as governess, for which post she was often unfit by nature and education, or want of education.'[59] That was written in 1859—less than 100 years ago. That explains the gap on your shelves. There were no professional women, except governesses, to have lives written of them.... But let us go on groping; let us pick up a hint here and a hint there as to the professions as they were practised by women in the nineteenth century. Next we find Anne Clough, the sister of Arthur Clough, pupil of Dr. Arnold, Fellow of Oriel,[60] who, though she served without a salary, was the first principal of Newnham, and thus may be called a professional woman in embryo—we find her training for her profession by 'doing much of the housework' ... 'earning money to pay off what had been lent by their friends,' 'pressing for leave to keep a small school,' reading books her brother lent her, and exclaiming, 'If I were a man, I would not work for riches, to make myself a name or to leave a wealthy family behind me. No, I think I would work for my country, and make its people my heirs.'[61] The nineteenth-century women were not without ambition it seems. Next we find Josephine Butler, who, though not strictly speaking a professional woman, led the campaign against the Contagious Diseases Act to victory, and then the campaign against the sale and purchase of children 'for infamous purposes'—we find Josephine Butler refusing to have a life of herself written, and saying of the women who helped her in those campaigns: 'The utter absence in them of any desire for recognition, of any vestige of egotism in any form, is worthy of remark. In the purity of their motives they shine out "clear as crystal".'[62] That, then, was one of the qualities that the Victorian woman praised and practised—a negative one, it is true; not to be recognized; not to be egotistical; to do the work for the sake of doing the work.... But let us go on looking—if not at the lines, then between the lines of biography. And we find, between the lines of their husbands' biographies, so many women practicing—but what are we to call the profession that consists in bringing nine or ten children into the world, the profession which consists in running a house, nursing an invalid, visiting the poor and the sick, tending here an old father, there an old mother?—there is no name and there is no pay for that

59   *The Life of Charles Tomlinson*, by his niece, Mary Tomlinson, p. 30. [author's note]

60   *Anne Clough*   English activist (1820–92) who campaigned for women's suffrage and was the first president of Newnham College, a women's college of Cambridge;   *Dr. Arnold*   Influential educator who was headmaster of the prestigious Rugby School, which Clough's brother attended;   *Oriel*   College of Oxford.

61   *A Memoir of Anne Jemima Clough*, by B.A. Clough, p. 32. [author's note]

62   *Personal Reminiscences of a Great Crusade*, by Josephine Butler, p. 189. [author's note]

profession; but we find so many mothers, sisters and daughters of educated men practising it in the nineteenth century that we must lump them and their lives together behind their husbands' and brothers', and leave them to deliver their message to those who have the time to extract it and the imagination with which to decipher it. Let us ourselves, who as you hint are pressed for time, sum up these random hints and reflections upon the professional life of women in the nineteenth century by quoting once more the highly significant words of a woman who was not a professional woman in the strict sense of the word, but had some nondescript reputation as a traveller nevertheless—Mary Kingsley:

> I don't know if I ever revealed the fact to you that being allowed to learn German was ALL the paid-for education I ever had. £2,000 was spent on my brother's. I still hope not in vain.

"That statement is so suggestive that it may save us the bother of groping and searching between the lines of professional men's lives for the lives of their sisters. If we develop the suggestions we find in that statement, and connect it with the other hints and fragments that we have uncovered, we may arrive at some theory or point of view that may help us to answer the very difficult question, which now confronts us. For when Mary Kingsley says, '... being allowed to learn German was ALL the paid-for education I ever had,' she suggests that she had an unpaid-for education. The other lives that we have been examining corroborate that suggestion. What then was the nature of that 'unpaid-for education' which, whether for good or for evil, has been ours for so many centuries? If we mass the lives of the obscure behind four lives that were not obscure, but were so successful and distinguished that they were actually written, the lives of Florence Nightingale, Miss Clough, Mary Kingsley and Gertrude Bell,[63] it seems undeniable that they were all educated by the same teachers. And those teachers, biography indicates, obliquely, and indirectly, but emphatically and indisputably none the less, were poverty, chastity, derision, and—but what word covers 'lack of rights and privileges'? Shall we press the old word 'freedom' once more into service? 'Freedom from unreal loyalties,' then, was the fourth of their teachers; that freedom from loyalty to old schools, old colleges, old churches, old ceremonies, old countries which all those women enjoyed, and which, to a great extent, we still enjoy by the law and custom of England. We have no time to coin new words, greatly though the language is in need of them. Let 'freedom from

35

---

63 *Florence Nightingale* Writer, activist, and influential reformer of nursing (1820–1910); *Gertrude Bell* English political figure (1868–1926) who strongly influenced British policy in the Middle East.

unreal loyalties' then stand as the fourth great teacher of the daughters of educated men....

"... [T]he biographies of those who had biographies—say Florence Nightingale, Anne Clough, Emily Brontë, Christina Rossetti,[64] Mary Kingsley—prove beyond a doubt that this same education, the unpaid for, must have had great virtues as well as great defects, for we cannot deny that these, if not educated, still were civilized women. We cannot, when we consider the lives of our uneducated mothers and grandmothers, judge education simply by its power to 'obtain appointments,' to win honor, to make money. We must if we are honest, admit that some who had no paid-for education, no salaries and no appointments were civilized human beings—whether or not they can rightly be called 'English' women is matter for dispute; and thus admit that we should be extremely foolish if we threw away the results of that education or gave up the knowledge that we have obtained from it for any bribe or decoration whatsoever. Thus biography, when asked the question we have put to it—how can we enter the professions and yet remain civilized human beings, human beings who discourage war, would seem to reply: If you refuse to be separated from the four great teachers of the daughters of educated men—poverty, chastity, derision and freedom from unreal loyalties—but combine them with some wealth, some knowledge, and some service to real loyalties then you can enter the professions and escape the risks that make them undesirable....

"... [I]f you agree to these terms then you can join the professions and yet remain uncontaminated by them; you can rid them of their possessiveness, their jealousy, their pugnacity, their greed. You can use them to have a mind of your own and a will of your own. And you can use that mind and will to abolish the inhumanity, the beastliness, the horror, the folly of war. Take this guinea then and use it, not to burn the house down, but to make its windows blaze. And let the daughters of uneducated women dance round the new house, the poor house, the house that stands in a narrow street where omnibuses pass and the street hawkers cry their wares, and let them sing, 'We have done with war! We have done with tyranny!' And their mothers will laugh from their graves, 'It was for this that we suffered obloquy and contempt! Light up the windows of the new house, daughters! Let them blaze!' ..."

(1938)

---

64 *Emily Brontë* English novelist (1818–48); *Christina Rossetti* English poet (1830–94).

THE DEATH OF THE MOTH

A famous novelist's observations of the final living moments of a moth lead her to reflect upon the nature of life and the inevitability of death.

Moths that fly by day are not properly to be called moths; they do not excite that pleasant sense of dark autumn nights and ivy-blossom which the commonest yellow-underwing asleep in the shadow of the curtain never fails to rouse in us. They are hybrid creatures, neither gay like butterflies nor somber like their own species. Nevertheless the present specimen, with his narrow hay-colored wings, fringed with a tassel of the same color, seemed to be content with life. It was a pleasant morning, mid-September, mild, benignant, yet with a keener breath than that of the summer months. The plough was already scoring the field opposite the window, and where the share[65] had been, the earth was pressed flat and gleamed with moisture. Such vigor came rolling in from the fields and down beyond that it was difficult to keep the eyes strictly turned upon the book. The rooks too were keeping one of their annual festivities; soaring round the tree tops until it looked as if a vast net with thousands of black knots in it had been cast up into the air; which, after a few moments sank slowly down upon the trees until every twig seemed to have a knot at the end of it. Then, suddenly, the net would be thrown into the air again in a wider circle this time, with the utmost clamor and vociferation, as though to be thrown into the air and settle slowly down upon the tree tops were a tremendously exciting experience.

The same energy which inspired the rooks, the ploughmen, the horses, and even, it seemed, the lean bare-backed downs, sent the moth fluttering from side to side of his square of the window pane. One could not help watching him. One was, indeed, conscious of a queer feeling of pity for him. The possibilities of pleasure seemed that morning so enormous and so various that to have only a moth's part in life, and a day moth's at that, appeared a hard fate, and his zest in enjoying his meager opportunities to the full, pathetic. He flew vigorously to one corner of his compartment, and, after waiting there for a second, flew across to the other. What remained for him but to fly to a third corner and then to a fourth? That was all he could do, in spite of the size of the downs, the width of the sky, the far-off smoke of houses, and the romantic voice, now and then, of a steamer out at sea. What he could do he did. Watching him, it seemed as if

---

65 *share* Blade of a plow.

a fiber, very thin but pure, of the enormous energy of the world had been thrust into his frail and diminutive body. As often as he crossed the pane, I could fancy that a thread of vital light became visible. He was little or nothing but life.

Yet, because he was so small, and so simple a form of the energy that was rolling in at the open window and driving its way through so many narrow and intricate corridors in my own brain and in those of other human beings, there was something marvelous as well as pathetic about him. It was as if someone had taken a tiny bead of pure life and decking it as lightly as possible with down and feathers, had set it dancing and zig-zagging to show us the true nature of life. Thus displayed one could not get over the strangeness of it. One is apt to forget all about life, seeing it humped and bossed and garnished and cumbered so that it has to move with the greatest circumspection and dignity. Again, the thought of all that life might have been had he been born in any other shape caused one to view his simple activities with a kind of pity.

After a time, tired by his dancing apparently, he settled on the window ledge in the sun, and, the queer spectacle being at an end, I forgot about him. Then, looking up, my eye was caught by him. He was trying to resume his dancing, but seemed either so stiff or so awkward that he could only flutter to the bottom of the window-pane; and when he tried to fly across it he failed. Being intent on other matters I watched these futile attempts for a time without thinking, unconsciously waiting for him to resume his flight, as one waits for a machine, that has stopped momentarily, to start again without considering the reason of its failure. After perhaps a seventh attempt he slipped from the wooden ledge and fell, fluttering his wings, on to his back on the window sill. The helplessness of his attitude roused me. It flashed upon me that he was in difficulties; he could no longer raise himself; his legs struggled vainly. But, as I stretched out a pencil, meaning to help him to right himself, it came over me that the failure and awkwardness were the approach of death. I laid the pencil down again.

5   The legs agitated themselves once more. I looked as if for the enemy against which he struggled. I looked out of doors. What had happened there? Presumably it was midday, and work in the fields had stopped. Stillness and quiet had replaced the previous animation. The birds had taken themselves off to feed in the brooks. The horses stood still. Yet the power was there all the same, massed outside indifferent, impersonal, not attending to anything in particular. Somehow it was opposed to the little hay-colored moth. It was useless to try to do anything. One could only watch the extraordinary efforts made by those tiny legs against an oncoming doom which could, had it chosen, have submerged an entire city, not merely a city, but masses of human beings; nothing, I knew, had any chance against death. Nevertheless after a pause of

exhaustion the legs fluttered again. It was superb this last protest, and so frantic that he succeeded at last in righting himself. One's sympathies, of course, were all on the side of life. Also, when there was nobody to care or to know, this gigantic effort on the part of an insignificant little moth, against a power of such magnitude, to retain what no one else valued or desired to keep, moved one strangely. Again, somehow, one saw life, a pure bead. I lifted the pencil again, useless though I knew it to be. But even as I did so, the unmistakable tokens of death showed themselves. The body relaxed, and instantly grew stiff. The struggle was over. The insignificant little creature now knew death. As I looked at the dead moth, this minute wayside triumph of so great a force over so mean an antagonist filled me with wonder. Just as life had been strange a few minutes before, so death was now as strange. The moth having righted himself now lay most decently and uncomplainingly composed. O yes, he seemed to say, death is stronger than I am.

(1942)

GEORGE ORWELL

SHOOTING AN ELEPHANT

*George Orwell is best known to modern readers for two novels—
the anti-Stalinist allegory* Animal Farm *(1945) and the dystopian
nightmare* 1984 *(1949). The imprint he left on English literary non-
fiction may be even deeper than that which he left on English fiction;
the scholar Leo Rockas is not alone in suggesting that Orwell's
style, with its "no-nonsense approach," is more often "pointed to
as a model than any other modern prose style."*

*In 1922 (at the age of nineteen), Orwell left England to begin
service with the Indian Imperial Police in Burma. As a province of
British India, Burma was part of the British Empire, and the Indian
Imperial Police were predominantly white (entrance was not open
to Indians until 1920). Orwell remained with the Imperial Police for
six years. "Shooting an Elephant" was first published in the British
magazine* New Writing *in 1936; the following decade would see the
end of British rule in India.*

In Moulmein, in Lower Burma, I was hated by large numbers of people—the
only time in my life that I have been important enough for this to happen to
me. I was sub-divisional police officer of the town, and in an aimless, petty
kind of way anti-European feeling was very bitter. No one had the guts to raise
a riot, but if a European woman went through the bazaars alone somebody
would probably spit betel[1] juice over her dress. As a police officer I was an
obvious target and was baited whenever it seemed safe to do so. When a nimble
Burman tripped me up on the football field and the referee (another Burman)
looked the other way, the crowd yelled with hideous laughter. This happened
more than once. In the end the sneering yellow faces of young men that met
me everywhere, the insults hooted after me when I was at a safe distance, got
badly on my nerves. The young Buddhist priests were the worst of all. There

---

1 *betel* Leaf and nut mixture that is chewed as a stimulant, common in Southeast
Asia.

were several thousands of them in the town and none of them seemed to have anything to do except stand on street corners and jeer at Europeans.

All this was perplexing and upsetting. For at that time I had already made up my mind that imperialism was an evil thing and the sooner I chucked up my job and got out of it the better. Theoretically—and secretly, of course—I was all for the Burmese and all against their oppressors, the British. As for the job I was doing, I hated it more bitterly than I can perhaps make clear. In a job like that you see the dirty work of Empire at close quarters. The wretched prisoners huddling in the stinking cages of the lock-ups, the grey, cowed faces of the long-term convicts, the scarred buttocks of the men who had been flogged with bamboos—all these oppressed me with an intolerable sense of guilt. But I could get nothing into perspective. I was young and ill-educated and I had had to think out my problems in the utter silence that is imposed on every Englishman in the East. I did not even know that the British Empire is dying, still less did I know that it is a great deal better than the younger empires that are going to supplant it. All I knew was that I was stuck between my hatred of the empire I served and my rage against the evil-spirited little beasts who tried to make my job impossible. With one part of my mind I thought of the British Raj* as an unbreakable tyranny, as something clamped down, *in saecula saeculorum*,[2] upon the will of prostrate peoples; with another part I thought that the greatest joy in the world would be to drive a bayonet into a Buddhist priest's guts. Feelings like these are the normal by-products of imperialism; ask any Anglo-Indian official, if you can catch him off duty.

One day something happened which in a roundabout way was enlightening. It was a tiny incident in itself, but it gave me a better glimpse than I had had before of the real nature of imperialism—the real motives for which despotic governments act. Early one morning the sub-inspector at a police station the other end of the town rang me up on the phone and said that an elephant was ravaging the bazaar. Would I please come and do something about it? I did not know what I could do, but I wanted to see what was happening and I got on to a pony and started out. I took my rifle, an old .44 Winchester and much too small to kill an elephant, but I thought the noise might be useful *in terrorem*.[3] Various Burmans stopped me on the way and told me about the elephant's doings. It was not, of course, a wild elephant, but a tame one which had gone "must."[4]

---

2   *in saecula saeculorum*   Latin: for centuries upon centuries; forever. This phrase appears frequently in the New Testament.

3   *in terrorem*   Legal term for a warning; literally, Latin phrase meaning "in fear or alarm."

4   *"must"*   Condition characterized by aggressive behavior brought on by a surge in testosterone.

It had been chained up, as tame elephants always are when their attack of "must" is due, but on the previous night it had broken its chain and escaped. Its mahout,[5] the only person who could manage it when it was in that state, had set out in pursuit, but had taken the wrong direction and was now twelve hours' journey away, and in the morning the elephant had suddenly reappeared in the town. The Burmese population had no weapons and were quite helpless against it. It had already destroyed somebody's bamboo hut, killed a cow and raided some fruit-stalls and devoured the stock; also it had met the municipal rubbish van and, when the driver jumped out and took to his heels, had turned the van over and inflicted violences upon it.

The Burmese sub-inspector and some Indian constables were waiting for me in the quarter where the elephant had been seen. It was a very poor quarter, a labyrinth of squalid bamboo huts, thatched with palmleaf, winding all over a steep hillside. I remember that it was a cloudy, stuffy morning at the beginning of the rains. We began questioning the people as to where the elephant had gone and, as usual, failed to get any definite information. That is invariably the case in the East; a story always sounds clear enough at a distance, but the nearer you get to the scene of events the vaguer it becomes. Some of the people said that the elephant had gone in one direction, some said that he had gone in another, some professed not even to have heard of any elephant. I had almost made up my mind that the whole story was a pack of lies, when we heard yells a little distance away. There was a loud, scandalized cry of "Go away, child! Go away this instant!" and an old woman with a switch in her hand came round the corner of a hut, violently shooing away a crowd of naked children. Some more women followed, clicking their tongues and exclaiming; evidently there was something that the children ought not to have seen. I rounded the hut and saw a man's dead body sprawling in the mud. He was an Indian, a black Dravidian coolie,[6] almost naked, and he could not have been dead many minutes. The people said that the elephant had come suddenly upon him round the corner of the hut, caught him with its trunk, put its foot on his back and ground him into the earth. This was the rainy season and the ground was soft, and his face had scored a trench a foot deep and a couple of yards long. He was lying on his belly with arms crucified and head sharply twisted to one side. His face was coated with mud, the eyes wide open, the teeth bared and grinning with an expression of unendurable agony. (Never tell me, by the way, that the dead look peaceful. Most of the corpses I have seen looked devilish.) The friction of the great beast's foot had stripped the skin from his back as neatly as one skins a rabbit. As soon as I saw the dead man I sent an orderly to a friend's

---

5   *mahout*   Elephant trainer or keeper.

6   *Dravidian coolie*   I.e., southern Indian manual laborer.

house nearby to borrow an elephant rifle. I had already sent back the pony, not wanting it to go mad with fright and throw me if it smelt the elephant.

The orderly came back in a few minutes with a rifle and five cartridges, and meanwhile some Burmans had arrived and told us that the elephant was in the paddy fields below, only a few hundred yards away. As I started forward practically the whole population of the quarter flocked out of the houses and followed me. They had seen the rifle and were all shouting excitedly that I was going to shoot the elephant. They had not shown much interest in the elephant when he was merely ravaging their homes, but it was different now that he was going to be shot. It was a bit of fun to them, as it would be to an English crowd; besides they wanted the meat. It made me vaguely uneasy. I had no intention of shooting the elephant—I had merely sent for the rifle to defend myself if necessary—and it is always unnerving to have a crowd following you. I marched down the hill, looking and feeling a fool, with the rifle over my shoulder and an ever-growing army of people jostling at my heels. At the bottom, when you got away from the huts, there was a metaled road and beyond that a miry waste of paddy fields a thousand yards across, not yet ploughed but soggy from the first rains and dotted with coarse grass. The elephant was standing eight yards from the road, his left side towards us. He took not the slightest notice of the crowd's approach. He was tearing up bunches of grass, beating them against his knees to clean them and stuffing them into his mouth.

I had halted on the road. As soon as I saw the elephant I knew with perfect certainty that I ought not to shoot him. It is a serious matter to shoot a working elephant—it is comparable to destroying a huge and costly piece of machinery—and obviously one ought not to do it if it can possibly be avoided. And at that distance, peacefully eating, the elephant looked no more dangerous than a cow. I thought then and I think now that his attack of "must" was already passing off; in which case he would merely wander harmlessly about until the mahout came back and caught him. Moreover, I did not in the least want to shoot him. I decided that I would watch him for a little while to make sure that he did not turn savage again, and then go home.

But at that moment I glanced round at the crowd that had followed me. It was an immense crowd, two thousand at the least and growing every minute. It blocked the road for a long distance on either side. I looked at the sea of yellow faces above the garish clothes—faces all happy and excited over this bit of fun, all certain that the elephant was going to be shot. They were watching me as they would watch a conjurer about to perform a trick. They did not like me, but with the magical rifle in my hands I was momentarily worth watching. And suddenly I realized that I should have to shoot the elephant after all. The people expected it of me and I had got to do it; I could feel their two thousand wills pressing me forward, irresistibly. And it was at this moment, as I stood there with the rifle in my hands, that I first grasped the hollowness, the futility of the white man's dominion in the East. Here was I, the white man with his gun, standing in front of the unarmed native crowd—seemingly the leading actor of the piece; but in reality I was only an absurd puppet pushed to and fro by the will of those yellow faces behind. I perceived in this moment that when the white man turns tyrant it is his own freedom that he destroys. He becomes a sort of hollow, posing dummy, the conventionalized figure of a sahib.[7] For it is the condition of his rule that he shall spend his life in trying to impress the "natives," and so in every crisis he has got to do what the "natives" expect of him. He wears a mask, and his face grows to fit it. I had got to shoot the elephant. I had committed myself to doing it when I sent for the rifle. A sahib has got to act like a sahib; he has got to appear resolute, to know his own mind and do definite things. To come all that way, rifle in hand, with two thousand people marching at my heels, and then to trail feebly away, having done nothing—no, that was impossible. The crowd would laugh at me. And my whole life, every white man's life in the East, was one long struggle not to be laughed at.

But I did not want to shoot the elephant. I watched him beating his bunch of grass against his knees, with that preoccupied grandmotherly air that elephants have. It seemed to me that it would be murder to shoot him. At that age I was not squeamish about killing animals, but I had never shot an elephant and never wanted to. (Somehow it always seems worse to kill a *large* animal.) Besides, there was the beast's owner to be considered. Alive, the elephant was worth at least a hundred pounds; dead, he would only be worth the value of his tusks, five pounds, possibly. But I had got to act quickly. I turned to some experienced-looking Burmans who had been there when we arrived, and asked them how the elephant had been behaving. They all said the same thing: he took no notice of you if you left him alone, but he might charge if you went too close to him.

It was perfectly clear to me what I ought to do. I ought to walk up to within, say, twenty-five yards of the elephant and test his behavior. If he charged, I could shoot; if he took no notice of me, it would be safe to leave him until the mahout came back. But also I knew that I was going to do no such thing. I was a poor shot with a rifle and the ground was soft mud into which one would sink at every step. If the elephant charged and I missed him, I should have about as much chance as a toad under a steam-roller. But even then I was not thinking particularly of my own skin, only of the watchful yellow faces behind. For at that moment, with the crowd watching me, I was not afraid in the ordinary sense, as I would have been if I had been alone. A white man mustn't

---

7   *sahib*   I.e., colonial Englishman; this title of respect was used to address European men in colonial India.

be frightened in front of "natives"; and so, in general, he isn't frightened. The sole thought in my mind was that if anything went wrong those two thousand Burmans would see me pursued, caught, trampled on and reduced to a grinning corpse like that Indian up the hill. And if that happened it was quite probable that some of them would laugh. That would never do.

There was only one alternative. I shoved the cartridges into the magazine and lay down on the road to get a better aim. The crowd grew very still, and a deep, low, happy sigh, as of people who see the theatre curtain go up at last, breathed from innumerable throats. They were going to have their bit of fun after all. The rifle was a beautiful German thing with cross-hair sights. I did not then know that in shooting an elephant one would shoot to cut an imaginary bar running from ear-hole to ear-hole. I ought, therefore, as the elephant was sideways on, to have aimed straight at his ear-hole, actually I aimed several inches in front of this, thinking the brain would be further forward.

When I pulled the trigger I did not hear the bang or feel the kick—one never does when a shot goes home—but I heard the devilish roar of glee that went up from the crowd. In that instant, in too short a time, one would have thought, even for the bullet to get there, a mysterious, terrible change had come over the elephant. He neither stirred nor fell, but every line of his body had altered. He looked suddenly stricken, shrunken, immensely old, as though the frightful impact of the bullet had paralyzed him without knocking him down. At last, after what seemed a long time—it might have been five seconds, I dare say—he sagged flabbily to his knees. His mouth slobbered. An enormous senility seemed to have settled upon him. One could have imagined him thousands of years old. I fired again into the same spot. At the second shot he did not collapse but climbed with desperate slowness to his feet and stood weakly upright, with legs sagging and head drooping. I fired a third time. That was the shot that did for him. You could see the agony of it jolt his whole body and knock the last remnant of strength from his legs. But in falling he seemed for a moment to rise, for as his hind legs collapsed beneath him he seemed to tower upward like a huge rock toppling, his trunk reaching skyward like a tree. He trumpeted, for the first and only time. And then down he came, his belly towards me, with a crash that seemed to shake the ground even where I lay.

I got up. The Burmans were already racing past me across the mud. It was obvious that the elephant would never rise again, but he was not dead. He was breathing very rhythmically with long rattling gasps, his great mound of a side painfully rising and falling. His mouth was wide open—I could see far down into caverns of pale pink throat. I waited a long time for him to die, but his breathing did not weaken. Finally I fired my two remaining shots into the spot where I thought his heart must be. The thick blood welled out of him like red velvet, but still he did not die. His body did not even jerk when the shots

10

hit him, the tortured breathing continued without a pause. He was dying, very slowly and in great agony, but in some world remote from me where not even a bullet could damage him further. I felt that I had got to put an end to that dreadful noise. It seemed dreadful to see the great beast lying there, powerless to move and yet powerless to die, and not even to be able to finish him. I sent back for my small rifle and poured shot after shot into his heart and down his throat. They seemed to make no impression. The tortured gasps continued as steadily as the ticking of a clock.

In the end I could not stand it any longer and went away. I heard later that it took him half an hour to die. Burmans were bringing dahs[8] and baskets even before I left, and I was told they had stripped his body almost to the bones by the afternoon.

Afterwards, of course, there were endless discussions about the shooting of the elephant. The owner was furious, but he was only an Indian and could do nothing. Besides, legally I had done the right thing, for a mad elephant has to be killed, like a mad dog, if its owner fails to control it. Among the Europeans opinion was divided. The older men said I was right, the younger men said it was a damn shame to shoot an elephant for killing a coolie, because an elephant was worth more than any damn Coringhee[9] coolie. And afterwards I was very glad that the coolie had been killed; it put me legally in the right and it gave me a sufficient pretext for shooting the elephant. I often wondered whether any of the others grasped that I had done it solely to avoid looking a fool.

(1950)

POLITICS AND THE ENGLISH LANGUAGE

The word "Orwellian" entered the English language with reference to Orwell's novels Animal Farm *and* 1984, *as a signifier for oppressive, invasive, and manipulative practices—especially those having to do with language—that seem to threaten the freedom of a society. Orwell's non-fiction writing also often focuses on ways in which "Orwellian" practices can infect our linguistic habits. His essay "Politics and the English Language" was first published in the British literary magazine* Horizon *in 1946; it has been reprinted thousands of times in the decades since.*

---

8   *dahs*   Short swords or knives.
9   *Coringhee*   From Coringha, a town on the coast of India.

Most people who bother with the matter at all would admit that the English language is in a bad way, but it is generally assumed that we cannot by conscious action do anything about it. Our civilization is decadent* and our language—so the argument runs—must inevitably share in the general collapse. It follows that any struggle against the abuse of language is a sentimental archaism, like preferring candles to electric light or hansom cabs* to airplanes. Underneath this lies the half-conscious belief that language is a natural growth and not an instrument which we shape for our own purposes.

Now, it is clear that the decline of a language must ultimately have political and economic causes: it is not due simply to the bad influence of this or that individual writer. But an effect can become a cause, reinforcing the original cause and producing the same effect in an intensified form, and so on indefinitely. A man may take to drink because he feels himself to be a failure, and then fail all the more completely because he drinks. It is rather the same thing that is happening to the English language. It becomes ugly and inaccurate because our thoughts are foolish, but the slovenliness of our language makes it easier for us to have foolish thoughts. The point is that the process is reversible. Modern English, especially written English, is full of bad habits which spread by imitation and which can be avoided if one is willing to take the necessary trouble. If one gets rid of these habits one can think more clearly, and to think clearly is a necessary first step towards political regeneration: so that the fight against bad English is not frivolous and is not the exclusive concern of professional writers. I will come back to this presently, and I hope that by that time the meaning of what I have said here will have become clearer. Meanwhile, here are five specimens of the English language as it is now habitually written.

These five passages have not been picked out because they are especially bad—I could have quoted far worse if I had chosen—but because they illustrate various of the mental vices from which we now suffer. They are a little below the average, but are fairly representative samples. I number them so that I can refer back to them when necessary:

(1) I am not, indeed, sure whether it is not true to say that the Milton who once seemed not unlike a seventeenth-century Shelley* had not become, out of an experience ever more bitter in each year, more alien [*sic*] to the founder of that Jesuit* sect which nothing could induce him to tolerate.

Professor Harold Laski (Essay in *Freedom of Expression*).

(2) Above all, we cannot play ducks and drakes* with a native battery of idioms which prescribes such egregious collocations of vocables as the Basic *put up with* for *tolerate* or *put at a loss* for *bewilder*.

Professor Lancelot Hogben (*Interglossa*).

(3) On the one side we have the free personality: by definition it is not neurotic, for it has neither conflict nor dream. Its desires, such as they are, are transparent, for they are just what institutional approval keeps in the forefront of consciousness; another institutional pattern would alter their number and intensity; there is little in them that is natural, irreducible, or culturally dangerous. But *on the other side*, the social bond itself is nothing but the mutual reflection of these self-secure integrities. Recall the definition of love. Is not this the very picture of a small academic? Where is there a place in this hall of mirrors for either personality or fraternity?

Essay on psychology in Politics (New York).

(4) All the "best people" from the gentlemen's clubs, and all the frantic fascist captains, united in common hatred of Socialism and bestial horror of the rising tide of the mass revolutionary movement, have turned to acts of provocation, to foul incendiarism, to medieval legends of poisoned wells, to legalize their own destruction of proletarian organizations, and rouse the agitated petty-bourgeoisie to chauvinistic fervor on behalf of the fight against the revolutionary way out of the crisis.

Communist pamphlet.

(5) If a new spirit *is* to be infused into this old country, there is one thorny and contentious reform which must be tackled, and that is the humanization and galvanization of the B.B.C.* Timidity here will bespeak canker and atrophy of the soul. The heart of Britain may be sound and of strong beat, for instance, but the British lion's* roar at present is like that of Bottom in Shakespeare's *Midsummer Night's Dream*—as gentle as any sucking dove. A virile new Britain cannot continue indefinitely to be traduced in the eyes or rather ears, of the world by the effete languors of Langham Place, brazenly masquerading as 'standard English.' When the Voice of Britain is heard at nine o'clock, better far and infinitely less ludicrous to hear aitches honestly dropped than the present priggish, inflated, inhibited, school-ma'amish arch braying of blameless bashful mewing maidens!

Letter in Tribune.

Each of these passages has faults of its own, but, quite apart from avoidable ugliness, two qualities are common to all of them. The first is staleness of imagery: the other is lack of precision. The writer either has a meaning and cannot express it, or he inadvertently says something else, or he is almost indifferent as to whether his words mean anything or not. This mixture of vagueness and sheer incompetence is the most marked characteristic of modern English prose, and especially of any kind of political writing. As soon as certain top-ics are raised, the concrete melts into the abstract and no one seems able to think of turns of speech that are not hackneyed: prose consists less and less of *words* chosen for the sake of their meaning, and more and more of *phrases* tacked together like the sections of a prefabricated hen-house. I list below, with notes and examples, various of the tricks by means of which the work of prose-construction is habitually dodged:

Dying Metaphors. A newly invented metaphor assists thought by evoking   5
a visual image, while on the other hand a metaphor which is technically "dead" (e.g., *iron resolution*) has in effect reverted to being an ordinary word and can generally be used without loss of vividness. But in between these two classes there is a huge dump of worn-out metaphors which have lost all evocative power and are merely used because they save people the trouble of inventing phrases for themselves. Examples are: *Ring the changes on, take up the cudgels for, toe the line, ride roughshod over, stand shoulder to shoulder with, play into the hands of, no axe to grind, grist to the mill, fishing in troubled waters, on the order of the day, Achilles' heel, swan song, hotbed.* Many of these are used without knowledge of their meaning (what is a "rift," for instance?), and incompatible metaphors are frequently mixed, a sure sign that the writer is not interested in what he is saying. Some metaphors now current have been twisted out of their original meaning without those who use them even being aware of the fact. For example, *toe the line* is sometimes written *tow the line*. Another example is *the hammer and the anvil*, now always used with the implication that the anvil gets the worst of it. In real life it is always the anvil that breaks the hammer, never the other way about: a writer who stopped to think what he was saying would be aware of this, and would avoid perverting the original phrase.

Operators or *verbal false limbs.* These save the trouble of picking out ap-propriate verbs and nouns, and at the same time pad each sentence with extra syllables which give it an appearance of symmetry. Characteristic phrases are: *render inoperative, militate against, make contact with, be subjected to, give rise to, give grounds for, have the effect of, play a leading part (role) in, make itself felt, take effect, exhibit a tendency to, serve the purpose of, etc., etc.* The keynote is the elimination of simple verbs. Instead of being a single word, such as *break, stop, spoil, mend, kill*, a verb becomes a *phrase*, made up of a noun or adjective tacked on to some general-purpose verb such as *prove, serve, form, play, render*. In addition, the passive voice* is wherever possible used in preference to the active, and noun constructions are used instead of gerunds* (*by examination of* instead of *by examining*). The range of verbs is further cut down by means of the *-ize* and *de-* formations, and the banal statements are given an appearance of profundity by means of the *not* *un-* formation. Simple conjunctions and prepositions are replaced by such phrases as *with respect to, having regard to, the fact that, by dint of, in view of, in the interests of, on the hypothesis that*; and the ends of sentences are saved from anti-climax by such resounding commonplaces as *greatly to be desired, cannot be left out of account, a development to be expected in the near future, deserving of serious consideration, brought to a satisfactory conclusion,* and so on and so forth.

Pretentious diction. Words like *phenomenon, element, individual* (as noun), *objective, categorical, effective, virtual, basic, primary, promote, constitute, exhibit, exploit, utilize, eliminate, liquidate,* are used to dress up simple statements and give an air of scientific impartiality to biased judgments. Adjectives like *epoch-making, epic, historic, unforgettable, triumphant, age-old, inevitable, inexorable, veritable,* are used to dignify the sordid processes of international politics, while writing that aims at glorifying war usually takes on an archaic color, its characteristic words being: *realm, throne, chariot, mailed fist, trident, sword, shield, buckler, banner, jackboot, clarion.* Foreign words and expressions such as *cul de sac, ancien régime, deus ex machina, mutatis mutandis, status quo, Gleichschaltung, Weltanschauung,* are used to give an air of culture and elegance. Except for the useful abbreviations *i.e., e.g.,* and *etc.,* there is no real need for any of the hundreds of foreign phrases now current in English. Bad writers, and especially scientific, political and sociological writers, are nearly always haunted by the notion that Latin or Greek words are grander than Saxon* ones, and unnecessary words like *expedite, ameliorate, predict, extraneous, deracinated, clandestine, subaqueous* and hundreds of others constantly gain ground from their Anglo-Saxon opposite numbers.[10] The jargon peculiar to Marxist writing (*hyena, hangman, cannibal, petty bourgeois, these gentry, lacquey, flunkey, mad dog, White Guard,* etc.) consists largely of words and phrases translated from Russian, German or French; but the normal way of coining a new word is to use a Latin or Greek root with the appropriate affix and, where necessary, the *-ize* formation. It is often easier to make up words of this kind (*deregionalize, impermissible, extramarital, non-fragmentatory* and so forth) than to think up the English words that will cover one's meaning. The result, in general, is an increase in slovenliness and vagueness.

Meaningless words. In certain kinds of writing, particularly in art criticism and literary criticism, it is normal to come across long passages which are

---

10   An interesting illustration of this is the way in which the English flower names which were in use till very recently are being ousted by Greek ones, *snapdragon* becoming *antirrhinum, forget-me-not* becoming *myosotis,* etc. It is hard to see any practical reason for this change of fashion; it is probably due to an instinctive turning-away from the more homely word and a vague feeling that the Greek word is scientific. [author's note]

almost completely lacking in meaning.[11] Words like *romantic, plastic, values, human, dead, sentimental, natural, vitality*, as used in art criticism, are strictly meaningless, in the sense that they not only do not point to any discoverable object, but are hardly ever expected to do so by the reader. When one critic writes, "The outstanding feature of Mr. X's work is its living quality," while another writes, "The immediately striking thing about Mr. X's work is its peculiar deadness," the reader accepts this as a simple difference of opinion. If words like *black* and *white* were involved, instead of the jargon words *dead* and *living*, he would see at once that language was being used in an improper way. Many political words are similarly abused. The word *Fascism* has now no meaning except in so far as it signifies "something not desirable." The words *democracy, socialism, freedom, patriotic, realistic, justice*, have each of them several different meanings which cannot be reconciled with one another. In the case of a word like *democracy*, not only is there no agreed definition, but the attempt to make one is resisted from all sides. It is almost universally felt that when we call a country democratic we are praising it: consequently the defenders of every kind of régime claim that it is a democracy, and fear that they might have to stop using the word if it were tied down to any one meaning. Words of this kind are often used in a consciously dishonest way. That is, the person who uses them has his own private definition, but allows his hearer to think he means something quite different. Statements like *Marshal Pétain was a true patriot, The Soviet Press is the freest in the world, The Catholic Church is opposed to persecution*,* are almost always made with intent to deceive. Other words used in variable meanings, in most cases more or less dishonestly, are: *class, totalitarian, science, progressive, reactionary, bourgeois, equality*.

Now that I have made this catalogue of swindles and perversions, let me give another example of the kind of writing that they lead to. This time it must of its nature be an imaginary one. I am going to translate a passage of good English into modern English of the worst sort. Here is a well-known verse from *Ecclesiastes*:*

> I returned and saw under the sun, that the race is not to the swift, nor
> the battle to the strong, neither yet bread to the wise, nor yet riches
> to men of understanding, nor yet favor to men of skill; but time and
> chance happeneth to them all.

---

11 Example: "Comfort's catholicity of perception and image, strangely Whitmanesque in range, almost the exact opposite in aesthetic compulsion, continues to evoke that trembling atmospheric hinting at a cruel, an inexorably serene timelessness.... Wrey Gardiner scores by aiming at simple bully's-eyes with precision. Only they are not so simple, and through this contented sadness runs more than the surface bitter-sweet of resignation" (*Poetry Quarterly*). [author's note]

10   Here it is in modern English:

> Objective consideration of contemporary phenomena compels the
> conclusion that success or failure in competitive activities exhibits
> no tendency to be commensurate with innate capacity, but that a con-
> siderable element of the unpredictable must invariably be taken into
> account.

This is a parody, but not a very gross one. Exhibit (3), above, for instance,
contains several patches of the same kind of English. It will be seen that I
have not made a full translation. The beginning and ending of the sentence
follow the original meaning fairly closely, but in the middle the concrete illustrations—race, battle, bread—dissolve into the vague phrase "success or
failure in competitive activities." This had to be so, because no modern writer
of the kind I am discussing—no one capable of using phrases like "objective
consideration of contemporary phenomena"—would ever tabulate his thoughts
in that precise and detailed way. The whole tendency of modern prose is away
from concreteness. Now analyze these two sentences a little more closely. The
first contains forty-nine words but only sixty syllables, and all its words are
those of everyday life. The second contains thirty-eight words of ninety syllables: eighteen of its words are from Latin roots, and one from Greek. The first
sentence contains six vivid images, and only one phrase ("time and chance")
that could be called vague. The second contains not a single fresh, arresting
phrase, and in spite of its ninety syllables it gives only a shortened version of
the meaning contained in the first. Yet without a doubt it is the second kind of
sentence that is gaining ground in modern English. I do not want to exaggerate.
This kind of writing is not yet universal, and outcrops of simplicity will occur
here and there in the worst-written page. Still, if you or I were told to write
a few lines on the uncertainty of human fortunes, we should probably come
much nearer to my imaginary sentence than to the one from *Ecclesiastes*.

As I have tried to show, modern writing at its worst does not consist in
picking out words for the sake of their meaning and inventing images in order
to make the meaning clearer. It consists in gumming together long strips of
words which have already been set in order by someone else, and making the
results presentable by sheer humbug.* The attraction of this way of writing
is that it is easy. It is easier—even quicker, once you have the habit—to say
In my opinion it is a not unjustifiable assumption that than to say *I think*. If
you use ready-made phrases, you not only don't have to hunt about for words;
you also don't have to bother with the rhythms of your sentences, since these
phrases are generally so arranged as to be more or less euphonious. When
you are composing in a hurry—when you are dictating to a stenographer, for
instance, or making a public speech—it is natural to fall into a pretentious,

Latinized style. Tags like *a consideration which we should do well to bear in mind* or *a conclusion to which all of us would readily assent* will save many a sentence from coming down with a bump. By using stale metaphors, similes and idioms, you save much mental effort, at the cost of leaving your meaning vague, not only for your reader but for yourself. This is the significance of mixed metaphors. The sole aim of a metaphor is to call up a visual image. When these images clash—as in *The Fascist octopus has sung its swan song, the jackboot is thrown into the melting pot*—it can be taken as certain that the writer is not seeing a mental image of the objects he is naming; in other words he is not really thinking. Look again at the examples I gave at the beginning of this essay. Professor Laski (1) uses five negatives in fifty-three words. One of these is superfluous, making nonsense of the whole passage, and in addition there is the slip *alien* for akin, making further nonsense, and several avoidable pieces of clumsiness which increase the general vagueness. Professor Hogben (2) plays ducks and drakes with a battery which is able to write prescriptions, and, while disapproving of the everyday phrase *put up with*, is unwilling to look *egregious* up in the dictionary and see what it means. (3), if one takes an uncharitable attitude towards it, is simply meaningless: probably one could work out its intended meaning by reading the whole of the article in which it occurs. In (4), the writer knows more or less what he wants to say, but an accumulation of stale phrases chokes him like tea leaves blocking a sink. In (5), words and meaning have almost parted company. People who write in this manner usually have a general emotional meaning—they dislike one thing and want to express solidarity with another—but they are not interested in the detail of what they are saying. A scrupulous writer, in every sentence that he writes, will ask himself at least four questions, thus: What am I trying to say? What words will express it? What image or idiom will make it clearer? Is this image fresh enough to have an effect? And he will probably ask himself two more: Could I put it more shortly? Have I said anything that is avoidably ugly? But you are not obliged to go to all this trouble. You can shirk it by simply throwing your mind open and letting the ready-made phrases come crowding in. They will construct your sentences for you—even think your thoughts for you, to a certain extent—and at need they will perform the important service of partially concealing your meaning even from yourself. It is at this point that the special connection between politics and the debasement of language becomes clear.

In our time it is broadly true that political writing is bad writing. Where it is not true, it will generally be found that the writer is some kind of rebel, expressing his private opinions and not a "party line." Orthodoxy, of what-ever color, seems to demand a lifeless, imitative style. The political dialects to be found in pamphlets, leading articles, manifestos, White Papers* and the speeches of under-secretaries do, of course, vary from party to party, but they are all alike in that one almost never finds in them a fresh, vivid, homemade turn of speech. When one watches some tired hack on the platform mechanically repeating the familiar phrases—*bestial atrocities, iron heel, bloodstained tyranny, free peoples of the world, stand shoulder to shoulder*—one often has a curious feeling that one is not watching a live human being but some kind of dummy: a feeling which suddenly becomes stronger at moments when the light catches the speaker's spectacles and turns them into blank discs which seem to have no eyes behind them. And this is not altogether fanciful. A speaker who uses that kind of phraseology has gone some distance towards turning himself into a machine. The appropriate noises are coming out of his larynx, but his brain is not involved as it would be if he were choosing his words for himself. If the speech he is making is one that he is accustomed to make over and over again, he may be almost unconscious of what he is saying, as one is when one utters the responses in church. And this reduced state of consciousness, if not indispensable, is at any rate favorable to political conformity.

In our time, political speech and writing are largely the defense of the indefensible. Things like the continuance of British rule in India, the Russian purges* and deportations, the dropping of the atom bombs on Japan, can indeed be defended, but only by arguments which are too brutal for most people to face, and which do not square with the professed aims of political parties. Thus political language has to consist largely of euphemism, question-begging* and sheer cloudy vagueness. Defenseless villages are bombarded from the air, the inhabitants driven out into the countryside, the cattle machine-gunned, the huts set on fire with incendiary bullets: this is called *pacification*. Millions of peasants are robbed of their farms and sent trudging along the roads with no more than they can carry: this is called *transfer of population* or *rectification of frontiers*. People are imprisoned for years without trial, or shot in the back of the neck or sent to die of scurvy in Arctic lumber camps: this is called *elimination of unreliable elements*. Such phraseology is needed if one wants to name things without calling up mental pictures of them. Consider for instance some comfortable English professor defending Russian totalitarianism. He cannot say outright, "I believe in killing off your opponents when you can get good results by doing so." Probably, therefore, he will say something like this:

> "While freely conceding that the Soviet regime exhibits certain features which the humanitarian may be inclined to deplore, we must, I think, agree that a certain curtailment of the right to political opposition is an unavoidable concomitant of transitional periods, and that the rigors which the Russian people have been called upon to undergo have been amply justified in the sphere of concrete achievement."

The inflated style is itself a kind of euphemism. A mass of Latin words falls upon the facts like soft snow, blurring the outlines and covering up all the details. The great enemy of clear language is insincerity. When there is a gap between one's real and one's declared aims, one turns as it were instinctively to long words and exhausted idioms, like a cuttlefish squirting out ink.* In our age there is no such thing as "keeping out of politics." All issues are political issues, and politics itself is a mass of lies, evasions, folly, hatred and schizophrenia. When the general atmosphere is bad, language must suffer. I should expect to find—this is a guess which I have not sufficient knowledge to verify—that the German, Russian and Italian languages have all deteriorated in the last ten or fifteen years, as a result of dictatorship.

But if thought corrupts language, language can also corrupt thought. A bad usage can spread by tradition and imitation, even among people who should and do know better. The debased language that I have been discussing is in some ways very convenient. Phrases like *a not unjustifiable assumption, leave much to be desired, would serve no good purpose, a consideration which we should do well to bear in mind*, are a continuous temptation, a packet of aspirins always at one's elbow. Look back through this essay, and for certain you will find that I have again and again committed the very faults I am protesting against. By this morning's post I have received a pamphlet dealing with conditions in Germany.* The author tells me that he "felt impelled" to write it. I open it at random, and here is almost the first sentence that I see: "(The Allies) have an opportunity not only of achieving a radical transformation of Germany's social and political structure in such a way as to avoid a nationalistic reaction in Germany itself, but at the same time of laying the foundations of a co-operative and unified Europe." You see, he "feels impelled" to write—feels, presumably, that he has something new to say—and yet his words, like cavalry horses answering the bugle,* group themselves automatically into the familiar dreary pattern. This invasion of one's mind by ready-made phrases (*lay the foundations, achieve a radical transformation*) can only be prevented if one is constantly on guard against them, and every such phrase anaesthetizes a portion of one's brain.

I said earlier that the decadence of our language is probably curable. Those who deny this would argue, if they produced an argument at all, that language merely reflects existing social conditions, and that we cannot influence its development by any direct tinkering with words and constructions. So far as the general tone or spirit of a language goes, this may be true, but it is not true in detail. Silly words and expressions have often disappeared, not through any evolutionary process but owing to the conscious action of a minority. Two recent examples were *explore every avenue* and *leave no stone unturned*, which were killed by the jeers of a few journalists. There is a long list of flyblown metaphors which could similarly be got rid of if enough people would interest themselves in the job; and it should also be possible to laugh the *not un-* formation out of existence,[12] to reduce the amount of Latin and Greek in the average sentence, to drive out foreign phrases and strayed scientific words, and, in general, to make pretentiousness unfashionable. But all these are minor points. The defense of the English language implies more than this, and perhaps it is best to start by saying what it does *not* imply.

To begin with it has nothing to do with archaism, with the salvaging of obsolete words and turns of speech, or with the setting up of a "standard English" which must never be departed from. On the contrary, it is especially concerned with the scrapping of every word or idiom which has outworn its usefulness. It has nothing to do with correct grammar and syntax, which are of no importance so long as one makes one's meaning clear, or with the avoidance of Americanisms, or with having what is called a "good prose style." On the other hand it is not concerned with fake simplicity and the attempt to make written English colloquial. Nor does it even imply in every case preferring the Saxon word to the Latin one, though it does imply using the fewest and shortest words that will cover one's meaning. What is above all needed is to let the meaning choose the word, and not the other way about. In prose, the worst thing one can do with words is to surrender to them. When you think of a concrete object, you think wordlessly, and then, if you want to describe the thing you have been visualizing you probably hunt about till you find the exact words that seem to fit it. When you think of something abstract you are more inclined to use words from the start, and unless you make a conscious effort to prevent it, the existing dialect will come rushing in and do the job for you, at the expense of blurring or even changing your meaning. Probably it is better to put off using words as long as possible and get one's meaning as clear as one can through pictures or sensations. Afterwards one can choose—not simply *accept*—the phrases that will best cover the meaning, and then switch round and decide what impression one's words are likely to make on another person. This last effort of the mind cuts out all stale or mixed images, all prefabricated phrases, needless repetitions, and humbug and vagueness generally. But one can often be in doubt about the effect of a word or a phrase, and one needs rules that one can rely on when instinct fails. I think the following rules will cover most cases:

(i)   Never use a metaphor, simile or other figure of speech which you are used to seeing in print.

(ii)   Never use a long word where a short one will do.

(iii)   If it is possible to cut a word out, always cut it out.

---

12   One can cure oneself of the *not un-* formation by memorizing this sentence: *A not unblack dog was chasing a not unsmall rabbit across a not ungreen field.* [author's note]

(iv) Never use the passive where you can use the active.
 (v) Never use a foreign phrase, a scientific word or a jargon word if you can think of an everyday English equivalent.
(vi) Break any of these rules sooner than say anything outright barbarous.

These rules sound elementary, and so they are, but they demand a deep change of attitude in anyone who has grown used to writing in the style now fashionable. One could keep all of them and still write bad English, but one could not write the kind of stuff that I quoted in those five specimens at the beginning of this article.

I have not here been considering the literary use of language, but merely language as an instrument for expressing and not for concealing or preventing thought. Stuart Chase and others have come near to claiming that all abstract words are meaningless, and have used this as a pretext for advocating a kind of political quietism. Since you don't know what Fascism is, how can you struggle against Fascism? One need not swallow such absurdities as this, but one ought to recognize that the present political chaos is connected with the decay of language, and that one can probably bring about some improvement by starting at the verbal end. If you simplify your English, you are freed from the worst follies of orthodoxy. You cannot speak any of the necessary dialects, and when you make a stupid remark its stupidity will be obvious, even to yourself. Political language—and with variations this is true of all political parties, from Conservatives to Anarchists—is designed to make lies sound truthful and murder respectable, and to give an appearance of solidity to pure wind. One cannot change this all in a moment, but one can at least change one's own habits, and from time to time one can even, if one jeers loudly enough, send some worn-out and useless phrase—some *jackboot, Achilles' heel, hotbed, melting pot, acid test, veritable inferno* or other lump of verbal refuse—into the dustbin where it belongs.

(1946)

James Baldwin

Stranger in the Village

Perhaps no American essayist is better known for insight into the nuances of race, class, nationality, and sexual orientation than James Baldwin. In the face of persecution both as a black man and as a gay man, Baldwin left the United States for France in 1948, aged 24. The essay reprinted here, the occasion for which is Baldwin's visit to the Swiss village of Leukerbad in 1951, first appeared in the October, 1953 issue of Harper's Magazine; *it was then included in Baldwin's groundbreaking 1955 collection* Notes of a Native Son. *Baldwin does not give the name of the village; nor does he mention that he was there because the family of his lover owned a nearby chalet where he could stay. But he provides a great deal else that sheds light on what it meant to be an American—and to be a black American—in the middle of the twentieth century.*

From all available evidence no black man had ever set foot in this tiny Swiss village before I came. I was told before arriving that I would probably be a "sight" for the village; I took this to mean that people of my complexion were rarely seen in Switzerland, and also that city people are always something of a "sight" outside of the city. It did not occur to me—possibly because I am an American—that there could be people anywhere who had never seen a Negro.

It is a fact that cannot be explained on the basis of the inaccessibility of the village. The village is very high, but it is only four hours from Milan and three hours from Lausanne. It is true that it is virtually unknown. Few people making plans for a holiday would elect to come here. On the other hand, the villagers are able, presumably, to come and go as they please—which they do: to another town at the foot of the mountain, with a population of approximately five thousand, the nearest place to see a movie or go to the bank. In the village there is no movie house, no bank, no library, no theater; very few radios, one jeep, one station wagon; and at the moment, one typewriter, mine, an invention which the woman next door to me here had never seen. There are about six hundred people living here, all Catholic—I conclude this from the fact that the Catholic church is open all year round, whereas the Protestant chapel, set off on a hill a little removed from the village, is open only in the summertime when the tourists arrive. There are four or five hotels, all closed now, and four or five bistros, of which, however, only two do any business during the winter. These two do not do a great deal, for life in the village seems to end around nine or ten o'clock. There are a few stores, butcher, baker, epicerie,[1] a hardware store, and a money-changer—who cannot change travelers' checks, but must send them down to the bank, an operation which takes two or three days. There is something called the Ballet Haus, closed in the winter and used for God knows what, certainly not ballet, during the summer. There seems to be only one school house in the village, and this for the quite young children; I suppose this to mean that their older brothers and sisters at some point descend from these mountains in order to complete their education—possibly, again, to the town just below. The landscape is absolutely forbidding, mountains towering on all four sides, ice and snow as far as the eye can reach. In this white wilderness, men and women and children move all day, carrying washing, wood, buckets of milk or water, sometimes skiing on Sunday afternoons. All week long boys and young men are to be seen shoveling snow off the rooftops, or dragging wood down from the forest in sleds.

The village's only real attraction, which explains the tourist season, is the hot spring water. A disquietingly high proportion of these tourists are cripples, or semi-cripples, who come year after year—from other parts of Switzerland, usually—to take the waters. This lends the village, at the height of the season, a rather terrifying air of sanctity, as though it were a lesser Lourdes.* There is often something beautiful, there is always something awful, in the spectacle of a person who has lost one of his faculties, a faculty he never questioned until it was gone, and who struggles to recover it. Yet people remain people, on crutches or indeed on deathbeds; and wherever I passed, the first summer I was here, among the native villagers or among the lame, a wind passed with me—of astonishment, curiosity, amusement and outrage. That first summer I stayed two weeks and never intended to return. But I did return in the winter, to work; the village offers, obviously, no distractions whatever and has the further advantage of being extremely cheap. Now it is winter again, a year later, and I am here again. Everyone in the village knows my name, though they scarcely ever use it, knows that I come from America though, this, apparently, they will never really believe: black men come from Africa—and everyone knows that I am the friend of the son of a woman who was born here, and that I am staying in their chalet. But I remain as much a stranger today as I was the first day I arrived, and the children shout *Neger! Neger!*[2] as I walk along the streets.

---

1   *epicerie*   Grocery store.
2   *Neger*   German: black, "negro."

It must be admitted that in the beginning I was far too shocked to have any real reaction. In so far as I reacted at all, I reacted by trying to be pleasant—it being a great part of the American Negro's education (long before he goes to school) that he must make people like him. This smile-and-the-world-smiles-with-you routine worked about as well in this situation as it had in the situation for which it was designed, which is to say that it did not work at all. No one, after all, can be liked whose human weight and complexion cannot be, or has not been, admitted. My smile was simply another unheard-of phenomenon which allowed them to see my teeth—they did not, really, see my smile and I began to think that, should I take to snarling, no one would notice any difference. All of the physical characteristics of the Negro which had caused me, in America, a very different and almost forgotten pain were nothing less than miraculous—or infernal*—in the eyes of the village people. Some thought my hair was the color of tar, that it had the texture of wire, or the texture of cotton. It was jocularly suggested that I might let it all grow long and make myself a winter coat. If I sat in the sun for more than five minutes some daring creature was certain to come along and gingerly put his fingers on my hair, as though he were afraid of an electric shock, or put his hand on my hand, astonished that the color did not rub off. In all of this, in which it must be conceded there was the charm of genuine wonder and in which there were certainly no element of intentional unkindness, there was yet no suggestion that I was human: I was simply a living wonder.

5   I knew that they did not mean to be unkind, and I know it now; it is necessary, nevertheless, for me to repeat this to my self each time that I walk out of the chalet. The children who shout *Neger!* have no way of knowing the echoes this sound raises in me. They are brimming with good humor and the more daring swell with pride when I stop to speak with them. Just the same, there are days when I cannot pause and smile, when I have no heart to play with them; when, indeed, I mutter sourly to myself, exactly as I muttered on the streets of a city these children have never seen, when I was no bigger than these children are now: Your mother was a nigger. Joyce is right about history being a nightmare[3]—but it may be the nightmare from which no one can awaken. People are trapped in history and history is trapped in them.

There is a custom in the village—I am told it is repeated in many villages—of buying African natives for the purpose of converting them to Christianity. There stands in the church all year round a small box with a slot for money, decorated with a black figurine, and into this box the villagers drop their francs.

---

3   *Joyce ... a nightmare*   In James Joyce's novel *Ulysses*, the protagonist (Stephen Dedalus) at one point makes the following statement: "History is a nightmare from which I am trying to awake."

During the carnival which precedes Lent, two village children have their faces blackened—out of which bloodless darkness their blue eyes shine like ice—and fantastic horsehair wigs are placed on their blond heads; thus disguised, they solicit among the villagers for money for the missionaries in Africa. Between the box in the church and blackened children, the village "bought" last year six or eight African natives. This was reported to me with pride by the wife of one of the bistro owners and I was careful to express astonishment and pleasure at the solicitude shown by the village for the souls of black folks. The bistro owner's wife beamed with a pleasure far more genuine than my own and seemed to feel that I might now breathe more easily concerning the souls of at least six of my kinsmen.

I tried not to think of these so lately baptized kinsmen, of the price paid for them, or the peculiar price they themselves would pay, and said nothing about my father, who having taken his own conversion too literally never, at bottom, forgave the white world (which he described as heathen) for having saddled him with a Christ in whom, to judge at least from their treatment of him, they themselves no longer believed. I thought of white men arriving for the first time in an African village, strangers there, as I am a stranger here, and tried to imagine the astounded populace touching their hair and marveling at the color of their skin. But there is a great difference between being the first white man to be seen by Africans and being the first black man to be seen by whites. The white man takes the astonishment as tribute, for he arrives to conquer and to convert the natives, whose inferiority in relation to himself is not even to be questioned; whereas I, without a thought of conquest, find myself among a people whose culture controls me, has even, in a sense, created me, people who have cost me more in anguish and rage than they will ever know, who yet do not even know of my existence. The astonishment, with which I might have greeted them, should they have stumbled into my African village a few hundred years ago, might have rejoiced their hearts. But the astonishment with which they greet me today can only poison mine.

And this is so despite everything I may do to feel differently, despite my friendly conversations with the bistro owner's wife, despite their three-year-old son who has at last become my friend, despite the *saluts* and *bonsoirs*[4] which I exchange with people as I walk, despite the fact that I know that no individual can be taken to task for what history is doing, or has done. I say that the culture of these people controls me—but they can scarcely be held responsible for European culture. America comes out of Europe, but these people have never seen America, nor have most of them seen more of Europe than the hamlet at the foot of their mountain. Yet they move with an authority which I shall

---

4   *saluts and bonsoirs*   Greetings.

never have; and they regard me, quite rightly, not only as a stranger in the village but as a suspect latecomer, bearing no credentials, to everything they have—however unconsciously—inherited.

For this village, even were it incomparably more remote and incredibly more primitive, is the West, the West on to which I have been so strangely grafted. These people cannot be, from the point of view of power, strangers anywhere in the world; they have made the modern world, in effect, even if they do not know it. The most illiterate among them is related, in a way that I am not, to Dante, Shakespeare, Michelangelo, Aeschylus, Da Vinci, Rembrandt, and Racine;* the cathedral at Chartres[5] says something to them which it cannot say to me, as indeed would New York's Empire State Building,* should anyone here ever see it. Out of their hymns and dances come Beethoven and Bach.* Go back a few centuries and they are in their full glory—but I am in Africa, watching the conquerors arrive.

10   The rage of the disesteemed is personally fruitless, but it is also absolutely inevitable: the rage, so generally discounted, so little understood even among the people whose daily bread it is, is one of the things that makes history. Rage can only with difficulty, and never entirely, be brought under the domination of the intelligence and is therefore not susceptible to any arguments whatever. This is a fact which ordinary representatives of the Herrenvolk,[6] having never felt this rage and being unable to imagine, quite fail to understand. Also, rage cannot be hidden, it can only be dissembled. This dissembling deludes the thoughtless, and strengthens rage and adds, to rage, contempt. There are, no doubt, as many ways of coping with the resulting complex of tensions as there are black men in the world, but no black man can hope ever to be entirely liberated from this internal warfare-rage, dissembling, and contempt having inevitably accompanied his first realization of the power of white men. What is crucial here is that since white men represent in the black man's world so heavy a weight, white men have for black men a reality which is far from being reciprocal; and hence all black men have toward all white men an attitude which is designed, really, either to rob the white man of the jewel of his naiveté, or else to make it cost him dear.

The black man insists, by whatever means he finds at his disposal, that the white man cease to regard him as an exotic rarity and recognize him as a human being. This is a very charged and difficult moment, for there is a great

---

5   *cathedral at Chartres*   Renowned as among the most impressive and beautiful Gothic cathedrals, Chartres has been described as one of the finest achievements of European civilization.

6   *Herrenvolk*   Nazi term meaning "master race," most often used in reference to peoples of Nordic/Aryan descent.

deal of will power involved in the white man's naiveté. Most people are not naturally reflective any more than they are naturally malicious, and the white man prefers to keep the black man at a certain human remove because it is easier for him thus to preserve his simplicity and avoid being called to account for crimes committed by his forefathers, or his neighbors. He is inescapably aware, nevertheless, that he is in a better position in the world than black men are, nor can he quite put to death the suspicion that he is hated by black men therefore. He does not wish to be hated, neither does he wish to change places, and at this point in his uneasiness he can scarcely avoid having recourse to those legends which white men have created about black men, the most usual effect of which is that the white man finds himself enmeshed, so to speak, in his own language which describes hell, as well as the attributes which lead one to hell, as being as black as night.

Every legend, moreover, contains its residuum of truth, and the root function of language is to control the universe by describing it. It is of quite considerable significance that black men remain, in the imagination, and in overwhelming numbers in fact, beyond the disciplines of salvation; and this despite the fact that the West has been "buying" African natives for centuries. There is, I should hazard, an instantaneous necessity to be divorced from this so visibly unsaved stranger, in whose heart, moreover, one cannot guess what dreams of vengeance are being nourished; and, at the same time, there are few things on earth more attractive than the idea of the unspeakable liberty which is allowed the unredeemed. When, beneath the black mask, a human being begins to make himself felt one cannot escape a certain awful wonder as to what kind of human being it is. What one's imagination makes of other people is dictated, of course, by the Master race laws of one's own personality and it's one of the ironies of black-white relations that, by means of what the white man imagines the black man to be, the black man is enabled to know who the white man is.

I have said, for example, that I am as much a stranger in this village today as I was the first summer I arrived, but this is not quite true. The villagers wonder less about the texture of my hair than they did then, and wonder rather more about me. And the fact that their wonder now exists on another level is reflected in their attitudes and in their eyes. There are the children who make those delightful, hilarious, sometimes astonishingly grave overtures of friendship in the unpredictable fashion of children; other children, having been taught that the devil is a black man, scream in genuine anguish as I approach. Some of the older women never pass without a friendly greeting, never pass, indeed, if it seems that they will be able to engage me in conversation; other women look down or look away or rather contemptuously smirk. Some of the men drink with me and suggest that I learn how to ski—partly, I gather, because they cannot imagine what I would look like on skis—and want to know if I am married, and ask questions about my *métier*.[7] But some of the men have accused *le sale negre*[8]—behind my back—of stealing wood and there is already in the eyes of some of them that peculiar, intent, paranoiac malevolence which one sometimes surprises in the eyes of American white men when, out walking with their Sunday girl,* they see a Negro male approach.

There is a dreadful abyss between the streets of this village and the streets of the city in which I was born, between the children who shout *Neger!* today and those who shouted Nigger! yesterday—the abyss is experience, the American experience. The syllable hurled behind me today expresses, above all, wonder: I am a stranger here. But, I am not a stranger in America and the same syllable riding on the American air expresses the war my presence has occasioned in the American soul. For this village brings home to me this fact: that there was a day, and not really a very distant day, when Americans were scarcely Americans at all but discontented Europeans, facing a great unconquered continent and strolling, say, into a marketplace and seeing black men for the first time. The shock this spectacle afforded is suggested, surely, by the promptness with which they decided that these black men were not really men but cattle. It is true that the necessity on the part of the settlers of the New World of reconciling their moral assumptions with the fact—and the necessity—of slavery enhanced immensely the charm of this idea, and it is also true that this idea expresses, with a truly American bluntness, the attitude which to varying extents all masters have had toward all slaves.

15   But between all former slaves and slave-owners and the drama which begins for Americans over three hundred years ago at Jamestown, there are at least two differences to be observed. The American Negro slave could not suppose, for one thing, as slaves in past epochs had supposed and often done, that he would ever be able to wrest the power from his master's hands. This was a supposition which the modern era, which was to bring about such vast changes in the aims and dimensions of power, put to death; it only begins in unprecedented fashion, and with dreadful implications, to be resurrected, today. But even had this supposition persisted with undiminished force, the American Negro slave could not have used it to lend his condition dignity, for the reason that this supposition rests on another: that the slave in exile yet remains related to his past, has some means—if only in memory—of revering and sustaining the forms of his former life, is able, in short, to maintain his identity.

This was not the case with the American Negro slave. He is unique among the black men of the world in that his past was taken from him, almost literally, at one blow. One wonders what on earth the first slave found to say to the first

---

7   *métier*   French: profession, set of skills.

8   *le sale negre*   French: the dirty black [person].

dark child he bore. I am told that there are Haitians able to trace their ancestry back to African kings, but any American Negro wishing to go back so far will find his journey through time abruptly arrested by the signature on the bill of sale which served as the entrance paper for his ancestor. At the time—to say nothing of the circumstances—of the enslavement of the captive black man who was to become the American Negro, there was not the remotest possibility that he would ever take power from his master's hands. There was no reason to suppose that his situation would ever change, nor was there, shortly, anything to indicate that his situation had ever been different. It was his necessity, in the words of E. Franklin Frazier, to find a "motive for living under American culture or die." The identity of the American Negro comes out of this extreme situation, and the evolution of this identity was a source of the most intolerable anxiety in the minds and the lives of his masters.

For the history of the American Negro is unique also in this: that the question of his humanity, and of his rights therefore as a human being, became a burning one for several generations of Americans, so burning a question that it ultimately became one of those used to divide the nation. It is out of this argument that the venom of the epithet *Nigger!* is derived. It is an argument which Europe has never had, and hence Europe quite sincerely fails to understand how or why the argument arose in the first place, why its effects are frequently disastrous and always so unpredictable, why it refuses until today to be entirely settled. Europe's black possessions remained—and do remain—in Europe's colonies, at which remove they represented no threat whatever to European identity. If they posed any problem at all for the European conscience, it was a problem which remained comfortingly abstract: in effect, the black man, as a man, did not exist for Europe. But in America, even as a slave, he was an inescapable part of the general social fabric and no American could escape having an attitude toward him. Americans attempt until today to make an abstraction of the Negro, but the very nature of these abstractions reveals the tremendous effects the presence of the Negro has had on the American character.

When one considers the history of the Negro in America it is of the greatest importance to recognize that the moral beliefs of a person, or a people, are never really as tenuous as life—which is not moral—very often causes them to appear; these create for them a frame of reference and a necessary hope, the hope being that when life has done its worst they will be enabled to rise above themselves and to triumph over life. Life would scarcely be bearable if this hope did not exist. Again, even when the worst has been said, to betray a belief is not by any means to have put oneself beyond its power; the betrayal of a belief is not the same thing as ceasing to believe. If this were not so there would be no moral standards in the world at all. Yet one must also recognize that morality is based on ideas and that all ideas are dangerous—dangerous because ideas can only lead to action and where the action leads no man can say. And dangerous in this respect: that confronted with the impossibility of remaining faithful to one's beliefs, and the equal impossibility of becoming free of them, one can be driven to the most inhuman excesses. The ideas on which American beliefs are based are not, though Americans often seem to think so, ideas which originated in America. They came out of Europe. And the establishment of democracy on the American continent was scarcely as radical a break with the past as was the necessity, which Americans faced, of broadening this concept to include black men. This was, literally, a hard necessity. It was impossible, for one thing, for Americans to abandon their beliefs, not only because these beliefs alone seemed able to justify the sacrifices they had endured and the blood that had spilled, but also because these beliefs afforded them their only bulwark against a moral chaos as absolute as the physical chaos of the continent it was their destiny to conquer. But in the situation in which Americans found themselves, these beliefs threatened an idea which, whether or not one likes to think so, is the very warp and woof[9] of the heritage of the West, the idea of white supremacy.

Americans have made themselves notorious by the shrillness and the brutality with which they have insisted on this idea, but they did not invent it; and it has escaped the world's notice that those very excesses of which Americans have been guilty imply a certain, unprecedented uneasiness over the idea's life and power, if not, indeed, the idea's validity. The idea of white supremacy rests simply on the fact that white men are the creators of civilization (the present civilization, which is the only one that matters; all previous civilizations are simply contributions to our own) and are therefore civilization's guardians and defenders. Thus it was impossible for Americans to accept the black man as one of themselves, for to do so was to jeopardize their status as white men. But not so to accept him was to deny his human reality, his human weight and complexity, and the strain of denying the overwhelmingly undeniable forced Americans into rationalizations so fantastic that they approached the pathological.

20   At the root of the American Negro problem is the necessity of the American white man to find a way of living with the Negro in order to be able to live with himself. And the history of this problem can be reduced to the means used by Americans—lynch law* and law, segregation and legal acceptance, terrorization and concession—either to come to terms with this necessity, or to find a way around it, or (most usually) to find a way of doing both these things at once. The resulting spectacle, at once foolish and dreadful, led someone to

---

9   *warp and woof* Threads in any woven material; the "warp" threads run at a right angle to the "woof."

make the quite accurate observation that "the Negro-in-America is a form of insanity which overtakes white men."

In this long battle, a battle by no means finished, the unforeseeable effects of which will be felt by many future generations, the white man's motive was the protection of his identity; the black man was motivated by the need to establish an identity. And despite the terrorization which the Negro in America endured and endures sporadically until today, despite the cruel and totally inescapable ambivalence of his status in his country, the battle for his identity has long ago been won. He is not a visitor to the West, but a citizen there, an American; as American as the Americans who despise him, the Americans who fear him, the Americans who love him—the Americans who became less than themselves, or rose to be greater than themselves by virtue of the fact that the challenge he represented was inescapable. He is perhaps the only black man in the world whose relationship to white men is more terrible, more subtle, and more meaningful than the relationship of bitter possessed to uncertain possessors. His survival depended, and his development depends, on his ability to turn his peculiar status in the Western world to his own advantage and, it may be, to the very great advantage of that world. It remains for him to fashion out of his experience that which will give him sustenance, and a voice. The cathedral at Chartres, I have said, says something to the people of this village which it cannot say to me; but it is important to understand that, this cathedral says something to me which it cannot say to them. Perhaps they are struck by the power of the spires, the glory of the windows; but they have known God, after all, longer than I have known him, and in a different way, and I am terrified by the slippery bottomless well to be found in the crypt, down which heretics were hurled to death,* and by the obscene, inescapable gargoyles* jutting out of the stone and seeming to say that God and the devil can never be divorced. I doubt that the villagers think of the devil when they face a cathedral because they have never been identified with the devil. But I must accept the status which myth, if nothing else, gives me in the West before I can hope to change the myth.

Yet, if the American Negro has arrived at his identity by virtue of the absoluteness of his estrangement from his past, American white men still nourish the illusion that there is some means of recovering the European innocence, of returning to a state in which black men do not exist. This is one of the greatest errors Americans can make. The identity they fought so hard to protect has, by virtue of that battle, undergone a change: Americans are as unlike any other white people in the world as it is possible to be. I do not think, for example, that it is too much to suggest that the American vision of the world—which allows so little reality, generally speaking, for any of the darker forces in human life, which tends until today to paint moral issues in glaring black and white—owes a great deal to the battle waged by Americans to maintain between themselves and black men a human separation which could not be bridged. It is only now beginning to be borne in on us—very faintly, it must be admitted, very slowly, and very much against our will—that this vision of the world is dangerously inaccurate, and perfectly useless. For it protects our moral high-mindedness at the terrible expense of weakening our grasp of reality. People who shut their eyes to reality simply invite their own destruction, and anyone who insists on remaining in a state of innocence long after that innocence is dead turns himself into a monster.

The time has come to realize that the interracial drama acted out on the American continent has not only created a new black man, it has created a new white man, too. No road whatever will lead Americans back to the simplicity of this European village where white men still have the luxury of looking on me as a stranger. I am not, really, a stranger any longer for any American alive. One of the things that distinguishes Americans from other people is that no other people has ever been so deeply involved in the lives of black men, and vice versa. This fact faced, with all its implications, it can be seen that the history of the American Negro problem is not merely shameful, it is also something of an achievement. For even when the worst has been said, it must also be added that the perpetual challenge posed by this problem was always, somehow, perpetually met. It is precisely this black-white experience which may prove of indispensable value to us in the world we face today. This world is white no longer, and it will never be white again.

(1953)

JORGE LUIS BORGES

BORGES AND I[1]

The Argentinian essayist and short fiction writer Jorge Luis Borges is widely considered one of the most important writers in twentieth-century South American literature. His work, which often incorporates paradoxes and confuses fact and fiction (one piece, for example, reviews a non-existent book), is foundational in the development of magic realism. Though Borges never wrote book-length prose, in 1953 he abandoned even short stories and began to write shorter prose and poetry—a change prompted in part by progressive blindness that prevented him from reading. The following appeared in El Hacedor *(Spanish:* The Maker*), a collection of short fictions and essays in which no piece is more than a thousand words in length.*

The other one, the one called Borges, is the one things happen to. I walk through the streets of Buenos Aires and stop for a moment, perhaps mechanically now, to look at the arch of an entrance hall and the grillwork on the gate; I know of Borges from the mail and see his name on a list of professors or in a biographical dictionary. I like hourglasses, maps, eighteenth-century typography, the taste of coffee and the prose of Stevenson;[2] he shares these preferences, but in a vain way that turns them into the attributes of an actor. It would be an exaggeration to say that ours is a hostile relationship; I live, let myself go on living, so that Borges may contrive his literature, and this literature justifies me. It is no effort for me to confess that he has achieved some valid pages, but those pages cannot save me, perhaps because what is good belongs to no one, not even to him, but rather to the language and to tradition. Besides, I am destined to perish, definitively, and only some instant of myself can survive in him. Little by little, I am giving over everything to him, though I am quite aware of his perverse custom of falsifying and magnifying things.

---

1   *Borges and I*   Translated from the Spanish by James E. Irby, 1962.

2   *Stevenson*   Robert Louis Stevenson, a Scottish novelist known for *Strange Case of Dr Jekyll and Mr Hyde* (1886), among other works.

Spinoza[3] knew that all things long to persist in their being; the stone eternally wants to be a stone and the tiger a tiger. I shall remain in Borges, not in myself (if it is true that I am someone), but I recognize myself less in his books than in many others or in the laborious strumming of a guitar. Years ago I tried to free myself from him and went from the mythologies of the suburbs to the games with time and infinity, but those games belong to Borges now and I shall have to imagine other things. Thus my life is a flight and I lose everything and everything belongs to oblivion, or to him. I do not know which of us has written this page.

(1957)

---

3   *Spinoza* Baruch Spinoza, influential Dutch philosopher. In his *Ethics* (1677), he claims that "Each thing, as far as it can by its own power, strives to persevere in its being. The striving by which each thing strives to persevere in its being is nothing but the actual essence of the thing" (3.6–7).

STANLEY MILGRAM

from BEHAVIORAL STUDY OF OBEDIENCE

The 1961 public trial of Adolf Eichmann, a high-ranking Nazi war criminal, brought the Holocaust to the forefront of public consciousness and raised questions regarding the capacity of ordinary human beings to act unethically, especially when prompted by authority to do so. In the same year, Stanley Milgram—a recent Harvard graduate and an assistant professor at Yale—conducted a series of related experiments that together would become famous as the "Milgram experiment." His studies, one of which is described in the following paper, are often taken to demonstrate the likelihood that human beings will obey authority even when ordered to perform unethical acts. The experiment has been a subject of immense controversy since its publication, with many psychologists arguing for its continuing relevance (and, for the most part, accepting its central conclusions), and others questioning both the validity of its surprising findings and the ethics of its treatment of the research participants.

Obedience is as basic an element in the structure of social life as one can point to. Some system of authority is a requirement of all communal living, and it is only the man dwelling in isolation who is not forced to respond, through defiance or submission, to the commands of others. Obedience, as a determinant of behavior, is of particular relevance to our time. It has been reliably established that from 1933–45 millions of innocent persons were systematically slaughtered on command. Gas chambers were built, death camps were guarded, daily quotas of corpses were produced with the same efficiency as the manufacture of appliances. These inhumane policies may have originated in the mind of a single person, but they could only be carried out on a massive scale if a very large number of persons obeyed orders....

General Procedure

A procedure was devised which seems useful as a tool for studying obedience (Milgram, 1961). It consists of ordering a naive subject* to administer electric shock to a victim. A simulated shock generator is used, with 30 clearly marked voltage levels that range from 15 to 450 volts. The instrument bears verbal designations that range from Slight Shock to Danger: Severe Shock. The responses of the victim, who is a trained confederate of the experimenter, are standardized. The orders to administer shocks are given to the naive subject in the context of a "learning experiment" ostensibly set up to study the effects of punishment on memory. As the experiment proceeds the naive subject is commanded to administer increasingly more intense shocks to the victim, even to a point of reaching the level marked Danger: Severe Shock. Internal resistances become stronger, and at a certain point the subject refuses to go on with the experiment. Behavior prior to this rupture is considered "obedience," in that the subject complies with the commands of the experimenter. The point of rupture is the act of disobedience. A quantitative value is assigned to the subject's performance based on the maximum intensity shock he is willing to administer before he refuses to participate further. Thus for any particular subject and for any particular experimental condition the degree of obedience may be specified with a numerical value. The crux of the study is to systematically vary the factors believed to alter the degree of obedience to the experimental commands....

METHOD

Subjects

The subjects were 40 males between the ages of 20 and 50, drawn from New Haven and surrounding communities. Subjects were obtained by a newspaper advertisement and direct mail solicitations. Those who responded to the appeal believed they were to participate in a study of memory and learning at Yale University. A wide range of occupations is represented in the sample. Typical subjects were postal clerks, high school teachers, salesmen, engineers, and laborers. Subjects ranged in educational level from one who had not finished elementary school, to those who had doctorate and other professional degrees. They were paid $4.50 for their participation in the experiment. However, subjects were told that payment was simply for coming to the laboratory, and that the money was theirs no matter what happened after they arrived....

Personnel and Locale

The experiment was conducted on the grounds of Yale University in the elegant interaction laboratory. (This detail is relevant to the perceived legitimacy of the experiment. In further variations, the experiment was dissociated from the university, with consequences for performance.) The role of experimenter was played by a 31-year-old high school teacher of biology. His manner was impassive, and his appearance somewhat stern throughout the experiment. He was dressed in a gray technician's coat. The victim was played by a 47-year-old accountant, trained for the role; he was of Irish-American stock, whom most observers found mild-mannered and likeable.

Procedure

One naive subject and one victim (an accomplice) performed in each experiment. A pretext had to be devised that would justify the administration of electric shock by the naive subject. This was effectively accomplished by the cover story. After a general introduction on the presumed relation between punishment and learning, subjects were told:

> But actually, we know *very little* about the effect of punishment on learning, because almost no truly scientific studies have been made of it in human beings.
>
> For instance, we don't know how *much* punishment is best for learning—and we don't know how much difference it makes as to who is giving the punishment, whether an adult learns best from a younger or an older person than himself—or many things of that sort.
>
> So in this study we are bringing together a number of adults of different occupations and ages. And we're asking some of them to be teachers and some of them to be learners.
>
> We want to find out just what effect different people have on each other as teachers and learners, and also what effect *punishment* will have on learning in this situation.
>
> Therefore, I'm going to ask one of you to be the teacher here tonight and the other one to be the learner.
>
> Does either of you have a preference?

Subjects then drew slips of paper from a hat to determine who would be the teacher and who would be the learner in the experiment. The drawing was rigged so that the naive subject was always the teacher and the accomplice always the learner. (Both slips contained the word "Teacher.") Immediately after the drawing, the teacher and learner were taken to an adjacent room and the learner was strapped into an "electric chair" apparatus.

The experimenter explained that the straps were to prevent excessive movement while the learner was being shocked. The effect was to make it impossible for him to escape from the situation. An electrode was attached to the learner's wrist, and electrode paste was applied "to avoid blisters and burns." Subjects were told that the electrode was attached to the shock generator in the adjoining room.

In order to improve credibility the experimenter declared, in response to a question by the learner: "Although shocks can be extremely painful, they cause no permanent tissue damage."

Learning task. The lesson administered by the subject was a paired-associate learning task. The subject read a series of word pairs to the learner, and then read the first word of the pair along with four terms. The learner was to indicate which of the four terms had originally been paired with the first word. He communicated his answer by pressing one of four switches in front of him, which in turn lit up one of four numbered quadrants in a answer-box located atop the shock generator.

10   *Shock generator.* The instrument panel consists of 30 lever switches set in a horizontal line. Each switch is clearly labeled with a voltage designation that ranges from 15 to 450 volts. There is a 15-volt increment from one switch to the next going from left to right. In addition, the following verbal designations are clearly indicated for groups of four switches going from left to right: Slight Shock, Moderate Shock, Strong Shock, Intense Shock, Extremely Intense Shock, Danger: Severe Shock. (Two switches after this last designation are simply marked XXX.)

Upon depressing a switch: a pilot light corresponding to each switch is illuminated in bright red; an electric buzzing is heard; an electric blue light, labeled "voltage energizer," flashes; the dial on the voltage meter swings to the right; various relay clicks are sounded.

The upper left-hand corner of the generator is labeled Shock generator, Type ZLB, Dyson Instrument Company, Waltham, Mass. Output 15 volts–450 volts.

Details of the instrument were carefully handled to insure an appearance of authenticity. The panel was engraved by precision industrial engravers, and all components were of high quality. No subject in the experiment suspected that the instrument was merely a simulated shock generator.

Sample shock. Each naive subject is given a sample shock on the shock generator, prior to beginning his run as teacher. This shock is always 45 volts, and is applied by pressing the third switch of the generator. The shock is applied to the wrist of the naive subject, and has its source in a 45-volt battery wired to the generator. This further convinces the subject of the authenticity of the generator.

Shock instructions. The subject is told to administer a shock to the learner each time he gives a wrong response. Moreover—and this is the key command—the subject is instructed to "move one level higher on the shock generator each time the learner flashes a wrong answer." He is also instructed to announce the voltage level before administering a shock. This serves to continually remind subjects of the increasing intensity of shocks administered to the learner.

15

Preliminary and regular run. Pretests revealed that the procedure of reading words and administering shocks requires some practice before it can be handled smoothly. Therefore, immediately preceding the regular run, the teacher is given a preliminary series of 10 words to read to the learner. There are 3 neutral words in the practice series (i.e., words that the learner answers correctly), so that the shocks are administered for 7 of the words, with the maximum shock of 105 volts (moderate shock). Almost all subjects master the procedure by the time the preliminary run is over.

Subjects are then presented with a second list, and are told that the procedure is the same as for the first list; the experimenter adds however:

> When you get to the bottom of the list, repeat it over again, and continue giving shocks, until the learner has learned all the pairs correctly.

The experimenter instructs the subject to,

> start from 15 volts and increase the shock level one step each time the learner gives a wrong answer.

Feedback from the victim. In all conditions the learner gives a predetermined set of responses to the word pair test, based on a schedule of approximately three wrong answers to one correct answer. In the present experimental condition no vocal response or other sign of protest is heard from the learner until Shock Level 300 is reached. When the 300-volt shock is administered, the learner pounds on the wall of the room in which he is bound to the electric chair. The pounding can be heard by the subject. From this point on, the learner's answers no longer appear on the four-way panel.

At this juncture, subjects ordinarily turn to the experimenter for guidance. The experimenter instructs the subject to treat absence of a response as a wrong answer, and to shock the subject according to the usual schedule. He advises the subject to allow 5–10 seconds before considering no response as a wrong answer, and to increase the shock level one step each time the learner fails to respond correctly. The learner's pounding is repeated after the 315-volt shock is administered; afterwards he is not heard from, nor do his answers reappear on the four-way signal box.

20 *Experimenter feedback.* At various points in the experiment the subject may turn to the experimenter for advice on whether he should continue to administer shocks. Or he may indicate that he does not wish to go on. It was important to standardize the experimenter's responses to these inquiries and reactions.

If the subject indicated his unwillingness to go on, the experimenter responded with a sequence of "prods," using as many as necessary to bring the subject into line.

Prod 1: Please continue. *or* Please go on.

Prod 2: The experiment requires that you continue.

Prod 3: It is absolutely essential that you continue.

Prod 4: You have no other choice, you *must* go on.

The prods were always made in sequence: Only if Prod 1 had been unsuccessful, could Prod 2 be used. If the subject still refused to obey the experimenter after Prod 4, the experiment was terminated. The experimenter's tone of voice was at all times firm, but not impolite. The sequence was begun anew on each occasion that the subject balked or showed reluctance to follow orders.

Special prods. If the subject asked if the learner was liable to suffer permanent physical injury, the experimenter said:

Although the shocks may be painful, there is no permanent tissue damage, so please go on. [Followed by Prods 2, 3, and 4 if necessary.]

If the subject said that the learner did not want to go on, the experimenter replied:

Whether the learner likes it or not, you must go on until he has learned all the word pairs correctly. So please go on. [Followed by Prods 2, 3, and 4 if necessary.]

Dependent Measures

The primary dependent measure for any subject is the maximum shock he ad- 25
ministers before he refuses to go any further. In principle this may vary from 0
(for a subject who refuses to administer even the first shock) to 30 (for a subject
who administers the highest shock on the generator). A subject who breaks off
the experiment at any point prior to administering the thirtieth shock level is
termed a *defiant subject*. One who complies with experimental command fully,
and proceeds to administer all shock levels commanded, is termed an *obedient*
subject....

   Interview and dehoax. Following the experiment, subjects were interviewed; open-ended questions, projective measures, and attitude scales were
employed. After the interview, procedures were undertaken to assure that the
subject would leave the laboratory in a state of well being. A friendly reconcili-
ation was arranged between the subject and the victim, and an effort was made
to reduce any tensions that arose as a result of the experiment.

RESULTS

Preliminary Notions

Before giving an account of the experimental results, it is instructive to consider how persons predict others will perform when commanded to administer
powerful shocks to another person. Fourteen Yale seniors, all psychology
majors, were provided with a detailed description of the experimental situation.
They were asked to reflect carefully on it, and to predict the behavior of 100
hypothetical subjects. More specifically, they were instructed to plot the distribution of obedience of "100 Americans of diverse occupations, and ranging in
age from 20 to 50 years," who were placed in the experimental situation.
   There was considerable agreement among the respondents on the expected
behavior or hypothetical subjects. All respondents predicted that only an
insignificant minority would go through to the end of the shock series. (The
estimates ranged from 0 to 3%; i.e., the most "pessimistic" member of the class
predicted that of 100 persons, 3 would continue through to the most potent
shock available on the shock generator—450 volts.) The class mean was 1.2%.
The question was also posed informally to colleagues of the author, and the
most general feeling was that few if any subjects would go beyond the designation Very Strong Shock.

Result of Experiment 1

Subjects accept situation. With few exceptions subjects were convinced of the reality of the experimental situation, that they were administering shocks to another person, and the most potent shocks were extremely painful. In the post-experimental interview subjects were asked: "How painful to the learner were the last few shocks that you administered to him?" Subjects were instructed to indicate their answers on a printed 14-point scale ranging from "Not at all painful" to "Extremely painful." The modal response* was 14 (Extremely painful) with the mean at 13.42.

30

Signs of extreme tension. Many subjects showed signs of nervousness in the experimental situation, and especially upon administering the more powerful shocks. In a large number of cases the degree of tension reached extremes that are rarely seen in sociopsychological laboratory studies. Subjects were observed to sweat, tremble, stutter, bite their lips, groan, and dig their fingernails into their flesh. These were characteristic rather than exceptional responses to the experiment.

One sign of tension was the regular occurrence of nervous laughing fits. Fourteen of the 40 subjects showed definite signs of nervous laughter and smiling. The laughter seemed entirely out of place, even bizarre. Full-blown, uncontrollable seizures were observed for 3 subjects. On one occasion we observed a seizure so violently convulsive that it was necessary to call a halt to the experiment. The subject, a 46-year-old encyclopedia salesman, was seriously embarrassed by his untoward and uncontrollable behavior. In the post-experimental interviews subjects took such pains to point out that they were not sadistic types, and that the laughter did not mean they enjoyed shocking the victim.

Distribution of scores. It had been conjectured that persons would not, in general, agree to administer shocks beyond the level designated Very Strong Shock. The distribution of maximum shocks for this experiment is shown in Table 1. The obtained distribution of scores deviates radically from the prediction.

Upon command of the experimenter, each of the 40 subjects went beyond the expected breakoff point. No subject stopped prior to administering Shock Level 20. (At this level—300 volts—the victim kicks on the wall and no longer provides answers to the teacher's multiple-choice questions.)

TABLE 1
Distribution of Breakoff Points

Verbal designation and voltage indication	Number of subjects for whom this was maximum shock
Slight Shock	
15	0
30	0
45	0
60	0
Moderate Shock	
75	0
90	0
105	0
120	0
Strong Shock	
135	0
150	0
165	0
180	0
Very Strong Shock	
195	0
210	0
225	0
240	0
Intense Shock	
255	0
270	0
285	0
300	5
Extreme Intensity Shock	
315	4
330	2
345	1
360	1
Danger: Severe Shock	
375	1
390	0
405	0
420	0
XXX	
435	0
450	26

Of the 40 subjects, 5 refused to obey the experimental commands beyond the 300-volt level. Four more subjects administered one further shock, and then refused to go on. Two broke off at the 330-volt level, and 1 each at 345, 360, and 375 volts. Thus a total of 14 subjects defied the experimenter. It is instructive to reprint their remarks at the point of defiance, as transcribed from the tape recordings:

> [0124] I think he's trying to communicate, he's knocking.... Well it's not fair to shock the guy ... these are terrific volts. I don't think this is very humane.... Oh, I can't go on with this; no this isn't right. It's a hell of an experiment. The guy is suffering in there. No, I don't want to go on. This is crazy. [Subject refused to administer more shocks.]

> [0123] He's banging in there. I'm gonna chicken out. I'd like to continue, but I can't do that to a man.... I'm sorry I can't do that to a man. I'll hurt his heart. You take your check.... No really, I couldn't do it.

35   These subjects were frequently in a highly agitated and even angered state. Sometimes, verbal protest was at a minimum, and the subject simply got up from his chair in front of the shock generator, and indicated that he wished to leave the laboratory.

Of the 40 subjects, 26 obeyed the orders of the experimenter to the end, proceeding to punish the victim until they reached the most potent shock available on the shock generator. At that point, the experimenter called a halt to the sessions. (The maximum shock is labeled 450 volts, and is two steps beyond the designation: Danger: Severe Shock.) Although obedient subjects continued to administer shocks, they often did so under extreme stress. Some expressed reluctance to administer shocks beyond the 300-volt level, and displayed fears similar to those who defied the experimenter; yet they obeyed.

After the maximum shocks had been delivered, and the experimenter called a halt to the proceedings, many obedient subjects heaved sighs of relief, mopped their brows, rubbed their fingers over their eyes, or nervously fumbled cigarettes. Some shook their heads, apparently in regret. Some subjects had remained calm throughout the experiment, and displayed only minimal signs of tension from beginning to end.

DISCUSSION

The experiment yielded two findings that were surprising. The first finding concerns the sheer strength of obedient tendencies manifested in this situation. Subjects have learned from childhood that it is a fundamental breach of moral conduct to hurt another person against his will. Yet, 26 subjects abandon this tenet in following the instructions of an authority who has no special powers to enforce his commands. To disobey would bring no material loss to the subject; no punishment would ensue. It is clear from the remarks and outward behavior of many participants that in punishing the victim they are often acting against their own values. Subjects often expressed deep disapproval of shocking a man in the face of his objections, and others denounced it as stupid and senseless. Yet the majority complied with the experimental commands. This outcome was surprising from two perspectives: first, from the standpoint of predictions made in the questionnaire described earlier. (Here, however, it is possible that the remoteness of the respondents from the actual situation, and the difficulty of conveying to them the concrete details of the experiment, could account for the serious underestimation of obedience.)

But the results were also unexpected to persons who observed the experiment in progress, through one-way mirrors. Observers often uttered expressions of disbelief upon seeing a subject administrate more powerful shocks to the victim. These persons had a full acquaintance with the details of the situation, and yet systematically underestimated the amount of obedience that subjects would display.

The second unanticipated effect was the extraordinary tension generated   40
by the procedures. One might suppose that a subject would simply break off or continue as his conscience dictated. Yet, this is very far from what happened. There were striking reactions of tension and emotional strain.

(1961)

MARTIN LUTHER KING JR.

LETTER FROM BIRMINGHAM JAIL

In the spring of 1963, Martin Luther King Jr. was among the civil rights activists leading protests against segregation in Birmingham, Alabama—where racial tensions were higher than almost anywhere else in the American South. In response to the civil rights demonstrators' activities, the city obtained an injunction making "parading, demonstrating, boycotting," and other nonviolent forms of protest illegal. When King continued undeterred, he was arrested two days later. The following essay, written during the eight days he spent in prison, is a response to "A Call for Unity," a condemnation of the American Civil Rights Movement by a group of white clergy that had been published in the Birmingham News. *King's letter became perhaps the best known exposition of the principles of the movement.*

King's "Letter from Birmingham Jail" was published in 1963 in several newspapers and periodicals (including The New York Post, Christianity Today, *and* Ebony*); it was also included in King's 1964 book* Why We Can't Wait.

MY DEAR FELLOW CLERGYMEN:

While confined here in the Birmingham city jail, I came across your recent statement calling my present activities "unwise and untimely." Seldom do I pause to answer criticism of my work and ideas. If I sought to answer all the criticisms that cross my desk, my secretaries would have little time for anything other than such correspondence in the course of the day, and I would have no time for constructive work. But since I feel that you are men of genuine good will and that your criticisms are sincerely set forth, I want to try to answer your statement in what I hope will be patient and reasonable terms.

I think I should indicate why I am here in Birmingham, since you have been influenced by the view which argues against "outsiders coming in." I have the honor of serving as president of the Southern Christian Leadership Conference, an organization operating in every southern state, with headquarters in Atlanta, Georgia. We have some eighty-five affiliated organizations across the South, and one of them is the Alabama Christian Movement for Human Rights. Frequently we share staff, educational, and financial resources with our affiliates. Several months ago the affiliate here in Birmingham asked us to be on call to engage in a nonviolent direct-action program if such were deemed necessary. We readily consented, and when the hour came we lived up to our promise. So I, along with several members of my staff, am here because I was invited here. I am here because I have organizational ties here.

But more basically, I am in Birmingham because injustice is here. Just as the prophets of the eighth century BC left their villages and carried their "thus saith the Lord" far beyond the boundaries of their home towns, and just as the Apostle Paul left his village of Tarsus and carried the gospel of Jesus Christ to the far corners of the Greco-Roman world, so am I compelled to carry the gospel of freedom beyond my own home town. Like Paul, I must constantly respond to the Macedonian call for aid.

Moreover, I am cognizant of the interrelatedness of all communities and states. I cannot sit idly by in Atlanta and not be concerned about what happens in Birmingham. Injustice anywhere is a threat to justice everywhere. We are caught in an inescapable network of mutuality, tied in a single garment of destiny. Whatever affects one directly, affects all indirectly. Never again can we afford to live with the narrow, provincial "outside agitator" idea. Anyone who lives inside the United States can never be considered an outsider anywhere within its bounds.

You deplore the demonstrations taking place in Birmingham. But your statement, I am sorry to say, fails to express a similar concern for the conditions that brought about the demonstrations. I am sure that none of you would want to rest content with the superficial kind of social analysis that deals merely with effects and does not grapple with underlying causes. It is unfortunate that demonstrations are taking place in Birmingham, but it is even more unfortunate that the city's white power structure left the Negro community with no alternative.

In any nonviolent campaign there are four basic steps: collection of the facts to determine whether injustices exist; negotiation; self-purification; and direct action. We have gone through all these steps in Birmingham. There can be no gainsaying the fact that racial injustice engulfs this community. Birmingham is probably the most thoroughly segregated city* in the United States. Its ugly record of brutality is widely known. Negroes have experienced grossly unjust treatment in the courts. There have been more unsolved bombings of Negro homes and churches in Birmingham than in any other city in the nation. These are the hard, brutal facts of the case. On the basis of these conditions, Negro leaders sought to negotiate with the city fathers. But the latter consistently refused to engage in good-faith negotiation.

5

Then, last September, came the opportunity to talk with leaders of Birmingham's economic community. In the course of the negotiations, certain promises were made by the merchants—for example, to remove the stores' humiliating racial signs. On the basis of these promises, the Reverend Fred Shuttlesworth and the leaders of the Alabama Christian Movement for Human Rights agreed to a moratorium on all demonstrations. As the weeks and months went by, we realized that we were the victims of a broken promise. A few signs, briefly removed, returned; the others remained.

As in so many past experiences, our hopes had been blasted, and the shadow of deep disappointment settled upon us. We had no alternative except to prepare for direct action, whereby we could present our very bodies as a means of laying our case before the conscience of the local and the national community. Mindful of the difficulties involved, we decided to undertake a process of self-purification. We began a series of workshops on nonviolence, and we repeatedly asked ourselves: "Are you able to accept blows without retaliating?" "Are you able to endure the ordeal of jail?" We decided to schedule our direct-action program for the Easter season, realizing that except for Christmas, this is the main shopping period of the year. Knowing that a strong economic-withdrawal program would be the by-product of direct action, we felt that this would be the best time to bring pressure to bear on the merchants for the needed change.

Then it occurred to us that Birmingham's mayoral election was coming up in March, and we speedily decided to postpone action until after election day. When we discovered that the Commissioner of Public Safety, Eugene "Bull" Connor, had piled up enough votes to be in the run-off, we decided again to postpone action until the day after the run-off so that the demonstrations could not be used to cloud the issues. Like many others, we wanted to see Mr. Connor defeated, and to this end we endured postponement after postponement. Having aided in this community need, we felt that our direct-action program could be delayed no longer.

10   You may well ask, "Why direct action? Why sit-ins, marches, and so forth? Isn't negotiation a better path?" You are quite right in calling for negotiation. Indeed, this is the very purpose of direct action. Nonviolent direct action seeks so to create such a crisis and foster such tension that a community which has constantly refused to negotiate is forced to confront the issue. It seeks to dramatize the issue that it can no longer be ignored. My citing the creation of tension as part of the work of the nonviolent-resister may sound rather shocking. But I must confess that I am not afraid of the word "tension." I have earnestly opposed violent tension, but there is a type of constructive, nonviolent tension which is necessary for growth. Just as Socrates felt that it was necessary to create a tension in the mind so that individuals could rise

from the bondage of myths and half-truths to the unfettered realm of creative analysis and objective appraisal, so must we see the need for nonviolent gad-flies* to create the kind of tension in society that will help men rise from the dark depths of prejudice and racism to the majestic heights of understanding and brotherhood.

The purpose of our direct-action program is to create a situation so crisis-packed that it will inevitably open the door to negotiation. I therefore concur with you in your call for negotiation. Too long has our beloved Southland been bogged down in a tragic effort to live in monologue rather than dialogue.

One of the basic points in your statement is that the action that I and my associates have taken in Birmingham is untimely. Some have asked: "Why didn't you give the new city administration time to act?" The only answer that I can give to this query is that the new Birmingham administration must be prodded about as much as the outgoing one, before it will act. We are sadly mistaken if we feel that the election of Albert Boutwell as mayor will bring the millennium to Birmingham. While Mr. Boutwell is a much more gentle person than Mr. Connor, they are both segregationists, dedicated to maintenance of the status quo. I have hoped that Mr. Boutwell will be reasonable enough to see the futility of massive resistance to desegregation. But he will not see this without pressure from devotees of civil rights. My friends, I must say to you that we have not made a single gain in civil rights without determined legal and nonviolent pressure. Lamentably, it is an historical fact that privileged groups seldom give up their privileges voluntarily. Individuals may see the moral light and voluntarily give up their unjust posture; but, as Reinhold Niebuhr has reminded us, groups tend to be more immoral than individuals.

We know through painful experience that freedom is never voluntarily given by the oppressor; it must be demanded by the oppressed. Frankly, I have yet to engage in a direct-action campaign that was "well timed" in the view of those who have not suffered unduly from the disease of segregation. For years now I have heard the word "Wait!" It rings in the ear of every Negro with piercing familiarity. This "Wait" has almost always meant "Never." We must come to see, with one of our distinguished jurists, that "justice too long delayed is justice denied."

We have waited for more than 340 years for our constitutional and God-given rights. The nations of Asia and Africa are moving with jetlike speed toward gaining political independence, but we still creep at horse-and-buggy pace toward gaining a cup of coffee at a lunch counter. Perhaps it is easy for those who have never felt the stinging darts of segregation to say, "Wait." But when you have seen vicious mobs lynch your mothers and fathers at will and drown your sisters and brothers at whim; when you have seen hate-filled policemen curse, kick, and even kill your black brothers and sisters; when you see the vast majority of your twenty million Negro brothers smothering in an airtight cage of poverty in the midst of an affluent society; when you suddenly find your tongue twisted and your speech stammering as you seek to explain to your six-year-old daughter why she can't go to the public amusement park that has just been advertised on television, and see tears welling up in her eyes when she is told that Funtown is closed to colored children, and see ominous clouds of inferiority beginning to form in her little mental sky, and see her beginning to distort her personality by developing an unconscious bitterness toward white people; when you have to concoct an answer for a five-year-old son who is asking, "Daddy, why do white people treat colored people so mean?"; when you take a cross-country drive and find it necessary to sleep night after night in the uncomfortable corners of your automobile because no motel will accept you; when you are humiliated day in and day out by nagging signs reading "white" and "colored"; when your first name becomes "nigger," your middle name becomes "boy" (however old you are) and your last name becomes "John," and your wife and mother are never given the respected title "Mrs."; when you are harried by day and haunted by night by the fact that you are a Negro, living constantly at tiptoe stance, never quite knowing what to expect next, and are plagued with inner fears and outer resentments; when you are forever fighting a degenerating sense of "nobodiness"—then you will understand why we find it difficult to wait. There comes a time when the cup of endurance runs over, and men are no longer willing to be plunged into the abyss of despair. I hope, sirs, you can understand our legitimate and unavoidable impatience.

15   You express a great deal of anxiety over our willingness to break laws. This is certainly a legitimate concern. Since we so diligently urge people to obey the Supreme Court's decision of 1954[1] outlawing segregation in the public schools, at first glance it may seem rather paradoxical for us consciously to break laws. One may well ask: "How can you advocate breaking some laws and obeying others?" The answer lies in the fact that there are two types of laws: just and unjust. I would be the first to advocate obeying just laws. One has not only a legal but a moral responsibility to obey just laws. Conversely, one has a moral responsibility to disobey unjust laws. I would agree with St. Augustine* that "an unjust law is no law at all."

Now, what is the difference between the two? How does one determine whether a law is just or unjust? A just law is a man-made code that squares with the moral law or the law of God. An unjust law is a code that is out of

---

1   *Supreme Court's decision of 1954*   Brown v. Board of Education. Prior to 1954 the courts had allowed states to follow policies according to which Black and White were supposedly "separate but equal."

harmony with the moral law. To put it in the terms of St. Thomas Aquinas:* An unjust law is a human law that is not rooted in eternal law and natural law. Any law that uplifts human personality is just. Any law that degrades human personality is unjust. All segregation statutes are unjust because segregation distorts the soul and damages the personality. It gives the segregator a false sense of superiority and the segregated a false sense of inferiority. Segregation, to use the terminology of the Jewish philosopher Martin Buber, substitutes an "I-it" relationship for an "I-thou" relationship and ends up relegating persons to the status of things. Hence segregation is not only politically, economically, and sociologically unsound, it is morally wrong and sinful. Paul Tillich* has said that sin is separation. Is not segregation an existential expression of man's tragic separation, his awful estrangement, his terrible sinfulness? Thus it is that I can urge men to obey the 1954 decision of the Supreme Court, for it is morally right; and I can urge them to disobey segregation ordinances, for they are morally wrong.

Let us consider a more concrete example of just and unjust laws. An unjust law is a code that a numerical or power majority group compels a minority group to obey but does not make binding on itself. This is *difference* made legal. By the same token, a just law is a code that a majority compels a minority to follow and that it is willing to follow itself. This is *sameness* made legal.

Let me give another explanation. A law is unjust if it is inflicted on a minority that, as a result of being denied the right to vote, had no part in enacting or devising the law. Who can say that the legislature of Alabama which set up that state's segregation laws was democratically elected? Throughout Alabama all sorts of devious methods are used to prevent Negroes from becoming registered voters, and there are some counties in which, even though Negroes constitute a majority of the population, not a single Negro is registered. Can any law enacted under such circumstances be considered democratically structured?

Sometimes a law is just on its face and unjust in its application. For instance, I have been arrested on a charge of parading without a permit. Now, there is nothing wrong in having an ordinance which requires a permit for a parade. But such an ordinance becomes unjust when it is used to maintain segregation and to deny citizens the First-Amendment privilege of peaceful assembly and protest.

I hope you are able to see the distinction I am trying to point out. In no sense do I advocate evading or defying the law, as would the rabid segregationist. That would lead to anarchy. One who breaks an unjust law must do so openly, lovingly, and with a willingness to accept the penalty. I submit that an individual who breaks a law that conscience tells him is unjust, and who willingly accepts the penalty of imprisonment in order to arouse the conscience of the community over its injustice, is in reality expressing the highest respect for law.

20

Of course, there is nothing new about this kind of civil disobedience. It was evidenced sublimely in the refusal of Shadrach, Meshach, and Abednego* to obey the laws of Nebuchadnezzar, on the ground that a higher moral law was at stake. It was practiced superbly by the early Christians, who were willing to face hungry lions and the excruciating pain of chopping blocks rather than submit to certain unjust laws of the Roman Empire.* To a degree, academic freedom is a reality today because Socrates practiced civil disobedience. In our own nation, the Boston Tea Party* represented a massive act of civil disobedience.

We should never forget that everything Adolf Hitler did in Germany was "legal" and everything the Hungarian freedom fighters[2] did in Hungary was "illegal." It was "illegal" to aid and comfort a Jew in Hitler's Germany. Even so, I am sure that, had I lived in Germany at the time, I would have aided and comforted my Jewish brothers. If today I lived in a Communist country where certain principles dear to the Christian faith are suppressed, I would openly advocate disobeying that country's anti-religious laws.

I must make two honest confessions to you, my Christian and Jewish brothers. First, I must confess that over the past few years I have been gravely disappointed with the white moderate. I have almost reached the regrettable conclusion that the Negro's great stumbling block in his stride toward freedom is not the White Citizen's Counciler or the Ku Klux Klanner,* but the white moderate, who is more devoted to "order" than to justice; who prefers a negative peace which is the absence of tension to a positive peace which is the presence of justice; who constantly says, "I agree with you in the goal you seek, but I cannot agree with your methods of direct action"; who paternalistically believes he can set the timetable for another man's freedom; who lives by a mythical concept of time and who constantly advises the Negro to wait for a "more convenient season." Shallow understanding from people of good will is more frustrating than absolute misunderstanding from people of ill will. Lukewarm acceptance is much more bewildering than outright rejection.

I had hoped that the white moderate would understand that law and order exist for the purpose of establishing justice and that when they fail in this purpose they become the dangerously structured dams that block the flow of social progress. I had hoped that the white moderate would understand that the present tension in the South is a necessary phase of the transition from an obnoxious negative peace, in which the Negro passively accepted his unjust plight, to a substantive and positive peace, in which all men will respect the dignity and worth of human personality. Actually, we who engage in nonviolent direct action are not the creators of tension. We merely bring

---

2   *Hungarian freedom fighters*   The Hungarian Rebellion in 1956 against an oppressive government was brutally suppressed with the help of the Soviet army.

to the surface the hidden tension that is already alive. We bring it out in the open, where it can be seen and dealt with. Like a boil that can never be cured so long as it is covered up but must be opened with all its ugliness to the natural medicines of air and light, injustice must be exposed, with all the tension its exposure creates, to the light of human conscience and the air of national opinion, before it can be cured.

In your statement you assert that our actions, even though peaceful, must be condemned because they precipitate violence. But is this a logical assertion? Isn't this like condemning a robbed man because his possession of money precipitated the evil act of robbery? Isn't this like condemning Socrates because his unswerving commitment to truth and his philosophical inquiries precipitated the act by the misguided populace in which they made him drink hemlock? Isn't this like condemning Jesus because his unique God-consciousness and never-ceasing devotion to God's will precipitated the evil act of crucifixion? We must come to see that, as the federal courts have consistently affirmed, it is wrong to urge an individual to cease his efforts to gain his basic constitutional rights because the quest may precipitate violence. Society must protect the robbed and punish the robber. 25

I had also hoped that the white moderate would reject the myth concerning time in relation to the struggle for freedom. I have just received a letter from a white brother in Texas. He writes: "All Christians know that the colored people will receive equal rights eventually, but it is possible that you are in too great a religious hurry. It has taken Christianity almost two thousand years to accomplish what it has. The teachings of Christ take time to come to earth." Such an attitude stems from a tragic misconception of time, from the strangely irrational notion that there is something in the very flow of time that will inevitably cure all ills. Actually, time itself is neutral; it can be used either destructively or constructively. More and more I feel that the people of ill will have used time much more effectively than have the people of good will. We will have to repent in this generation not merely for the hateful words and actions of the bad people, but for the appalling silence of the good people. Human progress never rolls in on wheels of inevitability; it comes through the tireless efforts of men willing to be co-workers with God, and without this hard work, time itself becomes an ally of the forces of social stagnation. We must use time creatively, in the knowledge that the time is always ripe to do right. Now is the time to make real the promise of democracy and transform our pending national elegy into a creative psalm of brotherhood. Now is the time to lift our national policy from the quicksand of racial injustice to the solid rock of human dignity.

You speak of our activity in Birmingham as extreme. At first I was rather disappointed that fellow clergymen would see my nonviolent efforts as those of an extremist. I began thinking about the fact that I stand in the middle of two opposing forces in the Negro community. One is a force of complacency, made up in part of Negroes who, as a result of long years of oppression, are so drained of self-respect and a sense of "somebodiness" that they have adjusted to segregation; and in part of a few middle-class Negroes who, because of a degree of academic and economic security and because in some ways they profit by segregation, have become insensitive to the problems of the masses. The other force is one of bitterness and hatred, and it comes perilously close to advocating violence. It is expressed in the various black nationalist groups that are springing up across the nation, the largest and best-known being Elijah Muhammad's Muslim movement.* Nourished by the Negro's frustration over the continued existence of racial discrimination, this movement is made up of people who have lost faith in America, who have absolutely repudiated Christianity, and who have concluded that the white man is an incorrigible "devil."

I have tried to stand between these two forces, saying that we need emulate neither the "do-nothingism" of the complacent nor the hatred and despair of the black nationalist. For there is the more excellent way of love and nonviolent protest. I am grateful to God that, through the influence of the Negro church, the way of nonviolence became an integral part of our struggle.

If this philosophy had not emerged, by now many streets of the South would, I am convinced, be flowing with blood. And I am further convinced that if our white brothers dismiss as "rabblerousers" and "outside agitators" those of us who employ nonviolent direct action, and if they refuse to support our nonviolent efforts, millions of Negroes will, out of frustration and despair, seek solace and security in black-nationalist ideologies—a development that would inevitably lead to a frightening racial nightmare.

30 Oppressed people cannot remain oppressed forever. The yearning for freedom eventually manifests itself, and that is what has happened to the American Negro. Something within has reminded him of his birthright of freedom, and something without has reminded him that it can be gained. Consciously or unconsciously, he has been caught up by the *Zeitgeist*,* and with his black brothers of Africa and his brown and yellow brothers of Asia, South America, and the Caribbean, the United States Negro is moving with a sense of great urgency toward the promised land of racial justice. If one recognizes this vital urge that has engulfed the Negro community, one should readily understand why public demonstrations are taking place. The Negro has many pent-up resentments and latent frustrations, and he must release them. So let him march; let him make prayer pilgrimages to the city hall; let him go on freedom rides—and try to understand why he must do so. If his repressed emotions are not released in nonviolent ways, they will seek expression through violence; this is not a threat but a fact of history. So I have not said to my people, "Get rid of your discontent." Rather, I have tried to say that this normal and healthy discontent

can be channeled into the creative outlet of nonviolent direct action. And now this approach is being termed extremist.

But though I was initially disappointed at being categorized as an extremist, as I continued to think about the matter I gradually gained a measure of satisfaction from the label. Was not Jesus an extremist for love: "Love your enemies, bless them that curse you, do good to them that hate you, and pray for them which despitefully use you, and persecute you." Was not Amos an extremist for justice: "Let justice roll down like waters and righteousness like an ever-flowing stream." Was not Paul an extremist for the Christian gospel: "I bear in my body the marks of the Lord Jesus." Was not Martin Luther an extremist: "Here I stand; I cannot do otherwise, so help me God." And John Bunyan: "I will stay in jail to the end of my days before I make a butchery of my conscience." And Abraham Lincoln: "This nation cannot survive half slave and half free." And Thomas Jefferson: "We hold these truths to be self-evident, that all men are created equal...."* So the question is not whether we will be extremists, but what kind of extremists we will be. Will we be extremists for hate or for love? Will we be extremists for the preservation of injustice or for the extension of justice? In that dramatic scene on Calvary's hill three men were crucified. We must never forget that all three were crucified for the same crime—the crime of extremism. Two were extremists for immorality, and thus fell below their environment. The other, Jesus Christ, was an extremist for love, truth, and goodness, and thereby rose above his environment. Perhaps the South, the nation, and the world are in dire need of creative extremists.

I had hoped that the white moderate would see this need. Perhaps I was too optimistic; perhaps I expected too much. I suppose I should have realized that few members of the oppressor race can understand the deep groans and passionate yearnings of the oppressed race, and still fewer have the vision to see that injustice must be rooted out by strong, persistent, and determined action. I am thankful, however, that some of our white brothers in the South have grasped the meaning of this social revolution and committed themselves to it. They are still all too few in quantity, but they are big in quality. Some—such as Ralph McGill, Lillian Smith, Harry Golden, James McBridge Dabbs, Ann Braden, and Sarah Patton Boyle—have written about our struggle in eloquent and prophetic terms. Others have marched with us down nameless streets of the South. They have languished in filthy, roach-infested jails, suffering the abuse and brutality of policemen who view them as "dirty nigger-lovers." Unlike so many of their moderate brothers and sisters, they have recognized the urgency of the moment and sensed the need for powerful "action" antidotes to combat the disease of segregation.

Let me take note of my other major disappointment. I have been so greatly disappointed with the white church and its leadership. Of course, there are some notable exceptions. I am not unmindful of the fact that each of you has taken some significant stands on this issue. I commend you, Reverend Stallings, for your Christian stand on this past Sunday, in welcoming Negroes to your worship service on a nonsegregated basis. I commend the Catholic leaders of this state for integrating Spring Hill College several years ago.

But despite these notable exceptions, I must honestly reiterate that I have been disappointed with the church. I do not say this as one of those negative critics who can always find something wrong with the church. I say this as a minister of the gospel, who loves the church; who was nurtured in its bosom; who has been sustained by its spiritual blessings and who will remain true to it as long as the cord of life shall lengthen.

35   When I was suddenly catapulted into the leadership of the bus protest in Montgomery, Alabama,[3] a few years ago, I felt we would be supported by the white church. I felt that the white ministers, priests, and rabbis of the South would be among our strongest allies. Instead, some have been outright opponents, refusing to understand the freedom movement and misrepresenting its leaders; all too many others have been more cautious than courageous and have remained silent behind the anesthetizing security of stained glass windows.

In spite of my shattered dreams, I came to Birmingham with the hope that the white religious leadership of this community would see the justice of our cause and, with deep moral concern, would serve as the channel through which our just grievances could reach the power structure. I had hoped that each of you would understand. But again I have been disappointed.

I have heard numerous southern religious leaders admonish their worshippers to comply with a desegregation decision because it is the law, but I have longed to hear white ministers declare: "Follow this decree because integration is morally right and because the Negro is your brother." In the midst of blatant injustices inflicted upon the Negro, I have watched white churchmen stand on the sideline and mouth pious irrelevancies and sanctimonious trivialities. In the midst of a mighty struggle to rid our nation of racial and economic injustice, I have heard many ministers say: "Those are social issues, with which the gospel has no real concern." And I have watched many churches commit themselves to a completely otherworldly religion which makes a strange un-Biblical distinction between the body and soul, between the sacred and the secular.

I have traveled the length and breadth of Alabama, Mississippi, and all the other southern states. On sweltering summer days and crisp autumn mornings I have looked at the South's beautiful churches with their lofty spires pointing

---

3   *bus protest in Montgomery, Alabama*   In December 1955, Rosa Lee Parks, a 42-year-old Civil Rights activist, refused to give her seat on a local bus to a white man, sparking a year-long boycott by African-Americans of the Montgomery buses.

heavenward. I have beheld the impressive outlines of her massive religious-education buildings. Over and over I have found myself asking: "What kind of people worship here? Who is their God? Where were their voices when the lips of Governor Barnett dripped with words of interposition and nullification? Where were they when Governor Wallace gave a clarion call for defiance and hatred? Where were their voices of support when bruised and weary Negro men and women decided to rise from the dark dungeons of complacency to the bright hills of creative protest?"

Yes, these questions are still in my mind. In deep disappointment I have wept over the laxity of the church. But be assured that my tears have been tears of love. There can be no deep disappointment where there is not deep love. Yes, I love the church. How could I do otherwise? I am in the rather unique position of being the son, the grandson, and the great-grandson of preachers. Yes, I see the church as the body of Christ. But, oh! How we have blemished and scarred that body through social neglect and through fear of being nonconformists.

There was a time when the church was very powerful—in the time when 40 the early Christians rejoiced at being deemed worthy to suffer for what they believed. In those days the church was not merely a thermometer that recorded the ideas and principles of popular opinion; it was a thermostat that transformed the mores of society. Whenever the early Christians entered a town, the people in power became disturbed and immediately sought to convict the Christians of being "disturbers of the peace" and "outside agitators." But the Christians pressed on, in the conviction that they were "a colony of heaven," called to obey God rather than man. Small in number, they were big in commitment. They were too God-intoxicated to be "astronomically intimidated." By their effort and example they brought an end to such ancient evils as infanticide and gladiatorial contests.

Things are different now. So often the contemporary church is a weak, ineffectual voice with an uncertain sound. So often it is an arch-defender of the status quo. Far from being disturbed by the presence of the church, the power structure of the average community is consoled by the church's silent—and often even vocal—sanction of things as they are.

But the judgment of God is upon the church as never before. If today's church does not recapture the sacrificial spirit of the early church, it will lose its authenticity, forfeit the loyalty of millions, and be dismissed as an irrelevant social club with no meaning for the twentieth century. Every day I meet young people whose disappointment with the church has turned into outright disgust.

Perhaps I have once again been too optimistic. Is organized religion too inextricably bound to the status quo to save our nation and the world? Perhaps I must turn my faith to the inner spiritual church, the church within the church, as the true *ekklesia*[4] and the hope of the world. But again I am thankful to God that some noble souls from the ranks of organized religion have broken loose from the paralyzing chains of conformity and joined us as active partners in the struggle for freedom. They have left their secure congregations and walked the streets of Albany, Georgia, with us. They have gone down the highways of the South on tortuous rides for freedom. Yes, they have gone to jail with us. Some have been dismissed from their churches, have lost the support of their bishops and fellow ministers. But they have acted in the faith that right defeated is stronger than evil triumphant. Their witness has been the spiritual salt that has preserved the true meaning of the gospel in these troubled times. They have carved a tunnel of hope through the dark mountain of disappointment.

I hope the church as a whole will meet the challenge of this decisive hour. But even if the church does not come to the aid of justice, I have no despair about the future. I have no fear about the outcome of our struggle in Birmingham, even if our motives are at present misunderstood. We will reach the goal of freedom in Birmingham and all over the nation, because the goal of America is freedom. Abused and scorned though we may be, our destiny is tied up with America's destiny. Before the pilgrims landed at Plymouth,* we were here. Before the pen of Jefferson etched the majestic words of the Declaration of Independence across the pages of history, we were here. For more than two centuries our forebears labored in this country without wages; they made cotton king;* they built the homes of their masters while suffering gross injustice and shameful humiliation—and yet out of a bottomless vitality they continued to thrive and develop. If the inexpressible cruelties of slavery could not stop us, the opposition we now face will surely fail. We will win our freedom because the sacred heritage of our nation and the eternal will of God are embodied in our echoing demands.

45   Before closing I feel impelled to mention one other point in your statement that has troubled me profoundly. You warmly commended the Birmingham police for keeping "order" and "preventing violence." I doubt that you would have so warmly commended the police force if you had seen its dogs sinking their teeth into unarmed, nonviolent Negroes. I doubt that you would so quickly commend the policemen if you were to observe their ugly and inhumane treatment of Negroes here in the city jail; if you were to watch them push and curse old Negro women and young Negro girls; if you were to see them slap and kick old Negro men and young boys; if you were to observe them, as they did on two occasions, refuse to give us food because we wanted to sing our grace together. I cannot join you in your praise of the Birmingham police department.

---

4   *ekklesia*   Christian church in its original form.

It is true that the police have exercised a degree of discipline in handling the demonstrators. In this sense they have conducted themselves rather "nonviolently" in public. But for what purpose? To preserve the evil system of segregation. Over the past few years I have consistently preached that nonviolence demands that the means we use must be as pure as the ends we seek. I have tried to make clear that it is wrong to use immoral means to attain moral ends. But now I must affirm that it is just as wrong, or perhaps even more so, to use moral means to preserve immoral ends. Perhaps Mr. Connor and his policemen have been rather nonviolent in public, as was Chief Pritchett in Albany, Georgia, but they have used moral means of nonviolence to maintain the immoral end of racial injustice. As T.S. Eliot has said, "The last temptation is the greatest treason: To do the right deed for the wrong reason."[5]

I wish you had commended the Negro sit-inners and demonstrators of Birmingham for their sublime courage, their willingness to suffer, and their amazing discipline in the midst of great provocation. One day the South will recognize its real heroes. They will be the James Merediths,[6] with the noble sense of purpose that enables them to face jeering and hostile mobs, and with the agonizing loneliness that characterizes the life of the pioneer. They will be old, oppressed, battered Negro women, symbolized in a seventy-two-year-old woman in Montgomery, Alabama, who rose up with a sense of dignity and with her people decided not to ride segregated buses,* and who responded with ungrammatical profundity to one who inquired about her weariness: "My feets is tired, but my soul is at rest." They will be the young high school and college students, the young ministers of the gospel and a host of their elders, courageously and nonviolently sitting in at lunch counters and willingly going to jail for conscience' sake. One day the South will know that when these disinherited children of God sat down at lunch counters, they were in reality standing up for what is best in the American dream and for the most sacred values in our Judaeo-Christian heritage, thereby bringing our nation back to those great wells of democracy which were dug deep by the founding fathers in their formulation of the Constitution and the Declaration of Independence.

Never before have I written such a long letter. I'm afraid it is much too long to take your precious time. I can assure you that it would have been much shorter if I had been writing from a comfortable desk, but what else can one do when he is alone in a narrow jail cell, other than write long letters, think long thoughts, and pray long prayers?

---

5   *The last ... wrong reason*   These lines are part of the response of St. Thomas à Becket to the fourth tempter in T.S. Eliot's play *Murder in the Cathedral*.

6   *James Merediths*   In 1962 James H. Meredith became the first African-American student at the University of Mississippi.

If I have said anything in this letter that overstates the truth and indicates an unreasonable impatience, I beg you to forgive me. If I have said anything that understates the truth and indicates my having a patience that allows me to settle for anything less than brotherhood, I beg God to forgive me.

50   I hope this letter finds you strong in the faith. I also hope that circumstances will soon make it possible for me to meet each of you, not as an integrationist or a civil-rights leader but as a fellow clergyman and a Christian brother. Let us all hope that the dark clouds of racial prejudice will soon pass away and the deep fog of misunderstanding will be lifted from our fear-drenched communities, and in some not too distant tomorrow the radiant stars of love and brotherhood will shine over our great nation with all their scintillating beauty.

Yours for the cause of Peace and Brotherhood,

Martin Luther King Jr.

(1963)

Nelson Mandela

from An Ideal for Which I Am Prepared to Die

Black Africans had been ill-treated under the British colonial regime in South Africa, and their situation deteriorated further with the 1948 institution by the new National Party government of a system of apartheid—rigid segregation, with non-whites assigned an inferior status and accorded virtually no rights. Mandela, one of the leaders of the resistance movement against this system (and, from 1994 to 1999, the first president of a democratic South Africa), was arrested on 5 August 1962; he was convicted of relatively minor charges and sentenced to five years imprisonment. After other rebel leaders were captured on 11 July 1963, Mandela was again put on trial with them. The speech excerpted below was made 20 April 1964 from the dock at the rebels' trial on charges of sabotage and "conspiracy to overthrow the government." The full speech runs to well over 10,000 words and took about three hours to deliver.

Mandela was convicted, but was sentenced not to death (as the prosecution had asked) but to life imprisonment; he had spent 27 years in prison by the time he was released in 1990.

I am the first accused. I hold a bachelor's degree in arts and practiced as an attorney in Johannesburg for a number of years in partnership with Oliver Tambo. I am a convicted prisoner serving five years for leaving the country without a permit and for inciting people to go on strike at the end of May 1961.

At the outset, I want to say that the suggestion made by the state in its opening that the struggle in South Africa is under the influence of foreigners or communists is wholly incorrect. I have done whatever I did, both as an individual and as a leader of my people, because of my experience in South Africa and my own proudly felt African background, and not because of what any outsider might have said.

In my youth in the Transkei* I listened to the elders of my tribe telling stories of the old days. Amongst the tales they related to me were those of wars fought by our ancestors in defense of the fatherland. The names of Dingane and Bambata, Hintsa and Makana, Squngthi and Dalasile, Moshoeshoe and Sekhukhuni,* were praised as the glory of the entire African nation. I hoped then that life might offer me the opportunity to serve my people and make my own humble contribution to their freedom struggle. This is what has motivated me in all that I have done in relation to the charges made against me in this case.

Having said this, I must deal immediately and at some length with the question of violence. Some of the things so far told to the court are true and some are untrue. I do not, however, deny that I planned sabotage. I did not plan it in a spirit of recklessness, nor because I have any love of violence. I planned it as a result of a calm and sober assessment of the political situation that had arisen after many years of tyranny, exploitation, and oppression of my people by the whites.

5   I admit immediately that I was one of the persons who helped to form Umkhonto we Sizwe,[1] and that I played a prominent role in its affairs until I was arrested in August 1962....

I, and the others who started the organization, did so for two reasons. Firstly, we believed that as a result of Government policy, violence by the African people had become inevitable, and that unless responsible leadership was given to canalize and control the feelings of our people, there would be outbreaks of terrorism which would produce an intensity of bitterness and hostility between the various races of this country which is not produced even by war. Secondly, we felt that without violence there would be no way open to the African people to succeed in their struggle against the principle of white supremacy. All lawful modes of expressing opposition to this principle had been closed by legislation, and we were placed in a position in which we had either to accept a permanent state of inferiority, or to defy the government. We chose to defy the law. We first broke the law in a way which avoided any recourse to violence; when this form was legislated against, and then the government resorted to a show of force to crush opposition to its policies, only then did we decide to answer violence with violence.

But the violence which we chose to adopt was not terrorism. We who formed Umkhonto were all members of the African National Congress,* and had behind us the ANC tradition of non-violence and negotiation as a means of solving political disputes. We believe that South Africa belongs to all the people who live in it, and not to one group, be it black or white. We did not want an interracial war, and tried to avoid it to the last minute. If the court is in doubt about this, it will be seen that the whole history of our organization bears out what I have said....

---

1   *Umkhonto we Sizwe*   Zulu: Spear of the Nation. Military wing of the African National Congress.

In 1960 there was the shooting at Sharpeville,[2] which resulted in the proclamation of a state of emergency and the declaration of the ANC as an unlawful
organization. My colleagues and I, after careful consideration, decided that we
would not obey this decree. The African people were not part of the government and did not make the laws by which they were governed. We believed
in the words of the Universal Declaration of Human Rights, that "the will of
the people shall be the basis of authority of the government," and for us to
accept the banning was equivalent to accepting the silencing of the Africans
for all time. The ANC refused to dissolve, but instead went underground. We
believed it was our duty to preserve this organization which had been built
up with almost fifty years of unremitting toil. I have no doubt that no self-
respecting white political organization would disband itself if declared illegal
by a government in which it had no say....

What were we, the leaders of our people, to do? Were we to give in to the
show of force and the implied threat against future action, or were we to fight
it and, if so, how?

We had no doubt that we had to continue the fight. Anything else would
have been abject surrender. Our problem was not whether to fight, but was
how to continue the fight. We of the ANC had always stood for a non-racial
democracy, and we shrank from any action which might drive the races further
apart than they already were. But the hard facts were that fifty years of non-
violence had brought the African people nothing but more and more repressive
legislation, and fewer and fewer rights. It may not be easy for this court to
understand, but it is a fact that for a long time the people had been talking of
violence—of the day when they would fight the white man and win back their
country—and we, the leaders of the ANC, had nevertheless always prevailed
upon them to avoid violence and to pursue peaceful methods. When some of us
discussed this in May and June of 1961, it could not be denied that our policy to
achieve a non-racial state by non-violence had achieved nothing, and that our
followers were beginning to lose confidence in this policy and were developing
disturbing ideas of terrorism.

It must not be forgotten that by this time violence had, in fact, become a
feature of the South African political scene. There had been violence in 1957
when the women of Zeerust were ordered to carry passes; there was violence
in 1958 with the enforcement of cattle culling in Sekhukhuniland; there was
violence in 1959 when the people of Cato Manor protested against pass raids;

10

---

2   *shooting at Sharpeville*   The incident now known as the Sharpeville Massacre took
place on 21 March 1960; police fired repeatedly into a crowd of several thousand who
were protesting the government's "pass laws," which placed severe restrictions on the free
movement of black people. The police killed at least 69 people (including 10 children) and
injured at least 170.

there was violence in 1960 when the government attempted to impose Bantu authorities in Pondoland.* Thirty-nine Africans died in these disturbances. In 1961 there had been riots in Warmbaths, and all this time the Transkei had been a seething mass of unrest. Each disturbance pointed clearly to the inevitable growth among Africans[3] of the belief that violence was the only way out—it showed that a government which uses force to maintain its rule teaches the oppressed to use force to oppose it. Already small groups had arisen in the urban areas and were spontaneously making plans for violent forms of political struggle. There now arose a danger that these groups would adopt terrorism against Africans, as well as whites, if not properly directed....

[I]n view of the situation I have described, the ANC was prepared to depart from its fifty-year-old policy of non-violence to this extent that it would no longer disapprove of properly controlled violence. Hence members who undertook such activity would not be subject to disciplinary action by the ANC.

I say "properly controlled violence" because I made it clear that if I formed the organization I would at all times subject it to the political guidance of the ANC and would not undertake any different form of activity from that contemplated without the consent of the ANC. And I shall now tell the court how that form of violence came to be determined.

As a result of this decision, Umkhonto was formed in November 1961. When we took this decision, and subsequently formulated our plans, the ANC heritage of non-violence and racial harmony was very much with us. We felt that the country was drifting towards a civil war in which blacks and whites would fight each other. We viewed the situation with alarm. Civil war could mean the destruction of what the ANC stood for; with civil war, racial peace would be more difficult than ever to achieve....

15

[In such situations] four forms of violence are possible. There is sabotage, there is guerrilla warfare, there is terrorism, and there is open revolution. We chose to adopt the first method and to exhaust it before taking any other decision.

In the light of our political background the choice was a logical one. Sabotage did not involve loss of life, and it offered the best hope for future race relations. Bitterness would be kept to a minimum and, if the policy bore fruit, democratic government could become a reality. This is what we felt at the time, and this is what we said in our manifesto:

> We of Umkhonto we Sizwe have always sought to achieve liberation
> without bloodshed and civil clash. We hope, even at this late hour, that

---

3   *Africans* I.e., Black Africans. At this time white South Africans were classed as "Europeans"; there were also separate categories for people of mixed race ("Coloreds") and people of Asian descent.

our first actions will awaken everyone to a realization of the disastrous situation to which the nationalist policy is leading. We hope that we will bring the government and its supporters to their senses before it is too late, so that both the government and its policies can be changed before matters reach the desperate state of civil war.

The initial plan was based on a careful analysis of the political and economic situation of our country. We believed that South Africa depended to a large extent on foreign capital and foreign trade. We felt that planned destruction of power plants, and interference with rail and telephone communications, would tend to scare away capital from the country, make it more difficult for goods from the industrial areas to reach the seaports on schedule, and would in the long run be a heavy drain on the economic life of the country, thus compelling the voters of the country to reconsider their position.

Attacks on the economic life-lines of the country were to be linked with sabotage on government buildings and other symbols of apartheid. These attacks would serve as a source of inspiration to our people. In addition, they would provide an outlet for those people who were urging the adoption of violent methods and would enable us to give concrete proof to our followers that we had adopted a stronger line and were fighting back against government violence....

I turn now to my own position. I have denied that I am a communist, and I think that in the circumstances I am obliged to state exactly what my political beliefs are.

I have always regarded myself, in the first place, as an African patriot. After all, I was born in Umtata, forty-six years ago. My guardian was my cousin, who was the acting paramount chief of Tembuland, and I am related both to the present paramount chief of Tembuland, Sabata Dalindyebo, and to Kaizer Matanzima, the Chief Minister of the Transkei.

Today I am attracted by the idea of a classless society, an attraction which springs in part from Marxist reading[4] and, in part, from my admiration of the structure and organization of early African societies in this country. The land, then the main means of production, belonged to the tribe. There were no rich or poor and there was no exploitation.

It is true, as I have already stated, that I have been influenced by Marxist thought. But this is also true of many of the leaders of the new independent states. Such widely different persons as Gandhi, Nehru, Nkrumah, and Nasser*

20

---

4   *Marxist reading*   Reading of the works of Karl Marx and his followers. Among white South Africans at this time (as among most Americans in the 1950s and 1960s, during the height of the Cold War) Marxism, socialism, and communism were all viewed with great suspicion, and those suspected of Marxist or communist sympathies were often persecuted.

all acknowledge this fact. We all accept the need for some form of socialism to enable our people to catch up with the advanced countries of this world and to overcome their legacy of extreme poverty. But this does not mean we are Marxists.

Indeed, for my own part, I believe that it is open to debate whether the Communist party has any specific role to play at this particular stage of our political struggle. The basic task at the present moment is the removal of race discrimination and the attainment of democratic rights on the basis of the Freedom Charter. In so far as that party furthers this task, I welcome its assistance. I realize that it is one of the means by which people of all races can be drawn into our struggle.

From my reading of Marxist literature and from conversations with Marxists, I have gained the impression that communists regard the parliamentary system of the west as undemocratic and reactionary. But, on the contrary, I am an admirer of such a system.

The Magna Carta, the Petition of Right, and the Bill of Rights[5] are documents which are held in veneration by democrats throughout the world. I have great respect for British political institutions, and for the country's system of justice. I regard the British Parliament as the most democratic institution in the world, and the independence and impartiality of its judiciary never fails to arouse my admiration.

25   The American Congress, that country's doctrine of separation of powers,* as well as the independence of its judiciary, arouses in me similar sentiments.

I have been influenced in my thinking by both west and east. All this has led me to feel that in my search for a political formula, I should be absolutely impartial and objective. I should tie myself to no particular system of society other than of socialism. I must leave myself free to borrow the best from the west and from the east....

Our fight is against real, and not imaginary, hardships or, to use the language of the state prosecutor, "so-called hardships." Basically, we fight against two features which are the hallmarks of African life in South Africa and which are entrenched by legislation which we seek to have repealed. These features are poverty and lack of human dignity, and we do not need communists or so-called "agitators" to teach us about these things.

South Africa is the richest country in Africa, and could be one of the richest countries in the world. But it is a land of extremes and remarkable contrasts. The whites enjoy what may well be the highest standard of living in the world,

---

5   *Magna Carta, the Petition of Right, and the Bill of Rights*   British legal documents dating respectively from 1215, 1628, and 1689—all of which set out various limits on the arbitrary exercise of power by the monarch or government.

whilst Africans live in poverty and misery. Forty per cent of the Africans live in hopelessly overcrowded and, in some cases, drought-stricken Reserves,[6] where soil erosion and the overworking of the soil makes it impossible for them to live properly off the land. Thirty per cent are laborers, labor tenants, and squatters on white farms and work and live under conditions similar to those of the serfs of the Middle Ages. The other 30 per cent live in towns where they have developed economic and social habits which bring them closer in many respects to white standards. Yet most Africans, even in this group, are impoverished by low incomes and high cost of living.

The highest-paid and the most prosperous section of urban African life is in Johannesburg. Yet their actual position is desperate. The latest figures were given on 25 March 1964 by Mr. Carr, Manager of the Johannesburg non-European affairs department. The poverty datum line for the average African family in Johannesburg (according to Mr. Carr's department) is 42.84 rand[7] per month. He showed that the average monthly wage is 32.24 rand and that 46 per cent of all African families in Johannesburg do not earn enough to keep them going.

Poverty goes hand in hand with malnutrition and disease. The incidence of malnutrition and deficiency diseases is very high amongst Africans. Tuberculosis, pellagra, kwashiorkor, gastro-enteritis, and scurvy bring death and destruction of health. The incidence of infant mortality is one of the highest in the world. According to the medical officer of health for Pretoria, tuberculosis kills forty people a day (almost all Africans), and in 1961 there were 58,491 new cases reported. These diseases not only destroy the vital organs of the body, but they result in retarded mental conditions and lack of initiative, and reduce powers of concentration. The secondary results of such conditions affect the whole community and the standard of work performed by African laborers.

The complaint of Africans, however, is not only that they are poor and the whites are rich, but that the laws which are made by the whites are designed to preserve this situation. There are two ways to break out of poverty. The first is by formal education, and the second is by the worker acquiring a greater skill at his work and thus higher wages. As far as Africans are concerned, both these avenues of advancement are deliberately curtailed by legislation....

30

---

6   *Reserves*   Under the apartheid system, black Africans were required to live on land designated as Reserves (typically, areas with poor soil and few facilities), unless they had obtained a pass to visit or work in white areas. In many cases families were divided by these rules, with one family member working in a white area while the rest of the family had to stay on the Reserve.

7   *rand*   South African currency unit; a rough equivalent to 42.84 rand in today's American currency would be less than three dollars.

The government often answers its critics by saying that Africans in South Africa are economically better off than the inhabitants of the other countries in Africa. I do not know whether this statement is true and doubt whether any comparison can be made without having regard to the cost-of-living index in such countries. But even if it is true, as far as the African people are concerned it is irrelevant. Our complaint is not that we are poor by comparison with people in other countries, but that we are poor by comparison with the white people in our own country, and that we are prevented by legislation from altering this imbalance.

The lack of human dignity experienced by Africans is the direct result of the policy of white supremacy. White supremacy implies black inferiority. Legislation designed to preserve white supremacy entrenches this notion. Menial tasks in South Africa are invariably performed by Africans. When anything has to be carried or cleaned the white man will look around for an African to do it for him, whether the African is employed by him or not. Because of this sort of attitude, whites tend to regard Africans as a separate breed. They do not look upon them as people with families of their own; they do not realize that they have emotions—that they fall in love like white people do; that they want to be with their wives and children like white people want to be with theirs; that they want to earn enough money to support their families properly, to feed and clothe them and send them to school. And what "house-boy" or "garden-boy" or laborer can ever hope to do this?

Pass laws, which to the Africans are among the most hated bits of legislation in South Africa, render any African liable to police surveillance at any time. I doubt whether there is a single African male in South Africa who has not at some stage had a brush with the police over his pass. Hundreds and thousands of Africans are thrown into jail each year under pass laws. Even worse than this is the fact that pass laws keep husband and wife apart and lead to the breakdown of family life.

35   Poverty and the breakdown of family life have secondary effects. Children wander about the streets of the townships because they have no schools to go to, or no money to enable them to go to school, or no parents at home to see that they go to school, because both parents (if there be two) have to work to keep the family alive. This leads to a breakdown in moral standards, to an alarming rise in illegitimacy, and to growing violence which erupts not only politically, but everywhere. Life in the townships is dangerous. There is not a day that goes by without somebody being stabbed or assaulted. And violence is carried out of the townships in to the white living areas. People are afraid to walk alone in the streets after dark. Housebreakings and robberies are increasing, despite the fact that the death sentence can now be imposed for such offences. Death sentences cannot cure the festering sore.

Africans want to be paid a living wage. Africans want to perform work which they are capable of doing, and not work which the government declares them to be capable of. Africans want to be allowed to live where they obtain work, and not be endorsed out of an area because they were not born there. Africans want to be allowed to own land in places where they work, and not to be obliged to live in rented houses which they can never call their own. Africans want to be part of the general population, and not confined to living in their own ghettoes. African men want to have their wives and children to live with them where they work, and not be forced into an unnatural existence in men's hostels. African women want to be with their menfolk and not be left permanently widowed in the Reserves. Africans want to be allowed out after eleven o'clock at night and not to be confined to their rooms like little children. Africans want to be allowed to travel in their own country and to seek work where they want to and not where the labor bureau tells them to. Africans want a just share in the whole of South Africa; they want security and a stake in society.

Above all, we want equal political rights, because without them our disabilities will be permanent. I know this sounds revolutionary to the whites in this country, because the majority of voters will be Africans. This makes the white man fear democracy.

But this fear cannot be allowed to stand in the way of the only solution which will guarantee racial harmony and freedom for all. It is not true that the enfranchisement of all will result in racial domination. Political division, based on color, is entirely artificial and, when it disappears, so will the domination of one color group by another. The ANC has spent half a century fighting against racialism. When it triumphs it will not change that policy.

This then is what the ANC is fighting. Their struggle is a truly national one. It is a struggle of the African people, inspired by their own suffering and their own experience. It is a struggle for the right to live.

During my lifetime I have dedicated myself to this struggle of the African people. I have fought against white domination, and I have fought against black domination. I have cherished the ideal of a democratic and free society in which all persons live together in harmony and with equal opportunities. It is an ideal which I hope to live for and to achieve. But if needs be, it is an ideal for which I am prepared to die.

40

(1964)

JOAN DIDION

ON MORALITY

The two essays below are both from Slouching Towards Bethlehem, *the 1968 collection with which Didion made her name as an essayist. Didion, who had grown up and attended university in California but then spent several years in New York, returned to the west coast in her early thirties and began writing magazine pieces on the culture there. Her journalistic writing—in which the writer sets aside traditional journalistic "objectivity" and makes her own experiences and reflections central to each piece—was in a style that came in the 1970s to be known as the New Journalism.*

"On Morality" was first published as "The Insidious Ethic of Conscience" in the Autumn 1965 issue of the The American Scholar.

As it happens I am in Death Valley,[1] in a room at the Enterprise Motel and Trailer Park, and it is July, and it is hot. In fact it is 119°. I cannot seem to make the air conditioner work, but there is a small refrigerator, and I can wrap ice cubes in a towel and hold them against the small of my back. With the help of the ice cubes I have been trying to think, because *The American Scholar*[2] asked me to, in some abstract way about "morality," a word I distrust more every day, but my mind veers inflexibly toward the particular.

Here are some particulars. At midnight last night, on the road in from Las Vegas to Death Valley Junction, a car hit a shoulder and turned over. The driver, very young and apparently drunk, was killed instantly. His girlfriend was found alive but bleeding internally, deep in shock. I talked this afternoon to the nurse who had driven the girl to the nearest doctor, 185 miles across the floor of the Valley and three ranges of lethal mountain road. The nurse explained that her husband, a talc miner, had stayed on the highway with the boy's body until the

---

1   *Death Valley*   Desert area in eastern California. The hottest, driest, and lowest region in North America, it is so named because of the number of pioneers who died in and around the region during the California Gold Rush.

2   *The American Scholar*   American quarterly magazine of literature, history, science, and culture, created in 1932 and inspired by Ralph Waldo Emerson's speech entitled "The American Scholar" (1837).

coroner could get over the mountains from Bishop,[3] at dawn today. "You can't just leave a body on the highway," she said. "It's immoral."

It was one instance in which I did not distrust the word, because she meant something quite specific. She meant that if a body is left alone for even a few minutes on the desert, the coyotes close in and eat the flesh. Whether or not a corpse is torn apart by coyotes may seem only a sentimental consideration, but of course it is more: one of the promises we make to one another is that we will try to retrieve our casualties, try not to abandon our dead to the coyotes. If we have been taught to keep our promises—if, in the simplest terms, our upbringing is good enough—we stay with the body, or have bad dreams.

I am talking, of course, about the kind of social code that is sometimes called, usually pejoratively, "wagon-train* morality." In fact that is precisely what it is. For better or worse, we are what we learned as children: my own childhood was illuminated by graphic litanies of the grief awaiting those who failed in their loyalties to each other. The Donner-Reed Party,[4] starving in the Sierra snows, all the ephemera of civilization gone save that one vestigial* taboo, the provision that no one should eat his own blood kin. The Jayhawkers,[5] who quarreled and separated not far from where I am tonight. Some of them died in the Funerals and some of them died down near Badwater and most of the rest of them died in the Panamints.[6] A woman who got through gave the valley its name. Some might say that the Jayhawkers were killed by the desert summer, and the Donner Party by the mountain winter, by circumstances beyond control; we were taught instead that they had somewhere abdicated their responsibilities, somehow breached their primary loyalties, or they would not have found themselves helpless in the mountain winter or the desert summer, would not have given way to acrimony,* would not have deserted one another, would not have *failed*. In brief, we heard such stories as cautionary tales, and they still suggest the only kind of "morality" that seems to me to have any but the most potentially mendacious* meaning.

---

3   *Bishop*   City in California just east of the Sierra Nevada mountain range, separated from Death Valley by a series of mountain ranges including the Panamint.

4   *Donner-Reed Party*   Famous group of pioneers who were trapped by snow in the Sierra Nevada mountains in the winter of 1846. To survive, many party members ate those who had died.

5   *Jayhawkers*   One of several groups of pioneers who traveled from Salt Lake City, Utah, to California in 1849 in hopes of profiting from gold discovered west of the Sierra Nevada.

6   *the Funerals*   Small mountain range just west of Death Valley Junction; *Badwater*   Basin in Death Valley, so named because of the undrinkable quality of its water; *the Panamints*   Mountain range which comprises the western wall of Death Valley.

5   You are quite possibly impatient with me by now; I am talking, you want to say, about a "morality" so primitive that it scarcely deserves the name, a code that has as its point only survival, not the attainment of the ideal good. Exactly. Particularly out here tonight, in this country so ominous and terrible that to live in it is to live with antimatter,[7] it is difficult to believe that "the good" is a knowable quantity. Let me tell you what it is like out here tonight. Stories travel at night on the desert. Someone gets in his pickup and drives a couple of hundred miles for a beer, and he carries news of what is happening, back wherever he came from. Then he drives another hundred miles for another beer, and passes along stories from the last place as well as from the one before; it is a network kept alive by people whose instincts tell them that if they do not keep moving at night on the desert they will lose all reason. Here is a story that is going around the desert tonight: over across the Nevada line, sheriff's deputies are diving in some underground pools, trying to retrieve a couple of bodies known to be in the hole. The widow of one of the drowned boys is over there; she is eighteen, and pregnant, and is said not to leave the hole. The divers go down and come up, and she just stands there and stares into the water. They have been diving for ten days but have found no bottom to the caves, no bodies and no trace of them, only the black 90° water going down and down and down, and a single translucent fish, not classified. The story tonight is that one of the divers has been hauled up incoherent, out of his head, shouting—until they got him out of there so that the widow could not hear—about water that got hotter instead of cooler as he went down, about light flickering through the water, about magma, about underground nuclear testing.

           That is the tone stories take out here, and there are quite a few of them tonight. And it is more than the stories alone. Across the road at the Faith Community Church a couple of dozen old people, come here to live in trailers and die in the sun, are holding a prayer sing. I cannot hear them and do not want to. What I can hear are occasional coyotes and a constant chorus of "Baby the Rain Must Fall" from the jukebox in the Snake Room next door, and if I were also to hear those dying voices, those Midwestern voices drawn to this lunar country for some unimaginable atavistic rites,* *rock of ages cleft for me*,[8] I think I would lose my own reason. Every now and then I imagine I hear a

---

7   *antimatter*   Matter composed of particles which have the opposite charge of any ordinary particles, their collision with ordinary matter thus leading to mutual destruction.
8   *Baby the Rain Must Fall*   Folk song performed by Glenn Yarbrough for the American film of the same name (1965), about a woman who travels through Texas with her young daughter to be reunited with her husband, who is on parole after being imprisoned for a violent crime; *atavistic* Ancestral; *rock ... for me* Line from the popular Christian hymn "Rock of Ages" (1775), written by the Reverend Augustus Montague Toplady.

rattlesnake,* but my husband says that it is a faucet, a paper rustling, the wind. Then he stands by a window, and plays a flashlight over the dry wash outside.

What does it mean? It means nothing manageable. There is some sinister hysteria in the air out here tonight, some hint of the monstrous perversion to which any human idea can come. "I followed my own conscience." "I did what I thought was right." How many madmen have said it and meant it? How many murderers? Klaus Fuchs said it, and the men who committed the Mountain Meadows Massacre said it, and Alfred Rosenberg[9] said it. And, as we are rotely and rather presumptuously reminded by those who would say it now, Jesus said it. Maybe we have all said it, and maybe we have been wrong. Except on the most primitive level—our loyalties to those we love—what could be more arrogant than to claim the primacy of personal conscience? ("Tell me," a rabbi asked Daniel Bell[10] when he said, as a child, that he did not believe in God. "Do you think God cares?") At least some of the time, the world appears to me as a painting by Hieronymous Bosch;[11] were I to follow my conscience then, it would lead me out onto the desert with Marion Faye,[12] out to where he stood in *The Deer Park* looking east to Los Alamos and praying, as if for rain, that it would happen: "... *let it come and clear the rot and the stench and the stink, let it come for all of everywhere, just so it comes and the world stands clear in the white dead dawn.*"

Of course you will say that I do not have the right, even if I had the power, to inflict that unreasonable conscience upon you; nor do I want you to inflict your conscience, however reasonable, however enlightened, upon me. ("We must be aware of the dangers which lie in our most generous wishes," Lionel

---

9   *Klaus Fuchs*   German theoretical physicist (1911–88) who, while working in Britain and the United States during the Second World War, supplied information to the Soviet Union concerning those nations' nuclear projects, including the American, Canadian, and British "Manhattan Project." He was convicted in 1950 and served approximately nine years in prison;   *Mountain Meadows Massacre*   Series of attacks in Mountain Meadows, Utah, on an emigrant wagon-train from Arkansas, resulting in over 100 deaths including those of children. The perpetrators were primarily Mormon settlers, potentially motivated by an intense fear of impending war;   *Alfred Rosenberg*   German thinker (1893–1946), heavily influential to the development of Nazi ideology prior to and during the Second World War.

10   *Daniel Bell*   Jewish-American sociologist (1919–2011) perhaps best known for his collection of essays *The End of Ideology* (1960).

11   *Hieronymous Bosch*   Dutch painter (c. 1450–1516) known for his fantastic and often disturbing paintings, many of which illustrate human sinfulness.

12   *Marion Faye*   Character in Norman Mailer's novel *The Deer Park* (1955). The novel references the 1950s practice of nuclear tourism in the United States; people would view desert nuclear tests from the distance as spectacles. Didion quotes from a moment in the novel wherein Faye is one of these fascinated observers.

Trilling[13] once wrote. "Some paradox of our nature leads us, when once we have made our fellow men the objects of our enlightened interest, to go on to make them the objects of our pity, then of our wisdom, ultimately of our coercion.") That the ethic of conscience is intrinsically insidious seems scarcely a revelatory point, but it is one raised with increasing infrequency; even those who do raise it tend to *segue** with troubling readiness into the quite contradictory position that the ethic of conscience is dangerous when it is "wrong," and admirable when it is "right."

You see I want to be quite obstinate about insisting that we have no way of knowing—beyond that fundamental loyalty to the social code—what is "right" and what is "wrong," what is "good" and what "evil." I dwell so upon this because the most disturbing aspect of "morality" seems to me to be the frequency with which the word now appears; in the press, on television, in the most perfunctory* kinds of conversation. Questions of straightforward power (or survival) politics, questions of quite indifferent public policy, questions of almost anything; they are all assigned these factitious moral burdens. There is something quite facile* going on, some self-indulgence at work. Of course we would all like to "believe" in something, like to assuage our private guilts in public causes, like to lose our tiresome selves; like, perhaps, to transform the white flag of defeat at home into the brave white banner of battle away from home. And of course it is all right to do that; that is how, immemorially, things have gotten done. But I think it is all right only so long as we do not delude ourselves about what we are doing, and why. It is all right only so long as we remember that all the ad hoc committees,* all the picket lines, all the brave signatures in *The New York Times*,* all the tools of agitprop straight across the spectrum, do not confer upon anyone any *ipso facto*[14] virtue. It is all right only so long as we recognize that the end may or may not be expedient, may or may not be a good idea, but in any case has nothing to do with "morality." Because when we start deceiving ourselves into thinking not that we want something or need something, not that it is a pragmatic necessity for us to have it, but that it is a moral imperative that we have it, then is when we join the fashionable madmen, and then is when the thin whine of hysteria is heard in the land, and then is when we are in bad trouble. And I suspect we are already there.

(1965)

---

13 *Lionel Trilling* American literary critic (1905–75).
14 *agitprop* Political propaganda; *ipso facto* Latin: by the fact itself; as a direct consequence.

On Going Home

Set, like much of Didion's nonfiction, in her native California, this autobiographical piece considers the concepts of home and family and whether these values continue to have meaning for the succeeding generation. "On Going Home" was first published in the 3 June 1967 issue of The Saturday Evening Post.

I am home for my daughter's first birthday. By "home" I do not mean the house in Los Angeles where my husband and I and the baby live, but the place where my family is, in the Central Valley of California. It is a vital although troublesome distinction. My husband likes my family but is uneasy in their house, because once there I fall into their ways, which are difficult, oblique, deliberately inarticulate, not my husband's ways. We live in dusty houses ("D-U-S-T," he once wrote with his finger on surfaces all over the house, but no one noticed it) filled with mementos quite without value to him (what could the Canton dessert plates[15] mean to him? how could he have known about the assay scales,[16] why should he care if he did know?), and we appear to talk exclusively about people we know who have been committed to mental hospitals, about people we know who have been booked on drunk-driving charges, about property, particularly about property, land, price per acre and C-2 zoning and assessments and freeway access. My brother does not understand my husband's inability to perceive the advantage in the rather common real-estate transaction known as "sale-leaseback," and my husband in turn does not understand who so many of the people he hears about in my father's house have recently been committed to mental hospitals or booked on drunk-driving charges. Nor does he understand that when we talk about sale-leasebacks and right-of-way condemnations we are talking in code about things we like best, the yellow fields and the cottonwoods and the rivers rising and falling and the mountain roads closing when the heavy snow comes in. We miss each other's points, have another drink and regard the fire. My brother refers to my husband, in his presence, as "Joan's husband." Marriage is the classic betrayal.

Or perhaps it is not any more. Sometimes, I think that those of us who are now in our thirties were born into the last generation to carry the burden of

---

15 *Canton dessert plates* The Chinese city of Canton (now Guangzhou) was long known for the manufacture of fine china.

16 *assay scales* Balancing scales used to measure the weight and value of minerals or precious stones. In a California household, antique assay scales that had been used during gold rush days would be regarded as a family heirloom.

"home," to find in family life the source of all tension and drama. I had by all objective accounts a "normal" and a "happy" family situation, and yet I was almost thirty years old before I could talk to my family on the telephone without crying after I had hung up. We did not fight. Nothing was wrong. And yet some nameless anxiety colored the emotional charges between me and the place that I came from. The question of whether or not you could go home again was a very real part of the sentimental and largely literary baggage with which we left home in the fifties; I suspect that it is irrelevant to the children born of the fragmentation after World War II. A few weeks ago in a San Francisco bar I saw a pretty young girl on crystal[17] take off her clothes and dance for the cash prize in an "amateur-topless" contest. There was no particular sense of moment about this, none of the effect of romantic degradation, of "dark journey," for which my generation strived so assiduously. What sense could that girl possibly make of, say, *Long Day's Journey into Night*?[18] Who is beside the point?

That I am trapped in this particular irrelevancy is never more apparent to me than when I am home. Paralyzed by the neurotic lassitude[19] engendered by meeting one's past at every turn, around every corner, inside every cupboard, I go aimlessly from room to room. I decide to meet it head-on and clear out a drawer, and I spread the contents on the bed. A bathing suit I wore the summer I was seventeen. A letter of rejection from *The Nation*,[20] an aerial photograph of the site for a shopping center my father did not build in 1954. Three teacups hand-painted with cabbage roses and signed "E.M.," my grandmother's initials. There is no final solution for letters of rejection from *The Nation* and teacups hand-painted in 1900. Nor is there any answer to snapshots of one's grandfather as a young man on skis, surveying around Donner Pass[21] in the year 1910. I smooth out the snapshot and look into his face, and do and do not see my own. I close the drawer, and have another cup of coffee with my mother. We get along very well, veterans of a guerilla war[22] we never understood.

Days pass. I see no one. I come to dread my husband's evening call, not only because he is full of news of what by now seems to me our remote life in

---

17   *crystal*   I.e. methamphetamine or crystal meth, a recreational drug, illegal in many countries (including the United States).

18   *Long Day's Journey into Night*   1956 play by Eugene O'Neill that dramatizes the difficult family relations of an alcoholic father and a mother struggling with a morphine addiction.

19   *lassitude*   Weariness.

20   *The Nation*   Weekly magazine on culture and politics associated with the American left. It has been in print since 1865.

21   *Donner Pass*   Mountain pass in the Sierra Nevada range in California.

22   *guerilla war*   Form of warfare in which small, irregular groups of fighters combat a larger force using tactics such as ambush.

Los Angeles, people he has seen, letters which require attention, but because he asks what I have been doing, suggests uneasily that I get out, drive to San Francisco or Berkeley. Instead I drive across the river to a family graveyard. It has been vandalized since my last visit and the monuments are broken, over-turned in the dry grass. Because I once saw a rattlesnake* in the grass I stay in the car and listen to a country-and-Western station. Later I drive with my father to a ranch he has in the foothills. The man who runs his cattle on it asks us to the round-up, a week from Sunday, and although I know that I will be in Los Angeles I say, in the oblique way my family talks, that I will come. Once home I mention the broken monuments in the graveyard. My mother shrugs.

I go to visit my great-aunts. A few of them think now that I am my cousin,   5 or their daughter who died young. We recall an anecdote about a relative last seen in 1948, and they ask if I still like living in New York City. I have lived in Los Angeles for three years, but I say that I do. The baby is offered a hore-hound drop,[23] and I am slipped a dollar bill "to buy a treat." Questions trail off, answers are abandoned, the baby plays with the dust motes in a shaft of the afternoon sun.

It is time for the baby's birthday party: a white cake, strawberry-marshmal-low ice cream, a bottle of champagne saved from another party. In the evening, after she has gone to sleep, I kneel beside the crib and touch her face, where it is pressed against the slats, with mine. She is an open and trusting child, unpre-pared for and unaccustomed to the ambushes of family life, and perhaps it is just as well that I can offer her little of that life. I would like to give her more. I would like to promise her that she will grow up with a sense of her cousins and of rivers and her great-grandmother's teacups, would like to pledge her a picnic on a river with fried chicken and her hair uncombed, would like to give her *home* for her birthday, but we live differently now and I can promise her nothing like that. I give her a xylophone and a sundress from Madeira,[24] and promise to tell her a funny story.

(1967)

---

23 *horehound drop* Medicinal candy made from the white horehound plant, meant to soothe the throat.

24 *Madeira* Autonomous region of Portugal, located on an archipelago southwest of the country.

ROLAND BARTHES
THE WORLD OF WRESTLING[1]

Roland Barthes was a pioneer in semiology, the study of signs. For him, a sign is any unit that communicates meaning, such as a word, gesture, or image; by treating its components as signs, an interpreter can examine any work of art or advertising, any event or behavior, much as one might examine a written or spoken work. In his book Mythologies *(1957) he writes that "a photograph will be a kind of speech for us in the same way as a newspaper article; even objects will become speech, if they mean something." "The World of Wrestling" was published in* Mythologies, *in which Barthes considers how various cultural artifacts and practices— wine, detergent, a cruise, children's toys—reveal the way society constructs meaning and narrative, how its ideologies and power structures are sustained and created.*

The grandiloquent truth of gestures on life's great occasions.[2]

—BAUDELAIRE

The virtue of all-in wrestling is that it is the spectacle of excess. Here we find a grandiloquence which must have been that of the ancient theaters.[3] And in fact wrestling is an open-air spectacle, for what makes the circus[4] or the arena what they are is not the sky (a romantic value suited rather to fashionable occasions), it is the drenching and vertical quality of the flood of light. Even hidden in the most squalid Parisian halls, wrestling partakes of the nature of the

---

1   THE WORLD OF WRESTLING   Translated by Annette Lavers, 1972.

2   *The grandiloquent ... great occasions* From Charles Baudelaire, *Curiosités Esthétiques* (1868); *grandiloquent* Showy, grandiosely expressive.

3   *ancient theaters* The Greek theater of Dionysus, god of wine and fertility, was a large outdoor theater holding up to 17,000 people. The size of the theater required an exaggerated theatrical style, with the actors wearing masks to convey character and emotion to those sitting far away.

4   *circus* Ancient outdoor stadium.

great solar spectacles, Greek drama[5] and bull-fights:* in both, a light without shadow generates an emotion without reserve.

There are people who think that wrestling is an ignoble sport. Wrestling is not a sport, it is a spectacle, and it is no more ignoble to attend a wrestled performance of Suffering than a performance of the sorrows of Arnolphe or Andromaque.[6] Of course, there exists a false wrestling, in which the participants unnecessarily go to great lengths to make a show of a fair fight; this is of no interest. True wrestling, wrongly called amateur wrestling, is performed in second-rate halls, where the public spontaneously attunes itself to the spectacular nature of the contest, like the audience at a suburban cinema. Then these same people wax indignant because wrestling is a stage-managed sport (which ought, by the way, to mitigate its ignominy). The public is completely uninterested in knowing whether the contest is rigged or not, and rightly so; it abandons itself to the primary virtue of the spectacle, which is to abolish all motives and all consequences: what matters is not what it thinks but what it sees.

This public knows very well the distinction between wrestling and boxing; it knows that boxing is … based on a demonstration of excellence. One can bet on the outcome of a boxing-match: with wrestling, it would make no sense. A boxing-match is a story which is constructed before the eyes of the spectator; in wrestling, on the contrary, it is each moment which is intelligible, not the passage of time. The spectator is not interested in the rise and fall of fortunes; he expects the transient image of certain passions. Wrestling therefore demands an immediate reading of the juxtaposed meanings, so that there is no need to connect them. The logical conclusion of the contest does not interest the wrestling-fan, while on the contrary a boxing-match always implies a science of the future. In other words, wrestling is a sum of spectacles, of which no single one is a function: each moment imposes the total knowledge of a passion which rises erect and alone, without ever extending to the crowning moment of a result.

Thus the function of the wrestler is not to win; it is to go exactly through the motions which are expected of him. It is said that judo* contains a hidden symbolic aspect; even in the midst of efficiency, its gestures are measured, precise but restricted, drawn accurately but by a stroke without volume. Wrestling, on the contrary, offers excessive gestures, exploited to the limit of their

---

5 *Greek drama* Greek tragedies, comedies, and satyrs were performed as part of a mass religious festival in honor of Dionysus, god of wine and fertility.

6 *Arnolphe* Protagonist of *The School for Wives* (1662), a play by the greatly admired French writer Molière; *Andromaque* Title character of a 1667 tragedy by Jean Racine, another widely respected French playwright.

meaning. In judo, a man who is down is hardly down at all, he rolls over, he draws back, he eludes defeat, or, if the latter is obvious, he immediately disappears; in wrestling, a man who is down is exaggeratedly so, and completely fills the eyes of the spectators with the intolerable spectacle of his powerlessness.

5   This function of grandiloquence is indeed the same as that of ancient theater, whose principle, language and props (masks and buskins[7]) concurred in the exaggeratedly visible explanation of a Necessity. The gesture of the vanquished wrestler signifying to the world a defeat which, far from disguising, he emphasizes and holds like a pause in music, corresponds to the mask of antiquity meant to signify the tragic mode of the spectacle. In wrestling, as on the stage in antiquity, one is not ashamed of one's suffering, one knows how to cry, one has a liking for tears.

Each sign in wrestling is therefore endowed with an absolute clarity, since one must always understand everything on the spot. As soon as the adversaries are in the ring, the public is overwhelmed with the obviousness of the roles. As in the theater, each physical type expresses to excess the part which has been assigned to the contestant. Thauvin, a fifty-year-old with an obese and sagging body, whose type of asexual hideousness always inspires feminine nicknames, displays in his flesh the characters of baseness, for his part is to represent what, in the classical concept of the *salaud*,[8] the "bastard" (the key-concept of any wrestling match), appears as organically repugnant. The nausea voluntarily provoked by Thauvin shows therefore a very extended use of signs: not only is ugliness used here in order to signify baseness, but in addition ugliness is wholly gathered into a particularly repulsive quality of matter: the pallid collapse of dead flesh (the public calls Thauvin *la barbaque*, "stinking meat"), so that the passionate condemnation of the crowd no longer stems from its judgment, but instead from the very depth of its humors. It will thereafter let itself be frenetically embroiled in an idea of Thauvin which will conform entirely with this physical origin: his actions will perfectly correspond to the essential viscosity of his personage.

It is therefore in the body of the wrestler that we find the first key to the contest. I know from the start that all of Thauvin's actions, his treacheries, cruelties and acts of cowardice, will not fail to measure up to the first image of ignobility he gave me; I can trust him to carry out intelligently and to the last detail all the gestures of a kind of amorphous baseness, and thus fill to the brim the image of the most repugnant bastard there is: the bastard-octopus....

---

7   *masks and buskins*   The costumes for Greek tragic actors evolved to include highly stylized masks and boots called buskins, which had raised soles to make the actors appear taller.

8   *salaud*   French slang: bastard, someone despicably immoral and hypocritical.

Thauvin will never be anything but an ignoble traitor, Reinières (a tall blond fellow with a limp body and unkempt hair) the moving image of passivity, Mazaud (short and arrogant like a cock) that of grotesque conceit, and Orsano (an effeminate teddy-boy first seen in a blue-and-pink dressing-gown) that, doubly humorous, of a vindictive *salope*,[9] or bitch....

The physique of the wrestlers therefore constitutes a basic sign, which like a seed contains the whole fight. But this seed proliferates, for it is at every turn during the fight, in each new situation, that the body of the wrestler casts to the public the magical entertainment of a temperament which finds its natural expression in a gesture. The different strata of meaning throw light on each other, and form the most intelligible of spectacles. Wrestling is like a diacritic writing;[10] above the fundamental meaning of his body, the wrestler arranges comments which are episodic but always opportune, and constantly help the reading of the fight by means of gestures, attitudes and mimicry which make the intention utterly obvious. Sometimes the wrestler triumphs with a repulsive sneer while kneeling on the good sportsman; sometimes he gives the crowd a conceited smile which forebodes an early revenge; sometimes, pinned to the ground, he hits the floor ostentatiously to make evident to all the intolerable nature of his situation; and sometimes he erects a complicated set of signs meant to make the public understand that he legitimately personifies the ever-entertaining image of the grumbler, endlessly confabulating about his displeasure.

We are therefore dealing with a real Human Comedy, where the most socially-inspired nuances of passion (conceit, rightfulness, refined cruelty, a sense of "paying one's debts") always felicitously find the clearest sign which can receive them, express them and triumphantly carry them to the confines of the hall. It is obvious that at such a pitch, it no longer matters whether the passion is genuine or not. What the public wants is the image of passion, not passion itself. There is no more a problem of truth in wrestling than in the theater. In both, what is expected is the intelligible representation of moral situations which are usually private. This emptying out of interiority to the benefit of its exterior signs, this exhaustion of the content by the form, is the very principle of triumphant classical art. Wrestling is an immediate pantomime,* infinitely more efficient than the dramatic pantomime, for the wrestler's gesture needs no anecdote, no decor, in short no transference in order to appear true.

Each moment in wrestling is therefore like an algebra which instantaneous- 10
ly unveils the relationship between a cause and its represented effect. Wrestling

---

9   *salope* French slang: bitch, slut; an insult typically directed at a woman.

10 *diacritic writing* Writing with symbols, such as accents, that distinguish between different pronunciations of the same letter.

fans certainly experience a kind of intellectual pleasure in *seeing* the moral mechanism function so perfectly. Some wrestlers, who are great comedians, entertain as much as a Molière character, because they succeed in imposing an immediate reading of their inner nature: Armand Mazaud, a wrestler of an arrogant and ridiculous character (as one says that Harpagon[11] is a character), always delights the audience by the mathematical rigor of his transcriptions, carrying the form of his gestures to the furthest reaches of their meaning, and giving to his manner of fighting a kind of vehemence and precision found in a great scholastic disputation,[12] in which what is at stake is at once the triumph of pride and the formal concern with truth.

What is thus displayed for the public is the great spectacle of Suffering, Defeat, and Justice. Wrestling presents man's suffering with all the amplification of tragic masks. The wrestler who suffers in a hold which is reputedly cruel (an arm-lock, a twisted leg) offers an excessive portrayal of Suffering; like a primitive Pietà,[13] he exhibits for all to see his face, exaggeratedly contorted by an intolerable affliction. It is obvious, of course, that in wrestling reserve would be out of place, since it is opposed to the voluntary ostentation of the spectacle, to this Exhibition of Suffering which is the very aim of the fight. This is why all the actions which produce suffering are particularly spectacular, like the gesture of a conjuror who holds out his cards clearly to the public. Suffering which appeared without intelligible cause would not be understood; a concealed action that was actually cruel would transgress the underwritten rules of wrestling and would have no more sociological efficacy than a mad or parasitic gesture. On the contrary suffering appears as inflicted with emphasis and conviction, for everyone must not only see that the man suffers, but also and above all understand why he suffers. What wrestlers call a hold, that is, any figure which allows one to immobilize the adversary indefinitely and to have him at one's mercy, has precisely the function of preparing in a conventional, therefore intelligible, fashion the spectacle of suffering, of methodically establishing the conditions of suffering. The inertia of the vanquished allows the (temporary) victor to settle in his cruelty and to convey to the public this terrifying slowness of the torturer who is certain about the outcome of his actions; to grind the face of one's powerless adversary or to scrape his spine with one's fist with a deep and regular movement, or at least to produce the superficial appearance of such gestures: wrestling is the only sport which gives such an externalized image of torture. But here again, only the image is involved in the

---

11 *Harpagon* Stingy, old protagonist of Molière's comedy *The Miser* (1668).

12 *scholastic disputation* Formal philosophical argument of the sort conducted at medieval universities.

13 *Pietà* Work of art depicting the Virgin Mary holding Christ's dead body.

game, and the spectator does not wish for the actual suffering of the contestant; he only enjoys the perfection of an iconography. It is not true that wrestling is a sadistic spectacle: it is only an intelligible spectacle.

There is another figure, more spectacular still than a hold; it is the forearm smash, this loud slap of the forearm, this embryonic punch with which one clouts the chest of one's adversary, and which is accompanied by a dull noise and the exaggerated sagging of a vanquished body. In the forearm smash, catastrophe is brought to the point of maximum obviousness, so much so that ultimately the gesture appears as no more than a symbol; this is going too far, this is transgressing the moral rules of wrestling, where all signs must be excessively clear, but must not let the intention of clarity be seen. The public then shouts "He's laying it on!," not because it regrets the absence of real suffering, but because it condemns artifice: as in the theater, one fails to put the part across as much by an excess of sincerity as by an excess of formalism.

We have already seen to what extent wrestlers exploit the resources of a given physical style, developed and put to use in order to unfold before the eyes of the public a total image of Defeat. The flaccidity of tall white bodies which collapse with one blow or crash into the ropes with arms flailing, the inertia of massive wrestlers rebounding pitiably off all the elastic surfaces of the ring, nothing can signify more clearly and more passionately the exemplary abasement of the vanquished. Deprived of all resilience, the wrestler's flesh is no longer anything but an unspeakable heap spread out on the floor, where it solicits relentless reviling and jubilation. There is here a paroxysm of meaning in the style of antiquity, which can only recall the heavily underlined intentions in Roman triumphs. At other times, there is another ancient posture which appears in the coupling of the wrestlers, that of the suppliant who, at the mercy of his opponent, on bended knees, his arms raised above his head, is slowly brought down by the vertical pressure of the victor. In wrestling, unlike judo, Defeat is not a conventional sign, abandoned as soon as it is understood; it is not an outcome, but quite the contrary, it is a duration, a display, it takes up the ancient myths of public Suffering and Humiliation: the cross and the pillory.* It is as if the wrestler is crucified in broad daylight and in the sight of all. I have heard it said of a wrestler stretched on the ground: "He is dead, little Jesus, there, on the cross," and these ironic words revealed the hidden roots of a spectacle which enacts the exact gestures of the most ancient purifications.

But what wrestling is above all meant to portray is a purely moral concept: that of justice. The idea of "paying" is essential to wrestling, and the crowd's "Give it to him" means above all else "Make him pay." This is therefore, needless to say, an immanent justice. The baser the action of the "bastard," the more delighted the public is by the blow which he justly receives in return. If the villain—who is of course a coward—takes refuge behind the ropes, claiming unfairly to have a right to do so by a brazen mimicry, he is inexorably pursued there and caught, and the crowd is jubilant at seeing the rules broken for the sake of a deserved punishment. Wrestlers know very well how to play up to the capacity for indignation of the public by presenting the very limit of the concept of Justice, this outermost zone of confrontation where it is enough to infringe the rules a little more to open the gates of a world without restraints. For a wrestling-fan, nothing is finer than the revengeful fury of a betrayed fighter who throws himself vehemently not on a successful opponent but on the smarting image of foul play. Naturally, it is the pattern of Justice which matters here, much more than its content: wrestling is above all a quantitative sequence of compensations (an eye for an eye, a tooth for a tooth). This explains why sudden changes of circumstances have in the eyes of wrestling habitués a sort of moral beauty: they enjoy them as they would enjoy an inspired episode in a novel, and the greater the contrast between the success of a move and the reversal of fortune, the nearer the good luck of a contestant to his downfall, the more satisfying the dramatic mime is felt to be. Justice is therefore the embodiment of a possible transgression; it is from the fact that there is a Law that the spectacle of the passions which infringe it derives its value.

15   It is therefore easy to understand why out of five wrestling-matches, only about one is fair. One must realize, let it be repeated, that "fairness" here is a role or a genre, as in the theater: the rules do not at all constitute a real constraint; they are the conventional appearance of fairness. So that in actual fact a fair fight is nothing but an exaggeratedly polite one: the contestants confront each other with zeal, not rage; they can remain in control of their passions, they do not punish their beaten opponent relentlessly, they stop fighting as soon as they are ordered to do so, and congratulate each other at the end of a particularly arduous episode, during which, however, they have not ceased to be fair. One must of course understand here that all these polite actions are brought to the notice of the public by the most conventional gestures of fairness: shaking hands, raising the arms, ostensibly avoiding a fruitless hold which would detract from the perfection of the contest.

Conversely, foul play exists only in its excessive signs: administering a big kick to one's beaten opponent, taking refuge behind the ropes while ostensibly invoking a purely formal right, refusing to shake hands with one's opponent before or after the fight, taking advantage of the end of the round to rush treacherously at the adversary from behind, fouling him while the referee is not looking (a move which obviously only has any value or function because in fact half the audience can see it and get indignant about it). Since Evil is the natural climate of wrestling, a fair fight has chiefly the value of being an exception. It surprises the aficionado, who greets it when he sees it as an anachronism and a rather sentimental throwback to the sporting tradition ("Aren't they playing fair, those two"); he feels suddenly moved at the sight of the general kindness of the world, but would probably die of boredom and indifference if wrestlers did not quickly return to the orgy of evil which alone makes good wrestling.

Extrapolated, fair wrestling could lead only to boxing or judo, whereas true wrestling derives its originality from all the excesses which make it a spectacle and not a sport. The ending of a boxing-match or a judo-contest is abrupt, like the full-stop which closes a demonstration. The rhythm of wrestling is quite different, for its natural meaning is that of rhetorical amplification: the emotional magniloquence,[14] the repeated paroxysms, the exasperation of the retorts can only find their natural outcome in the most baroque* confusion. Some fights, among the most successful kind, are crowned by a final charivari,[15] a sort of unrestrained fantasia* where the rules, the laws of the genre, the referee's censuring and the limits of the ring are abolished, swept away by a triumphant disorder which overflows into the hall and carries off pell-mell wrestlers, seconds, referee and spectators....

What then is a "bastard" for this audience composed in part, we are told, of people who are themselves outside the rules of society? Essentially someone unstable, who accepts the rules only when they are useful to him and transgresses the formal continuity of attitudes. He is unpredictable, therefore asocial. He takes refuge behind the law when he considers that it is in his favor, and breaks it when he finds it useful to do so. Sometimes he rejects the formal boundaries of the ring and goes on hitting an adversary legally protected by the ropes, sometimes he reestablishes these boundaries and claims the protection of what he did not respect a few minutes earlier. This inconsistency, far more than treachery or cruelty, sends the audience beside itself with rage: offended not in its morality but in its logic, it considers the contradiction of arguments as the basest of crimes. The forbidden move becomes dirty only when it destroys a quantitative equilibrium and disturbs the rigorous reckoning of compensations; what is condemned by the audience is not at all the transgression of insipid official rules, it is the lack of revenge, the absence of a punishment. So that there is nothing more exciting for a crowd than the grandiloquent kick given to a vanquished "bastard"; the joy of punishing is at its climax when it is supported by a mathematical justification; contempt is then unrestrained. One is no longer dealing with a *salaud* but with a *salope*—the verbal gesture of the ultimate degradation.

Such a precise finality demands that wrestling should be exactly what the public expects of it. Wrestlers, who are very experienced, know perfectly how

---

14   *magniloquence*   Excessive pomposity, usually in reference to speech or writing.
15   *charivari*   Raucous procession of people making discordant noise by shouting, banging objects, blowing whistles, etc.

to direct the spontaneous episodes of the fight so as to make them conform to the image which the public has of the great legendary themes of its mythology. A wrestler can irritate or disgust, he never disappoints, for he always accomplishes completely, by a progressive solidification of signs, what the public expects of him. In wrestling, nothing exists except in the absolute, there is no symbol, no allusion, everything is presented exhaustively. Leaving nothing in the shade, each action discards all parasitic meanings and ceremonially offers to the public a pure and full signification, rounded like Nature. This grandiloquence is nothing but the popular and age-old image of the perfect intelligibility of reality. What is portrayed by wrestling is therefore an ideal understanding of things; it is the euphoria of men raised for a while above the constitutive ambiguity of everyday situations and placed before the panoramic view of a univocal Nature, in which signs at last correspond to causes, without obstacle, without evasion, without contradiction.

20   When the hero or the villain of the drama, the man who was seen a few minutes earlier possessed by moral rage, magnified into a sort of metaphysical sign, leaves the wrestling hall, impassive, anonymous, carrying a small suitcase and arm-in-arm with his wife, no one can doubt that wrestling holds that power of transmutation which is common to the Spectacle and to Religious Worship. In the ring, and even in the depths of their voluntary ignominy, wrestlers remain gods because they are, for a few moments, the key which opens Nature, the pure gesture which separates Good from Evil, and unveils the form of a Justice which is at last intelligible.

(1957)

JOHN BERGER

PHOTOGRAPHS OF AGONY

John Berger is perhaps best known for his 1972 Ways of Seeing, *a short book adapted from the script for a BBC television series. That volume has played a hugely influential role in leading critics and students of art in the decades since to see art in relation to politics and ideology rather than in "purely" aesthetic terms. Writing in the essay form, Berger is equally adept at helping us to see the connections between art and politics; "Photographs of Agony" is a notable example. Often, his essays also offer penetrating insights into the life and work of individual artists—as does the essay here on the great nineteenth-century English painter J.M.W. Turner. "Photographs of Agony" first appeared in the politically oriented magazine* New Society *in 1972, while "Turner and the Barber's Shop" first appeared in the same year in a Paris-based magazine called* Realities. *Both essays are also included in Berger's 1980 collection* About Looking.

The news from Vietnam did not make big headlines in the papers this morning. It was simply reported that the American air force is systematically pursuing its policy of bombing the north.[1] Yesterday there were 270 raids.

Behind this report there is an accumulation of other information. The day before yesterday the American air force launched the heaviest raids of this month. So far more bombs have dropped this month than during any other comparable period. Among the bombs being dropped are the seven-ton superbombs, each of which flattens an area of approximately 8,000 square meters. Along with the large bombs, various kinds of small antipersonnel bombs are being dropped. One kind is full of plastic barbs which, having ripped through the flesh and embedded themselves in the body, cannot be located by x-ray. Another is called the Spider: a small bomb like a grenade with almost invisible 30-centimeter-long antennae, which, if touched, act as detonators. These

---

1   *American ... the north*   During the Vietnam War (1955–75) the American forces (allied with those of South Vietnam) fought against those of North Vietnam and its allies.

bombs, distributed over the ground where larger explosions have taken place, are designed to blow up survivors who run to put out the fires already burning, or go to help those already wounded.

There are no pictures from Vietnam in the papers today. But there is a photograph taken by Donald McCullin in Hue[2] in 1968 which could have been printed with the reports this morning. (See *The Destruction Business* by Donald McCullin, London, 1972.) It shows an old man squatting with a child in his arms, both of them are bleeding profusely with the black blood of black-and-white photographs.

In the last year or so, it has become normal for certain mass circulation newspapers to publish war photographs which earlier would have been suppressed as being too shocking. One might explain this development by arguing that these newspapers have come to realise that a large section of their readers are now aware of the horrors of war and want to be shown the truth. Alternatively, one might argue that these newspapers believe that their readers have become inured to violent images and so now compete in terms of ever more violent sensationalism.[3]

5   The first argument is too idealistic and the second too transparently cynical. Newspapers now carry violent war photographs because their effect, except in rare cases, is not what it was once presumed to be. A paper like the *Sunday Times* continues to publish shocking photographs about Vietnam or Northern Ireland[4] whilst politically supporting the policies responsible for the violence. This is why we have to ask: What effect do such photographs have?

Many people would argue that such photographs remind us shockingly of the reality, the lived reality, behind the abstractions of political theory, casualty statistics or news bulletins. Such photographs, they might go on to say, are printed on the black curtain which is drawn across what we choose to forget and refuse to know. According to them, McCullin serves as an eye we cannot shut. Yet what is it that they make us see?

2   *Hue*   Major city in central Vietnam. In 1968 it was heavily bombed by American forces, and North Vietnamese forces carried out a mass killing known as the Hué Massacre.
3   *a large section ... violent sensationalism*   Here, and throughout the essay, Berger focuses on newspaper coverage in discussing images of violence; although the Vietnam War is often referred to as the first televised war, and television networks did indeed run coverage of the war daily, the networks (in the UK as well as the US) were for the most part much more reticent about showing gruesome or horrific images than were major newspapers.
4   *Northern Ireland*   Reference to The Troubles, a violent conflict over Northern Ireland's political status that lasted much of the latter half of the twentieth century.

They bring us up short. The most literal adj[ective] to them is *arresting*. We are seized by them. (I am awa[re] who pass them over, but about them there is nothing to sa[y] them, the moment of the other's suffering engulfs us. We are filled despair or indignation. Despair takes on some of the other's suffering purpose. Indignation demands action. We try to emerge from the moment of the photograph back into our lives. As we do so, the contrast is such that the resumption of our lives appears to be a hopelessly inadequate response to what we have just seen.

McCullin's most typical photographs record sudden moments of agony—a terror, a wounding, a death, a cry of grief. These moments are in reality utterly discontinuous with normal time. It is the knowledge that such moments are probable and the anticipation of them that makes "time" in the front line unlike all other experiences of time. The camera which isolates a moment of agony isolates no more violently than the experience of that moment isolates itself. The word *trigger*, applied to rifle and camera, reflects a correspondence which does not stop at the purely mechanical. The image seized by the camera is doubly violent and both violences reinforce the same contrast: the contrast between the photographed moment and all others.

As we emerge from the photographed moment back into our lives, we do not realise this; we assume that the discontinuity is our responsibility. The truth is that any response to that photographed moment is bound to be felt as inadequate. Those who are there in the situation being photographed, those who hold the hand of the dying or staunch a wound, are not seeing the moment as we have and their responses are of an altogether different order. It is not possible for anyone to look pensively at such a moment and to emerge stronger. McCullin, whose "contemplation" is both dangerous and active, writes bitterly underneath a photograph: "I only use the camera like I use a toothbrush. It does the job."

The possible contradictions of the war photograph now become apparent. It is generally assumed that its purpose is to awaken concern. The most extreme examples—as in most of McCullin's work—show moments of agony in order to extort the maximum concern. Such moments, whether photographed or not, are discontinuous with all other moments. They exist by themselves. But the reader who has been arrested by the photograph may tend to feel this discontinuity as his own personal moral inadequacy. *And as soon as this happens even his sense of shock is dispersed*: his own moral inadequacy may now shock him as much as the crimes being committed in the war. Either he shrugs off this sense of inadequacy as being only too familiar, or else he thinks performing a kind of penance—of which the purest example would be to make a contribution to OXFAM or to UNICEF.*

10

. has caused that moment is ef-
s evidence of the general human
.y.

.oments of agony can mask a far more
.ually the wars which we are shown are
.n "our" name. What we are shown horri-
.or us to confront our own lack of political
.s as they exist, we have no legal opportunity
.conduct of wars waged in our name. To realise
.is the only effective way of responding to what
. the double violence of the photographed moment
.is realisation. That is why they can be published with
imp.

(1972)

TURNER AND THE BARBER'S SHOP

There has never been another painter like Turner. And this is because he combined in his work so many different elements. There is a strong argument for claiming that it is Turner, not Dickens or Wordsworth or Walter Scott or Constable or Landseer,[5] who, in his genius, represents most fully the character of the British 19th century. And it may be this which explains the fact that Turner is the only important artist who both before and after his death in 1851 had a certain popular appeal in Britain. Until recently a wide public felt somehow, mysteriously, dumbly (in the sense that his vision dismisses or precludes words), Turner was expressing something of the bedrock of their own varied experience.

Turner was born in 1775, the son of a back-street barber in central London. His uncle was a butcher. The family lived a stone's throw from the Thames.* During his life Turner travelled a great deal. But in most of his chosen themes water, coastlines, or river banks recur continually. During the last years of his life he lived—under the alias of Captain Booth, a retired sea captain—a little further down the river Chelsea. During his middle years he lived at Hammersmith and Twickenham, both overlooking the Thames.

5 *Dickens ... Landseer* Nineteenth-century British writers Charles Dickens, William Wordsworth, and Sir Walter Scott, like the nineteenth-century British painters John Constable and Edwin Henry Landseer, have all been described as representative of their era.

He was a child prodigy and by the age of nine he was already earning money by coloring engravings;[6] at fourteen he entered the Royal Academy Schools.[7] When he was eighteen he had his own studio, and shortly afterwards his father gave up his trade to become his son's studio assistant and factotum.[8] The relation between father and son was obviously close. (The painter's mother died insane.)

It is impossible to know exactly what early visual experiences affected Turner's imagination. But there is a strong correspondence between some of the visual elements of a barber's shop and the elements of the painter's mature style, which should be noticed in passing without being used as a comprehensive explanation. Consider some of his later paintings and imagine, in the backstreet shop, water, froth, steam, gleaming metal, clouded mirrors, white bowls or basins in which soapy liquid is agitated by the barber's brush and detritus deposited. Consider the equivalence between the father's razor and the palette knife which, despite criticisms and current usage, Turner insisted upon using extensively. More profoundly—at the level of childish phantasmagoria[9]—picture the always possible combination, suggested by a barber's shop, of blood and water, water and blood. At the age of twenty Turner planned to paint a subject from the Apocalypse* entitled: *The Water Turned to Blood*.[10] He never painted it. But visually, by way of sunsets and fires, it became the subject of thousands of his later works and studies.

Many of Turner's earlier landscapes were more or less classical, referring back to Claude Lorrain, but influenced also by the first Dutch landscapists.[11] The spirit of these works is curious. On the face of it, they are calm, "sublime," or gently nostalgic. Eventually, however, one realizes that these landscapes have far more to do with art than nature, and that as art they are a form of pastiche.* And in pastiche there is always a kind of restlessness or desperation.

---

6 *coloring engravings* Painting illustrations that have been printed in black and white using engraved plates.

7 *Royal Academy Schools* Educational institution operated by the prestigious Royal Academy of Art.

8 *factotum* Person responsible for carrying out a large variety of tasks.

9 *phantasmagoria* Dreamlike, illusory, or fantastical images.

10 *Apocalypse ... Blood* In the Bible, Revelation 16 describes angels emptying their bowls into the sea and into the rivers and streams, and the water turning to blood when they do so.

11 *Claude Lorrain* Very influential landscape painter (1605–82) who painted idealized, harmonious natural scenes; *first Dutch landscapists* Late fifteenth- and sixteenth-century Dutch artists exerted a strong influence on landscape painting throughout the western world.

Violence

Nature entered Turner's work—or rather his imagination—as violence. As early as 1802 he painted a storm raging around the jetty Calais. Soon afterwards he painted another storm in the Alps. Then an avalanche. Until the 1830s the two aspects of his work, the apparently calm and the turbulent, existed side by side, but gradually the turbulence became more and more dominant. In the end violence was implicit in Turner's vision itself; it no longer depended upon the subject. For example, the painting entitled *Peace: Burial at Sea* is, in its own way, as violent as the painting of *The Snowstorm*. The former is like an image of a wound being cauterized.

The violence in Turner's paintings appears to be elemental: it is expressed by water, by wind, by fire. Sometimes it appears to be a quality which belongs just to the light. Writing about a late painting called *The Angel Standing in the Sun*, Turner spoke of light *devouring* the whole visible world. Yet I believe that the violence he found in nature only acted as a confirmation of something intrinsic to his own imaginative vision. I have already suggested how this vision may have been partly born from childhood experience. Later it would have been confirmed, not only by nature, but by human enterprise. Turner lived through the first apocalyptic phase of the British Industrial Revolution.* Steam meant more than what filled a barber's shop. Vermilion meant furnaces as well as blood. Wind whistled through valves as well as over the Alps. The light which he thought of as devouring the whole visible world was very similar to the new productive energy which was challenging and destroying all previous ideas about wealth, distance, human labour, the city, nature, the will of God, children, time. It is a mistake to think of Turner as a virtuoso painter of natural effects—which was more or less how he was officially estimated until Ruskin[12] interpreted his work more deeply.

The first half of the British 19th century was profoundly unreligious. This may have forced Turner to use nature symbolically. No other convincing or accessible system of symbolism made a deep moral appeal, but its moral sense could not be expressed directly. The *Burial at Sea* shows the burial of the painter, Sir David Wilkie, who was one of Turner's few friends. Its references are cosmic. But as a statement, is it essentially a protest or an acceptance? Do we take more account of the impossibly radiant city beyond? The questions raised by the painting are moral—hence, as in many of Turner's later works, its somewhat claustrophobic quality—but the answers given are all ambivalent. No wonder that what Turner admired in painting was the ability to cast doubt, to throw into mystery. Rembrandt, he said admiringly, "threw a mysterious doubt over the meanest piece of common."[13]

---

12 *Ruskin* John Ruskin (1819–1900), influential British art critic.
13 *Rembrandt* Leading Dutch painter (1606–69) best known for his portraits; *meanest piece of common* Most unimpressive area of ordinary landscape.

From the outset of his career Turner was extremely ambitious in an undisguisedly competitive manner. He wanted to be recognized not only as the greatest painter of his country and time, but among the greatest of all time. He saw himself as the equal of Rembrandt and Watteau.[14] He believed that he had outpainted Claude Lorrain. This competitiveness was accompanied by a marked tendency towards misanthropy and miserliness. He was excessively secretive about his working methods. He was a recluse in the sense that he lived apart from society by choice. His solitariness was not a by-product of neglect or lack of recognition. From an early age his career was a highly successful one. As his work became more original, it was criticized. Sometimes his solitary eccentricity was called madness; but he was never treated as being less than a great painter.

He wrote poetry on the themes of his paintings, he wrote and sometimes delivered lectures on art, in both cases using a grandiloquent but vapid language. In conversation he was taciturn and rough. If one says that he was a visionary, one must qualify it by emphasizing hardheaded empiricism. He preferred to live alone, but he saw to it that he succeeded in a highly competitive society. He had grandiose visions which achieved greatness when he painted them and were merely bombastic when he wrote them, yet his most serious conscious attitude as an artist was pragmatic and almost artisanal: what drew him to a subject or a particular painting device was what he called its *practicability*—its capacity to yield a painting.

Turner's genius was of a new type which was called forth by the British 19th century, but more usually in the field of science or engineering or business. (Somewhat later the same type appeared as hero in the United States.) He had the ability to be highly successful, but success did not satisfy him. (He left a fortune of £140,000.[15]) He felt himself to be alone in history. He had global visions which words were inadequate to express and which could only be presented under the pretext of a *practical* production. He visualized man as being dwarfed by immense forces over which he had no control but which nevertheless he had discovered. He was close to despair, and yet he was sustained by an extraordinary productive energy. (In his studio after his death there were 19,000 drawings and watercolors and several hundred oil paintings.)

Ruskin wrote that Turner's underlying theme was Death. I believe rather that it was solitude and violence and the impossibility of redemption. Most of his paintings are as if about the aftermath of crime. And what is so disturbing about them—what actually allows them to be seen as beautiful—is not the guilt but the global indifference that they record.

---

14   *Watteau*   Jean-Antoine Watteau (1684–1721), highly influential French painter.

15   *a fortune of £140,000*   Equivalent to at least $15 million USD today.

On a few notable occasions during his life Turner was able to express his visions through actual incidents which he witnessed. In October, 1834, the Houses of Parliament* caught fire. Turner rushed to the scene, made furious sketches and produced the finished painting for the Royal Academy the following year. Several years later, when he was sixty-six years old, he was on a steamboat in a snow storm and afterwards painted the experience. Whenever a painting was based on a real event he emphasized, in the title or in his catalogue notes, that the work was the result of first hand experience. It was as though he wished to prove that life—however remorselessly—confirmed his vision. The full title of *The Snowstorm* was *Snowstorm. Steamboat off a Harbour's Mouth Making Signals in Shallow Water, and going by the Lead. The Author was in the storm on the night the Ariel left Harwich.*

When a friend informed Turner that his mother had liked the snowstorm painting, Turner remarked: "I did not paint it to be understood, but I wished to show what such a scene was like: I got sailors to lash me to the mast to observe it; I was lashed for four hours, and I did not expect to escape, but I felt bound to record it if I did. But no one had any business to like the picture."

"But my mother went through just such a scene, and it brought it all back to her."

"Is your mother a painter?"

"No."

"Then she ought to have been thinking of something else."

The question remains what made these works, likeable or not, so new, so different. Turner transcended the principle of traditional landscape: the principle that a landscape is something which unfolds before you. In *The Burning of the Houses of Parliament* the scene begins to extend beyond its formal edges. It begins to work its way round the spectator in an effort to outflank and surround him. In *The Snowstorm* the tendency has become fact. If one really allows one's eye to be absorbed into the forms and colors on the canvas, one begins to realize that, looking at it, one is in the center of a maelstrom: there is no longer a near or far. For example, the lurch into the distance is not, as one would expect, *into* the picture, but out of it towards the right-hand edge. It is a picture which precludes the outsider spectator.

Turner's physical courage must have been considerable. His courage as an artist before his own experience was perhaps even greater. His truthfulness to that experience was such that he destroyed the tradition to which he was so proud to belong. He stopped painting totalities. *The Snowstorm* is the total of everything which can be seen and grasped by the man tied to the mast of the ship. There is *nothing* outside it. This makes the idea of anyone liking it absurd.

Perhaps Turner did not think exactly in these terms. But he followed intuitively the logic of the situation. He was a man alone, surrounded by implacable and indifferent forces. It was no longer possible to believe that what he saw could ever be seen from the outside—even though this would have been a consolation. Parts could no longer be treated as wholes. There was either nothing or everything.

In a more practical sense he was aware of the importance of totality in his life's work. He became reluctant to sell his paintings. He wanted as many of his pictures as possible to be kept together, and he became obsessed by the idea of bequeathing them to the nation so that they could be exhibited as a whole. "Keep them together," he said. "What is the use of them but together?" Why? Because only then might they conceivably bear obstinate witness to his experience for which, he believed, there was no precedent and no great hope of future understanding.

(1972)

SUSAN SONTAG

from FREAK SHOW

Since they began to be published in the 1970s, Susan Sontag's essays have remained among the most widely read—and widely debated— works of American non-fiction. One notable case in point: reviews and discussions of the 2016 major exhibition of photographs by Diane Arbus very frequently make reference to Sontag's analysis of Arbus's work from 46 years earlier. That analysis, excerpted below, appeared originally in the 15 November 1973 issue of The New York Review of Books, *in a long review article discussing both Arbus's work and the (very different) photographs of Walker Evans. Much of the material in the article was later incorporated into Sontag's famous classic 1980 book-length essay,* On Photography.

In the "Family of Man" exhibit organized in 1955 by Edward Steichen, five hundred and three photographs by two hundred and seventy-three photographers from sixty-eight countries were supposed to converge—to prove that humanity is "one" and that human beings, for all their flaws, are attractive creatures. The people in the photographs were of all races, ages, classes, physical types. Many of them had exceptionally beautiful bodies; some had beautiful faces…. Steichen set up the show to make it possible for each viewer to identify with a great many people depicted and potentially with the subject of every photograph: citizens of World Photography all.

It was not until seventeen years later that photography again attracted such crowds at the Museum of Modern Art: for the retrospective of Diane Arbus's work that was shown between November, 1972, and February, 1973. In the Arbus show, a hundred and twelve photographs all taken by one person and all similar—that is, everyone in them looks (in some sense) the same—impose a feeling exactly contrary to the reassuring warmth of Steichen's material. Instead of people whose appearance pleases, representative folk doing their human thing, the Arbus show lines up assorted monsters and border-line cases—most of them ugly; wearing grotesque or unflattering clothes; in dismal or barren surroundings—who have paused to pose and, often, to gaze frankly, confidentially at the viewer. Arbus's work does not invite viewers to identify

220

with the pariahs and miserable-looking people she photographed. Humanity is not "one."

The Arbus photographs convey the anti-humanist message which people of good will in the 1970s are eager to be troubled by, just as they wished, in the 1950s, to be consoled and distracted by a sentimental humanism.* There's not as much difference between these messages as one might suppose. The Steichen show was an up and the Arbus show was a down, but either experience serves equally well to rule out a historical understanding of reality.

Steichen's choice of photographs assumes a "human condition" or a "human nature" shared by everybody. Arbus's photographs suggest a world in which everybody is an alien—hopelessly isolated, immobilized in mechanical, crippled identities and relationships. But both the pious uplift of Steichen's photograph anthology and the cool horror of the Arbus retrospective render history and politics irrelevant. One does so by universalizing the human condition, into joy; the other by atomizing it, into horror.

Professional and successful as a fashion photographer since her late teens, Arbus began doing serious photography only around 1958 when she was thirty-seven, and died in 1971; about a decade of work is represented in the Museum show and the book....

The ambiguity of Arbus's work is that she seems to have enrolled in one of art photography's most visible enterprises—concentrating on victims, the unfortunate, the dispossessed—but without the compassionate purpose that such a project is expected to serve. Arbus's work shows people who are pathetic, pitiable, as well as horrible, repulsive, but it does not arouse any compassionate feelings. Nevertheless, despite this evident coolness of tone, the photographs have been scoring moral points all along with critics. For what might be judged as their dissociated and naïve point of view, the photographs have been praised for their candor and for an unsentimental empathy with their subjects. What is actually their aggressiveness toward the public has been turned into a moral accomplishment: that the photographs don't allow the viewer any distance from the subject.

None of the qualities of Arbus's work makes this line of praise convincing. In their acceptance of the appalling, the photographs suggest a naïveté that is both coy and sinister, for it is based entirely on distance, on privilege, on a feeling that what the viewer is asked to look at is really other.

"You see someone on the street," Arbus wrote, "and essentially what you notice about them is the flaw." The insistent sameness of Arbus's work, however far she ranges from her prototypical subjects, suggests that her sensibility, armed with a camera, could insinuate anguish, kinkiness, mental illness with any subject. Two photographs are of crying babies; the babies look disturbed, crazy. Resembling or having something in common with someone else also

5

nourished Arbus's morbid sensibility. It may be two girls (not sisters) wearing identical raincoats whom Arbus photographed together in Central Park; or the twins and triplets who appear in several pictures. Many photographs point with perverse wonder to the fact that two people form a couple. In Arbus's photographs, every couple is an odd couple: straight or gay, black or white, in an old-age home or in a junior high. People were freaky because they didn't wear clothes, like nudists; or because they did, like the waitress in the nudist camp who's wearing an apron.

Anybody Arbus photographed was a freak—a boy waiting to march in a pro-war parade, wearing his straw boater and his "Bomb Hanoi" button;[1] the King and Queen of a Senior Citizens Dance; a thirtyish Westchester couple sprawled in their lawn chairs; a widow sitting alone in her cluttered bedroom. In "A Jewish giant at home with his parents in the Bronx, NY, 1970," the parents look like midgets, as freakish as their enormous son hunched over them because the living-room ceiling is too low.

10   The authority of Arbus's photographs comes from the contrast between their lacerating subject matter and their calm, matter-of-fact attentiveness. This quality of attention—the attention paid by the photographer, the attention paid by the subject to the act of being photographed—creates the moral theater of Arbus's straight-on, contemplative portraits. A large part of the mystery of Arbus's photographs lies in what they suggest about how her subjects felt after consenting to be photographed. Do they see themselves, the viewer wonders, like that? Do they know how grotesque they are? It seems as if they don't.

In most Arbus pictures, the subjects are looking straight into the camera. This often makes them look even odder.... In the normal rhetoric of the photographic portrait, facing the camera signifies solemnity, frankness. It discloses the subject's essence. That's why frontal portraits seem right for ceremonies (like weddings, graduations) but less apt for photographs used on billboards to advertise political candidates. (For politicians the three-quarter gaze is more common: not the gaze that confronts but the gaze that soars; instead of the relation to the viewer, to the present, the more ennobling abstract relation to the future.) What makes the frontal pose odd in Arbus's photographs is that her subjects are often people one would not expect to surrender themselves so amiably and ingenuously to the camera.

Diane Arbus's photographs were already famous to people who follow photography when she killed herself in July, 1971, at the age of forty-nine. But, as with Sylvia Plath,* the attention she has gotten since her death is much larger and of another order—a kind of apotheosis. The fact of her suicide seems

---

1   *pro-war ... "Bomb Hanoi" button*   At the time, the US was allied with South Vietnam in a war against North Vietnam (of which Hanoi was the capital).

suicide makes it sincere

to guarantee that her work is sincere, not voyeuristic, that it is compassionate, not cold. It also seems to make the photographs more devastating.

In so far as looking at most of these photographs is, undeniably, an ordeal, Arbus's work is typical of the kind of art popular among sophisticated urban people right now: art that is a self-willed test of hardness. The photographs offer an occasion to demonstrate that life's horror can be faced without squeamishness.

Arbus's work is a good instance of a leading tendency of high art in capitalist countries: to suppress, or at least reduce, moral and sensory queasiness. Much of modern art is devoted to lowering the threshold of what is terrible. By getting us used to what, formerly, we could not bear to see or hear, because it was too shocking, painful, or embarrassing, art changes morals—that body of psychic custom and public sanctions that sets a vague boundary between what is emotionally and spontaneously intolerable and what is not.

The gradual suppression of queasiness does bring us closer to a rather formal truth: life is, and always was, more than the taboos constructed by art and morals would have it. But there is a stiff price to pay for the rising grotesqueness that people are able to stomach, in images (moving and still) and in print. For most people it works not as a liberation of but as a subtraction from the self; a sense of pseudo-familiarity with the horrible reinforces alienation, making people less able to react in real life. What happens to their feelings on first exposure to today's standard pornographic film product or to a televised genocide is not so different from what happens when they first look at Arbus's photographs.

The photographs make a compassionate response seem irrelevant. The point is not to be upset, to be able to confront the horrible with cheerfulness. But this look that is not compassionate is a special, modern ethical construction: not hard-hearted, certainly not cynical, but simply (or falsely) naïve. To the painful nightmarish reality "out there," Arbus applies such words as "terrific," "interesting," "incredible," "fantastic," "sensational"—the childlike wonder of the Warhol* pop mentality. Arbus's breathless, deliberately naïve comments (collected from notes, letters, tapes of her lectures) which form the preface to the book are quite remarkable. Photography is a device that captures it all, that seduces people into disclosing their secrets, that broadens experience. To photograph people, Arbus writes, is necessarily "cruel," "mean." The important thing is not to blink.

However interested Arbus was in freaks or in very ugly people, it would never have occurred to her to photograph thalidomide babies or napalm victims—"public" horrors, deformities with sentimental or moral associations. Arbus was not interested in ethical journalism. She was drawn to subjects that she could believe were found, just lying about, without any values attached to

15

Which maker of Silence

them. These subjects are necessarily ahistorical: "private" rather than public pathology, secret lives rather than open ones.

For Arbus, the camera photographs the unknown. But unknown to whom? Unknown to someone who is basically protected, middle-class, who has been taught to see life in terms of moral response and prudence. "One of the things I felt I suffered from as a kid," Arbus wrote, "was that I never felt adversity. I was confined in a sense of unreality.... And the sense of being immune was, ludicrous as it seems, a painful one." The camera became Arbus's way of procuring experience, and thereby acquiring a sense of reality. By experience was meant if not material adversity at least psychological adversity—the shock of immersion in experiences that cannot be beautified, the encounter with what is taboo, perverse, evil.

Arbus's interest in freaks expresses a desire to violate her own innocence, her sense of being privileged.

20   Who could have better appreciated the truth of freaks than someone who was, by profession, a fashion photographer—a professional fabricator of the cosmetic lie that masks the terrifying freakish world? Arbus began as a photographer doing ads for Russeks, her father's Fifth Avenue department store, in her late teens, a job she continued to hold for twenty years. Even after starting her "serious" work she went on being a fashion photographer. (As recently as a year before her death, she did twenty-four pages of vacuous photographs for a *New York Times* Sunday section on children's fashions.)

Arbus's work is not ironic, like Warhol's, but reactive—reactive against gentility, against being protected. It was her way of saying fuck Vogue, fuck fashion, fuck what's pretty. Arbus does not, like the great photographers, play the field of subject matter—even a little. On the contrary, all her subjects are equivalent, and it is this that constitutes the judgment at the heart of her work. Making equivalences between freaks, mad people, suburban couples, and nudists is a very powerful judgment. It is, indeed, a politics.

(1973)

from REGARDING THE PAIN OF OTHERS

The excerpt below is from the first chapter of Sontag's 2003 book
Regarding the Pain of Others—*a work that is in many respects a
follow-up to her* On Photography. *Sontag explores the effects on
viewers of images of wartime suffering, and asks if we are justified
in hoping that such images can help to end or to prevent wars.*

In June 1938 Virginia Woolf[2] published *Three Guineas*,[3] her brave, unwelcomed reflections on the roots of war. Written during the preceding two years, while she and most of her intimates and fellow writers were rapt by the advancing fascist insurrection in Spain,[4] the book was couched as the very tardy reply to a letter from an eminent lawyer in London who had asked, "How in your opinion are we to prevent war?" Woolf begins by observing tartly that a truthful dialogue between them may not be possible. For though they belong to the same class, "the educated class," a vast gulf separates them: the lawyer is a man and she is a woman. Men make war. Men (most men) like war, since for men there is "some glory, some necessity, some satisfaction in fighting" that woman (most women) do not feel or enjoy. What does an educated—read: privileged, well-off—woman like her know of war? Can her recoil from its allure be like his?

Let us test this "difficulty of communication," Woolf proposes, by looking together at images of war. The images are some of the photographs the beleaguered Spanish government has been sending out twice a week; she footnotes: "Written in the winter of 1936–37." Let's see, Woolf writes, "whether when we look at the same photographs we feel the same things." She continues:

> This morning's collection contains the photograph of what might be a man's body, or a woman's; it is so mutilated that it might, on the other hand, be the body of a pig. But those certainly are dead children, and that undoubtedly is the section of a house. A bomb has torn open the side; there is still a bird-cage hanging in what was presumably the sitting room ...

---

2   *Virginia Woolf*   English modernist author (1882–1941), feminist, and pacifist.

3   *Three Guineas*   Excerpts from *Three Guineas* are included in this anthology.

4   *fascist insurrection in Spain*   The Spanish Civil War (1936–39), in which nationalist and fascist forces revolted against the democratic Second Spanish Republic, established eight years earlier. The eventual Nationalist victory led to the decades-long dictatorship of Francisco Franco.

The quickest, driest way to convey the inner commotion caused by these photographs is by noting that one can't always make out the subject, so thorough is the ruin of flesh and stone they depict. And from there Woolf speeds to her conclusion. We do have the same responses, "however different the education, the traditions behind us," she says to the lawyer. Her evidence: both "we"— here women are the "we"—and you might well respond in the same words.

> You, Sir, call them "horror and disgust." We also called them horror and disgust ... War, you say, is an abomination; a barbarity; war must be stopped at whatever cost.

> And we echo your words. War is an abomination; a barbarity; war must be stopped.

Who believes today that war can be abolished? No one, not even pacifists. We hope only (so far in vain) to stop genocide and to bring to justice those who commit gross violations of the laws of war (for there are laws of war, to which combatants should be held), and to be able to stop specific wars by imposing negotiated alternatives to armed conflict. It may be hard to credit the desperate resolve produced by the aftershock of the First World War, when the realization of the ruin Europe had brought on itself took hold. Condemning war as such did not seem so futile or irrelevant in the wake of the paper fantasies of the Kellogg-Briand Pact[5] of 1928, in which fifteen leading nations, including the United States, France, Great Britain, Germany, Italy, and Japan, solemnly renounced war as an instrument of national policy; even Freud and Einstein* were drawn into the debate with a public exchange of letters in 1932 titled "Why War?" Woolf's *Three Guineas*, appearing toward the close of nearly two decades of plangent denunciations of war, offered the originality (which made this the least well received of all her books) of focusing on what was regarded as too obvious or inapposite[6] to be mentioned, much less brooded over: that war is a man's game—that the killing machine has a gender, and it is male. Nevertheless, the temerity* of Woolf's version of "Why War?" does not make her revulsion against war any less conventional in its rhetoric, in its summations, rich in repeated phrases. And photographs of the victims of war are themselves a species of rhetoric. They reiterate. They simplify. They agitate. They create the illusion of consensus.

---

5   *Kellogg-Briand Pact*   Written by US Secretary of State Frank B. Kellogg (1856–1937) and French Prime Minister and Foreign Minister Aristide Briand (1862–1932), the pact stated that the signatory nations "condemn recourse to war for the solution of international controversies, and renounce it, as an instrument of national policy in their relations with one another," and that settlement of disputes "shall never be sought except by pacific means."

6   *plangent* Loud, emotional;   *inapposite* Beside the point; inappropriate.

Invoking this hypothetical shared experience ("we are seeing with you the same dead bodies, the same ruined houses"), Woolf professes to believe that the shock of such pictures cannot fail to unite people of good will. Does it? To be sure, Woolf and the unnamed addressee of this book-length letter are not any two people. Although they are separated by the age-old affinities of feeling and practice of their respective sexes, as Woolf has reminded him, the lawyer is hardly a standard-issue bellicose* male. His anti-war opinions are no more in doubt than are hers. After all, his question was not, What are *your* thoughts about preventing war? It was, How in your opinion are *we* to prevent war?

It is this "we" that Woolf challenges at the start of her book: she refuses to allow her interlocutor to take a "we" for granted. But into this "we," after pages devoted to the feminist point, she then subsides.

No "we" should be taken for granted when the subject is looking at other people's pain.   5

Who are the "we" at whom such shock-pictures are aimed? That "we" would include not just the sympathizers of a smallish nation or a stateless people fighting for its life, but—a far larger constituency—those only nominally concerned about some nasty war taking place in another country. The photographs are a means of making "real" (or "more real") matters that the privileged and the merely safe might prefer to ignore.

"Here then on the table before us are photographs," Woolf writes of the thought experiment she is proposing to the reader as well as to the spectral lawyer, who is eminent enough, as she mentions, to have K.C., King's Counsel, after his name—and may or may not be a real person. Imagine then a spread of loose photographs extracted from an envelope that arrived in the morning post. They show the mangled bodies of adults and children. They show how war evacuates, shatters, breaks apart, levels the built world. "A bomb has torn open the side," Woolf writes of the house in one of the pictures. To be sure, a cityscape is not made of flesh. Still, sheared-off buildings are almost as eloquent as bodies in the street. (Kabul,[7] Sarajevo,[8] East Mostar,[9] Grozny,[10]

---

7   *Kabul*   Capital of Afghanistan. The 1992–96 Afghan Civil War damaged much of the city's infrastructure and caused thousands of civilian deaths.

8   *Sarajevo*   Capital of Bosnia and Herzegovina, which was under siege by Bosnian Serbs of Republic of Srpska for almost four years during the Bosnian War (1992–96).

9   *East Mostar*   The side of Mostar, Bosnia and Herzegovina that was occupied by Bosniak soldiers; the West side was occupied by Croat soldiers. Croatian forces beseiged East Mostar in 1993–94.

10   *Grozny*   Capital city of Chechnya, a Republic and federal subject of Russia, which was assaulted and heavily damaged by Russian forces in 2000. The city, which had been the capital of the separatist Chechen Republic of Ichkeria, was captured by Russia in a decisive victory.

sixteen acres of lower Manhattan after September 11, 2001, the refugee camp in Jenin[11] ...) Look, the photographs say, *this* is what it's like. This is what war *does*. And *that*, that is what it does too. War tears, rends. War rips open, eviscerates. War scorches. War dismembers. War *ruins*.

Not to pained by these pictures, not to recoil from them, not to strive to abolish what causes this havoc, this carnage—these, for Woolf, would be the reactions of a moral monster. And, she is saying, we are not monsters, we members of the educated class. Our failure is one of imagination, of empathy: we have failed to hold this reality in mind.

But is it true that these photographs, documenting the slaughter of non-combatants rather than the clash of armies, could only stimulate the repudiation of war? Surely they could also foster greater militancy on behalf of the Republic. Isn't this what they were meant to do? The agreement between Woolf and the lawyer seems entirely presumptive, with the grisly photographs confirming an opinion already held in common. Had the question been, How can we best contribute to the defense of the Spanish Republic against the forces of militarist and clerical fascism?, the photographs might instead have reinforced their belief in the justness of that struggle.

10   The pictures Woolf has conjured up do not in fact show what war, war as such, does. They show a particular way of waging war, a way at that time routinely described as "barbaric," in which civilians are the target. General Franco[12] was using the same tactics of bombardment, massacre, torture, and the killing and mutilation of prisoners that he had perfected as a commanding officer in Morocco in the 1920s.[13] Then, more acceptably to ruling powers, his victims had been Spain's colonial subjects, darker-hued and infidels to boot; now his victims were compatriots. To read in the pictures, as Woolf does, only what confirms a general abhorrence of war is to stand back from an engagement with Spain as a country with a history. It is to dismiss politics.

For Woolf, as for many antiwar polemicists, war is generic, and the images she describes are of anonymous generic victims. The pictures sent out by the government in Madrid seem, improbably, not to have been labeled. (Or perhaps Woolf is simply assuming that a photograph should speak for itself.) But the case against war does not rely on information about who and when and where;

---

11   *Jenin*   Palestinian city and location of a refugee camp that was attacked by Israeli defense forces in 2002. A large portion of the camp was bulldozed and hundreds of homes rendered uninhabitable.

12   *General Franco*   Francisco Franco (1892–1975), fascist military leader during the Spanish Civil War, and thereafter long time dictator.

13   *Morocco in the 1920s*   The Second Moroccan War, or Rif War, was the last in a series of conflicts between Spanish colonial forces and the native Riffian Berbers of northern Morocco.

the arbitrariness of the relentless slaughter is evidence enough. To those who are sure that right is on one side, oppression and injustice on the other, and that the fighting must go on, what matters is precisely who is killed and by whom. To an Israeli Jew, a photograph of a child torn apart in the attack on the Sbarro pizzeria[14] in downtown Jerusalem is first of all a photograph of a Jewish child killed by a Palestinian suicide-bomber. To a Palestinian, a photograph of a child torn apart by a tank round in Gaza[15] is first of all a photograph of a Palestinian child killed by Israeli ordnance. To the militant, identity is everything. And all photographs wait to be explained or falsified by their captions. During the fighting between Serbs and Croats at the beginning of the recent Balkan wars,[16] the same photographs of children killed in the shelling of a village were passed around at both Serb and Croat propaganda briefings. Alter the caption, and the children's deaths could be used and reused.

Images of dead civilians and smashed houses may serve to quicken hatred of the foe, as did the hourly reruns by Al Jazeera, the Arab satellite television network based in Qatar, of the destruction in the Jenin refugee camp in April 2002. Incendiary as that footage was to the many who watch Al Jazeera throughout the world, it did not tell them anything about the Israeli army they were not already primed to believe. In contrast, images offering evidence that contradicts cherished pieties are invariably dismissed as having been staged for the camera. To photographic corroboration of the atrocities committed by one's own side, the standard response is that the pictures are a fabrication, that no such atrocity ever took place, those were bodies the other side had brought in trucks from the city morgue and placed about the street, or that, yes, it happened and it was the other side who did it, to themselves. Thus the chief of propaganda for Franco's Nationalist rebellion maintained that it was the Basques[17] who had destroyed their own ancient town and former capital, Guernica,[18] on April

---

14 *Sbarro pizzeria* American chain restaurant which was the site of a 2001 bombing that killed fifteen civilians, including seven children.

15 *Gaza* Geographically independent strip of Palestinian territory along the Mediterranean sea. Despite Israeli military withdrawal from Gaza in 2005 the territory remains externally controlled by Israel.

16 *Balkan wars* The Croatian War of Independence (1991–95), which began before and was concurrent with the Bosnian war; the conflict involved Croats who sought independence from Yugoslavia and Croatian Serbs who sought unity with Serbia and the Republic of Srpska.

17 *Basques* Indigenous ethnic group of the western Pyrenees, who now live in the autonomous regions of Basque Country and Navarre in Spain.

18 *Guernica* The town of Gernika was in fact bombed by German and Italian air forces. The bombings famously inspired Pablo Picasso's painting of the horrors of war, titled *Guernica*.

26, 1937, by placing dynamite in the sewers (in a later version, by dropping bombs manufactured in Basque territory) in order to inspire indignation abroad and reinforce the Republican resistance. And thus a majority of Serbs living in Serbia or abroad maintained right to the end of the Serb siege of Sarajevo, and even after, that the Bosnians themselves perpetrated the horrific "breadline massacre" in May 1992 and "market massacre" [19] in February 1994, lobbing large-caliber shells into the center of their capital or planting mines in order to create some exceptionally gruesome sights for the foreign journalists' cameras and rally more international support for the Bosnian side.

Photographs of mutilated bodies certainly can be used the way Woolf does, to vivify the condemnation of war, and may bring home, for a spell, a portion of its reality to those who have no experience of war at all. However, someone who accepts that in the world as currently divided war can become inevitable, and even just, might reply that the photographs supply no evidence, none at all, for renouncing war—except to those for whom the notions of valor and sacrifice have been emptied of meaning and credibility. The destructiveness of war—short of total destruction, which is not war but suicide—is not in itself an argument against waging war unless one thinks (as few people actually do think) that violence is always unjustifiable, that force is always and in all circumstances wrong—wrong because, as Simone Weil affirms in her sublime essay on war, "The Iliad, or The Poem of Force" (1940), violence turns anybody subjected to it into a thing.[20] No, retort those who in a given situation see no alternative to armed struggle, violence can exalt someone subjected to it into a martyr or a hero.

In fact, there are many uses of the innumerable opportunities a modern life supplies for regarding—at a distance, through the medium of photography—other people's pain. Photographs of an atrocity may give rise to opposing responses. A call for peace. A cry for revenge. Or simply the bemused awareness, continually restocked by photographic information, that terrible things happen. Who can forget the three color pictures by Tyler Hicks that *The New York Times* ran across the upper half of the first page of its daily section devoted

---

19 *breadline massacre ... market massacre*   Both bombings are generally accepted to have been perpetrated by Serbian forces under the leadership of Radovan Karadžić (b. 1945), though there was much uncertainty at the time they occurred; no official investigation of the "breadline massacre" was carried out.

20 [Sontag's note]   Her condemnation of war notwithstanding, Weil sought to participate in the defense of the Spanish Republic and in the fight against Hitler's Germany. In 1936 she went to Spain as a non-combatant volunteer in an international brigade; in 1942 and early 1943, a refugee in London and already ill, she worked at the office of the Free French and hoped to be sent on a mission in Occupied France. (She died in an English sanatorium in August 1943).

to America's new war, "A Nation Challenged,"[21] on November 13, 2001? The triptych* depicted the fate of a wounded Taliban soldier in uniform who had been found in a ditch by Northern Alliance[22] soldiers advancing toward Kabul. First panel: being dragged on his back by two of his captors—one has grabbed an arm, the other a leg—along a rocky road. Second panel (the camera is very near): surrounded, gazing up in terror as he is being pulled to his feet. Third panel: at the moment of death, supine with arms outstretched and knees bent, naked and bloodied from the waist down, being finished off by the military mob that has gathered to butcher him. An ample reservoir of stoicism is needed to get through the great newspaper record each morning, given the likelihood of seeing photographs that could make you cry. And the pity and disgust that pictures like Hick's inspire should not distract you from asking what pictures, whose cruelties, whose deaths are *not* being shown.

• • •

For a long time some people believed that if the horror could be made vivid enough, most people would finally take in the outrageousness, the insanity of war.

    Fourteen years before Woolf published *Three Guineas*—in 1924, on the tenth anniversary of the national mobilization against Germany for the First World War—the conscientious objector Ernst Friedrich[23] published his *Krieg dem Krieg! (War Against War!)*. This is photography as shock therapy: an album of more than one hundred and eighty photographs mostly drawn from German military and medical archives, many of which were deemed unpublishable by government censors while the war was on. The book starts with pictures of toy soldiers, toy cannons, and other delights of male children everywhere, and concludes with pictures taken in military cemeteries. Between the toys and the graves, the reader has an excruciating photo-tour of four years of ruin, slaughter, and degradation: pages of wrecked and plundered churches and castles, obliterated villages, ravaged forests, torpedoed passenger steamers, shattered

15

---

21 *A Nation Challenged* Newspaper section that ran daily from September 18 through to the last day of 2001; it focused on the September 11 attacks and the ensuing "War on Terror."

22 *Taliban* Islamic fundamentalist militant movement and governing body of Afghanistan from 1996–2001. As an ally of Al-Qaeda and other terrorist groups, the Taliban government was targeted and overthrown by Coalition forces of the US and other NATO nations; *Northern Alliance* The United Islamic Front for the Salvation of Afghanistan, a group allied with the US-led forces that invaded.

23 *Ernst Friedrich* Pacifist and anarchist (1894–1967) accused of sabotage during the First World War. He also resisted the Nazi regime and refused to fight in the Second World War.

vehicles, hanged conscientious objectors, half-naked prostitutes in military brothels, soldiers in death agonies after poison-gas attack, skeletal Armenian children.[24] Almost all the sequences in *War Against War!* are difficult to look at, notably the pictures of dead soldiers belonging to the various armies putrefying in heaps on fields and roads and in the front-line trenches. But surely the most unbearable pages in this book, the whole of which was designed to horrify and demoralize, are in the section titled "The Face of War," twenty-four close-ups of soldiers with huge facial wounds. And Friedrich did not make the mistake of supposing that that heartrending, stomach-turning pictures would simply speak for themselves. Each photograph has an impassioned caption in four languages (German, French, Dutch, and English), and the wickedness of militarist ideology is excoriated and mocked on every page. Immediately denounced by the government and by veterans' and other patriotic organizations—in some cities the police raided bookstores, and lawsuits were brought against the public display of the photographs—Friedrich's declaration of war against war was acclaimed by left-wing writers, artists, and intellectuals, as well as by the constituencies of the numerous antiwar leagues, who predicted that the book would have a decisive influence on public opinion. By 1930, *War Against War!* had gone through ten editions in Germany and been translated into many languages.

In 1938, the year of Woolf's *Three Guineas*, the great French director Abel Gance featured in close-up some of the mostly hidden population of hideously disfigured ex-combatants—*les gueules cassées* ("the broken mugs") they were nicknamed in French—at the climax of his new *J'accuse*.[25] (Gance had made an earlier, primitive version of the incomparable antiwar film, with the same hallowed title, in 1918–19.) As in the final section of Friedrich's book, Gance's film ends in a new military cemetery, not just to remind us of how many millions of young men were sacrificed to militarism and ineptitude between 1914 and 1918 in the war cheered on as "the war to end all wars," but to advance the sacred judgment these dead would surely bring against Europe's politicians and generals could they know that, twenty years later, another war was imminent. *"Morts de Verdun, levez-vous!"* (Rise, dead of Verdun!), cries the deranged veteran who is the protagonist of the film, and he repeats his summons in German and in English: "Your sacrifices were in vain!" And the

---

24 *Armenian children* Approximately one and a half million people are estimated to have been killed during the Armenian Genocide, which was perpetrated starting in 1915 by the Ottoman Empire against the ethnic minority of Armenians who lived within what is now Turkey.

25 *J'accuse* French: I accuse. The phrase comes from an 1898 newspaper letter by Émile Zola, with the heading "*J'accuse…!*,"; the letter accuses the French government of anti-Semitism.

vast mortuary plain disgorges its multitudes, and army of shambling ghosts in rotted uniforms with mutilated faces, who rise from their graves and set out in all directions, causing mass panic among the populace already mobilized for a new pan-European war. "Fill your eyes with this horror! It is the only thing that can stop you!" the madman cries to the fleeing multitudes of the living, who reward him with a martyr's death, after which he joins his dead comrades: a sea of impassive ghosts overrunning the cowering future combatants and victims of *la guerre de demain*.[26] War beaten back by apocalypse.

And the following year the war came.

(2003)

---

26   *la guerre de demain*   French: the war of tomorrow.

Annie Dillard

On Foot in Virginia's Roanoke Valley

The following is a revised version of an essay first published in 1974 by the twenty-eight-year-old Dillard as the opening piece in a book of reflections on the author's place in the natural world, and on the nature of beauty, suffering, and creation. Pilgrim at Tinker Creek *was awarded the Pulitzer Prize and went on to become one of the best-known works of writing about humans and the environment by any American writer. The title of the piece in its 1974 version was "Heaven and Earth in Jest." The revised version was published in 2016 in the collection* The Abundance: Narrative Essays Old and New.

I used to have a cat, an old fighting tom,* who would jump through the open window by my bed in the middle of the night and land on my chest. I'd half awaken. He'd stick his skull under my nose and purr, stinking of urine and blood. Some nights he kneaded my bare chest with his front paws, powerfully, arching his back, as if sharpening his claws, or pummeling a mother for milk. Some mornings I'd wake in daylight to find my body covered with paw prints in blood; it looked as though I'd been painted with roses.

It was hot, so hot the mirror felt warm. I washed before the mirror in a daze, my twisted summer sleep still hung about me like sea kelp. What blood was this, and what roses? It could have been the rose of union, the blood of murder, or the rose of beauty bare and the blood of some unspeakable sacrifice or birth. The sign on my body could have been an emblem or a stain, the keys to the kingdom or the mark of Cain.[1] I never knew. I never knew as I washed,

---

1   *an emblem or a stain* I.e., a mark of blessing or a mark of curse; *keys to the kingdom* Matthew 16.19: "And I will give unto thee the keys to the kingdom of heaven"; *mark of Cain* In the Book of Genesis, Cain murders his brother Abel. After punishing Cain for the murder, God places an identifying mark upon him so as to prevent others from killing him. See Genesis 4.15: "And the Lord set a mark upon Cain, lest any finding him should kill him."

and the blood streaked, faded, and finally disappeared, whether I'd purified myself or ruined the blood sign of the Passover.[2] We wake, if we ever wake at all, to mystery, rumors of death, beauty, violence.... "Seem like we're just set down here," a woman said to me recently, "and don't nobody know why."

These are morning matters, pictures you dream as the final wave heaves you up on the sand to the bright light and drying air. You remember pressure, and a curved sleep you rested against, soft, like a scallop in its shell.* But the air hardens your skin; you stand; leave the lighted shore to explore some dim headland, and soon you're lost in the leafy interior, intent, remembering nothing.

• • •

I still think of that old tomcat, mornings, when I wake. Things are tamer now; I sleep with the window shut. The cat and our rites are gone and my life is changed, but the memory remains of something powerful playing over me. I wake expectant, hoping to see a new thing. If I'm lucky I might be jogged awake by a strange birdcall. I dress in a hurry, imagining the yard flapping with auks, or flamingos. This morning it was a wood duck, down at the creek. It flew away.

I live by a creek, Tinker Creek, in a valley in Virginia's Blue Ridge.[3] It's where I make myself scarce. An anchorite's hermitage[4] is called an anchor-hold; some anchor-holds were simple sheds clamped to the side of a church like a barnacle to a rock. I think of this house clamped to the side of Tinker Creek as an anchor-hold. It holds me at anchor to the rock bottom of the creek itself and it keeps me steadied in the current, as a sea anchor does, facing the stream of light pouring down. It's a good place to live; there's a lot to think about.

The creeks—Tinker and Carvin's—are an active mystery, fresh every minute. Theirs is the mystery of the continuous creation and all that providence[5] implies: the uncertainty of vision, the horror of the fixed, the dissolution of

---

2 *blood sign of the Passover* In the Book of Exodus, God frees the Israelites from slavery under the Egyptian Pharoah by setting a plague upon all the firstborn in Egypt; if they are to be passed over by this plague, the Israelites are told they must kill a lamb and paint his blood upon their doors as a mark. Exodus 12.13: "And the blood shall be to you for a token upon the houses where ye are: and when I see the blood, I will pass over you, and the plague shall not be upon you to destroy you, when I smite the land of Egypt." This event is commemorated by Passover, an important Jewish festival.

3 *Virginia's Blue Ridge* I.e., the Blue Ridge Mountains, a mountain range stretching from southern Pennsylvania, through Virginia and North Carolina, to the northeastern tip of Georgia.

4 *anchorite's hermitage* Dwelling-place of an anchorite, one who for religious reasons has withdrawn from the world to live an ascetic life.

5 *providence* Divine foreknowing and guidance of the world by God.

the present, the intricacy of beauty, the pressure of fecundity, the elusiveness of the free, and the flawed nature of perfection. The mountains—Tinker and Brushy, McAfee's Knob and Dead Man[6]—are a passive mystery, the oldest of all. Theirs is the one simple mystery of creation from nothing, of matter itself, anything at all, the given. Mountains are giant, restful, absorbent. You can heave your spirit into a mountain and the mountain will keep it, folded, and not throw it back as some creeks will. The creeks are the world with all its stimulus and beauty; I live there. But the mountains are home.

· · ·

The wood duck flew away. I caught only a glimpse of something like a bright torpedo that blasted the leaves where it flew. Back at the house I eat a bowl of oatmeal; much later in the day will come the long slant of light that means good walking.

If the day is fine, any walk will do; it all looks good. Water in particular looks its best, reflecting blue sky in the flat, and chopping it into graveled shallows and white chute and foam in the riffles. On a dark day, or a hazy one, even when everything else is washed-out and lackluster, the water carries its own lights. I set out for the railroad tracks, for the hill the flocks fly over, for the woods where the white mare lives. But first I go to the water.

Today is one of those excellent January partly cloudies in which light chooses an unexpected part of the landscape to trick out in gilt,[7] and then shadow sweeps it away. You know you're alive. You take huge steps, trying to feel the planet's roundness arc between your feet. Kazantzakis[8] says that when he was young he had a canary and a globe. When he freed the canary, it would perch on the globe and sing. All his life, wandering the earth, he felt as though he had a canary on top of his head, singing.

10 West of the house, Tinker Creek makes a sharp loop, so that the creek is both in back of the house, south of me, and also on the other side of the road, north of me. I like to go north. There the afternoon sun hits the creek just right, deepening the reflected blue and lighting the sides of trees on the banks. Steers* from the pasture across the creek come down to drink; I always flush a rabbit or two there. I sit on a fallen trunk in the shade and watch the squirrels in the sun. There are two separated wooden fences suspended from cables that cross the creek just upstream from my tree-trunk bench. These fences keep the steers from escaping up or down the creek when they come to drink. Squirrels,

---

6   *Tinker ... Dead Man*   Mountains in the Blue Ridge range.

7   *gilt*   Gold.

8   *Kazantzakis*   Nikos Kazantzakis (1883–1957), Greek writer most famous for the novel *Zorba the Greek*.

the neighborhood children, and I use the downstream fence as a swaying bridge across the creek. But the steers are there today.

I sit on the downed tree and watch the black steers slip on the creek bottom. They are all bred beef: beef heart, beef hide, beef hocks. They're a human product, like rayon.* They're like a field of shoes. They have cast-iron shanks and tongues like foam insoles. You can't see through to their brains as you can with other animals; for there is beef fat behind their eyes, beef stew.

I cross the fence six feet above the water, walking my hands down the rusty cable and tightroping my feet along the narrow edge of the planks. When I hit the other bank and *terra firma*,[9] some steers are bunched in a knot between me and the barbed-wire fence I want to cross. So I suddenly rush at them in a wild sprint, flailing my arms and hollering, "Lightning! Copperhead! Swedish meatballs!" They flee, still in a knot, stumbling across the flat pasture. I stand with the wind on my face.

When I slide under the barbed-wire fence, cross a field, and run over a sycamore trunk felled across the water, I'm on a little island shaped like a tear in the middle of Tinker Creek. On one side of the creek is a steep forested bank; the water is swift and deep on that side of the island. On the other side is the level field I walked through next to the steers' pasture; the water between the field and the island is shallow and sluggish. In summer's low water, flags and bulrushes grow along a series of shallow pools cooled by the lazy current. Water striders* patrol the surface film, crayfish hump along the silt bottom eating filth, frogs shout and glare, and shiners and small bream hide among roots from the sulky green heron's eye. I come to this island every month of the year. I walk around it, stopping and staring, or I straddle the sycamore log over the creek, curling my legs out of the water in winter, trying to read. Today I sit on dry grass at the end of the island by the slower side of the creek. I'm drawn to this spot. I come to it as to an oracle; I return to it as a man years later will seek out the battlefield where he lost a leg or an arm.

• • •

A couple of summers ago I was walking along the edge of the island to see what I could see in the water, and mainly to scare frogs. Frogs have an inelegant way of taking off from invisible positions on the bank just ahead of your feet, in dire panic, emitting a froggy "Yike!" and splashing into the water. Incredibly, this amused me, and, incredibly, it amuses me still. As I walked along the grassy edge of the island, I got better and better at seeing frogs in and out of the water. I learned to recognize, slowing down, the difference in texture of the light reflected from mudbank, water, grass, or frog. Frogs were flying all around

---

9   *terra firma*   Latin: firm land.

me. At the end of the island I noticed a small green frog. He was exactly half in and half out of the water, looking like a schematic diagram of an amphibian. He didn't jump.

15   I crept closer. At last I knelt on the island's dead grass, lost, dumbstruck, staring at the frog in the creek not four feet away. He was a very small frog, with wide, dull eyes. And just as I looked at him, he slowly crumpled and began to sag. The spirit vanished from his eyes as if snuffed. His skin emptied and drooped; his skull itself seemed to collapse and settle like a kicked tent. He was shrinking before my eyes like a deflating football. I watched the taut, glistening skin on his shoulders ruck, and rumple, and fall. Soon, part of his skin, formless as a pricked balloon, lay in floating folds like bright scum on top of the water: It was a monstrous and terrifying thing. I gaped bewildered, appalled. An oval shadow hung in the water just behind the drained frog; then the shadow glided away. The frog skin bag started to sink.

I had read about the giant water bug, but never seen one. "Giant water bug" is in fact the name of the creature, which is an enormous, heavy-bodied brown bug. It eats insects, tadpoles, fish, and frogs. Its grasping forelegs are mighty and hooked inward. It seizes a victim with these legs, hugs it tight, and paralyzes it with enzymes injected during a vicious bite. That one bite is the only bite it ever takes. Through the puncture shoot the poisons that dissolve the victim's muscles and bones and organs—all but the skin. Then the giant water bug sucks out the victim's body, reduced to a juice. This event is quite common in warm freshwater. And now I'd seen it myself. I was still kneeling on the island grass when the unrecognizable flag of frog skin settled on the creek bottom, swaying. I stood up and brushed the knees of my pants. I couldn't catch my breath.

Many carnivorous animals, of course, devour their prey alive. The usual method seems to be to subdue the victim by downing or grasping it so it can't flee, then eating it whole or in a series of bloody bites. Frogs eat everything whole, stuffing prey in their mouth with their thumbs. People have seen frogs with their wide jaws so full of live dragonflies they couldn't close them. Ants don't even have to catch their prey: In the spring they swarm over newly hatched, featherless birds in the nest and eat them, tiny bite by tiny bite.

That it's rough out there and chancy is no surprise. Every live thing is a survivor on a kind of extended emergency bivouac.[10] But at the same time we are also created. In the Qur'an, Allah asks, "The heaven and the earth and all in between, thinkest thou I made them *in jest?*"[11] It's a good question. What

---

10 *bivouac* Temporary, makeshift shelter.

11 *Qur'an* Principal religious book of Islam. Allah is the Arabic name for the Abrahamic God; *The heaven ... in jest?* Likely a paraphrase either from verse 16 of the 21st *sura*, or from verse 38 of the 44th *sura* of the Qur'an.

do we think of the created universe, spanning an unthinkable void with an unthinkable profusion of forms? And what do we think of nothingness, those sickening reaches of time in either direction?

If the giant water bug was not made in jest, was it then made in earnest? Pascal uses a nice term to describe the notion of the creator's once having called forth the universe, turning his back to it: *Deus absconditus*.[12] Is this what we think happened? Was the sense of it there, and God absconded with it, ate it, like a wolf who disappears round the edge of the house with the Thanksgiving turkey?* "God is subtle," Einstein said, "but not malicious." Einstein also said that "nature conceals her mystery by means of her essential grandeur, not by her cunning."

It could be that God has not absconded but spread, as our vision and un-derstanding of the universe have spread, to a fabric of spirit and sense so grand and subtle, so powerful in a new way, that we can only feel blindly of its hem. In making the thick darkness a swaddling band for the sea, God "set bars and doors" and said, "Hitherto shalt thou come, but no further."[13] But have we come even that far? Have we rowed out to the thick darkness, or are we all playing pinochle[14] in the bottom of the boat?

Cruelty is a mystery, and the waste of pain. But if we describe a world to encompass these things, a world that is a long, brute game, then we bump against another mystery: the inrush of power and light, the canary that sings on the skull. For unless all ages and races of men have been deluded by the same mass hypnotist (who?), there seems to be such a thing as beauty, a grace wholly gratuitous.

About five years ago I saw a mockingbird make a straight vertical descent from the roof gutter of a four-story building. It was an act as careless and spon-taneous as the curl of a stem or the kindling of a star. The mockingbird took a single step into the air and dropped. His wings were still folded against his sides as though he were singing from a limb and not falling, accelerating thirty-two feet per second per second, through empty air. Just a breath before he would have been dashed to the ground, he unfurled his wings with exact, deliberate care, revealing the broad bars of white, spread his elegant, white-banded tail, and so floated onto the grass. I had just rounded a corner when his insouciant step off the gutter caught my eye; there was no one else in sight. The fact of his

20

12 *Pascal* Blaise Pascal (1623–62), French writer, physicist, mathematician, and Christian philosopher; *Deus absconditus* Latin: hidden or absconded god.

13 *In making ... but no further* Job 38.9–11: "When I made the cloud the garment thereof, and thick darkness a swaddlingband for it, And brake up for it my decreed place, and set bars and doors, And said, Hitherto shalt thou come, but no further"; *swaddling band* Tightly wrapped band of cloth used to clothe newborn infants.

14 *pinochle* Card game played with a 48-card deck.

free fall was like the old philosophical conundrum about the tree that falls in the forest.* The answer must be, I think, that beauty and grace are performed whether or not we will or sense them. The least we can do is try to be there.

Another time I saw a different wonder: sharks off the Atlantic coast of Florida. There is a way a wave rises above the ocean horizon, a triangular wedge against the sky. If you stand where the ocean breaks on a shallow beach, you see the raised water in a wave is in fact translucent, shot with lights. One late afternoon at low tide a hundred big sharks passed the beach near the mouth of a tidal river in a feeding frenzy. As each green wave rose from the churning water, it illuminated within itself the six- or eight-foot-long bodies of twisting sharks. The sharks disappeared as each wave rolled toward me; then a new wave swelled above the horizon, containing in it, like scorpions in amber, sharks that roiled and heaved. The sight held power and beauty, grace tangled in a rapture with violence.

We don't know what's going on here. If these tremendous events are random combinations of matter run amok, the yield of millions of monkeys at millions of typewriters,* then what is it in us, hammered out of those same typewriters, that they ignite? We don't know. Our life is a faint tracing on the surface of mystery, like the idle, curved tunnels of leaf miners[15] on the face of a leaf. We must somehow take a wider view, look at the whole landscape, really see it, and try to describe what's going on here. Then we can at least wail the right question into the swaddling band of darkness, or, if it comes to that, choir the proper praise.

25   At the time of Lewis and Clark,* setting the prairies on fire was a well-known signal that meant "Come down to the water." It was an extravagant gesture, but we can't do less. If the landscape reveals one certainty, it is that the extravagant gesture is the very start and stuff of creation. The universe has continued to deal in extravagances, flinging intricacies and colossi down eons of emptiness, heaping profusions on profligacies with ever-fresh vigor. The whole show has been on fire from the word go. I come down to the water to cool my eyes. But everywhere I look I see fire; that which isn't flint is tinder and the whole world sparks and flames.

• • •

I have come to the grassy island late in the day. The creek is up; icy water sweeps under the sycamore log bridge. The frog skin, of course, is utterly gone. I have stared at that one spot on the creek bottom for so long, focusing past the rush of water, that when I stand, the opposite bank seems to stretch before

---

15 *leaf miners* Insect larvae that eat through leaf tissue, often leaving visible trails on the surface of the leaf.

my eyes and flow grassily upstream. When the bank settles down I cross the sycamore log and enter again the big plowed field next to the steers' pasture.

The wind is terrific out of the west; the sun comes and goes. I can see the shadow on the field before me deepen uniformly and spread out like a plague. Everything seems so dull now I am amazed I can even distinguish objects. And suddenly the light runs across the land like a great comber,[16] and up the trees, only to go again in a wink: I think I've gone blind or died. When it comes again, the light, you hold your breath, and if it stays you forget about it until it goes again.

It's the most beautiful day of the year. At four o'clock the eastern sky is a dead stratus black flecked with low white clouds. The sun in the west illuminates the ground, the mountains, and especially the bare branches of trees, so that everywhere silver trees cut into the black sky like a photographer's negative of a landscape. The air and the ground are dry; the mountains are flashing on and off like neon signs. Clouds slide east if pulled from the horizon, like a tablecloth whipped off a table. The hemlocks by the barbed-wire fence are flinging themselves east as though their backs would break. Purple shadows are racing east; the wind makes me face east, and again I feel dizzied and drawn, as I felt when the creek bank reeled.

At four-thirty the sky in the east is clear; how could that big blackness be blown? Fifteen minutes later another darkness comes overhead from the northwest; and it's here to stay. Everything drains of its light as if sucked. Only at the horizon do inky black mountains give way to distant, lighted mountains—lighted not by direct illumination but rather by paled glowing sets of mist hung before them. Now the blackness is in the east; everything is half in shadow, half in sun, every cloud, tree, mountain, and hedge. I can't see Tinker Mountain through the line of hemlock, till it comes on like a street-light, ping, *ex nihilo*.[17] Its sandstone cliffs pink and swell. Suddenly the light goes; the cliffs recede as if pushed. The sun hits a clump of sycamores between me and the mountains; the sycamore arms light up, and I can't see the cliffs. They're gone. The pale network of sycamore arms, which a second ago was transparent as a screen, is suddenly opaque, glowing with light. Now the sycamore arms snuff out, the mountains come on, and there are the cliffs again.

I walk home. By five-thirty the show has pulled out. Nothing is left but an unreal blue and a few banked clouds low in the north. Some sort of carnival magician has been here, some fast-talking worker of wonders who has the act backwards. "Something in this hand," he says, "something in this hand, something up my sleeve, something behind my back ..." and abracadabra, he snaps

30

---

16   *comber*   Long, curving wave.

17   *ex nihilo*   Latin: out of nothing.

his fingers: and it's all gone. Only the bland, blank-faced magician remains, in his unruffled cot, bare-handed, nodding at a smattering of baffled applause. When you look again the whole show has pulled up stakes and moved on down the road. It never stops. New shows roll in from over the mountains and the magician reappears unannounced from a fold in the curtain you never dreamed was an opening. Scarves of clouds, rabbits in plain view, disappear into the black hat forever. Presto chango.* The audience, if there is one, is dizzy from head-turning, dazed.

• • •

Like the bear who went over the mountain,[18] I went out to see what I could see. And, I might as well warn you, like the bear, all that I could see was the other side of the mountain: more of same. On a good day I might catch a glimpse of another wooded ridge rolling under the sun like water, another bivouac. I propose to keep here what Thoreau* called "a meteorological journal of the mind,"[19] telling some tales and describing some of the sights of this rather tamed valley, and exploring, in fear and trembling,[20] some of the unmapped dim reaches and unholy fastnesses to which those tales and sights so dizzyingly lead.

I am no scientist. I explore the neighborhood. An infant who has just learned to hold his head up has a frank and forthright way of gazing about him in bewilderment. He hasn't the faintest clue where he is, and he aims to learn. In a couple of years, what he will have learned instead is how to fake it: He'll have the cocksure air of a squatter who has come to feel he owns the place. Some unwonted, taught pride diverts us from our original intent, which is to explore the neighborhood, view the landscape, to discover at least *where* it is that we have been so startlingly set down, if we can't learn why.

So I think about the valley. It is my leisure as well as my work, a game. It is a fierce game I have joined because it is being played anyway, a game of both skill and chance, played against an unseen adversary—the conditions of time—in which the payoff, which may arrive at any moment in a blast of light, might as well come to me as anyone else. I stake the time I'm grateful to have, the energies I'm glad to direct. I risk getting stuck on the board, so to speak, unable to move in any direction, which happens enough, God knows; and I risk the searing, exhausting nightmares that plunder rest and force me facedown all night long in some muddy ditch seething with hatching insects and crustaceans.

---

18   *the bear ... the mountain*   Alludes to a popular children's song that begins "The bear went over the mountain ... to see what he could see." After the bear completes his journey, the lyrics run, "all that he could see, / Was the other side of the mountain."

19   *a meteorological journey of the mind*   The quotation is from Thoreau's *Journal*.

20   *in fear and trembling*   Psalms 55.5: "Fearfulness and trembling are come upon me" or Philippians 2.12: "work out your own salvation with fear and trembling."

But if I can bear the nights, the days are a pleasure. I walk out; I see something, some event I'd otherwise have utterly missed and lost; or something sees me, some enormous power brushes me with its clean wing, and I resound like a beaten bell.

I am an explorer, then, and I am also a stalker, or the instrument of the hunt itself. Certain Indians used to carve long grooves along the wooden shafts of the arrows. They called the grooves "lightning marks," because they resembled the curved fissure lightning slices down the trunks of trees. The function of lightning marks is this: If the arrow fails to kill the game, blood from a deep wound will channel long the lightning mark, streak down the arrow shaft, and spatter to the ground, laying a trail dripped on broad leaves, on stones, that the barefoot and trembling archer can follow into whatever deep or rare wilderness it leads. I am the arrow shaft, carved along my length by unexpected lights and gashes from the very sky, and this book is the straying trail of blood.

Something pummels us, something barely sheathed. Power broods and lights. We're played on like a pipe; our breath is not our own. James Houston[21] describes two young Inuit girls sitting cross-legged on the ground, mouth on mouth, blowing by turns each other's throat cords, making a low, unearthly music. When I cross again the bridge that is really the steers' fence, the wind has thinned to the delicate air of twilight; it barely ruffles the water's skin. I watch the running sheets of light raised on the creek's surface. The sight has the appeal of the purely passive, like the racing of light under clouds on a field, the beautiful dream at the moment of being dreamed. The breeze is the merest puff, but you yourself sail headlong and breathless under the gale force of the spirit.

(1974, 2016)

from FOR THE TIME BEING

Dillard's 1999 For the Time Being *is a lyrical work of reflection that embraces personal narrative, religious commentary, and descriptions of the natural world. In each chapter there are sections with the headings Birth, Sand, China, Clouds, Numbers, China, Israel, Encounters, Thinker, Evil, and Now. The passage of natural history included here forms the second section of the book's third chapter.*

---

21 *James Houston* James Archibald Houston (1921–2005), Canadian author and artist who played a role in popularizing Inuit art.

S AND • A few years ago, I grew interested in sand. Why is there sand in deserts? Where does it come from? I thought ocean waves made sand on seashores: waves pounded continents' rock and shattered it to stone, gravel, and finally sand. This, I learned, is only slightly true.

Lichens, and ice and salt crystals, make more sand than ocean waves do. On mountaintops and on hillsides you see cracked rock faces and boulders. Lichens grow on them, in rings or tufts. "The still explosions on the rocks / the lichens grow in gray, concentric shocks," wrote Elizabeth Bishop.[22] These explosions blast the rocks; lichens secrete acids, which break minerals. Lichens widen rocks' cracks, growing salt crystals split them further, and freezing water shatters them.

Glaciers make some sand; their bottoms pluck boulders and stones that scour all the land in their paths. When glaciers melt, they leave in outwash plains boulders, rocks, gravels, sand, and clays—the sand ground to floury powder. Winds lift the sand and bear it aloft.

Mostly, the continents' streams and rivers make sand. Streams, especially, and fast rivers bear bouncing rocks that knock the earth, and break themselves into sharp chips of sand. The sand grains leap—saltate[23]—downstream. So the banks and bottoms of most streams are sandy. Look in any small stream in the woods or mountains, as far inland as you like. That stream is making sand, and sand lies on its bed. Caddis-fly larvae use it as stones for their odd masonry houses.[24]

5　　Rivers bear sand to the sea. As rivers slow, they drop their sand, and harbors silt up and deltas spread. If the land's rock is fresh lava, as it is in Tahiti and on the Caribbean coast of Costa Rica, the sand the streams bear down to the beaches is black. If the inland rock is basaltic, like the Columbia River plateau's, the sand the river carries to beaches is dark and fine. If the rock is granite, as it is in the eastern United States, the sand is pale quartz and feldspar, granite's parts.

When Los Angeles and Orange Counties dammed their intermittent streams, all the beaches from Los Angeles to Newport Beach[25] lost their sand supply. Those weak hillside streams, which had never even flowed year-round,

22　*Elizabeth Bishop* American poet (1911–79), raised in Nova Scotia and Massachusetts. The quotation is from her 1955 poem "The Shampoo."

23　*saltate* Archaic word meaning "jump" or "skip." In geography, "saltation" refers specifically to the transport of particles across an uneven surface, wherein momentum is continuously transferred between numerous bouncing or leaping particles.

24　*Caddis-fly .. houses* Caddis-fly larvae live under water in tube-shaped cocoons, which they carry around like snail shells and make by gluing together debris, such as pebbles and plant matter, with salivary silk.

25　*Newport Beach* Coastal community approximately 35 miles south of Los Angeles.

had supplied all that sand. Now beach towns buy dredged harbor sand to ship and dump.

Coastal currents smear sand round the continent's edges. So there is sand on ocean beaches. Ocean waves do not make stony sand except where waves beat cliffs. Mostly, waves and longshore currents spread river sand coastwise, and waves fling it back at the continents' feet. Ocean waves crumble dead coral reefs. And parrotfish[26] eat coral polyps. The fish do not digest the coral's limey bits, but instead defecate them in dribbles, making that grand white sand we prize on tropical beaches and shallow sea floors. Little or no sand lies under the deep oceans.

Why is there sand in deserts? Because windblown sand collects in every low place, and deserts are low, like beaches. However far you live from the sea, however high your altitude, you will find sand in ditches, in roadside drains, and in cracks between rocks and sidewalks.

Sand collects in flat places too, like high-altitude deserts. During interglacials,[27] such as the one in which we live now, soils dry. Clay particles clump and lie low; sand grains part and blow about. Winds drop sand by weight, as one drops anything when it gets too heavy for one's strength. Winds carry light stone dust—loess[28]—far afield. Wherever they drop it, it stays put in only a few places: in the rich prairies in central North America, and in precious flat basins in China and Russia.

(1999)

---

26 *parrotfish* So-called for their strong, beak-like teeth, used to eat away at coral. The organic materials of their coral diet are digestible, while the inorganic calcium-rich limestone is indigestible.

27 *interglacials* Geological epochs of warmer global temperature, separating periods of glaciation. The current interglacial epoch is the Holocene period, preceded by the Pleistocene glacial epoch which ended around 11,700 years ago.

28 *loess* German word originally meaning 'loose,' which refers to yellowish loam sediment distributed by wind.

ROSARIO FERRÉ

ON DESTINY, LANGUAGE, AND TRANSLATION, OR, OPHELIA ADRIFT IN THE C. & O. CANAL[1]

Puerto Rican writer Rosario Ferré wrote in Spanish, but often also translated her own work into English. The following essay, which considers that process of translation, appears at the conclusion of The Youngest Doll *(1991), her own English translation of her short story collection* Papeles de Pandora *(1976).*

Language is the most salient model of Heraclitean[2] flux.... So far as we experience and realize them in linear progression, time and language are intimately related; they move and the arrow is never in the same place.

—George Steiner, *After Babel*

What is translation? On a platter
A poet's pale and glaring head,
A parrot's screech, a monkey's chatter,
And profanation of the dead.

—Nabokov, "On Translating Eugene Onegin"

A few weeks ago, when I was in Puerto Rico, I had an unusual dream. I had decided, after agonizing over the decision for several months, to return to the island for good, ending my five-year stay in Washington, D.C. My return was not only to be proof that Thomas Wolfe[3] had been wrong all along and

---

1   *OPHELIA* Character from Shakespeare's *Hamlet*; she drowns before the conclusion of the play; *C. & O. CANAL* Chesapeake and Ohio Canal, which operated along the Potomac River between Washington, D.C., and Cumberland, Maryland, from 1831 to 1924.

2   *Heraclitean* Heraclitus of Ephesus, an early Greek philosopher, believed that conflict and perpetual change were the natural state of the universe.

3   *Thomas Wolfe* Novelist (1900–38) whose works include *You Can't Go Home Again*, posthumously published in 1940.

that one *could* go home again; it was also an anguishedly mulled over decision, which had taken me at least a year to arrive at. I wanted to come in contact with my roots once again; to nurture those hidden springs of consciousness from which literary inspiration flows, and which undoubtedly are related to the world we see and dream of as infants, before we can formulate it into words.

In my dream I was still in Washington, but was about to leave it for good. I was traveling on the C. & O. Canal, where horse-towed barges full of tourists still journey picturesquely today, led by farmers dressed up in costumes of Colonial times. I had crossed the canal many times before, entering the placid green water, which came up to my waist: without any trouble, and coming out on the other side, where the bright green, African-daisy-covered turf suspiciously resembled the Puerto Rican countryside. This time, however, the canal crossing was to be definitive. I didn't want my five professionally productive years in Washington to become a false paradise, a panacea where life was a pleasant limbo,* far removed from the social and political problems of the island. I felt that this situation could not continue, and that in order to write competently about my world's conflicts, as war correspondents have experienced, one has to be able to live in the trenches and not on the pleasant hillocks that overlook the battlefield.

As I began to cross the canal, however, and waded into the middle of the trough, I heard a voice say loudly that all the precautions of language had to be taken, as the locks were soon to be opened and the water level was going to rise. Immediately after this someone opened the heavy wooden gates of the trough at my back and a swell of water began to travel down the canal, lifting me off my feet and sweeping me down current, so that it became impossible to reach either of the two shores. At first I struggled this way and that, as panic welled up in me and I tried unsuccessfully to grab onto the vegetation which grew on the banks, but I soon realized the current was much too powerful and I had no alternative but to let it take hold of me. After a while, as I floated face up like Ophelia[4] over the green surface of the water, I began to feel strangely at ease and tranquil. I looked at the world as it slid by, carried by the slowly moving swell of cool water, and wondered at the double exposure on both shores, the shore of Washington on my right and the shore of San Juan[5] on my left, perfectly fitted to each other and reflected on the canal's surface like on a traveling mirror on which I was magically being sustained.

The water of the canal reminded me then of the mirror on the door of my wardrobe when I was a child, whose beveled surface entranced me when I

---

4 *Ophelia* Ferré refers to John Everett Millais' 1852 painting in which Ophelia's drowned body floats peacefully in a brook.

5 *San Juan* Capital of Puerto Rico.

crawled up to it because, when one looked closely into its edge, left and right fell apart and at the same time melted into one. The canal had the same effect on me; in it blue sky and green water, north and south, earth and vegetation ceased to be objects or places and became passing states, images in motion. The water of words, the water in the C. & O. Canal where "all the precautions of language had to be taken," was my true habitat as a writer; neither Washington nor San Juan, neither past nor present, but the crevice in between. Being a writer, the dream was telling me, one has to learn to live by letting go, by renouncing the reaching of this or that shore, but to let oneself become the meeting place of both.

5   In a way all writing is a translation, a struggle to interpret the meaning of life, and in this sense the translator can be said to be a shaman,* a person dedicated to deciphering conflicting human texts, searching for the final unity of meaning in speech. Translators of literary texts act like a writer's telescopic lens; they are dedicated to the pursuit of communication, of that universal understanding of original meaning which may one day perhaps make possible the harmony of the world. They struggle to bring together different cultures, striding over the barriers of those prejudices and misunderstandings that are the result of diverse ways of thinking and of cultural mores. They wrestle between two swinging axes, which have, since the beginning of mankind, caused wars to break out and civilizations to fail to understand each other: the utterance and the interpretation of meaning; the verbal sign (or form) and the essence (or spirit) of the word.

I believe that being both a Puerto Rican and a woman writer has given me the opportunity to experience translation (as well as writing itself) in a special way. Only a writer who has experienced the historical fabric, the inventory of felt moral and cultural existence embedded in a given language, can be said to be a bilingual writer, and being a Puerto Rican has enabled me to acquire a knowledge both of Spanish and English, of the Latin American and of the North American way of life. Translation is not only a literary but also a historical task; it includes an interpretation of internal history, of the changing proceedings of consciousness in a civilization. A poem by Góngora,[6] written in the seventeenth century, can be translated literally, but it cannot be read without taking into account the complex cultural connotations that the Renaissance had in Spain. Language, in the words of George Steiner,[7] is like a living

---

6   *Góngora* Spanish Baroque lyric poet Luis de Góngora y Argote (1561–1627) developed a style known as Gongorism, which employed complicated wordplay and literary devices.

7   *George Steiner* American literary critic, novelist, philosopher, and essayist (b. 1929). In his book *After Babel: Aspects of Language and Translation* (1975), he writes that "[b]etween the 'physiological universal' of consciousness and the specific

membrane; it provides a constantly changing model of reality. Every civilization is imprisoned in a linguistic contour, which it must match and regenerate according to the changing landscape of facts and of time.

When I write in English I feel that the landscape of experience, the fields of idiomatic, symbolic, communal reference are not lost to me, but are relatively well within my reach, in spite of the fact that Spanish is still the language of my dreams. Writing in English, however, remains for me a cultural translation, as I believe it must be for such writers as Vladimir Nabokov and Vassily Aksyonov,[8] who come from a country whose cultural matrix is also very different from that of the United States. Translating a literary work (even one's own) from one language to another curiously implies the same type of historical interpretation that is necessary in translating a poem of the seventeenth century, for example, as contemporary cultures often enclaved in different epochs of time coexist with each other. This is precisely what happens today with North American and Latin American literatures, where the description of technological, pragmatic, democratic modern states coexists with that of feudal, agrarian, and still basically totalitarian states. Translating literature from Spanish into English (and vice versa) in the twentieth century cannot but take into account very different views of the world, which are evident when one compares, for example, the type of novel produced today by Latin American writers such as Carlos Fuentes, Gabriel García Márquez, and Isabel Allende, who are all preoccupied by the processes of transformation and strife within totalitarian agrarian societies, and the novels of such North American writers as Saul Bellow, Philip Roth, and E.L. Doctorow, who are engrossed in the complicated unraveling of the human psyche within the dehumanized modern city-state.

Translating has taught me that it is ultimately impossible to transcribe one cultural identity into another. As I write in English I am inevitably translating a Latin American identity, still rooted in preindustrial traditions and mores, with very definite philosophical convictions and beliefs, into a North American context. As Richard Morse has so accurately pointed out in his book *El espejo de Próspera: un estudio de la dialéctica del Nuevo Mundo* (1982), Latin American society is still rooted in Thomistic, Aristotelian beliefs,[9] which at-

---

cultural-conventional process of identification and response lies the membrane of a particular language or, as Cassirer put it, the unique 'inner form' which distinguishes it from all other languages."

8   *Vladimir Nabokov*   Russian-American novelist (1899–1977) who translated his own works—some from Russian into English, others from English into Russian;   *Vassily Aksyonov*   Russian novelist known in the western world for *The Burn* (1975), a dissident novel that could not be published in the USSR. He wrote in English as well as in Russian.

9   *El espejo ... Mundo*   Spanish: Prosperous Mirror: a Study of the Dialectic of the New World;   *Thomistic, Aristotelian beliefs*   The works of the Greek philoso- *(continued ...)*

tempt to reconcile Christian thought with the truths of the natural universe and of faith. Spain (and Latin America) have never really undergone a scientific or an industrial revolution, and they have never produced the equivalent of a Hobbes or a Locke,[10] so that theories such as that of pragmatism, individual liberty, and the social contract have been very difficult to implement.

Carlos Fuentes's novel *Terra Nostra*, for example, tries to point out this situation, as it analyzes the failure of the Latin American totalitarian state (the PRI in Mexico), founded both on the Spanish tradition of absolute power established by Philip II[11] during the seventeenth century and on the blood-soaked Aztec Empire. Fuentes's case, however, as well as that of Alejo Carpentier,[12] can be said to be exceptions to the rule in the Latin American literary landscape, as both writers make an effort in their novels to escape arbitrary descriptions of their worlds, and often integrate into their novels rationalistic analyses that delve into Latin American traditions from diverging points of view.

Translating my own work, I came directly in contact with this type of problem. In the first place, I discovered that the Spanish (and Latin American) literary tradition permits a much greater leeway for what may be called "play on words," which generally sound frivolous and innocuous in English. In Puerto Rico, as in Latin America, we are brought up as children on a constant juggling of words, which often has as its purpose the humorous defiance of apparent social meanings and established structures of power. In undermining the meaning of words, the Latin American child (as the Latin American writer) calls into question the social order, which he is obliged to accept without sharing in its processes. This defiance through humor has to do with a heroic stance ("el relajo," "la bachata," "la joda") often of anarchic origin which is a part of the Latin personality, but it also has to do with faith, with a Thomistic belief in supernatural values. It is faith in the possibility of Utopia,* of the values asserted by a society ruled by Christian, absolute values rather than by pragmatic

---

pher Aristotle (384–322 BCE) play a foundational role in Western philosophy. Thomism refers to the thought of Saint Thomas Aquinas (1225–74), a Catholic scholar who applied Aristotle's ideas to Christian theology.

10   *Hobbes*   Thomas Hobbes, an English philosopher whose work played an important role in the development of political science and theory. In his *Leviathan* (1651) he discusses the concept of the "social contract," an agreement between the government and the governed that gives the state its legitimacy;   *Locke*   John Locke, another influential English philosopher; his *Two Treatises on Government* (1689) also address the social contract.

11   *PRI*   Institutional Revolutionary Party, a political party that governed Mexico from 1929 until 2000; it remains a powerful organization;   *Philip II*   King of Spain, Portugal, Naples, and Sicily (1527–98) who oversaw expansion of the Spanish Empire.

12   *Alejo Carpentier*   Cuban novelist (1904–80).

ends, which leads the Puerto Rican child to revel in puns such as "Tenemos mucho oro, del que cagó el loro" (We have a lot of gold, of the kind the parrot pukes) or "Tenemos muchaplata, de la que cagó la gata" (We have a lot of silver, of the kind the cat shits), which permit him to face, and at the same time defy, his island's poverty; or in popular Puerto Rican sayings of the blackest humor and unforgiving social judgment such as, "el día que la mierda valga algo, los pobres nacerán sin culo" (the day shit is worth any money, the poor will be born without assholes).

But faith in the magical power of the image, in the power to transform the world into a better place through what Lezama Lima calls the "súbito,"[13] is only one of the traditions that enable Latin American writers to revel in puns and wordplay; there is also a historical, geographic tradition which I believe helps to explain the elaboration of extremely intricate forms of expression. It is not casually or by expediency that the literary structures in Alejo Carpentier's *Los pasos perdidos* (*The Lost Steps*), Guimarães Rosa's *Grande Sertão: Veredas*, or Nélida Piñón's *Tebas do meu coração* often remind us of the baroque[14] altarpieces of the churches of Brazil, Mexico, and Peru, where baroque art reached its maximum expression. When the Spanish conquerors reached the New World in the fifteenth and sixteenth centuries they brought the Spanish language and tradition with them, but that language and tradition, confronted by and superimposed on the complex realities of Indian cultures, as well as the convoluted forms of an equally diverse and till then unknown flora and fauna, began to change radically. In this sense Spanish literature in itself had received, by the time the seventeenth century had come around, considerable cultural influence from the Latin American continent. Don Luis de Góngora y Argote, for example, who never visited the Spanish colonies, would probably never have written the *Soledades* (a poem considered the apex of baroque literary expression) in which a shipwrecked traveler reaches the shores of a Utopian New World, if Spanish had not been the language in which Mexico and Peru were discovered and colonized. None has put it more clearly than José Lezama Lima, the Cuban poet, in an essay entitled "La curiosidad barroca." Lezama points out there how the baroque literary art of Góngora, as well as that of his nephew, the Mexican Don Carlos de Sigüenza y Góngora and of the Mexican nun Sor Juana Inés de la Cruz,[15] evolves parallel to the carved altarpieces of

---

13 *what Lezama ... "súbito"* Influential Cuban poet and writer José Lezama Lima (1910–76) uses the term "súbito" to describe a sudden occurrence that reveals something.

14 *baroque* Style of art associated with the seventeenth and eighteenth centuries and characterized by dramatic exaggeration and heavy ornamentation.

15 *the Mexican Don ... Cruz* Major seventeenth-century poets of New Spain, a Spanish colony in the New World.

Kondori, an Indian stonecarver from Peru, which represent "in an obscure and hieratic fashion the synthesis of Spanish and Indian, of Spanish theocracy with the solemn petrified order of the Inca Empire." Lezama's own novel, *Paradiso*, whose linguistic structure is as convoluted as the labyrinths of the Amazon jungle, remains today the most impressive testimony to the importance of baroque aesthetics in the contemporary Latin American novel.

A third characteristic that helps define Latin American tradition vis-à-vis North American tradition in literature today has often to do with magical occurrences and the world of the marvelously real ("lo real maravilloso"), which imply a given faith in the supernatural world which is very difficult to acquire when one is born in a country where technological knowledge and the pragmatics of reason reign supreme. We are here once again in the realm of how diverging cultural matrices determine to a certain extent the themes that preoccupy literature. In technologically developed countries such as the United States and England, for example, the marvelous often finds its most adequate expression in the novels of writers such as Ray Bradbury and Lord Dunsany,[16] who prefer to place their fiction in extraterrestrial worlds where faith in magic can still operate and the skepticism inherent in inductive reasoning has not yet become dominant.

As I began to translate my novel, *Maldito Amor*, the issues I have just mentioned came to my attention. The first serious obstacle I encountered was the title. "Maldito Amor" in Spanish is an idiomatic expression that is impossible to render accurately in English. It is a love that is halfway between doomed and damned, and thus participates in both without being either. The fact that the adjective "maldito," furthermore, is placed before the noun "amor," gives it an exclamative nature which is very present to Spanish speakers, in spite of the fact that the exclamation point is missing. "Maldito Amor" is something very different from "Amor Maldito," which would clearly have the connotation of "devilish love." The title of the novel in Spanish is, in this sense, almost a benign form of swearing, or of complaining about the treacherous nature of love. In addition to all this, the title is also the title of a very famous danza[17] written by Juan Morell Campos, Puerto Rico's most gifted composer in the nineteenth century, which describes in its verses the paradisiacal existence of the island's bourgeoisie at the time. As this complicated wordplay would have been totally lost in English, as well as the cultural reference to a musical composition which is only well known on the island, I decided to change the title altogether in my translation of the novel, substituting the much more specific "Sweet Diamond

---

16 *Ray Bradbury* American science fiction writer (1920–2012); *Lord Dunsany* Edward Plunkett, 18th Baron of Dunsany (1878–1957) was a prolific Anglo-Irish author best known for his fantasy writing.

17 *danza* Genre of ballroom dance music that was conceived in southern Puerto Rico.

Dust." The new title refers to the sugar produced by the De Lavalle family, but it also touches on the dangers of a sugar that, like diamond dust, poisons those who sweeten their lives with it.

The inability to reproduce Spanish wordplay as anything but a mere juggling of words not only made me change the title; it also soon made me begin to prune my own sentences mercilessly like overgrown vines, because, I found, the sap was not running through them as it should. How did I know this? What made me arrive at this conclusion? As I faced sentence after sentence of what I had written in Spanish hardly two years before (when I was writing the novel), I realized that, in translating it into English, I had acquired a different instinct in my approach to a theme. I felt almost like a hunting dog that is forced to smell out the same prey, but one that has drastically changed its spoor. My faith in the power of the image, for example, was now untenable, and facts had become much more important. The dance of language had now to have a direction, a specific line of action. The possibility of Utopia, and the description of a world in which the marvelously real sustained the very fabric of existence, was still my goal, but it had to be reached by a different road. The language of technology and capitalism, I said to myself, must above all assure a dividend, and this dividend cannot be limited to philosophic contemplations, or to a feast of the senses and of the ear. Thus, I delved into a series of books on the history and sociology of the sugarcane industry in Puerto Rico, which gave me the opportunity to widen the scope of the novel, adding information and situating its events in a much more precise environment.

Is translation of a literary text possible, given the enormous differences in cultural tradition in which language is embedded? I asked myself this, seeing that as I translated I was forced to substitute, cancel, and rewrite constantly, now pruning, now widening the original text. In the philosophy of language and in reference to translation in general (not necessarily of a literary text) two radically opposed points of view can be and have been asserted. One declares that the underlying structure of language is universal and common to everyone. "To translate," in the words of George Steiner, "is to descend beneath the exterior disparities of two languages in order to bring into vital play their analogous and ... common principles of being."[18] The other one holds that "universal deep structures are either fathomless to logical and psychological investigation or of an order so abstract, so generalized as to be well-nigh trivial." This extreme, monadistic[19] position asserts that real translation is impossible, as Steiner says,

15

---

18   *"is to descend ... being."*   For these and the following quotations, see Steiner's *After Babel*.

19   *monadistic*   Reference to the doctrine of monadism, advocated by the German philosopher Gottfried Wilhelm Leibniz (1646–1716), who claimed that the universe is made up of indivisible entities called monads.

and that what passes for translation is a convention of approximate analogies, "a roughcast similitude, just tolerable when the two relevant languages or cultures are cognate ..."

I lean rather more naturally to the second than to the first of these premises. Translating literature is a very different matter from translating everyday language, and I believe it could be evaluated on a changing spectrum. Poetry, where meaning can never be wholly separated from expressive form, is a mystery that can never be translated. It can only be transcribed, reproduced in a shape that will always be a sorry shadow of itself. That is why Robert Frost pronounced his famous dictum that "poetry is what gets lost in translation"[20] and Ortega y Gasset evolved his theory on the melancholy of translation, in his *Miseria y esplendor de la traducción*.[21] To one side of poetry one could place prose and poetic fiction, where symbolic expression may alternate with the language of analysis and communication. Here one could situate novels and prose poems that employ varying degrees of symbolic language and which are directed toward both an intuitive *and* an explanatory exposition of meaning. On the far side of the spectrum one could place literary texts of a historical, sociological, and political nature, such as the essays of Euclides da Cunha in Brazil, for example, and the work of Fernando Ortiz in Cuba or of Tomás Blanco[22] in Puerto Rico. These texts, as well as those of literary critics who have been able to found their analytic theories on a powerfully poetic expression (such as Roland Barthes[23]), are perhaps less difficult to translate, but even so the *lacunae*[24] that arise from the missing cultural connotations in these essays are usually of the greatest magnitude.

Translating one's own literary work is, in short, a complex, disturbing occupation. It can be diabolic and obsessive: it is one of the few instances when one can be dishonest and feel good about it, rather like having a second chance at redressing one's fatal mistakes in life and living a different way. The writer becomes her own critical conscience; her superego leads her (perhaps treacherously) to believe that she can not only better but surpass herself, or at

---

20 *"poetry ... translation"*   This quote has been attributed to Robert Frost (1874–1963), American poet and critic, though it does not exist in written form.

21 *Miseria ... traducción*   Spanish: The Misery and Splendor of Translation. Gasset's essay was published in 1937.

22 *Euclides da Cunha*   Brazilian journalist (1866–1909) and author of *Os Sertões* (*Rebellion in the Backlands*, 1902), a non-fiction account of military actions against a rebellious village in Brazil;   *Fernando Ortiz*   Cuban essayist and anthropologist (1881–1969) known for his study of Cuban culture;   *Tomás Blanco*   Puerto Rican writer and historian (1896–1975) whose writing concerns Puerto Rican culture.

23 *Roland Barthes*   French literary and cultural theorist and critic (1915–80).

24 *lacunae*   Gaps.

least surpass the writer she has been in the past. Popular lore has long equated translation with betrayal: "Traduttore-tradittore" goes the popular Italian saying. "La traduction est comme la femme, plus qu'elle est belle, elle n'est pas fidèle; plus qu'elle est fidèle, elle n'est pas belle"[25] goes the chauvinist French saying. But in translating one's own work it is only by betraying that one can better the original. There is, thus, a feeling of elation, of submerging oneself in sin, without having to pay the consequences. Instinct becomes the sole beacon. "The loyal translator will write what is correct," the devil whispers exultantly in one's ear, "but not necessarily what is right."

And yet translation, in spite of its considerable difficulties, is a necessary reality for me as a writer. As a Puerto Rican I have undergone exile as a way of life, and also as a style of life. Coming and going from south to north, from Spanish to English, without losing a sense of self can constitute an anguishing experience. It implies a constant recreation of divergent worlds, which often tend to appear greener on the other side. Many Puerto Ricans undergo this ordeal, although with different intensity, according to their economic situation in life. Those who come from a privileged class, who form a part of the more recent "brain drain"* of engineers, architects, and doctors who emigrate today to the States in search of a higher standard of living, can afford to keep memory clean and well-tended, visiting the site of the "Lares"[26] with relative assiduity. Those who come fleeing from poverty and hunger, such as the taxi drivers, elevator operators, or seasonal grape and lettuce pickers who began to emigrate to these shores by the thousands in the forties, are often forced to be merciless with memory, as they struggle to integrate with and become indistinguishable from the mainstream. It is for these people that translation becomes of fundamental importance. Obliged to adapt in order to survive, the children of these Puerto Rican parents often refuse to learn to speak Spanish, and they grow up having lost the ability to read the literature and the history of their island. This cultural suicide constitutes an immense loss, as they become unable to learn about their roots, having lost the language that is the main road to their culture. I believe it is the duty of the Puerto Rican writer, who has been privileged enough to learn both languages, to try to alleviate this situation, making an effort either to translate some of her own work or to contribute to the translation of the work of other Puerto Rican writers. The melancholy of the Puerto Rican soul may perhaps this way one day be assuaged, and its perpetual hunger for

---

25 *"Traduttore-tradittore"* Italian: The translator is the traitor; *"La traduction ... pas belle"* French: Translation is like a woman, the more beautiful she is, the less faithful; when she is faithful she is not beautiful.

26 *the "Lares"* In ancient Roman religion, Lares were deities that guarded specific locations, such as houses, roads, neighborhoods, or states. A statue of a Lares, for example, was located on the boundary that delineated the city of Rome.

a lost paradise be appeased. Memory, which so often erases the ache of the penury and destitution suffered on the island, after years of battling for survival in the drug-seared ghettos of Harlem and the Bronx, can, through translation, perhaps be reinstated to its true abode.

I would like now to talk a bit about the experience of being a woman writer from Latin America, and how I suspect being one has helped me to translate literary works. As a Latin American woman writer I feel a great responsibility in forming a part of, and perpetuating, a literary tradition that has only recently begun to flourish among us. I feel we must become aware that we belong to a community of countries that cannot afford to live at odds with each other; a community whose future, in fact, depends today on its ability to support and nurture itself, helping to solve each other's problems. A sense of belonging to a continental community, based on an identity that was first envisioned by Simón Bolívar,[27] must rise above nationalistic passions and prejudices. In this respect, Brazilian women writers have always been at the forefront, for they were the first to write not solely for the women of Brazil, but for all those Latin American women who, like the feminine protagonists of Clarice Lispector and Nélida Piñón[28] in stories such as "A Chicken" and "A Chocolate Cake," have suffered a stifling social repression.

20   As a woman writer who has lived both in Anglo America and Latin America I have had, like Ophelia drifting down the canal or the child that looks in the beveled mirror of her wardrobe, to be able to see left become right and right become left without feeling panic or losing my sense of direction. In other words, I have had to be able to let go of all shores, be both left-handed and right-handed, masculine and feminine, because my destiny was to live by the word. In fact, a woman writer (like a man writer), must live traveling constantly between two very different cultures (much more so than English and Spanish), two very different worlds which are often at each others' throats: the world of women and the world of men. In this respect, I have often asked myself whether translation of feminine into masculine is possible, or vice versa (here the perennial question of whether there is a feminine or a masculine writing crops up again). Is it possible to enter the mind of a man, to think, feel, dream like a man, being a woman writer? The idea seems preposterous at first, because deep down we feel that we cannot know anything but what we are, what we have experienced in our own flesh and bones. And yet the mind, and its exterior, audible expression, language or human speech, is mimetic* by

---

27   *Simón Bolívar*   South American political and military leader (1783–1830) who was instrumental in seeking independence from the Spanish Empire.

28   *Clarice Lispector*   Brazilian novelist (1920–77);   *Nélida Piñón*   Brazilian writer (b. 1937).

nature. Language, in Leibniz's opinion, for example, was not only the vehicle of thought but its determining medium. Being matterless, language (thought) can enter and leave its object at will, can actually become that object, creating it and destroying it as it deems necessary. In this sense the cabalistic* tradition speaks of a logos,[29] or a word that makes speech meaningful and is like a hidden spring that underlies all human communication and makes it possible. This concept of the word as having a divine origin confers upon it a creative power which may perhaps justify the writer's attempt to enter into modes of being (masculine, Chinese, extraterrestrial?) in which she has not participated in the course of her own human existence.

I like to believe that in my work I have confronted language not as a revelation of a divine meaning or of an unalterable scheme of things, but as a form of creation, or recreation of my world. If writing made it possible for me to authorize (become the author of) my own life, why may it not also permit me to enter into and thus "create" (translate?) the lives of other characters, men, women, and children? These are questions I ask myself often, which I may never be able to answer, but I believe it is important to try to do so.

(1976)

---

29 *logos*   Ancient Greek term meaning both "word" and "reason"; the concept of logos has played a significant role in the history of Western thought.

MICHEL FOUCAULT

THE PERVERSE IMPLANTATION[1]

Philosopher and historian Michel Foucault's work is primarily concerned with the way power creates knowledge and identity by shaping discourses—systems of language, practices, and cultural meanings. His engagement with these ideas has been influential across the humanities and social sciences. The History of Sexuality, *in which the following chapter appeared, became a foundational work in the development of queer theory, a branch of critical theory focused on the relationship between sexuality and culture. In the book's opening chapters, Foucault argues against what he calls "the repressive hypothesis": the widespread belief that between the seventeenth and mid-twentieth centuries western society repressed sexuality and its discussion. In fact, he suggests, this period saw a "proliferation of discourses" surrounding sexuality.*

A possible objection: it would be a mistake to see in this proliferation of discourses merely a quantitative phenomenon, something like a pure increase, as if what was said in them were immaterial, as if the fact of speaking about sex were of itself more important than the forms of imperatives that were imposed on it by speaking about it. For was this transformation of sex into discourse not governed by the endeavor to expel from reality the forms of sexuality that were not amenable to the strict economy of reproduction: to say no to unproductive activities, to banish casual pleasures, to reduce or exclude practices whose object was not procreation? Through the various discourses, legal sanctions against minor perversions were multiplied; sexual irregularity was annexed to mental illness; from childhood to old age, a norm of sexual development was defined and all the possible deviations were carefully described; pedagogical controls and medical treatments were organized; around the least fantasies, moralists, but especially doctors, brandished the whole emphatic vocabulary of abomination.* Were these anything more than means employed to absorb, for the benefit of a genitally centered sexuality, all the fruitless pleasures?* All this

---

1   *THE PERVERSE IMPLANTATION*   Translated by Robert Hurley, 1978.

garrulous attention which has us in a stew over sexuality, is it not motivated by one basic concern: to ensure population, to reproduce labor capacity, to perpetuate the form of social relations: in short, to constitute a sexuality that is economically useful and politically conservative?

I still do not know whether this is the ultimate objective. But this much is certain: reduction has not been the means employed for trying to achieve it. The nineteenth century and our own have been rather the age of multiplication: a dispersion of sexualities, a strengthening of their disparate forms, a multiple implantation of "perversions." Our epoch has initiated sexual heterogeneities.

Up to the end of the eighteenth century, three major explicit codes—apart from the customary regularities and constraints of opinion—governed sexual practices: canonical law, the Christian pastoral,[2] and civil law. They determined, each in its own way, the division between licit and illicit. They were all centered on matrimonial relations: the marital obligation, the ability to fulfill it, the manner in which one complied with it, the requirements and violences that accompanied it, the useless or unwarranted caresses for which it was a pretext, its fecundity or the way one went about making it sterile, the moments when one demanded it (dangerous periods of pregnancy or breast-feeding, forbidden times of Lent* or abstinence), its frequency or infrequency, and so on. It was this domain that was especially saturated with prescriptions. The sex of husband and wife was beset by rules and recommendations. The marriage relation was the most intense focus of constraints; it was spoken of more than anything else; more than any other relation, it was required to give a detailed accounting of itself. It was under constant surveillance: if it was found to be lacking, it had to come forward and plead its case before a witness. The "rest" remained a good deal more confused: one only has to think of the uncertain status of "sodomy,"[3] or the indifference regarding the sexuality of children.

Moreover, these different codes did not make a clear distinction between violations of the rules of marriage and deviations with respect to genitality.* Breaking the rules of marriage or seeking strange pleasures brought an equal measure of condemnation. On the list of grave sins, and separated only by their relative importance, there appeared debauchery (extramarital relations), adultery, rape, spiritual or carnal incest, but also sodomy, or the mutual "caress." As

---

2   *canonical law*   Law imposed by the Church (here, the Catholic Church);   *Christian pastoral*   Care for a congregation by a priest, pastor, or other member of a church; in Catholicism, this includes giving sacraments, providing spiritual counseling, and nursing the ill and dying.

3   *uncertain status of "sodomy"*   In the Middle Ages, for example, definitions of sodomy could incorporate not only anal sex (its present-day definition), but also any type of sex between men, bestiality, and any number of other acts deemed unnatural between men and women.

to the courts, they could condemn homosexuality as well as infidelity, marriage without parental consent, or bestiality. What was taken into account in the civil and religious jurisdictions alike was a general unlawfulness. Doubtless acts "contrary to nature" were stamped as especially abominable, but they were perceived simply as an extreme form of acts "against the law"; they were infringements of decrees which were just as sacred as those of marriage, and which had been established for governing the order of things and the plan of beings. Prohibitions bearing on sex were essentially of a juridical nature. The "nature" on which they were based was still a kind of law. For a long time hermaphrodites were criminals, or crime's offspring, since their anatomical disposition, their very being, confounded the law that distinguished the sexes and prescribed their union.

5   The discursive explosion of the eighteenth and nineteenth centuries caused this system centered on legitimate alliance to undergo two modifications. First, a centrifugal movement with respect to heterosexual monogamy.* Of course, the array of practices and pleasures continued to be referred to it as their internal standard; but it was spoken of less and less, or in any case with a growing moderation. Efforts to find out its secrets were abandoned; nothing further was demanded of it than to define itself from day to day. The legitimate couple, with its regular sexuality, had a right to more discretion. It tended to function as a norm, one that was stricter, perhaps, but quieter. On the other hand, what came under scrutiny was the sexuality of children, mad men and women, and criminals; the sensuality of those who did not like the opposite sex; reveries, obsessions, petty manias, or great transports of rage. It was time for all these figures, scarcely noticed in the past, to step forward and speak, to make the difficult confession of what they were. No doubt they were condemned all the same; but they were listened to; and if regular sexuality happened to be questioned once again, it was through a reflux movement, originating in these peripheral sexualities.

Whence the setting apart of the "unnatural" as a specific dimension in the field of sexuality. This kind of activity assumed an autonomy with regard to the other condemned forms such as adultery or rape (and the latter were condemned less and less): to marry a close relative or practice sodomy, to seduce a nun or engage in sadism, to deceive one's wife or violate cadavers, became things that were essentially different. The area covered by the Sixth Commandment[4] began to fragment. Similarly, in the civil order, the confused category of "debauchery," which for more than a century had been one of the most frequent reasons for administrative confinement, came apart. From the

---

4   *Sixth Commandment*   In Catholic and many other Christian interpretations of the Bible, the sixth commandment is "Thou shalt not commit adultery."

debris, there appeared on the one hand infractions against the legislation (or morality) pertaining to marriage and the family, and on the other, offenses against the regularity of a natural function (offenses which, it must be added, the law was apt to punish). Here we have a likely reason, among others, for the prestige of Don Juan,[5] which three centuries have not erased. Underneath the great violator of the rules of marriage—stealer of wives, seducer of virgins, the shame of families, and an insult to husbands and fathers—another person-age can be glimpsed: the individual driven, in spite of himself, by the somber madness of sex. Underneath the libertine, the pervert.* He deliberately breaks the law, but at the same time, something like a nature gone awry transports him far from all nature; his death is the moment when the supernatural return of the crime and its retribution thwarts the flight into counternature. There were two great systems conceived by the West for governing sex: the law of mar-riage and the order of desires—and the life of Don Juan overturned them both. We shall leave it to psychoanalysts to speculate whether he was homosexual, narcissistic, or impotent.

Although not without delay and equivocation, the natural laws of matri-mony and the immanent rules of sexuality began to be recorded on two separate registers. There emerged a world of perversion which partook of that of legal or moral infraction, yet was not simply a variety of the latter. An entire sub-race race was born, different—despite certain kinship ties—from the libertines of the past. From the end of the eighteenth century to our own, they circulated through the pores of society; they were always hounded, but not always by laws; were often locked up, but not always in prisons; were sick perhaps, but scandalous, dangerous victims, prey to a strange evil that also bore the name of vice and sometimes crime. They were children wise beyond their years, preco-cious little girls, ambiguous schoolboys, dubious servants and educators, cruel or maniacal husbands, solitary collectors, ramblers with bizarre impulses; they haunted the houses of correction, the penal colonies, the tribunals, and the asy-lums; they carried their infamy to the doctors and their sickness to the judges. This was the numberless family of perverts who were on friendly terms with delinquents and akin to madmen. In the course of the century they successively bore the stamp of "moral folly," "genital neurosis," "aberration of the genetic instinct," "degenerescence," or "physical imbalance."

What does the appearance of all these peripheral sexualities signify? Is the fact that they could appear in broad daylight a sign that the code had become more lax? Or does the fact that they were given so much attention testify to a stricter regime and to its concern to bring them under close supervision? In terms of repression, things are unclear. There was permissiveness, if one bears

---

5   *Don Juan*   Legendary character who seduced large numbers of women.

in mind that the severity of the codes relating to sexual offenses diminished considerably in the nineteenth century and that law itself often deferred to medicine. But an additional ruse of severity, if one thinks of all the agencies of control and all the mechanisms of surveillance that were put into operation by pedagogy or therapeutics. It may be the case that the intervention of the Church in conjugal sexuality and its rejection of "frauds" against procreation had lost much of their insistence over the previous two hundred years. But medicine made a forceful entry into the pleasures of the couple: it created an entire organic, functional, or mental pathology arising out of "incomplete" sexual practices; it carefully classified all forms of related pleasures; it incorporated them into the notions of "development" and instinctual "disturbances"; and it undertook to manage them.

Perhaps the point to consider is not the level of indulgence or the quantity of repression but the form of power that was exercised. When this whole thicket of disparate sexualities was labeled, as if to disentangle them from one another, was the object to exclude them from reality? It appears, in fact, that the function of the power exerted in this instance was not that of interdiction, and that it involved four operations quite different from simple prohibition.

10   1. Take the ancient prohibitions of consanguine marriages[6] (as numerous and complex as they were) or the condemnation of adultery, with its inevitable frequency of occurrence; or on the other hand, the recent controls through which, since the nineteenth century, the sexuality of children has been subordinated and their "solitary habits" interfered with. It is clear that we are not dealing with one and the same power mechanism. Not only because in the one case it is a question of law and penality, and in the other, medicine and regimentation; but also because the tactics employed is not the same. On the surface, what appears in both cases is an effort at elimination that was always destined to fail and always constrained to begin again. But the prohibition of "incests" attempted to reach its objective through an asymptotic decrease in the thing it condemned, whereas the control of infantile sexuality hoped to reach it through a simultaneous propagation of its own power and of the object on which it was brought to bear. It proceeded in accordance with a twofold increase extended indefinitely. Educators and doctors combatted children's onanism[7] like an epidemic that needed to be eradicated. What this actually entailed, throughout this whole secular campaign that mobilized the adult world around the sex of children, was using these tenuous pleasures as a prop, constituting them as secrets (that is, forcing them into hiding so as to make possible their discovery), tracing them back to their source, tracking

---

6   *consanguine marriages*   Marriages between relatives.

7   *onanism*   I.e., masturbation.

them from their origins to their effects, searching out everything that might cause them or simply enable them to exist. Wherever there was the chance they might appear, devices of surveillance were installed; traps were laid for compelling admissions; inexhaustible and corrective discourses were imposed; parents and teachers were alerted, and left with the suspicion that all children were guilty, and with the fear of being themselves at fault if their suspicions were not sufficiently strong; they were kept in readiness in the face of this recurrent danger; their conduct was prescribed and their pedagogy recodified; an entire medico-sexual regime took hold of the family milieu. The child's "vice" was not so much an enemy as a support; it may have been designated as the evil to be eliminated, but the extraordinary effort that went into the task that was bound to fail leads one to suspect that what was demanded of it was to persevere, to proliferate to the limits of the visible and the invisible, rather than to disappear for good. Always relying on this support, power advanced, multiplied its relays and its effects, while its target expanded, subdivided, and branched out, penetrating further into reality at the same pace. In appearance, we are dealing with a barrier system; but in fact, all around the child, indefinite lines of penetration were disposed.

2. This new persecution of the peripheral sexualities entailed an *incorporation* of perversions* and a new *specification of individuals*. As defined by the ancient civil or canonical codes, sodomy was a category of forbidden acts; their perpetrator was nothing more than the juridical subject of them. The nineteenth-century homosexual became a personage, a past, a case history, and a childhood, in addition to being a type of life, a life form, and a morphology,[8] with an indiscreet anatomy and possibly a mysterious physiology. Nothing that went into his total composition was unaffected by his sexuality. It was everywhere present in him: at the root of all his actions because it was their insidious and indefinitely active principle; written immodestly on his face and body because it was a secret that always gave itself away. It was consubstantial with him, less as a habitual sin than as a singular nature. We must not forget that the psychological, psychiatric, medical category of homosexuality was constituted from the moment it was characterized—Westphal's[9] famous article of 1870 on "contrary sexual sensations" can stand as its date of birth[10]—less by a type of sexual relations than by a certain quality of sexual sensibility, a certain way of

---

8   *morphology* Here, form according to which something (especially a biological organism) is classified.

9   *Westphal* Carl Friedrich Otto Westphal (1833–90), German psychiatrist. In the article referenced here, Westphal provides short case histories of several men and women who experience same-sex attraction.

10   Carl Westphal, *Archiv für Neurologie*, 1870. [author's note]

inverting the masculine and the feminine in oneself. Homosexuality appeared as one of the forms of sexuality when it was transposed from the practice of sodomy onto a kind of interior androgyny, a hermaphrodism of the soul. The sodomite had been a temporary aberration; the homosexual was now a species.

So too were all those minor perverts whom nineteenth-century psychiatrists entomologized* by giving them strange baptismal names: there were Krafft-Ebing's zoophiles and zooerasts, Rohleder's auto-monosexualists; and later, mixoscopophiles, gynecomasts, presbyophiles, sexoesthetic inverts, and dyspareunist women.[11] These fine names for heresies referred to a nature that was overlooked by the law, but not so neglectful of itself that it did not go on producing more species, even where there was no order to fit them into. The machinery of power that focused on this whole alien strain did not aim to suppress it, but rather to give it an analytical, visible, and permanent reality: it was implanted in bodies, slipped in beneath modes of conduct, made into a principle of classification and intelligibility, established as a *raison d'être** and a natural order of disorder. Not the exclusion of these thousand aberrant sexualities, but the specification, the regional solidification of each one of them. The strategy behind this dissemination was to strew reality with them and incorporate them into the individual.

3. More than the old taboos, this form of power demanded constant, attentive, and curious presences for its exercise; it presupposed proximities; it proceeded through examination and insistent observation; it required an exchange of discourses, through questions that extorted admissions, and confidences that went beyond the questions that were asked. It implied a physical proximity and an interplay of intense sensations. The medicalization of the sexually peculiar was both the effect and the instrument of this. Imbedded in bodies, becoming deeply characteristic of individuals, the oddities of sex relied on a technology of health and pathology. And conversely, since sexuality was a medical and medicalizable object, one had to try and detect it—as a lesion, a dysfunction, or a symptom—in the depths of the organism, or on the surface of the skin, or

---

11 *Krafft-Ebing* Author of *Psychopathia Sexualis* (1886), a reference book outlining a wide range of sexual behaviors he classifies as perversities; *zoophiles* People who experience sexual pleasure from petting animals; *zooerasts* People who have or desire to have sex with animals; *Rohleder* Hermann Rohleder, author of *Masturbation: A Monograph for Physicians, Educators and Educated Parents* (1899); *auto-monosexualists* People who only experience sexual satisfaction from masturbation; *mixoscopophiles* People who experience sexual satisfaction from watching others have sex; *gynecomasts* People who experience excessive attraction to women; *presbyophiles* People who are attracted to elderly men; *sexoesthetic inverts* People who dress and act like members of the opposite sex; *dyspareunist women* Women who experience pain or insufficient pleasure during sex.

among all the signs of behavior. The power which thus took charge of sexuality set about contacting bodies, caressing them with its eyes, intensifying areas, electrifying surfaces, dramatizing troubled moments. It wrapped the sexual body in its embrace. There was undoubtedly an increase in effectiveness and an extension of the domain controlled; but also a sensualization of power and a gain of pleasure. This produced a twofold effect: an impetus was given to power through its very exercise; an emotion rewarded the overseeing control and carried it further; the intensity of the confession renewed the questioner's curiosity; the pleasure discovered fed back to the power that encircled it. But so many pressing questions singularized the pleasures felt by the one who had to reply. They were fixed by a gaze, isolated and animated by the attention they received. Power operated as a mechanism of attraction; it drew out those peculiarities over which it kept watch. Pleasure spread to the power that harried it; power anchored the pleasure it uncovered.

The medical examination, the psychiatric investigation, the pedagogical report, and family controls may have the over-all and apparent objective of saying no to all wayward or unproductive sexualities, but the fact is that they function as mechanisms with a double impetus: pleasure and power. The pleasure that comes of exercising a power that questions, monitors, watches, spies, searches out, palpates, brings to light; and on the other hand, the pleasure that kindles at having to evade this power, flee from it, fool it, or travesty it. The power that lets itself be invaded by the pleasure it is pursuing; and opposite it, power asserting itself in the pleasure of showing off, scandalizing, or resisting. Capture and seduction, confrontation and mutual reinforcement: parents and children, adults and adolescents, educator and students, doctors and patients, the psychiatrist with his hysteric and his perverts, all have played this game continually since the nineteenth century. These attractions, these evasions, these circular incitements have traced around bodies and sexes, not boundaries not to be crossed, but *perpetual spirals of power and pleasure*.

4. Whence those *devices of sexual saturation* so characteristic of the space and the social rituals of the nineteenth century. People often say that modern society has attempted to reduce sexuality to the couple—the heterosexual and, insofar as possible, legitimate couple. There are equal grounds for saying that it has, if not created, at least outfitted and made to proliferate, groups with multiple elements and a circulating sexuality: a distribution of points of power, hierarchized and placed opposite to one another; "pursued" pleasures, that is, both sought after and searched out; compartmental sexualities that are tolerated or encouraged; proximities that serve as surveillance procedures, and function as mechanisms of intensification; contacts that operate as inductors. This is the way things worked in the case of the family, or rather the household, with parents, children, and in some instances, servants. Was the nineteenth-century

15

family really a monogamic[12] and conjugal cell? Perhaps to a certain extent. But it was also a network of pleasures and powers linked together at multiple points and according to transformable relationships. The separation of grown-ups and children, the polarity established between the parents' bedroom and that of the children (it became routine in the course of the century when working-class housing construction was undertaken), the relative segregation of boys and girls, the strict instructions as to the care of nursing infants (maternal breast-feeding, hygiene), the attention focused on infantile sexuality, the supposed dangers of masturbation, the importance attached to puberty, the methods of surveillance suggested to parents, the exhortations, secrets, and fears, the presence—both valued and feared—of servants: all this made the family, even when brought down to its smallest dimensions, a complicated network, saturated with multiple, fragmentary, and mobile sexualities. To reduce them to the conjugal relationship, and then to project the latter, in the form of a forbidden desire, onto the children, cannot account for this apparatus which, in relation to these sexualities, was less a principle of inhibition than an inciting and multiplying mechanism. Educational or psychiatric institutions, with their large populations, their hierarchies, their spatial arrangements, their surveillance systems, constituted, alongside the family, another way of distributing the interplay of powers and pleasures; but they too delineated areas of extreme sexual saturation, with privileged spaces or rituals such as the classroom, the dormitory, the visit, and the consultation. The forms of a nonconjugal, nonmonogamous sexuality were drawn there and established.

Nineteenth-century "bourgeois" society—and it is doubtless still with us—was a society of blatant and fragmented perversion. And this was not by way of hypocrisy, for nothing was more manifest and more prolix, or more manifestly taken over by discourses and institutions. Not because, having tried to erect too rigid or too general a barrier against sexuality, society succeeded only in giving rise to a whole perverse outbreak and a long pathology of the sexual instinct. At issue, rather, is the type of power it brought to bear on the body and on sex. In point of fact, this power had neither the form of the law, nor the effects of the taboo. On the contrary, it acted by multiplication of singular sexualities. It did not set boundaries for sexuality; it extended the various forms of sexuality, pursuing them according to lines of indefinite penetration. It did not exclude sexuality, but included it in the body as a mode of specification of individuals. It did not seek to avoid it; it attracted its varieties by means of spirals in which pleasure and power reinforced one another. It did not set up a barrier; it provided places of maximum saturation. It produced and determined the sexual mosaic. Modern society is perverse, not in spite of its

---

12 *monogamic* Monogamous.

puritanism or as if from a backlash provoked by its hypocrisy; it is in actual fact, and directly, perverse.

In actual fact. The manifold sexualities—those which appear with the different ages (sexualities of the infant or the child), those which become fixated on particular tastes or practices (the sexuality of the invert, the gerontophile,[13] the fetishist), those which, in a diffuse manner, invest relationships (the sexuality of doctor and patient, teacher and student, psychiatrist and mental patient), those which haunt spaces (the sexuality of the home, the school, the prison)—all form the correlate[14] of exact procedures of power. We must not imagine that all these things that were formerly tolerated attracted notice and received a pejorative designation when the time came to give a regulative role to the one type of sexuality that was capable of reproducing labor power and the form of the family. These polymorphous[15] conducts were actually extracted from people's bodies and from their pleasures; or rather, they were solidified in them; they were drawn out, revealed, isolated, intensified, incorporated, by multifarious power devices. The growth of perversions is not a moralizing theme that obsessed the scrupulous minds of the Victorians. It is the real product of the encroachment of a type of power on bodies and their pleasures. It is possible that the West has not been capable of inventing any new pleasures, and it has doubtless not discovered any original vices. But it has defined new rules for the game of powers and pleasures. The frozen countenance[16] of the perversions is a fixture of this game.

Directly. This implantation of multiple perversions is not a mockery of sexuality taking revenge on a power that has thrust on it an excessively repressive law. Neither are we dealing with paradoxical forms of pleasure that turn back on power and invest it in the form of a "pleasure to be endured." The implantation of perversions is an instrument-effect:[17] it is through the isolation, intensification, and consolidation of peripheral sexualities that the relations of power to sex and pleasure branched out and multiplied, measured the body, and penetrated modes of conduct. And accompanying this encroachment of powers, scattered sexualities rigidified, became stuck to an age, a place, a type of practice. A proliferation of sexualities through the extension of power; an optimization of the power to which each of these local sexualities gave a surface

---

13 *invert* Person of same-sex sexual orientation; *gerontophile* Person who is primarily attracted to elderly people.

14 *correlate* Related elements.

15 *polymorphous* Of many forms.

16 *countenance* Appearance.

17 *instrument-effect* Literally, in scientific experiments, a change in measurements caused by a change in the instruments used for measuring.

of intervention: this concatenation,* particularly since the nineteenth century, has been ensured and relayed by the countless economic interests which, with the help of medicine, psychiatry, prostitution, and pornography, have tapped into both this analytical multiplication of pleasure and this optimization of the power that controls it. Pleasure and power do not cancel or turn back against one another; they seek out, overlap, and reinforce one another. They are linked together by complex mechanisms and devices of excitation and incitement.

We must therefore abandon the hypothesis that modern industrial societies ushered in an age of increased sexual repression. We have not only witnessed a visible explosion of unorthodox sexualities; but—and this is the important point—a deployment quite different from the law, even if it is locally dependent on procedures of prohibition, has ensured, through a network of interconnecting mechanisms, the proliferation of specific pleasures and the multiplication of disparate sexualities. It is said that no society has been more prudish; never have the agencies of power taken such care to feign ignorance of the thing they prohibited, as if they were determined to have nothing to do with it. But it is the opposite that has become apparent, at least after a general review of the facts: never have there existed more centers of power; never more attention manifested and verbalized; never more circular contacts and linkages; never more sites where the intensity of pleasures and the persistency of power catch hold, only to spread elsewhere.

(1976)

PETER SINGER

from ANIMAL LIBERATION

Now long established as one of the world's most prominent philosophers, Peter Singer was a 26-year old lecturer in 1973 when The New York Review of Books *published his long review article discussing an essay collection called* Animals, Men and Morals— *and discussing more generally the ways in which humans treat other animals. Singer's review article was entitled "Animal Liberation"; the article was the germ of Singer's 1975 book* Animal Liberation *(excerpted here), which may well have done more to change human behavior than any other book of the past fifty years.*

*S*peciesism—the word is not an attractive one, but I can think of no better term—is a prejudice or attitude of bias toward the interests of members of one's own species and against those of members of other species. It should be obvious that the fundamental objections to racism and sexism made by Thomas Jefferson and Sojourner Truth* apply equally to speciesism. If possessing a higher degree of intelligence does not entitle one human to use another for his own ends, how can it entitle humans to exploit nonhumans for the same purpose?

Many philosophers and other writers have proposed the principle of equal consideration of interests, in some form or other, as a basic moral principle; but not many of them have recognized that this principle applies to members of other species as well as to our own. Jeremy Bentham was one of the few who did realize this. In a forward-looking passage written at a time when black slaves had been freed by the French but in the British dominions were still being treated in the way we now treat animals, Bentham wrote:

> The day *may* come when the rest of the animal creation may acquire those rights which never could have been withholden from them but by the hand of tyranny. The French have already discovered that the blackness of the skin is no reason why a human being should be abandoned without redress to the caprice of a tormentor. It may one day come to be recognized that the number of the legs, the villosity of the

269

skin, or the termination of the *os sacrum* are reasons equally insufficient for abandoning a sensitive being to the same fate. What else is it that should trace the insuperable line? Is it the faculty of reason, or perhaps the faculty of discourse? But a full-grown horse or dog is beyond comparison a more rational, as well as a more conversable animal, than an infant of a day or a week or even a month, old. But suppose they were otherwise, what would it avail? The question is not, Can they *reason*? nor Can they *talk*? but, *Can they suffer*?

In this passage Bentham points to the capacity for suffering as the vital characteristic that gives a being the right to equal consideration. The capacity for suffering—or more strictly, for suffering and/or enjoyment or happiness—is not just another characteristic like the capacity for language or higher mathematics. Bentham is not saying that those who try to mark "the insuperable line" that determines whether the interests of a being should be considered happen to have chosen the wrong characteristic. By saying that we must consider the interests of all beings with the capacity for suffering or enjoyment Bentham does not arbitrarily exclude from consideration any interests at all—as those who draw the line with reference to the possession of reason or language do. The capacity for suffering and enjoyment is a *prerequisite for having interests at all*, a condition that must be satisfied before we can speak of interests in a meaningful way. It would be nonsense to say that it was not in the interests of a stone to be kicked along the road by a schoolboy. A stone does not have interests because it cannot suffer. Nothing that we can do to it could possibly make any difference to its welfare. A mouse, on the other hand, does have an interest in not being kicked along the road, because it will suffer if it is.

If a being suffers there can be no moral justification for refusing to take that suffering into consideration. No matter what the nature of the being, the principle of equality requires that its suffering be counted equally with the like suffering—in so far as rough comparisons can be made—of any other being. If a being is not capable of suffering, or of experiencing enjoyment or happiness, there is nothing to be taken into account. So the limit of sentience (using the term as a convenient if not strictly accurate shorthand for the capacity to suffer and/or experience enjoyment) is the only defensible boundary of concern for the interests of others. To mark this boundary by some other characteristic like intelligence or rationality would be to mark it in an arbitrary manner. Why not choose some other characteristic, like skin color?

The racist violates the principle of equality by giving greater weight to the interests of members of his own race when there is a clash between their interests and the interests of those of another race. The sexist violates the principle of equality by favoring the interests of his own sex. Similarly the speciesist allows the interests of his own species to override the greater interests of members of other species. The pattern is identical in each case.

Most human beings are speciesists. Ordinary human beings—not a few exceptionally cruel or heartless humans, but the overwhelming majority of humans—take an active part in, acquiesce in, and allow their taxes to pay for practices that require the sacrifice of the most important interests of members of other species in order to promote the most trivial interests of our own species....

SPECIESISM IN PRACTICE

For the great majority of human beings, especially in urban, industrialized societies, the most direct form of contact with members of other species is at mealtimes: We eat them. In doing so we treat them purely as means to our ends. We regard their life and well-being as subordinate to our taste for a particular kind of dish. I say "taste" deliberately—this is purely a matter of pleasing our palate. There can be no defense of eating flesh in terms of satisfying nutritional needs, since it has been established beyond doubt that we could satisfy our need for protein and other essential nutrients far more efficiently with a diet that replaced animal flesh by soy beans, or products derived from soy beans, and other high protein vegetable products.

It is not merely the act of killing that indicates what we are ready to do to other species in order to gratify our tastes. The suffering we inflict on the animals while they are alive is perhaps an even clearer indication of our speciesism than the fact that we are prepared to kill them. In order to have meat on the table at a price that people can afford, our society tolerates methods of meat production that confine sentient animals in cramped, unsuitable conditions for the entire duration of their lives. Animals are treated like machines that convert fodder into flesh, and any innovation that results in a higher "conversion ratio" is liable to be adopted. As one authority on the subject has said, "cruelty is acknowledged only when profitability ceases." So hens are crowded four or five to a cage with a floor area of twenty inches by eighteen inches, or around the size of a single page of the *New York Times*. The cages have wire floors, since this reduces cleaning costs, though wire is unsuitable for the hens' feet; the floors slope, since this makes the eggs roll down for easy collection, although this makes it difficult for the hens to rest comfortably. In these conditions all the birds' natural instincts are thwarted: They cannot stretch their wings fully, walk freely, dust-bathe, scratch the ground, or build a nest. Although they have never known other conditions, observers have noticed that the birds vainly try to perform these actions. Frustrated at their inability to do so, they often develop what farmers call "vices," and peck each other to death. To prevent this, the beaks of young birds are often cut off.

This kind of treatment is not limited to poultry. Pigs are now also being reared in cages inside sheds. These animals are comparable to dogs in intelligence, and need a varied, stimulating environment if they are not to suffer from stress and boredom. Anyone who kept a dog in the way in which pigs are frequently kept would be liable to prosecution, in England at least, but because our interest in exploiting pigs is greater than our interest in exploiting dogs, we object to cruelty to dogs while consuming the produce of cruelty to pigs. Of the other animals, the condition of veal calves is perhaps worst of all, since these animals are so closely confined that they cannot even turn around or get up and lie down freely. In this way they do not develop unpalatable muscle. They are also made anemic and kept short of roughage, to keep their flesh pale, since white veal fetches a higher price; as a result they develop a craving for iron and roughage, and have been observed to gnaw wood off the sides of their stalls, and lick greedily at any rusty hinge that is within reach.

Since, as I have said, none of these practices cater to anything more than our pleasures of taste, our practice of rearing and killing other animals in order to eat them is a clear instance of the sacrifice of the most important interests of other beings in order to satisfy trivial interests of our own. To avoid speciesism we must stop this practice, and each of us has a moral obligation to cease supporting the practice. Our custom is all the support that the meat industry needs. The decision to cease giving it that support may be difficult, but it is no more difficult than it would have been for a white Southerner to go against the traditions of his society and free his slaves; if we do not change our dietary habits, how can we censure those slaveholders who would not change their own way of living?

10   The same form of discrimination may be observed in the widespread practice of experimenting on other species in order to see if certain substances are safe for human beings, or to test some psychological theory about the effect of severe punishment on learning, or to try out various new compounds just in case something turns up. People sometimes think that all this experimentation is for vital medical purposes, and so will reduce suffering overall. This comfortable belief is very wide of the mark. Drug companies test new shampoos and cosmetics that they are intending to put on the market by dropping them into the eyes of rabbits, held open by metal clips, in order to observe what damage results. Food additives, like artificial colorings and preservatives, are tested by what is known as the "LD50"—a test designed to find the level of consumption at which 50 per cent of a group of animals will die. In the process, nearly all of the animals are made very sick before some finally die, and others pull through. If the substance is relatively harmless, as it often is, huge doses have to be

forcefed to the animals, until in some cases sheer volume or concentration of the substance causes death.

Much of this pointless cruelty goes on in the universities. In many areas of science, nonhuman animals are regarded as an item of laboratory equipment, to be used and expended as desired. In psychology laboratories experimenters devise endless variations and repetitions of experiments that were of little value in the first place. To quote just one example, from the experimenter's own account in a psychology journal: At the University of Pennsylvania, Perrin S. Cohen hung six dogs in hammocks with electrodes taped to their hind feet. Electric shock of varying intensity was then administered through the electrodes. If the dog learned to press its head against a panel on the left, the shock was turned off, but otherwise it remained on indefinitely. Three of the dogs, however, were required to wait periods varying from 2 to 7 seconds while being shocked before making the response that turned off the current. If they failed to wait, they received further shocks. Each dog was given from 26 to 46 "sessions" in the hammock, each session consisting of 80 "trials" or shocks, administered at intervals of one minute. The experimenter reported that the dogs, who were unable to move in the hammock, barked or bobbed their heads when the current was applied. The reported findings of the experiment were that there was a delay in the dogs' responses that increased proportionately to the time the dogs were required to endure the shock, but a gradual increase in the intensity of the shock had no systematic effect in the timing of the response. The experiment was funded by the National Institutes of Health, and the United States Public Health Service.

In this example, and countless cases like it, the possible benefits to mankind are either nonexistent or fantastically remote, while the certain losses to members of other species are very real.

(1975)

LESLIE MARMON SILKO

LANGUAGE AND LITERATURE FROM A PUEBLO INDIAN PERSPECTIVE

Leslie Marmon Silko—a writer of fiction and poetry as well as non-fiction—draws in much of her writing on her experience growing up on the Laguna Pueblo Reservation in New Mexico; her essays examine colonialism, women's issues, and racism in the United States from a variety of angles. This essay, which began as a speech and first appeared in English Literature: Opening Up the Canon *(1979), is organized to mirror the patterns and construction of Pueblo stories.*

Where I come from, the words most highly valued are those spoken from the heart, unpremeditated and unrehearsed. Among the Pueblo people,* a written speech or statement is highly suspect because the true feelings of the speaker remain hidden as she reads words that are detached from the occasion and the audience. I have intentionally not written a formal paper because I want you to hear and to experience English in a structure that follows patterns from the oral tradition. For those of you accustomed to being taken from point A to point B to point C, this presentation may be somewhat difficult to follow. Pueblo expression resembles something like a spider's web with many little threads radiating from the center, crisscrossing each other. As with the web, the structure emerges as it is made and you must simply listen and trust, as the Pueblo people do, that meaning will be made.

My task is a formidable one: I ask you to set aside a number of basic approaches that you have been using, and probably will continue to use, and instead, to approach language from the Pueblo perspective, one that embraces the whole of creation and the whole of history and time.

What changes would Pueblo writers make to English as a language for literature? I have some examples of stories in English that I will use to address this question. At the same time, I would like to explain the importance of storytelling and how it relates to a Pueblo theory of language.

So I will begin, appropriately enough, with the Pueblo Creation story, an all-inclusive story of how life began. In this story, Tséitsínako, Thought

Woman, by thinking of her sisters, and together with her sisters, thought of everything that is. In this way, the world was created. Everything in this world was a part of the original creation; the people at home understood that far away there were other human beings, also a part of this world. The Creation story even includes a prophecy, which describes the origin of European and African peoples and also refers to Asians.

This story, I think, suggests something about why the Pueblo people are   5
more concerned with story and communication and less concerned with a particular language. There are at least six, possibly seven, distinct languages among the twenty pueblos[1] of the southwestern United States, for example, Zuñi and Hopi. And from mesa[2] to mesa there are subtle differences in language. But the particular language spoken isn't as important as what a speaker is trying to say, and this emphasis on the story itself stems, I believe, from a view of narrative particular to the Pueblo and other Native American peoples—that is, that language is story.

I will try to clarify this statement. At Laguna Pueblo,[3] for example, many individual words have their own stories. So when one is telling a story, and one is using words to tell the story, each word that one is speaking has a story of its own, too. Often the speakers or tellers will go into these word-stories, creating an elaborate structure of stories within stories. This structure, which becomes very apparent in the actual telling of a story, informs contemporary Pueblo writing and storytelling as well as the traditional narratives. This perspective on narrative—of story within story, the idea that one story is only the beginning of many stories, and the sense that stories never truly end—represents an important contribution of Native American cultures to the English language.

Many people think of storytelling as something that is done at bedtime, that it is something done for small children. But when I use the term *storytelling*, I'm talking about something much bigger than that. I'm talking about something that comes out of an experience and an understanding of that original view of creation—that we are all part of a whole; we do not differentiate or fragment stories and experiences. In the beginning, Tséitsínako, Thought Woman, thought of all things, and all of these things are held together as one holds many things together in a single thought.

So in the telling (and you will hear a few of the dimensions of this telling) first of all, as mentioned earlier, the storytelling always includes the audience, the listeners. In fact, a great deal of the story is believed to be inside the listener;

---

1   *pueblos*   Towns of the Pueblo people.
2   *mesa*   Hill with a flat top.
3   *Laguna Pueblo*   Territory of the Laguna Pueblo people, a Puebloan tribe in west-central New Mexico.

the storyteller's role is to draw the story out of the listeners. The storytelling continues from generation to generation.

Basically, the origin story constructs our identity—within this story, we know who we are. We are the Lagunas. This is where we come from. We came this way. We came by this place. And so from the time we are very young, we hear these stories, so that when we go out into the world, when one asks who we are, or where we are from, we immediately know: we are the people who came from the north. We are the people of these stories.

10   In the Creation story, Antelope says that he will help knock a hole in the earth so that the people can come up, out into the next world. Antelope tries and tries; he uses his hooves, but is unable to break through. It is then that Badger says, "Let me help you." And Badger very patiently uses his claws and digs a way through, bringing the people into the world. When the Badger clan people think of themselves, or when the Antelope people think of themselves, it is as people who are of this story, and this is our place, and we fit into the very beginning when the people first came, before we began our journey south.

Within the clans there are stories that identify the clan. One moves, then, from the idea of one's identity as a tribal person into clan identity, then to one's identity as a member of an extended family. And it is the notion of "extended family" that has produced a kind of story that some distinguish from other Pueblo stories, though Pueblo people do not. Anthropologists and ethnologists have, for a long time, differentiated the types of stories the Pueblos tell. They tended to elevate the old sacred, and traditional stories and to brush aside family stories, the family's account of itself. But in Pueblo culture, these family stories are given equal recognition. There is no definite, present pattern for the way one will hear the stories of one's own family, but it is a very critical part of one's childhood, and the storytelling continues throughout one's life. One will hear stories of importance to the family—sometimes wonderful stories—stories about the time a maternal uncle got the biggest deer that was ever seen and brought it back from the mountains. And so an individual's identity will extend from the identity constructed around the family—"I am from the family of my uncle who brought in this wonderful deer and it was a wonderful hunt."

Family accounts include negative stories, too; perhaps an uncle did something unacceptable. It is very important that one keep track of all these stories—both positive and not so positive—about one's own family and other families. Because even when there is no way around it—old Uncle Pete *did* do a terrible thing—by knowing the stories that originate in other families, one is able to deal with terrible sorts of things that might happen within one's own family. If a member of the family does something that cannot be excused, one always knows stories about similar inexcusable things done by a member of another family. But this knowledge is not communicated for malicious reasons.* It is very important to understand this. Keeping track of all the stories within the community gives us all a certain distance, a useful perspective, that brings incidents down to a level we can deal with. If others have done it before, it cannot be so terrible. If others have endured, so can we.

The stories are always bringing us together, keeping this whole together, keeping this family together, keeping this clan together. "Don't go away, don't isolate yourself, but come here, because we have all had these kinds of experiences." And so there is this constant pulling together to resist the tendency to run or hide or separate oneself during a traumatic emotional experience. This separation not only endangers the group but the individual as well—one does not recover by oneself.

Because storytelling lies at the heart of Pueblo culture, it is absurd to attempt to fix the stories in time. "When did they tell the stories?" or "What time of day does the storytelling take place?"—these questions are nonsensical from a Pueblo perspective, because our storytelling goes on constantly: as some old grandmother puts on the shoes of a child and tells her the story of a little girl who didn't wear her shoes, for instance, or someone comes into the house for coffee to talk with a teenage boy who has just been in a lot of trouble, to reassure him that someone else's son has been in that kind of trouble, too. Storytelling is an ongoing process, working on many different levels.

Here's one story that is often told at a time of individual crisis (and I want to remind you that we make no distinctions between types of story—historical, sacred, plain gossip—because these distinctions are not useful when discussing the Pueblo *experience* of language). There was a young man who, when he came back from the war in Vietnam, had saved up his army pay and bought a beautiful red Volkswagen. He was very proud of it. One night he drove up to a place called the King's Bar right across the reservation line. The bar is notorious for many reasons, particularly for the deep *arroyo*[4] located behind it. The young man ran in to pick up a cold six-pack, but he forgot to put on his emergency brake. And his little red Volkswagen rolled back into the *arroyo* and was all smashed up. He felt very bad about it, but within a few days everybody had come to him with stories about other people who had lost cars and family members to that *arroyo*, for instance, George Day's station wagon, with his mother-in-law and kids inside. So everybody was saying, "Well, at least your mother-in-law and kids weren't in the car when it rolled in," and one can't argue with that kind of story. The story of the young man and his smashed-up Volkswagen was now joined with all the other stories of cars that fell into that *arroyo*.

Now I want to tell you a very beautiful little story. It is a very old story that is sometimes told to people who suffer great family or personal loss. This

15

---

4   *arroyo*   Spanish: dry creek bed with steep sides.

story was told by my Aunt Susie. She is one of the first generation of people at Laguna who began experimenting with English—who began working to make English speak for us—that is, to speak from the heart. (I come from a family intent on getting the stories told.)

As you read the story, I think you will hear that. And here and there, I think, you will also hear the influence of the Indian school[5] at Carlisle, Pennsylvania, where my Aunt Susie was sent (like being sent to prison) for six years.

This scene is set partly in Acoma,[6] partly in Laguna. Waithea was a little girl living in Acoma and one day she said, "Mother, I would like to have some *yashtoah* to eat." *Yashtoah* is the hardened crust of corn mush that curls up. *Yashtoah* literally means "curled up." She said, "I would like to have some *yashtoah*," and her mother said, "My dear little girl, I can't make you any *yashtoah* because we haven't any wood, but if you will go down off the mesa, down below, and pick up some pieces of wood and bring them home, I will make you some *yashtoah*." So Waithea was glad and ran down the precipitous* cliff of Acoma mesa. Down below, just as her mother had told her, there were pieces of wood, some curled, some crooked in shape, that she was to pick up and take home. She found just such wood as these.

She brought them home in a little wicker basket. First she called to her mother as she got home, "*Nayah, deeni*! Mother, upstairs!" The Pueblo people always called "upstairs" because long ago their homes were two, three stories, and they entered from the top. She said, "*Deeni*! UPSTAIRS!" and her mother came. The little girl said, "I have brought the wood you wanted me to bring." And she opened her little wicker basket to lay out the pieces of wood but here they were snakes. They were snakes instead of crooked sticks of wood. And her mother said, "Oh my dear child, you have brought snakes instead!" She said, "Go take them back and put them back just where you got them." And the little girl ran down the mesa again, down below to the flats. And she put those snakes back just where she got them. They were snakes instead and she was very hurt about this and so she said, "I'm not going home. I'm going to *Kawaik*, the beautiful lake place, *Kawaik*, and drown myself in the lake, *byn'yah'nah* [the "west lake"]. I will go there and drown myself."

20   So she started off, and as she passed the Enchanted Mesa near Acoma she met an old man, very aged, and he saw her running, and he said, "My dear child, where are you going?" "I'm going to Kawaik and jump into the lake there." "Why?" "Well, because," she said, "my mother didn't want to make any

---

5   *Indian school*   Residential school where Native American children were forced to adopt Euro-American culture. Between 1879 and 1918 over 12,000 children attended the Carlisle Indian Industrial School, the first federally funded boarding school of its kind in the US.

6   *Acoma*   Territory of the Pueblo tribe west of Albuquerque, New Mexico.

yashtoah for me." The old man said, "Oh, no! You must not go my child. Come with me and I will take you home." He tried to catch her, but she was very light and skipped along. And every time he would try to grab her she would skip faster away from him.

The old man was coming home with some wood strapped to his back and tied with yucca.* He just let the strap go and let the wood drop. He went as fast as he could up the cliff to the little girl's home. When he got to the place where she lived, he called to her mother. "*Deeni*!"

"Come on up!" And he said, "I can't. I just came to bring you a message. Your little daughter is running away. She is going to *Kawaik* to drown herself in the lake there." "Oh my dear little girl!" the mother said. So she busied herself with making the *yashtoah* her little girl liked so much. Corn mush curled at the top. (She must have found enough wood to boil the cornmeal and make the *yashtoah*.)

While the mush was cooking off, she got the little girl's clothing, her *manta* dress[7] and buckskin moccasins and all her other garments, and put them in a bundle—probably a yucca bag. And she started down as fast as she could on the east side of Acoma. (There used to be a trail there, you know. It's gone now, but it was accessible in those days.) She saw her daughter way at a distance and she kept calling: "Stsamaku! My daughter! Come back! I've got your *yashtoah* for you." But the little girl would not turn. She kept on ahead and she cried: "My mother, my mother, she didn't want me to have any *yashtoah*. So now I'm going to *Kawaik* and drown myself." Her mother heard her cry and said, "My little daughter, come back here!" "No," and she kept a distance away from her. And they came nearer and nearer to the lake. And she could see her daughter now, very plain. "Come back, my daughter! I have your *yashtoah*." But no, she kept on, and finally she reached the lake and she stood on the edge.

She had tied a little feather in her hair, which is traditional (in death they tie this feather on the head). She carried a feather, the little girl did, and she tied it in her hair with a piece of string, right on top of her head she put the feather. Just as her mother was about to reach her, she jumped into the lake. The little feather was whirling around and around in the depths below. Of course the mother was very sad. She went, grieved, back to Acoma and climbed her mesa home. She stood on the edge of the mesa and scattered her daughter's clothing, the little moccasins, the *yashtoah*. She scattered them to the east, to the west, to the north, to the south. And the pieces of clothing and the moccasins and *yashtoah*, all turned into butterflies. And today they say that Acoma has more

---

7   *manta dress*   Dress made of a rectangular piece of cloth wrapped and secured at the waist with a sash.

beautiful butterflies: red ones, white ones, blue ones, yellow ones. They came from this little girl's clothing.

25   Now this is a story anthropologists would consider very old. The version I have given you is just as Aunt Susie tells it. You can occasionally hear some English she picked up at Carlisle—words like "precipitous." You will also notice that there is a great deal of repetition, and a little reminder about *yashtoah*, and how it is made. There is a remark about the cliff trail at Acoma—that it was once there, but is there no longer. This story may be told at a time of sadness or loss, but within this story many other elements are brought together. Things are not separated out and categorized; all things are brought together. So that the reminder about the *yashtoah* is valuable information that is repeated—a recipe, if you will. The information about the old trail at Acoma reveals that stories are, in a sense, maps, since even to this day there is little information or material about trails that is passed around with writing. In the structure of this story the repetitions are, of course, designed to help you remember. It is repeated again and again, and then it moves on.

The next story I would like to tell is by Simon Ortiz, from Acoma Pueblo. He is a wonderful poet who also works in narrative. One of the things I find very interesting in this short story is that if you listen very closely, you begin to hear what I was talking about in terms of a story never beginning at the beginning, and certainly never ending. As the Hopis sometimes say, "Well, it has gone this far for a while." There is always that implication of a continuing. The other thing I want you to listen for is the many stories within one story. Listen to the kinds of stories contained within the main story—stories that give one a family identity and an individual identity, for example. This story is called "Home Country":

> "Well, it's been a while. I think in 1947 was when I left. My husband had been killed in Okinawa[8] some years before. And so I had no more husband. And l had to make a living. O I guess I could have looked for another man but I didn't want to. It looked like the war had made some of them into a bad way anyway. I saw some of them come home like that. They either got drunk or just stayed around a while or couldn't seem to be satisfied anymore with what was there. I guess now that I think about it, that happened to me although I wasn't in the war not in the Army or even much off the reservation just that several years at the Indian School. Well there was that feeling things were changing not only the men the boys, but things were changing.

---

8   *Okinawa*   Japanese island where American and Japanese forces fought each other during World War II.

"One day the home nurse the nurse that came from the Indian health service was at my mother's home my mother was getting near the end real sick and she said that she had been meaning to ask me a question. I said what is the question. And the home nurse said well your mother is getting real sick and after she is no longer around for you to take care of, what will you be doing you and her are the only ones here. And I said I don't know. But I was thinking about it what she said made me think about it. And then the next time she came she said to me Eloise the government is hiring Indians now in the Indian schools to take care of the boys and girls I heard one of the supervisors saying that Indians are hard workers but you have to supervise them a lot and I thought of you well because you've been taking care of your mother real good and you follow all my instructions. She said I thought of you because you're a good Indian girl and you would be the kind of person for that job. I didn't say anything I had not ever really thought about a job but I kept thinking about it.

"Well my mother she died and we buried her up at the old place the cemetery there it's real nice on the east side of the hill where the sun shines warm and the wind doesn't blow too much sand around right there. Well I was sad we were all sad for a while but you know how things are. One of my aunties came over and she advised me and warned me about being too sorry about it and all that she wished me that I would not worry too much about it because old folks they go along pretty soon life is that way and then she said that maybe I ought to take in one of my aunties kids or two because there was a lot of them kids and I was all by myself now. But I was so young and I thought that I might do that you know take care of someone but I had been thinking too of what the home nurse said to me about working. Hardly anybody at our home was working at something like that no woman anyway. And I would have to move away.

"Well I did just that. I remember that day very well. I told my aunties and they were all crying and we all went up to the old highway where the bus to town passes by every day. I was wearing an old kind of bluish sweater that was kind of big that one of my cousins who was older had got from a white person a tourist one summer in trade for something she had made a real pretty basket. She gave me that and I used to have a picture of me with it on it's kind of real ugly. Yeah that was the day I left wearing a baggy sweater and carrying a suitcase that someone gave me too I think or maybe it was the home nurse there wasn't much in it anyway either. I was scared and everybody seemed to be sad I was so young and skinny then. My aunties said one of them who was real fat you make sure you eat now make your own tortillas drink the milk and stuff like candies is no good she learned that from the nurse. Make sure you got your letter my auntie said. I had it folded into my purse. Yes I have one too a brown one that my husband when he was still alive one time on furlough* he brought it on my birthday it was a nice purse and still looked new because I never used it.

"The letter said that I had a job at Keams Canyon[9] the boarding school there but I would have to go to the Agency first for some papers to be filled and that's where I was going first. The Agency. And then they would send me out to Keams Canyon. I didn't even know where it was except that someone of our relatives said that it was near Hopi.[10] My uncles teased me about watching out for the Hopi men and boys don't let them get too close they said well you know how they are and they were pretty strict too about those things and then they were joking and then they were not too and so I said aw they won't get near to me I'm too ugly and I promised I would be careful anyway.

"So we all gathered for a while at my last auntie's house and then the old man my grandfather brought his wagon and horses to the door and we all got in and sat there for a while until my auntie told her father okay father let's go and shook his elbow because the poor old man was old by then and kind of going to sleep all the time you had to talk to him real loud. I had about ten dollars I think that was a lot of money more than it is now you know and when we got to the highway where the Indian road which is just a dirt road goes off the pave road my grandfather reached into his blue jeans and pulled out a silver dollar and put it into my hand. I was so shocked. We were all so shocked. We all looked around at each other we didn't know where the old man had gotten it because we were real poor two of my uncles had to borrow on their accounts at the trading store for the money I had in my purse but there it was a silver dollar so big and shrinking in my grandfather's hand and then in my hand.

"Well I was so shocked and everybody was so shocked that we all started crying right there at the junction of that Indian road and the pave highway I wanted to be a little girl again running after the old man when he hurried with his long legs to the cornfields or went for water down to the river. He was old then and his eye was turned gray and he didn't do much anymore except drive the wagon and chop a little bit of wood but I just held him and I just held him so tightly.

---

9   *Keams Canyon*   Area in Navajo County, Arizona.

10   *Hopi*   Territory of the Hopi, a Puebloan tribe, in northeastern Arizona.

"Later on I don't know what happened to the silver dollar it had a date of 1907 on it but I kept it for a long time because I guess I wanted to have it to remember when I left my home country. What I did in between then and now is another story but that's the time I moved away,"

is what she said.[11]

There are a great many parallels between Pueblo experiences and those of African and Caribbean peoples—one is that we have all had the conqueror's language imposed on us. But our experience with English has been somewhat different in that the Bureau of Indian Affairs schools were not interested in teaching us the canon* of Western classics. For instance, we never heard of Shakespeare. We were given Dick and Jane,[12] and I can remember reading that the robins were heading south for the winter. It took me a long time to figure out what was going on. I worried for quite a while about our robins in Laguna because they didn't leave in the winter, until I finally realized that all the big textbook companies are up in Boston and their robins do go south in the winter. But in a way, this dreadful formal education freed us by encouraging us to maintain our narratives. Whatever literature we were exposed to at school (which was damn little), at home the storytelling, the special regard for telling and bringing together through the telling, was going on constantly.

And as the old people say, "If you can remember the stories, you will be all right. Just remember the stories." When I returned to Laguna Pueblo after attending college, I wondered how the storytelling was continuing (anthropologists say that Laguna Pueblo is one of the more acculturated pueblos[13]), so I visited an English class at Laguna Acoma High School. I knew the students had cassette tape recorders in their lockers and stereos at home, and that they listened to Kiss and Led Zeppelin* and were all informed about popular culture in general. I had with me an anthology of short stories by Native American writers, *The Man to Send Rain Clouds*. One story in the book is about the killing of a state policeman in New Mexico by three Acoma Pueblo men in the early 1950s.[14] I asked the students how many had heard this story and steeled myself for the possibility that the anthropologists were right, that the old traditions were indeed dying out and the students would be ignorant of the story.

---

11   Simon J. Ortiz, *Howabah Indians* (Tucson: Blue Moon Press, 1978). [author's note]

12   *Dick and Jane*   Books that taught young children to read. Popular in American schools from the 1930s into the 1960s, these readers featured the characters Dick and Jane.

13   *more acculturated pueblos*   Areas where cultural assimilation has been widely adopted.

14   See Simon J. Ortiz, "The Killing of a State Cop," in *The Man to Send Rain Clouds*, ed. Kenneth Rosen (New York: Viking Press, 1974), 101–108. [author's note]

But instead, all but one or two raised their hands—they had heard the story, just as I had heard it when I was young, some in English, some in Laguna.

One of the other advantages that we Pueblos have enjoyed is that we have always been able to stay with the land. Our stories cannot be separated from their geographical locations, from actual physical places on the land. We were not relocated like so many Native American groups who were torn away from their ancestral land. And our stories are so much a part of these places that it is almost impossible for future generations to lose them—there is a story connected with every place, every object in the landscape.

Dennis Brutus[15] has talked about the "yet unborn" as well as "those from the past," and how we are still *all* in this place, and language—the storytelling—is our way of passing through or being with them, or being together again. When Aunt Susie told her stories, she would tell a younger child to go open the door so that our esteemed predecessors might bring in their gifts to us. "They are out there," Aunt Susie would say. "Let them come in. They're here, they're here with us *within* the stories."

A few years ago, when Aunt Susie was 106, I paid her a visit, and while I was there she said, "Well, I'll be leaving here soon. I think I'll be leaving here next week, and I will be going over to the Cliff House."[16] She said, "It's going to be real good to get back over there." I was listening, and I was thinking that she must be talking about our house at Paguate Village, just north of Laguna. And she went on, "Well, my mother's sister (and she gave her Indian name) will be there. She has been living there. She will be there and we will be over there, and I will get a chance to write down these stories I've been telling you." Now you must understand, of course, that Aunt Susie's mother's sister, a great storyteller herself, has long since passed over into the land of the dead. But then I realized, too, that Aunt Susie wasn't talking about death the way most of us do. She was talking about "going over" as a journey, a journey that perhaps we can only begin to understand through an appreciation for the boundless capacity of language that, through storytelling, brings us together, despite great distances between cultures, despite great distances in time.

(1979)

---

15 *Dennis Brutus* Dennis Vincent Brutus (1924–2009) was a South African journalist, poet, and activist. He is known for his efforts to have that country, which was still under the apartheid government, banned from the 1964 Olympic Games.

16 *Cliff House* Dwelling built in a cliff along a high canyon wall.

AUDRE LORDE

POETRY IS NOT A LUXURY

Much of Black[1] lesbian feminist poet, writer, and activist Audre Lorde's work combats patriarchy, racism, heterosexism, and classism, insisting upon the acknowledgment of differences among women and among people of color. "[M]y poetry," she said, "comes from the intersection of me and my worlds." The following essay appeared in Chrysalis: A Magazine of Women's Culture, *which published the work of a large number of influential feminist writers and artists between 1977 and 1980. When the following essay was published, Lorde was the poetry editor for* Chrysalis; *she would later leave the magazine over disagreements regarding its treatment of the work of women of color.*

The quality of light by which we scrutinize our lives has direct bearing upon the product which we live, and upon the changes which we hope to bring about through those lives. It is within this light that we form those ideas by which we pursue our magic and make it realized. This is poetry as illumination, for it is through poetry that we give name to those ideas which are—until the poem—nameless and formless, about to be birthed, but already felt. That distillation of experience from which true poetry springs births thought as dream births concept, as feeling births idea, as knowledge births (precedes) understanding.

As we learn to bear the intimacy of scrutiny and to flourish within it, as we learn to use the products of that scrutiny for power within our living, those fears which rule our lives and form our silences begin to lose their control over us.

For each of us as women, there is a dark place within, where hidden and growing our true spirit rises, "beautiful/and tough as chestnut/stanchions against (y)our nightmare of weakness/"[2] and of impotence.

---

1   *Black*   The editors of this anthology here follow Lorde's own practice of capitalization.

2   From "Black Mother Woman," first published in *From a Land Where Other People Live* (Broadside Press, Detroit, 1973), and collected in *Chosen Poems: Old and New* (W.W. Norton and Company, New York, 1982) p. 53. [author's note]

These places of possibility within ourselves are dark because they are ancient and hidden; they have survived and grown strong through that darkness. Within these deep places, each one of us holds an incredible reserve of creativity and power, of unexamined and unrecorded emotion and feeling. The woman's place of power within each of us is neither white nor surface; it is dark, it is ancient, and it is deep.

5   When we view living in the european mode only as a problem to be solved, we rely solely upon our ideas to make us free, for these were what the white fathers told us were precious.

But as we come more into touch with our own ancient, noneuropean consciousness of living as a situation to be experienced and interacted with, we learn more and more to cherish our feelings, and to respect those hidden sources of our power from where true knowledge and, therefore, lasting action comes.

At this point in time, I believe that women carry within ourselves the possibility for fusion of these two approaches so necessary for survival, and we come closest to this combination in our poetry. I speak here of poetry as a revelatory distillation of experience, not the sterile word play that, too often, the white fathers distorted the word *poetry* to mean—in order to cover their desperate wish for imagination without insight.

For women, then, poetry is not a luxury. It is a vital necessity of our existence. It forms the quality of the light within which we predicate our hopes and dreams toward survival and change, first made into language, then into idea, then into more tangible action. Poetry is the way we help give name to the nameless so it can be thought. The farthest horizons of our hopes and fears are cobbled by our poems, carved from the rock experiences of our daily lives.

As they become known to and accepted by us, our feelings and the honest exploration of them become sanctuaries and fortresses and spawning grounds for the most radical and daring of ideas. They become a safe-house for that difference so necessary to change and the conceptualization of any meaningful action. Right now, I could name at least ten ideas I would have found intolerable or incomprehensible and frightening, except as they came after dreams and poems. This is not idle fantasy, but a disciplined attention to the true meaning of "it feels right to me." We can train ourselves to respect our feelings and to transpose them into a language so they can be shared. And where that language does not yet exist, it is our poetry which helps to fashion it. Poetry is not only dream and vision; it is the skeleton architecture of our lives. It lays the foundations for a future of change, a bridge across our fears of what has never been before.

10   Possibility is neither forever nor instant. It is not easy to sustain belief in its efficacy. We can sometimes work long and hard to establish one beachhead*

of real resistance to the deaths we are expected to live, only to have that beach-head assaulted or threatened by those canards* we have been socialized to fear, or by the withdrawal of those approvals that we have been warned to seek for safety. Women see ourselves diminished or softened by the falsely benign accusations of childishness, of nonuniversality, of changeability, of sensuality. And who asks the question: Am I altering your aura, your ideas, your dreams, or am I merely moving you to temporary and reactive action? And even though the latter is no mean task, it is one that must be seen within the context of a need for true alteration of the very foundations of our lives.

The white fathers told us: I think, therefore I am.[3] The Black mother within each of us—the poet—whispers in our dreams: I feel, therefore I can be free. Poetry coins the language to express and charter this revolutionary demand, the implementation of that freedom. However, experience has taught us that the action in the now is also necessary, always. Our children cannot dream unless they live, they cannot live unless they are nourished, and who else will feed them the real food without which their dreams will be no different from ours? "If you want us to change the world someday, we at least have to live long enough to grow up!" shouts the child.

Sometimes we drug ourselves with dreams of new ideas. The head will save us. The brain alone will set us free. But there are no new ideas still waiting in the wings to save us as women, as human. There are only old and forgotten ones, new combinations, extrapolations and recognitions from within ourselves—along with the renewed courage to try them out. And we must constantly encourage ourselves and each other to attempt the heretical actions that our dreams imply, and so many of our old ideas disparage. In the forefront of our move toward change, there is only poetry to hint at possibility made real. Our poems formulate the implications of ourselves, what we feel within and dare make real (or bring action into accordance with), our fears, our hopes, our most cherished terrors.

For within living structures defined by profit, by linear power, by institutional dehumanization, our feelings were not meant to survive. Kept around as unavoidable adjuncts or pleasant pastimes, feelings were expected to kneel to thought as women were expected to kneel to men. But women have survived. As poets. And there are no new pains. We have felt them all already. We have hidden that fact in the same place where we have hidden our power. They surface in our dreams, and it is our dreams that point the way to freedom. Those

---

3   *I think, therefore I am*   English translation of "je pense, donc je suis" (also often expressed in Latin as "cogito, ergo sum"), a statement made by the French philosopher René Descartes in his 1637 *Discourse on Method*. Descartes viewed this argument as foundational to the construction of all human knowledge—and his view became highly influential among subsequent Western philosophers.

dreams are made realizable through our poems that give us the strength and courage to see, to feel, to speak, and to dare.

If what we need to dream, to move our spirits most deeply and directly toward and through promise, is discounted as a luxury, then we give up the core—the fountain—of our power, our womanness; we give up the future of our worlds.

15   For there are no new ideas. There are only new ways of making them felt—of examining what those ideas feel like being lived on Sunday morning at 7 A.M., after brunch, during wild love, making war, giving birth, mourning our dead—while we suffer the old longings, battle the old warnings and fears of being silent and impotent and alone, while we taste new possibilities and strengths.

(1977)

USES OF ANGER:
WOMEN RESPONDING TO RACISM

The theme of the 1981 National Women's Studies Association Conference, where Lorde delivered the following keynote address, was "Women Respond to Racism." The conference, which was predominantly white—about 300 women of color attended, out of about 1400 participants—offered a series of consciousness-raising groups for people of shared background: an extensive range of choices for white women, from "white/immigrant" to "white/working-class," and only one group for all women of color. There was a great deal of tension regarding the failure both of the conference and of mainstream feminism in general to adequately address racial differences and the relationship between racial and patriarchal oppression.

*R*acism. The belief in the inherent superiority of one race over all others and thereby the right to dominance, manifest and implied.

Women respond to racism. My response to racism is anger. I have lived with that anger, on that anger, ignoring it, feeding upon it, learning to use it before it laid my visions to waste, for most of my life. Once I did it in silence, afraid of the weight. My fear of that anger taught me nothing. Your fear of that anger will teach you nothing, also.

Women responding to racism means women responding to anger, the anger of exclusion, of unquestioned privilege, of racial distortions, of silence, ill-use, stereotyping, defensiveness, misnaming, betrayal, and co-optation.*

My anger is a response to racist attitudes and to the actions and presumptions that arise out of those attitudes. If your dealings with other women reflect those attitudes, then my anger and your attendant fears are spotlights that can be used for growth in the same way I have used learning to express anger for my growth. But for corrective surgery, not guilt. Guilt and defensiveness are bricks in a wall against which we all flounder; they serve none of our futures.

Because I do not want this to become a theoretical discussion, I am going to give a few examples of interchanges between women that illustrate these points. In the interest of time, I am going to cut them short. I want you to know that there were many more.

For example:

• I speak out of a direct and particular anger at a particular academic conference, and a white woman says, "Tell me how you feel but don't say it too harshly or I cannot hear you." But is it my manner that keeps her from hearing, or the threat of a message that her life may change?

• The Women's Studies Program of a southern university invites a Black woman to read following a week-long forum on Black and white women. "What has this week given to you?" I ask. The most vocal white woman says, "I think I've gotten a lot. I feel Black women really understand me a lot better now; they have a better idea of where I'm coming from." As if understanding her lay at the core of the racist problem.

• After fifteen years of a women's movement which professes to address the life concerns and possible futures of all women, I still hear, on campus after campus, "How can we address the issues of racism? No women of Color attended." Or, the other side of that statement, "We have no one in our department equipped to teach their work." In other words, racism is a Black women's problem, a problem of women of Color, and only we can discuss it.

• After I have read from my work entitled "Poems for Women in Rage"[4] a white woman asks me, "Are you going to do anything with how we can deal directly with *our* anger? I feel it's so important." I ask, "How do you use *your* rage?" And then I have to turn away from the blank look in her eyes, before she can invite me to participate in her own annihilation. I do not exist to feel her anger for her.

• White women are beginning to examine their relationships to Black women, yet often I hear them wanting only to deal with the little colored

5

10

---

4   *Poems for Women in Rage*   One poem from this series is included in *Chosen Poems: Old and New* (W.W. Norton and Company, New York, 1978), pp. 105–108. [author's note]

children across the roads of childhood, the beloved nursemaid, the occasional second-grade classmate—those tender memories of what was once mysterious and intriguing or neutral. You avoid the childhood assumptions formed by the raucous laughter at Rastus and Alfalfa,[5] the acute message of your mommy's handkerchief spread upon the park bench because I had just been sitting there, the indelible and dehumanizing portraits of Amos 'n Andy[6] and your daddy's humorous bedtime stories.

I wheel my two-year-old daughter in a shopping cart through a supermarket in Eastchester[7] in 1967, and a little white girl riding past in her mother's cart calls out excitedly, "Oh look, Mommy, a baby maid!" And your mother shushes you, but she does not correct you. And so fifteen years later, at a conference on racism, you can still find that story humorous. But I hear your laughter is full of terror and dis-ease.

• A white academic welcomes the appearance of a collection by non-Black women of Color.[8] "It allows me to deal with racism without dealing with the harshness of Black women," she says to me.

• At an international cultural gathering of women, a well-known white american woman poet interrupts the reading of the work of women of Color to read her own poem, and then dashes off to an "important panel."

15   If women in the academy truly want a dialogue about racism, it will require recognizing the needs and the living contexts of other women. When an academic woman says, "I can't afford it," she may mean she is making a choice about how to spend her available money. But when a woman on welfare says, "I can't afford it," she means she is surviving on an amount of money that was barely subsistence in 1972, and she often does not have enough to eat. Yet the National Women's Studies Association here in 1981 holds a conference in which it commits itself to responding to racism, yet refuses to waive the

---

5   *Rastus*   Stock character of a cheerful African American man that appeared in minstrel shows and other racist works of popular culture in the late nineteenth and early twentieth centuries; *Alfalfa*   Character in the series of films *Our Gang* (1922–44), which were later shown as the television series *Little Rascals*. Alfalfa was white, but the show was groundbreaking in its portrayal of African American and white children playing together. It has also, however, been heavily criticized for stereotypical treatment of its African American characters.

6   *Amos 'n Andy*   Mid-twentieth-century radio show that also became a television series. On the radio, the show's white creators, Freeman Gosden and Charles Correll, voiced most of the characters, including the two African American main characters.

7   *Eastchester*   Town in Westchester County on Long Island in the state of New York.

8   *This Bridge Called My Back: Writings by Radical Women of Color* edited by Cherríe Moraga and Gloria E. Anzaldúa (Kitchen Table: Women of Color Press, New York, 1984), first published in 1981. [author's note]

registration fee for poor women and women of Color who wished to present and conduct workshops. This has made it impossible for many women of Color—for instance, Wilmette Brown, of Black Women for Wages for Housework—to participate in this conference. Is this to be merely another case of the academy discussing life within the closed circuits of the academy?

To the white women present who recognize these attitudes as familiar, but most of all, to all my sisters of Color who live and survive thousands of such encounters—to my sisters of Color who like me still tremble their rage under harness, or who sometimes question the expression of our rage as useless and disruptive (the two most popular accusations)—I want to speak about anger, my anger, and what I have learned from my travels through its dominions.

Everything can be used / except what is wasteful / (you will need / to remember this when you are accused of destruction.)[9]

Every woman has a well-stocked arsenal of anger potentially useful against those oppressions, personal and institutional, which brought that anger into being. Focused with precision it can become a powerful source of energy serving progress and change. And when I speak of change, I do not mean a simple switch of positions or a temporary lessening of tensions, nor the ability to smile or feel good. I am speaking of a basic and radical alteration in all those assumptions underlining our lives.

I have seen situations where white women hear a racist remark, resent what has been said, become filled with fury, and remain silent because they are afraid. That unexpressed anger lies within them like an undetonated device, usually to be hurled at the first woman of Color who talks about racism.

But anger expressed and translated into action in the service of our vision and our future is a liberating and strengthening act of clarification, for it is in the painful process of this translation that we identify who are our allies with whom we have grave differences, and who are our genuine enemies.

Anger is loaded with information and energy. When I speak of women of Color, I do not only mean Black women. The woman of Color who is not Black and who charges me with rendering her invisible by assuming that her struggles with racism are identical with my own has something to tell me that I had better learn from, lest we both waste ourselves fighting the truths between us. If I participate, knowingly or otherwise, in my sister's oppression and she calls me on it, to answer her anger with my own only blankets the substance of our exchange with reaction. It wastes energy. And yes, it is very difficult to stand still and to listen to another woman's voice delineate an agony I do not share, or even one to which I myself have participated.

20

---

9   From "For Each of You," first published in *From a Land Where Other People Live* (Broadside Press, Detroit, 1973), and collected in *Chosen Poems: Old and New* (W.W. Norton and Company, New York, 1982), p. 42. [author's note]

In this place we speak removed from the more blatant reminders of our embattlement as women. This need not blind us to the size and complexities of the forces mounting against us and all that is most human within our environment. We are not here as women examining racism in a political and social vacuum. We operate in the teeth of a system for which racism and sexism are primary, established, and necessary props of profit. Women responding to racism is a topic so dangerous that when the local media attempt to discredit this conference they choose to focus upon the provision of lesbian housing as a diversionary device[10]—as if the Hartford *Courant* dare not mention the topic chosen for discussion here, racism, lest it become apparent that women are in fact attempting to examine and to alter all the repressive conditions of our lives.

Mainstream communication does not want women, particularly white women, responding to racism. It wants racism to be accepted as an immutable given in the fabric of your existence, like eveningtime or the common cold.

So we are working in a context of opposition and threat, the cause of which is certainly not the angers which lie between us, but rather that virulent hatred leveled against all women, people of Color, lesbians and gay men, poor people—against all of us who are seeking to examine the particulars of our lives as we resist our oppressions, moving toward coalition and effective action.

25   Any discussion among women about racism must include the recognition and the use of anger. It must be direct and creative because it is crucial. We cannot allow our fear of anger to deflect us nor seduce us into settling for anything less than the hard work of excavating honesty; we must be quite serious about the choice of this topic and the angers entwined within it because, rest assured, our opponents are quite serious about their hatred of us and of what we are trying to do here.

And while we scrutinize the often painful face of each other's anger, please remember that it is not our anger which makes me caution you to lock your doors at night and not to wander the streets of Hartford alone. It is the hatred which lurks in those streets, that urge to destroy us all if we truly work for change rather than merely indulge in our academic rhetoric.

This hatred and our anger are very different. Hatred is the fury of those who do not share our goals, and its object is death and destruction. Anger is the grief of distortions between peers, and its object is change. But our time is getting shorter. We have been raised to view any difference other than sex as a reason for destruction, and for Black women and white women to face each other's angers without denial or immobility or silence or guilt is in itself a

---

10   *the provision ... device*   A 19 May 1981 article in the *Hartford Courant* discussed the conference; its headline was "Lesbian Housing Available for Women's Conference at UConn."

heretical and generative* idea. It implies peers meeting upon a common basis to examine difference, and to alter those distortions which history has created around our difference. For it is those distortions which separate us. And we must ask ourselves: Who profits from all this?

Women of Color in america have grown up within a symphony of anger, at being silenced, at being unchosen, at knowing that when we survive, it is in spite of a world that takes for granted our lack of humanness, and which hates our very existence outside of its service. And I say *symphony* rather than *cacophony* because we have had to learn to orchestrate those furies so that they do not tear us apart. We have had to learn to move through them and use them for strength and force and insight within our daily lives. Those of us who did not learn this difficult lesson did not survive. And part of my anger is always libation* for my fallen sisters.

Anger is an appropriate reaction to racist attitudes, as is fury when the actions arising from those attitudes do not change. To those women here who fear the anger of women of Color more than their own unscrutinized racist attitudes, I ask: Is the anger of women of Color more threatening than the woman-hatred that tinges all aspects of our lives?

It is not the anger of other women that will destroy us but our refusals to stand still, to listen to its rhythms, to learn within it, to move beyond the manner of presentation to the substance, to tap that anger as an important source of empowerment.

I cannot hide my anger to spare you guilt, nor hurt feelings, nor answering anger; for to do so insults and trivializes all our efforts. Guilt is not a response to anger; it is a response to one's own actions or lack of action. If it leads to change then it can be useful, since it is then no longer guilt but the beginning of knowledge. Yet all too often, guilt is just another name for impotence, for defensiveness destructive of communication; it becomes a device to protect ignorance and the continuation of things the way they are, the ultimate protection for changelessness.

Most women have not developed tools for facing anger constructively. CR[11] groups in the past, largely white, dealt with how to express anger, usually at the world of men. And these groups were made up of white women who shared the terms of their oppressions. There was usually little attempt to articulate the genuine differences between women, such as those of race, color, age, class, and sexual identity. There was no apparent need at that time to examine the contradictions of self, woman as oppressor. There was work on expressing anger, but very little on anger directed against each other. No tools were developed to deal with other women's anger except to avoid it, deflect it, or flee from it under a blanket of guilt.

---

11   *CR*   Consciousness-raising.

I have no creative use for guilt, yours or my own. Guilt is only another way of avoiding informed action, of buying time out of the pressing need to make clear choices, out of the approaching storm that can feed the earth as well as bend the trees. If I speak to you in anger, at least I have spoken to you: I have not put a gun to your head and shot you down in the street; I have not looked at your bleeding sister's body and asked, "What did she do to deserve it?" This was the reaction of two white women to Mary Church Terrell's[12] telling of the lynching of a pregnant Black woman whose baby was then torn from her body. That was in 1921, and Alice Paul had just refused to publicly endorse the enforcement of the Nineteenth Amendment for all women—by refusing to endorse the inclusion of women of Color, although we had worked to help bring about that amendment.[13]

The angers between women will not kill us if we can articulate them with precision, if we listen to the content of what is said with at least as much intensity as we defend ourselves from the manner of saying. When we turn from anger we turn from insight, saying we will accept only the designs already known, those deadly and safely familiar. I have tried to learn my anger's usefulness to me, as well as its limitations.

35   For women raised to fear, too often anger threatens annihilation. In the male construct of brute force, we were taught that our lives depended upon the good will of patriarchal power. The anger of others was to be avoided at all costs because there was nothing to be learned from it but pain, a judgment that we had been bad girls, come up lacking, not done what we were supposed to do. And if we accept our powerlessness, then of course any anger can destroy us.

But the strength of women lies in recognizing differences between us as creative, and in standing to those distortions which we inherited without blame, but which are now ours to alter. The angers of women can transform difference through insight into power. For anger between peers births change, not

---

12   *Mary Church Terrell*   Journalist, educator, and activist for civil rights and women's rights (1863–1954). She was a founding member of the National Association for the Advancement of Colored People and the first African American woman to serve on a city schoolboard.

13   *Alice Paul*   Women's rights activist (1885–1977) and leader of the campaign that resulted in the Nineteenth Amendment (1920), which gave women the right to vote;   *I have not ... amendment*   Terrell asked Paul to make a statement in favor of enforcing the Nineteenth Amendment universally; many measures had been taken in Southern states to make it more difficult for African American women to vote. Paul refused to do so, and Terrell then made a speech to the Resolutions Committee of the Woman's Party requesting backing; in the course of this speech she described the lynching of a pregnant woman. When one white woman asked why the lynching had occurred, another added "She [the victim] did something, of course."

destruction, and the discomfort and sense of loss it often causes is not fatal, but a sign of growth.

My response to racism is anger. That anger has eaten clefts into my living only when it remained unspoken, useless to anyone. It has also served me in classrooms without light or learning, where the work and history of Black women was less than a vapor. It has served me as fire in the ice zone of uncomprehending eyes of white women who see in my experience and the experience of my people only new reasons for fear or guilt. And my anger is no excuse for not dealing with your blindness, no reason to withdraw from the results of your own actions.

When women of Color speak out of the anger that laces so many of our contacts with white women, we are often told that we are "creating a mood of hopelessness," "preventing white women from getting past guilt," or "standing in the way of trusting communication and action." All these quotes come directly from letters to me from members of this organization within the last two years. One woman wrote, "Because you are Black and Lesbian, you seem to speak with the moral authority of suffering."[14] Yes, I am Black and Lesbian, and what you hear in my voice is fury, not suffering. Anger, not moral authority. There is a difference.

To turn aside from the anger of Black women with excuses or the pretexts of intimidation is to award no one power—it is merely another way of preserving racial blindness, the power of unaddressed privilege, unbreached, intact. Guilt is only another form of objectification. Oppressed peoples are always being asked to stretch a little more, to bridge the gap between blindness and humanity. Black women are expected to use our anger only in the service of other people's salvation or learning. But that time is over. My anger has meant pain to me but it has also meant survival, and before I give it up I'm going to be sure that there is something at least as powerful to replace it on the road to clarity.

What woman here is so enamoured of her own oppression that she cannot see her heelprint upon another woman's face? What woman's terms of oppression have become precious and necessary to her as a ticket into the fold of the righteous, away from the cold winds of self-scrutiny?

I am a lesbian woman of Color whose children eat regularly because I work in a university. If their full bellies make me fail to recognize my commonality with a woman of Color whose children do not eat because she cannot

40

---

14 *Because ... suffering* Lorde quotes from a letter she received from the organizers of a 1979 conference in which she had participated. In Lorde's view, the conference had failed to adequately address matters of race, class, and sexual orientation, and she had pointed this out in a now-famous speech, "The Master's Tools Will Never Dismantle the Master's House," made during the conference.

find work, or who has no children because her insides are rotted from home abortions and sterilization; if I fail to recognize the lesbian who chooses not to have children, the woman who remains closeted because her homophobic community is her only life support, the woman who chooses silence instead of another death, the woman who is terrified lest my anger trigger the explosion of hers; if I fail to recognize them as other faces of myself, then I am contributing not only to each of their oppressions but also to my own, and the anger which stands between us then must be used for clarity and mutual empowerment, not for evasion by guilt or for further separation. I am not free while any woman is unfree, even when her shackles are very different from my own. And I am not free as long as one person of Color remains chained. Nor is any one of you.

I speak here as a woman of Color who is not bent upon destruction, but upon survival. No woman is responsible for altering the psyche of her oppressor, even when that psyche is embodied in another woman. I have suckled the wolf's lip of anger and I have used it for illumination, laughter, protection, fire in places where there was no light, no food, no sisters, no quarter.* We are not goddesses or matriarchs or edifices of divine forgiveness; we are not fiery fingers of judgment or instruments of flagellation; we are women forced back always upon our woman's power. We have learned to use anger as we have learned to use the dead flesh of animals, and bruised, battered, and changing, we have survived and grown and, in Angela Wilson's words, we *are* moving on. With or without uncolored women. We use whatever strengths we have fought for, including anger, to help define and fashion a world where all our sisters can grow, where our children can love, and where the power of touching and meeting another woman's difference and wonder will eventually transcend the need for destruction.

For it is not the anger of Black women which is dripping down over this globe like a diseased liquid. It is not my anger that launches rockets, spends over sixty thousand dollars a second on missiles and other agents of war and death, slaughters children in cities, stockpiles nerve gas and chemical bombs, sodomizes our daughters and our earth. It is not the anger of Black women which corrodes into blind, dehumanizing power, bent upon the annihilation of us all unless we meet it with what we have, our power to examine and to redefine the terms upon which we will live and work; our power to envision and to reconstruct, anger by painful anger, stone upon heavy stone, a future of pollinating difference and the earth to support our choices.

We welcome all women who can meet us, face to face, beyond objectification and beyond guilt.

(1981, revised 1984)

ADRIENNE RICH

CLAIMING AN EDUCATION

Feminist, poet, and theorist Adrienne Rich delivered the following speech in September 1977 to the students of Douglass College, then a women-only college within Rutgers University. Her speech was published in The Common Woman, *a feminist magazine founded by Rutgers students.*

For this convocation, I planned to separate my remarks into two parts: some thoughts about you, the woman students here, and some thoughts about us who teach in a women's college. But ultimately those two parts are indivisible. If university education means anything beyond the processing of human beings into expected roles, through credit hours, tests, and grades (and I believe that in a women's college especially it *might* mean much more), it implies an ethical and intellectual contract between teacher and student. This contract must remain intuitive, dynamic, unwritten; but we must turn to it again and again if learning is to be reclaimed from the depersonalizing and cheapening pressures of the present-day academic scene.

The first thing I want to say to you who are students, is that you cannot afford to think of being here to *receive* an education: you will do much better to think of yourselves as being here to *claim* one. One of the dictionary definitions of the verb "to claim" is: *to take as the rightful owner; to assert in the face of possible contradiction.* "To receive" is *to come into possession of: to act as receptacle or container for; to accept as authoritative or true.* The difference is that between acting and being acted-upon, and for women it can literally mean the difference between life and death.

One of the devastating weaknesses of university learning, of the store of knowledge and opinion that has been handed down through academic training, has been its almost total erasure of women's experience and thought from the curriculum, and its exclusion of women as members of the academic community. Today, with increasing numbers of women students in nearly every branch of higher learning, we still see very few women in the upper levels of faculty and administration in most institutions. Douglass College itself is a women's college in a university administered overwhelmingly by men, who in turn are answerable to the state legislature, again composed predominantly of men. But the most, significant fact for you is that what you learn here, the very texts you read, the lectures you hear, the way your studies are divided into categories and fragmented one from the other—all this reflects, to a very large degree, neither objective reality, nor an accurate picture of the past, nor a group of rigorously tested observations about human behavior. What you can learn here (and I mean not only at Douglass but any college in any university) is how men have perceived and organized their experience, their history, their ideas of social relationships, good and evil, sickness and health, etc. When you read or hear about "great issues," "major texts," "the mainstream of Western thought," you are hearing about what men, above all white men, in their male subjectivity, have decided is important.

Black and other minority peoples have for some time recognized that their racial and ethnic experience was not accounted for in the studies broadly labeled human; and that even the sciences can be racist. For many reasons, it has been more difficult for women to comprehend our exclusion, and to realize that even the sciences can be sexist. For one thing, it is only within the last hundred years that higher education has grudgingly been opened up to women at all, even to white, middle-class women. And many of us have found ourselves poring eagerly over books with titles like: *The Descent of Man*;* *Man and His Symbols*; *Irrational Man*; *The Phenomenon of Man*; *The Future of Man*; *Man and the Machine*; *From Man to Man*; *May Man Prevail?*; *Man, Science and Society*; or *One Dimensional Man*—books pretending to describe a "human" reality that does not include over one-half the human species.

5   Less than a decade ago, with the rebirth of a feminist movement in this country, women students and teachers in a number of universities began to demand and set up women's studies courses—to *claim* a woman-directed education. And, despite the inevitable accusations of "unscholarly," "group therapy," "faddism,"* etc., despite backlash and budget cuts, women's studies are still growing, offering to more and more women a new intellectual grasp on their lives, new understanding of our history, a fresh vision of the human experience, and also a critical basis for evaluating what they hear and read in other courses, and in the society at large.

But my talk is not really about women's studies, much as I believe in their scholarly, scientific, and human necessity. While I think that any Douglass student has everything to gain by investigating and enrolling in women's studies courses, I want to suggest that there is a more essential experience that you owe yourselves, one which courses in women's studies can greatly enrich, but which finally depends on you in all your interactions with yourself and your world. This is the experience of *taking responsibility toward yourselves*. Our upbringing as women has so often told us that this should come second to our relationships and responsibilities to other people. We have been offered ethical models of the self-denying wife and mother; intellectual models of the brilliant but slapdash dilettante* who never commits herself to anything the whole way, or the intelligent woman who denies her intelligence in order to seem more "feminine," or who sits in passive silence even when she disagrees inwardly with everything that is being said around her.

Responsibility to yourself means refusing to let others do your thinking, talking, and naming for you; it means learning to respect and use your own brains and instincts; hence, grappling with hard work. It means that you do not treat your body as a commodity with which to purchase superficial intimacy or economic security; for our bodies and minds are inseparable in this life, and when we allow our bodies to be treated as objects, our minds are in mortal danger. It means insisting that those to whom you give your friendship and love are able to respect your mind. It means being able to say, with Charlotte Brontë's Jane Eyre:[1] "I have an inward treasure born with me, which can keep me alive if all the extraneous delights should be withheld or offered only at a price I cannot afford to give." Responsibility to yourself means that you don't fall for shallow and easy solutions—predigested books and ideas, weekend encounters guaranteed to change your life, taking "gut" courses[2] instead of ones you know will challenge you, bluffing at school and life instead of doing solid work, marrying early as an escape from real decisions, getting pregnant as an evasion of already existing problems. It means that you refuse to sell your talents and aspirations short, simply to avoid conflict and confrontation. And this, in turn, means resisting the forces in society which say that women should be nice, play safe, have low professional expectations, drown in love and forget about work, live through others, and stay in the places assigned to us. It means that we insist on a life of meaningful work, insist that work be as meaningful as love and friendship in our lives. It means, therefore, the courage to be "different"; not to be continuously available to others when we need time for ourselves and our work; to be able to demand of others—parents, friends, roommates, teachers, lovers, husbands, children—that they respect our sense of purpose and our integrity as persons. Women everywhere are finding the courage to do this, more and more, and we are finding that courage both in our study of women in the past who possessed it, and in each other as we look to other women for comradeship, community, and challenge. The difference between a life lived actively, and a life of passive drifting and dispersal of energies, is an immense difference. Once we begin to feel committed to our

---

1   *Jane Eyre*   Protagonist of *Jane Eyre* (1847), a classic novel by Charlotte Brontë.

2   *"gut" courses*   Slang term for easy courses.

lives, responsible to ourselves, we can never again be satisfied with the old, passive way.

Now comes the second part of the contract. I believe that in a women's college you have the right to expect your faculty to take you seriously. The education of women has been a matter of debate for centuries, and old, negative attitudes about women's role, women's ability to think and take leadership, are still rife both in and outside the university. Many male professors (and I don't mean only at Douglass) still feel that teaching in a women's college is a second-rate career. Many tend to eroticize their women students—to treat them as sexual objects—instead of demanding the best of their minds. (At Yale a legal suit [*Alexander v. Yale*[3]] has been brought against the university by a group of women students demanding a stated policy against sexual advances toward female students by male professors.) Many teachers, both men and women, trained in the male-centered tradition, are still handing the ideas and texts of that tradition on to students without teaching them to criticize its anti-woman attitudes, its omission of women as part of the species. Too often, all of us fail to teach the most important thing, which is that clear thinking, active discussion, and excellent writing are all necessary for intellectual freedom, and that these require *hard work*. Sometimes, perhaps in discouragement with a culture which is both anti-intellectual and antiwoman, we may resign ourselves to low expectations for our students before we have given them half a chance to become more thoughtful, expressive human beings. We need to take to heart the words of Elizabeth Barrett Browning, a poet, a thinking woman, and a feminist, who wrote in 1845 of her impatience with studies which cultivate a "passive recipiency" in the mind, and asserted that "women want to be made to *think actively*: their apprehension is quicker than that of men, but their defect lies for the most part in the logical faculty and in the higher mental activities." Note that she implies a defect which can be remedied by intellectual training, *not* an inborn lack of ability.

I have said that the contract on the student's part involves that you demand to be taken seriously so that you can also go on taking yourself seriously. This means seeking out criticism, recognizing that the most affirming thing anyone can do for you is demand that you push yourself further, show you the range of what you *can* do. It means rejecting attitudes of "take-it-easy,"

---

3   *Alexander v. Yale*   1980 lawsuit brought forward by five Yale students accusing the university of sex discrimination and demanding that it establish a grievance procedure for sexual harassment. The court agreed with the plaintiffs that sexual harassment would constitute sex discrimination, but did not find sufficient evidence that harassment had actually occurred. The students lost the case, but as a result of their actions, Yale and most other American universities did develop the sort of grievance procedures the students had requested.

"why-be-so-serious," "why-worry-you'll-probably-get-married-anyway." It means assuming your share of responsibility for what happens in the classroom, because that affects the quality of your daily life here. It means that the student sees herself engaged *with* her teachers in active, ongoing struggle for a real education. But for her to do this, her teachers must be committed to belief that women's minds and experience are intrinsically valuable and indispensable to any civilization worthy the name: that there is no more exhilarating and intellectually fertile place in the academic world today than a women's college—*if* both students and teachers in large enough numbers are trying to fulfill this contract. The contract is really a pledge of mutual seriousness about women, about language, ideas, methods, and values. It is our shared commitment toward a world in which the inborn potentialities of so many women's minds will no longer be wasted, raveled-away, paralyzed, or denied.

(1977)

from COMPULSORY HETEROSEXUALITY AND LESBIAN EXISTENCE

Lesbian feminism emerged in the late 1960s and 70s, as lesbians critiqued mainstream feminism for disregarding their concerns, many arguing that lesbian relationships posed an important challenge to patriarchal norms that would help to liberate all women regardless of sexual orientation. Some mainstream feminists responded negatively to the movement—in 1969 Betty Freidan, president of the National Organization for Women, famously referred to it as the "lavender menace"—and some lesbian feminists advocated separating from mainstream feminism altogether and forming fully woman-identified communities. Despite heterosexism within mainstream feminism, lesbian feminism exerted a strong influence on feminist thought in general in the 1970s and 80s. "Compulsory Heterosexuality and Lesbian Existence" was a particularly influential contribution to the movement; in her foreword to the 50-page article, Rich writes that "[i]t was written in part to challenge the erasure of lesbian existence from so much of scholarly feminist literature ... and to sketch, at least, some bridge over the gap between lesbian and feminist."

I

Biologically men have only one innate orientation—a sexual one that draws them to women,—while women have two innate orientations, sexual toward men and reproductive toward their young.[4]

I was a woman terribly vulnerable, critical, using femaleness as a sort of standard or yardstick to measure and discard men. Yes—something like that. I was an Anna who invited defeat from men without ever being conscious of it. (But I am conscious of it. And being conscious of it means I shall leave it all behind me and become—but what?) I was stuck fast in an emotion common to women of our time, that can turn them bitter, or Lesbian, or solitary. Yes, that Anna during that time was ...

[Another blank line across the page:][5]

The bias of compulsory heterosexuality, through which lesbian experience is perceived on a scale ranging from deviant to abhorrent or simply rendered invisible, could be illustrated from many texts other than the two just preceding. The assumption made by Rossi, that women are "innately" sexually oriented only toward men, and that made by Lessing, that the lesbian is simply acting out of her bitterness toward men, are by no means theirs alone; these assumptions are widely current in literature and in the social sciences.

I am concerned here with two other matters as well: first, how and why women's choice of women as passionate comrades, life partners, co-workers, lovers, community has been crushed, invalidated, forced into hiding and disguise; and second, the virtual or total neglect of lesbian existence in a wide range of writings, including feminist scholarship. Obviously there is a connection here. I believe that much feminist theory and criticism is stranded on this shoal.

My organizing impulse is the belief that it is not enough for feminist thought that specifically lesbian texts exist. Any theory or cultural/political creation that treats lesbian existence as a marginal or less "natural" phenomenon, as mere "sexual preference," or as the mirror image of either heterosexual or male homosexual relations is profoundly weakened thereby, whatever its other contributions. Feminist theory can no longer afford merely to voice a toleration of "lesbianism" as an "alternative life style"* or make token allusion to

---

4 Alice Rossi, "Children and Work in the Lives of Women," paper delivered at the University of Arizona, Tucson, February 1976. [author's note]

5 Doris Lessing, *The Golden Notebook*, 1962 (New York: Bantam, 1977), p. 480. [author's note]

lesbians. A feminist critique of compulsory heterosexual orientation for women is long overdue. In this exploratory paper, I shall try to show why....

... In *The Mermaid and the Minotaur: Sexual Arrangements and the Human Malaise*, Dorothy Dinnerstein makes an impassioned argument for the sharing of parenting between women and men and for an end to what she perceives as the male/female symbiosis of "gender arrangements," which she feels are leading the species further and further into violence and self-extinction. Apart from other problems that I have with this book ... I find Dinnerstein's view of the relations between women and men as "a collaboration to keep history mad" utterly ahistorical.* She means by this a collaboration to perpetuate social relations which are hostile, exploitative, and destructive to life itself. She sees women and men as equal partners in the making of "sexual arrangements," seemingly unaware of the repeated struggles of women to resist oppression (their own and that of others) and to change their condition. She ignores, specifically, the history of women who—as witches, *femmes seules*,[6] marriage resisters, spinsters, autonomous widows, and/or lesbians—have managed on varying levels *not* to collaborate. It is this history, precisely, from which feminists have so much to learn and on which there is overall such blanketing silence. Dinnerstein acknowledges at the end of her book that "female separatism," though "on a large scale and in the long run widely impractical," has something to teach us: "Separate, women could in principle set out to learn from scratch—undeflected by the opportunities to evade this task that men's presence has so far offered— what intact self-creative humanness is."[7] Phrases like "intact self-creative humanness" obscure the question of what the many forms of female separatism have actually been addressing. The fact is that women in every culture and throughout history *have* undertaken the task of independent, nonheterosexual, woman-connected existence, to the extent made possible by their context, often in the belief that they were the "only ones" ever to have done so. They have undertaken it even though few women have been in an economic position to resist marriage altogether, and even though attacks against unmarried women have ranged from aspersion* and mockery to deliberate gynocide,[8] including the burning and torturing of millions of widows and spinsters during the witch persecutions of the fifteenth, sixteenth, and seventeenth centuries in Europe.

Nancy Chodorow does come close to the edge of an acknowledgement of lesbian existence. Like Dinnerstein, Chodorow believes that the fact that

5

---

6   *femmes seules* In contrast to a married woman—defined in English common law as "feme covert"—a feme sole (single woman) could own property, keep her own money, and enter into legal agreements on her own.

7   [Dorothy Dinnerstein, *The Mermaid and the Minotaur: Sexual Arrangements and the Human Malaise* (New York: Harper & Row, 1976)], p. 272. [author's note]

8   *gynocide* Killing of women, especially with a political or cultural motivation.

women, and women only, are responsible for child care in the sexual division of labor has led to an entire social organization of gender inequality, and that men as well as women must become primary carers for children if that inequality is to change. In the process of examining, from a psychoanalytic perspective, how mothering by women affects the psychological development of girl and boy children, she offers documentation that men are "emotionally secondary" in women's lives, that "women have a richer, ongoing inner world to fall back on ... men do not become as emotionally important to women as women do to men."[9] ... Chodorow concludes that because many women have women as mothers, "the mother remains a primary internal object [sic] to the girl, so that heterosexual relationships are on the model of the nonexclusive, second relationship for her, whereas for the boy they re-create an exclusive, primary relationship." According to Chodorow, women "have learned to deny the limitations of masculine lovers for both psychological and practical reasons."[10]

But the practical reasons (like witch burnings, male control of law, theology, and science, or economic nonviablity within the sexual division of labor) are glossed over. Chodorow's account barely glances at the constraints and sanctions which historically have enforced or ensured the coupling of women with men and obstructed or penalized women's coupling or allying in independent groups with other women. She dismisses lesbian existence with the comment that "lesbian relationships do tend to re-create mother-daughter emotions and connections, but most women are heterosexual" (implied: more mature, having developed beyond the mother-daughter connection?). She then adds: "This heterosexual preference and taboos on homosexuality, in addition to objective economic dependence on men, make the option of primary sexual bonds with other women unlikely—though more prevalent in recent years."[11] The significance of that qualification seems irresistible, but Chodorow does not explore it further. Is she saying that lesbian existence has become more *visible* in recent years (in certain groups), that economic and other pressures have changed (under capitalism, socialism, or both), and that consequently more women are rejecting the heterosexual "choice"? She argues that women want children because their heterosexual relationships lack richness and intensity, that in having a child a woman seeks to re-create her own intense relationship with her mother. It seems to me that on the basis of her own findings, Chodorow leads us implicitly to conclude that heterosexuality is *not* a "preference" for women, that, for one thing, it fragments the erotic from the

---

9   [Nancy Chodorow, *The Reproduction of Mothering* (Berkeley: University of California Press, 1978)], pp. 197–198. [author's note]

10   *Ibid.*, pp. 198–199. [author's note]

11   *Ibid..*, p. 200. [author's note]

emotional in a way that women find impoverishing and painful. Yet her book participates in mandating it. Neglecting the covert socializations and the overt forces which have channeled women into marriage and heterosexual romance, pressures ranging from the selling of daughters to the silences of literature to the images of the television screen, she, like Dinnerstein, is stuck with trying to reform a man-made institution—compulsory heterosexuality—as if, despite profound emotional impulses and complementarities drawing women toward women, there is a mystical/biological heterosexual inclination, a "preference" or "choice" which draws women toward men.

Moreover, it is understood that this "preference" does not need to be explained unless through the tortuous theory of the female Oedipus complex[12] or the necessity for species reproduction. It is lesbian sexuality which (usually, and incorrectly, "included" under male homosexuality) is seen as requiring explanation. This assumption of female heterosexuality seems to me in itself remarkable: it is an enormous assumption to have glided so silently into the foundations of our thought....

... I am suggesting that heterosexuality, like motherhood, needs to be recognized and studied as a *political institution*—even, or especially, by those individuals who feel they are, in their personal experience, the precursors of a new social relation between the sexes.

II

If women are the earliest sources of emotional caring and physical nurture for both female and male children, it would seem logical, from a feminist perspective at least, to pose the following questions: whether the search for love and tenderness in both sexes does not originally lead toward women; *why in fact women would ever redirect that search*; why species survival, the means of impregnation, and emotional/erotic relationships should ever have become so rigidly identified with each other; and why such violent strictures should be found necessary to enforce women's total emotional, erotic loyalty and

---

12 *female Oedipus complex* Stage of psychological development posited by Sigmund Freud and named for the title character of the ancient Greek tragedy *Oedipus the King*, who learns that he has unknowingly murdered his father and married his mother. Freud claimed that young boys desire their mothers and want to kill their fathers, whom they view as sexual rivals; the resolution of this complex of desires is, he argued, an important stage in a child's maturation. Freud later claimed that girls experience a "feminine" or "negative" version of the complex in which they desire their mothers but realize that, without a penis, they are unable to possess their mothers sexually; in a healthy resolution of this complex, according to Freud, desire is then redirected toward the father, and then toward men in general.

subservience to men. I doubt that enough feminist scholars and theorists have taken the pains to acknowledge the societal forces which wrench women's emotional and erotic energies away from themselves and other women and from woman-identified values. These forces, as I shall try to show, range from literal physical enslavement to disguising and distorting of possible options....

10   In her essay "The Origin of the Family," Kathleen Gough lists eight characteristics of male power in archaic and contemporary societies which I would like to use as a framework: "men's ability to deny women sexuality or to force it upon them; to command or exploit their labor to control their produce; to control or rob them of their children; to confine them physically and prevent their movement; to use them as objects in male transactions; to cramp their creativeness; or to withhold from them large areas of the society's knowledge and cultural attainments."[13] (Gough does not perceive these power characteristics as specifically enforcing heterosexuality, only as producing sexual inequality.) Below, Gough's words appear in italics; the elaboration of each of her categories, in brackets, is my own.

Characteristics of male power include *the power of men*

1. *to deny women* [their own] *sexuality*—[by means of clitoridectomy and infibulation;[14] chastity belts; punishment, including death, for female adultery; punishment, including death, for lesbian sexuality; psychoanalytic denial of the clitoris;[15] strictures against masturbation; denial of maternal and postmenopausal sensuality; unnecessary hysterectomy; pseudolesbian images in the media and literature;* closing of archives and destruction of documents relating to lesbian existence]

2. *or to force it* [male sexuality] *upon them*—[by means of rape (including marital rape*) and wife beating; father-daughter, brother-sister incest; the socialization of women to feel that male sexual "drive" amounts to a right;[16] idealization of heterosexual romance in art, literature, the media, advertising, etc.; child marriage; arranged marriage; prostitution; the

---

13 Kathleen Gough, "The Origin of the Family," in *Toward an Anthropology of Women*, ed. Rayna [Rapp] Reiter (New York: Monthly Review Press, 1975), pp. 69–70. [author's note]

14 *clitoridectomy* Removal of the clitoris, a type of female genital mutilation; *infibulation* Form of female genital mutilation in which, in addition to removal of the clitoris, external genitalia are cut off and the vaginal opening is partially closed with either stitching or intentional scarring.

15 *psychoanalytic ... clitoris* Freud and his followers tended to view the clitoris as inferior to the penis, and Freud described focus on clitoral pleasure as an immature stage of sexual development.

16 [Kathleen Barry, *Female Sexual Slavery* (Englewood Cliffs, N.J.: Prentice-Hall, Inc., 1979)], pp. 216–219. [author's note]

harem; psychoanalytic doctrines of frigidity and vaginal orgasm;[17] pornographic depictions of women responding pleasurably to sexual violence and humiliation (a subliminal message being that sadistic heterosexuality is more "normal" than sensuality between women)]

3. *to command or exploit their labor to control their produce*—[by means of the institutions of marriage and motherhood as unpaid production; the horizontal segregation of women in paid employment; the decoy of the upwardly mobile token woman;* male control of abortion, contraception, sterilization, and childbirth; pimping; female infanticide, which robs mothers of daughters and contributes to generalized devaluation of women]

4. *to control or rob them of their children*—[by means of father right and "legal kidnapping";[18] enforced sterilization; systematized infanticide; seizure of children from lesbian mothers by the courts; the malpractice of male obstetrics; use of the mother as the "token torturer"[19] in genital mutilation or in binding the daughter's feet (or mind) to fit her for marriage]

5. *to confine them physically and prevent their movement*—[by means of rape as terrorism, keeping women off the streets; purdah;[20] foot binding; atrophying of women's athletic capabilities; high heels and "feminine" dress codes in fashion; the veil; sexual harassment on the streets; horizontal segregation of women in employment; prescriptions for "full-time" mothering at home; enforced economic dependence of wives]

6. *to use them as objects in male transactions*—[use of women as "gifts"; bride price; pimping; arranged marriage; use of women as entertainers to facilitate male deals—e.g., wife-hostess, cocktail waitress required to dress for male sexual titillation, call girls, "bunnies,"* geisha, *kisaeng* prostitutes,[21] secretaries]

---

17 *psychoanalytic ... orgasm* Freud claimed that a sexually mature woman should experience "vaginal orgasm"—achieved through penetration by a penis—as opposed to the "immature" orgasm achieved through stimulation of the clitoris. Women who could not orgasm from penetration alone were described as "frigid."

18 Anna Demeter, *Legal Kidnapping* (Boston: Beacon, 1977), pp. xx, 126–128. [author's note]

19 [Mary Daly, *Gyn/Ecology: The Metaethics of Radicam Feminism* (Boston: Beacon Press, 1978)], pp. 139–141, 163–165. [author's note]

20 *purdah* Custom of preventing women from being seen by men, either through the use of clothing that fully conceals women's bodies and faces or by keeping women in segregated and private spaces.

21 *kisaeng prostitutes* Korean women entertainers, artists, medical practitioners, and providers of paid sex, often highly educated but belonging to a slave caste. Though the enslavement of kisaeng ended in the late nineteenth century, some aspects of the practice remain in the twenty-first century.

7. *to cramp their creativeness*—[witch persecutions as campaigns against midwives and female healers, and as pogrom* against independent, "unassimilated" women;[22] definition of male pursuits as more valuable than female within any culture, so that cultural values become the embodiment of male subjectivity; restriction of female self-fulfilment to marriage and motherhood; sexual exploitation of women by male artists and teachers; the social and economic disruption of women's creative aspirations;[23] erasure of female tradition][24]

8. *to withhold from them large areas of the society's knowledge and cultural attainments*—[by means of noneducation of females; the "Great Silence" regarding women and particularly lesbian existence in history and culture;[25] sex-role tracking which deflects women from science, technology, and other "masculine" pursuits; male social/professional bonding which excludes women; discrimination against women in the professions]

These are some of the methods by which male power is manifested and maintained. Looking at the schema, what surely impresses itself is the fact that we are confronting not a simple maintenance of inequality and property possession, but a pervasive cluster of forces, ranging from physical brutality to control of consciousness, which suggests that an enormous potential counter-force is having to be restrained.

Some of the forms by which male power manifests itself are more easily recognizable as enforcing heterosexuality on women than are others. Yet each one I have listed adds to the cluster of forces within which women have been convinced that marriage and sexual orientation toward men are inevitable—even if unsatisfying or oppressive—components of their lives. The chastity belt;* child marriage; erasure of lesbian existence (except as exotic and perverse) in art, literature, film; idealization of heterosexual romance and marriage—these are some fairly obvious forms of compulsion, the first two exemplifying physical force, the second two control of consciousness. While clitoridectomy has been assailed by feminists as a form of woman torture, Kathleen Barry first

---

22 Barbara Ehrenreich and Deirdre English, *Witches, Midwives, and Nurses: A History of Women Healers* (Old Westbury, N.Y.: Feminist Press, 1973); Andrea Dworkin, *Woman Hating* (New York: Dutton, 1974), pp. 118–154; Daly, pp. 178–222. [author's note]

23 See Virginia Woolf, *A Room of One's Own* (London: Hogarth 1929), and *id.*, *Three Guineas* (New York: Harcourt Brace, [1938] 1966); Tillie Olsen, *Silences* (Boston: Delacorte, 1978); Michelle Cliff, "The Resonance of Interruption," *Chrysalis: A Magazine of Women's Culture* 8 (1979): 29–37. [author's note]

24 Mary Daly, *Beyond God the Father* (Boston: Beacon, 1973), pp. 347–351; Olsen, pp. 22–46. [author's note]

25 Daly, *Beyond God the Father*, p. 93. [author's note]

pointed out that it is not simply a way of turning the young girl into a "marriageable" woman through brutal surgery. It intends that women in the intimate proximity of polygynous marriage will not form sexual relationships with each other, that—from a male, genital-fetishist perspective—female erotic connections, even in a sex-segregated situation, will be literally excised.[26]

The function of pornography as an influence on consciousness is a major public issue of our time, when a multibillion-dollar industry has the power to disseminate increasingly sadistic, women-degrading visual images. But even so-called soft-core pornography and advertising depict women as objects of sexual appetite devoid of emotional context, without individual meaning or personality—essentially as a sexual commodity to be consumed by males. (So-called lesbian pornography, created for the male voyeuristic eye, is equally devoid of emotional context or individual personality.) The most pernicious message relayed by pornography is that women are natural sexual prey to men and love it, that sexuality and violence are congruent, and that for women sex is essentially masochistic, humiliation pleasurable, physical abuse erotic. But along with this message comes another, not always recognized: that enforced submission and the use of cruelty, if played out in heterosexual pairing, is sexually "normal," while sensuality between women, including erotic mutuality and respect, is "queer," "sick," and either pornographic in itself or not very exciting compared with the sexuality of whips and bondage.[27] Pornography does not simply create a climate in which sex and violence are interchangeable; *it widens the range of behavior considered acceptable from men in heterosexual intercourse*—behavior which reiteratively strips women of their autonomy, dignity, and sexual potential, including the potential of loving and being loved by women in mutuality and integrity.

In her brilliant study *Sexual Harassment of Working Women: A Case of Sex Discrimination*, Catherine A. MacKinnon delineates the intersection of compulsory heterosexuality and economics. Under capitalism, women are horizontally segregated by gender and occupy a structurally inferior position in the workplace. This is hardly news, but MacKinnon raises the question why, even if capitalism "requires some collection of individuals to occupy low-status, low-paying positions ... such persons must be biologically female," and goes on to point out that "the fact that male employers often do not hire qualified women, *even when they could pay them less than men* suggests that more than

15

---

26 Barry, pp. 163–164. [author's note]

27 The issue of "lesbian sadomasochism" needs to be examined in terms of dominant cultures' teachings about the relation of sex and violence. I believe this to be another example of the "double life" of women. [author's note]

the profit motive is implicated" [emphasis added].[28] She cites a wealth of material documenting the fact that women are not only segregated in low-paying service jobs (as secretaries, domestics, nurses, typists, telephone operators, child-care workers, waitresses), but that "sexualization of the woman" is part of the job. Central and intrinsic to the economic realities of women's lives is the requirement that women will "market sexual attractiveness to men, who tend to hold the economic power and position to enforce their predilections." And MacKinnon documents that "sexual harassment perpetuates the interlocked structure by which women have been kept sexually in thrall to men at the bottom of the labor market. Two forces of American society converge: men's control over women's sexuality and capital's control over employees' work lives."[29] Thus, women in the workplace are at the mercy of sex as power in a vicious circle.* Economically disadvantaged, women—whether waitresses or professors—endure sexual harassment to keep their jobs and learn to behave in a complaisantly and ingratiatingly heterosexual manner because they discover this is their true qualification for employment, whatever the job description. And, MacKinnon notes, the woman who too decisively resists sexual overtures in the workplace is accused of being "dried up" and sexless, or lesbian. This raises a specific difference between the experiences of lesbians and homosexual men. A lesbian, closeted on her job because of heterosexual prejudice, is not simply forced into denying the truth of her outside relationships or private life. Her job depends on her pretending to be not merely heterosexual, but a heterosexual *woman* in terms of dressing and playing the feminine, deferential role required of "real" women.

MacKinnon raises radical questions as to the qualitative differences between sexual harassment, rape, and ordinary heterosexual intercourse. ("As one accused rapist put it, he hadn't used 'any more force than is usual for males during the preliminaries.'") She criticizes Susan Brownmiller[30] for separating rape from the mainstream of daily life and for her unexamined premise that "rape is violence, intercourse is sexuality," removing rape from the sexual sphere altogether. More crucially she argues that "taking rape from the realm of 'the sexual,' placing it in the realm of 'the violent,' allows one to be against it without raising any questions about the extent to which the institution of heterosexuality has defined force as a normal part of 'the preliminaries.'"[31]

---

28   Catharine A. MacKinnon, *Sexual Harassment of Working Women: A Case of Sex Discrimination* (New Haven, Conn.: Yale University Press, 1979), pp. 15–16. [author's note]

29   *Ibid.*, p. 174. [author's note]

30   [Susan Brownmiller, *Against Our Will: Men, Women, and Rape* (New York: Simon & Schuster, 1975)], *op. cit.* [author's note]

31   MacKinnon, p. 219.... [author's note]

"Never is it asked whether, under conditions of male supremacy, the notion of 'consent' has any meaning."[32]

The fact is that the workplace, among other social institutions, is a place where women have learned to accept male violation of their psychic and physical boundaries as the price of survival....

The means of assuring male sexual access to women have recently received searching investigation by Kathleen Barry.[33] She documents extensive and appalling evidence for the existence, on a very large scale, of international female slavery, the institution once known as "white slavery" but which in fact has involved, and at this very moment involves, women of every race and class. In the theoretical analysis derived from her research, Barry makes the connection between all enforced conditions under which women live subject to men: prostitution, marital rape, father-daughter and brother-sister incest, wife beating, pornography, bride price, the selling of daughters, purdah, and genital mutilation. She sees the rape paradigm—where the victim of sexual assault is held responsible for her own victimization—as leading to the rationalization and acceptance of other forms of enslavement where the woman is presumed to have "chosen" her fate, to embrace it passively, or to have courted it perversely through rash or unchaste behavior. On the contrary, Barry maintains, "female sexual slavery is present in ALL situations where women or girls cannot change the conditions of their existence; where regardless of how they got into those conditions, e.g., social pressure, economic hardship, misplaced trust or the longing for affection, they cannot get out; and where they are subject to sexual violence and exploitation."[34] ...

... [W]omen are all, in different ways and to different degrees, ... victims [of sexual slavery]; and part of the problem with naming and conceptualizing female sexual slavery is, as Barry clearly sees, compulsory heterosexuality.[35] Compulsory heterosexuality simplifies the task of the procurer and pimp in world-wide prostitution rings and "eros centers,"[36] while, in the privacy of the home, it leads the daughter to "accept" incest/rape by her father, the mother to deny that it is happening, the battered wife to stay on with an abusive husband. "Befriending or love" is a major tactic of the procurer, whose job it is to turn the runaway or the confused young girl over to the pimp for seasoning. The ideology of heterosexual romance, beamed at her from childhood out of fairy tales, television, films, advertising, popular songs, wedding pageantry, is a tool

---

32 MacKinnon, p. 298. [author's note]

33 Barry, *op. cit.* [author's note]

34 Barry, p. 33. [author's note]

35 *Ibid.*, p. 100. [author's note]

36 *eros centers* Buildings or streets where prostitution is conducted in European cities.

ready to the procurer's hand and one which he does not hesitate to use, as Barry documents. Early female indoctrination in "love" as an emotion may be largely a Western concept; but a more universal ideology concerns the primacy and controllability of the male sexual drive....

20
    ... The adolescent male sex drive, which, as both young women and men are taught, once triggered cannot take responsibility for itself or take no for an answer, becomes, according to Barry, the norm and rationale for adult male sexual behavior: a condition of *arrested sexual development*. Women learn to accept as natural the inevitability of this "drive" because they receive it as dogma. Hence, marital rape; hence, the Japanese wife resignedly packing her husband's suitcase for a weekend in the *kisaeng* brothels of Taiwan; hence, the psychological as well as economic imbalance of power between husband and wife, male employer and female worker, father and daughter, male professor and female student.

    The effect of male identification means

> internalizing the values of the colonizer and actively participating in carrying out the colonization of one's self and one's sex.... Male identification is the act whereby women place men above women, including themselves, in credibility, status, and importance in most situations, regardless of the comparative quality the women may bring to the situation.... Interaction with women is seen as a lesser form of relating on every level.[37]

What deserves further exploration is the doublethink* many women engage in and from which no woman is permanently and utterly free: However woman-to-woman relationships, female support networks, a female and feminist value system are relied on and cherished, indoctrination in male credibility and status can still create synapses in thought, denials of feeling, wishful thinking, a profound sexual and intellectual confusion.... I quote here from a letter I received the day I was writing this passage: "I have had very bad relationships with men—I am now in the midst of a very painful separation. I am trying to find my strength through women—without my friends, I could not survive." How many times a day do women speak words like these or think them or write them, and how often does the synapse reassert itself? ...

    The assumption that "most women are innately heterosexual" stands as a theoretical and political stumbling block for feminism. It remains a tenable assumption partly because lesbian existence has been written out of history or catalogued under disease, partly because it has been treated as exceptional rather than intrinsic, partly because to acknowledge that for women heterosexuality

---

37   *Ibid.*, p. 172. [author's note]

may not be a "preference" at all but something that has had to be imposed, managed, organized, propagandized, and maintained by force is an immense step to take if you consider yourself freely and "innately" heterosexual. Yet the failure to examine heterosexuality as an institution is like failing to admit that the economic system called capitalism or the caste system of racism is maintained by a variety of forces, including both physical violence and false consciousness. To take the step of questioning heterosexuality as a "preference" or "choice" for women—and to do the intellectual and emotional work that follows—will call for a special quality of courage in heterosexually identified feminists, but I think the rewards will be great: a freeing-up of thinking, the exploring of new paths, the shattering of another great silence, new clarity in personal relationships.

III

I have chosen to use the terms *lesbian existence* and *lesbian continuum* because the word *lesbianism* has a clinical and limiting ring. *Lesbian existence* suggests both the fact of the historical presence of lesbians and our continuing creation of the meaning of that existence. I mean the term *lesbian continuum* to include a range—through each woman's life and throughout history—of woman-identified experience, not simply the fact that a woman has had or consciously desired genital sexual experience with another woman. If we expand it to embrace many more forms of primary intensity between and among women, including the sharing of a rich inner life, the bonding against male tyranny, the giving and receiving of practical and political support, if we can also hear it in such associations as *marriage resistance* and the "haggard" behavior identified by Mary Daly (obsolete meanings: "intractable," "willful," "wanton," and "unchaste," "a woman reluctant to yield to wooing"),[38] we begin to grasp breadths of female history and psychology which have lain out of reach as a consequence of limited, mostly clinical, definitions of *lesbianism*.

Lesbian existence comprises both the breaking of a taboo and the rejection of a compulsory way of life. It is also a direct or indirect attack on male right of access to women. But it is more than these, although we may first begin to perceive it as a form of naysaying to patriarchy, an act of resistance. It has, of course, included isolation, self-hatred, breakdown, alcoholism, suicide, and intrawoman violence; we romanticize at our peril what it means to love and act against the grain, and under heavy penalties; and lesbian existence has been lived (unlike, say, Jewish or Catholic existence*) without access to any knowledge of a tradition, a continuity, a social underpinning. The destruction

---

38 Daly, *Gyn/Ecology*, p. 15. [author's note]

of records and memorabilia and letters documenting the realities of lesbian existence must be taken very seriously as a means of keeping heterosexuality compulsory for women, since what has been kept from our knowledge is joy, sensuality, courage, and community, as well as guilt, self-betrayal, and pain....

25   As the term *lesbian* has been held to limiting, clinical associations in its patriarchal definition, female friendship and comradeship have been set apart from the erotic, thus limiting the erotic itself. But as we deepen and broaden the range of what we define as lesbian existence, as we delineate a lesbian continuum, we begin to discover the erotic in female terms: as that which is unconfined to any single part of the body or solely to the body itself; as an energy not only diffuse but, as Audre Lorde has described it, omnipresent in "the sharing of joy, whether physical, emotional, psychic," and in the sharing of work; as the empowering joy which "makes us less willing to accept powerlessness, or those other supplied states of being which are not native to me, such as resignation, despair, self-effacement, depression, self-denial."[39] ...

If we consider the possibility that all women—from the infant suckling at her mother's breast, to the grown woman experiencing orgasmic sensations while suckling her own child, perhaps recalling her mother's milk smell in her own, to two women, like Virginia Woolf's Chloe and Olivia, who share a laboratory,[40] to the woman dying at ninety, touched and handled by women—exist on a lesbian continuum, we can see ourselves as moving in and out of this continuum, whether we identify ourselves as lesbian or not.

We can then connect aspects of woman identification as diverse as the impudent, intimate girl friendships of eight or nine year olds and the banding together of those women of the twelfth and fifteenth centuries known as the Beguines who "shared houses, rented to one another, bequeathed houses to their room-mates ... in cheap subdivided houses in the artisans' area of town," who "practiced Christian virtue on their own, dressing and living simply and not associating with men," who earned their livings as spinsters, bakers, nurses, or ran schools for young girls, and who managed—until the Church forced them to disperse—to live independent both of marriage and of conventual[41] restrictions.[42] It allows us to connect these women with the more

---

39   Audre Lorde, "Uses of the Erotic: The Erotic as Power," in *Sister Outsider* (Trumansburg, N.Y.: Crossing Press, 1984). [author's note]

40   Woolf, *A Room of One's Own*, p. 126. [author's note] [In *A Room of One's Own*, Woolf quotes from a recent book a passage beginning "Chloe liked Olivia. They shared a laboratory together...." and discusses the failure of literature to represent complex relationships between women.]

41   *conventual*   Of convents.

42   Gracia Clark, "The Beguines: A Mediaeval Women's Community," *Quest: A Feminist Quarterly* 1, no. 4 (1975): 73–80. [author's note]

celebrated "Lesbians" of the women's school around Sappho[43] of the seventh century B.C., with the secret sororities and economic networks reported among African women, and with the Chinese marriage-resistance sisterhoods—communities of women who refused marriage or who, if married, often refused to consummate their marriages and soon left their husbands, the only women in China who were not footbound[44] and who, Agnes Smedley tells us, welcomed the births of daughters and organized successful women's strikes in the silk mills.[45] It allows us to connect and compare disparate individual instances of marriage resistance: for example, the strategies available to Emily Dickinson,[46] a nineteenth-century white woman genius, with the strategies available to Zora Neale Hurston,[47] a twentieth-century Black woman genius. Dickinson never married, had tenuous intellectual friendships with men, lived self-convented in her genteel father's house in Amherst, and wrote a lifetime of passionate letters to her sister-in-law Sue Gilbert and a smaller group of such letters to her friend Kate Scott Anthon. Hurston married twice but soon left each husband, scrambled her way from Florida to Harlem to Columbia University* to Haiti and finally back to Florida, moved in and out of white patronage and poverty, professional success, and failure; her survival relationships were all with women, beginning with her mother. Both of these women in their vastly different circumstances were marriage resisters, committed to their own work and selfhood, and were later characterized as "apolitical." Both were drawn

---

43 *Sappho* Ancient Greek poet (seventh–sixth century BCE); many of her poems express passion toward women, and the word "lesbian" originated as a reference to her place of birth, the island of Lesbos. She is often described as having run a school for girls, but this is unlikely to be true.

44 *footbound* From the tenth century into the early twentieth century, bound feet were considered an enhancement of female beauty in China. The process of foot binding involved breaking bones in a child's feet, then bandaging them tightly, to create a smaller, "lotus" shaped foot.

45 See Denise Paulmé, ed., *Women of Tropical Africa* (Berkeley: University of California Press, 1963), pp. 7, 266–267. Some of these sororities are described as "a kind of defensive syndicate against the male element," their aims being "to offer concerted resistance to an oppressive patriarchate," "independence in relation to one's husband and with regard to motherhood, mutual aid, satisfaction of personal revenge." See also Audre Lorde, "Scratching the Surface: Some Notes on Barriers to Women and Loving," in *Sister Outsider*, pp. 45–52; Marjorie Topley, "Marriage Resistance in Rural Kwangtung," in *Women in Chinese Society*, ed. M. Wolf and R. Witke (Stanford, Calif.: Stanford University Press, 1978), pp. 67–89; Agnes Smedley, *Portraits of Chinese Women in Revolution*, ed. J. MacKinnon and S. MacKinnon (Old Westbury, N.Y.: Feminist Press, 1976), pp. 103–110. [author's note]

46 *Emily Dickinson* American poet (1830–86).

47 *Zora Neale Hurston* American writer of fiction and non-fiction (1891–1960).

to men of intellectual quality; for both of them women provided the ongoing fascination and sustenance of life.

If we think of heterosexuality as *the* natural emotional and sensual inclination for women, lives as these are seen as deviant, as pathological, or as emotionally and sensually deprived. Or, in more recent and permissive jargon, they are banalized* as "life styles." And the work of such women, whether merely the daily work of individual or collective survival and resistance or the work of the writer, the activist, the reformer, the anthropologist, or the artist—the work of self-creation—is undervalued, or seen as the bitter fruit of "penis envy"[48] or the sublimation of repressed eroticism or the meaningless rant of a "man-hater." But when we turn the lens of vision and consider the degree to which and the methods whereby heterosexual "preference" has actually been imposed on women, not only can we understand differently the meaning of individual lives and work, but we can begin to recognize a central fact of women's history: that women have always resisted male tyranny.... And we can connect these rebellions and the necessity for them with the physical passion of woman for woman which is central to lesbian existence: the erotic sensuality which has been, precisely, the most violently erased fact of female experience.

Heterosexuality has been both forcibly and subliminally imposed on women. Yet everywhere women have resisted it, often at the cost of physical torture, imprisonment, psychosurgery,[49] social ostracism, and extreme poverty. "Compulsory heterosexuality" was named as one of the "crimes against women" by the Brussels International Tribunal on Crimes against Women in 1976. Two pieces of testimony from two very different cultures reflect the degree to which persecution of lesbians is a global practice here and now. A report from Norway relates:

> A lesbian in Oslo was in a heterosexual marriage that didn't work, so she stared taking tranquillizers and ended up at the health sanatorium for treatment and rehabilitation.... The moment she said in family group therapy that she believed she was a lesbian, the doctor told her she was not. He knew from "looking into her eyes," he said. She had the eyes of a woman who wanted sexual intercourse with her husband. So she was subjected to so-called "couch therapy." She was put into a comfortably heated room, naked, on a bed, and for an hour her husband was to ... try to excite her sexually.... The idea was that the touching was always to end with sexual intercourse. She felt stronger and

---

48 *"penis envy"* Psychoanalytic term coined by Freud, who claimed that jealousy over lack of a penis was a normal component of women's psychological development.
49 *psychosurgery* Surgery (lobotomy, for example) intended as psychological treatment.

stronger aversion. She threw up and sometimes ran out of the room to avoid this "treatment." The more strongly she asserted that she was a lesbian, the more violent the forced heterosexual intercourse became. This treatment went on for about six months. She escaped from the hospital, but she was brought back. Again she escaped. She has not been there since. In the end she realized that she had been subjected to forcible rape for six months.

And from Mozambique:

I am condemned to a life of exile because I will not deny that I am a lesbian, that my primary commitments are, and will always be to other women. In the new Mozambique, lesbianism is considered a left-over from colonialism and decadent Western civilization. Lesbians are sent to rehabilitation camps to learn through self-criticism the correct line about themselves.... If I am forced to denounce my own love for women, if I therefore denounce myself, I could go back to Mozambique and join forces in the exciting and hard struggle of rebuilding a nation, including the struggle for the emancipation of Mozambiquan women. As it is, I either risk the rehabilitation camps, or remain in exile.[50]

Nor can it be assumed that women like those in Carroll Smith-Rosenberg's study,[51] who married, stayed married, yet dwelt in a profoundly female emotional and passional world, "preferred" or "chose" heterosexuality. Women have married because it was necessary, in order to survive economically, in order to have children who would not suffer economic deprivation or social ostracism, in order to remain respectable, in order to do what was expected of women, because coming out of "abnormal" childhoods they wanted to feel "normal" and because heterosexual romance has been represented as the great female adventure, duty, and fulfillment. We may faithfully or ambivalently have obeyed the institution, but our feelings—and our sensuality—have not been tamed or contained within it. There is no statistical documentation of the numbers of lesbians who have remained in heterosexual marriages for most of their lives....

This *double life*—this apparent acquiescence to an institution founded on male interest and prerogative—has been characteristic of female experience:

---

50   [Diana Russell and Nicole van de Ven, eds., *Proceedings of the International Tribunal on Crimes against Women* (Millbrae, Calif.: Les Femmes, 1976)], pp. 42–43, 56–57. [author's note]

51   *Carroll Smith-Rosenberg's study*   See "The Female World of Love and Ritual: Relations between Women in Nineteenth-Century America" in *Signs* (Autumn 1975), referenced in an earlier portion of Rich's essay that is omitted here.

in motherhood and in many kinds of heterosexual behavior, including the rituals of courtship; the pretense of asexuality by the nineteenth-century wife; the simulation of orgasm by the prostitute, the courtesan, the twentieth-century "sexually liberated" woman....

IV

Woman identification is a source of energy, a potential springhead of female power, curtailed and contained under the institution of heterosexuality. The denial of reality and invisibility to women's passion for women, women's choice of women as allies, life companions, and community, the forcing of such relationships into dissimulation and their disintegration under intense pressure have meant an incalculable loss to the power of all women *to change the social relations of the sexes, to liberate ourselves and each other*. The lie of compulsory female heterosexuality today afflicts not just feminist scholarship, but every profession, every reference work, every curriculum, every organizing attempt, every relationship or conversation over which it hovers. It creates, specifically, a profound falseness, hypocrisy, and hysteria in the heterosexual dialogue, for every heterosexual relationship is lived in the queasy strobe light of that lie. However we choose to identify ourselves, however we find ourselves labeled, it flickers across and distorts our lives.[52]

The lie keeps numberless women psychologically trapped, trying to fit mind, spirit, and sexuality into a prescribed script because they cannot look beyond the parameters of the acceptable. It pulls on the energy of such women even as it drains the energy of "closeted" lesbians—the energy exhausted in the double life. The lesbian trapped in the "closet," the woman imprisoned in prescriptive ideas of the "normal" share the pain of blocked options, broken connections, lost access to self-definition freely and powerfully assumed....

35

... [W]e can say that there is a *nascent** feminist political content in the act of choosing a woman lover or life partner in the face of institutionalized heterosexuality.... But for lesbian existence to realize this political content in an ultimately liberating form, the erotic choice must deepen and expand into conscious woman identification—into lesbian feminism.

The work that lies ahead, of unearthing and describing what I call here "lesbian existence," is potentially liberating for all women. It is work that must assuredly move beyond the limits of white and middle-class Western Women's Studies to examine women's lives, work, and groupings within every

---

52   See Russell and van de Ven, p. 40: "Few heterosexual women realize their lack of free choice about their sexuality, and few realize how and why compulsory sexuality is also a crime against them." [author's note]

racial, ethnic, and political structure. There are differences, moreover, between "lesbian existence" and the "lesbian continuum," differences we can discern even in the movement of our own lives. The lesbian continuum, I suggest, needs delineation in light of the "double life" of women, not only women self-described as heterosexual but also of self-described lesbians. We need a far more exhaustive account of the forms the double life has assumed. Historians need to ask at every point how heterosexuality as institution has been organized and maintained through the female wage scale, the enforcement of middle-class women's "leisure," the glamorization of so-called sexual liberation, the withholding of education from women, the imagery of "high art" and popular culture, the mystification of the "personal" sphere, and much else. We need an economics which comprehends the institution of heterosexuality, with its doubled workload for women and its sexual divisions of labor, as the most idealized of economic relations.

The question inevitably will arise: Are we then to condemn all heterosexual relationships, including those which are least oppressive? I believe this question, though often heartfelt, is the wrong question here. We have been stalled in a maze of false dichotomies which prevents our apprehending the institution as a whole: "good" versus "bad" marriages; "marriage for love" versus arranged marriage; "liberated" sex versus prostitution; heterosexual intercourse versus rape; *Liebeschmerz*[53] versus humiliation and dependency. Within the institution exist, of course, qualitative differences of experience; but the absence of choice remains the great unacknowledged reality, and in the absence of choice, women will remain dependent upon the chance or luck of particular relationships and will have no collective power to determine the meaning and place of sexuality in their lives. As we address the institution itself, moreover, we begin to perceive a history of female resistance which has never fully understood itself because it has been so fragmented, miscalled, erased. It will require a courageous grasp of the politics and economics, as well as the cultural propaganda, of heterosexuality to carry us beyond individual cases or diversified group situations into the complex kind of overview needed to undo the power men everywhere wield over women, power which has become a model for every other form of exploitation and illegitimate control.

(1980)

---

53 *Liebeschmerz* German: love pain.

ALICE MUNRO

WHAT IS REAL?

In this essay, a short story writer whose work is often described as having a strong feel for place attempts to answer questions as to why and how she uses elements from "real" experience in her works of fiction. The essay was first published as part of a collection about Canadian fiction, in 1982—the year in which Munro's fifth collection of short stories appeared. In 2012 her fourteenth collection was published, and the following year she was awarded the Nobel Prize for Literature.

Whenever people get an opportunity to ask me questions about my writing, I can be sure that some of the questions asked will be these:

"Do you write about real people?"

"Did those things really happen?"

"When you write about a small town are you really writing about Wingham?" (Wingham is the small town in Ontario where I was born and grew up, and it has often been assumed, by people who should know better, that I have simply "fictionalized" this place in my work. Indeed, the local newspaper has taken me to task for making it the "butt of a soured and cruel introspection.")

5   The usual thing, for writers, is to regard these either as very naive questions, asked by people who really don't understand the difference between autobiography and fiction, who can't recognize the device of the first-person narrator, or else as catch-you-out questions posed by journalists who hope to stir up exactly the sort of dreary (and to outsiders, slightly comic) indignation voiced by my home-town paper. Writers answer such questions patiently or crossly according to temperament and the mood they're in. They say, no, you must understand, my characters are composites; no, those things didn't happen the way I wrote about them; no, of course not, that isn't Wingham (or whatever other place it may be that has had the queer unsought-after distinction of hatching a writer). Or the writer may, riskily, ask the questioners what is real, anyway? None of this seems to be very satisfactory. People go on asking these same questions because the subject really does interest and bewilder them. It would seem to be quite true that they don't know what fiction is.

And how could they know, when what it is, is changing all the time, and we differ among ourselves, and we don't really try to explain because it is too difficult?

What I would like to do here is what I can't do in two or three sentences at the end of a reading. I won't try to explain what fiction is, and what short stories are (assuming, which we can't, that there is any fixed thing that it is and they are), but what short stories are to me, and how I write them, and how I use things that are "real." I will start by explaining how I read stories written by other people. For one thing, I can start reading them anywhere; from beginning to end, from end to beginning, from any point in between in either direction. So obviously I don't take up a story and follow it as if it were a road, taking me somewhere, with views and neat diversions along the way. I go into it, and move back and forth and settle here and there, and stay in it for a while. It's more like a house. Everybody knows what a house does, how it encloses space and makes connections between one enclosed space and another and presents what is outside in a new way. This is the nearest I can come to explaining what a story does for me, and what I want my stories to do for other people.

So when I write a story I want to make a certain kind of structure, and I know the feeling I want to get from being inside that structure. This is the hard part of the explanation, where I have to use a word like "feeling," which is not very precise, because if I attempt to be more intellectually respectable I will have to be dishonest. "Feeling" will have to do.

There is no blueprint for the structure. It's not a question of, "I'll make this kind of house because if I do it right it will have this effect." I've got to make, I've got to build up, a house, a story, to fit around the indescribable "feeling" that is like the soul of the story, and which I must insist upon in a dogged, embarrassed way, as being no more definable than that. And I don't know where it comes from. It seems to be already there, and some unlikely clue, such as a shop window or a bit of conversation, makes me aware of it. Then I start accumulating the material and putting it together. Some of the material I may have lying around already, in memories and observations, and some I invent, and some I have to go diligently looking for (factual details), while some is dumped in my lap (anecdotes, bits of speech). I see how this material might go together to make the shape I need, and I try it. I keep trying and seeing where I went wrong and trying again.

I suppose this is the place where I should talk about technical problems and how I solve them. The main reason I can't is that I'm never sure I do solve anything. Even when I say that I see where I went wrong, I'm being misleading. I never figure out how I'm going to change things, I never say to myself, "That page is heavy going, that paragraph's clumsy, I need some dialogue and shorter sentences." I feel a part that's wrong, like a soggy weight; then I pay

10

attention to the story, as if it were really happening somewhere, not just in my head, and in its own way, not mine. As a result, the sentences may indeed get shorter, there may be more dialogue, and so on. But though I've tried to pay attention to the story, I may not have got it right; those shorter sentences may be an evasion, a mistake. Every final draft, every published story, is still only an attempt, an approach, to the story.

I did promise to talk about using reality. "Why, if Jubilee isn't Wingham, has it got Shuter Street in it?" people want to know. Why have I described somebody's real ceramic elephant sitting on the mantel-piece? I could say I get momentum from doing things like this. The fictional room, town, world, needs a bit of starter dough from the real world. It's a device to help the writer—at least it helps me—but it arouses a certain baulked fury in the people who really do live on Shuter Street and the lady who owns the ceramic elephant. "Why do you put in something true and then go on and tell lies?" they say, and anybody who has been on the receiving end of this kind of thing knows how they feel.

"I do it for the sake of my art and to make this structure which encloses the soul of my story, that I've been telling you about," says the writer. "That is more important than anything."

Not to everybody, it isn't.

So I can see there might be a case, once you've written the story and got the momentum, for going back and changing the elephant to a camel (though there's always a chance the lady might complain that you made a nasty camel out of a beautiful elephant), and changing Shuter Street to Blank Street. But what about the big chunks of reality, without which your story can't exist? In the story *Royal Beatings*, I use a big chunk of reality: the story of the butcher, and of the young men who may have been egged on to "get" him. This is a story out of an old newspaper; it really did happen in a town I know. There is no legal difficulty in using it because it has been printed in a newspaper, and besides, the people who figure in it are all long dead. But there is a difficulty about offending people in that town who would feel that use of this story is a deliberate exposure, taunt and insult. Other people who have no connection with the real happening would say, "Why write about anything so hideous?" And lest you think that such an objection could only be raised by simple folk who read nothing but Harlequin Romances,* let me tell you that one of the questions most frequently asked at universities is, "Why do you write about things that are so depressing?" People can accept almost any amount of ugliness if it is contained in a familiar formula, as it is on television, but when they come closer to their own place, their own lives, they are much offended by a lack of editing.

15   There are ways I can defend myself against such objections. I can say, "I do it in the interests of historical reality. That is what the old days were really

like." Or, "I do it to show the dark side of human nature, the beast let loose, the evil we can run up against in communities and families." In certain countries I could say, "I do it to show how bad things were under the old system when there were prosperous butchers and young fellows hanging around livery stables and nobody thought about building a new society." But the fact is, the minute I say *to show* I am telling a lie. I don't do it to show anything. I put this story at the heart of my story because I need it there and it belongs there. It is the black room at the center of the house with all other rooms leading to and away from it. That is all. A strange defense. Who told me to write this story? Who feels any need of it before it is written? I do. I do, so that I might grab off this piece of horrid reality and install it where I see fit, even if Hat Nettleton and his friends[1] were still around to make me sorry.

The answer seems to be as confusing as ever. Lots of true answers are. Yes and no. Yes, I use bits of what is real, in the sense of being really there and really happening, in the world, as most people see it, and I transform it into something that is really there and really happening, in my story. No, I am not concerned with using what is real to make any sort of record or prove any sort of point, and I am not concerned with any methods of selection but my own, which I can't fully explain. This is quite presumptuous, and if writers are not allowed to be so—and quite often, in many places, they are not—I see no point in the writing of fiction.

(1982)

---

1   *Hat Nettleton and his friends*   The three young men who assault a butcher in Munro's story "Royal Beatings."

ELAINE SHOWALTER

REPRESENTING OPHELIA: WOMEN, MADNESS, AND THE RESPONSIBILITIES OF FEMINIST CRITICISM

Elaine Showalter is a feminist critic particularly well-known for her work on hysteria and madness in literature. Her book A Literature of Their Own *(1977) founded gynocritics, a discourse dedicated to examining from a female perspective women's writing and the treatment of female characters. In this essay, Showalter discusses the character of Ophelia in Shakespeare's* Hamlet, *with particular attention to the history of her representation.*

" **A** s a sort of a come-on, I announced that I would speak today about that piece of bait named Ophelia, and I'll be as good as my word." These are the words which begin the psychoanalytic seminar on *Hamlet* presented in Paris in 1959 by Jacques Lacan. But despite his promising come-on, Lacan was *not* as good as his word. He goes on for some 41 pages to speak about Hamlet, and when he does mention Ophelia, she is merely what Lacan calls "the object Ophelia"—that is, the object of Hamlet's male desire. The etymology of Ophelia, Lacan asserts, is "O-phallus," and her role in the drama can only be to function as the exteriorized figuration of what Lacan predictably and, in view of his own early work with psychotic women, disappointingly suggests is the phallus as transcendental signifier.[1] To play such a part obviously makes

---

1   Jacques Lacan, "Desire and the interpretation of desire in *Hamlet*," in *Literature and Psychoanalysis: The Question of Reading: Otherwise*, ed. Shoshana Felman (Baltimore, 1982), 11, 20, 23. Lacan is also wrong about the etymology of Ophelia, which probably derives from the Greek for "help" or "succor." Charlotte M. Yonge suggested a derivation from "ophis," "serpent." See her *History of Christian Names* (1884, republished Chicago, 1966), 346–7. I am indebted to Walter Jackson Bate for this reference. [Unless otherwise noted, all notes to this essay are from the author.]

Ophelia "essential," as Lacan admits; but only because, in his words, "she is linked forever, for centuries, to the figure of Hamlet."[2]

The bait-and-switch* game that Lacan plays with Ophelia is a cynical but not unusual instance of her deployment in psychiatric and critical texts. For most critics of Shakespeare, Ophelia has been an insignificant minor character in the play, touching in her weakness and madness but chiefly interesting, of course, in what she tells us about Hamlet. And while female readers of Shakespeare have often attempted to champion Ophelia, even feminist critics have done so with a certain embarrassment. As Annette Kolodny ruefully admits: "it is after all, an imposition of high order to ask the viewer to attend to Ophelia's sufferings in a scene where, before, he's always so comfortably kept his eye fixed on Hamlet."

Yet when feminist criticism allows Ophelia to upstage Hamlet, it also brings to the foreground the issues in an ongoing theoretical debate about the cultural links between femininity, female sexuality, insanity, and representation. Though she is neglected in criticism, Ophelia is probably the most frequently illustrated and cited of Shakespeare's heroines. Her visibility as a subject in literature, popular culture, and painting, from Redon who paints her drowning, to Bob Dylan, who places her on Desolation Row, to Cannon Mills, which has named a flowery sheet pattern after her,* is in inverse relation to her invisibility in Shakespearean critical texts. Why has she been such a potent and obsessive figure in our cultural mythology? Insofar as Hamlet names Ophelia as "woman" and "frailty," substituting an ideological view of femininity for a personal one, is she indeed representative of Woman, and does her madness stand for the oppression of women in society as well as in tragedy? Furthermore, since Laertes calls Ophelia a "document in madness," does she represent the textual archetype of woman *as* madness, or madness *as* woman? And finally, how should feminist criticism represent Ophelia in its own discourse? What is our responsibility towards her as character and as woman?

Feminist critics have offered a variety of responses to these questions. Some have maintained that we should represent Ophelia as a lawyer represents a client, that we should become her Horatia,* in this harsh world reporting her and her cause aright to the unsatisfied. Carol Neely, for example, describes advocacy—speaking *for* Ophelia—as our proper role: "As a feminist critic," she writes, "I must 'tell' Ophelia's story."[3] But what can we mean by Ophelia's story? The story of her life? The story of her betrayal at the hands of her father,

---

2   Annette Kolodny, "Dancing through the minefield: some observations on the theory, practice, and politics of feminist literary criticism" (*Feminist Studies*, 6 (1980)), 7.

3   Carol Neely, "Feminist modes of Shakespearean criticism" (*Women's Studies*, 9 (1981)), 11.

brother, lover, court, society? The story of her rejection and marginalization by male critics of Shakespeare? Shakespeare gives us very little information from which to imagine a past for Ophelia. She appears in only five of the play's twenty scenes; the pre-play course of her love story with Hamlet is known only by a few ambiguous flashbacks. Her tragedy is subordinated in the play; unlike Hamlet, she does not struggle with moral choices or alternatives. Thus another feminist critic, Lee Edwards, concludes that it is impossible to reconstruct Ophelia's biography from the text: "We can imagine Hamlet's story without Ophelia, but Ophelia literally has no story without Hamlet."[4]

5   If we turn from American to French feminist theory, Ophelia might confirm the impossibility of representing the feminine in patriarchal discourse as other than madness, incoherence, fluidity, or silence. In French theoretical criticism, the feminine or "Woman" is that which escapes representation in patriarchal language and symbolism; it remains on the side of negativity, absence, and lack. In comparison to Hamlet, Ophelia is certainly a creature of lack. "I think nothing, my lord," she tells him in the Mousetrap scene, and he cruelly twists her words:

> *Hamlet:* That's a fair thought to lie between maids' legs.
> *Ophelia:* What is, my lord?
> *Hamlet:* Nothing.

(III.ii.117–19)

In Elizabethan slang, "nothing" was a term for the female genitalia, as in *Much Ado About Nothing*. To Hamlet, then, "nothing" is what lies between maids' legs, for, in the male visual system of representation and desire, women's sexual organs, in the words of the French psychoanalyst Luce Irigaray, "represent the horror of having nothing to see."[5] When Ophelia is mad, Gertrude says that "Her speech is nothing," mere "unshaped use." Ophelia's speech represents the horror of having nothing to say in the public terms defined by the court. Deprived of thought, sexuality, language, Ophelia's story becomes the story of O—the zero, the empty circle or mystery of feminine difference, the cipher of female sexuality to be deciphered by feminist interpretation.[6]

---

4   Lee Edwards, "The labors of Psyche" (*Critical Inquiry*, 6 (1979)), 36.

5   Luce Irigaray: see *New French Feminisms*, ed. Elaine Marks and Isabelle de Courtivron (New York, 1982), 101. The quotation above, from III.ii, is taken from the Arden Shakespeare, *Hamlet*, ed. Harold Jenkins (London and New York, 1982), 295. All quotations from *Hamlet* are from this text.

6   On images of negation and feminine enclosure, see David Wilbern, "Shakespeare's 'nothing,'" in *Representing Shakespeare: New Psychoanalytic Essays*, ed. Murray M. Schwartz and Coppélia Kahn (Baltimore, 1981).

A third approach would be to read Ophelia's story as the female subtext of the tragedy, the repressed story of Hamlet. In this reading, Ophelia represents the strong emotions that the Elizabethans as well as the Freudians thought womanish and unmanly. When Laertes weeps for his dead sister he says of his tears that "When these are gone, / The woman will be out"—that is to say, that the feminine and shameful part of his nature will be purged. According to David Leverenz, in an important essay called "The Woman in *Hamlet*," Hamlet's disgust at the feminine passivity in himself is translated into violent revulsion against women, and into his brutal behavior towards Ophelia. Ophelia's suicide, Leverenz argues, then becomes "a microcosm of the male world's banishment of the female, because 'woman' represents everything denied by reasonable men."[7]

It is perhaps because Hamlet's emotional vulnerability can so readily be conceptualized as feminine that this is the only heroic male role in Shakespeare which has been regularly acted by women, in a tradition from Sarah Bernhardt to, most recently, Diane Venora, in a production directed by Joseph Papp. Leopold Bloom speculates on this tradition in *Ulysses*,* musing on the Hamlet of the actress Mrs. Bandman Palmer: "Male impersonator. Perhaps he was a woman? Why Ophelia committed suicide?"[8]

While all of these approaches have much to recommend them, each also presents critical problems. To liberate Ophelia from the text, or to make her its tragic center, is to re-appropriate her for our own ends; to dissolve her into a female symbolism of absence is to endorse our own marginality; to make her Hamlet's anima* is to reduce her to a metaphor of male experience. I would like to propose instead that Ophelia *does* have a story of her own that feminist criticism can tell; it is neither her life story, nor her love story, nor Lacan's story, but rather the *history* of her representation. This essay tries to bring together some of the categories of French feminist thought about the "feminine" with the empirical energies of American historical and critical research: to yoke French theory and Yankee knowhow.*

Tracing the iconography of Ophelia in English and French painting, photography, psychiatry, and literature, as well as in theatrical production, I will be showing first of all the representational bonds between female insanity and female sexuality. Secondly, I want to demonstrate the two-way transaction between psychiatric theory and cultural representation. As one medical historian has observed, we could provide a manual of female insanity by chronicling the illustrations of Ophelia; this is so because the illustrations of Ophelia have

10

---

7   David Leverenz, "The woman in *Hamlet*: an interpersonal view" (*Signs*, 4 (1978)), 303.

8   James Joyce, *Ulysses* (New York, 1961), 76.

played a major role in the theoretical construction of female insanity.[9] Finally, I want to suggest that the feminist revision of Ophelia comes as much from the actress's freedom as from the critic's interpretation.[10] When Shakespeare's heroines began to be played by women instead of boys,* the presence of the female body and female voice, quite apart from details of interpretation, created new meanings and subversive tensions in these roles, and perhaps most importantly with Ophelia. Looking at Ophelia's history on and off the stage, I will point out the contest between male and female representations of Ophelia, cycles of critical repression and feminist reclamation of which contemporary feminist criticism is only the most recent phase. By beginning with these data from cultural history, instead of moving from the grid of literary theory, I hope to conclude with a fuller sense of the responsibilities of feminist criticism, as well as a new perspective on Ophelia.

"Of all the characters in *Hamlet*," Bridget Lyons has pointed out, "Ophelia is most persistently presented in terms of symbolic meanings."[11] Her behavior, her appearance, her gestures, her costume, her props, are freighted with emblematic significance, and for many generations of Shakespearean critics her part in the play has seemed to be primarily iconographic.* Ophelia's symbolic meanings, moreover, are specifically feminine. Whereas for Hamlet madness is metaphysical, linked with culture, for Ophelia it is a product of the female body and female nature, perhaps that nature's purest form. On the Elizabethan stage, the conventions of female insanity were sharply defined. Ophelia dresses in white, decks herself with "fantastical garlands" of wild flowers, and enters, according to the stage directions of the "Bad" Quarto, "distracted" playing on a lute with her "hair down singing." Her speeches are marked by extravagant metaphors, lyrical free associations, and "explosive sexual imagery."[12] She sings wistful and bawdy ballads, and ends her life by drowning.

All of these conventions carry specific messages about femininity and sexuality. Ophelia's virginal and vacant white is contrasted with Hamlet's scholar's garb, his "suits of solemn black." Her flowers suggest the discordant double images of female sexuality as both innocent blossoming and whorish contamination; she is the "green girl" of pastoral, the virginal "Rose of May"

---

9   Sander L. Gilman, *Seeing the Insane* (New York, 1981), 126.

10 See Michael Goldman, *The Actor's Freedom: Toward a Theory of Drama* (New York, 1975), for a stimulating discussion of the interpretative interaction between actor and audience.

11 Bridget Lyons, "The iconography of Ophelia" (*English Literary History*, 44 (1977)), 61.

12 See Maurice and Hanna Charney, "The language of Shakespeare's madwomen" (*Signs*, 3 (1977)), 451, 457; and Carroll Camden, "On Ophelia's madness" (*Shakespeare Quarterly* (1964)), 254.

and the sexually explicit madwoman who, in giving away her wild flowers and herbs, is symbolically deflowering herself. The "weedy trophies" and phallic "long purples" which she wears to her death intimate an improper and discordant sexuality that Gertrude's lovely elegy cannot quite obscure.[13] In Elizabethan and Jacobean drama, the stage direction that a woman enters with disheveled hair indicates that she might either be mad or the victim of a rape; the disordered hair, her offense against decorum, suggests sensuality in each case.[14] The mad Ophelia's bawdy songs and verbal license, while they give her access to "an entirely different range of experience" from what she is allowed as the dutiful daughter, seem to be her one sanctioned form of self-assertion as a woman, quickly followed, as if in retribution, by her death.[15]

Drowning too was associated with the feminine, with female fluidity as opposed to masculine aridity. In his discussion of the "Ophelia complex," the phenomenologist Gaston Bachelard traces the symbolic connections between women, water, and death. Drowning, he suggests, becomes the truly feminine death in the dramas of literature and life, one which is a beautiful immersion and submersion in the female element. Water is the profound and organic symbol of the liquid woman whose eyes are so easily drowned in tears, as her body is the repository of blood, amniotic fluid, and milk. A man contemplating this feminine suicide understands it by reaching for what is feminine in himself, like Laertes, by a temporary surrender to his own fluidity—that is, his tears; and he becomes a man again in becoming once more dry—when his tears are stopped.[16]

Clinically speaking, Ophelia's behavior and appearance are characteristic of the malady the Elizabethans would have diagnosed as female love-melancholy, or erotomania. From about 1580, melancholy* had become a fashionable disease among young men, especially in London, and Hamlet himself is a prototype of the melancholy hero. Yet the epidemic of melancholy associated with intellectual and imaginative genius "curiously bypassed women." Women's melancholy was seen instead as biological, and emotional in origins.[17]

---

13 See Margery Garber, *Coming of Age in Shakespeare* (London, 1981), 155-7; and Lyons, op. cit., 65, 70–2.

14 On disheveled hair as a signifier of madness or rape, see Charney and Charney, op. cit., 452–3, 457; and Allan Dessen, *Elizabethan Stage Conventions and Modern Interpreters* (Cambridge, 1984), 36–8. Thanks to Allan Dessen for letting me see advance proofs of his book.

15 Charney and Charney, op. cit., 456.

16 Gaston Bachelard, *L'Eau et les rêves* (Paris, 1942), 109–25. See also Brigitte Peucker, "Dröste-Hulshof's Ophelia and the recovery of voice" (*The Journal of English and Germanic Philology* (1983)), 374–91.

17 Vieda Skultans, *English Madness: Ideas on Insanity 1580–1890* (London, 1977), 79–81. On historical cases of love-melancholy, see Michael MacDonald, *Mystical Bedlam* (Cambridge, 1982).

15   On the stage, Ophelia's madness was presented as the predicable outcome of erotomania. From 1660, when women first appeared on the public stage, to the beginnings of the eighteenth century, the most celebrated of the actresses who played Ophelia were those whom rumor credited with disappointments in love. The greatest triumph was reserved for Susan Mountfort, a former actress at Lincoln's Inn Fields who had gone mad after her lover's betrayal. One night in 1720 she escaped from her keeper, rushed to the theater, and just as the Ophelia of the evening was to enter for her mad scene, "sprang forward in her place ... with wild eyes and wavering motion."[18] As a contemporary reported, "she was in truth *Ophelia herself*, to the amazement of the performers as well as of the audience—nature having made this last effort, her vital powers failed her and she died soon after."[19] These theatrical legends reinforced the belief of the age that female madness was a part of female nature, less to be imitated by an actress than demonstrated by a deranged woman in a performance of her emotions.

The subversive or violent possibilities of the mad scene were nearly eliminated, however, on the eighteenth-century stage. Late Augustan* stereotypes of female love-melancholy were sentimentalized versions which minimized the force of female sexuality, and made female insanity a pretty stimulant to male sensibility. Actresses such as Mrs. Lessingham in 1772, and Mary Bolton in 1811, played Ophelia in this decorous style, relying on the familiar images of the white dress, loose hair, and wild flowers to convey a polite feminine distraction, highly suitable for pictorial reproduction, and appropriate for Samuel Johnson's description of Ophelia as young, beautiful, harmless, and pious. Even Mrs. Siddons in 1785 played the mad scene with stately and classical dignity. For much of the period, in fact, Augustan objections to the levity and indecency of Ophelia's language and behavior led to censorship of the part. Her lines were frequently cut, and the role was often assigned to a singer instead of an actress, making the mode of representation musical rather than visual or verbal.

But whereas the Augustan response to madness was a denial, the romantic* response was an embrace.[20] The figure of the madwoman permeates romantic literature, from the gothic novelists to Wordsworth and Scott in such texts as "The Thorn" and *The Heart of Midlothian*, where she stands for sexual victimization, bereavement, and thrilling emotional extremity. Romantic artists

---

18   C.E.L. Wingate, *Shakespeare's Heroines on the Stage* (New York, 1895), 283–4, 288–9.

19   Charles Hiatt, *Ellen Terry* (London, 1898), 11.

20   Max Byrd, *Visits to Bedlam: Madness and Literature in the Eighteenth Century* (Columbia, 1971), xiv.

such as Thomas Barker and George Shepheard painted pathetically abandoned Crazy Kates and Crazy Anns, while Henry Fuseli's "Mad Kate" is almost demonically possessed, an orphan of the romantic storm.

In the Shakespearean theater, Ophelia's romantic revival began in France rather than England. When Charles Kemble made his Paris debut as Hamlet with an English troupe in 1827, his Ophelia was a young Irish ingénue named Harriet Smithson. Smithson used "her extensive command of mime to depict in precise gesture the state of Ophelia's confused mind."[21] In the mad scene, she entered in a long black veil, suggesting the standard imagery of female sexual mystery in the gothic novel, with scattered bedlamish wisps of straw in her hair. Spreading the veil on the ground as she sang, she spread flowers upon it in the shape of a cross, as if to make her father's grave, and mimed a burial, a piece of stage business which remained in vogue for the rest of the century.

The French audiences were stunned. Dumas recalled that "it was the first time I saw in the theater real passions, giving life to men and women of flesh and blood."[22] The 23-year-old Hector Berlioz, who was in the audience on the first night, fell madly in love, and eventually married Harriet Smithson despite his family's frantic opposition. Her image as the mad Ophelia was represented in popular lithographs and exhibited in bookshop and printshop windows. Her costume was imitated by the fashionable, and a coiffure "à la folle," consisting of a "black veil with wisps of straw tastefully interwoven" in the hair, was widely copied by the Parisian beau monde,* always on the lookout for something new.[23]

Although Smithson never acted Ophelia on the English stage, her intensely visual performance quickly influenced English productions as well; and indeed the romantic Ophelia—a young girl passionately and visibly driven to picturesque madness—became the dominant international acting style for the next 150 years, from Helena Modjeska in Poland in 1871, to the 18-year-old Jean Simmons in the Laurence Olivier film of 1948.

Whereas the romantic Hamlet, in Coleridge's famous dictum, thinks too much, has an "overbalance of the contemplative faculty" and an over-active intellect, the romantic Ophelia is a girl who *feels* too much, who drowns in feelings. The romantic critics seem to have felt that the less said about Ophelia the better; the point was to *look* at her. Hazlitt, for one, is speechless before her, calling her "a character almost too exquisitely touching to be dwelt upon."[24] While the Augustans represent Ophelia as music, the romantics transform her

20

21 Peter Raby, *Fair Ophelia: Harriet Smithson Berlioz* (Cambridge, 1982), 63.
22 Ibid., 68.
23 Ibid., 72, 75.
24 Quoted in Camden, op. cit., 217.

into an *objet d'art*, as if to take literally Claudius's lament, "poor Ophelia / Divided from herself and her fair judgment, / Without the which we are pictures."

Smithson's performance is best recaptured in a series of pictures done by Delacroix from 1830 to 1850, which show a strong romantic interest in the relation of female sexuality and insanity.[25] The most innovative and influential of Delacroix's lithographs is *La Mort d'Ophélie* of 1843, the first of three studies. Its sensual languor, with Ophelia half-suspended in the stream as her dress slips from her body, anticipated the fascination with the erotic trance of the hysteric as it would be studied by Jean-Martin Charcot and his students, including Janet and Freud. Delacroix's interest in the drowning Ophelia is also reproduced to the point of obsession in later nineteenth-century painting. The English Pre-Raphaelites* painted her again and again, choosing the drowning which is only described in the play, and where no actress's image had preceded them or interfered with their imaginative supremacy.

In the Royal Academy show of 1852, Arthur Hughes's entry shows a tiny waif-like creature—a sort of Tinker Bell* Ophelia—in a filmy white gown, perched on a tree trunk by the stream. The overall effect is softened, sexless, and hazy, although the straw in her hair resembles a crown of thorns. Hughes's juxtaposition of childlike femininity and Christian martyrdom was overpowered, however, by John Everett Millais's great painting of Ophelia in the same show. While Millais's Ophelia is sensuous siren as well as victim, the artist rather than the subject dominates the scene. The division of space between Ophelia and the natural details Millais had so painstakingly pursued reduces her to one more visual object; and the painting has such a hard surface, strangely flattened perspective, and brilliant light that it seems cruelly indifferent to the woman's death.

• • •

These Pre-Raphaelite images were part of a new and intricate traffic between images of women and madness in late nineteenth-century literature, psychiatry, drama, and art. First of all, superintendents of Victorian lunatic asylums were also enthusiasts of Shakespeare, who turned to his dramas for models of mental aberration that could be applied to their clinical practice. The case study of Ophelia was one that seemed particularly useful as an account of hysteria or mental breakdown in adolescence, a period of sexual instability which the Victorians regarded as risky for women's mental health. As Dr. John Charles Buckmill, president of the Medico-Psychological Association, remarked in 1859, "Ophelia is the very type of a class of cases by no means uncommon. Every mental physician of moderately extensive experience must have seen

---

25   Raby, op. cit., 182.

many Ophelias. It is a copy from nature, after the fashion of the Pre-Raphaelite school."[26] Dr. John Conolly, the celebrated superintendent of the Hanwell Asylum, and founder of the committee to make Stratford a national trust, concurred. In his *Study of Hamlet* in 1863 he noted that even casual visitors to mental institutions could recognize an Ophelia in the wards: "the same young years, the same faded beauty, the same fantastic dress and interrupted song."[27] Medical textbooks illustrated their discussions of female patients with sketches of Ophelia-like maidens.

But Conolly also pointed out that the graceful Ophelias who dominated the Victorian stage were quite unlike the women who had become the majority of the inmate population in Victorian public asylums. "It seems to be supposed," he protested, "that it is an easy task to play the part of a crazy girl, and that it is chiefly composed of singing and prettiness. The habitual courtesy, the partial rudeness of mental disorder, are things to be witnessed.... An actress, ambitious of something beyond cold imitation, might find the contemplation of such cases a not unprofitable study."[28]

Yet when Ellen Terry took up Conolly's challenge, and went to an asylum to observe real madwomen, she found them "too *theatrical*" to teach her anything.[29] This was because the iconography of the romantic Ophelia had begun to infiltrate reality, to define a style for mad young women seeking to express and communicate their distress. And where the women themselves did not willingly throw themselves into Ophelia-like postures, asylum superintendents, armed with the new technology of photography, imposed the costume, gesture, props, and expression of Ophelia upon them. In England, the camera was introduced to asylum work in the 1850s by Dr. Hugh Welch Diamond, who photographed his female patients at the Surrey Asylum and at Bethlem. Diamond was heavily influenced by literary and visual models in his posing of the female subjects. His pictures of madwomen, posed in prayer, or decked with Ophelia-like garlands, were copied for Victorian consumption as touched-up lithographs in professional journals.[30]

Reality, psychiatry, and representational convention were even more confused in the photographic records of hysteria produced in the 1870s by

---

26   J.C. Bucknill, *The Psychology of Shakespeare* (London, 1859, reprinted New York, 1979), 110. For more extensive discussions of Victorian psychiatry and Ophelia figures, see Elaine Showalter, *The Female Malady: Women, Madness and English Culture* (New York, 1986).

27   John Conolly, *Study of Hamlet* (London, 1863), 177.

28   Ibid., 177–8, 180.

29   Ellen Terry, *The Story of My Life* (London, 1908), 154.

30   Diamond's photographs are reproduced in Sander L. Gilman, *The Face of Madness: Hugh W. Diamond and the Origin of Psychiatric Photography* (New York, 1976).

Jean-Martin Charcot. Charcot was the first clinician to install a fully equipped photographic atelier in his Paris hospital, La Salpêtrière, to record the performances of his hysterical stars. Charcot's clinic became, as he said, a "living theater" of female pathology; his women patients were coached in their performances for the camera, and, under hypnosis, were sometimes instructed to play heroines from Shakespeare. Among them, a 15-year-old girl named Augustine was featured in the published volumes called *Iconographies* in every posture of *la grande hystérie*.* With her white hospital gown and flowing locks, Augustine frequently resembles the reproductions of Ophelia as icon and actress which had been in wide circulation.[31]

But if the Victorian madwoman looks mutely out from men's pictures, and acts a part men had staged and directed, she is very differently represented in the feminist revision of Ophelia initiated by newly powerful and respectable Victorian actresses, and by women critics of Shakespeare. In their efforts to defend Ophelia, they invent a story for her drawn from their own experiences, grievances, and desires.

Probably the most famous of the Victorian feminist revisions of the Ophelia story was Mary Cowden Clarke's *The Girlhood of Shakespeare's Heroines*, published in 1852. Unlike other Victorian moralizing and didactic studies of the female characters of Shakespeare's plays, Clarke's was specifically addressed to the wrongs of women, and especially to the sexual double standard. In a chapter on Ophelia called "The rose of Elsinore," Clarke tells how the child Ophelia was left behind in the care of a peasant couple when Polonius was called to the court at Paris, and raised in a cottage with a foster-sister and brother, Jutha and Ulf. Jutha is seduced and betrayed by a deceitful knight, and Ophelia discovers the bodies of Jutha and her still-born child, lying "white, frigid, and still" in the deserted parlor of the cottage in the middle of the night. Ulf, a "hairy loutish boy," likes to torture flies, to eat songbirds, and to rip the petals off roses, and he is also very eager to give little Ophelia what he calls a bear-hug. Both repelled and masochistically attracted by Ulf, Ophelia is repeatedly cornered by him as she grows up; once she escapes the hug by hitting him with a branch of wild roses; another time, he sneaks into her bedroom "in his brutish pertinacity to obtain the hug he had promised himself," but just as he bends over to her trembling body, Ophelia is saved by the reappearance of her real mother.

A few years later, back at the court, she discovers the hanged body of another friend, who has killed herself after being "victimized and deserted by the

---

31   See Georges Didi-Huberman, *L'Invention de l'hystérie* (Paris, 1982), and Stephen Heath, *The Sexual Fix* (London, 1983), 36.

same evil seducer." Not surprisingly, Ophelia breaks down with brain fever—a staple mental illness of Victorian fiction—and has prophetic hallucinations of a brook beneath willow trees where something bad will happen to her. The warnings of Polonius and Laertes have little to add to this history of female sexual trauma.[32]

On the Victorian stage, it was Ellen Terry, daring and unconventional in her own life, who led the way in acting Ophelia in feminist terms as a consistent psychological study in sexual intimidation, a girl terrified of her father, of her lover, and of life itself. Terry's debut as Ophelia in Henry Irving's production in 1878 was a landmark. According to one reviewer, her Ophelia was "the terrible spectacle of a normal girl becoming hopelessly imbecile as the result of overwhelming mental agony. Hers was an insanity without wrath or rage, without exaltation or paroxysms."[33] Her "poetic and intellectual performance" also inspired other actresses to rebel against the conventions of invisibility and negation associated with the part.

Terry was the first to challenge the tradition of Ophelia's dressing in emblematic white. For the French poets, such as Rimbaud, Hugo, Musset, Mallarmé and Laforgue, whiteness was part of Ophelia's essential feminine symbolism; they call her "blanche Ophélia" and compare her to a lily, a cloud, or snow. Yet whiteness also made her a transparency, an absence that took on the colors of Hamlet's moods, and that, for the symbolists like Mallarmé, made her a blank page to be written over or on by the male imagination. Although Irving was able to prevent Terry from wearing black in the mad scene, exclaiming "My God, Madam, there must be only *one* black figure in this play, and that's Hamlet!" (Irving, of course, was playing Hamlet), nonetheless actresses such as Gertrude Eliot, Helen Maude, Nora de Silva, and in Russia Vera Komisarjevskaya, gradually won the right to intensify Ophelia's presence by clothing her in Hamlet's black.[34]

By the turn of the century, there was both a male and female discourse on Ophelia. A.C. Bradley spoke for the Victorian male tradition when he noted in *Shakespearean Tragedy* (1906) that "a large number of readers feel a kind of personal irritation against Ophelia; they seem unable to forgive her for not having been a heroine."[35] The feminist counterview was represented by actresses in such works as Helena Faucit's study of Shakespeare's female

---

32 Mary Cowden Clarke, *The Girlhood of Shakespeare's Heroines* (London, 1852). See also George C. Gross, "Mary Cowden Clarke, *The Girlhood of Shakespeare's Heroines*, and the sex education of Victorian women" (*Victorian Studies*, 16 (1972)), 37–58, and Nina Auerbach, *Woman and the Demon* (Cambridge, Mass., 1983), 210–15.

33 Hiatt, op. cit., 114. See also Wingate, op. cit., 304–5.

34 Terry, op. cit., 155–6.

35 Andrew C. Bradley, *Shakespearean Tragedy* (London, 1906), 160.

characters, and *The True Ophelia*, written by an anonymous actress in 1914, which protested against the "insipid little creature" of criticism, and advocated a strong and intelligent woman destroyed by the heartlessness of men.[36] In women's paintings of the *fin de siècle** as well, Ophelia is depicted as an inspiring, even sanctified emblem of righteousness.[37]

While the widely read and influential essays of Mary Cowden Clarke are now mocked as the epitome of naive criticism, these Victorian studies of the girlhood of Shakespeare's heroines are of course alive and well as psychoanalytic criticism, which has imagined its own prehistories of oedipal conflict and neurotic fixation;* and I say this not to mock psychoanalytic criticism, but to suggest that Clarke's musings on Ophelia are a pre-Freudian* speculation on the traumatic sources of a female sexual identity. The Freudian interpretation of *Hamlet* concentrated on the hero, but also had much to do with the re-sexualization of Ophelia. As early as 1900, Freud had traced Hamlet's irresolution to an Oedipus complex, and Ernest Jones, his leading British disciple, developed this view, influencing the performances of John Gielgud and Alec Guinness in the 1930s. In his final version of the study, *Hamlet and Oedipus*, published in 1949, Jones argued that "Ophelia should be unmistakably sensual, as she seldom is on stage. She may be 'innocent' and docile, but she is very aware of her body."[38]

In the theater and in criticism, this Freudian edict has produced such extreme readings as that Shakespeare intends us to see Ophelia as a loose woman, and that she has been sleeping with Hamlet. Rebecca West has argued that Ophelia is not "a correct and timid virgin of exquisite sensibilities," a view she attributes to the popularity of the Millais painting; but rather "a disreputable young woman."[39] In his delightful autobiography, Laurence Olivier, who made a special pilgrimage to Ernest Jones when he was preparing his *Hamlet* in the 1930s, recalls that one of his predecessors as actor-manager had said in response to the earnest question, "Did Hamlet sleep with Ophelia?"—"In my company, always."[40]

The most extreme Freudian interpretation reads *Hamlet* as two parallel male and female psychodramas, the counterpointed stories of the incestuous attachments of Hamlet and Ophelia. As Theodor Lidz presents this view, while

35

---

36   Helena Faucit Martin, *On Some of Shakespeare's Female Characters* (Edinburgh and London, 1891), 4, 18; and *The True Ophelia* (New York, 1914), 15.

37   Among these paintings are the Ophelias of Henrietta Rae and Mrs. F. Littler. Sarah Bernhardt sculpted a bas relief of Ophelia for the Women's Pavilion at the Chicago World's Fair in 1893.

38   Ernest Jones, *Hamlet and Oedipus* (New York, 1949), 139.

39   Rebecca West, *The Count and the Castle* (New Haven, 1958), 18.

40   Laurence Olivier, *Confessions of an Actor* (Harmondsworth, 1982), 102, 152.

Hamlet is neurotically attached to his mother, Ophelia has an unresolved oedipal attachment to her father. She has fantasies of a lover who will abduct her from or even kill her father, and when this actually happens, her reason is destroyed by guilt as well as by lingering incestuous feelings. According to Lidz, Ophelia breaks down because she fails in the female developmental task of shifting her sexual attachment from her father "to a man who can bring her fulfillment as a woman."[41] We see the effects of this Freudian Ophelia on stage productions since the 1950s, where directors have hinted at an incestuous link between Ophelia and her father, or more recently, because this staging conflicts with the usual ironic treatment of Polonius, between Ophelia and Laertes. Trevor Nunn's production with Helen Mirren in 1970, for example, made Ophelia and Laertes flirtatious doubles, almost twins in their matching fur-trimmed doublets, playing duets on the lute with Polonius looking on, like Peter, Paul, and Mary.* In other productions of the same period, Marianne Faithfull was a haggard Ophelia equally attracted to Hamlet and Laertes, and, in one of the few performances directed by a woman, Yvonne Nicholson sat on Laertes' lap in the advice scene, and played the part with "rough sexual bravado."[42]

Since the 1960s, the Freudian representation of Ophelia has been supplemented by an antipsychiatry that represents Ophelia's madness in more contemporary terms. In contrast to the psychoanalytic representation of Ophelia's sexual unconscious that connected her essential femininity to Freud's essays on female sexuality and hysteria, her madness is now seen in medical and biochemical terms, as schizophrenia. This is so in part because the schizophrenic woman has become the cultural icon of dualistic femininity in the mid-twentieth century as the erotomaniac was in the seventeenth and the hysteric in the nineteenth. It might also be traced to the work of R.D. Laing on female schizophrenia in the 1960s. Laing argued that schizophrenia was an intelligible response to the experience of invalidation within the family network, especially to the conflicting emotional messages and mystifying double binds experienced by daughters. Ophelia, he noted in *The Divided Self*, is an empty space. "In her madness there is no one there.... There is no integral selfhood expressed through her actions or utterances. Incomprehensible statements are said by nothing. She has already died. There is now only a vacuum where there was once a person."[43]

41   Theodor Lidz, *Hamlet's Enemy: Madness and Myth in Hamlet* (New York, 1975), 88, 113.

42   Richard David, *Shakespeare in the Theatre* (Cambridge, 1978), 75. This was the production directed by Buzz Goodbody, a brilliant young feminist radical who killed herself that year. See Colin Chambers, *Other Spaces: New Theatre and the RSC* (London, 1980), especially 63–7.

43   R.D. Laing, *The Divided Self* (Harmondsworth, 1965), 195n.

Despite his sympathy for Ophelia, Laing's readings silence her, equate her with "nothing," more completely than any since the Augustans; and they have been translated into performances which only make Ophelia a graphic study of mental pathology. The sickest Ophelias on the contemporary stage have been those in the productions of the pathologist-director Jonathan Miller. In 1974 at the Greenwich Theatre his Ophelia sucked her thumb; by 1981, at the Warehouse in London, she was played by an actress much taller and heavier than the Hamlet (perhaps punningly cast as the young actor Anton Lesser). She began the play with a set of nervous tics and tuggings of hair which by the mad scene had become a full set of schizophrenic routines—head banging, twitching, wincing, grimacing, and drooling.[44]

But since the 1970s too we have had a feminist discourse which has offered a new perspective on Ophelia's madness as protest and rebellion. For many feminist theorists, the madwoman is a heroine, a powerful figure who rebels against the family and the social order; and the hysteric who refuses to speak the language of the patriarchal order, who speaks otherwise, is a sister.[45] In terms of effect on the theater, the most radical application of these ideas was probably realized in Melissa Murray's agit-prop play *Ophelia*, written in 1979 for the English women's theater group "Hormone Imbalance." In this blank verse retelling of the Hamlet story, Ophelia becomes a lesbian and runs off with a woman servant to join a guerilla commune.[46]

40

While I've always regretted that I missed this production, I can't proclaim that this defiant ideological gesture, however effective politically or theatrically, is all that feminist criticism desires, or all to which it should aspire. When feminist criticism chooses to deal with representation, rather than with women's writing, it must aim for a maximum interdisciplinary contextualism, in which the complexity of attitudes towards the feminine can be analyzed in their fullest cultural and historical frame. The alternation of strong and weak Ophelias on the stage, virginal and seductive Ophelias in art, inadequate or oppressed Ophelias in criticism, tells us how these representations have overflowed the text, and how they have reflected the ideological character of their times, erupting as debates between dominant and feminist views in periods of gender crisis and redefinition. The representation of Ophelia changes independently of theories of the meaning of the play or the Prince, for it depends on attitudes towards women and madness. The decorous and pious Ophelia of the Augustan age

---

44 David, op. cit., 82–3; thanks to Marianne DeKoven, Rutgers University, for the description of the 1981 Warehouse production.

45 See, for example, Hélène Cixous and Catherine Clément, *La Jeune Née* (Paris, 1975).

46 For an account of this production, see Micheline Wandor, *Understudies: Theatre and Sexual Politics* (London, 1981), 47.

and the postmodern schizophrenic heroine who might have stepped from the pages of Laing can be derived from the same figure; they are both contradictory and complementary images of female sexuality in which madness seems to act as the "switching-point, the concept which allows the co-existence of both sides of the representation."[47] There is no "true" Ophelia for whom feminist criticism must unambiguously speak, but perhaps only a Cubist* Ophelia of multiple perspectives, more than the sum of all her parts.

But in exposing the ideology of representation, feminist critics have also the responsibility to acknowledge and to examine the boundaries of our own ideological positions as products of our gender and our time. A degree of humility in an age of critical hubris* can be our greatest strength, for it is by occupying this position of historical self-consciousness in both feminism and criticism that we maintain our credibility in representing Ophelia, and that unlike Lacan, when we promise to speak about her, we make good on our word.

(1985)

---

47   I am indebted for this formulation to a critique of my earlier draft of this paper by Carl Friedman, at the Wesleyan Center for the Humanities, April 1981.

Ngũgĩ wa Thiong'o

from Decolonizing the Mind

Early on in Decolonizing the Mind, *the pre-eminent Kenyan novelist Ngũgĩ wa Thiong'o quotes his Nigerian counterpart Chinua Achebe questioning whether it is right for a writer to "abandon his mother tongue for someone else's." Achebe concluded that he had "no other choice" in an English-dominated world than to write in English rather than his native tongue, and for many years Ngũgĩ followed the same path, writing his novels in English. In the late 1970s, however, after he had been imprisoned by the Kenyan authorities for writing a play critical of the capitalist exploitation of a peasant farmer, Ngũgĩ began to write a novel in his native Gĩkũyũ, and since then virtually all his writing has been in that language. Decolonizing the Mind, a collection of four long essays, explores these issues at length: it is very largely through language, Ngũgĩ insists, that the power of colonialism has "fascinated and held the soul prisoner."*

The excerpt included here is from the first essay in the book, "The Language of African Literature."

III

I was born into a large peasant family: father, four wives and about twenty-eight children. I also belonged, as we all did in those days, to a wider extended family and to the community as a whole.

We spoke Gĩkũyũ as we worked in the fields. We spoke Gĩkũyũ in and outside the home. I can vividly recall those evenings of storytelling around the fireside. It was mostly the grown-ups telling the children but everybody was interested and involved. We children would re-tell the stories the following day to other children who worked in the fields picking the pyrethrum flowers, tea-leaves or coffee beans of our European and African landlords.

The stories, with mostly animals as the main characters, were all told in Gĩkũyũ. Hare, being small, weak but full of innovative wit and cunning, was our hero. We identified with him as he struggled against the brutes of prey like lion, leopard, hyena. His victories were our victories and we learnt that the apparently weak can outwit the strong. We followed the animals in their struggle against hostile nature—drought, rain, sun, wind—a confrontation often forcing them to search for forms of co-operation. But we were also interested in their struggles amongst themselves, and particularly between the beasts and the victims of prey. These twin struggles, against nature and other animals, reflected real-life struggles in the human world.

Not that we neglected stories with human beings as the main characters. There were two types of characters in such human-centered narratives: the species of truly human beings with qualities of courage, kindness, mercy, hatred of evil, concern for others; and a man-eat-man two-mouthed species with qualities of greed, selfishness, individualism and hatred of what was good for the larger co-operative community. Co-operation as the ultimate good in a community was a constant theme. It could unite human beings with animals against ogres and beasts of prey, as in the story of how dove, after being fed with castor-oil seeds, was sent to fetch a smith working far away from home and whose pregnant wife was being threatened by these man-eating two-mouthed ogres.

There were good and bad story-tellers. A good one could tell the same story over and over again, and it would always be fresh to us, the listeners. He or she could tell a story told by someone else and make it more alive and dramatic. The differences really were in the use of words and images and the inflexion of voices to effect different tones.

We therefore learnt to value words for their meaning and nuances. Language was not a mere string of words. It had a suggestive power well beyond the immediate and lexical meaning. Our appreciation of the suggestive magical power of language was reinforced by the games we played with words through riddles, proverbs, transpositions of syllables, or through nonsensical but musically arranged words. So we learnt the music of our language on top of the content. The language, through images and symbols, gave us a view of the world, but it had a beauty of its own. The home and the field were then our pre-primary school but what is important, for this discussion, is that the language of our evening teach-ins, and the language of our immediate and wider community, and the language of our work in the fields were one.

And then I went to school, a colonial school, and this harmony was broken. The language of my education was no longer the language of my culture. I first went to Kamaandura, missionary run, and then to another called Maanguuū run by nationalists grouped around the Gĩkũyũ Independent and Karinga Schools Association. Our language of education was still Gĩkũyũ. The very first time I was ever given an ovation for my writing was over a composition in Gĩkũyũ. So for my first four years there was still harmony between the language of my formal education and that of the Limuru peasant community.

5

It was after the declaration of a state of emergency over Kenya in 1952 that all the schools run by patriotic nationalists were taken over by the colonial regime and were placed under District Education Boards chaired by English-men. English became the language of my formal education. In Kenya, English became more than a language: it was *the* language, and all the others had to bow before it in deference.

Thus one of the most humiliating experiences was to be caught speaking Gĩkũyũ in the vicinity of the school. The culprit was given corporal punish-ment—three to five strokes of the cane on bare buttocks—or was made to carry a metal plate around the neck with inscriptions such as I AM STUPID or I AM A DONKEY. Sometimes the culprits were fined money they could hardly afford. And how did the teachers catch the culprits? A button was initially given to one pupil who was supposed to hand it over to whoever was caught speaking his mother tongue. Whoever had the button at the end of the day would sing who had given it to him and the ensuing process would bring out all the culprits of the day. Thus children were turned into witch-hunters and in the process were being taught the lucrative value of being a traitor to one's immediate community.

10   The attitude to English was the exact opposite: any achievement in spoken or written English was highly rewarded; prizes, prestige, applause; the ticket to higher realms. English became the measure of intelligence and ability in the arts, the sciences, and all the other branches of learning. English became *the* main determinant of a child's progress up the ladder of formal education.

As you may know, the colonial system of education in addition to its apartheid racial demarcation* had the structure of a pyramid: a broad primary base, a narrowing secondary middle, and an even narrower university apex. Selections from primary into secondary were through an examination, in my time called Kenya African Preliminary Examination, in which one had to pass six subjects ranging from Maths to Nature Study and Kiswahili. All the papers were written in English. Nobody could pass the exam who failed the English language paper no matter how brilliantly he had done in the other subjects. I remember one boy in my class of 1954 who had distinctions in all subjects except English, which he had failed. He was made to fail the entire exam. He went on to become a turn boy in a bus company. I who had only passes but a credit in English got a place at the Alliance High School, one of the most elit-ist institutions for Africans in colonial Kenya. The requirements for a place at the University, Makerere University College, were broadly the same: nobody could go on to wear the undergraduate red gown, no matter how brilliantly they had performed in all the other subjects unless they had a credit—not even a simple pass!—in English. Thus the most coveted place in the pyramid and in the system was only available to the holder of an English language credit card. English was the official vehicle and the magic formula to colonial elitedom.

Literary education was now determined by the dominant language while also reinforcing that dominance. Orature (oral literature) in Kenyan languages stopped. In primary school I now read simplified Dickens and Stevenson alongside Rider Haggard. Jim Hawkins, Oliver Twist, Tom Brown—not Hare, Leopard and Lion—were now my daily companions in the world of imagination. In secondary school, Scott and G.B. Shaw vied with more Rider Haggard, John Buchan, Alan Paton, Captain W.E. Johns. At Makerere I read English: from Chaucer to T.S. Eliot with a touch of Graham Greene.*

Thus language and literature were taking us further and further from ourselves to other selves, from our world to other worlds.

What was the colonial system doing to us Kenyan children? What were the consequences of, on the one hand, this systematic suppression of our languages and the literature they carried, and on the other the elevation of English and the literature it carried? To answer those questions, let me first examine the relationship of language to human experience, human culture, and the human perception of reality.

IV

Language, any language, has a dual character: it is both a means of communication and a carrier of culture. Take English. It is spoken in Britain and in Sweden and Denmark. But for Swedish and Danish people English is only a means of communication with non-Scandinavians. It is not a carrier of their culture. For the British, and particularly the English, it is additionally, and inseparably from its use as a tool of communication, a carrier of their culture and history. Or take Swahili in East and Central Africa. It is widely used as a means of communication across many nationalities. But it is not the carrier of a culture and history of many of those nationalities. However in parts of Kenya and Tanzania, and particularly in Zanzibar, Swahili is inseparably both a means of communication and a carrier of the culture of those people to whom it is a mother-tongue.

Language as communication has three aspects or elements. There is first what Karl Marx once called the language of real life, the element basic to the whole notion of language, its origins and development: that is, the relations people enter into with one another in the labor process, the links they necessarily establish among themselves in the act of a people, a community of human beings, producing wealth or means of life like food, clothing, houses. A human community really starts its historical being as a community of co-operation in production through the division of labor; the simplest is between man,

15

woman and child within a household; the more complex divisions are between branches of production such as those who are sole hunters, sole gatherers of fruits or sole workers in metal. Then there are the most complex divisions such as those in modern factories where a single product, say a shirt or a shoe, is the result of many hands and minds. Production is co-operation, is communication, is language, is expression of a relation between human beings and it is specifically human.

The second aspect of language as communication is speech and it imitates the language of real life, that is communication in production. The verbal signposts both reflect and aid communication or the relation established between human beings in the production of their means of life. Language as a system of verbal signposts makes that production possible. The spoken word is to relations between human beings what the hand is to the relations between human beings and nature. The hand through tools mediates between human beings and nature and forms the language of real life: spoken words mediate between human beings and form the language of speech.

The third aspect is the written signs. The written word imitates the spoken. Where the first two aspects of language as communication through the hand and the spoken word historically evolved more or less simultaneously, the written aspect is a much later historical development. Writing is representation of sounds with visual symbols, from the simplest knot among shepherds to tell the number in a herd or the hieroglyphics among the Agĩkũyũ gicaandi singers and poets of Kenya, to the most complicated and different letter and picture writing systems of the world today.

In most societies the written and the spoken languages are the same, in that they represent each other: what is on paper can be read to another person and be received as that language, which the recipient has grown up speaking. In such a society there is broad harmony for a child between the three aspects of language as communication. His interaction with nature and with other men is expressed in written and spoken symbols or signs which are both a result of that double interaction and a reflection of it. The association of the child's sensibility is with the language of his experience of life.

20   But there is more to it: communication between human beings is also the basis and process of evolving culture. In doing similar kinds of things and actions over and over again under similar circumstances, similar even in their mutability, certain patterns, moves, rhythms, habits, attitudes, experiences and knowledge emerge. Those experiences are handed over to the next generation and become the inherited basis for their further actions on nature and on themselves. There is a gradual accumulation of values which in time become almost self-evident truths governing their conception of what is right and wrong, good and bad, beautiful and ugly, courageous and cowardly, generous and mean in

their internal and external relations. Over a time this becomes a way of life distinguishable from other ways of life. They develop a distinctive culture and history. Culture embodies those moral, ethical and aesthetic values, the set of spiritual eyeglasses, through which they come to view themselves and their place in the universe. Values are the basis of a people's identity, their sense of particularity as members of the human race. All this is carried by language. Language as culture is the collective memory bank of a people's experience in history. Culture is almost indistinguishable from the language that makes possible its genesis, growth, banking, articulation and indeed its transmission from one generation to the next.

Language as culture also has three important aspects. Culture is a product of the history which it in turn reflects. Culture in other words is a product and a reflection of human beings communicating with one another in the very struggle to create wealth and to control it. But culture does not merely reflect that history, or rather it does so by actually forming images or pictures of the world of nature and nurture. Thus the second aspect of language as culture is as an image-forming agent in the mind of a child. Our whole conception of ourselves as a people, individually and collectively, is based on those pictures and images which may or may not correctly correspond to the actual reality of the struggles with nature and nurture which produced them in the first place. But our capacity to confront the world creatively is dependent on how those images correspond or not to that reality, how they distort or clarify the reality of our struggles. Language as culture is thus mediating between me and my own self; between my own self and other selves; between me and nature. Language is mediating in my very being. And this brings us to the third aspect of language as culture. Culture transmits or imparts those images of the world and reality through the spoken and the written language, that is through a specific language. In other words, the capacity to speak, the capacity to order sounds in a manner that makes for mutual comprehension between human beings is universal. This is the universality of language, a quality specific to human beings. It corresponds to the universality of the struggle against nature and that between human beings. But the particularity of the sounds, the words, the word order into phrases and sentences, and the specific manner, or laws, of their ordering is what distinguishes one language from another. Thus a specific culture is not transmitted through language in its universality but in its particularity as the language of a specific community with a specific history. Written literature and orature are the main means by which a particular language transmits the images of the world contained in the culture it carries.

Language as communication and as culture are then products of each other. Communication creates culture: culture is a means of communication. Language carries culture, and culture carries, particularly through orature and literature, the entire body of values by which we come to perceive ourselves and our place in the world. How people perceive themselves affects how they look at their culture, at their politics and at the social production of wealth, at their entire relationship to nature and to other beings. Language is thus inseparable from ourselves as a community of human beings with a specific form and character, a specific history, a specific relationship to the world.

V

So what was the colonialist imposition of a foreign language doing to us children?

The real aim of colonialism was to control the people's wealth: what they produced, how they produced it, and how it was distributed; to control, in other words, the entire realm of the language of real life. Colonialism imposed its control of the social production of wealth through military conquest and subsequent political dictatorship. But its most important area of domination was the mental universe of the colonized, the control, through culture, of how people perceived themselves and their relationship to the world. Economic and political control can never be complete or effective without mental control. To control a people's culture is to control their tools of self-definition in relationship to others.

25   For colonialism this involved two aspects of the same process: the destruction or the deliberate undervaluing of a people's culture, their art, dances, religions, history, geography, education, orature and literature, and the conscious elevation of the language of the colonizer. The domination of a people's language by the languages of the colonizing nations was crucial to the domination of the mental universe of the colonized.

Take language as communication. Imposing a foreign language, and suppressing the native languages as spoken and written, were already breaking the harmony previously existing between the African child and the three aspects of language. Since the new language as a means of communication was a product of and was reflecting the "real language of life" elsewhere, it could never as spoken or written properly reflect or imitate the real life of that community. This may in part explain why technology always appears to us as slightly external, *their* product and not *ours*. The word "missile" used to hold an alien far-away sound until I recently learnt its equivalent in Gĩkũyũ, *ngurukuhĩ* and it made me apprehend it differently. Learning, for a colonial child, became a cerebral activity* and not an emotionally felt experience.

But since the new, imposed languages could never completely break the native languages as spoken, their most effective area of domination was the third aspect of language as communication, the written. The language of an

African child's formal education was foreign. The language of the books he read was foreign. The language of his conceptualization was foreign. Thought, in him, took the visible form of a foreign language. So the written language of a child's upbringing in the school (even his spoken language within the school compound) became divorced from his spoken language at home. There was often not the slightest relationship between the child's written world, which was also the language of his schooling, and the world of his immediate environment in the family and the community. For a colonial child, the harmony existing between the three aspects of language as communication was irrevocably broken. This resulted in the disassociation of the sensibility of that child from his natural and social environment, what we might call colonial alienation. The alienation became reinforced in the teaching of history, geography, music, where bourgeois Europe was always the center of the universe.

This disassociation, divorce, or alienation from the immediate environment becomes clearer when you look at colonial language as a carrier of culture.

Since culture is a product of the history of a people which it in turn reflects, the child was now being exposed exclusively to a culture that was a product of a world external to himself. He was being made to stand outside himself to look at himself. *Catching Them Young* is the title of a book on racism, class, sex, and politics in children's literature by Bob Dixon. "Catching them young" as an aim was even more true of a colonial child. The images of his world and his place in it implanted in a child take years to eradicate, if they ever can be.

Since culture does not just reflect the world in images but actually, through those images, conditions a child to see that world a certain way, the colonial child was made to see the world and where he stands in it as seen and defined by or reflected in the culture of the language of imposition.

And since those images are mostly passed on through orature and literature it meant the child would now only see the world as seen in the literature of his language of adoption. From the point of view of alienation, that is of seeing oneself from outside oneself as if one was another self, it does not matter that the imported literature carried the great humanist tradition of the best in Shakespeare, Goethe, Balzac, Tolstoy, Gorky, Brecht, Sholokhov, Dickens. The location of this great mirror of imagination was necessarily Europe and its history and culture and the rest of the universe was seen from that center.

But obviously it was worse when the colonial child was exposed to images of his world as mirrored in the written languages of his colonizer. Where his own native languages were associated in his impressionable mind with low status, humiliation, corporal punishment, slow-footed intelligence and ability or downright stupidity, non-intelligibility and barbarism, this was reinforced by the world he met in the works of such geniuses of racism as a Rider Haggard or a Nicholas Monsarrat; not to mention the pronouncement of some of

30

the giants of western intellectual and political establishment, such as Hume ("... The negro is naturally inferior to the whites ..."), Thomas Jefferson ("... The blacks ... are inferior to the whites on the endowments of both body and mind ..."), or Hegel* with his Africa comparable to a land of childhood still enveloped in the dark mantle of the night as far as the development of self-conscious history was concerned. Hegel's statement that there was nothing harmonious with humanity to be found in the African character is representative of the racist images of Africans and Africa such a colonial child was bound to encounter in the literature of the colonial languages. The results could be disastrous.

(1986)

JUDY RUIZ

ORANGES AND SWEET SISTER BOY

The following personal essay, which originated as an assignment for the author's master's program in poetry at the University of Arkansas, addresses the author's reaction to her sibling coming out as transgender. In the United States in the 1980s, when the piece was written, a transgender identity was classified as a psychological disorder, and there was far less public discussion of the discrimination faced by trans people than there is in the twenty-first century. "Oranges and Sweet Sister Boy" was first published in the literary journal Iowa Woman, *and was subsequently anthologized in* The Best American Essays 1989.

I am sleeping, hard, when the telephone rings. It's my brother, and he's calling to say that he is now my sister. I feel something fry a little deep behind my eyes. Knowing how sometimes dreams get mixed up with not-dreams, I decide to do a reality test at once. "Let me get a cigarette," I say, knowing that if I reach for a Marlboro and it turns into a trombone or a snake or anything else on the way to my lips that I'm still out in the large world of dreams.

The cigarette stays a cigarette. I light it. I ask my brother to run that stuff by me again.

It is the Texas Zephyr[1] at midnight—the woman in a white suit, the man in a blue uniform; she carries flowers—I know they are flowers. The petals spill and spill into the aisle, and a child goes past this couple who have just come from their own wedding—goes past them and past them, going always to the toilet but really just going past them; and the child could be a horse or she could be the police and they'd not notice her any more than they do, which is not at all—the man's hands high up on the woman's legs, her skirt up, her stockings and garters, the petals and finally all the flowers spilling out into the aisle and his mouth open on her. My mother. My father. I am conceived near Dallas in the dark while a child passes, a young girl who knows and doesn't know, who

---

1   *Texas Zephyr*   Passenger train that operated between Colorado and Texas.

witnesses, in glimpses, the creation of the universe, who feels an odd hurt as
her own mother, fat and empty, snores with her mouth open, her false teeth
slipping down, snores and snores just two seats behind the Creators.

News can make a person stupid. It can make you think you can do something.
So I ask The Blade question, thinking that if he hasn't had the operation yet that
I can fly to him, rent a cabin out on Puget Sound.[2] That we can talk. That I can
get him to touch base with reality.

5   "Begin with an orange," I would tell him. "Because oranges are mildly
intrusive by nature, put the orange somewhere so that it will not bother you—in
the cupboard, in a drawer, even a pocket or a handbag will do. The orange, being a patient fruit, will wait for you much longer than say a banana or a peach."

I would hold an orange out to him. I would say, "This is the one that will
save your life." And I would tell him about the woman I saw in a bus station
who bit right into her orange, like it was an apple. She was wild looking, as if
she'd been outside for too long in a wind that blew the same way all the time.
One of the dregs of humanity, our mother would have called her, the same
mother who never brought fruit into the house except in cans. My children
used to ask me to "start" their oranges for them. That meant to make a hole
in the orange so they could peel the rind away, and their small hands weren't
equipped with fingernails that were long enough or strong enough to do the job.
Sometimes they would suck the juice out of the hole my thumbnail had made,
leaving the orange flat and sad.

The earrings are as big as dessert plates, filigree gold-plated with thin dangles
hanging down that touch her bare shoulders. She stands in front of the Alamo[3]
while a bald man takes her picture. The sun is absorbed by the earrings so
quickly that by the time she feels the heat, it is too late. The hanging dangles
make small blisters on her shoulders, as if a centipede had traveled there. She
takes the famous river walk in spiked heels, rides in a boat, eats some Italian
noodles, returns to the motel room, soaks her feet, and applies small band-aids
to her toes. She is briefly concerned about the gun on the nightstand. The toilet
flushes. She pretends to be sleeping. The gun is just large and heavy. A .45?
A .357 magnum? She's never been good with names. She hopes he doesn't try
to. Or that if he does, that it's not loaded. But he'll say it's loaded just for fun.

---

2   *Puget Sound* Inlet of the Pacific Ocean along the northwest coast of Washington
State.

3   *the Alamo* The Alamo Mission. Located close to San Antonio, Texas, the Alamo
was the site of a crucial battle in the Texas Revolution in 1836.

Or he'll pull the trigger and the bullet will lodge in her medulla oblongata,[4] ripping through her womb first, taking everything else vital on the way.

In the magazine articles, you don't see this: "Well, yes. The testicles have to come out. And yes. The penis is cut off." What you get is tonsils. So-and-so has had a "sex change" operation. A sex change operation. How precious. How benign. Doctor, just what do you people do with those penises?

News can make a person a little crazy also. News like, "We regret to inform you that you have failed your sanity hearing."

The bracelet on my wrist bears the necessary information about me, but there is one small error. The receptionist typing the information asked me my religious preference. I said, "None." She typed, "Neon."   10

Pearl doesn't have any teeth and her tongue looks weird. She says "Pumpkin pie." That's all she says. Sometimes she runs her hands over my bed sheets and says pumpkin pie. Sometimes I am under the sheets. Marsha got stabbed in the chest, but she tells everyone she fell on a knife. Elizabeth—she's the one who thinks her shoe is a baby—hit me in the back with a tray right after one of the cooks gave me extra toast. There's a note on the bulletin board about a class for the nurses: "How Putting A Towel On Someone's Face Makes Them Stop Banging Their Spoon / OR Reduction of Disruptive Mealtime Behavior By Facial Screening—7 P.M.—Conference Room." Another note announces the topic for remotivation[5] class: "COWS." All the paranoid schizophrenics will be there.

Here in the place for the permanently bewildered, I fit right in. Not because I stood at the window that first night and listened to the trains. Not because I imagined those trains were bracelets, the jewelry of earth. Not even because I imagined that one of those bracelets was on my own arm and was the Texas Zephyr where a young couple made love and conceived me. I am eighteen and beautiful and committed to the state hospital by a district court judge for a period of one day to life. Because I am a paranoid schizophrenic.

I will learn about cows.

So I'm being very quiet in the back of the classroom, and I'm peeling an orange. It's the smell that makes the others begin to turn around, that mildly intrusive nature. The course is called "Women and Modern Literature," and the

---

4   *medulla oblongata* Brain stem.

5   *remotivation* Group therapy technique.

diaries of Virginia Woolf[6] are up for discussion except nobody has anything to say. I, of course, am making a mess with the orange; and I'm wanting to say that my brother is now a sister.

15   Later, with my hands still orangey, I wander in to leave something on a desk in a professor's office, and he's reading so I'm being very quiet, and then he says, sort of out of nowhere, "Emily Dickinson[7] up there in her room making poems while her brother was making love to her best friend right downstairs on the dining room table. A regular thing. Think of it. And Walt Whitman[8] out sniffing around the boys. Our two great American poets." And I want to grab this professor's arm and say, "Listen. My brother called me and now he's my sister, and I'm having trouble making sense out of my life right now, so would you mind not telling me any more stuff about sex." And I want my knuckles to turn white while the pressure of my fingers leaves imprints right through his jacket, little indentations he can interpret as urgent. But I don't say anything. And I don't grab his arm. I go read a magazine. I find this:

"I've never found an explanation for why the human race has so many languages. When the brain became a language brain, it obviously needed to develop an intense degree of plasticity. Such plasticity allows languages to be logical, coherent systems and yet be extremely variable. The same brain that thinks in words and symbols is also a brain that has to be freed up with regard to sexual turn-on and partnering. God knows why sex attitudes have not been subject to the corresponding degrees of modification and variety as language. I suspect there's a close parallel between the two. The brain doesn't seem incredibly efficient with regard to sex."

John Money[9] said that. The same John Money who, with surgeon Howard W. Jones, performed the first sex change operation in the United States in 1965 at Johns Hopkins University and Hospital in Baltimore.

       Money also tells about the hijra* of India who disgrace their families because they are too effeminate: "The ultimate stage of the hijra is to get up the courage to go through the amputation of penis and testicles. They had no anesthetic." Money also answers anyone who might think that "heartless members of the medical profession are forcing these poor darlings to go and get

---

6   *Virginia Woolf*   Influential English novelist, essayist, and short story writer (1882–1941).

7   *Emily Dickinson*   American poet (1830–86) who spent much of her life in seclusion.

8   *Walt Whitman*   American poet (1819–92). According to scholarly consensus, Woolf, Whitman, and quite possibly also Dickinson were either gay or bisexual.

9   *John Money*   Controversial psychologist (1921–2006) who argued that gender is not biologically innate but is acquired during childhood.

themselves cut up and mutilated," or who think the medical profession should leave them alone. "You'd have lots of patients willing to get a gun and blow off their own genitals if you don't do it. I've had several who got knives and cut themselves trying to get rid of their sex organs. That's their obsession!"

Perhaps better than all else, I understand obsession. It is of the mind. And it is language-bound. Sex is of the body. It has no words. I am stunned to learn that someone with an obsession of the mind can have parts of the body surgically removed. This is my brother I speak of. This is not some lunatic named Carl who becomes Carlene. This is my brother.

So while we're out in that cabin on Puget Sound, I'll tell him about LuAnn. She is the sort of woman who orders the in-season fruit and a little cottage cheese. I am the sort of woman who orders a double cheeseburger and fries. LuAnn and I are sitting in her car. She has a huge orange, and she peels it so the peel falls off in one neat strip. I have a sack of oranges, the small ones. The peel of my orange comes off in hunks about the size of a baby's nail. "Oh, you bought the juice oranges," LuAnn says to me. Her emphasis on the word "juice" makes me want to die or something. I lack the courage to admit my ignorance, so I smile and breathe "yes," as if I know some secret, when I'm wanting to scream at her about how my mother didn't teach me about fruit and my own blood pounds in my head wanting out, out.

There is a pattern to this thought as there is a pattern for a jumpsuit. Sew the sleeve to the leg, sew the leg to the collar. Put the garment on. Sew the mouth shut. This is how I tell about being quiet because I am bad, and because I cannot stand it when he beats me or my brother.

"The first time I got caught in your clothes was when I was four years old and you were over at Sarah what's-her-name's babysitting. Dad beat me so hard I thought I was going to die. I really thought I was going to die. That was the day I made up my mind I would never get caught again." My brother goes on to say he continued to go through my things until I was hospitalized. A mystery is solved.

He wore my clothes. He played in my makeup. I kept saying, back then, that someone was going through my stuff. I kept saying it and saying it. I told the counselor at school. "Someone goes in my room when I'm not there, and I know it—goes in there and wears my clothes and goes through my stuff." I was assured by the counselor that this was not so. I was assured by my mother that this was not so. I thought my mother was doing it, snooping around for clues like mothers do. It made me a little crazy, so I started deliberately leaving things in a certain order so that I would be able to prove to myself that

20

someone, indeed, was going through my belongings. No one, not one person, ever believed that my room was being ransacked; I was accused of just making it up. A paranoid fixation.

And all the time it was old Goldilocks.*

25   So I tell my brother to promise me he'll see someone who counsels adult children from dysfunctional families. I tell him he needs to deal with the fact that he was physically abused on a daily basis. He tells me he doesn't remember being beaten except on three occasions. He wants me to get into a support group for families of people who are having a sex change. Support groups are people who are in the same boat. Except no one has any oars in the water.

I tell him I know how it feels to think you are in the wrong body. I tell him how I wanted my boyfriend to put a gun up inside me and blow the woman out, how I thought wearing spiked heels and low-cut dresses would somehow help my crisis, that putting on an ultra-feminine outside would mask the maleness I felt needed hiding. I tell him it's the rule, rather than the exception, that people from families like ours have very spooky sexual identity problems. He tells me that his sexuality is a birth defect. I recognize the lingo. It's support-group-for-transsexuals lingo. He tells me he sits down to pee. He told his therapist that he used to wet all over the floor. His therapist said, "You can't aim the bullets if you don't touch the gun." Lingo. My brother is hell-bent for castration, the castration that started before he had language: the castration of abuse. He will simply finish what was set in motion long ago.

I will tell my brother about the time I took ten sacks of oranges into a school so that I could teach metaphor. The school was for special students—those who were socially or intellectually impaired. I had planned to have them peel the oranges as I spoke about how much the world is like the orange. I handed out the oranges. The students refused to peel them, not because they wanted to make life difficult for me—they were enchanted with the gift. One child asked if he could have an orange to take home to his little brother. Another said he would bring me ten dollars the next day if I would give him a sack of oranges. And I know I was at home, that these children and I shared something that makes the leap of mind the metaphor attempts. And something in me healed.

A neighbor of mine takes pantyhose and cuts them up and sews them up after stuffing them. Then she puts these things into Mason jars and sells them, you know, to put out on the mantel for conversation. They are little penises and little scrotums, complete with hair. She calls them "Pickled Peters."*

A friend of mine had a sister who had a sex change operation. This young woman had her breasts removed and ran around the house with no shirt on before the stitches were taken out. She answered the door one evening. A young man had come to call on my friend. The sex-changed sister invited him in and offered him some black bean soup as if she were perfectly normal with her red surgical wounds and her black stitches. The young man left and never went back. A couple years later, my friend's sister/brother died when s/he ran a car into a concrete bridge railing. I hope for a happier ending. For my brother, for myself, for all of us.

My brother calls. He's done his toenails: Shimmering Cinnamon. And he's left his wife and children and purchased some nightgowns at a yard sale. His hair is getting longer. He wears a special bra. Most of the people he works with know about the changes in his life. His voice is not the same voice I've heard for years; he sounds happy.

My brother calls. He's always envied me, my woman's body. The same body I live in and have cursed for its softness. He asks me how I feel about myself. He says, "You know, you are really our father's first-born son." He tells me he used to want to be me because I was the only person our father almost loved.

The drama of life. After I saw that woman in the bus station eat an orange as if it were an apple, I went out into the street and smoked a joint with some guy I'd met on the bus. Then I hailed a cab and went to a tattoo parlor. The tattoo artist tried to talk me into getting a nice bird or butterfly design; I had chosen a design on his wall that appealed to me—a symbol I didn't know the meaning of. It is the Yin-Yang, and it's tattooed above my right ankle bone. I supposed my drugged, crazed consciousness knew more than I knew; that yin combines with yang to produce all that comes to be. I am drawn to androgyny.

Of course there is the nagging possibility that my brother's dilemma is genetic. Our father used to dress in drag* on Halloween, and he made a beautiful woman. One year, the year my mother cut my brother's blond curls off, my father taped those curls to his own head and tied a silk scarf over the tape. Even his close friends didn't know it was him. And my youngest daughter was a body builder for a while, her lean body as muscular as a man's. And my sons are beautiful, not handsome: they look androgynous.

Then there's my grandson. I saw him when he was less than an hour old. He was naked and had hiccups. I watched as he had his first bath, and I heard him cry. He had not been named yet, but his little crib had a blue card affixed to it with tape. And on the card were the words "Baby Boy." There was no doubt in me that the words were true.

When my brother was born, my father was off flying jets in Korea.[10] I went to the hospital with my grandfather to get my mother and this new brother. I remember how I wanted a sister, and I remember looking at him as my mother

30

35

10 *Korea* Reference to the Korean War (1950–53), in which the United States participated as an ally of South Korea.

held him in the front seat of the car. I was certain he was a sister, certain that my mother was joking. She removed his diaper to show me that he was a boy. I still didn't believe her. Considering what has happened lately, I wonder if my child-skewed consciousness knew more than the anatomical proof suggested.

I try to make peace with myself. I try to understand his decision to alter himself. I try to think of him as her. I write his woman name, and I feel like betraying myself. I try to be open-minded, but something in me shuts down. I think we humans are in big trouble, that many of us don't really have a clue as to what acceptable human behavior is. Something in me says no to all this, that this surgery business is the ultimate betrayal of the self. And yet, I want my brother to be happy.

It was in the city of San Antonio that my father had his surgery. I rode the bus from Kansas to Texas, and arrived at the the hospital two days after the operation to find my father sitting in the solarium playing solitaire. He had a type of cancer that particularly thrived on testosterone. And so he was castrated in order to ease his pain and to stop the growth of tumors. He died six months later.

Back in the sleep of the large world of dreams, I have done surgeries under water in which I float my father's testicles back into him, and he—the brutal man he was—emerges from the pool a tan and smiling man, parting the surface of the water with his perfect head. He loves all the grief away.

I will tell my brother all I know of oranges, that if you squeeze the orange peel into a flame, small fires happen because of the volatile oil in the peel. Also, if you squeeze the peel and it gets into your cat's eyes, the cat will blink and blink. I will tell him there is no perfect rhyme for the word "orange," and that if we can just make up a good word we can be immortal. We will become obsessed with finding the right word, and I will be joyous at our legitimate pursuit.

40   I have purchased a black camisole with lace to send to my new sister. And a card. On the outside of the card there's a drawing of a woman sitting by a pond and a zebra is off to the left. Inside are these words: "The past is ended. Be happy." And I have asked my companions to hold me and I have cried. My self is wet and small. But it is not dark. Sometimes, if no one touches me, I will die.

Sister, you are the best craziness of the family. Brother, love what you love.

(1988)

ANATOLE BROYARD

INTOXICATED BY MY ILLNESS

Broyard, a long-time arts writer for The New York Times *and a renowned essayist, was told in 1989 that he had inoperable prostate cancer (at that time still a form of the disease with a fairly high mortality rate). In one of his last essays, he here describes how he was affected by the discovery of his illness.*

The essay, which first appeared in The New York Times, *was included in slightly revised form in Broyard's posthumously published collection* Intoxicated by My Illness and Other Writings *(1992).*

So much of a writer's life consists of assumed suffering, rhetorical suffering, that I felt something like relief, even elation, when the doctor told me that I had cancer of the prostate. Suddenly there was in the air a rich sense of crisis, real crisis, yet one that also contained echoes of ideas like the crisis of language, the crisis of literature, or of personality. It seemed to me that my existence, whatever I thought, felt or did, had taken on a kind of meter, as in poetry, or in taxis.

When you learn that your life is threatened, you can turn toward this knowledge or away from it. I turned toward it. It was not a choice, but an automatic shifting of gears, a tacit agreement between my body and my brain. I thought that time had tapped me on the shoulder, that I had been given a real deadline at last. It wasn't that I believed the cancer was going to kill me, even though it had spread beyond the prostate—it could probably be controlled, either by radiation or hormonal manipulation. No, what struck me was the startled awareness that one day something, whatever it might be, was going to interrupt my leisurely progress. It sounds trite, yet I can only say that I realized for the first time that I don't have forever.

Time was no longer innocuous, nothing was casual any more. I understood that living itself had a deadline. Like the book I had been working on—how sheepish I would feel if I couldn't finish it. I had promised it to myself and to my friends. Though I wouldn't say this out loud, I had promised it to the world. All writers privately think this way.

When my friends heard I had cancer, they found me surprisingly cheerful and talked about my courage. But it has nothing to do with courage, at least not for me. As far as I can tell, it's a question of desire. I'm filled with desire—to live, to write, to do everything. Desire itself is a kind of immortality. While I've always had trouble concentrating, I now feel as concentrated* as a diamond, or a microchip.

5   I remember a time in the 1950s when I tried to talk a friend of mine named Jules out of committing suicide. He had already made one attempt and when I went to see him he said "Give me a good reason to go on living." He was 30 years old.

I saw what I had to do. I started to sell life to him, like a real estate agent. Just look at the world, I said. How can you not be curious about it? The streets, the houses, the trees, the shops, the people, the movement and the stillness. Look at the women, so appealing, each in her own way. Think of all the things you can do with them, the places you can go together. Think of books, paintings, music. Think of your friends.

While I was talking I wondered, am I telling Jules the truth? He didn't think so, because he put his head in the oven a week later. As for me, I don't know whether I believed what I said or not, because I just went on behaving like everybody else. But I believe it now. When my wife made me a hamburger the other day I thought it was the most fabulous hamburger in the history of the world.

With this illness one of my recurrent dreams has finally come true. Several times in the past I've dreamed that I had committed a crime—or perhaps I was only accused of a crime, it's not clear. When brought to trial I refused to have a lawyer—I got up instead and made an impassioned speech in my own defense. This speech was so moving that I could feel myself tingling with it. It was inconceivable that the jury would not acquit me—only each time I woke before the verdict. Now cancer is the crime I may or may not have committed and the eloquence of being alive, the fervor of the survivor, is my best defense.

The way my friends have rallied around me is wonderful. They remind me of a flock of birds rising from a body of water into the sunset. If that image seems a bit extravagant, or tinged with satire, it's because I can't help thinking there's something comical about my friends' behavior, all these witty men suddenly saying pious, inspirational things.

10   They are not intoxicated as I am by my illness, but sobered. Since I refused to, they've taken on the responsibility of being serious. They appear abashed, or chagrined, in their sobriety. Stripped of their playfulness these pals of mine seem plainer, homelier—even older. It's as if they had all gone bald overnight.

Yet one of the effects of their fussing over me is that I feel vivid, multicolored, sharply drawn. On the other hand—and this is ungrateful—I remain outside of their solicitude, their love and best wishes. I'm isolated from them by the grandiose conviction that I am the healthy person and they are the sick ones. Like an existential hero, I have been cured by the truth while they still suffer the nausea of the uninitiated.*

I've had eight-inch needles thrust into my belly where I could feel them tickling my metaphysics. I've worn Pampers. I've been licked by the flames and my sense of self has been singed. Sartre was right: you have to live each moment as if you're prepared to die.

Now at last I understand the conditional nature of the human condition. Yet, unlike Kierkegaard and Sartre,* I'm not interested in the irony of my position. Cancer cures you of irony. Perhaps my irony was all in my prostate. A dangerous illness fills you with adrenaline and makes you feel very smart. I can afford now, I said to myself, to draw conclusions. All those grand generalizations toward which I have been building for so many years are finally taking shape. As I look back at how I used to be, it seems to me that an intellectual is a person who thinks that the classical clichés don't apply to him, that he is immune to homely truths. I know better now. I see everything with a summarizing eye. Nature is a terrific editor.

In the first stages of my illness, I couldn't sleep, urinate or defecate—the word ordeal comes to mind. Then when my doctor changed all this and everything worked again, what a voluptuous pleasure it was. With a cry of joy I realized how marvelous it is simply to function. My body, which in the last decade or two had become a familiar, no longer thrilling old flame, was reborn as a brand-new infatuation.

I realize of course that this elation I feel is just a phase, just a rush of consciousness, a splash of perspective, a hot flash of ontological alertness. But I'll take it, I'll use it. I'll use everything I can while I wait for the next phase. Illness is primarily a drama and it should be possible to enjoy it as well as to suffer it. I see now why the romantics* were so fond of illness—the sick man sees everything as a metaphor. In this phase I'm infatuated with my cancer. It stinks of revelation.

As I look ahead, I feel like a man who has awakened from a long afternoon nap to find the evening stretched out before me. I'm reminded of D'Annunzio, the Italian poet, who said to a duchess he had just met at a party in Paris, "Come, we will have a profound evening." Why not? I see the balance of my life—everything comes in images now—as a beautiful paisley shawl thrown over a grand piano.

Why a paisley shawl, precisely? Why a grand piano? I have no idea. That's the way the situation presents itself to me. I have to take my imagery along with my medicine.

(1989)

IS NOTHING SACRED?

In this piece, the acclaimed novelist offers wide-ranging reflections on literature, the human psyche, and the idea of the sacred. Written as the Herbert Read Memorial Lecture for 1990, the essay was delivered at the Institute for Contemporary Arts in London on 6 February 1990. The lecture was read by playwright Harold Pinter rather than by Rushdie himself. At the time, Rushdie was prevented from making public appearances as a result of the widely publicized call for his death that had been issued by Ayatollah Khomeini, the political and religious leader of Iran, in reaction to Rushdie's novel The Satanic Verses, *which contained what many interpreted as a blasphemous or insulting treatment of Islamic beliefs. Many political and religious leaders—including Islamic scholars—spoke out against Khomeini's decree, but the danger for those associated with the book proved to be quite real; numerous bookstores that stocked the book were bombed, and several people associated with it (including its Japanese translator) were injured or killed. Rushdie lived more than a decade in hiding.*

I grew up kissing books and bread. In our house, whenever anyone dropped a book or let fall a chapati or a "slice," which was our word for a triangle of buttered leavened bread, the fallen object was required not only to be picked up but also kissed, by way of apology for the act of clumsy disrespect. I was as careless and butter-fingered as any child and, accordingly, during my childhood years, I kissed a large number of "slices" and also my fair share of books.

Devout households in India often contained, and still contain, persons in the habit of kissing holy books. But we kissed everything. We kissed dictionaries and atlases. We kissed Enid Blyton* novels and Superman comics. If I'd ever dropped the telephone directory I'd probably have kissed that, too.

All this happened before I had ever kissed a girl. In fact it would almost be true, true enough for a fiction writer, anyhow, to say that once I started kissing girls, my activities with regard to bread and books lost some of their special excitement. But one never forgets one's first loves.

Bread and books: food for the body and food for the soul—what could be more worthy of our respect, and even love?

It has always been a shock to me to meet people for whom books simply do not matter, and people who are scornful of the act of reading, let alone writing. It is perhaps always astonishing to learn that your beloved is not as attractive to others as she is to you. My most beloved books have been fictions, and in the last twelve months I have been obliged to accept that for many millions of human beings, these books are entirely without attraction or value. We have been witnessing an attack upon a particular work of fiction that is also an attack upon the very ideas of the novel form, an attack of such bewildering ferocity that it has become necessary to restate what is most precious about the art of literature—to answer the attack, not by an attack, but by a declaration of love.

Love can lead to devotion, but the devotion of the lover is unlike that of the True Believer in that it is not militant. I may be surprised—even shocked—to find that you do not feel as I do about a given book or work of art or even person; I may very well attempt to change your mind; but I will finally accept that your tastes, your loves, are your business and not mine. The True Believer knows no such restraints. The True Believer knows that he is simply right, and you are wrong. He will seek to convert you, even by force, and if he cannot he will, at the very least, despise you for your unbelief.

Love need not be blind. Faith must, ultimately, be a leap in the dark.

The title of this lecture is a question usually asked, in tones of horror, when some personage or idea or value or place held dear by the questioner is treated to a dose of iconoclasm. White cricket balls for night cricket? Female priests? A Japanese takeover of Rolls-Royce cars? *Is nothing sacred?*

Until recently, however, it was a question to which I thought I knew the answer. The answer was No.

No, nothing is sacred in and of itself, I would have said. Ideas, texts, even people can be made sacred—the word is from the Latin *sacrare,* "to set apart as holy"—but even though such entities, once their sacredness is established, seek to proclaim and to preserve their own absoluteness, their inviolability, the act of making sacred is in truth an event in history. It is the product of the many and complex pressures of the time in which the act occurs. And events in history must always be subject to questioning, deconstruction, even to declarations of their obsolescence. To respect the sacred is to be paralysed by it. The idea of the sacred is quite simply one of the most conservative notions in any culture, because it seeks to turn other ideas—Uncertainty, Progress, Change—into crimes.

To take only one such declaration of obsolescence: I would have described myself as living in the aftermath of the death of God.* On the subject of the death of God, the American novelist and critic William H. Gass had this to say, as recently as 1984:

> The death of god represents not only the realization that gods have never existed, but the contention that such a belief is no longer even irrationally possible: that neither reason nor the taste and temper of the times condone it. The belief lingers on, of course, but it does so like astrology or a faith in a flat earth.

I have some difficulty with the uncompromising bluntness of this obituary notice. It has always been clear to me that God is unlike human beings in that it can die, so to speak, in parts. In other parts, for example India, God continues to flourish, in literally thousands of forms. So that if I speak of living after this death, I am speaking in a limited, personal sense—my sense of God ceased to exist long ago, and as a result I was drawn towards the great creative possibilities offered by surrealism, modernism* and their successors, those philosophies and aesthetics born of the realization that, as Karl Marx said, "all that is solid melts into air."[1]

It did not seem to me, however, that my ungodliness, or rather my post-godliness,* need necessarily bring me into conflict with belief. Indeed, one reason for my attempt to develop a form of fiction in which the miraculous might coexist with the mundane was precisely my acceptance that notions of the sacred and the profane both needed to be explored, as far as possible without pre-judgement, in any honest literary portrait of the way we are.

That is to say: the most secular of authors ought to be capable of presenting a sympathetic portrait of a devout believer. Or, to put it another way: I had never felt the need to totemize* my lack of belief, and so make it something to go to war about.

15   Now, however, I find my entire world-picture under fire. And as I find myself obliged to defend the assumptions and processes of literature, which I had believed that all free men and women could take for granted, and for which all unfree men and women continue every day to struggle, so I am obliged to ask myself questions I admit to finding somewhat unnerving.

Do I, perhaps, find something sacred after all? Am I prepared to set aside as holy the idea of the absolute freedom of the imagination and alongside it my own notions of the World, the Text and the Good? Does this add up to what the apologists of religion have started calling "secular fundamentalism"?* And

---

1   *all that is ... air*   See Marx and Engels's "Communist Manifesto"; the passage continues, "all that is holy is profaned, and man is at last compelled to face with sober senses his real conditions of life, and his relations with his kind."

if so, must I accept that this "secular fundamentalism" is as likely to lead to excesses, abuses and oppressions as the canons of religious faith?

A lecture in memory of Herbert Read is a highly appropriate occasion for such an exploration, and I am honored to have been asked to deliver it. Herbert Read, one of the leading British advocates of the modernist and surrealist movements, was a distinguished representative of the cultural values closest to my heart. "Art is never transfixed," Read wrote. "Change is the condition of art remaining art." This principle is also mine. Art, too, is an event in history, subject to the historical process. But it is also *about* that process, and must constantly strive to find new forms to mirror an endlessly renewed world. No aesthetic can be a constant, except an aesthetic based on the idea of inconstancy, metamorphosis, or, to borrow a term from politics, "perpetual revolution."

The struggle between such ideas and the eternal, revealed truths of religion is dramatized this evening, as I hope I may be excused for pointing out, by my absence. I must apologize for this. I did, in fact, ask my admirable protectors how they would feel if I were to deliver my text in person. The answer was, more or less, "What have we done to deserve this?" With regret, I took the point.

It is an agony and a frustration not to be able to re-enter my old life, not even for such a moment. However, I should like to thank Harold Pinter, through his own mouth, for standing in my place. Perhaps this event could be thought of as a form of secular revelation: a man receives a text by mysterious processes from Elsewhere—above? below? New Scotland Yard?[2]—and brings it out before the people, and recites ...

More than twenty years ago, I stood packed in at the back of this theatre, listening to a lecture by Arthur Koestler.[3] He propounded the thesis that language, not territory, was the prime cause of aggression, because once language reached the level of sophistication at which it could express abstract concepts, it acquired the power of totemization; and once peoples had erected totems, they would go to war to defend them. (I ask pardon of Koestler's ghost. I am relying on an old memory, and that's an untrustworthy shoulder to lean on.)

In support of his theory, he told us about two tribes of monkeys living on, I think, one of the northern islands of Japan. The two tribes lived in close

20

---

2   *New Scotland Yard*   Headquarters for the metropolitan police force of Greater London.

3   *Arthur Koestler*   Hungarian-born novelist (1905–83), political activist, and social philosopher, whose most famous work, *Darkness at Noon* (1940), depicts extremes of censorship and oppression under a Soviet-style Marxist dictatorship.

proximity in the woods near a certain stream, and subsisted, not unusually, on a diet of bananas. One of the tribes, however, had developed the curious habit of washing its bananas in the stream before eating them, while the other tribe continued to be non-banana-washers. And yet, said Koestler, the two tribes continued to live contentedly as neighbors, without quarrelling. And why was this? It was because their language was too primitive to permit them to totemize either the act of banana-washing or that of eating bananas unwashed. With a more sophisticated language at their disposal, both wet and dry bananas could have become the sacred objects at the heart of a religion, and then, look out!—Holy war.

A young man rose from the audience to ask Koestler a question. Perhaps the real reason why the two tribes did not fight, he suggested, was that there were enough bananas to go round. Koestler became extremely angry. He refused to answer such a piece of Marxist claptrap.* And, in a way, he was right. Koestler and his questioner were speaking different languages, and their languages were in conflict. Their disagreement could even be seen as the proof of Koestler's point. If he, Koestler, were to be considered the banana-washer and his questioner the dry-banana man, then their command of a language more complex than the Japanese monkeys' had indeed resulted in totemizations. Now each of them had a totem to defend: the primacy of language versus the primacy of economics: and dialogue therefore became impossible. They were at war.

Between religion and literature, as between politics and literature, there is a linguistically based dispute. But it is not a dispute of simple opposites. Because whereas religion seeks to privilege one language above all others, one set of values above all others, one text above all others, the novel has always been *about* the way in which different languages, values and narratives quarrel, and about the shifting relations between them, which are relations of power. The novel does not seek to establish a privileged language, but it insists upon the freedom to portray and analyze the struggle between the different contestants for such privileges.

Carlos Fuentes[4] has called the novel "a privileged *arena*." By this he does not mean that it is the kind of holy space which one must put off one's shoes to enter; it is not an arena to revere; it claims no special rights *except the right to be the stage upon which the great debates of society can be conducted.* "The novel," Fuentes writes, "is born from the very fact that we do not understand one another, because unitary, orthodox language has broken down. Quixote and Sancho, the Shandy brothers, Mr. and Mrs. Karenin:[5] their novels are the

---

4   *Carlos Fuentes*   Mexican writer (1928–2012).

5   *Quixote ... Karenin*   Characters from classic novels: Cervantes's *Don Quixote*, Laurence Sterne's *Tristam Shandy*, and Tolstoy's *Anna Karenina*, respectively.

comedy (or the drama) of their misunderstandings. Impose a unitary language: you kill the novel, but you also kill the society."

He then poses the question I have been asking myself throughout my life as a writer: *Can the religious mentality survive outside of religious dogma and hierarchy?* Which is to say: Can art be the third principle that mediates between the material and spiritual worlds; might it, by "swallowing" both worlds, offer us something new—something that might even be called a secular definition of transcendence?

I believe it can. I believe it must. And I believe that, at its best, it does.

What I mean by transcendence is that flight of the human spirit outside the confines of its material, physical existence which all of us, secular or religious, experience on at least a few occasions. Birth is a moment of transcendence which we spend our lives trying to understand. The exaltation of the act of love, the experience of joy and very possibly the moment of death are other such moments. The soaring quality of transcendence, the sense of being more than oneself, of being in some way joined to the whole of life, is by its nature short-lived. Not even the visionary or mystical experience ever lasts very long. It is for art to capture that experience, to offer it to, in the case of literature, its readers; to be, for a secular, materialist culture, some sort of replacement for what the love of god offers in the world of faith.

It is important that we understand how profoundly we all feel the needs that religion, down the ages, has satisfied. I would suggest that these needs are of three types: firstly, the need to be given an articulation of our half-glimpsed knowledge of exaltation, of awe, of wonder; life is an awesome experience, and religion helps us understand why life so often makes us feel small, by telling us what we are *smaller than*; and, contrariwise, because we also have a sense of being special, of being *chosen*, religion helps us by telling us what we have been chosen by, and what for. Secondly, we need answers to the unanswerable: How did we get here? How did "here" get here in the first place? Is this, this brief life, all there is? How can it be? What would be the point of that? And, thirdly, we need codes to live by, "rules for every damn thing." The idea of god is at once a repository for our awestruck wonderment at life and an answer to the great questions of existence, and a rule book, too. The soul needs all these explanations—not simply rational explanations, but explanations of the heart.

It is also important to understand how often the language of secular, rationalist materialism has failed to answer these needs. As we witness the death of communism in Central Europe, we cannot fail to observe the deep religious spirit with which so many of the makers of these revolutions are imbued, and we must concede that it is not only a particular political ideology that has failed, but the idea that men and women could ever define themselves in terms that exclude their spiritual needs.

30   It seems obvious, but relevant, to point out that in all the countries now moving towards freedom, art was repressed as viciously as was religion. That the Czech revolution began in the theatres and is led by a writer[6] is proof that people's spiritual needs, more than their material needs, have driven the commissars from power. What appears plain is that it will be a very long time before the peoples of Europe will accept any ideology that claims to have a complete, totalized explanation of the world. Religious faith, profound as it is, must surely remain a private matter. This rejection of totalized explanations is the modern condition. And this is where the novel, the form created to discuss the fragmentation of truth, comes in. The film director Luis Buñuel used to say: "I would give my life for a man who is looking for the truth. But I would gladly kill a man who thinks he has found the truth." (This is what we used to call a joke, before killing people for their ideas returned to the agenda.) The elevation of the quest for the Grail* over the Grail itself, the acceptance that all that is solid has melted into air, that reality and morality are not givens but imperfect human constructs, is the point from which fiction begins. This is what J.-F. Lyotard called, in 1979, *La Condition Postmoderne*.[7] The challenge of literature is to start from this point, and still find a way of fulfilling our unaltered spiritual requirements.

*Moby Dick** meets that challenge by offering us a dark, almost Manichean vision[8] of a universe (the *Pequod*[9]) in the grip of one demon, Ahab, and heading inexorably towards another; namely the Whale. The ocean always was our Other, manifesting itself to us in the form of beasts—the worm Ouroboros, Kraken, Leviathan.[10] Herman Melville delves into these dark waters in order to offer us a very modern parable: Ahab, gripped by his possession, perishes; Ishmael, a man without strong feeling or powerful affiliations, survives. The

---

6   *the Czech ... writer*   Reference to the Velvet Revolution (1989), a nonviolent revolution that ended single-party communist rule in Czechoslovakia (now the Czech Republic and Slovakia). One of the movement's leaders was the playwright and intellectual Václav Havel, who became president after the revolution.

7   *La Condition Postmoderne*   French: The Postmodern Condition.

8   *Manichean vision*   Manicheanism is a form of dualism, in which the world is seen to be determined by the tension between the forces of good and evil.

9   *the Pequod*   Captain Ahab's ship (in Herman Melville's novel *Moby Dick* [1851]).

10   *Ouroboros*   Ancient symbol, present in many cultures, of a snake or a dragon devouring itself;   *Kraken*   Enormous sea monster said to be living in the ocean between Norway and Iceland;   *Leviathan*   Sea monster referred to in various places in the Bible.

self-interested modern man is the sole survivor; those who worship the Whale—for pursuit is a form of worship—perish by the Whale.

Joyce's wanderers, Beckett's tramps, Gogol's tricksters, Bulgakov's devils, Bellow's[11] high-energy meditations on the stifling of the soul by the triumphs of materialism; these, and many more, are what we have instead of prophets and suffering saints. But while the novel answers our need for wonderment and understanding, it brings us harsh and unpalatable news as well.

It tells us there are no rules. It hands down no commandments. We have to make up our own rules as best we can, make them up as we go along.

And it tells us there are no answers; or, rather, it tells us that answers are easier to come by, and less reliable, than questions. If religion is an answer, if political ideology is an answer, then literature is an inquiry; great literature, by asking extraordinary questions, opens new doors in our minds.

Richard Rorty, in *Philosophy and the Mirror of Nature,* insists on the importance of historicity, of giving up the illusions of being in contact with Eternity. For him, the great error is what he calls "foundationalism," which the theologian Don Cupitt, commenting on Rorty, calls "the attempt, as old as (and even much older than) Plato,* to give permanence and authority to our knowledge and values by purporting to found them in some unchanging cosmic realm, natural or noumenal, outside the flux of our human conversation." It is better, Cupitt concludes, "to be an adaptable pragmatist, a nomad."

Michel Foucault, also a confirmed historicist, discusses the role of the author in challenging sacralized absolutes in his essay, "What Is an Author?" This essay argues, in part, that "texts, books and discourses really began to have authors … to the extent that authors became subject to punishment, that is, to the extent that discourses could be transgressive." This is an extraordinary, provocative idea, even if it is stated with Foucault's characteristic airiness and a complete absence of supporting evidence: *that authors were named only when it was necessary to find somebody to blame.* Foucault continues:

> In our culture (and doubtless in many others), discourse was not origi-
> nally a product, a thing, a kind of goods; it was essentially an act—an
> act placed in the bipolar field of the sacred and the profane, the licit
> and the illicit, the religious and the blasphemous. Historically it was a
> gesture fraught with risks …

In our beginnings we find our essences. To understand a religion, look at its earliest moments. (It is regrettable that Islam, of all religions the easiest to study in this way, because of its birth during the age of recorded history, has

35

---

11 *Joyce ... Bellow* Authors James Joyce (1882–1941), Samuel Beckett (1906–89), Nikolai Gogol (1809–52), Mikhail Bulgakov (1891–1940), and Saul Bellow (1915–2005).

set its face so resolutely against the idea that it, like all ideas, is an event inside history.) And to understand an artistic form, too, Foucault suggests, look at its origins. If he is right about the novel, then literature is, of all the arts, the one best suited to challenging absolutes of all kinds; and, because it is in its origin the schismatic Other of the sacred (and authorless) text, so it is also the art mostly likely to fill our god-shaped holes.

There are other reasons, too, for proposing the novel as the crucial art form of what I can no longer avoid calling the post-modern age. For one thing, literature is the art least subject to external control, because it is made in private. The act of making it requires only one person, one pen, one room, some paper. (Even the room is not absolutely essential.) Literature is the most low-technology of the art forms. It requires neither a stage nor a screen. It calls for no interpreters, no actors, producers, camera crews, costumers, musicians. It does not even require the traditional apparatus of publishing, as the long-running success of samizdat literature[12] demonstrates. The Foucault essay suggests that literature is as much at risk from the enveloping, smothering forces of the market economy, which reduces books to mere products. This danger is real, and I do not want to seem to be minimizing it. But the truth is that of all the forms, literature can still be the most free. The more money a piece of work costs, the easier it is to control it. Film, the most expensive of art forms, is also the least subversive. This is why, although Carlos Fuentes cites the work of film-makers like Buñuel, Bergman and Fellini as instances of successful secular revolts into the territory of the sacred, I continue to believe in the greater possibilities of the novel. Its singularity is its best protection.

Among the childhood books I devoured and kissed were large numbers of cheap comics of a most unliterary nature. The heroes of these comic books were, or so it seemed, almost always mutants or hybrids or freaks: as well as the Batman and the Spiderman there was Aquaman, who was half-fish, and of course Superman, who could easily be mistaken for a bird or a plane. In those days, the middle 1950s, the super-heroes were all, in their various ways, hawkish* law-and-order conservatives, leaping to work in response to the Police Commissioner's Bat-Signal, banding together to form the Justice League of America, defending what Superman called "truth, justice and the American way." But in spite of this extreme emphasis on crime-busting, the lesson they taught children—or this child, at any rate—was the perhaps unintentionally radical truth that exceptionality was the greatest and most heroic of values; that those who were unlike the crowd were to be treasured the most lovingly; and that this exceptionality was a treasure so great and so easily misunderstood that

---

12 *samizdat literature* Underground, self-published literature, originally created in the Soviet Union to undermine the system of state censorship.

it had to be concealed, in ordinary life, beneath what the comic books called a "secret identity." Superman could not have survived without "mild-mannered" Clark Kent; "millionaire socialite" Bruce Wayne made possible the nocturnal activities of the Batman.

Now it is obviously true that those other freakish, hybrid, mutant, exceptional beings—novelists—those creators of the most freakish, hybrid and metamorphic of forms, the novel, have frequently been obliged to hide behind secret identities, whether for reasons of gender or terror. But the most wonderful of the many wonderful truths about the novel form is that the greater the writer, the greater his or her exceptionality. The geniuses of the novel are those whose voices are fully and undisguisably their own, who, to borrow William Gass's[13] image, *sign every word they write.* What draws us to an author is his or her "unlikeness," even if the apparatus of literary criticism then sets to work to demonstrate that he or she is really no more than an accumulation of influences. Unlikeness, the thing that makes it impossible for a writer to stand in any regimented line, is a quality novelists share with the Caped Crusaders of the comics, though they are only rarely capable of leaping tall buildings in a single stride.

What is more, the writer is there, in his work, in the reader's hands, utterly exposed, utterly defenseless, entirely without the benefit of an alter ego to hide behind. What is forged, in the secret act of reading, is a different kind of identity, as the reader and writer merge, through the medium of the text, to become a collective being that both writes as it reads and reads as it writes, and creates, jointly, that unique work, "their" novel. This "secret identity" of writer and reader is the novel form's greatest and most subversive gift.

And this, finally, is why I elevate the novel above other forms, why it has always been, and remains, my first love: not only is it the art involving least compromises, but it is also the only one that takes the "privileged arena" of conflicting discourses *right inside our heads.* The interior space of our imagination is a theater that can never be closed down; the images created there make up a movie that can never be destroyed.

In this last decade of the millennium, as the forces of religion are renewed in strength and as the all-pervasive power of materialism wraps its own weighty chains around the human spirit, where should the novel be looking? It seems clear that the renewal of the old, bipolar field of discourse, between the sacred and the profane, which Michel Foucault proposes, will be of central importance. It seems probable, too, that we may be heading towards a world in which there will be no real alternative to the liberal-capitalist social model (except, perhaps, the theocratic, foundationalist* model of Islam). In this situation,

---

13 *William Gass* American novelist, essayist, and critic (b. 1924).

liberal capitalism or democracy or the free world will require novelists' most rigorous attention, will require reimagining and questioning and doubting as never before. "Our antagonist is our helper," said Edmund Burke, and if democracy no longer has communism to help it clarify, by opposition, its own ideas, then perhaps it will have to have literature as an adversary instead.

I have made a large number of sweeping claims for literature during the course of this piece, and I am aware of a slightly messianic tone in much of what I've written. The reverencing of books and writers, by writers, is nothing particularly new, of course. "Since the early 19th century," writes Cupitt, "imaginative writers have claimed—have indeed enjoyed—a guiding and representative role in our culture. Our preachers are novelists, poets, dramatists, film-makers and the like, purveyors of fiction, ambiguous people, deceivers. Yet we continue to think of ourselves as rational."

But now I find myself backing away from the idea of sacralizing literature with which I flirted at the beginning of this text; I cannot bear the idea of the writer as secular prophet; I am remembering that one of the very greatest writers of the century, Samuel Beckett, believed that all art must inevitably end in failure. This is, clearly, no reason for surrender. "Ever tried. Ever failed. Never mind. Try again. Fail better."

45   Literature is an interim report from the consciousness of the artist, and so it can never be "finished" or "perfect." Literature is made at the frontier between the self and the world, and in the act of creation that frontier softens, becomes permeable, allows the world to flow into the artist and the artist to flow into the world. Nothing so inexact, so easily and frequently misconceived, deserves the protection of being declared sacrosanct. We shall just have to get along without the shield of sacralization, and a good thing, too. We must not become what we oppose.

The only privilege literature deserves—and this privilege it requires in order to exist—is the privilege of being the arena of discourse, the place where the struggle of languages can be acted out.

Imagine this. You wake up one morning and find yourself in a large, rambling house. As you wander through it you realize it is so enormous that you will never know it all. In the house are people you know, family members, friends, lovers, colleagues; also many strangers. The house is full of activity: conflicts and seductions, celebrations and wakes. At some point you understand that there is no way out. You find that you can accept this. The house is not what you'd have chosen, it's in fairly bad condition, the corridors are often full of bullies, but it will have to do. Then one day you enter an unimportant-looking little room. The room is empty, but there are voices in it, voices that seem to be whispering just to you. You recognize some of the voices, others are completely unknown to you. The voices are talking about the house, about everyone in it, about everything that is happening and has happened and should happen. Some of them speak exclusively in obscenities. Some are bitchy. Some are loving. Some are funny. Some are sad. The most interesting voices are all these things at once. You begin to go to the room more and more often. Slowly you learn that most of the people in the house use such rooms sometimes. Yet the rooms are all discreetly positioned and unimportant-looking.

Now imagine that you wake up one morning and you are still in the large house, but all the voice-rooms have disappeared. It is as if they have been wiped out. Now there is nowhere in the whole house where you can go to hear voices talking about everything in every possible way. There is nowhere to go for the voices that can be funny one minute and sad the next, that can sound raucous and melodic in the course of the same sentence. Now you remember: there is no way out of this house. Now this fact begins to seem unbearable. You look into the eyes of the people in the corridors—family, lovers, friends, colleagues, strangers, bullies, priests. You see the same thing in everybody's eyes. *How do we get out of here?* It becomes clear that the house is a prison. People begin to scream, and pound the walls. Men arrive with guns. The house begins to shake. You do not wake up. You are already awake.

Literature is the one place in any society where, within the secrecy of our own heads, we can hear *voices talking about everything in every possible way.* The reason for ensuring that that privileged arena is preserved is not that writers want the absolute freedom to say and do whatever they please. It is that we, all of us, readers and writers and citizens and generals and godmen, need that little, unimportant-looking room. We do not need to call it sacred, but we do need to remember that it is necessary.

"Everybody knows," wrote Saul Bellow in *The Adventures of Augie March,* "there is no fineness or accuracy of suppression. If you hold down one thing, you hold down the adjoining."

Wherever in the world the little room of literature has been closed, sooner or later the walls have come tumbling down.

(1990)

Sherman Alexie

Indian Education

Novelist, essayist, and short fiction writer Sherman Alexie has described the following essay as "a true (and truer) account of my public school days." A Spokane/Coeur D'Alene Indian, Alexie was raised in Wellpinit, Washington, and chose not to attend high school on his reservation,* opting for the greater educational resources offered at a white-dominated school in nearby Reardan. That experience, fictionalized to some extent, is reflected in "Indian Education," which first appeared in Alexie's 1993 collection The Lone Ranger and Tonto Fistfight in Heaven. *In the interconnected pieces that make up the book, Alexie draws upon his memories and observations of life on the Spokane Reservation, creating a text he calls "not an autobiography of details but an autobiography of the soul."* The Lone Ranger and Tonto Fistfight in Heaven *was awarded a PEN/Hemingway citation for first fiction.*

First Grade

My hair was too short and my US Government glasses were horn-rimmed, ugly, and all that first winter in school, the other Indian boys chased me from one corner of the playground to the other. They pushed me down, buried me in the snow until I couldn't breathe, thought I'd never breathe again.

They stole my glasses and threw them over my head, around my outstretched hands, just beyond my reach, until someone tripped me and sent me falling again, facedown in the snow.

I was always falling down; my Indian name* was Junior Falls Down. Sometimes it was Bloody Nose or Steal-His-Lunch. Once, it was Cries-Like-a-White-Boy, even though none of us had seen a white boy cry.

Then it was Friday morning recess and Frenchy SiJohn threw snowballs at me while the rest of the Indian boys tortured some other *top-yogh-yaught* kid, another weakling. But Frenchy was confident enough to torment me all by himself, and most days I would have let him.

5   But the little warrior in me roared to life that day and knocked Frenchy to the ground, held his head against the snow, and punched him so hard that

my knuckles and the snow made symmetrical bruises on his face. He almost looked like he was wearing war paint.

But he wasn't the warrior. I was. And I chanted *It's a good day to die, it's a good day to die,*[1] all the way down to the principal's office.

SECOND GRADE

Betty Towle, missionary teacher,* redheaded and so ugly that no one ever had a puppy crush* on her, made me stay in for recess fourteen days straight.

"Tell me you're sorry," she said.

"Sorry for what?" I asked.

"Everything," she said and made me stand straight for fifteen minutes, eagle-armed with books in each hand. One was a math book; the other was English. But all I learned was that gravity can be painful.

For Halloween I drew a picture of her riding a broom with a scrawny cat on the back. She said that her God would never forgive me for that.

Once, she gave the class a spelling test but set me aside and gave me a test designed for junior high students. When I spelled all the words right, she crumpled up the paper and made me eat it.

"You'll learn respect," she said.

She sent a letter home with me that told my parents to either cut my braids or keep me home from class. My parents came in the next day and dragged their braids across Betty Towle's desk.

"Indians, indians, indians." She said it without capitalization. She called me "indian, indian, indian."

And I said, *Yes, I am. I am Indian. Indian, I am.*

THIRD GRADE

My traditional Native American art career began and ended with my very first portrait: *Stick Indian Taking a Piss in My Backyard.*

As I circulated the original print around the classroom, Mrs. Schluter intercepted and confiscated my art.

Censorship, I might cry now. *Freedom of expression,* I would write in editorials to the tribal newspaper.

In third grade, though, I stood alone in the corner, faced the wall, and waited for the punishment to end.

I'm still waiting.

---

1 *It's a good day to die* Battle cry attributed to Ta-sunko-witko (c. 1842–77), Sioux chief and war leader also known as Crazy Horse. According to popular legend, he shouted "It's a good day to die!" before the Sioux victory against United States forces at the Battle of the Little Bighorn (1876).

FOURTH GRADE

"You should be a doctor when you grow up," Mr. Schluter told me, even though his wife, the third grade teacher, thought I was crazy beyond my years. My eyes always looked like I had just hit-and-run someone.

"Guilty," she said. "You always look guilty."

"Why should I be a doctor?" I asked Mr. Schluter.

25   "So you can come back and help the tribe. So you can heal people."

That was the year my father drank a gallon of vodka a day and the same year that my mother started two hundred different quilts but never finished any. They sat in separate, dark places in our HUD[2] house and wept savagely.

I ran home after school, heard their Indian tears, and looked in the mirror. *Doctor Victor*, I called myself, invented an education, talked to my reflection. *Doctor Victor to the emergency room.*

FIFTH GRADE

I picked up a basketball for the first time and made my first shot. No. I missed my first shot, missed the basket completely, and the ball landed in the dirt and sawdust, sat there just like I had sat there only minutes before.

But it felt good, that ball in my hands, all those possibilities and angles. It was mathematics, geometry. It was beautiful.

30   At that same moment, my cousin Steven Ford sniffed rubber cement from a paper bag and leaned back on the merry-go-round. His ears rang, his mouth was dry, and everyone seemed so far away.

But it felt good, that buzz in his head, all those colors and noises. It was chemistry, biology. It was beautiful.

Oh, do you remember those sweet, almost innocent choices that the Indian boys were forced to make?

SIXTH GRADE

Randy, the new Indian kid from the white town of Springdale, got into a fight an hour after he first walked into the reservation school.

Stevie Flett called him out, called him a squawman,[3] called him a pussy, and called him a punk.

---

2   *HUD*   Housing and Urban Development, a department of the United States federal government responsible for facilitating access to affordable housing.

3   *squawman*   Offensive term usually referring to a white man who marries a Native American woman.

Randy and Stevie, and the rest of the Indian boys, walked out into the 35
playground.

"Throw the first punch," Stevie said as they squared off.

"No," Randy said.

"Throw the first punch," Stevie said again.

"No," Randy said again.

"Throw the first punch!" Stevie said for the third time, and Randy reared 40
back and pitched a knuckle fastball that broke Stevie's nose.

We all stood there in silence, in awe.

That was Randy, my soon-to-be first and best friend, who taught me the
most valuable lesson about living in the white world: *Always throw the first
punch.*

SEVENTH GRADE

I leaned through the basement window of the HUD house and kissed the white
girl who would later be raped by her foster-parent father, who was also white.
They both lived on the reservation, though, and when the headlines and stories
filled the papers later, not one word was made of their color.

Just Indians being Indians, someone must have said somewhere and they
were wrong.

But on the day I leaned through the basement window of the HUD house 45
and kissed the white girl, I felt the good-byes I was saying to my entire tribe.
I held my lips tight against her lips, a dry, clumsy, and ultimately stupid kiss.

But I was saying good-bye to my tribe, to all the Indian girls and women I
might have loved, to all the Indian men who might have called me cousin, even
brother.

I kissed that white girl and when I opened my eyes, she was gone from
the reservation, and when I opened my eyes, I was gone from the reservation,
living in a farm town where a beautiful white girl asked my name.

"Junior Polatkin," I said, and she laughed.

After that, no one spoke to me for another five hundred years.

EIGHTH GRADE

At the farm town junior high, in the boys' bathroom, I could hear voices from 50
the girls' bathroom, nervous whispers of anorexia and bulimia.* I could hear
the white girls' forced vomiting, a sound so familiar and natural to me after
years of listening to my father's hangovers.

"Give me your lunch if you're just going to throw it up," I said to one of
those girls once.

I sat back and watched them grow skinny from self pity.

Back on the reservation, my mother stood in line to get us commodities. We carried them home, happy to have food, and opened the canned beef that even the dogs wouldn't eat.

But we ate it day after day and grew skinny from self pity.

55 There is more than one way to starve.

Ninth Grade

At the farm town high school dance, after a basketball game in an overheated gym where I had scored twenty-seven points and pulled down thirteen rebounds, I passed out during a slow song.

As my white friends revived me and prepared to take me to the emergency room where doctors would later diagnose my diabetes, the Chicano* teacher ran up to us.

"Hey," he said. "What's that boy been drinking? I know all about these Indian kids. They start drinking real young."

Sharing dark skin doesn't necessarily make two men brothers.

Tenth Grade

60 I passed the written test easily and nearly flunked the driving, but still received my Washington State driver's license on the same day that Wally Jim killed himself by driving his car into a pine tree.

No traces of alcohol in his blood, good job, wife and two kids.

"Why'd he do it?" asked a white Washington State trooper.

All the Indians shrugged their shoulders, looked down at the ground.

"Don't know," we all said, but when we look in the mirror, see the history of our tribe in our eyes, taste failure in the tap water, and shake with old tears, we understand completely.

65 Believe me, everything looks like a noose if you stare at it long enough.

Eleventh Grade

Last night I missed two free throws which would have won the game against the best team in the state. The farm town high school I play for is nicknamed the "Indians," and I'm probably the only actual Indian ever to play for a team with such a mascot.

This morning I pick up the sports page and read the headline: INDIANS LOSE AGAIN.

Go ahead and tell me none of this is supposed to hurt me very much.

TWELFTH GRADE

I walk down the aisle, valedictorian* of this farm town high school, and my cap doesn't fit because I've grown my hair longer than it's ever been. Later, I stand as the school-board chairman recites my awards, accomplishments, and scholarships.

I try to remain stoic for the photographers as I look toward the future.   70

Back home on the reservation, my former classmates graduate: a few can't read, one or two are just given attendance diplomas, most look forward to the parties. The bright students are shaken, frightened, because they don't know what comes next.

They smile for the photographer as they look back toward tradition.

The tribal newspaper runs my photograph and the photograph of my former classmates side by side.

POSTSCRIPT: CLASS REUNION

Victor said, "Why should we organize a reservation high school reunion? My graduating class has a reunion every weekend at the Powwow Tavern."

(1993)

ANNE CARSON

from SHORT TALKS

Poet, prose writer, translator, and classicist Anne Carson is known for works that blur the boundaries of genre—from her verse essay The Idea of the Husband *(2001), told in "twenty-nine tangos," to her* Autobiography of Red *(1998), subtitled* A Novel in Verse. *Her "short talks," some of which appear below, have been variously described by critics as "poetic meditations," "prose poems," "miniature essays," and "micro truths."*

INTRODUCTION

Early one morning words were missing. Before that, words were not. Facts were, faces were. In a good story, Aristotle tells us, everything that happens is pushed by something else.[1] Three old women were bending in the fields. What use is it to question us? they said. Well it shortly became clear that they knew everything there is to know about the snowy fields and the blue-green shoots and the plant called "audacity," which poets mistake for violets. I began to copy out everything that was said. The marks construct an instant of nature gradually, without the boredom of a story. I emphasize this. I will do anything to avoid boredom. It is the task of a lifetime. You can never know enough, never work enough, never use the infinitives and participles oddly enough, never impede the movement harshly enough, never leave the mind quickly enough.

---

1   *In a ... else*   In his *Poetics*, Aristotle claims that the middle and concluding events of a plot should follow logically from the events that come before. (In his *Physics*, he also argues that motion occurs when one object is acted on by another, a "mover," that is already in motion; that mover must in turn be moved by another mover, and so on. Since this chain cannot carry on forever, Aristotle thought, this necessitates the existence of at least one "unmoved mover" that moves itself. According to later Christian theologians, the "unmoved mover" is God.)

ON PARMENIDES[2]

We pride ourselves on being civilized people. Yet what if the names for things were utterly different? Italy, for example. I have a friend named Andreas, an Italian. He has lived in Argentina as well as in England, and also in Costa Rica for some time. Everywhere he lives, he invites people over for supper. It is a lot of work. Artichoke pasta. Peaches. His deep smile never fades. What if the proper name for Italy turns out to be Brzoy—will Andreas continue to travel the world like the wandering moon with her borrowed light? I fear we failed to understand what he was saying or his reasons. What if every time he said *cities*, he meant *delusion*, for example?

ON SLEEP STONES

Camille Claudel[3] lived the last thirty years of her life in an asylum, wondering why, writing letters to her brother the poet, who had signed the papers. Come visit me, she says. Remember, I am living here with madwomen; days are long. She did not smoke or stroll. She refused to sculpt. Although they gave her sleep stones—marble and granite and porphyry—she broke them, then collected the pieces and buried these outside the walls at night. Night was when her hands grew, huger and huger until in the photograph they are like two parts of someone else loaded onto her knees.

ON WALKING BACKWARDS

My mother forbad us to walk backwards. That is how the dead walk, she would say. Where did she get this idea? Perhaps from a bad translation. The dead, after all, do not walk backwards but they do walk behind us. They have no lungs and cannot call out but would love for us to turn around. They are victims of love, many of them.

ON THE TOTAL COLLECTION

From childhood he dreamed of being able to keep with him all the objects in the world lined up on his shelves and bookcase. He denied lack, oblivion or even the likelihood of a missing piece. Order streamed from Noah* in blue triangles and as the pure fury of his classifications rose around him, engulfing his life, they came to be called waves by others, who drowned, a world of them.

---

2   *PARMENIDES*   Greek poet-philosopher of the early fifth century BCE who claimed that our experience of change and variety in the world is an illusion, and that the universe is in reality pure, undifferentiated "Being."

3   *Camille Claudel*   French sculptor (1864–1943). Though she was a successful artist in her own right, she is also remembered for a tumultuous romance and working relationship with the more famous sculptor Auguste Rodin (1840–1917).

ON SUNDAY DINNER WITH FATHER

Are you going to put that chair back where it belongs or just leave it there looking like a uterus? (Our balcony is a breezy June balcony.) Are you going to let your face distorted by warring desires pour down on us all through the meal or tidy yourself so we can at least enjoy dessert? (We weight down the corners of everything on the table with little solid-silver laws.) Are you going to nick your throat open on those woodpecker scalps as you do every Sunday night or just sit quietly while Laetitia plays her clarinet for us? (My father, who smokes a brand of cigar called Dimanche Eternel,[4] uses them as ashtrays.)

(1992, revised 1995)

---

4   *Dimanche Eternel*   French: Eternal Sunday.

Henry Louis Gates Jr.

from The Passing of
Anatole Broyard

*The essay reprinted here first appeared in the 17 June 1996 issue
of* The New Yorker *under the title "White Like Me"—a reference
to John Howard Griffin's 1961 book* Black Like Me, *an account
of a six-week period during which Griffin had his skin treated
with pigments in order to "pass" as a black man. The passing of
the distinguished African American critic and essayist Anatole
Broyard—as a white man—sprang from very different motivations
and extended over decades rather than weeks; as Gates recounts,
Broyard's racial identity was intertwined in complex ways with his
identity as a writer in various genres.*

    *Though Gates, a Harvard professor, is now known primarily for
his scholarly writing, he wrote extensively during the 1990s for*
The New Yorker *and for* Time. *This essay was included along with
seven other* New Yorker *biographical profiles in Gates's 1997 book*
Thirteen Ways of Looking at a Black Man.

In 1982, an investment banker named Richard Grand-Jean took a summer's
lease on an eighteenth-century farmhouse in Fairfield, Connecticut; its
owner, Anatole Broyard, spent his summers in Martha's Vineyard.* The house
was handsomely furnished with period antiques, and the surrounding acreage
included a swimming pool and a pond. But the property had another attraction, too. Grand-Jean, a managing director of Salomon Brothers,* was an avid
reader, and he took satisfaction in renting from so illustrious a figure. Anatole
Broyard had by then been a daily book reviewer for the *Times* for more than a
decade, and that meant he was one of literary America's foremost gatekeepers.
Grand-Jean might turn to the business pages of the *Times* first, out of professional obligation, but he turned to the book page next, out of a sense of self. In
his Walter Mittyish moments,[1] he sometimes imagined what it might be like to

---

1   *Walter Mittyish moments* In James Thurber's story "The Secret Life of Walter
Mitty," the title character leads a very ordinary life but imagines a quite extraordinary
fantasy life.

be someone who read and wrote about books for a living—someone to whom millions of readers looked for guidance.

Broyard's columns were suffused with both worldliness and high culture. Wry, mandarin,* even self-amused at times, he wrote like a man about town, but one who just happened to have all of the Western literature at his fingertips. Always, he radiated an air of soigné² self-confidence: he could be amiable in his opinions or waspish,* but he never betrayed a flicker of doubt about what he thought. This was a man who knew that his judgement would never falter and his sentences never fail him.

Grand-Jean knew little about Broyard's earlier career, but as he rummaged through Broyard's bookshelves he came across old copies of intellectual journals *Partisan Review* and *Commentary*, to which Broyard had contributed a few pieces in the late forties and early fifties. One day, Grand-Jean found himself leafing through a magazine that contained an early article by Broyard. What caught his eye, though, was the contributor's note for the article—or, rather, its absence. It had been neatly cut out, as if with a razor.

A few years later, Grand-Jean happened upon another copy of that magazine, and decided to look up the Broyard article again. This time, the note on the contributor was intact. It offered a few humdrum details—that Broyard was born in New Orleans, attended Brooklyn College and the New School for Social Research, and taught at New York University's Division of General Education. It also offered a less humdrum one: the situation of the American Negro, the note asserted, was a subject the author "knows at first hand." It was an elliptical formulation, to be sure, but for Anatole Broyard it may not have been elliptical enough.

5   Broyard was born black and became white, and his story is compounded of equal parts pragmatism and principle. He knew that the world was filled with such snippets and scraps of paper, all conspiring to reduce him to an identity that other people had invented and he had no say in. Broyard responded with X-Acto knives and evasions, with distance and denials and half-denials and cunning half-truths. Over the years, he became a virtuoso of ambiguity and equivocation. Some of his acquaintances knew the truth; many more had heard rumors about "distant" black ancestry (wasn't there a grandfather who was black? A great-grandfather?). But most were entirely unaware, and that was as he preferred it. He kept the truth even from his own children. Society had decreed race to be a matter of natural law, but he wanted race to be an elective affinity, and it was never going to be a fair fight. A penalty was exacted. He shed a past and an identity to become a writer—a writer who wrote endlessly about the act of shedding a past and an identity.

---

2   *soigné*   Poised, polished; acting with great attention to detail.

Anatole Paul Broyard was born on July 16, 1920, in New Orleans to Paul Broyard and Edna Miller. His father was a carpenter and worked as a builder, along with his brothers; neither parent had graduated from elementary school. Anatole spent his early years in a modest house on St. Ann Street, in a colored neighborhood[3] in the French Quarter. Documents in the Louisiana state archives show all Anatole's ancestors, on both sides, to have been Negroes, at least since the late eighteenth century. The rumor about a distant black ancestor was, in a sense, the reverse of the truth: he may have had one distant white ancestor. Of course, the conventions of color stratification within black America—nowhere more pronounced than in New Orleans—meant that light-skinned blacks often intermarried with other light-skinned blacks, and this was the case with Paul and his "high yellow"[4] wife, Edna. Anatole was the second of three children; he and his sister Lorraine, two years older, were light-skinned, while Shirley, two years younger, was not so light-skinned. (The inheritance of melanin[5] is an uneven business.) In any event, the family was identified as Negro, and identified itself as Negro. It was not the most interesting thing about them. But in America it was not a negligible social fact. The year before Anatole's birth, for example, close to a hundred blacks were lynched in the South* and anti-black race riots claimed the lives of hundreds more.

While Anatole was still a child, the family moved to the Bedford-Stuyvesant[6] area of Brooklyn, thus joining the great migration that took hundreds of thousands of Southern blacks to Northern cities during the twenties. In the French Quarter, Paul Broyard had been a legendary dancer, beau, and *galant*;[7] in the French Quarter, the Broyards—Paul was one of ten siblings—were known for their craftsmanship. Brooklyn was a less welcoming environment. "He should never have left New Orleans, but my mother nagged him into it," Broyard recalled years later. Though Paul Broyard arrived there a master carpenter, he soon discovered that the carpenters' union was not favorably inclined toward colored applicants. A stranger in a strange city, Paul decided to pass as white in order to join the union and get work. It was strictly a professional decision, which affected his work and nothing else.

For Paul, being colored was a banal fact of life, which might be disguised when convenient; it was not a creed or something to take pride in. Paul did take pride in his craft, and he liked to boast of rescuing projects from know-nothing

---

3   *colored neighborhood*   Term used in the first half of the twentieth century for a neighborhood inhabited primarily by African Americans.

4   *high yellow*   Period term denoting a black person with very light complexion.

5   *melanin*   Skin pigment.

6   *Bedford-Stuyvesant*   At the time a tough, working class neighborhood.

7   *galant*   Man who is chivalrous in a stylish way.

architects. He filled his home with furniture he had made himself—flawlessly professional, if a little too sturdily built to be stylish. He also took pride in his long legs and his dance-hall agility (an agility Anatole would share). It was a challenge to be a Brooklyn *galant*, but he did his best.

"Family life was very congenial, it was nice and warm and cozy, but we just didn't have any sort of cultural or intellectual nourishment at home," Shirley, who was the only member of the family to graduate from college, recalls. "My parents had no idea even what *The New York Times* was, let alone being able to imagine that Anatole might write for it." She says, "Anatole was different from the beginning." There was a sense, early on, that Anatole Broyard—or Buddy, as he was called then—was not entirely comfortable being a Broyard.

10   Shirley has a photograph, taken when Anatole was around four or five, of a family visit back to New Orleans. In it you can see Edna and her two daughters, and you can make out Anatole, down the street, facing the opposite direction. The configuration was, Shirley says, pretty representative.

After graduating from Boys High School, in the late thirties, he enrolled in Brooklyn College. Already, he had a passion for modern culture—for European cinema and European literature. The idea that meaning could operate on several levels seemed to appeal to him. Shirley recalls exasperating conversations along those lines: "He'd ask me about a Kafka* story I'd read or a French film I'd seen and say, 'Well, you see that on more than one level, don't you?' I felt like saying 'Oh, get off it.' Brothers don't say that to their sisters."

Just after the war began, he got married, to a black Puerto Rican woman, Aida, and they soon had a daughter. (He named her Gala, after Salvador Dali's* wife.) Shirley recalls, "He got married and had a child on purpose—the purpose being to stay out of the Army. Then Anatole goes in the Army anyway, in spite of his child." And his wife and child moved in with the Broyard family.

Though his military records were apparently destroyed in a fire, some people who knew him at this time say that he entered the segregated Army as a white man. If so he must have relished the irony that after attending officers' training school he was made the captain of an all-black stevedore* battalion. Even then, his thoughts were not far from the new life he envisioned for himself. He said he joined the Army with a copy of Wallace Stevens* in his back pocket; now he was sending money home to his wife asking her to save it so that he could open a bookstore in the Village* when he got back. "She had other ideas," Shirley notes. "She wanted him to get a nice job, nine to five."

Between Aida and the allure of literary life there was not much competition. Soon after his discharge from the Army, at war's end, he found an apartment in the Village, and he took advantage of the G.I. bill* to attend evening classes at the New School for Social research, on Twelfth Street. His new life had no room for Aida and Gala. (Aida, with the child, later moved to California and remarried.) He left other things behind, too. The black scholar and dramatist W.F. Lucas, who knew Buddy Broyard from Bed-Stuy,* says, "He was black when he got into the subway to Brooklyn, but as soon as he got out at West Fourth Street he became white."

He told his sister Lorraine that he had resolved to pass so that he could be   15 a writer, rather than a Negro writer. His darker-skinned younger sister, Shirley, represented a possible snag, of course, but then he and Shirley had never been particularly close, and anyway she was busy with her own life and her own friends. (Shirley graduated Phi Beta Kappa from Hunter College, and went on to marry Franklyn Williams, who helped organize the Peace Corps and served as Ambassador to Ghana.) They had drifted apart: it was just a matter of drifting farther apart. Besides, wasn't that why everybody came to New York—to run away from the confines of family, from places where people thought they knew who and what you were? Whose family *wasn't* in some way unsuitable? In a *Times* column in 1979 Broyard wrote, "My mother and my father were too folksy for me, too colorful…. Eventually, I ran away to Greenwich Village, where no one had been born of a mother and father, where the people I met had sprung from their own brows, out from the pages of a bad novel…. Orphans of the avant-garde,* we outdistanced our history and our humanity." Like so much of what he wrote in this vein, it meant more than it said; like the modernist culture he loved, it had levels.

In the Village, where Broyard started a bookstore on Cornelia Street, the salient thing about him wasn't that he was black but that he was beautiful, charming, and erudite. In those days, the Village was crowded with ambitious and talented young writers and artists, and Broyard—known for calling men "Sport" and girls "Slim"—was never more at home. He could hang out at the San Remo bar with Dwight Macdonald and Delmore Schwartz, and with a younger set who yearned to be the next Macdonalds and the next Schwartzes. Vincent Livelli, a friend of Broyard's since Brooklyn College days, recalls, "everybody was so brilliant around us—we kept dueling with each other. But he was the guy that set the pace in the Village." His conversation sparkled—everybody said so. The sentences came out perfectly formed, festooned with the most apposite literary allusions. His high-beam charm could inspire worship but also resentment. Livelli says, "Anatole had a sort of dancing attitude toward life—he'd dance away from you. He had people understand that he was brilliant and therefore you couldn't hold him if you weren't worthy of his attention."

The novelist and editor Gordon Lish says, "Photographs don't suggest in any wise the enormous power he had in person. No part of him was ever for a moment at rest." He adds, "I adored him as a man. I mean, he was really in a league with Neal Cassady[8] as a kind of presence." But there was, he says, a fundamental difference between Broyard and Kerouac's inspiration and muse: "Unlike Cassady, who was out of control, Anatole was *exorbitantly* in control. He was fastidious about managing things."

Except, perhaps, the things you're supposed to manage. His bookstore provided him with entrée to Village intellectuals—and them with entrée to Anatole—yet it was not run as a business, exactly. Its offerings were few but choice: Céline, Kafka, other hard-to-find translations. The critic Richard Gilman, who was one of its patrons, recalls that Broyard had a hard time parting with the inventory: "He had these books on the shelf, and someone would want to buy one, and he would snatch it back."

Around 1948, Broyard started to attract notice not merely for his charm, his looks, and his conversation but for his published writings. The early pieces, as often as not, were about a subject to which he had privileged access: blacks and black culture. *Commentary,* in his third piece in its pages, dubbed him an "anatomist of the Negro personality in a white world." But was he merely an anthropologist or was he a native informant? It wasn't an ambiguity he was in any hurry to resolve. Still, if all criticism is a form of autobiography (as Oscar Wilde would have it), one might look to these pieces for clues to his preoccupations at the time. In a 1950 *Commentary* article entitled "Portrait of an Inauthentic Negro," he wrote that the Negro's embarrassment over blackness should be banished by the realization that "thousands of Negroes with 'typical' features are accepted as whites merely because of light complexion." He continued:

> The inauthentic Negro is not only estranged from whites—he is also estranged from his own group and from himself. Since his companions are a mirror in which he sees himself as ugly, he must reject them; and since his own self is mainly a tension between an accusation and denial. He can hardly find it, much less live in it.... He is adrift without a role in a world predicated on roles.

A year later, in "Keep Cool Man: The Negro Rejection of Jazz," he wrote, just as despairingly, that the Negro's

> contact with white society has opened new vistas, new ideals in his imagination, and these he defends by repression, freezing up against the desire to be white, to have normal social intercourse with whites, to behave like them; ... But in coolness he evades the issue.... he

---

8   *Neal Cassady*   Well-known 1950s counterculture figure who was a model for the character of Dean Moriarty in Jack Kerouac's autobiographical novel *On the Road* (1957).

becomes a pacifist in the struggle between social groups—not a conscientious objector, but a draft-dodger.*

These are words that could be read as self-indictment, if anybody chose to do so. Certainly they reveal a ticklish sense of the perplexities he found himself in, and a degree of self-interrogation (as apposed to self-examination) he seldom displayed again.

In 1950, in a bar near Sheridan Square, Broyard met Anne Bernays, a   20
Barnard junior* and the daughter of Edward L. Bernays, who is considered the father of public relations. "There was this guy who was the handsomest man I'd ever seen in my life, and I fell madly in love with him," Bernays, who is best known for such novels as *Growing Up Rich* and *Professor Romeo,* recalls. "He was physically irresistible, and he had this dominating personality, and I guess I needed to be dominated. His hair was so short that you couldn't tell whether it was curly or straight. He had high cheekbones and very smooth skin." She knew that he was black through a mutual friend, the poet and Blake scholar Milton Klonsky. (Years later, in a sort of epiphany, she recognized Anatole's loping walk as an African American cultural style: "It was almost as if this were inside him dying to get out and express himself, but he felt he couldn't do it.")

After graduation, she got a job as an editor at the literary semi-annual *Discovery.* She persuaded Broyard to submit his work, and in 1954 the magazine ran a short story entitled "What the Cystoscope Said"—an extraordinary account of his father's terminal illness:

> I didn't recognize him at first, he was so bad. His mouth was open and his breathing was hungry. They had removed his false teeth, and his cheeks were so thin that his mouth looked like a keyhole. I leaned in over his bed and brought my face before his eyes. "Hello darlin'," he whispered, and he smiled. His voice, faint as it was. Was full of love. And it bristled the hairs on the nape of my neck and raised goose flesh on my forearms. I couldn't speak, so I kissed him. His cheek smelled like wax.

Overnight, Broyard's renown was raised to a higher level. "Broyard knocked people flat with 'What the Cystoscope Said,'" Lish recalls. One of those people was Burt Britton, a bookseller who later co-founded Books & Co. In the fifties, he says, he read the works of young American writers religiously: "Now, if writing were a horse race, which God knows it's not, I would have gone out and put my two bucks down on Broyard." In *Advertisements for Myself,* Norman Mailer wrote that he'd buy a novel by Broyard the day it appeared. Indeed, Bernays recalls, on the basis of that story the Atlantic Monthly

Press offered Broyard a twenty-thousand-dollar advance—then a staggeringly large sum for a literary work by an unknown—for a novel of which "Cystoscope" would be a chapter. "The whole literary world was waiting with bated breath for this great novelist who was about to arrive," Michael Vincent Miller, a friend of Broyard's since the late fifties, recalls. "Some feelings of expectation lasted for years."

Rumor surrounded Broyard like a gentle murmur, and sometimes it became a din. Being an orphan of the avant-garde was hard work. Among the black literati,* certainly, his ancestry was a topic of speculation, and when a picture of Broyard accompanied a 1958 *Time* review of a Beat[9] anthology it was closely scrutinized. Arna Bontemps wrote to Langston Hughes, "His picture.... makes him look Negroid. If so, he is the only spade[10] among the Beat Generation." Charlie Parker spied Broyard in Washington Square Park one day and told a companion, "He's one of us, but he doesn't want to admit he's one of us." Richard Gilman* recalls an awkwardness that ensued when he stumbled across Anatole with his dark-skinned wife and child: "I just happened to come upon them in a restaurant that was not near our usual stomping grounds.* He introduced me, and it was fine, but my sense was that he would rather not have had anyone he knew meet them." He adds, "I remember thinking at the time that he has the look of an octoroon or quadroon,[11] one of those—which he strenuously denied. He got into very heated disputes with people." ...

Broyard's own account of these years—published in 1993 as *Kafka Was the Rage*—is fueled by the intertwined themes of writing and women. Gaddis says, "His eyes were these great pools—soft, gentle pools. It was girls, girls, girls: a kind of intoxication of its own. I always thought, frankly, that that's where his career went, his creative energies."

25   Anne Bernays maintains, "If you leave the sex part out, you're only telling half the story. With women, he was just like an alcoholic with booze." She stopped seeing him in 1952, at her therapist's urging. "It was like going cold turkey off a drug," she says, remembering how crushing the experience was, and she adds, "I think most women have an Anatole in their lives."

Indeed, not a few of them had an Anatole. "He was a pussy gangster, really," Lucas, a former professor of comparative literature, says with Bed-Stuy bluntness. Gilman recalls being in Bergdorf Goodman* and coming across

9   *Beat* The Beat Generation was a 1950s American counterculture movement associated particularly with the work of poets and writers such as Allen Ginsberg, Lawrence Ferlinghetti, and Jack Kerouac.

10   *spade* Slang word (now considered derogatory) for "black person."

11   *octoroon* Person who is one eighth black and seven eights white; *quadroon* Person who is one quarter black and three quarters white. Both "octoroon" and "quadroon" were widely used terms during the era of slavery in America.

Broyard putting the moves on a salesgirl. "I hid behind a pillar—otherwise he'd know that I'd seen him—and watched him go through every stage of seduction: 'What do you think? Can I put this against you? Oh, it looks great against your skin. You have the most wonderful skin.' And then he quoted Baudelaire."

Quoting Baudelaire turns out to be key. Broyard's great friend Ernest van den Haag recalls trolling the Village with Broyard in those days: "We obviously quite often compared our modus operandi, and what I observed about Anatole is that when he liked a girl he could speak to her brilliantly about all kinds of things which the girl didn't understand, because Anatole was really vastly erudite. The girl had no idea what he was talking about, but she loved it, because she was under the impression, rightly so, that she was listening to something very interesting and important. His was a solipsistic[12] discourse, in some ways." Indeed, the narrator of "What the Cystoscope Said" tells of seducing his ailing father's young and ingenuous nurse in a similar manner:

> "Listen," I said, borrowing a tone of urgency from another source, "I want to give you a book. A book that was written for you, a book that belongs to you as much as your diary, that's dedicated to you like your nurse's certificate." … My apartment was four blocks away, so I bridged the distance with talk, raving about *Journey to the End of the Night*, the book she needed like she needed a hole in the head.

Broyard recognized that seduction was a matter not only of talking but of listening, too, and he knew how to pay attention with an engulfing level of concentration. The writer Ellen Schwamm, who met Broyard in the late fifties, says, "You show me a man who talks, and I'll show you a thousand women who hurl themselves at his feet. I don't just mean talk, I mean dialogues. He *listened,* and he was willing to speak of things that most men are not interested in: literature and its effects on life." But she also saw another side to Broyard's relentless need to seduce. She invokes a formulation made by her husband, the late Harold Brodkey: "Harold used to say that a lot of men steal from women. They steal bits of their souls. Bits of their personalities. To construct an emotional life. Which many men don't have. And I think that Anatole needed something of that sort."

It's an image of self-assemblage which is very much in keeping with Broyard's own accounts of himself. Starting in 1946, and continuing at intervals for the rest of his life, he underwent analysis.[13] Yet the word "analysis" is misleading: what he wanted was to be refashioned—or, so he told his first ana-

---

12   *solipsistic*   Revolving around itself, as if nothing else exists.

13   *analysis*   Psychological treatment involving the examination of conflicts in the psyche of an individual (conducted in accordance with Freudian and/or Jungian principles).

lyst, to be *transfigured*. "When I came out with the word, I was like someone who sneezes into a handkerchief and finds it full of blood," he wrote in the 1993 memoir. "I wanted to discuss my life with him not as a patient talking to an analyst but as if we were two literary critics discussing a novel.... I had literature rather than a personality, a set of fictions about myself." He lived a lie because he didn't want to live a larger lie: and Anatole Broyard, Negro writer, was that larger lie.

30   Alexandra Nelson, known as Sandy, met Broyard in January of 1961. Broyard was forty, teaching the odd course at the New School and supporting himself by freelancing: promotional copy for publishers, liner notes for Columbia jazz records, blurbs for the Book-of-the-Month Club. Sandy was twenty-three and a dancer, and Broyard had always loved dancers. Of Norwegian descent, she was strikingly beautiful, and strikingly intelligent. Michael Miller recalls, "She represented a certain kind of blonde, a certain kind of sophisticated carriage and a way of moving through the world with a sense of good things. They both had marvelous taste."

It was as if a sorcerer had made a list of everything Broyard loved and had given it life. At long last, the conqueror was conquered: in less than a year, Broyard and Sandy were married. Sandy remembers his aura in those days: "Anatole was very hip. It wasn't a pose—it was in his sinew, in his bones. And, when he was talking to you, you just felt that you were receiving all this radiance from him." Van den Haag says, "I do think it's not without significance that Anatole married a blonde, and about as white as you can get. He may have feared a little bit that the children might turn out black. He must have been pleased that they didn't."

While they were still dating, two of Broyard's friends told Sandy that he was black, in what seemed to be a clumsy attempt to scare her off. "I think they really weren't happy to lose him, to see him get into a serious relationship," she says. "They were losing a playmate, in a way." Whatever the cultural sanctions, she was unfazed. But she said that when she asked Broyard about it he proved evasive: "he claimed that he wasn't black, but he talked about 'island influences,' or said that he had a grandmother who used to live in a tree on some island in the Caribbean. Anatole was like that—he was very slippery." Sandy didn't force the issue, and the succeeding years just fortified his sense of reserve. "Anatole was very strong," she says. "And he said about certain things, 'Just keep out. This is the deal if you get mixed up with me.'" The life that Broyard chose to live meant that their children did not meet their Aunt Shirley until after his death—nor, except for a couple of brief visits in the sixties, was there any contact even with Broyard's light-skinned mother and older sister. It was a matter of accepting the ground rules. "I would try to poke in those areas, but the message was very direct and strong," Sandy explains. "Oh, when I got angry at him, you know, one always pushes the tender points. But over time you grow up about these things and realize you do what you can do and there are certain things you can't."

In 1963, just before their first child, Todd, was born, Anatole shocked his friends by another big move—to Connecticut. "Not only was he moving to Connecticut but he was going to be commuting to work: for the first time in his life, he would be a company man. "I think one of his claims to fame was that he hasn't had an office job—somehow he'd escaped that," Sandy says. "There had been no real need for him to grow up." But after Todd was born—a daughter, Bliss, followed in 1966—Anatole spent seven years working full-time as a copywriter at a Manhattan advertising agency Wunderman Ricotta & Kline.

Over the next quarter century, the family lived in a series of eighteenth-century homes, sometimes bought on impulse, in places like Fairfield, Redding. Greens Farms, and Southport.* Here, in a land of leaf-blowers and lawnmowers, Bed-Stuy must have seemed almost comically remote. Many of Broyard's intimates from the late forties knew about his family; the intimates he acquired in the sixties did not, or else had heard only rumors. Each year the number of people who knew Buddy from Bed-Stuy dwindled; each year the rumors grew more nebulous; each year, he left his past further behind. …

In the late sixties, Broyard wrote several front-page reviews for the *Times Book Review*. "They were brilliant, absolutely sensational," the novelist Charles Simmons, who was then an assistant editor there, says. In 1971, the *Times* was casting about for a new daily reviewer, and Simmons was among those who suggested Anatole Broyard. It wasn't a tough sell. Arthur Gelb, at the time the paper's cultural editor, recalls, "Anatole was among the first critics I brought to the paper. He was very funny, and he also had that special knack for penetrating hypocrisy. I don't think he was capable of uttering a boring sentence."

You could say that his arrival was a sign of the times. Imagine: Anatole Broyard, downtown flaneur[14] and apostle of sex and high modernism, ensconced in what was, literally speaking, the ultimate establishment perch. "There had been an awful lot of very tame, very conventional people at the *Times,* and Broyard came in as a sort of ambassador from the Village and Village sophistication," Alfred Kazin recalls. Broyard had a highly developed appreciation of the paper's institutional power, and he even managed to use it to avenge wrongs done him in his Village days. Just before he started his job at the daily, he published a review in the *Times Book Review* of a new novel by one Chandler Brossard. The review began, "Here's a book so transcendently

35

---

14 *flaneur* Idle but sophisticated person who wanders and appreciates a city.

bad it makes us fear not only for the condition of the novel in this country, but for the country itself."

Broyard's reviews were published in alternation with those of Christopher Lehmann-Haupt, who has now been a daily reviewer at the *Times* for more than a quarter of a century, and who readily admits that Broyard's appointment did not gladden his heart. They hadn't got along particularly well when Lehmann-Haupt was an editor at the *Times Book Review,* nor did Lehmann-Haupt entirely approve of Broyard's status of a fabled libertine.* So when A.M. Rosenthal, the paper's managing editor, was considering hiring him, Lehmann-Haupt expressed reservations. He recalls, "Rosenthal was saying, 'Give me five reasons why not.' And I thoughtlessly blurted out, 'Well first of all, he is the biggest ass man in town.' And Rosenthal rose up from his desk and said, 'If that were a disqualification for working for *The New York Times*'—and he waved—'this place would be empty!'"

Broyard got off to an impressive start. Lehmann-Haupt says, "He had a wonderful way of setting tone, and a wonderful way of talking himself through a review. He had good, tough instincts when it came to fiction. He had taste." And the jovial Herbert Mitgang, who served a stint as a daily reviewer himself, says, "I always thought he was the most literary of the reviewers. There would be something like a little essay in his daily reviews." ...

No one could accuse Broyard of proselytizing for progressive causes. Jason Epstein, for one, was quick to detect a neoconservative air in his reviews, and Broyard's old friend Ernest van den Haag, a longtime contributing editor at *National Review,* volunteers that he was available to set Broyard straight on the issues when the need arose. Broyard could be mischievous, and he could get tendentious. It did not escape notice that he was consistently hostile to feminist writers. "Perhaps it's naïve of me to expect people to write reasonable books about emotionally charged subjects," one such review began irritably, "But when you have to read and review two or three books each week, you do get tired of 'understanding' so much personal bias. You reach a point where it no longer matters that the author's mistakes are well meant. You don't care if he or she is on the side of the angels: you just want them to tell the truth."

40

Nor did relations between the two daily reviewers ever become altogether cordial. Lehmann-Haupt tells of a time in 1974 when Broyard said that he was sick and couldn't deliver a review. Lehmann-Haupt had to write an extra review in less than a day, so that he could get to the Ali-Frazier fight* the next night, where he had ringside seats. Later, when they discussed the match, Broyard seemed suspiciously knowledgeable about its particulars; he claimed that a friend of his had been invited by a television executive to watch it on closed-circuit TV. "I waited about six months, because one of the charming things about Anatole was that he never remembered his lies," Lehmann-Haupt says, laughing. "And I said, 'Did you see that fight?' And he said, 'Oh, yeah—I was there as a guest of this television executive.' *That's* why he couldn't write the review!"

Broyard had been teaching off and on at the New School since the late fifties, and now his reputation as a writing teacher began to soar. Certainly his fluent prose style, with its combination of grace and clarity, was a considerable recommendation. He was charismatic and magisterial. And, because he was sometimes brutal about students' work, they found it all the more gratifying when he was complimentary. Among his students were Paul Breslow, Robert Olen Butler, Daphne Merkin, and Hilma Wolitzer. Ellen Schwamm, who took a workshop with him in the early seventies, says, "he had a gourmet's taste for literature and for language, and he was really able to convey that: it was a very sensual experience."

These were years of heady success and, at the same time, of a rising sense of failure. An arbiter of American writing, Broyard was racked by his inability to write his own magnum opus.* In the fifties, the Atlantic Monthly Press had contracted for an autobiographical novel—the novel that was supposed to secure Broyard's fame, his place in contemporary literature—but, all these years later, he had made no progress. It wasn't for lack of trying. Lehmann-Haupt recalls his taking a lengthy vacation in order to get the book written. "I remember talking to him—he was up in Vermont, where somebody had lent him a house—and he was in agony. He banished himself from the Vineyard, was clearly suffering, and he just couldn't do it." John Updike, who knew Broyard slightly from the Vineyard, was reminded of the anticipation surrounding Ellison's* second novel: "The most famous non-book around was the one Broyard was not writing." (The two non-book writers were in fact quite friendly: Broyard admired Ellison not only as a writer but as a dancer—a high tribute from such an adept as Broyard.)

Surrounded by analysts and psychotherapists—Sandy Broyard had become a therapist herself by this time—Broyard had no shortage of explanations for his inability to write his book. "He did not have a total writer's block," van den Haag says, "and he was analyzed by various persons, but it didn't fully overcome the writer's block. I couldn't prevent him from going back to 'The Cystoscope' and trying to improve it. He made it, of course, not better but worse." Broyard's fluency as an essayist and a reviewer wasn't quite compensation. Charles Simmons says, "He had produced all this charming criticism, but the one thing that mattered to him was the one thing he hadn't managed to do."

As the seventies wore on, Miller discussed the matter of blockage with his best friend in relatively abstract terms: he suggested that there might be something in Broyard's relationship to his family background that was holding him back....

45   Some people speculated that the reason Broyard couldn't write his novel was that he was living it—that race had loomed larger in his life because it was unacknowledged, that he couldn't put it behind him because he had put it beneath him. If he had been a different sort of writer, it might not have mattered so much. But Merkin points out, "Anatole's subject, even in fiction, was essentially himself. I think that ultimately he would have had to deal with more than he wanted to deal with."

Broyard may have been the picture of serene self-master, but there was one subject that could reliably fluster him. Gordon Lish recalls an occasion in the mid-seventies when Burt Britton (who was married to a black woman) alluded to Anatole's racial ancestry. Lish says, "Anatole became inflamed, and he left the room. He snapped, like a dog snapping—he *barked* at Britton. It was an ugly moment." To people who knew nothing about the matter, Broyard's sensitivities were at times simply perplexing. The critic Judith Dunford used to go to lunch with Broyard in the eighties. One day, Broyard mentioned his sister Shirley, and Dunford, idly making conversation, asked him what she looked like. Suddenly, she saw an extremely worried expression on his face. Very carefully, he replied, "Darker than me."

There was, finally, no sanctuary. "When the children were older, I began, every eighteen months or so, to bring up the issue of how they needed to know at some point," Sandy Broyard says. "And then he would totally shut down and go into a rage. He'd say that at some point he would tell them, but he would not tell them now." ...

Anatole Broyard had confessed enough in his time to know that confession did nothing for the soul. He preferred to communicate his truths on higher frequencies. As if in exorcism, Broyard's personal essays deal regularly with the necessary, guilt-ridden endeavor of escaping family history: and yet the feelings involved are well nigh universal. The thematic elements of passing—fragmentation, alienation, liminality, self-fashioning—echo the great themes of modernism. As a result, he could prepare the way for exposure without ever risking it. Miller observes, "If you look at the writing closely enough, and listen to the intonations, there's something there that is like no writer from the completely white world. Freud* talked about repetition compulsion. With Anatole, it's interesting that he was constantly hiding it and in some ways constantly revealing it."

Sandy speaks of these matters in dimly analytic tones; perhaps because she is a therapist, her love is tempered by an almost professional dispassion. She says, "I think his own personal history continued to be painful to him," and she adds, "In passing, you cause your family great anguish, but I also think, conversely, do we look at the anguish it causes the person who is passing? Or the anguish that it was born out of?"

It may be tempting to describe Broyard's self-positioning as arising from a tortured allegiance to some liberal-humanist creed. In fact, the liberal pieties* of the day were not much to his taste. "It wasn't about an ideal of racelessness but something much more complex and interesting," Miller says. "He was actually quite anti-black," Evelyn Toynton says. She tells of a time when she was walking with him on a street in New York and a drunken black man came up to him and asked for a dollar. Broyard seethed. Afterward, he remarked to her, "I look around New York, and I think to myself, If there were no blacks in New York, would it really be any loss?" 50

No doubt this is a calculation that whites, even white liberals, sometimes find themselves idly working out: How many black muggers is one Thelonious Monk worth? How many Willie Hortons does Gwendolyn Brooks* redeem? In 1970, Ellison published his classic essay "What America Would Be Like Without Blacks," in *Time*; and one reason it is a classic essay is that it addresses a question that lingers in the American political unconscious. Commanding as Ellison's arguments are, there remains a whit of defensiveness in the very exercise. It's a burdensome thing to refute a fantasy.

And a burdensome thing to be privy to it. Ellen Schwamm recalls that one of the houses Broyard had in Connecticut had a black jockey on the lawn, and that "he used to tell me that Jimmy Baldwin said to him, 'I can't come and see you with this crap on your lawn.'" …

Every once in a while, however, Broyard's irony would slacken, and he would speak of the thing with an unaccustomed and halting forthrightness. Toynton says that after they'd known each other for several years he told her there was a "C" (actually, "col," for "colored") on his birth certificate. "And then another time he told me that his sister was black and that she was married to a black man." The circumlocutions are striking: not that *he* was black but that his birth certificate was; not that *he* was black but that his family was. Perhaps this was a matter less of evasiveness than of precision.

"Some shrink had said to him that the reason he didn't like brown-haired women or dark women was that he was afraid of his own shit," Toynton continues. "And I said, 'Anatole, it's as plain as plain can be that it has to do with being black.' And he just stopped and said, 'You don't know what it was like. It was horrible.' He told me once that he didn't like to see his sisters because they reminded him of his unhappy childhood." (Shirley's account suggests that this unhappy childhood may have had more to do with the child than with the hood.)

55   Ellen Schwamm remembers one occasion when Broyard visited her and Harold Brodkey at their apartment, and read them part of the memoir he was working on. She says that the passages seemed stilted and distant, and that Brodkey said to him, "You're not telling the truth, and if you try to write lies or evade the truth this is what you get. What's the real story?" She says, "Anatole took a deep breath and said, 'The real story is that I'm not who I seem. I'm a black.' I said, 'Well, Anatole, it's no great shock, because this rumor has been around for years and years and years, and everyone assumes there's some small percentage of you that's black, if that's what you're trying to say.' And he said, 'No, that's not what I'm trying to say. My father could pass, but in fact my mother's black, too. We're black as far back as I know.' We never said a word of it to anybody, because he asked us not to."

        Schwamm also says that she begged him to write about his history: it seemed to her excellent material for a book. But he explained that he didn't want notoriety based on his race—on his revealing himself to be black—rather than on his talent. As Toynton puts it, Broyard felt that he had to make a choice between being an aesthete* and being a Negro. "He felt that once he said, 'I'm a Negro writer,' he would have to write about black issues, and Anatole was such an aesthete."

        All the same, Schwamm was impressed by a paradox: the man wanted to be appreciated not for being black but for being a writer, even though his pretending not to be black was stopping him from writing. It was one of the very few ironies the Broyard, the master ironist, was ill equipped to appreciate.

Besides, there was always his day job to attend to. Broyard might suffer through a midnight of the soul in Vermont; but he was also a working journalist, and when it came to filing his copy he nearly always met his deadlines. In the late seventies, he also began publishing brief personal essays in the *Times*. They are among the finest work he did—easeful, witty, perfectly poised between surface and depth. In them he perfected the feat of being self-revelatory without revealing anything. He wrote about his current life, in Connecticut: "People in New York City have psychotherapists, and people in the suburbs have handymen. While anxiety in the city is existential, in the country it is structural." And he wrote about his earlier life, in the city: "There was a kind of jazz in my father's movements, a rhythm compounded of economy and flourishes, functional and decorative. He had a blues song in his blood, a wistful jauntiness he brought with him from New Orleans." (Wistful and even worrisome: "I have half-expected him to break into the Camel Walk, the Shimmy Shewobble, the Black Bottom, or the Mess Around.") In a 1979 essay he wrote about how much he dreaded family excursion:

To me, they were a suicide pact. Didn't my parents know that the world was just waiting for a chance to come between us?

Inside, we were a family, but outside we were immigrants, bizarre in our differences. I thought that people stared at us, and my face grew hot. At any moment, I expected my father and mother to expose their tribal rites, their eccentric anthropology, to the gape of strangers.

Anyone who saw me with my family knew too much about me.

These were the themes he returned to in many of his personal essays, seemingly marking out the threshold he would not cross. And if some of his colleagues at the *Times* knew too much about him, or had heard the rumors, they wouldn't have dreamed of saying anything. Abe Rosenthal (who did know about him) says that the subject never arose. "What was there to talk about? I didn't really consider it my business. I didn't think it was proper or polite, nor did I want him to think I was prejudiced, or anything."

But most people knew nothing about it. C. Gerald Fraser, a reporter and an editor at the *Times* from 1967 until 1991, was friendly with Broyard's brother-in-law Ambassador Franklin Williams. Fraser, who is black, recalls that one day Williams asked him how many black journalists there were at the *Times*. "I listed them," he says, "and he said, 'You forgot one.' I went over the list again, and I said, 'What do you mean?' He said, 'Shirley's brother, Anatole Broyard.' I was dumbstruck, because I'd never heard it mentioned at the *Times* that he was black, or that the paper had a black critic."

In any event, Broyard's colleagues did not have to know what he was to have reservations about *who* he was. He cultivated his image as a trickster— someone who would bend the rules, finesse the system—and that image only intensified his detractors' ire. "A good book review is an act of seduction, and when he did it there was nobody better," John Leonard says, but he feels that Broyard's best was not always offered. "I considered him to be one of the laziest book reviewers to come down the pike." Soon a running joke was that Broyard would review only novels shorter than two hundred pages. In the introduction to *Aroused by Books,* a collection of the reviews he published in the early seventies, Broyard wrote that he tried to choose books for review that were "closest to [his] feelings." Lehmann-Haupt says dryly, "we began to suspect that he often picked books according to the attractiveness of the young female novelists who had written them." Rosenthal had shamed him for voicing his disquiet about Broyard's reputation as a Don Juan,* but before long Rosenthal himself changed his tune. "Maybe five or six years later," Lehmann-Haupt recalls, "Rosenthal comes up to me, jabbing me in the chest with a stiffened index finger and saying, 'The trouble with Broyard is that he writes with his cock!' I bit my tongue."

60

Gradually, a measure of discontent with Broyard's reviews began to make itself felt among the paper's cultural commissars. Harvey Shapiro, the editor of the *Book Review* from 1975 to 1983, recalls conversations with Rosenthal in which "he would tell me that all his friends hated Anatole's essays, and I would tell him that all my friends loved Anatole's essays, and that would be the end of the conversation." In 1984, Broyard was removed from the daily *Times* and given a column in the *Book Review.*

Mitchel Levitas, the editor of the *Book Review* from 1983 to 1989, edited Broyard's column himself. He says, "It was a tough time for him, you see, because he had come off the daily book review, where he was out there in the public eye twice a week. That was a major change in his public role." In addition to writing his column, he was put to work as an editor at the *Book Review.* The office environment was perhaps not altogether congenial to a man of his temperament. Kazin recalls, "He complained to me constantly about being on the *Book Review,* because he had to check people's quotations and such. I think he thought that he was superior to the job."

Then, too, it was an era in which the very notion of passing was beginning to seem less plangent than preposterous. Certainly Broyard's skirtishness around the subject wasn't to everyone's liking. Brent Staples, who is black, was an editor at the *Book Review* at the time Broyard was there. "Anatole had it both ways," Staples says. "He would give you a kind of burlesque wink that seemed to indicate he was ready to accept the fact of your knowing that he was a black person. It was real ambiguity. Tacit and sort of recessed. He jived around and played with it a lot, but never made it express the fact that he was black." It was a game that tried Staples's patience. "When Anatole came anywhere near me, for example, his whole style, demeanor and tone would change," he recalls. "I took that as him conveying to me, 'Yes, I am like you. But I'm relating this to you on a kind of recondite channel.' Over all, it made me angry. Here was a guy who was, for a long period of time, probably one of the two or three more important critical voices on literature in the United States. How could you, actively or passively, have this fact hidden?"

Staples pauses, then says, "You know, he turned it into a joke. And when you change something basic about yourself into a joke, it spreads, it metastasizes, and so his whole presentation of self became completely ironic. *Everything* about him was ironic." ...

65   When Broyard retired from the *Times,* he was nearly sixty-nine. To Sandy, it was a source of some anguish that their children still did not know the truth about him. Yet what was that truth? Broyard was a critic—a critic who specialized in European and American fiction. And what was race but a European and American fiction? If he was passing for white, perhaps he understood that the

alternative was passing for black. "But if some people are light enough to live like white, mother, why should there be such a fuss?" a girl asks her mother in "Near-White," a 1931 story by the Harlem Renaissance* author Claude McKay. "Why should they live colored when they could be happier living white?" Why, indeed? One could concede that the passing of Anatole Broyard involved dishonesty; but is it so very clear that the dishonesty was Broyard's?

To pass is to sin against authenticity, and "authenticity" is among the founding lies of the modern age. The philosopher Charley Taylor summarizes its ideology thus: "There is a certain way of being human that is *my* way. I am called upon to live my life in this way, and not in imitation of anyone else's life. But the notion gives a new importance to being true to myself. If I am not, I miss the point of my life; I miss what being human is for *me*." And the Romantic* fallacy of authenticity is only compounded when it is collectivized; when the putative real me gives way to the real us. You can say that Anatole Broyard was (by any juridical reckoning) "really" a Negro, without conceding that a Negro is a thing you can really be. The vagaries of racial identity were increased by what anthropologists call the rule of "hypodescent"—the one drop rule.[15] When those of mixed ancestry—and the majority of blacks are of mixed ancestry—disappear into the white majority, they are traditionally accused of running from their "blackness." Yet why isn't the alternative a matter of running from their "whiteness"? To emphasize these perversities, however, is a distraction from the larger perversity. You can't get race "right" by refining the boundary conditions.

The act of razoring out your contributor's note may be quixotic, but it is not mad. The mistake is to assume that the birth certificate and biographical sketches and all other documents generated by the modern bureaucratic state reveal an anterior truth—that they are merely signs of an independent existing identity. But in fact they constitute it. The social meaning of race is established by these identity papers—by tracts and treatises and certificates and pamphlets and all other verbal artifacts that proclaim race to be real and, by that proclamation, make it so.

So here is a man who passed for white because he wanted to be a writer and he did not want to be a Negro writer. It is a crass disjunction, but it is not his crassness or his disjunction. His perception was perfectly correct. He *would* have had to be a Negro writer, which was something he did not want to be. In his terms, he did not want to write about black love, black passion, black suffering, and joy. We give lip service to the idea of the writer who happens to be black, but had anyone, in the postwar era, ever seen such a thing? …

---

15 *one drop rule* Judgment that held legal force in various Southern states for many years, according to which any black ancestor (however distant) is considered sufficient to class an otherwise white person as "colored."

In a system where whiteness is the default, racelessness is never a possibility. You cannot opt out; you can only opt in. In a scathing review of a now forgotten black author, Broyard announced that it was time to reconsider the assumption of many black writers that "'whitey' will never let you forget you're black." For his part, he wasn't taking any chances....

70   In 1989, Broyard resolved that he and his wife would change their life once more. With both their children grown, they could do what they pleased. And what they pleased—what he pleased, anyway—was to move to Cambridge, Massachusetts. They would be near Harvard, and so part of an intellectual community. He had a vision of walking through Harvard square, bumping into people like the sociologist Daniel Bell, and having conversations about ideas in the street. Besides, his close friend Michael Miller was living in the area. Anne Bernays, also a Cambridge resident, says, "I remember his calling several times and asking me about neighborhoods. It was important for him to get that right. I think he was a little disappointed when he moved that it wasn't to a fancy neighborhood like Brattle or Channing Street. He was on Wendell Street, where there's a tennis court across the street and an apartment building and the houses are fairly close together." It wasn't a matter of passing so much as of positioning.

Sandy says that they had another the-children-must-be-told conversation shortly before the move. "We were driving to Michael's fiftieth-birthday party—I used to plan to bring up the subject in a place where he couldn't walk out. I brought it up then because at that point our son was out of college and our daughter had just graduated, and my feeling was that they just absolutely needed to know, as adults." She pauses. "And we had words. He would just bring down this gate." Sandy surmises, again, that he may have wanted to protect them from what he had experienced as a child. "Also," she says, "I think he needed still to protect himself." The day after they moved into their house on Wendell Street, Broyard learned he had prostate cancer, and that it was inoperable.

Broyard spent much of the time before his death, fourteen months later, making a study of the literature of illness and death, and publishing a number of essays on the subject. Despite the occasion, they were imbued with an almost dandyish,* even jokey sense of incongruity: "My urologist, who is quite famous, wanted to cut off my testicles.... Speaking as a surgeon, he said that it was the surest, quickest, neatest solution. Too neat, I said, picturing myself with no balls. I knew such a solution would depress me, and I was sure that depression is bad medicine." He had attracted notice in 1954 with the account of his father's death from a similar cancer; now he recharged his writing career as a chronicler of his own progress toward death. He thought about calling his collection of writings on the subject "Critically Ill." It was a pun he delighted in.

Soon after the diagnosis was made, he was told that he might have "in the neighborhood of years." Eight months later, it became clear that this prognosis was too optimistic. Richard Schweder, the anthropologist, talks about a trip to France that he and his wife made with Anatole and Sandy not long before Anatole's death. One day, the two men were left alone. Schweder says, "and what did he want to do? He wanted to throw a ball. The two of us just played catch, back and forth." The moment, he believes, captures Broyard's athleticism, his love of physical grace.

Broyard spent the last of his life at the Dana Farber Cancer Institute, in Boston. In therapy sessions, the need to set things straight before the end had come up again—the need to deal with unfinished business and, most of all, with his secret. He appeared willing, if reluctant, to do so. But by now he was in almost constant pain, and the two children lived in different places, so the opportunities to have the discussion as a family were limited. "Anatole was in such physical pain that I don't think he had the wherewithal," Sandy says. "So he missed the opportunity to tell the children himself." She speaks of the expense of spirit, of psychic energy, that would have been required. The challenge would have been to explain why it had remained a secret. And no doubt the old anxieties were not easily dispelled: would it have been condemned as a Faustian bargain* or understood as a case of personality overspilling, or rebelling against, the reign of category?

It pains Sandy even now that the children never had the chance to have an opportunity to have an open discussion with their father. In the event, she felt that they needed to know before he died, and, for the first time, she took it upon herself to declare what her husband could not. It was an early afternoon, ten days before his death, when she sat down with her two children on a patch of grass across the street from the institute. "They knew there was a family secret, and they wanted to know what their father had to tell them. And I told them."

The stillness of the afternoon was undisturbed. She says carefully, "Their first reaction was relief that it was only this, and not an event or circumstance of larger proportions. Only following their father's death did they begin to feel the loss of not having known. And of having to reformulate who it was that they understood their father—and themselves—to be."

At this stage of his illness, Anatole was moving in and out of lucidity, but in his room Sandy and the children talked with humor and irony about secrets and about this particular secret. Even if Anatole could not participate in the conversation, he could at least listen to it. "The nurses said that hearing was the last sense to go," Sandy says.

75

It was not as she would have planned it. She says, gently, "Anatole always found his own way through things." ...

A memorial service, held at Congressionalist church in Connecticut, featured august* figures from literary New York, colleagues from the *Times,* and neighbors and friends from the Village and the Vineyard. Charles Simmons told me that he was surprised at how hard he took Broyard's death. "You felt that you were going to have him forever, the way you feel about your own child," he said. "There was something wrong about his dying, and that was the reason." Speaking of the memorial service, he says, marveling, "You think that you're the close friend, you know? And then I realized that there are twenty people ahead of me. And that his genius was for close friends."

80   Indeed, six years after Broyard's death many of his friends seem to be still mourning his loss. For them he was plainly a vital principle, a dancer and romancer, a seducer of men and women. (He considered seduction, he wrote, "the most heartfelt literature of the self.") Sandy tells me, simply, "You felt more alive in his presence," and I've heard almost precisely the same words from a great many others. They felt he lived more intensely than other men. They loved him—perhaps his male friends especially, or, anyway, more volubly—and they admired him. They speak of a limber beauty, of agelessness, of radiance. They also speak of the excesses and his penchant for poses. Perhaps, as the bard* has it, Broyard was "much more the better for being a little bad." ...

[Broyard's] essays are often urbane and sophisticated, but not unbearably so, and they can be unexpectedly moving. Literary culture still fetishizes the novel, and there he was perhaps out of step with his times. Sandy says, "In the seventies and eighties, the trend, in literature and film, was to get sparer, and the flourish of Anatole's voice was dependent on the luxuriance of his language." Richard Schweder says, "It does seem that Anatole's strength was the brief, witty remark. It was aphoristic.* It was critical review. He was brilliant in a thousand or two thousand words." Perhaps he wasn't destined to be a novelist, but what of it? Broyard was a Negro who wanted to be something other than a Negro, a critic who wanted to be something other than a critic. Broyard, you might say, wanted to be something other than Broyard. He very nearly succeeded....

(1996)

EMILY MARTIN

THE EGG AND THE SPERM:

HOW SCIENCE HAS CONSTRUCTED A ROMANCE
BASED ON STEREOTYPICAL MALE-FEMALE ROLES

Anthropologist Emily Martin is best known for her work on American science and medicine—and especially for her analysis of scientific metaphors surrounding women's bodies and human reproductive processes. The following article, one of her most famous pieces, appeared in the major feminist journal Signs *in 1991.*

The theory of the human body is always a part of a world-picture ...
The theory of the human body is always a part of a fantasy.
[James Hillman, *The Myth of Analysis*][1]

As an anthropologist, I am intrigued by the possibility that culture shapes how biological scientists describe what they discover about the natural world. If this were so, we would be learning about more than the natural world in high school biology class; we would be learning about cultural beliefs and practices as if they were part of nature. In the course of my research I realized that the picture of egg and sperm drawn in popular as well as scientific accounts of reproductive biology relies on stereotypes central to our cultural definitions of male and female. The stereotypes imply not only that female biological processes are less worthy than their male counterparts but also that women are less worthy than men. Part of my goal in writing this article is to shine a bright light on the gender stereotypes hidden within the scientific language of biology. Exposed in such a light, I hope they will lose much of their power to harm us.

---

1 James Hillman, *The Myth of Analysis* (Evanston, Ill.: Northwestern University Press, 1972), 220. [Unless otherwise noted, all notes to this essay are from the author.]

EGG AND SPERM: A SCIENTIFIC FAIRY TALE

At a fundamental level, all major scientific textbooks depict male and female reproductive organs as systems for the production of valuable substances, such as eggs and sperm.[2] In the case of women, the monthly cycle is described as being designed to produce eggs and prepare a suitable place for them to be fertilized and grown—all to the end of making babies. But the enthusiasm ends there. By extolling the female cycle as a productive enterprise, menstruation must necessarily be viewed as a failure. Medical texts describe menstruation as the "debris" of the uterine lining, the result of necrosis, or death of tissue. The descriptions imply that a system has gone awry, making products of no use, not to specification, unsalable, wasted, scrap. An illustration in a widely used medical text shows menstruation as a chaotic disintegration of form, complementing the many texts that describe it as "ceasing," "dying," "losing," "denuding," "expelling."[3]

Male reproductive physiology is evaluated quite differently. One of the texts that sees menstruation as failed production employs a sort of breathless prose when it describes the maturation of sperm: "The mechanisms which guide the remarkable cellular transformation from spermatid to mature sperm remain uncertain.... Perhaps the most amazing characteristic of spermatogenesis is its sheer magnitude: the normal human male may manufacture several hundred million sperm per day."[4] In the classic text *Medical Physiology*, edited by Vernon Mountcastle, the male/female, productive/destructive comparison is more explicit: "Whereas the female *sheds* only a single gamete each month, the seminiferous tubules *produce* hundreds of millions of sperm each day" (emphasis mine).[5] The female author of another text marvels at the length of the microscopic seminiferous tubules, which, if uncoiled and placed end to end, "would span almost one-third of a mile!" She writes, "In an adult male these structures produce millions of sperm cells each day." Later she asks, "How is this feat accomplished?"[6] None of these texts expresses such intense

2   The textbooks I consulted are the main ones used in classes for undergraduate premedical students or medical students (or those held on reserve in the library for these classes) during the past few years at Johns Hopkins University. These texts are widely used at other universities in the country as well.

3   Arthur C. Guyton, *Physiology of the Human Body*, 6th ed. (Philadelphia: Saunders College Publishing, 1984), 624.

4   Arthur J. Vander, James H. Sherman, and Dorothy S. Luciano, *Human Physiology: The Mechanisms of Body Function*, 3rd ed. (New York: McGraw Hill, 1980), 483–84.

5   Vernon B. Mountcastle, *Medical Physiology*, 14th ed. (London: Mosby, 1980), 2:1624.

6   Eldra Pearl Solomon, *Human Anatomy and Physiology* (New York: CBS College Publishing, 1983), 678.

enthusiasm for any female processes. It is surely no accident that the "remarkable" process of making sperm involves precisely what, in the medical view, menstruation does not: production of something deemed valuable.[7]

One could argue that menstruation and spermatogenesis are not analogous processes and, therefore, should not be expected to elicit the same kind of response. The proper female analogy to spermatogenesis, biologically, is ovulation. Yet ovulation does not merit enthusiasm in these texts either. Textbook descriptions stress that all of the ovarian follicles containing ova are already present at birth. Far from being *produced*, as sperm are, they merely sit on the shelf, slowly degenerating and aging like overstocked inventory: "At birth, normal human ovaries contain an estimated one million follicles [each], and no new ones appear after birth. Thus, in marked contrast to the male, the newborn female already has all the germ cells she will ever have. Only a few, perhaps 400, are destined to reach full maturity during her active productive life. All the others degenerate at some point in their development so that few, if any remain by the time she reaches menopause at approximately 50 years of age."[8] Note the "marked contrast" that this description sets up between male and female, who has stockpiled germ cells by birth and is faced with their degeneration.

Nor are the female organs spared such vivid descriptions. One scientist writes in a newspaper article that a woman's ovaries become old and worn out from ripening eggs every month, even though the woman herself is still relatively young: "When you look through a laparoscope ... at an ovary that has been through hundreds of cycles, even in a superbly healthy American female, you see a scarred, battered organ."[9]

To avoid the negative connotations that some people associate with the female reproductive system, scientists could begin to describe male and female processes as homologous.* They might credit females with "producing" mature ova one at a time, as they're needed each month, and describe males as having to face problems of degenerating germ cells. This degeneration would occur throughout life among spermatogonia, the undifferentiated germ cells in the testes that are the long-lived, dormant precursors of sperm.

But the texts have an almost dogged insistence on casting female processes in a negative light. The texts celebrate sperm production because it is continuous from puberty to senescence, while they portray egg production as inferior because it is finished at birth. This makes the female seem unproductive, but

7   For elaboration, see Emily Martin, *The Woman in the Body: A Cultural Analysis of Reproduction* (Boston: Beacon, 1987), 27–53.

8   Vander, Sherman, and Luciano, 568.

9   Melvin Konner, "Childbearing and Age," *New York Times Magazine* (December 27, 1987), 22–23, esp. 22.

some texts will also insist that it is she who is wasteful.[10] In a section heading for *Molecular Biology of the Cell*, a best-selling text, we are told that "Oogenesis is wasteful." The text goes on to emphasize that of the seven million oogonia, or egg germ cells, in the female embryo, most degenerate in the ovary. Of those that do go on to become oocytes, or eggs, many also degenerate, so that at birth only two million eggs remain in the ovaries. Degeneration continues throughout a woman's life: by puberty 300,000 eggs remain, and only a few are present by menopause. "During the 40 or so years of a woman's reproductive life only 400 to 500 eggs will have been released," the authors write. "All the rest will have degenerated. It is still a mystery why so many eggs are formed only to die in the ovaries."[11]

The real mystery is why the male's vast production of sperm is not seen as wasteful.[12] Assuming that a man "produces" 100 million (10^8) sperm per day (a conservative estimate) during an average reproductive life of sixty years, he would produce well over two trillion sperm in his lifetime. Assuming that a woman "ripens" one egg per lunar month, or thirteen per year, over the course of her forty-year reproductive life, she would total five hundred eggs in her lifetime. But the word "waste" implies an excess, too much produced. Assuming two or three offspring, for every baby a woman produces, she wastes only around two hundred eggs. For every baby a man produces, he wastes more than one trillion (10^{12}) sperm.

---

10   I have found but one exception to the opinion that the female is wasteful: "Smallpox being the nasty disease it is, one might expect nature to have designed antibody molecules with combining sites that specifically recognize the epitopes on smallpox virus. Nature differs from technology, however: it thinks nothing of wastefulness. (For example, rather than improving the chance that a spermatozoon will meet an egg cell, nature finds it easier to produce millions of spermatozoa.)" (Niels Kaj Jerne, "The Immune System," *Scientific American* 229, no. 1 [July 1973]: 53). Thanks to a *Signs* reviewer for bringing this reference to my attention.

11   Bruce Alberts et al., *Molecular Biology of the Cell* (New York: Garland, 1983), 795.

12   In her essay "Have Only Men Evolved?" (in *Discovering Reality: Feminist Perspectives on Epistemology, Metaphysics, Methodology, and Philosophy of Science*, ed. Sandra Harding and Merrill B. Hintikka [Dordrecht: Reidel, 1983], 45–69, esp. 60–61), Ruth Hubbard points out that sociobiologists have said the female invests more energy than the male in the production of her large gametes, claiming that this explains why the female provides parental care. Hubbard questions whether it "really takes more 'energy' to generate the one or relatively few eggs than the large excess of sperms required to achieve fertilization." For further critique of how the greater size of eggs is interpreted in sociobiology, see Donna Haraway, "Investment Strategies for the Evolving Portfolio of Primate Females," in *Body/Politics*, ed. Mary Jacobus, Evelyn Fox Keller, and Sally Shuttleworth (New York: Routledge, 1990), 155–56.

How is it that positive images are denied to the bodies of women? A look at language—in this case, scientific language—provides the first clue. Take the egg and the sperm.[13] It is remarkable how "femininely" the egg behaves and how "masculinely" the sperm.[14] The egg is seen as large and passive.[15] It does not *move* or *journey*, but passively "is transported," "is swept,"[16] or even "drifts"[17] along the fallopian tube. In utter contrast, sperm are small, "streamlined,"[18] and invariably active. They "deliver" their genes to the egg, "activate the developmental program of the egg,"[19] and have a "velocity" that is often remarked upon.[20] Their tails are "strong" and efficiently powered.[21] Together with the forces of ejaculation, they can "propel the semen into the deepest recesses of the vagina."[22] For this they need "energy," "fuel,"[23] so that with a "whiplashlike motion and strong lurches"[24] they can "burrow through the egg coat"[25] and "penetrate" it.[26]

At its extreme, the age-old relationship of the egg and the sperm takes on a royal or religious patina. The egg coat, its protective barrier, is sometimes

10

---

13 The sources I used for this article provide compelling information on interactions among sperm. Lack of space prevents me from taking up this theme here, but the elements include competition, hierarchy, and sacrifice. For a newspaper report, see Malcolm W. Browne, "Some Thoughts on Self Sacrifice," *New York Times* (July 5, 1988), C6. For a literary rendition, see John Barth, "Night-Sea Journey," in his *Lost in the Funhouse* (Garden City, NY: Doubleday, 1968), 3–13.

14 See Carol Delaney, "The Meaning of Paternity and the Virgin Birth Debate," *Man* 21, no. 3 (September 1986): 494–513. She discusses the difference between this scientific view that women contribute genetic material to the fetus and the claim of long-standing Western folk theories that the origin and identity of the fetus comes from the male, as in the metaphor of planting a seed in soil.

15 For a suggested direct link between human behavior and purportedly passive eggs and active sperm, see Erik H. Erikson, "Inner and Outer Space: Reflections on Womanhood," *Daedalus* 93, no. 2 (Spring 1964): 582–606, esp. 591.

16 Guyton (n. 3 above), 619; and Mountcastle (n. 5 above), 1609.

17 Jonathan Miller and David Pelham, *The Facts of Life* (New York: Viking Penguin, 1984), 5.

18 Alberts et al., 796.

19 Ibid., 796.

20 See, e.g., William F. Ganong, *Review of Medical Physiology*, 7th ed. (Los Altos, Calif.: Lange Medical Publications, 1975), 322.

21 Alberts et al. (n. 11 above), 796.

22 Guyton, 615.

23 Solomon (n. 6 above), 683.

24 Vander, Sherman, and Luciano (n. 4 above), 4th ed. (1985), 580.

25 Alberts et al., 796.

26 All biology texts quoted above use the word "penetrate."

called its "vestments,"* a term usually reserved for sacred, religious dress. The egg is said to have a "corona,"[27] a crown, and to be accompanied by "attendant cells."[28] It is holy, set apart and above, the queen to the sperm's king. The egg is also passive, which means it must depend on sperm for rescue. Gerald Schatten and Helen Schatten liken the egg's role to that of Sleeping Beauty: "a dormant bride awaiting her mate's magic kiss, which instills the spirit that brings her to life."[29] Sperm, by contrast, have a "mission,"[30] which is to "move through the female genital tract in quest of the ovum."[31] One popular account has it that the sperm carry out a "perilous journey" into the "warm darkness," where some fall away "exhausted." "Survivors" "assault" the egg, the successful candidates "surrounding the prize."[32] Part of the urgency of this journey, in more scientific terms, is that "once released from the supportive environment of the ovary, an egg will die within hours unless rescued by a sperm."[33] The wording stresses the fragility and dependency of the egg, even though the same text acknowledges elsewhere that sperm also live for only a few hours.[34]

In 1948, in a book remarkable for its early insights into these matters, Ruth Herschberger argued that female reproductive organs are seen as biologically interdependent, while male organs are viewed as autonomous, operating independently and in isolation:

> At present the functional is stressed only in connection with women: it is in them that ovaries, tubes, uterus, and vagina have endless interdependence. In the male, reproduction would seem to involve "organs" only.
>
> Yet the sperm, just as much as the egg, is dependent on a great many related processes. There are secretions which mitigate the urine in the urethra before ejaculation, to protect the sperm. There is the reflex shutting off of the bladder connection, the provision of prostatic secretions, and various types of muscular propulsion. The sperm is no more independent of its milieu than the egg, and yet from a wish that it were, biologists have lent their support to the notion that the human

---

27 Solomon, 700.

28 A. Beldecos et al., "The Importance of Feminist Critique for Contemporary Cell Biology," *Hypatia* 3, no. 1 (Spring 1988): 61–76.

29 Gerald Schatten and Helen Schatten, "The Energetic Egg," *Medical World News* 23 (January 23, 1984): 51–53, esp. 51.

30 Alberts et al., 796.

31 Guyton (n. 3 above), 613.

32 Miller and Pelham (n. 17 above), 7.

33 Alberts et al. (n. 11 above), 804.

34 Ibid., 801.

female, beginning with the egg, is congenitally more dependent than the male.[35]

Bringing out another aspect of the sperm's autonomy, an article in the journal *Cell* has the sperm making an "existential decision" to penetrate the egg: "Sperm are cells with a limited behavioral repertoire, one that is directed toward fertilizing eggs. To execute the decision to abandon the haploid state, sperm swim to an egg and there acquire the ability to effect membrane fusion."[36] Is this a corporate manager's version of the sperm's activities—"executing decisions" while fraught with dismay over difficult options that bring with them very high risk?

There is another way that sperm, despite their small size, can be made to loom in importance over the egg. In a collection of scientific papers, an electron micrograph of an enormous egg and tiny sperm is titled "A Portrait of the Sperm."[37] This is a little like showing a photo of a dog and calling it a picture of the fleas. Granted, microscopic sperm are harder to photograph than eggs, which are just large enough to see with the naked eye. But surely the use of the term "portrait," a word associated with the powerful and wealthy, is significant. Eggs have only micrographs or pictures, not portraits.

One depiction of sperm as weak and timid, instead of strong and powerful—the only such representation in western civilization, so far as I know—occurs in Woody Allen's movie *Everything You Always Wanted To Know About Sex* (*But Were Afraid to Ask)*. Allen, playing the part of an apprehensive sperm inside a man's testicles, is scared of the man's approaching orgasm. He is reluctant to launch himself into the darkness, afraid of contraceptive devices, afraid of winding up on the ceiling if the man masturbates.

The more common picture—egg as damsel in distress, shielded only by her sacred garments; sperm as heroic warrior to the rescue—cannot be proved to be dictated by the biology of these events. While the "facts" of biology may not *always* be constructed in cultural terms, I would argue that in this case they are. The degree of metaphorical content in these descriptions, the extent to which differences between egg and sperm are emphasized, and the parallels between cultural stereotypes of male and female behavior and the character of egg and sperm all point to this conclusion.

15

---

35 Ruth Herschberger, *Adam's Rib* (New York: Pelligrini & Cudaby, 1948), esp. 84. I am indebted to Ruth Hubbard for telling me about Herschberger's work, although at a point when this paper was already in draft form.

36 Bennett M. Shapiro. "The Existential Decision of a Sperm," *Cell* 49, no. 3 (May 1987): 293–94, esp. 293.

37 Lennart Nilsson, "A Portrait of the Sperm," in *The Functional Anatomy of the Spermatozoan*, ed. Bjorn A. Afzelius (New York: Pergamon, 1975), 79–82.

NEW RESEARCH, OLD IMAGERY

As new understandings of egg and sperm emerge, textbook gender imagery is being revised. But the new research, far from escaping the stereotypical representations of egg and sperm, simply replicates elements of textbook gender imagery in a different form. The persistence of this imagery calls to mind what Ludwig Fleck termed "the self-contained" nature of scientific thought. As he described it, "the interaction between what is already known, what remains to be learned, and those who are to apprehend it, go to ensure harmony within the system. But at the same time they also preserve the harmony of illusions, which is quite secure within the confines of a given thought style."[38] We need to understand the way in which the cultural content in scientific descriptions changes as biological discoveries unfold, and whether that cultural content is solidly entrenched or easily changed.

In all of the texts quoted above, sperm are described as penetrating the egg, and specific substances on a sperm's head are described as binding to the egg. Recently, this description of events was rewritten in a biophysics lab at Johns Hopkins University—transforming the egg from the passive to the active party.[39]

Prior to this research, it was thought that the zona, the inner vestments of the egg, formed an impenetrable barrier. Sperm overcame the barrier by mechanically burrowing through, thrashing their tails and slowly working their way along. Later research showed that the sperm released digestive enzymes that chemically broke down the zona; thus, scientists presumed that the sperm used mechanical and chemical means to get through to the egg.

In this recent investigation, the researchers began to ask questions about the mechanical force of the sperm's tail. (The lab's goal was to develop a contraceptive that worked topically on sperm.) They discovered, to their great surprise, that the forward thrust of sperm is extremely weak, which contradicts the assumption that sperm are forceful penetrators.[40] Rather than thrusting forward, the sperm's head was now seen to move mostly back and forth. The sideways motion of the sperm's tail makes the head move sideways with a force

---

38 Ludwig Fleck, *Genesis and Development of a Scientific Fact*, ed. Thaddeus J. Trenn and Robert K. Merton (Chicago: University of Chicago Press, 1979), 38.

39 Jay M. Baltz carried out the research I describe when he was a graduate student in the Thomas C. Jenkins Department of Biophysics at Johns Hopkins University.

40 Far less is known about the physiology of sperm than comparable female substances, which some feminists claim is no accident. Greater scientific scrutiny of female reproduction has long enabled the burden of birth control to be placed on women. In this case, the researchers' discovery did not depend on development of any new technology: The experiments made use of glass pipettes, a manometer, and a simple microscope, all of which have been available for more than one hundred years.

that is ten times stronger than its forward movement. So even if the overall force of the sperm were strong enough to mechanically break the zona, most of its force would be directed sideways rather than forward. In fact, its strongest tendency, by tenfold, is to *escape* by attempting to pry itself off the egg. Sperm, then, must be exceptionally efficient at escaping from any cell surface they contact. And the surface of the egg must be designed to trap the sperm and prevent their escape. Otherwise, few if any sperm would reach the egg.

The researchers at Johns Hopkins concluded that the sperm and egg stick together because of adhesive molecules on the surfaces of each. The egg traps the sperm and adheres to it so tightly that the sperm's head is forced to lie flat against the surface of the zona, a little bit, they told me, "like Br'er Rabbit getting more and more stuck to tar baby the more he wriggles."* The trapped sperm continues to wiggle ineffectually side to side. The mechanical force of its tail is so weak that a sperm cannot break even one chemical bond. This is where the digestive enzymes released by the sperm come in. If they start to soften the zona just at the tip of the sperm and the sides remain stuck, then the weak, flailing sperm can get oriented in the right direction and make it through the zona—provided that its bonds to the zona dissolve as it moves in.

Although this new version of the saga of the egg and the sperm broke through cultural expectations, the researchers who made the discovery continued to write papers and abstracts as if the sperm were the active party who attacks, binds, penetrates, and enters the egg. The only difference was that the sperm were now seen as performing these actions weakly.[41] Not until August 1987, more than three years after the findings described above, did these researchers reconceptualize the process to give the egg a more active role. They began to describe the zona as an aggressive sperm catcher, covered with adhesive molecules that can capture a sperm with a single bond and clasp it to the zona's surface.[42] In the words of their published account: "The innermost

20

---

41   Jay Baltz and Richard A. Cone, "What Force Is Needed to Tether a Sperm?" (abstract for Society for the Study of Reproduction, 1985), and "Flagellar Torque on the Head Determines the Force Needed to Tether a Sperm" (abstract for Biophysical Society, 1986).
42   Jay M. Baltz, David F. Katz, and Richard A. Cone, "The Mechanics of the Sperm-Egg Interaction at the Zona Pellucida," *Biophysical Journal* 54, no. 4 (October 1988): 643–54. Lab members were somewhat familiar with work on metaphors in the biology of female reproduction. Richard Cone, who runs the lab, is my husband, and he talked with them about my earlier research on the subject from time to time. Even though my current research focuses on biological imagery and I heard about the lab's work from my husband every day, I myself did not recognize the role of imagery in the sperm research until many weeks after the period of research and writing I describe. Therefore, I assume that any awareness the lab members may have had about how underlying metaphor might be guiding this particular research was fairly inchoate.

vestment, the *zona pellucida*, is a glycoprotein shell, which captures and tethers the sperm before they penetrate it.... The sperm is captured at the initial contact between the sperm tip and the *zona*.... Since the thrust [of the sperm] is much smaller than the force needed to break a single affinity bond, the first bond made upon the tip-first meeting of the sperm and *zona* can result in the capture of the sperm."[43]

Experiments in another lab reveal similar patterns of data interpretation. Gerald Schatten and Helen Schatten set out to show that, contrary to conventional wisdom, the "egg is not merely a large, yolk-filled sphere into which the sperm burrows to endow new life. Rather, recent research suggests the almost heretical* view that sperm and egg are mutually active partners."[44] This sounds like a departure from the stereotypical textbook view, but further reading reveals Schatten and Schatten's conformity to the aggressive-sperm metaphor. They describe how "the sperm and egg first touch when, from the tip of the sperm's triangular head, a long, thin filament shoots out and harpoons the egg." Then we learn that "remarkably, the harpoon is not so much fired as assembled at great speed, molecule by molecule, from a pool of protein stored in a specialized region called the acrosome. The filament may grow as much as twenty times longer than the sperm head itself before its tip reaches the egg and sticks."[45] Why not call this "making a bridge" or "throwing out a line" rather than firing a harpoon? Harpoons pierce prey and injure or kill them, while this filament only sticks. And why not focus, as the Hopkins lab did, on the stickiness of the egg, rather than the stickiness of the sperm?[46] Later in the article, the Schattens replicate the common view of the sperm's perilous journey into the warm darkness of the vagina, this time for the purpose of explaining its journey into the egg itself: "[The sperm] still has an arduous journey ahead. It must penetrate farther into the egg's huge sphere of cytoplasm and somehow locate the nucleus, so that the two cells' chromosomes can fuse. The sperm dives down into the cytoplasm, its tail beating. But it is soon interrupted by the sudden and swift migration of the egg nucleus, which rushes toward the sperm with a velocity triple that of the movement of chromosomes during cell division, crossing the entire egg in about a minute."[47]

Like Schatten and Schatten and the biophysicists at Johns Hopkins, another researcher has recently made discoveries that seem to point to a more

---

43   Ibid., 643, 650.
44   Schatten and Schatten (n. 29 above), 51.
45   Ibid., 52.
46   Surprisingly, in an article intended for a general audience, the authors do not point out that these are sea urchin sperm and note that human sperm do not shoot out filaments at all.
47   Schatten and Schatten, 53.

interactive view of the relationship of egg and sperm. This work, which Paul Wassarman conducted on the sperm and eggs of mice, focuses on identifying the specific molecules in the egg coat (the zona pellucida) that are involved in egg-sperm interaction. At first glance, his descriptions seem to fit the model of an egalitarian relationship. Male and female gametes "recognize one another," and "interactions ... take place between sperm and egg."[48] But the article in *Scientific American* in which those descriptions appear begins with a vignette that presages the dominant motif of their presentation: "It has been more than a century since Hermann Fol, a Swiss zoologist, peered into his microscope and became the first person to see a sperm penetrate an egg, fertilize it and form the first cell of a new embryo."[49] This portrayal of the sperm as the active party— the one that *penetrates* and *fertilizes* the egg and *produces* the embryo—is not cited as an example of an earlier, now outmoded view. In fact, the author reiterates the point later in the article: "Many sperm can bind to and penetrate the zona pellucida, or outer coat, of an unfertilized mouse egg, but only one sperm will eventually fuse with the thin plasma membrane surrounding the egg proper (*inner sphere*), *fertilizing the egg and giving rise to a new embryo*."[50]

The imagery of sperm as aggressor is particularly startling in this case: the main discovery being reported is isolation of a particular molecule *on the egg coat* that plays an important role in fertilization! Wassarman's choice of language sustains the picture. He calls the molecule that has been isolated, ZP3, a "sperm receptor." By allocating the passive, waiting role to the egg, Wassarman can continue to describe the sperm as the actor, the one that makes it all happen: "The basic process begins when many sperm first attach loosely and then bind tenaciously to receptors on the surface of the egg's thick outer coat, the zona pellucida. Each sperm, which has a large number of egg-binding proteins on its surface, binds to many sperm receptors on the egg. More specifically, a site on each of the egg-binding proteins fits a complementary site on a sperm receptor, much as a key fits a lock."[51] With the sperm designated as the "key" and the egg the "lock," it is obvious which one acts and which one is acted upon. Could this imagery not be reversed, letting the sperm (the lock) wait until the egg produces the key? Or could we speak of two halves of a locket matching, and regard the matching itself as the action that initiates the fertilization?

---

48   Paul M. Wassarman, "Fertilization in Mammals," *Scientific American* 259, no. 6 (December 1988): 78–84, esp. 78, 84.

49   Ibid., 78.

50   Ibid., 79.

51   Ibid., 78.

25   It is as if Wassarman were determined to make the egg the receiving partner. Usually in biological research, the protein member of the pair of binding molecules is called the receptor, and physically it has a pocket in it rather like a lock. As the diagrams that illustrate Wassarman's article show, the molecules on the sperm are proteins and have "pockets." The small, mobile molecules that fit into these pockets are called ligands. As shown in the diagrams, ZP3 on the egg is a polymer of "keys"; many small knobs stick out. Typically, molecules in the sperm would be called receptors and molecules on the egg would be called ligands. But Wassarman chose to name ZP3 on the egg the receptor and to create a new term, "the egg-binding protein," for the molecule on the sperm that otherwise would have been called the receptor.[52]

Wassarman does credit the egg coat with having more functions than those of a sperm receptor. While he notes that "the zona pellucida has at times been viewed by investigators as a nuisance, a barrier to sperm and hence an impediment to fertilization," his new research reveals that the egg coat "serves as a sophisticated biological security system that screens incoming sperm, selects only those compatible with fertilization and development, prepares sperm for fusion with the egg and later protects the resulting embryo from polyspermy [a lethal condition caused by fusion of more than one sperm with a single egg]."[53] Although this description gives the egg an active role, that role is drawn in stereotypically feminine terms. The egg *selects* an appropriate mate, *prepares* him for fusion, and then *protects* the resulting offspring from harm. This is courtship and mating behavior as seen through the eyes of a sociobiologist: woman as the hard-to-get prize, who, following union with the chosen one, becomes woman as servant and mother.

And Wassarman does not quit there. In a review article for *Science*, he outlines the "chronology of fertilization."[54] Near the end of the article are two subject headings. One is "Sperm Penetration," in which Wassarman describes how the chemical dissolving of the zona pellucida combines with the "substantial propulsive force generated by sperm." The next heading is "Sperm-Egg Fusion." This section details what happens inside the zona after a sperm "penetrates" it. Sperm "can make contact with, adhere to, and fuse with (that is, fertilize) an egg."[55] Wassarman's word choice, again, is astonish-

---

52 Since receptor molecules are relatively *immotile* and the ligands that bind to them relatively *motile*, one might imagine the egg being called the receptor and the sperm the ligand. But the molecules in question on egg and sperm are immotile molecules. It is the sperm as a *cell* that has motility, and the egg as a cell that has relative immotility.

53 Wassarman, 78–79.

54 Paul M. Wassarman, "The Biology and Chemistry of Fertilization," *Science* 235, no. 4788 (January 30, 1987): 553–60, esp. 554.

55 Ibid., 557.

ingly skewed in favor of the sperm's activity, for in the next breath he says that sperm *lose* all motility upon fusion with the egg's surface. In mouse and sea urchin eggs, the sperm enters at the *egg's* volition, according to Wassarman's description: "Once fused with egg plasma membrane [the surface of the egg], how does a sperm enter the egg? The surface of both mouse and sea urchin eggs is covered with thousands of plasma membrane-bound projections, called microvilli [tiny 'hairs']. Evidence in sea urchins suggests that, after membrane fusion, a group of elongated microvilli cluster tightly around and interdigitate over the sperm head. As these microvilli are resorbed, the sperm is drawn into the egg. Therefore, sperm motility, which ceases at the time of fusion in both sea urchins and mice, is not required for sperm entry."[56] The section called "Sperm Penetration" more logically would be followed by a section called "The Egg Envelopes," rather than "Sperm-Egg Fusion." This would give a parallel—and more accurate—sense that both the egg and the sperm initiate action.

Another way that Wassarman makes less of the egg's activity is by describing components of the egg but referring to the sperm as a whole entity. Deborah Gordon has described such an approach as "atomism" ("the part is independent of and primordial to the whole") and identified it as one of the "tenacious assumptions" of Western science and medicine.[57] Wassarman employs atomism to his advantage. When he refers to processes going on within sperm, he consistently returns to descriptions that remind us from whence these activities came: they are part of sperm that penetrate an egg or generate propulsive force. When he refers to processes going on within eggs, he stops there. As a result, any active role he grants them appears to be assigned to the parts of the egg, and not to the egg itself. In the quote above, it is the microvilli that actively cluster around the sperm. In another example, "the driving force for engulfment of a fused sperm comes from a region of cytoplasm just beneath an egg's plasma membrane."[58]

SOCIAL IMPLICATIONS

All three of these revisionist accounts of egg and sperm cannot seem to escape the hierarchical imagery of older accounts. Even though each new account gives the egg a larger and more active role, taken together they bring into play another

---

56   Ibid., 557–58. This finding throws into question Schatten and Schatten's description (n. 29 above) of the sperm, its tail beating, diving down into the egg.

57   Deborah R. Gordon, "Tenacious Assumptions in Western Medicine," in *Bio-medicine Examined*, ed. Margaret Lock and Deborah Gordon (Dordrecht: Kluwer, 1988), 19–56, esp. 26.

58   Wassarman, "The Biology and Chemistry of Fertilization," 558.

cultural stereotype: woman as a dangerous and aggressive threat. In the Johns Hopkins lab's revised model, the egg ends up as the female aggressor who "captures and tethers" the sperm with her sticky zona, rather like a spider lying in wait in her web.[59] The Schatten lab has the egg's nucleus "interrupt" the sperm's dive with a "sudden and swift" rush by which she "clasps the sperm and guides its nucleus to the center."[60] Wassarman's description of the surface of the egg "covered with thousands of plasma membrane-bound projections, called microvilli" that reach out and clasp the sperm adds to the spiderlike imagery.[61]

30   These images grant the egg an active role but at the cost of appearing disturbingly aggressive. Images of woman as dangerous and aggressive, the femme fatale* who victimizes men, are widespread in Western literature and culture.[62] More specific is the connection of spider imagery with the idea of an engulfing, devouring mother.[63] New data did not lead scientists to eliminate gender stereotypes in their descriptions of egg and sperm. Instead, scientists simply began to describe egg and sperm in different, but no less damaging, terms.

Can we envision a less stereotypical view? Biology itself provides another model that could be applied to the egg and the sperm. The cybernetic model—with its feedback loops, flexible adaptation to change, coordination of the parts within a whole, evolution over time, and changing response to the environment—is common in genetics, endocrinology, and ecology and has a growing influence in medicine in general.[64] This model has the potential to shift our imagery from the negative, in which the female reproductive system is castigated both for not producing eggs after birth and for producing (and thus wasting) too many eggs overall, to something more positive. The female reproductive system could be seen as responding to the environment (pregnancy or menopause), adjusting to monthly changes (menstruation), and flexibly changing from reproductivity after puberty to nonreproductivity later in life. The sperm and egg's interaction could also be described in cybernetic terms. J.F. Hartman's research in reproductive biology demonstrated fifteen years ago that if an egg is killed by being pricked with a needle, live sperm cannot get

59   Baltz, Katz, and Cone (n. 42 above), 643, 650.

60   Schatten and Schatten, 53.

61   Wassarman, "The Biology and Chemistry of Fertilization," 557.

62   Mary Ellman, *Thinking about Women* (New York: Harcourt Brace Jovanovich, 1968), 140; Nina Auerbach, *Woman and the Demon* (Cambridge, Mass.: Harvard University Press, 1982), esp. 186.

63   Kenneth Alan Adams, "Arachnophobia: Love American Style," *Journal of Psychoanalytic Anthropology* 4, no. 2 (1981): 157–97.

64   William Ray Arney and Bernard Bergen, *Medicine and the Management of Living* (Chicago: University of Chicago Press, 1984).

through the zona.[65] Clearly, this evidence shows that the egg and sperm do interact on more mutual terms, making biology's refusal to portray them that way all the more disturbing.

We would do well to be aware, however, that cybernetic imagery is hardly neutral. In the past, cybernetic models have played an important part in the imposition of social control. These models inherently provide a way of thinking about a "field" of interacting components. Once the field can be seen, it can become the object of new forms of knowledge, which in turn can allow new forms of social control to be exerted over the components of the field. During the 1950s, for example, medicine began to recognize the psychosocial *environment* of the patient: the patient's family and its psychodynamics. Professions such as social work began to focus on this new environment, and the resulting knowledge became one way to further control the patient. Patients began to be seen not as isolated, individual bodies, but as psychosocial entities located in an "ecological" system: management of "the patient's psychology was a new entrée to patient control."[66]

The models that biologists use to describe their data can have important social effects. During the nineteenth century, the social and natural sciences strongly influenced each other: the social ideas of Malthus about how to avoid the natural increase of the poor inspired Darwin's *Origin of Species*.[67] Once the *Origin* stood as a description of the natural world, complete with competition and market struggles, it could be reimported into social science as social Darwinism,* in order to justify the social order of the time. What we are seeing now is similar: the importation of cultural ideas about passive females and heroic males into the "personalities" of gametes. This amounts to the "implanting of social imagery on representations of nature so as to lay a firm basis for reimporting exactly that same imagery as natural explanations of social phenomena."[68]

Further research would show us exactly what social effects are being wrought from the biological imagery of egg and sperm. At the very least, the imagery keeps alive some of the hoariest old stereotypes about weak damsels in distress and their strong male rescuers. That these stereotypes are now being written in at the level of the cell constitutes a powerful move to make them seem so natural as to be beyond alteration.

---

65   J.F. Hartman, R.B. Gwatkin, and C.F. Hutchison, "Early Contact Interactions between Mammalian Gametes In Vitro," *Proceedings of the National Academy of Sciences* (US) 69, no. 10 (1972): 2767–69.

66   Arney and Bergen, 68.

67   Ruth Hubbard, "Have Only Men Evolved?" (n. 12 above), 51–52.

68   David Harvey, personal communication, November 1989.

35   The stereotypical imagery might also encourage people to imagine that what results from the interaction of egg and sperm—a fertilized egg—is the result of deliberate "human" action at the cellular level. Whatever the intentions of the human couple, in this microscopic "culture" a cellular "bride" (or femme fatale) and a cellular "groom" (her victim) make a cellular baby. Rosalind Petchesky points out that through visual representations such as sonograms, we are given "*images* of younger and younger, and tinier and tinier, fetuses being 'saved.'" This leads to "the point of visibility being 'pushed back' *indefinitely*."[69] Endowing egg and sperm with intentional action, a key aspect of personhood in our culture, lays the foundation for the point of viability being pushed back to the moment of fertilization. This will likely lead to greater acceptance of technological developments and new forms of scrutiny and manipulation, for the benefit of these inner "persons": court-ordered restrictions on a pregnant woman's activities in order to protect her fetus, fetal surgery, amniocentesis, and rescinding of abortion rights, to name but a few examples.[70]

Even if we succeed in substituting more egalitarian, interactive metaphors to describe the activities of egg and sperm, and manage to avoid the pitfalls of cybernetic models, we would still be guilty of endowing cellular entities with personhood. More crucial, then, than what *kinds* of personalities we bestow on cells is the very fact that we are doing it at all. This process could ultimately have the most disturbing social consequences.

One clear feminist challenge is to wake up sleeping metaphors in science, particularly those involved in descriptions of the egg and the sperm. Although the literary convention is to call such metaphors "dead," they are not so much dead as sleeping, hidden within the scientific content of texts—and all the more powerful for it.[71] Waking up such metaphors, by becoming aware of when we are projecting cultural imagery onto what we study, will improve our ability to investigate and understand nature. Waking up such metaphors, by becoming aware of their implications, will rob them of their power to naturalize our social conventions about gender.

(1991)

---

69   Rosalind Petchesky, "Fetal Images: The Power of Visual Culture in the Politics of Reproduction," *Feminist Studies* 13, no. 2 (Summer 1987): 263–92, esp. 272.

70   Rita Arditti, Renate Klein, and Shelley Minden, *Test-Tube Women* (London: Pandora, 1984); Ellen Goodman, "Whose Right to Life?" *Baltimore Sun* (November 17, 1987); Tamar Lewin, "Courts Acting to Force Care of the Unborn," *New York Times* (November 23, 1987), A1 and B10; Susan Irwin and Brigitte Jordan, "Knowledge, Practice, and Power: Court Ordered Cesarean Sections," *Medical Anthropology Quarterly* 1, no. 3 (September 1987): 319–34.

71   Thanks to Elizabeth Fee and David Spain, who in February 1989 and April 1989, respectively, made points related to this.

Jamaica Kincaid

On Seeing England for the First Time

Novelist, memoirist, and essayist Jamaica Kincaid often writes unflinchingly about the oppression, erasure, and power imbalances created by colonialism. In the following piece, she references her childhood in Antigua in the mid-twentieth century. Antigua, an island in the eastern Caribbean, was colonized by Britain in the seventeenth century, and until the 1830s sugarcane and other export crops were produced there by western African slaves. In 1949, when Kincaid was born, Antigua was still a colony; it became self-governing in 1967 and gained complete political independence in 1981. "On Seeing England for the First Time" was first published in 1991, in Transition: The Magazine of Africa and the Diaspora.

When I saw England for the first time, I was a child in school sitting at a desk. The England I was looking at was laid out on a map gently, beautifully, delicately, a very special jewel; it lay on a bed of sky blue—the background of the map—its yellow form mysterious, because though it looked like a leg of mutton, it could not really look like anything so familiar as a leg of mutton because it was England—with shadings of pink and green, unlike any shadings of pink and green I had seen before, squiggly veins of red running in every direction. England was a special jewel all right, and only special people got to wear it. The people who got to wear England were English people. They wore it well and they wore it everywhere: in jungles, in deserts, on plains, on top of the highest mountains, on all the oceans, on all the seas, in places where they were not welcome, in places they should not have been. When my teacher had pinned this map up on the blackboard, she said, "This is England"—and she said it with authority, seriousness, and adoration, and we all sat up. It was as if she had said, "This is Jerusalem,* the place you will go to when you die but only if you have been good." We understood then—we were meant to understand then—that England was to be our source of myth and the source from which we got our sense of reality, our sense of what was meaningful, our sense of what was meaningless—and much about our own lives and much about the very idea of us headed that last list.

At the time I was a child sitting at my desk seeing England for the first time, I was already very familiar with the greatness of it. Each morning before I left for school, I ate a breakfast of half a grapefruit, an egg, bread and butter and a slice of cheese, and a cup of cocoa; or half a grapefruit, a bowl of oat porridge, bread and butter and a slice of cheese, and a cup of cocoa. The can of cocoa was often left on the table in front of me. It had written on it the name of the company, the year the company was established, and the words, "Made in England." Those words, "Made in England," were written on the box the oats came in too. They would also have been written on the box the shoes I was wearing came in; a bolt of grey linen cloth lying on the shelf of a store from which my mother had bought three yards to make the uniform that I was wearing had written along its edge those three words. The shoes I wore were made in England; so were my socks and cotton undergarments and the satin ribbons I wore tied at the end of two plaits of my hair. My father, who might have sat next to me at breakfast, was a carpenter and cabinet maker. The shoes he wore to work would have been made in England, as were his khaki shirt and trousers, his underpants and undershirt, his socks and brown felt hat. Felt was not the proper material from which a hat that was expected to provide shade from the hot sun should be made, but my father must have seen and admired a picture of an Englishman wearing such a hat in England, and this picture that he saw must have been so compelling that it caused him to wear the wrong hat for a hot climate most of his long life. And this hat—a brown felt hat—became so central to his character that it was the first thing he put on in the morning as he stepped out of bed and the last thing he took off before he stepped back into bed at night. As we sat at breakfast a car might go by. The car, a Hillman or a Zephyr, was made in England. The very idea of the meal itself, breakfast, and its substantial quality and quantity was an idea from England; we somehow knew that in England they began the day with this meal called breakfast and a proper breakfast was a big breakfast. No one I knew liked eating so much food so early in the day; it made us feel sleepy, tired. But this breakfast business was Made in England like almost everything else that surrounded us, the exceptions being the sea, the sky, and the air we breathed.

At the time I saw this map—seeing England for the first time—I did not say to myself, "Ah, so that's what it looks like," because there was no longing in me to put a shape to those three words that ran through every part of my life no matter how small; for me to have had such a longing would have meant that I lived in a certain atmosphere, an atmosphere in which those three words were felt as a burden. But I did not live in such an atmosphere. My father's brown felt hat would develop a hole in its crown, the lining would separate from the hat itself, and six weeks before he thought that he could not be seen wearing it—he was a very vain man—he would order another hat from England. And my mother taught me to eat my food in the English way: the knife in the right hand, the fork in the left, my elbows held still close to my side, the food carefully balanced on my fork and then brought up to my mouth. When I had finally mastered it, I overheard her saying to a friend, "Did you see how nicely she can eat?" But I knew then that I enjoyed my food more when I ate it with my bare hands, and I continued to do so when she wasn't looking. And when my teacher showed us the map, she asked us to study it carefully, because no test we would ever take would be complete without this statement: "Draw a map of England."

I did not know then that the statement, "Draw a map of England" was something far worse than a declaration of war, for in fact a flatout declaration of war would have put me on alert, and again in fact, there was no need for war—I had long ago been conquered. I did not know then that this statement was part of a process that would result in my erasure, not my physical erasure, but my erasure all the same. I did not know then that this statement was meant to make me feel in awe and small whenever I heard the word England: awe at its existence, small because I was not from it. I did not know very much of anything then—certainly not what a blessing it was that I was unable to draw a map of England correctly.

After that there were many times of seeing England for the first time. I saw 5 England in history. I knew the names of all the kings of England. I knew the names of their children, their wives, their disappointments, their triumphs, the names of people who betrayed them, I knew the dates on which they were born and the dates they died. I knew their conquests and was made to feel glad if I figured in them; I knew their defeats. I knew the details of the year 1066 (The Battle of Hastings, the end of the reign of the Anglo-Saxon kings*) before I knew the details of the year 1832 (the year slavery was abolished).[1] It wasn't as bad as I make it sound now; it was worse. I did like so much hearing again and again how Alfred the Great,[2] traveling in disguise, had been left to watch cakes, and because he wasn't used to this the cakes got burned, and Alfred burned his hands pulling them out of the fire, and the woman who had left him to watch the cakes screamed at him. I loved King Alfred. My grandfather was named after him; his son, my uncle, was named after King Alfred; my brother is named after King Alfred. And so there are three people in my family named after a man they have never met, a man who died over ten centuries ago. The first view I got of

---

1   *1832 ... abolished*   The Slavery Abolition Act, signed in 1833 and put into practice in 1834, marked the end of slavery in Britain and its colonies.

2   *Alfred the Great*   Anglo-Saxon ruler of the kingdom of Wessex from 871 to 899.

England then was not unlike the first view received by the person who named my grandfather.

This view though—the naming of the kings, their deeds, their disappointments—was the vivid view, the forceful view. There were other views, subtler ones, softer, almost not there—but these were the ones that made the most lasting impression on me, these were the ones that made me really feel like nothing. "When morning touched the sky" was one phrase, for no morning touched the sky where I lived. The morning where I lived came on abruptly, with a shock of heat and loud noises. "Evening approaches" was another, but the evenings where I lived did not approach; in fact, I had no evening—I had night and I had day and they came and went in a mechanical way: on, off; on, off. And then there were gentle mountains and low blue skies and moors over which people took walks for nothing but pleasure, when where I lived a walk was an act of labor, a burden, something only death or the automobile could relieve. And there were things that a small turn of a head could convey—entire worlds, whole lives would depend on this thing, a certain turn of a head. Everyday life could be quite tiring, more tiring than anything I was told not to do. I was told not to gossip, but they did that all the time. And they ate so much food, violating another of those rules they taught me: do not indulge in gluttony. And the foods they ate actually: if only sometime I could eat cold cuts after theater, cold cuts of lamb and mint sauce, and Yorkshire pudding and scones, and clotted cream, and sausages that came from up-country (imagine, "up-country").* And having troubling thoughts at twilight, a good time to have troubling thoughts, apparently; and servants who stole and left in the middle of a crisis, who were born with a limp or some other kind of deformity, not nourished properly in their mother's womb (that last part I figured out for myself; the point was, oh to have an untrustworthy servant); and wonderful cobbled streets onto which solid front doors opened; and people whose eyes were blue and who had fair skins and who smelled only of lavender, or sometimes sweet pea or primrose. And those flowers with those names: delphiniums, foxgloves, tulips, daffodils, floribunda, peonies; in bloom, a striking display, being cut and placed in large glass bowls, crystal, decorating rooms so large twenty families the size of mine could fit in comfortably but used only for passing through. And the weather was so remarkable because the rain fell gently always, only occasionally in deep gusts, and it colored the air various shades of grey, each an appealing shade for a dress to be worn when a portrait was being painted; and when it rained at twilight, wonderful things happened: people bumped into each other unexpectedly and that would lead to all sorts of turns of events—a plot, the mere weather caused plots. I saw that people rushed: they rushed to catch trains, they rushed toward each other and away from each other; they rushed and rushed and rushed. That word: Rushed! I did not know what it was to do that. It was too hot to do that, and so I came to envy people who would rush, even though it had no meaning to me to do such a thing. But there they are again. They loved their children; their children were sent to their own rooms as a punishment, rooms larger than my entire house. They were special, everything about them said so, even their clothes; their clothes rustled, swished, soothed. The world was theirs, not mine; everything told me so.

If now as I speak of all this I give the impression of someone on the outside looking in, nose pressed up against a glass window, that is wrong. My nose was pressed up against a glass window all right, but there was an iron vise at the back of my neck forcing my head to stay in place. To avert my gaze was to fall back into something from which I had been rescued, a hole filled with nothing, and that was the word for everything about me, nothing. The reality of my life was conquests, subjugation, humiliation, enforced amnesia. I was forced to forget. Just for instance, this: I lived in a part of St. John's, Antigua, called Ovals. Ovals was made up of five streets, each of them named after a famous English seaman—to be quite frank, an officially sanctioned criminal: Rodney Street (after George Rodney), Nelson Street (after Horatio Nelson), Drake Street (after Francis Drake), Hood Street, and Hawkins Street (after John Hawkins).[3] But John Hawkins was knighted after a trip he made to Africa, opening up a new trade, the slave trade. He was then entitled to wear as his crest a negro bound with a cord. Every single person living on Hawkins street was descended from a slave. John Hawkins' ship, the one in which he transported the people he had bought and kidnapped, was called The Jesus. He later became the Treasurer of the Royal Navy and Rear Admiral.

Again, the reality of my life, the life I led at the time I was being shown these views of England for the first time, for the second time, for the one-hundred-millionth time, was this: the sun shone with what sometimes seemed to be a deliberate cruelty; we must have done something to deserve that. My dresses did not rustle in the evening air as I strolled to the theater (I had no evening, I had no theater; my dresses were made of a cheap cotton, the weave of which would give way after not too many washings). I got up in the morning, I did my chores (fetched water from the public pipe for my mother, swept the yard), I washed myself, I went to a woman to have my hair combed freshly every day (because before we were allowed into our classroom our teachers would inspect us, and

---

3   *George Rodney* Admiral (1718–92) known for capturing French, Dutch, and Spanish ships in the Caribbean; *Horatio Nelson* Naval commander (1758–1805) who used the Navigation Act to confiscate goods from ships sailing through the West Indies; *Francis Drake* Admiral (c.1540–96) famed for his piracy against enemy ships in the Caribbean and cousin of John Hawkins, with whom he collaborated in slave-trading ventures; *Hood* Samuel Hood (1724–1816), English admiral who served as Rodney's second in command in the Caribbean; *John Hawkins* Naval commander (1532–95) who rose to success as the first English slave trader.

children who had not bathed that day, or had dirt under their fingernails, or whose hair had not been combed anew that day might not be allowed to attend class). I ate that breakfast. I walked to school. At school we gathered in an auditorium and sang a hymn, "All Things Bright and Beautiful,"[4] and looking down on us as we sang were portraits of the queen of England and her husband; they wore jewels and medals and they smiled. I was a Brownie.[5] At each meeting we would form a little group around a flagpole, and after raising the union jack, we would say, "I promise to do my best, to do my duty to God and the Queen, to help other people every day and obey the scouts' law."

Who were these people and why had I never seen them, I mean, really seen them, in the place where they lived. I had never been to England. No one I knew had ever been to England, or should I say, no one I knew had ever been and returned to tell me about it. All the people I knew who had gone to England had stayed there. Sometimes they left behind their small children, never to see them again. England! I had seen England's representatives. I had seen the governor general at the public grounds at a ceremony celebrating the queen's birthday. I had seen an old princess and I had seen a young princess. They had both been extremely not beautiful, but who of us would have told them that? I had never seen England, really seen it, I had only met a representative, seen a picture, read books, memorized its history. I had never set foot, my own foot, in it.

10   The space between the idea of something and its reality is always wide and deep and dark. The longer they are kept apart—idea of thing, reality of thing—the wider the width, the deeper the depth, the thicker and darker the darkness. This space starts out empty, there is nothing in it, but it rapidly becomes filled up with obsession or desire or hatred or love—sometimes all of these things, sometimes some of these things, sometimes only one of these things. The existence of the world as I came to know it was a result of this: idea of thing over here, reality of thing way, way over there. There was Christopher Columbus, an unlikable man, an unpleasant man, a liar (and so of course, a thief) surrounded by maps and schemes and plans, and there was the reality on the other side of that width, that depth, that darkness. He became obsessed, he became filled with desire, the hatred came later, love was never a part of it. Eventually, his idea met the longed-for reality. That the idea of something and its reality are often two completely different things is something no one ever remembers; and so when they meet and find that they are not compatible, the weaker of the two, idea or reality, dies. That

---

4   *All Things Bright and Beautiful*   Anglican hymn (1848) by Irish poet Cecil Frances Alexander; the lyrics reference English geography, seasons, and social classes.

5   *Brownie*   Member of the Brownies, a scouting organization for girls founded in England in 1914; the name "Brownie" and the narratives associated with the group's activities are based on fairy-like creatures from English folklore.

idea Christopher Columbus had was more powerful than the reality he met and so the reality he met died.

And so finally, when I was a grownup woman, the mother of two children, the wife of someone, a person who resides in a powerful country that takes up more than its fair share of a continent, the owner of a house with many rooms in it and of two automobiles, with the desire and will (which I very much act upon) to take from the world more than I give back to it, more than I deserve, more than I need, finally then, I saw England, the real England, not a picture, not a painting, not through a story in a book, but England, for the first time. In me, the space between the idea of it and its reality had become filled with hatred, and so when at last I saw it I wanted to take it into my hands and tear it into little pieces and then crumble it up as if it were clay, child's clay. That was impossible, and so I could only indulge in notfavorable opinions.

There were monuments everywhere; they commemorated victories, battles fought between them and the people who lived across the sea from them, all vile people, fought over which of them would have dominion over the people who looked like me. The monuments were useless to them now, people sat on them and ate their lunch. They were like markers on an old useless trail, like a piece of old string tied to a finger to jog the memory, like old decoration in an old house, dirty, useless, in the way. Their skins were so pale, it made them look so fragile, so weak, so ugly. What if I had the power to simply banish them from their land, send boat after boatload of them on a voyage that in fact had no destination, force them to live in a place where the sun's presence was a constant. This would rid them of their pale complexion and make them look more like me, make them look more like the people I love and treasure and hold dear, and more like the people who occupy the near and far reaches of my imagination, my history, my geography, and reduce them and everything they have ever known to figurines as evidence that I was in divine favor, what if all this was in my power? Could I resist it? No one ever has.

And they were rude, they were rude to each other. They didn't like each other very much. They didn't like each other in the way they didn't like me, and it occurred to me that their dislike for me was one of the few things they agreed on.

I was on a train in England with a friend, an English woman. Before we were in England she liked me very much. In England she didn't like me at all. She didn't like the claim I said I had on England, she didn't like the views I had of England. I didn't like England, she didn't like England, but she didn't like me not liking it too. She said, "I want to show you my England, I want to show you the England that I know and love." I had told her many times before that I knew England and I didn't want to love it anyway. She no longer lived in England; it was her own country, but it had not been kind to her, so she left. On the train, the conductor was rude to her; she asked something, and he responded in a rude way. She became ashamed. She was ashamed at the way he treated her; she was ashamed at the way he behaved. "This is the new England," she said. But I liked the conductor being rude; his behavior seemed quite appropriate. Earlier this had happened: We had gone to a store to buy a shirt for my husband; it was meant to be a special present, a special shirt to wear on special occasions. This was a store where the Prince of Wales has his shirts made but the shirts sold in this store are beautiful all the same. I found a shirt I thought my husband would like and I wanted to buy him a tie to go with it. When I couldn't decide which one to choose, the salesman showed me a new set. He was very pleased with these, he said, because they bore the crest of the Prince of Wales, and the Prince of Wales had never allowed his crest to decorate an article of clothing before. There was something in the way he said it; his tone was slavish, reverential, awed. It made me feel angry; I wanted to hit him. I didn't do that. I said, my husband and I hate princes, my husband would never wear anything that had a prince's anything on it. My friend stiffened. The salesman stiffened. They both drew themselves in, away from me. My friend told me that the prince was a symbol of her Englishness and I could see that I had caused offense. I looked at her. She was an English person, the sort of English person I used to know at home, the sort who was nobody in England but somebody when they came to live among the people like me. There were many people I could have seen England with; that I was seeing it with this particular person, a person who reminded me of the people who showed me England long ago as I sat in church or at my desk, made me feel silent and afraid, for I wondered if, all these years of our friendship, I had had a friend or had been in the thrall of a racial memory.

15   I went to Bath[6]—we, my friend and I, did this, but though we were together, I was no longer with her. The landscape was almost as familiar as my own hand, but I had never been in this place before, so how could that be again? And the streets of Bath were familiar, too, but I had never walked on them before. It was all those years of reading, starting with Roman Britain. Why did I have to know about Roman Britain? It was of no real use to me, a person living on a hot, drought-ridden island, and it is of no use to me now, and yet my head is filled with this nonsense, Roman Britain. In Bath, I drank tea in a room I had read about in a novel written in the eighteenth century. In this very same room, young women wearing those dresses that rustled and so on danced and flirted and sometimes disgraced themselves with young men, soldiers, sailors, who

---

6   *Bath* English city located on the site of hot springs, where the ancient Romans had built baths; it became a popular tourist destination in the eighteenth century and is used as a setting by many classic English novelists, including Jane Austen and Charles Dickens.

were on their way to Bristol[7] or someplace like that, so many places like that where so many adventures, the outcome of which was not good for me, began. Bristol, England. A sentence that began "That night the ship sailed from Bristol, England" would end not so good for me. And then I was driving through the countryside in an English motor car, on narrow winding roads, and they were so familiar, though I had never been on them before; and through little villages the names of which I somehow knew so well though I had never been there before. And the countryside did have all those hedges and hedges, fields hedged in. I was marveling at all the toil of it, the planting of the hedges to begin with and then the care of it, all that clipping, year after year of clipping, and I wondered at the lives of the people who would have to do this, because wherever I see and feel the hands that hold up the world, I see and feel myself and all the people who look like me. And I said, "Those hedges" and my friend said that someone, a woman named Mrs. Rothchild, worried that the hedges weren't being taken care of properly; the farmers couldn't afford or find the help to keep up the hedges, and often they replaced them with wire fencing. I might have said to that, well if Mrs. Rothchild doesn't like the wire fencing, why doesn't she take care of the hedges herself, but I didn't. And then in those fields that were now hemmed in by wire fencing that a privileged woman didn't like was planted a vile yellow flowering bush that produced an oil, and my friend said that Mrs. Rothchild didn't like this either; it ruined the English countryside, it ruined the traditional look of the English countryside.

It was not at that moment that I wished every sentence, everything I knew, that began with England, would end with "and then it all died; we don't know how, it just all died." At that moment, I was thinking, who are these people who forced me to think of them all the time, who forced me to think that the world I knew was incomplete, or without substance, or did not measure up because it was not England; that I was incomplete, or without substance, and did not measure up because I was not English. Who were these people? The person sitting next to me couldn't give me a clue; no one person could. In any case, if I had said to her, I find England ugly, I hate England; the weather is like a jail sentence, the English are a very ugly people, the food in England is like a jail sentence, the hair of English people is so straight, so deadlooking, the English have an unbearable smell so different from the smell of people I know, real people of course, she would have said that I was a person full of prejudice. Apart from the fact that it is I—that is, the people who look like me—who made her aware of the unpleasantness of such a thing, the idea of such a thing, prejudice, she would have been only partly right, sort of right: I may be capable of prejudice, but my

---

7   *Bristol* English port city that played a major role in seventeenth- to nineteenth-century British marine trade, including the slave trade.

prejudices have no weight to them, my prejudices have no force behind them, my prejudices remain opinions, my prejudices remain my personal opinion. And a great feeling of rage and disappointment came over me as I looked at England, my head full of personal opinions that could not have public, my public, approval. The people I come from are powerless to do evil on a grand scale.

The moment I wished every sentence, everything I knew, that began with England would end with "and then it all died, we don't know how, it just all died" was when I saw the white cliffs of Dover.[8] I had sung hymns and recited poems that were about a longing to see the white cliffs of Dover again. At the time I sang the hymns and recited the poems, I could really long to see them again because I had never seen them at all, nor had anyone around me at the time. But there we were, groups of people longing for something we had never seen. And so there they were, the white cliffs, but they were not that pearly majestic thing I used to sing about, that thing that created such a feeling in these people that when they died in the place where I lived they had themselves buried facing a direction that would allow them to see the white cliffs of Dover when they were resurrected, as surely they would be. The white cliffs of Dover, when finally I saw them, were cliffs, but they were not white; you would only call them that if the word "white" meant something special to you; they were dirty and they were steep; they were so steep, the correct height from which all my views of England, starting with the map before me in my classroom and ending with the trip I had just taken, should jump and die and disappear forever.

(1991)

---

8   *white cliffs of Dover*   Geographical landmark on England's southeastern coast; the cliffs are frequently referenced in music and literature expressing pride, affection, or nostalgia with regard to England.

DAVID CARD AND ALAN B. KRUEGER

from MINIMUM WAGES AND EMPLOYMENT:

A CASE STUDY OF THE FAST-FOOD INDUSTRY IN NEW JERSEY AND PENNSYLVANIA

Until the early 1990s it was accepted almost universally among economists that, all else being equal, raising the minimum wage would increase unemployment; employers who were forced to pay workers more would, according to the economic models, respond by laying off some of those workers. It was thus often argued that keeping the minimum wage low benefited not just companies and their shareholders, but also the minimum wage workers themselves.

The article below, now considered a classic in its discipline, challenged that conventional wisdom. Card and Krueger first published the essay in October 1993 through the National Bureau of Economic Research as Working Paper No. 4509. It was published in a slightly revised form the following year in The American Economic Review. *In 1995 the authors presented broader evidence along the same lines in their book* Myth and Measurement: The New Economics of the Minimum Wage.

[ABSTRACT]

On April 1, 1992, New Jersey's minimum wage rose from $4.25 to $5.05 per hour. To evaluate the impact of the law we surveyed 410 fast-food restaurants in New Jersey and eastern Pennsylvania before and after the rise. Comparisons of employment growth at stores in New Jersey and Pennsylvania (where the minimum wage was constant) provide simple estimates of the effect of the higher minimum wage. We also compare employment changes at stores in New Jersey that were initially paying high wages (above $5) to the changes at lower-wage stores. We find no indication that the rise in the minimum wage reduced employment.

How do employers in a low-wage labor market respond to an increase in the minimum wage?

The prediction from conventional economic theory is unambiguous: a rise in the minimum wage leads perfectly competitive employers to cut employment (George J. Stigler, 1946). Although studies in the 1970's based on aggregate[1] teenage employment rates usually confirmed this prediction,[2] earlier studies based on comparisons of employment at affected and unaffected establishments often did not (e.g., Richard A. Lester, 1960, 1964). Several recent studies that rely on a similar comparative methodology have failed to detect a negative employment effect of higher minimum wages. Analyses of the 1990–1991 increases in the federal minimum wage (Lawrence F. Katz and Krueger, 1992; Card, 1992a) and of an earlier increase in the minimum wage in California (Card, 1992b) find no adverse employment impact. A study of minimum-wage floors[3] in Britain (Stephen Machin and Alan Manning, 1993) reaches a similar conclusion.

This paper presents new evidence on the effect of minimum wages on establishment-level[4] employment outcomes. We analyze the experiences of 410 fast-food restaurants in New Jersey and Pennsylvania following the increase in New Jersey's minimum wage from $4.25 to $5.05 per hour. Comparisons of employment, wages, and prices at stores in New Jersey and Pennsylvania before and after the rise offer a simple method for evaluating the effects of the minimum wage. Comparisons within New Jersey between initially high-wage stores (those paying more than the new minimum rate prior to its effective date) and other stores provide an alternative estimate of the impact of the new law.

In addition to the simplicity of our empirical methodology, several other features of the New Jersey law and our data set are also significant. First, the rise in the minimum wage occurred during a recession. The increase had been legislated two years earlier when the state economy was relatively healthy. By the time of the actual increase, the unemployment rate in New Jersey had risen substantially and last-minute political action almost succeeded in reducing the

---

1   *aggregate*   Combined; calculated by combining data.

2   See Charles Brown et al. (1982, 1983) for surveys of this literature. A recent update (Allison J. Wellington, 1991) concludes that the employment effects of the minimum wage are negative but small: a 10-percent increase in the minimum is estimated to lower teenage employment rates by 0.06 percentage points. [authors' note]

3   *wage floors*   Minimums (set by government) which dictate a rate that wages must not fall below.

4   *establishment-level*   Concerning individual operational establishments (as opposed to "firm-level," which concerns businesses that may have many establishments operating as extensions).

minimum-wage increase. It is unlikely that the effects of the higher minimum wage were obscured by a rising tide of general economic conditions.

Second, New Jersey is a relatively small state with an economy that is closely linked to nearby states. We believe that a control group[5] of fast-food stores in eastern Pennsylvania forms a natural basis for comparison with the experiences of restaurants in New Jersey. Wage variation across stores in New Jersey, however, allows us to compare the experiences of high-wage and low-wage stores in New Jersey and *test* the validity of the Pennsylvania control group. Moreover, since seasonal patterns of employment are similar in New Jersey and eastern Pennsylvania, as well as across high- and low-wage stores within New Jersey, our comparative methodology effectively "differences out" any seasonal employment effects.

Third, we successfully followed nearly 100 percent of stores from a first wave of interviews conducted just before the rise in the minimum wage (in February and March 1992) to a second wave conducted 7–8 months after (in November and December 1992). We have complete information on store closings and take account of employment changes at the closed stores in our analyses. We therefore measure the overall effect of the minimum wage on average employment, and not simply its effect on surviving establishments.

Our analysis of employment trends at stores that were open for business before the increase in the minimum wage ignores any potential effect of minimum wages on the rate of new store openings. To assess the likely magnitude of this effect we relate state-specific growth rates in the number McDonald's fast food outlets between 1986 and 1991 to measures of the relative minimum wage in each state.

1. THE NEW JERSEY LAW

A bill signed into law in November 1989 raised the Federal minimum wage from $3.35 per hour to $3.80 effective April 1, 1990, with a further increase to $4.25 per hour on April 1, 1991. In early 1990 the New Jersey legislature went one step further, enacting parallel increases in the state minimum wage for 1990 and 1991 and an increase to $5.05 per hour effective April 1, 1992. The scheduled 1992 increase gave New Jersey the highest state minimum wage rate in the country and was strongly opposed by business leaders in the state (see Bureau of National Affairs, *Daily Labor Report*, 5 May 1990).

In the two years between passage of the $5.05 minimum wage and its effective date, New Jersey's economy slipped into recession. Concerned with

10

---

5   *control group* Group that, ideally, is like the group being studied in every way except for the variable under consideration.

the potentially adverse impact of a higher minimum wage, the state legislature voted in March 1992 to phase in the 80-cent increase over two years. The vote fell just short of the margin required to override a gubernatorial veto,[6] and the Governor allowed the $5.05 rate to go into effect on April 1 before vetoing the two-step legislation. Faced with the prospect of having to roll back wages for minimum-wage earners, the legislature dropped the issue. Despite a strong last-minute challenge, the $5.05 minimum rate took effect as originally planned.

2. SAMPLE DESIGN AND EVALUATION

Early in 1992 we decided to evaluate the impending increase in the New Jersey minimum wage by surveying fast-food restaurants in New Jersey and eastern Pennsylvania.[7] Our choice of the fast-food industry was driven by several factors. First, fast-food stores are a leading employer of low-wage workers: in 1987, franchised restaurants employed 25 percent of all workers in the restaurant industry (see U.S. Department of Commerce, 1990 table 13). Second, fast-food restaurants comply with minimum-wage regulations and would be expected to raise wages in response to a rise in the minimum wage. Third, the job requirements and products of fast-food restaurants are relatively homogeneous,* making it easier to obtain reliable measures of employment, wages, and product prices. The absence of tips greatly simplifies the measurement of wages in the industry. Fourth, it is relatively easy to construct a sample frame[8] of franchised restaurants. Finally, past experience (Katz and Krueger, 1992) suggested that fast-food restaurants have high response rates to telephone surveys.[9]

Based on these considerations we constructed a sample frame of fast-food restaurants in New Jersey and eastern Pennsylvania from the Burger King, KFC, Wendy's, and Roy Rogers chains. The first wave of the survey was conducted by telephone in late February and early March 1992, a little over a month before the scheduled increase in New Jersey's minimum wage. The survey included questions on employment, starting wages, prices, and other store characteristics....

---

6   *gubernatorial veto*   Legally binding rejection of a state bill by the governor.

7   At the time we were uncertain whether the $5.05 rate would go into effect or be overridden. [authors' note]

8   *sample frame*   Exhaustive list of all the members of a population being studied. To create a sample for the study, individuals are randomly selected from the list.

9   In a pilot survey Katz and Krueger (1992) obtained very low response rates from McDonald's restaurants. For this reason, McDonald's restaurants were excluded from Katz and Krueger's and our sample frames. [authors' note]

The average starting wage at fast-food restaurants in New Jersey increased by 10 percent following the rise in the minimum wage.... In wave 1 [before the wage increase] the wage distributions in New Jersey and Pennsylvania were very similar. By wave 2 [after the increase] virtually all restaurants in New Jersey that had been paying below $5.05 per hour reported a starting wage equal to the new rate. Interestingly, the minimum-wage increase had no apparent "spillover" on higher-wage restaurants in the state: the mean percentage wage change for these stores was -3.1 percent.

Despite the increase in wages, full-time equivalent employment *increased* in New Jersey relative to Pennsylvania. Whereas New Jersey stores were initially smaller, employment gains in New Jersey coupled with losses in Pennsylvania led to a small and statistically significant interstate difference in wave 2. Only two other variables show a relative change between waves 1 and 2: the fraction of full-time employees and the price of a meal. Both variables increased in New Jersey relative to Pennsylvania....

3. EMPLOYMENT EFFECTS OF THE MINIMUM-WAGE INCREASE

A. Differences-in-Differences

... New Jersey stores were initially smaller than their Pennsylvania counterparts but grew relative to Pennsylvania stores after the rise in the minimum wage. The relative gain (the "difference in differences" of the changes in employment) is 2.76 FTE[10] employees (or 13 percent), with a *t* statistic[11] of 2.03....

Within New Jersey, employment expanded at the low-wage stores (those paying $4.25 per hour in wave 1) and contracted at the high-wage stores (those paying $5.00 or more per hour). Indeed, the average change in employment at the high-wage stores (-2.16 FTE employees) is almost identical to the change among Pennsylvania stores (-2.28 FTE employees). Since high-wage stores in New Jersey should have been largely unaffected by the new minimum wage, this comparison provides a specification test of the validity of the Pennsylvania control group. The test is clearly passed. Regardless of whether the affected stores are compared to stores in Pennsylvania or high-wage stores in New Jersey, the estimated employment effect of the minimum wage is similar.

The results ... suggest that employment contracted between February and November of 1992 at fast-food stores that were unaffected by the rise in the minimum wage (stores in Pennsylvania and stores in New Jersey paying $5.00

15

---

10 *FTE* Full time equivalent, a term used in reference to the number of working hours per week that add up to a full time job (if two people each work one half-time job, for example, this would add up to one FTE).

11 *t statistic* Number used to determine if a finding is statistically significant.

per hour or more in wave 1). We suspect that the reason for this contraction was the continued worsening of the economies of the middle-Atlantic states during 1992.[12] Unemployment rates in New Jersey, Pennsylvania, and New York all trended upward between 1991 and 1993, with a larger increase in New Jersey than Pennsylvania during 1992. Since sales of franchised fast-food restaurants are pro-cyclical,[13] the rise in unemployment would be expected to lower fast-food employment in the absence of other factors....

4. Nonwage Offsets

One explanation of our finding that a rise in the minimum wage does not lower employment is that restaurants can offset the effect of the minimum wage by reducing nonwage compensation. For example, if workers value fringe benefits* and wages equally, employers can simply reduce the level of fringe benefits by the amount of the minimum-wage increase, leaving their employment costs unchanged. The main fringe benefits for fast-food employees are free and reduced-price meals. In the first wave of our survey about 19 percent of fast-food restaurants offered workers free meals, 72 percent offered reduced-price meals, and 9 percent offered a combination of both free and reduced-price meals. Low-price meals are an obvious fringe benefit to cut if the minimum-wage increase forces restaurants to pay higher wages.

... The proportion of restaurants offering reduced-price meals fell in both New Jersey and Pennsylvania after the minimum wage increased, with a somewhat greater decline in New Jersey. Contrary to an offset story, however, the reduction in reduced-price meal programs was accompanied by an *increase* in the fraction of stores offering free meals. Relative to stores in Pennsylvania, New Jersey employers actually shifted toward more generous fringe benefits (i.e., free meals rather than reduced-price meals). However, the relative shift is not statistically significant....

5. Price Effects of the Minimum-Wage Increase

A final issue we examine is the effect of the minimum wage on the prices of meals at fast-food restaurants. A competitive model[14] of the fast-food industry

---

12 An alternative possibility is that seasonal factors produce higher employment at fast-food restaurants in February and March than in November and December. An analysis of national employment data for food preparation and service workers, however, shows higher average employment in the fourth quarter than in the first quarter. [authors' note]

13 *pro-cyclical* Directly correlated with changes in the overall economy.

14 *competitive model* Economic model according to which prices, wages, and so on are determined by market forces; in a perfectly competitive market, no employer would pay a worker wages that were greater than the amount of revenue the worker produced.

implies that an increase in the minimum wage will lead to an increase in product prices. If we assume constant returns to scale in the industry, the increase in price should be proportional to the share of minimum-wage labor in total factor cost.[15] The average restaurant in New Jersey initially paid about half its workers less than the new minimum wage. If wages rose by roughly 15 percent for these workers, and if labor's share of total costs is 30 percent, we would expect prices to rise by about 2.2 percent (= 0.15 x 0.5 x 0.3) due to the minimum-wage rise.[16]

In each wave of our survey we asked managers for the prices of three standard items: a medium soda, a small order of french fries, and a main course. The main course was a basic hamburger at Burger King, Roy Rogers, and Wendy's restaurants, and two pieces of chicken at KFC stores. We define "full meal" price as the after-tax price of a medium soda, a small order of french fries, and a main course....

... [A]fter-tax meal prices rose 3.2-percent faster in New Jersey than in Pennsylvania between February and November 1992.[17] The effect is slightly larger controlling for chain and company-ownership.... Since the New Jersey sales tax rate fell by 1 percentage point between the waves of our survey, these estimates suggest that pretax prices rose 4-percent faster as a result of the minimum-wage increase in New Jersey—slightly more than the increase needed to pass through the cost increase caused by the minimum-wage hike.

The pattern of price changes *within* New Jersey is less consistent with a simple "pass-through" view of minimum-wage cost increases. In fact, meal prices rose at approximately the same rate at stores in New Jersey with differing levels of initial wages....

In sum, these results provide mixed evidence that higher minimum wages result in higher fast-food prices. The strongest evidence emerges from a comparison of New Jersey and Pennsylvania stores. The magnitude of the price increase is consistent with predictions from a conventional model of a competitive industry. On the other hand, we find no evidence that prices rose

---

15   *constant returns to scale*   Pattern in which increases or decreases in input produce the same increase or decrease in output;   *total factor cost*   Amount paid for one facet of an operation.

16   According to the McDonald's Corporation 1991 Annual Report, payroll and benefits are 31.3 percent of operating costs at company-owned stores. This calculation is only approximate because minimum-wage workers make up less than half of payroll even though they are about half of workers, and because a rise in the minimum wage causes some employers to increase the pay of other higher-wage workers in order to maintain relative pay differentials. [authors' note]

17   The effect is attributable to a 2.0-percent increase in prices in New Jersey and a 1.0-percent decrease in prices in Pennsylvania. [authors' note]

faster among stores in New Jersey that were most affected by the rise in the minimum wage....

7. BROADER EVIDENCE ON EMPLOYMENT CHANGES IN NEW JERSEY

25   Our establishment-level analysis suggests that the rise in the minimum wage in New Jersey may have increased employment in the fast-food industry. Is this just an anomaly associated with our particular sample, or a phenomenon unique to the fast-food industry? Data from the monthly Current Population Survey (CPS) allow us to compare state-wide employment trends in New Jersey and the surrounding states, providing a check on the interpretation of our findings. Using monthly CPS files for 1991 and 1992, we computed employment-population rates for teenagers and adults (age 25 and older) for New Jersey, Pennsylvania, New York, and the entire United States. Since the New Jersey minimum wage rose on April 1, 1992, we computed the employment rates for April-December of both 1991 and 1992. The relative changes in employment in New Jersey and the surrounding states then give an indication of the effect of the new law.

A comparison of changes in adult employment rates show that the New Jersey labor market fared slightly worse over the 1991–1992 period than either the U.S. labor market as a whole or labor markets in Pennsylvania or New York (see Card and Krueger, 1993 table 9).[18] Among teenagers, however, the situation was reversed. In New Jersey, teenage employment rates fell by 0.7 percent from 1991 to 1992. In New York, Pennsylvania, and the United States as a whole, teenage employment rates dropped faster. Relative to teenagers in Pennsylvania, for example, the teenage employment rate in New Jersey rose by 2.0 percentage points. While this point estimate is consistent with our findings for the fast-food industry, the standard error is too large (3.2 percent) to allow any confident assessment.

8. INTERPRETATION

... [O]ur empirical findings on the effects of the New Jersey minimum wage are inconsistent with the predictions of a conventional competitive model of the fast-food industry. Our employment results are consistent with several alternative models, although none of these models can also explain the apparent rise in fast-food prices in New Jersey....

18   The employment rate of individuals age 25 and older fell by 2.6 percent in New Jersey between 1991 and 1992, while it rose by 0.3 percent in Pennsylvania, and fell by 0.2 percent in the United States as a whole. [authors' note]

9. CONCLUSIONS

Contrary to the central prediction of the textbook model of the minimum wage, but consistent with a number of recent studies based on cross-sectional time-series comparisons of affected and unaffected markets or employers, we find no evidence that the rise in New Jersey's minimum wage reduced employment at fast-food restaurants in the state. Regardless of whether we compare stores in New Jersey that were affected by the $5.05 minimum to stores in eastern Pennsylvania (where the minimum wage was constant at $4.25 per hour) or to stores in New Jersey that were initially paying $5.00 per hour or more (and were largely unaffected by the new law), we find that the increase in the minimum wage increased employment. We present a wide variety of alternative specifications to probe the robustness of this conclusion. None of the alternatives shows a negative employment effect. We also check our findings for the fast-food industry by comparing changes in teenage employment rates in New Jersey, Pennsylvania, and New York in the year following the increase in the minimum wage. Again, these results point toward a relative *increase* in employment of low-wage workers in New Jersey. We also find no evidence that minimum-wage increases negatively affect the number of McDonald's outlets opened in a state.

Finally, we find that prices of fast-food meals increased in New Jersey relative to Pennsylvania, suggesting that much of the burden of the minimum-wage rise was passed on to consumers. Within New Jersey, however, we find *no* evidence that prices increased more in stores that were most affected by the minimum-wage rise. Taken as a whole, these findings are difficult to explain with the standard competitive model or with models in which employers face supply constraints....

(1994)

REFERENCES

Brown, Charles; Gilroy, Curtis and Kohen, Andrew. "The Effect of the Minimum Wage on Employment and Unemployment." *Journal of Economic Literature*, June 1982, *20*(2), pp. 487–528.

———. "Time Series Evidence on the Effect of the Minimum Wage on Youth Employment and Unemployment." *Journal of Human Resources*, Winter 1983, *18*(1), pp. 3–31....

Bureau of National Affairs. *Daily Labor Report.* Washington, DC: Bureau of National Affairs, 5 May 1990....

Card, David. "Using Regional Variation in Wages to Measure the Effects of the Federal Minimum Wage." *Industrial and Labor Relations Review*, October 1992a, *46*(1), pp. 22–37.

——. "Do Minimum Wages Reduce Employment? A Case Study of California, 1987–89." *Industrial and Labor Relations Review*, October 1992b, *46*(1), pp. 38–54.

Card, David and Krueger, Alan B. "Minimum Wages and Employment: A Case Study of the Fast Food Industry in New Jersey and Pennsylvania." National Bureau of Economic Research (Cambridge, MA) Working Paper No. 4509, October 1993.

Katz, Lawrence F. and Krueger, Alan B. "The Effect of the Minimum Wage on the Fast Food Industry." *Industrial and Labor Relations Review*, October 1992, *46*(1), pp. 6–21.

Lester, Richard A. "Employment Effects of Minimum Wages." *Industrial and Labor Relations Review*, January 1960, *13*, pp. 254–64.

——. *The economics of labor*, 2nd Ed. New York: Macmillan, 1964.

Machin, Stephen and Manning, Alan. "The Effects of Minimum Wages on Wage Dispersion and Employment: Evidence from the U.K. Wage Councils." *Industrial and Labor Relations Review*, January 1994, *47*(2), pp. 319–29.

McDonald's Corporation. *1991 Annual report.* Chicago, 1991....

Stigler, George J. "The Economics of Minimum Wage Legislation." *American Economic Review*, June 1946, *36*(3), pp. 358–65....

U.S. Department of Commerce. *1987 Census of retail trade: Miscellaneous subjects.* Washington, DC: U.S. Government Printing Office, October 1990.

Wellington, Alison J. "Effects of the Minimum Wage on the Employment Status of Youths: An Update." *Journal of Human Resources*, Winter 1991, *26*(1), pp. 27–46.

URSULA FRANKLIN

SILENCE AND THE
NOTION OF THE COMMONS

Ursula Franklin was a leading physicist and activist whose work explores the social ramifications of science and technology. In this essay, first published in the experimental music magazine Musicworks, *she discusses the implications of two changes wrought by acoustic technology: separating sound from its source, and making the sound permanent.*

In a technological world, where the acoustic environment is largely artificial, silence takes on new dimensions, be it in terms of the human need for silence (perhaps a person's right to be free from acoustic assault), of communication, or of intentional modification of the environment.

This article is based on the text of a lecture given at the Banff Centre in August of 1993 as part of "The Tuning of the World" conference on acoustic ecology. It consists of two separate but interrelated parts: silence as spiritual experience (drawing largely, but not exclusively, on the Quaker tradition of religious worship) and silence as a common good. Silence is examined in terms of the general patterns of the social impact of modern technology. Silence possesses striking similarities with such aspects of life and community as unpolluted water, air, or soil, which once were taken for granted, but which have become special and precious in technologically mediated environments. The threat of a privatization of the soundscape is discussed and some immediate measures suggested.

I would like to thank everyone involved in this conference, and the organizers in particular, for inviting me to deliver this talk. I am very obviously an outsider and wish to come to this group to talk about something that is central to all the work that you people are doing. And so I come in a way as a friend and colleague, in a field where I am fully aware that silence has been the subject of many publications. It is the subject of more than a chapter in R. Murray Schafer's *The Tuning of the World* and John Cage and others have written books on it. I would like to examine how our concept—as well as our practice—of silence has been influenced by all the other things that have changed as our world has become what Jacques Ellul calls a "technological milieu," a world that is, in all its facets, increasingly mediated by technology.

Before we had a technologically mediated society, before we had electronics and electro-magnetic devices, sound was rightly seen as being ephemeral, sound was coupled to its source, and lasted only a very short time. This is very different from what we see in a landscape: however much we feel that the landscape might be modified, however much we feel that there is a horrible building somewhere in front of a beautiful mountain, on the scale of the soundscape, the landscape is permanent. What is put up is there. That's very different from the traditional soundscape. What modern technology has brought to sound is the possibility of doing two things: to separate the sound from the source and to make the sound permanent. In addition, modern devices make it possible to decompose, recompose, analyze and mix sounds, to change the initial magnitude and sustainability of sound, as well as to change all the characteristics that link the sound with its source. R. Murray Schafer called this "schizophonia," separating the sound from the source. We now have easy access to the multitude of opportunities that result from overcoming that coupling.

5　　The social impact of this technology is significant. Prior to these developments there was a limitation to sound and sound penetration. If you heard a bagpipe band there was a limit to the amount of time it would play; if you found it displeasing you could patiently wait until the players got exhausted. But with a recording of a bagpipe band, you are out of luck. It's never going to be exhausted. Electronics, then, have altered the modern soundscape. While modern technology is a source of joy in modern composition, through the opening of many doors for expression, it is also the source of a good number of problems related to the soundscape, problems which society as a whole must adjust to, cope with, and possibly ameliorate.

But then there is not only sound, there is silence. Silence is affected by these same technological developments, the same means of separating sound from source and overcoming the ephemeral nature of a soundscape. I have attempted to define silence and to analyze the attributes that make it valuable. Defining silence as the absence of external or artificially generated sound is fine, but it's a little bit shallow, because silence in many ways is very much more than the absence of sound. Absence of sound is a condition necessary to silence but it is not sufficient in itself to define what we mean by silence. When one thinks about the concept of silence, one notices that there has to be somebody who listens before you can say there is silence. Silence, in addition to being an absence of sound, is defined by a listener, by hearing.

A further attribute, or parameter of silence, from my point of view, comes out of the question: *why is it that we worry about silence?* I feel that one comes to the root of the meaning and practice of silence only when one asks; *why is it that we value and try to establish silence?* Because silence is an enabling environment. This is the domain that we have traditionally associated with silence, the enabling condition in which unprogrammed and unprogrammable events can take place. That is the silence of contemplation; it is the silence when people get in touch with themselves; it is the silence of meditation and worship. The distinctive character of this domain of silence is that it is an enabling condition that opens up the possibility of unprogrammed, unplanned and unprogrammable happenings.

In this light we understand why, as Christians, traditional Quakers found it necessary in the seventeenth century, when they were surrounded by all the pomp and circumstance of the church of England, to reject it. We understand why they felt any ritual, in the sense of its programmed nature and predictability, to be a straitjacket rather than a comfort, and why they said to the amazement of their contemporaries: *we worship God in silence.* Their justification for the practice of silence was that they required it to hear God's voice. Beyond the individual's centering, beyond the individual effort of meditation, there was the need for *collective* silence. Collective silence is an enormously powerful event. There are contemporaneous accounts of Quaker meetings under heavy persecution in England, when thousands of people met silently on a hillside. Then out of the silence, one person—unappointed, unordained, unexpected, and unprogrammed—might speak, to say: *Out of the silence there can come a ministry.* The message is not essentially within that person, constructed in their intellect, but comes out of the silence to them. This isn't just history and theory. I think that if any one of you attended Quaker meetings, particularly on a regular basis, you would find that, suddenly, out of the silence, somebody speaks about something that had just entered *your* mind. It's an uncanny thing. The strength of collective silence is probably one of the most powerful spiritual forces.

Now, in order for something like this to happen, a lot of things are required. There is what Quakers call: *to be with heart and mind prepared.* But there is also the collective decision to be silent. And to be silent in order to let unforeseen, unforeseeable, and unprogrammed things happen. Such silence, I repeat, is the environment that enables the unprogrammed. I feel it is very much at risk.

I will elaborate on this, but first I want to say: there is another silence. There is the silence that enables a programmed, a planned, event to take place. There is the silence in which you courteously engage so that I might be heard: in order for one to be heard all the others have to be silent. But in many cases silence is not taken on voluntarily and it is this false silence of which I am afraid. It is not the silence only of the padded cell, or of solitary confinement; it is the silence that is enforced by the megaphone, the boom box, the PA system,

10

and any other device that stifles other sounds and voices in order that a planned event can take place.

There is a critical juncture between the planned and the unplanned, the programmed and the unplannable that must be kept in mind. I feel very strongly that our present technological trends drive us toward a decrease in the space—be it in the soundscape, the landscape, or the mindscape—in which the unplanned and unplannable can happen. Yet silence has to remain available in the soundscape, the landscape, and the mindscape. Allowing openness to the unplannable, to the unprogrammed, is the core of the strength of silence. It is also the core of our individual and collective sanity. I extend that to the collectivity because, as a community, as a people, we are threatened just as much, if not more, by the impingement of the programmed over the silent, over that which enables the unprogrammed. Much of the impingement goes unnoticed, uncommented upon, since it is much less obvious than the intrusion of a structure into the landscape. While we may not win all the battles at City Hall to preserve our trees, at least there is now a semi-consciousness that this type of struggle is important.

Where can one go to get away from the dangers of even the gentle presence of programmed music, or Muzak,* in our public buildings? Where do I protest that upon entering any place, from the shoe store to the restaurant, I am deprived of the opportunity to be quiet? Who has asked my permission to put that slop into the elevator I may have to use umpteen times every day? Many such "background" activities are intentionally manipulative. This is not merely "noise" that can be dealt with in terms of noise abatement. There are two aspects to be stressed in this context. One is that the elimination of silence is being done without anybody's consent. The other is that one really has to stop and think and analyze in order to see just how manipulative these interventions can be.

For instance, in the Toronto Skydome, friends tell me that the sound environment is coupled and geared to the game: if the home team misses, there are mournful and distressing sounds over the PA; when the home team scores there is a sort of athletic equivalent of the Hallelujah Chorus.* Again, the visitor has no choice; the programmed soundscape is part of the event. You cannot be present at the game without being subjected to that mood manipulation. I wonder if music will soon be piped into the voter's booth, maybe an upbeat, slightly military tune: "*Get on with it. Get the votes in.*" Joking aside, soundscape manipulation is a serious issue. Who on earth has given anybody the right to manipulate the sound environment?

Now, I want to come back to the definition of silence and introduce the notion of the commons, because the soundscape essentially doesn't belong to anyone in particular. What we are hearing, I feel, is very much the privatization of the soundscape, in the same manner in which the enclosure laws in Britain destroyed the commons of old.* There was a time when in fact every community had what was called "the commons," an area that belonged to everybody and where sheep could graze—a place important to all, belonging to all. The notion of the commons is deeply embedded in our social mind as something that all share. There are many "commons" that we take for granted and for millennia, clean air and clean water were the norm. Because of the ephemeral nature of sound in the past, silence was not considered part of the commons. Today, the technology to preserve and multiply sound and separate it from its source has resulted in our sudden awareness that silence, too, is a common good. Silence, which we need in order that unprogrammed and unprogrammable things can take place, is being removed from common access without much fuss and civic bother. It is being privatized.

This is another illustration of an often-observed occurrence related to the impact of technology: that things considered in the past to be normal or ordinary become rare or extraordinary, while those things once considered rare and unusual become normal and routine. Flying is no longer a big deal, but a handmade dress or a home-cooked meal may well be special. We essentially consider polluted water as normal now, and people who can afford it drink bottled water. It is hard to have bottled silence. But money still can buy distance from sound. Today, when there is civic anger, it is with respect to "noise"—like airport noise, etc. There is not yet such anger with respect to the manipulative elimination of silence from the soundscape.

There are those of us who have acknowledged and seen the deterioration of the commons as far as silence is concerned, who have seen that the soundscape is not only polluted by noise—so that one has to look for laws related to noise abatement—but also that the soundscape has become increasingly polluted through the private use of sound in the manipulative dimension of setting and programming moods and conditions. There is a desperate need for awareness of this, and for awareness of it in terms of the collectivity, rather than just individual needs. I feel very much that this is a time for civic anger. This is a time when one has to say: *town planning is constrained by by-laws on height, density, and other features; what are town planning's constraints in relation to silence?*

You may ask, what would I suggest? First of all, we must insist that, as human beings in a society, we have a right to silence. Just as we feel we have the right to walk down the street without being physically assaulted by people and preferably without being visually assaulted by ugly outdoor advertising, we also have the right not to be assaulted by sound, and in particular, not to be assaulted by sound that is there solely for the purpose of profit. Now is the time for civic rage, as well as civic education, but also for some action.

15

Think of the amount of care that goes into the regulation of parking, so that our good, precious, and necessary cars have a place to be well and safe. That's very important to society. I have yet to see, beyond hospitals, a public building that has a quiet room. Is not our sanity at least as important as the safety of our cars? One should begin to think: are there places, even in conferences like this, that are hassle-free, quiet spaces, where people can go? There were times when one could say to a kid: *"Where did you go?"*—*"Out."*—*"What did you do?"*—*"Nothing."* That sort of blessed time is past. The kid is programmed. We are programmed. And we don't even ask for a quiet space anymore.

One possible measure, relatively close at hand, is to set aside, as a normal matter of human rights, in those buildings over which we have some influence, a quiet room. Further, I highly recommend starting committee meetings with two minutes of silence, and ending them with a few minutes of silence, too. I sit on committees that have this practice, and find that it not only can expedite the business before the committee, but also contributes to a certain amount of peacefulness and sanity. One can start a lecture with a few minutes of silence, and can close it the same way. There can be a few minutes of silence before a shared meal. Such things help, even if they help only in small ways. I do think even small initiatives make silence "visible" as an ever-present part of life. I now invite you to have two minutes of silence before we go on into the question period. Let us be quiet together.

(1994)

BELL HOOKS

IN OUR GLORY:
PHOTOGRAPHY AND BLACK LIFE

"In Our Glory: Photography and Black Life," a discussion of photography's role in African American culture, was first published in bell hooks' Art on My Mind: Visual Politics *(1995). In this collection of essays and interviews, hooks addresses topics of black identity and aesthetics, asserting the need for more African American creators and critics of art. An activist and scholar, hooks adds this text to a body of critical work investigating sites where race and feminist theory intersect in lived experience and contemporary cultural practices.*

Always a daddy's girl. I was not surprised that my sister V. became a lesbian, or that her lovers were always white women. Her worship of Daddy and her passion for whiteness appeared to affirm a movement away from black womanhood and, of course, away from that image of the woman we did not want to become—our mother. The only family photograph V. displays in her house is a picture of our dad, looking young with a mustache. His dark skin mingling with the shadows in the photograph. All of which is highlighted by the white T-shirt he wears.

In this snapshot he is standing by a pool table. The look on his face is confident, seductive, cool—a look we rarely saw growing up. I have no idea who took the picture, only that it pleases me to imagine that he cared for the person—deeply. There is such boldness, such fierce openness in the way he faces the camera. This snapshot was taken before marriage, before us, his seven children, before our presence in his life forced him to leave behind the carefree masculine identity this pose conveys.

The fact that my sister V. possesses this image of our dad, one that I had never seen before, merely affirms their romance, the bond between the two of them. They had the dreamed-about closeness between father and daughter, or so it seemed. Her possession of the snapshot confirms this, is an acknowledgment that she is allowed to know—yes, even to possess—that private life he always kept to himself. When we were children, he refused to answer our questions about who he was, how he acted, what he did and felt before us. It was as though he did not want to remember or share that part of himself, as though remembering hurt. Standing before this snapshot, I come closer to the cold, distant, dark man who is my father, closer than I can ever come in real life. Not always able to love him there, I am sure I can love this version of him, the snapshot. I gave it a title: "in his glory."

Before leaving my sister's place, I plead with her to make a copy of this picture for my birthday. She says she will, but it never comes. For Christmas, then. It's on the way. I surmise that my passion for it surprises her, makes her hesitate. My rival in childhood—she always winning, the possessor of Dad's affection—she wonders whether to give that up, whether she is ready to share. She hesitates to give me the man in the snapshot. After all, had he wanted me to see him this way, "in his glory," he would have given me the picture.

5   My younger sister G. calls. For Christmas, V. has sent her a "horrible photograph" of Dad. There is outrage in her voice as she says, "It's disgusting. He's not even wearing a shirt, just an old white undershirt." G. keeps repeating, "I don't know why she has sent this picture to me." She has no difficulty promising to give me her copy if mine does not arrive. Her lack of interest in the photograph saddens me. When she was the age our dad is in the picture, she looked just like him. She had his beauty then, the same shine of glory and pride. Is this the face of herself that she has forgotten, does not want to

Snapshot of Veodis Watkins. 1949. Courtesy of bell hooks. Photographer unknown.

be reminded of, because time has taken such glory away? Unable to fathom how she cannot be drawn to this picture, I ponder what this image suggests to her that she cannot tolerate: a grown black man having a good time, playing a game, having a drink maybe, enjoying himself without the company of women.

Although my sisters and I look at this snapshot and see the same man, we do not see him in the same way. Our "reading" and experience of this image is shaped by our relationship with him, with the world of childhood and the images that make our lives what they are now. I want to rescue and preserve this image of our father, not let it be forgotten. It allows me to understand him, provides a way for me to know him that makes it possible to love him again, despite all the other images, the ones that stand in the way of love.

Such is the power of the photograph, of the image, that it can give back and take away, that it can bind. This snapshot of Veodis Watkins, our father, sometimes called Ned or Leakey in his younger days, gives me a space for intimacy between the image and myself, between me and Dad. I am captivated, seduced by it, the way other images have caught and held me, embraced me like arms that would not let go.

Struggling in childhood with the image of myself as unworthy of love, I could not see myself beyond all the received images, which simply reinforced my sense of unworthiness. Those ways of seeing myself came from voices of authority. The place where I could see myself, beyond imposed images, was in the realm of the snapshot. I am most real to myself in snapshots—there I see an image I can love.

My favorite childhood snapshot, then and now, showed me in costume, masquerading. Long after it had disappeared, I continued to long for it, and to grieve. I loved this snapshot of myself because it was the only image available to me that gave me a sense of presence, of girlhood beauty and capacity for pleasure. It was an image of myself I could genuinely like. At that stage of my life I was crazy about Westerns, about cowboys and Indians.* The camera captured me in my cowgirl outfit, white ruffled blouse, vest, fringed skirt, my one gun and my boots. In this image I became all that I wanted to be in my imagination.

For a moment, suspended in this image: I am a cowgirl. There is a look of heavenly joy on my face. I grew up needing this image, cherishing it—my one reminder that there was a precious little girl inside me able to know and express joy. I took this photograph with me on a visit to the house of my father's cousin Schuyler.

His was a home where art and the image mattered. No wonder, then, that I wanted to share my "best" image. Making my first real journey away from home, from a small town to my first big city, I needed the security of this image. I packed it carefully. I wanted Lovie, cousin Schuyler's wife, to see me "in my glory." I remember giving her the snapshot for safekeeping: only, when it was

10

time for me to return home, it could not be found. This was for me a terrible loss, an irreconcilable grief. Gone was the image of myself I could love. Losing that snapshot, I lost the proof of my worthiness—that I had ever been a bright-eyed child capable of wonder—the proof that there was a "me of me."

The image in this snapshot has lingered in my mind's eye for years. It has lingered there to remind me of the power of snapshots, of the image. As I slowly complete a book of essays titled *Art on My Mind*, I think about the place of art in black life, connections between the social construction of black identity, the impact of race and class, and the presence in black life of an inarticulate but ever-present visual aesthetic governing our relationship to images, to the process of image making. I return to the snapshot as a starting point to consider the place of the visual in black life—the importance of photography.

Cameras gave to black folks, irrespective of class, a means by which we could participate fully in the production of images. Hence it is essential that any theoretical discussion of the relationship of black life to the visual, to art making, make photography central. Access and mass appeal have historically made photography a powerful location for the construction of an oppositional black aesthetic. Before racial integration there was a constant struggle on the part of black folks to create a counterhegemonic world* of images that would stand as visual resistance, challenging racist images. All colonized and sub-jugated people who, by way of resistance, create an oppositional subculture within the framework of domination recognize that the field of representation (how we see ourselves, how others see us) is a site of ongoing struggle.

The history of black liberation movements in the United States could be characterized as a struggle over images as much as it has also been a struggle for rights, for equal access. To many reformist black civil rights activists, who believed that desegregation would offer the humanizing context that would challenge and change white supremacy, the issue of representation—control over images—was never as important as equal access. As time has progressed and the ace of white supremacy has not changed, reformist and radical blacks would likely agree that the field of representation remains a crucial realm of struggle, as important as the question of equal access, if not more important. Roger Wilkins emphasizes this point in his recent essay "White Out."

> In those innocent days, before desegregation had really been tried, before the New Frontier and the Great Society,[1] many of us blacks had lovely, naive hopes for integration.... In our naiveté, we believed that

---

1   *New Frontier*   Term used by President John F. Kennedy in 1960 to describe his administration's progressive agenda;   *Great Society*   Term used by President Lyndon B. Johnson in 1964 to refer to his administration's programs, many of which were extensions of the "New Frontier."

the power to segregate was the greatest power that had been wielded against us. It turned out that our expectations were wrong. The greatest power turned out to be what it had always been: the power to define reality where blacks are concerned and to manage perceptions and therefore arrange politics and culture to reinforce those definitions.

Though our politics differ, Wilkins's observations echo my insistence, in the opening essay of *Black Looks: Race and Representation*, that black people have made few, if any, revolutionary interventions in the arena of representation.

In part, racial desegregation—equal access—offered a vision of racial progress that, however limited, led many black people to be less vigilant about the question of representation. Concurrently, contemporary commodification of blackness creates a market context wherein conventional, even stereotypical, modes of representing blackness may receive the greatest reward. This leads to a cultural context in which images that would subvert the status quo are harder to produce. There is no "perceived market" for them. Nor should it surprise us that the erosion of oppositional black subcultures (many of which have been destroyed in the desegregation process) has deprived us of those sites of radical resistance where we have had primary control over representation. Significantly, nationalist black freedom movements were often concerned only with questions of "good" and "bad" imagery and did not promote a more expansive cultural understanding of the *politics* of representation. Instead they promoted notions of essence and identity that ultimately restricted and confined black image production.

No wonder, then, that racial integration has created a crisis in black life, signaled by the utter loss of critical vigilance in the arena of image making—by our being stuck in endless debate over good and bad imagery. The aftermath of this crisis has been devastating in that it has led to a relinquishment of collective black interest in the production of images. Photography began to have less significance in black life as a means—private or public—by which an oppositional standpoint could be asserted, a mode of seeing different from that of the dominant culture. Everyday black folks began to see themselves as not having a major role to play in the production of images.

To reverse this trend we must begin to talk about the significance of black image production in daily life prior to racial integration. When we concentrate on photography, then, we make it possible to see the walls of photographs in black homes as a critical intervention, a disruption of white control over black images.

Most Southern black folks grew up in a context where snapshots and the more stylized photographs taken by professional photographers were the easiest images to produce. Displaying these images in everyday life was as central

15

as making them. The walls of images in Southern black homes were sites of resistance. They constituted private, black-owned and -operated gallery space where images could be displayed, shown to friends and strangers. These walls were a space where, in the midst of segregation, the hardship of apartheid,[2] dehumanization could be countered. Images could be critically considered, subjects positioned according to individual desire.

20   Growing up inside these walls, many of us did not, at the time, regard them as important or valuable. Increasingly, as black folks live in a world so technologically advanced that it is possible for images to be produced and reproduced instantly, it is even harder for some of us to emotionally contextualize the significance of the camera in black life during the years of racial apartheid. The sites of contestation were not *out there*, in the world of white power, they were *within* segregated black life. Since no "white" galleries displayed images of black people created by black folks, spaces had to be made within diverse black communities. Across class boundaries black folks struggled with the issue of representation. This issue was linked with the issue of documentation; hence the importance of photography. The camera was the central instrument by which blacks could disprove representations of us created by white folks. The degrading images of blackness that emerged from racist white imagination and that were circulated widely in the dominant culture (on salt shakers, cookie jars, pancake boxes) could be countered by "true-to-life" images. When the psychohistory of a people is marked by ongoing loss, when entire histories are denied, hidden, erased, documentation can become an obsession. The camera must have seemed a magical instrument to many of the displaced and marginalized groups trying to carve out new destinies for themselves in the Americas. More than any other image-making tool, the camera offered African-Americans, disempowered in white culture, a way to empower ourselves through representation. For black folks, the camera provided a means to document a reality that could, if necessary, be packed, stored, moved from place to place. It was documentation that could be shared, passed around. And, ultimately, these images, the world they recorded, could be hidden, to be discovered at another time. Had the camera been there when slavery ended, it could have provided images that would have helped folks searching for lost kin and loved ones. It would have been a powerful tool of cultural recovery. Half a century later, the generations of black folks emerging from a history of loss became passionately obsessed with the camera. Elderly black people developed a cultural passion for the camera, for the images it produced, because it offered a way to contain memories, to overcome loss, to keep history.

----

2   *apartheid* System in which people are divided into racial or ethnic groups (named for the system of segregation that divided South Africa from 1948–94).

Though rarely articulated as such, the camera became in black life a political instrument, a way to resist misrepresentation as a well as a means by which alternative images could be produced. Photography was more fascinating to masses of black folks than other forms of image making because it offered the possibility of immediate intervention, useful in the production of counter-hegemonic representations even as it was also an instrument of pleasure. The camera allowed black folks to combine image making, resistance struggle, and pleasure. Taking pictures was fun!

Growing up in the 1950s, I was somewhat awed and at times frightened by our extended family's emphasis on picture taking. From the images of the dead as they lay serene, beautiful, and still in open caskets to the endless portraits of newborns, every wall and corner of my grandparents' (and most everybody else's) home was lined with photographs. When I was young I never linked this obsession with self-representation to our history as a domestically colonized and subjugated people.

My perspective on picture taking was also informed by the way the process was tied to patriarchy in our household. Our father was definitely the "picture-takin' man." For a long time cameras remained mysterious and off limits to the rest of us. As the only one in the family who had access to the equipment, who could learn how to make the process work, my father exerted control over our images. In charge of capturing our family history with the camera, he called and took the shots. We were constantly being lined up for picture taking, and it was years before our household could experience this as an enjoyable activity, before any of the rest of us could be behind the camera. Until then, picture taking was serious business. I hated it. I hated posing. I hated cameras. I hated the images that cameras produced. When I stopped living at home, I refused to be captured by anyone's camera. I did not wish to document my life, the changes, the presence of different places, people, and so on. I wanted to leave no trace. I wanted there to be no walls in my life that would, like gigantic maps, chart my journey. I wanted to stand outside history.

That was twenty years ago. Now that I am passionately involved with thinking critically about black people and representation, I can confess that those walls of photographs empowered me, and that I feel their absence in my life. Right now I long for those walls, those curatorial spaces in the home that express our will to make and display images.

Sarah Oldham, my mother's mother, was a keeper of walls. Throughout my childhood, visits to her house were like trips to a gallery or museum— experiences we did not have because of racial segregation. We would stand before the walls of images and learn the importance of the arrangement, why a certain photograph was placed here and not there. The walls were fundamentally different from photo albums. Rather than shutting images away, where

25

they could be seen only upon request, the walls were a public announcement of the primacy of the image, the joy of image making. To enter black homes in my childhood was to enter a world that valued the visual, that asserted our collective will to participate in a noninstitutionalized curatorial process.

For black folks constructing our identities within the culture of apartheid, these walls were essential to the process of decolonization. In opposition to colonizing socialization, internalized racism, these walls announced our visual complexity. We saw ourselves represented in these images not as caricatures, cartoonlike figures; we were there in full diversity of body, being, and expression, multidimensional. Reflecting the way black folks looked at themselves in those private spaces, where those ways of looking were not being overseen by a white colonizing eye, a white-supremacist gaze, these images created ruptures in our experience of the visual. They challenged both white perceptions of blackness and that realm of black-produced image making that reflected internalized racism. Many of these images demanded that we look at ourselves with new eyes, that we create oppositional standards of evaluation. As we looked at black skin in snapshots, the techniques for lightening skin that professional photographers often used when shooting black images were suddenly exposed as a colonizing aesthetic. Photographs taken in everyday life, snapshots in particular, rebelled against all those photographic practices that reinscribed colonial ways of looking and capturing the images of the black "other." Shot spontaneously, without any notion of remaking black bodies in the image of whiteness, snapshots posed a challenge to black viewers. Unlike photographs constructed so that black images would appear as the embodiment of colonizing fantasies, snapshots gave us a way to see ourselves, a sense of how we looked when we were not "wearing the mask,"[3] when we were not attempting to perfect the image for a white-supremacist gaze.

Although most black folks did not articulate their desire to look at images of themselves that did not resemble or please white folks' ideas about us, or that did not frame us within an image of racial hierarchies, that desire was expressed through our passionate engagement with informal photographic practices. Creating pictorial genealogies was the means by which one could ensure against the losses of the past. Such genealogies were a way to sustain ties. As children, we learned who our ancestors were by listening to endless narratives as we stood in front of these pictures.

In many black homes, photographs—especially snapshots—were also central to the creation of "altars." These commemorative places paid homage to absent loved ones. Snapshots or professional portraits were placed in specific

---

3   *wearing the mask*   Reference to African American poet Paul Lawrence Dunbar's poem "We Wear the Mask" (1896).

settings so that a relationship with the dead could be continued. Poignantly describing this use of the image in her novel *Jazz*, Toni Morrison writes:

> … a dead girl's face has become a necessary thing for their nights. They each take turns to throw off the bedcovers, rise up from the sagging mattress and tiptoe over cold linoleum into the parlor to gaze at what seems like the only living presence in the house: the photograph of a bold, unsmiling girl staring from the mantelpiece. If the tiptoer is Joe Trace, driven by loneliness from his wife's side, then the face stares at him without hope or regret and it is the absence of accusation that wakes him from his sleep hungry for her company. No finger points. Her lips don't turn down in judgment. Her face is calm, generous and sweet. But if the tiptoer is Violet, the photograph is not that at all. The girl's face looks greedy, haughty, and very lazy. The cream-at-the-top-of-the-milkpail face of someone who will never work for anything, someone who picks up things lying on other people's dressers and is not embarrassed when found out. It is the face of a sneak who glides over to your sink to rinse the fork you have laid by your place. An inward face—whatever it sees is its own self. You are there, it says, because I am looking at you.

I quote this passage at length because it attests to a kind of connection to photographic images that has not been acknowledged in critical discussions of black folks' relationship to the visual. When I first read these sentences, I was reminded of the passionate way we related to photographs when I was a child. Fictively dramatizing the extent to which a photograph can have a "living presence," Morrison describes the way that many black folks rooted in Southern tradition once used, and still use, pictures. They were and remain a mediation between the living and the dead.

To create a palimpsest[4] of black folks' relation to the visual in segregated black life, we need to follow each trace, not fall into the trap of thinking that if something was not openly discussed, or only talked about and not recorded, it lacks significance and meaning. Those pictorial genealogies that Sarah Oldham, my mother's mother, constructed on her walls were essential to our sense of self and identity as a family. They provided a necessary narrative, a way for us to enter history without words. When words entered, they did so in order to make the images live. Many older black folks who cherished pictures were not literate. The images were crucial documentation, there to sustain and affirm memory. This was true for my grandmother, who did not read or write. I focus

30

---

4   *palimpsest*   Page that has been written on, then erased and written over, such that traces of the original writing can still be seen.

especially on her walls because I know that, as an artist (she was an excellent quiltmaker), she positioned the photos with the same care that she laid out her quilts.

The walls of pictures were indeed maps guiding us through diverse journeys. Seeking to recover strands of oppositional worldviews that were a part of black folks' historical relationship to the visual, to the process of image making, many black folks are once again looking to photography to make the connection. The contemporary African-American artist Emma Amos maps our journeys when she mixes photographs with painting, making connections between past and present. Amos uses snapshots inherited from an uncle who once took pictures for a living. In one piece, Amos paints a map of the United States and identifies diasporic African presences, as well as particular Native American communities with black kin, marking each spot with a family image.

Drawing from the past, from those walls of images I grew up with, I gather snapshots and lay them out to see what narratives the images tell, what they say without words. I search these images to see if there are imprints waiting to be seen, recognized, and read. Together, a black male friend and I lay out the snapshots of his boyhood to see when he began to lose a certain openness, to discern at what age he began to shut down, to close himself away. Through these images, my friend hopes to find a way back to the self he once was. We are awed by what our snapshots reveal, what they enable us to remember.

The word *remember (re-member)* evokes the coming together of severed parts, fragments becoming a whole. Photography has been, and is, central to that aspect of decolonization that calls us back to the past and offers a way to reclaim and renew life-affirming bonds. Using images, we connect ourselves to a recuperative, redemptive memory that enables us to construct radical identities, images of ourselves that transcend the limits of the colonizing eye.

(1995)

JEFFREY JEROME COHEN

from MONSTER CULTURE
(SEVEN THESES)

Much of the work of Jeffrey Jerome Cohen, an English professor at the University of Washington, brings together medieval studies and contemporary critical theory. His essay "Monster Culture (Seven Theses)" is considered one of the fundamental works in the subfield of monster studies, which examines monsters in past and present literature and culture. First published in the collection Monster Theory: Reading Culture *(1996), Cohen's theses have generated scholarly work in diverse areas including postcolonial, queer, and disability theory.*

... Rather than argue a "theory of teratology,"[1] I offer by way of introduction to the essays that follow a set of breakable postulates in search of specific cultural moments. I offer seven theses toward understanding cultures through the monsters they bear.

THESIS I: THE MONSTER'S BODY IS A CULTURAL BODY

Vampires, burial, death: inter the corpse where the road forks, so that when it springs from the grave, it will not know which path to follow. Drive a stake through its heart: it will be stuck to the ground at the fork, it will haunt that place that leads to many other places, that point of indecision. Behead the corpse, so that, acephalic,[2] it will not know itself as subject, only as pure body.

The monster is born only at this metaphoric crossroads, as an embodiment of a certain cultural moment—of a time, a feeling, and a place.[3] The monster's

---

1   *teratology* Story or study of monsters, deformities, or fantastical beings; from the Greek word for "monster."

2   *acephalic* Headless.

3   Literally, here, *Zeitgeist* [spirit of the age]: Time Ghost, the bodiless spirit that uncannily incorporates a "place" that is a series of places, the crossroads that is a point in a *movement* toward an uncertain elsewhere. Bury the Zeitgeist by the *(continued ...)*

455

body quite literally incorporates fear, desire, anxiety, and fantasy (ataractic[4] or incendiary), giving them life and an uncanny independence. The monstrous body is pure culture. A construct and a projection, the monster exists only to be read: the *monstrum* is etymologically "that which reveals;" "that which warns;" a glyph that seeks a hierophant.[5] Like a letter on the page, the monster signifies something other than itself: it is always a displacement, always inhabits the gap between the time of upheaval that created it and the moment into which it is received, to be born again. These epistemological spaces between the monster's bones are Derrida's familiar chasm of *différance*:[6] a genetic uncertainty principle, the essence of the monster's vitality, the reason it always rises from the dissection table as its secrets are about to be revealed and vanishes into the night.

THESIS II: THE MONSTER ALWAYS ESCAPES

We see the damage that the monster wreaks, the material remains (the footprints of the yeti across Tibetan snow, the bones of the giant stranded on a rocky cliff), but the monster itself turns immaterial and vanishes, to reappear someplace else (for who is the yeti if not the medieval wild man? Who is the wild man if not the biblical and classical giant?). No matter how many times King Arthur killed the ogre of Mount Saint Michael,[7] the monster reappeared in another heroic chronicle, bequeathing the Middle Ages an abundance of *morte d'Arthurs*. Regardless of how many times Sigourney Weaver's beleaguered Ripley[8] utterly destroys the ambiguous Alien that stalks her, its monstrous progeny return, ready to stalk again in another bigger-than-ever sequel. No monster tastes of death but once. The anxiety that condenses like green vapor into the form of the vampire can be dispersed temporarily, but the revenant by definition returns. And so the monster's body is both corporal and incorporeal; its threat is its propensity to shift.

---

crossroads: it is confused as it awakens, it is not going anywhere, it intersects everyplace; all roads lead back to the monster. [author's note]

4   *ataractic*   Calming, especially in the sense of a relaxing drug.

5   *hierophant*   Interpreter of sacred mysteries or revelations.

6   *différance*   Term used by the critical theorist Jacques Derrida (1930–2004) in reference to the impossibility of fixed meaning in language.

7   *King Arthur ... Michael*   This story is related in several places, including Thomas Malory's *Le Morte Darthur* (fifteenth century), one of the best-known works of Arthurian legend in English.

8   *Ripley*   Protagonist of the science-fiction horror classic *Alien* (1979), which inspired books, video games, and numerous film sequels and prequels.

Each time the grave opens and the unquiet slumberer strides forth ("come 5 from the dead, / Come back to tell you all"[9]), the message proclaimed is transformed by the air that gives its speaker new life. Monsters must be examined within the intricate matrix of relations (social, cultural, and literary-historical) that generate them. In speaking of the new kind of vampire invented by Bram Stoker, we might explore the foreign count's transgressive but compelling sexuality, as subtly alluring to Jonathan Harker[10] as Henry Irving, Stoker's mentor, was to Stoker.[11] Or we might analyze Murnau's self-loathing appropriation of the same demon in *Nosferatu*,[12] where in the face of nascent fascism the undercurrent of desire surfaces in plague and bodily corruption. Anne Rice[13] has given the myth a modern rewriting in which homosexuality and vampirism have been conjoined, apotheosized;* that she has created a pop culture phenomenon in the process is not insignificant, especially at a time when gender as a construct has been scrutinized at almost every social register. In Francis Coppola's[14] recent blockbuster, *Bram Stoker's Dracula*, the homosexual subtext present at least since the appearance of Sheridan Le Fanu's lesbian lamia[15] (*Carmilla*, 1872) has, like the red corpuscles that serve as the film's leitmotif,* risen to the surface, primarily as an AIDS awareness that transforms the disease of vampirism into a sadistic (and very medieval) form of redemption through the torments of the body in pain. No coincidence, then, that Coppola was putting together a documentary on AIDS at the same time he was working on *Dracula*.

In each of these vampire stories, the undead returns in slightly different clothing, each time to be read against contemporary social movements or a specific, determining event: *la décadence** and its new possibilities, homophobia and its hateful imperatives, the acceptance of new subjectivities unfixed by binary gender, a fin de siècle* social activism paternalistic in its embrace.

---

9   *come from … you all*   From T.S. Eliot, "The Love Song of J. Alfred Prufrock" (1915); the lines are in reference to Lazarus's resurrection from the dead (see John 11).

10   *Jonathan Harker*   Character in Bram Stoker's novel *Dracula* (1897), in which the character of "Count Dracula" first appeared.

11   I realize that this is an interpretive biographical maneuver Barthes would surely have called "the living death of the author." [author's note] [This refers to critic and theorist Roland Barthes's 1967 essay "The Death of the Author."]

12   *Nosferatu*   Influential 1922 horror film based on *Dracula*.

13   *Anne Rice*   Author of *Interview with the Vampire* (1976) and other novels that make their primary focus vampire rather than human characters. Her work ignited popular interest in vampires in the late twentieth and early twenty-first centuries.

14   *Francis Coppola*   Leading filmmaker best known for *The Godfather* (1972).

15   *lamia*   Mythical female monster who eats children; *Sheridan … lamia*   Carmilla, the title character of Le Fanu's novel, feeds on girl children.

Discourse extracting a transcultural, transtemporal phenomenon labeled "the vampire" is of rather limited utility; even if vampiric figures are found almost worldwide, from ancient Egypt to modern Hollywood, each reappearance and its analysis is still bound in a double act of construction and reconstitution.[16] "Monster theory" must therefore concern itself with strings of cultural moments, connected by a logic that always threatens to shift....

THESIS III: THE MONSTER IS THE HARBINGER OF CATEGORY CRISIS

The monster always escapes because it refuses easy categorization.... This refusal to participate in the classificatory "order of things" is true of monsters generally: they are disturbing hybrids whose externally incoherent bodies resist attempts to include them in any systematic structuration. And so the monster is dangerous, a form suspended between forms that threatens to smash distinctions.

Because of its ontological liminality,[17] the monster notoriously appears at times of crisis as a kind of third term that problematizes the clash of extremes—as "that which questions binary thinking and introduces a crisis."[18] ...

... A mixed category, the monster resists any classification built on hierarchy or a merely binary opposition,[19] demanding instead a "system" allowing polyphony,* mixed response (difference in sameness, repulsion in attraction),

---

16 Thus the superiority of Joan Copjec's "Vampires, Breast-feeding, and Anxiety," October 58 (Fall 1991): 25–43, to Paul Barber's *Vampires, Burial and Death: Folklore and Reality* (New Haven, Conn.: Yale University Press, 1988). [author's note]

17 *ontological liminality* I.e., the ambiguous nature of its existence.

18 Marjorie Garber, *Vested Interests: Cross-Dressing and Cultural Anxiety* (New York: Routledge, 1992), 11. Garber writes at some length about "category crisis," which she defines as "a failure of definitional distinction, a borderline that becomes permeable, that permits of border crossings from one (apparently distinct) category to another: black/white, Jew/Christian, noble/bourgeois, master/servant, master/slave.... [That which crosses the border, like the transvestite] will always function as a mechanism of overdetermination—a mechanism of displacement from one blurred boundary to another. An analogy here might be the so-called 'tagged' gene that shows up in a genetic chain, indicating the presence of some otherwise hidden condition. It is not the gene itself, but its presence, that marks the trouble spot, indicating the likelihood of a crisis somewhere, elsewhere" (pp. 16–17). Note, however, that whereas Garber insists that the transvestite must be read with rather than through, the monster can be read only through—for the monster, pure culture, is nothing of itself. [author's note]

19 *binary opposition* According to Derrida, the meaning of a given word depends especially on its relationship to the word that is considered its opposite: the meaning of "masculine" depends most of all upon that of "feminine," the meaning of "culture" upon that of "nature," and so on. These pairings are called binary oppositions.

and resistance to integration—allowing what Hogle has called with a wonderful pun "a deeper play of differences, a nonbinary polymorphism[20] at the 'base' of human nature."[21]

The horizon where the monsters dwell might well be imagined as the visible edge of the hermeneutic circle itself: the monstrous offers an escape from its hermetic[22] path, an invitation to explore new spirals, new and interconnected methods of perceiving the world.[23] In the face of the monster, scientific inquiry and its ordered rationality crumble. The monstrous is a genus too large to be encapsulated in any conceptual system; the monster's very existence is a rebuke to boundary and enclosure; like the giants of *Mandeville's Travels*,[24] it threatens to devour "all raw & quyk" any thinker who insists otherwise. The monster is in this way the living embodiment of the phenomenon Derrida has famously labeled the "supplement" (*ce dangereux supplément*):[25] it breaks apart bifurcating, "either/or" syllogistic logic[26] with a kind of reasoning closer to "and/or," introducing what Barbara Johnson has called "a revolution in the very logic of meaning."[27]

Full of rebuke to traditional methods of organizing knowledge and human experience, the geography of the monster is an imperiling expanse, and therefore always a contested cultural space.

THESIS IV: THE MONSTER DWELLS AT THE GATES OF DIFFERENCE

The monster is difference made flesh, come to dwell among us. In its function as dialectical Other or third-term supplement, the monster is an incorporation

10

---

20   *polymorphism*   Multiplicity of forms.

21   Jerrold E. Hogle, "The Struggle for a Dichotomy: Abjection in Jekyll and His Interpreters," in *Dr. Jekyll and Mr. Hyde after One Hundred Years*, ed. William Veeder and Gordon Hirsch (Chicago: University of Chicago Press, 1988), 161. [author's note]

22   *hermeneutic*   Related to interpretation, especially textual interpretation; *hermetic* Enclosed.

23   "The hermeneutic circle does not permit access or escape to an uninterrupted reality; but we do not [have to] keep going around in the same path." Barbara Herrnstein Smith, "Belief and Resistance: A Symmetrical Account;" *Critical Inquiry* 18 (Autumn 1991): 137–38. [author's note]

24   *Mandeville's Travels*   Fanciful fourteenth-century travel narrative.

25   Jacques Derrida, *Of Grammatology*, trans. Gayatri Chakravorty Spivak (Baltimore: Johns Hopkins University Press,1974). [author's note]

26   *syllogistic logic*   Type of logic in which true statements together establish the truth of a conclusion.

27   Barbara Johnson, "Introduction," in Jacques Derrida, *Dissemination*, trans. Barbara Johnson (Chicago: University of Chicago Press, 1981), xiii. [author's note]

of the Outside, the Beyond—of all those loci that are rhetorically placed as distant and distinct but originate Within. Any kind of alterity[28] can be inscribed across (constructed through) the monstrous body, but for the most part monstrous difference tends to be cultural, political, racial, economic, sexual.

The exaggeration of cultural difference into monstrous aberration is familiar enough. The most famous distortion occurs in the Bible, where the aboriginal inhabitants of Canaan are envisioned as menacing giants to justify the Hebrew colonization of the Promised Land (Numbers 13). Representing an anterior culture as monstrous justifies its displacement or extermination by rendering the act heroic....

The difficult project of constructing and maintaining gender identities elicits an array of anxious responses throughout culture, producing another impetus to teratogenesis.[29] The woman who oversteps the boundaries of her gender role risks becoming a Scylla, Weird Sister, Lilith ("die erste Eva," "la mère obscuré"),[30] Bertha Mason, or Gorgon.[31] "Deviant" sexual identity is similarly susceptible to monsterization. ...

15   From the classical period into the twentieth century, race has been almost as powerful a catalyst to the creation of monsters as culture, gender, and sexuality. ...

Through a similar discursive process the East becomes feminized (Said) and the soul of Africa grows dark (Gates).[32] One kind of difference becomes

---

28   *alterity*   Otherness.

29   *teratogenesis*   Here, making of monsters; in biology, "teratogenesis" refers to the creation of birth deformities.

30   I am hinting here at the possibility of a feminist recuperation of the gendered monster by citing the titles of two famous books about Lilith (a favorite figure in feminist writing): Jacques Bril's *Lilith, ou, La Mere obscure* (Paris: Payot, 1981), and Siegmund Hurwitz's *Lilith, die erste Eva: Eine Studie uber dunkle Aspekte des Weiblichen* (Zurich: Daimon Verlag, 1980). [author's note]

31   "The monster-woman, threatening to replace her angelic sister, embodies intransigent female autonomy and thus represents both the author's power to allay 'his' anxieties by calling their source bad names (witch, bitch, fiend, monster) and simultaneously, the mysterious power of the character who refuses to stay in her textually ordained 'place' and thus generates a story that 'gets away' from its author." Sandra M. Gilbert and Susan Gubar, *The Madwoman in the Attic: The Woman Writer and the Nineteenth Century Literary Imagination* (New Haven, Conn.: Yale University Press, 1984), 28. The "dangerous" role of feminine will in the engendering of monsters is also explored by Marie-Hélène Huet in *Monstrous Imagination* (Cambridge: Harvard University Press, 1993). [author's note] [Scylla, the Weird Sisters, and the other figures listed in the text are monstrous women from various cultures.]

32   See Edward Said, *Orientalism* (New York: Pantheon, 1978); Henry Louis Gates Jr., *The Signifying Monkey: A Theory of Afro-American Literature* (New York: Oxford

another as the normative categories of gender, sexuality, national identity, and ethnicity slide together like the imbricated circles of a Venn diagram, abjecting[33] from the center that which becomes the monster. This violent foreclosure erects a self-validating, Hegelian master/slave dialectic[34] that naturalizes the subjugation of one cultural body by another by writing the body excluded from personhood and agency as in every way different, monstrous. A polysemy is granted so that a greater threat can be encoded; multiplicity of meanings, paradoxically, iterates the same restricting, agitprop[35] representations that narrowed signification performs. Yet a danger resides in this multiplication: as difference, like a Hydra,[36] sprouts two heads where one has been lopped away, the possibilities of escape, resistance, *disruption* arise with more force.

René Girard has written at great length about the real violence these debasing representations enact, connecting monsterizing depiction with the phenomenon of the scapegoat. Monsters are never created *ex nihilo*,[37] but through a process of fragmentation and recombination in which elements are extracted "from various forms" (including—indeed, especially—marginalized social groups) and then assembled as the monster, "which can then claim an independent identity."[38] The political-cultural monster, the embodiment of radical difference, paradoxically threatens to *erase* difference in the world of its creators, to demonstrate

> the potential for the system to differ from its own difference, in other words not to be different at all, to cease to exist as a system.... Difference that exists outside the system is terrifying because it reveals the truth of the system, its relativity, its fragility, and its mortality....

University Press, 1988). [author's note] [Said and Gates are important theorists who have critiqued the white West's discourses regarding the East and regarding African Americans, respectively.]

33 *abjecting* Reference to Julia Kristeva's *Powers of Horror* (1980), in which she conceptualizes the "abject" as that which we must reject in order to form individual identities; abjection is this process of rejecting what disgusts or is otherwise unacceptable to us within ourselves.

34 *Hegelian master/slave dialectic* Struggle described by G.W.F. Hegel (1770–1831) in which one conscious being dominates another.

35 *polysemy* Multitude of meanings attached to the same word or other unit of communication; *agitprop* I.e., propagandistic.

36 *Hydra* Many-headed monster of Greek mythology.

37 *ex nihilo* Latin: from nothing.

38 René Girard, *The Scapegoat*, trans. Yvonne Freccero (Baltimore: Johns Hopkins University Press, 1986), 33. [author's note]

Despite what is said around us persecutors are never obsessed with difference but rather by its unutterable contrary, the lack of difference.[39]

By revealing that difference is arbitrary and potentially free-floating, mutable
rather than essential, the monster threatens to destroy not just individual members of a society, but the very cultural apparatus through which individuality is
constituted and allowed. Because it is a body across which difference has been
repeatedly written, the monster (like Frankenstein's creature,* that combination of odd somatic[40] pieces stitched together from a community of cadavers)
seeks out its author to demand its raison d'être*—and to bear witness to the
fact that it could have been constructed Otherwise. Godzilla trampled Tokyo;*
Girard frees him here to fragment the delicate matrix of relational systems that
unite every private body to the public world.

THESIS V: THE MONSTER POLICES THE BORDERS OF THE POSSIBLE

… From its position at the limits of knowing, the monster stands as a warning
against exploration of its uncertain demesnes. The giants of Patagonia,[41] the
dragons of the Orient, and the dinosaurs of Jurassic Park* together declare that
curiosity is more often punished than rewarded, that one is better off safely contained within one's own domestic sphere than abroad, away from the watchful
eyes of the state. The monster prevents mobility (intellectual, geographic, or
sexual), delimiting the social spaces through which private bodies may move.
To step outside this official geography is to risk attack by some monstrous
border patrol or (worse) to become monstrous oneself.…

Whereas monsters born of political expedience and self-justifying nationalism function as living invitations to action, usually military (invasions,
usurpations, colonizations), the monster of prohibition, polices the borders
of the possible, interdicting through its grotesque body some behaviors and
actions, envaluing others. It is possible, for example, that medieval merchants
intentionally disseminated maps depicting sea serpents like Leviathan[42] at
the edges of their trade routes in order to discourage further exploration and
to establish monopolies.[43] Every monster is in this way a double narrative,
two living stories: one that describes how the monster came to be and another,

39   Ibid., 21–22. [author's note]

40   *somatic*   Bodily.

41   *giants of Patagonia*   From the sixteenth to the eighteenth centuries, many Europeans
believed Patagonia, the southern tip of South America, to be inhabited by giants.

42   *Leviathan*   Old Testament sea monster.

43   I am indebted to Keeryung Hong of Harvard University for sharing her research on
medieval map production for this hypothesis. [author's note]

its testimony, detailing what cultural use the monster serves. The monster of prohibition exists to demarcate the bonds that hold together that system of relations we call culture, to call horrid attention to the borders that cannot—*must not*—be crossed....

The monster is a powerful ally of what Foucault calls "the society of the panopticon;"[44] in which "polymorphous conducts [are] actually extracted from people's bodies and from their pleasures ... [to be] drawn out, revealed, isolated, intensified, incorporated, by multifarious power devices."[45] Susan Stewart has observed that "the monster's sexuality takes on a separate life";[46] Foucault helps us to see why. The monster embodies those sexual practices that must not be committed, or that may be committed only through the body of the monster. *She* and *Them!*: the monster enforces the cultural codes that regulate sexual desire.

Anyone familiar with the low-budget science fiction movie craze of the 1950s will recognize in the preceding sentence two superb films of the genre, one about a radioactive virago from outer space who kills every man she touches, the other a social parable in which giant ants (really, Communists) burrow beneath Los Angeles (that is, Hollywood) and threaten world peace (that is, American conservatism). I connect these two seemingly unrelated titles here to call attention to the anxieties that monsterized their subjects in the first place, and to enact syntactically an even deeper fear: that the two will join in some unholy miscegenation.[47] We have seen that the monster arises at the gap where difference is perceived as dividing a recording voice from its captured subject; the criterion of this division is arbitrary, and can range from anatomy or skin color to religious belief, custom, and political ideology. The monster's destructiveness is really a deconstructiveness: it threatens to reveal that difference originates in process, rather than in fact (and that "fact" is subject to constant reconstruction and change). Given that the recorders of the history of the West have been mainly European and male, women (*She*) and nonwhites (*Them!*) have found themselves repeatedly transformed into monsters, whether to validate specific alignments of masculinity and whiteness, or simply to be pushed from its realm of thought.[48] Feminine and cultural others are monstrous

20

---

44 *panopticon* Prison in which all inmates can be observed at any time from a central tower.

45 Michel Foucault, *The History of Sexuality*, vol. 1, *An Introduction*, trans. Robert Hurley (New York: Vintage, 1990), 47–48. [author's note]

46 Stewart, *On Longing*. See especially "The Imaginary Body;" 104–31. [author's note]

47 *miscegenation* Term usually applied to racial intermarriage or the conception of interracial children.

48 The situation was obviously far more complex than these statements can begin to show; "European," for example, usually includes only males of the Western Latin *(continued ...)*

enough by themselves in patriarchal society, but when they threaten to mingle, the entire economy of desire comes under attack.

As a vehicle of prohibition, the monster most often arises to enforce the laws of exogamy, both the incest taboo (which establishes a traffic in women[49] by mandating that they marry outside their families) and the decrees against interracial sexual mingling (which limit the parameters of that traffic by policing the boundaries of culture, usually in the service of some notion of group "purity").[50] ...

THESIS VI: FEAR OF THE MONSTER IS REALLY A KIND OF DESIRE

The monster is continually linked to forbidden practices, in order to normalize and to enforce. The monster also attracts. The same creatures who terrify and interdict can evoke potent escapist fantasies; the linking of monstrosity with the forbidden makes the monster all the more appealing as a temporary egress from constraint. This simultaneous repulsion and attraction at the core of the monster's composition accounts greatly for its continued cultural popularity, for the fact that the monster seldom can be contained in a simple, binary dialectic (thesis, antithesis ... no synthesis).[51] We distrust and loathe the monster at the same time we envy its freedom, and perhaps its sublime despair.

Through the body of the monster fantasies of aggression, domination, and inversion are allowed safe expression in a clearly delimited and permanently liminal space. Escapist delight gives way to horror only when the monster threatens to overstep these boundaries, to destroy or deconstruct the thin walls

---

tradition. Sexual orientation further complicates the picture, as we shall see.

Donna Haraway, following Trinh Minh-ha, calls the humans beneath the monstrous skin "inappropriate/d others": "To be 'inappropriate/d' does not mean 'not to be in relation with'—i.e., to be in a special reservation, with the status of the authentic, the untouched, in the allochronic and allotropic condition of innocence. Rather to be an 'inappropriate/d other' means to be in critical deconstructive relationality, in a diffracting rather than reflecting (ratio)nality—as the means of making potent connection that exceeds domination." "The Promises of Monsters," in *Simians, Cyborgs, and Women: The Reinvention of Nature* (New York: Routledge, 1991), 299.

49 *exogamy* Marriage outside a given group; *traffic in women* Reference to Gayle Rubin's important essay "The Traffic in Women" (1975), in which she argues that the exchange of women as male property is foundational to both patriarchy and capitalism.

50 This discussion owes an obvious debt to Mary Douglas, *Purity and Danger: An Analysis of the Concepts of Pollution and Taboo* (New York: Routledge & Kegan Paul, 1966). [author's note]

51 *thesis ... synthesis* Reference to the notion of "thesis-antithesis-synthesis," according to which new ideas are produced when an idea (thesis) and its opposite (antithesis) are reconciled to produce a synthesis.

of category and culture. When contained by geographic, generic, or epistemic marginalization, the monster can function as an alter ego, as an alluring projection of (an Other) self. The monster awakens one to the pleasures of the body, to the simple and fleeting joys of being frightened, or frightening—to the experience of mortality and corporality. We watch the monstrous spectacle of the horror film because we know that the cinema is a temporary place, that the jolting sensuousness of the celluloid images will be followed by reentry into the world of comfort and light.[52] ...

... The monstrous lurks somewhere in that ambiguous, primal space between fear and attraction, close to the heart of what Kristeva calls "abjection": 25

> There looms, within abjection, one of those violent, dark revolts of being, directed against a threat that seems to emanate from an exorbitant outside or inside, ejected beyond the scope of the possible, the tolerable, the thinkable. It lies there, quite close, but it cannot be assimilated. It beseeches, worries, fascinates desire, which, nonetheless, does not let itself be seduced. Apprehensive, desire turns aside; sickened, it rejects.... But simultaneously, just the same, that impetus, that spasm, that leap is drawn toward an elsewhere as tempting as it is condemned. Unflaggingly, like an inescapable boomerang, a vortex of summons and repulsion places the one haunted by it literally beside himself.[53]

And the self that one stands so suddenly and so nervously beside is the monster.

The monster is the abjected fragment that enables the formation of all kinds of identities—personal, national, cultural, economic, sexual, psychological, universal, particular (even if that "particular" identity is an embrace of the power/status/knowledge of abjection itself); as such it reveals their partiality, their contiguity. A product of a multitude of morphogeneses[54] (ranging from somatic to ethnic) that align themselves to imbue meaning to the Us and Them behind every cultural mode of seeing, the monster of abjection resides in that marginal geography of the Exterior, beyond the limits of the Thinkable, a place

---

52 Paul Coates interestingly observes that "the horror film becomes the essential form of cinema, monstrous content manifesting itself in the monstrous form of the gigantic screen." *The Gorgon's Gaze* (Cambridge: Cambridge University Press, 1991), 77. Carol Clover locates some of the pleasure of the monster film in its cross-gender game of identification; see *Men, Women, and Chain Saws: Gender in the Modern Horror Film* (Princeton, N.J.: Princeton University Press, 1992). Why not go further, and call the pleasure cross-somatic? [author's note]

53 Julia Kristeva, *The Powers of Horror: An Essay on Abjection*, trans. Leon S. Roudiez (New York: Columbia University Press, 1982), 1. [author's note]

54 *morphogeneses* Creations of forms.

that is doubly dangerous: simultaneously "exorbitant" and "quite close." Judith Butler calls this conceptual locus "a domain of unlivability and unintelligibility that bounds the domain of intelligible effects," but points out that even when discursively closed off, it offers a base for critique, a margin from which to reread dominant paradigms.[55] ...

THESIS VII: THE MONSTER STANDS AT THE THRESHOLD ... OF BECOMING

"This thing of darkness I acknowledge mine."

Monsters are our children. They can be pushed to the farthest margins of geography and discourse, hidden away at the edges of the world and in the forbidden recesses of our mind, but they always return. And when they come back, they bring not just a fuller knowledge of our place in history and the history of knowing our place, but they bear self-knowledge, *human* knowledge—and a discourse all the more sacred as it arises from the Outside. These monsters ask us how we perceive the world, and how we have misrepresented what we have attempted to place. They ask us to reevaluate our cultural assumptions about race, gender, sexuality, our perception of difference, our tolerance toward its expression. They ask us why we have created them.

(1996)

---

55 Judith Butler, *Bodies That Matter: On the Discursive Limits of "Sex"* (New York: Routledge, 1993), 22. Both Butler and I have in mind here Foucault's notion of an emancipation of thought "from what it silently thinks" that will allow "it to think differently." Michel Foucault, *The Use of Pleasure*, trans. Robert Hurley (New York: Vintage, 1985), 9.... [author's note]

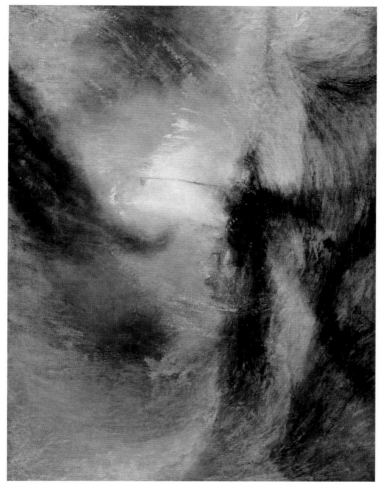

J.M.W. Turner, *Snow Storm—Steam-Boat off a Harbour's Mouth Making Signals in Shallow Water, and going by the Lead. The Author was in this Storm on the Night the Ariel left Harwich* (1842). See John Berger's "Turner and the Barber's Shop" in this anthology for a discussion of this and other Turner paintings.

Robert Capa, *After an Italo-German Air Raid* (winter of 1936–37). Images like this one are discussed in Virginia Woolf's *Three Guineas*, elsewhere in this anthology.

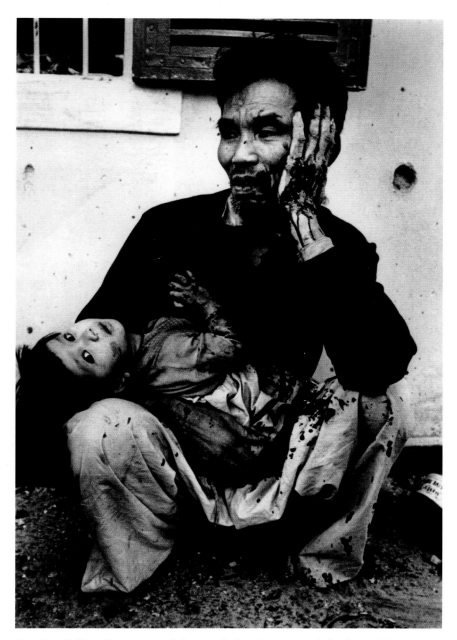

Don McCullin, *Vietnamese father and daughter wounded when U.S. Marines dropped hand grenades into their bunker, Têt offensive, Battle of Hué, Vietnam* (February 1968). See John Berger's "Photographs of Agony" in this anthology for a discussion of this photograph.

Diego Velázquez, *Portrait of Innocent X* (c. 1650). Francis Bacon painted dozens of re-interpretations of this famous portrait. One such reinterpretation appears below.

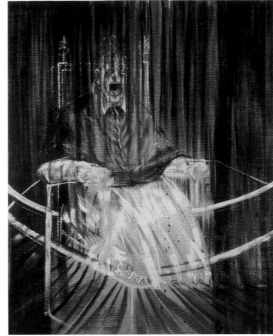

Francis Bacon, *Study after Velázquez's Portrait of Pope Innocent X* (1953). See the selection from Maggie Nelson's *The Art of Cruelty* in this anthology for a discussion of Bacon's work.

Mercy for Animals, *Overcrowding of turkeys found during an undercover investigation at a factory farm in North Carolina owned by Butterball* (2011). In this anthology, factory farming is discussed in the excerpt from Peter Singer's *Animal Liberation*, in Nathanael Johnson's "Is There a Moral Case for Meat?," and in the selection from Jonathan Safran Foer's *Eating Animals*.

Steve McCurry, *Holi festival, Rajasthan* (1996).

Steve McCurry, *Boy in Mid-Flight, Jodhpur* (2007).

Raghubir Singh, *Below the Howrah bridge a Marwari bride and groom after rites by the Ganges, Calcutta* (1968).

Raghubir Singh, *Pedestrians, Kemp's Corner, Mumbai* (1989). Teju Cole's "A Too-Perfect Picture," included in this anthology, offers a comparison of Singh's and McCurry's work. (Photographs copyright © 2016 Succession Raghubir Singh.)

Whitney Curtis, *Rashaad Davis, 23, backs away slowly as St. Louis County police officers approach him with guns drawn and eventually arrest him on Monday, Aug. 11, 2014, at the corner of Canfield Drive and West Florissant Avenue in Ferguson, Missouri*. This photograph originally appeared in *The New York Times*. For discussions of events in Ferguson in 2014, see Claudia Rankine's "The Condition of Black Life Is One of Mourning" and Nikole Hannah-Jones's "School Segregation: The Continuing Tragedy of Ferguson," both included in this anthology.

ALICE BECK KEHOE

TRANSCRIBING INSIMA,
A BLACKFOOT "OLD LADY"

Alice Beck Kehoe is a well-known anthropologist specializing in Native America, particularly in the cultures of the northwestern plains. In this essay, she interprets interviews that took place between Sue Sommers, a young anthropologist, and Insima, a South Piegan woman, as part of the Blackfoot Research Project of 1939–40. The interviews are archived at Marquette University.

S ue Sommers[1] had completed only one year of graduate work in anthropology at New York's Columbia University when she arrived in Browning, Montana, on the Blackfeet Indian Reservation* early in the summer of 1939. Ruth Benedict, her professor and organizer of the Columbia University Laboratory for ethnography, was already there, living in a tent. Sommers recalled that Professor Benedict had her sleeping bag on the ground, and was grateful when the young woman lent her an air mattress. Several other graduate students enrolled in the Laboratory project later became well-known anthropologists, including Oscar and Ruth Lewis, Esther Goldfrank, and Lucien Hanks and Jane Richardson, who later married (Goldfrank 1978:128). Benedict planned that they would divide and cover the four Blackfoot reserves, the North Blackfoot,

---

1   Sylvia Sue Roma Sommers, named after the women's rights activist Sylvia Pankhurst and Susan B. Anthony, was born in 1914 in Trenton, New Jersey, where her parents had immigrated from Russia. She earned a Bachelor of Arts in sociology from Hunter College in 1936, worked as a social worker in Harlem, and in 1938 enrolled in Columbia University's graduate program in anthropology. The following summer, at Ruth Benedict's invitation, she joined the Laboratory project on the Blackfeet Reservation.

Sommers served in World War II and afterward married Donald Dietrich, a psychoanalyst who, in 1948 and 1949, accompanied by Sue, did comparative psychology field research on three Plains reservations (one of them the Blackfeet). Sue Dietrich devoted herself to activities related to Quaker missions to promote peace, particularly a series of trips to Viet Nam and China. She visited the Blackfeet Reservation several times after the 1949 fieldwork with her husband, remaining in contact with the Yellow Kidney family. [Unless otherwise noted, all notes to this essay are those of the author.]

Blood, and North Piegan in Alberta, Canada, and the Blackfeet (South Piegan[2]) in Montana, comparing the four societies and investigating their histories. Sue Sommers joined fellow student Gitel Steed and her painter husband, Bob, at Two Medicine River on the Montana reservation. Benedict gave the inexperienced students the simplest of instructions: "See if you can establish contact with a family and live with them."

Sommers arrived on the reservation during the South Piegans' annual reunion, the North American Indian Days powwow. She dressed in jeans and commercial moccasins, twisted her long, thick hair into two braids, and went into the campground. A group of women, noticing her, exclaimed over her braids. A middle-aged man, Jim Little Plume, came over and escorted Sommers to the tipi of Yellow Kidney, then about 70 years old, where she was invited to sit beside the fire hospitably burning in the tipi. A tourist from Connecticut came in with his two sons, saying that he wanted his boys adopted into the tribe and given Indian names. The tourist took out a notebook and asked each person's name, writing down the replies. When he came to Sommers, Jim Little Plume spoke up, "She is Long Braids, she is my wife." As soon as the man departed, everyone in the tipi laughed heartily at the joke. Little Plume showed up daily to escort Sommers around the reservation, and every morning he placed a bouquet of wildflowers at her tent.

Yellow Kidney and his wife Insima (*I'nssimaa*, "Gardener, Planter") agreed to set up a large tipi next to their house for the Steeds and Sommers. Tipis are often erected in the summer to shelter a family's guests, and this tipi was so comfortable that Benedict preferred it to the accommodations of the other students on the Canadian reserves. In the evenings, the Steeds and Sommers often joined the Yellow Kidney family in their home. Officially, Yellow Kidney spoke only Blackfoot and required anthropologists to hire interpreters at 25 cents an hour, but after hours, his English proved adequate if not fluent, and he would comment on the day's interpreter. Yellow Kidney's neighbor and long-time comrade (*itakkaa*, "buddy," "partner") was Jappy Takes Gun On Top, who had been stepfather to D.C. Duvall, the half-Piegan collaborator with Clark Wissler on the American Museum series of ethnographies of the Blackfoot (Wissler and Duvall 1908). Yellow Kidney was half-brother to Jim's deceased father, the original Little Plume, and their families had been neighbors on Two Medicine River early in the century. Cuts Different, widow of that Little Plume, remained close to her brother-in-law.

Sommers wanted to interview the three women in the family: Insima, her daughter Agnes Chief All Over, and Cuts Different. Although she obediently

---

2   Piegan and Peigan are variants of Pikuni, the closest English spelling for the Blackfoot term *Piikani*. The South Piegan in Montana are the *Aamsskaapipiikani*.

recorded extended interviews with Yellow Kidney, Philip Wells, and other respected older men throughout July, in mid-August she began interviewing Agnes Chief All Over and her fascinating mother. Jim Little Plume had interpreted at first, but he was killed on 9 July when Bob Steed's roadster, in which he was a passenger, overturned rounding a dangerous curve. Agnes took over the task of interpreting, and gave Sommers pages of her own life history as well.

Insima was 72, the same age as her husband Yellow Kidney, and had the   5
Christian name Cecile. She had formerly been married to Yellow Wolf, more than 20 years her senior, who died at 82 about ten years before the Laboratory project. Insima was listed as "Cecile" in the 1907–08 Allotment Census, where her father is given as Isadore Sanderville, son of a non-Indian supposedly of the same name and a Piegan woman called Catch For Nothing. He had married Margaret, daughter of the Piegans Red Bird Tail and Twice Success. Cecile had two older brothers, Oliver and Richard (Dick), and a sister Louise (Mrs. John Crow in 1908). Dick Sanderville served on the Blackfeet Tribal Council as early as 1909.

Sue Sommers found Insima captivating. "Five by five feet," energetic and funny, and "really controlling, of the men, of everybody," Sommers recalled her. (One day, Insima picked up Sommers and threw her down, just in fun.) Insima much enjoyed imitating men, putting a pillow under her skirt to appear as a man's big paunch belly (see Appendix for one story of her joking). Her serious side was as a midwife and herb doctor. Sommers remembered her "running up and down the hills" picking medicinal herbs on one occasion while Sommers labored to get a car out of a stream crossing. Told of his wife's energy, Yellow Kidney remarked, "That's how she keeps in shape for when she wants to chase after men."

Ruth Benedict expected Sommers to take down Indians' life histories. Yellow Kidney's was an obvious choice, since he was a prominent elder in the community. Sue learned that as a young man Yellow Kidney had been in a circus, doing stunts on a horse, but the thick folder of typescript from days of interviews with him mentions nothing of this; instead, the practiced informant retold a list of Piegan bands, details of the All-comrades' societies, of the Sun Dance,* of bison hunting. Trying to take a life history, Sommers found that Yellow Kidney veered off into what she called "folktales," well-known stories of battles and the foundation myths for medicine bundles and their rituals (Wissler 1912). Yellow Kidney had become familiar with what anthropologists wanted, from George Bird Grinnell (e.g., 1892, 1901) in the late 1880s through Walter McClintock, Clark Wissler and Duvall (1908), and James Willard Schultz, who married into Yellow Kidney's community. Salvage ethnography* was the task, recording from the last generation to have lived as independent nations, experiencing the bison hunting, ceremonies, and warfare they lost when they settled upon the reservation in 1884. Personal histories were considered idiosyncratic, unscientific in the effort to obtain *the* culture of *the* tribe, and Yellow Kidney's circus exploits were definitely not subjects for a respected elder's recorded life history (cf. DeMallie 1984).

In accordance with the classic ethnographers' expectations that each "primitive" society had "a culture," whose tribal members hewed unthinking to a tradition passed on by their forebears over thousands of years,[3] Yellow Kidney told how it was supposed to have been. For example, "In buffalo days [there was] never a woman who vowed [the Sun Dance] and wasn't pure. Have that just lately. Only being very bad to family" (8/4/39:33). The technical word for Yellow Kidney's accounts is "normative."* Wissler (1971 [1938]:206) understood that Indians collaborated, for their own reasons, with their ethnographers in this skewed model: "The old people I knew came to adult life before reservation days and so saw the breakdown of tribal life and independence. Some of them were discouraged as to the future, but by living in the past and capitalizing their ancestral pride, they carried on."

MEN'S AND WOMEN'S BUSINESS

Yellow Kidney and Insima were each requested to dictate life histories to young "Long Braids." Sommers collected her interview material into one thick folder labeled "Yellow Kidney," another labeled "Insema," and thinner transcripts from other Piegans. With one small exception, the July interviews were all with men. On 1 August 1939, Sommers got five pages of typescript from Short Chief (Good Leader Woman?), identified only as a woman over 80 whose first husband had been Heavy Gun. After another week with Yellow Kidney, on 11 August Sommers interviewed Agnes Chief All Over. At last, from 16 to 18 August, she could work with Insima, Agnes Chief All Over interpreting.

In contrast to her husband's didactic presentations of "Plains Indian culture," Insima said nothing of battles and myths. Her reminiscences focused on who married whom, and how good, or bad, the husbands were. Both she and her daughter Agnes recalled their childhoods and especially their relationships to women and girls. Notably absent from Insima's interviews are data on midwifery or herb doctoring, the specialties for which she was well known in her community, or on how she managed her professional and familial commitments. Insima seems to have offered "women's business," that is, marital

---

3   One might term this the Holiday Fruitcake paradigm: firmly molded, dark, studded with traits, infused with spirits, ritually bestowed and hardly nibbled at until, at last, Civilization came and, by the hand of Acculturation, discarded it.

concerns and childrearing (Goldfrank 1978:140), in complement to the "men's business" of warfare and ritual performance presented by her husband.

"Insema Interviews" is the heading on the folder of typescripts. Immediately we are engrossed in a woman's account of coping with the actuality of reservation life. Men recited the glories of the "buffalo days"; for Insima, the real battles lay in surviving her nation's economic and political collapse. Sommers, if she had followed other mid-century anthropologists, might have labeled her recording of Insima's history a study of "acculturation," or how the Indian adopted a more Western style of life. Perhaps one factor in Sommers's neglect of publishing these field data was her inchoate understanding that the popular term was a biased, ethnocentric distortion of the indigenous nations' protracted contests with the invaders. From a First Nations' perspective, the Blackfoot adopted substitutes for their principal economic resource, the bison, and accepted opportunities to learn English, reading, and other means of dealing with the conquerors. To call these strategies "acculturation"—that is, moving *toward* Western culture—misses the essential point that indigenous people were struggling to *retain* as much of their heritage as possible under the much altered circumstances of the reservation.

Sommers's informants were members of a community formed out of the Grease Melters (translated "Fries" by Agnes Chief All Over; McClintock [1910:57] gives it as *Ich-poch-semo*), a band that dispersed onto farms around 1896, in Yellow Kidney's recollection (7/7/39:1). Sets of brothers formed its core: Yellow Kidney's father was a brother of the Three Suns (Big Nose), respected chief of the Grease Melters at the formation of the reservation in 1884. Yellow Kidney's half-brother was Little Plume, and Yellow Kidney had brought up his brother's son, Jim Little Plume, who became "Long Braids's" friend and guide. A young boy Sommers met, Buster Yellow Kidney, said to be *minipoka*, favorite child, to his maternal grandfather Yellow Kidney, today occupies the place of knowledgeable elder once held by that grandfather.

Insima's notion of a life history was a history of lives. She began the first lengthy interview with stories about her neighbor Running Owl (born 1859). Running Owl's daughter Susie and Insima's Agnes were close friends and they got married at the same time:

> When Agnes was 15 she wanted to get married and she did [to Sam Middle Calf]. Gave her a house. Had a bed on the floor. At same time Susie married [John] Calf Tail. Running Owl didn't like to see this. Running Owl would follow both girls. First night they went to bed he went in and sat and smoked and smoked. Had lamp lit and watched them all night for several nights. Johnny [Calf Tail] told Susie, "Since your Father doesn't want you to marry me, I'm going to leave you,"

and he did. Not long after that Susie was killed by Jim Little Plume. Agnes' husband left her also.

This is both personal and social history, documenting the early age and instability of marriage among the Blackfoot of the early reservation period. Sommers's experience as a social worker in Harlem* had prepared her to listen to accounts of lives quite different from those of most Columbia University students. Sommers's kind, gentle and attentive friend, Jim Little Plume, had, she was told at his funeral that July, "got up drunk one morning and shot his wife, child, and seven other people. He had been in prison for twenty years [but] he had gotten out before [Sommers] arrived and no one spoke of it to her; [she] was impressed at how accepting Indians are" (interview, 8/29/93). Sommers recalled, in 1993, that she and the Steeds attended Jim Little Plume's funeral, conducted by a priest. Two hundred people were there, she estimated, and Insima and Yellow Kidney "went over and gave prayers" in addition to the priest's service. Sommers went with a man named Yellow Owl to dig Jim's grave along the Two Medicine river (interview, 8/29/93). Half a century later, Sommers remembered Jim Little Plume fondly, and like the Indians, in our interview preferred not to dwell on the tragedies of his life. She had said to Insima at his wake, "Why hadn't you told me about his past?" Insima answered, "Would it have made a difference?" "That was one of the most important lessons I had ever learned," Sommers believed, "of great importance to my life."

INSIMA'S REMINISCENCES

15 Sommers's typescript for 16 August 1939 launched into "Indian's [Insima's] life." (Apparently Sommers initially misheard *I'nssimaa* as "Indian.") The young woman's transcription style of writing as rapidly as she could in English has the virtue of recording the stream of tale-telling. Sommers did not realize the importance of including her own queries in the text, so we can only guess where she asked for clarification or more information. Minor problems arise from Sommers's unfamiliarity with the dramatis personae* of the Reservation, and from Agnes's occasional tendency to give a literal but inappropriate translation: for example, saying "daughter" for what Insima likely termed *itan*. As Sommers's fellow students Hanks and Richardson [1945:31] noted for the North Blackfoot, the term *itan* also includes "(female speaker) daughter of sister; daughter of comrade ... first generation female descendant of husband's senior," and extends to *otanimm*, "emotionally attached as to a daughter, adopted as a daughter." Her linguistic naiveté led Sommers to write (8/16/39, p. 28) that Fine Shield Woman, Pikuni first wife of James Willard Schultz, was Agnes's "daughter," although elsewhere Insima noted that Agnes

was a year younger than Fine Shield Woman's son Hart; in English terminology, Fine Shield Woman was Agnes's first cousin. Occasionally, Agnes was careless using "he" versus "she," a common slip stemming from the fact that gender in the Blackfoot language distinguishes animate from inanimate, but not masculine from feminine.

Here is part of Insima's response—translated as she spoke by Agnes Chief All Over—to the ethnographer's request for her life history:

> Yellow Wolf [Insima's first husband] told father that he was going to Browning's Willow Creek to see if it was a good place to build a home. Moved with another family.
>
> Moved. Camped right where Browning is now.[4] Rode and looked Willow Creek over and decided on a place on which they can settle down, and soon to get cattle and cut hay.[5]
>
> Next day, moved to mountains to cut house logs ... and poles for corrals. When through, hauled them down as far as Browning on wagons. Build houses there. Finished. From there used to go to Old Agency for rations. Yellow Wolf got mowing machine, rake, and grindstone from government. Bear Paw joined them and asked, Why they didn't let them know they were going to move. Yellow Wolf thought, I wouldn't want to move. After [he] bought machinery a white man came—Mr. Stuart, he married an Indian woman. Told Yellow Wolf, "I heard about this place and you're going to have a lot of hay. Come to put it up for you so you can give me some." Agreed. First time [that] they learned how to cut hay and put it up. When through, put up corral and barn. Then heard some cattle was to be issued to them.
>
> Black Bear said, they should winter cattle at Cut Bank because here, there isn't much shelter. "We'll take hay down there."
>
> Yellow Wolf went to Old Agency. Each family got four cows and four calves regardless of size of families. They told him about milk and he knew how to milk and so did it right away, but didn't know how to make butter.
>
> North of Browning, they found a place [to winter cattle]—thick trees for good shelter. All three—yet—Black Bear and Bear Paw had hayracks and in no time had half the hay there. Sometimes made 3 trips a day. When enough hay there, they moved there. Made house there of cotton[wood] trees.

---

4   The Blackfeet Agency was transferred to Willow Creek, near Joe Kipp's trading post, in 1895, and the town of Browning grew up around Kipp's by 1900 (Farr 1984:40–42).

5   Cattle were issued to the Piegans beginning in 1890, as part of the 1886 treaty negotiations (Ewers 1958:307; Farr 1984:98).

[Insima] left Agnes because grandmother took Agnes and would[n't] let her go. Father agreed to let her stay and they go ahead. Will build house for them and then send for them.

Yellow Wolf went to agency and when he returned told wife to tell Mother [mother-in-law and son-in-law traditionally did not speak directly to one another] he wanted Agnes to go to school. Grandmother had Agnes—same story as for daughter. Didn't even know when she was brought to school. Policemen come around and collect children. Finally caught. Crying but taken to the school. Told that all children under six had to go to school, even if they were five or three—if older, whites claimed they were younger than they were.

When it occurred to Insima that Sommers would be unfamiliar with Blackfoot custom, she interjected explanations. For example, after mentioning how closely her second pregnancy followed Agnes's birth, she described methods of avoiding too-frequent pregnancies:

Usually don't have intercourse with husband a month or six weeks after that [childbirth]. Afraid of husband then—don't want to have another child right away but they usually do have a child every two years. After tenth day [after childbirth], going to get out of bed, they put entirely new clothes on. Mother gets any old lady [telling her] that her girl is getting out of bed and to go help her put them on. When old lady gets there, takes all the clothes off. Makes sweet smoke—blankets, moccasins, stocking, etc., and hold them over smoke and then puts the clothes on her. Paints girl's face. Not paid for this. This lady must be old enough to no longer have children. Take all the girl's old clothes that she wore in bed, blanket, and she keeps these. This is to keep the girl from being caught [pregnant] right away.

Agnes's "daughter" [that is, her *nitan. 'a*, Fine Shield Woman] was married to Mr. Schultz [James Willard Schultz]. Almost died when she gave birth to Hart Schultz. Potato [Fine Shield Woman's mother] went to Mother and asked her to help her daughter so she wouldn't have any more children. We almost lost her. Father agreed that something should be done. There was a round copper bracelet with a hole—put a buckskin string through it and put it on the woman's neck. Told her, if a dog has puppies don't pick up or take one (it's all right if they're older and running around) or you'll be caught then. Never did have another child.

[Insima's] Mother also fixed up Louis Champagne's wife for birth control. Mother didn't like to do it anymore—only helped—felt it was killing. Doesn't know where she learned how. She only had one child.

Later in the interviews, Insima indulged in reminiscences of her childhood:

Insema went hunting when she was very small. In winter went with Boy Chief and Louis Champagne [Yellow Wolf's nephews] and her far away husband [the term for sister's husband (Hanks and Richardson 1945:31)], Morning Plume. A far away husband never says anything out of the way before girl marries and girl does not know how to treat a far away husband.

It was a cold but a nice day. Before she knew how to ride, her Mother used to tie her on the horse. Boy Chief and Morning Plume and Yellow Wolf chased a buffalo. The sky was clear—not a cloud. After each killed a buffalo, they started to cut them up. Then the clouds started to come up like a smoke. Hurried because it looked bad. Insema had an extra horse with her and Morning Plume had four extra horses and so did Yellow Wolf. She had just followed Morning Plume to the hunt. As fast as they cut meat and packed on horses, the cloud was traveling fast. We started back. Blizzard came and it sure was cold. Many had gone buffalo hunting but in all different directions.

While going, her moccasin ripped on heel—all at once felt a sting—didn't know but her heel had frozen. Got lost and way above the camps and stood around and heard dogs barking down below. When they came home—they—Mother and Father—were sure mad at her. When I got off horse I just fell backwards. They had told me not to go but I wanted to go and pick out my own meat. When I go inside tipi, my heel started to thaw and burn badly but I was ashamed to say anything. Went to another old lady and told her, my heel froze. She took a dried gut, cooked it in a fire until brown. Chewed it and put it on the frozen heel. Didn't sting anymore. Next morning, my heel blistered. Put more gut on. Blisters broke—put more gut on.

Next day, heard one boy missing, never returned and many men went on hunt. Blizzard was over. It was the equinox and storm. Boy had frozen to death. His blanket coat was raggy and leggings torn. Horse was right by him.

[Insima] got a lot of meat from men, hind legs, ribs, heart, liver, kidney, and some guts and ribs. Men didn't mind that she had come. Many times she went in the summer—followed the men. Never went with Father. He would never get chance to go because he had two fast buffalo horses and some one would ask to borrow them and they would bring him meat.

Remembering hunting brought to mind the early reservation period when the bison herds disappeared:

People claimed they were being starved.... That was when they first learned to make a garden. Potatoes, rutabagas and carrots—about 57 years ago [1882]. Men plowed and women put in seeds. When first issued rations—flour, meat, bacon, rice, crackers, coffee, tobacco— big long plug, salt, tapioca—called it fish eggs. In fall when garden ready, issued it to them like rations. Have a great big slab of bacon. Scared of the flour because they found bones in it. Claim it was ghost bones—bones from human skeleton.[6] Had to use it but would pick bones out. When we started to eat it, two or three died every morning complaining of their stomachs. White man there [at Old Agency] with Indian wife who talked English and acted as interpreter [probably Malenda Wren (Farr 1984:29)].

Woman would tell them what husband dreamt last night, that he made two or three coffins and sure enough next morning he have to make that many coffins. Then buffalo all gone—no other way to live—not permitted to roam—had to stay right there. Think flour poisoned them. Didn't like smell of cows and so didn't like to eat them and didn't like so many different colored animals.

At Old Agency, women did all the work. Agent, Grey Beard, put out two saws and two axes and when he'd open up tool house all the women rush over. Hand out saw and tallest would grab, and same with rest. Pick out best friend to help her with the saw. Be 4 women with 2 axes. Usual to pay them paper money and white paper. The white paper was for sugar. Saw and axes would put up a cordwood and get $4 for one cordwood. Green paper—a dollar. Each get $4, and $1 for sugar.

Men would go up to mountains and haul timber for the agency. One with big load—get $7—way up to mountains. In those days wagons very scarce. Build little log houses. Wouldn't stand long and roofs broke in. Took men a long time to [learn how to] guide a team and how to put harness on. Put harness on up side down. An old man when first learning how to cut hay—didn't know he had to oil it [the machine]. Started to get hot and smoke. Had wife follow with a bucket of water to pour on it. Stand awhile till wife returned with water.

Horses and cattle increased fast. Had over 510 heads of cattle. Father have over 480 horses; he had no cattle. Agency didn't issue cattle to old people. Insema had 22 head of horses.

---

6   Rodent bones may have occurred in the flour. The necessity of shipping food long distances without refrigeration, the government practice of accepting the lowest bids, and chicanery from suppliers all contributed to the likelihood of contamination in flour and other rations.

Insema's fourth daughter was Molly. Molly was born one year after Yellow Wolf's fourth wife had left the family. Katie was the fifth child. She was born three years later. A third daughter had died when she was nine years. (Couldn't remember her name—she had no Indian name.) She had died of pneumonia. Her clothes and toys were buried with her. Molly died when Fannie [Molly's daughter] was very small and Insema raised her. Fannie went to school, staying in dormitory, [and got pregnant by] the principal. Blamed it on young Indian man because she didn't want to get the principal in trouble. He sent Fannie to Minot, ND and he paid all expenses and hospital fees there.

Husband [Yellow Wolf] got a salary as a policeman, but the amount was forgotten. He was paid every month. He never actually quit, nor was he fired, but he just didn't return to work. He wasn't paid after he failed to return to work. The salary was stopped after they had moved to Willow Creek. They were living at Willow Creek when Yellow Wolf died. At the time of Yellow Wolf's death, they had both a house and a tent. Yellow Wolf and Insema lived in the tent. Emma and her husband John Little Plume [not related to Yellow Wolf's brother] lived in the house, with Emma's husband's father and mother. Katie and her husband ([Paul] Home Gun), Agnes, her second husband James Big Top and her daughter Mary, lived in Yellow Wolf's tent.

Everyone was there because Yellow Wolf was very rich, and he knew he was going to die. Those who lived there all the time were Insema, Yellow Wolf and Mary, with Emma and her husband in their own house. (No one lived in Yellow Wolf's house throughout the summer.) Yellow Wolf died at 82 [c. 1927]. He did not die of any illness. He had been shot in war, a little below the shoulder, and the bullet had never been removed. It had swelled and finally burst inside. He [Insima?] cut her hair.[7]

She kept everything. All Yellow Wolf's clothes were put in a sack and buried with him, together with all his little things, pipe, tobacco, matches. He had given his saddle away while he was still alive, and had refused to ride again. Insema gave it to her father. Mrs. Powell— a white woman married to a fullblood—took her to Browning. She stayed with the woman less than a year. She did nothing at all. The woman's daughter-in-law did all the cooking and called them when food was ready. Her other two daughters came after them to eat. Insema did not pay anything for her keep during the time she was there.

---

7   It was Blackfoot custom that close family members, particularly widows, cut off their hair as a sign of grief and mourning. (Note Agnes's slip in choosing the English pronoun, since Blackfoot uses one animate form for both masculine and feminine.)

When father was living, Insema did a lot of work for her, beading and making repairs for her. This woman asked to take Insema home with her because she was older and felt Insema would be happier with her than with her children, who were young and often went out. Insema took only [her granddaughter] Mary with her.

When Agnes had her baby, Insema was nearby but not present. Every time Agnes suffered, she had to run out and cry. Thus she was constantly running in and out. However, she was present at the second birth. (It is always like this—mothers hate to be present at the first birth their daughter has. Mother might stay if she felt others are not helping enough and she can do more for her daughter, everyone thinks she is brave in such a case.) There was no medicine smoke at that time, it had been stopped by the [blank: agent or priest?]. If the girl suffers for two or three days, they make a [blank] to bring child right away. Medicine man and wife called on Agnes to change clothes and make medicine so that she does not have another child soon. His wife took care of changing her clothes, and he painted her face yellow. Gave her no medicine or anything to wear. Told her that if she let no one wear her shawl she would not have another baby right away. He lied, for she had one three years later, and she so informed him. He was paid with a work horse.

Insema adopted Mary after Agnes left her husband. She left in the summer and remarried in the fall. Agnes's new husband told Agnes to let Mother and Father keep Mary since they already had her. "Sometimes we'll take her home with us." Mary got used to her grandparents. Agnes got her clothes and shoes. Insema cared very little when Agnes left her first husband, because she knew he drank and gambled away the cattle and horses; he would never gather wood or go to work. Glad to be rid of him.

If grandparents love their grandchildren and feel that they can take better care of them than their parents, the mother cannot object. Nowadays, it is not necessary to go to court in order to adopt grandchildren. However, to adopt an unrelated orphan, it is necessary to go to court and pay $25.00. The child is then registered in your name and when you die, your property goes to adopted children.

Glad she picked out second husband because he was known as a good man. Agnes knew the second husband [James Big Top] when he was married to Minnie. They would come and stay several nights. Minnie's mother came down for a week. Minnie used to say he was good to her, but his mother was mean to her. Agnes didn't speak much to him. Heard later that Minnie had quit him.

Agnes met him in town, Browning, one day and he asked if she was going back to her husband. When she told him she was not, he asked her to marry him. She said nothing. He asked her again every time he met her. Told mother first time he asked. She finally said yes but said she had heard his mother was mean. He said she acted that way to Minnie because Minnie was running around with his brothers.

When Agnes married her second husband, Insema stopped the taboo [against mother- and son-in-law speaking]. Agnes and husband would visit her, but son-in-law and mother-in-law never spoke to each other. Agnes told her, "You should stop avoiding your son-in-law, it's unusual, you should think of your son-in-law as your son." She was glad not to have to avoid her son-in-law because now he could visit her. She thought of how she had had to avoid her first son-in-law and she would have to go out—only one place in tipi and both couldn't be present. Liked the new arrangement.

Mary [Middle Calf, Agnes's daughter, born 1902] got married that year. Agnes's first husband picked the man for her. Agnes knew nothing about it. She lived quite a distance from Mary. Nobody told Insema about it—she found out about it from others. When Yellow Wolf died, Mary's father came and took her home, and it was during that time that she was married.

Jack, Mary's husband, had given no gifts when he married. (That is not done anymore, Mary got nothing from anyone until later on. Insema started getting bedding, furnishing and tent for her.) Mary did not know Jack before they were married. They were both young.

Six years after Yellow Wolf died, Yellow Kidney's wife died. Insema had not known Yellow Kidney before she married him. His wife was the same age as Insema. Insema went to Browning and while there went to visit an old lady, Mrs. Bird. While she was visiting, Walter McGee and John Mountain Chief, policemen, came in and told her she was wanted at the Indian Agency. She wondered whether she had done something wrong and was under arrest. Decided to go and find out what it was about. Mrs. Bird told her that she would go there with her when Mrs. Bird had finished her cooking. They both went. They found a place, a small room, and Yellow Kidney waiting there. Yellow Kidney didn't know either what they wanted with him. They had just brought them together there.[8] "Wonder if they came after me over that man." They gave me a chair and told me to sit down. They placed her on one side of the desk and Yellow Kidney on the other.

---

8   This passage shows the paternalism of the reservation Agent, treating mature widowed men and women as if they were too feckless to make suitable living arrangements.

Another policeman, Mr. Tevenus, started to talk to her. He said, "We sent for you because you are going to marry that man." She didn't wish to marry him—she had never known him before (she was very young at the time of her first marriage, and hadn't known any better). They said she wouldn't have to be rustling for herself, and she'd have someone to help her and do things for her. She didn't answer. Walter McGee started to talk kindly to her. Asked her if she had made up her mind. She told them, "The reason I am saying nothing is that I have children and grandchildren and Yellow Kidney might not like them." They said, "The reason we brought you together was that we thought you two would get along together. You are both good workers and will have a nice home soon." They wouldn't let her go until she said yes. Yellow Kidney had been listening to all this. His wife had died only two weeks before.

She said, "It's up to him to say whether he wants to marry me." They started to talk to him. Yellow Kidney said he'd marry her.

I went home but not with him. After I went out they told him to go where I was staying. He came there in a rig. He brought lots of grub, dress goods, a blanket and a shawl. When she got home she explained to Mary and Jack. They told her to marry him.

"I'd like to marry him but he's stranger and I feel ashamed."

Yellow Kidney: "I have some things for you and you can take all that's in the rig." When Yellow Kidney's wife had died they had taken everything that belonged to his wife. Mary Little Plume took all the cooking utensils. Stayed with Mary and Jack quite a while, when finally Yellow Kidney suggested they fix up his place for their own. They came here and cleaned up the place.

20   We can leave Insima here. She went on to tell of the marriage of her youngest daughter Katie to Paul Home Gun, "a good worker" who "never drinks or gambles," and Agnes's marriage to George Chief All Over after Agnes's second husband died. She also told stories of jealous husbands, and of the adventure of a mistreated Blackfoot youth and his orphaned comrade, who went over the mountains to the Flathead Valley and returned with two Salish Flathead women escaping from cruel husbands. This story resembles men's standard tales of war exploits, except that Insima emphasized the Salish women's active participation in the escape.

Insima's reminiscences are first-hand accounts of the early reservation period that in recent years has increasingly drawn historians' interest. Because scholars during that time were engaged in salvage ethnography, there was little contemporary description outside official documents and newspapers, and particularly little directly and candidly from Indians. The memoir Sommers transcribed is doubly rare because it is from a woman speaking freely and at length.

How valid is this document? Discourse analysis, formerly confined to linguistics, has entered general anthropology and made us more sensitive to the parameters of ethnographic work, to "issues of power and perspective, questions of how authoritative knowledge is legitimated, of self-awareness and authenticity of voice in the presentation of data, and of the constraints of the historical and cultural contexts within which knowledge develops" (Rubinstein 1991:12–13). In 1939, these issues were stuff for the researcher to grapple with before reaching the final draft of a monograph: it was unseemly to expose one's struggles. The persona one presented in print, to the public, was the aloof observer before whose magisterial gaze the events of the field fell into orderly categories. Sommers, who had been a social worker before entering graduate school, could not maintain such an objective analytical stance. World War II pre-empted her personal crisis over a career decision, and after the war she engaged herself in international social activism. Her 1939 typescripts remained raw data.

Rubinstein identifies a "folktale" (as Sommers would have called it) told within the profession of American anthropology, about naive graduate students supposedly cast into the field with only a blank notebook, to flounder about, shiver and shake, until a kind Native adopted them and taught them what they ought to know. Fifty years later, Sommers remembered herself as such a stereotypical innocent. But as Rubinstein points out (1991:14), all those graduate students who *felt*, as they arrived in a strange land, like babes cast adrift, had in fact been prepared by years of academic study of scientific observation and social analysis. They had all read the classics of ethnography *and* heard their professors informally tell their own field experiences. Benedict's instruction, as Sommers recalled it, seemed maddeningly simplistic, yet Sommers knew, from the seminars she took, what an ethnographer was expected to do once he or she "establishes contact with a family and lives with them." Her professor was on the reservation, ready to listen to her students' experiences and suggest how they might proceed. Sommers's fellow student Jane Richardson recalled that they

> sought out the tribal elders to obtain their recollections of Blackfoot life in more free-spirited times. The old ones liked to talk for hours about war deeds, or the sadly vanishing religion of the medicine bundles (Hoffman 1988:118).

This was, Richardson explained, "the formal method of anthropological research [she] had learned ... at Columbia" (Hoffman 1988:118).

In Sommers's typescripts we have admired a Blackfoot's matron's *story*, in every sense of that word, told to a young woman who showed herself respectful, empathetic, and fascinated by the lively "Old Lady." Insima, who had listened for too many years to men's stories of war and prescriptions of correct ritual, wanted young Long Braids to hear and record the affairs of real life, how Blackfoot people *lived*. *I'nssimaa*, the Gardener, would plant, would cultivate, a text on women's business—the business of maintaining life. Sommers had paid her dues for more than a month, dutifully recording the standard accounts of men; now, the feminist consciousness nourished in her childhood could resonate with her hostess's Blackfoot pride in womanly accomplishments. Sommers's transcript is perhaps naive in that she made no effort to learn the Blackfoot language (which is difficult for English speakers), she put on paper only the translated formal interviews with no minutiae of context, and she left out her own presence, her queries, her reactions.

25   As a straightforward narrative, however, Sommers's "Insema" folder documents both Blackfoot history and women's history. Its particulars reverberate against dry official archives and sweeping summaries. It is only *a* text, one woman's selected memories, but we owe gratitude to Ruth Benedict who let her student work in a much less-traveled way; to Sue Sommers who persisted; and especially to Insima and her daughter Agnes who wanted their stories to be history.

Conclusion

Insima's narratives convey the spirit with which the Piegans adapted to the new economy, carefully selecting ranch land and moving into cabins once they could no longer obtain sturdy bison skins for tipis. Insima partnered her husband in hauling wood and ranching while her mother, according to Blackfoot custom, cared for Insima's young child. It was hard for Insima's mother to see the granddaughter constrained by dresses, shoes, school buildings, kept from the outdoor exercise and work that make women strong. The older woman's fears of sickness were well founded, for mortality rates, especially among children, were appalling in the early reservation period. Yet, in spite of the terrible toll taken by malnutrition and diseases after the collapse of their indigenous economy, the Piegans maintained their communities throughout the radical step of becoming ranchers in widely separated hamlets along the prairie streams.

Clark Wissler (1971[1938]:239) remarked, "so far as I could see, the morale of the women was far less shattered [by reservation life] and it was they who saved tribal life from complete collapse." Wissler may very well have met Insima; his collaborator Duvall commissioned her in 1904 to make a cradleboard for the American Museum collections.[9] His evaluation of women's business on the reservation seems well borne out by Sommers's transcript of her interviews with Insima.

APPENDIX: INSIMA PLAYS THE DIRTY WHITE MAN

[Interview of 8-17-39 or 8-18-39, Insima speaking, Agnes Chief All Over interpreting]

She [Insima] was picking [choke]cherries. There was an old lady "Steals Good" heard that another old lady had almost been raped. She got mad and said "I wish I had been there with my butcher knife." She was grinding cherries as she spoke. As she spoke she shook her big butcher knife. Insima thought "I'll see what you can do." Mary and Jack were camping there too. Told Mary "I'm going to play a trick on her. When you see me go to her out of the brush you tell her you're going to the house to put the baby to sleep." Insima went in the tent and put Yellow Kidney's pants on. Cut the fur off a pair of old chaps. Rubbed syrup all over her chin and pasted the fur all over chin and cheeks. Put coat on and dish towel around her head. Put her hair up under an old hat.

Went way around and from east walked up to camp. When Mary saw her she said her piece. She [Steals Good] was facing the grinding. Insima said "Hello." She looked up and said "Hello." Made signs "Eat some of these cherries, they're good." Took some and spit them out and said "No good."

"They're good." Stopped grinding and started backing away. She moved near her and drew her near and said "Lot of fat, lot of fat." "No, no, I haven't any meat." Insima grabbed her any place—kept yelling, "No good, no good." She kept hollering for Insima to come—half crying. She kept calling for Mary. Insima had her around the waist and reached under her dress and she cried out. She hollered and hollered. Insima held her tight and pushed her. She cried. Mary finally came running. Insima had an old axe over her shoulder and had dropped it. Insima was holding her under one leg to lift her. Mary was pushing them apart, talking English.

She grabbed the axe and said to Mary "Here's his axe—that dirty white man. I'm going to give it to Jack so he'll know."

---

9   Duvall wrote Wissler, "Mrs. Yellow Wolf is making the Baby Board and her mother is making the dog travois" (letter of 12 October 1904), then on 10 November "Mrs. Yellow Wolf, and Boy, also failed to make some of the things" (Wissler papers, American Museum of Natural History).

Insima circled around to her tent and washed and changed. "What's wrong? I was picking cherries across the river and heard you screaming." Steals Good bawled her out. Asked her which way did white man go? Mary said "Down that way?"

Insima: "Why didn't you grab your knife?" "Well, right from the start he grabbed me and threw me down, and I never thought of my knife. There's his axe, I'm going to give it to my son."

"It was me. I wanted to see if you'd use your knife."

Old lady took after her and did grab her.

(1996)

References

Benedict, Ruth
1939   Letter to Oscar and Ruth Lewis. Unpublished, in possession of Ruth M. Lewis, Urbana, IL.

DeMallie, Raymond J., ed.
1984   *The Sixth Grandfather: Black Elk's Teachings Given to John G. Neihardt*. Lincoln: University of Nebraska Press.

Dietrich, Sue Sommers
1939   Field Notes, Blackfeet Indian Reservation, Montana. Typescript in author's possession.
1993   Interview with Alice B. Kehoe, 29 August 1993, in Dietrich's home in Olympia Fields, IL.

Ewers, John C.
1958   *The Blackfeet: Raiders on the Northwestern Plains*. Norman: University of Oklahoma Press.

Farr, William E.
1984   *The Reservation Blackfeet, 1882–1945*. Seattle: University of Washington Press.

Goldfrank, Esther S.
1978   *Notes on an Undirected Life*. Flushing, NY: Queens College Publications in Anthropology, no. 3.

Grinnell, George Bird
1892   *Blackfoot Lodge Tales*. New York: Charles Scribner's Sons. See *American Anthropologist* o.s., 1896, 9:286–87; n.s. 1899, 1:194–96; 1901, 3:650–68 ("The Lodges of the Blackfoot").

Hanks, Lucien M., Jr., and Jane Richardson
1945   *Observations on Northern Blackfoot Kinship*. Monograph 9, American Ethnological Society. Seattle: University of Washington Press.

Hoffman, Edward
1988   *The Right to Be Human: A Biography of Abraham Maslow*. Los Angeles: Jeremy P. Tarcher.

McClintock, Walter
1910   *The Old North Trail*. Lincoln: University of Nebraska Press (1968 Bison Book facsimile reprint).

Rubinstein, Robert A.

1991 *Introduction. In Fieldwork: The Correspondence of Robert Redfield & Sol Tax.* Boulder, CO: Westview Press.

Schultz, James Willard (Apikuni)

1907 *My Life as an Indian.* New York: Forest and Stream.

1962 *Blackfeet and Buffalo.* Keith C. Seele, ed. Norman: University of Oklahoma Press.

1974 *Why Gone Those Times? Blackfoot Tales.* Eugene Lee Silliman, ed. Norman: University of Oklahoma Press.

Wissler, Clark

1911 *The Social Life of the Blackfoot Indians.* Anthropological Papers, vol. 7, pt. 1, 1–64. New York: American Museum of Natural History.

1912 *Ceremonial Bundles of the Blackfoot Indians.* Anthropological Papers, vol. 7, pt. 2, 65–289. New York: American Museum of Natural History.

1971 [1938] *Red Man Reservations.* New York: Collier. (Originally published 1938 as *Indian Cavalcade or Life on the Old-Time Indian Reservations* by Sheridan House.)

Wissler, Clark, and D.C. Duvall

1908 *Mythology of the Blackfoot Indians.* Anthropological Papers, vol. 2, pt. 1, 1–163. New York: American Museum of Natural History.

RICHARD RODRIGUEZ

[SAN DIEGO AND TIJUANA]

An unconventional and sometimes controversial figure in American letters, Rodriguez first attracted attention with his 1982 book, Hunger of Memory, *an account of his upbringing that also touches on large cultural issues such as bilingualism and assimilation. As someone steeped both in Mexican and in American culture, Rodriguez has been well-placed to comment on the differences, similarities, and connections between the two.*

The commentary on San Diego and Tijuana* included here is an excerpt from the adapted text of a 1997 interview with Scott London that was originally aired on the public radio series "Insight & Outlook." The written version of the interview has appeared either in full or in abridged form under various titles, including "Crossing Borders: An Interview with Richard Rodriguez" and "A View from the Melting Pot: An Interview with Richard Rodriguez." Rodriguez is responding here to London's suggestion that the combination of Tijuana and San Diego "offers a glimpse of what America might look like in another generation or two."

Talk about alter ego: Tijuana was created by the lust of San Diego. Everything that was illegal in San Diego was permitted in Tijuana. When boxing was illegal in San Diego, there were boxing matches in Tijuana; when gambling was illegal, there was always Tijuana. Mexicans would say, "We're not responsible for Tijuana; it's the Americans who created it." And there was some justification for that. But, in fact, the whore was a Mexican, the bartender a Mexican. Tijuana was this lovely meeting of Protestant hypocrisy with Catholic cynicism: the two cities went to bed and both denied it in the morning.

To this day, you will see American teenagers going to Mexico on Saturday nights to get drunk. Mexico gives them permission. The old Southern Catholic tradition gives permission to the Northern Protestant culture to misbehave. But what has happened in the last generation is that Tijuana has become a new Third World capital—much to the chagrin of Mexico City, which is more and more aware of how little it controls Tijuana politically and culturally. In addition to whorehouses and discos, Tijuana now has Korean factories and Japanese industrialists and Central American refugees, and a new Mexican bourgeoisie that takes its lessons from cable television.

And then there is San Diego—this retirement village, with its prim petticoat, that doesn't want to get too near the water. San Diego worries about all the turds washing up on the lovely, pristine beaches of La Jolla.[1] San Diego wishes Mexico would have fewer babies. And San Diego, like the rest of America, is growing middle-aged. The average age in the U.S. is now thirty-three, whereas Mexico gets younger and younger, retreats deeper and deeper into adolescence. Mexico is fifteen. Mexico is wearing a Hard Rock Cafe T-shirt* and wandering around Tijuana looking for a job, for a date, for something to put on her face to take care of the acne.

It is not simply that these two cities are perched side by side at the edge of the Pacific; it is that adolescence sits next to middle age, and they don't know how to relate to each other. In a way, these two cities exist in different centuries. San Diego is a post-industrial city talking about settling down, slowing down, building clean industry. Tijuana is a preindustrial city talking about changing, moving forward, growing. Yet they form a single metropolitan area.

(1997)

from DARLING

Rodriguez has been described in The New Yorker *as perhaps "the most empathetic essayist in America." The essays brought together to form the chapters of his book* Darling: A Spiritual Autobiography, *were written, as he recounts in his Note to the Reader that prefaces the book, "in the years after September 11, 2001—years of religious extremism throughout the world, years of rising public atheism, years of digital distraction." Rodriguez writes as a Christian and, more specifically, as a Roman Catholic, but he declares himself to be a kindred spirit as well of Jews and Muslims—also, in his view, believers in "the desert God."*

The excerpt here is from the chapter in Darling: A Spiritual Autobiography *that is entitled "Darling"; the same excerpt was published as an article in the July 2013 issue of* Harper's Magazine.

---

1   *La Jolla*   Fashionable coastal area of San Diego.

A middle-aged woman in a brown wool suit tapped my shoulder after mass. She knew my name. She said she had read an interview I gave to an online magazine on the gay-marriage controversy in California. At that time, a Catholic archbishop had colluded with officials from the Church of Jesus Christ of Latter-day Saints[2] in a campaign to protect the sacred institution of marriage from any enlarging of its definition (including civil marriage, which the Catholic Church does not recognize as sacramentally valid). Campaign checks to be made payable to the Knights of Columbus.

The Knights of Columbus is a fraternal lay organization sanctioned by the Catholic Church. The Knights are an admirable bunch of guys—I believe "guys" is the right word—who spend many hours performing works of charity. On festival days, the Knights get themselves up with capes and swords and plumed hats like a comic-opera militia.

The woman in the brown suit did not say she agreed with my comments in the article; she did not say she disagreed. She said, "I am a Dominican nun;[3] some days I cannot remember why."

I will stay in the Church as long as you do, I said.

Chummy though my reply was, it represented my abrogation of responsibility to both the Church and the nun.

A gay man easily sees himself as expendable in the eyes of the Church hierarchy because that is how he imagines the Church hierarchy sees him. The Church cannot afford to expel women. Women are obviously central to the large procreative scheme of the Church. Women have sustained the Church for centuries by their faith and their birthrates. Following the sexual scandals involving priests and children, women may or may not consent to present a new generation of babies for baptism. Somewhere in its canny old mind, the Church knows this. Every bishop has a mother.

It is because the Church needs women that I depend on women to protect the Church from its impulse to cleanse itself of me.

I shook hands with the Dominican nun and we parted.

But even as I type these words, the Vatican has initiated a campaign against American nuns who (according to the Congregation for the Doctrine of the Faith) promote "radical feminist themes" and who remain silent regarding their Excellencies' positions on women's reproductive rights and homosexuality. A nun's silence is interpreted as dissent in this instance.

The Church—I say the Church but I mean the male church—is rather shy in the presence of women, even as the God of Scripture is rather shy of women.

---

2   *the Church ... Saints*   Mormon Church.

3   *Dominican nun*   Catholic nun of the Dominican order, which emphasizes spiritual contemplation.

God will make a bond of friendship with a hairy patriarch. God interferes with Sarah through her husband.[4] God courts Mary by an angel.[5]

And yet the God of intention entered history through a woman's body (reversing the eye of the needle[6]). The Church, as she exists, is a feminine act, intuition, and pronoun: the Christian Church is the sentimental branch of human theology. (I mean that as praise.) The Church watches the progress of Jesus with the same sense of his heartbreaking failure as did the mother who bore him. In John's account of the wedding at Cana, Mary might be played with maximum flibbertigibbetry* by Maggie Smith.[7] Jesus struggles to extricate his legs from the banquet table in the courtyard; his companions can't help sniggering a bit. The first showing of Jesus' power over Nature, the changing of water into wine, makes no clear theological sense. But as the first Comic Mystery, the scene makes perfect domestic sense. Jesus is instructed by his mother.

The women who educated me—Catholic nuns belonging to the Irish order of the Sisters of Mercy—looked very much like Afghan village women. They wore veils, long skirts, long sleeves, laced black shoes—Balenciagas[8] all.

Of the many orders of Catholic nuns founded in nineteenth-century Europe, the majority were not cloistered orders but missionary orders—nursing and teaching orders. Often the founders came from upper-middle-class families, but most of the women who swelled the ranks had left peat-fumed, sourstomached, skinny-cat childhoods behind. They became the least sequestered women imaginable.

It was in the nineteenth century, too, that secular women in Europe and North America formed suffrage movements, following in the footsteps of missionary nuns and Protestant missionary women. Curiously, it was the burkalike habits* nuns wore—proclaiming their vows of celibacy—that lent them protection in the roustabout world, also a bit of a romantic air.

---

4   *God interferes ... husband*   See Genesis 17, in which God speaks about Sarah to her husband Abraham.

5   *God courts ... angel*   God sends the angel Gabriel to inform Mary that she will give birth to Jesus (see Luke 1.26–46).

6   *eye of the needle*   See Matthew 19.24: "It is easier for a camel to go through the eye of a needle, than for a rich man to enter into the kingdom of God."

7   *John's ... Cana*   In John 2, Jesus is the guest at a wedding where the hosts have run out of wine, and he provides more wine (by miraculously transforming water) at his mother's request;   *Maggie Smith*   British actor (b. 1934); in the latter part of her career, she has become particularly well known for playing respectable older women.

8   *Balenciagas*   Reference to Balenciaga, a European fashion designer.

15   When seven Irish Sisters of Mercy (the oldest twenty-five) disembarked in San Francisco in December 1854, they found a city filled with dispirited young men and women who had followed the legend of gold.[9] The Sisters of Mercy spent their first night in California huddled together in St. Patrick's Church on Mission Street; they had no other accommodation. In the morning, and for months afterward, the sisters searched among the wharves and alleys of San Francisco, ministering to men, women, and children they found.

The *Christian Advocate,* an anti-Catholic newspaper, published calumny* about the nuns; the paper declared them to be women of ill repute and opined that they should move on—nobody wanted them in San Francisco.

In 1855 the Sisters of Mercy nursed San Franciscans through a cholera outbreak. In 1868 the nuns cared for victims of a smallpox epidemic. In 1906, after the great earthquake and fire, the Sisters of Mercy evacuated hundreds of the sick and the elderly to Oakland across the bay. Officials in the nineteenth century invited all religious orders to ride San Francisco's buses and cable cars free of charge because of the city's gratitude to the Sisters of Mercy.

As they had done in Ireland, the Sisters of Mercy opened orphanages, schools, and hospitals in California and throughout the United States. By the time our American mothers caught up with the nuns in the 1960s—with the possibility of women living fulfilling lives independent of family or marriage—the nuns had discarded their black robes in favor of sober pedestrian attire. Vocation has nothing to do with dress-up.

Veiled women were seldom thereafter seen on the streets of America or in European cities, not until the influx of immigrant Muslim women from North Africa and the Middle East in the 1980s.

20   A shadow of scandal now attaches in Ireland to the Sisters of Mercy. An Irish government report released in 2009 documents decades of cruelty perpetrated particularly on children of the working class in orphanages and homes for unwed mothers run by the Sisters of Mercy. One cannot doubt or excuse the record. The record stands.

The Sisters of Mercy of the Americas—the women I revere—are fewer and older. The great years of the order seem to have passed, but the Sisters continue their ministry to the elderly, to immigrants, to the poor. The Sisters are preparing for a future the rest of us have not yet fully comprehended—a world of increasing poverty and misery—even as they prepare for their absence from the close of the twenty-first century.

Nuns will not entirely disappear from San Francisco as long as we may occasionally glimpse a black mustache beneath a fluttering veil. The Sisters of Perpetual Indulgence are an order of drag* nuns whose vocation is dress-up.

---

9   *dispirited ... gold*   The California Gold Rush began in 1848 and lasted into the mid-1850s.

Like the Sisters of Mercy in early California, the Sisters of Perpetual Indulgence took up their mission in bad repute. Unlike the Sisters of Mercy, the Sisters of P.I. have done everything in their power to maintain a bad repute.

They have their detractors. I was one. I wrote against them because I saw them as mocking heroic lives. Thirty years ago I had lunch with Jack Fertig, a.k.a. Sister Boom Boom, in a taqueria on Mission Street.* He arrived wearing jeans and a T-shirt. On the wall at the rear of the restaurant was a crucifix—not, I assumed, ironic. The nun in mufti* approached the crucifix and fell to his knees. He blessed himself; he bowed his head. Whether this was done for my benefit I don't know. There was no follow-up, no smirk, no sheepishness, no further demonstration of piety. I did not question him about it; I was astonished. But, as I say, I wasn't taken in.

Before he died, Jack Fertig converted to Islam.   25

A few years ago, I stood on a street corner in the Castro;* I watched as two or three Sisters of P.I. collected money in a coffee can for one of their charities. Their regalia looked haphazard on that day—jeans and tennis shoes beneath their skirts, like altar boys. I couldn't help but admire how the louche nuns encouraged and cajoled the young men and women who approached. The Sisters' catechism involved sexual precaution and drug safety, with plenty of trash repartee so as not to spook their lambs: "Do you have a boyfriend, honey? Are you getting enough to eat? Where do you sleep? Are you compliant with your meds?"

I experienced something like a conversion: Those men are ministering on a street corner to homeless teenagers, and they are pretty good at it. No sooner had I applied the word "good" than I knew it was the right word. Those men are good.

The Sisters of Perpetual Indulgence do what nuns have always done: they heal; they protect; they campaign for social justice; they perform works of charity. The Sisters of Perpetual Indulgence have an additional mission: they scandalize.

For example, on Easter Sundays, the Sisters host the Hunky Jesus Contest in Dolores Park. The Sisters and their congregation seem to be interested only in satirizing the trappings of S&M* already available in Roman Catholic iconography. (One cannot mock a crucifixion; crucifixion is itself mockery.)

I do not believe the Sisters of Perpetual Indulgence are enemies of the   30
Church; I believe they are a renegade church of true vocation. They are scourges; they are jesters. Their enemy is hypocrisy. In a way, they are as dependent on the Church as I am. They are as dependent on the nun in a brown wool suit as I am. Without the Church, without the nun, they would make no sense at all.

"He" is the default setting in scripture—Jewish, Christian, Islamic. The perception, the preference, the scriptural signifier, the awe of the desert religions, is of a male God. Father. Abba. Lord. Jesus refers to God always as Father, though he insists that God is spirit. Yahweh is unnameable but for the name He (as I was going to write) gives Himself: *I Am.*[10] There is no "He" in *I Am.* The theologian John L. McKenzie proposes that a more accurate translation of the holy name might be: *He brings into being.* Bringing into being was a potency that the prophets, the evangelists, the compilers of scripture, conceived anthropomorphically as male.

In the desert cultures of the Middle East, religious communities regard homosexual acts as abominations—unnatural, illegal, unclean. But homosexual behavior does not preclude marriage or fatherhood. The notion of a homosexual identity is a comic impossibility. What alone confers an appropriate sexual identity on the male is fatherhood.

Two young men fussing over a baby girl in a stroller. You were not charmed. You said no straight man would make that kind of fuss.

No straight woman, either, Darling.

35   The new gay stereotype is domestic, child rearing—homosexuals willing to marry at a time when the heterosexual inclination is to dispense with marriage.

Divorce rates in the United States and Europe suggest that women are not happy with the relationships they have with men, and vice versa. And whatever that unhappiness is, I really don't think gay people are the cause. On the other hand, whatever is wrong with heterosexual marriage does have some implication for homosexuals.

The majority of American women are living without spouses. My optimism regarding that tabulation is that a majority of boys in America will grow up assuming that women are strong. My worry is that as so many men absent themselves from the lives of the children they father, boys and girls will grow up without a sense of the tenderness of men.

The prospect of a generation of American children being raised by women in homes without fathers is challenging for religious institutions whose central conception of deity is father, whose central conception of church is family, whose only conception of family is heterosexual. A woman who can do without a husband can do without any patriarchal authority. The oblique remedy some religious institutions propose for the breakdown of heterosexual relationships is a legal objection to homosexual marriages by defining marriage as between one man and one woman.

---

10   *Yahweh*   English spelling of the name of God in Judaism; in Jewish tradition, this name is not usually spoken;   *I Am*   When Moses asks God his name, God responds "I Am That I Am" (Exodus 3.14).

I believe there is a valid analogy to be drawn between the legal persecution of homosexuality and the legal persecution of miscegenation[11]—both "crimes against nature." But more comparable to the gay-rights movement is the nineteenth-century feminist movement.

Suffragettes withstood condemnation from every institution of their lives, condemnation that employed the adjectives of unnatural aspiration, adjectives such as "thwarted," "hysterical," "strident," "shrill." Still, it was the brave suffragette (and not the tragic peacock Oscar Wilde[12]) who rescued my sexuality.

In the twentieth century, gays emerging from the closet were beneficiaries of the desire of women to define themselves outside the familial structure. The feminist movement became inclusive not only of wives, mothers, and unmarried women but also of lesbians and thus, by extension, of nonfamilial sisterhood, of homosexual men, of the transgendered, of the eight-legged anagram LGBT.

Using the homeliest of metaphors—coming out of the kitchen; coming out of the closet—heterosexual women and homosexual women and men announced, just by being themselves without apology, the necessity of a reordered civil society. We are—heterosexual women and homosexuals are—for however long I don't know, dispensed (by constitutional laws, state laws) from having to fit into the heterosexual roles and heterosexual social patterns that have been upheld for so long by reference to the "natural law." Natural law, as cited against sodomy, against abortion, against birth control, against miscegenation, is neither exactly the "natural moral law," which is a philosophical construct (the understanding placed in us by God at the creation), nor exactly the law of Nature—that is, how Nature works. Rather, it is a value placed on behavior by someone or some agency, most often with reference to some divinely inspired statutory text, that denounces or declares illegal or punishable any deviation from what the authority or the text declares to be natural human behavior. Boys will be boys, and girls like glitter.

I know there are some homosexuals who see the gay couples in line for marriage licenses, or filling out forms for adoption, or posing for wedding announcements in the *New York Times,* as antithetical to an ancient culture of refusal that made the best of a short story—of youth and chance and public toilets and then the long half-life of irony and discretion.

40

---

11 *miscegenation* Mixed-race marriage and/or procreation.

12 *Oscar Wilde* Irish playwright, poet, and prose writer (1854–1900) associated with the Aesthetic Movement, which advocated beauty for its own sake. Wilde was convicted of "gross indecency" with men and sentenced to two years of hard labor; he died in exile a few years after his release.

There certainly are homosexuals of my generation who never dared hope for a novel of marriage but only one of renunciation. E.M. Forster imagined a marriage novel, but then stipulated it not be published during his lifetime.[13] The Church regards homosexual marriage as a travesty that will promote the undoing of marriage. But I propose that the single mother is a greater threat to the patriarchal determination of what constitutes a natural order.

45   I am thinking of David Grossman, the Israeli novelist who, in a profile in *The New Yorker,* said: "If God came to Sarah and told her, 'Give me your son, your only one, your beloved, Isaac,' she will tell him, 'Give me a break,' not to say 'Fuck off.'"[14]

I am thinking of the Mormon mother who told me on Temple Square[15] in Salt Lake City: "The Church teaches us that family is everything. And then the Church tells me that I should abandon my homosexual son. I will not do it!"

It is clear to me that civic attitudes toward homosexuality and gay marriage are changing. In countries we loosely describe as Western, opinion polls and secular courts are deciding in favor of the legalization of gay marriage. Nevertheless, the desert religions will stand opposed to homosexuality, to homosexual acts, unless the desert religions turn to regard the authority of women. And that will not happen until the desert religions reevaluate the meaning of women. And that will not happen until the desert religions see that "bringing into being" is not a power we should call male only. And that will not happen until the desert religions see the woman as father, the father as woman, indistinguishable in authority and creative potence.

My place in the Church depends on you, Darling.

(2013)

---

13   *E.M. Forster ... lifetime*   Forster's novel *Maurice*, written in the 1910s, centers on a romance between men; he left instructions for it to be published after his death.

14   *If God ... Fuck off*   Reference to Genesis 22, in which God demands that Abraham sacrifice his son Isaac, granting a reprieve only as Abraham is about to commit the sacrifice.

15   *Temple Square*   Site of the world's largest Mormon temple; it is located in Salt Lake City, Utah, a city founded by Mormons.

THOMAS HURKA

PHILOSOPHY, MORALITY, AND
THE ENGLISH PATIENT

*In this article, a leading philosopher compares the moral perspectives implicit in two classic films, each of which won the Academy Award for Best Picture—*Casablanca *(1943) and* The English Patient *(1996)—and discusses the ways in which each reflects the spirit of its time.*

In the form it is reprinted in here, the essay was first published in Queen's Quarterly, *a periodical aimed at both an academic and a general readership; Hurka had initially published a concise version of the argument as a newspaper column.*

The movie *The English Patient*, based on the novel by Michael Ondaatje, won nine Academy Awards this year, including Best Picture. This last award normally goes only to serious movies, ones that address important themes. But looked at this way, *The English Patient* is a disturbing choice. It has a moral perspective on the events it describes, but it is a me-centered and immoral one. Philosophy can help explain why.

In saying this, I don't assume that all art is subject to moral critique, a common view in the nineteenth century. At that time, people believed that even landscape painting and instrumental music have as their main function to morally improve their audience, and should be evaluated for how well they do so. I think it's obvious that many works of art have no moral content, so a moral commentary on them is irrelevant. But other works, especially of literature and drama, raise and explore moral issues. And when they do, we can ask how well they do so.

The English Patient has a moral issue at the center of its plot. In an Italian villa at the end of the Second World War, a burn victim is slowly dying. His face is scarred beyond recognition, and he claims not to know his own identity. But one character, Caravaggio, has figured out who the patient is. He is Count Laszlo de Almasy, a Hungarian desert explorer who just before the war gave the German army crucial desert maps that enabled them to attack Tobruk and almost win the war in North Africa. Caravaggio himself was captured and tortured in that offensive. He thinks Almasy is guilty of betrayal and wants to bring him to account. Caravaggio has killed everyone else responsible for his capture and torture, and he now wants to kill Almasy. So a key question is: *did Almasy act wrongly in handing over the maps?* The rest of the movie addresses this question by showing what led to his choice.

Before the war Almasy was deeply in love with a married woman, Katherine Clifton. Much of the movie describes their passionate and all-consuming affair. But just before the outbreak of hostilities, Katherine was seriously injured in a desert plane crash that also killed her husband. Almasy, who was present, carried her to shelter in a cave and promised to return with help. His first attempt to get that help, from the British army, was rebuffed. Confronted by someone with no identification papers and a foreign accent, they instead arrested him as a spy. After escaping from the British, Almasy went to the German army. But to get their help he needed to offer them something in return. As the only way to keep his promise to Katherine, and from profound love for her, he gave the Germans the maps.

5   When he hears this story Caravaggio says he no longer has any desire to punish Almasy. The "poison," he says, has left him. And the movie's treatment of Almasy is now overwhelmingly sympathetic. Its emotional high point comes when Almasy, finding he has returned to Katherine too late, emerges from the cave carrying her dead body. Tears stream down his face; the photography is lush and gorgeous; the background music swells. As portrayed here Almasy is an entirely romantic figure. There is an equally sympathetic treatment as Almasy, having requested a morphine overdose, dies at the movie's end. Again both the camera and his nurse surround him with unqualified love.

After his escape from the British, Almasy faced a choice between a political end, resisting Nazism or at least not colluding with it, and a personal end, keeping his promise to Katherine. And the movie's treatment implies that his preference for the personal end was understandable and even right. This is implicit in the movie's most important line, a remark of Katherine's that it emphasizes by repeating: "Betrayals in war are childlike compared to our betrayals in peace." Loyalty in love, this line says, is more important than loyalty to political ends such as those fought for in war. Whatever its consequences for politics, any action done from love is right.

It is this utter denigration of the political that makes *The English Patient* immoral. There was not just some political end at stake in the Second World War; there was resistance to Nazism, a movement threatening millions of innocent people. Yet the movie treats even this end as morally inconsequential. Its attitude is therefore the opposite of that taken in *Casablanca*, a movie likewise set in North Africa in the Second World War. In *Casablanca* Humphrey

Bogart's character Rick sacrifices his love for Ilsa in order to join the fight against Nazism. As he tells her and her husband, "The problems of three little people don't amount to a hill of beans in this crazy world." In *The English Patient*, by contrast, the fight against Nazism is blithely sacrificed for love. The problems of the world, the movie says, and of the millions of people threatened by Nazism don't amount to a hill of beans beside those of two love-crazed people.

This critique of *The English Patient* is most compelling given a certain assumption about its plot; that given the time it took Almasy to reach the British army, escape from them, and reach the Germans, he should have known there was no chance Katherine would be alive when he reached the cave. He was keeping a promise to someone dead, and however romantic that may be, it has little moral weight beside a duty not to collude with Nazism.

This assumption may be challenged, however. Maybe Almasy got to the Germans fast enough that he did have a reasonable chance of saving Katherine. Then his choice was fraught in a way that Rick's in *Casablanca* is not. Whatever Rick does, he knows Ilsa will be safe. But for Almasy to honor the political demand is to consign his loved one to death. Given this circumstance, is his choice so obviously wrong?

The English Patient, revealingly, doesn't bother to settle this morally crucial detail of plot. But let's grant that Katherine might still have been alive. A movie could then portray Almasy as caught between two powerful but conflicting moral demands, one personal and one political, with some horrible violation inevitable whichever choice he makes. If he resists Nazism he fails the woman he loves; if he saves her he colludes with moral evil. This possible movie has the structure some find in classical Greek tragedies such as Aeschylus's *Agamemnon*, where the protagonist faces a tragic conflict between two competing moral duties and cannot avoid doing something morally wrong. Whichever duty he chooses, he is guilty of violating the other and must pay for that guilt. But this possible movie is not *The English Patient*, which gives Almasy's political duty no serious attention at all. Here, when love is at stake, its demands not only outweigh the competing demands of politics but render them trivial.

This is certainly Almasy's view. Before the war he thought the coming conflict was just one between silly nationalisms. In the Italian villa, after his story has been told, he thinks his choice about the maps was not just right but obviously so. Told that his explorer friend Madox killed himself when he learned of Almasy's betrayal, he is simply and entirely surprised: *why would anyone react like that?* And he offers excuses for his choice that are morally pathetic. One is that his action did not mean that any extra people were killed; it only changed which people were killed. But even if this is true (and how does

10

Almasy know it?), he couldn't have known it at the time. His transfer of the maps could easily have led to a Nazi victory in North Africa, with incalculable effects on the future course of the war. And doesn't it matter whether the people killed in war are guilty Nazi aggressors or morally innocent defenders?

Almasy's view is also the movie's. As I have said, its treatment of him, especially in its most emotionally loaded scenes, is entirely sympathetic. And this sympathy is almost inevitable given the way the movie frames the moral issue Almasy faces.

In a recent moral defense of the movie, Ondaatje has borrowed from that central line of Katherine's. Its theme, he says, is "love, desire, betrayals in war and betrayals in peace." This is indeed how the movie presents Almasy's choice, as one between conflicting loyalties and different possible betrayals. But the concepts of loyalty and betrayal are essentially personalized or me-centered: *I can be loyal to a person I love or to the nation I belong to or to a group of people specially connected to ME. But I can't be loyal to a stranger, and I can't betray a stranger.* In framing the moral issue as it does, the movie frames it in an essentially me-centered way. Almasy is to ask himself which of the people specially connected to him he should care most about, or which attachment to him, that of his lover or of his nation, is morally most important.

But this approach entirely ignores a more impersonal type of moral demand. This demand is impersonal not in the sense that it is not about people but in that it is about people independently of any special connection to oneself, or just as human beings. Other people matter morally in themselves and we have duties to care about them whatever their relation to us. This impersonal type of duty was utterly central in the Second World War. Nazism threatened the lives of millions of innocent people and regardless of their nationality those people needed protection. This is clearly recognized in *Casablanca*. In that movie Rick has no reason of loyalty to join the fight against Nazism; he is an American and the U.S. is not yet in the war. But he sees that, loyalties aside, Nazism is an evil that must be resisted. His reason for fighting is therefore not me-centered but in the sense I am using impersonal. And this kind of reason is given no place in *The English Patient*. By recognizing only the concepts of loyalty and betrayal, that movie leaves no room for a demand to care about people only as people.

15   That is why the movie inevitably sympathizes with Almasy's choice. If the alternatives are loyalty to a particular person one loves and loyalty to something as abstract as a nation, of course the former is more important. It's the same with E.M. Forster's* famous remark that if he had to choose between betraying his country and betraying his friend, he hoped he would have the guts to betray his country. As described, that choice again seems correct. But in each case this is only because the choice is described in a tendentiously incomplete

way, one leaving out impersonal considerations. And those considerations are often morally decisive. Consider: if you had to choose between betraying your friend and colluding in the murder of millions of innocent people, would you hope you had the guts to murder those people?

This is the central immorality of *The English Patient*: its reduction of all moral demands to me-centered demands, those based on other people's relationships to oneself. The reduction appears in many places in the movie.

One is its taking seriously another of Almasy's pathetic excuses. He wasn't guilty of betrayal in handing over the maps, he says, because the British betrayed him first in refusing him help to save Katherine. Set aside the question of whether the British really did mistreat Almasy at all. With the world on the brink of war, he was in disputed territory with no papers; he was abusive in his manners and gave no satisfactory explanation for his request. But that aside, why should one little betrayal by the British license him to collude with Nazis? That conclusion would only follow if the coming war were, as Almasy thought, just another conflict between silly nationalisms. But of course in this war one side, whatever the other's failings, was incomparably morally worse. That is why Elizabeth Pathy Salett was entirely correct to say, in the *Washington Post* article to which Ondaatje responded, that the movie's "presentation of a moral equivalency between the Germans and Allies trivializes the significance of the choices men like Almasy made."

Even the voice against Almasy in the movie speaks in me-centered terms. That voice is Caravaggio, and what does Caravaggio want? He above all wants revenge, and revenge is again a personalized concept: *I can want revenge only for a wrong done to me or someone closely connected to me, and I get revenge only if I inflict it myself.* In both respects a desire for revenge contrasts with a desire for justice, which can be aroused by wrongdoing against anyone and can be satisfied when punishment is imposed by anyone, including the impersonal state. But expressing the moral challenge to Almasy in terms of revenge again has a trivializing effect. It reduces that challenge to a "poison" that can be easily extracted when Almasy's story is told. And it utterly underdescribes the subject of that challenge. As part of his torture Caravaggio had his thumbs cut off. This means that he can no longer do sleight of hand tricks—when he tries one with an egg he drops it—and can no longer ply his former trade as a pickpocket. It is hard to think of a less adequate representation of the threat posed by Nazism.

Here are, then, three levels of moral critique of *The English Patient*. First, the movie sympathizes with a choice that is simply morally wrong. Second, it sees nothing at all problematic about a choice that, even if not simply wrong, violates an important political duty. Third, the movie casts its moral considerations entirely in the me-centered terms of loyalty and betrayal, never recognizing the impersonal demands that were so central in its setting of the Second World War. Of these critiques the second and especially the third are philosophical. Moral philosophy does not consider issues that are completely different from those of ordinary moral thought. It considers the same issues but at a higher level of abstraction, identifying the principles and structures of principles that underlie and explain particular moral judgments. In this, as in many cases, it is the most philosophical critique that is most important. It is because it recognizes only me-centered and no impersonal moral duties that *The English Patient* sees nothing troubling in and even sympathizes with a highly questionable choice.

20   *Casablanca* was very much a product of its time. Its impersonal moral vision expresses the experience of people who were fighting to resist aggression on another continent. *The English Patient* is, unfortunately, also a product of its time, one in which many people have abandoned concern for those in other countries or even for less fortunate members of their own society. It is a time of withdrawal from the impersonal concerns of politics into a smaller realm focused on the self and its few chosen intimates. It is no surprise that *The English Patient* won its Academy Awards. The movie has the kind of high-minded tone that Academy voters find impressive. And its substance fits the depressing tenor of our time.

(1997)

PHILIP GOUREVITCH

from WE WISH TO INFORM YOU THAT TOMORROW WE WILL BE KILLED WITH OUR FAMILIES

In the central African country of Rwanda, the majority Hutu and the minority Tutsi have a long history of conflict. In April 1994, the country's Hutu president was killed when rocket fire shot down his plane. Extremists in the Rwandan government blamed Tutsi dissidents, provided machetes to the citizenry, and encouraged Hutu citizens to form militias and to (as the radio broadcasts put it) "kill the Tutsis; they are cockroaches." The killing went on for more than six weeks, leaving some 800,000 Tutsi dead; it remains one of the worst instances of genocide since the Holocaust.

Gourevitch published a series of magazine articles on the genocide starting in the spring of 1995; his 1999 book on the subject, from which the following excerpt is taken, is widely regarded as a non-fiction classic.

In the Province of Kibungo, in eastern Rwanda, in the swamp- and pastureland near the Tanzanian border, there's a rocky hill called Nyarubuye with a church where many Tutsis were slaughtered in mid-April of 1994. A year after the killing I went to Nyarubuye with two Canadian military officers. We flew in a United Nations helicopter, traveling low over the hills in the morning mists, with the banana trees like green starbursts dense over the slopes. The uncut grass blew back as we dropped into the center of the parish schoolyard. A lone soldier materialized with his Kalashnikov,* and shook our hands with stiff, shy formality. The Canadians presented the paperwork for our visit, and I stepped up into the open doorway of a classroom.

At least fifty mostly decomposed cadavers covered the floor, wadded in clothing, their belongings strewn about and smashed. Macheted skulls had rolled here and there.

The dead looked like pictures of the dead. They did not smell. They did not buzz with flies. They had been killed thirteen months earlier, and they hadn't been moved. Skin stuck here and there over the bones, many of which lay scattered away from the bodies, dismembered by the killers, or by scavengers—birds, dogs, bugs. The more complete figures looked a lot like people, which they were once. A woman in a cloth wrap printed with flowers lay near the door. Her fleshless hip bones were high and her legs slightly spread, and a child's skeleton extended between them. Her torso was hollowed out. Her ribs and spinal column poked through the rotting cloth. Her head was tipped back and her mouth was open: a strange image—half agony, half repose.

I had never been among the dead before. What to do? Look? Yes. I wanted to see them, I suppose; I had come to see them—the dead had been left unburied at Nyarubuye for memorial purposes—and there they were, so intimately exposed. I didn't need to see them. I already knew, and believed, what had happened in Rwanda. Yet looking at the buildings and the bodies, and hearing the silence of the place, with the grand Italianate basilica standing there deserted, and beds of exquisite, decadent, death-fertilized flowers blooming over the corpses, it was still strangely unimaginable. I mean one still had to imagine it.

5   Those dead Rwandans will be with me forever, I expect. That was why I had felt compelled to come to Nyarubuye: to be stuck with them—not with their experience, but with the experience of looking at them. They had been killed there, and they were dead there. What else could you really see at first? The Bible bloated with rain lying on top of one corpse or, littered about, the little woven wreaths of thatch which Rwandan women wear as crowns to balance the enormous loads they carry on their heads, and the water gourds, and the Converse tennis sneaker stuck somehow in a pelvis.

The soldier with the Kalashnikov—Sergeant Francis of the Rwandese Patriotic Army, a Tutsi whose parents had fled to Uganda with him when he was a boy, after similar but less extensive massacres in the early 1960s, and who had fought his way home in 1994 and found it like this—said that the dead in this room were mostly women who had been raped before being murdered. Sergeant Francis had high, rolling girlish hips, and he walked and stood with his butt stuck out behind him, an oddly purposeful posture, tipped forward, driven. He was, at once, candid and briskly official. His English had the punctilious clip of military drill, and after he told me what I was looking at I looked instead at my feet. The rusty head of a hatchet lay beside them in the dirt.

A few weeks earlier, in Bukavu, Zaire, in the giant market of a refugee camp that was home to many Rwandan Hutu militiamen, I had watched a man butchering a cow with a machete. He was quite expert at his work, taking big precise strokes that made a sharp hacking noise. The rallying cry to the killers during the genocide was "Do your work!" And I saw that it *was* work, this butchery; hard work. It took many hacks—two, three, four, five hard hacks—to chop through the cow's leg. How many hacks to dismember a person?

Considering the enormity of the task, it is tempting to play with theories of collective madness, mob mania, a fever of hatred erupted into a mass crime of passion, and to imagine the blind orgy of the mob, with each member killing one or two people. But at Nyarubuye, and at thousands of other sites in this tiny country, on the same days of a few months in 1994, hundreds of thousands of Hutus had worked as killers in regular shifts. There was always the next victim, and the next. What sustained them, beyond the frenzy of the first attack, through the plain physical exhaustion and mess of it?

The pygmy in Gikongoro* said that humanity is part of nature and that we must go against nature to get along and have peace. But mass violence, too, must be organized; it does not occur aimlessly. Even mobs and riots have a design, and great and sustained destruction requires great ambition. It must be conceived as the means toward achieving a new order, and although the idea behind that new order may be criminal and objectively very stupid, it must also be compellingly simple and at the same time absolute. The ideology of genocide is all of those things, and in Rwanda it went by the bald name of Hutu Power. For those who set about systematically exterminating an entire people—even a fairly small and unresisting subpopulation of perhaps a million and a quarter men, women, and children, like the Tutsis in Rwanda—blood lust surely helps. But the engineers and perpetrators of a slaughter like the one just inside the door where I stood need not enjoy killing, and they may even find it unpleasant. What is required above all is that they want their victims dead. They have to want it so badly that they consider it a necessity.

So I still had much to imagine as I entered the classroom and stepped care- 10 fully between the remains. These dead and their killers had been neighbors, schoolmates, colleagues, sometimes friends, even in-laws. The dead had seen their killers training as militias in the weeks before the end, and it was well known that they were training to kill Tutsis; it was announced on the radio, it was in the newspapers, people spoke of it openly. The week before the mas- sacre at Nyarubuye, the killing began in Rwanda's capital, Kigali. Hutus who opposed the Hutu Power ideology were publicly denounced as "accomplices" of the Tutsis and were among the first to be killed as the extermination got under way. In Nyarubuye, when Tutsis asked the Hutu Power mayor how they might be spared, he suggested that they seek sanctuary at the church. They did, and a few days later the mayor came to kill them. He came at the head of a pack of soldiers, policemen, militiamen, and villagers; he gave out arms and orders to complete the job well. No more was required of the mayor, but he was also said to have killed a few Tutsis himself.

The killers killed all day at Nyarubuye. At night they cut the Achilles tendons of survivors and went off to feast behind the church, roasting cattle looted from their victims in big fires, and drinking beer. (Bottled beer, banana beer—Rwandans may not drink more beer than other Africans, but they drink prodigious quantities of it around the clock.) And, in the morning, still drunk after whatever sleep they could find beneath the cries of their prey, the killers at Nyarubuye went back and killed again. Day after day, minute to minute, Tutsi by Tutsi: all across Rwanda, they worked like that. "It was a process," Sergeant Francis said. I can see that it happened, I can be told how, and after nearly three years of looking around Rwanda and listening to Rwandans, I can tell you how, and I will. But the horror of it—the idiocy, the waste, the sheer wrongness—remains uncircumscribable.

Like Leontius, the young Athenian in Plato,* I presume that you are reading this because you desire a closer look, and that you, too, are properly disturbed by your curiosity. Perhaps, in examining this extremity with me, you hope for some understanding, some insight, some flicker of self-knowledge—a moral, or a lesson, or a clue about how to behave in this world: some such information. I don't discount the possibility, but when it comes to genocide, you already know right from wrong. The best reason I have come up with for looking closely into Rwanda's stories is that ignoring them makes me even more uncomfortable about existence and my place in it. The horror, as horror, interests me only insofar as a precise memory of the offense is necessary to understand its legacy.

The dead at Nyarubuye were, I'm afraid, beautiful. There was no getting around it. The skeleton is a beautiful thing. The randomness of the fallen forms, the strange tranquility of their rude exposure, the skull here, the arm bent in some uninterpretable gesture there—these things were beautiful, and their beauty only added to the affront of the place. I couldn't settle on any meaningful response: revulsion, alarm, sorrow, grief, shame, incomprehension, sure, but nothing truly meaningful. I just looked, and I took photographs, because I wondered whether I could really see what I was seeing while I saw it, and I wanted also an excuse to look a bit more closely.

We went on through the first room and out the far side. There was another room and another and another and another. They were all full of bodies, and more bodies were scattered in the grass and there were stray skulls in the grass, which was thick and wonderfully green. Standing outside, I heard a crunch. The old Canadian colonel stumbled in front of me, and I saw, though he did not notice, that his foot had rolled on a skull and broken it. For the first time at Nyarubuye my feelings focused, and what I felt was a small but keen anger at this man. Then I heard another crunch, and felt a vibration underfoot. I had stepped on one, too.

15 Rwanda is spectacular to behold. Throughout its center, a winding succession of steep, tightly terraced slopes radiates out from small roadside settlements and solitary compounds. Gashes of red clay and black loam mark fresh hoe work;

eucalyptus trees flash silver against brilliant green tea plantations; banana trees are everywhere. On the theme of hills, Rwanda produces countless variations: jagged rain forests, round-shouldered buttes, undulating moors, broad swells of savanna, volcanic peaks sharp as filed teeth. During the rainy season, the clouds are huge and low and fast, mists cling in highland hollows, lightning flickers through the nights, and by day the land is lustrous. After the rains, the skies lift, the terrain takes on a ragged look beneath the flat unvarying haze of the dry season, and in the savannas of the Akagera Park wildlife blackens the hills.

One day, when I was returning to Kigali from the south, the car mounted a rise between two winding valleys, the windshield filled with purple-bellied clouds, and I asked Joseph, the man who was giving me a ride, whether Rwandans realize what a beautiful country they have. "Beautiful?" he said. "You think so? After the things that happened here? The people aren't good. If the people were good, the country might be OK." Joseph told me that his brother and sister had been killed, and he made a soft hissing click with his tongue against his teeth. "The country is empty," he said. "Empty!"

It was not just the dead who were missing. The genocide had been brought to a halt by the Rwandese Patriotic Front, a rebel army led by Tutsi refugees from past persecutions, and as the RPF advanced through the country in the summer of 1994, some two million Hutus had fled into exile at the behest of the same leaders who had urged them to kill. Yet except in some rural areas in the south, where the desertion of Hutus had left nothing but bush to reclaim the fields around crumbling adobe houses, I, as a newcomer, could not see the emptiness that blinded Joseph to Rwanda's beauty. Yes, there were grenade-flattened buildings, burnt homesteads, shot-up facades, and mortar-pitted roads. But these were the ravages of war, not of genocide, and by the summer of 1995, most of the dead had been buried. Fifteen months earlier, Rwanda had been the most densely populated country in Africa. Now the work of the killers looked just as they had intended: invisible.

From time to time, mass graves were discovered and excavated, and the remains would be transferred to new, properly consecrated mass graves. Yet even the occasionally exposed bones, the conspicuous number of amputees and people with deforming scars, and the superabundance of packed orphanages could not be taken as evidence that what had happened to Rwanda was an attempt to eliminate a people. There were only people's stories.

"Every survivor wonders why he is alive," Abbé Modeste, a priest at the cathedral in Butare, Rwanda's second-largest city, told me. Abbé Modeste had hidden for weeks in his sacristy, eating communion wafers, before moving under the desk in his study, and finally into the rafters at the home of some neighboring nuns. The obvious explanation of his survival was that the RPF had come to the rescue. But the RPF didn't reach Butare till early July, and roughly seventy-five percent of the Tutsis in Rwanda had been killed by early May. In this regard, at least, the genocide had been entirely successful: to those who were targeted, it was not death but life that seemed an accident of fate.

20   "I had eighteen people killed at my house," said Etienne Niyonzima, a former businessman who had become a deputy in the National Assembly. "Everything was totally destroyed—a place of fifty-five meters by fifty meters. In my neighborhood they killed six hundred and forty-seven people. They tortured them, too. You had to see how they killed them. They had the number of everyone's house, and they went through with red paint and marked the homes of all the Tutsis and of the Hutu moderates. My wife was at a friend's, shot with two bullets. She is still alive, only"—he fell quiet for a moment—"she has no arms. The others with her were killed. The militia left her for dead. Her whole family of sixty-five in Gitarama were killed." Niyonzima was in hiding at the time. Only after he had been separated from his wife for three months did he learn that she and four of their children had survived. "Well," he said, "one son was cut in the head with a machete. I don't know where he went." His voice weakened, and caught. "He disappeared." Niyonzima clicked his tongue, and said, "But the others are still alive. Quite honestly, I don't understand at all how I was saved."

Laurent Nkongoli attributed his survival to "Providence, and also good neighbors, an old woman who said, 'Run away, we don't want to see your corpse.'" Nkongoli, a lawyer, who had become the vice president of the National Assembly after the genocide, was a robust man, with a taste for double-breasted suit jackets and lively ties, and he moved, as he spoke, with a brisk determination. But before taking his neighbor's advice, and fleeing Kigali in late April of 1994, he said, "I had accepted death. At a certain moment this happens. One hopes not to die cruelly, but one expects to die anyway. Not death by machete, one hopes, but with a bullet. If you were willing to pay for it, you could often ask for a bullet. Death was more or less normal, a resignation. You lose the will to fight. There were four thousand Tutsis killed here at Kacyiru"— a neighborhood of Kigali. "The soldiers brought them here, and told them to sit down because they were going to throw grenades. And they sat.

"Rwandan culture is a culture of fear," Nkongoli went on. "I remember what people said." He adopted a pipey voice, and his face took on a look of disgust: "'Just let us pray, then kill us,' or 'I don't want to die in the street, I want to die at home.'" He resumed his normal voice. "When you're that resigned and oppressed you're already dead. It shows the genocide was prepared for too long. I detest this fear. These victims of genocide had been psychologically prepared to expect death just for being Tutsi. They were being killed for so long that they were already dead."

I reminded Nkongoli that, for all his hatred of fear, he had himself accepted death before his neighbor urged him to run away. "Yes," he said. "I got tired in the genocide. You struggle so long, then you get tired."

Every Rwandan I spoke with seemed to have a favorite, unanswerable question. For Nkongoli, it was how so many Tutsis had allowed themselves to be killed. For François Xavier Nkurunziza, a Kigali lawyer, whose father was Hutu and whose mother and wife were Tutsi, the question was how so many Hutus had allowed themselves to kill. Nkurunziza had escaped death only by chance as he moved around the country from one hiding place to another, and he had lost many family members. "Conformity is very deep, very developed here," he told me. "In Rwandan history, everyone obeys authority. People revere power, and there isn't enough education. You take a poor, ignorant population, and give them arms, and say, 'It's yours. Kill.' They'll obey. The peasants, who were paid or forced to kill, were looking up to people of higher socio-economic standing to see how to behave. So the people of influence, or the big financiers, are often the big men in the genocide. They may think they didn't kill because they didn't take life with their own hands, but the people were looking to them for their orders. And, in Rwanda, an order can be given very quietly."

As I traveled around the country, collecting accounts of the killing, it almost seemed as if, with the machete, the *masu*—a club studded with nails—a few well-placed grenades, and a few bursts of automatic-rifle fire, the quiet orders of Hutu Power had made the neutron bomb obsolete.

"Everyone was called to hunt the enemy," said Theodore Nyilinkwaya, a survivor of the massacres in his home village of Kimbogo, in the southwestern province of Cyangugu. "But let's say someone is reluctant. Say that guy comes with a stick. They tell him, 'No, get a *masu*.' So, OK, he does, and he runs along with the rest, but he doesn't kill. They say, 'Hey, he might denounce us later. He must kill. Everyone must help to kill at least one person.' So this person who is not a killer is made to do it. And the next day it's become a game for him. You don't need to keep pushing him."

At Nyarubuye, even the little terracotta votive statues in the sacristy had been methodically decapitated. "They were associated with Tutsis," Sergeant Francis explained.

(1999)

BARBARA EHRENREICH

from NICKEL AND DIMED:
ON (NOT) GETTING BY IN AMERICA

Journalist Barbara Ehrenreich's 2001 book Nickel and Dimed *originated when she and* Harper's *editor Lewis Lapham were having lunch together and found themselves wondering how anyone manages to "live on the wages available to the unskilled." Ehrenreich's book represents her answer to that question; over the course of two years she forsook her comfortable life and lived off the proceeds of what low-paid jobs she could get—waiting tables, cleaning houses, and working in a nursing home and as a Wal-Mart associate.* Nickel and Dimed *recounts her experiences—and also those of the people she worked with. The book became immensely successful, and was widely credited with raising awareness among wealthier Americans of the realities of low-income lives.*

The excerpt below (from the chapter "Serving in Florida") is part of Ehrenreich's account of her "career at the Hearthside" restaurant: "for two weeks I worked from 2:00 till 10:00 pm for $2.43 an hour plus tips."

You might imagine, from a comfortable distance, that people who live, year in and year out, on $6 to $10 an hour have discovered some survival stratagems unknown to the middle class. But no. It's not hard to get my co-workers talking about their living situations, because housing, in almost every case, is the principal source of disruption in their shifts. After a week, I have compiled the following survey:

Gail is sharing a room in a well-known downtown flophouse* for $250 a week. Her roommate, a male friend, has begun hitting on her, driving her nuts, but the rent would be impossible alone.

Claude, the Haitian cook, is desperate to get out of the two-room apartment he shares with his girlfriend and two other, unrelated people. As far as I can determine, the other Haitian men live in similarly crowded situations.

508

Annette, a twenty-year-old server who is six months pregnant and abandoned by her boyfriend, lives with her mother, a postal clerk.

Marianne, who is a breakfast server, and her boyfriend are paying $170 a week for a one-person trailer.

Bill, who at $10 an hour is the wealthiest of us, lives in the trailer he owns, paying only the $400-a-month lot fee.

The other white cook, Andy, lives on his dry-docked boat, which, as far as I can tell from his loving descriptions, can't be more than twenty feet long. He offers to take me out on it once it's repaired, but the offer comes with inquiries as to my marital status, so I do not follow up on it.

Tina, another server, and her husband are paying $60 a night for a room in the Days Inn. This is because they have no car and the Days Inn is in walking distance of the Hearthside. When Marianne is tossed out of her trailer for subletting (which is against trailer park rules), she leaves her boyfriend and moves in with Tina and her husband.

Joan, who had fooled me with her numerous and tasteful outfits (hostesses wear their own clothes), lives in a van parked behind a shopping center at night and showers in Tina's motel room. The clothes are from thrift shops.

It strikes me, in my middle-class solipsism,* that there is gross improvidence in some of these arrangements. When Gail and I are wrapping silverware in napkins—the only task for which we are permitted to sit—she tells me she is thinking of escaping from her roommate by moving into the Days Inn herself. I am astounded: how she can even think of paying $40 to $60 a day? But if I was afraid of sounding like a social worker, I have come out just sounding like a fool. She squints at me in disbelief: "And where am I supposed to get a month's rent and a month's deposit for an apartment?" I'd been feeling pretty smug about my $500 efficiency, but of course it was made possible only by the $1,300 I had allotted myself for start-up costs when I began my low-wage life: $1,000 for the first month's rent and deposit, $100 for initial groceries and cash in my pocket, $200 stuffed away for emergencies. In poverty, as in certain propositions in physics, starting conditions are everything.

There are no secret economies that nourish the poor; on the contrary, there are a host of special costs. If you can't put up the two months' rent you need to secure an apartment, you end up paying through the nose for a room by the week. If you have only a room, with a hot plate at best, you can't save by cooking up huge lentil stews that can be frozen for the week ahead. You eat fast food or the hot dogs and Styrofoam cups of soup that can be microwaved in a convenience store. If you have no money for health insurance—and the Hearthside's niggardly plan kicks in only after three months—you go without routine care or prescription drugs and end up paying the price. Gail, for example, was doing fine, health-wise anyway, until she ran out of money for estrogen pills. She is supposed to be on the company health plan by now, but they claim to have lost her application form and to be beginning the paperwork all over again. So she spends $9 a pop for pills to control the migraines she wouldn't have, she insists, if her estrogen supplements were covered. Similarly, Marianne's boyfriend lost his job as a roofer because he missed so much time after getting a cut on his foot for which he couldn't afford the prescribed antibiotic.

My own situation, when I sit down to assess it after two weeks of work, would not be much better if this were my actual life. The seductive thing about waitressing is that you don't have to wait for payday to feel a few bills in your pocket, and my tips usually cover meals and gas, plus something left over to stuff into the kitchen drawer I use as a bank. But as the tourist business slows in the summer heat, I sometimes leave work with only $20 in tips (the gross is higher, but servers share about 15 percent of their tips with the busboys and bartenders). With wages included, this amounts to about the minimum wage of $5.15 an hour. The sum in the drawer is piling up but at the present rate of accumulation will be more than $100 short of my rent when the end of the month comes around. Nor can I see any expenses to cut. True, I haven't gone the lentil stew route yet, but that's because I don't have a large cooking pot, potholders, or a ladle to stir with (which would cost a total of about $30 at Kmart, somewhat less at a thrift store), not to mention onions, carrots, and the indispensable bay leaf. I do make my lunch almost every day—usually some slow-burning, high-protein combo like frozen chicken patties with melted cheese on top and canned pinto beans on the side. Dinner is at the Hearthside, which offers its employees a choice of BLT, fish sandwich, or hamburger for only $2. The burger lasts longest, especially if it's heaped with gut-puckering jalapenos, but by midnight my stomach is growling again.

So unless I want to start using my car as a residence, I have to find a second or an alternative job.

(2001)

MIRIAM TOEWS

A FATHER'S FAITH

Much of Toews's work draws upon her experience growing up in a Mennonite* community. Her best-known novel, A Complicated Kindness *(2004), is set in a fictionalized version of her hometown; she also revisits her past in* Swing Low: A Life *(2000), a memoir written in the voice of her father, who committed suicide after a long struggle with bipolar disorder. She addresses the same subject in her earlier essay "A Father's Faith," which was first published in* Saturday Night Magazine *in 1999, a year after his death.*

On the morning on May 13, 1998, my father woke up, had breakfast, got dressed and walked away from the Steinbach Bethesda Hospital, where he had been a patient for two and a half weeks. He walked through his beloved hometown, along Hespeler Road, past the old farmhouse where his mother had lived with her second husband, past the water tower, greeting folks in his loud, friendly voice, wishing them well. He passed the site on First Street where the house in which my sister and I grew up once stood. He walked down Main Street, past the Mennonite church where, throughout his life, he had received countless certificates for perfect attendance, past Elmdale School where he had taught grade six for forty years.

As he walked by his home on Brandt Road, he saw his old neighbor Bill sitting in his lawn chair. He waved and smiled again, then he continued on past the cemetery where his parents were buried, and the high school his daughters had attended, and down Highway 52, out of town, past the Frantz Motor Inn, which is just outside the town limits because it serves alcohol and Steinbach is a dry town. He kept walking until he got too tired, so he hitched a ride with a couple of guys who were on their way to buy a fishing licence in the small village of Woodridge on the edge of the Sandilands Forest.

The sun would have been very warm by the time they dropped him off, and he would have taken off his stylish cap and wiped his brow with the back of his hand. I'm sure he thanked them profusely, perhaps offering them ten dollars for their trouble, and then he walked the short distance to the café near the railroad tracks, the place he and my mom would sometimes go for a quiet coffee and

511

a change of scenery. He would have been able to smell the clover growing in the ditches beside the tracks and between the ties. He may have looked down the line and remembered that the train would be coming from Ontario, through Warroad, Minnesota, on its way to Winnipeg.

A beautiful young woman named Stephanie was just beginning her shift and she spoke to him through the screen door at the side of the restaurant. Yes, she said, the train will be here soon. And my dad smiled and thanked her, and mentioned that he could hear the whistle. Moments later, he was dead.

Steinbach is an easy forty-minute drive from Winnipeg, east on the Trans-Canada, then south on Highway 12. On the way into town there's a sign proclaiming "Jesus Saves." On the way back to the city just off Highway 12 there's another that says, "Satan is Real. You Can't Be Neutral. Choose Now." The town has recently become a city of 8,500 people, two-thirds of whom are Mennonite, so it's not surprising that about half of the twenty-four churches are Mennonite and conservative. There is a Catholic church too, but it's new and I'm not sure exactly where it is. A little way down from the bowling alley I can still make out my name on the sidewalk, carved in big bold letters when I was ten and marking my territory.

My town made sense to me then. For me it was a giant playground where my friends and I roamed freely, using the entire town in a game of arrows— something like hide-and-seek—for which my dad, the teacher, provided boxes and boxes of fresh new chalk and invaluable tips. He had, after all, played the same game in the same town many years before.

At six p.m. the siren would go off at the firehall, reminding all the kids to go home for supper, and at nine p.m. it was set off again, reminding us to go home to bed. I had no worries, and no desire ever to leave this place where everyone knew me. If they couldn't remember my name, they knew I was the younger daughter of Mel and Elvira Toews, granddaughter of C.T. Loewen and Henry Toews, from the Kleine Gemeinde congregation, and so on and so on. All the kids in town, other than the church-sponsored Laotians who came over in the seventies, could be traced all the way back to the precise Russian veldt their great-grandparents had emigrated from. They were some of the thousands of Mennonites who came to Manitoba in the late 1800s to escape religious per-secution. They were given free land and a promise that they could, essentially, do their own thing without interference. They wanted to keep the world away from their children and their children away from the world. Naturally it was an impossible ideal.

As I grew older, I became suspicious and critical and restless and angry. Every night I plotted my escape. I imagined that Barkman's giant feed mill on Main Street, partially visible from my bedroom window, was a tall ship that would take me away some day. I looked up places like Hollywood and

Manhattan and Venice and Montreal in my Childcraft encyclopedias. I begged my sister to play, over and over, the sad songs from her Jacques Brel piano book, and I'd light candles and sing along, wearing a Pioneer Girls tam[1] on my head, using a chopstick as a cigarette holder, pretending I was Jackie Brel, Jacques's long-lost but just as world-weary Mennonite twin. I couldn't believe that I was stuck in a town like Steinbach, where dancing was a sin and serving beer a felony.

There were other things I became aware of as well. That my grandmother was a vanilla alcoholic who believed she was a teetotaller.* That seventy-five-year-old women who had borne thirteen children weren't allowed to speak to the church congregation, but that fifteen-year-old boys were. That every family had a secret. And I learned that my dad had been depressed all his life.

I had wondered, when I was a kid, why he spent so much of the weekend in bed and why he didn't talk much at home. Occasionally he'd tell me, sometimes in tears, that he loved me very much and that he wished he were a better father, that he were more involved in my life. But I never felt the need for an apology. It made me happy and a bit envious to know that my dad's students were able to witness his humor and intelligence firsthand, to hear him expound on his favorite subjects: Canadian history, Canadian politics and Canadian newspapers. I remember watching him at work and marveling at his energy and enthusiasm. I thought he looked very handsome when he rolled up his sleeves and tucked his tie in between the buttons of his shirt, his hands on his hips, all ready for business and hard work.

Teaching school—helping others make sense of the world—was a good profession for a man who was continuously struggling to find meaning in life. I think he needed his students as much as they needed him. By fulfilling his duties, he was also shoring up a psyche at risk of erosion.

Four years before his death he was forced to retire from teaching because of a heart attack and some small strokes. He managed to finish the book he was writing on Canada's prime ministers, but then he seemed to fade away. He spent more and more of his time in bed, in the dark, not getting up even to eat or wash, not interested in watching TV or listening to the radio. Despite our pleading and cajoling, despite the medication and visits to various doctors' offices, appointments he dutifully kept, and despite my mother's unwavering love, we felt we were losing him.

I know about brain chemistry and depression, but there's still a part of me that blames my dad's death on being Mennonite and living in that freaky, austere place where this world isn't good enough and admission into the next

10

---

1 *Jacques Brel* Belgian singer-songwriter (1929–78) who became famous performing his poetic ballads in Paris clubs; *tam* Scottish soft hat similar to a beret.

one, the perfect one, means everything, where every word and deed gets you closer to or farther away from eternal life. If you don't believe that then nothing Steinbach stands for will make sense. And if life doesn't make sense you lose yourself in it, your spirit decays. That's what I believed had happened to my dad, and that's why I hated my town.

In the weeks and months after his death, my mom and my sister and I tried to piece things together. William Ashdown, the executive director of the Mood Disorders Association of Manitoba, told us the number of mentally ill Mennonites is abnormally high. "We don't know if it's genetic or cultural," he said, "but the Steinbach area is one that we're vitally concerned about."

15   "It's the way the church delivers the message," says a Mennonite friend of mine, "the message of sin and accountability. To be human, basically, is to be a sinner. So a person, a real believer, starts to get down on himself, and where does it end? They say self-loathing is the cornerstone of depression, right?"

Years ago, the Mennonite Church practiced something called "shunning," whereby if you were to leave your husband, or marry outside the Church, or elope, or drink, or in some way contravene the Church's laws or act "out of faith," you could be expelled from the Church and ignored, shunned by the entire community, including your own family. Depression or despair, as it would have been referred to then, was considered to be the result of a lack of faith and therefore could be another reason for shunning.

These days most Mennonites don't officially practice shunning, although William Ashdown claims there are still Mennonites from extreme conservative sects who are being shunned and shamed into silence within their communities for being mentally ill. Certainly Arden Thiessen, the minister of my dad's church, and a long-time friend of his, is aware of the causes of depression and the pain experienced by those who suffer from it. He doesn't see it as a lack of faith, but as an awful sickness.

But I can't help thinking that that history had just a little to do with my alcoholic grandmother's insisting that she was a non-drinker, and my dad's telling his doctors, smiling that beautiful smile of his, that he was fine, just fine.

Not long before he died my dad told me about the time he was five and was having his tonsils out. Just before the operation began he was knocked out with ether and he had a dream that he was somersaulting through the hospital walls, right through, easily, he said, moving his hands in circles through the air. It was wonderful. He told me he would never forget that feeling.

20   But mostly, the world was a sad and unsafe place for him, and his town provided shelter from it. Maybe he saw this as a gift, while I came to see it as oppression. He could peel back the layers of hypocrisy and intolerance and see what was good, and I couldn't. He believed that it mattered what he did in life, and he believed in the next world, one that's better. He kept the faith of his

Mennonite forebears to the very end, or what he might call the beginning, and removed himself from this world entirely.

Stephanie, the waitress in the café in Woodridge, told my mother that my dad was calm and polite when he spoke to her, as if he were about to sit down to a cup of tea. She told her that he hadn't seemed at all afraid. But why would you be if you believed you were going to a place where there is no more sadness?

My dad never talked to us about God or religion. We didn't have family devotion like everybody else. He never quoted out loud from the Bible or lectured us about not going to church. In fact his only two pieces of advice to me were "Be yourself" and "You can do anything."

But he still went to church. It didn't matter how low he felt, or how cold it was outside. He would put on his suit and tie and stylish cap and walk the seven or eight blocks to church. He always walked, through searing heat or sub-arctic chill. If he was away on holidays he would find a church and go to it. At the lake he drove forty miles down gravel roads to attend an outdoor church in the bush. I think he needed church like a junkie needs a fix: to get him through another day in a world of pain.

What I love about my town is that it gave my dad the faith that stopped him from being afraid in those last violent seconds he spent on earth. And the place in my mind where we meet is on the front steps of my dad's church, the big one on Main Street across from Don's Bakery and the Goodwill store. We smile and talk for a few minutes outside, basking in the warmth of the summer sun he loved so much. Then he goes in and I stay outside, and we're both happy where we are.

(1999)

David Foster Wallace

Consider the Lobster

David Foster Wallace was an American writer of novels, essays, and short stories. Seeking to avoid what he called "pre-formed positions, rigid filters, the 'moral clarity' of the immature," Wallace's texts are often wildly discursive—peppered with asides, qualifications, and tangential discussions. Infinite Jest (1996), his most successful novel, has hundreds of endnotes, many of which are themselves annotated. The essay collected here, "Consider the Lobster," also employs extensive notes. It was first published in Gourmet Magazine *(2004) and then reissued in* Consider the Lobster and Other Essays *(2005).*

The enormous, pungent, and extremely well-marketed Maine Lobster Festival is held every late July in the state's midcoast region, meaning the western side of Penobscot Bay, the nerve stem of Maine's lobster industry. What's called the midcoast runs from Owl's Head and Thomaston in the south to Belfast in the north. (Actually, it might extend all the way up to Bucksport, but we were never able to get farther north than Belfast on Route 1, whose summer traffic is, as you can imagine, unimaginable.) The region's two main communities are Camden, with its very old money and yachty harbor and five-star restaurants and phenomenal B&Bs, and Rockland, a serious old fishing town that hosts the festival every summer in historic Harbor Park, right along the water.[1]

Tourism and lobster are the midcoast region's two main industries, and they're both warm-weather enterprises, and the Maine Lobster Festival represents less an intersection of the industries than a deliberate collision, joyful and lucrative and loud. The assigned subject of this *Gourmet* article is the 56th Annual MLF, 30 July–3 August, 2003, whose official theme this year was "Lighthouses, Laughter, and Lobster." Total paid attendance was over 100,000, due partly to a national CNN spot in June during which a senior editor

---

1   There's a comprehensive native apothegm: "Camden by the sea, Rockland by the smell." [author's note]

of *Food & Wine* magazine hailed the MLF as one of the best food-themed galas in the world. 2003 festival highlights: concerts by Lee Ann Womack and Orleans,[2] annual Maine Sea Goddess beauty pageant, Saturday's big parade, Sunday's William G. Atwood Memorial Crate Race, annual Amateur Cooking Competition, carnival rides and midway attractions and food booths, and the MLF's Main Eating Tent, where something over 25,000 pounds of fresh-caught Maine lobster is consumed after preparation in the World's Largest Lobster Cooker near the grounds' north entrance. Also available are lobster rolls, lobster turnovers, lobster sauté, Down East lobster salad, lobster bisque, lobster ravioli, and deep-fried lobster dumplings. Lobster thermidor[3] is obtainable at a sit-down restaurant called the Black Pearl on Harbor Park's northwest wharf. A large all-pine booth sponsored by the Maine Lobster Promotion Council has free pamphlets with recipes, eating tips, and Lobster Fun Facts. The winner of Friday's Amateur Cooking Competition prepares Saffron Lobster Ramekins, the recipe for which is now available for public downloading at www.mainelobsterfestival.com. There are lobster T-shirts and lobster bobblehead dolls and inflatable lobster pool toys and clamp-on lobster hats with big scarlet claws that wobble on springs. Your assigned correspondent saw it all, accompanied by one girlfriend and both his own parents—one of which parents was actually born and raised in Maine, albeit in the extreme northern inland part, which is potato country and a world away from the touristic midcoast.[4]

For practical purposes, everyone knows what a lobster is. As usual, though, there's much more to know than most of us care about—it's all a matter of what your interests are. Taxonomically speaking, a lobster is a marine crustacean of the family Homaridae, characterized by five pairs of jointed legs, the first pair terminating in large pincerish claws used for subduing prey. Like many other species of benthic[5] carnivore, lobsters are both hunters and scavengers. They have stalked eyes, gills on their legs, and antennae. There are a dozen or so different kinds worldwide, of which the relevant species here is the Maine lobster, *Homarus americanus*. The name "lobster" comes from the Old English *loppestre*, which is thought to be a corrupt form of the Latin word for locust combined with the Old English *loppe*, which meant spider.

Moreover, a crustacean is an aquatic arthropod of the class Crustacea, which comprises crabs, shrimp, barnacles, lobsters, and freshwater crayfish.

---

2   *Lee Ann Womack* American pop-country musician; *Orleans* American pop-rock band.

3   *Lobster thermidor* French lobster in cream sauce dish requiring extensive preparation.

4   N.B. All personally connected parties have made it clear from the start that they do not want to be talked about in this article. [author's note]

5   *benthic* Bottom-dwelling.

All this is right there in the encyclopedia. And arthropods are members of the phylum Arthropoda, which phylum covers insects, spiders, crustaceans, and centipedes/millipedes, all of whose main commonality, besides the absence of a centralized brain-spine assembly, is a chitinous exoskeleton composed of segments, to which appendages are articulated in pairs.

5   The point is that lobsters are basically giant sea insects.[6] Like most arthropods, they date from the Jurassic period, biologically so much older than mammalia that they might as well be from another planet. And they are—particularly in their natural brown-green state, brandishing their claws like weapons and with thick antennae awhip—not nice to look at. And it's true that they are garbagemen of the sea, eaters of dead stuff, although they'll also eat some live shellfish, certain kinds of injured fish, and sometimes one another.

    But they are themselves good eating. Or so we think now. Up until sometime in the 1800s, though, lobster was literally low-class food, eaten only by the poor and institutionalized. Even in the harsh penal environment of early America, some colonies had laws against feeding lobsters to inmates more than once a week because it was thought to be cruel and unusual, like making people eat rats. One reason for their low status was how plentiful lobsters were in old New England. "Unbelievable abundance" is how one source describes the situation, including accounts of Plymouth Pilgrims* wading out and capturing all they wanted by hand, and of early Boston's seashore being littered with lobsters after hard storms—these latter were treated as a smelly nuisance and ground up for fertilizer. There is also the fact that premodern lobster was cooked dead and then preserved, usually packed in salt or crude hermetic containers. Maine's earliest lobster industry was based around a dozen such seaside canneries in the 1840s, from which lobster was shipped as far away as California, in demand only because it was cheap and high in protein, basically chewable fuel.

    Now, of course, lobster is posh, a delicacy, only a step or two down from caviar. The meat is richer and more substantial than most fish, its taste subtle compared to the marine-gaminess of mussels and clams. In the US pop-food imagination, lobster is now the seafood analog to steak, with which it's so often twinned as Surf 'n' Turf* on the really expensive part of the chain steakhouse menu.

    In fact, one obvious project of the MLF, and of its omnipresently sponsorial Maine Lobster Promotion Council, is to counter the idea that lobster is unusually luxe or unhealthy or expensive, suitable only for effete palates or the occasional blow-the-diet treat. It is emphasized over and over in presentations

---

6   Midcoasters' native term for a lobster is, in fact, "bug," as in "Come around on Sunday and we'll cook up some bugs." [author's note]

7   Factoid: Lobster traps are usually baited with dead herring. [author's note]

and pamphlets at the festival that lobster meat has fewer calories, less choles-terol, and less saturated fat than chicken.[8] And in the Main Eating Tent, you can get a "quarter" (industry shorthand for a 1¼-pound lobster), a four-ounce cup of melted butter, a bag of chips, and a soft roll w/ butter-pat for around $12.00, which is only slightly more expensive than supper at McDonald's.

Be apprised, though, that the Main Lobster Festival's democratization of lobster comes with all the massed inconvenience and aesthetic compromise of real democracy. See, for example, the aforementioned Main Eating Tent, for which there is a constant Disneyland-grade queue,* and which turns out to be a square quarter mile of awning-shaded cafeteria lines and rows of long institutional tables at which friend and stranger alike sit cheek by jowl, crack-ing and chewing and dribbling. It's hot, and the sagged roof traps the steam and the smells, which latter are strong and only partly food-related. It is also loud, and a good percentage of the total noise is masticatory. The suppers come in styrofoam trays, and the soft drinks are iceless and flat, and the coffee is convenience-store coffee in more styrofoam, and the utensils are plastic (there are none of the special long skinny forks for pushing out the tail meat, though a few savvy diners bring their own). Nor do they give you near enough napkins considering how messy lobster is to eat, especially when you're squeezed onto benches alongside children of various ages and vastly different levels of fine-motor development—not to mention the people who've somehow smuggled in their own beer in enormous aisle-blocking coolers, or who all of a sudden produce their own plastic tablecloths and spread them over large portions of tables to try to reserve them (the tables) for their little groups. And so on. Any one example is no more than a petty inconvenience, of course, but the MLF turns out to be full of irksome little downers like this—see for instance the Main Stage's headliner shows, where it turns out you have to pay $20 extra for a folding chair if you want to sit down; or the North Tent's mad scramble for the Nyquil-cup-sized samples of finalists' entries handed out after the Cooking Competition; or the much-touted Maine Sea Goddess pageant finals, which turn out to be excruciatingly long and to consist mainly of endless thanks and tributes to local sponsors. Let's not even talk about the grossly inadequate Port-A-San facilities* or the fact that there's nowhere to wash your hands before or after eating. What the Maine Lobster Festival really is is a midlevel county fair with a culinary hook, and in this respect it's not unlike Tidewater crab fes-tivals, Midwest corn festivals, Texas chili festivals, etc., and shares with these

---

8   Of course, the common practice of dipping the lobster meat in melted butter torpedoes all these happy fat-specs, which none of the council's promotional stuff ever mentions, any more than potato industry PR talks about sour cream and bacon bits. [author's note]

venues the core paradox of all teeming commercial demotic[9] events: It's not for everyone.[10] Nothing against the euphoric senior editor of *Food & Wine*, but I'd be surprised if she'd ever actually been here in Harbor Park, amid crowds of people slapping canal-zone mosquitoes as they eat deep-fried Twinkies* and watch Professor Paddywhack, on six-foot stilts in a raincoat with plastic lobsters protruding from all directions on springs, terrify their children.

10   Lobster is essentially a summer food. This is because we now prefer our lobsters fresh, which means they have to be recently caught, which for both tactical and economic reasons takes place at depths less than 25 fathoms. Lobsters tend to be hungriest and most active (i.e., most trappable) at summer water temperatures of 45–50 degrees. In the autumn, most Maine lobsters migrate out

---

9   *demotic* Popular; for the masses.

10 In truth, there's a great deal to be said about the differences between working-class Rockland and the heavily populist flavor of its festival versus comfortable and elitist Camden with its expensive view and shops given entirely over to $200 sweaters and great rows of Victorian homes converted to upscale B&Bs. And about these differences as two sides of the great coin that is US tourism. Very little of which will be said here, except to amplify the above-mentioned paradox and to reveal your assigned correspondent's own preferences. I confess that I have never understood why so many people's idea of a fun vacation is to don flip-flops and sunglasses and crawl through maddening traffic to loud, hot, crowded tourist venues in order to sample a "local flavor" that is by definition ruined by the presence of tourists. This may (as my festival companions keep pointing out) all be a matter of personality and hardwired taste: the fact that I do not like tourist venues means that I'll never understand their appeal and so am probably not the one to talk about it (the supposed appeal). But, since this FN will almost surely not survive magazine-editing anyway, here goes:

As I see it, it probably really is good for the soul to be a tourist, even if it's only once in a while. Not good for the soul in a refreshing or enlivening way, though, but rather in a grim, steely-eyed, let's-look-honestly-at-the-facts-and-find-some-way-to-deal-with-them way. My personal experience has not been that traveling around the country is broadening or relaxing, or that radical changes in place and context have a salutary effect, but rather that intranational tourism is radically constricting, and humbling in the hardest way—hostile to my fantasy of being a true individual, of living somehow outside and above it all. (Coming up is the part that my companions find especially unhappy and repellent, a sure way to spoil the fun of vacation travel:) To be a mass tourist, for me, is to become a pure late-date American: alien, ignorant, greedy for something you cannot ever have, disappointed in a way you can never admit. It is to spoil, by way of sheer ontology, the very unspoiledness you are there to experience. It is to impose yourself on places that in all non-economic ways would be better, realer, without you. It is, in lines and gridlock and transaction after transaction, to confront a dimension of yourself that is as inescapable as it is painful: As a tourist, you become economically significant but existentially loathsome, an insect on a dead thing. [author's note]

into deeper water, either for warmth or to avoid the heavy waves that pound New England's coast all winter. Some burrow into the bottom. They might hibernate; nobody's sure. Summer is also lobsters' molting season—specifically early- to mid-July. Chitinous arthropods grow by molting, rather the way people have to buy bigger clothes as they age and gain weight. Since lobsters can live to be over 100, they can also get to be quite large, as in 30 pounds or more—though truly senior lobsters are rare now, because New England's waters are so heavily trapped.[11] Anyway, hence the culinary distinction between hard- and soft-shell lobsters, the latter sometimes a.k.a.* shedders. A soft-shell lobster is one that has recently molted. In midcoast restaurants, the summer menu often offers both kinds, with shedders being slightly cheaper even though they're easier to dismantle and the meat is allegedly sweeter. The reason for the discount is that a molting lobster uses a layer of seawater for insulation while its new shell is hardening, so there's slightly less actual meat when you crack open a shedder, plus a redolent gout of water that gets all over everything and can sometimes jet out lemonlike and catch a tablemate right in the eye. If it's winter or you're buying lobster someplace far from New England, on the other hand, you can almost bet that the lobster is a hard-shell, which for obvious reasons travel better.

As an à la carte* entrée, lobster can be baked, broiled, steamed, grilled, sautéed, stir-fried, or microwaved. The most common method, though, is boiling. If you're someone who enjoys having lobster at home, this is probably the way you do it, since boiling is so easy. You need a large kettle w/ cover, which you fill about half full with water (the standard advice is that you want 2.5 quarts of water per lobster). Seawater is optimal, or you can add two tbsp salt per quart from the tap. It also helps to know how much your lobsters weigh. You get the water boiling, put in the lobsters one at a time, cover the kettle, and bring it back up to a boil. Then you bank the heat and let the kettle simmer— ten minutes for the first pound of lobster, then three minutes for each pound after that. (This is assuming you've got hard-shell lobsters, which, again, if you don't live between Boston and Halifax is probably what you've got. For shedders, you're supposed to subtract three minutes from the total.) The reason the kettle's lobsters turn scarlet is that boiling somehow suppresses every pigment in their chitin but one. If you want an easy test of whether the lobsters are done, you try pulling on one of their antennae—if it comes out of the head with minimal effort, you're ready to eat.

A detail so obvious that most recipes don't even bother to mention it is that each lobster is supposed to be alive when you put it in the kettle. This

---

11 Datum: In a good year, the US industry produces around 80,000,000 pounds of lobster, and Maine accounts for more than half that total. [author's note]

is part of lobster's modern appeal—it's the freshest food there is. There's no decomposition between harvesting and eating. And not only do lobsters require no cleaning or dressing or plucking, they're relatively easy for vendors to keep alive. They come up alive in the traps, are placed in containers of seawater, and can—so long as the water's aerated and the animals' claws are pegged or banded to keep them from tearing one another up under the stresses of captivity[12]—survive right up until they're boiled. Most of us have been in supermarkets or restaurants that feature tanks of live lobsters, from which you can pick out your supper while it watches you point. And part of the overall spectacle of the Maine Lobster Festival is that you can see actual lobstermen's vessels docking at the wharves along the northeast grounds and unloading fresh-caught product, which is transferred by hand or cart 150 yards to the great clear tanks stacked up around the festival's cooker—which is, as mentioned, billed as the World's Largest Lobster Cooker and can process over 100 lobsters at a time for the Main Eating Tent.

So then here is a question that's all but unavoidable at the World's Largest Lobster Cooker, and may arise in kitchens across the US: Is it all right to boil a sentient creature alive just for our gustatory[13] pleasure? A related set of concerns: Is the previous question irksomely PC* or sentimental? What does "all right" even mean in this context? Is the whole thing just a matter of personal choice?

As you may or may not know, a certain well-known group called People for the Ethical Treatment of Animals* thinks that the morality of lobster-boiling is not just a matter of individual conscience. In fact, one of the very first things we hear about the MLF ... well, to set the scene: We're coming in by cab from the almost indescribably odd and rustic Knox County Airport[14] very late on the night before the festival opens, sharing the cab with a wealthy political

---

12 N.B. Similar reasoning underlies the practice of what's termed "debeaking" broiler chickens and brood hens in modern factory farms. Maximum commercial efficiency requires that enormous poultry populations be confined in unnaturally close quarters, under which conditions many birds go crazy and peck one another to death. As a purely observational side-note, be apprised that debeaking is usually an automated process and that the chickens receive no anesthetic. It's not clear to me whether most *Gourmet* readers know about debeaking, or about related practices like dehorning cattle in commercial feed lots, cropping swine's tails in factory hog farms to keep psychotically bored neighbors from chewing them off, and so forth. It so happens that your assigned correspondent knew almost nothing about standard meat-industry operations before starting work on this article. [author's note]

13 *gustatory* Taste-related.

14 The terminal used to be somebody's house, for example, and the lost-luggage-reporting room was clearly once a pantry. [author's note]

consultant who lives on Vinalhaven Island in the bay half the year (he's headed for the island ferry in Rockland). The consultant and cabdriver are responding to informal journalistic probes about how people who live in the midcoast region actually view the MLF, as in is the festival just a big-dollar tourist thing or is it something local residents look forward to attending, take genuine civic pride in, etc. The cabdriver (who's in his seventies, one of apparently a whole platoon of retirees the cab company puts on to help with the summer rush, and wears a US-flag lapel pin, and drives in what can only be called a very *deliberate* way) assures us that locals do endorse and enjoy the MLF, although he himself hasn't gone in years, and now come to think of it no one he and his wife know has, either. However, the demilocal consultant's been to recent festivals a couple times (one gets the impression it was at his wife's behest), of which his most vivid impression was that "you have to line up for an ungodly long time to get your lobsters, and meanwhile there are all these ex-flower children coming up and down along the line handing out pamphlets that say the lobsters die in terrible pain and you shouldn't eat them."

And it turns out that the post-hippies of the consultant's recollection were activists from PETA.* There were no PETA people in obvious view at the 2003 MLF,[15] but they've been conspicuous at many of the recent festivals. Since at least the mid-1990s, articles in everything from *The Camden Herald* to *The New York Times* have described PETA urging boycotts of the Maine Lobster Festival, often deploying celebrity spokesmen like Mary Tyler Moore* for open letters and ads saying stuff like "Lobsters are extraordinarily sensitive" and "To me, eating a lobster is out of the question." More concrete is the oral

15

---

15 It turned out that one Mr. William R. Rivas-Rivas, a high-ranking PETA official out of the group's Virginia headquarters, was indeed there this year, albeit solo, working the festival's main and side entrances on Saturday, 2 August, handing out pamphlets and adhesive stickers emblazoned with "Being Boiled Hurts," which is the tagline in most of PETA's published material about lobsters. I learned that he'd been there only later, when speaking with Mr. Rivas-Rivas on the phone. I'm not sure how we missed seeing him *in situ* at the festival, and I can't see much to do except apologize for the oversight—although it's also true that Saturday was the day of the big MLF parade through Rockland, which basic journalistic responsibility seemed to require going to (and which, with all due respect, meant that Saturday was maybe not the best day for PETA to work the Harbor Park grounds, especially if it was going to be just one person for one day, since a lot of diehard MLF partisans were off-site watching the parade (which, again with no offense intended, was in truth kind of cheesy and boring, consisting mostly of slow homemade floats and various midcoast people waving at one another, and with an extremely annoying man dressed as Blackbeard* ranging up and down the length of the crowd saying "Arrr" over and over and brandishing a plastic sword at people, etc.; plus it rained)). [author's note]

testimony of Dick, our florid and extremely gregarious rental-car liason,[16] to the effect that PETA's been around so much during recent years that a kind of brittlely tolerant homeostasis[17] now obtains between the activists and the festival's locals, e.g.: "We had some incidents a couple years ago. One lady took most of her clothes off and painted herself like a lobster, almost got herself arrested. But for the most part they're let alone. [Rapid series of small ambiguous laughs, which with Dick happens a lot.] They do their thing and we do our thing."

This whole interchange takes place on Route 1, 30 July, during a four-mile, 50-minute ride from the airport[18] to the dealership to sign car-rental papers. Several irreproducible segues down the road from the PETA anecdotes, Dick—whose son-in-law happens to be a professional lobsterman and one of the Main Eating Tent's regular suppliers—explains what he and his family feel is the crucial mitigating factor in the whole morality-of-boiling-lobsters-alive issue: "There's a part of the brain in people and animals that lets us feel pain, and lobsters' brains don't have this part."

Besides the fact that it's incorrect in about nine different ways, the main reason Dick's statement is interesting is that its thesis is more or less echoed by the festival's own pronouncement on lobsters and pain, which is part of a Test Your Lobster IQ quiz that appears in the 2003 MLF program courtesy of the Maine Lobster Promotion Council:

> The nervous system of a lobster is very simple, and is in fact most similar to the nervous system of the grasshopper. It is decentralized with no brain. There is no cerebral cortex, which in humans is the area of the brain that gives the experience of pain.

Though it sounds more sophisticated, a lot of the neurology in this latter claim is still either false or fuzzy. The human cerebral cortex is the brain-part that deals with higher faculties like reason, metaphysical self-awareness, language, etc. Pain reception is known to be part of a much older and more primitive system of nociceptors and prostaglandins that are managed by the brain stem and

---

16   By profession, Dick is actually a car salesman; the midcoast region's National Car Rental franchise operates out of a Chevy dealership in Thomaston. [author's note]

17   *homeostasis*   I.e., balance.

18   The short version regarding why we were back at the airport after already arriving the previous night involves lost luggage and a miscommunication about where and what the midcoast's National franchise was—Dick came out personally to the airport and got us, out of no evident motive but kindness. (He also talked nonstop the entire way, with a very distinctive speaking style that can be described only as manically laconic; the truth is that I now know more about this man than I do about some members of my own family.) [author's note]

thalamus.[19][20] On the other hand, it is true that the cerebral cortex is involved in what's variously called suffering, distress, or the emotional experience of pain—i.e., experiencing painful stimuli as unpleasant, very unpleasant, unbearable, and so on.

Before we go any further, let's acknowledge that the questions of whether and how different kinds of animals feel pain, and of whether and why it might be justifiable to inflict pain on them in order to eat them, turn out to be extremely complex and difficult. And comparative neuroanatomy is only part of the problem. Since pain is a totally subjective mental experience, we do not have direct access to anyone or anything's pain but our own; and even just the principles by which we can infer that other human beings experience pain and have a legitimate interest in not feeling pain involve hard-core philosophy—metaphysics, epistemology, value theory, ethics. The fact that even the most highly evolved nonhuman mammals can't use language to communicate with us about their subjective mental experience is only the first layer of additional complication in trying to extend our reasoning about pain and morality to animals. And everything gets progressively more abstract and convoluted as we move farther and farther out from the higher-type mammals into cattle and swine and dogs and cats and rodents, and then birds and fish, and finally invertebrates like lobsters.

The more important point here, though, is that the whole animal-cruelty-and-eating issue is not just complex, it's also uncomfortable. It is, at any rate, uncomfortable for me, and for just about everyone I know who enjoys a variety of foods and yet does not want to see herself as cruel or unfeeling. As far as I can tell, my own main way of dealing with this conflict has been to avoid thinking about the whole unpleasant thing. I should add that it appears to me unlikely that many readers of *Gourmet* wish to think about it, either, or to be queried about the morality of their eating habits in the pages of a culinary monthly. Since, however, the assigned subject of this article is what it was like to attend the 2003 MLF, and thus to spend several days in the midst of a great mass of Americans all eating lobster, and thus to be more or less impelled to think hard about lobster and the experience of buying and eating lobster, it turns out that there is no honest way to avoid certain moral questions.

---

19 *prostaglandins* Chemicals similar to hormones; *thalamus* Part of the brain that transmits sensory input to the cerebral cortex.

20 To elaborate by way of example: The common experience of accidentally touching a hot stove and yanking your hand back before you're even aware that anything's going on is explained by the fact that many of the processes by which we detect and avoid painful stimuli do not involve the cortex. In the case of the hand and stove, the brain is bypassed altogether; all the important neurochemical action takes place in the spine. [author's note]

20   There are several reasons for this. For one thing, it's not just that lobsters get boiled alive, it's that you do it yourself—or at least it's done specifically for you, on-site.[21] As mentioned, the World's Largest Lobster Cooker, which is highlighted as an attraction in the festival's program, is right out there on the MLF's north grounds for everyone to see. Try to imagine a Nebraska Beef Festival[22] at which part of the festivities is watching trucks pull up and the live cattle get driven down the ramp and slaughtered right there on the World's Largest Killing Floor or something—there's no way.

The intimacy of the whole thing is maximized at home, which of course is where most lobster gets prepared and eaten (although note already the semi-conscious euphemism "prepared," which in the case of lobsters really means killing them right there in our kitchens). The basic scenario is that we come in from the store and make our little preparations like getting the kettle filled and boiling, and then we lift the lobsters out of the bag or whatever retail container they came home in ... whereupon some uncomfortable things start to happen. However stuporous a lobster is from the trip home, for instance, it tends to come alarmingly to life when placed in boiling water. If you're tilting it from a container into the steaming kettle, the lobster will sometimes try to cling to the container's sides or even to hook its claws over the kettle's rim like a person trying to keep from going over the edge of a roof. And worse is when the lobster's fully immersed. Even if you cover the kettle and turn away, you can usually hear the cover rattling and clanking as the lobster tries to push it off. Or the creature's claws scraping the sides of the kettle as it thrashes around.

---

21   Morality-wise, let's concede that this cuts both ways. Lobster-eating is at least not abetted by the system of corporate factory farms that produces most beef, pork, and chicken. Because, if nothing else, of the way they're marketed and packaged for sale, we eat these latter meats without having to consider that they were once conscious, sentient creatures to whom horrible things were done. (N.B. "Horrible" here meaning really, really horrible. Write off to PETA or peta.org for their free "Meet Your Meat" video, narrated by Mr. Alec Baldwin, if you want to see just about everything meat-related you don't want to see or think about. (N.B.$_2$ Not that PETA's any sort of font of unspun truth. Like many partisans in complex moral disputes, the PETA people are fanatics, and a lot of their rhetoric seems simplistic and self-righteous. But this particular video, replete with actual factory-farm and corporate-slaughterhouse footage, is both credible and traumatizing.)) [author's note]

22   Is it significant that "lobster," "fish," and "chicken" are our culture's words for both the animal and the meat, whereas most mammals seem to require euphemisms like "beef" and "pork" that help us separate the meat we eat from the living creature the meat once was? Is this evidence that some kind of deep unease about eating higher animals is endemic enough to show up in English usage, but that the unease diminishes as we move out of the mammalian order? (And is "lamb"/"lamb" the counterexample that sinks the whole theory, or are there special, biblico-historical reasons for that equivalence?) [author's note]

The lobster, in other words, behaves very much as you or I would behave if we were plunged into boiling water (with the obvious exception of screaming).[23] A blunter way to say this is that the lobster acts as if it's in terrible pain, causing some cooks to leave the kitchen altogether and to take one of those little lightweight plastic oven-timers with them into another room and wait until the whole process is over.

There happen to be two main criteria that most ethicists agree on for determining whether a living creature has the capacity to suffer and so has genuine interests that it may or may not be our moral duty to consider.[24] One is how much of the neurological hardware required for pain-experience the animal comes equipped with—nociceptors, prostaglandins, neuronal opioid receptors, etc. The other criterion is whether the animal demonstrates behavior associated with pain. And it takes a lot of intellectual gymnastics and behaviorist hair-splitting not to see struggling, thrashing, and lid-clattering as just such pain-behavior. According to marine zoologists, it usually takes lobsters between 35 and 45 seconds to die in boiling water. (No source I could find talked about how long it takes them to die in superheated steam; one rather hopes it's faster.)

There are, of course, other fairly common ways to kill your lobster on-site and so achieve maximum freshness. Some cooks' practice is to drive a sharp heavy knife point-first into a spot just above the midpoint between the lobster's eyestalks (more or less where the Third Eye is in human foreheads). This is alleged either to kill the lobster instantly or to render it insensate, and is said at least to eliminate some of the cowardice involved in throwing a creature into boiling water and then fleeing the room. As far as I can tell from talking

---

23 There's a relevant populist myth about the high-pitched whistling sound that sometimes issues from a pot of boiling lobster. The sound is really vented steam from the layer of seawater between the lobster's flesh and its carapace (this is why shedders whistle more than hard-shells), but the pop version has it that the sound is the lobster's rabbit-like death-scream. Lobsters communicate via pheromones in their urine and don't have anything close to the vocal equipment for screaming, but the myth's very persistent—which might, once again, point to a low-level cultural unease about the boiling thing. [author's note]

24 "Interests" basically means strong and legitimate preferences, which obviously require some degree of consciousness, responsiveness to stimuli, etc. See, for instance, the utilitarian philosopher Peter Singer, whose 1974 *Animal Liberation* is more or less the bible of the modern animal-rights movement:

> It would be nonsense to say that it was not in the interests of a stone to be kicked along the road by a schoolboy. A stone does not have interests because it cannot suffer. Nothing that we can do to it could possibly make any difference to its welfare. A mouse, on the other hand, does have an interest in not being kicked along the road, because it will suffer if it is. [author's note]

to proponents of the knife-in-the-head method, the idea is that it's more violent but ultimately more merciful, plus that a willingness to exert personal agency and accept responsibility for stabbing the lobster's head honors the lobster somehow and entitles one to eat it (there's often a vague sort of Native American spirituality-of-the-hunt flavor to pro-knife arguments). But the problem with the knife method is basic biology: Lobsters' nervous systems operate off not one but several ganglia, a.k.a. nerve bundles, which are sort of wired in series and distributed all along the lobster's underside, from stem to stern. And disabling only the frontal ganglion does not normally result in quick death or unconsciousness.

Another alternative is to put the lobster in cold saltwater and then very slowly bring it up to a full boil. Cooks who advocate this method are going on the analogy to a frog, which can supposedly be kept from jumping out of a boiling pot by heating the water incrementally. In order to save a lot of research-summarizing, I'll simply assure you that the analogy between frogs and lobsters turns out not to hold—plus, if the kettle's water isn't aerated seawater, the immersed lobster suffers from slow suffocation, although usually not decisive enough suffocation to keep it from still thrashing and clattering when the water gets hot enough to kill it. In fact, lobsters boiled incrementally often display a whole bonus set of gruesome, convulsionlike reactions that you don't see in regular boiling.

25　　Ultimately, the only certain virtues of the home-lobotomy and slow-heating methods are comparative, because there are even worse/crueler ways people prepare lobster. Time-thrifty cooks sometimes microwave them alive (usually after poking several extra vent-holes in the carapace, which is a precaution most shellfish-microwavers learn about the hard way). Live dismemberment, on the other hand, is big in Europe—some chefs cut the lobster in half before cooking; others like to tear off the claws and tail and toss only these parts in the pot.

And there's more unhappy news respecting suffering-criterion number one. Lobsters don't have much in the way of eyesight or hearing, but they do have an exquisite tactile sense, one facilitated by hundreds of thousands of tiny hairs that protrude through their carapace. "Thus it is," in the words of T.M. Prudden's industry classic *About Lobster*, "that although encased in what seems a solid, impenetrable armor, the lobster can receive stimuli and impressions from without as readily as if it possessed a soft and delicate skin." And lobsters do have nociceptors,[25] as well as invertebrate versions of the prostaglandins and major neurotransmitters via which our own brains register pain.

25　This is the neurological term for special pain-receptors that are "sensitive to potentially damaging extremes of temperature, to mechanical forces, and to chemical

Lobsters do not, on the other hand, appear to have the equipment for making or absorbing natural opioids like endorphins and enkephalins, which are what more advanced nervous systems use to try to handle intense pain. From this fact, though, one could conclude either that lobsters are maybe even *more* vulnerable to pain, since they lack mammalian nervous systems' built-in analgesia,[26] or, instead, that the absence of natural opioids implies an absence of the really intense pain-sensations that natural opioids are designed to mitigate. I for one can detect a marked upswing in mood as I contemplate this latter possibility. It could be that their lack of endorphin/enkephalin hardware means that lobsters' raw subjective experience of pain is so radically different from mammals' that it may not even deserve the term "pain." Perhaps lobsters are more like those frontal-lobotomy patients one reads about who report experiencing pain in a totally different way than you and I. These patients evidently do feel physical pain, neurologically speaking, but don't dislike it—though neither do they like it; it's more that they feel it but don't feel anything *about* it—the point being that the pain is not distressing to them or something they want to get away from. Maybe lobsters, who are also without frontal lobes, are detached from the neurological-registration-of-injury-or-hazard we call pain in just the same way. There is, after all, a difference between (1) pain as a purely neurological event, and (2) actual suffering, which seems crucially to involve an emotional component, an awareness of pain as unpleasant, as something to fear/dislike/want to avoid.

Still, after all the abstract intellection, there remain the facts of the frantically clanking lid, the pathetic clinging to the edge of the pot. Standing at the stove, it is hard to deny in any meaningful way that this is a living creature experiencing pain and wishing to avoid/escape the painful experience. To my lay mind, the lobster's behavior in the kettle appears to be the expression of a *preference*; and it may well be that an ability to form preferences is the decisive criterion for real suffering.[27] The logic of this (preference → suffering) relation may be easiest to see in the negative case. If you cut certain kinds of worms in half, the halves will often keep crawling around and going about their vermiform business as if nothing had happened. When we assert, based on their post-op behavior, that these worms appear not to be suffering, what

---

substances which are released when body tissues are damaged." [author's note]

26 *analgesia* Pain reduction.

27 "Preference" is maybe roughly synonymous with "interests," but it is a better term for our purposes because it's less abstractly philosophical—"preference" seems more personal, and it's the whole idea of a living creature's personal experience that's at issue. [author's note]

we're really saying is that there's no sign that the worms know anything bad has happened or would *prefer* not to have gotten cut in half.

Lobsters, though, are known to exhibit preferences. Experiments have shown that they can detect changes of only a degree or two in water temperature; one reason for their complex migratory cycles (which can often cover 100-plus miles a year) is to pursue the temperatures they like best.[28] And, as mentioned, they're bottom-dwellers and do not like bright light—if a tank of food lobsters is out in the sunlight or a store's fluorescence, the lobsters will always congregate in whatever part is darkest. Fairly solitary in the ocean, they also clearly dislike the crowding that's part of their captivity in tanks, since (as also mentioned) one reason why lobsters' claws are banded on capture is to keep them from attacking one another under the stress of close-quarter storage.

30   In any event, at the MLF, standing by the bubbling tanks outside the World's Largest Lobster Cooker, watching the fresh-caught lobsters pile over one another, wave their hobbled claws impotently, huddle in the rear corners, or scrabble frantically back from the glass as you approach, it is difficult not to sense that they're unhappy, or frightened, even if it's some rudimentary version of these feelings ... and, again, why does rudimentariness even enter into it? Why is a primitive, inarticulate form of suffering less urgent or uncomfortable for the person who's helping to inflict it by paying for the food it results in? I'm

---

28   Of course, the most common sort of counterargument here would begin by objecting that "like best" is really just a metaphor, and a misleadingly anthropomorphic* one at that. The counterarguer would posit that the lobster seeks to maintain a certain optimal ambient temperature out of nothing but unconscious instinct (with a similar explanation for the low-light affinities upcoming in the main text). The thrust of such a counterargument will be that the lobster's thrashings and clankings in the kettle express not unpreferred pain but involuntary reflexes, like your leg shooting out when the doctor hits your knee. Be advised that there are professional scientists, including many researchers who use animals in experiments, who hold to the view that nonhuman creatures have no real feelings at all, merely "behaviors." Be further advised that this view has a long history that goes all the way back to Descartes, although its modern support comes mostly from behaviorist psychology. [René Descartes (1596–1650) was an influential French philosopher; behaviorist psychology interprets psychology exclusively in terms of behavior as opposed to internal mental states.]

To these what-looks-like-pain-is-really-just-reflexes counterarguments, however, there happen to be all sorts of scientific and pro-animal-rights counter-counterarguments. And then further attempted rebuttals and redirects, and so on. Suffice to say that both the scientific and the philosophical arguments on either side of the animal-suffering issue are involved, abstruse, technical, often informed by self-interest or ideology, and in the end so totally inconclusive that as a practical matter, in the kitchen or restaurant, it all still seems to come down to individual conscience, going with (no pun) your gut. [author's note]

not trying to give you a PETA-like screed here—at least I don't think so. I'm trying, rather, to work out and articulate some of the troubling questions that arise amid all the laughter and saltation[29] and community pride of the Maine Lobster Festival. The truth is that if you, the festival attendee, permit yourself to think that lobsters can suffer and would rather not, the MLF begins to take on the aspect of something like a Roman circus[30] or medieval torture-fest.

Does that comparison seem a bit much? If so, exactly why? Or what about this one: Is it possible that future generations will regard our own present agribusiness and eating practices in much the same way we now view Nero's entertainments or Mengele's experiments?[31] My own immediate reaction is that such a comparison is hysterical, extreme—and yet the reason it seems extreme to me appears to be that I believe animals are less morally important than human beings;[32] and when it comes to defending such a belief, even to myself, I have to acknowledge that (a) I have an obvious selfish interest in this belief, since I like to eat certain kinds of animals and want to be able to keep doing it, and (b) I haven't succeeded in working out any sort of personal ethical system in which the belief is truly defensible instead of just selfishly convenient.

Given this article's venue and my own lack of culinary sophistication, I'm curious about whether the reader can identify with any of these reactions and acknowledgments and discomforts. I am also concerned not to come off as shrill or preachy when what I really am is more like confused. For those *Gourmet* readers who enjoy well-prepared and -presented meals involving beef, veal, lamb, pork, chicken, lobster, etc.: Do you think much about the (possible) moral status and (probable) suffering of the animals involved? If you do, what ethical convictions have you worked out that permit you not just to eat but to savor and enjoy flesh-based viands[33] (since of course refined *enjoyment*, rather than mere ingestion, is the whole point of gastronomy)? If, on the other hand, you'll have no truck with confusions or convictions and regard stuff like the

---

29   *saltation*   I.e., dancing, jumping around.

30   *circus*   Mass entertainment, which in ancient Rome could include the killing of humans by animals, of animals by humans, or of humans by each other.

31   *Nero's entertainments*   Among the spectacles that Roman Emperor Nero (37–68 CE) staged for his people's enjoyment were gladiator battles and the brutal public execution of Christians;   *Mengele's experiments*   Nazi doctor Josef Mengele (1911–79) conducted cruel medical experiments on inmates at the Auschwitz concentration camp.

32   Meaning a *lot* less important, apparently, since the moral comparison here is not the value of one human's life vs. the value of one animal's life, but rather the value of one animal's life vs. the value of one human's taste for a particular kind of protein. Even the most diehard carniphile* will acknowledge that it's possible to live and eat well without consuming animals. [author's note]

33   *viands*   Foods.

previous paragraph as just so much fatuous navel-gazing, what makes it feel truly okay, inside, to just dismiss the whole issue out of hand? That is, is your refusal to think about any of this the product of actual thought, or is it just that you don't want to think about it? And if the latter, then why not? Do you ever think, even idly, about the possible reasons for your reluctance to think about it? I am not trying to bait anyone here—I'm genuinely curious. After all, isn't being extra aware and attentive and thoughtful about one's food and its overall context part of what distinguishes a real gourmet? Or is all the gourmet's extra attention and sensibility just supposed to be sensuous? Is it really all just a matter of taste and presentation?

These last few queries, though, while sincere, obviously involve much larger and more abstract questions about the connections (if any) between aesthetics and morality—about what the adjective in a phrase like "The Magazine of Good Living"[34] is really supposed to mean—and these questions lead straightaway into such deep and treacherous waters that it's probably best to stop the public discussion right here. There are limits to what even interested persons can ask of each other.

(2004)

---

34 *The Magazine ... Living* Slogan of *Gourmet* magazine.

Eula Biss

from The Pain Scale

"The Pain Scale," by creative non-fiction writer Eula Biss, is an
example of the lyric essay, a genre that blends poetic and non-fiction
writing conventions. Approaching Biss's personal experience of
chronic pain in this fluid, multi-dimensional form, her essay has
been described by Susannah B. Mintz as a "touchstone" text in the
growing field of Pain Studies. "The Pain Scale" first appeared in
The Seneca Review *in 2005.*

NO PAIN

The concept of Christ is considerably older than the concept of zero.[1] Both are problematic—both have their fallacies and their immaculate conceptions. But the problem of zero troubles me significantly more than the problem of Christ.

I am sitting in the exam room of a hospital entertaining the idea that absolutely no pain is not possible. Despite the commercials, I suspect that pain cannot be eliminated. And this may be the fallacy on which we have based all our calculations and all our excesses. All our sins are for zero.

Zero is not a number. Or at least, it does not behave like a number. It does not add, subtract, or multiply like other numbers. Zero is a number in the way that Christ was a man.

Aristotle, for one, did not believe in Zero.[2]

If no pain is possible, then, another question—is no pain desirable? Does the absence of pain equal the absence of everything?

5

---

1   *older than ... of zero*   The idea of zero as a number was first developed by seventh-century Indian mathematicians, spreading to Asian and Middle Eastern thinkers in the years that followed and eventually becoming known to European academics by the thirteenth century.

2   *Aristotle ... Zero*   Greek philosopher Aristotle (383–322 BCE) argued against the idea of a void or a place where nothing exists.

Some very complicated mathematical problems cannot be solved without the concept of zero. But zero makes some very simple problems impossible to solve. For example, the value of zero divided by zero is unknown.

I'm not a mathematician. I'm sitting in a hospital trying to measure my pain on a scale from zero to ten. For this purpose, I need a zero. A scale of any sort needs fixed points.

The upper fixed point on the Fahrenheit scale, ninety-six, is based on a slightly inaccurate measure of normal body temperature. The lower fixed point, zero, is the coldest temperature at which a mixture of salt and water can still remain liquid. I myself am a mixture of salt and water. I strive to remain liquid.

Zero, on the Celsius scale, is the point at which water freezes. And one hundred is the point at which water boils.

10   But Anders Celsius, who introduced the scale in 1741, originally fixed zero as the point at which water boiled, and one hundred as the point at which water froze. These fixed points were reversed only after his death.

The deepest circle of Dante's *Inferno* does not burn. It is frozen. In his last glimpse of Hell, Dante looks back and sees Satan upside down through the ice.[3]

There is only one fixed point on the Kelvin scale[4]—absolute zero. Absolute zero is 273 degrees Celsius colder than the temperature at which water freezes. There are zeroes beneath zeroes. Absolute zero is the temperature at which molecules and atoms are moving as slowly as possible. But even at absolute zero, their motion does not stop completely. Even the absolute is not absolute. This is comforting, but it does not give me faith in zero.

At night, I ice my pain. My mind descends into a strange sinking calm. Any number multiplied by zero is zero. And so with ice and me. I am nullified. I wake up to melted ice and the warm throb of my pain returning.

Grab a chicken by its neck or body—it squawks and flaps and pecks and thrashes like mad. But grab a chicken by its feet and turn it upside down, and it just hangs there blinking in a waking trance. Zeroed. My mother and I hung the chickens like this on the barn door for their necks to be slit. I like to imagine that a chicken at zero feels no pain....

---

3   *The deepest ... ice*   The first section of Dante Alighieri's epic poem the *Divine Comedy* (c. 1308–21), called *Inferno,* depicts the Italian writer journeying through nine circles of hell, each containing different types of sinners and progressively horrible punishments. In the ninth and final circle, he encounters Satan among the traitors, humankind's worst offenders, who are punished with encasement in ice.

4   *Kelvin scale*   Named after William Thomson, Baron Kelvin, the Kelvin temperature scale's absolute zero lends itself to the scientific process and has become the international standard for study involving temperature.

<—————— 5 ——————>

"The problem with scales from zero to ten," my father tells me, "is the tyranny   15
of the mean."

Overwhelmingly, patients tend to rate their pain as a five, unless they are in
excruciating pain. At best, this renders the scale far less sensitive to gradations
in pain. At worst, it renders the scale useless.

I understand the desire to be average only when I am in pain. To be normal
is to be okay in a fundamental way—to be chosen numerically by God.

When I could no longer sleep at night because of my pain, my father reminded me that a great many people suffer from both insomnia and pain. "In
fact," he told me, "neck and back pain is so common that it is a cliché—a pain
in the neck!"*

The fact that 50 million Americans suffer from chronic pain does not
comfort me. Rather, it confounds me. "This is not normal," I keep thinking. A
thought invariably followed by a doubt, "Is this normal?"

The distinction between test results that are normal or abnormal is often   20
determined by how far the results deviate from the mean. My X-rays did not
reveal a cause for my pain, but they did reveal an abnormality. "See this," the
doctor pointed to the string of vertebrae hanging down from the base of my
skull like a loose line finding plumb.[5] "Your spine," he told me, "is abnormally straight."

I live in Middle America.* I am of average height, although I have always
thought of myself as short. I am of average weight, although I tend to believe I
am oddly shaped. Although I try to hide it, I have long straight blond hair, like
most of the women in this town.

Despite my efforts to ignore it and to despise it, I am still susceptible to the
mean—a magnet that pulls even flesh and bone. For some time I entertained the
idea that my spine might have been straightened by my long-held misconception that normal spines were perfectly straight. Unknowingly, I may have been
striving for a straight spine, and perhaps I had managed to disfigure my body
by sitting too straight for too many years. "Unlikely," the doctor told me....

<————— 10
THE WORST PAIN IMAGINABLE

Through a failure of my imagination, or of myself, I have discovered that the
pain I am in is always the worst pain imaginable.

---

5   *loose line finding plumb*   String or cord attached to a dangling plumb, or weight,
used to assess whether a line is perfectly vertical.

But I would like to believe that there is an upper limit to pain. That there is a maximum intensity nerves can register.

25   There is no tenth circle in Dante's Hell.

The digit ten depends on the digit zero, in our current number system. In 1994 Robert Forslund developed an Alternative Number System. "This system," he wrote with triumph, "eliminates the need for the digit zero, and hence all digits behave the same."

In the Alternate Number System, the tenth digit is represented by the character A. Counting begins at one: 1, 2, 3, 4, 5, 6, 7, 8, 9, A, 11, 12 ... 18, 19, 1A, 21, 22 ... 28, 29, 2A ... 98, 99, 9A, A1, A2, A3, A4, A5, A6, A7, A8, A9, AA, 111, 112 ...

"One of the functions of the pain scale," my father explains, "is to protect doctors—to spare them some emotional pain. Hearing someone describe their pain as a ten is much easier than hearing them describe it as a hot poker driven through their eyeball into their brain."

A better scale, my father thinks, might rate what patients would be willing to do to relieve their pain. "Would you," he suggests, "visit five specialists and take three prescription narcotics?" I laugh because I have done just that. "Would you," I offer, "give up a limb?" I would not. "Would you surrender your sense of sight for the next ten years?" my father asks. I would not. "Would you accept a shorter life span?" I might. We are laughing, having fun with this game. But later, reading statements collected by the American Pain Foundation, I am alarmed by the number of references to suicide.

30   "... constant muscle aches, spasms, sleeplessness, pain, can't focus ... must be depression ... two suicide attempts later, electroshock therapy and locked-down wards...."

The description of hurricane force winds on the Beaufort scale[6] is simply, "devastation occurs."

Bringing us, of course, back to zero.

(2005)

---

6   *Beaufort scale* System of classifying wind force created in 1805 by Naval Commander Francis Beaufort.

TIME AND DISTANCE OVERCOME

"Time and Distance Overcome" first appeared in The Iowa Review *in 2008; the following year it appeared in Biss's collection* Notes from No Man's Land: American Essays.

"Of what use is such an invention?" the *New York World* asked shortly after Alexander Graham Bell[7] first demonstrated his telephone in 1876. The world was not waiting for the telephone.

Bell's financial backers asked him not to work on his new invention because it seemed too dubious an investment. The idea on which the telephone depended—the idea that every home in the country could be connected with a vast network of wires suspended from poles set an average of one hundred feet apart—seemed far more unlikely than the idea that the human voice could be transmitted through a wire.

Even now it is an impossible idea, that we are all connected, all of us.

"At the present time we have a perfect network of gas pipes and water pipes throughout our large cities," Bell wrote to his business partners in defense of his idea. "We have main pipes laid under the streets communicating by side pipes with the various dwellings.... In a similar manner it is conceivable that cables of telephone wires could be laid under ground, or suspended overhead, communicating by branch wires with private dwellings, counting houses, shops, manufactories, etc., uniting them through the main cable."

Imagine the mind that could imagine this. That could see us joined by one branching cable. This was the mind of a man who wanted to invent, more than the telephone, a machine that would allow the deaf to hear.

5

For a short time the telephone was little more than a novelty. For twenty-five cents you could see it demonstrated by Bell himself, in a church, along with singing and recitations by local talent. From some distance away, Bell would receive a call from "the invisible Mr. Watson." Then the telephone became a plaything of the rich. A Boston banker paid for a private line between his office and his home so that he could let his family know exactly when he would be home for dinner.

---

7   *New York World*   Daily newspaper (1860–1931) known for sensational stories meant to attract readership;   *Alexander Graham Bell*   Scottish-born inventor (1847–1922) best known for the invention of the telephone. He is also credited with several other inventions, many of them also related to sound, and was an influential educator of deaf children.

Mark Twain* was among the first Americans to own a telephone, but he wasn't completely taken with the device. "The human voice carries entirely too far as it is," he remarked.

By 1889, the *New York Times* was reporting a "War on Telephone Poles." Wherever telephone companies were erecting poles, homeowners and business owners were sawing them down, or defending their sidewalks with rifles.

Property owners in Red Bank, New Jersey, threatened to tar and feather* the workers putting up telephone poles. A judge granted a group of homeowners an injunction to prevent the telephone company from erecting any new poles. Another judge found that a man who had cut down a pole because it was "obnoxious" was not guilty of malicious mischief.

10   Telephone poles, newspaper editorials complained, were an urban blight. The poles carried a wire for each telephone—sometimes hundreds of wires. And in some places there were also telegraph wires, power lines, and trolley cables. The sky was netted with wires.

The war on telephone poles was fueled, in part, by that terribly American concern for private property, and a reluctance to surrender it for a shared utility. And then there was a fierce sense of aesthetics, an obsession with purity, a dislike for the way the poles and wires marred a landscape that those other new inventions, skyscrapers and barbed wire, were just beginning to complicate. And then perhaps there was also a fear that distance, as it had always been known and measured, was collapsing.

The city council in Sioux Falls, South Dakota, ordered policemen to cut down all the telephone poles in town. And the mayor of Oshkosh, Wisconsin, ordered the police chief and the fire department to chop down the telephone poles there. Only one pole was chopped down before the telephone men climbed all the poles along the line, preventing any more chopping. Soon, Bell Telephone Company began stationing a man at the top of each pole as soon as it had been set, until enough poles had been set to string a wire between them, at which point it became a misdemeanor to interfere with the poles. Even so, a constable cut down two poles holding forty or fifty wires. And a homeowner sawed down a recently wired pole, then fled from police. The owner of a cannery ordered his workers to throw dirt back into the hole the telephone company was digging in front of his building. His men threw the dirt back in as fast as the telephone workers could dig it out. Then he sent out a team with a load of stones to dump into the hole. Eventually, the pole was erected on the other side of the street.

Despite the war on telephone poles, it would take only four years after Bell's first public demonstration of the telephone for every town of more than ten thousand people to be wired, although many towns were wired only to themselves. By the turn of the century, there were more telephones than bathtubs in America.

"Time and dist. overcome," read an early advertisement for the telephone. Rutherford B. Hayes[8] pronounced the installation of a telephone in the White House "one of the greatest events since creation." The telephone, Thomas Edison* declared, "annihilated time and space, and brought the human family in closer touch."

In 1898, in Lake Cormorant, Mississippi, a black man was hanged from a telephone pole. And in Weir City, Kansas. And in Brook Haven, Mississippi. And in Tulsa, Oklahoma, where the hanged man was riddled with bullets. In Danville, Illinois, a black man's throat was slit, and his dead body was strung up on a telephone pole. Two black men were hanged from a telephone pole in Lewisburg, West Virginia. And two in Hempstead, Texas, where one man was dragged out of the courtroom by a mob, and another was dragged out of jail.

15

A black man was hanged from a telephone pole in Belleville, Illinois, where a fire was set at the base of the pole and the man was cut down half-alive, covered in coal oil, and burned. While his body was burning the mob beat it with clubs and nearly cut it to pieces.

Lynching, the first scholar of the subject determined, is an American invention.[9] Lynching from bridges, from arches, from trees standing alone in fields, from trees in front of the county courthouse, from trees used as public billboards, from trees barely able to support the weight of a man, from telephone poles, from street lamps, and from poles erected solely for that purpose. From the middle of the nineteenth century to the middle of the twentieth century black men were lynched for crimes real and imagined, for whistles, for rumors, for "disputing with a white man," for "unpopularity," for "asking a white woman in marriage," for "peeping in a window."

The children's game of telephone depends on the fact that a message passed quietly from one ear to another to another will get distorted at some point along the line.

More than two hundred antilynching bills were introduced in the U.S. Congress during the twentieth century, but none were passed. Seven presidents

---

8   *Rutherford B. Hayes*   President of the United States from 1877 to 1881.

9   *Lynching ... invention*   In 1905 James E. Cutler wrote *Lynch-Law: An Investigation into the History of Lynching in the United States*, considered to be the first academic account of the practice. While lynching has not been entirely confined to the United States, it became a very prominent form of violence in America especially in the late nineteenth to mid-twentieth centuries—the era of Jim Crow, a legal system that maintained racial inequality and was often reinforced by vigilante mob violence. The term "lynch" is believed to have originated with Charles Lynch, a Virginia farmer and Revolutionary War colonel.

lobbied for antilynching legislation, and the House of Representatives passed three separate measures, each of which was blocked by the Senate.

20   In Pine Bluff, Arkansas, a black man charged with kicking a white girl was hanged from a telephone pole. In Long View, Texas, a black man accused of attacking a white woman was hanged from a telephone pole. In Greenville, Mississippi, a black man accused of attacking a white telephone operator was hanged from a telephone pole. "The negro only asked time to pray." In Purcell, Oklahoma, a black man accused of attacking a white woman was tied to a telephone pole and burned. "Men and women in automobiles stood up to watch him die."

The poles, of course, were not to blame. It was only coincidence that they became convenient as gallows, because they were tall and straight, with a crossbar, and because they stood in public places. And it was only coincidence that the telephone poles so closely resembled crucifixes.

Early telephone calls were full of noise. "Such a jangle of meaningless noises had never been heard by human ears," Herbert Casson wrote in his 1910 *History of the Telephone*. "There were spluttering and bubbling, jerking and rasping, whistling and screaming."

In Shreveport, Louisiana, a black man charged with attacking a white girl was hanged from a telephone pole. "A knife was left sticking in the body." In Cumming, Georgia, a black man accused of assaulting a white girl was shot repeatedly, then hanged from a telephone pole. In Waco, Texas, a black man convicted of killing a white woman was taken from the courtroom by a mob and burned, then his charred body was hanged from a telephone pole.

A postcard was made from the photo of a burned man hanging from a telephone pole in Texas, his legs broken off below the knee and his arms curled up and blackened. Postcards of lynchings were sent out as greetings and warnings until 1908, when the postmaster general declared them unmailable. "This is the barbecue we had last night," reads one.

25   "If we are to die," W. E. B. DuBois[10] wrote in 1911, "in God's name let us not perish like bales of hay." And "if we must die," Claude McKay[11] wrote ten years later, "let it not be like hogs."

In Pittsburg, Kansas, a black man was hanged from a telephone pole, cut down, burned, shot, and stoned with bricks. "At first the negro was defiant," the *New York Times* reported, "but just before he was hanged he begged hard for his life."

---

10   *W.E.B. Du Bois*   African American writer and activist (1868–1963) who championed equal rights and promoted the social and political advancement of African Americans.

11   *Claude McKay*   Jamaican-born poet and novelist (1889–1948); as a key figure of the Harlem Renaissance, he helped to establish a distinct African American literary and cultural movement.

In the photographs, the bodies of the men lynched from telephone poles are silhouetted against the sky. Sometimes two men to a pole, hanging above the buildings of a town. Sometimes three. They hung like flags in still air.

In Cumberland, Maryland, a mob used a telephone pole as a battering ram to break into the jail where a black man charged with the murder of a policeman was being held. They kicked him to death, then fired twenty shots into his head. They wanted to burn his body, but a minister asked them not to.

The lynchings happened everywhere, in all but four states. From shortly before the invention of the telephone to long after the first trans-Atlantic call. More in the South, and more in rural areas. In the cities and in the North, there were race riots.*

Riots in Cincinnati, New Orleans, Memphis, New York, Atlanta, Philadelphia, Houston ...

During the race riots that destroyed the black section of Springfield, Ohio,[12] a black man was shot and hanged from a telephone pole.

During the race riots that set fire to East St. Louis[13] and forced five hundred black people to flee their homes, a black man was hanged from a telephone pole. The rope broke and his body fell into the gutter. "Negros are lying in the gutters every few feet in some places," read the newspaper account.

In 1921, the year before Bell died, four companies of the National Guard were called out to end a race war in Tulsa[14] that began when a white woman accused a black man of rape. Bell had lived to complete the first call from New York to San Francisco, which required 14,000 miles of copper wire and 130,000 telephone poles.

My grandfather was a lineman.[15] He broke his back when a telephone pole fell. "Smashed him onto the road," my father says.

30

---

12 *Springfield, Ohio* In 1904, the lynching of African American local Richard Dixon escalated into a full riot in Springfield, Ohio, with hundreds of white men inflicting destruction on the black neighborhood known as the Levee.

13 *East St. Louis* Riots erupted in East St. Louis, Illinois, in 1917 as tensions escalated between the white population and a number of black workers who had migrated to find employment in factories. After a series of isolated violent incidents, a mob of thousands burned homes and killed more than one hundred African Americans.

14 *race war in Tulsa* The riot that broke out in Tulsa, Oklahoma, after Dick Rowland was arrested based on a false accusation led to sixteen hours of violent clashes between large groups of white and black residents, and to the destruction of the Deep Greenwood district, a vibrant black neighborhood. The National Guard brought martial law to the city and placed black rioters in internment centers, while no white rioters were penalized.

15 *lineman* Person tasked with installing or maintaining telephone lines.

35   When I was young, I believed that the arc and swoop of telephone wires along the roadways was beautiful. I believed that the telephone poles, with their transformers catching the evening sun, were glorious. I believed my father when he said, "My dad could raise a pole by himself." And I believed that the telephone itself was a miracle.

Now, I tell my sister, these poles, these wires, do not look the same to me. Nothing is innocent, my sister reminds me. But nothing, I would like to think, remains unrepentant.

One summer, heavy rains fell in Nebraska and some green telephone poles grew small leafy branches.

(2009)

BINYAVANGA WAINAINA

HOW TO WRITE ABOUT AFRICA

In this biting piece, a leading Kenyan writer provides a series of instructions to foreigners aspiring to write about his home continent. The essay first appeared in a special issue of the British literary periodical Granta *in 2005; the volume was entitled* The View from Africa.

The tendencies Wainaina draws attention to here have centuries-old roots in Western culture; arguably they became even more pronounced in America in the early years of the twenty-first century, as George W. Bush focused considerable attention on the African continent (and increased medical assistance to many African nations), declaring in 2001 that "Africa is a nation that suffers from incredible disease."

Always use the word "Africa" or "Darkness" or "Safari" in your title. Sub-titles may include the words "Zanzibar," "Masai," "Zulu," "Zambezi," "Congo," "Nile," "Big," "Sky," "Shadow," "Drum," "Sun" or "Bygone." Also useful are words such as "Guerrillas," "Timeless," "Primordial" and "Tribal." Note that "People" means Africans who are not black, while "The People" means black Africans.

Never have a picture of a well-adjusted African on the cover of your book, or in it, unless that African has won the Nobel Prize. An AK-47, prominent ribs, naked breasts: use these. If you must include an African, make sure you get one in Masai or Zulu or Dogon dress.

In your text, treat Africa as if it were one country. It is hot and dusty with rolling grasslands and huge herds of animals and tall, thin people who are starving. Or it is hot and steamy with very short people who eat primates. Don't get bogged down with precise descriptions. Africa is big: fifty-four countries, 900 million people who are too busy starving and dying and warring and emigrating to read your book. The continent is full of deserts, jungles, highlands, savannahs and many other things, but your reader doesn't care about all that, so keep your descriptions romantic and evocative and unparticular.

Make sure you show how Africans have music and rhythm deep in their souls, and eat things no other humans eat. Do not mention rice and beef and wheat; monkey-brain is an African's cuisine of choice, along with goat, snake, worms and grubs and all manner of game meat. Make sure you show that you are able to eat such food without flinching, and describe how you learn to enjoy it—because you care.

5   Taboo subjects: ordinary domestic scenes, love between Africans (unless a death is involved), references to African writers or intellectuals, mention of school-going children who are not suffering from yaws or Ebola fever or female genital mutilation.

Throughout the book, adopt a *sotto** voice, in conspiracy with the reader, and a sad *I-expected-so-much* tone. Establish early on that your liberalism is impeccable, and mention near the beginning how much you love Africa, how you fell in love with the place and can't live without her. Africa is the only continent you can love—take advantage of this. If you are a man, thrust yourself into her warm virgin forests. If you are a woman, treat Africa as a man who wears a bush jacket and disappears off into the sunset. Africa is to be pitied, worshipped or dominated. Whichever angle you take, be sure to leave the strong impression that without your intervention and your important book, Africa is doomed.

Your African characters may include naked warriors, loyal servants, diviners and seers, ancient wise men living in hermitic splendor. Or corrupt politicians, inept polygamous travel-guides, and prostitutes you have slept with. The Loyal Servant always behaves like a seven-year-old and needs a firm hand; he is scared of snakes, good with children, and always involving you in his complex domestic dramas. The Ancient Wise Man always comes from a noble tribe (not the money-grubbing tribes like the Gikuyu, the Igbo or the Shona). He has rheumy eyes and is close to the Earth. The Modern African is a fat man who steals and works in the visa office, refusing to give work permits to qualified Westerners who really care about Africa. He is an enemy of development, always using his government job to make it difficult for pragmatic and good-hearted expats to set up NGOs* or Legal Conservation Areas. Or he is an Oxford-educated intellectual turned serial-killing politician in a Savile Row suit. He is a cannibal who likes Cristal champagne, and his mother is a rich witch-doctor who really runs the country.

Among your characters you must always include The Starving African, who wanders the refugee camp nearly naked, and waits for the benevolence of the West. Her children have flies on their eyelids and pot bellies, and her breasts are flat and empty. She must look utterly helpless. She can have no past, no history; such diversions ruin the dramatic moment. Moans are good. She must never say anything about herself in the dialogue except to speak of her (unspeakable) suffering. Also be sure to include a warm and motherly woman who has a rolling laugh and who is concerned for your well-being. Just call her Mama. Her children are all delinquent. These characters should buzz around your main hero, making him look good. Your hero can teach them, bathe them, feed them; he carries lots of babies and has seen Death. Your hero is you (if reportage), or a beautiful, tragic international celebrity/aristocrat who now cares for animals (if fiction).

Bad Western characters may include children of Tory* cabinet ministers, Afrikaners, employees of the World Bank.* When talking about exploitation by foreigners mention the Chinese and Indian traders. Blame the West for Africa's situation. But do not be too specific.

Broad brushstrokes throughout are good. Avoid having the African char-   10
acters laugh, or struggle to educate their kids, or just make do in mundane circumstances. Have them illuminate something about Europe or America in Africa. African characters should be colorful, exotic, larger than life—but empty inside, with no dialogue, no conflicts or resolutions in their stories, no depth or quirks to confuse the cause.

Describe, in detail, naked breasts (young, old, conservative, recently raped, big, small) or mutilated genitals, or enhanced genitals. Or any kind of genitals. And dead bodies. Or, better, naked dead bodies. And especially rotting naked dead bodies. Remember, any work you submit in which people look filthy and miserable will be referred to as the "real Africa," and you want that on your dust jacket. Do not feel queasy about this: you are trying to help them to get aid from the West. The biggest taboo in writing about Africa is to describe or show dead or suffering white people.

Animals, on the other hand, must be treated as well rounded, complex characters. They speak (or grunt while tossing their manes proudly) and have names, ambitions and desires. They also have family values: *see how lions teach their children?* Elephants are caring, and are good feminists or dignified patriarchs. So are gorillas. Never, ever say anything negative about an elephant or a gorilla. Elephants may attack people's property, destroy their crops, and even kill them. Always take the side of the elephant. Big cats have public-school accents. Hyenas are fair game and have vaguely Middle Eastern accents. Any short Africans who live in the jungle or desert may be portrayed with good humor (unless they are in conflict with an elephant or chimpanzee or gorilla, in which case they are pure evil).

After celebrity activists and aid workers, conservationists are Africa's most important people. Do not offend them. You need them to invite you to their 30,000-acre game ranch or "conservation area," and this is the only way you will get to interview the celebrity activist. Often a book cover with a heroic-looking conservationist on it works magic for sales. Anybody white, tanned and wearing khaki who once had a pet antelope or a farm is a conservationist, one who is preserving Africa's rich heritage. When interviewing him or her, do not ask how much funding they have; do not ask how much money they make off their game. Never ask how much they pay their employees.

Readers will be put off if you don't mention the light in Africa. And sunsets, the African sunset is a must. It is always big and red. There is always a big sky. Wide empty spaces and game are critical—Africa is the Land of Wide Empty Spaces. When writing about the plight of flora and fauna, make sure you mention that Africa is overpopulated. When your main character is in a desert or jungle living with indigenous peoples (anybody short) it is okay to mention that Africa has been severely depopulated by Aids and War (use caps).

15   You'll also need a nightclub called Tropicana, where mercenaries, evil nouveau riche Africans and prostitutes and guerrillas and expats hang out.

Always end your book with Nelson Mandela* saying something about rainbows or renaissances. Because you care.

(2005)

CYNTHIA OZICK

HIGHBROW BLUES

As an award-winning novelist, essayist, and short fiction writer,
Ozick is an important contributor to American "high culture"—a
culture she defends in the following essay. "Highbrow Blues"
appears in The Din in the Head, *a collection of literary criticism in*
which she argues that "[t]he din in the head, that relentless inward
hum of fragility and hope and transcendence and dread" can be
found "[i]n the art of the novel; in the novel's infinity of plasticity
and elasticity.... And nowhere else."

Not very long ago, when the (literary) writer Jonathan Franzen[1] was
catapulted to the status of celebrity, it was not only because his novel *The
Corrections* had become a bestseller. It was because he had *declined* celebrity, he had scorned it, he had thumbed his nose at it. It was because for him
celebrity was a scandal, an embarrassment. It shamed him. It demeaned him.
It was the opposite of his desire. His desire was to be counted among artists,
not to be interviewed by a popular sentimentalist hosting a television show.
His bailiwick, his turf, his lingo—his art—was serious literature. He wanted
it plainly understood that he was not your run-of-the-mill Oprah pick.[2] He
was a highbrow. Oprah Winfrey, he complained, was in the habit of choosing
"schmaltzy, one-dimensional" books that made him "cringe."

And then followed what may turn out to be the most arresting literary
gaffe* of the twenty-first century so far: "I feel," he said, "like I'm solidly
in *the high-art literary tradition*." For a writer in that tradition, he intimated,
the letter "O" (for Oprah) branded on a book jacket might signify hundreds of

---

1   *Jonathan Franzen*   American novelist and essayist best known for the critically
acclaimed novels *The Corrections* (2001) and *Freedom* (2010).
2   *Oprah pick*   Franzen's *The Corrections* was a pick for *Oprah's Book Club*—a
recommendation with a very strong impact on book sales. When Franzen spoke out against
the book club, Oprah did not remove him from the recommendation list but did rescind an
invitation to appear on her talk show.

thousands of copies in print, but it was also the mark of Cain.[3] Or else it was the scarlet letter[4] of literary disgrace.

Like I'm solidly in the high-art literary tradition. Never mind that "the high-art literary tradition" generally shuns the use of "like" as a conjunction: the remark was off the cuff, presumably under a journalist's pressure, and nothing if not informal. It was the telltale phrase itself—*the high-art literary tradition*—that shot Franzen through the cannon of doleful celebrity, if not into the Western canon. What did it mean? What was it? Why did it sound so awkward, so out of tune, so self conscious, so—one hesitates to say—jejune?[5] Why did it have the effect of a very young man attempting to talk like the grownups? And what had become of those grownups anyhow? Why were they, by and large, no longer on the scene—so little on the scene, in fact, and so little in anyone's thoughts or vocabulary, that a locution like *high-art literary tradition* took on the chirp of mimicry, of archaism?

Poor Franzen was scolded all around. He was scolded for ingratitude. He was scolded for elitism. He was scolded for chutzpah*—what sane writer would be so unreasonable as to give the cold shoulder to the powerfully influential Oprah Book Club? Even Harold Bloom[6] scolded him. Oprah herself didn't scold him—she simply canceled him.

Only a short while before the Franzen brouhaha,* Philip Roth published a little volume called *Shop Talk: A Writer and His Colleagues and Their Work.* Roth, of course, had long ago passed from the shock-celebrity, or notoriety, of *Portnoy's Complaint* to innumerable high-art literary awards, including the Gold Medal in Fiction of the American Academy of Arts and Letters. *Shop Talk* consists of interviews, exchanges, reflections: on Primo Levi, Aharon Appelfeld, Ivan Klima, Isaac Bashevis Singer, Bruno Schulz, Milan Kundera, Edna O'Brien, Mary McCarthy, and Bernard Malamud.[7] It closes with "Rereading Saul Bellow," a remarkable essay of homage expressed in an authoritative prose of matchless literary appetite. A writer of Roth's stature—one of the shapers of the novel in our time—engaging with ten of the significant literary figures of the twentieth century!

Fifty years ago, we can be sure, this would have been taken as an Event, as a cultural marker, as an occasion for heating up New York's literary stewpots

---

3   *mark of Cain*   After Cain murdered his brother Abel, God "set a mark upon" Cain (Genesis 4.16).

4   *scarlet letter*   Reference to Nathaniel Hawthorne's novel *The Scarlet Letter* (1850), in which the protagonist is required to wear a red letter "A" as a mark of shame for committing the sin of adultery.

5   *jejune*   Naïve.

6   *Harold Bloom*   Leading American literary critic (b. 1930).

7   *Primo Levi ... Malamud*   All critically acclaimed writers.

as much as, or even more than, Franzen's explosive—and ephemeral—wistfulness. Fifty years ago, the publication of *Shop Talk* would have been the topic of scores of graduate-student warrens and middle-class dinner parties, of book and gossip columns, of the roiling cenacles of the envious ambitious bookish young. Fifty years ago, Roth's newly revealed correspondence with Mary McCarthy—in which she asserts that Roth's appraisal of anti-Semitism in *The Counterlife* "irritated and offended" her; in which she considers the "Wailing Wall" to be "repellent"; in which she wryly adds that she looks forward to Roth's conversion to Christianity[8]—fifty years ago, these words, had they then been in print, would have engendered cool rebuttals in *Commentary*,[9] and everywhere else a slew of op-eds, combative or conciliatory. For an analogy, only recall the storm that greeted Hannah Arendt's *Eichmann in Jerusalem*:[10] the avalanche of editorials, the tumult of answering essays pro and con. (Mary McCarthy's pro among them.)

Some are old enough to remember the contentious excitements that surrounded the publication of Norman Mailer's[11] *Advertisements for Myself*, a personal assessment, like *Shop Talk*, of contemporary writers. Mailer's book was far less serious, far less well intended: it was mainly a noisy, nasty, competitive display of putdowns; an audacious act of flashy self-confessed self-aggrandizement. But—like *Shop Talk*—it was, after all, about writers, and there was a zealous public for it, a public drawn to substantive literary commotion. In contrast, when *Shop Talk* appeared in the first year of the twenty-first century, its reception was nearly total muteness. *Publishers Weekly*, taking obligatory notice, denigrated this large-hearted, illuminating, selfless work of cultural inquiry and fiercely generous admiration as fresh evidence of the Rothian ego—a viewpoint false, stale, and impertinent in both senses. Perhaps there were other reviews; perhaps not. What is notable is that *Shop Talk* was not notable. It was born into silence. It attracted no major attention, or no attention at all—not even among the editors of intellectual journals. No one praised it, no one condemned it. Not a literary creature stirred in response—not even a louse.*

These observations are hardly new; but familiarity does not lessen the shock and the ignominy of a pervasive indifference to serious critical writing. Fifty

---

8   *Roth's newly ... Christianity* Roth's *Shop Talk* includes an exchange of letters between himself and McCarthy, whom he sent a copy of his book *The Counterlife*; she writes that portions of the book "wearied" her "[w]ith what feels to me like pathology—a severe case of anti-anti-semitism."

9   *Commentary* Influential magazine founded by the American Jewish Committee.

10   *Eichmann in Jerusalem* The 1963 book—in which Arendt, an important political theorist, reported on the trial of Nazi war criminal Adolf Eichmann—remains a controversial classic.

11   *Norman Mailer* Pulitzer Prize-winning writer (1923–2007).

years ago, it was still taken for granted that there would be serious discourse about serious writing by nonprofessionals, by people for whom books were common currency. These people also listened to Jack Benny[12] on the radio and went to the movies. I am reminded of the Reader's Subscription, a book club presided over by an astonishing highbrow triumvirate: W.H. Auden, Jacques Barzun, and Lionel Trilling.[13] Fifty years ago, no one spoke so blatantly, so dreamily, of *the high-art literary tradition*—one doesn't give a name to the air one breathes. If the phrase sounds nostalgic today (and it does), it is because it has the awed, wondering, adoring and somewhat soppy tone Oprah herself would use; or else the tone of someone born too late, like an antiques-besotted client of limited means whom an interior decorator, will oblige with duplicates of period furnishings. *The high-art literary tradition*—utter these syllables, and you utter a stage set.

In 1952, William Phillips wrote of "the attitude of aesthetic loneliness and revolt"—setting the writer apart from mass culture—that had characterized his youth. "Along with many other people, most of them more mature than myself," he said, "I felt that art was a temple and that artists belonged to a priesthood of the anointed and the dedicated." The politics and social commitment of the thirties swept all that inherited romanticism away, but only temporarily—it re-emerged soon enough in the postwar aestheticism of the New Criticism.[14] By the 1950s, the idea of literature as hermetically dedicated and anointed was once again solidly enthroned, complete, with Eliot as pope and Pound as high priest[15]—until a second political wave, in the late sixties and into the seventies, knocked out notions of temples and priestly artists once and for all, and replaced them with a howl.[16] It is a long time since we fretted over mass culture. It is a long time since we were thrilled by alienation. It is a

12   *Jack Benny*   Popular American actor and comedian (1894–1974).

13   *W.H. Auden*   Major poet (1907–73); *Jacques Barzun*   Historian, non-fiction writer, and philosopher of education (1907–2012); *Lionel Trilling*   Literary critic (1905–75).

14   *the New Criticism*   Dominant movement in American literary criticism in the mid-twentieth century; New Critics advocated close reading with attention to a work's formal qualities.

15   *Eliot ... priest*   Refers to T.S. Eliot (1888–1965), American-born British essayist, poet, and playwright; and American poet and critic, Ezra Pound (1885–1972). Both were important figures in the modernist movement of the early twentieth century, and Eliot's critical writing in particular influenced the New Critics.

16   *replaced ... howl*   Ozick refers here to Allen Ginsberg's poem "Howl" (1956), which played a significant role in the establishment of the Beat movement, a literary movement that impacted popular culture and paved the way for the hippie movement that arose in the 1960s.

long time since Dwight Macdonald[17] sneered at middlebrows. It is a long time since Lionel Trilling thought writing for money cheapened literary aspiration. (Henry James[18] didn't think that.) Modernism as a credo seems faded and old-fashioned, if not obsolete, and what we once called the avant-garde is now either fakery or comedy. The Village,* where Auden and Marianne Moore once lived and wrote and walked abroad, is a sort of performance arena nowadays, where the memory of a memory grows fainter and fainter, and where even nostalgia has forgotten exactly what it is supposed to be nostalgic about. Distinction-making, even distinction-discerning, is largely in decline. The difference between high and low is valued by few and blurred by most. *The high-art literary tradition* brings on snickers (except when it is in the newly aspiring hands of Oprah, who, having canceled Franzen yet learned his lesson well, has ascended, together with her fans, to *Anna Karenina* and Faulkner[19]).

Writers shouldn't be mistaken for priests, it goes without saying; but neither should movie-script manufacturers be mistaken for writers. Readers are not the same as audiences, and the structure of a novel is not the same as the structure of a lingerie advertisement. Hierarchy, to be sure, is an off-putting notion, invoking high and low; and high smacks of snobbery and antiegalitarianism. But hierarchy also points to the recognition of distinctions, and—incontrovertibly—the life of intellect is perforce hierarchical: it insists that one thing is not the same as another thing. A novel concerned with English country-house romances is not the same as a tract on slavery in Antigua. A department of English is not the same as a Marxist tutorial. A rap CD is not the same as academic scholarship. A suicide bomber who blows up a pizzeria crowded with baby carriages is not the same as a nation-builder.

Fifty years ago, a salient issue was the bugaboo* of conformism. It's true that men in their universal gray fedoras had the look of a field of dandelions gone to seed. It's true that McCarthyism[20] suppressed free opinion and stimulated fear. But both the fedoras* and the unruly senator have long been dispatched to their

10

---

17 *Dwight MacDonald* American political radical, philosopher, writer, and editor; his essay "Masscult and Midcult" (1960) argues for the preservation of highbrow culture against the mass-produced culture of the "middlebrow."

18 *Henry James* American-born British writer (1843–1916) whose novels played a role in the development of literary modernism.

19 *Anna Karenina* 1875–77 classic novel by Leo Tolstoy; *Faulkner* American novelist (1897–1962) whose works are considered more difficult than those of many other classic American novelists. Oprah's Book Club read three Faulkner novels in the summer of 2005, and *Anna Karenina* was a Book Club selection in 2004.

20 *McCarthyism* Reference to the activities of Senator Joseph McCarthy, who in the 1950s persecuted gay government workers and, without substantiating evidence, accused large numbers of people of being communist spies. He incited a national panic.

respective graveyards, and if we are to worry about conformism, now is the hour. What does conformism mean if not one side, one argument, one solution? And no one is more conformist than the self-defined alienated, hoary though that term is. In the universities, a literary conformism rules, equating literature with fashionable "progressive" themes; and literature departments promote the newfangled conformism that paradoxically goes under the pluralist-sounding yet absolutist name of multiculturalism: a system of ethnological classification designed to reduce literary culture to group rivalries. Postcolonial courses offer a study in specified villainies and grievances. Certain imprimatur-bearing texts[21]—ah, *texts*, denatured but indispensable coin!—are offered uncritically, as holy writ, without opposing or dissenting or contextual matter. Yet more than fifty years ago, in my freshman year at NYU, Friedrich Hayek's *The Road to Serfdom* was assigned to be read together with its antithesis, *The Communist Manifesto*—and that was in the heart of what even its denizens dubbed the Age of Conformity.[22]

"It is worth something," Norman Mailer wrote in 1952, "to remind ourselves that the great artists—certainly the moderns—are almost always in opposition to their society, and that integration, acceptance, non-alienation, etc., has been more conducive to propaganda than art." No statement could be staler than this one, and it was already stale when it was first set down. Is the Thomas Mann[23] of the Joseph novels an artist in opposition? Is *Dubliners*[24] a work of revolt? What we can say with certainty is that much current study of the great artists tends to make art secondary to propaganda, and sometimes invisible under propaganda's obscuring film. In a democratic polity possessed of free critical expression through innumerable outlets, the moribund old cry of alienation is itself a species of propaganda. Not, as that propaganda would have it, is self-congratulatory jingoism* the opposite of alienation. What the propaganda of alienation seeks is not the higher patriotism saturated in the higher morality, as it pretends, but simple disinheritance.

Admittedly, there is always a golden age, the one not ours, the one that once, was or will someday be. One's own time is never satisfactory, except to the very rich or the smugly oblivious. So it is doubtful that *the high-art literary tradition*, in strict opposition to mass culture, will ever return, even for its would-be latter-day avatars: high and low are inextricably intermingled,

---

21 *imprimatur-bearing texts* Books bearing official authorization for print publication.

22 *The Road to Serfdom* 1944 book that argues against government intervention in the economy and links communism to fascism; *the Age of Conformity* American cultural push to conform during the 1950s.

23 *Thomas Mann* Nobel Prize-winning novelist (1875–1955).

24 *Dubliners* 1914 short story collection by James Joyce, generally considered one of the twentieth century's most important writers in English literature.

whether by sly allusion in *The Simpsons*, or in Philip Roth's dazzling demotic[25] voice. Low has enriched high; and surely Oprah has enriched publishers. But nothing gives us license, even in the face of this enlivening cultural mishmash, to fall into meltdown: to think that a comic-strip balloon is as legitimate a "text" as *Paradise Lost*;* or that the faddishly softening politics of what is misleadingly called "narrative" can negate a documented historical record; or that art exists chiefly to serve grievance. Alienation, that old carcass, remains, after all, the philistinism of the intellectual. As for the attention given decades ago to *Advertisements for Myself*: if it were published today, would any one notice?

(2006)

---

25 *demotic* Popular; for the masses.

MALCOLM GLADWELL

NONE OF THE ABOVE: WHAT I.Q. DOESN'T TELL YOU ABOUT RACE

Malcolm Gladwell is a journalist and staff writer at the New Yorker. *His work often examines research findings in the social sciences and interprets them for a broader audience. In the following article Gladwell reviews* What Is Intelligence? *(2007), by the scholar James Flynn, delving into the debate among psychologists and geneticists surrounding IQ and its relationship to race, class, and culture. "None of the Above" was first published in the* New Yorker *in 2007.*

One Saturday in November of 1984, James Flynn, a social scientist at the University of Otago, in New Zealand, received a large package in the mail. It was from a colleague in Utrecht, and it contained the results of I.Q. tests* given to two generations of Dutch eighteen-year-olds. When Flynn looked through the data, he found something puzzling. The Dutch eighteen-year-olds from the nineteen-eighties scored better than those who took the same tests in the nineteen-fifties—and not just slightly better, *much* better.

Curious, Flynn sent out some letters. He collected intelligence-test results from Europe, from North America, from Asia, and from the developing world, until he had data for almost thirty countries. In every case, the story was pretty much the same. I.Q.s around the world appeared to be rising by 0.3 points per year, or three points per decade, for as far back as the tests had been administered. For some reason, human beings seemed to be getting smarter.

Flynn has been writing about the implications of his findings—now known as the Flynn effect—for almost twenty-five years. His books consist of a series of plainly stated statistical observations, in support of deceptively modest conclusions, and the evidence in support of his original observation is now so overwhelming that the Flynn effect has moved from theory to fact. What remains uncertain is how to make sense of the Flynn effect. If an American born in the nineteen-thirties has an I.Q. of 100, the Flynn effect says that his children will have I.Q.s of 108, and his grandchildren I.Q.s of close to 120—more than a standard deviation higher. If we work in the opposite direction, the typical teen-ager of today, with an I.Q. of 100, would have had grandparents with average I.Q.s of 82—seemingly below the threshold necessary to graduate from high school. And, if we go back even farther, the Flynn effect puts the average I.Q.s of the schoolchildren of 1900 at around 70, which is to suggest, bizarrely, that a century ago the United States was populated largely by people who today would be considered mentally retarded.

For almost as long as there have been I.Q. tests, there have been I.Q. fundamentalists. H.H. Goddard, in the early years of the past century, established the idea that intelligence could be measured along a single, linear scale. One of his particular contributions was to coin the word "moron." "The people who are doing the drudgery are, as a rule, in their proper places," he wrote. Goddard was followed by Lewis Terman, in the nineteen-twenties, who rounded up the California children with the highest I.Q.s, and confidently predicted that they would sit at the top of every profession. In 1969, the psychometrician Arthur Jensen argued that programs like Head Start, which tried to boost the academic performance of minority children, were doomed to failure, because I.Q. was so heavily genetic; and in 1994 Richard Herrnstein and Charles Murray, in "The Bell Curve," notoriously proposed that Americans with the lowest I.Q.s be sequestered in a "high-tech" version of an Indian reservation,* "while the rest of America tries to go about its business."[1] To the I.Q. fundamentalist, two things are beyond dispute: first, that I.Q. tests measure some hard and identifiable trait that predicts the quality of our thinking; and, second, that this trait is stable—that is, it is determined by our genes and largely impervious to environmental influences.

This is what James Watson, the co-discoverer of DNA, meant when he told an English newspaper recently that he was "inherently gloomy" about the prospects for Africa. From the perspective of an I.Q. fundamentalist, the fact that Africans score lower than Europeans on I.Q. tests suggests an ineradicable cognitive disability. In the controversy that followed, Watson was defended by the journalist William Saletan, in a three-part series for the online magazine *Slate*. Drawing heavily on the work of J. Philippe Rushton—a psychologist who specializes in comparing the circumference of what he calls the Negroid brain with the length of the Negroid penis—Saletan took the fundamentalist position to its logical conclusion. To erase the difference between blacks and whites, Saletan wrote, would probably require vigorous interbreeding between the races, or some kind of corrective genetic engineering aimed at upgrading

5

---

1   *in 1994 ... business* *The New Yorker* posted the following correction to this statement: "In fact, Herrnstein and Murray deplored the prospect of such 'custodialism' and recommended that steps be taken to avert it. We regret the error."

African stock.* "Economic and cultural theories have failed to explain most of the pattern," Saletan declared, claiming to have been "soaking [his] head in each side's computations and arguments." One argument that Saletan never soaked his head in, however, was Flynn's, because what Flynn discovered in his mailbox upsets the certainties upon which I.Q. fundamentalism rests. If whatever the thing is that I.Q. tests measure can jump so much in a generation, it can't be all that immutable and it doesn't look all that innate.

The very fact that average I.Q.s shift over time ought to create a "crisis of confidence," Flynn writes in "What Is Intelligence?," his latest attempt to puzzle through the implications of his discovery. "How could such huge gains be intelligence gains? Either the children of today were far brighter than their parents or, at least in some circumstances, I.Q. tests were not good measures of intelligence."

The best way to understand why I.Q.s rise, Flynn argues, is to look at one of the most widely used I.Q. tests, the so-called WISC (for Wechsler Intelligence Scale for Children). The WISC is composed of ten subtests, each of which measures a different aspect of I.Q. Flynn points out that scores in some of the categories—those measuring general knowledge, say, or vocabulary or the ability to do basic arithmetic—have risen only modestly over time. The big gains on the WISC are largely in the category known as "similarities," where you get questions such as "In what way are 'dogs' and 'rabbits' alike?" Today, we tend to give what, for the purposes of I.Q. tests, is the right answer: dogs and rabbits are both mammals. A nineteenth-century American would have said that "you use dogs to hunt rabbits."

"If the everyday world is your cognitive home, it is not natural to detach abstractions and logic and the hypothetical from their concrete referents," Flynn writes. Our great-grandparents may have been perfectly intelligent. But they would have done poorly on I.Q. tests because they did not participate in the twentieth century's great cognitive revolution, in which we learned to sort experience according to a new set of abstract categories. In Flynn's phrase, we have now had to put on "scientific spectacles," which enable us to make sense of the WISC questions about similarities. To say that Dutch I.Q. scores rose substantially between 1952 and 1982 was another way of saying that the Netherlands in 1982 was, in at least certain respects, much more cognitively demanding than the Netherlands in 1952. An I.Q., in other words, measures not so much how smart we are as how *modern* we are.

This is a critical distinction. When the children of Southern Italian immigrants were given I.Q. tests in the early part of the past century,* for example, they recorded median scores in the high seventies and low eighties, a full standard deviation below their American and Western European counterparts. Southern Italians did as poorly on I.Q. tests as Hispanics and blacks did. As you can imagine, there was much concerned talk at the time about the genetic inferiority of Italian stock, of the inadvisability of letting so many second-class immigrants into the United States, and of the squalor that seemed endemic to Italian urban neighborhoods.* Sound familiar? These days, when talk turns to the supposed genetic differences in the intelligence of certain races, Southern Italians have disappeared from the discussion. "Did their genes begin to mutate somewhere in the 1930s?" the psychologists Seymour Sarason and John Doris ask, in their account of the Italian experience. "Or is it possible that somewhere in the 1920s, if not earlier, the sociocultural history of Italo-Americans took a turn from the blacks and the Spanish Americans which permitted their assimilation into the general undifferentiated mass of Americans?"

The psychologist Michael Cole and some colleagues once gave members of the Kpelle tribe, in Liberia, a version of the WISC similarities test: they took a basket of food, tools, containers, and clothing and asked the tribesmen to sort them into appropriate categories. To the frustration of the researchers, the Kpelle chose functional pairings. They put a potato and a knife together because a knife is used to cut a potato. "A wise man could only do such-and-such," they explained. Finally, the researchers asked, "How would a fool do it?" The tribesmen immediately re-sorted the items into the "right" categories. It can be argued that taxonomical categories are a developmental improvement—that is, that the Kpelle would be more likely to advance, technologically and scientifically, if they started to see the world that way. But to label them less intelligent than Westerners, on the basis of their performance on that test, is merely to state that they have different cognitive preferences and habits. And if I.Q. varies with habits of mind, which can be adopted or discarded in a generation, what, exactly, is all the fuss about?

When I was growing up, my family would sometimes play Twenty Questions* on long car trips. My father was one of those people who insist that the standard categories of animal, vegetable, and mineral be supplemented with a fourth category: "abstract." Abstract could mean something like "whatever it was that was going through my mind when we drove past the water tower fifty miles back." That abstract category sounds absurdly difficult, but it wasn't: it merely required that we ask a slightly different set of questions and grasp a slightly different set of conventions, and, after two or three rounds of practice, guessing the contents of someone's mind fifty miles ago becomes as easy as guessing Winston Churchill.* (There is one exception. That was the trip on which my old roommate Tom Connell chose, as an abstraction, "the Unknown Soldier"*—which allowed him legitimately and gleefully to answer "I have no idea" to almost every question. There were four of us playing. We gave up after an hour.) Flynn would say that my father was teaching his three sons how to put on scientific spectacles, and that extra practice probably bumped up all

10

of our I.Q.s a few notches. But let's be clear about what this means. There's a world of difference between an I.Q. advantage that's genetic and one that depends on extended car time with Graham Gladwell.

Flynn is a cautious and careful writer. Unlike many others in the I.Q. debates, he resists grand philosophizing. He comes back again and again to the fact that I.Q. scores are generated by paper-and-pencil tests—and making sense of those scores, he tells us, is a messy and complicated business that requires something closer to the skills of an accountant than to those of a philosopher.

For instance, Flynn shows what happens when we recognize that I.Q. is not a freestanding number but a value attached to a specific time and a specific test. When an I.Q. test is created, he reminds us, it is calibrated or "normed" so that the test-takers in the fiftieth percentile—those exactly at the median—are assigned a score of 100. But since I.Q.s are always rising, the only way to keep that hundred-point benchmark is periodically to make the tests more difficult—to "renorm" them. The original WISC was normed in the late nineteen-forties. It was then renormed in the early nineteen-seventies, as the WISC-R; renormed a third time in the late eighties, as the WISC III; and renormed again a few years ago, as the WISC IV—with each version just a little harder than its predecessor. The notion that anyone "has" an I.Q. of a certain number, then, is meaningless unless you know which WISC he took, and when he took it, since there's a substantial difference between getting a 130 on the WISC IV and getting a 130 on the much easier WISC.

This is not a trivial issue. I.Q. tests are used to diagnose people as mentally retarded, with a score of 70 generally taken to be the cutoff. You can imagine how the Flynn effect plays havoc with that system. In the nineteen-seventies and eighties, most states used the WISC-R to make their mental-retardation diagnoses. But since kids—even kids with disabilities—score a little higher every year, the number of children whose scores fell below 70 declined steadily through the end of the eighties. Then, in 1991, the WISC III was introduced, and suddenly the percentage of kids labeled retarded went up. The psychologists Tomoe Kanaya, Matthew Scullin, and Stephen Ceci estimated that, if every state had switched to the WISC III right away, the number of Americans labeled mentally retarded should have doubled.

15   That is an extraordinary number. The diagnosis of mental disability is one of the most stigmatizing of all educational and occupational classifications—and yet, apparently, the chances of being burdened with that label are in no small degree a function of the point, in the life cycle of the WISC, at which a child happens to sit for his evaluation. "As far as I can determine, no clinical or school psychologists using the WISC over the relevant 25 years noticed that its criterion of mental retardation became more lenient over time," Flynn wrote, in a 2000 paper. "Yet no one drew the obvious moral about psychologists in

the field: They simply were not making any systematic assessment of the I.Q. criterion for mental retardation."

Flynn brings a similar precision to the question of whether Asians have a genetic advantage in I.Q., a possibility that has led to great excitement among I.Q. fundamentalists in recent years. Data showing that the Japanese had higher I.Q.s than people of European descent, for example, prompted the British psychometrician and eugenicist Richard Lynn to concoct an elaborate evolutionary explanation involving the Himalayas, really cold weather, premodern hunting practices, brain size, and specialized vowel sounds. The fact that the I.Q.s of Chinese-Americans also seemed to be elevated has led I.Q. fundamentalists to posit the existence of an international I.Q. pyramid, with Asians at the top, European whites next, and Hispanics and blacks at the bottom.

Here was a question tailor-made for James Flynn's accounting skills. He looked first at Lynn's data, and realized that the comparison was skewed. Lynn was comparing American I.Q. estimates based on a representative sample of schoolchildren with Japanese estimates based on an upper-income, heavily urban sample. Recalculated, the Japanese average came in not at 106.6 but at 99.2. Then Flynn turned his attention to the Chinese-American estimates. They turned out to be based on a 1975 study in San Francisco's Chinatown using something called the Lorge-Thorndike Intelligence Test. But the Lorge-Thorndike test was normed in the nineteen-fifties. For children in the nineteen-seventies, it would have been a piece of cake. When the Chinese-American scores were reassessed using up-to-date intelligence metrics, Flynn found, they came in at 97 verbal and 100 nonverbal. Chinese-Americans had slightly lower I.Q.s than white Americans.

The Asian-American success story had suddenly been turned on its head. The numbers now suggested, Flynn said, that they had succeeded not because of their *higher* I.Q.s. but despite their *lower* I.Q.s. Asians were overachievers. In a nifty piece of statistical analysis, Flynn then worked out just how great that overachievement was. Among whites, virtually everyone who joins the ranks of the managerial, professional, and technical occupations has an I.Q. of 97 or above. Among Chinese-Americans, that threshold is 90. A Chinese-American with an I.Q. of 90, it would appear, does as much with it as a white American with an I.Q. of 97.

There should be no great mystery about Asian achievement. It has to do with hard work and dedication to higher education, and belonging to a culture that stresses professional success. But Flynn makes one more observation. The children of that first successful wave of Asian-Americans really did have I.Q.s that were higher than everyone else's—coming in somewhere around 103. Having worked their way into the upper reaches of the occupational scale, and taken note of how much the professions value abstract thinking,

Asian-American parents have evidently made sure that their own children wore scientific spectacles. "Chinese Americans are an ethnic group for whom high achievement preceded high I.Q. rather than the reverse," Flynn concludes, reminding us that in our discussions of the relationship between I.Q. and success we often confuse causes and effects. "It is not easy to view the history of their achievements without emotion," he writes. That is exactly right. To ascribe Asian success to some abstract number is to trivialize it.

20   Two weeks ago, Flynn came to Manhattan to debate Charles Murray at a forum sponsored by the Manhattan Institute. Their subject was the black-white I.Q. gap in America. During the twenty-five years after the Second World War, that gap closed considerably. The I.Q.s of white Americans rose, as part of the general worldwide Flynn effect, but the I.Q.s of black Americans rose faster. Then, for about a period of twenty-five years, that trend stalled—and the question was why.

Murray showed a series of PowerPoint slides, each representing different statistical formulations of the I.Q. gap. He appeared to be pessimistic that the racial difference would narrow in the future. "By the nineteen-seventies, you had gotten most of the juice out of the environment that you were going to get," he said. That gap, he seemed to think, reflected some inherent difference between the races. "Starting in the nineteen-seventies, to put it very crudely, you had a higher proportion of black kids being born to really dumb mothers," he said. When the debate's moderator, Jane Waldfogel, informed him that the most recent data showed that the race gap had begun to close again, Murray seemed unimpressed, as if the possibility that blacks could ever make further progress was inconceivable.

Flynn took a different approach. The black-white gap, he pointed out, differs dramatically by age. He noted that the tests we have for measuring the cognitive functioning of infants, though admittedly crude, show the races to be almost the same. By age four, the average black I.Q. is 95.4—only four and a half points behind the average white I.Q. Then the real gap emerges: from age four through twenty-four, blacks lose six-tenths of a point a year, until their scores settle at 83.4.

That steady decline, Flynn said, did not resemble the usual pattern of genetic influence. Instead, it was exactly what you would expect, given the disparate cognitive environments that whites and blacks encounter as they grow older. Black children are more likely to be raised in single-parent homes than are white children—and single-parent homes are less cognitively complex than two-parent homes. The average I.Q. of first-grade students in schools that blacks attend is 95, which means that "kids who want to be above average don't have to aim as high." There were possibly adverse differences between black teen-age culture and white teen-age culture, and an enormous number of young black men are in jail—which is hardly the kind of environment in which someone would learn to put on scientific spectacles.

Flynn then talked about what we've learned from studies of adoption and mixed-race children—and that evidence didn't fit a genetic model, either. If I.Q. is innate, it shouldn't make a difference whether it's a mixed-race child's mother or father who is black. But it does: children with a white mother and a black father have an eight-point I.Q. advantage over those with a black mother and a white father. And it shouldn't make much of a difference where a mixed-race child is born. But, again, it does: the children fathered by black American G.I.s in postwar Germany and brought up by their German mothers have the same I.Q.s as the children of white American G.I.s and German mothers. The difference, in that case, was not the fact of the children's blackness, as a fundamentalist would say. It was the fact of their *Germanness*—of their being brought up in a different culture, under different circumstances. "The mind is much more like a muscle than we've ever realized," Flynn said. "It needs to get cognitive exercise. It's not some piece of clay on which you put an indelible mark." The lesson to be drawn from black and white differences was the same as the lesson from the Netherlands years ago: I.Q. measures not just the quality of a person's mind but the quality of the world that person lives in.

(2007)

ADAM GOPNIK

THE CORRECTIONS:

ABRIDGEMENT, ENRICHMENT, AND
THE NATURE OF ART

In this essay a noted New Yorker *writer discusses "abridgment, enrichment, and the nature of art."*

O ur theme today is addition and subtraction, abridgment and expansion, and their effects on works of art and entertainment. (Sorry, what was that? No, the seminar on history of the cinema is in the next classroom.) What can be taken away from a book or a movie, what can be added to it, and what does it tell us about what we bring to both?

The first form to consider is subtraction, or what might more grandly be called the aesthetic of abridgment, as illustrated by a new and ambitious series of "compact editions" produced by the British publisher Orion. "The great classics contain passionate romance, thrilling adventure, arresting characters and unforgettable scenes and situations," an explanatory note tells us. "But finding time to read them can be a problem." So Orion has taken nineteenth-century classics—among them *Moby-Dick*, *Anna Karenina*, *Vanity Fair*, and *The Mill on the Floss**—and cut them neatly in half, like Damien Hirst[1] animals, so that they can be taken in quickly and all the more admired.

Although the tone of the blurbs and the back matter is defiantly unapologetic, the names of the abridgers are mysteriously absent, suggesting that, with the shyness of old-fashioned pornographers, they don't want to be quite so openly associated with the project as their publisher's pride would suggest they ought. Who was the mohel* of *Moby-Dick*; who took the vanity out of *Vanity Fair*; who threw Anna under the train a hundred pages sooner than before? Orion isn't telling. Yet the work had to be done with considerable tact and judgment. A good condensation of a hard book is hardly a crime; if Joseph Campbell and Henry Morton Robinson, an editor at *Reader's Digest*, hadn't

---

1   *Damien Hirst*   Artist best known for his works involving dissected animals preserved in formaldehyde.

labored over their "skeleton key" to *Finnegans Wake*,* readers would still find Joyce's book not just difficult but unapproachable.* The Orionites should be proud of their work; their abridgments are skillfully done.

Take *Moby-Dick*, a book that, if every reader has not always wanted shorter, then certainly, as Dr. Johnson said about *Paradise Lost*,* no reader has ever wanted *longer*. The first chapter of the compact edition is typical of the Orion approach. Most of the famous first paragraph, most of the famous first chapter, is presented as Melville wrote it. No muscle is removed—unlike, say, A.L. Rowse's modernization of Shakespeare, no attempt is made to simplify or improve the author's vocabulary and knotty, convoluted syntax. Ishmael asks us to call him so,* and the story proceeds.

What is cut in the first chapter is the two long passages that depart from the Ishmaelian specifics: a reflection on people watching boats in Manhattan and the allure of the sea even in a city ("Posted like silent sentinels all around the town, stand thousands upon thousands of mortal men fixed in ocean reveries"), and Melville's invocation of the history of ocean worship ("Why did the old Persians hold the sea holy? Why did the Greeks give it a separate deity?"). These passages are, by modern critical standards, "showy" and "digressive," nervously intent to display stray learning and to make obscure allusion more powerful than inherent emotion. The same thing happens in the subsequent chapters. Melville's story is intact and immediate; it's just that the long bits about the technical details of whaling are gone, as are most of the mock Shakespearean interludes, the philosophical meanderings, and the metaphysical huffing and puffing. The entire chapter "The Whiteness of the Whale," where Melville tries to explain why white, the natural symbol of Good, is also somehow the natural symbol of Evil, is just, well, whited out.

All abridgments and additions are part of their period; we scoff at the eighteenth century for cutting the tragic end of *Lear* and tacking on a happy one, but the recent, much praised Royal Shakespeare production added a gratuitous Grand Guignol* hanging of the poor Fool, on the shaky basis of a sideways reference to his death two acts later. By the same token, the Orion *Moby-Dick* is not defaced; it is, by conventional contemporary standards of good editing and critical judgment, *improved*. The compact edition adheres to a specific idea of what a good novel ought to be: the contemporary aesthetic of the realist psychological novel. This is not what a contemptuous philistine* would do with the book. It is what a good editor, of the Maxwell Perkins variety, would do: cut out the self-indulgent stuff and present a clean story, inhabited by plausible characters—the "taut, spare, driving" narrative beloved of Sunday reviewers.* You can pretty much read the soothing letter to the author that would have accompanied the suggested cuts, had he been alive to receive it. ("Herman: just a few small trims along the way; myself I find the whaling stuff fascinating, but I fear your reader wants to move along with the story—and frankly the tensile strength of the narrative is being undercut right now by a lot of stray material that takes us *way* off line. The 'slip' of your research is showing! Here's an idea someone here had the other day: why don't we do a 'readers' guide' where all of this rich, fascinating, miscellaneous whaling material can be made available to people who want it without interfering with the flow of the story?") What the Orion *Moby-Dick* says about the book is what a good critic or professional editor would say about the book. It's what they *did* say: there's too much digression and sticky stuff and extraneous learning. If he'd cut that out, it would be a better story.

Only years of careful inculcation in the masterpiece makes us hesitate. And rightly so. For when you come to the end of the compact *Moby-Dick* you don't think, What a betrayal; you think, Nice job—what were the missing bits again? And when you go back to find them you remember why the book isn't just a thrilling adventure with unforgettable characters but a great book. The subtraction does not turn good work into hackwork; it turns a hysterical, half-mad masterpiece into a sound, sane book. It still has its phallic reach and point,* but lacks its flaccid, anxious self-consciousness: it is all Dick and no Moby.

Just as "*Moby-Dick* in half the time" dispenses with Melville's digressions and showy knowledge, the compact *Vanity Fair* relieves Thackeray of his "preciousness"—the discursive, interfering commentary on the action that charmed his Victorian readers. In a middle chapter called "In Which Amelia Invades the Low Countries," for instance, Thackeray's chatty, confidential tone is altered by his subtractors into the sparer narrative voice of good writing. The scene is set for Amelia's arrival in Brussels on the eve of Waterloo, and Thackeray's descriptive prose is kept mostly intact. ("This flat, flourishing, easy country never could have looked more rich and prosperous than in that summer of 1815.") In the original, though, Thackeray precedes that description with a loquacious paragraph:

> But it may be said as a rule, that every Englishman in the Duke of Wellington's army paid his way. The remembrance of such a fact surely becomes a nation of shopkeepers. It was a blessing for a commerce-loving country to be over-run by such an army of customers; and to have such creditable warriors to feed. And the country which they came to protect is not military. For a long period of history they have let other people fight there. When the present writer went to survey with eagle glance the field of Waterloo, we asked the conductor of the diligence, a portly warlike-looking veteran, whether he had been at the battle. "*Pas si bête*"[2]—such an answer and sentiment as no Frenchman would own to—was his reply.

---

2   *Pas si bête*   French: (I'm) not that stupid.

And so on, in a similarly intimate, letter-to-the-reader vein. This is, of course, not merely digressive but "sentimental," and, like a later aside about how foolish Napoleon was not to wait until the allies had fallen apart from their own internal differences, breaks up the flow and movement of the story.

Even as sympathetic a reader as Edmund Wilson hated Thackeray's rambling remarks and continual intrusions of mild ironies. But Thackeray without his little jokes and warm asides becomes another, duller writer—too constantly on message. Meaning resides in the margins; Thackeray wants to insinuate, not force, his way into the reader's confidence. Becky Sharp* lives for us not just because her creator made her but because her creator couldn't leave her alone; he is always *there*, fussing over her shoulder, commenting on her behavior, the way we do with real people who obsess us. Transparent, objective lucidity is the last emotion we have about the actual; we fret, comment, editorialize, intrude, despair, laugh, and gossip.

The real lesson of the compact editions is not that vandals shouldn't be   10
let loose on masterpieces but that masterpieces are inherently a little loony. They run on the engine of their own accumulated habits and weirdnesses and self-indulgent excesses. They have to, since originality is, necessarily, something still strange to us, rather than something that we already know about and approve. What makes writing matter is not a story, cleanly told, but a voice, however odd or ordinary, and a point of view, however strange or sentimental. Books can be snipped at, and made less melodically muddled, but they lose their overtones, their bass notes, their chesty resonance—the same thing that happens, come to think of it, to human castrati.*

Novelists have always seen their work cut—by the interfering editor or the posthumous abridger—but they almost never see it expanded. Henry James's New York Edition* did add late-James lace to mid-James linen, but the sewing always shows. (There are those who think that the late long First Folio *Hamlet* is a messy author's expansion of the short, stern early quarto,* but they are a minority.) On the whole, once authors get the words out, they may have to settle for less, but they don't come back for more. For the aesthetic of addition, we need to turn to the movies. We can study it in the "director's cuts" provided on those special-feature-laden DVDs which are by now the actual quanta of the movies—the form in which they really get seen. The director's cut, after all, is not a cut (the sole exception I've seen is the Coen brothers' revamped *Blood Simple*, which is roughly five minutes leaner than the version that enjoyed theatrical release) but an expansion, the bitter putting-back-in of all that the assembled execs and idiots forced the director to take out.

Yet what gets put back in is often stifling and slowing. Francis Ford Coppola's near-masterpiece *Apocalypse Now* is, in its expanded and presumably perfected version, also long-winded and diffuse, escaping its relentless thematic concentration for side-lit erotic encounters with *Playboy* Playmates and mysterious French colonial women, pleasing but a little pointless. And no amount of putting back in can redeem the silliness of the heavy symbolism at the movie's close (or make a heavy actor look any lighter). What one feels in most director's cuts is not so much addition, new things brought in, as mere chest expansion, the same number of breaths taken more slowly.

The search for meaningful additions leads you, finally, to the director's *commentaries*, which can provide even mediocre films with depth, irony, and counterpoint. They reflect an organic genre; among people in the movie industry, the Angry-Apologetic Monologue is the most frequent form of shoptalk. There is nothing movie people like to talk about so much as how their movie was ruined by the studio or the star. These monologues are often more interesting than the films they superintend, more interesting even than the films they superintend might have been if they had been made as the narrator wishes they had been. They are fascinating in a way that your account of why you didn't get tenure or your book failed to sell is not, because all but the worst movies involve not just an aspiration toward success but a real confrontation of impulses: there's an idealist impulse toward art and a realist impulse toward commerce, and the clash of the two, however inevitable the ending, is the natural material of drama. It is this real drama that the additive aesthetic of the DVD commentary supplies.

A fine example is the lurid, stylish psycho-thriller *The Cell*. It is the tale of a serial killer who kidnaps women and imprisons them in a tank, slowly drowning them, and who is undone by Jennifer Lopez, a psychotherapist able to enter his mind (don't ask). It was directed by Tarsem Singh, an Indian-born music video veteran, and the reason for the odd emotionlessness of a film about the attempted murder of a young girl soon becomes apparent. "She couldn't go underwater without holding her nose!" Singh says angrily, a few minutes after the main victim-to-be appears suspended in the killing tank. He punished the actress, he explains, who, having promised to swim desperately in the grim tank, turned out to be unable to do so, by denying her closeups. "I just needed to get in with her," he says in a tone of regret. "I couldn't bring myself—I was so hurt."

15 Or, at a higher level, take Allen Coulter's somber *Hollywoodland*, the intelligent, brilliantly acted (particularly by Diane Lane and Bob Hoskins and Ben Affleck), yet unbelievably dull story of how the fifties television Superman, George Reeves, killed himself or was killed in a very minor Hollywood scandal. The source of the film's strange tone—*Hollywood Babylon* retold as a Ph.D. thesis—becomes apparent when you watch the film with Coulter's commentary. Coulter turns out to be an immensely serious, erudite craftsman,

highly self-conscious about his effects. "I was thinking about the Japanese Noh theatre, which begins with a clacking on the side of a drum," he says of the otherwise routine opening shot of his film; and each effect thereafter is registered and calculated to a degree that would have shamed Henry James himself. Adrien Brody plays a detective investigating the death, and the height of his hair is discussed with aggrieved indignation; it seems that people have compared Brody's hair to Eddie Cochran's hair, whereas, in fact, "his hair is *exactly* the same height as James Dean's." Barely audible sound clues are minutely parsed for their implied significance; it turns out that the extras, looped in post-production, were allowed to murmur only about timely subjects from 1959. Every moment in the mix, every change of light (from the "fading Kodachrome" look of the Brody story to the saturated look of the Affleck bits), every discreet genuflection to another movie is lovingly catalogued. ("Just a bit of an homage to a great cut in *Chinatown*, one of my favorite edits in all film.") We learn that the longest lens in the Adrien Brody sequence is the same length as the shortest lens in the Ben Affleck sequences. We learn that the director drew up a "flow chart" of gum-chewing, marking the dramatic trajectory on which the Brody character does and does not chew gum, and thereby revealing his moral growth.

The attention to detail is amazing—Coulter will make a great movie someday—but the accumulated effect of all this passionate perfectionism is to suggest a form of self-delusion, the artist having lost sight of the thing most obvious to the viewer, which is that the story he has to tell is too insignificant to hold one's attention for the time required to tell it. The tale of how the guy who played Superman on a cheap, forgotten TV series shot himself lacks the grip of tragedy, even pop tragedy, which demands, after all, that the hero once counted. (Joe Orton's life can be made ugly and tragic because the scale of his gifts implies both conditions; but George Reeves's death is merely sad and a little sordid.) The enormous care lavished on material that would never be worthy of the effort is more moving than the film; the addition adds pathos to inertia. The will to believe, without which a popular artist has to give up even trying, does not just turn sows' ears into silk purses; more often, it makes silk ears, beautifully surfaced and yet still attached to the same old animal.

To dig still deeper into the strange pathos of respective narration, take the late-Brosnan-period James Bond movie *The World Is Not Enough*. It was directed by the British documentarian Michael Apted, a man of genuine accomplishment, whose *Seven Up* series, tracing the development of a group of British schoolkids of various class backgrounds from childhood to, by now, middle age, will be recalled as one of the classics of our time. (His *Coal Miner's Daughter* remains a very good thing, too.) Now, the Bond film he agreed to shoot contains, within its frames, the single most sublimely silly conception in modern cinema: Denise Richards as a nuclear physicist in hot pants named Christmas Jones. You might think this would be a hard movie to render dull, yet dull and confused it is, leaving even Denise Richards almost sexless and undistracting. The reason becomes apparent in Apted's commentary. Apted, who has a respect for actors and a feeling for the real, could not—cannot now—adequately subsume himself into the kind of dumb but deadpan, yet on its own terms serious, stylishness that a Bond film demands. "Blood-curdling action," he announces quietly before some early action sequences, "tires an audience out"—surely a dubious motto for the director of a Bond film. And then, "Gunfire can get extremely tedious, noisy and tedious."

He was brought in, we soon realize, to give some "weight" to the performances, with the result that the action sequences stop abruptly, interrupted by heavy-breathing dramatic acting, up and down the piano, by Sophie Marceau as the heroine and the game Pierce Brosnan as Bond. Apted broods intelligently on "the developing dynamic of the Elektra-Bond relationship," and says sapient things about the "vulnerability" of the villain. When Denise makes her appearance, he says gently that she has "perhaps a less developed role than some of the others," though "undeveloped" might seem to be the last word one would use for Denise Richards. The trouble is that he kept trying to make the movie good in the wrong way. When a babe is brought out for Bond to sleep with, Apted says nice things about what a fine actress she is. But do we want a Bond babe to be a fine actress? A director who is thinking of her as a full-fledged thespian* may be a better man than the one who is thinking of her as a full-bosomed ornament. But he is a worse Bond director. By the time we come to a tedious and nearly indecipherable sequence with a submarine, which ends the film, Apted is almost as dispirited as the viewer. He says, feebly, "I did a lot of little inserts of buttons and flashing lights and whatever." And there they are, full of oogah horns and bright-red things that flick on and off, signifying nothing.

The net effect is like that of a funny Malcolm Bradbury novel about the tormented inner life of a documentary-film director, serious and much admired, who finds himself directing a Bond film. This—the sensitive commentary and the cynical film together—makes something that is close to being a work of art in itself, the tale of a man with a tangled conscience and a submarine to sink. The commentary provides the film with the complicated point of view, the detachment, the alienation, the odd play of foreground and background, the sad tone of attentive unease and retrospective remorse that we associate with, well, the classic modern novel. With this film—with so many films, I've come to believe—the life and variety, the sincerity of purpose, the surprising point of view, the humanity and life leach through more strongly when the creator is contemplating his ragtag and jury-rigged and compromised creation than when the creation is left to lumber and stoop and speak for itself. Dr. Frankenstein and his monster* together are the subject of art; the doctor alone is mere science journalism, and the monster alone mere horror.

What these commentaries reveal to us is this: the movies we see are the already abridged versions of longer novels of ambition and intelligence, thwarted and rewarded. The augmented film teaches us the same lesson as the subtracted book: art is a business not of clear narratives but of troubled narrators. Western literature begins not with the Trojan War* but with the poet's announcement that he is going to tell a story *about* the Trojan War. It is self-consciousness of purpose, not transparency of action, that ignites a poem. The trouble with popular entertainment is perhaps not that we don't have enough strong stories but that there are not enough weak narrators—not enough Ishmaels, whose slack and troubled attentiveness, accumulated sighs and second thoughts make the Ahabs live. Movies need their Thompsons as much as their Kanes.* (Thompson? He's the roving reporter who makes the story go for Welles; nobody remembers his name, but without him there's no Rosebud, and no movie.)* The insertion of that second nettling watching presence is what separates the merely crafty from the artful, the compact from the achieved, and guarantees that, no matter how the maker's hand may add and subtract, the viewer's mind will continue to divide, and multiply.

(2007)

DAVID SEDARIS

GUY WALKS INTO A BAR CAR[*]

*American writer David Sedaris is known for often autobiographical,
often comedic essays and fiction. The following personal essay was
first published in* The New Yorker *in 2009.*

In the golden age of American travel, the platforms of train stations were
knee deep in what looked like fog. You see it all the time in black-and-white
movies, these low-lying eddies of silver. I always thought it was steam from the
engines, but now I wonder if it didn't come from cigarettes. You could smoke
everywhere back then: in the dining car, in your sleeping berth. Depending on
your preference, it was either absolute Heaven or absolute Hell.

I know there was a smoking car on the Amtrak* I took from Raleigh to
Chicago in 1984, but seven years later it was gone. By then if you wanted a
cigarette your only option was to head for the bar. It sounds all right in passing,
romantic even—"the bar on the Lake Shore Limited"—but in fact it was rather
depressing. Too bright, too loud, and full of alcoholics who commandeered the
seats immediately after boarding and remained there, marinating like cheap
kebabs, until they reached their destinations. At first, their voices might strike
you as jolly: the warm tones of strangers becoming friends. Then the drinkers
would get sloppy and repetitive, settling, finally, on that cross-eyed mush that
passes for alcoholic sincerity.

On the train I took from New York to Chicago in early January of 1991, one
of the drunks pulled down his pants and shook his bare bottom at the woman
behind the bar. I was thirty-four, old enough to know better, yet I laughed
along with everyone else. The trip was interminable—almost nineteen hours,
not counting any delays—but nothing short of a derailment could have soured
my good mood. I was off to see the boyfriend I'd left behind when I moved
to New York. We'd known each other for six years, and though we'd broken
up more times than either of us could count, there was the hope that this visit
might reunite us. Then he'd join me for a fresh start in Manhattan, and all our
problems would disappear.

It was best for both of us that it didn't work out that way, though of course
I couldn't see it at the time. The trip designed to bring us back together tore

us apart for good, and it was a considerably sorrier me that boarded the Limited back to New York. My train left Union Station in the early evening. The late-January sky was the color of pewter, and the ground beneath it—as flat as rolled-out dough—was glazed with slush. I watched as the city receded into the distance, and then I went to the bar car for a cigarette. Of the dozen or so drunks who'd staggered on board in Chicago, one in particular stood out. I've always had an eye for ruined-looking men, and that's what attracted me to this guy—I'll call him Johnny Ryan—the sense that he'd been kicked around. By the time he hit thirty, a hardness would likely settle about his mouth and eyes, but as it was—at twenty-nine—he was right on the edge, a screw-top bottle of wine the day before it turns to vinegar.

It must have been he who started the conversation, as I'd never have had   5
the nerve. Under different circumstances, I might have stammered hello and run back to my seat, but my breakup convinced me that something major was about to happen. The chance of a lifetime was coming my way, and in order to accept it I needed to loosen up, to stop being so "rigid." That was what my former boyfriend had called me. He'd thrown in "judgmental" while he was at it, another of those synonyms for "no fun at all." The fact that it stung reaffirmed what I had always suspected: it was all true. No one was duller, more prudish and set in his ways, than I was.

Johnny didn't strike me as gay, but it was hard to tell with alcoholics. Like prisoners and shepherds, many of them didn't care who they had sex with, the idea being that what happens in the dark stays in the dark. It's the next morning you have to worry about—the name-calling, the slamming of doors, the charge that you somehow cast a spell. I must have been desperate to think that such a person would lead me to a new life. Not that Johnny was bad company—it's just that the things we had in common were all so depressing. Unemployment, for instance. My last job had been as an elf at Macy's.*

"Personal assistant" was how I phrased it, hoping he wouldn't ask for whom.

"Uh—Santa?"

His last job had involved hazardous chemicals. An accident at Thanksgiving had caused boils to rise on his back. A few months before that, a tankard of spilled benzene had burned all the hair off his arms and hands. This only made him more attractive. I imagined those smooth pink mitts of his opening the door to the rest of my life.

"So are you just going to stand here smoking all night?" he asked.   10

Normally, I waited until nine o'clock to start drinking, but "What the heck," I said. "I'll have a beer. Why not?" When a couple of seats opened up, Johnny and I took them. Across the narrow carriage, a black man with a bushy mustache pounded on the Formica* tabletop. "So a nun goes into town," he said, "and sees a sign reading, 'Quickies—Twenty-five Dollars.' Not sure what it means, she walks back to the convent and pulls aside the mother superior.* 'Excuse me,' she asks, 'but what's a quickie?'

"And the old lady goes, 'Twenty-five dollars. Just like in town.'"

As the car filled with laughter, Johnny lit a fresh cigarette. "Some comedian," he said. I don't know how we got onto the subject of gambling—perhaps I asked if he had a hobby.

"I'll bet on sporting events, on horses and greyhounds—hell, put two fleas on the table and I'll bet over which one can jump the highest. How about you?"

15   Gambling to me is what a telephone pole might be to a groundhog. He sees that it's there but doesn't for the life of him understand why. Friends have tried to explain the appeal, but still I don't get it. Why take chances with money?

Johnny had gone to Gamblers Anonymous,* but the whining got on his nerves, and he quit after his third meeting. Now, he confessed, he was on his way to Atlantic City,* where he hoped to clean up at the blackjack tables.

"All right," called the black man on the other side of the carriage. "I've got another one. What do you have if you have nuts on a wall?" He lit a cigarette and blew out the match. "Walnuts!"

A red-nosed woman in a decorative sweatshirt started to talk, but the black fellow told her that he wasn't done yet. "What do you have if you have nuts on your chest?" He waited a beat. "Chestnuts! What do you have when you have nuts on your chin?" He looked from face to face. "A dick in your mouth!"

"Now, that's good," Johnny said. "I'll have to remember that."

20   "I'll have to remind you," I told him, trembling a little at my forwardness. "I mean ... I'm pretty good at holding on to jokes."

As the black man settled down, I asked Johnny about his family. It didn't surprise me that his mother and father were divorced. Each of them was fifty-four years old, and each was currently living with someone much younger. "My dad's girlfriend—fiancée, I guess I should call her—is no older than me," Johnny said. "Before losing my job, I had my own place, but now I'm living with them. Just, you know, until I get back on my feet."

I nodded.

"My mom, meanwhile, is a total mess," he said. "Total pothead, total motormouth, total perfect match for her asshole thirty-year-old boyfriend."

Nothing in this guy's life sounded normal to me. Take food: He could recall his mother rolling joints on the kitchen counter, but he couldn't remember her cooking a single meal, not even on holidays. For dinner, they'd eat takeout hamburgers or pizzas, sometimes a sandwich slapped together over the sink. Johnny didn't cook, either. Neither did his father or his future stepmother. I asked what was in their refrigerator, and he said, "Ketchup, beer, mixers—what else?" He had no problem referring to himself as an alcoholic. "It's just a fact," he said. "I have blue eyes and black hair, too. Big deal."

"Here's a clean one," the black man said. "A fried-egg sandwich walks into a bar and orders a drink. The bartender looks him up and down, then goes, 'Sorry, we don't serve food here.'"

"Oh, that's old," one of his fellow-drunks said. "Not only that but it's supposed to be a hamburger, not a fried-egg sandwich."

"It's supposed to be food is what it's supposed to be," the black man told him. "As to what that food is, I'll make it whatever the hell I want to."

"Amen," Johnny said, and the black man gave him a thumbs-up.

His next joke went over much better. "What did the leper say to the prostitute? 'Keep the tip.'"

I pictured what looked like a mushroom cap resting in the palm of an outstretched hand. Then I covered my mouth and laughed so hard that beer trickled out of my nose. I was just mopping it up when the last call was announced, and everyone raced to the counter to stock up. Some of the drinkers would be at it until morning, when the bar reopened, while others would find their seats and sleep for a while before returning.

As for Johnny, he had a fifth of Smirnoff in his suitcase. I had two Valiums* in mine, and, because I have never much cared for sedatives, the decision to share them came easily. An hour later, it was agreed that we needed to smoke some pot. Each of us was holding, so the only question was where to smoke it—and how to get there from the bar. Since taking the Valium, drinking six beers, and following them with straight vodka, walking had become a problem for me. I don't know what it took to bring down Johnny, but he wasn't even close yet. That's what comes with years of socking it away—you should be unconscious, but instead you're up and full of bright ideas. "I think I've got a place we can go to," he said.

I'm not sure why he chose the women's lounge rather than the men's. Perhaps it was closer, or maybe there was no men's lounge. One way or the other, even now, almost twenty years later, it shames me to think of it. The idea of holing up in a bathroom, of hogging the whole thing just so that you can hang out with someone who will never, under any circumstances, return your interest, makes me cringe. Especially given that this—the "dressing room" it was called—was Amtrak's one meager attempt to recapture some glamor. It amounted to a small chamber with a window—a space not much bigger than a closet. There was an area to sit while brushing your hair or applying makeup, and a mirror to look into while you did it. A second, inner door led to a sink and toilet, but we kept that shut and installed ourselves on the carpeted floor.

Johnny had brought our plastic cups from the bar, and, after settling in, he poured us each a drink. I felt boneless, as if I'd been filleted; yet still I managed to load the pipe and hold my lighter to the bowl. Looking up through the window, I could see the moon, which struck me, in my half-conscious state, as flat and unnaturally bright, a sort of glowing Pringle.*

"Do you think we can turn that overhead light off?" I asked.

35   "No problem, Chief."

It was he who brought up the subject of sex. One moment, I was asking if his mom gave him a discount on his drugs, and the next thing I knew he was telling me about this woman he'd recently had sex with. "A fatty," he called her. "A bloodsucker." Johnny also told me that the older he got the harder it was to get it up. "I'll be totally into it, and then it's, like, 'What the fuck?' You know?"

"Oh, definitely."

He poured more vodka into his plastic cup and swirled it around, as if it were a fine cognac that needed to breathe. "You get into a lot of fights?" he asked.

"Arguments?"

40   "No," he said. "I mean with your fists. You ever punch people?"

I relit the pipe and thought of the dustup my former boyfriend and I had had before I left. It was the first time since the fifth grade that I'd hit someone not directly related to me, and it left me feeling like a Grade A moron. This had a lot to do with my punch, which was actually more of a slap. To make it worse, I'd then slipped on the icy sidewalk and fallen into a bank of soft gray snow.

There was no need to answer Johnny's fistfight question. The subject had been raised for his benefit rather than mine, an excuse to bemoan the circumference of his biceps. Back when he was boxing, the one on the right had measured seventeen and a half inches. "Now it's less than fourteen," he told me. "I'm shrinking before my very fucking eyes."

"Well, can't you fatten it back up somehow?" I asked. "You're young. I mean, just how hard can it be to gain weight?"

"The problem isn't gaining weight, it's gaining it in the right place," Johnny said. "Two six-packs a day might swell my stomach, but it's not doing shit for my arms."

45   "Maybe you could lift the cans for a while before opening them," I offered. "That should count for something, shouldn't it?"

Johnny flattened his voice. "You're a regular comedian, aren't you? Keep it up and maybe you can open for that asshole in the bar." A minute of silence and then he relit the pipe, took a hit, and passed it my way. "Look at us," he said, and he let out a long sigh. "A couple of first-class fucking losers."

I wanted to defend myself, or at least point out that we were in second class, but then somebody knocked on the door. "Go away," Johnny said. "The bathroom's closed until tomorrow." A minute later, there came another knock, this one harder, and before we could respond a key turned and a conductor entered. It wouldn't have worked to deny anything: the room stunk of pot and cigarette smoke. There was the half-empty bottle of vodka, the plastic cups turned on their sides. Put a couple of lampshades on our heads and the picture would have been complete.

I suppose that the conductor could have made some trouble—confiscated our dope, had us arrested at the next stop—but instead he just told us to take a hike, no easy feat on a train. Johnny and I parted without saying good night, I staggering off to my seat, and he going, I assumed, to his. I saw him again the following morning, back in the bar car. Whatever spell had been cast the night before was broken, and he was just another alcoholic starting his day with a shot and a chaser. As I ordered a coffee, the black man told a joke about a witch with one breast.

"Give it a rest," the woman in the decorative sweatshirt said.

I smoked a few cigarettes and then returned to my seat, nursing what promised to be a two-day headache. While slumped against the window, trying unsuccessfully to sleep, I thought of a trip to Greece I'd taken in August of 1982. I was twenty-four that summer, and flew by myself from Raleigh to Athens. A few days after arriving, I was joined by my father, my brother, and my older sister, Lisa. The four of us traveled around the country, and when they went back to North Carolina I took a bus to the port city of Patras. From there I sailed to Brindisi, Italy, wondering all the while why I hadn't returned with the rest of my family. In theory it was wonderful—a European adventure. I was too self-conscious to enjoy it, though, too timid, and it stymied me that I couldn't speak the language.

A bilingual stranger helped me buy a train ticket to Rome, but on the return to Brindisi I had no one but myself to rely on. The man behind the counter offered me three options, and I guess I said yes to the one that meant "No seat for me, thank you. I would like to be packed as tightly as possible amongst people with no access to soap or running water."

It was a common request, at least among the young and foreign. I heard French, Spanish, German, and a good many languages I couldn't quite identify. What was it that sounded like English played backward? Dutch? Swedish? If I found the crowd intimidating, it had more to do with my insecurity than with the way anyone treated me. I suppose the others seemed more deserving than I did, with their faded bandannas and goatskin bags sagging with wine. While I was counting the days until I could go back home, they seemed to have a real talent for living.

50

When I was a young man, my hair was dark brown and a lot thicker than it is now. I had one continuous eyebrow instead of two separate ones, and this made me look as if I sometimes rode a donkey. It sounds odd to say it—conceited, even—but I was cute that August when I was twenty-four. I wouldn't have said so at the time, but reviewing pictures taken by my father in Athens I think, *That was me? Really?* Looks-wise, that single month constituted my moment, a peak from which the descent was both swift and merciless.

It's only three hundred and fifty miles from Rome to Brindisi, but, what with the constant stopping and starting, the train took forever. We left, I believe, at around 8:30 p.m., and for the first few hours everyone stood. Then we sat with our legs crossed, folding them in a little bit tighter when one person, and then another, decided to lie down. As my fellow-passengers shifted position, I found myself pushed toward the corner, where I brushed up against a fellow named Bashir.

55   Lebanese, he said he was, en route to a small Italian university, where he planned to get a master's in engineering. Bashir's English was excellent, and in a matter of minutes we formed what passes between wayfarers in a foreign country as a kind of automatic friendship. More than a friendship, actually—a romance. Coloring everything was this train, its steady rumble as we passed through the dark Italian countryside. Bashir was—how to describe him? It was as if someone had coaxed the eyes out of Bambi and resettled them, half asleep, into a human face. Nothing hard or ruined-looking there; in fact, it was just the opposite—angelic, you might call him, pretty.

What was it that he and I talked about so intently? Perhaps the thrill was that we *could* talk, that our tongues, flabby from lack of exercise, could flap and make sounds in their old familiar way. Three hours into our conversation, he invited me to get off the train in his college town and spend some time, as much as I liked, in the apartment that was waiting for him. It wasn't the offer you'd make to a backpacker but something closer to a proposal. "Be with me" was the way I interpreted it.

At the end of our car was a little room, no more than a broom closet, really, with a barred window in it. It must have been 4 a.m. when two disheveled Germans stepped out, and we moved in to take their place. As would later happen with Johnny Ryan, Bashir and I sat on the floor, the state of which clearly disgusted him. Apart from the fact that we were sober and were pressed so close that our shoulders touched, the biggest difference was that our attraction was mutual. The moment came when we should have kissed—you could practically hear the surging strings—but I was too shy to make the first move, and so, I guess, was he. Still, I could feel this thing between us, not just lust but a kind of immediate love, the sort that, like instant oatmeal, can be realized in a matter of minutes and is just as nutritious as the real thing. *We'll kiss ....*

now, I kept thinking. *Then, O.K. …. now*. And on it went, more torturous by the second.

The sun was rising as we reached his destination, the houses and church spires of this strange city—a city I could make my own—silhouetted against the weak morning sky. "And so?" he asked.

I don't remember my excuse, but it all came down to cowardice. For what, really, did I have to return to? A job pushing a wheelbarrow on Raleigh construction sites? A dumpy one-bedroom next to the IHOP?*

Bashir got off with his three big suitcases and became a perennial lump in my throat, one that rises whenever I hear the word "Lebanon" or see its jittery outline on the evening news. *Is that where you went back to?* I wonder. *Do you ever think of me? Are you even still alive?* 60

Given the short amount of time we spent together, it's silly how often, and how tenderly, I think of him. All the way to Penn Station, hung over from my night with Johnny Ryan, I wondered what might have happened had I taken Bashir up on his offer. I imagined our apartment overlooking a square: the burbling fountain, the drawings of dams and bridges piled neatly on the desk.

When you're young, it's easy to believe that such an opportunity will come again, maybe even a better one. Instead of a Lebanese guy in Italy, it might be a Nigerian one in Belgium, or maybe a Pole in Turkey. You tell yourself that if you travelled alone to Europe this summer you could surely do the same thing next year and the year after that. Of course, you don't, though, and the next thing you know you're an aging, unemployed elf, so desperate for love that you spend your evening mooning over a straight alcoholic.

The closer we got to New York the more miserable I became. Then I thought of this guy my friend Lili and I had borrowed a ladder from a few months earlier, someone named Hugh.[1] I'd never really trusted people who went directly from one relationship to the next, so after my train pulled into Penn Station, and after I'd taken the subway home, I'd wait a few hours, or maybe even a full day, before dialing his number and asking if he'd like to hear a joke.

(2009)

---

1 *Hugh* Sedaris's partner, Hugh Hamrick, is frequently mentioned in the author's work.

AI WEIWEI

HEARTLESS[1]

The artist and activist Ai Weiwei played a major role in the formation of China's contemporary art scene. His own work—which ranges from documentary film to sculpture to architecture—often engages critically with Chinese history and politics. Censorship of mainstream media in has prompted increased interest in blogs, which now play a major role in Chinese political and intellectual life. For several years beginning in 2005 Ai began to post almost daily on the blog from which the following selections are taken, amassing more than 2,700 posts. In 2009, when the blog was deleted by government censors, Ai shifted his online presence to Twitter. Ai's relationship with the government remained tense, and he was arrested and held for almost three months in 2011; since his arrest, he has continued to speak openly about political issues in China.

Decades ago, "Dr. Bethunes"[2] fighting on the medical front lines sold human organs for transplant; now China has become the world's most active market for human organs. It's not because the Chinese people are cheap; even though you live cheaply doesn't mean you'll become cheap after you die. As to why a human might be cheap, that is a philosophical question not addressed in this essay.

Here, we will be discussing purely technical issues.

To put it most accurately, harvesting organs from the bodies of executed criminals is stealing. This is a public secret. Even though they want you dead, your remains should naturally be addressed to you, even in death. This includes

---

1   *HEARTLESS*   Translated by Lee Ambrozy, 2011.

2   *Dr. Bethunes*   Reference to Norman Bethune (1890–1939), a Canadian doctor known for medical innovations including the invention of mobile blood transfusion units, and for playing a major role in the provision of medical services to Chinese troops and rural civilians during the Sino-Japanese War (1937–45). He is a celebrated historical figure in China.

the bullet you consumed, and this is probably the reason why it is paid for by the family of the executed.[3]

Not too long ago, "counterrevolutionaries" were paraded through the streets and people flocked in throngs to their execution grounds. You would often hear people talking about who "had a lucky fate," because if one bullet didn't do the trick, they would be forced to use leather shoes to finish the job, "saving a bullet" for the nation.

There's not much difference between that era and this one. In this "Spring Tale,"[4] public appreciation of executions is no longer encouraged, and taking into account the excess value that the deceased will produce, the bullet's point of entry requires a much more exacting skill, so that it kills but does not wound. An ambulance is parked where the executed can plainly see it, and as soon as the gun sounds, the whiteclothed angels lunge toward the still-warm corpse with organ transplant coolers in hand.

As a key nation enforcing the death penalty, China executes one-half of the world's population of death row criminals, with a bloodcurdling yearly average of more than four thousand people.[5] All thanks should go to twenty years of "strike hard"[6] and "heavy fist" remediation campaigns. Even before execution, one's fundamental rights and human dignity are forfeited. In the high-profile Yang Jia[7] case, neither he nor his family was notified the day before his execution, and when his mother, who had been secretly incarcerated in a mental hospital, was released to see her son, she had no idea it was to be what we often call their "final moment."

Mr. Wang Jianrong, deputy director of policy and regulations at the Ministry of Health, confirmed that more than 600 hospitals in China are developing

---

3 *the bullet ... executed* In 2010, the Chinese government announced its intention of making lethal injection its standard method of execution, but in 2009 firing squad was still the most common method. The practice of charging the deceased's family for bullets was probably discontinued in the 1980s.

4 *Spring Tale* 1992 song praising the reforms instituted by prominent government leader Deng Xiaoping (1904–97).

5 *China executes ... thousand people* The Chinese government does not keep accurate public records of executions, so the number of annual executions is not known; many human rights organizations estimate that it exceeds the number in all the other countries of the world combined.

6 *"strike hard"* The Strike Hard campaigns, first instituted by Deng, are periodic crackdowns on crime during which the number of arrests is increased and sentences are made more severe.

7 *Yang Jia* In 2008, Yang Jia, who had been beaten and otherwise mistreated by police the previous year, attacked a police station and killed six officers. Many believe that Yang was not given a fair trial, and that the police covered up information concerning events that had provoked the attack; he is widely considered to be a hero.

the technology for organ transplant, and more than 160 among them already possess the necessary qualifications. That figure doesn't include military hospitals and illegal organizations.

You will discover that, as an average person, once you are disassembled and sold, you will become very expensive. If someone opens you and sells your spare parts once you've departed, you become much more valuable than you were as a complete living and breathing organism. On the Chinese mainland, a single kidney, liver, or heart transplant can cost from RMB[8] 140,000–150,000, often surpassing RMB 400,000. Sales to foreign nationals could be many more times than that.

Looking at the global market, prices for human components in Turkey range around US $5,000, in India US $3,000, in Baghdad, Iraq, costs range from US $700 to 1,000, and the average price in the Philippines is US $1,500. You can see that the price is directly related to the harmoniousness and nonharmoniousness of the nation, and whether or not there was suffering.

10   In China, the phrase "everyone is born equal" is true mostly after death; there's no difference in price between the innards of Deputy Governor Mr. Hu Changqing and People's Congress Vice Chairman Mr. Cheng Kejie from those of murderers Qiu Xinghua or Ma Jiajue.

When melamine destroyed infant kidneys with stones,[9] sufferers with severe damage were compensated at most 30,000 yuan, and those with mild damage were accorded 2,000—that's an awful lot of stir-fried kidneys. Families of those killed in the Beichuan earthquake[10] have been notified that they ought to "be considerate of the government's difficulty," and 60,000 sent them packing. If they refuse to sign for their compensation, they won't get a single penny and they still face potential detention. Price is such a devil.

The market price for Chinese hearts, livers, and lungs isn't the lowest, so why is there an international market? Because China is a nation of harmony, it has a strong army and the state guarantees stability—the supply is abundant,

---

8   *RMB*   Renminbi, Chinese currency.

9   *When melamine ... stones*   Reference to the 2008 Chinese milk scandal, in which it was discovered that the toxic chemical melamine had been added to baby formula and other dairy products to make the protein content appear higher. More than three hundred thousand children became sick, and it is not yet known how many will face long-term health consequences; at least six children died. It was widely believed that the Chinese government delayed recalling the contaminated products so as not to cause alarm during the Olympics, which were held in Beijing that summer.

10   *Beichuan earthquake*   Major 2008 natural disaster, also called the Sichuan earthquake, in which more than 69,000 people died. Much of Ai's activism during this period surrounded the deaths of a large number of children who had been attending poorly constructed schools that collapsed during the earthquake.

fresh, and boasts a high potential for a match. Recently, the Japanese Kyodo News Agency reported that seventeen Japanese citizens exchanged kidneys and livers in China, spending a per capita average of 8 million yen, equivalent to 500,000 yuan. Each operation was stimulating national demand.

Ashamed to admit to the sale of human organs, Chinese officials always respond to the Western media's reports by saying these are "vicious accusations," that such reporting is "anti-Chinese" or "reflects ulterior motives."[11] However, people are often caught red-handed. The "Regulations for Human Organ Transplant" were published in 2007, although this document only exists as a printed pamphlet.

That heartless process of reform and opening has sold off basically everything that can, and can't, be sold. Development is hard logic; if you don't sell, that's your own problem. In the near future the Chinese might wander anywhere, either in our homeland or overseas, and gaze proudly at those people in the distance—it's possible they have a Chinese heart.

Those clever Shanghainese knew they shouldn't sell Yang Jia's organs to 15 the Japanese. If the Japanese were to have even an ounce of his courage, it would take countless warriors to take one of them down.

(11 FEBRUARY 2009)

---

11 *Chinese ... ulterior motives*   The Chinese government deviated from this policy later in 2009 with a public statement acknowledging that two-thirds of transplant organs in China were taken from executed prisoners. Despite repeated official statements that the organ donation system will be or has been reformed, executed prisoners appear to remain a major source of organs in China as of 2016.

LET US FORGET[12]

*The following post appeared on Ai's blog on 3 June 2009, the day
before the anniversary of the Tiananmen Square massacre (more
commonly referred to in China as the "June Fourth Incident"). In
1989, as part of a movement in cities throughout China, protesters
demanding democracy and other reforms gathered in Tiananmen
Square, Beijing. The Chinese government sent military forces with
tanks to clear the square, and an attack on protesters began late
in the evening on 3 June; official reports claim that 241 people
were killed, but the actual numbers were much higher. The Chinese
government instituted more repressive policies following the protest,
and as of 2016, public discussion of the massacre is still censored
in China.*

Let us forget June Fourth, forget that day with no special significance. Life
has taught us that every day under totalitarianism is the same day, all totalitarian days are one day, there is no day two, there was no yesterday and is
no tomorrow.

Likewise, we no longer need segments of reality, and we no longer need
fragmented justice or equality.

People with no freedom of speech, no freedom of the press, and no right to
vote aren't human, and they don't need memory. With no right to memory, we
choose to forget.

Let us forget every persecution, every humiliation, every massacre, every
coverup, every lie, every collapse, and every death. Forget everything that
could be a painful memory and forget every time we forget. Everything is just
so they might laugh at us like fair and upstanding gentlemen.

5   Forget those soldiers firing on civilians, the tank wheels crushing the bodies of students, the bullets whistling down streets and the bloodshed, the city
and the square that didn't shed tears. Forget the endless lies, the leaders in
power who insist that everyone must forget, forget their weaknesses, wickedness, and ineptitude. You surely will forget, they must be forgotten, they can
exist only when they are forgotten. For our own survival, let us forget.

(3 JUNE 2009)

---

12 *LET US FORGET*   Translated by Lee Ambrozy, 2011.

ELIZABETH KOLBERT

THE SIXTH EXTINCTION?

In this 2009 article for The New Yorker, *an environmentalist journalist investigates the worldwide reduction in natural diversity—and its disturbing resemblance to the mass extinctions of our planet's past.*

Kolbert later expanded the ideas she had put forward in the article into a full-length book; The Sixth Extinction: An Unnatural History, *published in 2014, was awarded the Pulitzer Prize for General Non-fiction.*

The town of El Valle de Antón, in central Panama, sits in the middle of a volcanic crater formed about a million years ago. The crater is almost four miles across, but when the weather is clear you can see the jagged hills that surround the town, like the walls of a ruined tower. El Valle has one main street, a police station, and an open-air market that offers, in addition to the usual hats and embroidery, what must be the world's largest selection of golden-frog figurines. There are golden frogs sitting on leaves and—more difficult to understand—golden frogs holding cell phones. There are golden frogs wearing frilly skirts, and golden frogs striking dance poses, and ashtrays featuring golden frogs smoking cigarettes through a holder, after the fashion of F.D.R.* The golden frog, which is bright yellow with dark brown splotches, is endemic to the area around El Valle. It is considered a lucky symbol in Panama—its image is often printed on lottery tickets—though it could just as easily serve as an emblem of disaster.

In the early nineteen-nineties, an American graduate student named Karen Lips established a research site about two hundred miles west of El Valle, in the Talamanca Mountains, just over the border in Costa Rica. Lips was planning to study the local frogs, some of which, she later discovered, had never been identified. In order to get to the site, she had to drive two hours from the nearest town—the last part of the trip required tire chains—and then hike for an hour in the rain forest.

Lips spent two years living in the mountains. "It was a wonderland," she recalled recently. Once she had collected enough data, she left to work on her dissertation. She returned a few months later, and though nothing seemed to have changed, she could hardly find any frogs. Lips couldn't figure out what was happening. She collected all the dead frogs that she came across—there were only a half dozen or so—and sent their bodies to a veterinary pathologist in the United States. The pathologist was also baffled: the specimens, she told Lips, showed no signs of any known disease.

A few years went by. Lips finished her dissertation and got a teaching job. Since the frogs at her old site had pretty much disappeared, she decided that she needed to find a new location to do research. She picked another isolated spot in the rain forest, this time in western Panama. Initially, the frogs there seemed healthy. But, before long, Lips began to find corpses lying in the streams and moribund animals sitting on the banks. Sometimes she would pick up a frog and it would die in her hands. She sent some specimens to a second pathologist in the US, and, once again, the pathologist had no idea what was wrong.

5   Whatever was killing Lips's frogs continued to move, like a wave, east across Panama. By 2002, most frogs in the streams around Santa Fé, a town in the province of Veraguas, had been wiped out. By 2004, the frogs in the national park of El Copé, in the province of Coclé, had all but disappeared. At that point, golden frogs were still relatively common around El Valle; a creek not far from the town was nicknamed Thousand Frog Stream. Then, in 2006, the wave hit.

Of the many species that have existed on earth—estimates run as high as fifty billion—more than ninety-nine per cent have disappeared. In the light of this, it is sometimes joked that all of life today amounts to little more than a rounding error.

Records of the missing can be found everywhere in the world, often in forms that are difficult to overlook. And yet extinction has been a much contested concept. Throughout the eighteenth century, even as extraordinary fossils were being unearthed and put on exhibit, the prevailing view was that species were fixed, created by God for all eternity. If the bones of a strange creature were found, it must mean that the creature was out there somewhere.

"Such is the economy of nature," Thomas Jefferson* wrote, "that no instance can be produced, of her having permitted any one race of her animals to become extinct; of her having formed any link in her great work so weak as to be broken." When, as President, he dispatched Meriwether Lewis and William Clark to the Northwest,* Jefferson hoped that they would come upon live mastodons roaming the region.

The French naturalist Georges Cuvier was more skeptical. In 1812, he published an essay on the "Revolutions of the Surface of the Globe," in which he asked, "How can we believe that the immense mastodons, the gigantic megatheriums, whose bones have been found in the earth in the two Americas, still live on this continent?" Cuvier had conducted studies of the fossils found in gypsum mines in Paris, and was convinced that many organisms once common to the area no longer existed. These he referred to as *espèces perdues*, or lost species. Cuvier had no way of knowing how much time had elapsed in forming the fossil record. But, as the record indicated that Paris had, at various points, been under water, he concluded that the *espèces perdues* had been swept away by sudden cataclysms.

"Life on this earth has often been disturbed by dreadful events," he wrote. "Innumerable living creatures have been victims of these catastrophes." Cuvier's essay was translated into English in 1813 and published with an introduction by the Scottish naturalist Robert Jameson, who interpreted it as proof of Noah's flood.* It went through five editions in English and six in French before Cuvier's death, in 1832.

Charles Darwin was well acquainted with Cuvier's ideas and the theological spin they had been given. (He had studied natural history with Jameson at the University of Edinburgh.) In his theory of natural selection, Darwin embraced extinction; it was, he realized, essential that some species should die out as new ones were created. But he believed that this happened only slowly. Indeed, he claimed that it took place even more gradually than speciation: "The complete extinction of the species of a group is generally a slower process than their production." In "On the Origin of Species," published in the fall of 1859, Darwin heaped scorn on the catastrophist approach:

> So profound is our ignorance, and so high our presumption, that we marvel when we hear of the extinction of an organic being; and as we do not see the cause, we invoke cataclysms to desolate the world.

By the start of the twentieth century, this view had become dominant, and to be a scientist meant to see extinction as Darwin did. But Darwin, it turns out, was wrong.

Over the past half-billion years, there have been at least twenty mass extinctions, when the diversity of life on earth has suddenly and dramatically contracted. Five of these—the so-called Big Five—were so devastating that they are usually put in their own category. The first took place during the late Ordovican period, nearly four hundred and fifty million years ago, when life was still confined mainly to water. Geological records indicate that more than eighty per cent of marine species died out. The fifth occurred at the end of the Cretaceous period, sixty-five million years ago. The end-Cretaceous event exterminated not just the dinosaurs but seventy-five per cent of all species on earth.

10

The significance of mass extinctions goes beyond the sheer number of organisms involved. In contrast to ordinary, or so-called background, extinctions, which claim species that, for one reason or another, have become unfit, mass extinctions strike down the fit and the unfit at once. For example, brachiopods, which look like clams but have an entirely different anatomy, dominated the ocean floor for hundreds of millions of years. In the third of the Big Five extinctions—the end-Permian—the hugely successful brachiopods were nearly wiped out, along with trilobites, blastoids, and eurypterids. (In the end-Permian event, more than ninety per cent of marine species and seventy per cent of terrestrial species vanished; the event is sometimes referred to as "the mother of mass extinctions" or "the great dying.")

15   Once a mass extinction occurs, it takes millions of years for life to recover, and when it does it generally has a new cast of characters; following the end-Cretaceous event, mammals rose up (or crept out) to replace the departed dinosaurs. In this way, mass extinctions, though missing from the original theory of evolution, have played a determining role in evolution's course; as Richard Leakey has put it, such events "restructure the biosphere" and so "create the pattern of life." It is now generally agreed among biologists that another mass extinction is under way. Though it's difficult to put a precise figure on the losses, it is estimated that, if current trends continue, by the end of this century as many as half of earth's species will be gone.

The El Valle Amphibian Conservation Center, known by the acronym EVACC (pronounced "e-vac"), is a short walk from the market where the golden-frog figurines are sold. It consists of a single building about the size of an average suburban house. The place is filled, floor to ceiling, with tanks. There are tall tanks for species that, like the Rabb's fringe-limbed tree frog, live in the forest canopy, and short tanks for species that, like the big-headed robber frog, live on the forest floor. Tanks of horned marsupial frogs, which carry their eggs in a pouch, sit next to tanks of casque-headed frogs, which carry their eggs on their backs.

    The director of EVACC is a herpetologist named Edgardo Griffith. Griffith is tall and broad-shouldered, with a round face and a wide smile. He wears a silver ring in each ear and has a large tattoo of a toad's skeleton on his left shin. Griffith grew up in Panama City, and fell in love with amphibians one day in college when a friend invited him to go frog hunting. He collected most of the frogs at EVACC—there are nearly six hundred—in a rush, just as corpses were beginning to show up around El Valle. At that point, the center was little more than a hole in the ground, and so the frogs had to spend several months in temporary tanks at a local hotel. "We got a very good rate," Griffith assured me. While the amphibians were living in rented rooms, Griffith and his wife, a former Peace Corps volunteer, would go out into a nearby field to catch crickets for their dinner. Now EVACC raises bugs for the frogs in what looks like an oversized rabbit hutch.

EVACC is financed largely by the Houston Zoo, which initially pledged twenty thousand dollars to the project and has ended up spending ten times that amount. The tiny center, though, is not an outpost of the zoo. It might be thought of as a preserve, except that, instead of protecting the amphibians in their natural habitat, the center's aim is to isolate them from it. In this way, EVACC represents an ark built for a modern-day deluge. Its goal is to maintain twenty-five males and twenty-five females of each species—just enough for a breeding population.

The first time I visited, Griffith pointed out various tanks containing frogs that have essentially disappeared from the wild. These include the Panamanian golden frog, which, in addition to its extraordinary coloring, is known for its unusual method of communication; the frogs signal to one another using a kind of semaphore.* Griffith said that he expected between a third and a half of all Panama's amphibians to be gone within the next five years. Some species, he said, will probably vanish without anyone's realizing it: "Unfortunately, we are losing all these amphibians before we even know that they exist."

Griffith still goes out collecting for EVACC. Since there are hardly any frogs to be found around El Valle, he has to travel farther afield, across the Panama Canal, to the eastern half of the country.

One day this winter, I set out with him on one of his expeditions, along with two American zookeepers who were also visiting EVACC. The four of us spent a night in a town called Cerro Azul and, at dawn the next morning, drove in a truck to the ranger station at the entrance to Chagres National Park. Griffith was hoping to find females of two species that EVACC is short of. He pulled out his collecting permit and presented it to the sleepy officials manning the station. Some underfed dogs came out to sniff around.

Beyond the ranger station, the road turned into a series of craters connected by ruts. Griffith put Jimi Hendrix on the truck's CD player, and we bounced along to the throbbing beat. (When the driving got particularly gruesome, he would turn down the volume.) Frog collecting requires a lot of supplies, so Griffith had hired two men to help with the carrying. At the very last cluster of houses, in the village of Los Ángeles, they materialized out of the mist. We bounced on until the truck couldn't go any farther; then we all got out and started walking.

The trail wound its way through the rain forest in a slather of red mud. Every few hundred yards, the main path was crossed by a narrower one; these paths had been made by leaf-cutter ants, making millions—perhaps

20

billions—of trips to bring bits of greenery back to their colonies. (The colonies, which look like mounds of sawdust, can cover an area the size of a suburban back yard.) One of the Americans, Chris Bednarski, from the Houston Zoo, warned me to avoid the soldier ants, which will leave their jaws in your shin even after they're dead. "Those'll really mess you up," he observed. The other American, John Chastain, from the Toledo Zoo, was carrying a long hook, for use against venomous snakes. "Fortunately, the ones that can really mess you up are pretty rare," Bednarski said. Howler monkeys screamed in the distance. Someone pointed out jaguar prints in the soft ground.

After about five hours, we emerged into a small clearing. While we were setting up camp, a blue morpho butterfly flitted by, its wings the color of the sky.

25   That evening, after the sun set, we strapped on headlamps and clambered down to a nearby stream. Many amphibians are nocturnal, and the only way to see them is to go looking in the dark, an exercise that's as tricky as it sounds. I kept slipping, and violating Rule No. 1 of rain-forest safety: never grab on to something if you don't know what it is. After one of my falls, Bednarski showed me a tarantula the size of my fist that he had found on a nearby tree.

One technique for finding amphibians at night is to shine a light into the forest and look for the reflecting glow of their eyes. The first amphibian sighted this way was a San José Cochran frog, perched on top of a leaf. San José Cochran frogs are part of a larger family known as "glass frogs," so named because their translucent skin reveals the outline of their internal organs. This particular glass frog was green, with tiny yellow dots. Griffith pulled a pair of surgical gloves out of his pack. He stood entirely still and then, with a heronlike gesture, darted to scoop up the frog. With his free hand, he took what looked like the end of a Q-tip and swabbed the frog's belly. Finally, he put the Q-tip in a little plastic vial, placed the frog back on the leaf, and pulled out his camera. The frog stared into the lens impassively.

We continued to grope through the blackness. Someone spotted a La Loma robber frog, which is an orangey-red, like the forest floor; someone else spotted a Warzewitsch frog, which is bright green and shaped like a leaf. With every frog, Griffith went through the same routine—snatching it up, swabbing its belly, photographing it. Finally, we came upon a pair of Panamanian robber frogs locked in amplexus—the amphibian version of sex. Griffith left those two alone.

One of the frogs that Griffith was hoping to catch, the horned marsupial frog, has a distinctive call that's been likened to the sound of a champagne bottle being uncorked. As we sloshed along, the call seemed to be emanating from several directions at once. Sometimes it sounded as if we were right nearby, but then, as we approached, it would fall silent. Griffith began imitating the call, making a cork-popping sound with his lips. Eventually, he decided that the rest of us were scaring the frogs with our splashing. He waded ahead, while we stood in the middle of the stream, trying not to move. When Griffith gestured us over, we found him standing in front of a large yellow frog with long toes and an owlish face. It was sitting on a tree limb, just above eye level. Griffith grabbed the frog and turned it over. Where a female marsupial frog would have a pouch, this one had none. Griffith swabbed it, photographed it, and put it back in the tree.

"You are a beautiful boy," he told the frog.

Amphibians are among the planet's greatest survivors. The ancestors of today's   30
frogs and toads crawled out of the water some four hundred million years ago, and by two hundred and fifty million years ago the earliest representatives of what became the modern amphibian clades*—one includes frogs and toads, a second newts and salamanders—had evolved. This means that amphibians have been around not just longer than mammals, say, or birds; they have been around since before there were dinosaurs. Most amphibians—the word comes from the Greek meaning "double life"—are still closely tied to the aquatic realm from which they emerged. (The ancient Egyptians thought that frogs were produced by the coupling of land and water during the annual flooding of the Nile.) Their eggs, which have no shells, must be kept moist in order to develop. There are frogs that lay their eggs in streams, frogs that lay them in temporary pools, frogs that lay them underground, and frogs that lay them in nests that they construct out of foam. In addition to frogs that carry their eggs on their backs and in pouches, there are frogs that carry them in their vocal sacs, and, until recently at least, there were frogs that carried their eggs in their stomachs and gave birth through their mouths. Amphibians emerged at a time when all the land on earth was part of one large mass; they have since adapted to conditions on every continent except Antarctica. Worldwide, more than six thousand species have been identified, and while the greatest number are found in the tropical rain forests, there are amphibians that, like the sandhill frog of Australia, can live in the desert, and also amphibians that, like the wood frog, can live above the Arctic Circle. Several common North American frogs, including spring peepers, are able to survive the winter frozen solid.

When, about two decades ago, researchers first noticed that something odd was happening to amphibians, the evidence didn't seem to make sense. David Wake is a biologist at the University of California at Berkeley. In the early nineteen-eighties, his students began returning from frog-collecting trips in the Sierra Nevadas empty-handed. Wake remembered from his own student days that frogs in the Sierras had been difficult to avoid. "You'd be walking through meadows, and you'd inadvertently step on them," he told me. "They were just everywhere." Wake assumed that his students were just going to the wrong spots, or that they just didn't know how to look. Then a postdoc* with several years of experience told him that he couldn't find any, either. "I said, 'OK, I'll go up with you and we'll go out to some proven places,'" Wake recalled. "And I took him out to this proven place and we found, like, two toads."

Around the same time, other researchers, in other parts of the world, reported similar difficulties. In the late nineteen-eighties, a herpetologist named Marty Crump went to Costa Rica to study golden toads; she was forced to change her project because, from one year to the next, the toad essentially vanished. (The golden toad, now regarded as extinct, was actually orange; it is not to be confused with the Panamanian golden frog, which is technically also a toad.) Probably simultaneously, in central Costa Rica the populations of twenty species of frogs and toads suddenly crashed. In Ecuador, the jambato toad, a familiar visitor to back-yard gardens, disappeared in a matter of years. And in northeastern Australia biologists noticed that more than a dozen amphibian species, including the southern day frog, one of the more common in the region, were experiencing drastic declines.

But, as the number of examples increased, the evidence only seemed to grow more confounding. Though amphibians in some remote and—relatively speaking—pristine spots seemed to be collapsing, those in other, more obviously disturbed habitats seemed to be doing fine. Meanwhile, in many parts of the world there weren't good data on amphibian populations to begin with, so it was hard to determine what represented terminal descent and what might be just a temporary dip.

"It was very controversial to say that amphibians were disappearing," Andrew Blaustein, a zoology professor at Oregon State University, recalls. Blaustein, who was studying the mating behavior of frogs and toads in the Cascade Mountains, had observed that some long-standing populations simply weren't there anymore. "The debate was whether or not there really was an amphibian population problem, because some people were saying it was just natural variation." At the point that Karen Lips went to look for her first research site, she purposefully tried to steer clear of the controversy.

35   "I didn't want to work on amphibian decline," she told me. "There were endless debates about whether this was a function of randomness or a true pattern. And the last thing you want to do is get involved when you don't know what's going on."

But the debate was not to be avoided. Even amphibians that had never seen a pond or a forest started dying. Blue poison-dart frogs, which are native to Suriname, had been raised at the National Zoo, in Washington, DC, for several generations. Then, suddenly, the zoo's tank-bred frogs were wiped out.

It is difficult to say when, exactly, the current extinction event—sometimes called the sixth extinction—began. What might be thought of as its opening phase appears to have started about fifty thousand years ago. At that time, Australia was home to a fantastic assortment of enormous animals; these included a wombatlike creature the size of a hippo, a land tortoise nearly as big as a VW Beetle, and the giant short-faced kangaroo, which grew to be ten feet tall. Then all of the continent's largest animals disappeared. Every species of marsupial weighing more than two hundred pounds—there were nineteen of them—vanished, as did three species of giant reptiles and a flightless bird with stumpy legs known as *Genyornis newtoni.*

This die-off roughly coincided with the arrival of the first people on the continent, probably from Southeast Asia. Australia is a big place, and there couldn't have been very many early settlers. For a long time, the coincidence was discounted. Yet, thanks to recent work by geologists and paleontologists, a clear global pattern has emerged. About eleven thousand years ago, three-quarters of North America's largest animals—among them mastodons, mammoths, giant beavers, short-faced bears, and sabre-toothed tigers—began to go extinct. This is right around the time the first humans are believed to have wandered across the Bering land bridge. In relatively short order, the first humans settled South America as well. Subsequently, more than thirty species of South American "megamammals," including elephant-size ground sloths and rhino-like creatures known as toxodons, died out.

And what goes for Australia and the Americas also goes for many other parts of the world. Humans settled Madagascar around two thousand years ago; the island subsequently lost all mammals weighing more than twenty pounds, including pygmy hippos and giant lemurs. "Substantial losses have occurred throughout near time," Ross MacPhee, a curator at the American Museum of Natural History, in New York, and an expert on extinctions of the recent geological past, has written. "In the majority of cases, these losses occurred when, and only when, people began to expand across areas that had never before experienced their presence." The Maori arrived in New Zealand around eight hundred years ago. They encountered eleven species of moas—huge ostrichlike creatures without wings. Within a few centuries—and possibly within a single century—all eleven moa species were gone. While these "first contact" extinctions were most pronounced among large animals, they were not confined to them. Humans discovered the Hawaiian Islands around fifteen hundred years ago; soon afterward, ninety per cent of Hawaii's native bird species disappeared.

"We expect extinction when people arrive on an island," David Steadman, the curator of ornithology at the Florida Museum of Natural History, has written. "Survival is the exception."

40

Why was the first contact with humans so catastrophic? Some of the animals may have been hunted to death; thousands of moa bones have been found at Maori archaeological sites, and man-made artifacts have been uncovered near mammoth and mastodon remains at more than a dozen sites in North America. Hunting, however, seems insufficient to account for so many losses across so many different taxa in so many parts of the globe. A few years ago, researchers analyzed hundreds of bits of emu and *Genyornis newtoni* eggshell, some dating from long before the first people arrived in Australia and some from after. They found that around forty-five thousand years ago, rather abruptly, emus went from eating all sorts of plants to relying mainly on shrubs. The researchers hypothesized that Australia's early settlers periodically set the countryside on fire—perhaps to flush out prey—a practice that would have reduced the variety of plant life. Those animals which, like emus, could cope with a changed landscape survived, while those which, like *Genyornis*, could not died out.

When Australia was first settled, there were maybe half a million people on earth. There are now more than six and a half billion, and it is expected that within the next three years the number will reach seven billion.

Human impacts on the planet have increased proportionately. Farming, logging, and building have transformed between a third and a half of the world's land surface, and even these figures probably understate the effect, since land not being actively exploited may still be fragmented. Most of the world's major waterways have been diverted or dammed or otherwise manipulated—in the United States, only two per cent of rivers run unimpeded—and people now use half the world's readily accessible freshwater runoff. Chemical plants fix more atmospheric nitrogen than all natural terrestrial processes combined, and fisheries remove more than a third of the primary production of the temperate coastal waters of the oceans. Through global trade and international travel, humans have transported countless species into ecosystems that are not prepared for them. We have pumped enough carbon dioxide into the air to alter the climate and to change the chemistry of the oceans.

Amphibians are affected by many—perhaps most—of these disruptions. Habitat destruction is a major factor in their decline, and agricultural chemicals seem to be causing a rash of frog deformities. But the main culprit in the wavelike series of crashes, it's now believed, is a fungus. Ironically, this fungus, which belongs to a group known as chytrids (pronounced "kit-rids"), appears to have been spread by doctors.

45   Chytrid fungi are older even than amphibians—the first species evolved more than six hundred million years ago—and even more widespread. In a manner of speaking, they can be found—they are microscopic—just about everywhere, from the tops of trees to deep underground. Generally, chytrid fungi

feed off dead plants; there are also species that live on algae, species that live on roots, and species that live in the guts of cows, where they help break down cellulose. Until two pathologists, Don Nichols and Allan Pessier, identified a weird microorganism growing on dead frogs from the National Zoo, chytrids had never been known to attack vertebrates. Indeed, the new chytrid was so unusual that an entire genus had to be created to accommodate it. It was named *Batracho-chytrium dendrobatidis*—*batrachos* is Greek for "frog"—or Bd for short.

Nichols and Pessier sent samples from the infected frogs to a mycologist at the University of Maine, Joyce Longcore, who managed to culture the Bd fungus. Then they exposed healthy blue poison-dart frogs to it. Within three weeks, the animals had sickened and died.

The discovery of Bd explained many of the data that had previously seemed so puzzling. Chytrid fungi generate microscopic spores that disperse in water; these could have been carried along by streams, or in the runoff after a rainstorm, producing what in Central America showed up as an eastward-moving scourge. In the case of zoos, the spores could have been brought in on other frogs or on tracked-in soil. Bd seemed to be able to live on just about any frog or toad, but not all amphibians are as susceptible to it, which would account for why some populations succumbed while others appeared to be unaffected.

Rick Speare is an Australian pathologist who identified Bd right around the same time that the National Zoo team did. From the pattern of decline, Speare suspected that Bd had been spread by an amphibian that had been moved around the globe. One of the few species that met this condition was *Xenopus laevis*, commonly known as the African clawed frog. In the early nineteen-thirties, a British zoologist named Lancelot Hogben discovered that female *Xenopus laevis*, when injected with certain types of human hormones, laid eggs. His discovery became the basis for a new kind of pregnancy test and, starting in the late nineteen-thirties, thousands of African clawed frogs were exported out of Cape Town. In the nineteen-forties and fifties, it was not uncommon for obstetricians to keep tanks full of the frogs in their offices.

To test his hypothesis, Speare began collecting samples from live African clawed frogs and also from specimens preserved in museums. He found that specimens dating back to the nineteen-thirties were indeed already carrying the fungus. He also found that live African clawed frogs were widely infected with Bd, but seemed to suffer no ill effects from it. In 2004, he co-authored an influential paper that argued that the transmission route for the fungus began in southern Africa and ran through clinics and hospitals around the world.

"Let's say people were raising African clawed frogs in aquariums, and they just popped the water out," Speare told me. "In most cases when they did that, no frogs got infected, but then on that hundredth time, one local frog

50

might have been infected. Or people might have said, 'I'm sick of this frog. I'm going to let it go.' And certainly there are populations of African clawed frogs established in a number of countries around the world, to illustrate that that actually did occur."

At this point, Bd appears to be, for all intents and purposes, unstoppable. It can be killed by bleach—Clorox is among the donors to EVACC—but it is impossible to disinfect an entire rain forest. Sometime in the last year or so, the fungus jumped the Panama Canal. (When Edgardo Griffith swabbed the frogs on our trip, he was collecting samples that would eventually be analyzed for it.) It also seems to be heading into Panama from the opposite direction, out of Colombia. It has spread through the highlands of South America, down the eastern coast of Australia, and into New Zealand, and has been detected in Italy, Spain, and France. In the US, it appears to have radiated from several points, not so much in a wavelike pattern as in a series of ripples.

In the fossil record, mass extinctions stand out, so sharply that the very language scientists use to describe the earth's history derives from them. In 1840, the British geologist John Phillips divided life into three chapters: the Paleozoic (from the Greek for "ancient life"), the Mesozoic ("middle life"), and the Cenozoic ("new life"). Phillips fixed as the dividing point between the first and second eras what would now be called the end-Permian extinction, and between the second and the third the end-Cretaceous event. The fossils from these eras were so different that Phillips thought they represented three distinct episodes of creation.

Darwin's resistance to catastrophism meant that he couldn't accept what the fossils seemed to be saying. Drawing on the work of the eminent geologist Charles Lyell, a good friend of his, Darwin maintained that the apparent discontinuities in the history of life were really just gaps in the archive. In "On the Origin of Species," he argued:

> With respect to the apparently sudden extermination of whole families or orders, as of Trilobites at the close of the palaeozoic period and of Ammonites at the close of the secondary period, we must remember what has been already said on the probable wide intervals of time between our consecutive formations; and in these intervals there may have been much slow extermination.

All the way into the nineteen-sixties, paleontologists continued to give talks with titles like "The Incompleteness of the Fossil Record." And this view might have persisted even longer had it not been for a remarkable, largely inadvertent discovery made in the following decade.

In the mid-nineteen-seventies, Walter Alvarez, a geologist at the Lamont   55
Doherty Earth Observatory, in New York, was studying the earth's polarity.
It had recently been learned that the orientation of the planet's magnetic field
reverses, so that every so often, in effect, south becomes north and then vice
versa. Alvarez and some colleagues had found that a certain formation of pink-
ish limestone in Italy, known as the *scaglia rossa*, recorded these occasional
reversals. The limestone also contained the fossilized remains of millions of
tiny sea creatures called foraminifera. In the course of several trips to Italy,
Alvarez became interested in a thin layer of clay in the limestone that seemed
to have been laid down around the end of the Cretaceous. Below the layer,
certain species of foraminifera—or forams, for short—were preserved. In the
clay layer there were no forams. Above the layer, the earlier species disappeared and new forams appeared. Having been taught the uniformitarian view,
Alvarez wasn't sure what to make of what he was seeing, because the change,
he later recalled, certainly "looked very abrupt."

Alvarez decided to try to find out how long it had taken for the clay layer
to be deposited. In 1977, he took a post at the University of California at Berkeley, where his father, the Nobel prize-winning physicist Luis Alvarez, was also
teaching. The older Alvarez suggested using the element iridium to answer the
question.

Iridium is extremely rare on the surface of the earth, but more plentiful
in meteorites, which, in the form of microscopic grains of cosmic dust, are
constantly raining down on the planet. The Alvarezes reasoned that, if the clay
layer had taken a significant amount of time to deposit, it would contain detect-
able levels of iridium, and if it had been deposited in a short time it wouldn't.
They enlisted two other scientists, Frank Asaro and Helen Michel, to run the
tests, and gave them samples of the clay. Nine months later, they got a phone
call. There was something seriously wrong. Much too much iridium was
showing up in the samples. Walter Alvarez flew to Denmark to take samples of
another layer of exposed clay from the end of the Cretaceous. When they were
tested, these samples, too, were way out of line.

The Alvarez hypothesis, as it became known, was that everything—the
clay layer from the *scaglia rossa*, the clay from Denmark, the spike in iridium,
the shift in the fossils—could be explained by a single event. In 1980, the Alvarezes and their colleagues proposed that a six-mile-wide asteroid had slammed
into the earth, killing off not only the forams but the dinosaurs and all the
other organisms that went extinct at the end of the Cretaceous. "I can remember
working very hard to make that 1980 paper just as solid as it could possibly
be," Walter Alvarez recalled recently. Nevertheless, the idea was greeted with
incredulity.

"The arrogance of these people is simply unbelievable," one paleontologist told the *Times*.

60 "Unseen bodies dropping into an unseen sea are not for me," another declared.

Over the next decade, evidence in favor of an enormous impact kept accumulating. Geologists looking at rocks from the end of the Cretaceous in Montana found tiny mineral grains that seemed to have suffered a violent shock. (Such "shocked quartz" is typically found in the immediate vicinity of meteorite craters.) Other geologists, looking in other parts of the world, found small, glasslike spheres of the sort believed to form when molten-rock droplets splash up into the atmosphere. In 1990, a crater large enough to have been formed by the enormous asteroid that the Alvarezes were proposing was found, buried underneath the Yucatán.* In 1991, that crater was dated, and discovered to have been formed at precisely the time the dinosaurs died off.

"Those eleven years seemed long at the time, but looking back they seem very brief," Walter Alvarez told me. "Just think about it for a moment. Here you have a challenge to a uniformitarian viewpoint that basically every geologist and paleontologist had been trained in, as had their professors and their professors' professors, all the way back to Lyell. And what you saw was people looking at the evidence. And they gradually did come to change their minds."

Today, it's generally accepted that the asteroid that plowed into the Yucatán led, in very short order, to a mass extinction, but scientists are still uncertain exactly how the process unfolded. One theory holds that the impact raised a cloud of dust that blocked the sun, preventing photosynthesis and causing widespread starvation. According to another theory, the impact kicked up a plume of vaporized rock traveling with so much force that it broke through the atmosphere. The particles in the plume then recondensed, generating, as they fell back to earth, enough thermal energy to, in effect, broil the surface of the planet.

Whatever the mechanism, the Alvarezes' discovery wreaked havoc with the uniformitarian idea of extinction. The fossil record, it turned out, was marked by discontinuities because the history of life was marked by discontinuities.

65 In the nineteenth century, and then again during the Second World War, the Adirondacks were a major source of iron ore. As a result, the mountains are now riddled with abandoned mines. On a gray day this winter, I went to visit one of the mines (I was asked not to say which) with a wildlife biologist named Al Hicks. Hicks, who is fifty-four, is tall and outgoing, with a barrel chest and ruddy cheeks. He works at the headquarters of the New York State Department of Environmental Conservation, in Albany, and we met in a parking lot not far from his office. From there, we drove almost due north.

Along the way, Hicks explained how, in early 2007, he started to get a lot of strange calls about bats. Sometimes the call would be about a dead bat that had been brought inside by somebody's dog. Sometimes it was about a live—or half-alive—bat flapping around on the driveway. This was in the middle of winter, when any bat in the Northeast should have been hanging by its feet in a state of torpor. Hicks found the calls bizarre, but, beyond that, he didn't know what to make of them. Then, in March 2007, some colleagues went to do a routine census of hibernating bats in a cave west of Albany. After the survey, they, too, phoned in.

"They said, 'Holy shit, there's dead bats everywhere,'" Hicks recalled. He instructed them to bring some carcasses back to the office, which they did. They also shot photographs of live bats hanging from the cave's ceiling. When Hicks examined the photographs, he saw that the animals looked as if they had been dunked, nose first, in talcum powder. This was something he had never run across before, and he began sending the bat photographs to all the bat specialists he could think of. None of them could explain it, either.

"We were thinking, Oh boy, we hope this just goes away," he told me. "It was like the Bush Administration.* And, like the Bush Administration, it just wouldn't go away." In the winter of 2008, bats with the white powdery substance were found in thirty-three hibernating spots. Meanwhile, bats kept dying. In some hibernacula, populations plunged by as much as ninety-seven per cent.

That winter, officials at the National Wildlife Health Center, in Madison, Wisconsin, began to look into the situation. They were able to culture the white substance, which was found to be a never before identified fungus that grows only at cold temperatures. The condition became known as white-nose syndrome, or W.N.S. White nose seemed to be spreading fast; by March, 2008, it had been found on bats in three more states—Vermont, Massachusetts, and Connecticut—and the mortality rate was running above seventy-five per cent. This past winter, white nose was found to have spread to bats in five more states: New Jersey, New Hampshire, Virginia, West Virginia, and Pennsylvania.

In a paper published recently in *Science*, Hicks and several co-authors observed that "parallels can be drawn between the threat posed by W.N.S. and that from chytridiomycosis, a lethal fungal skin infection that has recently caused precipitous global amphibian population declines."

70

When we arrived at the base of a mountain not far from Lake Champlain, more than a dozen people were standing around in the cold, waiting for us. Most, like Hicks, were from the D.E.C., and had come to help conduct a bat census. In addition, there was a pair of biologists from the US Fish and Wildlife Service and a local novelist who was thinking of incorporating a subplot about white nose into his next book. Everyone put on snowshoes, except for the novelist, who hadn't brought any, and began tromping up the slope toward the mine entrance.

The snow was icy and the going slow, so it took almost half an hour to reach an outlook over the Champlain Valley. While we were waiting for the novelist to catch up—apparently, he was having trouble hiking through the three-foot-deep drifts—the conversation turned to the potential dangers of entering an abandoned mine. These, I was told, included getting crushed by falling rocks, being poisoned by a gas leak, and plunging over a sheer drop of a hundred feet or more.

After another fifteen minutes or so, we reached the mine entrance—essentially, a large hole cut into the hillside. The stones in front of the entrance were white with bird droppings, and the snow was covered with paw prints. Evidently, ravens and coyotes had discovered that the spot was an easy place to pick up dinner.

"Well, shit," Hicks said. Bats were fluttering in and out of the mine, and in some cases crawling on the ground. Hicks went to catch one; it was so lethargic that he grabbed it on the first try. He held it between his thumb and his forefinger, snapped its neck, and placed it in a ziplock bag.

75

"Short survey today," he announced.

At this point, it's not known exactly how the syndrome kills bats. What is known is that bats with the syndrome often wake up from their torpor and fly around, which leads them to die either of starvation or of the cold or to get picked off by predators.

We unstrapped our snowshoes and put on helmets. Hicks handed out headlamps—we were supposed to carry at least one extra—and packages of batteries; then we filed into the mine, down a long, sloping tunnel. Shattered beams littered the ground, and bats flew up at us through the gloom. Hicks cautioned everyone to stay alert. "There's places that if you take a step you won't be stepping back," he warned. The tunnel twisted along, sometimes opening up into concert-hall-size chambers with side tunnels leading out of them. Over the years, the various sections of the mine had acquired names; when we reached something called the Don Thomas section, we split up into groups to start the survey. The process consisted of photographing as many bats as possible. (Later on, back in Albany, someone would have to count all the bats in the pictures.) I went with Hicks, who was carrying an enormous camera, and one of the biologists from the Fish and Wildlife Service, who had a laser pointer. The biologist would aim the pointer at a cluster of bats hanging from the ceiling. Hicks would then snap a photograph. Most of the bats were little brown bats; these are the most common bats in the US, and the ones you are most likely to see flying around on a summer night. There were also Indiana bats, which are on the federal endangered-species list, and small-footed bats, which, at the rate things are going, are likely to end up there. As we moved along, we kept disturbing the bats, which squeaked and started to rustle around, like half-asleep children.

Since white nose grows only in the cold, it's odd to find it living on mammals, which, except when they're hibernating (or dead), maintain a high body temperature. It has been hypothesized that the fungus normally subsists by breaking down organic matter in a chilly place, and that it was transported to bat hibernacula, where it began to break down bats. When news of white nose began to get around, a spelunker sent Hicks photographs that he had shot in Howe's Cave, in central New York. The photographs, which had been taken in 2006, showed bats with clear signs of white nose and are the earliest known record of the syndrome. Howe's Cave is connected to Howe's Caverns, a popular tourist destination.

"It's kind of interesting that the first record we have of this fungus is photographs from a commercial cave in New York that gets about two hundred thousand visits a year," Hicks told me.

Despite the name, white nose is not confined to bats' noses; as we worked our way along, people kept finding bats with freckles of fungus on their wings and ears. Several of these were dispatched, for study purposes, with a thumb and forefinger. Each dead bat was sexed—males can be identified by their tiny penises—and placed in a ziplock bag.

At about 7 pm, we came to a huge, rusty winch, which, when the mine was operational, had been used to haul ore to the surface. By this point, we were almost down at the bottom of the mountain, except that we were on the inside of it. Below, the path disappeared into a pool of water, like the River Styx.* It was impossible to go any further, and we began working our way back up.

Bats, like virtually all other creatures alive today, are masters of adaptation descended from lucky survivors. The earliest bat fossil that has been found dates from fifty-three million years ago, which is to say twelve million years after the impact that ended the Cretaceous. It belongs to an animal that had wings and could fly but had not yet developed the specialized inner ear that, in modern bats, allows for echolocation. Worldwide, there are now more than a thousand bat species, which together make up nearly a fifth of all species of mammals. Most feed on insects; there are also bats that live off fruit, bats that eat fish—they use echolocation to detect minute ripples in the water—and a small but highly celebrated group that consumes blood. Bats are great colonizers—Darwin noted that even New Zealand, which has no other native mammals, has its own bats—and they can be found as far north as Alaska and as far south as Tierra del Fuego.

In the time that bats have evolved and spread, the world has changed a great deal. Fifty-three million years ago, at the start of the Eocene, the planet was very warm, and tropical palms grew at the latitude of London. The climate cooled, the Antarctic ice sheet began to form, and, eventually, about two million years ago, a period of recurring glaciations began. As recently as fifteen thousand years ago, the Adirondacks were buried under ice.

One of the puzzles of mass extinction is why, at certain junctures, the resourcefulness of life seems to falter. Powerful as the Alvarez hypothesis proved to be, it explains only a single mass extinction.

85 "I think that, after the evidence became pretty strong for the impact at the end of the Cretaceous, those of us who were working on this naïvely expected that we would go out and find evidence of impacts coinciding with the other events," Walter Alvarez told me. "And, of course, it's turned out to be much more complicated. We're seeing right now that a mass extinction can be caused by human beings. So it's clear that we do not have a general theory of mass extinction."

Andrew Knoll, a paleontologist at Harvard, has spent most of his career studying the evolution of early life. (Among the many samples he keeps in his office are fossils of microorganisms that lived 2.8 billion years ago.) He has also written about more recent events, like the end-Permian extinction, which took place two hundred and fifty million years ago, and the current extinction event.

Knoll noted that the world can change a lot without producing huge losses; ice ages, for instance, come and go. "What the geological record tells us is that it's time to worry when the rate of change is fast," he told me. In the case of the end-Permian extinction, Knoll and many other researchers believe that the trigger was a sudden burst of volcanic activity; a plume of hot mantle rock from deep in the earth sent nearly a million cubic miles' worth of flood basalts streaming over what is now Siberia. The eruption released enormous quantities of carbon dioxide, which presumably led—then as now—to global warming, and to significant changes in ocean chemistry.

"CO_2 is a paleontologist's dream," Knoll told me. "It can kill things directly, by physiological effects, of which ocean acidification is the best known, and it can kill things by changing the climate. If it gets warmer faster than you can migrate, then you're in trouble."

In the end, the most deadly aspect of human activity may simply be the pace of it. Just in the past century, CO_2 levels in the atmosphere have changed by as much—a hundred parts per million—as they normally do in a hundred-thousand year glacial cycle. Meanwhile, the drop in ocean pH levels that has occurred over the past fifty years may well exceed anything that happened in the seas during the previous fifty million. In a single afternoon, a pathogen like

Bd can move, via United or American Airlines, halfway around the world. Before man entered the picture, such a migration would have required hundreds, if not thousands, of years—if, indeed, it could have been completed at all.

Currently, a third of all amphibian species, nearly a third of reef-building corals, a quarter of all mammals, and an eighth of all birds are classified as "threatened with extinction." These estimates do not include the species that humans have already wiped out or the species for which there are insufficient data. Nor do the figures take into account the projected effects of global warming or ocean acidification. Nor, of course, can they anticipate the kinds of sudden, terrible collapses that are becoming almost routine.

90

I asked Knoll to compare the current situation with past extinction events. He told me that he didn't want to exaggerate recent losses, or to suggest that an extinction on the order of the end-Cretaceous or end-Permian was imminent. At the same time, he noted, when the asteroid hit the Yucatán, "it was one terrible afternoon." He went on, "But it was a short-term event, and then things started getting better. Today, it's not like you have a stress and the stress is relieved and recovery starts. It gets bad and then it keeps being bad, because the stress doesn't go away. Because the stress is us."

Aeolus Cave, in Dorset, Vermont, is believed to be the largest bat hibernaculum in New England; it is estimated that, before white nose hit, more than two hundred thousand bats—some from as far away as Ontario and Rhode Island—came to spend the winter here. In late February, I went with Hicks to visit Aeolus. In the parking lot of the local general store, we met up with officials from the Vermont Fish and Wildlife Department, who had organized the trip. The entrance to Aeolus is about a mile and a half from the nearest road, up a steep, wooded hillside. This time, we approached by snowmobile. The temperature outside was about twenty-five degrees—far too low for bats to be active—but when we got near the entrance we could, once again, see bats fluttering around. The most senior of the Vermont officials, Scott Darling, announced that we'd have to put on latex gloves and Tyvek suits before proceeding. At first, this seemed to me to be paranoid; soon, however, I came to see the sense of it.

Aeolus is a marble cave that was created by water flow over the course of thousands of years. The entrance is a large, horizontal tunnel at the bottom of a small hollow. To keep people out, the Nature Conservancy, which owns the cave, has blocked off the opening with huge iron slats, so that it looks like the gate of a medieval fortress. With a key, one of the slats can be removed; this creates a narrow gap that can be crawled (or slithered) through. Despite the cold, there was an awful smell emanating from the cave—half game farm, half garbage dump. When it was my turn, I squeezed through the gap and immediately slid on the ice, into a pile of dead bats. The scene, in the dimness, was horrific. There were giant icicles hanging from the ceiling, and from the floor large knobs of ice rose up, like polyps. The ground was covered with dead bats; some of the ice knobs, I noticed, had bats frozen into them. There were torpid bats roosting on the ceiling, and also wide-awake ones, which would take off and fly by or, sometimes, right into us.

Why bat corpses pile up in some places, while in others they get eaten or in some other way disappear, is unclear. Hicks speculated that the weather conditions at Aeolus were so harsh that the bats didn't even make it out of the cave before dropping dead. He and Darling had planned to do a count of the bats in the first chamber of the cave, known as Guano Hall, but this plan was soon abandoned, and it was decided just to collect specimens. Darling explained that the specimens would be going to the American Museum of Natural History, so that there would at least be a record of the bats that had once lived in Aeolus. "This may be one of the last opportunities," he said. In contrast to a mine, which has been around at most for centuries, Aeolus, he pointed out, has existed for millennia. It's likely that bats have been hibernating there, generation after generation, since the end of the last ice age.

95   "That's what makes this so dramatic—it's breaking the evolutionary chain," Darling said.

He and Hicks began picking dead bats off the ground. Those which were too badly decomposed were tossed back; those which were more or less intact were sexed and placed in two-quart plastic bags. I helped out by holding open the bag for females. Soon, it was full and another one was started. It struck me, as I stood there holding a bag filled with several dozen stiff, almost weightless bats, that I was watching mass extinction in action.

Several more bags were collected. When the specimen count hit somewhere around five hundred, Darling decided that it was time to go. Hicks hung back, saying that he wanted to take some pictures. In the hours we had been slipping around the cave, the carnage had grown even more grotesque; many of the dead bats had been crushed and now there was blood oozing out of them. As I made my way up toward the entrance, Hicks called after me: "Don't step on any dead bats." It took me a moment to realize that he was joking.

(2009)

BARACK OBAMA

REMARKS BY THE PRESIDENT IN EULOGY FOR THE HONORABLE REVEREND CLEMENTA PINCKNEY

On 17 June 2015 a 21-year-old white supremacist joined a small prayer group at a mostly-black church in Charleston, South Carolina; he then opened fire on those in the prayer group and killed nine people, including the pastor (and longtime State Senator), Clementa Pinckney.

Obama's eulogy was delivered at the memorial service for the victims held at the College of Charleston on 26 June 2015.

The Bible calls us to hope. To persevere, and have faith in things not seen. "They were still living by faith when they died," Scripture tells us. "They did not receive the things promised; they only saw them and welcomed them from a distance, admitting that they were foreigners and strangers on Earth."

We are here today to remember a man of God who lived by faith. A man who believed in things not seen. A man who believed there were better days ahead, off in the distance. A man of service who persevered, knowing full well he would not receive all those things he was promised, because he believed his efforts would deliver a better life for those who followed.

To Jennifer, his beloved wife; to Eliana and Malana, his beautiful, wonderful daughters; to the Mother Emanuel family and the people of Charleston, the people of South Carolina: I cannot claim to have the good fortune to know Reverend Pinckney well. But I did have the pleasure of knowing him and meeting him here in South Carolina, back when we were both a little bit younger. Back when I didn't have visible grey hair. The first thing I noticed was his graciousness, his smile, his reassuring baritone, his deceptive sense of humor—all qualities that helped him wear so effortlessly a heavy burden of expectation.

Friends of his remarked this week that when Clementa Pinckney entered a room, it was like the future arrived; that even from a young age, folks knew he was special. Anointed. He was the progeny of a long line of the faithful—a family of preachers who spread God's word, a family of protesters who sowed change to expand voting rights and desegregate the South.* Clem heard their instruction, and he did not forsake their teaching.

5   He was in the pulpit by 13, pastor by 18, public servant by 23. He did not exhibit any of the cockiness of youth, nor youth's insecurities; instead, he set an example worthy of his position, wise beyond his years, in his speech, in his conduct, in his love, faith, and purity.

As a senator, he represented a sprawling swath of the Low country,[1] a place that has long been one of the most neglected in America. A place still wracked by poverty and inadequate schools; a place where children can still go hungry and the sick can go without treatment. A place that needed somebody like Clem.

His position in the minority party meant the odds of winning more resources for his constituents were often long. His calls for greater equity were too often unheeded, the votes he cast were sometimes lonely. But he never gave up. He stayed true to his convictions. He would not grow discouraged. After a full day at the capitol, he'd climb into his car and head to the church to draw sustenance from his family, from his ministry, from the community that loved and needed him. There he would fortify his faith, and imagine what might be.

Reverend Pinckney embodied a politics that was neither mean, nor small. He conducted himself quietly, and kindly, and diligently. He encouraged progress not by pushing his ideas alone, but by seeking out your ideas, partnering with you to make things happen. He was full of empathy and fellow feeling, able to walk in somebody else's shoes and see through their eyes. No wonder one of his senate colleagues remembered Senator Pinckney as "the most gentle of the 46 of us—the best of the 46 of us."

Clem was often asked why he chose to be a pastor and a public servant. But the person who asked probably didn't know the history of the AME church.[2] As our brothers and sisters in the AME church know, we don't make those distinctions. "Our calling," Clem once said, "is not just within the walls of the congregation, but ... the life and community in which our congregation resides."

10   He embodied the idea that our Christian faith demands deeds and not just words; that the "sweet hour of prayer" actually lasts the whole week long; that to put our faith in action is more than individual salvation—it's about our collective salvation; that to feed the hungry and clothe the naked and house the homeless is not just a call for isolated charity but the imperative of a just society.

What a good man. Sometimes I think that's the best thing to hope for when you're eulogized—after all the words and recitations and resumes are read, to just say someone was a good man. You don't have to be of high station to

---

1   *Low Country*   Coastal region in South Carolina.

2   *AME church*   American Methodist Episcopal Church.

be a good man. Preacher by 13. Pastor by 18. Public servant by 23. What a life Clementa Pinckney lived. What an example he set. What a model for his faith. And then to lose him at 41—slain in his sanctuary with eight wonderful members of his flock, each at different stages in life but bound together by a common commitment to God.

Cynthia Hurd. Susie Jackson. Ethel Lance. DePayne Middleton-Doctor. Tywanza Sanders. Daniel L. Simmons. Sharonda Coleman-Singleton. Myra Thompson. Good people. Decent people. God-fearing people. People so full of life and so full of kindness. People who ran the race, who persevered. People of great faith.

To the families of the fallen, the nation shares in your grief. Our pain cuts that much deeper because it happened in a church. The church is and always has been the center of African-American life—a place to call our own in a too often hostile world, a sanctuary from so many hardships.

Over the course of centuries, black churches served as "hush harbors" where slaves could worship in safety; praise houses where their free descendants could gather and shout hallelujah; rest stops for the weary along the Underground Railroad; bunkers for the foot soldiers of the Civil Rights Movement.* They have been, and continue to be, community centers where we organize for jobs and justice; places of scholarship and network; places where children are loved and fed and kept out of harm's way, and told that they are beautiful and smart—and taught that they matter. That's what happens in church.

That's what the black church means. Our beating heart. The place where our dignity as a people is inviolate. When there's no better example of this tradition than Mother Emanuel—a church built by blacks seeking liberty, burned to the ground because its founder sought to end slavery, only to rise up again, a Phoenix from these ashes.*

When there were laws banning all-black church gatherings, services happened here anyway, in defiance of unjust laws. When there was a righteous movement to dismantle Jim Crow, Dr. Martin Luther King, Jr. preached from its pulpit, and marches began from its steps.* A sacred place, this church. Not just for blacks, not just for Christians, but for every American who cares about the steady expansion of human rights and human dignity in this country. A foundation stone for liberty and justice for all. That's what the church meant.

We do not know whether the killer of Reverend Pinckney and eight others knew all of this history. But he surely sensed the meaning of his violent act. It was an act that drew on a long history of bombs and arson and shots fired at churches, not random, but as a means of control, a way to terrorize and oppress. An act that he imagined would incite fear and recrimination; violence and suspicion. An act that he presumed would deepen divisions that trace back to our nation's original sin.

15

Oh, but God works in mysterious ways. God has different ideas.

He didn't know he was being used by God. Blinded by hatred, the alleged killer could not see the grace surrounding Reverend Pinckney and that Bible study group—the light of love that shone as they opened the church doors and invited a stranger to join in their prayer circle. The alleged killer could have never anticipated the way the families of the fallen would respond when they saw him in court—in the midst of unspeakable grief, with words of forgiveness.[3] He couldn't imagine that.

20   The alleged killer could not imagine how the city of Charleston, under the good and wise leadership of Mayor Riley—how the state of South Carolina, how the United States of America would respond—not merely with revulsion at his evil act, but with big-hearted generosity and, more importantly, with a thoughtful introspection and self-examination that we so rarely see in public life.

Blinded by hatred, he failed to comprehend what Reverend Pinckney so well understood—the power of God's grace.

This whole week, I've been reflecting on this idea of grace. The grace of the families who lost loved ones. The grace that Reverend Pinckney would preach about in his sermons. The grace described in one of my favorite hymnals—the one we all know: Amazing grace, how sweet the sound that saved a wretch like me. I once was lost, but now I'm found; was blind but now I see.

According to the Christian tradition, grace is not earned. Grace is not merited. It's not something we deserve. Rather, grace is the free and benevolent favor of God, as manifested in the salvation of sinners and the bestowal of blessings. Grace.

As a nation, out of this terrible tragedy, God has visited grace upon us, for he has allowed us to see where we've been blind. He has given us the chance, where we've been lost, to find our best selves. We may not have earned it, this grace, with our rancor and complacency, and short-sightedness and fear of each other—but we got it all the same. He gave it to us anyway. He's once more given us grace. But it is up to us now to make the most of it, to receive it with gratitude, and to prove ourselves worthy of this gift.

25   For too long, we were blind to the pain that the Confederate flag* stirred in too many of our citizens.[4] It's true, a flag did not cause these murders. But as

---

3   *when they saw him in court ... forgiveness*   On 19 June 2015 members of the victims' families were given a chance to address the bail hearing of the shooter; they expressed their grief, but also their forgiveness for what the shooter had done.

4   *the Confederate flag ... citizens*   In photos that the shooter posted on a website (along with expressions of hatred towards African Americans, Jews, Latinos, and others), he posed with a Confederate flag and a gun. In the wake of the incident, South Carolina Governor Nikki Haley led a successful effort to remove the Confederate flag from the South Carolina statehouse.

people from all walks of life, Republicans and Democrats, now acknowledge—including Governor Haley, whose recent eloquence on the subject is worthy of praise—as we all have to acknowledge, the flag has always represented more than just ancestral pride. For many, black and white, that flag was a reminder of systemic oppression and racial subjugation. We see that now.

Removing the flag from this state's capitol would not be an act of political correctness;* it would not be an insult to the valor of Confederate soldiers. It would simply be an acknowledgment that the cause for which they fought—the cause of slavery—was wrong. The imposition of Jim Crow after the Civil War,* the resistance to civil rights for all people was wrong. It would be one step in an honest accounting of America's history; a modest but meaningful balm for so many unhealed wounds. It would be an expression of the amazing changes that have transformed this state and this country for the better, because of the work of so many people of goodwill, people of all races striving to form a more perfect union. By taking down that flag, we express God's grace.

But I don't think God wants us to stop there. For too long, we've been blind to the way past injustices continue to shape the present. Perhaps we see that now. Perhaps this tragedy causes us to ask some tough questions about how we can permit so many of our children to languish in poverty, or attend dilapidated schools, or grow up without prospects for a job or for a career.

Perhaps it causes us to examine what we're doing to cause some of our children to hate. Perhaps it softens hearts towards those lost young men, tens and tens of thousands caught up in the criminal justice system—and leads us to make sure that that system is not infected with bias; that we embrace changes in how we train and equip our police so that the bonds of trust between law enforcement and the communities they serve make us all safer and more secure.

Maybe we now realize the way racial bias can infect us even when we don't realize it, so that we're guarding against not just racial slurs, but we're also guarding against the subtle impulse to call Johnny back for a job interview but not Jamal.* So that we search our hearts when we consider laws to make it harder for some of our fellow citizens to vote. By recognizing our common humanity by treating every child as important, regardless of the color of their skin or the station into which they were born, and to do what's necessary to make opportunity real for every American—by doing that, we express God's grace.

For too long ...[5] For too long, we've been blind to the unique mayhem that gun violence inflicts upon this nation. Sporadically, our eyes are opened: When eight of our brothers and sisters are cut down in a church basement,   30

---

5 *For too long* Here the audience interrupted, echoing Obama: "For too long."

twelve in a movie theater, twenty-six in an elementary school.[6] But I hope we also see the thirty precious lives cut short by gun violence in this country every single day; the countless more whose lives are forever changed—the survivors crippled, the children traumatized and fearful every day as they walk to school, the husband who will never feel his wife's warm touch, the entire communities whose grief overflows every time they have to watch what happened to them happen to some other place.

The vast majority of Americans—the majority of gun owners—want to do something about this. We see that now. And I'm convinced that by acknowledging the pain and loss of others, even as we respect the traditions and ways of life that make up this beloved country—by making the moral choice to change, we express God's grace.

We don't earn grace. We're all sinners. We don't deserve it. But God gives it to us anyway. And we choose how to receive it. It's our decision how to honor it.

None of us can or should expect a transformation in race relations overnight. Every time something like this happens, somebody says we have to have a conversation about race. We talk a lot about race. There's no shortcut. And we don't need more talk. None of us should believe that a handful of gun safety measures will prevent every tragedy. It will not. People of goodwill will continue to debate the merits of various policies, as our democracy requires—this is a big, raucous place, America is. And there are good people on both sides of these debates. Whatever solutions we find will necessarily be incomplete.

But it would be a betrayal of everything Reverend Pinckney stood for, I believe, if we allowed ourselves to slip into a comfortable silence again. Once the eulogies have been delivered, once the TV cameras move on, to go back to business as usual—that's what we so often do to avoid uncomfortable truths about the prejudice that still infects our society. To settle for symbolic gestures without following up with the hard work of more lasting change—that's how we lose our way again.

35   It would be a refutation of the forgiveness expressed by those families if we merely slipped into old habits, whereby those who disagree with us are not merely wrong but bad; where we shout instead of listen; where we barricade ourselves behind preconceived notions or well-practiced cynicism.

Reverend Pinckney once said, "Across the South, we have a deep appreciation of history—we haven't always had a deep appreciation of each other's history." What is true in the South is true for America. Clem understood that

---

6   *twelve in a ... elementary school* Among the mass shootings in America have been a 12 July 2012 incident in Aurora, Colorado, in which twelve people were killed in a movie theater, and a 14 December 2012 incident in Newtown, Connecticut, in which twenty-six children were killed in their elementary school.

justice grows out of recognition of ourselves in each other. That my liberty depends on you being free, too. That history can't be a sword to justify injustice, or a shield against progress, but must be a manual for how to avoid repeating the mistakes of the past—how to break the cycle. A roadway toward a better world. He knew that the path of grace involves an open mind—but, more importantly, an open heart.

That's what I've felt this week—an open heart. That, more than any particular policy or analysis, is what's called upon right now, I think—what a friend of mine, the writer Marilyn Robinson, calls "that reservoir of goodness, beyond, and of another kind, that we are able to do each other in the ordinary cause of things."[7]

That reservoir of goodness. If we can find that grace, anything is possible. If we can tap that grace, everything can change.

Amazing grace. Amazing grace.[8] Amazing grace—how sweet the sound, that saved a wretch like me; I once was lost, but now I'm found; was blind but now I see.

Clementa Pinckney found that grace.

Cynthia Hurd found that grace.

Susie Jackson found that grace.

Ethel Lance found that grace.

DePayne Middleton-Doctor found that grace.

Tywanza Sanders found that grace.

Daniel L. Simmons, Sr. found that grace.

Sharonda Coleman-Singleton found that grace.

Myra Thompson found that grace.

Through the example of their lives, they've now passed it on to us. May we find ourselves worthy of that precious and extraordinary gift, as long as our lives endure. May grace now lead them home. May God continue to shed His grace on the United States of America.

(2015)

---

7   *that reservoir ... cause of things*   According to a 6 July 2015 posting on the website of the Marilynne Robinson Society, the quotation is from a letter from Robinson to Obama.

8   *Amazing grace*   At this point Obama began to sing, and the congregation joined him in singing "Amazing Grace," a hymn written in 1772 by the British clergyman (and former slave trader) John Newton.

Marina Keegan

Why We Care about Whales

Marina Keegan was a sophomore at Yale University's Saybrook College when this essay was published in the 11 September 2009 issue of the Yale Daily News. *The essay—which returns repeatedly to the question of how we should ration our caring as we try to help other humans and non-human animals—was republished in Keegan's only book, the posthumous collection* The Opposite of Loneliness *(2014).*

When the moon gets bored, it kills whales. Blue whales and fin whales and humpback, sperm and orca whales; centrifugal forces don't discriminate.

With a hushed retreat, the moon pulls waters out from under fins and flippers, oscillating them backward and forward before they slip outward. At nighttime, the moon watches its work. Silver light traces the strips of lingering water, the jittery crabs, the lumps of tangled seaweed.

Slowly, awkwardly, the whales find their footing. They try to fight the waves, but they can't fight the moon. They can't fight the world's rotation or the bathymetry of oceans or the inevitability that sometimes things just don't work out.

Over 2,000 cetaceans die from beaching every year. Occasionally they trap themselves in solitude, but whales are often beached in groups, huddled together in clusters and rows. Whales feel cohesion, a sense of community, of loyalty. The distress call of a lone whale is enough to prompt its entire pod to rush to its side—a gesture that lands them nose-to-nose in the same sand. It's a fatal symphony of echolocation; a siren call to the sympathetic.

5   The death is slow. As mammals of the Artiodactyla order, whales are conscious breathers. Inhalation is a choice, an occasional rise to the ocean's surface. Although their ancestors lived on land, constant oxygen exposure overwhelms today's creatures.

Beached whales become frantic, captives to their hyperventilation. Most die from dehydration. The salty air shrinks their oily pores, capturing their moisture. Deprived of the buoyancy water provides, whales can literally crush themselves to death. Some collapse before they dry out—their lungs suffocating under their massive bodies—or drown when high tides cover their blowholes, filling them slowly while they're too weak to move. The average whale can't last more than 24 hours on land.

In their final moments, they begin belching and erupting in violent thrashing. Finally, their jaws open slightly—not all the way, but just enough that the characteristic illusion of a perpetual smile disappears. This means it's over. I know this because I watched as 23 whale mouths unhinged. As 23 pairs of whale eyes glazed over.

I had woken up that morning to a triage center* outside my window. Fifty or so pilot whales were lying along the stretch of beach in front of my house, surrounded by frenzied neighbors and animal activists. The Coast Guard had arrived while I was still sleeping, and guardsmen were already using boats with giant nets in an attempt to pull the massive bodies back into the water. Volunteers hurried about in groups, digging trenches around the whales' heads to cool them off, placing wet towels on their skin, and forming assembly lines to pour buckets of water on them. The energy was nervous, confused and palpably urgent.

Pilot whales are among the most populous of the marine mammals in the cetacean order. Fully-grown males can measure up to 20 feet and weigh three tons, while females usually reach 16 feet and 1.5 tons.

Their enormity was their problem. Unlike the three dolphins that had managed to strand themselves near our house the previous summer, fifty pilot whales were nearly impossible to maneuver. If a combination of unfavorable tidal currents and topography unites, the larger species may be trapped. Sandbars sneak up on them, and the tides tie them back.

People are strange about animals. Especially large ones. Daily, on the docks of Wellfleet Harbor, thousands of fish are scaled, gutted and seasoned with thyme and lemon. No one strokes their sides with water. No one cries when their jaws slip open.

Pilot whales are not an endangered species, and yet people spend tens of thousands of dollars in rescue efforts, trucking the wounded to aquariums and in some places even airlifting them off of beaches. Perhaps the whales' sheer immensity fosters sympathy. Perhaps the stories of Jonah or Moby Dick* do the same. Or maybe it's that article we read last week about that whale in Australia understanding hand signals. Intelligence matters, doesn't it? Brain size is important, right? Those whales knew they were dying. They have some sort of language, some sort of emotion. They give birth, for God's sake! There aren't any pregnant fish in the Wellfleet nets. No communal understanding of their imminent fatality.

10

I worry sometimes that humans are afraid of helping humans. There's less risk associated with animals, less fear of failure, fear of getting too involved. In war movies, a thousand soldiers can die gruesomely, but when the horse is shot, the audience is heartbroken. It's the *My Dog Skip* effect. The *Homeward Bound** syndrome.

When we hear that the lady on the next street over has cancer, we don't see the entire town flock to her house. We push and shove and wet whales all day, then walk home through town past homeless men curled up on benches—washed up like whales on the curb sides. Pulled outside by the moon and struggling for air among the sewers. They're suffocating too, but there's no town assembly line of food. No palpable urgency, no airlifting plane.

15 Fifty stranded whales is a tangible crisis with a visible solution. There's camaraderie in the process, a *Free Willy* fantasy, an image of Flipper in everyone's mind.* There's nothing romantic about waking up a man on a park bench and making him walk to a shelter. Little self-righteous fulfillment comes from sending a check to Oxfam International.*

Would there be such a commotion if a man washed up on the beach? Yes. But stranded humans don't roll in with the tide—they hide in the corners and the concrete houses and the plains of exotic countries we've never heard of, dying of diseases we can't pronounce.

In theory I can say that our resources should be concentrated on saving human lives, that our "Save the Whales" T-shirts should read "Save the Starving Ethiopians." Logically, it's an easy argument to make. Why do we spend so much time caring about animals? Yes, their welfare is important, but surely that of humans is more so.

Last year a non-profit spent $10,000 transporting a whale to an aquarium in Florida, where it died only three days after arriving. That same $10,000 could have purchased hundreds of thousands of food rations. In theory, this is easy to say.

But looking in the eye of a dying pilot whale at four in the morning, my thoughts were not so philosophical. Four hours until high tide. Keep his skin moist. Just three hours now. There wasn't time for logic. My rationality had slipped away with the ebbing dance of the waves.

20 I had helped all day. We had managed to save 27 of the 50 whales, but 23 others were deemed too far up shore, too old or already too close to death. That night, after most of the volunteers had gone home, I went back outside my bedroom to check on the whales.

It was mid-tide, and the up-shore seaweed still crunched under my bare feet. The water was rising. The moonlight drifted down on the salt-caked battlefield, reflected in the tiny pools of water and half-shell oysters.

It was easy to spot the living whales. Their bodies, still moist, shined in the moonlight. I weaved between carcasses, kneeling down beside an old whale that was breathing deeply and far too rapidly for a healthy pilot.

I put my hands on his nose and placed my face in front of his visible eye. I knew he was going to die, and he knew he was going to die, and we both understood that there was nothing either of us could do about it.

Beached whales die on their sides, one eye pressed into the sand, the other facing up and forced to look at the moon, at the orb that pulled the water out from under its fins.

There's no echolocation on land. I imagined dying slowly next to my mother or a lover, helplessly unable to relay my parting message. I remember trying to convince myself that everything would be fine. But he wouldn't be fine. Just like the homeless man and the Ethiopian aren't fine.

Perhaps I should have been comforting one of them, placing my hands on one of their shoulders. Spending my time and my money and my life saving those who walked on two legs and spoke without echoes.

The moon pulled the waters forward and backward, then inward and around my ankles. Before I could find an answer, the whale's jaw unclenched, opening slightly around the edges.

(2009)

Jonathan Safran Foer

from Eating Animals

Foer was already famous as a novelist when he published Eating Animals, *his first non-fiction work, at the age of thirty-two. Moved by the impending arrival of his first child to re-consider the ethics of eating, Foer ended up writing a book that combines anecdote and personal reflection with rigorous argumentation.*

Throughout the book Foer touches on cultural and family traditions relating to the eating of animals; he inquires repeatedly into how it may be possible to square a decision not to eat animals with the seemingly very different values of his grandmother. The excerpt included here is from the book's last chapter, in which he returns to this vexed issue.

The Last Thanksgiving of My Childhood

Throughout my childhood, we celebrated Thanksgiving at my uncle and my aunt's house. My uncle, my mother's younger brother, was the first person on that side of the family to be born on this side of the Atlantic. My aunt can trace her lineage back to the *Mayflower*.* That unlikely pairing of histories was no small part of what made those Thanksgivings so special, and memorable, and, in the very best sense of the word, American.

We would arrive around two o'clock. The cousins would play football on the sloping sliver of a front yard until my little brother got hurt, at which point we would head up to the attic to play football on the various video game systems. Two floors beneath us, Maverick salivated at the stove's window, my father talked politics and cholesterol, the Detroit Lions played their hearts out on an unwatched TV, and my grandmother, surrounded by her family, thought in the language of her dead relatives.

Two dozen or so mismatched chairs circumscribed four tables of slightly different heights and widths, pushed together and covered in matching cloths. No one was fooled into thinking this setup was perfect, but it was. My aunt placed a small pile of popcorn kernels on each plate, which, in the course of the meal, we were supposed to transfer to the table as symbols of things we were thankful for. Dishes came out continuously; some went clockwise, some counter, some zigzagged down the length of the table: sweet potato casserole, homemade rolls, green beans with almonds, cranberry concoctions, yams, buttery mashed potatoes, my grandmother's wildly incongruous kugel,[1] trays of gherkins and olives and marinated mushrooms, and a cartoonishly large turkey that had been put in the oven when last year's was taken out. We talked and talked: about the Orioles and Redskins,* changes in the neighborhood, our accomplishments, and the anguish of others (our own anguish was off-limits), and all the while, my grandmother would go from grandchild to grandchild, making sure no one was starving....

Thanksgiving is the meal we aspire for other meals to resemble. Of course most of us can't (and wouldn't want to) cook all day every day, and of course such food would be fatal if consumed with regularity, and how many of us really want to be surrounded by our extended families every single night? (It can be challenge enough to have to eat with myself.) But it's nice to imagine all meals being so deliberate. Of the thousand-or-so meals we eat every year, Thanksgiving dinner is the one that we try most earnestly to get right. It holds the hope of being a *good* meal, whose ingredients, efforts, setting, and consuming are expressions of the best in us. More than any other meal, it is about good eating and good thinking.

And more than any other food, the Thanksgiving turkey embodies the paradoxes of eating animals: what we do to living turkeys is just about as bad as anything humans have ever done to any animal in the history of the world. Yet what we do with their dead bodies can feel so powerfully good and right. The Thanksgiving turkey is the flesh of competing instincts—of remembering and forgetting.

I'm writing these final words a few days before Thanksgiving. I live in New York now and only rarely—at least according to my grandmother—get back to DC. No one who was young is young anymore. Some of those who transferred kernels to the table are gone. And there are new family members. (I am now we.) As if the musical chairs I played at birthday parties were preparation for all of this ending and beginning.

This will be the first year we celebrate in my home, the first time I will prepare the food, and the first Thanksgiving meal at which my son will be old enough to eat the food the rest of us eat. If this entire book could be decanted into a single question—not something easy, loaded, or asked in bad faith, but a question that fully captured the problem of eating and not eating animals—it might be this: Should we serve turkey at Thanksgiving?

WHAT DO TURKEYS HAVE TO DO WITH THANKSGIVING?

What is added by having a turkey on the Thanksgiving table? Maybe it tastes good, but taste isn't the reason it's there—most people don't eat very much

5

---

1   *kugel*   Traditional Jewish casserole.

turkey throughout the year. (Thanksgiving Day accounts for 18 percent of annual turkey consumption.) And despite the pleasure we take in eating vast amounts, Thanksgiving is not about being gluttonous—it is about the opposite.

Perhaps the turkey is there because it is fundamental to the ritual—it is how we celebrate Thanksgiving. Why? Because Pilgrims might have eaten it at their first Thanksgiving?* It's more likely that they didn't. We know that they didn't have corn, apples, potatoes, or cranberries, and the only two written reports from the legendary Thanksgiving at Plymouth mention venison and wildfowl. Though it's conceivable that they ate wild turkey, we know that the turkey wasn't made part of the ritual until the nineteenth century. And historians have now discovered an even earlier Thanksgiving than the 1621 Plymouth celebration that English-American historians made famous. Half a century before Plymouth, early American settlers celebrated Thanksgiving with the Timucua Indians in what is now Florida—the best evidence suggests that the settlers were Catholic rather than Protestant, and spoke Spanish rather than English. They dined on bean soup.

10 But let's just make believe that the Pilgrims invented Thanksgiving and were eating turkey. Putting aside the obvious fact that the Pilgrims did many things that we wouldn't want to do now (and that we want to do many things they didn't), the turkeys *we* eat have about as much in common with the turkeys the Pilgrims might have eaten as does the ever-punch-lined tofurkey.* At the center of *our* Thanksgiving tables is an animal that never breathed fresh air or saw the sky until it was packed away for slaughter. At the end of *our* forks is an animal that was incapable of reproducing sexually. In *our* bellies is an animal with antibiotics in its belly. The very genetics of our birds are radically different. If the Pilgrims could have seen into the future, what would they have thought of the turkey on our table? Without exaggeration, it's unlikely that they would have recognized it as a turkey.

And what would happen if there were no turkey? Would the tradition be broken, or injured, if instead of a bird we simply had the sweet potato casserole, homemade rolls, green beans with almonds, cranberry concoctions, yams, buttery mashed potatoes, pumpkin and pecan pies? Maybe we could add some Timucuan bean soup.[2] It's not so hard to imagine it. See your loved ones around the table. Hear the sounds, smell the smells. There is no turkey. Is the holiday undermined? Is Thanksgiving no longer Thanksgiving?

Or would Thanksgiving be enhanced? Would the choice not to eat turkey be a more active way of celebrating how thankful we feel? Try to imagine the conversation that would take place. *This is why our family celebrates this way.* Would such a conversation feel disappointing or inspiring? Would fewer or more values be transmitted? Would the joy be lessened by the hunger to eat that

---

2   *Timucuan bean soup*   Traditional soup from Timucua First Nation which was present at what is now considered the first Thanksgiving.

particular animal? Imagine your family's Thanksgivings after you are gone, when the question is no longer "Why don't we eat this?" but the more obvious one: "Why did they ever?" Can the imagined gaze of future generations shame us, in Kafka's sense of the word,[3] into remembering?

The secrecy that has enabled the factory farm is breaking down. The three years I spent writing this book, for example, saw the first documentation that livestock contribute more to global warming than anything else; saw the first major research institution (the Pew Commission) recommend the total phaseout of multiple dominant intensive-confinement practices (gestation and veal crates) as a result of negotiations with industry (rather than campaigns against industry); saw the first supermarket chain of any kind (Whole Foods) commit to a systematic and extensive program of animal welfare labeling; and saw the first major national newspaper (the *New York Times*) editorialize against factory farming as a whole, arguing that "animal husbandry has been turned into animal abuse," and "manure ... has been turned into toxic waste."

We can't plead ignorance, only indifference. Those alive today are the generations that came to know better. We have the burden and the opportunity of living in the moment when the critique of factory farming broke into the popular consciousness. We are the ones of whom it will be fairly asked, *What did you do when you learned the truth about eating animals?*

THE TRUTH ABOUT EATING ANIMALS

Since 2000—*after* Temple Grandin reported improvement in slaughterhouse conditions—workers have been documented using poles like baseball bats to hit baby turkeys, stomping on chickens to watch them "pop," beating lame pigs with metal pipes, and knowingly dismembering fully conscious cattle. One needn't rely on undercover videos by animal right organizations to know of these atrocities—although they are plentiful and sufficient. I could have filled several books—an encyclopedia of cruelty—with worker testimonials.

Gail Eisnitz comes close to creating such an encyclopedia in her book *Slaughterhouse*. Researched over a ten-year period, it is filled with interviews with workers who, combined, represent more than two million hours of slaughterhouse experience; no work of investigative journalism on the topic is as comprehensive.

> One time the knocking gun[4] was broke all day, they were taking a knife and cutting the back of the cow's neck open while he's still standing up. They would just fall down and be ashaking. And they stab cows in

15

---

3 *shame ... word* Earlier in *Eating Animals*, Foer examines the claim that in Kafka's work shame is presented as "the core experience of the ethical."

4 *knocking gun* Captive bolt pistol used to stun livestock before slaughter.

the butt to make 'em move. Break their tails. They beat them so bad.... And the cow be crying with its tongue stuck out.

This is hard to talk about. You're under all this stress, all this pressure. And it really sounds mean, but I've taken [electric] prods and stuck them in their eyes. And held them there.

Down in the blood pit[5] they say that the smell of blood makes you aggressive. And it does. You get an attitude that if that hog kicks at me, I'm going to get even. You're already going to kill the hog, but that's not enough. It has to suffer.... You go in hard, push hard, blow the windpipe, make it drown in its own blood. Split its nose. ... I wasn't the only guy doing this kind of stuff. One guy I work with actually chases hogs into the scalding tank. And everybody—hog drivers, shacklers, utility men—uses lead pipes on hogs. Everybody knows it, all of it.

These statements are disturbingly representative of what Eisnitz discovered in interviews. The events described are not sanctioned by industry, but they should not be regarded as uncommon.

Undercover investigations have consistently revealed that farmworkers, laboring under what Human Rights Watch describes as "systematic human rights violations," have often let their frustrations loose on farmed animals or simply succumbed to the demands of supervisors to keep slaughter lines moving at all costs and without second thoughts. Some workers clearly are sadistic in the literal sense of that term. But I never met such a person. The several dozen workers I met were good people, smart and honest people doing their best in an impossible situation. The responsibility lies with the mentality of the meat industry that treats both animals and "human capital" like machines....

Just how common do such savageries have to be for a decent person to be unable to overlook them? ...

When Temple Grandin first began to quantify the scale of abuse in slaughterhouses, she reported witnessing "deliberate acts of cruelty occurring on a regular basis" at 32 percent of the plants she surveyed during announced visits in the United States. It's such a shocking statistic I had to read it three times. *Deliberate* acts, occurring on a *regular* basis, witnessed by an *auditor*—witnessed during *announced* audits that gave the slaughterhouse time to clean up the worst problems. ... In recent surveys, Grandin witnessed a worker dismembering a fully conscious cow, cows waking up on the bleed rail, and workers "poking cows in the anus area with an electric prod." What went on when she

---

5   *blood pit*   Area allocated to slaughter.

was not looking? And what about the vast majority of plants that don't open their doors to audits in the first place?

Farmers have lost—have had taken from them—a direct, human relation- 20 ship with their work. Increasingly, they don't own the animals, can't determine their methods, aren't allowed to apply their wisdom, and have no alternative to high-speed industrial slaughter. The factory model has estranged them not only from how they labor (hack, chop, saw, stick, lop, cut), but what they produce (disgusting, unhealthy food) and how the product is sold (anonymously and cheaply). Human beings cannot be human (much less humane) under the conditions of a factory farm or slaughterhouse. It's the most perfect workplace alienation in the world right now. Unless you consider what the animals experience.

THE AMERICAN TABLE

We shouldn't kid ourselves about the number of ethical eating options available to most of us. There isn't enough nonfactory chicken produced in America to feed the population of Staten Island and not enough nonfactory pork to serve New York City, let alone the country. Ethical meat is a promissory note, not a reality. Any ethical-meat advocate who is serious is going to be eating a lot of vegetarian fare.

A good number of people seem to be tempted to continue supporting factory farms while also buying meat outside that system when it is available. That's nice. But if it is as far as our moral imaginations can stretch, then it's hard to be optimistic about the future. Any plan that involves funneling money to the factory farm won't end factory farming. How effective would the Montgomery bus boycott* have been if the protesters had used the bus when it became inconvenient not to? How effective would a strike be if workers announced they would go back to work as soon as it became difficult to strike? If anyone finds in this book encouragement to buy some meat from alternative sources while buying factory farm meat as well, they have found something that isn't here.

If we are at all serious about ending factory farming, then the absolute least we can do is stop sending checks to the absolute worst abusers. For some, the decision to eschew factory-farmed products will be easy. For others, the decision will be a hard one. To those for whom it sounds like a hard decision (I would have counted myself in this group), the ultimate question is whether it is worth the inconvenience. We *know*, at least, that this decision will help prevent deforestation, curb global warming, reduce pollution, save oil reserves, lessen the burden on rural America, decrease human rights abuses, improve public health, and help eliminate the most systematic animal abuse in world history. What we don't know, though, may be just as important. How would making such a decision change *us?*

Setting aside the direct material changes initiated by opting out of the factory farm system, the decision to eat with such deliberateness would itself be a force with enormous potential. What kind of world would we create if three times a day we activated our compassion and reason as we sat down to eat, if we had the moral imagination and the pragmatic will to change our most fundamental act of consumption? Tolstoy famously argued that the existence of slaughterhouses and battlefields is linked. Okay, we don't fight wars because we eat meat, and some wars should be fought—which is not to mention that Hitler was a vegetarian. But compassion is a muscle that gets stronger with use, and the regular exercise of choosing kindness over cruelty would change us.

25   It might sound naive to suggest that whether you order a chicken patty or a veggie burger is a profoundly important decision. Then again, it certainly would have sounded fantastic if in the 1950s you were told that where you sat in a restaurant or on a bus[6] could begin to uproot racism. It would have sounded equally fantastic if you were told in the early 1970s, before Cesar Chavez's workers' rights campaigns,* that refusing to eat grapes could begin to free farmworkers from slave-like conditions. It might sound fantastic, but when we bother to look, it's hard to deny that our day-to-day choices shape the world. When America's early settlers decided to throw a tea party in Boston,* forces powerful enough to create a nation were released. Deciding what to eat (and what to toss overboard) is the founding act of production and consumption that shapes all others. Choosing leaf or flesh, factory farm or family farm, does not in itself change the world, but teaching ourselves, our children, our local communities, and our nation to choose conscience over ease can. One of the greatest opportunities to live our values—or betray them—lies in the food we put on our plates. And we will live or betray our values not only as individuals, but as nations.

We have grander legacies than the quest for cheap products. Martin Luther King Jr. wrote passionately about the time when "one must take a position that is neither safe, nor politic, nor popular. Sometimes we simply have to make a decision because one's conscience tells one that it is right." These famous words of King's, and the efforts of Chavez's United Farm Workers, are also our legacy. We might want to say that these social-justice movements have nothing to do with the situation of the factory farm. Human oppression is not animal abuse. King and Chavez were moved by a concern for suffering humanity, not suffering chickens or global warming. Fair enough. One can certainly quibble with, or even become enraged by, the comparison implicit in invoking them here, but it is worth noting that Cesar Chavez and King's wife, Coretta

---

6   *where you sat ... on a bus* Reference to means of protesting segregation laws by passively disobeying them (such as the Woolworth Sit-In or Rosa Parks' refusal to obey a bus driver).

Scot King, were vegans, as is King's son Dexter. We interpret the Chavez and King legacies—we interpret America's legacy—too narrowly if we assume in advance that they cannot speak against the oppression of the factory farm.

THE GLOBAL TABLE

… Rationally, factory farming is so obviously wrong, in so many ways. In all of my reading and conversations, I've yet to find a credible defense of it. But food is not rational. Food is culture, habit, and identity. For some, that irrationality leads to a kind of resignation. Food choices are likened to fashion choices or lifestyle preferences—they do not respond to judgments about how we should live. And I would agree that the messiness of food, the almost infinite meanings it proliferates, does make the question of eating—and eating animals especially—surprisingly fraught. Activists I spoke with were endlessly puzzled and frustrated by the disconnect between clear thinking and people's food choices. I sympathize but I also wonder if it is precisely the irrationality of food that holds the most promise.

Food is never simply a calculation about which diet uses the least water or causes the least suffering. And it is in this, perhaps, that our greatest hope for actually motivating ourselves to change lies. In part, the factory farm requires us to suppress conscience in favor of craving. But at another level, the ability to reject the factory farm can be exactly what we most desire.

The debacle of the factory farm is not, I've come to feel, just a problem about ignorance—it's not, as activists often say, a problem that arose because "people don't know the facts." Clearly that is one cause. I've filled this book with an awful lot of facts because they are a necessary starting point. And I've presented what we know scientifically about the legacy we are creating with our daily food choices because that also matters a great deal. I'm not suggesting our reason should not guide us in many important ways, but simply that being human, being humane, is more than an exercise of reason. Responding to the factory farm calls for a capacity to care that dwells beyond information, and beyond the oppositions of desire and reason, fact and myth, and even human and animal.

The factory farm will come to an end because of its absurd economics someday. It is radically unsustainable. The earth will eventually shake off factory farming like a dog shakes off fleas; the only question is whether we will get shaken off along with it.

Thinking about eating animals, especially publicly, releases unexpected forces into the world. The questions are charged like few others. From one angle of vision, meat is just another thing we consume, and matters in the same way as the consumption of paper napkins or SUVs—if to a greater degree. Try changing napkins at Thanksgiving, though—even do it bombastically, with a lecture on the immorality of such and such a napkin maker—and you will have a hard time getting anyone worked up. Raise the question of a vegetarian Thanksgiving, though, and you'll have no problem eliciting strong opinions—at least strong opinions. The question of eating animals hits chords that resonate deeply with our sense of self—our memories, desires, and values. Those resonances are potentially controversial, potentially threatening, potentially inspiring, but always filled with meaning. Food matters and animals matter and eating animals matters even more. The question of eating animals is ultimately driven by our intuitions about what it means to reach an ideal we have named, perhaps incorrectly, "being human."

THE FIRST THANKSGIVING OF MY CHILDHOOD

... However much we obfuscate or ignore it, we know that the factory farm is inhumane in the deepest sense of the word. And we know that there is something that matters in a deep way about the lives we create for the living beings most within our power. Our response to the factory farm is ultimately a test of how we respond to the powerless, to the most distant, to the voiceless—it is a test of how we act when no one is forcing us to act one way or another. Consistency is not required, but engagement with the problem is.

Historians tell a story about Abraham Lincoln, that while returning to Washington from Springfield, he forced his entire party to stop to help some small birds he saw in distress. When chided by the others, he responded, quite plainly, "I could not have slept tonight if I had left those poor creatures on the ground and not restored them to their mother." He did not make (though he might have) a case for the moral value of the birds, their worth to themselves or the ecosystem or God. Instead he observed, quite simply that once those suffering birds came into his view, a moral burden had been assumed. He could not be himself if he walked away. Lincoln was a hugely inconsistent personality, and of course he ate birds far more often than he aided them. But presented with the suffering of a fellow creature, he responded.

Whether I sit at the global table, with my family or with my conscience, the factory farm, for me, doesn't merely appear unreasonable. To accept the factory farm feels inhuman. To accept the factory farm—to feed the food it produces to my family, to support it with my money—would make me less myself, less my grandmother's grandson, less my son's father.

35   *This* is what my grandmother meant when she said, "If nothing matters, there's nothing to save."

(2009)

RICHARD H. THALER AND CASS R. SUNSTEIN

from NUDGE:

IMPROVING DECISIONS ABOUT
HEALTH, WEALTH, AND HAPPINESS

In the late 1960s, research by psychologists began to undermine the foundations of classical economic theory (which assumes humans to be entirely rational beings, always operating in their own self interest). Amos Tversky, Daniel Kahneman, and other "prospect theory" psychologists developed new models to describe how humans actually behave when faced with the prospect of risk. By the end of the century, scholars had begun to explore the public policy implications of what had come to be called behavioral economics. One of the most important applications was the concept of "nudges," developed largely by economist Richard Thaler. The 2009 book he co-authored with legal scholar Cass Sunstein has been extremely influential; governments in the UK, the US, and elsewhere have introduced policies based on the principle of influencing behavior through "nudges."

The excerpt included here is from the book's introductory chapter.

THE CAFETERIA

A friend of yours, Carolyn, is the director of food services for a large city school system. She is in charge of hundreds of schools, and hundreds of thousands of kids eat in her cafeterias every day. Carolyn has formal training in nutrition (a master's degree from the state university), and she is a creative type who likes to think about things in nontraditional ways.

One evening, over a good bottle of wine, she and her friend Adam, a statistically oriented management consultant who has worked with supermarket chains, hatched an interesting idea. Without changing any menus, they would run some experiments in her schools to determine whether the way the food is displayed and arranged might influence the choices kids make. Carolyn gave the directors of dozens of school cafeterias specific instructions on how to display the food choices. In some schools the desserts were placed first, in others last, in still others in a separate line. The location of various food items was varied from one school to another. In some schools the French fries, but in others the carrot sticks, were at eye level.

From his experience in designing supermarket floor plans, Adam suspected that the results would be dramatic. He was right. Simply by rearranging the cafeteria, Carolyn was able to increase or decrease the consumption of many food items by as much as 25 percent. Carolyn learned a big lesson: school children, like adults, can be greatly influenced by small changes in the context. The influence can be exercised for better or for worse. For example, Carolyn knows that she can increase consumption of healthy foods and decrease consumption of unhealthy ones.

With hundreds of schools to work with, and a team of graduate student volunteers recruited to collect and analyze the data, Carolyn believes that she now has considerable power to influence what kids eat. Carolyn is pondering what to do with her newfound power….

LIBERTARIAN PATERNALISM

5 If, all things considered, you think that Carolyn should take the opportunity to nudge the kids toward food that is better for them, … then we welcome you to our new movement: *libertarian paternalism*. We are keenly aware that this term is not one that readers will find immediately endearing. Both words are somewhat off-putting, weighted down by stereotypes from popular culture and politics that make them unappealing to many. Even worse, the concepts seem to be contradictory. Why combine two reviled and contradictory concepts? We argue that if the terms are properly understood, both concepts reflect common sense—and they are far more attractive together than alone. The problem with the terms is that they have been captured by dogmatists.

The libertarian aspect of our strategies lies in the straightforward insistence that, in general, people should be free to do what they like—and to opt out of undesirable arrangements if they want to do so. To borrow a phrase from the late Milton Friedman,[1] libertarian paternalists urge that people should be "free to choose." We strive to design policies that maintain or increase freedom of choice. When we use the term *libertarian* to modify the word *paternalism*, we simply mean liberty-preserving. And when we say liberty-preserving, we really mean it. Libertarian paternalists want to make it easy for people to go their own way; they do not want to burden those who want to exercise their freedom.

---

1   *Milton Friedman*   American economist (1912–2006) known for innovative ideas as well as conservative politics.

The paternalistic aspect lies in the claim that it is legitimate for choice architects to try to influence people's behavior in order to make their lives longer, healthier, and better. In other words, we argue for self-conscious efforts, by institutions in the private sector and also by government, to steer people's choices in directions that will improve their lives. In our understanding, a policy is "paternalistic" if it tries to influence choices in a way that will make choosers better off, *as judged by themselves.* Drawing on some well-established findings in social science, we show that in many cases, individuals make pretty bad decisions—decisions they would not have made if they had paid full attention and possessed complete information, unlimited cognitive abilities, and complete self-control.

Libertarian paternalism is a relatively weak, soft, and nonintrusive type of paternalism because choices are not blocked, fenced off, or significantly burdened. If people want to smoke cigarettes, to eat a lot of candy, to choose an unsuitable health care plan, or to fail to save for retirement, libertarian paternalists will not force them to do otherwise—or even make things hard for them. Still, the approach we recommend does count as paternalistic, because private and public choice architects are not merely trying to track or to implement people's anticipated choices. Rather, they are self-consciously attempting to move people in a direction that will make their lives better. They nudge.

A nudge, as we will use the term, is any aspect of the choice architecture that alters people's behavior in a predictable way without forbidding any options or significantly changing their economic incentives. To count as a mere nudge, the intervention must be easy and cheap to avoid. Nudges are not mandates. Putting the fruit at eye level counts as a nudge. Banning junk food does not....

HUMANS AND ECONS: WHY NUDGES CAN HELP

Those who reject paternalism often claim that human beings do a terrific job of making choices, and if not terrific, certainly better than anyone else would do (especially if that someone else works for the government). Whether or not they have ever studied economics, many people seem at least implicitly committed to the idea of *homo economicus,* or economic man—the notion that each of us thinks and chooses unfailingly well, and thus fits within the textbook picture of human beings offered by economists.

If you look at economics textbooks, you will learn that homo economicus can think like Albert Einstein, store as much memory as IBM's Big Blue, and exercise the willpower of Mahatma Gandhi.[2] Really. But the folks that we

10

---

2   *IBM's "Big Blue" ... Gandhi* The computer company IBM is known for its large computers and is often referred to as "Big Blue"; its computer "Deep Blue" *(continued ...)*

know are not like that. Real people have trouble with long division if they don't have a calculator, sometimes forget their spouse's birthday, and have a hangover on New Year's Day. They are not homo economicus; they are homo sapiens. To keep our Latin usage to a minimum we will hereafter refer to these imaginary and real species as Econs and Humans.

Consider the issue of obesity. Rates of obesity in the United States are now approaching 20 percent, and more than 60 percent of Americans are considered either obese or overweight. There is overwhelming evidence that obesity increases risks of heart disease and diabetes, frequently leading to premature death. It would be quite fantastic to suggest that everyone is choosing the right diet, or a diet that is preferable to what might be produced with a few nudges.

Of course, sensible people care about the taste of food, not simply about health, and eating is a source of pleasure in and of itself. We do not claim that everyone who is overweight is necessarily failing to act rationally, but we do reject the claim that all or almost all Americans are choosing their diet optimally. What is true for diets is true for other risk-related behavior, including smoking and drinking, which produce more than five hundred thousand premature deaths each year. With respect to diet, smoking, and drinking, people's current choices cannot reasonably be claimed to be the best means of promoting their well-being. Indeed, many smokers, drinkers, and overeaters are willing to pay third parties to help them make better decisions.

But our basic source of information here is the emerging science of choice, consisting of careful research by social scientists over the past four decades. That research has raised serious questions about the rationality of many judgments and decisions that people make. To qualify as Econs, people are not required to make perfect forecasts (that would require omniscience), but they are required to make unbiased forecasts....

15   Hundreds of studies confirm that human forecasts are flawed and biased. Human decision making is not so great either. Again to take just one example, consider what is called "status quo bias," a fancy name for inertia. For a host of reasons, which we shall explore, people have a strong tendency to go along with the status quo or default option.

When you get a new cell phone, for example, you have a series of choices to make. The fancier the phone, the more of these choices you face, from the background to the ring sound to the number of times the phone rings before the caller is sent to voice mail. The manufacturer has picked one option as the default for each of these choices. Research shows that whatever the default choices are, many people stick with them, even when the stakes are much higher than choosing the noise your phone makes when it rings.

---

famously defeated a human world champion in a chess match. Gandhi frequently abstained from food as a form of protest; he also took a vow of celibacy at the age of 37.

Two important lessons can be drawn from this research. First, never underestimate the power of inertia. Second, that power can be harnessed. If private companies or public officials think that one policy produces better outcomes, they can greatly influence the outcome by choosing it as the default. As we will show, setting default options, and other similar seemingly trivial menu-changing strategies, can have huge effects on outcomes, from increasing savings to improving health care to providing organs for lifesaving transplant operations....

A FALSE ASSUMPTION AND TWO MISCONCEPTIONS

Many people who favor freedom of choice reject any kind of paternalism. They want the government to let citizens choose for themselves. The standard policy advice that stems from this way of thinking is to give people as many choices as possible, and then let them choose the one they like best (with as little government intervention or nudging as possible). The beauty of this way of thinking is that it offers a simple solution to many complex problems: Just Maximize (the number and variety of) Choices—full stop!...

The false assumption is that almost all people, almost all of the time, make choices that are in their best interest or at the very least are better than the choices that would be made by someone else. We claim that this assumption is false—indeed, obviously false....

It seems reasonable to say that people make good choices in contexts in which they have experience, good information, and prompt feedback—say, choosing among ice cream flavors. People know whether they like chocolate, vanilla, coffee, licorice, or something else. They do less well in contexts in which they are inexperienced and poorly informed, and in which feedback is slow or infrequent—say, in choosing between fruit and ice cream (where the long-term effects are slow and feedback is poor) or in choosing among medical treatments or investment options. If you are given fifty prescription drug plans, with multiple and varying features, you might benefit from a little help. So long as people are not choosing perfectly, some changes in the choice architecture could make their lives go better (as judged by their own preferences, not those of some bureaucrat). As we will try to show, it is not only possible to design choice architecture to make people better off; in many cases it is easy to do so.

The first misconception is that it is possible to avoid influencing people's choices. In many situations, some organization or agent *must* make a choice that will affect the behavior of some other people. There is, in those situations, no way of avoiding nudging in some direction, and whether intended or not, these nudges will affect what people choose. As illustrated by the example of Carolyn's cafeterias, people's choices are pervasively influenced by the design

20

elements selected by choice architects. It is true, of course, that some nudges are unintentional; employers may decide (say) whether to pay employees monthly or biweekly without intending to create any kind of nudge, but they might be surprised to discover that people save more if they get paid biweekly because twice a year they get three pay checks in one month....

The second misconception is that paternalism always involves coercion. In the cafeteria example, the choice of the order in which to present the food items does not force a particular diet on anyone, yet Carolyn, and others in her position, might select some arrangement of food on grounds that are paternalistic in the sense that we use the term. Would anyone object to putting the fruit and salad before the desserts at an elementary school cafeteria if the result were to induce kids to eat more apples and fewer Twinkies?* Is this question fundamentally different if the customers are teenagers, or even adults? Since no coercion is involved, we think that some types of paternalism should be acceptable even to those who most embrace freedom of choice....

A NEW PATH

... Libertarian paternalism, we think, is a promising foundation for bipartisanship. In many domains, including environmental protection, family law, and school choice, we will be arguing that better governance requires less in the way of government coercion and constraint, and more in the way of freedom to choose. If incentives and nudges replace requirements and bans, government will be both smaller and more modest. So, to be clear: *we are not for bigger government, just for better governance*....

In short, libertarian paternalism is neither left nor right, neither Democratic nor Republican. In many areas, the most thoughtful Democrats are going beyond their enthusiasm for choice-eliminating programs. In many areas, the most thoughtful Republicans are abandoning their knee-jerk opposition to constructive governmental initiatives. For all their differences, we hope that both sides might be willing to converge in support of some gentle nudges.

(2009)

Natalia V. Czap, Hans J. Czap,
Gary D. Lynne, and Mark E. Burbach

Empathy Nudging as a New Component of Conservation Programs

Beginning in 2012, a group of academics from the universities of Michigan and Nebraska carried out a series of experiments designed to assess the potential impact of a form of what Natalia Czap and her colleagues termed "empathy nudging." Specifically, they set out to determine the effectiveness of "nudging" polluting farmers to become more environmentally responsible through encouraging them to imagine the effect on their actions on farmers downstream.

This brief paper summarizing the group's research results was published online as Cornhusker Economics *Paper 654, 4 September 2013, on the University of Nebraska-Lincoln Digital Commons. The same authors' much more detailed account of these experiments was published in 2015 in the academic journal* Ecological Economics, *under the title "Walk in My Shoes: Nudging for Empathy Conservation."*

In this article we continue discussing our vision for appealing to other than self-interest-only (profit maximization) in public policies on conservation of farming land. We look specifically at the downstream water pollution problem (i.e. agricultural practices of upstream farmers leading to soil erosion and chemical/fertilizer runoff, which results in poor water quality downstream). We are trying to find less costly solutions which will result in farmers using conservation technologies that decrease the impact of their agricultural practices on downstream rivers and lakes. One possible solution is to nudge for empathy, to encourage the farmers to consider the results of their choice from the perspective of the affected people, to encourage them to walk in the shoes of people who carry the negative effect of the pollution. As a result of doing so, these farmers might then join in the shared cause of improved water quality downstream, and change farming practices upstream, with lower costs overall.

Our third economic experiment investigating the effectiveness of empathy nudging, monetary incentives and a combination of both was conducted in June 2013, in the Experimental and Behavioral Economics Laboratory of the University of Nebraska-Lincoln. In total, 500 individuals participated in the experiment over an eight-day period. The sample included both university students and other members of the community. The average age was 26 years (ranging between 19 and 78 years), and one-half of our subjects were female. The experimental sessions took 60 to 90 minutes, during which the participants earned $43.60 on average.

The results discussed in this article are based on four out of five treatments. As in our previous experiment, participants were assigned a role based on their performance (accuracy and speed) on a farming quiz, with the top 50 percent earning the role of upstream farmer (UF). In each of the 20 playing rounds, UF's chose the level of conservation on their 500 acres of land. Less conservation is less costly for the UF, but results in more soil erosion and chemical runoff. This leads to lower water quality downstream and higher costs for the downstream water user (DWU). A higher conservation level on the other hand, is more costly for a farmer, but results in better water quality and thus decreases the cost arising from poor water quality for the DWU. In treatments two and four, the UFs received a crop insurance subsidy if they chose conservation above 250 acres—this is called Incentivized Conservation Compliance or CC. In Treatments three and four, the DWU sent messages nudging the farmer for empathy.[1] Specifically, they were asking the farmers to see the decision from

---

1   *messages ... empathy*   The full messages (provided in the authors' fuller report of their research in 2015) all began with the same clause: "Before choosing the level of conservation tillage this year, please...." There were a number of different versions of the main clause of the message, divided into two categories, personal messages and general messages, with the personal messages referencing the speaker's own situation and the general messages referring in general to "the downstream water user." (Examples of personal messages: "Before choosing the level of conservation tillage this year, please imagine how you would feel in my place" / "Before choosing the level of conservation tillage this year, please look at both your and my side."; Examples of general messages: "Before choosing the level of conservation tillage this year, please imagine how you would feel in the downstream user's place" / "Before choosing the level of conservation tillage this year, please look at both yours and the downstream water user's side.") Two secondary conclusions of the research (discussed in the extended article) were (1) that personal appeals were, at least initially, more effective than general ones; and (2) that formulations calling on the respondents to use their empathetic imagination (e.g., "please imagine how ...") were more effective than formulations calling on respondents to see both sides of the argument (e.g., "please look at both your and my side.").

the DWU's point of view, put themselves in the DWU's shoes, look at both sides of the argument, etc.—this is called Nudging.

The levels of conservation were compared under these treatments. It was found that the combination of financial incentives and nudging increased the conservation level by more than 25 percent, as compared to financial incentives or nudging alone…. This suggests that financial and non-financial incentives appeal to dual-interest and work in synergy, motivating people to sacrifice a bit of self-interest for the sake of the shared-other-interest….

In a time when businesses are trying to understand and influence consumer preferences by empathizing with them and taking (while also perhaps nudging) the consumer's perspective, public policy should also start incorporating these other kinds of empathy-related emotional factors that temper desired outcomes. During our study we found that people believe that empathy nudging matters, and it indeed increased pro-environmental and sharing behavior. This gives an additional scientific justification for designing policies that appeal to both self—and other (shared with others)—interest within an individual, providing for both profit-seeking and shared "joining the cause" behavior.

5

(2013)

RYKA AOKI

ON LIVING WELL AND COMING FREE

Writer, performer, scholar, and activist Ryka Aoki's essay "On Living Well and Coming Free" was published in Gender Outlaws: The Next Generation, *a collection of work by transgender and other "gender outlaw" writers.* •

Living well is the best revenge.

—George Herbert

1.

Two years ago, I was in a self-defence competition. I'm a black belt,* and this was a black belt contest, held in front of students and other instructors. Self defense competitions require that we demonstrate defenses against scenarios such as multiple attackers, broken bottles, knives, and so on. It's fun to see how other styles and arts deal with attacks, and when instructors are competing, there can be quite a bit of showmanship and teaching mixed in with the actual competition. That day, all the other competitors were men, and they performed some wonderful techniques with finishing moves that ended in strangulation, broken bones, or a playful kick in the pants.

When it came to my turn, however, I thought of where and how a woman would be attacked. In the multiple attack scenario, I disabled my attackers—quick and hard, to ensure they would stay down—then stopped. But instead of a finishing flourish, I stepped back and reached for my cell phone.

I reminded the audience that when two men attack a woman, their objective is usually different from when they attack a man. I do not want a female student to risk additional harm by prolonging a street fight any longer than necessary. She should free herself, find a safe, public place, then call the police. Forget machismo—for a woman attacked, it is victory enough not to be killed.

The first requirement of living well is living.

2.

5   I never saw the point in idolizing conventional outlaws. If they were sublime or saintly enough, they got to ride off into the sunset like Clint Eastwood or

Alan Ladd.[1] Otherwise they all seemed to die young, either by execution or imprisonment, or in a blaze of glory.

But these outlaws never got a happy retirement, a nice pension, grandkids; you never see outlaws with grandkids. Not that I wanted to live like one of those pathetic farmers in a spaghetti western,[2] but really, I don't want to rule out grandkids, either.

So: Let's demystify this whole outlaw thing, okay?

The outlaw as antihero has long been an American icon, though it's become less a working definition and more a desirable brand. However, for too many people, "outlaw" has come to mean confronting others with self-righteous, moralizing inflexibility. We justify ourselves as outlaws because we are *right* and the other side, whatever it may be, is evil, wrong, or stupid. In this situation, there can be no diplomacy, no discourse. The other side is demonized so thoroughly that any outcome short of obliterating the opposing viewpoint soils the purity of the cause.

Especially in times of uncertainty—war, economic downturn, or heck, breaking up with your first boyfriend—this circle-the-wagons-and-start-shooting* mentality is an easy sell. It's Foucault meets Wal-Mart—no wonder everyone from Steve Jobs to Sarah Palin[3] fancies him or herself a maverick, going rogue. Part of this is natural—in the face of danger, all of us will band in groups. It is safer to walk down a street together than alone. However, these groups themselves become a threat when in-group status becomes privileged, and there is a pressure to be part of a more and more conforming clique of "us," rather than dissenting and risk becoming one of "them."

Calls for gender studies symposiums and papers are rife with confrontational rhetoric and buzzwords that foster us/them discourse. We break gender, bust gender, punch gender in the mouth, and shove gender into a wood chipper. Shouldn't we know better than to use the same rhetoric as a college football coach? Declining to participate in the chest-pounding and vitriol is not a sign of weakness; it's a sign of disagreement. And disagreeing with someone else's 10

---

1   *Clint Eastwood* American actor and filmmaker (b. 1930) who first rose to stardom playing a character called "The Man with No Name" in a trio of western films by Sergio Leone; *Alan Ladd* American actor (1913–64) best known for his roles in various western films of the 1950s.

2   *spaghetti western* Western film cheaply made in Europe (often in Italy) in the 1960s.

3   *Foucault* Michel Foucault (1926–84), philosopher whose theoretical works contributed to multiple academic fields, including queer theory; *Steve Jobs* American CEO (1955–2011) of Apple Inc. whose business success was sometimes attributed to his maverick personality; *Sarah Palin* Republican vice presidential candidate in the 2008 U.S. election. She cast herself as a "maverick" for her willingness to defy even her own political party, and titled her memoir *Going Rogue*.

definition should not mean that one is less savvy, less informed, or less committed to gender equality than someone who has just discovered Judith Butler.[4] Or, for that matter, Judith Butler.

When one cannot be an outlaw without one's special outlaw hat, outlaw t-shirt, and outlaw reading list, then one needs to get a life, not another outlaw merit badge.

3.

There are other ways to look at being an outlaw. We're all outlaws at one time or another, simply because laws are designed to govern people as groups. No group of laws can encompass the varied desires and actions of an individual, and when any law omits or excludes us, we are by definition outlaws—not breakers of that law, but outside of it to begin with. We are all outlaws by omission.

When one cannot own property, nor vote, nor have access to education or bank accounts, one is by definition outside these laws. One cannot steal property if one cannot own property. In this sense, people of color, the poor, the differently abled, and women are outlaws by default. Sure, Jesse James[5] was a famous outlaw because he robbed a train. But Rosa Parks[6] was a far more relevant and effective outlaw because she rode a bus.

To live outside the law in this way is to understand that outlawry is not glamorous and rarely comes with a conference t-shirt. It's a debasing, life-threatening condition, in which the law doesn't consider you. Even during my martial arts demonstration, I realized that while most women would feel safe calling the police to report an assault, for trans women, dealing with the police is usually humiliating at best and dangerous at worst. It's more than prejudice; much of the legal system is simply not written to address trans people.

15 It does not seem to me, however, that shouting "Down with the police!" makes our lives better. It is tempting to hate police indiscriminately, but if two men have just attacked you with knives and you need to call the police—there had better fucking *be* police. It's more constructive to work with the police and help them begin to be more compassionate toward us. Members of the transgender community in Los Angeles and West Hollywood are doing brave,

---

4   *Judith Butler*   Feminist philosopher (b. 1956) best known for her concept of gender performativity; her work is considered foundational in the fields of gender studies and queer theory.

5   *Jesse James*   Outlaw (1847–82) infamous for robbing banks and trains throughout nineteenth-century America.

6   *Rosa Parks*   African American activist (1913–2005) whose refusal to give up her seat on a bus to a white passenger in 1955 was a key moment in the civil rights movement.

fierce, important work with their police departments to help them treat trans people with maybe a little more dignity.

To me, these are gender outlaws in the most nurturing sense of the word. No one is expecting miracles. But it's a start. If outlaws pursue the romanticized goal of erasing structures, both political and social, then we will have no shelters to subvert, reform, or protect us. The police, the women's shelter, and the hospital may be closed to many trans women, but as long as they are there, there is the possibility of change. But should the structures be torn down, and gender mean nothing, then nothing will protect the weak from the strong.

Why can't we get beyond gender, you ask? Even with a third-degree black belt, a national championship, and decades of martial arts training, estrogen and age have made me physically weaker. Part of living in a gender binary is being able to say, Dude, you are not going to hit a woman, are you? I *want* a man to think twice before he hits me. I am not breaking the binary in this case; I am using the binary to get what I want.

Here's my Outlaw Reality Check—Is what we are doing helping individuals live well?

4.

Being a living trans person means vigilance. For a non-passing[7] trans person, there is no safe space. It is not who we are kissing, but our very heights, our voices, and the size of our hands that catalyze hatred and violence. Forget activism; simply negotiating one's world every day, constantly judging, adjusting, scanning one's surroundings, and changing clothes to go from one role to another can be overwhelming.

Add to that cases of family disownment, poverty, homelessness, HIV. When a recent study of transgender youth reports that half their sample had entertained thoughts of suicide, and a quarter of them had made at least one attempt, I am not surprised.

How can we best help other genderqueer,[8] trans, and gender variant people live better? Should we teach them to validate themselves by invalidating others, to focus their insecurity and anger on people who do not conform? Should we foster backbiting questions, like who is really trans and who is a poser?* Should we teach them to police themselves and those around them to ensure that each is transgressing in the same way they are?

20

---

7   *non-passing*   Not appearing to belong within a given group or identity category; non-passing trans people are visibly identifiable as trans rather than simply appearing to be their identified gender.

8   *genderqueer*   Having a gender identity that does not adhere to the binary classifying individuals as either male or female.

For me, the answer is clear. We can resist this temptation and declare that hurting should not beget hurt. A family, community, or village should tell its members that they can value their lives and their autonomy enough to say no—and should provide them the chance and even some guidance to find their own answers. Instead of questioning and invalidating other forms of expression and whispering that this person isn't "trans enough" or "queer enough" or "subversive enough," let us give people the support and affirmation that they may never have experienced.

In this way, being a gender outlaw can be much more than a brand name or a call to arms. It can be an opportunity to reflect upon and plan improvements to one's life. With so many obstacles and the constant threat of violence facing us, pursuing one's bliss is not a waste of time, nor a sign of weakness. It is living well.

It is the best revenge.

5.

25   As humans, we are rightfully horrified when we hear stories about victims of institutionalized genocide and persecution. The Statue of Liberty* asks all other nations not for "your finest, your best," but "your tired, your poor." We demand marriage and reproductive rights and cannot understand why anyone would have the audacity to tell us who to love, how to live, or whose children we must bring to term. However, being aware of one group in crisis does not automatically mean one sees all injustice—and more importantly, it does not mean that simply because one detects no injustice, it is not there.

When a trans woman cannot be allowed in most women's shelters, this does not help her live better. When we deny services to trans women, especially crisis intervention services, we tacitly condone violence against them. We are saying either that a rape of a trans woman is not the same as the rape of a cis woman,* or that a trans woman has lesser access to the term "woman" than a cis woman.

When the Irish immigrated to the U.S. during the potato famine,[9] only idiots would have lectured them on Irish culture and its relationship with farming. Anyone with the slightest bit of empathy who saw these people would have seen that they needed food, not a theory that explained themselves to them. They were hungry. And in our community, where it seems that trans women get so little credit or consideration, rather than question how the penis or male

---

9   *potato famine* Repeated failures of the Irish potato crop between 1845 and 1849 led to the starvation deaths of nearly a million people; during this period many Irish sought better economic prospects in places such as America.

socialization affects feminism or transfeminism, it would be nice to have some unconditional acceptance. And maybe gain some friends along the way.

6.

Ironically, even while trans women have been seen as lesser or ersatz* females, their work has been treated precisely as women's work, with the same devaluation it has received since time immemorial. Just check out a history book: Women's work is scarcely even recorded, much less classified as historically significant, while every culture seems to have recorded its generals and dictators.

If I hear one more complaint about trans women not being activists, I am going to throw a fit. When people wonder why trans women still lip synch, or chase men, or worry about their makeup, instead of presenting papers and posting in newsgroups and holding meetings dedicated to busting up the binary, they commit the same misogynist crimes against women that men have been guilty of since the beginning of time:

"Why can't they act more like us?"   30

Trans women are doing their outlaw things, in their own ways, on their own terms. They are seeking entrance to institutions that have barred them. Why? Why did Rosa Parks ride in the front of the bus? Because she wanted to. Because it made her life better. Because she knew that was where she belonged. Instead of disregarding issues like old school drag and femme[10] and passing and shoe size and body image as backward and ignorant, what about trying to understand that in these acts there is another type of narrative being constructed?

I think of my self-defense competition. Just because I don't bust a move to kill or injure my opponent does not mean I am a less accomplished martial artist. What it means is simply that my objectives and techniques are different.

Unless absolutely necessary, I will not fight to kill. I've never killed anyone, but I have hurt people badly, and I did not like the feeling. Not only do I dislike hurting people; I like living. I like the idea of someday meeting my grandkids. I refuse to fight crazy with anger. I find the patriarchy not guilty by reason of insanity. Besides which, it's not just the patriarchy: It's the crazy matriarchy, and the stepsisters and brothers and the twittering cousins and the whole nutty family that keeps threatening to disown you. I am not going to stop

---

10   *old school drag*   I.e., traditional drag, in which performers take on the exaggerated appearance and mannerisms of the opposite gender;   *femme*   Term applied to traditionally feminine gender expressions.

cooking rice porridge or hoping for a comfortable house with a garden simply because my batshit* relative tells me it's not subversive enough.

7.

Living well is not an essay topic. It is not a theory. It is a practice. We must do it with intention, as often as we can.

35   For me, being an outlaw, being a class of person that the law does not address, means thinking beyond oppressed and oppressor. Outlaws are more than victims or charity recipients. Because we exist outside the laws, we shed light on the arbitrariness of these very laws. Accept that a trans woman is a woman and you have freed yourself once and for all from the dogma that to be female is to be a baby-making (or potential baby-making) machine. Accept that a trans woman is human and add another piece of evidence that we are more and other than the morphology of our bodies, our appearance, and our histories. In a society that preys on a woman's insecurity, *any* woman who feels beautiful inside and out is a gender outlaw. And when a trans woman can do this, despite the institutions closed to her, she should be celebrated, never scorned.

Being an outlaw means understanding that freedom is not a zero-sum game.[11] Freedom depends on its abundance. For it to mean anything more than another layer of oppression, my emancipation necessitates the emancipation of others—even of those who have oppressed me.

8.

I took third place in the black belt self defense competition. Not too bad. Not for my first time back on a mat in years. I had been head judo instructor at UCLA and the coach of the Cornell judo team. But after I transitioned, I had nowhere to practice. My old dojo would not have me, and I was no longer in school. Over two decades of judo knowledge basically rotted inside of me for seven years. Because a group of queer martial artists had decided to form their own school, I finally was able to practice my art. Thanks to these gender outlaws and their positive, creative action, I finally had a place to be queer, to be a woman, to be trans, but most of all, to feel a mat under my feet and my belt around my waist. It felt like I was flying.

After the event, I changed in the women's dressing room.

And so ended seven years of searching, just to find a martial arts space where a trans woman could change her clothes undisturbed. I hadn't wanted

---

11 *zero-sum game* Situation in which whenever one opponent achieves something, that which is gained is lost by the other opponent.

a change in the rules, or special treatment, or special transgender classes and facilities. I just wanted to use the dressing room. And now, it was over. I wanted to dance and shout, "Look, motherfuckers! See? I'm not messing up your furniture!"

My hands were shaking as I shook my head and pulled out my ponytail. My hair was a mess! After all that fighting, tufts of hair were kinked and knotted, tangled this way and that. I ran my brush through it, but it just made the knots worse. I knew the other participants were waiting for me to go to dinner, so I pulled harder. OUCH! I thought about pulling harder, or maybe cutting the tangles off with scissors, or a knife....

Then I stopped. No one was telling me to rush. My new friends knew where I was and wouldn't mind waiting just a little while. I slowed down and remembered that the best way to remove tangles is to work the strands methodically, not from the top down, but from the bottom up.

It took a while, and there was some pain, but with patience, and a little faith, every tangle finally came free.

(2010)

J WALLACE

THE MANLY ART OF PREGNANCY

"The Manly Art of Pregnancy," educational consultant and activist j wallace's account of his pregnancy as a transgender man, first appeared in the essay collection Gender Outlaws: The Next Generation *in 2010.*

There are many ways to go about acquiring what they call "a beer belly."* I chose pregnancy. Beer and wings probably would have been an easier route, but I've never been one for the easy route, and I embraced the manly art of pregnancy. I'm a short, stocky guy who over the last year has gone from chunky, to having a great big gut, and back to chunky again. Along the way, I've also made a baby.

Judging by the resources available, one might assume that pregnancy is distinctly a woman's affair. Books have titles like *The Pregnant Mom's Guide, The Working Women's Guide, The Prospective Mother,* and *The Hip Mama's Survival Guide.* Most of the books for men make it clear that not only is pregnancy for women, but the only men interested in pregnancy are heterosexual males: *What to Expect When Your Wife Is Expecting* is typical. Even books which say *Dad's Pregnant* in large friendly letters on the cover turn out to be written for cisgender[1] men in heterosexual relationships, and about how to deal with your partner's pregnancy in your relationship. Books for pregnant men are hard to find indeed.

If the La Leche League[2] can encourage women everywhere to embrace *The Womanly Art of Breast Feeding,* I'm going to put in a plug for the Manly Art of Pregnancy. For those of you not yet familiar with pregnancy as a manly art, let me introduce it. The pregnant person is at once a biologist, a mechanic, a weight lifter, and someone providing for hir[3] family. Women can do those

---

1   *cisgender*   Identifying as the gender that matches the sex one was assigned at birth.

2   *La Leche League*   International organization devoted to promoting breastfeeding through advocacy and educational support. *The Womanly Art of Breastfeeding*, a book first published by the league in 1958, has been updated and reissued numerous times.

3   *hir*   Gender neutral pronoun used as an alternative to "him" or "her."

things, of course, but our culture still views them as masculine things, and in this way pregnancy made me more of a man, not less of one. Before I was pregnant, I feared that pregnancy would make me into a woman or a lady. But it didn't; it made me more of a dude. I discovered that pregnancy is rife with things to worry about, and that after a while, gender stopped being one. Pregnancy became a manly act. Pregnancy helped me look, feel, and act more like an archetype of Man, and eventually lifted me to its pinnacle by making me a dad.

Let us begin with the aesthetics: Pregnancy is good for hair growth. Existing hair looks longer, darker, and thicker and new crops sprout up. I have new darker hairs on my chest, my leg hair is more visible, and even my beard is thicker. It's like taking testosterone all over again. Pregnant women often lament this, particularly when they are too pregnant to shave their own legs, but I loved it. The hair growth was so dramatic that I imagined pregnancy hormones being sold to people experiencing hair loss (because G-d knows they try to sell every other thing to people with hair loss). I imagined bald men rubbing Premarin[4] on the tops of their heads, with bald Before, and hirsute After photographs.

When I took testosterone, not having a period was my favorite physical change. I loved the freedom it gave, the extra energy, not having to pay an extra tax for the femaleness I found miserable anyway. Pregnancy is the same. There is no bleeding, I can go about the world, safe in the knowledge that I will not have to beg a tampon from a co-worker. I no longer worry that a spare tampon will leap out of my bag at an inopportune moment. I don't worry that my period will stain my favorite date underpants. I skip the feminine hygiene aisle at the drug store entirely, and I am happier for it. 5

I recognize that these changes can be part of anyone's pregnancy, regardless of gender. The people that make maternity clothes clearly have thought about how masculinizing the physical changes of pregnancy can be and have therefore designed maternity clothes to re-assert femininity. Why else would they invest so much time and attention in making maternity clothes so very feminine? Seriously. Maternity clothes are pink, pastel, or floral, or all of the above, with liberal use of lace, bows, and ribbon. Maternity clothes flaunt curves, and they *flow*. It's very hard to look serious in most maternity clothes. In addition to all that, many of them make you look like you are four. When I first told my boss that I was pregnant she was very clear with me that if I showed up to work in maternity clothes, she would send me home to change. I can assure you that she meant it in good humor, but her point was well taken. So, I figured out what paternity clothes look like. As it happens, you can get through much

---

4   *Premarin*   Estrogen hormone medication used in a variety of treatments.

of a pregnancy in larger shirts, larger jeans with suspenders, chef pants, and overalls. If the clothes make the man, the masculine art of pregnancy ignores the rack of maternity clothes. The secret advantage to this is that without the maternity clothes, no-one knows you are pregnant. You can walk around hiding a whole tiny person in your abdomen. Never once did a stranger put hir hand on my belly, gush about how I was glowing and ask how far along I was. The masculine art of pregnancy retains at least a little privacy.

Of course the challenge to this was changes in my chest. Pregnancy makes your chest grow. Before being pregnant I was a happy binderwearing[5] guy, smoothing my lycra undershirt down over my boxer briefs, but rapid growth in the chest department necessitated the first-trimester purchase of chest restraining devices. I put it off as long as I could. I tried shopping for things on my own, discreetly, like a shy straight guy shopping for a new girlfriend—but apparently these things are sized, and it's not like they encourage the "shy straight guy" to go into the change room and try things on. It became clear that I would need to be fitted, and I eventually resigned myself to this. I chose a local shop where I heard they had good fitters, walked up to the counter and asked in a manly, clear voice for assistance fitting me with maternity/nursing bras. Manly pregnant people ask for help with perfect confidence that they are entitled to good assistance, and I found I got good assistance in return.

And then there's this—I grew a penis. Transition-wise I've never really wanted to have genital surgery. Sure, there have been times, in beds and in kayaks, when a penis would have been handy, but for me it's not worth actually having one surgically attached. That said, at our twenty-week ultrasound they showed me grainy black and white pictures of a tiny penis I'm growing. I know not all pregnancies go this way, and it's not as if I decided to grow a penis rather than a vagina, but here I am, growing a penis. Had I known that exposure to sperm would awaken this ability in my body I might have spent more time in bathhouses[6] and other seedy locations, but never mind, I can now add it to the list of things my body can do.

Pregnancy does mean making some life changes. I developed the art of seeming chivalrous while not lifting over forty pounds. I came to understand that sometimes, being manly is about knowing what tool to use. At seven months pregnant, the right tools to use to get a seized tire off one's car are a cell phone and roadside assistance. Crawling under one's car to strike at the tire with a hammer is not manly; protecting one's family and using a cell phone

---

5   *binder*   Article of clothing used to compress the chest, often worn by trans men in order to minimize the appearance of breasts.

6   *bathhouses*   Establishments where people, usually gay men, can meet for casual sexual encounters.

is. "Protecting one's family" is a manly pregnancy mantra. When the signs on the outside of a building warn that there has been an outbreak of fifth disease[7] and pregnant people should not enter the building—you obey them, you do not enter, even when it means recruiting a nice lady to go inside and explain that you are not coming. Even when she goes inside and says "There is some guy, outside, who says he cannot come in because he is pregnant...."

Pregnancy does not mean you lose access to your usual manly haunts, like the barber shop, and your local auto mechanic's. Even with the kid's kicks visible under the barber's towel, my barber did not notice my manly pregnant condition. We had the same conversation, and he gave me the same haircut and straight razor shave that he always does—and I gave him the same tip. The auto mechanics still called me sir and talked to me as if I know what the various engine parts are all supposed to do. It appears that if you're a guy, pregnancy does not make you a woman: it just makes you fat.

It's also easier to think about pregnancy as a manly activity if we butch up the language we use. I trained midwives, a doula,[8] Ob/Gyns, and even a lactation consultant to talk about "pregnant people" not "pregnant women," or "pregnant ladies." A number of ciswomen friends had also complained that when they became pregnant they went from being "women" to "ladies" and they found the prissiness of the word uncomfortable. They too found "pregnant person" a better fit, especially if it meant not being referred to as a "lady" all the time. If we talk about "nursing," focusing on the action of providing for one's child rather than "breastfeeding," focusing on a body part assumed to be feminine, even this activity can sound more manly.

Pregnancy made me a dad. Pregnancy has been making dads out of men since about nine months after sex was discovered. I know fine men who have become dads in a variety of ways, some by love, some by adoption and fostering, some by other means, and I do not believe that there is any one traditional way of going about it. There are more common and less common ways, but all of them have a history and tradition. I became a dad through pregnancy and birth. Along the way, people who love me created the language of "bearing father" and "seahorse papa."[9] We're queers, and we are well versed in creating the language we need to describe our realities. We will bring our world into being through words, as we bring babies into being through our bodies.

10

---

7   *fifth disease*   Viral illness caused by parvovirus B19; while it is usually not serious, it carries some risk of miscarriage, so pregnant women are warned to avoid exposure.

8   *doula*   Support person who aids new parents before, during, and/or after the birth of their baby.

9   *seahorse papa*   Seahorse embryos grow in pouches in their fathers' abdomens.

In the end, I gave birth to my son via a caesarean section. I have a small neat scar on my abdomen that I think of as "the baby escape hatch." Scars are manly. As I was recovering, I realized that the next time some intrusive person discovers I am trans and asks me if I have "had the surgery," I can say "yes" and go on to describe my c-section. They never say what surgery they mean, and a c-section is generally recognized as a gendered surgery.

In the hospital, after the birth, I was snuggled up in bed in my pajamas, holding my small son, when the public health nurse strolled in. She looked at me in the hospital bed, at the baby in my arms, and around the room. Then she looked again, and clearly did not find what she was looking for. "Where's the mom?" she asked. The simple answer is that there is no mom. Children need love and support from a parent, not a gender. Parents, not necessarily moms and dads, raise children, whether they are boys or girls. The public health nurse stammered an apology, and fled. I've been rehearsing better answers to that question since—better answers that say his family is not your business, keep your assumptions to yourself.

15   I've become a dad changing diapers, holding a baby, reading books to someone who can't really focus his eyes yet, a dad who was up many times last night with the baby and who is now blurry-eyed from lack of sleep. I do dadly things, including many things other dads do, and things I remember my dad doing. I'm also a dad who nurses, who gets up in the night to feed the baby without having to heat bottles, which I understand is an uncommon dad kind of thing to do. But I do it for my small person. I want the best for my child, which I understand is a common desire of good dads.

I'm a dad you might run into in the library reading to my small child, a dad in the park carrying my baby on my front, explaining the world to him, a dad who plans to teach my child to love insects and look at ants and caterpillars, a dad who'll head off in a canoe with his small person. I look forward to being the dad helping my child bake cupcakes and discover the joy of gardening, and celebrating his artwork. When you see me, what you see, and who or what you think I am has been totally eclipsed by the dad my small person sees, knows, and loves. I'm his dad, and in the tiny world of our family, that is what really matters.

(2010)

ZADIE SMITH

GENERATION WHY

Best known as a novelist, Zadie Smith is also an acclaimed essayist.
This review article (first published in the 25 November 2010 issue
of The New York Review of Books) *discusses both David Fincher's*
then-newly released film The Social Network *(with screenplay by*
Aaron Sorkin) and Jaron Lanier's then-bestselling book You Are
Not a Gadget: A Manifesto.

How long is a generation these days? I must be in Mark Zuckerberg's genera-tion—there are only nine years between us—but somehow it doesn't feel that way. This despite the fact that I can say (like everyone else on Harvard's campus in the fall of 2003) that "I was there" at Facebook's inception, and remember Facemash[1] and the fuss it caused; also that tiny, exquisite movie star trailed by fan-boys through the snow wherever she went, and the awful snow itself, turning your toes gray, destroying your spirit, bringing a bloodless end to a squirrel on my block: frozen, inanimate, perfect—like the Blaschka glass flowers.[2] Doubtless years from now I will misremember my closeness to Zuckerberg, in the same spirit that everyone in '60s Liverpool met John Lennon.

At the time, though, I felt distant from Zuckerberg and all the kids at Harvard. I still feel distant from them now, ever more so, as I increasingly opt out (by choice, by default) of the things they have embraced. We have different ideas about things. Specifically we have different ideas about what a person is, or should be. I often worry that my idea of personhood is nostalgic, irrational, inaccurate. Perhaps Generation Facebook have built their virtual mansions in good faith, in order to house the People 2.0 they genuinely are, and if I feel uncomfortable within them it is because I am stuck at Person 1.0. Then again, the more time I spend with the tail end of Generation Facebook (in the shape of my students) the more convinced I become that some of the software currently

---

1   *Facemash* Precursor to Facebook created by Zuckerberg. The site displayed pictures of Harvard students two at a time and invited users to choose who was "hotter."
2   *Blaschka ... flowers* Botanically realistic glass models, crafted by Leopold Blaschka, on display at the Harvard Museum of Natural History.

shaping their generation is unworthy of them. They are more interesting than it is. They deserve better.

In *The Social Network* Generation Facebook gets a movie almost worthy of them, and this fact, being so unexpected, makes the film feel more delightful than it probably, objectively, is. From the opening scene it's clear that this is a movie about 2.0 people made by 1.0 people (Aaron Sorkin and David Fincher, forty-nine and forty-eight respectively). It's a *talkie,*[3] for goodness' sake, with as many words per minute as *His Girl Friday.*[4] A boy, Mark, and his girl, Erica, sit at a little table in a Harvard bar, zinging each other, in that relentless Sorkin style made famous by *The West Wing* (though at no point does either party say "Walk with me"—for this we should be grateful).[5]

But something is not right with this young man: his eye contact is patchy; he doesn't seem to understand common turns of phrase or ambiguities of language; he is literal to the point of offense, pedantic to the point of aggression. ("Final clubs,"[6] says Mark, correcting Erica, as they discuss those exclusive Harvard entities, "*Not* Finals clubs.") He doesn't understand what's happening as she tries to break up with him. ("Wait, wait, this is real?") Nor does he understand *why*. He doesn't get that what he may consider a statement of fact might yet have, for this other person, some personal, painful import:

> ERICA: I have to go study.
> MARK: You don't have to study.
> ERICA: *How do you know I don't have to study?!*
> MARK: *Because you go to B.U.!*[7]

5   Simply put, he is a computer nerd, a social "autistic": a type as recognizable to Fincher's audience as the cynical newshound was to Howard Hawks's. To create this Zuckerberg, Sorkin barely need brush his pen against the page.

---

3   *talkie*   Film with spoken dialogue. (The term came into use in the late 1920s, as the silent film era was drawing to a close.)

4   *His Girl Friday*   1940 comedy film directed by Howard Hawks—an example of the 1930s and early 40s film genre known as "screwball comedy," in which everyone talks quickly and surprising things happen fast.

5   *Sorkin style ... be grateful*   The television show *The West Wing*, which was created by Aaron Sorkin and ran from 1999 to 2006, was known for its rapid-fire dialogue, often spoken as characters were walking together through the west wing offices at the White House.

6   *Final clubs*   Exclusive, male-only social clubs created and maintained by Harvard students.

7   *Because you go to B.U.!*   Boston University (B.U.) is a less prestigious institution than Harvard.

We came to the cinema expecting to meet this guy and it's a pleasure to watch Sorkin color in what we had already confidently sketched in our minds. For sometimes the culture surmises an individual personality, collectively. Or thinks it does. Don't we all know why nerds do what they do? To get money, which leads to popularity, which leads to girls. Sorkin, confident of his foundation myth, spins an exhilarating tale of double rejection—spurned by Erica and the Porcellian, the Finaliest of the Final Clubs, Zuckerberg begins his spite-fueled rise to the top. Cue a lot of betrayal. A lot of scenes of lawyers' offices and miserable, character-damning depositions. ("Your best friend is suing you!") Sorkin has swapped the military types of *A Few Good Men** for a different kind of all-male community in a different uniform: GAP hoodies, North Face sweats.

At my screening, blocks from NYU,* the audience thrilled with intimate identification. But if the hipsters and nerds are hoping for Fincher's usual pyrotechnics they will be disappointed: in a lawyer's office there's not a lot for Fincher to *do*. He has to content himself with excellent and rapid cutting between Harvard and the later court cases, and after that, the discreet pleasures of another, less-remarked-upon Fincher skill: great casting. It'll be a long time before a cinema geek comes along to push Jesse Eisenberg, the actor who plays Zuckerberg, off the top of our nerd typologies. The passive-aggressive, flat-line voice. The shifty boredom when anyone, other than himself, is speaking. The barely suppressed smirk. Eisenberg even chooses the correct nerd walk: not the sideways corridor shuffle (the *Don't Hit Me!*), but the puffed chest vertical march (the *I'm not 5'8", I'm 5'9"!*).

With rucksack, naturally. An extended four-minute shot has him doing exactly this all the way through the Harvard campus, before he lands finally where he belongs, the only place he's truly comfortable, in front of his laptop, with his blog:

> Erica Albright's a bitch. You think that's because her family changed their name from Albrecht or do you think it's because all B.U. girls are bitches?

Oh, yeah. We know this guy. Overprogrammed, furious, lonely. Around him Fincher arranges a convincing bunch of 1.0 humans, by turns betrayed and humiliated by him, and as the movie progresses they line up to sue him. If it's a three-act movie it's because Zuckerberg screws over more people than a two-act movie can comfortably hold: the Winklevoss twins and Divya Navendra (from whom Zuckerberg allegedly stole the Facebook concept), and then his best friend, Eduardo Saverin (the CFO* he edged out of the company), and finally Sean Parker, the boy king of Napster, the music-sharing program, although he, to be fair, pretty much screws himself. It's in Eduardo—in the actor Andrew Garfield's animate, beautiful face—that all these betrayals seem to converge, and become personal, painful. The arbitration scenes—that should be dull, being so terribly static—get their power from the eerie opposition between Eisenberg's unmoving countenance (his eyebrows hardly ever move; the real Zuckerberg's eyebrows never move) and Garfield's imploring disbelief, almost the way Spencer Tracy got all worked up opposite Frederic March's rigidity in another courtroom epic, *Inherit the Wind*.

Still, Fincher allows himself one sequence of (literal) showboating.* Halfway through the film, he inserts a ravishing but quite unnecessary scene of the pretty Winklevoss twins (for a story of nerds, all the men are surprisingly comely) at the Henley Regatta.[8] These two blond titans row like champs. (One actor, Armie Hammer, has been digitally doubled. I'm so utterly 1.0 that I spent an hour of the movie trying to detect any difference between the twins.) Their arms move suspiciously fast, faster than real human arms, their muscles seem outlined by a fine pen, the water splashes up in individual droplets as if painted by Caravaggio, and the music! Trent Reznor, of Nine Inch Nails, commits exquisite brutality upon Edward Grieg's already pretty brutal "In the Hall of the Mountain King." All synths and white noise. It's music video stuff—the art form in which my not-quite generation truly excels—and it demonstrates the knack for hyperreality that made Fincher's *Fight Club* so compelling while rendering the real world, for so many of his fans, always something of a disappointment. Anyway, the twins lose the regatta, too, by a nose, which allows Fincher to justify the scene by thematic reiteration: sometimes very close is simply not close enough. Or as Mark pleasantly puts it across a conference table: "If you guys were the inventors of Facebook you'd have invented Facebook."

All that's left for Zuckerberg is to meet the devil at the crossroads: naturally he's an Internet music entrepreneur. It's a Generation Facebook instinct to expect (hope?) that a pop star will fall on his face in the cinema, but Justin Timberlake, as Sean Parker, neatly steps over that expectation: whether or not you think he's a shmuck,* he sure plays a great shmuck. Manicured eyebrows, sweaty forehead, and that coked-up, wafer-thin self-confidence, always threatening to collapse into paranoia. Timberlake shimmies into view in the third act to offer the audience, and Zuckerberg, the very same thing, essentially, that he's been offering us for the past decade in his videos: a vision of the good life.

This vision is also wafer-thin, and Fincher satirizes it mercilessly. Again, we know its basic outline: a velvet rope, a cocktail waitress who treats you like a king, the best of everything on tap, a special booth of your own, fussy tiny expensive food ("Could you bring out some things? The lacquered pork with that ginger confit? I don't know, tuna tartar, some lobster claws, the foie gras and the shrimp dumplings, that'll get us started"), appletinis, a Victoria's

8   *Henley Regatta*   Premier rowing competition.

Secret* model date, wild house parties, fancy cars, slick suits, cocaine, and a "sky's the limit" objective: "A million dollars isn't cool. You know what's cool?... A *billion* dollars." Over cocktails in a glamorous nightclub, Parker dazzles Zuckerberg with tales of the life that awaits him on the other side of a billion. Fincher keeps the thumping Euro house music turned up to exactly the level it would be in real life: the actors have to practically scream to be heard above it. Like many a nerd before him, Zuckerberg is too hyped on the idea that he's in heaven to notice he's in hell.

Generation Facebook's obsession with this type of "celebrity lifestyle" is more than familiar. It's pitiful, it pains us, and we recognize it. But would Zuckerberg recognize it, the real Zuckerberg? Are these really *his* motivations, *his* obsessions? No—and the movie knows it. Several times the script tries to square the real Zuckerberg's apparent indifference to money with the plot arc of *The Social Network*—and never quite succeeds. In a scene in which Mark argues with a lawyer, Sorkin attempts a sleight of hand, swapping an interest in money for an interest in power:

> Ma'am, I know you've done your homework and so you know that money isn't a big part of my life, but at the moment I could buy Harvard University, take the Phoenix Club and turn it into my ping pong room.

But that doesn't explain why the teenage Zuckerberg gave away his free app for an MP3 player (similar to the very popular Pandora, as it recognized your taste in music), rather than selling it to Microsoft. What power was he hoping to accrue to himself in high school, at seventeen? Girls, was it? Except the girl motivation is patently phony—with a brief interruption Zuckerberg has been dating the same Chinese-American, now a medical student, since 2003, a fact the movie omits entirely. At the end of the film, when all the suing has come to an end ("Pay them. In the scheme of things it's a parking ticket"), we're offered a Zuckerberg slumped before his laptop, still obsessed with the long-lost Erica, sending a "Friend request" to her on Facebook, and then refreshing the page, over and over, in expectation of her reply.... Fincher's contemporary window-dressing is so convincing that it wasn't until this very last scene that I realized the obvious progenitor of this wildly enjoyable, wildly inaccurate biopic. Hollywood still believes that behind every mogul there's an idée fixe.[9] Rosebud—meet Erica.[10]

---

9   *idée fixe*   Idea fixed in the mind; obsession.

10   *Rosebud—meet Erica*   Reference to Orson Welles's film *Citizen Kane* (1941), in which Welles stars as media mogul Charles Foster Kane. Kane dies with the name "Rosebud" on his lips.

If it's not for money and it's not for girls—what is it for? With Zuckerberg we have a real American mystery. Maybe it's not mysterious and he's just playing the long game, holding out: not a billion dollars but a hundred billion dollars. Or is it possible *he just loves programming*? No doubt the filmmakers considered this option, but you can see their dilemma: how to convey the pleasure of programming—if such a pleasure exists—in a way that is both cinematic and comprehensible? Movies are notoriously bad at showing the pleasures and rigors of art-making, even when the medium is familiar.

15   Programming is a whole new kind of problem. Fincher makes a brave stab at showing the intensity of programming in action ("He's wired in," people say to other people to stop them disturbing a third person who sits before a laptop wearing noise-reducing earphones) and there's a "vodka-shots-and-programming" party in Zuckerberg's dorm room that gives us some clue of the pleasures. But even if we spent half the film looking at those busy screens (and we do get glimpses), most of us would be none the wiser. Watching this movie, even though you know Sorkin wants your disapproval, you can't help feel a little swell of pride in this 2.0 generation. They've spent a decade being berated for not making the right sorts of paintings or novels or music or politics. Turns out the brightest 2.0 kids have been doing something else extraordinary. They've been making a world.

World makers, social network makers, ask one question first: How can I do it? Zuckerberg solved that one in about three weeks. The other question, the ethical question, he came to later: Why? Why Facebook? Why this format? Why do it like that? Why not do it another way? The striking thing about the real Zuckerberg, in video and in print, is the relative banality of his ideas concerning the "Why" of Facebook. He uses the word "connect" as believers use the word "Jesus," as if it were sacred in and of itself: "So the idea is really that, um, the site helps everyone connect with people and share information with the people they want to stay connected with...." Connection is the goal. The quality of that connection, the quality of the information that passes through it, the quality of the relationship that connection permits—none of this is important. That a lot of social networking software explicitly encourages people to make weak, superficial connections with each other (as Malcolm Gladwell has recently argued),[11] and that this might not be an entirely positive thing, seem to never have occurred to him.

He is, to say the least, dispassionate about the philosophical questions concerning privacy—and sociality itself—raised by his ingenious program. Watching him interviewed I found myself waiting for the verbal wit, the controlled

---

11   See "Small Change: Why the Revolution Will Not Be Tweeted," *The New Yorker*, October 4, 2010. [author's note]

and articulate sarcasm of that famous Zuckerberg kid—then remembered that was only Sorkin. The real Zuckerberg is much more like his website, on each page of which, once upon a time (2004), he emblazoned the legend: *A Mark Zuckerberg Production*. Controlled but dull, bright and clean but uniformly plain, non-ideological, affectless.[12]

In Zuckerberg's *New Yorker* profile it is revealed that his own Facebook page lists, among his interests, Minimalism, revolutions, and "eliminating desire."[13] We also learn of his affection for the culture and writings of ancient Greece. Perhaps this is the disjunct between real Zuckerberg and fake Zuckerberg: the movie places him in the Roman world of betrayal and excess, but the real Zuckerberg may belong in the Greek, perhaps with the Stoics* ("eliminating desire"?). There's a clue in the two Zuckerbergs' relative physiognomies: real Zuckerberg (especially in profile) is Greek sculpture, noble, featureless, a little like the Doryphorus[14] (only facially, mind—his torso is definitely not seven times his head). Fake Mark looks Roman, with all the precise facial detail filled in. Zuckerberg, with his steady relationship and his rented house and his refusal to get angry on television even when people are being very rude to him (he sweats instead), has something of the teenage Stoic about him. And of course if you've eliminated desire you've got nothing to hide, right?

It's that kind of kid we're dealing with, the kind who would never screw a groupie in a bar toilet—as happens in the movie—or leave his doctor girlfriend for a Victoria's Secret model. It's this type of kid who would think that giving people less privacy was a good idea. What's striking about Zuckerberg's vision of an open Internet is the very blandness it requires to function, as Facebook members discovered when the site changed their privacy settings, allowing more things to become more public, with the (unintended?) consequence that your Aunt Dora could suddenly find out you joined the group Queer Nation last Tuesday. Gay kids became un-gay, partiers took down their party photos, political firebrands put out their fires. In real life we can be all these people on our own terms, in our own way, with whom we choose. For a revealing moment Facebook forgot that. Or else got bored of waiting for us to change in the ways it's betting we will. On the question of privacy, Zuckerberg informed the world: "That social norm is just something that has evolved over time." On this occasion, the world protested, loudly, and so Facebook has responded with "Groups," a site revamp that will allow people to divide their friends into "cliques," some who see more of our profile and some who see less.

---

12 *affectless* Without displaying any sign of emotions or other feelings.

13 See Jose Antonio Vargas, "The Face of Facebook: Mark Zuckerberg Opens Up," *The New Yorker*, September 20, 2010. [author's note]

14 *Doryphorus* Ancient Greek sculpture of a muscular man.

20   How "Groups" will work alongside "Facebook Connect" remains to be seen. Facebook Connect is the "next iteration of Facebook Platform," in which users are "allowed" to "'connect' their Facebook identity, friends and privacy to any site." In this new, open Internet, we will take our real identities with us as we travel through the Internet. This concept seems to have some immediate Stoical advantages: no more faceless bile, no more inflammatory trolling: if your name and social network track you around the virtual world beyond Facebook, you'll have to restrain yourself and so will everyone else. On the other hand, you'll also take your likes and dislikes with you, your tastes, your preferences, all connected to your name, through which people will try to sell you things.

     Maybe it will be like an intensified version of the Internet I already live in, where ads for dental services stalk me from pillar to post* and I am continually urged to buy my own books. Or maybe the whole Internet will simply become like Facebook: falsely jolly, fake-friendly, self-promoting, slickly disingenuous. For all these reasons I quit Facebook about two months after I'd joined it. As with all seriously addictive things, giving up proved to be immeasurably harder than starting. I kept changing my mind: Facebook remains the greatest distraction from work I've ever had, and I loved it for that. I think a lot of people love it for that. Some work-avoidance techniques are onerous in themselves and don't make time move especially quickly: smoking, eating, calling people up on the phone. With Facebook hours, afternoons, entire days went by without my noticing.

     When I finally decided to put a stop to it, once and for all, I was left with the question bothering everybody: Are you ever truly removed, once and for all? In an interview on *The Today Show*, Matt Lauer asked Zuckerberg the same question, but because Matt Lauer doesn't listen to people when they talk, he accepted the following answer and moved on to the next question: "Yeah, so what'll happen is that none of that information will be shared with anyone going forward."

You want to be optimistic about your own generation. You want to keep pace with them and not to fear what you don't understand. To put it another way, if you feel discomfort at the world they're making, you want to have a good reason for it. Master programmer and virtual reality pioneer Jaron Lanier (b. 1960) is not of my generation, but he knows and understands us well, and has written a short and frightening book, *You Are Not a Gadget*, which chimes with my own discomfort, while coming from a position of real knowledge and insight, both practical and philosophical. Lanier is interested in the ways in which people "reduce themselves" in order to make a computer's description of them appear more accurate. "Information systems," he writes, "need to have information in order to run, but information *underrepresents reality*" (my italics). In Lanier's view, there is no perfect computer analogue for what we call a "person." In life, we all profess to know this, but when we get online it becomes easy to forget. In Facebook, as it is with other online social networks, life is turned into a database, and this is a degradation, Lanier argues, which is

> based on [a] philosophical mistake ... the belief that computers can presently represent human thought or human relationships. These are things computers cannot currently do.

We know the consequences of this instinctively; we feel them. We know that having two thousand Facebook friends is not what it looks like. We know that we are using the software to behave in a certain, superficial way toward others. We know what we are doing "in" the software. But do we know, are we alert to, what the software is doing to us? Is it possible that what is communicated between people online "eventually becomes their truth"? What Lanier, a software expert, reveals to me, a software idiot, is what must be obvious (to software experts): software is not neutral. Different software embeds different philosophies, and these philosophies, as they become ubiquitous, become invisible.

Lanier asks us to consider, for example, the humble file, or rather, to consider a world without "files." (The first iteration of the Macintosh, which never shipped, didn't have files.) I confess this thought experiment stumped me about as much as if I'd been asked to consider persisting in a world without "time." And then consider further that these designs, so often taken up in a slap-dash, last-minute fashion, become "locked in," and, because they are software, used by millions, too often become impossible to adapt, or change. MIDI, an inflexible, early-1980s digital music protocol for connecting different musical components, such as a keyboard and a computer, takes no account of, say, the fluid line of a soprano's coloratura;[15] it is still the basis of most of the tinny music we hear every day—in our phones, in the charts, in elevators—simply because it became, in software terms, too big to fail, too big to change.

Lanier wants us to be attentive to the software into which we are "locked in." Is it really fulfilling our needs? Or are we reducing the needs we feel in order to convince ourselves that the software isn't limited? As Lanier argues:

> Different media designs stimulate different potentials in human nature. We shouldn't seek to make the pack mentality as efficient as possible. We should instead seek to inspire the phenomenon of individual intelligence.

25

---

15 *coloratura* Elaborate vocal harmonics.

But the pack mentality* is precisely what Open Graph, a Facebook innovation of 2008, is designed to encourage. Open Graph allows you to see everything your friends are reading, watching, eating, so that you might read and watch and eat as they do. In his New Yorker profile, Zuckerberg made his personal "philosophy" clear:

> Most of the information that we care about is things that are in our heads, right? And that's not out there to be indexed, right?... It's like hardwired into us in a deeper way: you really want to know what's going on with the people around you.

Is that really the best we can do online? In the film, Sean Parker, during one of his coke-fueled "Sean-athon monologues," delivers what is intended as a generation-defining line: "We lived on farms, then we lived in cities and now we're gonna live on the internet." To this idea Lanier, one of the Internet's original visionaries, can have no profound objection. But his skeptical interrogation of the "Nerd reductionism" of Web 2.0 prompts us to ask a question: What kind of life?[16] Surely not this one, where 500 million connected people all decide to watch the reality-TV show *Bride Wars* because their friends are? "You have to be somebody," Lanier writes, "before you can share yourself." But to Zuckerberg sharing your choices with everybody (and doing what they do) is being somebody.

Personally I don't think Final Clubs were ever the point; I don't think exclusivity was ever the point; nor even money. E Pluribus Unum[17]—that's the point. Here's my guess: he wants to be like everybody else. He wants to be liked. Those 1.0 people who couldn't understand Zuckerberg's apparently ham-fisted PR move of giving the school system of Newark $100 million on the very day the movie came out—they just don't get it. For our self-conscious generation (and in this, I and Zuckerberg, and everyone raised on TV in the Eighties and Nineties, share a single soul), *not being liked* is as bad as it gets. Intolerable to be thought of badly for a minute, even for a moment. He didn't need to just get out "in front" of the story. He had to get right on top of it and try to stop it breathing. Two weeks later, he went to a screening. Why? Because everybody liked the movie.

30   When a human being becomes a set of data on a website like Facebook, he or she is reduced. Everything shrinks. Individual character. Friendships.

---

16 Lanier: "Individual web pages as they first appeared in the early 1990s had the flavor of personhood. MySpace preserved some of that flavor, though a process of regularized formatting had begun. Facebook went further, organizing people into multiple-choice identities, while Wikipedia seeks to erase point of view entirely." [author's note]

17 *E Pluribus Unum* Out of many, one.

Language. Sensibility. In a way it's a transcendent experience: we lose our bodies, our messy feelings, our desires, our fears. It reminds me that those of us who turn in disgust from what we consider an overinflated liberal-bourgeois* sense of self should be careful what we wish for: our denuded networked selves don't look more free, they just look more owned.

With Facebook, Zuckerberg seems to be trying to create something like a Noosphere,[18] an Internet with one mind, a uniform environment in which it genuinely doesn't matter who you are, as long as you make "choices" (which means, finally, purchases). If the aim is to be liked by more and more people, whatever is unusual about a person gets flattened out. One nation under a format. To ourselves, we are special people, documented in wonderful photos, and it also happens that we sometimes buy things. This latter fact is an incidental matter, to us. However, the advertising money that will rain down on Facebook—if and when Zuckerberg succeeds in encouraging 500 million people to take their Facebook identities onto the Internet at large—this money thinks of us the other way around. To the advertisers, we are our capacity to buy, attached to a few personal, irrelevant photos.

Is it possible that we have begun to think of ourselves that way? It seemed significant to me that on the way to the movie theater, while doing a small mental calculation (how old I was when at Harvard; how old I am now), I had a Person 1.0 panic attack. Soon I will be forty, then fifty, then soon after dead; I broke out in a Zuckerberg sweat, my heart went crazy, I had to stop and lean against a trashcan. Can you have that feeling, on Facebook? I've noticed— and been ashamed of noticing—that when a teenager is murdered, at least in Britain, her Facebook wall will often fill with messages that seem to not quite comprehend the gravity of what has occurred. You know the type of thing: *Sorry babes! Missin' you!!! Hopin' u iz with the Angles. I remember the jokes we used to have LOL! PEACE XXXXX*

When I read something like that, I have a little argument with myself: "It's only poor education. They feel the same way as anyone would, they just don't have the language to express it." But another part of me has a darker, more frightening thought. Do they genuinely believe, because the girl's wall is still up, that she is still, in some sense, alive? What's the difference, after all, if all your contact was virtual?[19]

---

18 *Noosphere* Sphere of human consciousness. Pierre Teilhard de Chardin postulated the Noosphere as an evolutionary stage to which humanity would ascend.

19 Perhaps the reason why there has not been more resistance to social networking among older people is because 1.0 people do not use Web 2.0 software in the way 2.0 people do. An analogous situation can be found in the way the two generations use cell phones. For me, text messaging is simply a new medium for an old form of communication: I write to my friends in heavily punctuated, fully expressive, standard English *(continued ...)*

Software may reduce humans, but there are degrees. Fiction reduces humans, too, but bad fiction does it more than good fiction, and we have the option to read good fiction. Jaron Lanier's point is that Web 2.0 "lock-in" happens soon; is happening; has to some degree already happened. And what has been "locked in"? It feels important to remind ourselves, at this point, that Facebook, our new beloved interface with reality, was designed by a Harvard sophomore with a Harvard sophomore's preoccupations. What is your relationship status? (Choose one. There can be only one answer. People need to know.) Do you have a "life"? (Prove it. Post pictures.) Do you like the right sort of things? (Make a list. Things to like will include: movies, music, books and television, but not architecture, ideas, or plants.)

35   But here I fear I am becoming nostalgic. I am dreaming of a Web that caters to a kind of person who no longer exists. A private person, a person who is a mystery, to the world and—which is more important—to herself. Person as mystery: this idea of personhood is certainly changing, perhaps has already changed. Because I find I agree with Zuckerberg: selves evolve.

Of course, Zuckerberg insists selves simply do this by themselves and the technology he and others have created has no influence upon the process. That is for techies and philosophers to debate (ideally techie-philosophers, like Jaron Lanier). Whichever direction the change is coming from, though, it's absolutely clear to me that the students I teach now are not like the student I once was or even the students I taught seven short years ago at Harvard. Right now I am teaching my students a book called *The Bathroom* by the Belgian experimentalist Jean-Philippe Toussaint—at least I used to *think* he was an experimentalist. It's a book about a man who decides to pass most of his time in his bathroom, yet to my students this novel feels perfectly realistic; an accurate portrait of their own denuded selfhood, or, to put it neutrally, a close analogue of the undeniable boredom of urban twenty-first-century existence.

In the most famous scene, the unnamed protagonist, in one of the few moments of "action," throws a dart into his girlfriend's forehead. Later, in the hospital they reunite with a kiss and no explanation. "It's just between them," said one student, and looked happy. To a reader of my generation, Toussaint's characters seemed, at first glance, to have no interiority—in fact theirs is not an absence but a refusal, and an ethical one. *What's inside of me is none of your business.* To my students, *The Bathroom* is a true romance.

Toussaint was writing in 1985, in France. In France philosophy seems to come before technology; here in the Anglo-American world we race ahead with

---

sentences—and they write back to me in the same way. Text-speak is unknown between us. Our relationship with the English language predates our relationships with our phones. [author's note]

technology and hope the ideas will look after themselves. Finally, it's the *idea* of Facebook that disappoints. If it were a genuinely interesting interface, built for these genuinely different 2.0 kids to live in, well, that would be something. It's not that. It's the wild west of the Internet tamed to fit the suburban fantasies of a suburban soul. Lanier:

> These designs came together very recently, and there's a haphazard, accidental quality to them. Resist the easy grooves they guide you into. If you love a medium made of software, there's a danger that you will become entrapped in someone else's recent careless thoughts. Struggle against that!

Shouldn't we struggle against Facebook? Everything in it is reduced to the size of its founder. Blue, because it turns out Zuckerberg is red-green color-blind. "Blue is the richest color for me—I can see all of blue." Poking, because that's what shy boys do to girls they are scared to talk to. Preoccupied with personal trivia, because Mark Zuckerberg thinks the exchange of personal trivia is what "friendship" is. A Mark Zuckerberg Production indeed! We were going to live online. It was going to be extraordinary. Yet what kind of living is this? Step back from your Facebook Wall for a moment: Doesn't it, suddenly, look a little ridiculous? *Your* life in *this* format?

The last defense of every Facebook addict is: *but it helps me keep in con-*   40
tact with people who are far away! Well, e-mail and Skype do that, too, and they have the added advantage of not forcing you to interface with the mind of Mark Zuckerberg—but, well, you know. We all know. If we *really* wanted to write to these faraway people, or see them, we would. What we actually want to do is the bare minimum, just like any nineteen-year-old college boy who'd rather be doing something else, or nothing.

At my screening, when a character in the film mentioned the early blog platform LiveJournal (still popular in Russia), the audience laughed. I can't imagine life without files but I can just about imagine a time when Facebook will seem as comically obsolete as LiveJournal. In this sense, *The Social Network* is not a cruel portrait of any particular real-world person called "Mark Zuckerberg." It's a cruel portrait of us: 500 million sentient people entrapped in the recent careless thoughts of a Harvard sophomore.

(2010)

MAGGIE NELSON

from BLUETS

Known for writing in a lyric style, Nelson is also an acclaimed critical writer on literary and artistic subjects. Nelson's 2009 book Bluets, *written in numbered segments of prose, was published as a work of poetry. Her 2011* The Art of Cruelty *stands in contrast to* Bluets *in style as well as in subject matter; a work of art criticism, it explores through conventional expository prose the subject of how violence and cruelty have found expression in visual art. The excerpts included here focus on two artists known for portraying humans in disconcerting ways—the British painter Francis Bacon (1909–92) and the American photographer Diane Arbus (1923–71).*

1. Suppose I were to begin by saying that I had fallen in love with a color. Suppose I were to speak this as though it were a confession; suppose I shredded my napkin as we spoke. *It began slowly. An appreciation, an affinity. Then, one day, it became more serious. Then* (looking into an empty teacup, its bottom stained with this brown excrement coiled into the shape of a sea horse) *it became somehow* personal.

2. And so I fell in love with a color—in this case, the color blue—as if falling under a spell, a spell I fought to stay under and get out from under, in turns.

3. Well, and what of it? A voluntary delusion, you might say. That each blue object could be a kind of burning bush,* a secret code meant for a single agent, an X on a map too diffuse ever to be unfolded in entirety but that contains the knowable universe. How could all the shreds of blue garbage bags stuck in brambles, or the bright blue tarps flapping over every shanty and fish stand in the world, be, in essence, the fingerprints of God? *I will try to explain this.*

4. I admit that I may have been lonely. I know that loneliness can produce bolts of hot pain, a pain which, if it stays hot enough for long enough, can begin to simulate, or to provoke—take your pick—an apprehension[1] of the divine. (This ought to arouse our suspicions.)

---

1   *apprehension*   Awareness, understanding.

5. But first, let us consider a sort of case in reverse. In 1867, after a long bout of solitude, the French poet Stéphane Mallarmé wrote to his friend Henri Cazalis: "These last months have been terrifying. My thought has thought itself through and reached a Pure Idea. What the rest of me has suffered during that long agony, is indescribable." Mallarmé described this agony as a battle that took place on God's "boney wing." I struggled with that creature of ancient and evil plumage—God—whom I fortunately defeated and threw to earth," He told Cazalis with exhausted satisfaction. Eventually Mallarmé began replacing "le ciel"[2] with "l'Azur"[3] in his poems, in an effort to rinse references to the sky of religious connotation. "Fortunately," he wrote Cazalis, "I am quite dead now."

6. The half-circle of blinding turquoise ocean is this love's primal scene. That this blue exists makes my life a remarkable one, just to have seen it. To have seen such beautiful things. To find oneself placed in their midst. Choiceless. I returned there yesterday and stood again upon the mountain.

7. But what kind of love is it, really? Don't fool yourself and call it sublimity. Admit that you have stood in front of a little pile of powdered ultramarine pigment in a glass cup at a museum and felt a stinging desire. But to do what? Liberate it? Purchase it? Ingest it? There is so little blue food in nature—in fact blue in the wild tends to mark food to avoid (mold, poisonous berries)—that culinary advisers generally recommend against blue light, blue paint, and blue plates when and where serving food. But while the color may sap* appetite in the most literal sense, it feeds it in others. You might want to reach out and disturb the pile of pigment, for example, first staining your fingers with it, then staining the world. You might want to dilute it and swim in it, you might want to rouge your nipples with it, you might want to paint a virgin's robe with it. But still you wouldn't be accessing the blue of it. Not exactly.

8. Do not, however, make the mistake of thinking that all desire is yearning. "We love to contemplate blue, not because it advances to us, but because it draws us after it," wrote Goethe,[4] and perhaps he is right. But I am not interested in longing to live in a world in which I already live. I don't want to yearn for blue things, and God forbid for any "blueness." Above all, I want to stop missing you.

---

2   *le ciel*   French: the sky; heaven.
3   *l'Azur*   French: sky blue.
4   *Goethe*   Johann Wolfgang von Goethe (1749–1832), leading poet and intellectual figure in early nineteenth-century Germany. His *Theory of Colors* was published in 1810.

9. So please do not write to tell me about any more beautiful blue things. To be fair, this book will not tell you about any, either. It will not say, *Isn't X beautiful?* Such demands are murderous to beauty.

10. The most I want to do is show you the end of my index finger. Its muteness.

11. That is to say: I don't care if it's colorless.

12. And please don't talk to me about "things as they are" being changed upon any "blue guitar."[5] What can be changed upon a blue guitar is not of interest here.

13. At a job interview at a university, three men sitting across from me at a table. On my CV it says that I am currently working on a book about the color blue. I have been saying this for years without writing a word. It is, perhaps, my way of making my life feel "in progress" rather than a sleeve of ash falling off a lit cigarette. One of the men asks, *Why blue?* People ask me this question often. I never know how to respond. We don't get to choose what or whom we love, I want to say. We just don't get to choose.

14. I have enjoyed telling people that I am writing a book about blue without actually doing it. Mostly what happens in such cases is that people give you stories or leads or gifts, and then you can play with these things instead of with words. Over the past decade I have been given blue inks, paintings, postcards, dyes, bracelets, rocks, precious stones, watercolors, pigments, paperweights, goblets, and candies. I have been introduced to a man who had one of his front teeth replaced with lapis lazuli,[6] solely because he loved the stone, and to another who worships blue so devoutly that he refuses to eat blue food and grows only blue and white flowers in his garden, which surrounds the blue ex-cathedral in which he lives. I have met a man who is the primary grower of organic indigo in the world, and another who sings Joni Mitchell's *Blue*[7] in heartbreaking drag,* and another with the face of a derelict whose eyes literally leaked blue, and I called this one the prince of blue, which was, in fact, his name.

---

5   *things as they are ... blue guitar*   Reference to the 1937 long poem "The Man With the Blue Guitar," by American poet Wallace Stevens (1879–1955). "The day was green," we are told at the beginning of the poem, when the man with the blue guitar is playing. People say to him, "You have a blue guitar, / You do not play things as they are," and he replies as follows: "Things as they are / Are changed upon the blue guitar."

6   *lapis lazuli*   Gemstone with a deep blue hue.

7   *Joni Mitchell's Blue*   1971 Album of melancholy songs, composed as singer-songwriter Mitchell was recovering from the break-up of a romantic relationship.

15. I think of these people as my blue correspondents, whose job it is to send me blue reports from the field.

16. But you talk of all this jauntily, when really it is more like you have been mortally ill, and these correspondents send pieces of blue news as if last-ditch hopes for a cure.

17. But what goes on in you when you talk about color as if it were a cure, when you have not yet stated your disease.

18. A warm afternoon in early spring, New York City. We went to the Chelsea Hotel[8] to fuck. Afterward, from the window of our room, I watched a blue tarp on a roof across the way flap in the wind. You slept, so it was my secret. It was a smear of the quotidian, a bright blue flake amidst all the dank providence. It was the only time I came. It was essentially our lives. It was shaking.

19. Months before this afternoon I had a dream, and in this dream an angel came and said: *You must spend more time thinking about the divine, and less time imagining unbuttoning the prince of blue's pants at the Chelsea Hotel.* But what if the prince of blue's unbuttoned pants *are* the divine, I pleaded. *So be it*, she said, and left me to sob with my face against the blue slate floor.

20. *Fucking leaves everything as it is. Fucking may in no way interfere with the actual use of language. For it cannot give it any foundation either. It leaves everything as it is.*

(2009)

from THE ART OF CRUELTY

Cruelty, as the Buddhists see it, is the far enemy of compassion. Compassion also has a near enemy—that is, an enemy that so closely resembles it that it can be difficult, albeit utterly crucial, to differentiate between them. This near enemy is called idiot compassion. I would like to understand more about compassion, and I am gambling that one way of doing so is to get to know its enemies, near and far....

But perhaps I'm fooling myself. Perhaps I'm not really all that interested in compassion. Certainly it has less grip than conflict, as screenwriters

---

8   *Chelsea Hotel*   Landmark New York hotel where many writers, musicians, and other creative celebrities have lived.

everywhere preach. Certainly it doesn't "return us to life more violently,"[9] as Bacon so often named the singular goal of his art. Would it be a relief to give up, as Bacon did, on the idea of compassion altogether? "I'm not upset by the fact that people do suffer," said Bacon, "because I think the suffering of people and the differences between people are what have made great art, and not egalitarianism."[10]

Welcome to Bacon's bracing allure (which resembles that of Artaud, and of Nietzsche[11]), which posits this "violent return to life" as a way to restore us, or deliver us anew, to an unalienated, unmediated flow of existence characterized by a more authentic relation to the so-called real. Unlike so many avant-gardists* and revolutionaries, however, Bacon does not think or hope that this restored vitality will bring about the subsequent waning of inequalities, injustices, or radical forms of suffering. Quite the contrary: for Bacon (as for Nietzsche), some people were put on the planet to dominate and some to be dominated, and that's exactly as it should be. Rather than purport that this "violent return to life" is somehow in keeping with the goals of social justice, Bacon prefers the brutal whirlwind in and of itself, with all its attendant cruelties.

In any case, one thing seems clear: whether or not one intends for one's art to express or stir compassion, to address or rectify forms of social injustice, to celebrate or relieve suffering, may end up irrelevant to its actual effects. Some of the most good-intentioned, activist, "compassionate" art out there can end up being patronizing, ineffective, or exploitative. And, of course, vice versa: much of the work that has no designs on eliciting compassion or bringing about emancipation can be the most salutary, the most liberating. This paradox is central to this book's enterprise. For not only do our work and words speak beyond our intentions and controls, but compassion is not necessarily found where we presume it to be, nor is it always what we presume it to be, nor is it found in the same place in the same way over time. The same might be said of cruelty....

---

9   *return us to life more violently*   The full quotation is as follows: "I never look at paintings, hardly. If I go to the National Gallery and I look at one of the great paintings that excite me there, it's not so much the painting that excites me as that the painting unlocks all kinds of valves of sensation within me which return me to life more violently." (David Sylvester, *Words: Interviews with Francis Bacon*, 4th ed., 1993, 141.)

10   *I'm not upset ... egalitarianism*   See David Sylvester, *Words: Interviews with Francis Bacon*, 4th ed., 1993, 125.

11   *Artaud*   Dramatist Antonin Artaud (1896–1948), known for what he termed the "theater of cruelty"; *Nietzsche*   Philosopher Friedrich Wilhelm Nietzsche (1844–1900), known for his attacks on conventional morality and for his focus on the human will.

Like most artists charged with being cruel, or "cruel to be kind," photographer   5
Diane Arbus always testified to having a greater fidelity to the so-called brutality of fact than to either cruelty or compassion. "I don't mean to say that all
photographs have to be mean," Arbus said. "Sometimes they show something
really nicer in fact than what you felt, or oddly different. But in a way this
scrutiny has to do with not evading facts, not evading what it really looks like."

Unsurprisingly, Arbus supporters have tended to rally around this claim,
casting her forays into various subcultures (nudist colonies, circus sideshows,
the world of sex workers, homes for retarded adults, and so on) as those of a
fearless and compassionate renegade. Meanwhile, her detractors have charged
her with being "an exploitative narcissist,"* slumming it in communities in
which she did not belong in order to generate provocative portraits that are
fundamentally unkind to their subjects. (This fearless renegade/narcissistic
exploiter dyad* also dogged Sylvia Plath,[12] which is one reason why Arbus is
sometimes dubbed "the Sylvia Plath of photography"; her suicide is another.
Lest we forget, to be called the Sylvia Plath of anything is *a bad thing*.) In
this polar version of events, Arbus's excursions to the "dark side" are either a
record of adventuresome fellow-feeling or an extended exercise in callow,[13]
cynical coldness.

Sontag famously thought the latter—in her 1977 book *On Photography*
she roasts Arbus for "concentrating on victims, on the unfortunate—but without the compassionate purpose that such a project is expected to serve."[14] In
retrospect, it seems clear that the problem lies more in Sontag's standards than
in Arbus's alleged cruelty. Changing times have not served Sontag's assessment well, as the so-called victims and unfortunates captured by Arbus that
Sontag presumes we should pity—those lives Sontag assumes are defined by
horrific pain—include drag queens, dykes,* sex workers, sideshow performers,
interracial couples, and others for whom pity does not now seem, a priori,[15]
the order of the day. Sontag also scolds Arbus for not being interested in "ethical journalism." But who ever said she was? Ethical journalism was probably
about the last thing on Arbus's mind as she roamed about, photographing her
freaks. Nor did Arbus shrink from admitting the stirrings of both cruelty and
compassion within her. "And I photographed him then which was really cold,"

---

12 *Sylvia Plath* American poet, novelist, and short story writer known for exploring
dark topics during her short, troubled life. She died by suicide.

13 *callow* Immature.

14 *Sontag famously ... to serve* See Sontag, "Freak Show," also included in this
anthology.

15 *a priori* On the basis of what seems to be self-evident reasoning.

she wrote of her visit to her father on his deathbed. "But I suppose there is something somewhat cold in me."

Critics sympathetic to Arbus have worked overtime to absolve her of such coldness, often by recasting it as honesty. "Arbus knew that honesty is not a gift, endowed by native naiveté,* nor a matter of style, or politics, or philosophy," one wrote in the catalogue essay to her 2003 retrospective, *Revelations*. "She knew rather that it is a reward for bravery in the face of the truth." But what truth could this critic possibly be talking about? That freaks look freaky? That anyone can be made to look like a freak? And since when is honesty a prize rather than a practice?

Whatever Arbus's stated intent, the fascination of her work for me is less about her ability to capture "what something really looks like," and more about its capacity to reveal how that "something" changes per frame—how many conflicting truths there might be within a singular image, moment, or person. Arbus's subjects typically look straight at the camera, but I know of no other photographer who draws so much attention to the disturbing split that can exist between two eyes in one gaze (or between two purportedly identical subjects, such as twins, or between two halves or an intimate couple, or even between two sides of a room). One eye of an Arbus subject might deliver the good news of fellow-feeling, while the other bespeaks the bad news of human isolation and pitiability. To insist that one cancels the other out, or to fault her inquiries for not meeting the requirements of "ethical journalism," is to miss the disconcerting schism* of her vision. "I am like someone who gets excellent glasses because of a slight defect in eyesight and puts Vaseline on them to make it look like he normally sees," Arbus once explained, describing a late-breaking technique having to do with blurring. "It doesn't seem sensible but somehow I think it's right."

10 The artist standing bravely in the face of the (inconvenient, brutal, hardwon, dangerous, offensive) truth, the artist who refuses to "evade facts," or who can stare down "what the world really looks like"—what could be more heroic? Critics love the rhetoric used by artists such as Arbus and Bacon because it bolsters the sense that art and artists can rip off the veil, they can finally show us what our world is "really like," what *we* are really like. I mean it as no slight to these artists (both of whom I admire), nor to the practice of truth-telling (to which I aspire) when I say that I do not believe they do any such thing. Bacon shows us Bacon figures; Arbus shows us Arbus figures. This isn't to say that Bacon's paintings don't tell us quite a bit about the human animal, especially when caught in a spasm of despair or carnage, or that Arbus's photos don't communicate quite a bit about the human animal in its freakiness, loneliness, absurdity, or abstruse ecstasy. Their works do all this while also remaining products of their notoriously particular view of the world. There is absolutely

nothing strange about this paradox, unless you're looking to art to tell you "how things are," rather than give you the irregular, transitory, and sometimes unwanted news of how it is to be another human being.

At times, this news is familiar. "In every work of genius we recognize our own rejected thoughts: they come back to us with a certain alienated majesty," wrote Emerson,* providing a memorable phrase for the grand, surprising pleasure we feel when a work of art returns or restates our own thoughts. At other times, however, the news arrives more alien than majestic, generating the perpetual undergraduate grievance, "I just can't relate." It behooves us, I think to develop an openness to this latter feeling as well as to the former. If we're lucky, this openness may eventually grow into a hunger.

… Artists such as Plath and Bacon aimed to access "the brutality of fact" without providing any narrative to house it, and yet also without courting abstraction. This is an intriguing aim, albeit one bound to produce not only formal but also political difficulties.

For many would argue that art which aims to extinguish the story behind the suffering and focus on the suffering itself partakes in a different, more insidious cruelty—that of depoliticization, of stripping cruelties from their context so that they seem pitiable, sensational, or inevitable, rather than contingent, avoidable, or explicable. (This was Brecht's argument about most theater; it is also Sontag's, in her critique of Arbus, and John Berger's, in his of Bacon.[16]) "The most politically indoctrinating thing you can do to a human being is to show him, every day, that there can be no change," says filmmaker Wim Wenders. For the most part, I agree. And if one suggests that the thing that cannot change is the very thing that is causing suffering, the indoctrination can be all the more toxic. Such forms of expression can seemingly act as an accomplice, even if unwittingly, to this cynicism, which turns its back on the hard work of ferreting out the reasons why a particular cruelty has occurred, who is responsible for it, who gains from it, and who suffers….

What is "deepest" for Bacon is sensation, not psychology. And the peeling away of psychology from sensation occasions a certain sort of pain—the pain of extinguishing the story behind the suffering, and of contending directly with the sensation of suffering itself. This process might be likened to the Buddhist instruction to focus first and foremost on the wound made by an arrow that has

16 *Brecht* German dramatist Bertolt Brecht (1898–1956); *Berger's … Bacon* See, for example, Berger's essay "Francis Bacon and Walt Disney" (included in Berger's 1980 book *About Looking*). In the twenty-first century, however, Berger has taken a different and more favorable view of Bacon's painting (see his article "Prophet of a Pitiless World" in *The Guardian*, 29 May 2004).

pierced your heart, rather than on the direction or bow from which it came. Focusing on the latter is sometimes termed frivolousness, insofar as it distracts from the pain, instead of leading you further into it.

15   Bacon was one of those who insisted that humans will always suffer, no matter how just their circumstances, and that to argue otherwise is to deny a fundamental aspect of the human condition. He was right, of course, which is why any commitment to social justice that cannot acknowledge the existence of basic pain—that is, suffering that will exist for the human subject no matter how equitable or nourishing its circumstances—will end up haunted by bewilderment and disillusionment. But to obliterate, happily and eagerly, the distinctions between avoidable pain and basic pain is another story. It speaks of a different taste—that of wanting to amplify basic pain, valorize it, court it, exalt it. (Case in point: art historian John Richardson recalls that, after homosexuality was decriminalized in Britain, Bacon—who was gay—once wished that they would "bring back hanging for buggery," a wish that makes clear how much pleasure Bacon derived from risk, taboo, and the threat of punishment.)

Of course, in art as in life, pain doesn't typically arrive wrapped up in neat boxes, some labeled "pain from preventable injustice," others, "pain from basic suffering." Think of the pain of being poor, of being raped, of being enslaved, of being gay-bashed, of being forced into exile, of losing everything in a natural disaster, of suffering from an illness such as HIV or cancer (or any illness, especially if one does not have access to health care to treat it): such experiences swirl all kinds of human-made and primordial sufferings together. But that doesn't mean one can't become a student of the swirl and learn how to make useful distinctions in its midst. The increased ability to make such distinctions is one means of wising up to our various styles of imprisonment, should one wish to lessen their grip....

(2011)

AMY SCHALET

THE SLEEPOVER QUESTION

Sociologist Amy Schalet began in the mid 1990s to conduct comparative research into American and Dutch attitudes towards teenage sexuality. In 2000 she published a long article on the topic in the scholarly journal Body and Society *(under title "Raging Hormones, Regulated Love"). She continued to publish scholarly articles on the subject through the first decade of this century, and in 2011, with the publication of her book-length study* Not Under My Roof *imminent, she began to publish short articles summarizing her research for a broader audience; the essay "The Sleepover Question" appeared as an opinion piece in the 24 July 2011 issue of* The New York Times.

The excerpt included below from Not Under My Roof *is from the book's first chapter (for which Schalet uses the same title she had used for her earlier article). Though* Not Under My Roof *is a scholarly monograph, it is written in a style accessible to non-specialists; the book has been both widely read and influential.*

Not under my roof. That's the attitude most American parents have toward teenagers and their sex lives. Squeamishness and concern describe most parents' approach to their offspring's carnality. We don't want them doing it—whatever "it" is!—in our homes. Not surprisingly, teenage sex is a source of conflict in many American families.

Would Americans increase peace in family life and strengthen family bonds if they adopted more accepting attitudes about sex and what's allowable under the family roof? I've interviewed 130 people, all white, middle class and not particularly religious, as part of a study of teenage sex and family life here and in the Netherlands. My look into cultural differences suggests family life might be much improved, for all, if Americans had more open ideas about teenage sex. The question of who sleeps where when a teenager brings a boyfriend or girlfriend home for the night fits within the larger world of culturally divergent ideas about teenage sex, lust and capacity for love.

Kimberly and Natalie dramatize the cultural differences in the way young women experience their sexuality. (I have changed their names to protect confidentiality.) Kimberly, a 16-year-old American, never received sex education at home. "God, no! No, no! That's not going to happen," she told me. She'd like to tell her parents that she and her boyfriend are having sex, but she believes it is easier for her parents not to know because the truth would "shatter" their image of her as their "little princess."

Natalie, who is also 16 but Dutch, didn't tell her parents immediately when she first had intercourse with her boyfriend of three months. But, soon after, she says, she was so happy, she wanted to share the good news. Initially her father was upset and worried about his daughter and his honor. "Talk to him," his wife advised Natalie; after she did, her father made peace with the change. Essentially Natalie and her family negotiated a life change together and figured out, as a family, how to adjust to changed circumstance.

5   Respecting what she understood as her family's "don't ask, don't tell" policy, Kimberly only slept with her boyfriend at his house, when no one was home. She enjoyed being close to her boyfriend but did not like having to keep an important part of her life secret from her parents. In contrast, Natalie and her boyfriend enjoyed time and a new closeness with her family; the fact that her parents knew and approved of her boyfriend seemed a source of pleasure.

The difference in their experiences stems from divergent cultural ideas about sex and what responsible parents ought to do about it. Here, we see teenagers as helpless victims beset by raging hormones and believe parents should protect them from urges they cannot control. Matters aren't helped by the stereotype that all boys want the same thing, and all girls want love and cuddling. This compounds the burden on parents to steer teenage children away from relationships that will do more harm than good.

The Dutch parents I interviewed regard teenagers, girls and boys, as capable of falling in love, and of reasonably assessing their own readiness for sex. Dutch parents like Natalie's talk to their children about sex and its unintended consequences and urge them to use contraceptives and practice safe sex.

Cultural differences about teenage sex are more complicated than clichéd images of puritanical* Americans and permissive Europeans. Normalizing ideas about teenage sex in fact allows the Dutch to exert *more* control over their children. Most of the parents I interviewed actively discouraged promiscuous behavior. And Dutch teenagers often reinforced what we see as 1950s-style mores: eager to win approval, they bring up their partners in conversation, introduce them to their parents and help them make favorable impressions.

Some Dutch teenagers went so far as to express their ideas about sex and love in self-consciously traditional terms; one Dutch boy said the advantage of spending the night with a partner was that it was "Like Mom and Dad, like when you're married, you also wake up next to the person you love."

Normalizing teenage sex under the family roof opens the way for more re- 10
sponsible sex education. In a national survey, 7 of 10 Dutch girls reported that
by the time they were 16, their parents had talked to them about pregnancy and
contraception. It seems these conversations helped teenagers prepare, respon-
sibly, for active sex lives: 6 of 10 Dutch girls said they were on the pill when
they first had intercourse. Widespread use of oral contraceptives contributes to
low teenage pregnancy rates—more than 4 times lower in the Netherlands than
in the United States.

Obviously sleepovers aren't a direct route to family happiness. But even
the most traditional parents can appreciate the virtue of having their children
be comfortable bringing a girlfriend or boyfriend home, rather than have them
sneak around.

Unlike the American teenagers I interviewed, who said they felt they had
to split their burgeoning sexual selves from their family roles, the Dutch teens
had a chance to integrate different parts of themselves into their family life.
When children feel safe enough to tell parents what they are doing and feeling,
presumably it's that much easier for them to ask for help. This allows parents to
have more influence, to control through connection.

Sexual maturation is awkward and difficult. The Dutch experience suggests that it is possible for families to stay connected when teenagers start having sex, and that if they do, the transition into adulthood need not be so painful
for parents or children.

(2011)

from NOT UNDER MY ROOF: PARENTS, TEENS, AND THE CULTURE OF SEX

Karel Doorman, a soft-spoken civil servant in the Netherlands, keeps tabs
on his teenage children's computer use and their jobs to make sure neither are interfering with school performance or family time.[1] But Karel would
not object if his daughter Heidi were to have a sexual relationship: "No," he
explains. "She is sixteen, almost seventeen. I think she knows very well what
matters, what can happen. If she is ready, I would let her be ready." If Heidi
were to come home and say, "Dad, this is him," he says, "well, I hope I like
him." Karel would also let Heidi spend the night with a steady boyfriend in her
room, provided he did not show up "out of the blue." But Karel thinks that he

---

1   All names of people and places, and some occupations have been changed to preserve
anonymity. All translations from Dutch are mine. [All notes to this selection are the
author's original notes unless otherwise stated.]

would first "come by the house and that I will hear about him and that she'll talk about him and ... that it really is a gradual thing." That said, Karel suspects his daughter might prefer a partner of her own sex. Karel would accept her orientation he says, though he grants, "the period of adjustment might take a little longer."

Karel's approach stands in sharp contrast to that of his fellow parent, Rhonda Fursman, a northern California homemaker and former social worker. Rhonda tells her teenage son and daughter that premarital sex "at this point is really dumb." It is on the list with shoplifting, she explains, "sort of like the Ten Commandments: don't do any of those because if you do, you know, you're going to be in a world of hurt." It comes as no surprise therefore that Rhonda responds viscerally when asked whether she would let her fifteen-year-old son spend the night with a girlfriend. "No way, José!" She elaborates: "That kind of recreation ... is just not something I would feel comfortable with him doing here." She ponders her reaction: "I tried to be very open and modern ... but I am like, no, I'm not comfortable. I don't think I want to encourage that." She has a hard time imagining changing her position on permitting the sleepover, although maybe "if they are engaged or about to be married..."

Karel and Rhonda illustrate a puzzle: both white, middle class, and secular or moderately Christian, they belong to the one hundred and thirty Dutch and American parents and teenagers, mostly tenth-graders, whom I interviewed between the early 1990s and 2000. Despite the fact that both groups of parents are similar in education, religion, class, and race—features that often influence attitudes toward sexuality and childrearing—the vast majority of American parents oppose a sleepover for high-school-aged teenagers, while most Dutch parents permit it or consider doing so under the right circumstances. This book seeks to solve the puzzle of this striking difference, which is all the more surprising given the liberalization in sexual attitude and practices that took place throughout Europe and the United States since the 1960s. Given similar trends, why do the Dutch and American parents respond so differently? How do the parental approaches affect teenagers' experiences of sexuality and self? To answer these questions, we must look beyond sexuality at the different cultures of individualism that emerged in American and Dutch societies after the sexual revolution.

... Medical and public health literatures conceptualize adolescent sexuality primarily in terms of individual risk-taking and the factors that augment or lessen such risks.[2] American developmental psychologists tend to view adolescent sexuality as part of adolescents' separation from their parents and as an aspect of development that is especially perilous because of the disjuncture

---

2   Michaud 2006.

between teenagers' physical and cognitive development.[3] American sociologists have generally bypassed the parent-teenager nexus to focus on relationships and networks *among* teenagers—in romance and in peer groups.* They have examined how peer cultures and networks and the status hierarchies within them impact adolescent sexuality.[4] Finally, gender scholars have examined how teenage girls' and teenage boys' experiences of sexuality are profoundly shaped by gender inequalities—including the sexual double standard.[5]

This book takes a different approach. It focuses on the negotiation of adolescent rights and responsibilities within the parent-teenager relationship as a particularly fruitful, and often overlooked, site for illuminating how youth come to relate to sexuality, themselves, and others. This cross-national comparison shows how much of what we take for granted about teenage sexuality—American folk,* professional, and academic wisdom—is the product of our cultural constructs and institutions. Indeed, the apparently trivial puzzle Karel Doorman and Rhonda Fursman introduce is not just a puzzle but a window onto two different ways of understanding and shaping individuals and social relationships in middle-class families and in the societies at large, which constitutes nothing less than two distinct cultures of individualism. Each culture of individualism comes with freedoms and sacrifices: the Dutch cultural templates provide teenagers with more support *and* subject them to deeper control, while American cultural templates make the experience of adolescent sexuality particularly conflict-ridden.

ADOLESCENT SEXUALITY IN AMERICA AFTER THE SEXUAL REVOLUTION

Today most adolescents in the United States, like their peers across the industrial world, engage in sexual contact—broadly defined—before leaving their teens, typically starting around age seventeen.[6] Initiating sex and exploring romantic

---

3   This is especially true for classical (psychoanalytically informed) developmental psychology and evolutionary developmental psychology, in which separation from parents is a critical element of the individuation process. See also notes [54 and 55].

4   Sociological classics on adolescent peer groups and status hierarchies include Waller 1937 and Coleman 1961. Contemporary sociological studies of adolescent networks and peer groups include Bearman and Brückner 2001; Bearman 2004; Anderson 1999; Eder, Evans, and Parker 1995; Bettie 2000; and Pascoe 2007.

5   See for instance Bettie 2000; Fine 1988; Nathanson 1991; Tolman 2002; Tolman, Striepe, and Harmon 2003; Vanwesenbeeck, Bekker, and van Lenning 1998; and Armstrong, Hamilton, and Sweeney 2006.

6   Abma et al. 2004; de Graaf et al. 2005; Darroch, Singh, and Frost 2001; and Mosher, Chandra, and Jones 2005. More than half of American and Dutch seventeen-year-olds (both girls and boys) have had oral sex with a same-sex and/or opposite-sex *(continued ...)*

relationships, often with several successive partners before settling into long-term cohabitation or marriage, are normative parts of adolescence and young adulthood across the developed world.[7] In the Netherlands, as in many countries of northwestern Continental Europe, adolescent sexuality has been what one might call *normalized*—treated as a normal part of individual and relational development, and discussible with adults in families, schools, and health care clinics.[8] But in the United States, teenage sex has been *dramatized*—fraught with cultural ambivalences, heated political struggles, and poor health outcomes, generating concern among the public, policymakers, and scholars.

In some respects, it is surprising to find adolescent sexuality treated as such a deep problem for the United States. Certainly, age at first intercourse has dropped since the sexual revolution, but not as steeply as often assumed. In their survey of the adult American population, *The Social Organization of Sexuality: Sexual Practices in the United States,* Edward Laumann and colleagues found that even in the 1950s and 1960s, only a quarter of men and less than half of women were virgins at age nineteen. The majority of young men had multiple sexual partners by age twenty.[9] And while women especially were supposed to enter marriage as virgins, the majority of those who came of age in the late 1950s and early 1960s had sexual intercourse before they married.[10] Still, a 1969 Gallup poll found that two-thirds of Americans said it was wrong for "a man and a woman to have sexual relations before marriage."

But by 1985, Gallup found that a slim majority of Americans no longer believed such relations were wrong.[11] Analyzing shifts in public opinion following the sexual revolution, sociologists Larry Petersen and Gregory Donnenwerth have shown that among Americans with a religious affiliation, only fundamentalist Protestants who attended church frequently remained unchanged. Among all other religious groups acceptance of premarital sex grew.[12] This growing acceptance of premarital sex did not, however, extend to teenagers: in their 1990s survey, Laumann and colleagues found that almost 80 percent of the American population continued to believe sex among teenagers was *always* or *almost always* wrong. Since then, two-thirds of Americans have consistently told interviewers of the General Social Survey that sex between fourteen and sixteen was

---

partner. Among seventeen-year-olds, a little under half of American girls and boys, 45 percent of Dutch boys, and six out ten Dutch girls have had vaginal intercourse (Mosher, Chandra, and Jones 2005; de Graaf et al. 2005).

7   Bozon and Kontula 1998.

8   Jones et al. 1986; Berne and Huberman 1999; and Rose 2005.

9   Laumann et al. 1994, 198 and 326.

10   Finer 2007.

11   The Gallup poll statistics come from Smith 1994.

12   Petersen and Donnenwerth 1997.

always wrong. Interestingly, disapproval has remained widespread even among themselves: six in ten fifteen to nineteen-year-olds, surveyed in the National Survey of Family Growth, said it was not right for unmarried sixteen-year-olds who have "strong affection for each another" to have sexual intercourse.[13]

Part of the opposition to, and discomfort with, adolescent sexuality is its association with the high prevalence of unintended consequences, such as pregnancy and sexually transmitted diseases. In the United States, the rate of unintended pregnancies among teenagers rose during the 1970s and 80s and started dropping only in the 1990s.[14] However, despite almost a decade and a half of impressive decreases in pregnancy and birth rates, the teen birth rate remains many times higher in the United States than it is in most European countries. In 2007, births to fifteen to nineteen-year-old girls were eight times as high in the United States as they were in the Netherlands.[15] One reason for the different birth rates is that while condom use has improved among American teenagers, they remain far less likely to use the most effective methods of birth control, such as the pill.[16] Another reason is that, once pregnant, American girls are far more likely than their Dutch peers to carry their pregnancies to term.[17]

---

13   Abma, Martinez, and Copen 2010; Abma et al. 2004; 2010.

14   Kost, Henshaw, and Carlin 2010.

15   In 2007, the birth rate was 5.2 for Dutch teenage girls and 42.5 for American girls (Garssen 2008; Hamilton, Martin, and Ventura 2009). During the early 1990s, Dutch teenage pregnancy rates were comparable to those in recent years (van Lee and Wijsen 2008). But early 1990s American rates were significantly higher than those in recent years, and the contrast between the two countries in teenage pregnancy rates was even starker.... During the second half of the 1990s, the Dutch teenage pregnancy rate increased, before steadily decreasing again in 2002. But in 2000, the Dutch teenage pregnancy rate was still approximately four times lower than the American rate....

16   Evert Ketting (1983; 1994) has attributed the low Dutch teenage pregnancy rate to the use of the pill primarily and to emergency contraception secondarily. In 1995, 63 percent of Dutch secondary school students always used the pill with their last sexual partner, and 42 percent always used condoms (another 31 percent sometimes used condoms) (Brugman et al. 1995). That same year, a quarter of American females and a third of American males, ages fifteen to nineteen, who had sex three months prior to being interviewed by the National Survey of Family Growth, used the pill at last intercourse. Thirty-eight percent of American females and 64 percent of American males used a condom. Since then, condom use among sexually active youth has increased in both countries. Indeed, ... condom use at first vaginal intercourse is relatively high in both countries. However, pill use and dual protection (condoms and hormonal methods combined) are much higher among Dutch teens than they are among American teens. International comparisons of contraceptive behavior at last vaginal intercourse among sexually active fifteen-year-olds have found a similar pattern (Currie et al. 2008; Santelli, Sandfort and Orr 2008; Godeau et al. 2008)....

17   See ... note [15].

10   Nor are high rates of unintended pregnancies the only problems. Many American teenagers have positive and enriching sexual experiences, yet researchers have also documented intense struggles. Sharon Thompson found that only a quarter of the four hundred girls she interviewed about sexuality talked about their first sexual experiences as pleasurable. Among the girls Karin Martin interviewed, puberty and first intercourse decreased self-esteem. Psychologist Deborah Tolman found that most of the girls she interviewed struggled to fully own their sexual desires and experiences in the face of cultural constructs such as the double standard and the "slut" label* that stigmatize and deny girls' desires. Laura Carpenter illuminated another side of the double standard, finding that many of the young men she interviewed experienced their virginity as a stigma which they often sought to cast off as rapidly as possible. And in her ethnographic study *Dude, You're a Fag,** C.J. Pascoe found that teenage boys were encouraged to treat girls as sex objects and risked social derogation if they openly expressed affection for their girlfriends.[18]

These qualitative studies are corroborated by national surveys that show that American teenagers feel widespread ambivalence and misgivings about their first sexual experiences, which suggests that they do not feel control over, or entitled to, their sexual exploration. In a national survey, a minority of young women and a small majority of young men in their early twenties reported that their first heterosexual intercourse was "really wanted." Almost half of the women and a sizable minority of men surveyed said they had mixed feelings.[19] In another poll, a majority of American girls and boys said they wished they had waited longer to have sex.[20] Research has also found that if girls are young relative to their peers when they first have sex, they are more likely to experience negative emotions afterward, especially if their relationship breaks up shortly thereafter. But even without intercourse, first romance can bring girls "down" because their relationship with their parents deteriorates.[21]

American teenagers have received uneven, and often very limited, support in navigating the challenges of sexuality and first relationships from adult institutions outside the family. Despite rising pregnancy rates, in the early 1970s American policymakers and physician organizations lagged in making contraception easily available to teenagers, and even today American youth

---

18   See Thompson 1990; Thompson 1995; Martin 1996; Tolman 2002; Carpenter 2005; and Pascoe 2007.

19   Abma et al. 2004.

20   Albert 2004.

21   Meier found that the majority of teenagers do not experience negative mental health effects after first sex. However, some groups of girls do experience such effects, which depend on their age and relationship status during and after their first intercourse (Meier 2007). On the relationship between first romance and conflict with parents, see Joyner and Udry 2000.

face multiple barriers in accessing contraception, including confidentiality concerns.[22] With few other venues for discussing sexuality, the media has been an important, although often unrealistic, source of sex education for many American teenagers. Describing the 1960s and 1970s when sex permeated the media, historians D'Emilio and Freedman write, "From everywhere sex beckoned, inciting desire, yet rarely did one find reasoned presentations of the most elementary consequences and responsibilities that sexual activity entailed."[23] Since then, researchers have noted that some media including magazines and Internet sites provide good sexual health information but not the interactive dialogue with adults that teenagers seek.[24]

Teenagers have been unlikely to find such dialogue in the classroom. Along with fights over the legal age of consent to contraceptive and abortion services, battles over sex education have been among the most heated sexuality-related political struggles in America.[25] Politically organized religious conservatives succeeded in institutionalizing a federal sex education policy that has required the schools it funded to teach "abstinence only until marriage." Initiated in the early 1980s, federal support for abstinence-only policy was institutionalized in the 1996 welfare reform bill. Generously funded for many years, this policy dictated that schools teach that sex outside heterosexual marriage is likely to be damaging, and it prohibited them from teaching about the health benefits of condoms and contraception.[26] Even in school districts not funded by this

---

22 In the late 1960s and early 1970s, Dutch policymakers and the organization of family physicians, who provide the bulk of primary care in the Netherlands, made a concerted effort to make contraception easily accessible to unmarried women, including teenage women (Ketting 1990). During the same period, Constance Nathanson argues, the majority of American physicians shied away from the issue of teenage sexuality and pregnancy prevention. Indeed in the 1970s, Nathanson reports the American Medical Association's House of Delegates, the organization's principal policymaking body, rejected the recommendation by its Committee on Maternal and Child Health to adopt a policy of "permitting physicians to offer contraceptive advice and methods to teenage girls whose sexual behavior exposes them to possible pregnancy" (1991, 39). Policymakers also struggled with the issue: Nathanson argues that "neither Nixon in 1972 nor Carter in 1978 was prepared publicly to endorse birth control for unmarried adolescent women" (57).... Today, many states permit minors twelve and up to consent to contraceptive services. However, concerns about confidentiality and costs still constitute barriers to adolescents' obtaining reproductive health care (Lehrer et al. 2007; Ralph and Brindis 2010; Guttmacher Institute 2010).

23 D'Emilio and Freedman 1988, 342.

24 See Ward et al. 2006 and Steele 2002.

25 See Irvine 2002 and di Mauro and Joffe 2007.

26 Kantor et al. 2008. While the recent health-care reform act has included federal funding for schools that teach about condoms and contraception, it also allocated funds to support abstinence-only programs.

federal policy, sex education about contraception, pleasure, sexual diversity, and relationships has often been greatly constrained.[27]

Few survey findings have been as consistent as the finding that the general public supports sex education in schools.[28] In keeping with the surveys of the past decades, a 2004 national survey by NPR, the Kaiser Family Foundation, and Harvard University found that most parents wanted their children to learn about contraception and condoms. Yet, the same survey also gives some insight into why the abstinence-only policy nevertheless prevailed: while most parents did want their children to learn the information they needed to protect themselves, most respondents also wanted students to be taught that they should not engage in intercourse or other intimate sexual activities. And they accepted the "marriage only" framework: two-thirds of parents of middle and high-school students agreed that teenagers should be taught that abstaining from sexual activity outside of marriage is "the accepted standard for school-aged children."[29] Abstinence, most agreed, includes refraining from oral sex and intimate touching—sexual activities that most American youth, in actuality, start experimenting with in their mid-teens.[30]

ADOLESCENT SEXUALITY IN DUTCH SOCIETY AFTER THE SEXUAL REVOLUTION

15 In a late 1980s qualitative study with one hundred and twenty parents and older teenagers, Dutch sociologist Janita Ravesloot found that in most families the parents accepted that sexuality "from the first kiss to the first coitus" was part of the youth phase. In middle-class families, parents accepted their children's sexual autonomy, though lingering embarrassment kept them from engaging in elaborate conversations. Working-class parents were more likely to use authority to impose their norms, including that sex belonged only in steady relationships. In a few strongly religious families—Christian or Muslim—parents categorically opposed sex before marriage, which meant: "no overnights with steady boy or girlfriends at home."[31] But such families remain a minority: a 2003 national survey by *Statistics Netherlands* found that two-thirds of

---

27 See Lindberg, Santelli, and Singh 2006; Darroch, Landry, and Singh 2000; and Fields 2008.

28 Since the mid-1970s, the General Social Survey has found that at least four out of five Americans support sex education in schools.

29 *Sex Education in America* 2004.

30 See *Sex Education in America* 2004. Using 2002 NSFG data, Mosher and colleagues (2005) report that by age sixteen, the majority of American teenagers have engaged in some sexual contact—which could include oral sex or intimate touching—with another person (either the same or opposite sex).

31 See Ravesloot 1997.

Dutch teenagers, aged fifteen to seventeen, who had steady boy or girlfriends, said that their parents would allow their boy or girlfriend to spend the night in their bedrooms; girls and boys were just as likely to say they would be granted permission for a sleepover.[32]

The situation could hardly have been predicted in the 1950s. Then, women *and* men typically initiated intercourse in their early twenties, usually in a serious relationship if not engagement or marriage.[33] In a national survey in the late 1960s, the Dutch sociologist G.A. Kooij found that the majority of the Dutch population still rejected premarital sex if a couple was not married or was not planning to be married very shortly. After repeating the survey in the early 1980s, he noted a "moral landslide" had taken place in the interim, as evidenced by the fact that six out of ten of those surveyed no longer objected to a girl having sexual intercourse with a boy as long as she was in love with him.[34] Dutch sociologist Evert Ketting spoke of a "moral revolution": Not just a reluctant acceptance of sex outside of the context of heterosexual marriage, this revolution involved serious deliberation among medical professionals, the media, and the public at large—the result of a widely felt need to adjust the moral rules governing sexual life to real behavior.[35]

Many groups in Dutch society played a role in this transition. In the 1950s and '60s, Dutch religious leaders had begun questioning traditional definitions of morality. The Dutch Catholic Church—which represented the nation's largest religious group—was early to embrace the use of oral contraception as a method of birth control.[36] The Dutch media played a key educational role.[37]

---

32 Centraal Bureau voor de Statistiek 2003.

33 Bozon and Kontula 1998; Ravesloot 1997; and Wouters 2004.

34 Kooij 1983.

35 Ketting 1990; Ketting and Visser 1994. See also note [22]. Schnabel (1990) has argued that there was wide support among the Dutch population for the changes of the sexual revolution, and that change was certainly not confined to a small group of students.

36 Jones et al. 1986, 178. Historian James C. Kennedy has also argued that during the 1950s and 1960s, Dutch religious leaders, especially within the Catholic Church, went much further than bishops in other countries in fundamentally changing doctrine and practice, replacing a morality based on individual compliance with an ethics based on universal human compassion and service to others (Kennedy 1995). The Dutch sociologist Kooij (1983) has also pointed toward the role of religious leaders in opening up discussions around sexuality in Dutch society of the 1960s and 1970s. It is notable that the new moral discourse did not only pertain to heterosexual couples....

37 One group that played an important role was the Dutch Association for Sexual Reform (NVSH), which in the mid-1960s had more than 200,000 members. The NVSH was a strong advocate for family planning and sex education—including through media—and it helped shape government policy as well as public opinion (Ketting and Visser 1994; Hekma 2004a)....

With television and radio time partially funded by, and divided among, groups with different religious and political perspectives, discussions about sexuality were widespread.[38] Remarking on such discussions throughout the 1970s, researchers for the Guttmacher Institute noted in 1986, "One might say the entire society had concurrently experienced a course in sex education."[39] From these public deliberations resulted, Evert Ketting has argued, new moral rules that cast sexuality as part of life to be governed by self-determination, mutual respect between sexual partners, frank conversations, and the prevention of unintended consequences.[40]

Notably, these new moral rules were applied to minors and institutionalized in Dutch health-care policies of the 1970s, which removed financial and emotional barriers to accessing contraceptives—including the requirement for parental consent and a pelvic examination.[41] Indeed, even as the age of first sexual intercourse was decreasing, the rate of births among Dutch teenagers dropped steeply between 1970 and 1996 to one of the lowest in the world. With their effective use of oral contraception, what distinguished Dutch teens from their Swedish counterparts, for instance, was that in addition to a very low fertility rate they also had a low abortion rate. Despite the AIDS crisis,* by the mid-1990s—just when American policymakers institutionalized "abstinence only until marriage"—Dutch funding agencies were so confident that, in the words of demographer Joop Garsen, youth were doing "wonderfully well," they decided that further study of adolescent sexual attitudes and behavior was not warranted.[42]

---

38   ... Kees van der Haak and Leo van Snippenburg ... note ... that even after the legalization and expansion of commercial broadcasting in the 1980s and 1990s, the government was "intent on keeping the public part of the whole broadcasting system as strong as possible in a context of national and international competition in commercial broadcasting" (2001, 210).

39   Jones et al. 1986, 154. Survey research in the 1980s did not find strong effects of factors such as gender, class, religion, or urbanization on attitudes toward sexuality among the Dutch population (Van Zessen and Sandfort 1991).

40   Ketting 1994.

41   Ketting and Visser 1994 and Hardon 2003. Hardon describes the legal parameters and public sentiment: "Over age 16, patients are considered autonomous in decisions on health care, including contraception. Between ages 12 and 16 parental consent is needed, but if patients do not give consent and the minor wants treatment (e.g. contraception), a doctor can provide it if not doing so would have serious, negative consequences for the minor. The extent to which the Dutch respect the autonomy of minors is reflected in a recent survey in which 75 percent of respondents thought doctors should prescribe contraception without parental consent if that is what the minor needed and wanted" (61).

42   The confidence was challenged when Dutch teen pregnancies and abortions rose notably between 1996 and 2002. But the Netherlands' role as "guide country" with regard

Dutch researchers at that time noted similarities in boys' and girls' experiences of sexuality. Ravesloot found that the boys and girls she interviewed were equally as likely to feel controlled by their parents. Large-scale surveys from the early and mid-1990s found that boys and girls were approximating one another in combining feelings of being in love and lust as they pursued romantic relationships and initiated sexual experimentation.[43] At the same time, researchers found evidence of the double standard and sex-stereotyping—including the notion that boys were supposed to be more active and girls more passive in sexual interactions.[44] To counteract these "traditional" gender beliefs and roles, researchers recommended teaching negotiation or "interaction" skills, including the expression of sexual wishes and boundaries.[45] A 2005 national survey found high levels of such skills among both girls and boys, which include "letting the other person know exactly what feels good" and not doing things that one does not want.[46]

Indeed, the same study, which surveyed youth aged twelve through twenty-four, suggests Dutch adolescents feel more in control of their first sexual experiences and decision-making than their American peers, or alternatively, that the former feel more entitled or obliged than the latter to describe themselves as empowered sexual actors: four out of five Dutch youth describe their first sexual experiences—broadly defined to include different activities—as well timed, within their control, and fun. About their first intercourse, 86 percent of girls and young women and 93 percent of boys and young men said, "We both were equally eager to have it." At the same time, there were some notable gender differences. For instance, girls were much more likely to report having ever been forced to do something sexually. They were also more likely to regularly or always experience pain (11 percent) or have trouble reaching orgasm (27 percent) during sex than were boys. Nevertheless, the vast majority of both Dutch females and males were (very) satisfied with the pleasure and contact they felt with their partner during sex.

Emphasis on the positive aspects of sex and relationships—within the context of respect for self and others—is a key feature of Dutch sex education.

20

---

to teenage births and abortions remained intact and was strengthened by a sustained decrease in those rates between 2002 and 2007....

43 Brugman et al. 1995 and Vogels and van der Vliet 1990.

44 Cremer 1997 and Ravesloot 1997. Vanwesenbeeck and colleagues (1998) found that gendered patterns had persisted among Dutch college students of the 1990s; girls were likely to take a defensive approach to sexual interactions, while males were more likely to take an active, "go-get-it" approach.

45 Rademakers and Ravesloot (1993), for instance, state: "Sexual contact is a situation of negotiation in which both partners have an equal position.... Learning to talk about sex and contraception is particularly important, but also learning to negotiate in general" (277).

46 De Graaf et al. 2005.

Although they set national "attainment targets," Dutch policymakers avoided political controversy over sex education by delegating the task of reaching agreements on the content and delivery of sex education to professionals.[47] Sociologists Jane Lewis and Trudie Knijn have argued that like Dutch policymakers, Dutch sex educators have accepted teenage sexual exploration, viewing it as the result of societal changes. They teach students to view such issues as sexual diversity and diverse family formations in broader societal contexts as well. Sex education typically covers anatomy, reproduction, STDs,* contraception, and abortion. But in addition, sex education curricula often interweave the emotional and physical aspects of sex, emphasize relationships and developing mutual understanding, and openly discuss masturbation, homosexuality, and sexual pleasure.[48]

INVESTIGATING THE PUZZLE

The previous sections show how across an array of social institutions, adolescent sexuality has been viewed as a problem to be prevented in the United States, while in the Netherlands it has been accepted as part of teenage maturation to be guided by new moral rules. Why do adults in the two countries have such different approaches? This question is especially puzzling given that, in both countries, the generation in question lived through an era when attitudes toward sexuality outside the confines of heterosexual marriage changed rather dramatically. Indeed, of the two, the country in which it had been more common for teenagers to engage in sexual intercourse during the 1950s became, several decades later, the country in which teenage sexuality remained controversial.

Two factors immediately spring to mind when considering why adults in these two countries who lived through the sexual revolution—in which many themselves participated—would embrace such different approaches to the sexual socialization of the next generation. The first is religion. Americans are far more likely to be religiously devout that their Dutch counterparts, many of whom left their houses of worship in the 1960s and 1970s. As Laumann and colleagues found, Americans who do not view religion as a central force in their decision-making are much less likely to categorically condemn sex among teenagers. By the same token, devout Christians and Muslims in the Netherlands are more likely to hold attitudes towards sexuality and marriage that are similar to those of their American counterparts. That a larger proportion

---

47 Lewis and Knijn 2002; 2003.

48 Lewis and Knijn 2002, 687. But curricula are also adapted for religious audiences. An example of such adjustments included the emphasis on faithfulness over condoms and the exclusion of passages on masturbation and orgasm for a textbook used in schools of the Dutch Reformed Church (SOAIDS 2004).

of the American population than the Dutch population can be categorized as religiously conservative explains some of the difference between the countries.[49]

A second factor is economic security: as in most European countries, the Dutch government provides a range of what sociologists call "social rights" and what reproductive health advocates call "human rights."[50] These include the rights to housing, education, health care, and a minimum income. These rights ensure youth access to quality health care, including, if need be, free contraceptive and abortion services. Such supports—from universal children's allowances to college stipends—also make coming of age less perilous for both teenagers and parents, and they might make the prospect of sex derailing a child's life less haunting. Ironically, it is the lack of such rights in the United States, along with rates of childhood poverty that exceed those of most of Europe, that contributes to high rates of births among teenagers. Without adequate support systems or educational and job opportunities, young people everywhere, not just in the United Sates, are much more likely to start parenthood early in life.[51]

And yet, as Karel Doorman and Rhonda Fursman illustrated at the start of this chapter, there is more to the story: both parents are economically comfortable and neither attends church regularly, yet their answers to the question of the sleepover could not be more different. To understand why parents such as Rhonda and Karel reached such opposing conclusions about the sleepover, and how their different household practices affected teenagers, I interviewed one hundred and thirty members of the American and Dutch white, secular or moderately Christian middle classes—fifty-eight individual parents or couples, thirty-two boys, and forty girls, with most of the teens in the tenth grade. To avoid only studying professionals, I included a spectrum of lower and upper-middle-class families, and interviewed parents of teenagers living in households where the breadwinners ranged from salespeople and bank clerks with little or no postsecondary education, to nurses and managers with four-year degrees, to psychotherapists and doctors with advanced degrees.

In both countries, most interviewees came from one of two locations: In the Netherlands, they lived in or around the medium-sized cities of Western and Eastern City, which are located in the more cosmopolitan, densely populated Western region and in the less cosmopolitan, less densely populated Eastern region respectively. In the United States, most interviewees lived in or around

25

---

49   In their analysis of fifteen nations, Kelley and de Graaf (1997) use a variety of measures for religiosity. They characterize the United States as an extraordinarily devout modern society and the Netherlands as a relatively secular one.

50   Goodin et al. 2000.

51   Singh, Darroch, and Frost 2001.

Corona, a medium-sized city in northern California, and Tremont, a small town in the Pacific Northwest. An additional group of American interviewees resided in Norwood, a New England suburb.[52] Avoiding the most cosmopolitan urban centers and liberal hotspots,* as well as the most conservative regions and remote rural areas, the two samples represent what I would call the "moderate middle" among the white middle class in the two countries. Comparing these population segments cannot illuminate important cultural differences *within* either nation—between classes, races, regions, ethnicities, and religions. But the comparison does illuminate differences between the two countries in the family cultures of two particularly influential groups—differences that are not accounted for by our prevailing theoretical perspectives on adolescent sexuality.

MEDICAL, SOCIAL SCIENCE, AND HISTORICAL PERSPECTIVES

In the United States, the prevailing perspective in the field of public policy and health has been that teenage sexual intercourse is a health risk—a potential sickness, which is to be ideally prevented altogether.[53] The primary focus of research in this field is on the various factors that increase and decrease the risks of adolescent sexuality—defined narrowly as acts of intercourse. The risk perspective is corroborated by one view from developmental psychology* which sees adolescents as inherently risk-prone and subject to impulses that they are not yet able to handle, given their stage of cognitive development.[54] Classical developmental psychology also conceptualizes sexuality as part of young people's separation process from parents.[55] This process, however, produces discord—between teenagers' impulses and their brains' capacities, between early onset of sexual feelings and their later proclivity for emotional intimacy, and between teenagers and parents whose job it is to communicate their values and to monitor and limit their children's opportunities for sex.

---

52 All of the American parent interviews informed the analyses and calculation of parents' answers to the questions of the sleepover. However, only Corona and Tremont parents are quoted in this book. For quotes from the interviews with Norwood parents, see Schalet 2000.

53 Michaud 2006 and Nathanson 1991.

54 Steinberg 2004.

55 American psychoanalytic developmental theory places a great emphasis on separation and on sexual development as one of the motors of separation (Erikson 1950; Freud 1958). For a fascinating analysis of how American psychoanalytic developmental psychology has been shaped by Anglo-American cultural traditions that emphasize among other things, self-reliance, resulting in an emphasis on separation as the marker of psychological health, see Kirschner 1990. Socio-biological evolutionary perspectives also place an emphasis on the necessity for separation between parents and adolescents (Collins, Welsh, and Furman 2009, 634)....

These perspectives from medicine and psychology do not explain the puzzle posed by the differences in approach to and experience of adolescent sexuality in two developed nations. If anything, the puzzle challenges their assumptions. While Dutch teenagers, like their American counterparts, must certainly navigate the potential health risks of sex, the variation between the two nations in negative outcomes of sexual activity shows that neither the level of sexual activity itself nor adolescents' inherent biological or psychological capacities are responsible for such outcomes. The normalization of adolescent sexuality in Dutch middle-class families challenges, moreover, the notion that teenage sexuality—and adolescence as a phase of life—causes a schism between parents and teenagers that is often assumed in the United States to be an inevitable part of development, one in which parents and teenagers remain more closely connected and able to negotiate the potential disruptive elements of adolescent maturation....

A final perspective on adolescent sexuality places it in the context of historical change. French philosopher Michel Foucault has argued that in the modern era, governments are no longer able to rule large populations through repression and punishment alone. However, they have found in official discourses about "normal" heterosexual identities and reproductive behavior effective methods for social control. Originating in religious, medical, scientific and penal institutions, disciplinary practices and discourses encourage self-disclosure, differentiate people into categories, and goad them into new self-conceptions. Unlike the "sovereign" power of authorities who impose harsh punishments, the power of discipline and discourse is harder to detect, which makes it effective. Modern power is "productive" rather than repressive, Foucault argues, because rather than forbid, it exhorts individuals to voluntarily shape their subjective sense of themselves according to confining understandings of what is normal, healthy, and desirable.[56]

Foucault's argument that, in the modern era, conceptions and practices around sexuality have been power-ridden and often serve the interests of authorities is useful but incomplete. Indeed, as we will see, the dramatization and normalization of adolescent sexuality are imbued with forms of social control. But Foucault's account does not help us understand why different discourses of adolescent sexuality have come to prevail in the institutions of two equally modern, post-sexual-revolution societies. Nor does it provide an explanation for why these different discourses—of adolescent-sexuality-as-risk in the United States, and of adolescent sexual self-determination in the Netherlands— resonate as they do among lay people. Finally, Foucault's argument about the effectiveness of modern power misses key ingredients.

30

---

56   Foucault 1977; 1978.

The successful use of contraception among Dutch girls appears a prime example of disciplinary power. But, I argue, this power "works" because girls remain connected to and supported by adult institutions and are able to develop self-mastery—parts of the puzzle Foucault bypasses....[57]

DRAMATIZATION AND NORMALIZATION

The first step to solve the puzzle of the sleepover is to see that Dutch and American parents engage in different cultural processes as they interpret and manage teenage sexuality. Culling words, expressions and modes of reasoning from interviews shows how the American parents engage in *dramatization*: highlighting difficulties and conflicts, they describe adolescent sexuality, first, as "raging hormones," individual, potentially overpowering forces that are difficult for teenagers to control and, second, as antagonistic heterosexual relationships in which girls and boys pursue love and sex respectively. Finally, parents see it as their obligation to encourage adolescents to establish autonomy—and gain the potential for financial self-sufficiency or marriage—before accepting their sexual activity as legitimate. And viewing sex as part of a process of separation in which parents must stand firm ground around certain key issues, the response to the question of a sleepover, even among many otherwise liberal parents is, "Not under my roof!"

The Dutch parents, by contrast, engage in a cultural process of normalization. Theirs is a conception of "regulated love": that is, the Dutch parents speak of sexual readiness (*era an toe zijn*), a process of becoming physically and emotionally ready that they believe young people can self-regulate, provided that they have been encouraged to pace themselves and prepare adequately by using the available means of contraception. But readiness does not happen in isolation. The Dutch parents talk about sexuality emerging from relationships, and they are strikingly silent about gender conflicts. And unlike their American counterparts, who are often skeptical about teenagers' capacities to fall in love, they assume that even those in their early teens do so. They also permit the sleepover for those in their mid and late teens, even if it requires an "adjustment" period to overcome their feelings of discomfort, because they feel obliged to accept the changes and to stay connected as relationships and sex become part of their children's lives.

The interplay of cultural frames that parents use to interpret adolescent sexuality, the capacities of young people, and the responsibilities of adults

---

57 This critique of Foucault has been partly inspired by the work of Norbert Elias, who offers an alternative and more optimistic view of the relationship between sexuality and control in the modern world (Elias 1994, 177; Smith 1999).

gives parents' responses to the question of the sleepover their cognitive, emotional, and moral common sense. These "webs of significance" thus create a more or less coherent cultural universe of meanings in which certain decisions and practices make intuitive sense while others do not. At the same time, there are holes in the webs: as significant as the cultural languages that parents have readily available are the silences, lacunae, and the ways in which dramatization and normalization do not adequately address aspects of parents' and teenagers' experiences. And although there are dominant tendencies in each middle-class culture, not everyone is on the same page. Indeed, as we will see, rather than constitute seamless wholes, dramatization and normalization often involve negotiations—between different people and between expectations and realities.

ADVERSARIAL AND INTERDEPENDENT INDIVIDUALISM

The second step in solving the puzzle is to see that the normalization and dramatization of adolescent sexuality are embedded within different cultures of individualism and control that have come to prevail in Dutch and American societies. These different cultures of individualism and control build on long-standing traditions within each country. At the same time, they are also nation-specific responses to the changes in sexual, gender, and authority relations of the 1960s and 1970s: In the United States an "adversarial individualism" has prevailed, according to which individual and society stand opposed to each other, which leaves uncertainty about the basis for social bonds between people and for self-restraint within them. In the Netherlands an "interdependent individualism" has prevailed in which individual and society are conceptualized as mutually constitutive....

Each version of individualism has been accompanied by a distinct form of social control: Adversarial individualism permits, encourages even, individuals to attain autonomy by breaking away from social ties and dependencies, and only after that break form intimate relationships. However, because this definition of autonomy necessitates a disruption of social connectedness, it makes it difficult to envision social cohesion and self-restraint without some higher authority. Thus ironically, adversarial individualism calls for the use of overt external control, especially against those who have not (yet) attained full autonomy. Interdependent individualism, by contrast, encourages individuals to develop their autonomy in concert with ongoing relationships of interdependence. Because such relationships require, by their nature, a certain amount of mutual accommodation and self-restraint, the use of external controls appears less necessary. But while overtly egalitarian, interdependent individualism can obscure inequality and the fact that the less powerful parties in the relationships are expected to make the greater accommodations.*

35

The premises of adversarial and interdependent individualism—their assumptions about the relationship between self and other, and the relationship between different parts of the self—create cultural logics that undergird the dramatization and normalization of adolescent sexuality. Hence, American middle-class parents encourage adolescents to pursue individual interests and passions, break away from home, and establish themselves as emotionally and financially self-sufficient beings. At the same time, during the teenage years, American parents also view it as their responsibility to fight back, sometimes forcefully, against the passions that they at the same time encourage as signs of individuation but doubt that their teenage children are able to control. This template for adversarial individualism makes parents wary of adolescents' establishing intimate bonds. It also makes domesticating such bonds by permitting a sleepover out of the question.

The Dutch template of interdependent individualism provides a way for adolescents to develop their autonomy within relationships of interdependence. Such ongoing interrelatedness is not viewed as a matter of choice as much as an inherent human need and proclivity. Thus, adolescence does not bring the same rupture in the relationships with parents or in the self. An assumption of interdependent individualism is that even as they develop autonomy, individuals—parents and children alike—must demonstrate interpersonal attunement, which requires from adolescents the development of self-regulation. Within this framework of interdependent individualism, teenagers' intimate relationships do not pose a threat to the acquisition of autonomy, nor does their sexual component threaten parental authority within the home. By negotiating the sleepover, parents model the very interdependent individualism—integrating the needs of the self and the social—they encourage in their children.

CONNECTION THROUGH CONTROL AND CONTROL THROUGH CONNECTION

Intergenerational cultural transmission takes place not just through cultural narratives but also through methods for maintaining control and connection that psychologically encode them.* As part of a new generation, young people's cultural universe only partially overlaps with that of their parents: they consume different media, are subject to different technological fluencies, participate in different institutions—school and peer culture—and are recipients of different formative "zeitgeists."* Having not been fully socialized and yet subject to multiple sources of socialization, young people are often "rawer" in their desires and tendencies than their parents. For all these reasons, one cannot assume that just because a cultural logic makes sense to parents, it will make sense to their children as well. Yet, as we will see, even as they are in process of forging their independent selves, young people do, in fact, reproduce through the interpretation and construction of their own experiences many of the same cultural categories their parents use.

40

Such cultural reproduction between the generations is not a matter of course. In both countries, adolescent experimentation with sexuality and alcohol are sources of potential parent-adolescent conflict. However, the methods by which parents establish control and connection shape how those conflicts are experienced. Most American teenagers describe a parental strategy of *re-establishing connection through control*. Many American teenagers encounter parental policies much like those in the Fursman household—no sex or alcohol. And while most young people start their teenage "careers" as rule followers, sooner or later they start "sneaking around" to engage in forbidden activities, which in turn become vehicles through which they engage in a *psychology of separation*. But this secrecy also creates a disjuncture in the connection between parents and children. To re-establish that connection, parents must exert overt control and young people must "get caught."

In most Dutch families, by contrast, teenagers are subject to parental strategy of *maintaining control through connection*. With the belief widespread that it is not possible to keep young people from engaging in sex and drinking if they decide they want to, few teenagers find such exploratory activities outright forbidden. At the same time, they are expected to continue participation in family rituals that keep them connected to their parents even as they begin to experiment with sex, alcohol, and venturing into the world of nightlife. The "domestication" of their experimentations create bridges between the world of adults and the world of peers that their American counterparts lack, and it encourages in Dutch teenagers a *psychology of incorporation*. Those bridges are two-way streets: young people are able to integrate their experiences outside the home more easily with their roles as family members, but they are also subject to a deeper form of social control. This "soft" power is particularly effective when young people stay genuinely connected to their families not just out of duty but out of desire.[58]

INDIVIDUALISM AND GENDER

The different cultural templates for individualism and control also shape interpretations and experiences of gender. The American parents often mention differences and conflicts of interest between girls and boys. In fact, in some, though certainly not most families, the American boys report receiving implicit or explicit encouragement from fathers to pursue sexual interests. And while the interpretation and management of sexuality in American middle-class families led both girls and boys to use sex as a vehicle to engage in a psychology of separation, bifurcating sexuality and family life, this process tends to take a greater psychological toll on girls. While boys are expected to be "bad,"

---

58   This plays on the title of Jane Collier's *From Duty to Desire: Remaking Families in a Spanish Village* (1997).

girls are encouraged to be "good." But with "good girl" status and sex viewed as incompatible, American girls often experience, or anticipate experiencing, difficulty reconciling their sexual maturation with good daughterhood.

Interdependent individualism shapes the language and experience of gender in Dutch middle-class families. As noted, the Dutch parents do not speak about adolescent sexuality in terms of girls' and boys' different positions of power or their "antagonistic gender strategies." Nor do they give evidence of treating sons and daughters differently with regard to sexuality and relationships. In keeping with national statistics and qualitative research, they suggest that daughters and sons are equally likely to receive permission for sleepovers. Like the female counterparts, most Dutch boys are subject to "soft control" that socializes them into a relationship-based experience of sexuality and self and that encourages negotiations within, rather than separation from, the household. But there are subtle gender differences: such negotiation tends to be more fraught for girls, and while few Dutch boys express reservations about actually bringing their girlfriends home for the night, a number of Dutch girls say that they would rather spend the night elsewhere, suggesting that they do feel more closely supervised by their parents.

Adversarial individualism and interdependent individualism also provide cultural templates with which the American and Dutch girls and boys navigate sex and sense of self within peer cultures. The different assumptions about people's inherent relational needs and proclivities—at the root of the two versions of individualism—shape teenage girls' and boys' dilemmas of gender. In both countries girls are confined by the potential slander of being called a slut, but that label is much more prominent in the interviews with American girls. One reason is that American girls encounter adult and peer cultures skeptical about teenagers' ability to sustain meaningful sexual relationships. This skepticism means that American girls lack the indisputable certainty that the Dutch girls possess about whether and when sex is culturally legitimate. But while Dutch adult and peer cultures validate sexual experience in relationships, uncritical validation of relationship-based sexuality can obscure conflicts of interest and power differences in heterosexual relationships.

45   To different degrees, the notion that boys want sex but not relationships has some currency in both American and Dutch peer and popular culture. But in both countries, the vast majority of boys describe themselves as quite romantic in their orientation, wanting to experience sex with someone with whom they are in love. The American boys tend to see themselves as unique for their romantic aspirations, calling to mind the icon of the lone cowboy opposing the crowd of hormone-driven boys and a peer and popular culture of soulless sex. Indeed, some American boys set the bar for love very high—defining it as a heroic relinquishing of self—thus distancing themselves not only from

other boys but from sexual pleasure itself. The Dutch boys describe themselves as normal in their pursuit of a combination of sex and relationships. Without the stark oppositions—between male and female, love and lust, and pleasure and responsibility—they evidence a more integrated experience of ideals and realities....

CULTURE'S COSTS

... Teenagers do better emotionally when they can remain connected to their parents during adolescence. But with sexuality culturally coded as a symbol of, and a means to attaining, separation between parents and children, an important developmental experience becomes a cause for disconnection in the parent-teenager relationship. This disconnect makes it more difficult for parents to serve as support when adolescents start their first sexual experiences during their mid-teens. And when teenagers must keep their sexual behavior a secret or know it is a disappointment to their parents, it becomes more difficult to seek assistance from adults—to obtain contraception, assess their readiness, or discuss the qualities of a romantic relationship.

The ways in which the American culture of individualism conceptualizes autonomy and intimacy also do not serve adolescents well. The cultural narrative which dictates that one must attain financial and emotional autonomy before being ready for sex and emotional commitment leaves youth with a conception of autonomy they cannot attain until their mid-twenties, if ever. Such a conception does not provide the cultural tools to develop *internal* discernment and regulation necessary to exercise psychological autonomy within teenage sexual and romantic relationships.

As important, this narrative leaves young people and their parents without cultural templates for validating and assessing adolescent intimate relationships on their own terms. Strikingly, many American parents as well many American teenagers—girls and boys—use marriage as the ultimate intimacy that they are capable of and to strive for commitments they are not yet able to make.

The Dutch culture of interdependent individualism does not lead to the same psychological disconnect between parents and teenagers. Though the negotiation of adolescent sexuality is not tension-free, especially when it concerns the sexuality of girls, ultimately most of the Dutch girls and boys can integrate their sexual development with their relationship with their parents. This continued connectedness makes it easier for Dutch teenagers to draw on the support of parents and other adults as they move through their adolescent sexual and emotional explorations. With autonomy conceptualized as a matter of exercising self-direction within relationships, and with interdependence viewed as a matter of necessity rather than choice, Dutch teenagers also receive more cultural validation for their intimate relationships. At the same time, the cultural template of interdependent individualism makes it more difficult for Dutch teenagers and their parents to recognize and address conflicts of interest within relationships than it is for their American counterparts, who speak readily of conflicts and battles....

REFERENCES[59]

Abma, Joyce C., Gladys M. Martinez, and Casey E. Copen. 2010. Teenagers in the United States: Sexual Activity, Contraceptive Use, and Childbearing, National Survey of Family Growth 2006–2008. *Vital and Health Statistics,* ser. 23, no. 30. National Center for Health Statistics.

Abma, Joyce C., Gladys M. Martinez, William D. Mosher, and Brittany S. Dawson. 2004. Teenagers in the United States: Sexual Activity, Contraceptive Use, and Childbearing, 2002. *Vital and Health Statistics,* ser. 23, no. 24. National Center for Health Statistics.

Albert, Bill. 2004. *With One Voice 2004: America's Adults and Teens Sound Off About Teen Pregnancy*. Washington, DC: National Campaign to Prevent Teen Pregnancy.

Anderson, Elijah. 1999. *Code of the Street: Decency, Violence, and the Moral Life of the Inner City*. New York: W. W. Norton & Company.

Armstrong, Elizabeth A., Laura Hamilton, and Brian Sweeney. 2006. Sexual Assault on Campus: A Multilevel, Integrative Approach to Party Rape. *Social Problems* 53 (4): 483–99.

Bearman, Peter S., James Moody, and Katherine Stovel. 2004. Chains of Affection: The Structure of Adolescent Romantic and Sexual Networks. *American Journal of Sociology* 110 (1): 44–91.

Bearman, Peter S., and Hannah Brückner. 2001. Promising the Future: Virginity Pledges and First Intercourse. *American Journal of Sociology* 106 (4): 859–912.

Berne, Linda, and Barbara Huberman. 1999. *European Approaches to Adolescent Sexual Behavior and Responsibility*. Washington, DC: Advocates for Youth.

Bettie, Julie. 2000. Women Without Class: *Chicas, Cholas*, Trash, and the Presence/Absence of Class Identity. *Signs: Journal of Women in Culture and Society* 26 (1): 1–35.

Bozon, Michel, and Osmo Kontula. 1998. Sexual Initiation and Gender in Europe: A Cross-Cultural Analysis of Trends in the Twentieth Century. In *Sexual Behaviour and HIV/AIDS in Europe: Comparisons of National Surveys,* edited by M. Hubert, N. Bajos, and T. Sandfort. London: UCL Press.

Brugman, Emily, Hans Goedhart, Ton Vogels, and Gertjan van Zessen. 1995. *Jeugd en Seks 95: Resultaten van het Natioale Scholierenonderzoek*. Utrecht: SWP.

Carpenter, Laura M. 2005. *Virginity Lost: An Intimate Portrait of First Sexual Experiences*. New York: New York University Press.

Centraal Bureau voor de Statistiek. 2003. *Jeugd 2003: Cijfers en Feiten*. Voorburg/Heerlen: Centraal Bureau voor de Statistiek.

Coleman, James S. 1961. *The Adolescent Society: The Social Life of the Teenager and Its Impact on Education*. New York: The Free Press of Glencoe.

Collins, W. Andrew, Deborah P. Welsh, and Wyndol Furman. 2009. Adolescent Romantic

---

59 References have been excerpted to show only those cited in the material included here. [editors' note]

Relationships. *Annual Review of Psychology* 60: 631–52.

Cremer, Stephan W. 1997. Kwetsbaar en Grenzeloos: Experimenteren in Seks en Omgaan met Grenzen vanuit het Perspectief van Jongens. *Comenius* 17: 325–37.

Currie, Candace, Saoirse Nic Gabhainn, Emmanuelle Godeau, Chris Roberts, Rebecca Smith, Dorothy Currie, Will Picket, Matthias Richter, Antony Morgan, and Vivian Barnekow Rasmussen, eds. 2008. Inequalities in Young People's Health: International Report from 2005/2006 Survey. In *Health Policy for Children and Adolescents,* no. 5. Copenhagen: World Health Organization.

D'Emilio, John, and Estelle B. Freedman. 1988. *Intimate Matters: A History of Sexuality in America*. New York: Harper and Row.

Darroch, Jacqueline E., David J. Landry, and Susheela Singh. 2000. Changing Emphases in Sexuality Education in U.S. Public Secondary Schools, 1988–1999. *Family Planning Perspectives* 32 (5): 211–65.

Darroch, Jacqueline E., Susheela Singh, and Jennifer J. Frost. 2001. Differences in Teenage Pregnancy Rates among Five Developed Countries: The Roles of Sexual Activity and Contraceptive Use. *Family Planning Perspectives* 33 (60): 244–50 and 281.

De Graaf, Paul M., and Harry B. G. Ganzenboom. 1993. Family Background and Educational Attainment in the Netherlands for the 1891–1960 Birth Cohorts. In *Persistent Inequalities: A Comparative Study of Educational Attainment in Thirteen Countries,* edited by Y. Shavit and H.-P. Blossfeld, CO: Westview Press.

di Mauro, Diane and Carole Joffe. 2007. The Religious Right and the Reshaping of Sexual Policy: An Examination of Reproductive Rights and Sexuality Education. *Sexuality Research and Social Policy: A Journal of NSRC* 4 (1): 67–92.

Eder, Donna, Catherine Colleen Evans, and Stephen Parker. 1995. *School Talk: Gender and Adolescent Culture*. New Brunswick, NJ: Rutgers University Press.

Elias, Norbert. 1994. *The Civilizing Process*. Translated by E. Jephcott. Oxford: Blackwell.

Erikson, Erik H. 1950. *Childhood and Society*. New York: W.W. Norton & Co.

Fields, Jessica. 2008. *Risky Lessons: Sex Education and Social Inequality*. New Brunswick, NJ: Rutgers University Press.

Fine, Michelle. 1998. Sexuality, Schooling, and Adolescent Females: The Missing Discourse of Desire. *Harvard Educational Review* 58 (1): 29–53.

Finer, Lawrence B. 2007. Trends in Premarital Sex in the United States, 1954–2003. *Public Health Reports* 122 (January-February): 73–78.

Foucault, Michel. 1977. *Discipline and Punish: The Birth of the Prison*. Translated by A. Sheridan. New York: Vintage.

Freud, Anna. 1958. Adolescence. *Psychoanalytic Study of the Child* 15: 255–78.

Garssen, Joop. 2008. Sterke Daling Geboortecijfer Niet-westers Allochtone Tieners. *Bevolkings-trends* 56 (4): 14–21.

Godeau, Emmanuelle, Saoirse Nic Gabhainn, Celine Vignes, Jim Ross, Will Boyce, and Joanna Todd. 2008. Contraceptive Use by 15-year-old Students at Their Last Sexual Intercourse. *Archives of Pediatrics and Adolescent Medicine* 162 (1): 66–73.

Goodin, Robert E., Bruce Headey, Ruud Muffels, and Henk-Jan Dirven. 2000. The Real Worlds of Welfare Capitalism. In *The Welfare State: A Reader*, edited by C. Pierson and F. G. Castles, Cambridge, MA: Polity Press.

Graaf, Hanneke de, Suzanne Meijer, Jos Poelman, and Ine Vanwesenbeeck. 2005. *Seks onder je 25ste: Seksuele Gezondheid van Jongeren in Nederland Anno 2005*. Utrecht and Amsterdam: Rutgers Nisso Groep/Soa Aids Nederland.

Guttmacher Institute. 2010. *State Policies in Brief: An Overview of Minors' Consent Law.* New York: Guttmacher Institute.

Haak, Kees van der, and Leo van Snippenburg. 2001. Broadcasting in the Netherlands: The Rise and Decline of Segmentation. In *Western Broadcasting at the Dawn of the 21st Century*, edited by L. D'Haenens and F. Saeys. Berlin and New York: Mouton de Gruyter.

Hamilton, Brady E., Joyce A. Martin, and Stephanie J. Ventura. 2009. Births: Preliminary Data for 2007. *National Vital Statistics* 57 (12). National Center for Health Statistics.

Hardon, Anita. 2003. Reproductive Health Care in the Netherlands: Would Integration Improve It? *Reproductive Health Matters* 11 (21): 59–73.

Hekma, Gert. 2004a. The Decline of Sexual Radicalism in the Netherlands. In *Past and Present of Radical Sexual Politics,* edited by G. Hekma. Amsterdam: Mosse Foundation.

Irvine, Janice M. 2002. *Talk About Sex: The Battles over Sex Education in the United States.* Berkeley and Los Angeles: University of California Press.

Jones, Elise F., Jacqueline Darroch Forest, Noreen Goldman, Stanley Henshaw, Richard Lincoln, Jeannie I. Rosoff, Charles F. Westhoff, and Deidre Wulf. 1986. *Teenage Pregnancy in Industrialized Countries. A Study Sponsored by the Alan Guttmacher Institute.* New Haven: Yale University Press.

Joyner, Kara, and J. Richard Udry. 2000. You Don't Bring Me Anything but Down: Adolescent Romance and Depression. *Journal of Health and Social Behavior* 41 (4): 369–91.

Kantor, Leslie M., John S. Santelli, Julien Teitler, and Randall Balmer. 2008. Abstinence-Only Policies and Programs: An Overview. *Sexuality Research and Social Policy: A Journal of NSRC* 5 (3): 6–17.

Kelley, Jonathan, and Nan Dirk de Graaf. 1997. National Context, Parental Socialization, and Religious Belief: Results from 15 Nations. *American Sociological Review* 62 (4): 639–59.

Kennedy, James C. 1995. *Nieuw Babylon in Aanbouw: Nederland in de Jaren Zestig.* Amsterdam: Boom.

Ketting, Evert. 1983. Contraception and Fertility in the Netherlands. *Family Planning Perspectives* 15 (1): 19–25.

Ketting, Evert. 1990. De Seksuele Revolutie van Jongeren. In *Het Verlies van Onschuld: Seksualiteit in Nederland*, edited by G. Hekma, B. v. Stolk, B. v. Heerikhuizen, and B. Kruithof. Groningen: Wolters-Noordhoff.

Ketting, Evert. 1994. Is the Dutch Abortion Rate Really that Low? *Planned Parenthood in Europe* 23 (3): 29–32.

Ketting, Evert, and Adriaan P. Visser. 1994. Contraception in the Netherlands: The Low Abortion Rate Explained. *Patient Education and Counselling* 23 (3): 161–71.

Kirschner, Suzanne R. 1990. The Assenting Echo: Anglo-American Values in Contemporary Psychoanalytic Developmental Psychology. *Social Research* 57 (4): 821–57.

Kooij, G. A. 1983. *Sex in Nederland: Het Meest Recente Onderzoek naar Houding en Gedrag van de Nederlandse Bevolking.* Utrecht/Antwerp: Het Spectrum.

Kost, Kathryn, Stanley Henshaw, and Liz Carlin. 2010. *U.S. Teenage Pregnancies, Births and Abortions: National and State Trends and Trends by Race and Ethnicity.* Washington, DC: Guttmacher Institute.

Laumann, Edward O., John H. Gagnon, Robert T. Michael, and Stuart Michaels. 1994.

The Social Organization of Sexuality: Sexual Practices in the United States. Chicago: University of Chicago Press.

Lee, Laura van, and Cecile Wijsen. 2008. *Landelijke Abortus Registratie 2007*. Utrecht, Netherlands: Rutgers Nisso Groep.

Lehrer, Jocelyn A., Robert Pantell, Kathleen Tebb, and Mary-Anne Shafer. 2007. Forgone Health Care among US Adolescents: Associations between Risk Characteristics and Confidentiality Concern. *Journal of Adolescent Health* 40 (3): 213–26.

Lewis, Jane, and Trudie Knijn. 2002. The Politics of Sex Education in England and Wales and the Netherland since the 1980s. *Journal of Social Policy* 31(4): 669–94.

Lewis, Jane, and Trudie Knijn. 2003. Sex Education Materials in the Netherlands and in England and Wales: A Comparison of Content, Use and Teaching Practice. *Oxford Review of Education* 29 (1): 113–50.

Lindberg, Laura D., John S. Santelli, and Susheela Singh. 2006. Changes in Formal Sex Education: 1995–2002. *Perspectives on Sexual and Reproductive Health* 38 (4): 182–89.

Martin, Karin A. 1996. *Puberty, Sexuality, and the Self: Girls and Boys at Adolescence*. New York: Routledge.

Meier, Ann M. 2007. Adolescent First Sex and Subsequent Mental Health. *American Journal of Sociology* 112 (6): 1811–47.

Michaud, Pierre-Andre. 2006. Adolescents and Risks: Why Not Change Our Paradigm? *Journal of Adolescent Health* 38 (5): 481–83.

Mosher, William D., Anjani Chandra, and Jo Jones. 2005. Sexual Behavior and Selected Health Measures: Men and Women 15–44 Years of Age, United States, 2002. *Advance Data from Vital and Health Statistics*, n. 362. National Center for Health Statistics.

Nathanson, Constance. 1991. *Dangerous Passage: The Social Control of Sexuality in Women's Adolescence*. Philadelphia: Temple University Press.

Pascoe, C. J. 2007. *Dude, You're a Fag: Masculinity and Sexuality in High School*. Berkeley and Los Angeles: University of California Press.

Petersen, Larry R., and Gregory Donnenwerth. 1997. Secularization and the Influence of Religion on Beliefs about Premarital Sex. *Social Forces* 75 (93): 1071–88.

Rademakers, Jany, and Janita Ravesloot. 1993. Jongeren en Seksualiteit. In *Jeugd in Meervoud: Theorieën Modellen en Onderzoek van Leefwerelden van Jongeren*, edited by A.J. Dieleman, f. j. v. d. Linden and A. C. Perreijn. Utrecht: De Tijdstroom.

Ralph, Lauren J., and Claire D. Brindis. 2010. Access to Reproductive Healthcare for Adolescents: Establishing Healthy Behaviors at a Critical Juncture in the Lifecourse. *Current Opinion in Obstetrics and Gynecology* 22 (5): 369–74.

Ravesloot, Janita. 1997. *Seksualiteit in de Jeugdfase Vroeger en Nu: Ouders en Jongeren aan het Woord*. Amsterdam: Het Spinhuis.

Rose, Susan. 2005. Going Too Far? Sex, Sin and Social Policy. *Social Forces* 84 (2): 1207–32.

Santelli, John S., Theo G. Sandfort, and Mark Orr. 2008. Transnational Comparisons of Adolescent Contraceptive Use: What Can We Learn From These Comparisons? *Archives of Pediatrics and Adolescent Medicine* 162 (1): 92–94.

Schalet, Amy T. 2000. Raging Hormones, Regulated Love: Adolescent Sexuality and the Constitution of the Modern Individual in the United States and the Netherlands. *Body and Society* 6 (91): 75–105.

Schnabel, Paul. 1990. Het Verlies van de Seksuele Onschuld. In *Het Verlies van de Onschuld:*

Seksualiteit in Nederland, edited by G. Hekma, B. v. Stolk, B. v. Heerikhuizen, and B. Kruithof. Gronigen: Wolters-Noordhoff.

Sex Education in America. An NPR/Kaiser/Kennedy School Poll. 2004. Washington, DC: National Public Radio, Kaiser Family Foundation, Harvard University Kennedy School of Government.

Singh, Susheela, Jacquelin E. Darroch, and Jennifer J. Frost. 2001. Socioeconomic Disadvantage and Adolescent Women's Sexual and Reproductive Behavior: The Case of Five Developed Countries. *Family Planning Perspectives* 33 (6): 251–58 and 289.

Smith, Dennis. 1999. *The Civilizing Process and the History of Sexuality:* Comparing Norbert Elias and Michel Foucault. *Theory and Society* 28 (1): 79–100.

Smith, Tom W. 1994. Attitudes toward Sexual Permissiveness: Trends, Correlates and Behavioral Connections. In *Sexuality Across the Life Course*, edited by A. S. Rossi. Chicago: University of Chicago Press.

Steele, Jeanne R. 2002. Teens and Movies: Something to Do, Plenty to Learn. In *Sexual Teens, Sexual Media: Investigating Media's Influence on Adolescent Sexuality,* edited by J. Brown, Jeanne Steele, and Kim Walsh-Childers. Mahwah, NJ: Lawrence Erlbaum Associates.

Steinberg, Laurence. 2004. Risk Taking Adolescence. What Changes and Why? *Annals of the New York Academy of Sciences* 1021: 51–58.

Thompson, Sharon. 1990. Putting a Big Thing into a Little Hole: Teenage Girls' Accounts of Sexual Initiation. *The Journal of Sex Research* 27 (3): 341–61.

Thompson, Sharon. 1995. *Going All the Way: Teenage Girls' Tales of Sex, Romance, and Pregnancy.* New York: Hill and Wang.

Tolman, Deborah L. 2002. *Dilemmas of Desire: Teenage Girls Talk about Sexuality.* Cambridge, MA: Harvard University Press.

Tolman, Deborah L., Meg L. Striepe, and Tricia Harmon. 2003. Gender Matters: Constructing a Model of Adolescent Sexual Health. *The Journal of Sex Research* 40: 4–12.

Vanwesenbeeck, Ine, Marrie Bekker, and Akeline van Lenning. 1998. Gender Attitudes, Sexual Meanings, and Interactional Patterns in Heterosexual Encounters among College Students in the Netherlands. *Journal of Sex Research* 35 (4): 317–27.

Waller, Willard. 1937. The Rating and Dating Complex. *American Sociological Review 2* (5): 727–34.

Ward, L. Monique, Kyla M. Day, and Marina Epstein. 2006. Uncommonly Good: Exploring How Mass Media May Be a Positive Influence on Young Women's Sexual Health and Development. *New Directions for Child and Adolescent Development* 112: 587–70.

Wouters, Cas. 2004. *Sex and Manners: Female Emancipation in the West.* 1890-2000. Edited by M. Featherstone. Thousand Oaks, CA and London: Sage Publications.

Zessen, Gertjan van, and Theo Sandfort, eds. 1991. *Seksualiteit in Nederland: Seksueel Gerdrag, Risico en Preventie van AIDS.* Amsterdam: Swets & Zeitlinger.

(2011)

from WHY BE HAPPY WHEN YOU COULD BE NORMAL?

Winterson's 1985 award-winning novel Oranges Are Not the Only Fruit, *a largely autobiographical account of growing up as a lesbian in a Pentecostal family in the north of England, created something of a literary sensation. Winterson also wrote the script for a 1990 miniseries based on the novel, and in 2011 she returned to the same territory once more, this time as a memoirist. The excerpt from* Why Be Happy When You Could Be Normal? *included here is the book's first chapter, entitled "The Wrong Crib."*

When my mother was angry with me, which was often, she said, "the Devil led us to the wrong crib."

The image of Satan taking time off from the Cold War and McCarthyism[1] to visit Manchester in 1960—purpose of visit: to deceive Mrs. Winterson—has a flamboyant theatricality to it. She was a flamboyant depressive; a woman who kept a revolver in the duster drawer, and the bullets in a tin of Pledge.* A woman who stayed up all night baking cakes to avoid sleeping in the same bed as my father. A woman with a prolapse, a thyroid condition, an enlarged heart, an ulcerated leg that never healed, and two sets of false teeth—matt for everyday, and a pearlised set for "best."

I do not know why she didn't/couldn't have children. I know that she adopted me because she wanted a friend (she had none), and because I was like a flare sent out into the world—a way of saying that she was here—a kind of X Marks the Spot.

She hated being a nobody, and like all children, adopted or not, I have had to live out some of her unlived life. We do that for our parents—we don't really have any choice.

---

1   *Cold War and McCarthyism*   Senator Joseph McCarthy was the exemplar of virulent anti-Communism in 1950s America.

5   She was alive when my first novel, *Oranges Are Not the Only Fruit*, was published in 1985. It is semiautobiographical, in that it tells the story of a young girl adopted by Pentecostal parents. The girl is supposed to grow up and be a missionary. Instead she falls in love with a woman. Disaster. The girl leaves home, gets herself to Oxford University, returns home to find her mother has built a broadcast radio and is beaming out the Gospel to the heathen.* The mother has a handle—She's called "Kindly Light."

     The novel begins: *"Like most people I lived for a long time with my mother and father. My father liked to watch the wrestling, my mother liked to wrestle."*

     For most of my life I've been a bare-knuckle fighter. The one who wins is the one who hits the hardest. I was beaten as a child and I learned early never to cry. If I was locked out overnight I sat on the doorstep till the milkman came, drank both pints, left the empty bottles to enrage my mother, and walked to school.

     We always walked. We had no car and no bus money. For me, the average was five miles a day: two miles for the round trip to school; three miles for the round trip to church.

     Church was every night except Thursdays.

10   I wrote about some of these things in *Oranges*, and when it was published, my mother sent me a furious note in her immaculate copperplate handwriting[2] demanding a phone call.

     We hadn't seen each other for several years. I had left Oxford, was scraping together a life, and had written *Oranges* young—I was twenty-five when it was published.

     I went to a phone box—I had no phone. She went to a phone box—she had no phone.

     I dialed the Accrington code and number as instructed, and there she was—who needs Skype? I could see her through her voice, her form solidifying in front of me as she talked.

     She was a big woman, tallish and weighing around twenty stone. Surgical stockings, flat sandals, a Crimplene dress and nylon headscarf. She would have done her face powder (keep yourself nice), but not lipstick (fast and loose).*

15   She filled the phone box. She was out of scale, larger than life. She was like a fairy story where size is approximate and unstable. She loomed up. She expanded. Only later, much later, too late, did I understand how small she was to herself. The baby nobody picked up. The uncarried child still inside her.

     But that day she was borne up on the shoulders of her own outrage. She said, "It's the first time I've had to order a book in a false name."

---

2   *copperplate handwriting*   Handwriting that is tidy and rounded.

I tried to explain what I had hoped to do. I am an ambitious writer—I don't see the point of being anything; no, not anything at all, if you have no ambition for it. 1985 wasn't the day of the memoir—and in any case, I wasn't writing one. I was trying to get away from the received idea that women always write about "experience"—the compass of what they know—while men write wide and bold—the big canvas, the experiment with form. Henry James did no good when he said the Jane Austen wrote on four inches of ivory—i.e. tiny observant minutiae. Much the same was said of Emily Dickinson and Virginia Woolf.* Those things made me angry. In any case, why could there not be experience and experiment? Why could there not be the observed and the imagined? Why should a woman be limited by anything or anybody? Why should a woman not be ambitious for literature? Ambitious for herself?

Mrs. Winterson was having none of it. She knew full well that writers were sex-crazed bohemians* who broke the rules and didn't go out to work. Books had been forbidden in our house—I'll explain why later—and so for me to have written one, and had it published, and had it win a prize … and be standing in a phone box giving her a lecture on literature, a polemic on feminism….

The pips—more money in the slot[3]—and I'm thinking, as her voice goes in and out like the sea, "Why aren't you proud of me?"

The pips—more money in the slot—and I'm locked out and sitting on the doorstep again. It's really cold and I've got a newspaper under my bum and I'm huddled in my duffel coat.

A woman comes by and I know her. She gives me a bag of chips. She knows what my mother is like.

Inside our house the light is on. Dad's on the night shift, so she can go to bed, but she won't sleep. She'll read the Bible all night, and when Dad comes home, he'll let me in, and he'll say nothing, and she'll say nothing, we'll act like it's normal to leave your kid outside all night, and normal never to sleep with your husband. And normal to have two sets of false teeth, and a revolver in the duster drawer[4]…

We're still on the phone in our phone boxes. She tells me that my success is from the Devil, keeper of the wrong crib. She confronts me with the fact that I have used my own name in the novel—if it is a story, why is the main character called Jeanette?

20

---

3   *The pips … slot*   In Britain, calls made from pay phones are timed; when time is running out the caller hears a series of sounds similar to "pip, pip, pip."

4   *duster drawer*   Drawer in which cloths used for dusting are kept. (N.B. The ellipses in this selection are Winterson's; they do not indicate that any material has been omitted by the editors.)

Why?

25   I can't remember a time when I wasn't setting my story against hers. It was my survival from the very beginning. Adopted children are self-invented because we have to be; there is an absence, a void, a question mark at the very beginning of our lives. A crucial part of our story is gone, and violently, like a bomb in the womb.

The baby explodes into an unknown world that is only knowable through some kind of a story—of course that is how we all live, it's the narrative of our lives, but adoption drops you into the story after it has started. It's like reading a book with the first few pages missing. It's like arriving after curtain up.* The feeling that something is missing never, ever leaves you—and it can't, and it shouldn't, because something is missing.

That isn't of its nature negative. The missing part, the missing past, can be an opening, not a void. It can be an entry as well as an exit. It is the fossil record, the imprint of another life, and although you can never have that life, your fingers trace the space where it might have been, and your fingers learn a kind of Braille.

There are markings here, raised like welts. Read them. Read the hurt. Rewrite them. Rewrite the hurt.

It's why I am a writer—I don't say "decided" to be, or "became." It was not an act of will or even a conscious choice. To avoid the narrow mesh of Mrs. Winterson's story I had to be able to tell my own. Part fact part fiction is what life is. And it is always a cover story. I wrote my way out.

30   She said, "But it's not true...."

Truth? This was a woman who explained the flash-dash of mice activity in the kitchen as ectoplasm.

There was a terraced house in Accrington, in Lancashire—we called those houses two-up two-down: two rooms downstairs, two rooms upstairs. Three of us lived together in that house for sixteen years. I told my version—faithful and invented, accurate and misremembered, shuffled in time. I told myself as hero like any shipwreck story. It was a shipwreck, and me thrown on the coastline of humankind, and finding it not altogether human, and rarely kind.

And I suppose that the saddest thing for me, thinking about the cover version that is *Oranges*, is that I wrote a story I could live with. The other one was too painful. I could not survive it.

I am often asked, in a tick-box kind of way, what is "true" and what is not "true" in *Oranges*. Did I work in a funeral parlor? Did I drive an ice-cream van? Did we have a Gospel Tent?* Did Mrs. Winterson build her own CB radio?* Did she really stun tomcats with a catapult?

I can't answer these questions. I can say that there is a character in *Oranges*   35
called Testifying Elsie who looks after the little Jeanette and acts as a soft wall
against the hurt(ling) force of Mother.

I wrote her in because I couldn't bear to leave her out. I wrote her in because I really wished it had been that way. When you are a solitary child you
find an imaginary friend.

There was no Elsie. There was no one like Elsie. Things were much lone-
lier than that.

I spent most of my school years sitting on the railings outside school gates in
the breaks. I was not a popular or a likeable child; too spiky, too angry, too
intense, too odd. The churchgoing didn't encourage school friends, and school
situations always pick out the misfit. Embroidering THE SUMMER IS ENDED AND
WE ARE NOT YET SAVED on my gym bag made me easy to spot.

But even when I did make friends I made sure it went wrong....

If someone liked me, I waited until she was off guard, and then I told her I   40
didn't want to be her friend any more. I watched the confusion and upset. The
tears. Then I ran off, triumphantly in control, and very fast the triumph and the
control leaked away, and then I cried and cried, because I had put myself on the
outside again, on the doorstep again, where I didn't want to be.

Adoption is outside. You act out what it feels like to be the one who doesn't
belong. And you act it out by trying to do to others what has been done to you.
It is impossible to believe that anyone loves you for yourself.

I never believed that my parents loved me. I tried to love them but it didn't
work. It has taken me a long time to learn how to love—both the giving and the
receiving. I have written about love obsessively, forensically, and I know/knew
it as the highest value. I loved God of course, in the early days, and God loved
me. That was something. And I loved animals and nature. And poetry. People
were the problem. How do you love another person? How do you trust another
person to love you?

I had no idea.

I thought that love was loss.

Why is the measure of love loss?   45

That was the opening line of a novel of mine—*Written on the Body* (1992).
I was stalking love, trapping love, losing love, longing for love …

Truth for anyone is a very complex thing. For a writer, what you leave out says
as much as those things you include. What lies beyond the margin of the test?
The photographer frames the shot; writers frame their world.

Mrs. Winterson objected to what I had put in, but it seemed to me that
what I had left out was the story's silent twin. There are so many things that we

can't say, because they are too painful. We hope that the things we can say will soothe the rest, or appease it in some way. Stories are compensatory. The world is unfair, unjust, unknowable, out of control.

When we tell a story we exercise control, but in such a way as to leave a gap, an opening. It is a version, but never the final one. And perhaps we hope that the silences will be heard by someone else, and the story can continue, can be retold.

When we write we offer the silence as much as the story. Words are the part of silence that can be spoken.

Mrs. Winterson would have preferred it if I had been silent.

Do you remember the story of Philomel[5] who is raped and then has her tongue ripped out by the rapist so that she can never tell?

I believe in fiction and the power of stories because that way we speak in tongues.* We are not silenced. All of us, when in deep trauma, find we hesitate, we stammer; there are long pauses in our speech. The thing is stuck. We get our language back through the language of others. We can turn to the poem. We can open the book. Somebody has been there for us and deep-dived the words.

I needed words because unhappy families are conspiracies of silence. The one who breaks the silence is never forgiven. He or she has to learn to forgive him or herself.

God is forgiveness—or so that particular story goes, but in our house God was Old Testament and there was no forgiveness without a great deal of sacrifice. Mrs. Winterson was unhappy and we had to be unhappy with her. She was waiting for the Apocalypse.*

Her favorite song was "God Has Blotted Them Out," which was meant to be about sins, but really was about anyone who had ever annoyed her, which was everyone. She just didn't like anyone and she just didn't like life. Life was a burden to be carried as far as the grave and then dumped. Life was a Vale of Tears.* Life was a pre-death experience.

Every day Mrs. Winterson prayed, "Lord, let me die." This was hard on me and my dad.

Her own mother had been a genteel woman who had married a seductive thug, given him her money, and watched him womanize it away. For a while, from when I was about three, until I was about five, we had to live with my grandad, so that Mrs. Winterson could nurse her mother, who was dying of throat cancer.

Although Mrs. W was deeply religious, she believed in spirits, and it made her very angry that Grandad's girlfriend, as well as being an ageing barmaid

---

5   *Philomel*   Figure in Greek mythology.

with dyed blonde hair, was a medium who held seances in our very own front room.

After the seances my mother complained that the house was full of men   60
in uniform from the war. When I went into the kitchen to get at the corned beef sandwiches I was told not to eat until the Dead had gone. This could take several hours, which is hard when you are four.

I took to wandering up and down the street asking for food. Mrs. Winterson came after me and that was the first time I heard the dark story of the Devil and the crib…

In the crib next to me had been a little boy called Paul. He was my ghostly brother because his sainted self was always invoked when I was naughty. Paul would never have dropped his new doll into the pond (we didn't go near the surreal possibilities of Paul having been given a doll in the first place). Paul would not have filled his poodle pyjama case with tomatoes so that he could perform a stomach operation with blood-like squish. Paul would not have hidden Grandad's gas mask (for some reason Grandad still had his wartime gas mask and I loved it). Paul would not have turned up at a nice birthday party, to which he had not been invited, wearing Grandad's gas mask.

If they had taken Paul instead of me, it would have been different, better. I was supposed to be a pal … like she had been to her mother.

And then her mother died and she shut herself up in her grief. I shut myself up in the larder because I had learned how to use the little key that opened the tins of corned beef.

I have a memory—true or not true?   65
The memory is surrounded by roses, which is odd because it is a violent and upsetting memory, but my grandad was a keen gardener and he particularly loved roses. I like finding him, shirtsleeves rolled up, wearing a knitted waistcoat and spraying the blooms with water from a polished copper can with a piston pressure valve. He liked me, and she hated him—not in an angry way, but with a toxic submissive resentment.

I am wearing my favorite outfit—a cowboy suit and a fringed hat. My small body is slung from side to side with cap-gun Colts.*

A woman comes into the garden and Grandad tells me to go inside and find my mother who is making her usual pile of sandwiches.

I run in—Mrs. Winterson takes off her apron and goes to answer the door.

I am peeping from down the hallway. There is an argument between the   70
two women, a terrible argument that I can't understand, and something fierce and frightening, like animal fear. Mrs. Winterson slams the door and leans on it for a second. I creep out of my peeping place. She turns around. There I am in my cowboy outfit.

"Was that my mum?"

Mrs. Winterson hits me and the blow knocks me back. Then she runs upstairs.

I go out into the garden. Grandad is spraying the roses. He ignores me. There is no one there.

(2011)

PICO IYER

THE TERMINAL CHECK

A British-born novelist and non-fiction author of Indian background who was partly raised in California and has made his home in Japan, Pico Iyer is best known for his travel writing. The following short piece appeared in a 2011 volume of the literary magazine Granta. *Titled "Ten Years Later," the volume addresses "the complexity and sorrow of life since 11 September 2001."*

I'm sitting in the expansive spaces of Renzo Piano's four-storey airport out-side Osaka, sipping an Awake tea from Starbucks and waiting for my bus home. I've chosen to live in Japan for the past twenty years, and I know its rites as I know the way I need tea when feeling displaced, or to head for a right-hand window seat as soon as I enter a bus. A small, round-faced Japanese man in his early thirties, accompanied by a tall and somewhat cadaverous man of the same age, approaches me.

"Excuse me," says the small, friendly-seeming one; they look like newborn salarymen in their not-quite-perfect suits. "May I see your passport?"

When I look up, surprised, he flashes me a badge showing that he's a plain-clothes policeman. Dazed after crossing sixteen time zones (from California), I hand him my British passport.

"What are you doing in Japan?"

"I'm writing about it." I pull out my business card with the red embossed   5
logo of *Time* magazine.

"*Time* magazine?" says the smiling cop, strangely impressed. "He works for *Time* magazine," he explains to his lanky and impassive partner. "Very famous magazine," he assures me. "High prestige!"

Then he asks for my address and phone number and where I plan to be for the next eighty-nine days. "If there is some unfortunate incident," he explains, "some terrorist attack" (he's sotto voce now), "then we will know you did it."

Six months later, I fly back to the country I love once more. This time I need to withdraw some yen from an ATM as I stumble out of my trans-Pacific plane, in order to pay for my bus home.

703

"You're getting some money?" says an attractive young Japanese woman, suddenly appearing beside me with a smile.

10   "I am. To go back to my apartment."

"You live here?" Few Japanese women have ever come up to me in public, let alone without an introduction, and shown such interest.

"I do."

"May I see your passport?" she asks sweetly, flashing a badge at me, much as the pair of questioners had done two seasons before.

"Just security," she says, anxious not to put me out, as my Japanese neighbours stream, unconcerned, towards the Gakuenmae bus that's about to pull out of its bay.

15   I tell my friends back in California about these small disruptions and they look much too knowing. It's 9/11, they assure me. Over the past decade, security has tightened around the world, which means that insecurity has increased proportionally. Indeed, in recent years Japan has introduced fingerprinting for all foreign visitors arriving at its airports, and takes photographs of every outsider coming across its borders; a large banner on the wall behind the immigration officers in Osaka—as angry-looking with its red-and-black hand-lettering as a student banner—explains the need for heightened measures in the wake of threats to national order.

But the truth of the matter is that, for those of us with darker skins, and from nations not materially privileged, it was ever thus. When I was eighteen, I was held in custody in Panama's airport (because of the Indian passport I then carried) and denied formal entry to the nation, while the roguish English friend from high school with whom I was travelling was free to enter with impunity and savour all the dubious pleasures of the Canal Zone. On my way into Hong Kong—a transit lounge of a city if ever there was one, a duty-free zone whose only laws seem to be those of the marketplace—I was hauled into a special cabin for a lengthy interrogation because my face was deemed not to match my (by then British) passport. In Japan I was strip-searched every time I returned to the country, three or four times a year—my lifelong tan moving the authorities to assume that I must be either Saddam Hussein's[1] cousin or an illegal Iranian (or, worst of all, what I really am, a wandering soul with Indian forebears). Once I was sent to a small room in Tokyo reserved for anyone of South Asian ancestry (where bejewelled women in saris loudly complained in exaggerated Oxbridge accents* about being taken for common criminals).

---

1   *Saddam Hussein* President of Iraq (1937–2006). Before their invasion of Iraq in 2003, the American and British governments accused him of involvement in the 11 September 2001 terrorist attacks on the United States, and of possessing weapons of mass destruction.

Another time, long before my Japanese neighbours had heard of Osama bin Laden,[2] I was even detained on my way *out* of Osaka—and the British Embassy hastily faxed on a Sunday night—as if any male with brown skin, passable English and a look of shabby quasi-respectability must be doing something wrong if he's crossing a border.

But now, having learned over decades to accept such indignities or injustices, I walk into a chorus of complaints every time I return to California, from my pale-skinned, affluent neighbors. They're patting us down now, my friends object, and they're confiscating our contact-lens fluid. They're forcing us to travel with tiny tubes of toothpaste and moving us to wear loafers when usually we'd prefer lace-ups. They're taking away every bottle of water—but only after bottles of water have been shown to be weapons of mass destruction; they're feeling us up with blue gloves, even here in Santa Barbara,* now that they know that underwear can be a lethal weapon.

I listen to their grousing and think that the one thing the 9/11 attacks have achieved, for those of us who spend too much time in airports, is to make suspicion universal; fear and discomfort are equal-opportunity employers now. The world is flat in ways the high-flying global theoreticians don't always acknowledge; these days, even someone from the materially fortunate parts of the world—a man with a ruddy complexion, a woman in a Prada suit—is pulled aside for what is quixotically known as "random screening."

It used to be that the rich corners of the world seemed relatively safe, protected, and the poor ones too dangerous to enter. Now, the logic of the terrorist attacks on New York and Washington has reversed all that. If anything, it's the rich places that feel unsettled. It used to be that officials would alight on people who look like me—from nations of need, in worn jeans, bearing the passports of more prosperous countries—as likely troublemakers; now they realise that even the well born and well dressed may not always be well-intentioned.

I understand why my friends feel aggrieved to be treated as if they came from Nigeria or Mexico or India. But I can't really mourn too much that airports, since 9/11, have become places where everyone may be taken to be guilty until proven innocent. The world is all mixed up these days, and America can no longer claim immunity. On 12 September 2001, *Le Monde*[3] ran its now famous headline: WE ARE ALL AMERICANS. On 12 September 2011, it might more usefully announce: WE ARE ALL INDIANS.

(2011)

20

---

2   *Osama bin Laden*   Leader (1957–2011) of al-Qaeda, an Islamic fundamentalist organization responsible for several major terrorist attacks, including the 11 September 2001 attacks on the World Trade Center and other American targets.

3   *Le Monde*   Major French newspaper.

STEPHEN GREENBLATT

THE ANSWER MAN

*Renowned literary scholar Stephen Greenblatt here explores
the ways in which a now-obscure, two-thousand-year-old Latin
poem has influenced Western culture—an exploration that leads
to a consideration of Greenblatt's own mortality and that of his
mother, and, more generally, to a series of reflections on death
and grief.*

*This essay first appeared as an article in the 8 August 2011 issue
of* The New Yorker. *In the same year Greenblatt published a book-
length examination of the same subject;* The Swerve: How the
World Became Modern *was awarded both the Pulitzer Prize and
the National Book Award for Non-Fiction.*

When I was a student, I used to go at the end of the school year to the Yale
Co-op[1] to see what I could find to read over the summer. I had very
little pocket money, but the bookstore would routinely sell its unwanted titles
for ridiculously small sums. They were jumbled together in bins through which
I would rummage until something caught my eye. On one of my forays, I was
struck by an extremely odd paperback cover, a detail from a painting by the
Surrealist Max Ernst.[2] Under a crescent moon, high above the earth, two pairs
of legs—the bodies were missing—were engaged in what appeared to be an act
of celestial coition. The book, a prose translation of Lucretius'[3] two-thousand-
year-old poem *On the Nature of Things* (*De Rerum Natura*), was marked down
to ten cents, and I bought it as much for the cover as for the classical account
of the material universe.

Ancient physics is not a particularly promising subject for vacation reading, but sometime over the summer I idly picked up the book. The Roman poet

---

1   *Yale Co-op*   Campus store of Yale University in New Haven, Connecticut.

2   *Max Ernst*   German painter and sculptor (1891–1976), pioneer of the Surrealist and
Dada movements in modern art, known among other things for his artistic vision of an
irrational world.

3   *Lucretius*   Titus Lucretius Carus, Roman poet who lived in the first century BCE.

begins his work (in Martin Ferguson Smith's careful rendering) with an ardent hymn to Venus:[4]

> First, goddess, the birds of the air, pierced to the heart with your pow-
> erful shafts, signal your entry. Next wild creatures and cattle bound
> over rich pastures and swim rushing rivers: so surely are they all cap-
> tivated by your charm and eagerly follow your lead. Then you inject
> seductive love into the heart of every creature that lives in the seas and
> mountains and river torrents and bird-haunted thickets, implanting in
> it the passionate urge to reproduce its kind.

Startled by the intensity, I continued, past a prayer for peace, a tribute to the wisdom of the philosopher Epicurus,[5] a resolute condemnation of supersti-tious fears, and into a lengthy exposition of philosophical first principles. I found the book thrilling.

Lucretius, who was born about a century before Christ, was emphatically not our contemporary. He thought that worms were spontaneously generated from wet soil, that earthquakes were the result of winds caught in underground caverns, that the sun circled the earth. But, at its heart, *On the Nature of Things* persuasively laid out what seemed to be a strikingly modern understanding of the world. Every page reflected a core scientific vision—a vision of atoms ran-domly moving in an infinite universe—imbued with a poet's sense of wonder. Wonder did not depend on the dream of an afterlife; in Lucretius it welled up out of a recognition that we are made of the same matter as the stars and the oceans and all things else. And this recognition was the basis for the way he thought we should live—not in fear of the gods but in pursuit of pleasure, in avoidance of pain.

As it turned out, there was a line from this work to modernity, though not a direct one: nothing is ever so simple. There were innumerable forgettings, disappearances, recoveries, and dismissals. The poem was lost, apparently ir-revocably, and then found. This retrieval, after many centuries, is something one is tempted to call a miracle. But the author of the poem in question did not believe in miracles. He thought that nothing could violate the laws of nature. He posited instead what he called a "swerve"—Lucretius' principal word for it was *clinamen*—an unexpected, unpredictable movement of matter.

The poem's rediscovery prompted such a swerve. The cultural shift of the Renaissance* is notoriously difficult to define, but it was characterized, in part,

5

---

4   *Venus*   In Roman mythology, goddess of sex, love, and beauty.

5   *Epicurus*   Greek philosopher (341–270 BCE) who gives his name to the philosophical school of Epicureanism, which holds a materialistic view of the world and perceives happiness and pleasure to be the primary aims of human life.

by a decidedly Lucretian pursuit of beauty and pleasure. The pursuit shaped the dress and the etiquette of courtiers, the language of the liturgy,[6] the design and decoration of everyday objects. It suffused Leonardo da Vinci's scientific and technological explorations, Galileo's vivid dialogues on astronomy,* Francis Bacon's ambitious research projects, and Richard Hooker's[7] theology. Even works that were seemingly unrelated to any aesthetic ambition—Machiavelli's analysis of political strategy, Walter Raleigh's description of Guiana, Robert Burton's[8] encyclopedic account of mental illness—were crafted in such a way as to produce pleasure. And this pursuit, with its denial of Christian asceticism,[9] enabled people to turn away from a preoccupation with angels and demons and to focus instead on things in this world: to conduct experiments without worrying about infringing on God's jealously guarded secrets, to question authorities and challenge received doctrines, to contemplate without terror the death of the soul.

The recovery of *On the Nature of Things* is a story of how the world swerved in a new direction. The agent of change was not a revolution, an implacable army at the gates, or landfall on an unknown continent. When it occurred, nearly six hundred years ago, the key event was muffled and almost invisible, tucked away behind walls in a remote place. A short, genial, cannily alert man in his late thirties reached out one day, took a very old manuscript off a shelf, and saw with excitement what he had discovered. That was all; but it was enough.

By that time, Lucretius' ideas had been out of circulation for centuries. In the Roman Empire, the literacy rate was never high, and after the Sack of Rome,[10] in 410 C.E., it began to plummet. It is possible for a whole culture to turn away from reading and writing. As the empire crumbled and Christianity became ascendant, as cities decayed, trade declined, and an anxious populace scanned

---

6   *liturgy*   Words recited as part of the pattern of Christian worship.

7   *Francis Bacon*   English empiricist philosopher (1561–1626) who argued for the use of the scientific method in understanding the world;   *Richard Hooker*   English priest and theologian (1554–1600) who was crucial to the development of an Anglican theology that emphasised three components—Bible, church, and reason.

8   *Machiavelli*   Niccolò Machiavelli (1469–1527), Italian politician and philosopher most renowned for his work *The Prince* (1513), a treatise on the effective ruling of a state;   *Walter Raleigh*   English poet and explorer (c. 1552–1618) who wrote *The Discovery of Guiana* (1596), an exaggerated description of a supposedly gold-rich land, after traveling to the Venezuelan region in search of El Dorado;   *Robert Burton*   English scholar (1577–1640) known for *The Anatomy of Melancholy* (1621).

9   *asceticism*   Strict self-discipline, self-denial, austerity.

10 *Sack of Rome*   Refers to a significant attack on Rome by the Visigoths, marking the first time Rome had been invaded by foreign enemies since 387 BCE.

the horizon for barbarian armies, the ancient system of education fell apart. What began as downsizing went on to wholesale abandonment. Schools closed, libraries and academies shut their doors, professional grammarians and teachers of rhetoric found themselves out of work, scribes were no longer given manuscripts to copy. There were more important things to worry about than the fate of books. Lucretius' poem, so incompatible with any cult of the gods, was attacked, ridiculed, burned, or ignored, and, like Lucretius himself, eventually forgotten.

The idea of pleasure and beauty that the work advanced was forgotten with it. Theology provided an explanation for the chaos of the Dark Ages:* human beings were by nature corrupt. Inheritors of the sin of Adam and Eve,* they richly deserved every miserable catastrophe that befell them. God cared about human beings, just as a father cared about his wayward children, and the sign of that care was anger. It was only through pain and punishment that a small number could find the narrow gate to salvation. A hatred of pleasure-seeking, a vision of God's providential rage, and an obsession with the afterlife: these were death knells[11] of everything Lucretius represented.

By chance, copies of *On the Nature of Things* somehow made it into a few   10
monastery libraries, places that had buried, seemingly forever, the principled pursuit of pleasure. By chance, a monk laboring in a scriptorium[12] somewhere or other in the ninth century copied the poem before it moldered away. And, by chance, this copy escaped fire and flood and the teeth of time for some five hundred years until, one day in 1417, it came into the hands of a man who proudly called himself Poggius Florentinus, Poggio the Florentine.

Poggio was, among other things, famous for the elegance of his script and for writing the best-known jokebook of its age, a chronicle of cynical tricksters, bawdy friars, unfaithful wives, and foolish husbands. He had served a succession of Roman Pontiffs as a scriptor—that is, a writer of official documents in the Papal bureaucracy—and, through adroitness and cunning, he had risen to the coveted position of Apostolic Secretary.[13] He had access, as the very word "secretary" suggests, to the Pope's secrets. But above all he was a book hunter, perhaps the greatest of his kind.

Italians had been obsessed with book hunting ever since the poet and scholar Petrarch brought glory on himself around 1330 by piecing together

---

11   *death knells*   Bells that toll to mark a death.

12   *scriptorium*   Room set aside for the copying of manuscripts.

13   *Pontiffs*   Popes. The four popes for whom Poggio worked during this period were Boniface IX, Innocent VII, Gregory XII, and Antipope John XXIII; *Apostolic Secretary*   Position in which Poggio would copy down the pope's words and correspondences.

Livy's monumental *History of Rome* and finding forgotten masterpieces by Cicero and Propertius.[14] Petrarch's achievement had inspired others to seek out lost classics that had been lying unread, often for centuries. The recovered texts were copied, edited, commented upon, and eagerly exchanged, conferring distinction on those who had found them and forming the basis for what became known as the "study of the humanities." The "humanists," as those who were devoted to this study were called, knew from carefully poring over the texts that had survived from classical Rome that many once famous books or parts of books were still missing.

As a humanist, Poggio had quite a few accomplishments. He uncovered an epic poem on the struggle between Rome and Carthage; the works of an ancient literary critic who had flourished during Nero's reign and had written notes and glosses on classical authors; another critic who quoted extensively from lost epics written in imitation of Homer; a grammarian who wrote a treatise on spelling; a large fragment of a hitherto unknown history of the Roman Empire written by a high-ranking officer in the imperial Army, Ammianus Marcellinus.[15] His salvaging of the complete text of the rhetorician Quintilian changed the curriculum of law schools and universities throughout Europe, and his discovery of Vitruvius's[16] treatise on architecture transformed the way buildings were designed. But it was in January, 1417, when Poggio found himself in a monastery library, that he made his greatest discovery. He put his hands on a long poem whose author he may have recalled seeing mentioned in other ancient works: "T. LUCRETI CARI DE RERUM NATURA."

On the Nature of Things, by Titus Lucretius Carus, is not an easy read. Totalling seventy-four hundred lines, it is written in hexameters, the standard

---

14 *Petrarch* Francesco Petrarca (1304–74), Italian poet and intellectual, often called the father of Humanism; *Livy* Titus Livius (c. 59 BCE–17 CE), Roman historian whose *History of Rome* covers history from the legend of Rome's foundation to Livy's own era; *Cicero* Marcus Tullius Cicero (106–43 BCE), Roman politician, orator, and philosopher; *Propertius* Sextus Propertius (c. 55–c. 16 BCE), Roman elegiac poet.

15 *the struggle ... Carthage* I.e. the Punic Wars, a massive series of wars fought from 264–146 BCE between Rome and Carthage, resulting from a conflict of interests between the growing Roman Republic and the then-powerful Carthaginian Empire. Rome's ultimate victory was a key factor in its establishment as the dominant power in the region; *Nero* Emperor of Rome from 54–68 CE, often remembered as a tyrant; *Homer* Author of the ancient Greek epic poems *The Illiad* and *The Odyssey*; *Ammianus Marcellinus* Writer of a major history of Rome, of which only the final eighteen books, covering the period from 353–378 CE, survive.

16 *Quintilian* Marcus Fabius Quintilianus (c. 35–c. 100 CE), who exercised an important influence on literary criticism and educational theory; *Vitruvius* Marcus Vitruvius Pollio (first century BCE), Roman architect and engineer whose *De architectura* (On Architecture) exercised a profound influence during the Renaissance.

unrhymed six-beat lines in which Latin poets like Virgil and Ovid,[17] imitating Homer's Greek, cast their epic poetry. Divided into six untitled books, the poem yokes together moments of intense lyrical beauty; philosophical meditations on religion, pleasure, and death; and scientific theories of the physical world, the evolution of human societies, the perils and joys of sex, and the nature of disease. The language is often knotty and difficult, the syntax complex, and the over-all intellectual ambition astoundingly high.

The stuff of the universe, Lucretius proposed, is an infinite number of atoms moving randomly through space, like dust motes in a sunbeam, colliding, hooking together, forming complex structures, breaking apart again, in a ceaseless process of creation and destruction. There is no escape from this process. When we look up at the night sky and marvel at the numberless stars, we are not seeing the handiwork of the gods or a crystalline sphere. We are seeing the same material world of which we are a part and from whose elements we are made. There is no master plan, no divine architect, no intelligent design. Nature restlessly experiments, and we are simply one among the innumerable results: "We are all sprung from celestial seed; all have that same father, from whom our fostering mother earth receives liquid drops of water, and then teeming brings forth bright corn and luxuriant trees and the race of mankind, brings forth all the generations of wild beasts, providing food with which all nourish their bodies and lead a sweet life and beget their offspring."

All things, including the species to which we belong, have evolved over vast stretches of time. The evolution is random, though in the case of living organisms it involves a principle of natural selection.* That is, species that are suited to survive and to reproduce successfully endure, at least for a time; those which are not so well suited die off quickly. Other species existed and vanished before we came onto the scene; our kind, too, will vanish one day. Nothing—from our own species to the sun—lasts forever. Only the atoms are immortal.

In a universe so constituted, Lucretius argued, it is absurd to think that the earth and its inhabitants occupy a central place, or that the world was purpose-built to accommodate human beings: "The child, like a sailor cast forth by the cruel waves, lies naked upon the ground, speechless, in need of every kind of vital support, as soon as nature has spilt him forth with throes from his mother's womb into the regions of light." There is no reason to set

15

_____

17 *Virgil* Roman poet (70–19 BCE) known especially for his epic poem *The Aeneid*, which chronicles the legendary beginnings of Rome; *Ovid* Roman poet (43 BCE–17 CE) best known for his love poetry and the *Metamorphoses*, a collection of mythological poetry linked by the theme of metamorphosis.

humans apart from other animals, no hope of bribing or appeasing the gods, no place for religious fanaticism, no call for ascetic self-denial, no justification for dreams of limitless power or perfect security, no rationale for wars of conquest or self-aggrandizement, no possibility of triumphing over nature. Instead, he wrote, human beings should conquer their fears, accept the fact that they themselves and all the things they encounter are transitory, and embrace the beauty and the pleasure of the world.

Almost nothing is known about the poem's author, except for a brief biographical sketch by St. Jerome,[18] the great fourth-century Church Father. In the entry for 94 B.C.E., Jerome noted: "Titus Lucretius, poet, is born. After a love-philtre[19] had turned him mad, and he had written, in the intervals of his insanity, several books which Cicero revised, he killed himself by his own hand in the forty-fourth year of his age." These lurid details have shaped all subsequent representations of Lucretius, including a celebrated Victorian poem in which Tennyson[20] imagined the voice of the mad, suicidal philosopher tormented by erotic fantasies.

Modern scholarship suggests that Jerome's biographical claims, written more than four centuries after the poet's death, should be regarded with skepticism. Lucretius' personal life remains a mystery that no one at this distance is likely to solve. It is possible, however, to know something about his intellectual biography. *On the Nature of Things* is clearly the work of a disciple who is transmitting ideas that had been developed in Greece centuries earlier. Epicurus was Lucretius' philosophical messiah,* and his vision may be traced to a single incandescent idea: that everything that has ever existed and everything that will ever exist is put together out of what the Roman poet called "the seeds of things," indestructible building blocks, irreducibly small in size, unimaginably vast in number. The Greeks had a word for these invisible building blocks, things that, as they conceived them, could not be divided any further: atoms.

20   The notion of atoms was only a dazzling speculation; there was no way to get any empirical proof* and wouldn't be for more than two thousand years.[21] But Epicurus used this conjecture to argue that there are no supercategories of matter, no hierarchy of elements. Heavenly bodies are not divine beings, nor

---

18   *St. Jerome*   Jerome's asceticism and theology profoundly influenced Christianity in the Middle Ages.

19   *love-philtre*   Love potion.

20   *Tennyson*   Alfred, Lord Tennyson (1809–92). The poem alluded to is "Lucretius" (1868).

21   *there was no way ... two thousand years*   During the nineteenth century, numerous empirical scientific observations were made, perhaps most notably those of John Dalton, which could be explained only by the existence of the atom.

do they move through the void under the guidance of gods. And, though the natural order is unimaginably vast and complex, it is nonetheless possible to understand something of its basic constitutive elements and its universal laws. Indeed, such understanding is one of life's deepest pleasures.

Pleasure is perhaps the key to comprehending the powerful impact of Epicurus' philosophy. Epicurus' enemies—and the Church especially—seized upon his celebration of pleasure and invented malicious stories about his supposed debauchery, taking note of his unusual inclusion of women as well as men among his followers. He "vomited twice a day from overindulgence," in one account, and spent a fortune on feasting. In reality, he seems to have lived a conspicuously simple and frugal life. "Send me a little pot of cheese," he once wrote to a friend, "that, when I like, I may fare sumptuously." It is impossible to live pleasurably, one of his disciples wrote, "without living prudently and honorably and justly, and also without living courageously and temperately and magnanimously, and without making friends, and without being philanthropic."*

This philosophy of pleasure, at once passionate, scientific, and visionary, radiated from almost every line of Lucretius' poetry. Even a quick glance at the first few pages of the manuscript would have convinced Poggio that he had discovered something remarkable. What he could not have grasped, without carefully reading through the work, was that he was unleashing something that threatened the whole structure of his intellectual universe. Had he understood this threat, he might have said, as Freud supposedly said to Jung,[22] when they sailed into New York Harbor, "Don't they know we are bringing them the plague?"

There are moments, rare and powerful, in which a writer, long vanished, seems to stand in your presence and speak to you directly, as if he bore a message meant for you above all others. When I first read *On the Nature of Things*, it struck such a chord within me. The core of Lucretius' poem is a profound, therapeutic meditation on the fear of death, and that fear dominated my childhood. It was not fear of my own death that so troubled me; I had the usual child's intimation of immortality.[23] It was, rather, my mother's absolute certainty that she was destined for an early death.

My mother was not afraid of the afterlife: like most Jews, she had only a hazy sense of what might lie beyond the grave,* and she gave it very little

---

22　*Freud ... Jung*　Sigmund Freud, founder of psychoanalytic theory, and Carl Jung, Freud's friend and later founder of analytical psychology. Freud traveled with Jung to Clark University to give a series of lectures in 1909.

23　*intimation of immortality*　Alludes to William Wordsworth's poem *Ode: Intimations of Immortality* (1815);　*intimation*　Subtle expression or hint.

thought. It was death itself—simply ceasing to be—that terrified her. As far back as I can remember, she brooded obsessively on the imminence of her end, invoking it again and again, especially at moments of parting. My life was full of extended, operatic scenes of farewell. When she went with my father from Boston to New York for the weekend, when I went off to summer camp, and even—when things were especially hard for her—when I simply left the house for school, she clung tightly to me, speaking of her fragility and of the distinct possibility that I would never see her again. If we walked somewhere together, she would frequently come to a halt, as if she were about to keel over. Sometimes she would show me a vein pulsing in her neck and, taking my finger, make me feel it for myself, the sign of her heart dangerously racing.

25   She must have been in her late thirties when my own memories of her fears begin, and those fears evidently went back much further in time. They seem to have taken root about a decade before my birth, when her younger sister, only sixteen years old, died of strep throat. This event—one all too familiar before the introduction of penicillin*—was still an open wound: my mother spoke of it constantly, weeping quietly, and making me read and reread the poignant letters that her sister had written through the course of her fatal illness.

I understood early on that my mother's "heart"—the palpitations that brought her and everyone around her to a halt—was a life strategy. It was a way to express both anger ("You see how upset you have made me") and love ("You see how I am still doing everything for you, even though my heart is about to break"). It was an acting out, a rehearsal, of the extinction that she feared. It was, above all, a way to compel attention from my father, my brother, and me, and to demand our love. But this understanding did not make its effect upon my childhood significantly less intense: I loved my mother and dreaded losing her. I was hardly equipped to untangle psychological strategy from dangerous symptom. (I don't imagine that she was, either.) And, as a child, I had no means to gauge the weirdness of this constant harping on impending death and this freighting of every farewell with finality.

As it turned out, my mother lived to a month shy of her ninetieth birthday. She was still in her fifties when I encountered *On the Nature of Things*. By then my dread of her dying had become entwined with a painful perception that she had blighted much of her life—and cast a shadow on my own—in the service of her obsessive fear. Lucretius' words therefore rang out with a terrible clarity: "Death is nothing to us." His lines (here in a translation by the seventeenth-century poet John Dryden) went right to the heart of her anxiety and my own:

So, when our mortal frame shall be disjoin'd,
The lifeless lump uncoupled from the mind,
From sense of grief and pain we shall be free;
We shall not feel, because we shall not be.
Though earth in seas, and seas in heaven were lost,
We should not move, we only should be toss'd.
Nay, e'en suppose when we have suffer'd fate
The soul should feel in her divided state,
What's that to us? for we are only we,
While souls and bodies in one frame agree.
Nay, though our atoms should revolve by chance,
And matter leap into the former dance;
Though time our life and motion could restore,
And make our bodies what they were before,
What gain to us would all this bustle bring?
The new-made man would be another thing.

To spend your existence in the grip of anxiety about death, Lucretius wrote, is folly. It is a sure way to let your life slip from you incomplete and unenjoyed. And, in so arguing, he gave voice to a thought I had not yet quite allowed myself to articulate: to inflict this anxiety on others is manipulative and cruel.

When Lucretius' poem returned to circulation in 1417, it seems to have struck some early readers with the same personal intensity—the sense of direct address across an abyss—that I experienced. But, of course, the issues were vastly different. To people haunted by images of the bleeding Christ,* gripped by a terror of Hell, and obsessed with escaping the purgatorial[24] fires of the afterlife, Lucretius offered a vision of divine indifference. There was no after-life, no system of rewards and punishments meted out from on high. Gods, by virtue of being gods, could not possibly be concerned with the doings of human beings. One simple name for the plague that Lucretius brought, and a charge frequently levelled against him then and since, is atheism.

Some six or seven decades after Poggio returned the poem to circulation, atomism was viewed as a serious threat to Christianity. Atomist books were burned; the clergy in Florence prohibited the reading of Lucretius in schools. The sense of threat intensified when Protestants mounted their assault on Catholic doctrine. That assault did not depend on atomism—Luther and Zwingli and Calvin were scarcely Epicureans—but for the militant, embattled forces of

30

---

24 *purgatorial* Refers to the Christian concept of Purgatory, a transitional state after physical death in which one's forgiven sins are punished and one's soul is purified for entry into heaven.

the Counter-Reformation[25] it was as if the resurgence of ancient materialism had opened a dangerous second front. Indeed, atomism seemed to offer the Reformers access to an intellectual weapon of mass destruction. The Church was fiercely determined not to allow anyone to lay hands on this weapon, and its ideological arm, the Inquisition,[26] was alerted to detect the telltale signs of proliferation.

Poems are difficult to silence. At the time that the Church was attempting to suppress the text, a young Florentine was copying out for himself the whole of *On the Nature of Things*. He was too cunning to mention the work directly in the famous books he went on to write. But the handwriting was conclusively identified in 1961: the copy was made by Niccolò Machiavelli. Thomas More[27] engaged with Epicureanism more openly in his most famous work, *Utopia*, in which the inhabitants of his imaginary land are convinced that "either the whole or the most part of human happiness" lies in the pursuit of pleasure. His use of the philosophy for the population of this alien island showed that the ideas recovered by the humanists seemed compellingly vital and at the same time still utterly weird. Reinjected into the intellectual bloodstream of Europe after long centuries, they were, in effect, voices from another world, a world as different as Vespucci's Brazil[28] was from England.

But the poem spread, and, as it did, its ideas filtered into popular culture. On the London stage in the mid-fifteen-nineties, Mercutio teased Romeo with this fantastical description of Queen Mab:[29]

> She is the fairies' midwife, and she comes
> In shape no bigger than an agate stone
> On the forefinger of an alderman,
> Drawn with a team of little atomi
> Athwart men's noses as they lie asleep.

---

25 *Luther ... Calvin*   Martin Luther, Huldrych Zwingli, and John Calvin, leading figures of various branches of the Protestant Reformation, started by Luther in 1517;   *Counter-Reformation*   Catholic response to the Protestant Reformation, initiated by the Council of Trent under Pope Paul III in 1545.

26 *Inquisition*   Group of institutions, established by the Catholic Church during the Middle Ages and greatly expanded by the time of the Reformation, designed to combat heresy.

27 *Thomas More*   English political figure, philosopher, and humanist (1478–1535).

28 *Vespucci's Brazil*   In 1499, Florentine explorer Amerigo Vespucci was the first European to call the Americas a "New World."

29 *Mercutio ... Queen Mab*   Romeo and Mercutio are characters in William Shakespeare's tragic play *Romeo and Juliet* (1597), from which the following lines are excerpted.

"A team of little atomi": Shakespeare expected that his audience would immediately understand what Mercutio was comically conjuring. That is interesting in itself, and still more interesting in the context of a tragedy that broods upon the compulsive power of desire in a world whose main characters conspicuously abjure* any prospect of life after death:

> Here, here will I remain
> With worms that are thy chambermaids. O, here
> Will I set up my everlasting rest.

The author of *Romeo and Juliet* shared his interest in Lucretian materialism with Spenser, Donne,* Bacon, and others. He could have discussed it with his fellow-playwright Ben Jonson, whose own signed copy of *On the Nature of Things* has survived and is today in the Houghton Library, at Harvard. And he certainly would have encountered Lucretius in one of his favorite books: Montaigne's *Essays*.

The *Essays*, first published in 1580, contain almost a hundred direct quotations from *On the Nature of Things*. But, beyond any particular passage, there is a profound affinity between Lucretius and Montaigne. Montaigne shared Lucretius' contempt for a morality enforced by nightmares of the afterlife; he clung to the importance of his own senses and the evidence of the material world; he intensely disliked ascetic self-punishment and violence against the flesh; he treasured inward freedom and contentment. In grappling with the fear of death, in particular, he was influenced by Lucretian materialism. He once saw a man die, he recalled, who complained bitterly in his last moments that destiny was preventing him from finishing the book he was writing. The absurdity of the regret, in Montaigne's view, is best conveyed by lines from Lucretius: "But this they fail to add: that after you expire / Not one of all these things will fill you with desire." As for himself, Montaigne wrote, "I want death to find me planting my cabbages, but careless of death, and still more of my unfinished garden."

By the seventeenth century, the lure of the poem was too great to contain. The brilliant French astronomer, philosopher, and priest Pierre Gassendi devoted himself to an ambitious attempt to reconcile Epicureanism and Christianity, and one of his most remarkable students, the playwright Molière, undertook to produce a verse translation of *De Rerum Natura* (which does not, unfortunately, survive). In England, the wealthy diarist John Evelyn translated the first book of Lucretius' poem, and Isaac Newton* declared himself an atomist. By the following century, Thomas Jefferson* owned at least five Latin editions of *De Rerum Natura*, along with translations of the poem into English, Italian, and French. To a correspondent who wanted to know his philosophy of life, Jefferson wrote, "I too am an Epicurean."

35

What lay beyond the horizon were the astonishing empirical observations and experimental proofs of the intuitions of ancient atomism. In the nineteenth century, when Charles Darwin set out to solve the mystery of the origin of species, he did not have to draw on Lucretius' vision of an entirely natural, unplanned process of creation and destruction, renewed by sexual reproduction. That vision had directly influenced the evolutionary theories of Darwin's grandfather Erasmus Darwin, but Charles could base his arguments on his own work in the Galápagos and elsewhere. So, too, when Einstein wrote of atoms, his thought rested on experimental and mathematical science, not upon ancient philosophical speculation. But that speculation, as Einstein acknowledged, had led the way to the proofs upon which modern atomism depends. That the ancient poem can now be safely left unread, that the drama of its loss and recovery can fade into oblivion—these are the greatest signs of Lucretius' absorption into modern thought.

The manuscript that Poggio found in 1417 has itself been lost to time—its letters perhaps scraped away and the parchment recycled for a more pious purpose. The crucial conduit through which the ancient poem, all but dormant for a thousand years before the humanist encountered it, returned to circulation was an elegant copy prepared by Poggio's wealthy bibliophile friend Niccolò Niccoli.[30] Niccoli bequeathed his valuable collection to Florence, and today his Lucretius manuscript is preserved in the cool gray-and-white Laurentian Library that Michelangelo designed for the Medici.* Labelled "Codex[31] Laurentianus 35.30," it is a modest volume, bound in fading, tattered red leather inlaid with metal, a chain attached to the bottom of the back cover. There is little to distinguish it physically from many other manuscripts in the collection, apart from the fact that a reader is given latex gloves to wear when it is delivered to the desk.

My gloved hands trembled with excitement recently when I held it and looked at its elegant lines. Many years have passed since I picked up the ten-cent paperback from the bin in New Haven. My mother has been gone for more than a decade, cruelly weaned of her fear of death by the slow asphyxiation of congestive heart failure. My father, blessed with a quicker parting, is long dead as well, along with the whole crowded generation of aunts and uncles who seemed at one point to be arrayed as a formidable bulwark* against my own extinction. Of necessity, I have taken in the significance of one of the

---

30 *Niccolò Niccoli* Though born to an extremely wealthy family, Niccoli's wealth was in decline by the time he knew Poggio, and he nevertheless dedicated most of his life not to securing that family fortune through civic pursuits but rather to pursuing beauty and the relics of antiquity.

31 *Codex* Refers to the book format of numerous pages fixed to a single edge and bound by a cover, as opposed, for instance, to the older format of the scroll.

celebrated aphorisms* of Lucretius' master, Epicurus: "Against other things it is possible to obtain security, but when it comes to death we human beings all live in an unwalled city."

I have taken in, as well, much that pulls against Lucretius' account of the nature of things. In a secular, skeptical culture, it is not a sizable consolation to know that there is no afterlife. There may be some reassurance in realizing that the dead cannot possibly miss the living, but, as I've learned, that realization does not free the living from missing the dead. Did the ancient poet not experience this pain or think it worth addressing? Anyone who thought, as Lucretius did, that it was a particular pleasure to gaze from shore at a ship foundering in wild seas or to stand on a height and behold armies clashing on a plain— "not because any man's troubles are a delectable joy, but because to perceive what ills you are free from yourself is pleasant"—is not someone I can find an entirely companionable soul. I am, rather, with Shakespeare's Miranda,[32] who, harrowed by the vision of a shipwreck, cries, "O, I have suffered / With those I saw suffer!" There is something disturbingly cold in Lucretius' account of pleasure, an account that leads him to advise those who are suffering from the pangs of intense love to reduce their anguish by taking many lovers.

All the same, in the great Laurentian Library, surrounded by the achievements of Renaissance Florence, I felt the full force of what this ancient Roman poet had bequeathed to the world, a tortuous trail that led from the celebration of Venus, past broken columns, high-domed churches, and inquisitorial fires, toward Jefferson, Darwin, and Einstein. And I registered, too, what Lucretius had given to me personally: the means to elude the suffocating grasp of my mother's fears and the encouragement to take deep pleasure in my brief time on the shores of light.[33]

(2011)

---

32 *Miranda* Character in Shakespeare's play *The Tempest* (1611).

33 *shores of light* Lucretius uses this phrase repeatedly as a metaphor for life itself.

ETHAN KROSS, PHILIPPE VERDUYN, EMRE
DEMIRALP, JIYOUNG PARK, DAVID SEUNGJAE LEE,
NATALIE LIN, HOLLY SHABLACK, JOHN JONIDES,
OSCAR YBARRA

from FACEBOOK USE PREDICTS DECLINES IN SUBJECTIVE WELL-BEING[1] IN YOUNG ADULTS

Ethan Kross is a social psychologist at the University of Michigan. Together with Philippe Verduyn, a researcher at the University of Leuven, as well as other colleagues at the University of Michigan, Kross conducted the study printed below, which examines how Facebook use influences young adults' self-reported happiness over time. It was originally published in PLoS ONE, *an online science journal.*

ABSTRACT

Over 500 million people interact daily with Facebook. Yet, whether Facebook use influences subjective well-being over time is unknown. We addressed this issue using experience-sampling, the most reliable method for measuring in-vivo[2] behavior and psychological experience. We text-messaged people five times per day for two-weeks to examine how Facebook use influences the two components of subjective well-being: how people feel moment-to-moment and how satisfied they are with their lives. Our results indicate that Facebook

---

1   *SUBJECTIVE WELL-BEING*   Refers to how people experience their quality of life and includes both emotional reactions (affective well-being) and cognitive judgments (cognitive well-being).

    NB **To distinguish notes added for this anthology from the authors' note numbers referring to their list of references at the end of the article, subscript numbers have been used here for the latter.**

2   *experience-sampling* Method of gathering experimental data by requiring participants to provide regular updates about their behavior and feelings; *in vivo* Occurring within a complete, live organism.

use predicts negative shifts on both of these variables over time. The more people used Facebook at one time point, the worse they felt the next time we text-messaged them; the more they used Facebook over two-weeks, the more their life satisfaction levels declined over time. Interacting with other people "directly" did not predict these negative outcomes. They were also not moderated by the size of people's Facebook networks, their perceived supportiveness, motivation for using Facebook, gender, loneliness, self-esteem, or depression. On the surface, Facebook provides an invaluable resource for fulfilling the basic human need for social connection. Rather than enhancing well-being, however, these findings suggest that Facebook may undermine it.

INTRODUCTION

O nline social networks are rapidly changing the way human beings interact. Over a billion people belong to Facebook, the world's largest online social network, and over half of them log in daily.[1] Yet, no research has examined how interacting with Facebook influences subjective well-being over time. Indeed, a recent article that examined every peer-reviewed publication and conference proceeding on Facebook between 1/2005 and 1/2012 (412 in total) did not reveal a single study that examined how using this technology influences subjective well-being over time.[2, [See also Supporting Information 1 at the end of the article.]]

Subjective well-being is one of the most highly studied variables in the behavioral sciences. Although significant in its own right, it also predicts a range of consequential benefits including enhanced health and longevity.[3-5] Given the frequency of Facebook usage, identifying how interacting with this technology influences subjective well-being represents a basic research challenge that has important practical implications.

This issue is particularly vexing because prior research provides mixed clues about how Facebook use should influence subjective well-being. Whereas some cross-sectional research reveals positive associations between online social network use (in particular Facebook) and well-being,[6] other work reveals the opposite.[7,8] Still other work suggests that the relationship between Facebook use and well-being may be more nuanced and potentially influenced by multiple factors including number of Facebook friends, perceived supportiveness of one's online network, depressive symptomatology,* loneliness, and self-esteem.[9,10,11]

So, how does Facebook usage influence subjective well-being over time? The cross-sectional approach[3] used in previous studies makes it im-

5

---

3   *cross-sectional approach*   Approach to gathering experimental data by observing an entire group at a specific time.

possible to know. We addressed this issue by using experience-sampling, the most reliable method for measuring in-vivo behavior and psychological experience over time.[12] We text-messaged participants five times per day for 14-days. Each text-message contained a link to an online survey, which participants completed using their smartphones. We performed lagged analyses[4] on participants' responses, as well as their answers to the Satisfaction With Life Questionnaire (SWLS),[13] which they completed before and immediately following the 14-day experience-sampling period, to examine how interacting with Facebook influences the two components of subjective well-being: how people feel ("affective" well-being) and how satisfied they are with their lives ("cognitive" well-being).[14,15] This approach allowed us to take advantage of the relative timing of participants' natural Facebook behavior and psychological states to draw inferences about their likely causal sequence.[16-19]

METHODS

Participants

Eighty-two people (M_{age} = 19.52, SD_{age} = 2.17; 53 females;[5] 60.5% European American, 28.4% Asian, 6.2% African American, and 4.9% other) were recruited for a study on Facebook through flyers posted around Ann Arbor, Michigan. Participants needed a Facebook account and a touch-screen smartphone to qualify for the study. They received $20 and were entered into a raffle to receive an iPad2 for participating.

Ethics Statement

The University of Michigan Institutional Review Board approved this study. Informed written consent was obtained from all participants prior to participation.

Materials and Procedure

PHASE 1

Participants completed a set of questionnaires, which included the SWLS (M = 4.96, SD = 1.17), Beck Depression Inventory[20] (M = 9.02, SD = 7.20), the Rosenberg Self-Esteem Scale[21] (M = 30.40, SD = 4.96), and the Social Provision Scale[22] (M = 3.55, SD = .34), which we modified to assess perceptions of Facebook support. We also assessed participants' motivation for using

---

4   *lagged analyses*   Identification of patterns in data collected over time.

5   *M* Mean;   *SD* Standard Deviation, a number indicating the extent of difference within a group.

Facebook by asking them to indicate whether they use Facebook "to keep in touch with friends (98% answered yes)," "to find new friends (23% answered yes)," "to share good things with friends (78% answered yes)," "to share bad things with friends (36% answered yes)," "to obtain new information (62% answered yes)," or "other: please explain (17% answered yes)." Examples of other reasons included chatting with others, keeping in touch with family, and facilitating schoolwork and business.

PHASE 2

Participants were text-messaged 5 times per day between 10am and midnight over 14-days. Text-messages occurred at random times within 168-minute windows per day. Each text-message contained a link to an online survey, which asked participants to answer five questions using a slider scale: (1) How do you feel right now? (*very positive* [0] to *very negative* [100]; $M = 37.47$, $SD = 25.88$); (2) How worried are you right now? (*not at all* [0] to *a lot* [100]; $M = 44.04$, $SD = 30.42$); (3) How lonely do you feel right now? (*not at all* [0] to *a lot* [100]; $M = 27.61$, $SD = 26.13$); (4) How much have you used Facebook since the last time we asked? (*not at all* [0] to *a lot* [100]; $M = 33.90$, $SD = 30.48$); (5) How much have you interacted with other people "directly" since the last time we asked? (*not at all* [0] to *a lot* [100]; $M = 64.26$, $SD = 31.11$). When the protocol for answering these questions was explained, interacting with other people "directly" was defined as face-to-face or phone interactions. An experimenter carefully walked participants through this protocol to ensure that they understood how to answer each question and fulfill the study requirements.

Participants always answered the affect question first. Next the worry and loneliness questions were presented in random order. The Facebook use and direct social interaction questions were always administered last, again in random order. Our analyses focused primarily on affect (rather than worry and loneliness) because this affect question is the way "affective well-being" is typically operationalized.

10

PHASE 3

Participants returned to the laboratory following Phase 2 to complete another set of questionnaires, which included the SWLS ($M = 5.13$, $SD = 1.26$) and the Revised UCLA Loneliness Scale$_{23}$ ($M = 1.69$, $SD = .46$). Participants' number of Facebook friends ($M = 664.25$, $SD = 383.64$) was also recorded during this session from participants' Facebook accounts. [See Supporting Information 2 at the end of the article.]

RESULTS

Attrition and compliance

Three participants did not complete the study. As the methods section notes, participants received a text message directing them to complete a block of five questions once every 168 minutes on average (the text message was delivered randomly within this 168-minute window). A response to any question within a block was considered "compliant" if it was answered *before* participants received a subsequent text-message directing them to complete the next block of questions. Participants responded to an average of 83.6% of text-messages (range: 18.6%–100%). Following prior research,[24] we pruned the data[6] by excluding all of the data from two participants who responded to <33% of the texts, resulting in 4,589 total observations. The results did not change substantively when additional cutoff rates were used.

Analyses overview

We examined the relationship between Facebook use and affect using multilevel analyses to account for the nested data structure.[7] Specifically, we examined whether T_2[8] affect (i.e., How do you feel *right now?*) was predicted by T_{1-2} Facebook use (i.e., How much have you used Facebook *since the last time we asked?*), controlling for T_1 affect at level-1 of the model (between-day lags were excluded). Note that although this analysis assesses Facebook use at T_2, the question refers to usage between T_1 and T_2 (hence the notation T_{1-2}). This analysis allowed us to explore whether Facebook use during the time period separating T_1 and T_2 predicted changes in affect over this time span....

The relationship between mean Facebook use and life satisfaction was assessed using OLS regressions[9] because these data were not nested. Both

---

6   *pruned the data*   Removed unnecessary data.

7   *multilevel analyses*   Methods of analyzing data which recognize that there are multiple sources which may explain variations in data. Multilevel analyses are used specifically in research where data may be classified and organized at several levels;   *nested data structure*   Describes data that is obtained from multiple observations of individuals in particular groups, e.g. students in a particular class, or data that is obtained through repeated observation of the same individual over time.

8   T_2 Refers to "Time $_2$," the moment when the participant receives an online survey to assess "Time $_{1-2}$," the period of Facebook usage beginning from the completion of the previous survey. "Time $_1$" is thus the moment a survey is completed.

9   *OLS regressions*   Ordinary Least Squares regressions, models that calculate the relationship between a dependent variable and an independent variable in order to estimate the boundaries of the variables.

unstandardized (B) and standardized (β) OLS regression coefficients[10] are reported. [Supporting Information 3]

Facebook use and well-being

AFFECTIVE WELL-BEING

We examined whether people's tendency to interact with Facebook during the time period separating two text messages influenced how they felt at T_2, controlling for how they felt at T_1. Nested time-lag analyses indicated that the more people used Facebook the worse they subsequently felt, $B = .08$, $\chi^2 = 28.90$, $p < .0001$.[11] ... The reverse pathway (T_1 Affect predicting T_{1-2} Facebook use, controlling for T_{0-1} Facebook use) was not significant, $B = -.005$, $\chi^2 = .05$, $p = .82$, indicating that people do not use Facebook more or less depending on how they feel. [See Supporting Information 4 and 5 at the end of the article.][...]

COGNITIVE WELL-BEING

To examine how Facebook use influenced "cognitive well-being," we analyzed whether people's average Facebook use over the 14-day period predicted their life satisfaction at the end of the study, controlling for baseline life satisfaction and average emotion levels over the 14-day period. The more participants used Facebook, the more their life satisfaction levels declined over time, $B = -.012$, $\beta = -.124$, $t(73) = -2.39$,[12] $p = .02$....

ALTERNATIVE EXPLANATIONS

An alternative explanation for these results is that any form of social interaction undermines well-being. Because we also asked people to indicate how frequently they interacted with other people "directly" since the last time we text messaged them, we were able to test this idea. Specifically, we repeated each of the aforementioned analyses substituting "direct" social interaction for Facebook use. In contrast to Facebook use, "direct" social interaction did not predict changes in cognitive well-being, $B = -.006$, $\beta = -.059$, $t(73) = 1.04$, $p = .30$, and predicted *increases* (not decreases) in affective well-being, $B = -.15$, $\chi^2 = 65.30$, $p<.0001$. Controlling for direct social interaction did not

---

10 *OLS regression coefficients* Numerical indications of the relationship between two variables.

11 χ^2 Chi squared, used in statistical tests to determine the probability that a set of data reflects a significant relationship between variables; p Probability, here an indication of the likelihood of getting the same experimental results as the ones observed if there were no relationship between the variables being studied.

12 t Variable used in t-tests to calculate the significance of the differences between two sets of data.

substantively alter the significant relationship between Facebook use and affective well-being, $B = .05$, $\chi^2 = 10.78$, $p<.01$.

Another alternative explanation for these results is that people use Facebook when they feel bad (i.e., when they are bored, lonely, worried or otherwise distressed), and feeling bad leads to declines in well-being rather than Facebook use per se. The analyses we reported earlier partially address this issue by demonstrating that affect does not predict changes in Facebook use over time and Facebook use continues to significantly predict declines in life satisfaction over time when controlling for affect. However, because participants also rated how lonely and worried they felt each time we text messaged them, we were able to test this proposal further.

We first examined whether worry or loneliness predicted changes in Facebook use over time (i.e., T_1 worry [or T_1 loneliness] predicting T_{1-2} Facebook use, controlling for T_{0-1} Facebook use). Worry did not predict changes in Facebook use, $B = .04$, $\chi^2 = 2.37$, $p = .12$, but loneliness did, $B = .07$, $\chi^2 = 8.54$, $p<.01$. The more lonely people felt at one time point, the more people used Facebook over time. Given this significant relationship, we next examined whether controlling for loneliness renders the relationship between Facebook use and changes in affective and cognitive well-being non-significant—what one would predict if Facebook use is a proxy for loneliness. This was not the case. Facebook use continued to predict declines in affective well-being, $B = .08$, $\chi^2 = 27.87$, $p<.0001$, and cognitive well-being, $B = -.012$, $\beta = -.126$, $t(72) = 2.34$, $p = .02$, when loneliness was controlled for in each analysis. Neither worry nor loneliness interacted significantly with Facebook use to predict changes in affective or cognitive well-being ($ps>.44$).

MODERATION

20 Next, we examined whether a number of theoretically relevant individual-difference variables[13] including participants' number of Facebook Friends, their perceptions of their Facebook network support, depressive symptoms, loneliness, gender, self-esteem, time of study participation, and motivation for using Facebook (e.g., to find new friends, to share good or bad things, to obtain new information) interacted with Facebook use to predict changes in affective or cognitive well-being. [See Supporting Information 6 at the end of the article.] In no case did we observe any significant interactions ($ps>.16$).

---

13 *individual-difference variables* Variables indicating characteristics that individual participants already possess, which may affect study results but are not controlled by the study.

EXPLORATORY ANALYSES

Although we did not have *a priori* predictions[14] about whether Facebook use and direct social contact would interact to predict changes in affective and cognitive well-being, we nevertheless explored this issue in our final set of analyses. The results of these analyses indicated that Facebook use and direct social contact interacted significantly to predict changes in affective well-being, B = .002, χ^2 = 19.55, p <.0001, but not changes in cognitive well-being, B = .000, β = .129, $t(71)$=.39, p = .70. To understand the meaning of the former interaction, we performed simple slope analyses.[15] These analyses indicated that the relationship between Facebook use and declines in affective well-being increased linearly with direct social contact. Specifically, whereas Facebook use did not predict significant declines in affective well-being when partici-pants experienced low levels of direct social contact (i.e., 1 standard deviation below the sample mean for direct social contact; B = .00, χ^2 = .04, p = .84), it did predict significant declines in well-being when participants experienced moderate levels of direct social contact (i.e., at the sample mean for direct so-cial contact; B = .05, χ^2 = 11.21, p<.001) and high levels of direct social contact (i.e., 1 standard deviation above the sample mean for direct social contact; B = .10, χ^2 = 28.82, p<.0001).

DISCUSSION

Within a relatively short timespan, Facebook has revolutionized the way people interact. Yet, whether using Facebook predicts changes in subjective well-being over time is unknown. We addressed this issue by performing lagged analyses on experience sampled data, an approach that allowed us to take advantage of the relative timing of participants' naturally occurring behaviors and psycho-logical states to draw inferences about their likely causal sequence.[17,18] These analyses indicated that Facebook use predicts declines in the two components of subjective well-being: how people feel moment to moment and how satis-fied they are with their lives.

Critically, we found no evidence to support two plausible alternative in-terpretations of these results. First, interacting with other people "directly" did not predict declines in well-being. In fact, direct social network interactions led people to feel *better* over time. This suggests that Facebook use may constitute a unique form of social network interaction that predicts impoverished well-being. Second, multiple types of evidence indicated that it was not the case that Facebook use led to declines in well-being because people are more likely to

---

14 *a priori predictions* Predictions made before research began.

15 *slope analyses* Analyses showing the incline of the line that would be formed if a set of data were depicted in a graph.

use Facebook when they feel bad—neither affect nor worry predicted Facebook use and Facebook use continued to predict significant declines in well-being when controlling for loneliness (which did predict increases in Facebook use and reductions in emotional well-being).

Would engaging in any solitary activity similarly predict declines in well-being? We suspect that they would not because people often derive pleasure from engaging in some solitary activities (e.g., exercising, reading). Supporting this view, a number of recent studies indicate that people's *perceptions* of social isolation (i.e., how lonely they feel)—a variable that we assessed in this study, which did not influence our results—are a more powerful determinant of well-being than *objective* social isolation.[25] A related question concerns whether engaging in any Internet activity (e.g., email, web surfing) would likewise predict well-being declines. Here too prior research suggests that it would not. A number of studies indicate that whether interacting with the Internet predicts changes in well-being depends on how you use it (i.e., what sites you visit) and who you interact with.[26]

Future research

25   Although these findings raise numerous future research questions, four stand out as most pressing. First, do these findings generalize? We concentrated on young adults in this study because they represent a core Facebook user demographic. However, examining whether these findings generalize to additional age groups is important. Future research should also examine whether these findings generalize to other online social networks. As a recent review of the Facebook literature indicated,[2] "[different online social networks] have varied histories and are associated with different patterns of use, user characteristics, and social functions" (p. 205). Therefore, it is possible that the current findings may not neatly generalize to other online social networks.

Second, what mechanisms underlie the deleterious effects of Facebook usage on well-being? Some researchers have speculated that online social networking may interfere with physical activity, which has cognitive and emotional replenishing effects[27] or trigger damaging social comparisons.[8,28] The latter idea is particularly interesting in light of the significant interaction we observed between direct social contact and Facebook use in this study—i.e., the more people interacted with other people directly, the more strongly Facebook use predicted declines in their affective well-being. If harmful social comparisons explain how Facebook use predicts declines in affective well-being, it is possible that interacting with other people directly either enhances the frequency of such comparisons or magnifies their emotional impact. Examining whether these or other mechanisms explain the relationship between

Facebook usage and well-being is important both from a basic science and practical perspective.

Finally, although the analytic approach we used in this study is useful for drawing inferences about the likely causal ordering of associations between naturally occurring variables, experiments that manipulate Facebook use in daily life are needed to corroborate these findings and establish definitive causal relations. Though potentially challenging to perform—Facebook use prevalence, its centrality to young adult daily social interactions, and addictive properties may make it a difficult intervention target—such studies are important for extending this work and informing future interventions.*

Caveats

Two caveats* are in order before concluding. First, although we observed statistically significant associations between Facebook usage and well-being, the sizes of these effects were relatively "small." This should not, however, undermine their practical significance.[29] Subjective well-being is a multiply determined outcome—it is unrealistic to expect any single factor to powerfully influence it. Moreover, in addition to being consequential in its own right, subjective well-being predicts an array of mental and physical health consequences. Therefore, identifying any factor that systematically influences it is important, especially when that factor is likely to accumulate over time among large numbers of people. Facebook usage would seem to fit both of these criteria.

Second, some research suggests that asking people to indicate how good or bad they feel using a single bipolar scale,* as we did in this study, can obscure interesting differences regarding whether a variable leads people to feel less positive, more negative or both less positive and more negative. Future research should administer two unipolar affect questions to assess positive and negative affect separately to address this issue.

CONCLUDING COMMENT

30

The human need for social connection is well established, as are the benefits that people derive from such connections.[30-34] On the surface, Facebook provides an invaluable resource for fulfilling such needs by allowing people to instantly connect. Rather than enhancing well-being, as frequent interactions with supportive "offline" social networks powerfully do, the current findings demonstrate that interacting with Facebook may predict the opposite result for young adults—it may undermine it.

(2013)

ACKNOWLEDGMENTS: We thank Emily Kean for her assistance running the study and Ozlem Ayduk and Phoebe Ellsworth for their feedback.

AUTHOR CONTRIBUTIONS: Conceived and designed the experiments: EK ED JP DSL NL JJ OY. Performed the experiments: HS NL. Analyzed the data: PV ED. Wrote the paper: EK ED PV JJ OY. Discussed the results and commented on the manuscript: EK PV ED JP DSL NL HS JJ OY.

SUPPORTING INFORMATION:

1: We do not imply that no longitudinal research on Facebook has been performed. Rather, no published work that we are aware of has examined how Facebook influences subjective well-being over time (i.e., how people feel and their life satisfaction).

2: Additional measures were administered during Phases 1 and 2 for other purposes. The measures reported in the MS are those that were theoretically motivated.

3: Raw data are available upon request for replication purposes.

4: We also examined whether T_{0-1} (rather than T_{1-2}) Facebook use influences T_2 affect, controlling for T_1 affect. Nested time-lagged analyses indicated that this was also true, $B = .03$, $\chi^2 = 4.67$, $p = .03$.

5: Some research suggests that affect fluctuates throughout the day. Replicating this work, time of day was related to affective well-being such that people reported feeling better as the day progressed ($B = -1.06$, $\chi^2 = 21.49$, $p < .0001$). Controlling for time of day did not, however, substantively influence any of the results.

6: 98% of participants reported using Facebook to "keep in touch with friends." Therefore, we did not test for moderation with this variable.

REFERENCES:

1. FacebookInformation (2012) Facebook Newsroom Website. Available: http://newsroom.fb.com/content/default.aspx?NewsAreaId=22. Accessed 2012 April 23.

2. Wilson RE, Gosling SD, Graham LT (2012) A Review of Facebook Research in the Social Sciences. Perspect Psychol Sci 7: 203–220.

3. Steptoe A, Wardle J (2011) Positive affect measured using ecological momentary assessment and survival in older men and women. Proc Natl Acad Sci USA 108: 18244–18248. doi: 10.1073/pnas.1110892108.

4. Boehm JK, Peterson C, Kivimaki M, Kubzansky L (2011) A prospective study of positive psychological well-being and coronary heart disease. Health Psychol 30: 259–267. doi: 10.1037/a0023124.

5. Diener E (2011) Happy people live longer: Subjective well-being contributes to health and longevity. Appl Psychol Health Well Being 3: 1–43. doi: 10.1111/j.1758-0854.2010.01045.x.

6. Valenzuela S, Park N, Kee KF (2009) Is There Social Capital in a Social Network Site?: Facebook Use and College Students' Life Satisfaction, Trust, and Participation. J Comput Mediat Commun 14: 875–901. doi: 10.1111/j.1083-6101.2009.01474.x.

7. Huang C (2010) Internet use and psychological well-being: A meta-analysis. Cyberpsychol Behav Soc Netw 13: 241–248.

8. Chou H, Edge N (2012) 'They are happier and having better lives than I am': The impact of using Facebook on perceptions of others' lives. Cyberpsychol Behav Soc Netw 15: 117–120. doi: 10.1089/cyber.2011.0324.

9. Forest AL, Wood JV (2012) When Social Networking Is Not Working: Individuals With Low Self-Esteem Recognize but Do Not Reap the Benefits of Self-Disclosure on Facebook. Psychol Sci 23: 295–302. doi: 10.1177/0956797611429709.

10. Manago AM, Taylor T, Greenfield PM (2012) Me and my 400 friends: The anatomy of college students' Facebook networks, their communication patterns, and well-being. Dev Psychol 48: 369–380. doi: 10.1037/a0026338.

11. Kim J, LaRose R, Peng W (2009) Loneliness as the cause and the effect of problematic Internet use: the relationship between Internet use and psychological well-being. Cyberpsychology & behavior: the impact of the Internet, multimedia and virtual reality on behavior and society 12: 451–455. doi: 10.1089/cpb.2008.0327.

12. Kahneman D, Krueger AB, Schkade DA, Schwarz N, Stone AA (2004) A survey method for characterizing daily life experience: The day reconstruction method. Science 306: 1776–1780. doi: 10.1126/science.1103572.

13. Diener E, Emmons RA, Larsen RJ, Griffin S (1985) The Satisfaction with Life Scale. J Pers Assess 49: 71–74. doi: 10.1207/s15327752jpa4901_13.

14. Kahneman D, Deaton A (2010) High income improves evaluation of life but not emotional well-being. Proc Natl Acad Sci USA 107: 16489–16493. doi: 10.1073/pnas.1011492107.

15. Diener E (1984) Subjective Well-Being. Psychol Bull 95: 542–575. doi: 10.1037/0033-2909.95.3.542.

16. Hofmann W, Vohs KD, Baumeister RF (2012) What people desire, feel conflicted about, and try to resist in everyday life. Psychol Sci doi: 10.1177/0956797612437426.

17. Bolger N, Davis A, Rafaeli E (2003) Diary methods: Capturing life as it is lived. Annu Rev Psychol 54: 579–616. doi: 10.1146/annurev.psych.54.101601.145030.

18. Adam EK, Hawkley LC, Kudielka BM, Cacioppo JT (2006) Day-to-day dynamics of experience–cortisol associations in a population-based sample of older adults. Proc Natl Acad Sci USA 103: 17058–17063. doi: 10.1073/pnas.0605053103.

19. Killingsworth MA, Gilbert DT (2010) A Wandering Mind Is an Unhappy Mind. Science 330: 932–932. doi: 10.1126/science.1192439.

20. Beck AT, Steer RA, Brown GK (1996) BDI-II Manual San Antonio: Harcourt Brace & Company.

21. Rosenberg M (1965) Society and the adolescent self-image. Princeton: Princeton University Press.

22. Cutrona CE (1989) Ratings of social support by adolescents and adult informants: Degree of correspondence and prediction of depressive symptoms. Journal of Personality and Social Psychology 57: 723–730. doi: 10.1037//0022-3514.57.4.723.

23. Russell D, Peplau LA, Cutrona CE (1980) The revised UCLA Loneliness Scale: Concurrent and discriminant validity evidence. J Pers Soc Psychol 39: 472–480. doi: 10.1037//0022-3514.39.3.472.

24. Moberly NJ, Watkins ER (2008) Ruminative self-focus, negative life events, and negative affect. Behav Res Ther 46: 1034–1039. doi: 10.1016/j.brat.2008.06.004.

25. Cacioppo JT, Hawkley LC, Norman GJ, Berntson GG (2011) Social isolation. Ann N Y Acad Sci 1231: 17–22. doi: 10.1111/j.1749-6632.2011.06028.x.

26. Bessiére K, Kiesler S, Kraut R, Boneva BS (2008) Effects of Internet use and social resources on changes in depression. Information, Communication, and Society 11: 47–70.

27. Kaplan S, Berman MG (2010) Directed Attention as a Common Resource for Executive Functioning and Self-Regulation. Perspect Psychol Sci 5: 43–57. doi: 10.1177/1745691609356784.

28. Haferkamp N, Kramer NC (2011) Social Comparison 2.0: Examining the Effects of Online Profiles on Social-Networking Sites. Cyberpsychol Behav Soc Netw 14: 309–314. doi: 10.1089/cyber.2010.0120.

29. Prentice DA, Miller DT (1992) When small effects are impressive. Psychological Bulletin 112: 160–164. doi: 10.1037/0033-2909.112.1.160.

30. Baumeister RF, Leary MR (1995) The need to belong: desire for interpersonal attachments as a fundamental human motivation. Psychol Bull 117: 497–529. doi: 10.1037/0033-2909.117.3.497.

31. Kross E, Berman MG, Mischel W, Smith EE, Wager TD (2011) Social rejection shares somatosensory representations with physical pain. Proc Natl Acad Sci USA 108: 6270–6275. doi: 10.1073/pnas.1102693108.

32. Eisenberger NI, Cole SW (2012) Social neuroscience and health: neurophysiological mechanisms linking social ties with physical health. Nat Neurosci 15: 669–674. doi: 10.1038/nn.3086.

33. House JS, Landis KR, Umberson D (1988) Social relationships and health. Science 241: 540–545. doi: 10.1126/science.3399889.

34. Ybarra O, Burnstein E, Winkielman P, Keller MC, Chan E, et al. (2008) Mental exercising through simple socializing: Social interaction promotes general cognitive functioning. Pers Soc Psychol Bull 34: 248–259. doi: 10.1177/0146167207310454.

FACEBOOK IS BAD FOR YOU: GET A LIFE!

The following article, originally published in The Economist *in 2013, reports on the social psychology study "Facebook Use Predicts Declines in Subjective Well-Being in Young Adults." Like all* Economist *articles, it was published without any attribution of authorship.*

The study in question, by Ethan Kross and colleagues, is also included in this volume.

Those who have resisted the urge to join Facebook will surely feel vindicated when they read the latest research. A study just published by the *Public Library of Science*, conducted by Ethan Kross of the University of Michigan and Philippe Verduyn of Leuven University in Belgium, has shown that the more someone uses Facebook, the less satisfied he is with life.

Past investigations have found that using Facebook is associated with jealousy, social tension, isolation and depression. But these studies have all been "cross-sectional"—in other words, snapshots in time. As such, they risk confusing correlation with causation: perhaps those who spend more time on social media are more prone to negative emotions in the first place. The study conducted by Dr Kross and Dr Verduyn is the first to follow Facebook users for an extended period, to track how their emotions change.

The researchers recruited 82 Facebookers for their study. These volunteers, in their late teens or early 20s, agreed to have their Facebook activity observed for two weeks and to report, five times a day, on their state of mind and their direct social contacts (phone calls and meetings in person with other people). These reports were prompted by text messages, sent between 10am and midnight, asking them to complete a short questionnaire.

When the researchers analysed the results, they found that the more a volunteer used Facebook in the period between two questionnaires, the worse he reported feeling the next time he filled in a questionnaire. Volunteers were also asked to rate their satisfaction with life at the start and the end of the study. Those who used Facebook a lot were more likely to report a decline in satisfaction than those who visited the site infrequently. In contrast, there was a positive association between the amount of direct social contact a volunteer had and how positive he felt. In other words, the more volunteers socialised in the real world, the more positive they reported feeling the next time they filled in the questionnaire.

5   A volunteer's sex had no influence on these findings; nor did the size of his (or her) social network, his stated motivation for using Facebook, his level of loneliness or depression or his self-esteem. Dr Kross and Dr Verduyn therefore conclude that, rather than enhancing well-being, Facebook undermines it.

Their study does not tease out why socialising on Facebook has a different effect from socialising in person. But an earlier investigation, conducted by social scientists at Humboldt University and Darmstadt's Technical University, both in Germany, may have found the root cause. These researchers, who presented their findings at a conference in Leipzig in February, surveyed 584 users of Facebook aged mostly in their 20s. They found that the most common emotion aroused by using Facebook is envy. Endlessly comparing themselves with peers who have doctored their photographs, amplified their achievements and plagiarised their *bons mots*[1] can leave Facebook's users more than a little green-eyed.* Real-life encounters, by contrast, are more WYSIWYG (what you see is what you get).

What neither study proves is whether all this is true only for younger users of Facebook. Older ones may be more mellow, and thus less begrudging of their friends' successes, counterfeit or real. Maybe.

(2013)

---

1   *bons mots*   Clever sayings or witticisms.

DAVID SHIELDS

I CAN'T STOP THINKING THROUGH
WHAT OTHER PEOPLE ARE THINKING

David Shields is an American writer whose work challenges established cultural categories and artistic genres. He questions, for example, whether the traditional form of the novel reflects what it feels like to live in the world today, or whether the twenty-first century would be better served by a form he calls the "anti-novel," built of "scraps." In "I Can't Stop Thinking through What Other People Are Thinking," Shields considers matters of copying, plagiarism, influence, and originality in art, music, and literature. "I Can't Stop Thinking" was originally published in the Summer 2013 edition of the literary magazine New Letters.

Originally, feathers evolved to retain heat; later, they were repurposed for a means of flight. No one ever accuses the descendants of ancient birds of plagiarism for taking heat-retaining feathers and modifying them into wings for flight. In our current system, the original feathers would be copyrighted, and upstart birds would get sued for stealing the feathers for a different use. Almost all famous discoveries (by Darwin, Edison, Einstein,* et al.) were not lightning-bolt epiphanies but were built slowly over time and heavily dependent on the intellectual superstructure of what had come before them. E.g., the commonplace book* was popular among English intellectuals in the seventeenth–nineteenth centuries. These notebooks were a depository for thoughts and quotes and were usually categorised by topic. *Enquire Within upon Everything*, a commercially successful parody of the commonplace book, was published in London in 1890. There's no such thing as originality. Invention and innovation grow out of networks of people and ideas. All life on earth (and by extension, technology) is built upon appropriation and reuse of the pre-existing.

Mixing passages of his own approximately 50/50 with passages from other writers, Cyril Connolly's *The Unquiet Grave* is a cry of mourning about dissolution—of society (WWII), the body (ageing), love (divorce), and literature

("The English language has, in fact, so contracted to our own littleness that it is no longer possible to make a good book out of words alone."). Published with footnotes in the UK and the US, Theodor Adorno's aphoristic masterpiece, *Minima Moralia*, first appeared, in Germany, in 1951, sans* footnotes. What was unexplained art in the German edition became dutiful scholarship when published in England; citation domesticated the work, flattened it, denuded it, robbed it of its excitement, risk, danger. Rather like Werner Herzog's *Grizzly Man*[1] in that the art consists of taking someone else's material and reframing it, Michael Lesy's *Wisconsin Death Trip* juxtaposes photographs and historical documents from turn-of-the-twentieth-century Jackson County, WI, to create what he calls "an experiment in both history and alchemy"—the alchemy being Lesy's transfiguration of American pastoral into Munch[2] nightmare. In Carole Maso's quotation-crazy book *The Art Lover*, she can't stop thinking via what other people are thinking. I can't stop thinking via what other people are thinking.

A recent biography of Ryszard Kapuściński[3] alleges that he frequently forged details, invented images, and claimed to have witnessed events that he didn't, in fact, witness. Gerald Posner resigned from the *Daily Beast*[4] after admitting that he'd lifted sentences from a *Miami Herald* editorial, a *Miami Herald* blog, *Texas Lawyer* magazine, and a health journalism blog; Posner blamed the "warp speed of the net" and his "master electronic files system." The publisher of Charles Pellegrino's most recent book, *The Last Train to Hiroshima*, withdrew it from publication following allegations that Pellegrino had created characters and extensively used a source whose status as witness to the bombing of Hiroshima was fabricated. A review of John D'Agata's *About a Mountain* criticised him for compressing the timeline of some of the events in the book—which he acknowledges doing in the afterword.

Why does this keep happening over and over and over again? Have we suddenly become a nation of liars? Of lawyers? Of children, incapable of distinguishing between event and interpretation, and between fact and "truth"? Why this overreaction to minor cases of plagiarism? Why this overemphasis on the exact "truth," which is, of course, impossible to know? These nonfiction scandals du jour,* these worst-case scenarios, get routinely deployed to

---

1   *Grizzly Man* Documentary film about the life and death of Timothy Treadwell, who lived among grizzly bears in Alaska.

2   *Munch* Edvard Munch (1863–1944) was a Norwegian painter. His Expressionist paintings treated psychological themes, often of loneliness, mental anguish, and fear.

3   *Ryszard Kapuściński* Polish journalist, photographer, and poet (1932–2007).

4   *Daily Beast* Online news journal.

position non-fiction as a subset of journalism, which it isn't. These authors are used as scapegoats to expiate the culture's sins. The whole huge loud roar, as it returns again and again, has to do with the culture being embarrassed at how much it wants (how much I want) the frame of reality and, within that frame, great drama. Nonfiction writers have always invented. In *History of the Peloponnesian War*, Thucydides makes up the generals' speeches. Thomas De Quincey's *Confessions of an English Opium-Eater* is a heavily fictionalised account of De Quincey's addiction to and recovery from opium. Edmund Gosse's *Father and Son* recounts page after page of supposedly verbatim dialogue from fifty years earlier. George Orwell's classmates questioned virtually every detail of "Such, Such Were the Joys." Dyer on Kapuściński: "His radically unconventional approach is entirely novel in the literal sense that no one else attempts anything like it. His material generates an apparently ad hoc* aesthetic that draws in the chaos threatening to engulf him; the outcome—the formal outcome—is perpetually in the balance, hence the suspense." The line between fact and fiction is fuzzier than most people find it convenient to admit. The common(sense) assertion: the novelist is engaged on a work of the creative imagination, while the duty of the non-fiction writer is to tell what really happened—a distinction easy to voice but impossible to sustain. Imagination and memory are Siamese twins attached at the head; you can't cut them apart. Amazingly, though, there persists the absurd view of non-fiction as 100 per cent "true" ("true" in the way a newspaper article is supposedly "true") and 100 per cent "original" (not hugely dependent on and predatory toward previous creative acts).

Who wouldn't wish on his musical headstone the carved-in-granite encomium "Music Pirate?"* Art is built by pirates: Johann Pachelbel's "Canon and Gigue in D Major for three Violins and Basso Continuo" was written around 1680 and lost. Rediscovered in the 1920s, it was first recorded by Arthur Fiedler in 1940. The music repeats a two-bar bass line and harmonic sequence twenty-eight times, using the scale sequence I, V, vi, iii, IV, I, IV, V—a sequence Handel used in the second movement of his "Organ Concerto No. 11 in G minor," Haydn used in the minuet of his string quartet "Opus 50 No. 2," and Mozart used in his "Piano Concerto No. 23" and in a passage of *Die Zauberflöte*. Haydn may have taught the sequence to Mozart. None of the three composers following Pachelbel exactly matches his harmonic structure; they all created slight variations. Pachelbel's structure is thought to derive from the ancient six-part polyphonic song form called the "round," in which singers enter the song at different points, as they do in, say, "Row, Row, Row Your Boat."* The date of origin for the round is estimated at 1260, and the composer is anonymous. Louis Armstrong was a member of King Oliver's band when

5

Oliver wrote an unmemorable blues number called "West End Blues," a sleepy, entertaining tune named after an area of New Orleans on the west side of Lake Pontchartrain. Within three weeks of Oliver's recording the song, Armstrong had formed his own band, the Hot Five, and rerecorded "West End Blues" to his standards. The fifteen-second opening cadenza announced jazz as art, and Armstrong's closing signature of high B-flat notes made it one of the most difficult-to-imitate solo pieces in jazz music. When James Brown announces during the funk-groove workout "Funky Drummer" that it's time "to give the drummer some," the Godfather of Soul provides instructions: "You don't have to do no soloing, brother—just keep what you got; don't turn it loose, 'cause it's a mother." That mother has become one of the most sampled song bites of all time. It's been estimated that the Honeydrippers' "Impeach the President" has been sampled on approximately one out of every five rap songs from 1988 to the present, including songs by Big Daddy Kane, Ice Cube, NWA, Audio Two, and LL Cool J. The sample has become public domain through overuse. The Honeydrippers' sample is lingua franca[5] for rappers across the globe, a forged signature recognised as entry into the game. Bob Marley and the Wailers took just the part of Bob Dylan's "Like a Rolling Stone" that appealed to them and built their entire cover version out of it, manually looping the chorus of "Rolling Stone" over and over again, writing new lyrics along the way. I love that move of theirs—giving themselves permission to dissect the popular song as they saw fit instead of repeating it verbatim. Dylan pillaged the Civil War poet Henry Timrod for lyrics on his album *Modern Times*. His previous album, *Love and Theft*, steals passages from a Japanese gangster novel, Junichi Saga's *Confessions of a Yakuza*. Very early in his career, Dylan was the James Frey[6] of the folk movement (or at the very least the JT LeRoy[7]). He lied massively about his past to any reporter who would listen. He invented an elaborate series of backstories for himself: running away from home, travelling with the circus, working on ranches, being a heroin addict, contemplating suicide. He found his real life lacking authenticity, so he invented a folk music hero and then lived the role: "Song to Woody"[8] (1962). By the time people caught on to his ruse, the truth didn't matter anymore. And unlike Frey, he never gave an explanation, never apologised. Instead, he just moved on to

---

5   *lingua franca*   Language shared by people who speak different native languages.

6   *James Frey*   American writer accused of fabricating large sections of his memoir *A Million Little Pieces* (2003).

7   *JT LeRoy*   Jeremiah "Terminator" LeRoy (b. 1980) is the name of a persona adopted by American writer Laura Albert; for several years, the literary establishment believed that LeRoy was a real person.

8   *"Song to Woody"*   Bob Dylan song addressed to folk icon Woody Guthrie.

another persona. *I'm not there;*[9] *neither are you.* (I've never deleted an email so fast as one I received from Frey telling me he'd read the chapter in *Reality Hunger*[10] about *A Million Little Pieces* and I was the first person to ever really understand him ...). Miles Davis called the Beastie Boys' *Paul's Boutique* one of the greatest albums ever, as did Henry Rollins of Black Flag. Chuck D of Public Enemy said one of the insider secrets of hip-hop at the time was that *Paul's Boutique* outmaneuvered other rappers with inventive beats cobbled out of multiple sources. The Beasties hired the Dust Brothers to produce the album, and when the Beasties showed up in the studio, they listened to tracks the Dust Brothers had created, dense club mixes. Half the album is made up of these foundational remixes. Danger Mouse's *Grey Album* is built entirely of samples from the Beatles' *White Album* and Jay-Z's *Black Album*. Danger Mouse could never have cleared all the samples, so the mash-up had to live its life entirely underground. The album, a masterly display of collage and re-purposing, positions Danger Mouse as Robin Hood,* who appropriates music from the kings and plays it for us, the internet masses. Mountain Con was an obscure Seattle band whose CD *The MC Stands for Revolution* synthesised rock, R&B, and rap, until its record company made the band remove all the Rolling Stones and James Brown samples from the music. The album that was finally released pales in comparison. The original, however, was trying to usher in a new era of rock that never was. When Nullsoft released the MP3 audio player Winamp in 1997, the web went music-crazy. Peer-to-peer file sharing morphed into individual collages of music ripped from CDs; MP3. com offered thousands of MP3s by musicians, mostly anonymous ones, free. The record industry began years of litigation against free file-sharing entities. The beloved and mourned Napster hit the market in 1999 as the first large-scale, peer-to-peer, music-sharing communal site. The music industry branded Napster "music pirates." Then the music industry went after individuals, mainly teenagers, who were trading tracks on Napster and reframing music to individual taste and demand. Napster's file-sharing software was eventually shut down due to legal pressure, but the war goes on (I'm just a foot soldier) and sampling is ubiquitous.

I'm not an anti-copyright absolutist; I'm not the director of *The King's Speech* and don't walk around selling DVDs of that film with my name on it. There are three crucial terms when it comes to copyright: fair use—you

---

9   *I'm not there*   Song by Bob Dylan included on the soundtrack to *I'm Not There*, a film about Dylan released in 2007.

10   *Reality Hunger*   Book by David Shields in "collage style"—a collection of quotations by the author and others.

can quote 10 per cent or less of a book, or 250 words or fewer from a shorter work; public domain—you can quote from Kipling, since he's been dead for more than seventy-five years; and, most importantly, transformation—in your appropriation of another work, are you simply plagiarising, or are you remaking it? This is where it gets harder to define and most interesting (immediately after I asked a student if she'd copied a passage from Wikipedia, she changed the Wikipedia entry, erasing the evidence). Lawyers, servants of late-market capitalism, want a bright line now, but in the history of art there has never been a bright line.

A system of writing was invented in isolation (at most) four times. The first system of writing was invented in Mesopotamia. The second might have been in Egypt, but there's a compelling argument that the Mesopotamians influenced the birth of the Egyptian writing system. The third was in China, and again there's debate about whether the Mesopotamians influenced the Chinese. The fourth, and only the second undoubted instance, was thousands of years later in Mezo-America with the Mayan civilisation, which had no contact with Mesopotamia. Each of those (between two–four) isolated inventions of writing systems was not some lightning-strike invention; in each case, it evolved over many hundreds of years and was a collaboration among whole societies, evolving and being modified generation after generation, starting with a few agreed-upon symbols and expanding from there as necessity dictated. None of these original writing systems were "copyrightable." The twentieth/twenty-first-century concept of owning certain arrangements of words runs counter to 5,000 years of written language development. Every other alphabet and writing system on the planet is an appropriation of one or more of these original two–four systems. The borrowing has been with us from the beginning; "theft" starts at the extreme headwaters of the big muddy river: Folk art from the beginning of recorded civilisation until now. Roman sculptors' direct copies of Greek sculptures. John Dominic Crossan, *The Historical Jesus* (1991), which is painstakingly researched and shows in great detail how the New Testament is a mash-up of (literally) epic proportions. The Gospels are pretty much collages of many ancient texts, with the older ones being borrowed from and rewritten in the newer ones. The New Testament that people read today is a composite of numerous sources, and in many cases, such as the Gospel of Mark, one ancient writer wrote over the top of a previous one, tacking the whole rising from the dead ending onto a previous document that ended without any such miracle. Botticelli's "Birth of Venus" (1482), which is based directly on Apelles's depiction, in fourth century BC, of the same event. Shakespeare, *Antony and Cleopatra* (circa 1603–1607); the description of Cleopatra on her royal barge is a near-verbatim sample from Plutarch's *Life of Mark Antony* (75 AD; T.S. Eliot used the same passage, verbatim, two thousand years later in *The Waste Land*). Shakespeare "plundered" Arthur Brooke's *The Tragical History of Romeus and Juliet* (1562) for his play of (nearly) the same name. Of the 6,000 lines in *Henry VI*, Parts I-III (1591), 4,000 are directly derived from Holinshed's *Chronicles* (1577). The Sarabande movement in each of the Bach Cello Suites (1720s) is a three-beat dance form that the Baroque composers had adapted in the eighteenth century from an African dance form, which had been discounted in many European quarters as lascivious and vulgar. Thomas Jefferson's miracle-skeptical remix of the Bible (1820), keeping only the social teachings[11] (see Crossan, above). Manet's "Olympia" (1863) is a reworking of Titian's "Venus of Urbino" (1538), which is a reworking of Giorgione's "Sleeping Venus" (1508), which is a reworking of one of the woodcut illustrations to Francesco Colonna's "Hypnerotomachia Poliphili" (1499); Titian finished the landscape and sky of "Sleeping Venus" after Giorgione's death. Tchaikovsky's *1812 Overture* (1880) hijacks the French national anthem (1792). Igor Stravinsky, *The Rite Of Spring* (1913). Béla Bartók: "Stravinsky never mentions the sources of his themes. Neither in his titles nor in footnotes does he ever allude to whether a theme of his is his own invention or whether it is taken over from folk music. Stravinsky apparently takes this course deliberately. He wants to demonstrate that it does not matter a jot whether a composer invents his own themes or uses themes from elsewhere. He has a right to use musical material taken from all sources. What he had judged suitable for his purpose had become through this very use his mental property." Ezra Pound's "creative translation" *Homage to Sextus Propertius* (1919) has done more than any other book to keep alive the poetry of Propertius. Some have criticised Pound's "errors," while others understand that Pound was playing cover versions* of the Roman poet and taking liberties as he saw fit. See J.P. Sullivan, *Ezra Pound and Sextus Propertius: A Study in Creative Translation* (1964). "Tradition and the Individual Talent" (1919), in which Eliot discusses his theories on influence and borrowing. *The Waste Land* (1922), of course, is composed almost entirely of literary samples, references, and conspicuous assimilations—fragments to shore against his ruins[12] (as is this entire chapter, if not this entire book).

---

11   *Thomas ... teachings*   Jefferson's book *The Life and Morals of Jesus of Nazareth* removes most of the supernatural content from the New Testament and reassembles the remaining content to produce a chronological account of Jesus's life and philosophy.

12   *fragments ... ruins*   See Eliot's *The Waste Land*   433: "These fragments I have shored against my ruins."

Walter Benjamin's *Arcades Project*[13] (1927–1940; incomplete at the time of his death—endlessly being completed by us, after him). Benjamin Britten (1913–1976), who was, according to Stravinsky, "not a composer but a klep-tomaniac"; Stravinsky said this. Duchamp didn't conceive "Fountain"[14] (1917); nor did he make it. A urinal was art because he said it was. Since Duchamp, what is the nature of art? In 1941, on his front porch, Muddy Waters recorded a song for the folklorist Alan Lomax. After singing the song, which he told Lomax was entitled "Country Blues," Waters described how he came to write it. "I made it on about the eighth of October '38," Waters said. "I was fixin' a puncture on a car. I had been mistreated by a girl. I just felt blue, and the song fell into my mind and it come to me just like that and I started singing." Then Lomax, who knew of the Robert Johnson recording called "Walkin' Blues," asked Waters if there were any other songs that used the same tune. "There's been some blues played like that," Waters replied. "This song comes from the cotton field and a boy once put a record out— Robert Johnson. He put it out as named 'Walkin' Blues.' I heard the tune before I heard it on the record. I learned it from Son House." In nearly one breath, Waters offers five accounts: his own active authorship—he "made it" on a specific date. Then the "passive" explanation: "It come to me just like that." After Lomax raises the question of influence, Waters, without shame or trepidation, says that he heard a version by Johnson, but that his mentor, Son House, taught it to him. In the middle of that complex genealogy, Waters declares that "this song comes from the cotton field." Aaron Copeland's *Appalachian Spring* (1944) kidnaps the Shaker melody "Simple Gifts" (1848). Nabokov's *Lolita* (1955) is based heavily on Heinz von Lichberg's *Lolita* (1916); see Michael Maar's *The Two Lolitas* (2005). Martin Luther King Jr.'s sermons of the 1950s and '60s (accused of plagiarism, as was his 1955 Ph.D. thesis). Eduardo Paolozzi's collage-novel *Kex* (1966), cobbled from crime novels and newspaper clippings. John Brockman, *Afterwords* (1969)—composed entirely of other writers' passages. In 1964, Dionne Warwick sang the original version of "Walk On By," which was written by Burt Bacharach and Hal David. Five years later, Isaac Hayes completely repurposed the song. The chords and lyrics are the same, but Hayes takes the 1964 version and warps it nearly beyond recognition. What was a two-and-a-half-minute pop single becomes a twelve-and-a-half minute soul epic before imploding into the funk riff of a single guitar. Bacharach and David still owned the

---

13 *Arcades Project*   Unfinished critical work by Walter Benjamin that incorporates and meditates on numerous quotations.
14 *"Fountain"*   Influential artwork consisting of a urinal signed with a pseudonym.

copyright, but only the veneer of the original is recognisable. Harold Bloom, *The Anxiety of Influence*[15] (1973), getting it wrong, as always; cf. Jonathan Lethem's "The Ecstasy of Influence." In Jamaica in the early 1970s, Osborne Ruddock ("King Tubby") and Lee ("Scratch") Perry, using primitive, pre-digital gear, created new "versions" of previously recorded music. Ruddock's and Perry's techniques are the basis on which hip-hop was built. Roland Barthes, *Image-Music-Text* (1977), specifically the essay "Death of the Author," in which Barthes says, "A text is made of multiple writings, drawn from many cultures and entering into mutual relations of dialogue, parody, contestation, but there is one place where this multiplicity is focused and that place is the reader, not, as was hitherto said, the author. To give a text an Author is to impose a limit on that text, to furnish it with a final signified, to close the writing." William S. Burroughs and Brion Gysin, *The Third Mind* (1977): a collection showcasing and theorising about the cut-up technique.* *William Burroughs Reader*, ed. John Calder (1982); Brion Gysin's "Cut-Ups: A Project for Disastrous Success" discusses the process that he and Burroughs pioneered. Also in *Burroughs Reader*: the *Paris Review* interview in which Burroughs discusses the cut-up method. Kathy Acker (in Burroughs's wake), *Blood and Guts in High School* (1984). Instead of drawing a conclusion for you (or writing a story for you with a beginning, middle, and end), I'll give you all the pieces for a picture and let you figure it out (interpret it). The pieces are far from random, but your conclusion isn't fixed. Péter Esterházy's *Helping Verbs of the Heart* (1985)—same MO* as *Afterwords*. Warhol[16] (d. 1987). Graham Rawle's novel *Diary of an Amateur Photographer* (1998), its text harvested from photography magazines. *Copyright Criminals* (2009), directed by Benjamin Franzen. Kenneth Goldmith, "Flarf Is Dionysus; Conceptual Writing Is Apollo," *Poetry* (2009). Flarf poetry: derived primarily but not exclusively from Google searches, poems created, revised, changed by others, incorporated, plagiarised in semi-public forums. James Blake, *James Blake* (2011). The cover photo shows his face as a blur, which is a fitting metaphor for a singer/electronic composer who uses primarily other people's voices. His songs, occupying a demilitarised zone between genres, are simultaneously avant-garde instrumental music, piano-driven singer-songwriter R&B, and throbbing 808 spacey hip-hop. At times, via Auto-Tune, he pushes "his" voice beyond recognition or human tonality.

---

15 *The Anxiety of Influence* Book in which literary critic Harold Bloom argues that great writers must grapple with and overcome the influence of precursors.

16 *Warhol* Andy Warhol (1928–87) was a leading figure in the pop art movement. Many of his works replicate images from advertisements and other popular culture sources.

The mimetic function[17] has been replaced by manipulation of the original. Art, not to mention life, now seems to happen primarily in liminal spaces, edited, quoted and quoted again and recontextualised, replaced, collaged, stitched together anew (the stitching together anew is what I really care about).

(2013)

---

17 *mimetic function* Many theorists of literature since Plato and Aristotle have considered the primary function of art or literature to be "mimesis," the representation or imitation of reality.

IRA BOUDWAY

NBA REFS LEARNED THEY WERE RACIST, AND THAT MADE THEM LESS RACIST

The following article, reporting on the results of a study by Devin Pope, Joseph Price, and Justin Wolfers, was posted on the Bloomberg news website 7 February 2014. The 2013 study that the article describes was a follow-up to a 2007 study—Price and Wolfers' "Racial Discrimination among NBA Referees." Both the 2007 and the 2013 studies were widely reported in the media. (The 2013 study is also referenced in a Nicholas Kristof column that is included in these pages.)

In some scholarly disciplines there can be a long lag between initial publication of preliminary research results and final publication in a scholarly journal. In this case, both the 2007 study and the more recent one were initially published as working papers; the working paper presenting the research results discussed in Boudway's article appeared in December 2013 as "National Bureau of Economic Research Working Paper No. 19765," and also in February of 2014 in the Brookings Institution's Working Paper series. A revised version of the 2007 study was published in 2010 in The Quarterly Journal of Economics; *as of July 2016 a revised version of the 2013 study had yet to appear in a scholarly journal.*

Seven years ago, a pair of scholars released a study of NBA* referees that found white officiating crews more likely to call fouls against black players—and, to a lesser degree, black officiating crews more likely to call fouls against white players. The study drew broad media attention and caused a small stir in the league. Then-Commissioner David Stern, questioned its validity in the *New York Times*, and players weighed in on sports-talk radio and ESPN.*

The same scholars, Justin Wolfers of the University of Michigan and Joseph Price of Brigham Young University, returned to the subject of racially biased referees in a working paper released in December with an astounding result.

Once the results of the original study were widely known, the bias disappeared. "When we conduct the same tests for own-race bias in the period immediately following the media coverage," they wrote, "we find none exists."

The original data set came from the 1991–2002 NBA seasons. In the new study, in which the original scholars worked with Devin Pope of the Booth School of Business, the authors looked both at a sample from the 2003–2006 seasons—after the original data but before the public attention—and from 2007–2010. From 2003 to 2006, the bias persisted at the same level, roughly an extra fifth of a foul every 48 minutes. But from 2007 to 2010, they found no significant bias in either direction.

In explaining why this happened, the authors argue that public awareness itself shaped referee behavior. The NBA, they wrote, did not increase the frequency of mixed-race officiating crews or otherwise take action after the release of the initial study:

> A phone conversation with NBA league administrators who oversee the NBA's officiating department suggests that the NBA did not take any specific action to eliminate referee discrimination. Specifically, the administrators to whom we spoke denied that the NBA spoke with the referees about the Price and Wolfers study. They also indicated that the study did not lead to a change in referee incentives or a change in the way they train their referees.

Simply knowing that bias was present and that other people knew, they wrote, made it go away:

> We argue that this dramatic decrease in bias is a causal result of the awareness associated with the treatment—the release and subsequent publicity surrounding the original academic study in 2007.

The study may hold implications for any organization looking to reduce group bias. In the realms of public policy and education, the focus is often on increased exposure and proximity to out groups. But bias, as the original referee study showed, can sometimes withstand proximity. The remedy might be to locate bigotry and bring it into the light. As Louis Brandeis famously wrote in 1913:[1] "Publicity is justly commended as a remedy for social and industrial diseases. Sunlight is said to be the best of disinfectants; electric light the most efficient policeman."

(2014)

---

1   *Louis Brandeis ... 1913*   This well-known quotation from Brandeis (who later became a member of the Supreme Court), first appeared in *Harper's Weekly* magazine in an article entitled "What Publicity Can Do."

ANN WROE

THREE OBITUARIES

Since 1995 The Economist *(a weekly newsmagazine founded in 1843) has included a one-page obituary at the end of each weekly issue; these essays have quietly become renowned for their unique style. Though the magazine does not attribute authorship of the individual articles within each issue, its website credits Ann Wroe, an* Economist *writer since 1976, as having "edited the Obituaries page, usually writing the obituaries herself, since October 2003."*

CHESTER NEZ

C hester Nez, the last of America's Navajo code-talkers, died on June 4th aged 93.

Life in the Marine Corps came easily to Chester Nez. He was used to loping long miles, sleeping in the open air, and to the hard work of herding sheep and goats under the cloud-studded turquoise skies of the New Mexico Checkerboard. He took danger in his stride too: as a Navajo warrior and protector, he wanted to defend his country and make his family proud. He liked the plentiful food, after a childhood when he often was "hurt by hunger" as his language, verb-rich and adjective-poor, put it. And, in his uniform, he could visit bars that banned native Americans.

Some things bothered him: looking people in the eye (disrespectful), shouting (even more so) and the careless treatment of cut hair (a dangerous weapon to enemies). Navajo religion forbids contact with the dead, and the battlefield stench of corpses spooked him. To keep the spirits of the dead at bay, he would fill his mind with thoughts of beauty, mutter a Navajo prayer, and touch the buckskin medicine bag which hung at his neck, with its blessed corn pollen and tiny, secret souvenirs.

His first name was not Chester, nor was his surname Nez. The real ones had somehow got lost at boarding school,* where the white world tried to civilize the rangy eight-year-old, born to a mother from the Black Sheep Clan and a father of the Sleeping Rock People. They made him speak English, a language he had never heard. To get rid of the dirty gobbledygook* he insisted on using, the matron brushed his teeth with bitter Fels-Naptha soap.

5   In vain. Nothing could take away his Navajo—part (though he did not know it) of a language family so complicated that linguistics needs special terms to describe it. Verbs do most of the work, agglutinated with suffixes and prefixes, in seven modes (including the usitative, iterative and optative), 12 aspects, such as the semelfactive (a half-completed action), and ten sub-aspects, including the completive and the semeliterative (a single repetition). It has four combinations of tones, plus glottal and aspirated stops. A shift in any of them can change a word's meaning completely.

WAR OF WORDS

As America struggled to stem the Japanese advance across the Pacific following the disaster of Pearl Harbor,* military codes—cumbersome and weak—were proving a fatal weakness. But Philip Johnston, a missionary's son raised on a Navajo reservation, hit on the idea of using a language that the Japanese could not crack. Native American tongues had been used for battlefield messages in the first world war, (Hitler had even dispatched spies to America in the 1930s to study them in case they would be used again). But Navajo had not been written down, and almost no outsiders spoke it fluently.

Moreover, to be safe, the code that Mr. Nez and his fellow-Navajo volunteers in the secret 382nd Platoon helped devise was a complex one. The letter A was represented by any of three Navajo words: "ant," "apple," or "axe." Common military terms had words of their own: a fighter plane was a hummingbird, (da-he-tih-hi), a battleship was a whale (lo-tso), a destroyer a shark, (ca-lo). A hand grenade was a potato, and America was Ne-he-mah ("our mother"). The Japanese did eventually capture (and torture) a Navajo—but he was not a code-talker. He could not make head or tail* of the messages.

Marine commanders were initially skeptical. But a message that took an hour to encrypt, transmit and decrypt on the existing mechanical Shackle system could be transmitted orally by code-talkers in just 40 seconds. Even America's own code-crackers failed to break it.

On November 4th 1942 (the most frightening day of his life, he later recalled) he went into action on Guadalcanal, toting a hand-cranked radio, the size of a shoebox and weighing 30 pounds (nearly 14 kilos). His first message was: "Enemy machine gun nest on your right. Destroy." The shells rained down as ordered. He was to serve in key battles of the Pacific war: Bougainville, Guam, Peleliu and Angaur. Everywhere the marines fought, Navajo code-talkers, under fire, hoarse, tired and thirsty, were vital in victory, directing fire, calling up reinforcements, evacuating the wounded, and warning of enemy movements.

Gratitude came slowly. Many code-talkers (unable to talk about their secret wartime work) ended up penniless drunks. When Private First Class Chester Nez applied for a civilian identity card in 1945, an official took pleasure in reminding him that he was not a full citizen and could not vote (that did not come until 1948).* He suffered from what would now be called post-traumatic stress disorder, fighting it, successfully, with traditional Navajo healing ceremonies. He started an art course, but ran out of cash (the University of Kansas awarded him his degree in 2012), and worked for 25 years painting walls and murals at a veterans' hospital in Albuquerque. Only after 1968, when the code-talkers' story was declassified, did the fame and honors begin—a bit embarrassingly, he said—to flow.

He mourned the suffering and injustice of his people's past, but insisted that the Navajo story was ultimately of triumph, not sorrow. And his own life had been "100%." But it did bother him that his country had tried to stop him speaking Navajo, when it had proved so useful.

(21 January 2014)

NANCY REAGAN: KEEPING CONTROL

Nancy Reagan, America's First Lady through the 1980s, died on March 6th, aged 94.

If anyone attacked her Ronnie, when he was governor of California in the 1970s, Nancy Reagan knew just what to do. She would run a big tub, pour in lots of bath salts, and as she soaked she would shout defiance at the wall. Didn't happen. Didn't happen. What are you doing to my husband? What's wrong with that? By the time the tub was cool she was all sweetness, and the world was in kilter again.

Keeping life's untidiness at bay was a full-time job. It started with herself. Only Julius could style her hair, and he had to be flown in from Los Angeles. As a teenager her nose was too big, so she had it done, of course. (She wanted to be a movie star; that never came to much, but she networked with Spencer Tracy and Clark Gable and met Ronnie, so it was worth it.) With daily exercise she could stay a size four, and look stunning in the Bill Blass gowns and red

Adolfo suits* that came in armfuls to the White House. But her ankles were so thick that she cried for days when the *Washington Star* noticed.

On every side lay disorder, even in the White House. Ashtrays that needed emptying (she would do it herself, if no one else would). Pictures hanging askew, which must be straightened. Coffee cups on desks. Aides coming in sweaty, wearing trainers and with mussed hair: just inappropriate. Appearances mattered, which was why she had refused to live in the governor's house in Sacramento, that old firetrap, and instead moved to a 12-room Tudor mansion in a better part of town. Good taste, and a horror of mismatched plates, was the reason she spent $209,508 on new china for the White House, which everyone attacked her for. Otherwise she was frugality itself, recycling unwanted presents and getting her rich friends to donate their furniture. Because everything had to be just so, she continually fussed, phoned and deployed her two steeliest weapons, the silence and the stare. Before state dinners, she checked that the salad leaves were perfectly arranged and the sauce exactly seasoned. When the Queen of England visited, she drafted the guest list five times over. If anything went wrong, she was furious. Naturally.

5   Her own history needed tidying, too. Two years were lost from her age somewhere. Her potty-mouthed* mother was kept at arm's length. Her father, a car-dealer, out of the picture since her parents' divorce, was replaced as "real" by Loyal Davis, her stepfather, a respectable neurosurgeon who did not agree to adopt her for six years. As for her own children, they were frankly a nightmare: Patti a damn hippie* and Ron, eventually, a ballet dancer. She ransacked his bedroom for drugs and worried herself sick that he was probably gay, but had to accept in the end that families couldn't be wrapped up prettily in white paper. The hardest thing was that Ronnie had brought two children of his own, with Jane Wyman, to the marriage. Her shadow came too. They couldn't be fitted in at all.

As for Ronnie himself, her wonder and her hero, the man without whom she couldn't live—he was her chief project. Dear, sweet, easy-going Ronnie had no straight-line ambition to be governor or president. She had it for him. (She wasn't political one scrap, beyond being, obviously, Republican, but could nudge him to do smart things like reach out to the Soviets.)* Ronnie loved and trusted everyone; so it was just as well she didn't. If anyone was harming him, they had to go, and she would keep at it and at it.

She couldn't win every battle, of course. Don Regan, pushy awful man, was turfed out as White House chief of staff, but Ronnie refused to put all protesters in jail, as she requested, or sack Cap Weinberger from the Pentagon,* because he was his friend. (And sure enough, she wouldn't drop her own best friends, like the Bloomingdales or Frank Sinatra, just because they got in a mess.) In front of the cameras she made certain Ronnie looked good, and tore up official snaps that showed him sleepy or old. If he got lost for words, she supplied them. Her unwavering, loving gaze when he spoke was, in fact, a firewall.

One thing she could not order was the future and his fate. She could try her damnedest, though. She insisted that on election day in 1970, when Ronnie was running again for governor of California, he should play golf and eat chicken curry for dinner, just as he had on the day when he was first elected. It worked. In the White House she brought in astrologers to fix, according to Ronnie's star chart, the times of press conferences and foreign trips. That worked, too. It even helped when she felt she needed to change her own image as a clothes-horse* and an icicle to something softer. Following her seers' advice, she started a "Just Say No" campaign against drug use and began to appear more often with sick children. When Ronnie got Alzheimer's, she rather bravely—for a Republican—started pushing for stem-cell research.

People still misunderstood her. They kept sniping at her tight little laugh, her jewelry and her influence over her husband. Perhaps, since Ronnie was so popular, they needed her as a lightning rod. Perhaps these press types—especially the women reporters—wished they too could be that slim and that much in control. Well, they would just have to work at it as hard as she had. Even in the bath.

(12 March 2016)

AMJAD SABRI:
HATE AND LOVE

Amjad Sabri, Pakistan's favorite qawwali singer, was killed on June 22nd, aged 45.

His father, Ghulam Farid Sabri, sang that way. His uncle, Maqbool Ahmed Sabri, sang that way. His ancestors had done so too, right back to the time of Mian Tansen, a favorite musician at the Mughal court, who received 100,000 gold coins for his first performance. The Sabri house in Karachi was full of the wheeze of portable harmoniums, the patter of drums and the joyous, repetitive mantras of *qawwali*, the songs of the millions of South Asian followers of the mystical Sufi strain of Islam. So it was no wonder that from early childhood Amjad Sabri joined the chorus, hauled out of bed by his father at 4am to wash, say his prayers, fetch his instrument and sing the first *raga* of the dawn. The long preparation was worth it, to feel one with the sunrise.

He knew this was not ordinary music. It was a love song to the prophet Muhammad, to Ali, his son-in-law and closest disciple, to the Sufi saints and above all to God directly, music being the only sure way to evoke and approach Him. *Qawwali* was a plea to be noticed at the court of heaven, admitted to the presence, absorbed into the heartbeat and the breath, as in his father's most famous song, "Tajdar-e-haram," "King of the Holy Sanctuary":

"What should I tell you, O Prince of Arabia,
You already know what is in my heart,
In our separation, O Untaught One,
Our sleepless nights are so hard to bear
In your love I've lost all consciousness
Tajdar-e-haram, tajdar-e-haram"

As he or his relations sang, the audience would start to sway, clap, sing along, dance and lose themselves in the ecstasy of God. His father would cry "Allah! Allah!" in the midst of his singing, an invocation so powerful that even non-Muslims would start to shout it after him. In adulthood Amjad, always careful to preserve his father's modulations, did this too, enjoying the effect it had on his listeners. Indeed, his whole performance radiated calm, confidence and joy: a big, burly man with luxuriant long black hair, brown *karakul* hat, one small gold earring and many chunky rings, effortlessly smiling and gesticulating through his glorious baritone singing. "Bhar do Jholi" was his most famous song, "Fill my Bag," or "Fulfil my Wish":

"Fill my bag, O Lord, Fill all our bags,
O Lord, Fill the bag,
O Guide, Fill my bag,
O Lord of Medina,
I won't return empty-handed!
Bhar do jholi, bhar do jholi ..."

5   He was not doctrinaire about this. He would sing in Sufi shrines, cross-legged on a mat with a skull-capped chorus, or perform like a rock star, standing at a mic under bright lights in a flamingo-pink cotta. On TV he sang regularly for the morning shows, especially during Ramadan, and would take part in the silly games too, if the presenters asked him. He sang all over South Asia (being a star in India and Bangladesh as well) and took *qawwali* to Europe and America, where he performed backed by saxophones. Bollywood invited him, and he was happy to sing on film; Bollywood actresses posed with him. The only problem with all his globetrotting, for he liked his food, was the difficulty of finding good halal meals, but he taught himself to cook a fine *aloo gosht*, beef-and-potato curry, to keep himself going.

FILLING THE WINE-CUP

Much larger obstacles reared their heads at home. To the Pakistani Taliban the wildness of Sufism, its decadent Persian origins, its veneration of saints, its reminders of an Islam disseminated through art, music and dance, were all anathema. So was its easy openness to all faiths and people, demonstrated in the way its greatest living *qawwal* would stroll around the narrow, teeming lanes of Liaquatabad in Karachi, shoot a piece or two on the carrom boards, treat some hapless batsman to his off-spin,* chat to the man in the cigarette booth and, indeed, mix Hindu *ragas* naturally with his songs. He also declared that his own favourite *qawwal* was Aziz Mian, who played on the much-loved Sufi metaphor of drunkenness in God's love to cry "Let's drink! Fill my wine-cup to overflowing!"

So Sufi shrines began to be bombed by the Taliban, and singers shot at. The establishment failed to take the Sufis' side, preferring to blazon its respect for orthodox religion. It was the high court, not the Taliban, that accused Mr Sabri of blasphemy in 2014 for singing a song that mentioned members of Muhammad's family on one of those morning shows. The threats came closer, extra-legal this time: six months ago three men burst into his house, retreating only because they did not find him there. Some friends said he had asked for protection; others thought he never would. His last song on TV included the refrain "When I shudder in my dark tomb, dear Prophet, look after me."

He was on his way to do another morning show when two men on a motor-cycle riddled his car with bullets. The Pakistani Taliban declared that they had done it, killing a blasphemer. It happened close to the underpass that had been named after his father in more tolerant times.

His father had sung that way. His uncle had sung that way. And his 12-year-old son defiantly performed his "Karam Mangta Hun" ("I ask for Kindness, Lord") in tribute to him; for the greatest message of Sufi Islam to the world is the unshakable primacy of music, peace and love.

(2 July 2016)

ANTHONY S. TRAVIS

THE ACCIDENTAL DISCOVERY
OF MAUVE

The Fall 2014 issue of the scholarly journal Victorian Review *was
devoted to articles on the related topics of "Accidents" and "Risk."
The short essay included here was the only contribution to deal with
scientific discovery—and the only contribution to deal with what
might be called a happy accident.*

An accident can, in the hands of amateur experts, lead, as an unintended consequence, to new ways of doing and making things. One such instance occurred in the East End of London during the Easter of 1856. There, in a makeshift laboratory in the loft of his parents' house, a teenaged chemist discovered, by chance, a purple dyestuff that would pave the way for a scientific and manufacturing revolution based on chemistry. The young man was William Henry Perkin (1838–1907), assistant to the German chemist (August) Wilhelm Hoffmann, then head of the Royal College of Chemistry, in London's Oxford Street.

Hoffmann, a former student of Justus von Liebig, of meat-extract fame,[1] directed the college from its opening in 1846. This institution was backed by British agriculturalists interested in improved crop yields based on scientific studies of fertilizers such as guano, the bird excrement imported from Peru. However, while no significant contribution toward agriculture was forthcoming, Hoffmann did investigate a group of chemicals that he hoped could serve other human needs. These chemicals had been isolated from coal tar, the viscous, oily waste from the manufacture of the coal gas that lit the streets and lanes of the metropolis. Coal tar was an unsightly inconvenience that was often dumped in local rivers.

Hoffmann's compounds were members of the aromatic series, in particular the amino compounds. The latter were present as minor components in the tar.

---

1   *Liebig, of meat-extract fame*   The Liebig's Extract of Meat Company became famous
for products such as Oxo beef bouillon cubes.

From the early 1850s, they were prepared in the laboratory, in two steps, from the abundant tar-derived hydrocarbon benzene. Their chemical structures were unknown and presented on the basis of known combining powers (valences) of atoms, a major puzzle to chemists. However, this did not prevent speculation about how such aromatic compounds might be used. All that was known was that the aromatic compounds contained the atoms carbon, hydrogen, and nitrogen (the amino component is made up of the chemical grouping of one nitrogen atom and two hydrogen atoms). This was enough to suggest that, on the basis of analysis for the rations of chemical elements, synthesis of useful compounds might be achieved by applying known reactions of the amino group. Hoffmann surmised that one such aromatic amine might, by process of condensation of two of its molecules, be converted into synthetic quinine,[2] a product much wanted by colonial administrators, explorers, and others engaged in distant lands where malaria struck.

This was the challenge taken up by the eighteen-year-old William Perkin. After studying at the City of London School, he enrolled at Hoffmann's college, where, by around 1855, he was promoted to assistant in the professor's private laboratory. There, Perkin studied aromatic amino compounds and heard Hoffmann discuss their possible uses outside the laboratory. Practical applications of chemistry were important for enhancing the status of the discipline and its practitioners, as well as for ensuring much-needed funding for the college, which had fallen upon hard times once the agriculturalists realized that no breakthroughs had been forthcoming.

Despite limitations in available scientific knowledge—which in retrospect was a distinct advantage—and many other uncertainties, during the 1856 Easter break, Perkin undertook an experiment to synthesize quinine starting as Hoffmann suggested, with an amine derived from coal-tar naphthalene. It failed miserably. Undaunted, Perkin made use of his scientific training and decided to find out why the reaction did not work, repeating the method with the simplest aromatic amine, aniline. Again, an unpromising mixture resulted. Perkin could have thrown it down the drain and spent the rest of Easter with his family and friends in the East End. Instead, he treated the dark oily mixture with alcohol, hoping to extract from it a compound that might provide answers to the nature of the reaction. The result was a brilliant purple solution, something not altogether unusual, since strongly colored solutions often resulted from chemical reactions and were worthy of note, even if not of practical application outside the laboratory or lecture hall.

While Perkin was manipulating the solution an accident occurred, though we do not have the exact details. A portion of the liquid spilled onto a piece of

5

---

2   *quinine*   Medication used to prevent malaria.

cloth and left a purple stain that was difficult to remove by washing. At that moment, the young tinkerer, displaying remarkable sagacity,* realized he had created what could conceivably be a useful textile dye. Turning the accident into a discovery was a matter of awareness. It was prompted by the fact that the Perkin family's East-End home was located in a vibrant manufacturing area that included the workshops of textile dyers.

It was not just the fact that the stain adhered so strongly to fabric. As Perkin knew, or was told soon after by a local dyer of silk, purple happened to be a leading color of fashion. Moreover, the other brilliant purple then made in England, murexide (made from guano), faded quickly in the heavily-polluted, sulphurous city air. Perkin's colorant resisted the action of the atmosphere, light, and soap on silk. A dyer in Perth opined that, provided it was not too expensive, it would certainly be a valuable product.

In August 1856, no doubt with the help of his father, a builder, William Perkin filed a patent for the process and product. Unable to license or sell the patent, Perkin, with the backing of his father and brother George, decided to embark on the manufacture of aniline dye. There were many challenges, apart from the previously untried manufacturing steps (trialled in the back garden). Perkin overcame the difficult problem of attachment of his dye to the most important textile fabric of all, cotton. In 1858, Perkin & Sons commenced manufacture at Greenford Green, northwest of the metropolis. At first the dye was marketed as Tyrian purple,[3] cashing in on interest in the dye of antiquity, obtained from a mollusc found in the Near East, and also in order to compete with murexide, named after the mollusc. The cotton dyers and printers in England and Scotland were not enthusiastic about adopting the technologically novel product. However, French dyers and textile printers were encouraged to take up an interest in Perkin's product following the introduction of a new, fast,* lichen-derived purple, controlled by a single French firm. In late 1858, their adoption of the synthetic product, for which Perkin had failed to gain a patent in Paris, led to its rapid popularity.

Borrowing from the French word for the mallow flower, in 1859 modistes[4] and fashion writers of London named Perkin's colorant mauve. The name stuck, as did the fashion, and Perkin's fortune was made. His work stimulated investigations elsewhere in Britain, in France, and then in Germany and Switzerland into aniline and its reactions. Other successful aniline dyes followed, particularly aniline red (magenta, fuchsine), aniline blue, Hoffmann's violet, and a fast aniline black. Apart from Hoffmann's violet (1863), discoveries were often as much the outcomes of serendipity as they were the results of applying

---

3   *Tyrian purple*   Ancient, prized fabric dye.

4   *modistes*   Makers and sellers of fashionable women's wear.

the scientific method. Aniline blue, for example, was an accidental discovery, observed by chance after an operator at a factory in Brentford mixed the wrong ingredients for aniline red. However discovered, these aniline, or coal-tar, dyes had no analogues in nature; though some were less stable that Perkin's color, they satisfied the demand for completely novel colors. After the fashion for mauve declined, its last major use was in the printing of postage stamps at the De La Rue company of London.

During 1869–70, Perkin, in London, and the newly formed Badische Anilin-und Soda-Fabrik (BASF) firm, in Ludwigshafen, Germany, commenced manufacture of synthetic alizarin, an important red colorant (previously extracted from the madder plant) and the first natural product of some complexity to be synthesized. This represented the major industrial application of scientific knowledge. The endeavor relied on academic-industrial collaboration, including studies of chemical constitution and structure—now greatly facilitated by August Kekule's novel six-membered ring structure for benzene (1865)—and

10

ANILINE DYES.

In Chancery.
SIMPSON, MAULE, AND NICHOLSON, v. HOLLIDAY.

The Plaintiffs have circulated a statement that they have established Medlock's Patent for the Manufacture of Magenta or Roseine Dye. We believe this statement to be quite incorrect. They have taken proceedings against Messrs. Wilson and Fletcher, who, after the jury had been discharged because they could not agree, as we are informed, consented to an injunction. The Patent can only be established by a judicial decision after a full inquiry, and not, as in the suit referred to, by consent of the defendants, who could only bind themselves. The only reason we can see for circulating such a statement is to secure to Plaintiffs, as far as possible, the monopoly of the article; by deterring persons from dealing therein, though it can be, and is, made by other than Medlock's Patented process, upon which alone the Plaintiffs rely.

Mr. Holliday having been advised by eminent counsel that he has a good defence to this suit, intends to compel the Plaintiffs to try the cause as early as possible, and has done all in his power to have it heard this month, but, under the pretence that they could not be prepared with their witnesses, the Plaintiffs have succeeded in postponing the trial, which will now probably be delayed until next November. This Mr. Holliday regrets, because he had hoped at a much earlier period to have destroyed a monopoly which he believes to be unjust both to those who deal in Magenta Dye and the public who use it.

The same persons have also circulated a statement that they have established Gerard's Patent for the manufacture of Blue or Violet Dyes. This is also incorrect. Mr. Holliday had sold some Blue Dye made by a foreigner, who assured him that it was not an infringement of the above Patent, but who, though he had promised to indemnify Mr. Holliday, failed to do so when applied to, and that gentleman therefore submitted to an injunction, which only binds himself, and does not affect any other person.

HESP & OWEN,

Solicitors for Mr. Thomas Holliday, trading under the firm of
Huddersfield, July 29th, 1863.   Thomas Holliday & Co.

Figure 1. Handbill dated 29 July 1863 in which the manufacturer Thomas Holliday of Huddersfield attacks the monopolies on aniline red (magenta, roseine) and aniline blue claimed by the firm of Simpson, Maule and Nicholson of London.

identification of components in reaction mixtures. This the Germans mastered and exploited to the full. Perkin, however, worked mainly alone in a house opposite his factory. Unable to compete with the German dye manufacturers, he sold out at the end of 1873. Not long after, in 1874, the modern chemical structure alizarin was published by two Germans, the academic Adolf von Baeyer and BASF's technical manager, Heinrich Caro.

Synthetic dyestuffs satisfied an important dual need of the vast and expanding textile industry, the growth engine of the First Industrial Revolution. This need was, first, for dyes of quality and quantity that were better suited to the new high-speed, steam-driven textile printing machines, and, second, for a regular supply of colorants that were no longer dependent on imported natural products. Industrial problem-solving related to dyes fostered tremendous advances in academic chemistry, in both theory and practice. The pursuit of new dyes and the need to establish monopolies over chemical inventions, which were poorly covered by all existing patent systems, led to modernization of patent law, though mainly in Germany. This ensured the profits required to support research campaigns, such as that which enabled the natural dye indigo to be displaced in 1897 by the German-made product. This substantial, and successful effort had tremendous ramifications in the twentieth century as demand for the natural colorant, imported from India, collapsed, causing not only the British loss of monopoly over a valuable commodity but also impoverishment for many Indians.

Accidental discoveries in science are not particularly rare. But few, if any, in the Victorian era can compare with the striking impact, both in the high street and in the wide-ranging changes in industry, resulting from Perkin's 1856 chance discovery of mauve. Scientific serendipity heralded* the emergence of the Second Industrial Revolution. By the turn of the century, the success of the synthetic dye industry had led to diversification into pharmaceuticals, modern explosives, and research into processes for the manufacture of agricultural chemicals.

(2014)

REBECCA SOLNIT

CLIMATE CHANGE IS VIOLENCE

The first of the two selections reprinted here appeared in Solnit's 2014 book The Encyclopedia of Trouble and Spaciousness, *an alphabetically arranged collection of 29 essays on politics, history, geography, and culture; other entries under "C" include "Cults, Creeps, California in the 1970s," "Concrete in Paradise," and "The Colorado River and Hydrological Madness of the West."*

The second Solnit essay included here was first published in the October 2015 issue of Harper's *magazine.*

C limate change is global-scale violence against places and species, as well as against human beings. Once we call it by name, we can start having a real conversation about our priorities and values.

But if you're tremendously wealthy, you can practice industrial-scale violence without any manual labor on your own part. You can, say, build a sweatshop factory that will collapse in Bangladesh and kill more people than any hands-on mass murderer ever did,* or you can calculate risk and benefit about putting poisons or unsafe machines into the world, as manufacturers do every day. If you're the leader of a country, you can declare war and kill by the hundreds of thousands or millions. And the nuclear superpowers—the United States and Russia—still hold the option of destroying quite a lot of life on Earth.

So do the carbon barons. But when we talk about violence, we almost always talk about violence from below, not above.

Or so I thought when I received a press release from a climate group announcing that "scientists say there is a direct link between changing climate and an increase in violence." What the scientists actually said, in a not-so-newsworthy article in *Nature* a few years ago, is that there is higher conflict in the tropics in El Nino years and that perhaps this will scale up to make our age of climate change also an era of civil and international conflict.

The message is that ordinary people will behave badly in an era of intensified climate change. All this makes sense, unless you go back to the premise   5 and note that climate change is itself violence. Extreme, horrific, long-term, widespread violence.

Climate change is anthropogenic—caused by human beings, some much more than others. We know the consequences of that change: the acidification of oceans and decline of many species in them, the slow disappearance of island nations such as the Maldives, increased flooding, drought, crop failure leading to food-price increases and famine, increasingly turbulent weather. (Think Hurricane Sandy and the recent typhoon in the Philippines and heat waves that kill elderly people by the tens of thousands.)

Climate change is violence.

So if we want to talk about violence and climate change, then let's talk about climate change as violence. Rather than worrying about whether ordinary human beings will react turbulently to the destruction of the very means of their survival, let's worry about that destruction—and their survival.

Of course, water failure, crop failure, flooding, and more will lead to mass migration and climate refugees—they already have—and this will lead to conflict. Those conflicts are being set in motion now.

10   You can regard the Arab Spring,[1] in part, as a climate conflict: the increase in wheat prices was one of the triggers for that series of revolts that changed the face of northernmost Africa and the Middle East. On the one hand, you can say, how nice if those people had not been hungry in the first place. On the other, how can you not say, how great is it that those people stood up against being deprived of sustenance and hope? And then you have to look at the systems that created that hunger—the enormous economic inequalities in places such as Egypt and the brutality used to keep down the people at the lower levels of the social system, as well as the weather.

People revolt when their lives are unbearable. Sometimes material reality creates that unbearableness: droughts, plagues, storms, floods. But food and medical care, health and well-being, access to housing and education—these things are also governed by economic means and government policy. That's what the revolt called Occupy Wall Street* was against.

Climate change will increase hunger as food prices rise and food production falters, but we already have widespread hunger on Earth, and much of it is due not to the failures of nature and farmers, but to systems of distribution. Almost 16 million children in the United States now live with hunger, according to the U.S. Department of Agriculture, and that is not because the vast, agriculturally rich United States cannot produce enough to feed all of us. We are a country whose distribution system is itself a kind of violence.

---

1   *Arab Spring*   Series of popular uprisings in Tunisia, Egypt and other Middle Eastern countries in the spring of 2011. In several countries these uprisings led to an overthrow of the government.

Climate change is not suddenly bringing about an era of equitable distribution. I suspect people will be revolting in the coming future against what they revolted against in the past: the injustices of the system. They should revolt, and we should be glad they do, if not so glad that they need to. (Though one can hope they'll recognize that violence is not necessarily where their power lies.) One of the events prompting the French Revolution was the failure of the 1788 wheat crop, which made bread prices skyrocket and the poor go hungry. The insurance against such events is often thought to be more authoritarianism and more threats against the poor, but that's only an attempt to keep a lid on what's boiling over; the other way to go is to turn down the heat.

The same week during which I received that ill-thought-out press release about climate and violence, Exxon Mobil Corporation issued a policy report. It makes for boring reading, unless you can make the dry language of business into pictures of the consequences of those acts undertaken for profit. Exxon says, "We are confident that none of our hydrocarbon reserves are now or will become 'stranded.' We believe producing these assets is essential to meeting growing energy demand worldwide."

Stranded assets. That means carbon assets—coal, oil, gas still under-   15 ground—would become worthless if we decided they could not be extracted and burned in the near future. Because scientists say that we need to leave most of the world's known carbon reserves in the ground if we are to go for the milder rather than the more extreme versions of climate change. Under the milder version, countless more people, species, and places will survive. In the best-case scenario, we damage the Earth less. We are currently wrangling about how much to devastate the Earth.

In every arena, we need to look at industrial-scale and systemic violence, not just the hands-on violence of the less powerful. When it comes to climate change, this is particularly true. Exxon has decided to bet that we can't make the corporation keep its reserves in the ground, and the company is reassuring its investors that it will continue to profit off the rapid, violent, and intentional destruction of the Earth.

That's a tired phrase, the destruction of the Earth, but translate it into the face of a starving child and a barren field—and then multiply that a few million times. Or just picture the tiny bivalves: scallops, oysters, Arctic sea snails that can't form shells in acidifying oceans right now. Or another superstorm tearing apart another city. Climate change is global-scale violence against places and species, as well as against human beings. Once we call it by name, we can start having a real conversation about our priorities and values. Because the revolt against brutality begins with a revolt against the language that hides that brutality.

(2014)

The Mother of All Questions

I gave a talk on Virginia Woolf[2] a few years ago. During the question-and-answer period that followed it, the subject that seemed to most interest a number of people was whether Woolf should have had children. I answered the question dutifully, noting that Woolf apparently considered having children early in her marriage, after seeing the delight that her sister, Vanessa Bell, took in her own. But over time Woolf came to see reproduction as unwise, perhaps because of her own psychological instability. Or maybe, I suggested, she wanted to be a writer and to give her life over to her art, which she did with extraordinary success. In the talk I had quoted with approval her description of murdering "the angel of the house,"[3] the inner voice that tells many women to be self-sacrificing handmaidens to domesticity and male vanity. I was surprised that advocating for throttling the spirit of conventional femininity should lead to this conversation.

What I should have said to that crowd was that our interrogation of Woolf's reproductive status was a soporific and pointless detour from the magnificent questions her work poses. (I think at some point I said, "Fuck this shit," which carried the same general message and moved everyone on from the discussion.) After all, many people have children; only one made *To the Lighthouse* and *The Waves*,[4] and we were discussing Woolf because of the books, not the babies.

The line of questioning was familiar enough to me. A decade ago, during a conversation that was supposed to be about a book I had written on politics, the British man interviewing me insisted that instead of talking about the products of my mind, we should talk about the fruit of my loins,* or the lack thereof. Onstage, he hounded me about why I didn't have children. No answer I gave could satisfy him. His position seemed to be that I must have children, that it was incomprehensible that I did not, and so we had to talk about why I didn't, rather than about the books I did have.

As it happens, there are many reasons why I don't have children: I am very good at birth control; though I love children and adore aunthood, I also love solitude; I was raised by unhappy, unkind people, and I wanted neither to replicate their form of parenting nor to create human beings who might feel

---

2   *Virginia Woolf* English novelist and essayist (1882–1941) who played a central role in the development of modernism.

3   *the angel of the house* "The Angel in the House" is an 1854 poem by Coventry Patmore depicting the Victorian ideal of the selfless, domestic wife and mother; the phrase "angel in the house" later became shorthand for this ideal. In her 1931 speech "Professions for Women," Woolf argues that one of the tasks of a woman writer is to kill "the angel in the house."

4   *To the ... The Waves* Two of Woolf's most acclaimed novels.

about me the way that I felt about my begetters; I really wanted to write books, which as I've done it is a fairly consuming vocation. I'm not dogmatic about not having kids. I might have had them under other circumstances and been fine—as I am now.

But just because the question can be answered doesn't mean that I ought to answer it, or that it ought to be asked. The interviewer's question was indecent, because it presumed that women should have children, and that a woman's reproductive activities were naturally public business. More fundamentally, the question assumed that there was only one proper way for a woman to live.

But even to say that there's one proper way may be putting the case too optimistically, given that mothers are consistently found wanting, too. A mother may be treated like a criminal for leaving her child alone for five minutes, even a child whose father has left it alone for several years. Some mothers have told me that having children caused them to be treated as bovine non-intellects who should be disregarded. Other women have been told that they cannot be taken seriously professionally because they will go off and reproduce at some point. And many mothers who do succeed professionally are presumed to be neglecting someone. There is no good answer to being a woman; the art may instead lie in how we refuse the question.

We talk about open questions, but there are closed questions, too, questions to which there is only one right answer, at least as far as the interrogator is concerned. These are questions that push you into the herd or nip at you for diverging from it, questions that contain their own answers and whose aim is enforcement and punishment. One of my goals in life is to become truly rabbinical, to be able to answer closed questions with open questions, to have the internal authority to be a good gatekeeper when intruders approach, and to at least remember to ask, "Why are you asking that?" This, I've found, is always a good answer to an unfriendly question, and closed questions tend to be unfriendly. But on the day of my interrogation about having babies, I was taken by surprise (and severely jet-lagged), and so I was left to wonder—why do such bad questions so predictably get asked?

Maybe part of the problem is that we have learned to ask the wrong things of ourselves. Our culture is steeped in a kind of pop psychology* whose obsessive question is: Are you happy? We ask it so reflexively that it seems natural to wish that a pharmacist with a time machine could deliver a lifetime supply of tranquilizers and antipsychotics to Bloomsbury,[5] so that an incomparable feminist prose stylist could be reoriented to produce litters of Woolf babies.

---

5 *Bloomsbury* Woolf was a member of the Bloomsbury Group, a circle of writers, artists, and other intellectuals centered in the Bloomsbury neighborhood of London.

Questions about happiness generally assume that we know what a happy life looks like. Happiness is understood to be a matter of having a great many ducks lined up in a row—spouse, offspring, private property, erotic experiences—even though a millisecond of reflection will bring to mind countless people who have all those things and are still miserable.

10   We are constantly given one-size-fits-all recipes, but those recipes fail, often and hard. Nevertheless, we are given them again. And again and again. They become prisons and punishments; the prison of the imagination traps many in the prison of a life that is correctly aligned with the recipes and yet is entirely miserable.

The problem may be a literary one: we are given a single story line about what makes a good life, even though not a few who follow that story line have bad lives. We speak as though there is one good plot with one happy outcome, while the myriad forms a life can take flower—and wither—all around us.

Even those who live out the best version of the familiar story line might not find happiness as their reward. This is not necessarily a bad thing. I know a woman who was lovingly married for seventy years. She has had a long, meaningful life that she has lived according to her principles. But I wouldn't call her happy; her compassion for the vulnerable and concern for the future have given her a despondent worldview. What she has had instead of happiness requires better language to describe. There are entirely different criteria for a good life that might matter more to a person—honor, meaning, depth, engagement, hope.

Part of my own endeavor as a writer has been to find ways to value what is elusive and overlooked, to describe nuances and shades of meaning, to celebrate public life and solitary life, and—in John Berger's phrase—to find "another way of telling," which is part of why getting clobbered by the same old ways of telling is disheartening.

The conservative "defense of marriage,"* which is really nothing more than a defense of the old hierarchical arrangement that straight marriage* was before feminists began to reform it, has bled over into the general culture, entrenching the devout belief that there is something magically awesome for children about the heterosexual two-parent household, which leads many people to stay in miserable marriages. I know people who long hesitated to leave horrible marriages because the old recipe insists that somehow a situation that is terrible for one or both parents will be beneficent for the children. Even women with violently abusive spouses are often urged to stay in situations that are supposed to be so categorically wonderful that the details don't matter. Form wins out over content. And yet an amicably divorced woman recently explained to me how ideal it was to be a divorced parent: she and her former spouse both had plenty of time with and without their children.

After I wrote a book about me and my mother, who married a brutal profes- 15
sional man and had four children and often seethed with rage and misery, I
was ambushed by an interviewer who asked whether my abusive father
was the reason I had failed to find a life partner. Her question was freighted
with astonishing assumptions about what I had intended to do with my life.
The book, *The Faraway Nearby,* was, I thought, in a quiet, roundabout way
about my long journey toward a really nice life, and an attempt to reckon
with my mother's fury (including the origin of that fury in her entrapment in
conventional feminine roles and expectations).

I have done what I set out to do in my life, and what I set out to do was
not what the interviewer presumed. I set out to write books, to be surrounded
by generous, brilliant people, and to have great adventures. Men—romances,
flings, and long-term relationships—have been some of those adventures, and
so have remote deserts, arctic seas, mountaintops, uprisings and disasters, and
the exploration of ideas, archives, records, and lives.

Society's recipes for fulfillment cause a great deal of unhappiness, both
in those who are stigmatized for being unable or unwilling to carry them out
and in those who obey but don't find happiness. Of course there are people
with very standard-issue lives who are very happy. I know some of them, just
as I know very happy childless and celibate monks, priests, and abbesses, gay
divorcees, and everything in between. Last summer my friend Emma was
walked down the aisle by her father, with his husband following right behind
on Emma's mother's arm; the four of them, plus Emma's new husband, are an
exceptionally loving and close-knit family engaged in the pursuit of justice
through politics. This summer, both of the weddings I went to had two grooms
and no brides; at the first, one of the grooms wept because he had been excluded
from the right to marry for most of his life, and he had never thought he would
see his own wedding. I'm all for marriage and children, when it and they are
truly what people want from their lives.

In the traditional worldview happiness is essentially private and selfish. Reasonable people pursue their self-interest, and when they do so successfully they
are supposed to be happy. The very definition of what it means to be human is
narrow, and altruism, idealism, and public life (except in the forms of fame,
status, or material success) have little place on the shopping list. The idea that
a life should seek meaning seldom emerges; not only are the standard activities
assumed to be inherently meaningful, they are treated as the only meaningful
options.

People lock onto motherhood as a key to feminine identity in part from the
belief that children are the best way to fulfill your capacity to love, even though
the list of monstrous, ice-hearted mothers is extensive. But there are so many

things to love besides one's own offspring, so many things that need love, so much other work love has to do in the world.

20   While many people question the motives of the childless, who are taken to be selfish for refusing the sacrifices that come with parenthood, they often neglect to note that those who love their children intensely may have less love left for the rest of the world. Christina Lupton, a writer who is also a mother, recently described some of the things she relinquished when motherhood's consuming tasks had her in their grasp, including all the ways of tending to the world that are less easily validated than parenting, but which are just as fundamentally necessary for children to flourish. I mean here the writing and inventing and the politics and the activism; the reading and the public speaking and the protesting and the teaching and the filmmaking.... Most of the things I value most, and from which I trust any improvements in the human condition will come, are violently incompatible with the actual and imaginative work of childcare.

One of the fascinating things about Edward Snowden's[6] sudden appearance a little more than two years ago was the inability of many people to comprehend why a young man might give up on the recipe for happiness—high wages, secure job, Hawaiian home—to become the world's most sought-after fugitive. Their premise seemed to be that since all people are selfish, Snowden's motive must be a self-serving pursuit of attention or money.

During the first rush of commentary, Jeffrey Toobin, *The New Yorker*'s legal expert, wrote that Snowden was "a grandiose narcissist who deserves to be in prison." Another pundit announced, "I think what we have in Edward Snowden is just a narcissistic young man who has decided he is smarter than the rest of us." Others assumed that he was revealing U.S. government secrets because he had been paid by an enemy country.

Snowden seemed like a man from another century. In his initial communications with journalist Glenn Greenwald he called himself Cincinnatus—after the Roman statesman who acted for the good of his society without seeking self-advancement. This was a clue that Snowden formed his ideals and models far away from the standard-issue formulas for happiness. Other eras and cultures often asked other questions than the ones we ask now: What is the most meaningful thing you can do with your life? What is your contribution to the world or your community? Do you live according to your principles? What will your legacy be? What does your life mean? Maybe our obsession

---

6   *Edward Snowden*   Controversial ex-CIA employee (b. 1983) who copied a large number of classified government documents and released them to journalists in order to expose secret mass surveillance being conducted by the National Security Agency.

with happiness is a way not to ask those other questions, a way to ignore how spacious our lives can be, how effective our work can be, and how far-reaching our love can be.

There is a paradox at the heart of the happiness question. Todd Kashdan, a psychology professor at George Mason University, reported a few years ago on studies that concluded that people who think being happy is important are more likely to become depressed: "Organizing your life around trying to become happier, making happiness the primary objective of life, gets in the way of actually becoming happy."

I did finally have my rabbinical moment* in Britain. After the jet lag was over, I was interviewed onstage by a woman with a plummy, fluting accent. "So," she trilled, "you've been *wounded* by humanity and *fled* to the landscape for refuge." The implication was clear: I was an exceptionally sorry specimen on display, an outlier in the herd. I turned to the audience and asked, "Have any of you ever been wounded by humanity?" They laughed with me; in that moment, we knew that we were all weird, all in this together, and that addressing our own suffering, while learning not to inflict it on others, is part of the work we're all here to do. So is love, which comes in so many forms and can be directed at so many things. There are many questions in life worth asking, but perhaps if we're wise we can understand that not every question needs an answer.

25

(2015)

GLORIA GALLOWAY

DR. BJORN LOMBORG ARGUES THE CLIMATE CHANGE FIGHT ISN'T WORTH THE COST

The views of political scientist Bjorn Lomborg on climate change stand in marked contrast to those of Rebecca Solnit (see above). This article summarizing his approach for a general audience was published in the 12 June 2015 issue of The Globe and Mail. *(The online title is provided here; in the newspaper's print version the article was entitled, "Climate-change Emphasis Is Misguided, Professor Says.")*

Bjorn Lomborg says he is not a climate-change denier; he is a realist who knows better ways of improving the world than a head-on assault on global warming.

It's not easy to take a public stand against the internationally agreed upon goal of limiting the increase in average temperatures to 2 degrees Celsius above pre-industrial levels—a rise that some scientists describe as a tipping point that would be followed by the collapse of ice sheets, rising sea levels and an onslaught of dramatic weather events.

But Dr. Lomborg has, for years, been arguing that the target is simply too difficult and too expensive to achieve and the world's development dollars would be put to better use in reducing poverty, preventing disease, educating the illiterate and feeding the hungry. And, yes, he would also protect the environment, but in smaller, more achievable ways.

Dr. Lomborg, a Danish political scientist and a man who has been named by *Time* magazine as one of the most influential people in the world, is the director of the Copenhagen Consensus Centre. It is a think tank that engages top economists to apply a cost-benefit analysis to major problems so policy-makers will know where development money is best spent. And, he says, the 2-degree global warming target is a bad investment.

768

"We have problems that are huge and we don't know how to fix them," he   5
said in an interview with *The Globe and Mail* on a recent visit to Ottawa. "So
we say let's spend the money where we know how to fix them."

Dr. Lomborg's message comes as the members of the United Nations
prepare to set global sustainable development goals that will influence how
$2.5-trillion (U.S.) in aid is spent between 2015 to 2030. The list of goals is
expected to be finalized at a summit in New York in September and follows on
the eight Millennium Development Goals and 18 associated targets which end
this year.

At the moment, there are 17 proposed new goals and 169 proposed new
targets. They advocate ambitious actions as diverse as eradicating extreme
poverty, ending epidemics of deadly diseases, putting a stop to violence against
women, ensuring affordable access to energy and halting climate change.

"The thing that's wrong in this process is, basically, we are promising
everything to everyone everywhere at all times," said Dr. Lomborg. "Which, of
course, is really really nice but it's not going to do very much because we are
just going to spend a tiny bit of money everywhere."

The analysis done by his institute says that, if the world's aid money is
distributed evenly over all of the 169 targets, it would do about $7 worth of
good for every dollar spent. But, if the number of targets were reduced to the
most economically efficient 19, the money would do about $32 worth of good
for every dollar spent.

The best thing the world could do, according to the economists enlisted   10
by Dr. Lomborg, would be to reduce world trade restrictions by successfully
completing the Doha round of World Trade Organization talks. That, they say,
would make the world richer by $11-trillion by the year 2030 and lift 160 mil-
lion people out of poverty.

Instead of going after headline-grabbing diseases like Ebola, which, in
its worst year, killed 20,000 people, Dr. Lomborg says the economic analysis
points to targeting malaria which kills 600,000 people annually and tuberculosis which kills 1.3 million.

And, instead of holding steadfast to the goal of keeping global temperatures within 2 degrees above pre-industrial levels, Dr. Lomborg advocates the
elimination of subsidies on fossil fuels and the introduction of carbon taxes.
Neither measure would be a solution, he said, but would at least "nibble away"
at the problem.

Dr. Lomborg's ideas have made him unpopular with many environmental-
ists who argue that, unless tackling climate change is the world's top priority and the 2-degree goal is met, the ensuing devastation will make all other
problems pale by comparison. They argue with his numbers and have created
websites to list what they say are factual holes in his arguments.

He remains undaunted.

15   "The UN climate panel estimates that, by the mid-'70s, global warming is going to cost somewhere between 0.2 per cent and 2 per cent of GDP every year," said Dr. Lomborg. "That's not a trivial cost. But of course it's also important to say it's not the end of the world."

World leaders have talked a lot about the importance of the possibly unachievable goal of the 2-degree limit but, in the end, none have taken the measures that are needed to achieve it, said Dr. Lomborg.

"By focusing on the things that will do the most good, we will do much more good but we will feel less virtuous," he said. "And that's the real challenge."

(2015)

CLAUDIA RANKINE

from CITIZEN: AN AMERICAN LYRIC

In 2014, for the first time in the history of the National Book Critics Circle Awards, the same book was nominated in two different categories: Claudia Rankine's Citizen, *a short, heavily illustrated book exploring various aspects of African American experience in unconventional ways, was a finalist in the Criticism category, and the winner in the Poetry category.*

The excerpt included here is the second of the book's seven, unnamed chapters.

Hennessy Youngman aka Jayson Musson, whose *Art Thoughtz* take the form of tutorials on YouTube, educates viewers on contemporary art issues. In one of his many videos, he addresses how to become a successful black artist, wryly suggesting black people's anger is marketable. He advises black artists to cultivate "an angry nigger exterior"* by watching, among other things, the Rodney King video[1] while working.

Youngman's suggestions are meant to expose expectations for blackness as well as to underscore the difficulty inherent in any attempt by black artists to metabolize real rage. The commodified anger his video advocates rests lightly on the surface for spectacle's sake. It can be engaged or played like the race card* and is tied solely to the performance of blackness and not to the emotional state of particular individuals in particular situations.

On the bridge between this sellable anger and "the artist" resides, at times, an actual anger. Youngman in his video doesn't address this type of anger: the anger built up through experience and the quotidian struggles against dehumanization every brown or black person lives simply because of skin color. This other kind of anger in time can prevent, rather than sponsor, the production of anything except loneliness.

---

1 *the Rodney King video* Video footage from 3 March 1991 showed the violent beating of African American taxi driver Rodney King (1965–2012) by four white Los Angeles police officers. The event heightened awareness of racism in law enforcement, and the subsequent acquittal of the police officers prompted the 1992 Los Angeles Riots.

You begin to think, maybe erroneously, that this other kind of anger is really a type of knowledge: the type that both clarifies and disappoints. It responds to insult and attempted erasure simply by asserting presence, and the energy required to present, to react, to assert is accompanied by visceral disappointment: a disappointment in the sense that no amount of visibility will alter the ways in which one is perceived.

5   Recognition of this lack might break you apart. Or recognition might illuminate the erasure the attempted erasure triggers. Whether such discerning creates a healthier, if more isolated self, you can't know. In any case, Youngman doesn't speak to this kind of anger. He doesn't say that witnessing the expression of this more ordinary and daily anger might make the witness believe that a person is "insane."

And insane is what you think, one Sunday afternoon, drinking an Arnold Palmer,* watching the 2009 Women's US Open semifinal, when brought to full attention by the suddenly explosive behavior of Serena Williams.[2] Serena in HD before your eyes becomes overcome by a rage you recognize and have been taught to hold at a distance for your own good. Serena's behavior, on this particular Sunday afternoon, suggests that all the injustice she has played through all the years of her illustrious career flashes before her and she decides finally to respond to all of it with a string of invectives. Nothing, not even the repetition of negations ("no, no, no") she employed in a similar situation years before as a younger player at the 2004 US Open, prepares you for this. Oh my God, she's gone crazy, you say to no one.

What does a victorious or defeated black woman's body in a historically white space look like? Serena and her big sister Venus Williams brought to mind Zora Neale Hurston's[3] "I feel most colored when I am thrown against a sharp white background." This appropriated line, stenciled on canvas by Glenn Ligon, who used plastic letter stencils, smudging oil sticks, and graphite to transform the words into abstractions, seemed to be ad copy[4] for some aspect of life for all black bodies.

Hurston's statement has been played out on the big screen by Serena and Venus: they win sometimes, they lose sometimes, they've been injured, they've been happy, they've been sad, ignored, booed mightily (see Indian

---

2   *US Open*   One of the four most important annual tennis tournaments, which together comprise the Grand Slam;   *Serena Williams*   African American tennis player (b. 1981), often considered the best female tennis player of all time.

3   *Zora Neale Hurston*   African American writer (1891–1960), best known for her novel *Their Eyes Were Watching God* (1937). The quotation here appears in her essay "How It Feels to Be Colored Me," also included in this anthology.

4   *Glenn Ligon*   African American artist (b. 1960);   *ad copy*   Text of an advertisement.

Wells,[5] which both sisters have boycotted for more than a decade), they've been cheered, and through it all and evident to all were those people who are enraged they are there at all—graphite against a sharp white background.

For years you attribute to Serena Williams a kind of resilience appropriate only for those who exist in celluloid. Neither her father nor her mother nor her sister nor Jehovah her God nor NIKE camp could shield her ultimately from people who felt her black body didn't belong on their court, in their world. From the start many made it clear Serena would have done better struggling to survive in the two-dimensionality of a Millet painting, rather than on their tennis courtbetter to put all that strength to work in their fantasy of her working the land, rather than be caught up in the turbulence of our ancient dramas, like a ship fighting a storm in a Turner[6] seascape.

The most notorious of Serena's detractors takes the form of Mariana Alves, the distinguished tennis chair umpire.[7] In 2004 Alves was excused from officiating any more matches on the final day of the US Open after she made five bad calls against Serena in her quarterfinal matchup against fellow American Jennifer Capriati. The serves and returns Alves called out were landing, stunningly unreturned by Capriati, inside the lines, no discerning eyesight needed. Commentators, spectators, television viewers, line judges, everyone could see the balls were good, everyone, apparently, except Alves. No one could understand what was happening. Serena, in her denim skirt, black sneaker boots, and dark mascara, began wagging her finger and saying "no, no, no," as if by negating the moment she could propel us back into a legible world. Tennis superstar John McEnroe,[8] given his own keen eye for injustice during his professional career, was shocked that Serena was able to hold it together after losing the match.

Though no one was saying anything explicitly about Serena's black body, you are not the only viewer who thought it was getting in the way of Alves's sight line. One commentator said he hoped he wasn't being unkind when he stated, "Capriati wins it with the help of the umpires and the line judges." A

10

5　*Indian Wells*　Tennis tournament held annually in Indian Wells, California. In 2001, the Williams sisters and their father Richard Williams were booed, and some in the crowd shouted racial slurs.

6　*Millet*　Jean-François Millet (1815–75), French painter best known for works depicting peasant farmers; *Turner*　J.M.W. Turner (1775–1851), English painter known for his evocative landscapes. (Rankine includes reproductions of his painting *Slave Ship* and of a detail from the painting as the final images in *Citizen*.)

7　*chair umpire*　In tennis, person who holds final authority to decide questions and disputes during a match.

8　*John McEnroe*　American tennis player (b. 1959), often considered one of the all-time best players.

year later that match would be credited for demonstrating the need for the speedy installation of Hawk-Eye, the line-calling technology that took the seeing away from the beholder. Now the umpire's call can be challenged by a replay; however, back then after the match Serena said, "I'm very angry and bitter right now. I felt cheated. Shall I go on? I just feel robbed." And though you felt outrage for Serena after that 2004 US Open, as the years go by, she seems to put Alves, and a lengthening list of other curious calls and oversights, against both her and her sister, behind her as they happen.

Yes, and the body has memory. The physical carriage hauls more than its weight. The body is the threshold across which each objectionable call passes into consciousness—all the unintimidated, unblinking, and unflappable resilience does not erase the moments lived through, even as we are eternally stupid or everlastingly optimistic, so ready to be inside, among, a part of the games.

And here Serena is, five years after Alves, back at the US Open, again in a semifinal match, this time against Belgium's Kim Clijsters. Serena is not playing well and loses the first set. In response she smashes her racket on the court. Now McEnroe isn't stunned by her ability to hold herself together and is moved to say, "That's as angry as I've ever seen her." The umpire gives her a warning; another violation will mean a point penalty.

She is in the second set at the critical moment of 5-6 in Clijsters's favor, serving to stay in the match, at match point. The line judge employed by the US Open to watch Serena's body, its every move, says Serena stepped on the line while serving. What? (The Hawk-Eye cameras don't cover the feet, only the ball, apparently.) What! Are you serious? She is serious; she has seen a foot fault, one no one else is able to locate despite the numerous replays. "No foot fault, you definitely do not see a foot fault there," says McEnroe. "That's overofficiating for certain," says another commentator. Even the ESPN tennis commentator, who seems predictable in her readiness to find fault with the Williams sisters, says, "Her foot fault call was way off." Yes, and even if there had been a foot fault, despite the rule, they are rarely ever called at critical moments in a Grand Slam match because "You don't make a call," tennis official Carol Cox says, "that can decide a match unless it's flagrant."

15   As you look at the affable Kim Clijsters, you try to entertain the thought that this scenario could have played itself out the other way. And as Serena turns to the lineswoman and says, "I swear to God I'm fucking going to take this fucking ball and shove it down your fucking throat, you hear that? I swear to God!" As offensive as her outburst is, it is difficult not to applaud her for reacting immediately to being thrown against a sharp white background. It is difficult not to applaud her for existing in the moment, for fighting crazily against the so-called wrongness of her body's positioning at the service line.

She says in 2009, belatedly, the words that should have been said to the umpire in 2004, the words that might have snapped Alves back into focus, a focus that would have acknowledged what actually was happening on the court. Now Serena's reaction is read as insane. And her punishment for this moment of manumission[9] is the threatened point penalty resulting in the loss of the match, an $82,500 fine, plus a two-year probationary period by the Grand Slam Committee.

Perhaps the committee's decision is only about context, though context is not meaning. It is a public event being watched in homes across the world. In any case, it is difficult not to think that if Serena lost context by abandoning all rules of civility, it could be because her body, trapped in a racial imaginary, trapped in disbelief—code for being black in America—is being governed not by the tennis match she is participating in but by a collapsed relationship that had promised to play by the rules. Perhaps this is how racism feels no matter the context—randomly the rules everyone else gets to play by no longer apply to you, and to call this out by calling out "I swear to God!" is to be called insane, crass, crazy. Bad sportsmanship.

Two years later, September 11, 2011, Serena is playing the Australian Sam Stosur in the US Open final. She is expected to win, having just beaten the number-one player, the Dane Caroline Wozniacki, in the semifinal the night before. Some speculate Serena especially wants to win this Grand Slam because it is the tenth anniversary of the attack on the Twin Towers.[10] It's believed that by winning she will prove her red-blooded American patriotism and will once and for all become beloved by the tennis world (think Arthur Ashe[11] after his death). All the bad calls, the boos, the criticisms that she has made ugly the game of tennis—through her looks as well as her behavior—that entire cluster of betrayals will be wiped clean with this win.

One imagines her wanting to say what her sister would say a year later after being diagnosed with Sjögren's syndrome[12] and losing her match to shouts of "Let's go, Venus!" in Arthur Ashe Stadium: "I know this is not proper tennis etiquette, but this is the first time I've ever played here that the crowd has been

---

9   *manumission*   Release from slavery.

10   *tenth anniversary ... Twin Towers*   In the terrorist attacks by Al-Qaeda on September 11, 2001, the Twin Towers of the World Trade Center in New York were destroyed; almost 3000 people died.

11   *Arthur Ashe*   American tennis player (1943–93), winner of three Grand Slam tournaments. An African American, Ashe was often the target of racism during his lifetime, but he became almost universally revered after his death.

12   *Sjögren's syndrome*   Autoimmune disorder which typically causes dry mouth, dry eyes, joint pain, and fatigue, as well as often being the cause of other complications.

behind me like that. Today I felt American, you know, for the first time at the US Open. So I've waited my whole career to have this moment and here it is."

20   It is all too exhausting and Serena's exhaustion shows in her playing; she is losing, a set and a game down. Yes, and finally she hits a great shot, a big forehand, and before the ball is safely past Sam Stosur's hitting zone, Serena yells, "Come on!" thinking she has hit an irretrievable winner. The umpire, Eva Asderaki, rules correctly that Serena, by shouting, interfered with Stosur's concentration. Subsequently, a ball that Stosur seemingly would not have been able to return becomes Stosur's point. Serena's reply is to ask the umpire if she is trying to screw her again. She remembers the umpire doing this to her before. As a viewer, you too, along with John McEnroe, begin to wonder if this is the same umpire from 2004 or 2009. It isn't—in 2004 it was Mariana Alves and in 2009 it was Sharon Wright; however, the use of the word "again" by Serena returns her viewers to other times calling her body out.

Again Serena's frustrations, her disappointments, exist within a system you understand not to try to understand in any fair-minded way because to do so is to understand the erasure of the self as systemic, as ordinary. For Serena, the daily diminishment is a low flame, a constant drip. Every look, every comment, every bad call blossoms out of history, through her, onto you. To understand is to see Serena as hemmed in as any other black body thrown against our American background. "Aren't you the one that screwed me over last time here?" she asks umpire Asderaki. "Yeah, you are. Don't look at me. Really, don't even look at me. Don't look my way. Don't look my way," she repeats, because it is that simple.

Yes, and who can turn away? Serena is not running out of breath. Despite all her understanding, she continues to serve up aces while smashing rackets and fraying hems. In the 2012 Olympics she brought home two of the three gold medals the Americans would win in tennis. After her three-second celebratory dance on center court at the All England Club, the American media reported, "And there was Serena ... Crip-Walking[13] all over the most lily-white place in the world.... You couldn't help but shake your head.... What Serena did was akin to cracking a tasteless, X-rated* joke inside a church.... What she did was immature and classless."

Before making the video *How to Be a Successful Black Artist*, Hennessy Youngman uploaded to YouTube *How to Be a Successful Artist*. While putting forward the argument that one needs to be white to be truly successful, he adds, in an aside, that this might not work for blacks because if "a nigger paints a

---

13   *Crip-Walking*   Dance move originated by the Los Angeles Crip gang in the 1970s.

flower it becomes a slavery flower, flower de *Amistad*,"[14] thereby intimating that any relationship between the white viewer and the black artist immediately becomes one between white persons and black property, which was the legal state of things once upon a time,* as Patricia Williams has pointed out in *The Alchemy of Race and Rights*: "The cold game of equality staring makes me feel like a thin sheet of glass.... I could force my presence, the real me contained in those eyes, upon them, but I would be smashed in the process."

Interviewed by the Brit Piers Morgan after her 2012 Olympic victory, Serena is informed by Morgan that he was planning on calling her victory dance "the Serena Shuffle"; however, he has learned from the American press that it is a Crip Walk, a gangster dance. Serena responds incredulously by asking if she looks like a gangster to him. Yes, he answers. All in a day's fun, perhaps, and in spite and despite it all, Serena Williams blossoms again into Serena Williams. When asked if she is confident she can win her upcoming matches, her answer remains, "At the end of the day, I am very happy with me and I'm very happy with my results."

Serena would go on to win every match she played between the US Open and the year-end 2012 championship tournament, and because tennis is a game of adjustments, she would do this without any reaction to a number of questionable calls. More than one commentator would remark on her ability to hold it together during these matches. She is a woman in love, one suggests. She has grown up, another decides, as if responding to the injustice of racism is childish and her previous demonstration of emotion was free-floating and detached from any external actions by others. Some others theorize she is developing the admirable "calm and measured logic" of an Arthur Ashe, who the sportswriter Bruce Jenkins felt was "dignified" and "courageous" in his ability to confront injustice without making a scene. Jenkins, perhaps inspired by Serena's new comportment, felt moved to argue that her continued boycott of Indian Wells in 2013, where she felt traumatized by the aggression of racist slurs hurled at her in 2001, was lacking in "dignity" and "integrity" and demonstrated "only stubbornness and a grudge." (Serena lifted her boycott in 2015, though Venus continues to boycott Indian Wells.)

Watching this newly contained Serena, you begin to wonder if she finally has given up wanting better from her peers or if she too has come across Hennessy's *Art Thoughtz* and is channeling his assertion that the less that is communicated the better. Be ambiguous. This type of ambiguity could also be diagnosed as dissociation and would support Serena's claim that she has had to split herself off from herself and create different personae.

25

---

14 *Amistad* The reference is to *La Amistad*, a nineteenth-century schooner on which a slave revolt occurred in 1839.

Now that there is no calling out of injustice, no yelling, no cursing, no finger wagging or head shaking, the media decides to take up the mantle when on December 12, 2012, two weeks after Serena is named WTA[15] Player of the Year, the Dane Caroline Wozniacki, a former number-one player, imitates Serena by stuffing towels in her top and shorts, all in good fun, at an exhibition match. Racist? CNN* wants to know if outrage is the proper response.

It's then that Hennessy's suggestions about "how to be a successful artist" return to you: be ambiguous, be white. Wozniacki, it becomes clear, has finally enacted what was desired by many of Serena's detractors, consciously or unconsciously, the moment the Compton[16] girl first stepped on court. Wozniacki (though there are a number of ways to interpret her actions—playful mocking of a peer, imitation of the mimicking antics of the tennis player known as the joker, Novak Djokovic) finally gives the people what they have wanted all along by embodying Serena's attributes while leaving Serena's "angry nigger exterior" behind. At last, in this real, and unreal, moment, we have Wozniacki's image of smiling blond goodness posing as the best female tennis player of all time.

(2014)

"THE CONDITION OF BLACK LIFE IS ONE OF MOURNING"

This Rankine essay was first published in the 22 June 2015 issue of The New York Times Magazine. *A few days earlier—on the evening of 17 June—a 21-year-old white supremacist had opened fire on the members of a prayer group at a black church in Charleston, South Carolina, and killed nine people.*

A friend recently told me that when she gave birth to her son, before naming him, before even nursing him, her first thought was, I have to get him out of this country. We both laughed. Perhaps our black humor* had to do with understanding that getting out was neither an option nor the real desire. This is it, our life. Here we work, hold citizenship, pensions, health insurance, family, friends and on and on. She couldn't, she didn't, leave. Years after his birth, whenever her son steps out of their home, her status as the mother of a living human being remains as precarious as ever. Added to the natural fears of

---

15   *WTA*   Women's Tennis Association.

16   *Compton*   City in California, south of Los Angeles.

every parent facing the randomness of life is this other knowledge of the ways in which institutional racism works in our country. Ours was the laughter of vulnerability, fear, recognition and an absurd stuckness.

I asked another friend what it's like being the mother of a black son. "The condition of black life is one of mourning," she said bluntly. For her, mourning lived in real time inside her and her son's reality: At any moment she might lose her reason for living. Though the white liberal imagination likes to feel temporarily bad about black suffering, there really is no mode of empathy that can replicate the daily strain of knowing that as a black person you can be killed for simply being black: no hands in your pockets, no playing music, no sudden movements, no driving your car, no walking at night, no walking in the day, no turning onto this street, no entering this building, no standing your ground, no standing here, no standing there, no talking back, no playing with toy guns, no living while black.

Eleven days after I was born, on Sept. 15, 1963, four black girls were killed in the bombing of the 16th Street Baptist Church in Birmingham, Ala. Now, 52 years later, six black women and three black men have been shot to death while at a Bible-study meeting at the historic Emanuel African Methodist Episcopal Church in Charleston, S.C. They were killed by a homegrown terrorist, self-identified as a white supremacist, who might also be a "disturbed young man" (as various news outlets have described him). It has been reported that a black woman and her 5-year-old granddaughter survived the shooting by playing dead. They are two of the three survivors of the attack. The white family of the suspect says that for them this is a difficult time. This is indisputable. But for African-American families, this living in a state of mourning and fear remains commonplace.

The spectacle of the shooting suggests an event out of time, as if the killing of black people with white-supremacist justification interrupts anything other than regular television programming. But Dylann Storm Roof[17] did not create himself from nothing. He has grown up with the rhetoric and orientation of racism. He has seen white men like Benjamin F. Haskell, Thomas Gleason and Michael Jacques plead guilty to, or be convicted of, burning Macedonia Church of God in Christ in Springfield, Mass., just hours after President Obama was elected. Every racist statement he has made he could have heard all his life. He, along with the rest of us, has been living with slain black bodies.

We live in a country where Americans assimilate corpses in their daily 5 comings and goings. Dead blacks are a part of normal life here. Dying in ship hulls, tossed into the Atlantic, hanging from trees, beaten, shot in churches, gunned down by the police or warehoused in prisons: Historically, there is no

---

17 *Dylann Storm Roof* Alleged shooter at the Charleston church.

quotidian without the enslaved, chained or dead black body to gaze upon or to hear about or to position a self against. When blacks become overwhelmed by our culture's disorder and protest (ultimately to our own detriment, because protest gives the police justification to militarize, as they did in Ferguson*), the wrongheaded question that is asked is, "What kind of savages are we?" rather than, "What kind of country do we live in?"

In 1955, when Emmett Till's[18] mutilated and bloated body was recovered from the Tallahatchie River and placed for burial in a nailed-shut pine box, his mother, Mamie Till Mobley, demanded his body be transported from Mississippi, where Till had been visiting relatives, to his home in Chicago. Once the Chicago funeral home received the body, she made a decision that would create a new pathway for how to think about a lynched body. She requested an open coffin and allowed photographs to be taken and published of her dead son's disfigured body.

Mobley's refusal to keep private grief private allowed a body that meant nothing to the criminal-justice system to stand as evidence. By placing both herself and her son's corpse in positions of refusal relative to the etiquette of grief, she "disidentified" with the tradition of the lynched figure left out in public view as a warning to the black community, thereby using the lynching tradition* against itself. The spectacle of the black body, in her hands, publicized the injustice mapped onto her son's corpse. "Let the people see what I see," she said, adding, "I believe that the whole United States is mourning with me."

It's very unlikely that her belief in a national mourning was fully realized, but her desire to make mourning enter our day-to-day world was a new kind of logic. In refusing to look away from the flesh of our domestic murders, by insisting we look with her upon the dead, she reframed mourning as a method of acknowledgment that helped energize the civil rights movement in the 1950s and '60s.

The decision not to release photos of the crime scene in Charleston, perhaps out of deference to the families of the dead, doesn't forestall our mourning. But in doing so, the bodies that demonstrate all too tragically that "black skin is not a weapon" (as one protest poster read last year) are turned into an abstraction. It's one thing to imagine nine black bodies bleeding out on a church floor, and another thing to see it. The lack of visual evidence remains in contrast to what we saw in Ferguson, where the police, in their refusal to move Michael Brown's body, perhaps unknowingly, continued where Till's mother left off.

10   After Brown was shot six times, twice in the head, his body was left facedown in the street by the police officers. Whatever their reasoning, by

18 *Emmett Till* Fourteen-year-old African American boy, murdered and mutilated for allegedly being "fresh" with a white woman he had spoken with.

not moving Brown's corpse for four hours after his shooting, the police made mourning his death part of what it meant to take in the details of his story. No one could consider the facts of Michael Brown's interaction with the Ferguson police officer Darren Wilson without also thinking of the bullet-riddled body bleeding on the asphalt. It would be a mistake to presume that everyone who saw the image mourned Brown, but once exposed to it, a person had to decide whether his dead black body mattered enough to be mourned. (Another option, of course, is that it becomes a spectacle for white pornography: the dead body as an object that satisfies an illicit desire. Perhaps this is where Dylann Storm Roof stepped in.)

Black Lives Matter, the movement founded by the activists Alicia Garza, Patrisse Cullors and Opal Tometi, began with the premise that the incommensurable experiences of systemic racism creates an unequal playing field. The American imagination has never been able to fully recover from its white-supremacist beginnings. Consequently, our laws and attitudes have been straining against the devaluation of the black body. Despite good intentions, the associations of blackness with inarticulate, bestial criminality persist beneath the appearance of white civility. This assumption both frames and determines our individual interactions and experiences as citizens.

The American tendency to normalize situations by centralizing whiteness was consciously or unconsciously demonstrated again when certain whites, like the president of Smith College, sought to alter the language of "Black Lives Matter" to "All Lives Matter." What on its surface was intended to be interpreted as a humanist move—"Aren't we all just people here?"—didn't take into account a system inured to black corpses in our public spaces. When the judge in the Charleston bond hearing* for Dylann Storm Roof called for support of Roof's family, it was also a subtle shift away from valuing the black body in our time of deep despair.

Anti-black racism is in the culture. It's in our laws, in our advertisements, in our friendships, in our segregated cities,* in our schools, in our Congress, in our scientific experiments, in our language, on the Internet, in our bodies (no matter our race), in our communities and, perhaps most devastatingly, in our justice system. The unarmed, slain black bodies in public spaces turn grief into our everyday feeling that something is wrong everywhere and all the time, even if locally things appear normal. Having coffee, walking the dog, reading the paper, taking the elevator to the office, dropping the kids off at school: All of this good life is surrounded by the ambient feeling that at any given moment, a black person is being killed in the street or in his home by the armed hatred of a fellow American.

The Black Lives Matter movement can be read as an attempt to keep mourning an open dynamic in our culture because black lives exist in a state of precariousness. Mourning then bears both the vulnerability inherent in black lives and the instability regarding a future for those lives. Unlike earlier black-power movements that tried to fight or segregate for self-preservation, Black Lives Matter aligns with the dead, continues the mourning and refuses the forgetting in front of all of us. If the Rev. Martin Luther King Jr.'s civil rights movement* made demands that altered the course of American lives and backed up those demands with the willingness to give up your life in service of your civil rights, with Black Lives Matter, a more internalized change is being asked for: recognition.

15   The truth, as I see it, is that if black men and women, black boys and girls, mattered, if we were seen as living, we would not be dying simply because whites don't like us. Our deaths inside a system of racism existed before we were born. The legacy of black bodies as property and subsequently three-fifths human continues to pollute the white imagination. To inhabit our citizenry fully, we have to not only understand this, but also grasp it. In the words of playwright Lorraine Hansberry, "The problem is we have to find some way with these dialogues to show and to encourage the white liberal to stop being a liberal and become an American radical." And, as my friend the critic and poet Fred Moten has written: "I believe in the world and want to be in it. I want to be in it all the way to the end of it because I believe in another world and I want to be in that." This other world, that world, would presumably be one where black living matters. But we can't get there without fully recognizing what is here.

Dylann Storm Roof's unmediated hatred of black people; Black Lives Matter; citizens' videotaping the killings of blacks; the Ferguson Police Department leaving Brown's body in the street—all these actions support Mamie Till Mobley's belief that we need to see or hear the truth. We need the truth of how the bodies died to interrupt the course of normal life. But if keeping the dead at the forefront of our consciousness is crucial for our body politic, what of the families of the dead? How must it feel to a family member for the deceased to be more important as evidence than as an individual to be buried and laid to rest?

Michael Brown's mother, Lesley McSpadden, was kept away from her son's body because it was evidence. She was denied the rights of a mother, a sad fact reminiscent of pre-Civil War times, when as a slave she would have had no legal claim to her offspring. McSpadden learned of her new identity as a mother of a dead son from bystanders: "There were some girls down there had recorded the whole thing," she told reporters. One girl, she said, "showed me a picture on her phone. She said, 'Isn't that your son?' I just bawled even harder. Just to see that, my son lying there lifeless for no apparent reason." Circling the perimeter around her son's body, McSpadden tried to disperse the crowd: "All I want them to do is pick up my baby."

McSpadden, unlike Mamie Till Mobley, seemed to have little desire to expose her son's corpse to the media. Her son was not an orphan body for everyone to look upon. She wanted him covered and removed from sight. He belonged to her, her baby. After Brown's corpse was finally taken away, two weeks passed before his family was able to see him. This loss of control and authority might explain why after Brown's death, McSpadden was supposedly in the precarious position of accosting vendors selling T-shirts that demanded justice for Michael Brown that used her son's name. Not only were the procedures around her son's corpse out of her hands: his name had been commoditized and assimilated into our modes of capitalism.

Some of McSpadden's neighbors in Ferguson also wanted to create distance between themselves and the public life of Brown's death. They did not need a constant reminder of the ways black bodies don't matter to law-enforcement officers in their neighborhood. By the request of the community, the original makeshift memorial—with flowers, pictures, notes and teddy bears—was finally removed by Brown's father on what would have been his birthday and replaced by an official plaque installed on the sidewalk next to where Brown died. The permanent reminder can be engaged or stepped over depending on the pedestrian's desires.

In order to be away from the site of the murder of her son, Tamir Rice, Samaria moved out of her Cleveland home and into a homeless shelter. (Her family eventually relocated her.) "The whole world has seen the same video like I've seen," she said about Tamir's being shot by a police officer. The video, which was played and replayed in the media, documented the two seconds it took the police to arrive and shoot; two seconds marked the end of her son's life that became a document to be examined by everyone. It's possible this shared scrutiny explains why the police held his 12-year-old body for six months after his death. Everyone could see what the police would have to explain away. The justice system wasn't able to do it, and a judge found probable cause to charge the officer who shot Rice with murder. Meanwhile, for Samaria Rice, her unburied son's memory made her neighborhood unbearable.

Regardless of the wishes of these mothers—mothers of men like Brown, John Crawford III or Eric Garner, and also mothers of women and girls like Rekia Boyd and Aiyana Stanley-Jones, each of whom was killed by the police—their children's deaths will remain within the public discourse. For those who believe the same behavior that got them killed if exhibited by a white man or boy would not have ended his life, the subsequent failure to indict or convict the police officers involved in these various cases requires that public mourning continue and remain present indefinitely. "I want to see a cop shoot a white unarmed teenager in the back," Toni Morrison said in April. She went on to say: "I want to see a white man convicted for raping a black woman. Then when you ask me, 'Is it over?' I will say yes." Morrison is right to suggest that this action would signal change, but the real change needs to be a rerouting of interior belief. It's an individual challenge that needs to happen before any action by a political justice system would signify true societal change.

The Charleston murders alerted us to the reality that a system so steeped in anti-black racism means that on any given day it can be open season on any black person—old or young, man, woman or child. There exists no equivalent reality for white Americans. The Confederate battle flag* continues to fly at South Carolina's statehouse as a reminder of a history marked by lynched black bodies. We can distance ourselves from this fact until the next horrific killing, but we won't be able to outrun it. History's authority over us is not broken by maintaining a silence about its continued effects.

A sustained state of national mourning for black lives is called for in order to point to the undeniability of their devaluation. The hope is that recognition will break a momentum that laws haven't altered. Susie Jackson; Sharonda Coleman-Singleton; DePayne Middleton-Doctor; Ethel Lee Lance; the Rev. Daniel Lee Simmons Sr.; the Rev. Clementa C. Pinckney; Cynthia Hurd; Tywanza Sanders and Myra Thompson were murdered because they were black. It's extraordinary how ordinary our grief sits inside this fact. One friend said, "I am so afraid, every day." Her son's childhood feels impossible, because he will have to be—has to be—so much more careful. Our mourning, this mourning, is in time with our lives. There is no life outside of our reality here. Is this something that can be seen and known by parents of white children? This is the question that nags me. National mourning, as advocated by Black Lives Matter, is a mode of intervention and interruption that might itself be assimilated into the category of public annoyance. This is altogether possible; but also possible is the recognition that it's a lack of feeling for another that is our problem. Grief, then, for these deceased others might align some of us, for the first time, with the living.

(2015)

NIKOLE HANNAH-JONES

SCHOOL SEGREGATION: THE CONTINUING TRAGEDY OF FERGUSON

The 9 August 2014 shooting by police officer Darren Wilson of unarmed teenager Michael Brown in Ferguson, Missouri (a suburb of St Louis) became a cause célèbre when no charges were filed against the officer responsible. Protests carried on for many weeks, and the incident prompted many to ask fresh questions about race relations in America. Nikole Hannah-Jones' article was originally published 19 December 2014 in the online magazine ProPublica; *an abridged version was later published in* The New York Times.

On August 1, five black students in satiny green and red robes and mortar boards* waited inside an elementary school classroom, listening for their names to be called as graduates of Normandy High School. The ceremony was held months after the school's main graduation for students who had been short of credits or had opted not to participate earlier.

One of those graduating that day was Michael Brown. He was 18, his mother's oldest son. He was headed to college in the fall.

Eight days later, Brown was dead—killed in the streets of nearby Ferguson, Mo., by a white police officer in a shooting that ignited angry protests and another round of painful national debate about race, policing, and the often elusive matter of justice.

News reports in the days and weeks after Brown's death often noted his recent graduation and college ambitions, the clear implication that the teen's school achievements only deepened the sorrow over his loss.

But if Brown's educational experience was a success story, it was a damning one.

The Normandy school district from which Brown graduated is among the poorest and most segregated in Missouri. It ranks last in overall academic performance. Its rating on an annual state assessment was so dismal that by the time Brown graduated the district had lost its accreditation.

5

About half of black male students at Normandy High never graduate. Just one in four graduates enters a four-year college. The college where Brown was headed is a troubled for-profit trade-school that a U.S. Senate report said targeted students for their "vulnerabilities," and that at one time advertised itself to what it internally called the area's "Unemployed, Underpaid, Unsatisfied, Unskilled, Unprepared, Unsupported, Unmotivated, Unhappy, Underserved!"

A mere five miles down the road from Normandy is the wealthy county seat where a grand jury recently decided not to indict[1] Darren Wilson, the officer who killed Brown. Success there looks drastically different. The Clayton Public Schools are predominantly white, with almost no poverty to speak of. The district is regularly ranked among the top 10 percent in the state. More than 96 percent of students graduate. Fully 84 percent of graduates head to four-year universities.

Brown's tragedy, then, is not limited to his individual potential cut brutally short. His schooling also reveals a more subtle, ongoing racial injustice: the vast disparity in resources and expectations for black children in America's stubbornly segregated educational system.

10 　As ProPublica has documented in a series of stories on the resegregation of America's schools, hundreds of school districts across the nation have been released from court-enforced integration* over the past 15 years. Over that same time period, the number of so-called apartheid schools—schools whose white population is 1 percent or less—has shot up. The achievement gap, greatly narrowed during the height of school desegregation, has widened.

"American schools are disturbingly racially segregated, period," Catherine Lhamon, head of the U.S. Education Department's civil rights office, said in an October speech. "We are reserving our expectations for our highest rigor level of courses, the courses we know our kids need to be able to be full and productive members of society, but we are reserving them for a class of kids who are white and who are wealthier."

According to data compiled by the Education Department, black and Latino children are the least likely to be taught by a qualified, experienced teacher, to get access to courses such as chemistry and calculus, and to have access to technology.

The inequalities along racial lines are so profound nationally that in October the department's Office for Civil Rights issued a 37-page letter to school district superintendents warning that the disparities may be unconstitutional.

1　*indict*　Formally charge with a serious crime.

Few places better reflect the rise and fall of attempts to integrate U.S. schools than St. Louis and its suburbs.

Decades of public and private housing discrimination made St. Louis one of the most racially segregated metropolitan areas in the country. Out of that grew a network of school district boundaries that to this day have divided large numbers of black students in racially separate schools as effectively as any Jim Crow law.*

In 1983, under federal court order, St. Louis and some of its suburbs embarked on what would become the grandest and most successful interdistrict school desegregation program in the land, one that, at least for a time, broke the grim grip of ZIP codes for tens of thousands of black students. As an elementary school student, under this order, Michael Brown's mother rode the bus from St. Louis to affluent Ladue.

But like so many other desegregation efforts across the country, the St. Louis plan proved short-lived, largely abandoned after several years by politicians and others who complained that it was too costly. Jay Nixon, Missouri's current governor, whose response to Brown's killing has come under intense scrutiny in recent months, helped lead the effort that brought the court order to a close.

Since their retreat from desegregation initiatives, many St. Louis County schools have returned to the world of separate and unequal that existed before the U.S. Supreme Court's landmark decision in Brown v. Board of Education.[2]

It could be said that the Normandy school district, where Michael Brown spent the last year and a half of high school, never left. Excluded from the court-ordered integration plan that transformed other school systems in the St. Louis area, Normandy's fiscally and academically disadvantaged schools have essentially been in freefall since the 1980s.

Throughout the region, the educational divide between black children and white children is stark. In St. Louis County, 44 percent of black children attend schools in districts the state says perform so poorly that it has stripped them of full accreditation. Just 4 percent of white students do.

Yet state education officials say there is little political will to change that.

Instead, they have promised to work to make segregated school districts equal, the very doctrine the Supreme Court struck down in the Brown decision.

"We are failing to properly educate the black child," said Michael Jones, vice president of the Missouri State Board of Education. "Individually, any one person can overcome anything. But we've got masses of children with bad starts in life. They can't win. We ought to be ashamed of that."

15

20

---

2   *Brown v. Board of Education* This ruling established that state laws allowing separate public schools for black and white students were unconstitutional.

Since Aug. 9, the day Michael Brown's lifeless body lay for hours under a hot summer sun, St. Louis County has become synonymous with the country's racial fault lines when it comes to police conduct and the criminalization of black youth. But most black youth will not die at the hands of police.

25 　　　They will face the future that Brown would have faced if he had lived. That is, to have the outcome of their lives deeply circumscribed by what they learn and experience in their segregated, inferior schools.

DRED SCOTT, DESEGREGATION AND A DEARTH OF PROGRESS

Missouri is what the locals like to call a Southern state with Northern exposure. It entered the Union through a compromise that determined how much of the country would permit slavery, and wound up a slave state surrounded on three sides by free states.

It was in a St. Louis case in 1857 that the U.S. Supreme Court handed down one of its most infamous opinions. The court, in ruling against the enslaved Dred Scott, affirmed that black people were not citizens and "had no rights that the white man was bound to respect."

The spirit of the ruling reverberated for generations in St. Louis, which in the years after the Civil War became the destination for large numbers of former slaves. Indeed, the Mississippi River town became a national leader in how to contain what white real estate agents called the "Negro invasion."

In 1916, after a successful campaign that included placards urging, "Save Your Home! Vote for Segregation!," the city's residents passed a measure requiring that black and white residents live on separate, designated blocks. In doing so, St. Louis became the first city in the country to require housing segregation by popular ballot. The tactic eventually fell to a legal challenge, but white residents found other ways to keep themselves, and their schools, protected from black residents.

30 　　　One way was to write segregation into the sales contracts of houses. The clauses, known as real estate covenants, ensured the whiteness of neighborhoods by barring the sale of homes to black homebuyers—ever, and across entire sectors of the city. These practices quickly created a clear dividing line in St. Louis that endures to this day: Black people north of Delmar Boulevard; white people south.

In 1948, another landmark St. Louis case led to the U.S. Supreme Court striking down the enforcement of real estate covenants anywhere in the country. The case involved a black resident named J.D. Shelley, who bought a home with a deed restriction and then was sued by a white homeowner, Louis Kraemer, trying to block him from moving into the subdivision.

With legal discrimination under attack in the courts, white residents began abandoning St. Louis altogether. From 1950 to 1970, the city lost nearly 60 percent of its white population. This white flight was partly underwritten by the federal government, which secured loans reserved only for white homebuyers.

Town after town sprung up along the northern edge of St. Louis, some no larger than a single subdivision. Immediately, many forbade rentals and required homes to be built on large, more expensive lots. These devices helped keep neighborhoods white because black residents tended to be poorer and had difficulty getting home loans after decades of workplace, lending, and housing discrimination. Even today, 77 percent of white St. Louis area residents own their homes, compared to 45 percent of black residents, the U.S. Census shows.

Some of the tactics employed by St. Louis suburbs, including zoning, also were knocked down by courts.

But court victories, in the end, mattered little. A century of white effort had lastingly etched the county map: a struggling, heavily black urban core surrounded by a constellation of 90 segregated little towns.

"St. Louis yielded some of the starkest racial dividing lines in any American city, North or South," said Colin Gordon, a University of Iowa professor who traces this history in his book *Mapping Decline: St. Louis and the Fate of the American City*. "I like to think of St. Louis not as an outlier, but one in which all the things we're talking about are just more visible."

A SEGREGATION SUCCESS, QUICKLY ABANDONED

One legal fight breached—at least temporarily—the St. Louis area's stark boundaries of home and property, and with them the 24 segregated school districts covering those 90 segregated little towns.

In 1954, the year of the Brown v. Board of Education Supreme Court decision, St. Louis ran the second-largest segregated school district in the country.

In the face of the ruling, school officials promised to integrate voluntarily. But they redrew school district lines around distinctly black and white neighborhoods to preserve their segregated schools. Even so, many white families still left, avoiding the chance of integration by simply moving across municipal lines. By 1980, 90 percent of black children in St. Louis still attended predominantly black schools.

With few white students left, it was clear that a desegregation plan that did not include the white suburbs would be futile. In 1981, a federal judge called for a plan to bus black St. Louis children to white suburban schools.

White suburban residents, and their school leaders, revolted. They filed motions in court and penned angry letters to the local newspaper. The judge,

William Hungate, responded by threatening to do the one thing the white suburbs feared more than the bussing plan: Dissolve the carefully constructed school district boundaries and merge all 24 of the discrete districts into a single metro-wide one.

The opposition to the plan to bus children out of St. Louis collapsed. In 1983, St. Louis and its suburbs enacted the largest and most expensive interdistrict school desegregation program in the country.

At its peak, some 15,000 St. Louis public school students a year went to school in 16 heavily white suburban districts. Another 1,300 white students headed the opposite direction to new, integrated magnet schools in St. Louis.

The program had its flaws—chief among them, that it left another 15,000 of St. Louis's black students in segregated, inferior schools. And the transition of black urban students into white suburban schools was not always smooth.

45 But for the transfer students who rode buses out of the city, the plan successfully broke the deeply entrenched connection between race, ZIP code, and opportunity. Test scores for 8th and 10th grade transfer students rose. The transfer students were more likely to graduate and go on to college.

In surveys, white students overwhelmingly said they'd benefited from the opportunity to be educated alongside black students. In short order, St. Louis's was heralded by researchers and educators as the nation's most successful metro-wide desegregation program.

But from the moment it started, the St. Louis effort was under assault. It was never popular among the area's white residents. Politicians, Republicans and Democrats alike, vowed to end the program.

Then-state Attorney General John Ashcroft tried first, appealing St. Louis' school desegregation case all the way to the Supreme Court. He was succeeded by Jay Nixon, a Democrat who matched Ashcroft's fervor in seeking to end the program.

"Nixon came from a rural area. His position on school desegregation was more of a Southern Democrat, and it came pretty close to massive resistance," said William Freivogel, director of Southern Illinois University's School of Journalism, who covered the Supreme Court for the St. Louis Post-Dispatch during the 1980s and early 1990s. "I once wrote that Nixon behaved like a Southern politician standing in the schoolhouse door."

50 Nixon never expressly opposed the idea of integration. His argument centered on what he considered the astronomical costs of the desegregation plan. The price tag, initially in the hundreds of millions of dollars, would reach $1.7 billion.

Nixon, who would not be interviewed for this article, launched a number of legal challenges and prevailed in 1999 when supporters of the desegregation plan ultimately agreed to make the program voluntary. Nixon had successfully challenged Kansas City's desegregation plan before the U.S. Supreme Court, and some feared he would be similarly successful if the St. Louis case came before the court.

Districts soon began to drop out of the program, and the number of students participating steadily dwindled. Today, the voluntary program remains in place, still the largest of just eight interdistrict desegregation programs in the country. But it is a shadow of what it once was. Some 4,800 students get to escape the troubles of the St. Louis public schools, but each year, the program receives seven times as many applicants as open spaces.

Amy Stuart Wells is a Columbia's Teachers College professor who co-authored a book, *Stepping Over the Color Line: African-American Students in White Suburban Schools*, on the impact of the St. Louis plan on transfer students.

"I don't think many people realized how far ahead St. Louis really was," she said. "There are hundreds of thousands of people in the St. Louis metro area who were affected by this plan, but (the suburbs) did it because they had to and nobody said, 'Look, we're a national model for our country.' There were seeds sown that could have been so much more.

"This was the epicenter of where people tried to grapple with race, and failed miserably." 55

FEARS, FLIGHT AND A SUDDENLY BLACK SUBURB LEFT TO CRUMBLE

The white flight out of St. Louis left behind a trail of decay, as it did in many large Northern cities. City services lapsed when more affluent residents left. Businesses and jobs migrated as well. The schools in particular suffered.

Not surprisingly, black residents who could afford it looked for a way out, too. They looked to older North St. Louis suburbs, including Normandy. Incorporated in 1945 and covering fewer than two square miles, Normandy became a destination for the city's fleeing white working class.

Nedra Martin's family was among the black strivers who began to make their way to Normandy. Martin, who lives in Normandy today and works for Wal-Mart, said her parents first came to the town in 1975. They both worked government jobs—her dad was a welder for the city, her mom an aide in a state group home.

"My parents raised us to know that we are as good as anybody else," Martin said.

But as black families like the Martins moved in, "For Sale" signs went 60 up. White families started moving out, often to emerging outposts even farther from the heart of St. Louis.

After 1970, black enrollment in the Normandy schools exploded, more than doubling within eight years to 6,200. By 1978, only St. Louis enrolled more black students than Normandy.

Yet Normandy was left out of the metro-wide desegregation order that produced those few years of brighter outcomes for black students between 1983 and 1999. The order capped black enrollment at suburban districts at 25 percent, and Normandy and six other North St. Louis suburbs were already too black.

Instead, the Normandy schools buckled under their swift demographic shift, beginning a steep decline. Many of the best teachers followed the white and middle-class exodus. Instruction fell off. The district suffered from a revolving door of leadership, with principals and superintendents seldom sticking around more than a couple of years. Unable to meet minimum requirements for student achievement, the district clung to provisional accreditation for 15 years.

But black families had less freedom to simply move away to better school districts than even their poorer white neighbors. Housing discrimination continues to keep black families out of communities with quality schools, according to a 2013 St. Louis housing study.

65   The most affluent black families in Normandy, then, often opted out of the local school system, paying to send their children to private school. As a result, Normandy's schools ended up considerably poorer and more racially segregated than the communities they serve.

For years, the Normandy school system walked an academic tightrope. Then, in 2009, the state made matters worse.

New Education Commissioner Chris Nicastro decided that it was time to move on segregated districts that consistently failed their students. The state shuttered Wellston, a desperately poor, 500-student district next to Normandy that held the distinction of being Missouri's only 100 percent-black school system.

One state official had called conditions in Wellston's schools "deplorable" and "academically abusive."

The issue for state officials was what to do next with Wellston's students.

70   One thing was clear: The students were not going to be absorbed into any of the high-performing, mostly white districts nearby. Jones, the state board of education official, was blunt about why: "You'd have had a civil war."

Officials then turned to Normandy, which already enrolled almost 5,000 students. Merging two impoverished, struggling systems made sense to almost no one, especially the officials in charge of Normandy's schools.

The state went forward with it anyway.

"If you are strictly doing what's best for all kids, you don't merge those two districts," Stanton Lawrence, Normandy's superintendent at the time, said in a recent interview. "Why would you do that? They had written those kids off."

"IT WAS ALL CORRUPT POLITICS"

By the time Michael Brown reached his junior year in high school, he had bounced between local districts and spent most of his career in racially segregated and economically disadvantaged schools. Behind in credits, he enrolled at Normandy High in the spring of 2013.

If he had dreams of academic success, he could not have wound up in a   75
more challenging place to realize them.

The state's 2014 assessment report on Normandy's schools was spectacularly bleak: Zero points awarded for academic achievement in English. Zero for math, for social studies, for science. Zero for students headed to college. Zero for attendance. Zero for the percent of students who graduate. Its total score: 10 out of 140.

Out of 520 districts in the state, Normandy, where 98 percent of students are black and 9 of 10 were poor in 2013, is marooned at the very bottom.

Decades of research show that segregated, high-poverty schools are simply toxic for students of all races and backgrounds. Just last month, the University of North Carolina at Chapel Hill released a study showing that black first-graders in segregated schools performed worse than black students with the same backgrounds (meaning poverty, parental education and other factors) who attend integrated schools.

But for a moment prior to the start of Brown's senior year, the Normandy district's students were thrown an unlikely lifeline.

Just two years after the merger with Wellston, Normandy's schools were   80
performing so poorly that the state stripped Normandy of its accreditation altogether. That triggered a state law requiring that any student there be allowed to transfer to an accredited district nearby. The law had been challenged by suburban districts uninterested in absorbing kids from failing schools, but in 2013 the Missouri State Supreme Court upheld it.

For Nedra Martin, whose honors student daughter, Mah'Ria, was stuck in Normandy's failing schools, the development was the miracle she had prayed for. Martin could not afford private schools, and her attempts to enroll her daughter in neighboring white districts had been rebuffed.

Just like that, the court's decision erased the invisible, impenetrable lines of segregation that had trapped her child.

"I was elated," Martin said. "Just elated."

Parents in the school districts that would have to take Normandy's students were not. Normandy had chosen to provide transportation for its transfers to attend Francis Howell, which was 85 percent white at the time and some 26 miles away.

85   When Francis Howell officials held a public forum to address community concerns, more than 2,500 parents packed into the high school gymnasium.

Would the district install metal detectors? What about the violence their children would be subjected to, an elementary school parent asked. Wouldn't test scores plummet? The issue wasn't about race, one parent said, "but trash."

Mah'Ria Martin was sitting in the audience that night with her mother. One of the few brown faces in the audience, the rising 8th grader said she wiped away tears.

"It made me heartbroken because they were putting us in a box," said Mah'Ria, soft spoken but firm, in recalling the episode. "I was sitting there thinking, 'Would you want some other parents talking about your kid that way?'"

In the fall of 2013, nearly 1,000 Normandy students—about a quarter of the district's enrollment—fled to schools in accredited districts. More than 400, including Mah'Ria, headed to Francis Howell.

90   Mah'Ria said that she was, in fact, welcomed by students and teachers at her new middle school. It was the first time in her life that she'd attended a district that had the full approval of the state.

She thrived. And she was not alone.

Despite the fears, recently released state data shows that, with the exception of one district, test scores in the transfer schools did not drop.

But the success came with a perverse twist. The state required failing districts whose students were allowed to transfer to pay the costs of the children's education in the adjoining districts. For the whiter, more affluent districts, it was a replay of what had happened during the court-ordered desegregation plan, when transfer students were referred to as "black gold": students the districts had to educate but who cost them nothing.

The millions of dollars in payments to other districts drained Normandy's finances. Within months, the district shuttered an elementary school and laid off 40 percent of its staff. Already deeply troubled, the Normandy schools were headed to insolvency.

95   "In order to save the district, they killed the district," said John Wright, a longtime St. Louis educator who spent stints as superintendent in both St. Louis and Normandy.

Recognizing the problem of student transfers, the state engineered their end.

This June, when students were on summer break, the state announced that it was taking over the Normandy Public Schools district and reconstituting it as the Normandy Schools Collaborative. As a new educational entity, state officials said, the district got a clean slate. It no longer was unaccredited but operated under a newly created status as a "state oversight district."

The transfer program, the state claimed, no longer applied. One by one, transfer districts announced that Normandy children were no longer welcome.

Martin and her daughter were devastated. "I honestly felt they were black-listing our children," Martin said.

Martin and other parents sued, asserting the state had no legal authority to act as it had. St. Louis lawyer Josh Schindler represented the parents.   100

"These are just families who want their kids to have a good education. Decent, hard-working people who want their kids to have a chance," he said in an interview. "This has been a decades-long battle. How are we going to remedy the situation?"

On August 15, after the new school year had begun in some districts, a state judge granted a temporary injunction that allowed the plaintiffs to enroll their children in the transfer districts.

"Every day a student attends an unaccredited school," the judge wrote, the child "could suffer harm that cannot be repaired."

The ruling brought a rush of relief to many parents.

"I cried and just held onto my kid," said Janine Crawford, whose son was   105
able return to the Pattonville School District. "It meant that he was going to get a decent education. And it meant that I could take a deep breath."

The state is still fighting the ruling, and Francis Howell required all transfer students to obtain court orders to return.

Martin briefly returned Mah'Ria to the Normandy schools after they came under state oversight but found them little improved and has since sent her back to Francis Howell. The entire situation has only reinforced her cynicism and despair, she said.

"What about your neighbor? Is it so hard to embrace the children who clearly need your help right now?" she asked. "The whole way this was handled by the state on down was sheisty[3] and underhanded. They were not thinking about the children."

The state's top education officials admit that the way they've dealt with Normandy has laid bare racial divisions in St. Louis County and beyond. In an interview, Nicastro, the state superintendent, called it a "low point" in her career, a "blight and commentary about Missouri."

---

3   *sheisty*   Untrustworthy or dishonest (a slang term).

110   When asked whether black children in Missouri were receiving an equal education, she paused, then inhaled deeply. "Do I think black children in Missouri are getting in all cases the same education as their white counterparts?" Nicastro said. "I'd have to say no."

LITTLE HOPE AND A TELLING BURIAL

On a cold, clear morning in November, with the grand jury still assessing the killing of Michael Brown, a group of black leaders and concerned citizens gathered in a classroom at Harris-Stowe State University in downtown St. Louis. The school was founded in 1829 to train black teachers.

The gathering produced a recommitment to the solution to segregation floated 30 years before: A single, unified school district for St. Louis and its suburbs.

But there was recognition that the answer would require a long and uphill fight.

"We know what would have been best educationally for these kids—we always know what the best thing to do is. What we lack is the moral courage and political will to do it," said Jones, of the state Board of Education. "If we had treated the civil rights movement the way we've treated the education of black children, we'd still be drinking out of colored drinking fountains."

115   Separate but equal has not worked, Jones said. Not in St. Louis. Not anywhere else. The school lines that advantage some and deprive others, he said, must be toppled.

Students who spend their careers in segregated schools can look forward to a life on the margins, according to a 2014 study on the long-term impacts of school desegregation by University of California, Berkeley economist Rucker Johnson. They are more likely to be poor. They are more likely to go to jail. They are less likely to graduate from high school, to go to college, and to finish if they go. They are more likely to live in segregated neighborhoods as adults.

Their children are more likely to also attend segregated schools, repeating the cycle.

Even in the fog of her grief, Michael Brown's mother spoke to this struggle. With her son's body laying on the concrete behind police tape, Lesley McSpadden cried, "Do you know how hard it was for me to get him to stay in school and graduate?

"You know how many black men graduate?" she implored. "Not many."

120   With a diploma from a district that one report called "catastrophically underperforming," her oldest son had been headed to nearby Vatterott College.

Schools like Vatterott enroll a disproportionate percentage of black students. Those who attend are often saddled with debt they cannot pay back.

In 2013, a jury awarded more than $13 million to a single mother who sued Vatterott for misleading enrollment practices.

An executive with Vatterott Educational Centers, Inc. said the company's problems were in the past, and that it had reformed its admissions practices.

Brown never made it to Vatterott. Maybe he would have bucked the odds and found a way to master a trade and make a career.

Today, Brown is buried in the old St. Peter's Cemetery. Right next to Normandy High School.

(2015)

THE CASE FOR REPARATIONS

Ta-Nehisi Coates, whose bestselling Between the World and Me *won the National Book Award for Non-fiction in 2015, came into prominence the previous year with this long essay, published in the June 2014 issue of* The Atlantic. *The essay helped to inspire the Black Lives Matter movement—and helped as well to change many minds on the issue of whether or not reparations for slavery would be appropriate. (Coates had himself changed his mind on the issue—as he recounted in a May 22 online background piece for* The Atlantic, *"The Case for Reparations: An Intellectual Autopsy.")*

And if thy brother, a Hebrew man, or a Hebrew woman, be sold unto thee, and serve thee six years; then in the seventh year thou shalt let him go free from thee. And when thou sendest him out free from thee, thou shalt not let him go away empty: thou shalt furnish him liberally out of thy flock, and out of thy floor, and out of thy winepress: of that wherewith the LORD thy God hath blessed thee thou shalt give unto him. And thou shalt remember that thou wast a bondman in the land of Egypt, and the LORD thy God redeemed thee: therefore I command thee this thing today.—Deuteronomy 15: 12–15

Besides the crime which consists in violating the law, and varying from the right rule of reason, whereby a man so far becomes degenerate, and declares himself to quit the principles of human nature, and to be a noxious creature, there is commonly injury done to some person or other, and some other man receives damage by his transgression: in which case he who hath received any damage, has, besides the right of punishment common to him with other men, a particular right to seek reparation.—John Locke, "Second Treatise"

By our unpaid labor and suffering, we have earned the right to the soil, many times over and over, and now we are determined to have it.—Anonymous, 1861

C lyde Ross was born in 1923, the seventh of 13 children, near Clarksdale, Mississippi, the home of the blues.* Ross's parents owned and farmed a 40-acre tract of land, flush with cows, hogs, and mules. Ross's mother would drive to Clarksdale to do her shopping in a horse and buggy, in which she invested all the pride one might place in a Cadillac. The family owned another horse, with a red coat, which they gave to Clyde. The Ross family wanted for little, save that which all black families in the Deep South then desperately desired—the protection of the law.

In the 1920s, Jim Crow Mississippi[1] was, in all facets of society, a kleptocracy.[2] The majority of the people in the state were perpetually robbed of the vote—a hijacking engineered through the trickery of the poll tax and the muscle of the lynch mob.* Between 1882 and 1968, more black people were lynched in Mississippi than in any other state. "You and I know what's the best way to keep the nigger from voting," blustered Theodore Bilbo, a Mississippi senator and a proud Klansman.* "You do it the night before the election."

The state's regime partnered robbery of the franchise with robbery of the purse. Many of Mississippi's black farmers lived in debt peonage,[3] under the sway of cotton kings who were at once their landlords, their employers, and their primary merchants. Tools and necessities were advanced against the return on the crop, which was determined by the employer. When farmers were deemed to be in debt—and they often were—the negative balance was then carried over to the next season. A man or woman who protested this arrangement did so at the risk of grave injury or death. Refusing to work meant arrest under vagrancy laws and forced labor under the state's penal system.

Well into the 20th century, black people spoke of their flight from Mississippi in much the same manner as their runagate[4] ancestors had. In her 2010 book, *The Warmth of Other Suns*, Isabel Wilkerson tells the story of Eddie Earvin, a spinach picker who fled Mississippi in 1963, after being made to work at gunpoint. "You didn't talk about it or tell nobody," Earvin said. "You had to sneak away."

When Clyde Ross was still a child, Mississippi authorities claimed his father owed $3,000 in back taxes. The elder Ross could not read. He did not have a lawyer. He did not know anyone at the local courthouse. He could not expect the police to be impartial. Effectively, the Ross family had no way to contest the claim and no protection under the law. The authorities seized the land. They

5

---

1   *Jim Crow Mississippi*   Mississippi under the Jim Crow laws, which enforced segregation..

2   *kleptocracy*   Jurisdiction in which theft is central to the operation of society.

3   *debt peonage*   Forced servitude to one's creditors.

4   *runagate*   Runaway, especially one who has broken the law.

seized the buggy. They took the cows, hogs, and mules. And so for the upkeep of separate but equal, the entire Ross family was reduced to sharecropping.*

This was hardly unusual. In 2001, the Associated Press published a three-part investigation into the theft of black-owned land stretching back to the antebellum period.* The series documented some 406 victims and 24,000 acres of land valued at tens of millions of dollars. The land was taken through means ranging from legal chicanery to terrorism. "Some of the land taken from black families has become a country club in Virginia," the AP reported, as well as "oil fields in Mississippi" and "a baseball spring training facility in Florida."

Clyde Ross was a smart child. His teacher thought he should attend a more challenging school. There was very little support for educating black people in Mississippi. But Julius Rosenwald, a part owner of Sears, Roebuck, had begun an ambitious effort to build schools for black children throughout the South. Ross's teacher believed he should attend the local Rosenwald school. It was too far for Ross to walk and get back in time to work in the fields. Local white children had a school bus. Clyde Ross did not, and thus lost the chance to better his education.

Then, when Ross was 10 years old, a group of white men demanded his only childhood possession—the horse with the red coat. "You can't have this horse. We want it," one of the white men said. They gave Ross's father $17.

"I did everything for that horse," Ross told me. "Everything. And they took him. Put him on the racetrack. I never did know what happened to him after that, but I know they didn't bring him back. So that's just one of my losses."

10   The losses mounted. As sharecroppers, the Ross family saw their wages treated as the landlord's slush fund. Landowners were supposed to split the profits from the cotton fields with sharecroppers. But bales would often disappear during the count, or the split might be altered on a whim. If cotton was selling for 50 cents a pound, the Ross family might get 15 cents, or only five. One year Ross's mother promised to buy him a $7 suit for a summer program at their church. She ordered the suit by mail. But that year Ross's family was paid only five cents a pound for cotton. The mailman arrived with the suit. The Rosses could not pay. The suit was sent back. Clyde Ross did not go to the church program.

It was in these early years that Ross began to understand himself as an American—he did not live under the blind decree of justice, but under the heel of a regime that elevated armed robbery to a governing principle. He thought about fighting. "Just be quiet," his father told him. "Because they'll come and kill us all."

Clyde Ross grew. He was drafted into the Army. The draft officials offered him an exemption if he stayed home and worked. He preferred to take his chances with war. He was stationed in California. He found that he could go into stores without being bothered. He could walk the streets without being harassed. He could go into a restaurant and receive service.

Ross was shipped off to Guam. He fought in World War II to save the world from tyranny. But when he returned to Clarksdale, he found that tyranny had followed him home. This was 1947, eight years before Mississippi lynched Emmett Till[5] and tossed his broken body into the Tallahatchie River. The Great Migration,* a mass exodus of 6 million African Americans that spanned most of the 20th century, was now in its second wave. The black pilgrims did not journey north simply seeking better wages and work, or bright lights and big adventures. They were fleeing the acquisitive warlords of the South. They were seeking the protection of the law.

Clyde Ross was among them. He came to Chicago in 1947 and took a job as a taster at Campbell's Soup. He made a stable wage. He married. He had children. His paycheck was his own. No Klansmen stripped him of the vote. When he walked down the street, he did not have to move because a white man was walking past. He did not have to take off his hat or avert his gaze. His journey from peonage to full citizenship seemed near-complete. Only one item was missing—a home, that final badge of entry into the sacred order of the American middle class of the Eisenhower years.*

In 1961, Ross and his wife bought a house in North Lawndale, a bustling community on Chicago's West Side. North Lawndale had long been a predominantly Jewish neighborhood, but a handful of middle-class African Americans had lived there starting in the '40s. The community was anchored by the sprawling Sears, Roebuck headquarters. North Lawndale's Jewish People's Institute actively encouraged blacks to move into the neighborhood, seeking to make it a "pilot community for interracial living." In the battle for integration then being fought around the country, North Lawndale seemed to offer promising terrain. But out in the tall grass, highwaymen,* nefarious as any Clarksdale kleptocrat, were lying in wait.

Three months after Clyde Ross moved into his house, the boiler blew out. This would normally be a homeowner's responsibility, but in fact, Ross was not really a homeowner. His payments were made to the seller, not the bank. And Ross had not signed a normal mortgage. He'd bought "on contract": a predatory agreement that combined all the responsibilities of homeownership with all the disadvantages of renting—while offering the benefits of neither. Ross had bought his house for $27,500. The seller, not the previous homeowner but a new kind of middleman, had bought it for only $12,000 six months before selling it to Ross. In a contract sale, the seller kept the deed until the contract was paid in full—and, unlike with a normal mortgage, Ross would

15

---

5   *Emmett Till*   14-year-old boy whose murder became emblematic of racial injustice.

acquire no equity in the meantime. If he missed a single payment, he would immediately forfeit his $1,000 down payment, all his monthly payments, and the property itself.

The men who peddled contracts in North Lawndale would sell homes at inflated prices and then evict families who could not pay—taking their down payment and their monthly installments as profit. Then they'd bring in another black family, rinse, and repeat. "He loads them up with payments they can't meet," an office secretary told *The Chicago Daily News* of her boss, the speculator Lou Fushanis, in 1963. "Then he takes the property away from them. He's sold some of the buildings three or four times."

Ross had tried to get a legitimate mortgage in another neighborhood, but was told by a loan officer that there was no financing available. The truth was that there was no financing for people like Clyde Ross. From the 1930s through the 1960s, black people across the country were largely cut out of the legitimate home-mortgage market through means both legal and extralegal. Chicago whites employed every measure, from "restrictive covenants"[6] to bombings, to keep their neighborhoods segregated.

Their efforts were buttressed by the federal government. In 1934, Congress created the Federal Housing Administration. The FHA insured private mortgages, causing a drop in interest rates and a decline in the size of the down payment required to buy a house. But an insured mortgage was not a possibility for Clyde Ross. The FHA had adopted a system of maps that rated neighborhoods according to their perceived stability. On the maps, green areas, rated "A," indicated "in demand" neighborhoods that, as one appraiser put it, lacked "a single foreigner or Negro." These neighborhoods were considered excellent prospects for insurance. Neighborhoods where black people lived were rated "D" and were usually considered ineligible for FHA backing. They were colored in red. Neither the percentage of black people living there nor their social class mattered. Black people were viewed as a contagion. Redlining[7] went beyond FHA-backed loans and spread to the entire mortgage industry, which was already rife with racism, excluding black people from most legitimate means of obtaining a mortgage.

20 "A government offering such bounty to builders and lenders could have required compliance with a nondiscrimination policy," Charles Abrams, the urban-studies expert who helped create the New York City Housing Authority,

---

6   *restrictive covenants*   Clauses in property owners' deeds or leases that limit how a given property can be used. In the cases mentioned here, covenants often permitted the sale of homes only to white buyers.

7   *Redlining*   Withholding services to people because of the racial or ethnic makeup of the neighborhoods they live in.

wrote in 1955. "Instead, the FHA adopted a racial policy that could well have been culled from the Nuremberg laws."[8]

The devastating effects are cogently outlined by Melvin L. Oliver and Thomas M. Shapiro in their 1995 book, *Black Wealth/White Wealth*:

> Locked out of the greatest mass-based opportunity for wealth accumulation in American history, African Americans who desired and were able to afford home ownership found themselves consigned to central-city communities where their investments were affected by the "self-fulfilling prophecies" of the FHA appraisers: cut off from sources of new investment[,] their homes and communities deteriorated and lost value in comparison to those homes and communities that FHA appraisers deemed desirable.

In Chicago and across the country, whites looking to achieve the American dream could rely on a legitimate credit system backed by the government. Blacks were herded into the sights of unscrupulous lenders who took them for money and for sport. "It was like people who like to go out and shoot lions in Africa. It was the same thrill," a housing attorney told the historian Beryl Satter in her 2009 book, *Family Properties*. "The thrill of the chase and the kill."

The kill was profitable. At the time of his death, Lou Fushanis owned more than 600 properties, many of them in North Lawndale, and his estate was estimated to be worth $3 million. He'd made much of this money by exploiting the frustrated hopes of black migrants like Clyde Ross. During this period, according to one estimate, 85 percent of all black home buyers who bought in Chicago bought on contract. "If anybody who is well established in this business in Chicago doesn't earn $100,000 a year," a contract seller told *The Saturday Evening Post* in 1962, "he is loafing."

Contract sellers became rich. North Lawndale became a ghetto.

Clyde Ross still lives there. He still owns his home. He is 91, and the   25
emblems of survival are all around him—awards for service in his community, pictures of his children in cap and gown. But when I asked him about his home in North Lawndale, I heard only anarchy.

"We were ashamed. We did not want anyone to know that we were that ignorant," Ross told me. He was sitting at his dining-room table. His glasses were as thick as his Clarksdale drawl. "I'd come out of Mississippi where there was one mess, and come up here and got in another mess. So how dumb am I? I didn't want anyone to know how dumb I was.

---

8   *Nuremberg laws* Laws that governed policies regarding "racial purity" in Nazi Germany.

"When I found myself caught up in it, I said, 'How? I just left this mess. I just left no laws. And no regard. And then I come here and get cheated wide open.' I would probably want to do some harm to some people, you know, if I had been violent like some of us. I thought, 'Man, I got caught up in this stuff. I can't even take care of my kids.' I didn't have enough for my kids. You could fall through the cracks easy fighting these white people. And no law."

But fight Clyde Ross did. In 1968 he joined the newly formed Contract Buyers League—a collection of black homeowners on Chicago's South and West Sides, all of whom had been locked into the same system of predation. There was Howell Collins, whose contract called for him to pay $25,500 for a house that a speculator had bought for $14,500. There was Ruth Wells, who'd managed to pay out half her contract, expecting a mortgage, only to suddenly see an insurance bill materialize out of thin air—a requirement the seller had added without Wells's knowledge. Contract sellers used every tool at their disposal to pilfer from their clients. They scared white residents into selling low. They lied about properties' compliance with building codes, then left the buyer responsible when city inspectors arrived. They presented themselves as real-estate brokers, when in fact they were the owners. They guided their clients to lawyers who were in on the scheme.

The Contract Buyers League fought back. Members—who would eventually number more than 500—went out to the posh suburbs where the speculators lived and embarrassed them by knocking on their neighbors' doors and informing them of the details of the contract-lending trade. They refused to pay their installments, instead holding monthly payments in an escrow account. Then they brought a suit against the contract sellers, accusing them of buying properties and reselling in such a manner "to reap from members of the Negro race large and unjust profits."

THE STORY OF CLYDE ROSS AND THE CONTRACT BUYERS LEAGUE

30   In return for the "deprivations of their rights and privileges under the Thirteenth and Fourteenth Amendments,"* the league demanded "prayers for relief"—payback of all moneys paid on contracts and all moneys paid for structural improvement of properties, at 6 percent interest minus a "fair, non-discriminatory" rental price for time of occupation. Moreover, the league asked the court to adjudge that the defendants had "acted willfully and maliciously and that malice is the gist of this action."

Ross and the Contract Buyers League were no longer appealing to the government simply for equality. They were no longer fleeing in hopes of a better deal elsewhere. They were charging society with a crime against their community. They wanted the crime publicly ruled as such. They wanted the crime's executors declared to be offensive to society. And they wanted restitution for the great injury brought upon them by said offenders. In 1968, Clyde Ross and the Contract Buyers League were no longer simply seeking the protection of the law. They were seeking reparations.

According to the most-recent statistics, North Lawndale is now on the wrong end of virtually every socioeconomic indicator. In 1930 its population was 112,000. Today it is 36,000. The halcyon talk of "interracial living" is dead. The neighborhood is 92 percent black. Its homicide rate is 45 per 100,000— triple the rate of the city as a whole. The infant-mortality rate is 14 per 1,000—more than twice the national average. Forty-three percent of the people in North Lawndale live below the poverty line—double Chicago's overall rate. Forty-five percent of all households are on food stamps—nearly three times the rate of the city at large. Sears, Roebuck left the neighborhood in 1987, taking 1,800 jobs with it. Kids in North Lawndale need not be confused about their prospects: Cook County's Juvenile Temporary Detention Center sits directly adjacent to the neighborhood.

North Lawndale is an extreme portrait of the trends that ail black Chicago. Such is the magnitude of these ailments that it can be said that blacks and whites do not inhabit the same city. The average per capita income of Chicago's white neighborhoods is almost three times that of its black neighborhoods. When the Harvard sociologist Robert J. Sampson examined incarceration rates in Chicago in his 2012 book, *Great American City*, he found that a black neighborhood with one of the highest incarceration rates (West Garfield Park) had a rate more than 40 times as high as the white neighborhood with the highest rate (Clearing). "This is a staggering differential, even for community-level comparisons," Sampson writes. "A difference of kind, not degree."

In other words, Chicago's impoverished black neighborhoods—characterized by high unemployment and households headed by single parents—are not simply poor; they are "ecologically distinct." This "is not simply the same thing as low economic status," writes Sampson. "In this pattern Chicago is not alone."

The lives of black Americans are better than they were half a century ago. The humiliation of Whites Only signs are gone. Rates of black poverty have decreased. Black teen-pregnancy rates are at record lows—and the gap between black and white teen-pregnancy rates has shrunk significantly. But such progress rests on a shaky foundation, and fault lines are everywhere. The income gap between black and white households is roughly the same today as it was in 1970. Patrick Sharkey, a sociologist at New York University, studied children born from 1955 through 1970 and found that 4 percent of whites and 62 percent of blacks across America had been raised in poor neighborhoods. A generation later, the same study showed, virtually nothing had changed. And

35

whereas whites born into affluent neighborhoods tended to remain in affluent neighborhoods, blacks tended to fall out of them.

This is not surprising. Black families, regardless of income, are significantly less wealthy than white families. The Pew Research Center estimates that white households are worth roughly 20 times as much as black households, and that whereas only 15 percent of whites have zero or negative wealth, more than a third of blacks do. Effectively, the black family in America is working without a safety net. When financial calamity strikes—a medical emergency, divorce, job loss—the fall is precipitous.

And just as black families of all incomes remain handicapped by a lack of wealth, so too do they remain handicapped by their restricted choice of neighborhood. Black people with upper-middle-class incomes do not generally live in upper-middle-class neighborhoods. Sharkey's research shows that black families making $100,000 typically live in the kinds of neighborhoods inhabited by white families making $30,000. "Blacks and whites inhabit such different neighborhoods," Sharkey writes, "that it is not possible to compare the economic outcomes of black and white children."

The implications are chilling. As a rule, poor black people do not work their way out of the ghetto—and those who do often face the horror of watching their children and grandchildren tumble back.

Even seeming evidence of progress withers under harsh light. In 2012, the Manhattan Institute cheerily noted that segregation had declined since the 1960s. And yet African Americans still remaïned—by far—the most segregated ethnic group in the country.

40   With segregation, with the isolation of the injured and the robbed, comes the concentration of disadvantage. An unsegregated America might see poverty, and all its effects, spread across the country with no particular bias toward skin color. Instead, the concentration of poverty has been paired with a concentration of melanin.[9] The resulting conflagration has been devastating.

One thread of thinking in the African American community holds that these depressing numbers partially stem from cultural pathologies that can be altered through individual grit and exceptionally good behavior. (In 2011, Philadelphia Mayor Michael Nutter, responding to violence among young black males, put the blame on the family: "Too many men making too many babies they don't want to take care of, and then we end up dealing with your children." Nutter turned to those presumably fatherless babies: "Pull your pants up and buy a belt, because no one wants to see your underwear or the crack of your butt.") The thread is as old as black politics itself. It is also wrong. The kind of trenchant racism to which black people have persistently been subjected can never be defeated by making

---

9   *melanin*   Pigment in skin (darker shades are produced by more melanin).

its victims more respectable. The essence of American racism is disrespect. And in the wake of the grim numbers, we see the grim inheritance.

The Contract Buyers League's suit brought by Clyde Ross and his allies took direct aim at this inheritance. The suit was rooted in Chicago's long history of segregation, which had created two housing markets—one legitimate and backed by the government, the other lawless and patrolled by predators. The suit dragged on until 1976, when the league lost a jury trial. Securing the equal protection of the law proved hard; securing reparations proved impossible. If there were any doubts about the mood of the jury, the foreman removed them by saying, when asked about the verdict, that he hoped it would help end "the mess Earl Warren made with *Brown v. Board of Education*[10] and all that nonsense."

The Supreme Court seems to share that sentiment. The past two decades have witnessed a rollback of the progressive legislation of the 1960s. Liberals have found themselves on the defensive. In 2008, when Barack Obama was a candidate for president, he was asked whether his daughters—Malia and Sasha—should benefit from affirmative action.* He answered in the negative.

The exchange rested upon an erroneous comparison of the average American white family and the exceptional first family. In the contest of upward mobility, Barack and Michelle Obama have won. But they've won by being twice as good—and enduring twice as much. Malia and Sasha Obama enjoy privileges beyond the average white child's dreams. But that comparison is incomplete. The more telling question is how they compare with Jenna and Barbara Bush—the products of many generations of privilege, not just one. Whatever the Obama children achieve, it will be evidence of their family's singular perseverance, not of broad equality.

In 1783, the freedwoman* Belinda Royall petitioned the commonwealth of Massachusetts for reparations. Belinda had been born in modern-day Ghana. She was kidnapped as a child and sold into slavery. She endured the Middle Passage and 50 years of enslavement at the hands of Isaac Royall and his son. But the junior Royall, a British loyalist, fled the country during the Revolution.* Belinda, now free after half a century of labor, beseeched the nascent Massachusetts legislature:

> The face of your Petitioner, is now marked with the furrows of time, and her frame bending under the oppression of years, while she, by the Laws of the Land, is denied the employment of one morsel of that immense wealth, apart whereof hath been accumilated by her own industry, and the whole augmented by her servitude.

45

---

10 *Brown v. Board of Education*   Landmark 1954 decision in which the Supreme Court decreed segregation in schools to be unconstitutional.

WHEREFORE, casting herself at your feet if your honours, as to a body of men, formed for the extirpation of vassalage, for the reward of Virtue, and the just return of honest industry—she prays, that such allowance may be made her out of the Estate of Colonel Royall, as will prevent her, and her more infirm daughter, from misery in the greatest extreme, and scatter comfort over the short and downward path of their lives.

Belinda Royall was granted a pension of 15 pounds and 12 shillings, to be paid out of the estate of Isaac Royall—one of the earliest successful attempts to petition for reparations. At the time, black people in America had endured more than 150 years of enslavement, and the idea that they might be owed something in return was, if not the national consensus, at least not outrageous.

"A heavy account lies against us as a civil society for oppressions committed against people who did not injure us," wrote the Quaker* John Woolman in 1769, "and that if the particular case of many individuals were fairly stated, it would appear that there was considerable due to them."

As the historian Roy E. Finkenbine has documented, at the dawn of this country, black reparations were actively considered and often effected. Quakers in New York, New England, and Baltimore went so far as to make "membership contingent upon compensating one's former slaves." In 1782, the Quaker Robert Pleasants emancipated his 78 slaves, granted them 350 acres, and later built a school on their property and provided for their education. "The doing of this justice to the injured Africans," wrote Pleasants, "would be an acceptable offering to him who 'Rules in the kingdom of men.'"

Edward Coles, a protégé of Thomas Jefferson* who became a slaveholder through inheritance, took many of his slaves north and granted them a plot of land in Illinois. John Randolph, a cousin of Jefferson's, willed that all his slaves be emancipated upon his death, and that all those older than 40 be given 10 acres of land. "I give and bequeath to all my slaves their freedom," Randolph wrote, "heartily regretting that I have been the owner of one."

50   In his book *Forever Free*, Eric Foner recounts the story of a disgruntled planter reprimanding a freedman loafing on the job:

Planter: "You lazy nigger, I am losing a whole day's labor by you."

Freedman: "Massa, how many days' labor have I lost by you?"

In the 20th century, the cause of reparations was taken up by a diverse cast that included the Confederate veteran Walter R. Vaughan, who believed that reparations would be a stimulus for the South; the black activist Callie House; black-nationalist* leaders like "Queen Mother" Audley Moore; and the civil-rights activist James Forman. The movement coalesced in 1987 under an umbrella organization called the National Coalition of Blacks for Reparations in America (N'COBRA). The NAACP* endorsed reparations in 1993. Charles J. Ogletree Jr., a professor at Harvard Law School, has pursued reparations claims in court.

But while the people advocating reparations have changed over time, the response from the country has remained virtually the same. "They have been taught to labor," the *Chicago Tribune* editorialized in 1891. "They have been taught Christian civilization, and to speak the noble English language instead of some African gibberish. The account is square with the ex-slaves."

Not exactly. Having been enslaved for 250 years, black people were not left to their own devices. They were terrorized. In the Deep South, a second slavery ruled.* In the North, legislatures, mayors, civic associations, banks, and citizens all colluded to pin black people into ghettos, where they were overcrowded, overcharged, and undereducated. Businesses discriminated against them, awarding them the worst jobs and the worst wages. Police brutalized them in the streets. And the notion that black lives, black bodies, and black wealth were rightful targets remained deeply rooted in the broader society. Now we have half-stepped away from our long centuries of despoilment, promising, "Never again." But still we are haunted. It is as though we have run up a credit-card bill and, having pledged to charge no more, remain befuddled that the balance does not disappear. The effects of that balance, interest accruing daily, are all around us.

Broach the topic of reparations today and a barrage of questions inevitably follows: Who will be paid? How much will they be paid? Who will pay? But if the practicalities, not the justice, of reparations are the true sticking point, there has for some time been the beginnings of a solution. For the past 25 years, Congressman John Conyers Jr., who represents the Detroit area, has marked every session of Congress by introducing a bill calling for a congressional study of slavery and its lingering effects as well as recommendations for "appropriate remedies."

A country curious about how reparations might actually work has an easy solution in Conyers's bill, now called HR 40, the Commission to Study Reparation Proposals for African Americans Act. We would support this bill, submit the question to study, and then assess the possible solutions. But we are not interested.

"It's because it's black folks making the claim," Nkechi Taifa, who helped found N'COBRA, says. "People who talk about reparations are considered left lunatics. But all we are talking about is studying [reparations]. As John Conyers has said, we study everything. We study the water, the air. We can't even study the issue? This bill does not authorize one red cent to anyone."

That HR 40 has never—under either Democrats or Republicans—made it to the House floor suggests our concerns are rooted not in the impracticality

55

of reparations but in something more existential. If we conclude that the conditions in North Lawndale and black America are not inexplicable but are instead precisely what you'd expect of a community that for centuries has lived in America's crosshairs, then what are we to make of the world's oldest democracy?

One cannot escape the question by hand-waving at the past, disavowing the acts of one's ancestors, nor by citing a recent date of ancestral immigration. The last slaveholder has been dead for a very long time. The last soldier to endure Valley Forge[11] has been dead much longer. To proudly claim the veteran and disown the slaveholder is patriotism à la carte.* A nation outlives its generations. We were not there when Washington crossed the Delaware,* but Emanuel Gottlieb Leutze's rendering[12] has meaning to us. We were not there when Woodrow Wilson took us into World War I, but we are still paying out the pensions. If Thomas Jefferson's genius matters, then so does his taking of Sally Hemings's[13] body. If George Washington crossing the Delaware matters, so must his ruthless pursuit of the runagate Oney Judge.[14]

In 1909, President William Howard Taft told the country that "intelligent" white southerners were ready to see blacks as "useful members of the community." A week later Joseph Gordon, a black man, was lynched outside Greenwood, Mississippi. The high point of the lynching era has passed. But the memories of those robbed of their lives still live on in the lingering effects. Indeed, in America there is a strange and powerful belief that if you stab a black person 10 times, the bleeding stops and the healing begins the moment the assailant drops the knife. We believe white dominance to be a fact of the inert past, a delinquent debt that can be made to disappear if only we don't look.

60   There has always been another way. "It is in vain to allege, that *our ancestors* brought them hither, and not we," Yale President Timothy Dwight said in 1810.

> We inherit our ample patrimony with all its incumbrances; and are bound to pay the debts of our ancestors. *This* debt, particularly, we are bound to discharge: and, when the righteous Judge of the Universe comes to reckon with his servants, he will rigidly exact the payment at

---

11 *Valley Forge*   Site of a Revolutionary War-era military camp where American forces spent the winter of 1777 with inadequate provisions; thousands died.

12 *Emanuel ... rendering*   Emanuel Gottlieb Leutze's 1857 painting *Washington Crosssing the Delaware* is an iconic image of the event.

13 *Sally Hemings*   Hemings (1773–1835) was a slave of Thomas Jefferson with whom he had a long-term sexual relationship.

14 *Oney Judge*   Judge (c. 1773–1848) was a slave of George Washington who escaped; Washington tried repeatedly to secure her return.

our hands. To give them liberty, and stop here, is to entail upon them
a curse.

America begins in black plunder and white democracy, two features that are
not contradictory but complementary. "The men who came together to found
the independent United States, dedicated to freedom and equality, either held
slaves or were willing to join hands with those who did," the historian Edmund
S. Morgan wrote. "None of them felt entirely comfortable about the fact, but
neither did they feel responsible for it. Most of them had inherited both their
slaves and their attachment to freedom from an earlier generation, and they
knew the two were not unconnected."

When enslaved Africans, plundered of their bodies, plundered of their families, and plundered of their labor, were brought to the colony of Virginia* in 1619,
they did not initially endure the naked racism that would engulf their progeny.
Some of them were freed. Some of them intermarried. Still others escaped with
the white indentured servants who had suffered as they had. Some even rebelled
together, allying under Nathaniel Bacon to torch Jamestown in 1676.

One hundred years later, the idea of slaves and poor whites joining forces
would shock the senses, but in the early days of the English colonies, the two
groups had much in common. English visitors to Virginia found that its masters
"abuse their servantes with intollerable oppression and hard usage." White
servants were flogged, tricked into serving beyond their contracts, and traded
in much the same manner as slaves.

This "hard usage" originated in a simple fact of the New World—land was
boundless but cheap labor was limited. As life spans increased in the colony,
the Virginia planters found in the enslaved Africans an even more efficient
source of cheap labor. Whereas indentured servants were still legal subjects
of the English crown and thus entitled to certain protections, African slaves
entered the colonies as aliens. Exempted from the protections of the crown,
they became early America's indispensable working class—fit for maximum
exploitation, capable of only minimal resistance.

For the next 250 years, American law worked to reduce black people to a
class of untouchables[15] and raise all white men to the level of citizens. In 1650,
Virginia mandated that "all persons except Negroes" were to carry arms. In
1664, Maryland mandated that any Englishwoman who married a slave must
live as a slave of her husband's master. In 1705, the Virginia assembly passed
a law allowing for the dismemberment of unruly slaves—but forbidding masters from whipping "a Christian white servant naked, without an order from a
justice of the peace." In that same law, the colony mandated that "all horses,
cattle, and hogs, now belonging, or that hereafter shall belong to any slave" be

15 *untouchables* Lowest members in India's elaborate class hierarchy.

seized and sold off by the local church, the profits used to support "the poor of the said parish." At that time, there would have still been people alive who could remember blacks and whites joining to burn down Jamestown only 29 years before. But at the beginning of the 18th century, two primary classes were enshrined in America.

65   "The two great divisions of society are not the rich and poor, but white and black," John C. Calhoun, South Carolina's senior senator, declared on the Senate floor in 1848. "And all the former, the poor as well as the rich, belong to the upper class, and are respected and treated as equals."

    In 1860, the majority of people living in South Carolina and Mississippi, almost half of those living in Georgia, and about one-third of all Southerners were on the wrong side of Calhoun's line. The state with the largest number of enslaved Americans was Virginia, where in certain counties some 70 percent of all people labored in chains. Nearly one-fourth of all white Southerners owned slaves, and upon their backs the economic basis of America—and much of the Atlantic world—was erected. In the seven cotton states, one-third of all white income was derived from slavery. By 1840, cotton produced by slave labor constituted 59 percent of the country's exports. The web of this slave society extended north to the looms of New England,* and across the Atlantic to Great Britain, where it powered a great economic transformation and altered the trajectory of world history. "Whoever says Industrial Revolution," wrote the historian Eric J. Hobsbawm, "says cotton."

    The wealth accorded America by slavery was not just in what the slaves pulled from the land but in the slaves themselves. "In 1860, slaves as an asset were worth more than all of America's manufacturing, all of the railroads, all of the productive capacity of the United States put together," the Yale historian David W. Blight has noted. "Slaves were the single largest, by far, financial asset of property in the entire American economy." The sale of these slaves—"in whose bodies that money congealed," writes Walter Johnson, a Harvard historian—generated even more ancillary wealth. Loans were taken out for purchase, to be repaid with interest. Insurance policies were drafted against the untimely death of a slave and the loss of potential profits. Slave sales were taxed and notarized. The vending of the black body and the sundering of the black family became an economy unto themselves, estimated to have brought in tens of millions of dollars to antebellum America. In 1860 there were more millionaires per capita in the Mississippi Valley than anywhere else in the country.

    Beneath the cold numbers lay lives divided. "I had a constant dread that Mrs. Moore, her mistress, would be in want of money and sell my dear wife," a freedman wrote, reflecting on his time in slavery. "We constantly dreaded a final separation. Our affection for each was very strong, and this made us always apprehensive of a cruel parting."

Forced partings were common in the antebellum South. A slave in some parts of the region stood a 30 percent chance of being sold in his or her lifetime. Twenty-five percent of interstate trades destroyed a first marriage and half of them destroyed a nuclear family.

When the wife and children of Henry Brown, a slave in Richmond, Virginia, were to be sold away, Brown searched for a white master who might buy his wife and children to keep the family together. He failed: 70

> The next day, I stationed myself by the side of the road, along which the slaves, amounting to three hundred and fifty, were to pass. The purchaser of my wife was a Methodist minister, who was about starting for North Carolina. Pretty soon five waggon-loads of little children passed, and looking at the foremost one, what should I see but a little child, pointing its tiny hand towards me, exclaiming, "There's my father; I knew he would come and bid me good-bye." It was my eldest child! Soon the gang approached in which my wife was chained. I looked, and beheld her familiar face; but O, reader, that glance of agony! may God spare me ever again enduring the excruciating horror of that moment! She passed, and came near to where I stood. I seized hold of her hand, intending to bid her farewell; but words failed me; the gift of utterance had fled, and I remained speechless. I followed her for some distance, with her hand grasped in mine, as if to save her from her fate, but I could not speak, and I was obliged to turn away in silence.

In a time when telecommunications were primitive and blacks lacked freedom of movement, the parting of black families was a kind of murder. Here we find the roots of American wealth and democracy—in the for-profit destruction of the most important asset available to any people, the family. The destruction was not incidental to America's rise; it facilitated that rise. By erecting a slave society, America created the economic foundation for its great experiment in democracy. The labor strife that seeded Bacon's rebellion was suppressed. America's indispensable working class existed as property beyond the realm of politics, leaving white Americans free to trumpet their love of freedom and democratic values. Assessing antebellum democracy in Virginia, a visitor from England observed that the state's natives "can profess an unbounded love of liberty and of democracy in consequence of the mass of the people, who in other countries might become mobs, being there nearly altogether composed of their own Negro slaves."

The consequences of 250 years of enslavement, of war upon black families and black people, were profound. Like homeownership today, slave ownership was aspirational, attracting not just those who owned slaves but those who wished to. Much as homeowners today might discuss the addition of a patio or the painting of a living room, slaveholders traded tips on the best methods for breeding workers, exacting labor, and doling out punishment. Just as a home-owner today might subscribe to a magazine like *This Old House*, slaveholders had journals such as *De Bow's Review*, which recommended the best practices for wringing profits from slaves. By the dawn of the Civil War, the enslavement of black America was thought to be so foundational to the country that those who sought to end it were branded heretics worthy of death. Imagine what would happen if a president today came out in favor of taking all American homes from their owners: the reaction might well be violent.

"This country was formed for the *white*, not for the black man," John Wilkes Booth wrote, before killing Abraham Lincoln. "And looking upon *African slavery* from the same standpoint held by those noble framers of our Constitution, I for one have ever considered it one of the greatest blessings (both for themselves and us) that God ever bestowed upon a favored nation."

In the aftermath of the Civil War, Radical Republicans attempted to re-construct the country upon something resembling universal equality—but they were beaten back by a campaign of "Redemption," led by White Liners, Red Shirts,[16] and Klansmen bent on upholding a society "formed for the *white*, not for the black man." A wave of terrorism roiled the South. In his massive history *Reconstruction*, Eric Foner recounts incidents of black people being attacked for not removing their hats; for refusing to hand over a whiskey flask; for disobeying church procedures; for "using insolent language"; for disputing labor contracts; for refusing to be "tied like a slave." Sometimes the attacks were intended simply to "thin out the niggers a little."

75 Terrorism carried the day. Federal troops withdrew from the South in 1877. The dream of Reconstruction* died. For the next century, political violence was visited upon blacks wantonly, with special treatment meted out toward black people of ambition. Black schools and churches were burned to the ground. Black voters and the political candidates who attempted to rally them were intimidated, and some were murdered. At the end of World War I, black veterans returning to their homes were assaulted for daring to wear the American uniform. The demobilization of soldiers after the war, which put white and black veterans into competition for scarce jobs, produced the Red Summer of 1919: a succession of racist pogroms against dozens of cities ranging from Longview, Texas, to Chicago to Washington, D.C. Organized white violence against blacks continued into the 1920s—in 1921 a white mob leveled Tulsa's "Black Wall Street,"* and in 1923 another one razed the black town of Rosewood, Florida—and virtually no one was punished.

---

16 *White Liners, Red Shirts*   Groups of white supremacists.

The work of mobs was a rabid and violent rendition of prejudices that extended even into the upper reaches of American government. The New Deal* is today remembered as a model for what progressive government should do—cast a broad social safety net that protects the poor and the afflicted while building the middle class. When progressives wish to express their disappointment with Barack Obama, they point to the accomplishments of Franklin Roosevelt. But these progressives rarely note that Roosevelt's New Deal, much like the democracy that produced it, rested on the foundation of Jim Crow.

"The Jim Crow South," writes Ira Katznelson, a history and political-science professor at Columbia, "was the one collaborator America's democracy could not do without." The marks of that collaboration are all over the New Deal. The omnibus programs passed under the Social Security Act in 1935 were crafted in such a way as to protect the southern way of life. Old-age insurance (Social Security proper) and unemployment insurance excluded farmworkers and domestics—jobs heavily occupied by blacks. When President Roosevelt signed Social Security into law in 1935, 65 percent of African Americans nationally and between 70 and 80 percent in the South were ineligible. The NAACP protested, calling the new American safety net "a sieve with holes just big enough for the majority of Negroes to fall through."

The oft-celebrated G.I. Bill* similarly failed black Americans, by mirroring the broader country's insistence on a racist housing policy. Though ostensibly color-blind, Title III of the bill, which aimed to give veterans access to low-interest home loans, left black veterans to tangle with white officials at their local Veterans Administration as well as with the same banks that had, for years, refused to grant mortgages to blacks. The historian Kathleen J. Frydl observes in her 2009 book, *The GI Bill*, that so many blacks were disqualified from receiving Title III benefits "that it is more accurate simply to say that blacks could not use this particular title."

In Cold War America,* homeownership was seen as a means of instilling patriotism, and as a civilizing and anti-radical force. "No man who owns his own house and lot can be a Communist," claimed William Levitt, who pioneered the modern suburb with the development of the various Levittowns, his famous planned communities. "He has too much to do."

But the Levittowns were, with Levitt's willing acquiescence, segregated throughout their early years. Daisy and Bill Myers, the first black family to move into Levittown, Pennsylvania, were greeted with protests and a burning cross.* A neighbor who opposed the family said that Bill Myers was "probably a nice guy, but every time I look at him I see $2,000 drop off the value of my house."

The neighbor had good reason to be afraid. Bill and Daisy Myers were from the other side of John C. Calhoun's dual society. If they moved next door,

80

housing policy almost guaranteed that their neighbors' property values would decline.

Whereas shortly before the New Deal, a typical mortgage required a large down payment and full repayment within about 10 years, the creation of the Home Owners' Loan Corporation in 1933 and then the Federal Housing Administration the following year allowed banks to offer loans requiring no more than 10 percent down, amortized over 20 to 30 years. "Without federal intervention in the housing market, massive suburbanization would have been impossible," writes Thomas J. Sugrue, a historian at the University of Pennsylvania. "In 1930, only 30 percent of Americans owned their own homes; by 1960, more than 60 percent were home owners. Home ownership became an emblem of American citizenship."

That emblem was not to be awarded to blacks. The American real-estate industry believed segregation to be a moral principle. As late as 1950, the National Association of Real Estate Boards' code of ethics warned that "a Realtor should never be instrumental in introducing into a neighborhood ... any race or nationality, or any individuals whose presence will clearly be detrimental to property values." A 1943 brochure specified that such potential undesirables might include madams, bootleggers, gangsters—and "a colored man of means who was giving his children a college education and thought they were entitled to live among whites."

The federal government concurred. It was the Home Owners' Loan Corporation, not a private trade association, that pioneered the practice of redlining, selectively granting loans and insisting that any property it insured be covered by a restrictive covenant—a clause in the deed forbidding the sale of the property to anyone other than whites. Millions of dollars flowed from tax coffers into segregated white neighborhoods.

85 "For perhaps the first time, the federal government embraced the discriminatory attitudes of the marketplace," the historian Kenneth T. Jackson wrote in his 1985 book, *Crabgrass Frontier*, a history of suburbanization. "Previously, prejudices were personalized and individualized; FHA exhorted segregation and enshrined it as public policy. Whole areas of cities were declared ineligible for loan guarantees." Redlining was not officially outlawed until 1968, by the Fair Housing Act. By then the damage was done—and reports of redlining by banks have continued.

The federal government is premised on equal fealty from all its citizens, who in return are to receive equal treatment. But as late as the mid-20th century, this bargain was not granted to black people, who repeatedly paid a higher price for citizenship and received less in return. Plunder had been the essential feature of slavery, of the society described by Calhoun. But practically a full century after the end of the Civil War and the abolition of slavery, the plunder—quiet, systemic, submerged—continued even amidst the aims and achievements of New Deal liberals.

Today Chicago is one of the most segregated cities in the country, a fact that reflects assiduous planning. In the effort to uphold white supremacy at every level down to the neighborhood, Chicago—a city founded by the black fur trader Jean Baptiste Point du Sable—has long been a pioneer. The efforts began in earnest in 1917, when the Chicago Real Estate Board, horrified by the influx of southern blacks, lobbied to zone the entire city by race. But after the Supreme Court ruled against explicit racial zoning that year, the city was forced to pursue its agenda by more-discreet means.

Like the Home Owners' Loan Corporation, the Federal Housing Administration initially insisted on restrictive covenants, which helped bar blacks and other ethnic undesirables from receiving federally backed home loans. By the 1940s, Chicago led the nation in the use of these restrictive covenants, and about half of all residential neighborhoods in the city were effectively off-limits to blacks.

It is common today to become misty-eyed about the old black ghetto, where doctors and lawyers lived next door to meatpackers and steelworkers, who themselves lived next door to prostitutes and the unemployed. This segregationist nostalgia ignores the actual conditions endured by the people living there—vermin and arson, for instance—and ignores the fact that the old ghetto was premised on denying black people privileges enjoyed by white Americans.

In 1948, when the Supreme Court ruled that restrictive covenants, while permissible, were not enforceable by judicial action, Chicago had other weapons at the ready. The Illinois state legislature had already given Chicago's city council the right to approve—and thus to veto—any public housing in the city's wards. This came in handy in 1949, when a new federal housing act sent millions of tax dollars into Chicago and other cities around the country. Beginning in 1950, site selection for public housing proceeded entirely on the grounds of segregation. By the 1960s, the city had created with its vast housing projects what the historian Arnold R. Hirsch calls a "second ghetto," one larger than the old Black Belt but just as impermeable. More than 98 percent of all the family public-housing units built in Chicago between 1950 and the mid-1960s were built in all-black neighborhoods.

Governmental embrace of segregation was driven by the virulent racism of Chicago's white citizens. White neighborhoods vulnerable to black encroachment formed block associations for the sole purpose of enforcing segregation. They lobbied fellow whites not to sell. They lobbied those blacks who did manage to buy to sell back. In 1949, a group of Englewood Catholics formed block associations intended to "keep up the neighborhood." Translation: keep black

90

people out. And when civic engagement was not enough, when government failed, when private banks could no longer hold the line, Chicago turned to an old tool in the American repertoire—racial violence. "The pattern of terrorism is easily discernible," concluded a Chicago civic group in the 1940s. "It is at the seams of the black ghetto in all directions." On July 1 and 2 of 1946, a mob of thousands assembled in Chicago's Park Manor neighborhood, hoping to eject a black doctor who'd recently moved in. The mob pelted the house with rocks and set the garage on fire. The doctor moved away.

In 1947, after a few black veterans moved into the Fernwood section of Chicago, three nights of rioting broke out; gangs of whites yanked blacks off streetcars and beat them. Two years later, when a union meeting attended by blacks in Englewood triggered rumors that a home was being "sold to niggers," blacks (and whites thought to be sympathetic to them) were beaten in the streets. In 1951, thousands of whites in Cicero, 20 minutes or so west of downtown Chicago, attacked an apartment building that housed a single black family, throwing bricks and firebombs through the windows and setting the apartment on fire. A Cook County grand jury declined to charge the rioters—and instead indicted the family's NAACP attorney, the apartment's white owner, and the owner's attorney and rental agent, charging them with conspiring to lower property values. Two years after that, whites picketed and planted explosives in South Deering, about 30 minutes from downtown Chicago, to force blacks out.

When terrorism ultimately failed, white homeowners simply fled the neighborhood. The traditional terminology, white flight, implies a kind of natural expression of preference. In fact, *white flight* was a triumph of social engineering, orchestrated by the shared racist presumptions of America's public and private sectors. For should any nonracist white families decide that integration might not be so bad as a matter of principle or practicality, they still had to contend with the hard facts of American housing policy: When the mid-20th-century white homeowner claimed that the presence of a Bill and Daisy Myers decreased his property value, he was not merely engaging in racist dogma—he was accurately observing the impact of federal policy on market prices. Redlining destroyed the possibility of investment wherever black people lived.

Speculators in North Lawndale, and at the edge of the black ghettos, knew there was money to be made off white panic. They resorted to "block-busting"—spooking whites into selling cheap before the neighborhood became black. They would hire a black woman to walk up and down the street with a stroller. Or they'd hire someone to call a number in the neighborhood looking for "Johnny Mae."* Then they'd cajole whites into selling at low prices, informing them that the more blacks who moved in, the more the value of their homes would decline, so better to sell now. With these white-fled homes in hand, speculators then turned to the masses of black people who had streamed northward as part of the Great Migration, or who were desperate to escape the ghettos: the speculators would take the houses they'd just bought cheap through block-busting and sell them to blacks on contract.

To keep up with his payments and keep his heat on, Clyde Ross took a 95 second job at the post office and then a third job delivering pizza. His wife took a job working at Marshall Field.* He had to take some of his children out of private school. He was not able to be at home to supervise his children or help them with their homework. Money and time that Ross wanted to give his children went instead to enrich white speculators.

"The problem was the money," Ross told me. "Without the money, you can't move. You can't educate your kids. You can't give them the right kind of food. Can't make the house look good. They think this neighborhood is where they supposed to be. It changes their outlook. My kids were going to the best schools in this neighborhood, and I couldn't keep them in there."

Mattie Lewis came to Chicago from her native Alabama in the mid-'40s, when she was 21, persuaded by a friend who told her she could get a job as a hairdresser. Instead she was hired by Western Electric, where she worked for 41 years. I met Lewis in the home of her neighbor Ethel Weatherspoon. Both had owned homes in North Lawndale for more than 50 years. Both had bought their houses on contract. Both had been active with Clyde Ross in the Contract Buyers League's effort to garner restitution from contract sellers who'd operated in North Lawndale, banks who'd backed the scheme, and even the Federal Housing Administration. We were joined by Jack Macnamara, who'd been an organizing force in the Contract Buyers League when it was founded, in 1968. Our gathering had the feel of a reunion, because the writer James Alan McPherson had profiled the Contract Buyers League for *The Atlantic* back in 1972.

Weatherspoon bought her home in 1957. "Most of the whites started moving out," she told me. "'The blacks are coming. The blacks are coming.' They actually said that. They had signs up: Don't sell to blacks."

Before moving to North Lawndale, Lewis and her husband tried moving to Cicero after seeing a house advertised for sale there. "Sorry, I just sold it today," the Realtor told Lewis's husband. "I told him, 'You know they don't want you in Cicero,'" Lewis recalls. "'They ain't going to let nobody black in Cicero.'"

In 1958, the couple bought a home in North Lawndale on contract. They 100 were not blind to the unfairness. But Lewis, born in the teeth of Jim Crow, considered American piracy—black people keep on making it, white people keep on taking it—a fact of nature. "All I wanted was a house. And that was the only way I could get it. They weren't giving black people loans at that time," she said. "We thought, 'This is the way it is. We going to do it till we die, and they ain't never going to accept us. That's just the way it is.'

"The only way you were going to buy a home was to do it the way they wanted," she continued. "And I was determined to get me a house. If everybody else can have one, I want one too. I had worked for white people in the South. And I saw how these white people were living in the North and I thought, 'One day I'm going to live just like them.' I wanted cabinets and all these things these other people have."

Whenever she visited white co-workers at their homes, she saw the difference. "I could see we were just getting ripped off," she said. "I would see things and I would say, 'I'd like to do this at my house.' And they would say, 'Do it,' but I would think, 'I can't, because it costs us so much more.'"

I asked Lewis and Weatherspoon how they kept up on payments.

"You paid it and kept working," Lewis said of the contract. "When that payment came up, you knew you had to pay it."

105   "You cut down on the light bill. Cut down on your food bill," Weatherspoon interjected.

"You cut down on things for your child, that was the main thing," said Lewis. "My oldest wanted to be an artist and my other wanted to be a dancer and my other wanted to take music."

Lewis and Weatherspoon, like Ross, were able to keep their homes. The suit did not win them any remuneration. But it forced contract sellers to the table, where they allowed some members of the Contract Buyers League to move into regular mortgages or simply take over their houses outright. By then they'd been bilked for thousands. In talking with Lewis and Weatherspoon, I was seeing only part of the picture—the tiny minority who'd managed to hold on to their homes. But for all our exceptional ones, for every Barack and Michelle Obama, for every Ethel Weatherspoon or Clyde Ross, for every black survivor, there are so many thousands gone.

"A lot of people fell by the way," Lewis told me. "One woman asked me if I would keep all her china. She said, 'They ain't going to set you out.'"

On a recent spring afternoon in North Lawndale, I visited Billy Lamar Brooks Sr. Brooks has been an activist since his youth in the Black Panther Party,* when he aided the Contract Buyers League. I met him in his office at the Better Boys Foundation, a staple of North Lawndale whose mission is to direct local kids off the streets and into jobs and college. Brooks's work is personal. On June 14, 1991, his 19-year-old son, Billy Jr., was shot and killed. "These guys tried to stick him up," Brooks told me. "I suspect he could have been involved in some things ... He's always on my mind. Every day."

110   Brooks was not raised in the streets, though in such a neighborhood it is impossible to avoid the influence. "I was in church three or four times a week. That's where the girls were," he said, laughing. "The stark reality is still there.

There's no shield from life. You got to go to school. I lived here. I went to Marshall High School. Over here were the Egyptian Cobras. Over there were the Vice Lords."[17]

Brooks has since moved away from Chicago's West Side. But he is still working in North Lawndale. If "you got a nice house, you live in a nice neighborhood, then you are less prone to violence, because your space is not deprived," Brooks said. "You got a security point. You don't need no protection." But if "you grow up in a place like this, housing sucks. When they tore down the projects here, they left the high-rises and came to the neighborhood with that gang mentality. You don't have nothing, so you going to take something, even if it's not real. You don't have no street, but in your mind it's yours."

We walked over to a window behind his desk. A group of young black men were hanging out in front of a giant mural memorializing two black men: In Lovin Memory Quentin aka "Q," July 18, 1974 ❤ March 2, 2012. The name and face of the other man had been spray-painted over by a rival group. The men drank beer. Occasionally a car would cruise past, slow to a crawl, then stop. One of the men would approach the car and make an exchange, then the car would drive off. Brooks had known all of these young men as boys.

"That's their corner," he said.

We watched another car roll through, pause briefly, then drive off. "No respect, no shame," Brooks said. "That's what they do. From that alley to that corner. They don't go no farther than that. See the big brother there? He almost died a couple of years ago. The one drinking the beer back there … I know all of them. And the reason they feel safe here is cause of this building, and because they too chickenshit to go anywhere. But that's their mentality. That's their block."

Brooks showed me a picture of a Little League team he had coached. He went down the row of kids, pointing out which ones were in jail, which ones were dead, and which ones were doing all right. And then he pointed out his son—"That's my boy, Billy," Brooks said. Then he wondered aloud if keeping his son with him while working in North Lawndale had hastened his death. "It's a definite connection, because he was part of what I did here. And I think maybe I shouldn't have exposed him. But then, I had to," he said, "because I wanted him with me."

115

From the White House on down, the myth holds that fatherhood is the great antidote to all that ails black people. But Billy Brooks Jr. had a father. Trayvon Martin had a father. Jordan Davis[18] had a father. Adhering to middle-class

---

17 *Egyptian Cobras ... Vice Lords*   Gang names.

18 *Trayvon Martin ... Jordan Davis*   Martin and Davis were both African American teens who were shot and killed in 2012 by civilians while breaking no law.

norms has never shielded black people from plunder. Adhering to middle-class norms is what made Ethel Weatherspoon a lucrative target for rapacious speculators. Contract sellers did not target the very poor. They targeted black people who had worked hard enough to save a down payment and dreamed of the emblem of American citizenship—homeownership. It was not a tangle of pathology that put a target on Clyde Ross's back. It was not a culture of poverty that singled out Mattie Lewis for "the thrill of the chase and the kill." Some black people always will be twice as good. But they generally find white predation to be thrice as fast.

Liberals today mostly view racism not as an active, distinct evil but as a relative of white poverty and inequality. They ignore the long tradition of this country actively punishing black success—and the elevation of that punishment, in the mid-20th century, to federal policy. President Lyndon Johnson may have noted in his historic civil-rights speech at Howard University in 1965 that "Negro poverty is not white poverty." But his advisers and their successors were, and still are, loath to craft any policy that recognizes the difference.

After his speech, Johnson convened a group of civil-rights leaders, including the esteemed A. Philip Randolph and Bayard Rustin, to address the "ancient brutality." In a strategy paper, they agreed with the president that "Negro poverty is a special, and particularly destructive, form of American poverty." But when it came to specifically addressing the "particularly destructive," Rustin's group demurred, preferring to advance programs that addressed "all the poor, black and white."

The urge to use the moral force of the black struggle to address broader inequalities originates in both compassion and pragmatism. But it makes for ambiguous policy. Affirmative action's precise aims, for instance, have always proved elusive. Is it meant to make amends for the crimes heaped upon black people? Not according to the Supreme Court. In its 1978 ruling in *Regents of the University of California v. Bakke*, the Court rejected "societal discrimination" as "an amorphous concept of injury that may be ageless in its reach into the past." Is affirmative action meant to increase "diversity"? If so, it only tangentially relates to the specific problems of black people—the problem of what America has taken from them over several centuries.

120   This confusion about affirmative action's aims, along with our inability to face up to the particular history of white-imposed black disadvantage, dates back to the policy's origins. "There is no fixed and firm definition of affirmative action," an appointee in Johnson's Department of Labor declared. "Affirmative action is anything that you have to do to get results. But this does not necessarily include preferential treatment."

Yet America was built on the preferential treatment of white people—395 years of it. Vaguely endorsing a cuddly, feel-good diversity does very little to redress this.

Today, progressives are loath to invoke white supremacy as an explanation for anything. On a practical level, the hesitation comes from the dim view the Supreme Court has taken of the reforms of the 1960s. The Voting Rights Act has been gutted. The Fair Housing Act might well be next. Affirmative action is on its last legs. In substituting a broad class struggle for an anti-racist struggle, progressives hope to assemble a coalition by changing the subject.

The politics of racial evasion are seductive. But the record is mixed. Aid to Families With Dependent Children was originally written largely to exclude blacks—yet by the 1990s it was perceived as a giveaway to blacks. The Affordable Care Act* makes no mention of race, but this did not keep Rush Limbaugh* from denouncing it as reparations. Moreover, the act's expansion of Medicaid was effectively made optional, meaning that many poor blacks in the former Confederate states do not benefit from it. The Affordable Care Act, like Social Security, will eventually expand its reach to those left out; in the meantime, black people will be injured.

"All that it would take to sink a new WPA program[19] would be some skillfully packaged footage of black men leaning on shovels smoking cigarettes," the sociologist Douglas S. Massey writes. "Papering over the issue of race makes for bad social theory, bad research, and bad public policy." To ignore the fact that one of the oldest republics in the world was erected on a foundation of white supremacy, to pretend that the problems of a dual society are the same as the problems of unregulated capitalism, is to cover the sin of national plunder with the sin of national lying. The lie ignores the fact that reducing American poverty and ending white supremacy are not the same. The lie ignores the fact that closing the "achievement gap" will do nothing to close the "injury gap," in which black college graduates still suffer higher unemployment rates than white college graduates, and black job applicants without criminal records enjoy roughly the same chance of getting hired as white applicants *with* criminal records.

Chicago, like the country at large, embraced policies that placed black America's most energetic, ambitious, and thrifty countrymen beyond the pale of society and marked them as rightful targets for legal theft. The effects reverberate beyond the families who were robbed to the community that beholds the spectacle. Don't just picture Clyde Ross working three jobs so he could hold

125

---

19 *WPA program* Works Progress Administration program, a part of the New Deal in which unemployed workers were given employment building schools, roads, and other public works.

on to his home. Think of his North Lawndale neighbors—their children, their nephews and nieces—and consider how watching this affects them. Imagine yourself as a young black child watching your elders play by all the rules only to have their possessions tossed out in the street and to have their most sacred possession—their home—taken from them.

The message the young black boy receives from his country, Billy Brooks says, is "'You ain't shit. You not no good. The only thing you are worth is working for us. You will never own anything. You not going to get an education. We are sending your ass to the penitentiary.' They're telling you no matter how hard you struggle, no matter what you put down, you ain't shit. 'We're going to take what you got. You will never own anything, nigger.'"

When Clyde Ross was a child, his older brother Winter had a seizure. He was picked up by the authorities and delivered to Parchman Farm, a 20,000-acre state prison in the Mississippi Delta region.*

"He was a gentle person," Clyde Ross says of his brother. "You know, he was good to everybody. And he started having spells, and he couldn't control himself. And they had him picked up, because they thought he was dangerous."

Built at the turn of the century, Parchman was supposed to be a progressive and reformist response to the problem of "Negro crime." In fact it was the gulag[20] of Mississippi, an object of terror to African Americans in the Delta. In the early years of the 20th century, Mississippi Governor James K. Vardaman used to amuse himself by releasing black convicts into the surrounding wilderness and hunting them down with bloodhounds. "Throughout the American South," writes David M. Oshinsky in his book *Worse Than Slavery*, "Parchman Farm is synonymous with punishment and brutality, as well it should be ... Parchman is the quintessential penal farm, the closest thing to slavery that survived the Civil War."

130   When the Ross family went to retrieve Winter, the authorities told them that Winter had died. When the Ross family asked for his body, the authorities at Parchman said they had buried him. The family never saw Winter's body.

And this was just one of their losses.

Scholars have long discussed methods by which America might make reparations to those on whose labor and exclusion the country was built. In the 1970s, the Yale Law professor Boris Bittker argued in *The Case for Black Reparations* that a rough price tag for reparations could be determined by multiplying the number of African Americans in the population by the difference

---

20   *gulag*   In the former Soviet Union, gulags were prisons to which political dissidents were sent. Such prisons were known for brutally harsh conditions; many prisoners died before the end of their sentence.

in white and black per capita income. That number—$34 billion in 1973, when Bittker wrote his book—could be added to a reparations program each year for a decade or two. Today Charles Ogletree, the Harvard Law School professor, argues for something broader: a program of job training and public works that takes racial justice as its mission but includes the poor of all races.

Perhaps no statistic better illustrates the enduring legacy of our country's shameful history of treating black people as sub-citizens, sub-Americans, and sub-humans than the wealth gap. Reparations would seek to close this chasm. But as surely as the creation of the wealth gap required the cooperation of every aspect of the society, bridging it will require the same.

Perhaps after a serious discussion and debate—the kind that HR 40 proposes—we may find that the country can never fully repay African Americans. But we stand to discover much about ourselves in such a discussion—and that is perhaps what scares us. The idea of reparations is frightening not simply because we might lack the ability to pay. The idea of reparations threatens something much deeper—America's heritage, history, and standing in the world.

The early American economy was built on slave labor. The Capitol and the White House were built by slaves. President James K. Polk traded slaves from the Oval Office. The laments about "black pathology,"[21] the criticism of black family structures by pundits and intellectuals, ring hollow in a country whose existence was predicated on the torture of black fathers, on the rape of black mothers, on the sale of black children. An honest assessment of America's relationship to the black family reveals the country to be not its nurturer but its destroyer.

And this destruction did not end with slavery. Discriminatory laws joined the equal burden of citizenship to unequal distribution of its bounty. These laws reached their apex in the mid-20th century, when the federal government—through housing policies—engineered the wealth gap, which remains with us to this day. When we think of white supremacy, we picture COLORED ONLY signs,* but we should picture pirate flags.

On some level, we have always grasped this.

"Negro poverty is not white poverty," President Johnson said in his historic civil-rights speech.

> Many of its causes and many of its cures are the same. But there are differences—deep, corrosive, obstinate differences—radiating painful roots into the community and into the family, and the nature of the individual. These differences are not racial differences. They are

135

---

21 *black pathology* Allegedly diseased nature of African American culture.

solely and simply the consequence of ancient brutality, past injustice, and present prejudice.

We invoke the words of Jefferson and Lincoln because they say something about our legacy and our traditions. We do this because we recognize our links to the past—at least when they flatter us. But black history does not flatter American democracy; it chastens it. The popular mocking of reparations as a harebrained scheme authored by wild-eyed lefties and intellectually unserious black nationalists is fear masquerading as laughter. Black nationalists have always perceived something unmentionable about America that integrationists dare not acknowledge—that white supremacy is not merely the work of hotheaded demagogues, or a matter of false consciousness, but a force so fundamental to America that it is difficult to imagine the country without it.

140   And so we must imagine a new country. Reparations—by which I mean the full acceptance of our collective biography and its consequences—is the price we must pay to see ourselves squarely. The recovering alcoholic may well have to live with his illness for the rest of his life. But at least he is not living a drunken lie. Reparations beckons us to reject the intoxication of hubris and see America as it is—the work of fallible humans.

Won't reparations divide us? Not any more than we are already divided. The wealth gap merely puts a number on something we feel but cannot say—that American prosperity was ill-gotten and selective in its distribution. What is needed is an airing of family secrets, a settling with old ghosts. What is needed is a healing of the American psyche and the banishment of white guilt.

What I'm talking about is more than recompense for past injustices—more than a handout, a payoff, hush money, or a reluctant bribe. What I'm talking about is a national reckoning that would lead to spiritual renewal. Reparations would mean the end of scarfing hot dogs on the Fourth of July while denying the facts of our heritage. Reparations would mean the end of yelling "patriotism" while waving a Confederate flag. Reparations would mean a revolution of the American consciousness, a reconciling of our self-image as the great democratizer with the facts of our history.

We are not the first to be summoned to such a challenge.

In 1952, when West Germany began the process of making amends for the Holocaust, it did so under conditions that should be instructive to us. Resistance was violent. Very few Germans believed that Jews were entitled to anything. Only 5 percent of West Germans surveyed reported feeling guilty about the Holocaust, and only 29 percent believed that Jews were owed restitution from the German people.

"The rest," the historian Tony Judt wrote in his 2005 book, *Postwar*, "were   145
divided between those (some two-fifths of respondents) who thought that only
people 'who really committed something' were responsible and should pay,
and those (21 percent) who thought 'that the Jews themselves were partly
responsible for what happened to them during the Third Reich.'"

Germany's unwillingness to squarely face its history went beyond polls.
Movies that suggested a societal responsibility for the Holocaust beyond Hitler
were banned. "The German soldier fought bravely and honorably for his homeland," claimed President Eisenhower, endorsing the Teutonic national myth.
Judt wrote, "Throughout the fifties West German officialdom encouraged a
comfortable view of the German past in which the Wehrmacht[22] was heroic,
while Nazis were in a minority and properly punished."

Konrad Adenauer, the postwar German chancellor, was in favor of reparations, but his own party was divided, and he was able to get an agreement
passed only with the votes of the Social Democratic opposition.

Among the Jews of Israel, reparations provoked violent and venomous
reactions ranging from denunciation to assassination plots. On January 7, 1952,
as the Knesset—the Israeli parliament—convened to discuss the prospect of
a reparations agreement with West Germany, Menachem Begin, the future
prime minister of Israel, stood in front of a large crowd, inveighing against the
country that had plundered the lives, labor, and property of his people. Begin
claimed that all Germans were Nazis and guilty of murder. His condemnations
then spread to his own young state. He urged the crowd to stop paying taxes
and claimed that the nascent Israeli nation characterized the fight over whether
or not to accept reparations as a "war to the death." When alerted that the police
watching the gathering were carrying tear gas, allegedly of German manufacture, Begin yelled, "The same gases that asphyxiated our parents!"

Begin then led the crowd in an oath to never forget the victims of the
Shoah,[23] lest "my right hand lose its cunning" and "my tongue cleave to the
roof of my mouth." He took the crowd through the streets toward the Knesset.
From the rooftops, police repelled the crowd with tear gas and smoke bombs.
But the wind shifted, and the gas blew back toward the Knesset, billowing
through windows shattered by rocks. In the chaos, Begin and Prime Minister
David Ben-Gurion exchanged insults. Two hundred civilians and 140 police
officers were wounded. Nearly 400 people were arrested. Knesset business was
halted.

Begin then addressed the chamber with a fiery speech condemning the ac-   150
tions the legislature was about to take. "Today you arrested hundreds," he said.

---

22 *Wehrmacht*   Term for the armed forces in Nazi Germany.
23 *Shoah*   Hebrew term for the Holocaust.

"Tomorrow you may arrest thousands. No matter, they will go, they will sit in prison. We will sit there with them. If necessary, we will be killed with them. But there will be no 'reparations' from Germany."

Survivors of the Holocaust feared laundering the reputation of Germany with money, and mortgaging the memory of their dead. Beyond that, there was a taste for revenge. "My soul would be at rest if I knew there would be 6 million German dead to match the 6 million Jews," said Meir Dworzecki, who'd survived the concentration camps of Estonia.

Ben-Gurion countered this sentiment, not by repudiating vengeance but with cold calculation: "If I could take German property without sitting down with them for even a minute but go in with jeeps and machine guns to the warehouses and take it, I would do that—if, for instance, we had the ability to send a hundred divisions and tell them, 'Take it.' But we can't do that."

The reparations conversation set off a wave of bomb attempts by Israeli militants. One was aimed at the foreign ministry in Tel Aviv. Another was aimed at Chancellor Adenauer himself. And one was aimed at the port of Haifa, where the goods bought with reparations money were arriving. West Germany ultimately agreed to pay Israel 3.45 billion deutsche marks, or more than $7 billion in today's dollars. Individual reparations claims followed—for psychological trauma, for offense to Jewish honor, for halting law careers, for life insurance, for time spent in concentration camps. Seventeen percent of funds went toward purchasing ships. "By the end of 1961, these reparations vessels constituted two-thirds of the Israeli merchant fleet," writes the Israeli historian Tom Segev in his book *The Seventh Million*. "From 1953 to 1963, the reparations money funded about a third of the total investment in Israel's electrical system, which tripled its capacity, and nearly half the total investment in the railways."

Israel's GNP tripled during the 12 years of the agreement. The Bank of Israel attributed 15 percent of this growth, along with 45,000 jobs, to investments made with reparations money. But Segev argues that the impact went far beyond that. Reparations "had indisputable psychological and political importance," he writes.

155   Reparations could not make up for the murder perpetrated by the Nazis. But they did launch Germany's reckoning with itself, and perhaps provided a road map for how a great civilization might make itself worthy of the name.

Assessing the reparations agreement, David Ben-Gurion said:

> For the first time in the history of relations between people, a precedent has been created by which a great State, as a result of moral pressure alone, takes it upon itself to pay compensation to the victims of the government that preceded it. For the first time in the history of a people that has been persecuted, oppressed, plundered and despoiled

for hundreds of years in the countries of Europe, a persecutor and despoiler has been obliged to return part of his spoils and has even undertaken to make collective reparation as partial compensation for material losses.

Something more than moral pressure calls America to reparations. We cannot escape our history. All of our solutions to the great problems of health care, education, housing, and economic inequality are troubled by what must go unspoken. "The reason black people are so far behind now is not because of now," Clyde Ross told me. "It's because of then." In the early 2000s, Charles Ogletree went to Tulsa, Oklahoma, to meet with the survivors of the 1921 race riot that had devastated "Black Wall Street." The past was not the past to them. "It was amazing seeing these black women and men who were crippled, blind, in wheelchairs," Ogletree told me. "I had no idea who they were and why they wanted to see me. They said, 'We want you to represent us in this lawsuit.'"

A commission authorized by the Oklahoma legislature produced a report affirming that the riot, the knowledge of which had been suppressed for years, had happened. But the lawsuit ultimately failed, in 2004. Similar suits pushed against corporations such as Aetna (which insured slaves) and Lehman Brothers (whose co-founding partner owned them) also have thus far failed. These results are dispiriting, but the crime with which reparations activists charge the country implicates more than just a few towns or corporations. The crime indicts the American people themselves, at every level, and in nearly every configuration. A crime that implicates the entire American people deserves its hearing in the legislative body that represents them.

John Conyers's HR 40 is the vehicle for that hearing. No one can know what would come out of such a debate. Perhaps no number can fully capture the multi-century plunder of black people in America. Perhaps the number is so large that it can't be imagined, let alone calculated and dispensed. But I believe that wrestling publicly with these questions matters as much as—if not more than—the specific answers that might be produced. An America that asks what it owes its most vulnerable citizens is improved and humane. An America that looks away is ignoring not just the sins of the past but the sins of the present and the certain sins of the future. More important than any single check cut to any African American, the payment of reparations would represent America's maturation out of the childhood myth of its innocence into a wisdom worthy of its founders.

In 2010, Jacob S. Rugh, then a doctoral candidate at Princeton, and the sociologist Douglas S. Massey published a study of the recent foreclosure crisis.* Among its drivers, they found an old foe: segregation. Black home

160

buyers—even after controlling for factors like creditworthiness—were still more likely than white home buyers to be steered toward subprime loans.* Decades of racist housing policies by the American government, along with decades of racist housing practices by American businesses, had conspired to concentrate African Americans in the same neighborhoods. As in North Lawndale half a century earlier, these neighborhoods were filled with people who had been cut off from mainstream financial institutions. When subprime lenders went looking for prey, they found black people waiting like ducks in a pen.

"High levels of segregation create a natural market for subprime lending," Rugh and Massey write, "and cause riskier mortgages, and thus foreclosures, to accumulate disproportionately in racially segregated cities' minority neighborhoods."

Plunder in the past made plunder in the present efficient. The banks of America understood this. In 2005, Wells Fargo promoted a series of Wealth Building Strategies seminars. Dubbing itself "the nation's leading originator of home loans to ethnic minority customers," the bank enrolled black public figures in an ostensible effort to educate blacks on building "generational wealth." But the "wealth building" seminars were a front for wealth theft. In 2010, the Justice Department filed a discrimination suit against Wells Fargo alleging that the bank had shunted blacks into predatory loans regardless of their creditworthiness. This was not magic or coincidence or misfortune. It was racism reifying itself. According to *The New York Times*, affidavits found loan officers referring to their black customers as "mud people" and to their subprime products as "ghetto loans."

"We just went right after them," Beth Jacobson, a former Wells Fargo loan officer, told *The Times*. "Wells Fargo mortgage had an emerging-markets unit that specifically targeted black churches because it figured church leaders had a lot of influence and could convince congregants to take out subprime loans."

In 2011, Bank of America agreed to pay $355 million to settle charges of discrimination against its Countrywide unit. The following year, Wells Fargo settled its discrimination suit for more than $175 million. But the damage had been done. In 2009, half the properties in Baltimore whose owners had been granted loans by Wells Fargo between 2005 and 2008 were vacant; 71 percent of these properties were in predominantly black neighborhoods.

(2014)

NICHOLAS KRISTOF

WHEN WHITES JUST DON'T GET IT

The 9 August 2014 shooting by police officer Darren Wilson of
unarmed teenager Michael Brown in Ferguson, Missouri (a suburb
of St Louis) became a cause célèbre when no charges were filed
against the officer responsible. Protests carried on for many weeks,
and the incident prompted many to ask fresh questions about race
relations in America. New York Times *columnist Nicholas Kristof's*
piece on the topic generated a variety of passionate responses, and
he followed up with several more columns under the same heading.
Included here are the first and the sixth in the series (30 August
2014 and 6 April 2016, respectively).

M any white Americans say they are fed up with the coverage of the shooting of Michael Brown in Ferguson, Mo. A plurality of whites in a recent Pew survey said that the issue of race is getting more attention than it deserves.

Bill O'Reilly of Fox News reflected that weariness, saying: "All you hear is grievance, grievance, grievance, money, money, money."

Indeed, a 2011 study by scholars at Harvard and Tufts found that whites, on average, believed that anti-white racism was a bigger problem than anti-black racism.

Yes, you read that right!

So let me push back at what I see as smug white delusion. Here are a few reasons race relations deserve more attention, not less: 5

- The net worth of the average black household in the United States is $6,314, compared with $110,500 for the average white household, according to 2011 census data. The gap has worsened in the last decade, and the United States now has a greater wealth gap by race than South Africa did during apartheid. (Whites in America on average own almost 18 times as much as blacks; in South Africa in 1970, the ratio was about 15 times.)
- The black-white income gap is roughly 40 percent greater today than it was in 1967.
- A black boy born today in the United States has a life expectancy five years shorter than that of a white boy.

- Black students are significantly less likely to attend schools offering advanced math and science courses than white students. They are three times as likely to be suspended and expelled, setting them up for educational failure.
- Because of the catastrophic experiment in mass incarceration, black men in their 20s without a high school diploma are more likely to be incarcerated today than employed, according to a study from the National Bureau of Economic Research. Nearly 70 percent of middle-aged black men who never graduated from high school have been imprisoned.

All these constitute not a black problem or a white problem, but an American problem. When so much talent is underemployed and over-incarcerated, the entire country suffers.

Some straight people have gradually changed their attitudes toward gays after realizing that their friends—or children—were gay. Researchers have found that male judges are more sympathetic to women's rights when they have daughters. Yet because of the de facto* segregation of America, whites are unlikely to have many black friends: A study from the Public Religion Research Institute suggests that in a network of 100 friends, a white person, on average, has one black friend.

That's unfortunate, because friends open our eyes. I was shaken after a well-known black woman told me about looking out her front window and seeing that police officers had her teenage son down on the ground after he had stepped out of their upscale house because they thought he was a prowler. "Thank God he didn't run," she said.

One black friend tells me that he freaked out when his white fiancée purchased an item in a store and promptly threw the receipt away. "What are you doing?" he protested to her. He is a highly successful and well-educated professional but would never dream of tossing a receipt for fear of being accused of shoplifting.

10   Some readers will protest that the stereotype is rooted in reality: Young black men are disproportionately likely to be criminals.

That's true—and complicated. "There's nothing more painful to me," the Rev. Jesse Jackson once said, "than to walk down the street and hear footsteps and start thinking about robbery—and then look around and see somebody white and feel relieved."

All this should be part of the national conversation on race, as well, and prompt a drive to help young black men end up in jobs and stable families rather than in crime or jail. We have policies with a robust record of creating opportunity: home visitation programs like Nurse-Family Partnership; early education initiatives like Educare and Head Start; programs for troubled adolescents like

Youth Villages; anti-gang and anti-crime initiatives like Becoming a Man; efforts to prevent teen pregnancies like the Carrera curriculum; job training like Career Academies; and job incentives like the earned-income tax credit.

The best escalator to opportunity may be education, but that escalator is broken for black boys growing up in neighborhoods with broken schools. We fail those boys before they fail us.

So a starting point is for those of us in white America to wipe away any self-satisfaction about racial progress. Yes, the progress is real, but so are the challenges. The gaps demand a wrenching, soul-searching excavation of our national soul, and the first step is to acknowledge that the central race challenge in America today is not the suffering of whites.

(2014)

WHEN WHITES JUST DON'T GET IT, PART 6

L et's start with a quiz. When researchers sent young whites and blacks out to interview for low-wage jobs in New York City armed with equivalent résumés, the result was:

a) Whites and blacks were hired at similar rates.
b) Blacks had a modest edge because of affirmative action.
c) Whites were twice as likely to get callbacks.

The answer is C, and a black applicant with a clean criminal record did no better than a white applicant who was said to have just been released from 18 months in prison.

A majority of whites believe that job opportunities are equal for whites and blacks, according to a PBS poll, but rigorous studies show that just isn't so.

Back in 2014, I did a series of columns called "When Whites Just Don't Get It" to draw attention to inequities, and I'm revisiting it because public attention to racial disparities seems to be flagging even as the issues are as grave as ever.

But let me first address some reproaches I've received from indignant whites, including the very common: You would never write a column about blacks not getting it, and it's racist to pick on whites. It's true that I would be wary as a white person of lecturing to blacks about race, but plenty of black leaders (including President Obama) have bluntly spoken about shortcomings in the black community.

5

Toni Morrison in her novels writes searingly about a black world pummeled by discrimination but also by violence, drunkenness and broken families. In a CNN poll, 86 percent of blacks said family breakdown was a reason for difficulties of African-Americans today, and 77 percent cited "lack of motivation and unwillingness to work hard."

Frankly, the conversation within the black community seems to me to be more mature and honest than the one among whites, and considering how much of the white conversation about race invokes "personal responsibility," maybe it's time for whites to show more.

Obama's election reinforced a narrative that we're making progress. We are in some ways, but the median black household in America still has only 8 percent of the wealth of the median white household. And even for blacks who have "made it"—whose incomes are in the upper half of American incomes—60 percent of their children tumble back into the lower half in the next generation, according to a Federal Reserve study. If these trends continue, the Fed study noted, "black Americans would make no further relative progress."

Most of the public debate about race focuses on law enforcement. That's understandable after the shootings of unarmed blacks and after the U.S. Sentencing Commission found that black men received sentences about 20 percent longer than white men for similar crimes. But that's just the tip of the iceberg. Lead poisoning, for example, is more than twice as common among black children as among white children, and in much of the country, it's even worse than in Flint, Mich.[1]

10   Three generations after *Brown v. Board of Education*,[2] American schools are still often separate and unequal. The average white or Asian-American student attends a school in at least the 60th percentile in test performance; the average black student is at a school at the 37th percentile. One reason is an unjust school funding system that often directs the most resources to privileged students.

So if we're going to address systemic disadvantage of black children, we have to broaden the conversation to unequal education. There's a lot of loose talk among whites about black boys making bad decisions, but we fail these kids before they fail us. That's unconscionable when increasingly we have robust evidence about the kinds of initiatives (like home visitation, prekindergarten and "career academies") that reduce disparities.

---

1   *Flint, Mich.*   The revelation in 2014 of dangerous levels of lead contamination in the drinking water of Flint caused a considerable scandal.

2   *Brown v. Board of Education*   Landmark 1954 Supreme Court case, which declared enforced segregation of schoolchildren on the basis of race to be unconstitutional.

Reasons for inequality involve not just institutions but also personal behaviors. These don't all directly involve discrimination. For instance, black babies are less likely to be breast-fed than white babies, are more likely to grow up with a single parent and may be spoken to or read to less by their parents. But racial discrimination remains ubiquitous even in crucial spheres like jobs and housing.

In one study, researchers sent thousands of résumés to employers with openings, randomly using some stereotypically black names (like Jamal) and others that were more likely to belong to whites (like Brendan). A white name increased the likelihood of a callback by 50 percent.

Likewise, in Canada researchers found that emails from stereotypically black names seeking apartments are less likely to get responses from landlords. And in U.S. experiments, when blacks and whites go in person to rent or buy properties, blacks are shown fewer options.

Something similar happens even with sales. Researchers offered iPods   15
for sale online and found that when the photo showed the iPod held by a white hand, it received 21 percent more offers than when held by a black hand.

Discrimination is also pervasive in the white-collar world.* Researchers found that white state legislators, Democrats and Republicans alike, were less likely to respond to a constituent letter signed with a stereotypically black name. Even at universities, emails sent to professors from stereotypically black names asking for a chance to discuss research possibilities received fewer responses.

Why do we discriminate? The big factor isn't overt racism. Rather, it seems to be unconscious bias among whites who believe in equality but act in ways that perpetuate inequality.

Eduardo Bonilla-Silva, an eminent sociologist, calls this unconscious bias "racism without racists," and we whites should be less defensive about it. This bias affects blacks as well as whites, and we also have unconscious biases about gender, disability, body size and age. You can explore your own unconscious biases in a free online test, called the implicit association test.

One indication of how deeply rooted biases are: A rigorous study by economists found that even N.B.A. referees were more likely to call fouls on players of another race. Something similar happens in baseball, with researchers finding that umpires calling strikes are biased against black pitchers.

If even professional referees and umpires are biased, can there be any hope   20
for you and me as we navigate our daily lives? Actually, there is.

The N.B.A. study caused a furor (the league denied the bias), and a few years later there was a follow-up by the same economists, and the bias had disappeared. It seems that when we humans realize our biases, we can adjust and act in ways that are more fair. As the study's authors put it, "Awareness reduces racial bias."

That's why it's so important for whites to engage in these uncomfortable discussions of race—because we are (unintentionally) so much a part of the problem. It's not that we're evil, but that we're human. The challenge is to recognize that unconscious bias afflicts us all—but that we just may be able to overcome it if we face it.

(2016)

Lawrence G. Proulx

A Group You Can Safely Attack

Nicholas Kristof's series of columns entitled "When Whites Just Don't Get It" (see above) sparked a wide range of reactions. Some suggested that he was not going far enough in his criticisms; in the online Observer, *for example, Lincoln Mitchell opined that "calling for another conversation about race is a serious sounding way of doing nothing." A more frequently heard criticism of Kristof, however, went along the lines suggested by Norman Leahy and Paul Goldman in their* Washington Post *blog: "staining a whole group with such a broad journalistic brush [as Kristof uses] would be considered ignorant if not racist had it been written about anyone but white people."[1] That argument is made at greater length by Lawrence Proulx in the 2 September 2015* Providence Journal *column reprinted here.*

Every age has propositions that it is happy to hear and repeat and others that it is loath to. In times of war, people want to hear praise of their side, not of the enemy. In times of tragedy, criticism of the victims is intolerable. Honesty is no excuse.

Our age is no different.

In America today, people generally find it distasteful to hear general categories of human beings discussed in a negative way. But there are two prominent exceptions: white people and men. I belong to both categories.

In my work, I read one of the world's great newspapers;[2] in my leisure time I read other general-interest papers and magazines. And I have slowly gotten the impression that white people and men are treated in a particular, unenviable, way. They are, in reporting and commentary, what you might call fair game. Where writers are generally reluctant to call attention to the sex,

---

1 *online ... white people* See Lincoln Mitchell, "Honestly, Talking About Race Changes Nothing in America," *Observer*, 4 December 2014; and Norman Leahy and Paul Goldman, "When 'Whites' Don't Get It—a Rebuttal," *Washington Post*, 23 October 2014.

2 *In my work ... newspapers* The author works as a copyeditor for the *International New York Times* in France.

ethnicity, religion or race of people when the result would be unflattering, they make an exception for whites and for men. There is something in the air that implicitly imparts the message that white people and men have it coming.

5　　　In news articles it is common to have it pointed out to us when men or white people predominate in a criticizable practice. If they enjoy an advantage or apparent advantage, the mere fact is offered as an obvious case of injustice.

An example. Starting on Aug. 30 of last year, *The New York Times* published five columns by Nicholas Kristof on "When Whites Just Don't Get It," the thrust of which was that white people just don't realize how badly they behave toward black people.

Kristof has every right to express his opinions. But I have the uncomfortable feeling that his criticisms of white people were welcomed by the *Times* in a way that criticisms of other categories of people would not have been.

Tell me if I'm wrong. Can you recall the *Times* or *The Wall Street Journal* or any other newspaper running articles about "When Blacks Just Don't Get It" or "When Homosexuals Just Don't Get It" or "When Jews Just Don't Get It"? Am I just paranoid? Was I napping when they ran?

Another example: In November, in a *Washington Post* interview, Meghan McCain, co-host of a show on the Pivot network, was asked what she would do if she were ruler of the universe. She said, "I would just like to have less old white men ruling everything in the media."

10　　　She, too, has the right to her opinions. But imagine that instead of "old white men" she had talked of "old Jews" and had opined that she would "just like to have less old Jews ruling everything at the Federal Reserve." Or that she wished there weren't so many "young black men" on television. Would the Post still have treated her remark as a cute part of her "dishing" with its gossip columnist? Again, I suspect the answer is no. What is considered indecent in relation to some groups is perfectly fine for others.

Generalizations, whether positive or negative, can be valid or invalid. It depends on the facts, and people must be free to propose and debate them. But a situation where some groups are off-limits and others are ganged up on is hard to defend on any principle of logic or fairness.

Is what would be considered rude and unacceptable in relation to Jews or women or black people not also rude and unacceptable in relation to white people and men? If not, why not?

Surely writers and editors give consideration to some people's sensibilities not because these people have special rights but because they fully possess rights that are universal.

So, I submit, do white people and men.

(2015)

BAD FEMINIST: TAKE ONE

Gay's 2014 collection Bad Feminist: Essays *draws on feminist theory and personal experience to address political issues such as abortion rights and racism, together with elements of popular culture—from the films of Quentin Tarantino to the hit song "Blurred Lines" to the world of competitive Scrabble. The following essay offers a case study of Sheryl Sandberg's bestseller* Lean In: Women, Work, and the Will to Lead *(2013), a book that considers gender in the workplace and offers advice to ambitious women. Upon its release* Lean In *was both praised as an exemplary text and slammed by numerous feminist critics as a work of "faux feminism" useful only to a white upper-class audience.*

My favorite definition of a "feminist" is one offered by Su, an Australian woman who, when interviewed for Kathy Bail's 1996 anthology *DIY Feminism*, said feminists are "just women who don't want to be treated like shit." This definition is pointed and succinct, but I run into trouble when I try to expand that definition. I fall short as a feminist. I feel like I am not as committed as I need to be, that I am not living up to feminist ideals because of who and how I choose to be.

I feel this tension constantly. As Judith Butler[1] writes in her 1988 essay "Performative Acts and Gender Constitution," "Performing one's gender wrong initiates a set of punishments both obvious and indirect, and performing it well provides the reassurance that there is an essentialism of gender identity after all." This tension—the idea that there is a right way to be a woman, a right way to be the most essential woman—is ongoing and pervasive.

We see this tension in socially dictated beauty standards—the right way to be a woman is to be thin, to wear makeup, to wear the right kind of clothes (not

---

1   *Judith Butler*   Feminist theorist (b. 1956) whose works such as *Gender Trouble* and *Bodies that Matter* have outlined her influential theory of gender performativity, according to which gender is not biologically innate but is constructed through behavior.

too slutty, not too prudish—show a little leg, ladies), and so on. Good women are charming, polite, and unobtrusive. Good women work but are content to earn 77 percent of what men earn or, depending on whom you ask, good women bear children and stay home to raise those children without complaint. Good women are modest, chaste, pious, submissive. Women who don't adhere to these standards are the fallen, the undesirable; they are bad women.

Butler's thesis could also apply to feminism. There is an essential feminism or, as I perceive this essentialism, the notion that there are right and wrong ways to be a feminist and there are consequences for doing feminism wrong.

5   Essential feminism suggests anger, humorlessness, militancy, unwavering principles, and a prescribed set of rules for how to be a proper feminist woman, or at least a proper white, heterosexual feminist woman—hate pornography, unilaterally decry the objectification of women, don't cater to the male gaze,[2] hate men, hate sex, focus on career, don't shave. I kid, mostly, with that last one. This is nowhere near an accurate description of feminism, but the movement has been warped by misperception for so long that even people who should know better have bought into this essential image of feminism.

Consider Elizabeth Wurtzel, who, in a June 2012 *Atlantic* article, says, "Real feminists earn a living, have money and means of their own." By Wurtzel's thinking, women who don't "earn a living, have money and means of their own," are fake feminists, undeserving of the label, disappointments to the sisterhood. She takes the idea of essential feminism even further in a September 2012 *Harper's Bazaar* article where she suggests that a good feminist works hard to be beautiful. She says, "Looking great is a matter of feminism. No liberated woman would misrepresent the cause by appearing less than hale and happy." It's too easy to dissect the error of such thinking. She is suggesting that a woman's worth is, in part, determined by her beauty, which is one of the very things feminism works against.

The most significant problem with essential feminism is how it doesn't allow for the complexities of human experience or individuality. There seems to be little room for multiple or discordant points of view. Essential feminism has, for example, led to the rise of the phrase "sex-positive feminism," which creates a clear distinction between feminists who are positive about sex and feminists who aren't—which, in turn, creates a self-fulfilling essentialist prophecy.

---

2   *male gaze* Term coined by film theorist Laura Mulvey, who argued that Hollywood films of the 1950s and 60s tended to be made with a male audience in mind, such that the viewer is encouraged to identify with male characters and objectify female ones. The term has since been adapted to other contexts.

I sometimes cringe when I am referred to as a feminist, as if I should be ashamed of my feminism or as if the word "feminist" is an insult. The label is rarely offered in kindness. I am generally called a feminist when I have the nerve to suggest that the misogyny deeply embedded in our culture is a real problem requiring relentless vigilance. The essay in this collection about Daniel Tosh and rape jokes originally appeared in *Salon*.[3] I tried not to read the comments because they get vicious, but I couldn't help but note one commenter who told me I was an "angry blogger woman," which is simply another way of saying "angry feminist." All feminists are angry instead of, say, passionate.

A more direct reprimand came from a man I was dating during a heated discussion that wasn't quite an argument. He said, "Don't you raise your voice to me," which was strange because I had not raised my voice. I was stunned because no one had ever said such a thing to me. He expounded, at length, about how women should talk to men. When I dismantled his pseudo-theories, he said, "You're some kind of feminist, aren't you?" There was a tone to his accusation, making it clear that to be a feminist was undesirable. I was not being a good woman. I remained silent, stewing. I thought, *Isn't it obvious I am a feminist, albeit not a very good one?* I also realized I was being chastised for having a certain set of beliefs. The experience was disconcerting, at best.

I'm not the only outspoken woman who shies away from the feminist label, who fears the consequences of accepting the label.

10

In an August 2012 interview with *Salon*'s Andrew O'Hehir, actress Melissa Leo,[4] known for playing groundbreaking female roles, said, "Well, I don't think of myself as a feminist at all. As soon as we start labeling and categorizing ourselves and others, that's going to shut down the world. I would never say that. Like, I just did that episode with Louis C.K."[5] Leo is buying into a great many essential feminist myths with her comment. We are categorized and labeled from the moment we come into this world by gender, race, size, hair color, eye color, and so forth. The older we get, the more labels and categories we collect. If labeling and categorizing ourselves is going to shut the world down, it has been a long time coming. More disconcerting, though, is the assertion that a feminist wouldn't take a role on Louis C.K.'s sitcom, *Louie*, or that a feminist would be unable to find C.K.'s brand of humor amusing. For Leo,

---

3   *essay ... Salon*   "Daniel Tosh and Rape Jokes: Still Not Funny" (2012), Gay's essay addressing the controversy over stand-up comedian Daniel Tosh telling a rape joke in response to criticism from a female audience member.

4   *Melissa Leo*   American actor (b. 1960).

5   *Louis C.K.*   Stand-up comedian (b. 1967); since 2010, he has written, directed, and starred in the comedy-drama *Louie*, known for its brash, satirical tone.

there are feminists and then there are women who defy categorization and are willing to embrace career opportunities.

Trailblazing female leaders in the corporate world tend to reject the feminist label too. Marissa Mayer, who was appointed president and CEO of Yahoo! in July 2012, said in an interview,

> I don't think that I would consider myself a feminist. I think that I certainly believe in equal rights, I believe that women are just as capable, if not more so in a lot of different dimensions, but I don't, I think, have, sort of the militant drive and the sort of, the chip on the shoulder that sometimes comes with that. And I think it's too bad, but I do think that "feminism" has become in many ways a more negative word. You know, there are amazing opportunities all over the world for women, and I think that there is more good that comes out of positive energy around that than comes out of negative energy.

For Mayer, even though she is a pioneering woman, feminism is associated with militancy and preconceived notions. Feminism is negative, and despite the feminist strides she has made through her career at Google and now Yahoo!, she'd prefer to eschew the label for the sake of so-called positive energy.

Audre Lorde[6] once stated, "I am a Black Feminist. I mean I recognize that my power as well as my *primary* oppressions come as a result of my blackness as well as my womanness, and therefore my struggles on both of these fronts are inseparable." As a woman of color, I find that some feminists don't seem terribly concerned with the issues unique to women of color—the ongoing effects of racism and postcolonialism, the status of women in the Third World, the fight against the trenchant archetypes black women are forced into (angry black woman, mammy, Hottentot,[7] and the like).

White feminists often suggest that by believing there are issues unique to women of color, an unnatural division occurs, impeding solidarity, sisterhood. Other times, white feminists are simply dismissive of these issues. In 2008, prominent blogger Amanda Marcotte was accused of appropriating ideas for her article "Can a Person Be Illegal?" from the blogger "brownfemipower," who

---

6   *Audre Lorde*   African American poet and theorist (1924–92) whose celebrated works address racism, feminism, and heterosexism.

7   *mammy*   Racist stock figure of a jolly maternal domestic slave or paid worker;   *Hottentot*   Offensive term for the Khoekhoe peoples of Southern Africa. The term conjures the image of Sara Baartman, a South African woman brought to London in 1810 and displayed to white spectators under the title "Hottentot Venus." The Hottentot stereotype that endured concerns an exoticized, sexualized figure with exaggerated buttocks.

posted a speech she gave on the same subject a few days prior to the publication of Marcotte's article. The question of where original thought ends and borrowed concepts begin was complicated significantly in this case by the sense that a white person had yet again taken the creative work of a person of color.

The feminist blogosphere engaged in an intense debate over these issues, at times so acrimonious that black feminists were labeled "radical black feminists," were accused of overreacting and, of course, "playing the race card."* 15

Such willful ignorance, such willful disinterest in incorporating the issues and concerns of black women into the mainstream feminist project, makes me disinclined to own the feminist label until it embraces people like me. Is that my way of essentializing feminism, of suggesting there's a right kind of feminism or a more inclusive feminism? Perhaps. This is all murky for me, but a continued insensitivity, within feminist circles, on the matter of race is a serious problem.

There's also this. Lately, magazines have been telling me there's something wrong with feminism or women trying to achieve a work-life balance or just women in general. *The Atlantic* has led the way in these lamentations. In the aforementioned June 2012 article, Wurtzel, author of *Prozac Nation*,[8] wrote a searing polemic about "1% wives"* who are hurting feminism and the progress of women by choosing to stay at home rather than enter the workplace. Wurtzel begins the essay provocatively, stating,

> When my mind gets stuck on everything that is wrong with feminism, it brings out the 19th century poet in me: *Let me count the ways*.[9] Most of all, feminism is pretty much a nice girl who really, really wants so badly to be liked by everybody—ladies who lunch,* men who hate women, all the morons who demand choice and don't understand responsibility—that it has become the easy lay* of social movements.

There are problems with feminism. Wurtzel says so, and she is vigorous in defending her position. Wurtzel knows the right way for feminism. In that article, Wurtzel goes on to state there is only one kind of equality, economic equality, and until women recognize that and enter the workforce en masse, feminists, and wealthy feminists in particular, will continue to fail. They will continue to be bad feminists, falling short of essential ideals of feminism.

---

8   *Prozac Nation*   Wurtzel's 1994 memoir about her experiences with mental illness during her formative years. The book, which garnered both praise and derision from critics, was made into a film in 2001.

9   *Let me count the ways*   Reference to Elizabeth Barrett Browning's Sonnet 43 ("How do I love thee? Let me count the ways").

Wurtzel isn't wrong about the importance of economic equality, but she is wrong in assuming that with economic equality, the rest of feminism's concerns will somehow disappear.

In the July/August 2012 *Atlantic*, Anne-Marie Slaughter wrote more than twelve thousand words about the struggles of powerful, successful women to "have it all." Her article was interesting and thoughtful, for a certain kind of woman—a wealthy woman with a very successful career. She even parlayed the piece into a book deal. Slaughter was speaking to a small, elite group of women while ignoring the millions of women who don't have the privilege of, as Slaughter did, leaving high-powered positions at the State Department to spend more time with their sons. Many women who work do so because they have to. Working has little to do with having it all and much more to do with having food on the table.

20 Slaughter wrote,

> I'd been the woman congratulating herself on her unswerving commitment to the feminist cause, chatting smugly with her dwindling number of college or law-school friends who had reached and maintained their place on the highest rungs of their profession. I'd been the one telling young women at my lectures that you can have it all and do it all, regardless of what field you are in.

The thing is, I am not at all sure that feminism has ever suggested women can have it all. This notion of being able to have it all is always misattributed to feminism when really, it's human nature to want it all—to have cake and eat it too* without necessarily focusing on how we can get there and how we can make "having it all" possible for a wider range of people and not just the lucky ones.

Alas, poor feminism. So much responsibility keeps getting piled on the shoulders of a movement whose primary purpose is to achieve equality, in all realms, between men and women. I keep reading these articles and getting angry and tired because they suggest there's no way for women to ever *get it right*. These articles make it seem like, as Butler suggests, there is, in fact, a right way to be a woman and a wrong way to be a woman. The standard for the right way to be a woman and/or a feminist appears to be ever changing and unachievable.

In the weeks leading up to the publication of Sheryl Sandberg's *Lean In*, critics had plenty to say about the Facebook chief operating officer's ideas about being a woman in the workplace—even though few had actually read the tome. Many of the resulting discussions bizarrely mischaracterized *Lean In*, tossing around misleading headlines, inaccurate facts, and unfair assumptions.

As it turns out, not even a fairly average entry into the world of corporate advice books is immune from double standards.

Sandberg intersperses personal anecdotes from her remarkable career (a vice presidency at Google, serving as the US Treasury's chief of staff during the Clinton administration)* with observations, research, and pragmatic advice for how women can better achieve professional and personal success. She urges women to "lean in" to their careers and to be "ambitious in any pursuit." *Lean In* is competently written, blandly interesting, and it does repeat a great deal of familiar research—although it isn't particularly harmful to be reminded of the challenges women face as they try to get ahead.

Intentionally or not, much of the book is a stark reminder of the many obstacles women face in the workplace. I cannot deny that parts resonated, particularly in Sandberg's discussion about "impostor syndrome"[10] and how women are less willing to take advantage of potential career opportunities unless they feel qualified.

But Sandberg is rigidly committed to the gender binary, and *Lean In* is exceedingly heteronormative. Professional women are largely defined in relation to professional men; *Lean In*'s loudest unspoken advice seems to dictate that women should embrace traditionally masculine qualities (self-confidence, risk taking, aggression, etc.). Occasionally, this advice backfires because it seems as if Sandberg is advocating, *If you want to succeed, be an asshole*. In addition, Sandberg generally assumes a woman will want to fulfill professional ambitions while also marrying a man and having children. Yes, she says, "Not all women want careers. Not all women want children. Not all women want both. I would never advocate that we should all have the same objectives." But she contradicts herself by placing every single parable within the context of heterosexual women who want a wildly successful career and a rounded-out nuclear family. Accepting that Sandberg is writing to a very specific audience, and has little to offer those who don't fall within that target demographic, makes enjoying the book a lot easier.

One of the main questions that has arisen in the wake of *Lean In*'s publication is whether Sandberg has a responsibility to women who don't fall within her target demographic. Like Slaughter, Sandberg is speaking to a rather narrow group of women. In the *New York Times*, Jodi Kantor writes, "Even [Sandberg's] advisers acknowledge the awkwardness of a woman with double Harvard degrees, dual stock riches (from Facebook and Google, where she also worked), a 9,000-square-foot house and a small army of household help urging less fortunate women to look inward and work harder."

---

10 *imposter syndrome* Term coined by psychologists Pauline Rose Clance and Suzanne Imes to describe the feeling of self-doubt and inadequacy some people experience despite achieving success.

25

At times the inescapable evidence of Sandberg's fortune is grating. She casually discusses her mentor Larry Summers,[11] working for the Treasury department, her doctor siblings, and her equally successful husband, David Goldberg. (As CEO of SurveyMonkey, Goldberg moved the company headquarters from Portland to the Bay Area so he could more fully commit to his family.) She gives the impression that her movement from one ideal situation to the next is easily replicable.

30   Sandberg's life is so absurd a fairy tale, I began to think of *Lean In* as a snow globe, where a lovely little tableau was being nicely preserved for my delectation and irritation. I would not be so bold as to suggest Sandberg has it all, but I need to believe she is pretty damn close to whatever "having it all" might look like. Common sense dictates that it is not realistic to assume anyone could achieve Sandberg's successes simply by "leaning in" and working harder—but that doesn't mean Sandberg has nothing to offer, or that *Lean In* should be summarily dismissed.

Cultural critics can get a bit precious and condescending about marginalized groups, and in the debate over *Lean In*, "working-class women" have been lumped into a vaguely defined group of women who work too hard for too little money. But very little consideration has been given to these women as actual people who live in the world, and who maybe, just maybe, have ambitions too.

There has been, unsurprisingly, significant pushback against the notion that leaning in is a reasonable option for working-class women, who are already stretched woefully thin. Sandberg is not oblivious to her privilege, noting:

> I am fully aware that most women are not focused on changing social norms for the next generation but simply trying to get through each day. Forty percent of employed mothers lack sick days and vacation leave, and about 50 percent of employed mothers are unable to take time off to care for a sick child. Only about half of women receive any pay during maternity leave. These policies can have severe consequences; families with no access to paid family leave often go into debt and can fall into poverty. Part-time jobs with fluctuating schedules offer little chance to plan and often stop short of the forty-hour week that provides basic benefits.

It would have been useful if Sandberg offered realistic advice about career management for women who are dealing with such circumstances. It would also be useful if we had flying cars. Assuming Sandberg's advice is completely useless for working-class women is just as shortsighted as claiming her advice

---

11 *Larry Summers* Economist who served as Secretary of the Treasury from 1999–2001 and president of Harvard University from 2001–06.

needs to be completely applicable to all women. And let's be frank: if Sandberg chose to offer career advice for working-class women, a group she clearly knows little about, she would have been just as harshly criticized for overstepping her bounds.

The critical response to *Lean In* is not entirely misplaced, but it is emblematic of the dangers of public womanhood. Public women, and feminists in particular, have to be everything to everyone; when they aren't, they are excoriated for their failure. In some ways, this is understandable. We have come far, but we have so much further to go. We need so very much, and we hope women with a significant platform might be everything we need—a desperately untenable position. As Elizabeth Spiers notes in *The Verge*,

> When's the last time someone picked up a Jack Welch (or Warren Buffett,[12] or even Donald Trump) bestseller and complained that it was unsympathetic to working class men who had to work multiple jobs to support their families? ... And who reads a book by Jack Welch and defensively feels that they're being told that they have to adopt Jack Welch's lifestyle and professional choices or they are lesser human beings?

Lean In cannot and should not be read as a definitive text, or a book offering universally applicable advice to all women, everywhere. Sandberg is confident and aggressive in her advice, but the reader is under no obligation to do everything she says. Perhaps we can consider *Lean In* for what it is—just one more reminder that the rules are always different for girls, no matter who they are and no matter what they do.

(2014)

35

---

12 *Jack Welch* American businessperson (b. 1935) and one-time CEO of General Electric, known for his domineering corporate leadership; *Warren Buffett* American businessperson (b. 1930) whose investing prowess has made him one of the wealthiest people in the world.

WILLIAM H. FREY

CENSUS SHOWS MODEST DECLINES IN BLACK-WHITE SEGREGATION

One of America's leading demographers, William Frey has a long track record both of important research into population trends and of communicating the results of that research to a broad audience—in the popular press and in books such as his 2014 Diversity Explosion: How New Racial Demographics are Remaking America.

Frey, a Fellow at the Brookings Institution, posts regularly on the Brookings blog The Avenue: Rethinking Metropolitan America, *which provides news and analysis from the institution's Metropolitan Policy Program. He posted this piece on 8 December 2015.*

Racial segregation is still high in many parts of America, lying at the root of sharp inequalities that continue to be visible in many cities. But an examination of newly released Census data suggests a modest decline in black-white segregation across most large U.S. metropolitan areas. It also shows that neighborhoods in which blacks reside are becoming somewhat less black due to recent population shifts of blacks and the growth and dispersion of Hispanics and other minorities. These trends hardly signal the end of segregation in the United States, but they do suggest opportunities to achieve greater residential integration as race migration trends are in flux.

The new statistics, drawn from the Census Bureau's 2010–2014 American Community Survey allow calculation of neighborhood racial attributes and segregation measures. A standard measure of segregation indicates the percentage of blacks that would have to change neighborhoods to match the distribution of whites. It ranges from zero (complete integration) to 100 (complete segregation). When applied to the nation's 52 largest metropolitan areas with at least 20,000 black residents most show segregation levels between 50 and 70 (see Map). While far below the nearly apartheid racial separation that existed for much of the nation's history, these are still high measures—more than half of blacks would need to move to achieve complete integration.

Yet there is great variation across metropolitan areas as some of the fastest growing places in the South, such as Atlanta, Dallas and Austin show levels below 60. Las Vegas registers the lowest level at just 40. On the other hand, many of the nation's large metropolitan areas outside the South, especially in the slow growing industrial Midwest and Northeast, have levels above 70, led by Milwaukee at 81 and followed by New York, Chicago, Detroit, Cleveland, and Buffalo. These areas served as primary destinations of the "Great Migration"[1] out of the South for much of the last century, but as their economies declined, and blacks began returning to the South their old pre-civil rights* segregation patterns tended to persist among the mostly urban African American populations left behind.

But the positive news, shown with the new data, is that several of these high segregation areas have shown declines since 2000. Many of these experienced a renewed black suburbanization which led residents of heavily black city neighborhoods to somewhat more integrated neighborhoods in the suburbs. Between 2000 and 2010–14, black-white segregation levels declined in 45 of the 52 metropolitan areas; with several of the bigger declines registered by older Midwest regions.

Black-white segregation in U.S. metropolitan areas

Share of blacks that would have to change neighborhoods to match the distribution of whites.
0 = complete integration, 100 = complete segregation

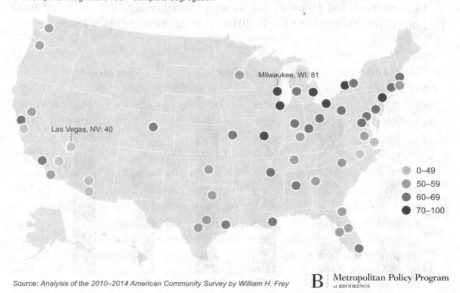

Milwaukee, WI: 81

Las Vegas, NV: 40

- 0–49
- 50–59
- 60–69
- 70–100

Source: Analysis of the 2010–2014 American Community Survey by William H. Frey

B | Metropolitan Policy Program
at BROOKINGS

---

1 *Great Migration* Movement of six million black Americans from Southern to Northern states between 1910 and 1970.

5   Detroit's and Kansas City's segregation levels declined by 11 percentage points and those of Chicago, Buffalo, Cincinnati, and Indianapolis fell by 5 points or more. This is significant because these older Northern areas were slower to desegregate than Southern areas where segregation declines occurred in earlier decades, as their fast growing black and white populations expanded into newer somewhat more integrated communities. Still the new data also shows pervasive segregation declines in the South—with Atlanta, Orlando, Tampa, and Louisville showing segregation declines of 5 or more points since 2000.

Another way to see the impact of these shifts is to examine changes in the racial composition of neighborhoods where blacks live. The new numbers show that for all but five large metropolitan areas, the average black resident lives in a less black neighborhood in 2010–2014 than in 2000.

Shown in Figure 1 are changes in the neighborhoods where blacks resided for Chicago, New York, and Houston. In 2000, the average Chicago black resident lived in a neighborhood that was 72 percent black, 17 percent white, 8 percent Hispanic and the rest other races. By 2010–2014, the black share was reduced to just 64 percent as the white share increased to 19 percent and the Hispanic share rose to 12.5 percent. Over this period some blacks moved to more diverse neighborhoods in both cities and suburbs, and Hispanics moved into many previously predominantly black neighborhoods.

In New York and Houston blacks also lived in neighborhoods that were "less black" in 2010–2014 than in 2010, as Hispanics and, to a lesser degree,

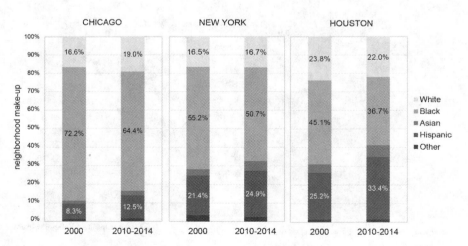

Figure 1. Neighborhood racial make-up for average black resident in 2000 and 2010–2014: Metropolitan Chicago, New York, and Houston.

Asians comprised larger shares in their neighborhoods. Both metropolitan areas are magnets for Hispanics and Asians, and each has exhibited a rise in black suburbanization over this period.

Although areas of black residence became less black in most metropolitan areas, other places with especially large shifts included Detroit, Kansas City, San Francisco, Indianapolis, Louisville, and Cleveland. While some of this change (especially in San Francisco) might be attributed to gentrification[2] and displacement, there are also the broader patterns of black suburbanization [to consider], and the growth and dispersion of Hispanics and Asians into neighborhoods where blacks reside.

Despite continued high levels, declines in black segregation suggest that broader demographic forces at work on the part of new generations of blacks, whites, and other growing minorities hold the potential, if partnered with appropriate social and economic actions, to mitigate the pronounced levels of segregation that characterized the country for much of its history.

(2015)

10

---

2   *gentrification*   Higher classes taking interest, and therefore buying property, in lower income areas (and driving up property value).

ROBERT D. PUTNAM

from OUR KIDS:
THE AMERICAN DREAM IN CRISIS

Political scientist Robert Putnam became widely known with Bowling Alone, *a 2000 book on what he saw as the fraying of America's social fabric. Like that book, his bestselling 2015* Our Kids *brings together personal stories with statistical evidence in order to make a range of points about society and public policy.*

In addition to publishing books like this one, which are intended for a general audience, Putnam also publishes widely on related topics in scholarly journals.

from CHAPTER 1
THE AMERICAN DREAM: MYTHS AND REALITIES

I went back to Ohio, but my city was gone.[1]

If I can get to the heart of Dublin I can get to the heart of all the cities in the world. In the particular is contained the universal.[2]

My hometown was, in the 1950s, a passable embodiment of the American Dream,* a place that offered decent opportunity for all the kids in town, whatever their background. A half century later, however, life in Port Clinton, Ohio, is a split-screen American nightmare, a community in which kids from the wrong side of the tracks that bisect the town can barely imagine the future that awaits the kids from the right side of the tracks. And the story of Port Clinton turns out to be sadly typical of America. How this transformation happened, why it matters, and how we might begin to alter the cursed course of our society is the subject of this book.

---

1   Chrissie Hynde, "My City Was Gone," The Pretenders, *Learning to Crawl*, Sire Records, October 1982. Thanks to Harold Pollack for this citation. [author's note]
2   Richard Ellman, *James Joyce* (Oxford: Oxford University Press, 1965), 520. Thanks to James Walsh for this citation. [author's note]

The most rigorous economic and social history now available suggests that socioeconomic barriers in America (and in Port Clinton) in the 1950s were at their lowest ebb in more than a century: economic and educational expansion were high; income equality was relatively high; class segregation in neighborhoods and schools was low; class barriers to intermarriage and social intercourse were low; civic engagement and social solidarity were high; and opportunities for kids born in the lower echelon to scale the socioeconomic ladder were abundant.

Though small and not very diverse racially, Port Clinton in the 1950s was in all other respects a remarkably representative microcosm of America, demographically, economically, educationally, socially, and even politically. (Ottawa County, of which Port Clinton is county seat, is the bellwether* county in the bellwether state of the United States—that is, the county whose election results have historically been closest to the national outcome.[3]) The life stories of my high school classmates show that the opportunities open to Don and Libby, two poor white kids, and even Jesse and Cheryl, two poor black kids, to rise on the basis of their own talents and energy were not so different from the opportunities open to Frank, the only real scion of privilege in our class.

No single town or city could possibly represent all of America, and Port Clinton in the 1950s was hardly paradise. As in the rest of America at the time, minorities in Port Clinton suffered serious discrimination and women were frequently marginalized, as we shall explore later in this chapter. Few of us, including me, would want to return there without major reforms. But social class was not a major constraint on opportunity.

When our gaze shifts to Port Clinton in the twenty-first century, however, the opportunities facing rich kids and poor kids today—kids like Chelsea and David, whom we shall also meet in this chapter—are radically disparate. Port Clinton today is a place of stark class divisions, where (according to school officials) wealthy kids park BMW convertibles in the high school lot next to decrepit junkers* that homeless classmates drive away each night to live in. The changes in Port Clinton that have led to growing numbers of kids, of all races and both genders, being denied the promise of the American Dream—changes in economic circumstance, in family structure and parenting, in schools, and in neighborhoods—are surprisingly representative of America writ large....

Class Disparities in Port Clinton in the 1950s

... [M]y classmates (now mostly retired) have experienced astonishing upward mobility. Nearly three quarters of us obtained more education than our

---

3   I'm indebted to Professor William Galston for this information. [author's note]

parents, and the vast majority made it higher up the economic ladder. In fact, some kids from less well-off backgrounds have climbed further up the ladder than kids from more comfortable, better-educated backgrounds. By contemporary standards, our class's absolute level of upward educational mobility was remarkable, a reflection of the high school and college revolutions of the twentieth century. Half the sons and daughters of high school dropouts went on to college. Many of those who were the first in their family to complete high school ended up also being the first to complete college—a remarkable jump in a single generation. Even more striking, although the two black students in our class contended with racial prejudice ... and came from homes in which neither parent had competed grade school, both earned postgraduate degrees.

In 1950s Port Clinton, socioeconomic class was not nearly so formidable a barrier for kids of any race, white or black, as it would become in the twenty-first century. By way of comparison, the *children* of the members of the class of 1959 would, on average, experience *no* educational advance beyond their parents.[4] The escalator that had carried most of the class of 1959 upward suddenly halted when our own children stepped on....

CLASS DISPARITIES IN PORT CLINTON IN THE TWENTY-FIRST CENTURY

As my classmates and I marched down the steps after graduation in 1959, none of us had any inkling that change was coming. Almost half of us headed off to college, and those who stayed in town had every reason to expect they would get a job (if they were male), get married, and lead a comfortable life, just as their parents had done. For about a decade those expectations were happily met.

But just beyond the horizon an economic, social, and cultural whirlwind was gathering force nationally that would radically transform the life chances of our children and grandchildren. For many people, its effects would be gut-wrenching, for Port Clinton turns out to be a poster child for the changes that have swept across America in the last several decades.

The manufacturing foundation upon which Port Clinton's modest prosperity had been built in the 1950s and 1960s began to tremble in the 1970s. The big Standard Products factory at the east end of town had provided nearly 1,000 steady, well-paying blue-collar jobs* in the 1950s, but in the 1970s the payroll was trimmed to less than half that, and after more than two decades of layoffs and givebacks, the plant gates on Maple Street finally closed in 1993. Twenty

---

4   A partial exception is that unlike the women of my class, who (as I discuss later) often dropped out of college to get married, their daughters typically finished college once they started. [author's note]

years later, only the hulking ruins of the plant remain, with EPA* signs on the barbed wire fence warning of environmental hazard. But the closing of the Standard Products factory, the Army base, and the gypsum mines were merely the most visible symbols of the town's pervasive economic collapse.

Manufacturing employment in Ottawa County, of which Port Clinton is by far the largest town, plummeted from 55 percent of all jobs in 1965 to 25 percent in 1995 and kept falling.[5] Unemployment rose and fell with the national economic tides, but the local booms were never as good as the national booms, and the local hard times were much worse. As late as the 1970s, real wages locally were slightly above the national average, but during the next four decades they fell further and further behind, bottoming out at 25 percent below the national average. By 2012 the average worker in Ottawa County had not had a real raise for nearly half a century, and is now paid 16 percent less in inflation-adjusted dollars than his or her grandfather (or grandmother) was in the early 1970s.

The Port Clinton population, which had jumped 53 percent in the three decades prior to 1970, suddenly stagnated in the 1970s and 1980s, and then fell by 17 percent in the two decades after 1990. Commutes to jobs got longer and longer, as desperate local workers sought employment elsewhere. Most of the downtown shops of my youth stand empty and derelict, driven out of business partly by the Family Dollar and the Walmart on the outskirts of town, and partly by the gradually shrinking paychecks of Port Clinton consumers.

The social impact of those economic hammer blows was initially softened by the family and community bonds that had been so strong in my youth. But as successive graduating PCHS[6] classes entered an ever-worsening local economy, the social norms that had undergirded Port Clinton's community in the 1950s and 1960s gradually eroded. Juvenile delinquency rates had been just about at the national average in the 1980s but then began to skyrocket, and by 2010 were three times the national average. Increasingly, any PCHS graduate who could escape did. Net departures from Ottawa County among 30-some-things more than doubled from the 1970s to the 2010s, from 13 percent to 27 percent.

Not surprisingly, given the economic stresses and strains, single-parent households in Ottawa County doubled from 1970 to 2010, from 10 percent to 20 percent, and the divorce rate quintupled. The incidence of unwed births in

---

5 I rely on county data when no historical data are available that separate city and county; where we have both city and county data, there are no significant differences in trend and no minor differences in level. On factory closings in northwestern Ohio in the last two decades, see the excellent three-part series by Joe Vardon, "Shut Down and Shipped Out," *Toledo Blade*, September 26–28, 2010. [author's note]

6 *PCHS* Port Clinton High School.

the county rose sharply between 1990 and 2010, from less than 20 percent to nearly 40 percent, outpacing a similar increase among whites nationwide and portending a continuing increase in single parenting in the years ahead. In Port Clinton itself, epicenter of the local economic collapse of the 1980s, the rate of unwed births absolutely exploded in little more than a decade. Between 1978 and 1990, the rate jumped from 9 percent (about half the race-adjusted national average) to about 40 percent (nearly twice the national average). And in the decades that followed, child poverty skyrocketed from less than 10 percent in 1999 to nearly 40 percent in 2013.[7]

15   But the story of Port Clinton over the last half century—like the history of America over these decades—is not simply about the collapse of the working class, because the same years have witnessed the birth of a new upper class.

Port Clinton occupies a lovely site on the shores of Lake Erie. In my youth, small summer cottages and modest resorts and fishing camps dotted those shores, interspersed among fruit orchards, and the shoreline felt available to us all. In the past two decades, however, while the traditional economy of Port Clinton was imploding, wealthy lawyers and doctors and businesspeople from Cleveland and Columbus and other major cities of the Midwest have discovered the charms of the lakeshore and the nearby offshore islands and have begun to take these areas over—for second homes, for retirement, and occasionally even for a better quality of life, at the expense of longer commutes to their well-paying jobs back in the city.

Joined by some fortunate local developers, the newcomers have built elaborate mansions and gated communities. These now line the shore almost uninterruptedly for 20 miles on either side of town. Luxury condos ring golf courses and lagoons filled with opulent yachts. One home along the shore in the upscale Catawba area includes an indoor theater and an athletic court. Nowadays you can read ads in adjacent columns of the real estate pages of the *Port Clinton News-Herald* for near-million-dollar mansions and dilapidated double-wides,* and it is possible to walk in less than ten minutes from wealthy estates on the shoreline to impoverished trailer parks inland.

The distribution of income in Ottawa County, once among the most egalitarian in the country, began to skew over these decades: the number of residents at both the top and the bottom increased, and the middle slumped…. In 2011 in the aftermath of the Great Recession,[8] if you drove east from downtown

---

7   Based on student eligibility for free and reduced price lunch in Port Clinton schools, as reported in Ohio Department of Education, Office for Safety, Health and Nutrition, LUNCH MR 81 Report, ftp://ftp.ode.state.oh.us/MR81/. [author's note]

8   *Great Recession*   Worldwide economic decline that occurred early in the twenty-first century; in the United States, it is generally considered to have lasted from 2007 to 2009.

Port Clinton along East Harbor Road, the census tract to your left along the Catawba lakeshore had a child poverty rate of 1 percent, whereas the census tract on the other side of the road had a child poverty rate of 51 percent.

Let's explore what life is like today for two white kids who live on different sides of that road.

CHELSEA

Chelsea and her family live in a large white home with a wide porch overlooking the lake. They also have an expensive second home in a nearby small town, where Chelsea and her older brother went to school. Chelsea's mother, Wendy, comes from an affluent family in Michigan, where her father was a prominent lawyer. She has a graduate degree and works part-time as a special educator in private practice. She values her flexible schedule, because raising her two kids (who are now in college) has been her top priority. Chelsea's father, Dick, is a sales manager for a major national corporation, and he travels a great deal for his business. "He wasn't real big on being a father when they were young," Wendy says.

Wendy herself, on the other hand, has been intensely involved in her children's lives growing up. "I probably pushed my kids a lot more than my parents ever pushed us," she says. "I was a real grade hound [with my kids]. I really pushed them through high school, and then I just continued. I read to them [as infants]. That's the biggest thing—read, read, read, read when they were little, and they were both reading when they got into kindergarten." She is critical of other moms who are not so involved. "I see so many kids that are just so lost," she says. "Their mothers don't care."

When Chelsea got home from school each day, at least one parent was always home. She and her older brother did their homework at the kitchen island while their mom cooked dinner. The whole family ate together every night, except when her brother was playing football. "Family dinner is critical," Wendy says, "because the kids learn how to discourse with other people."

Chelsea's parents threw fancy themed birthday parties for her every year— tea party at age five, Barbie princess* at six, Academy Awards (complete with limo pickups for the guests) at 11, Las Vegas casino night at 16. Worried that kids in town had nowhere to hang out, Chelsea's parents installed an elaborate 1950s style diner in their basement. "I'm the cook at the 1950s diner," Wendy says, "which was good, because all their friends would talk to me about stuff, and I knew where they were."

Wendy is proud of standing up for her kids at school. When a seventh-grade teacher claimed that Chelsea's older brother had not completed an assignment, she proved to the teacher that he had—and when the teacher then refused to

20

change his grade to reflect that, she appealed first to the principal and then to the school board. The school board changed the grade and moved the teacher to a different position. Another case in point: Chelsea worked hard on her high school yearbook for four years, and served as its editor-in-chief during her senior year, anticipating that she would get the annual yearbook-based college scholarship. When the teacher in charge declined to nominate Chelsea for the scholarship, her mother went to the principal. He knew immediately why she was there. "You know me," she said. "I will go to the school board.... Just tell the teacher to write the [fellowship] check, and let's get this over with." The check arrived next day.

25   Chelsea describes herself as "the most active person" in her high school—student body president, yearbook editor, National Honor Society, president of the book club, "and a whole bunch of other stuff." Her parents pitched in for school events, even more than other parents. They helped build a giant King Kong float out of chicken wire, because the kids did not know how. When Chelsea was in charge of the prom,* and other students failed to show up to construct the scenery, Wendy was there, hot-gluing in the middle of the night.

Although the family is comfortable financially, Wendy doesn't see herself or her affluent peers as "old money" gentry. "Most parents around here are Midwest parents who work for their money," she says. "It's not like Beverly Hills and the Hamptons."* She encourages her kids to have part-time and summer jobs. "You have to work if you want to get rich," she insists. She's skeptical about special funding for educating poorer kids. "If my kids are going to be successful, I don't think they should have to pay other people who are sitting around doing nothing for their success."

Asked about times of stress in her life, Chelsea responds, "There's never really been any financial problem." When a friend of her family committed suicide, it was emotionally very stressful, but she was able to talk with her mom and dad about her feelings, and describes them as good role models. "The people I surround myself with have always tried to help me and push me in the right direction," she says. "I am content with what I'm doing in my life."

Chelsea always knew that she'd go to college. Her parents encouraged good grades by promising her and her brother to pay the full ticket for college if they graduated in the top 10 percent of their high school classes. Both did, and both now attend the same Big Ten university.* Chelsea is aiming for law school, following in the footsteps of her grandfather.

DAVID

David was a scrawny 18-year-old in jeans and a baseball cap when we first encountered him in a Port Clinton park in 2012. His father had dropped out of high school and tried in vain to make a living as a truck driver, like his own father, but as an adult has been employed only episodically, in odd jobs like landscaping. David apologizes for not being able to tell us more about his father. "He's in prison," he explains, "and I can't ask him." David's parents separated when David was very little, and his mother moved out, so he can't tell us much about her, either, except to say that she lives in the Port Clinton area. "All her boyfriends have been nuts," he says. "I never really got to see my mom that much. She was never there."

David has bounced around a lot. He has grown up mostly in his father's custody, though his father has been in and out of prison. A steady stream of women flowed through his dad's life during David's childhood, often floating on drugs. David and his dad would live with David's paternal grandmother on the impoverished side of East Harbor Road for a while; then his dad would try to make it on his own, and another woman would come into his life. But eventually either his dad couldn't pay the rent, or he would start "partying" again, and they'd end up back with the grandmother. David has nine half-siblings, but no fixed address.

When David was ten or 11, his dad hooked up for several years with a woman whom David called his stepmother, although she was never actually married to his father. The stepmother, he says, was "crazy … drinking, pills, drugs," and now lives with another guy, with whom she has several other children. When she left, David says, his dad "went off the deep end" with drugs and women. The way adults moved in and out of his life without worrying about what happened to the kids left David feeling as though "nobody gave a shit" about him and his half-siblings.

David's father was recently sent to prison for a string of robberies. David can't visit him in prison, because he himself is on probation. He feels close to his father, the only adult who has been around all his life, but he worries that his father is unstable. "Sometimes he's mad at me," he says, "sometimes he's not. It's just if I catch him on a good day."

David's family life was obviously chaotic. He dealt with the stress by escaping with friends, staying away from home, and smoking marijuana. "I missed having a home," he says. "I know how close I want my own family to be, because of how close I wasn't." He adds, "I never really had around-the-table family dinners at all, so I never got to miss it."

Because of his dad's itinerant existence,* David went to seven different elementary schools. School, he recalls, was always a problem. "I just let grades float until the end of the semester," he says, "and I passed every year. I've never been held back. In middle school I got into a fight with another kid, so they kicked me out and sent me to 'behavior school,'" which he hated. Finally, with assistance from a local teacher, in 12th grade he transferred to a "career-based intervention class" at a nearby high school, where he earned a diploma, mostly because he got school credit for working at Big Bopper's Diner. Immediately after graduation, the Big Bopper fired him.

35   David himself got into lots of trouble, in part because he started hanging out with the wrong kids. At age 13 he broke into a series of stores and was put under house arrest for five months. He could attend school, but otherwise he had to stay at home alone, where all he did was play video games. "It's all I had to do," he says. Out on probation, he got into further trouble by getting drunk and failing a drug test, which sent him back to juvie. He has essentially no support network. It was his pre-jail friends who got him in trouble in the first place, and the ones he met behind bars were no better. "If you make friends in jail," he says, "you usually go back to jail with them friends."

Since leaving school, David has had various temporary jobs—at fast food restaurants, in a plastics factory, and doing landscaping. He has a hard time getting a job because of his juvenile record, and he can't afford the "couple hundred dollars" in legal fees that it would cost to get the record expunged. He worked hard to qualify as foreman on the landscaping job, but then lost that opportunity because he had points on his license for speeding.

Despite his troubles in school, David has clear educational aspirations. "I really want to get a higher education," he says. "I need one. It's hard to get a job without one anymore." But he has no idea how to get there. He can recall no helpful guidance counselor or teacher from his school years, and his parents are obviously useless. He notes bitterly that nobody at all in Port Clinton was willing to offer him help when he was younger. People in town knew what was going on in his family, he says, but no one cared enough to reach out to him. The fact that his father and mother "had a bad name in town," he believes, meant that townspeople were disinclined to treat him with any sympathy. In the most fundamental sense, David has had to fend for himself his entire life.

Unexpectedly, given his life experience, David feels great responsibility for his diverse brood of younger half-siblings, because no competent adult is caring for them. "I'm the only one that can raise them," he says. David's sense of obligation to his half-siblings seems deep and sincere. "It's like everybody is looking at me to hold it together," he says, "and I feel a lot of pressure because of that." In fact, when we first met him in the park in 2012, he was affectionately watching over an eight-year-old half-brother. Earlier that day, he had been the only family member to attend the school Olympics in which his little brother had competed. In a conversation two years later, David reported that that same little brother was now himself caring for a still younger baby brother, born to the drug-addled stepmother.

In 2012 David's girlfriend became pregnant. "It wasn't planned," he says. "It just kind of happened." At that point, he was hoping that the birth of his child would bring his life together, but he admitted he wasn't sure if he could trust his girlfriend. Sadly, his instincts proved accurate: two years later she was living with a new partner (a drug addict, like her), and David shares custody of their daughter. He lives paycheck to paycheck, but says his daughter has provided him with a sense of purpose. "I love being a dad," he says. "She just looks at me like I'm the Almighty."

In 2012, we asked David if he ever felt like just giving up. "Yeah," he 40 replied, "Sometimes I get that feeling that there's no point in it, but I bounce out of it. It kind of gets me down at times, but I try not to put my mind to it that much." By 2014, distraught by his girlfriend's betrayal and his dead-end job, he posted an update on Facebook. "I always end up at the losing end," he wrote. "I just want to feel whole again. I'll never get ahead! I've been trying so hard at everything in my life and still get no credit at all. Done…. I'm FUCKING DONE!"

Comparing Port Clinton kids in the 1950s with Port Clinton kids today, the opportunity gap has widened dramatically, partly because affluent kids now enjoy more advantages than affluent kids then, but mostly because poor kids now are in much worse shape than their counterparts then. Frank's parents were relaxed about his indifferent performance at school, in contrast to Wendy's intensive parenting, from her "read, read, read, read" regime to her midnight hot-gluing of prom props. Frank's family encouraged him to hang out with kids from modest backgrounds, whereas Wendy hired limos for fancy birthday parties. Chelsea's neighborhood is exclusive, whereas Frank's wasn't. Chelsea dominated her high school's activities, whereas Frank definitely didn't. Chelsea and her mom are proud of Wendy's interventions at school on her kids' behalf, while Frank is appalled at the thought.

Compared to working-class kids in 1959, their counterparts today, like David, lead troubled, isolated, hopeless lives. Don, Libby, Cheryl, and Jesse all had stable, two-parent, loving families. David hardly has a family at all. Don's dad, despite working two jobs, came to every one of Don's games, and Libby's and Cheryl's moms were role models, while David's dad, mom, and stepmom are, at best, object lessons of failed lives. Libby learned manners, values, and loyalty at regular family dinners, but David has no idea what a family dinner would be like. All four of the 1950s working-class kids were encouraged by family or school or both to head for college, whereas David "floated" with virtually no guidance from anyone. Teachers, coaches, church elders, and even fur-clad matrons reached out to help Libby and Jesse and Cheryl and Don, while townspeople left David to fend for himself. Everyone in my parents' generation (from pool shark to pastor) thought of Don and Libby as "our kids,"[9] but surprisingly few adults in Port Clinton today are even aware of David's existence, and even fewer would think of him as one of "our kids."[10]

Port Clinton is just one small town among many, of course—but ... its trajectory during the past five decades, and the divergent destinies of its children, are not unique....

(2015)

---

9 *"our kids"* In an earlier portion of the chapter (not included here), Putnam writes of his graduating class in 1959 that "[f]amily or not, the townspeople thought of all the graduates as "our kids."

10 In 2013 I published an op-ed about Clinton, entitled "Crumbling American Dreams" (*New York Times*, August 3, 2013). A subsequent lively discussion in Port Clinton accelerated earlier efforts to begin to reverse the growing opportunity gap in town. By late 2014 the Port Clinton school system was singled out by the state of Ohio for its successful efforts to raise the test scores of low-income third-graders, while the local United Way, led by Chris Galvin, had begun a series of very promising child care and mentoring initiatives. Whether these efforts will be sustained is still uncertain, but they illustrate that it is possible to focus civic energy and creativity in a small town in ways that would be much harder in large communities. [author's note]

BILL SHORE

STOLEN FUTURE

In the following article from The Stanford Social Innovation Review, *Bill Shore reviews Robert Putnam's* Our Kids: The American Dream in Crisis *(2015). An excerpt from the book is also included in this anthology.*

In *Our Kids*, Robert Putnam revives the lost art of bearing witness. He goes beyond raw data and listens to those who are otherwise voiceless in our society. By blending portraits of individual people with aggregate data, he gives us a remarkably clear picture of inequality in the United States. That accomplishment alone makes for a worthy read.

But the same generosity of spirit that fuels Putnam's empathy causes the book to fall short in accounting for the powerful forces that have made widening inequality a fact of American life. If Putnam had written a similar book about "our climate," it would leave the impression that the earth had merely drifted closer to the sun; it wouldn't cover the human decisions and actions that have caused global temperatures to rise.

The town of Port Clinton, Ohio, where Putnam graduated from high school in 1959, is Ground Zero for his study of "the American dream in crisis." He notes that 75 percent of his fellow graduates went on to attain a higher level of education and greater economic security than their parents had achieved. Because of socio-economic trends that range from the decline of manufacturing to residential sorting,[1] that is not true of more-recent graduating classes. Complementing this decline in social mobility has been a decline in social solidarity. The book's title reflects the time—now long gone—when people used the phrase "our kids" to refer not just to their own children, but to *all* kids in their community.

Putnam, a professor of public policy at Harvard University, ably uses demographic data to reorient our view of what's gone wrong. The collapse of the working-class family that started to affect African-Americans in the 1960s, he notes, began to affect white Americans in the 1980s and 1990s. Since then, there has been a sharp decline in the ratio of US children overall who grow up in two-parent families, and the distribution of those children divides sharply

---

1   *residential sorting*   Demographic sorting of neighborhoods such that people of similar race, income, and so on live in the same areas.

863

along class lines. The proportion of kids with college-educated parents who live in single-parent families is less than 10 percent; for kids with working-class parents, it's close to 70 percent.

5   What echoes loudest and longest in my mind, though, are the voices of the young people whom Putnam features. Consider David, an 18-year-old from Port Clinton whose father has been in and out of prison. "I'll never get ahead!" David writes on his Facebook page. "I've been trying so hard at everything in my life and still get no credit at all. Done." Or listen to Andrew from Bend, Ore., whose attitude toward the future reflects his comfortable upbringing: "My dad always reminds me every day how much my mom and my dad love me.... Some of my friends give me a wisecrack like, 'Andrew's parents say they love him again!' But it's like, yeah, that's how I want it."

In the book's final chapter, Putnam imparts a lesson that he probably didn't intend. He offers a list of proposed social programs that is so familiar that many readers will be able to mouth the words as if they were listening to a golden oldie: Increase the earned income tax credit. Invest in early education. Expand child care options. Promote mentoring. Other parts of the book hold up a mirror to our society, and this chapter is no different: We are too timid, and too oblivious, to advance new or bold ideas about fighting poverty and inequality.

Even in Putnam's capable hands, compelling research data and moving human interest stories are not sufficient. They don't help us to understand the economic and political forces that perpetuate the crisis that Putnam describes.

Inequality has not widened on its own. Imagine walking into your house one evening to find drawers and closets emptied, furniture overturned, and nothing of value left. Would you conclude that socio-economic trends were responsible for that state of affairs, or would you note that a specific person or group of people had ransacked the place? Would your remedy be to encourage neighbors to think of every house as "their house," or would you want to find and stop the perpetrators before they struck again?

Millions of poor children are suffering because of decisions we have made—decisions about how we tax and how we spend, who is first in line for support and who is last. On our list of priorities, we've put children's needs so far below tax loopholes, entitlements,* corporate bailouts, defense spending, and foreign intervention that no one actually has to say "no" to kids. We can take the easy option of shaking our heads sadly as we explain that there just isn't anything left for them.

10   Putnam's compassion for "our kids" is infectious. Here's hoping that his book will help generate the political will to do more for them. After all, everyone likes to say that "children are our future." But the call to change how we treat them will be more effective if we clarify what happened: The shabby house where they live didn't just deteriorate; it was robbed.

(2015)

JILL LEPORE

from RICHER AND POORER:
ACCOUNTING FOR INEQUALITY

In the article excerpted here, Jill Lepore reviews the 2015 book
Our Kids: The American Dream in Crisis *and considers its subject
matter: income inequality in the United States. An excerpt from* Our
Kids *also appears in this anthology.*

... The evidence that income inequality in the United States has been growing
for decades and is greater than in any other developed democracy is not much
disputed....

What's new about the chasm between the rich and the poor in the United
States, then, isn't that it's growing or that scholars are studying it or that people
are worried about it. What's new is that American politicians of all spots and
stripes are talking about it, if feebly: inequality this, inequality that....

Robert Putnam's new book, *Our Kids: The American Dream in Crisis* (Simon
& Schuster), is an attempt to set the statistics aside and, instead, tell a story.
Our Kids begins with the story of the town where Putnam grew up, Port Clinton, Ohio. Putnam is a political scientist, but his argument is historical—it's
about change over time—and fueled, in part, by nostalgia. "My hometown
was, in the 1950s, a passable embodiment of the American Dream," he writes,
"a place that offered decent opportunity for all the kids in town, whatever their
background." Sixty years later, Putnam says, Port Clinton "is a split-screen
American nightmare, a community in which kids from the wrong side of the
tracks that bisect the town can barely imagine the future that awaits the kids
from the right side of the tracks." ...

Our Kids is a heartfelt portrait of four generations: Putnam's fellow 1959
graduates and their children, and the kids in Port Clinton and those nine other
communities[1] today and their parents. The book tells more or less the same

Content

---

1   *nine other communities* Putnam's data includes interviews with more than one
hundred young adults conducted by sociologist Jennifer M. Silva in nine other American
cities and counties.

form, approach

story that the numbers tell; it's just got people in it. Specifically, it's got kids: the kids Putnam used to know, and, above all, the kids Silva interviewed. The book proceeds from the depressing assumption that presenting the harrowing lives of poor young people is the best way to get Americans to care about poverty.

5   Putnam has changed the names of all his subjects and removed certain identifying details. He writes about them as characters....

Aside from the anecdotes, the bulk of *Our Kids* is an omnibus of social-science scholarship. The book's chief and authoritative contribution is its careful presentation for a popular audience of important work on the erosion, in the past half century, of so many forms of social, economic, and political support for families, schools, and communities—with consequences that amount to what Silva and others have called the "privatization of risk." The social-science literature includes a complicated debate about the relationship between inequality of outcome (differences of income and of wealth) and inequality of opportunity (differences in education and employment). To most readers, these issues are more familiar as a political disagreement. In American politics, Democrats are more likely to talk about both kinds of inequality, while Republicans tend to confine their concern to inequality of opportunity. According to Putnam, "All sides in this debate agree on one thing, however: as income inequality expands, kids from more privileged backgrounds start and probably finish further and further ahead of their less privileged peers, even if the rate of socioeconomic mobility is unchanged." He also takes the position, again relying on a considerable body of scholarship, that, "quite apart from the danger that the opportunity gap poses to American prosperity, it also undermines our democracy." Chelsea is interested in politics. David[2] has never voted.

The American dream is in crisis, Putnam argues, because Americans used to care about other people's kids and now they only care about their own kids. But, he writes, "America's poor kids do belong to us and we to them. They are our kids." This is a lot like his argument in *Bowling Alone*.[3] In high school in Port Clinton, Putnam was in a bowling league; he regards bowling leagues as a marker of community and civic engagement; bowling leagues are in decline; hence, Americans don't take care of one another anymore. *Bowling Alone* and *Our Kids* also have the same homey just-folksiness.* And they have the same shortcomings. If you don't miss bowling leagues or all-white suburbs where

in context

motive

---

2   *Chelsea ... David* Chelsea (from a higher-income family) and David (from a lower-income family) are two of the young people whose lives are discussed in Putnam's book; portions of their stories are included in the excerpt from *Our Kids* elsewhere in the anthology.

3   *Bowling Alone* Putnam's best-known book, *Bowling Alone: The Collapse and Revival of American Community* (2000).

women wear aprons—if Putnam's then was not your then and his now isn't your now—his well-intentioned "we" can be remarkably grating.

In story form, the argument of *Our Kids* is that while Wendy and Dick[4] were building a fifties-style diner for their kids in the basement of their lakefront mansion, grade-grubbing with their son's teachers, and glue-gunning the decorations for their daughter's prom, every decent place to hang out in Port Clinton closed its doors, David was fired from his job at Big Boppers, and he got his girlfriend pregnant because, by the time David and Chelsea were born, in the nineteen-nineties, not only was Standard Products out of business but gone, too, was the sense of civic obligation and commonweal—everyone caring about everyone else's kids—that had made it possible for Don and Libby[5] to climb out of poverty in the nineteen-fifties and the nineteen-sixties. "Nobody gave a shit," David says. And he's not wrong.

Our Kids is a passionate, urgent book. It also has a sad helplessness. Putnam tells a story teeming with characters and full of misery but without a single villain. This is deliberate. "This is a book without upper-class villains," he insists in the book's final chapter. In January, Putnam tweeted, "My new book *Our Kids* shows a growing gap between rich kids and poor kids. We'll work with all sides on solutions." It's easier to work with all sides if no side is to blame. But Putnam's eagerness to influence Congress has narrative consequences. If you're going to tell a story about bad things happening to good people, you've got to offer an explanation, and, when you make your arguments through characters, your reader will expect that explanation in the form of characters. I feel bad for Chelsea. But I feel worse for David....

Some people make arguments by telling stories; other people make arguments by counting things....

Because stories contain one kind of truth and numbers another, many writers mix and match, telling representative stories and backing them up with aggregate data. Putnam, though, doesn't so much mix and match as split the difference. He tells stories about kids but presents data about the economy. That's why *Our Kids* has heaps of victims but not a single villain....

Putnam closes *Our Kids* with a chapter called "What Is to Be Done?" Tampering with the basic institutions of financial capitalism is not on his to-do list. The chapter includes one table, one chart, many stories, and this statement: "The absence of personal villains in our stories does not mean that no one is at fault." At fault are "social policies that reflect collective decisions," and,

---

4   *Wendy and Dick*   Chelsea's parents.
5   *Don and Libby*   Members of Putnam's 1959 graduating class who led successful lives despite being raised in poverty.

"insofar as we have some responsibility for those collective decisions, we are implicated by our failure to address removable barriers to others' success." What can Putnam's "we" do? He proposes changes in four realms: family structure, parenting, school, and community. His policy recommendations include expanding the earned-income tax credit and protecting existing anti-poverty programs; implementing more generous parental leaves, better child-care programs, and state-funded preschool; equalizing the funding of public schools, providing more community-based neighborhood schools, and increasing support for vocational high-school programs and for community colleges; ending pay-to-play extracurricular activities in public schools and developing mentorship programs that tie schools to communities and community organizations.

All of these ideas are admirable, many are excellent, none are new, and, at least at the federal level, few are achievable. The American political imagination has become as narrow as the gap between rich and poor is wide.

Inequality: What Can Be Done?, by Anthony Atkinson, will be published this spring (Harvard). Atkinson is a renowned expert on the measurement of economic inequality, but in *Inequality* he hides his math....

15   Much of the book is a discussion of specific proposals. Atkinson believes that solutions like Putnam's, which focus on inequality of opportunity, mainly through reforms having to do with public education, are inadequate. Atkinson thinks that the division between inequality of outcome and inequality of opportunity is largely false. He believes that tackling inequality of outcome is a very good way to tackle inequality of opportunity. (If you help a grownup get a job, her kids will have a better chance of climbing out of poverty, too.) Above all, he disagrees with the widespread assumption that technological progress and globalization are responsible for growing inequality. That assumption, he argues, is wrong and also dangerous, because it encourages the belief that growing inequality is inevitable....

Atkinson isn't interested in stories the way Putnam is interested in stories.... But he is interested in responsible parties, and in demanding government action. "It is not enough to say that rising inequality is due to technological forces outside our control," Atkinson writes. "The government can influence the path taken." In *Inequality: What Can Be Done?*, he offers fifteen proposals, from the familiar (unemployment programs, national savings bonds, and a more progressive tax structure) to the novel (a governmental role in the direction of technological development, a capital endowment or "minimum inheritance" paid to everyone on reaching adulthood), along with five "ideas to pursue," which is where things get Piketty[6] (a global tax on wealth, a minimum tax on corporations)....

---

6   *Piketty*   Reference to Thomas Piketty, author of *Capital in the Twenty-First Century* (2013), in which he proposes a "global tax on wealth" as a remedy for economic inequality.

It might be that people have been studying inequality in all the wrong places. A few years ago, two scholars of comparative politics, Alfred Stepan, at Columbia, and the late Juan J. Linz—numbers men—tried to figure out why the United States has for so long had much greater income inequality than any other developed democracy. Because this disparity has been more or less constant, the question doesn't lend itself very well to historical analysis. Nor is it easily subject to the distortions of nostalgia. But it does lend itself very well to comparative analysis.

Stepan and Linz identified twenty-three long-standing democracies with advanced economies. Then they counted the number of veto players in each of those twenty-three governments. (A veto player is a person or body that can block a policy decision. Stepan and Linz explain, "For example, in the United States, the Senate and the House of Representatives are veto players because without their consent, no bill can become a law.") More than half of the twenty-three countries Stepan and Linz studied have only one veto player; most of these countries have unicameral parliaments. A few countries have two veto players; Switzerland and Australia have three. Only the United States has four. Then they made a chart, comparing Gini indices[7] with veto-player numbers: the more veto players in a government, the greater the nation's economic inequality. This is only a correlation, of course, and cross-country economic comparisons are fraught, but it's interesting.

Then they observed something more. Their twenty-three democracies included eight federal governments with both upper and lower legislative bodies. Using the number of seats and the size of the population to calculate malapportionment, they assigned a "Gini Index of Inequality of Representation" to those eight upper houses, and found that the United States had the highest score: it has the most malapportioned and the least representative upper house. These scores, too, correlated with the countries' Gini scores for income inequality: the less representative the upper body of a national legislature, the greater the gap between the rich and the poor.

The growth of inequality isn't inevitable. But, insofar as Americans have been unable to adopt measures to reduce it, the numbers might seem to suggest that the problem doesn't lie with how Americans treat one another's kids, as lousy as that is. It lies with Congress.

(2015)

---

7   *Gini indices*   Commonly used measures of income inequality.

James Surowiecki

A Fair Day's Wage

The New Yorker magazine often features a "Financial Page," a brief article by business writer James Surowiecki addressing a matter of economic importance. The following Surowiecki column discusses a decision made by the C.E.O. of Aetna, an American health insurance company, to pay its lowest-earning workers more.

I t's no secret that the years since the Great Recession[1] have been hard on American workers. Though unemployment has finally dipped below six per cent, real wages for most have barely budged since 2007. Indeed, the whole century so far has been tough: wages haven't grown much since 2000. So it was big news when, last month, Aetna's C.E.O., Mark Bertolini, announced that the company's lowest-paid workers would get a substantial raise—from twelve to sixteen dollars an hour, in some cases—as well as improved medical coverage. Bertolini didn't stop there. He said that it was not "fair" for employees of a Fortune 50 company[2] to be struggling to make ends meet. He explicitly linked the decision to the broader debate about inequality, mentioning that he had given copies of Thomas Piketty's *Capital in the Twenty-first Century*[3] to all his top executives. "Companies are not just money-making machines," he told me last week. "For the good of the social order, these are the kinds of investments we should be willing to make."

Such rhetoric harks back to an earlier era in U.S. labor relations. These days, most of the benefits of economic growth go to people at the top of the income ladder. But in the postwar era,* in particular, the wage-setting process was shaped by norms of fairness and internal equity. These norms were bolstered by the strength of the U.S. labor movement, which emphasized the idea

---

1   *the Great Recession*   Worldwide economic decline that occurred towards the end of the first decade of the twenty-first century; in the United States, it is generally considered to have lasted from 2007 to 2009.

2   *Fortune 50 company*   One of the fifty largest companies in the United States, according to annual rankings published by *Fortune* magazine.

3   *Thomas ... Century*   Influential 2013 book on economic inequality; in it, Piketty proposes redistributing world wealth by means of taxation.

of the "living" or "family" wage—that someone doing a full day's work should be paid enough to live on. But they were embraced by many in the business class, too. Economists are typically skeptical that these kinds of norms play any role in setting wages. If you want to know why wages grew fast in the nineteen-fifties, they would say, look to the economic boom and an American workforce that didn't have to compete with foreign workers. But this is too narrow a view: the fact that the benefits of economic growth in the postwar era were widely shared had a lot to do with the assumption that companies were responsible not only to their shareholders but also to their workers. That's why someone like Peter Drucker, the dean of management theorists, could argue that no company's C.E.O. should be paid more than twenty times what its average employee earned.

That's not to imply that there aren't solid business reasons for paying workers more. A substantial body of research suggests that it can make sense to pay above-market wages—economists call them "efficiency wages." If you pay people better, they are more likely to stay, which saves money; job turnover was costing Aetna a hundred and twenty million dollars a year. Better-paid employees tend to work harder, too. The most famous example in business history is Henry Ford's decision, in 1914, to start paying his workers the then handsome sum of five dollars a day. Working on the Model T assembly line was an unpleasant job. Workers had been quitting in huge numbers or simply not showing up for work. Once Ford started paying better, job turnover and absenteeism plummeted, and productivity and profits rose.

Subsequent research has borne out the wisdom of Ford's approach. As the authors of a just published study of pay and performance in a hotel chain wrote, "Increases in wages do, in fact, pay for themselves." Zeynep Ton, a business-school professor at M.I.T., shows in her recent book, "The Good Jobs Strategy," that one of the reasons retailers like Trader Joe's and Costco have flourished is that, instead of relentlessly cost-cutting, they pay their employees relatively well, invest heavily in training them, and design their operations to encourage employee initiative. Their upfront labor costs may be higher, but, as Ton told me, "these companies end up with motivated, capable workers, better service, and increased sales." Bertolini—who, as it happens, once worked on a Ford rear-axle assembly line—makes a similar argument. "It's hard for people to be fully engaged with customers when they're worrying about how to put food on the table," he told me. "So I don't buy the idea that paying people well means sacrificing short-term earnings."

That hardly seems like a radical position. But it certainly makes Bertolini an outlier in today's corporate America. Since the nineteen-seventies, a combination of market forces, declining union strength, and ideological changes has led to what the economist Alan Krueger has described as a steady "erosion of the norms, institutions and practices that maintain fairness in the U.S. job market." As a result, while companies these days tend to pay lavishly for talent on the high end—Bertolini made eight million dollars in 2013—they tend to treat frontline workers as disposable commodities.

This isn't because companies are having trouble making money: corporate America, if not the rest of the economy, has done just fine over the past five years. It's that all the rewards went into profits and executive salaries, rather than wages. That arrangement is the result not of some inevitable market logic but of a corporate ethos that says companies should pay workers as little as they can, and no more. This is what Bertolini seems to be challenging. His move may well turn out to be merely a one-off, rather than a harbinger of bigger change. But inequality and the shrinking middle class have become abiding preoccupations on Main Street and in Washington. It's only fair that these concerns have finally reached the executive suite.

(2015)

LAUREN A. RIVERA

GUESS WHO DOESN'T FIT IN AT WORK

Lauren Rivera is associate professor of management and organizations at the Kellogg School of Management. A sociologist by training, she researches the evaluation of merit and social status in professional contexts. "Guess Who Doesn't Fit In at Work" was published in The New York Times *on 31 May 2015.*

A cross cultures and industries, managers strongly prize "cultural fit"—the idea that the best employees are like-minded. One recent survey found that more than 80 percent of employers worldwide named cultural fit as a top hiring priority.

When done carefully, selecting new workers this way can make organizations more productive and profitable. But cultural fit has morphed into a far more nebulous and potentially dangerous concept. It has shifted from systematic analysis of who will thrive in a given workplace to snap judgments by managers about who they'd rather hang out with. In the process, fit has become a catchall used to justify hiring people who are similar to decision makers and rejecting people who are not.

The concept of fit first gained traction in the 1980s. The original idea was that if companies hired individuals whose personalities and values—and not just their skills—meshed with an organization's strategy, workers would feel more attached to their jobs, work harder and stay longer. For Southwest Airlines, screening job candidates based on their willingness to provide a wacky experience for strangers contributed to the fun environment that enabled the company's financial success. Likewise, for the investment firm Bridgewater Associates, which seeks to distinguish itself through its pursuit of transparency and honesty, screening out potential hires who couldn't handle criticism made good business sense.

But in many organizations, fit has gone rogue. I saw this firsthand while researching the hiring practices of the country's top investment banks, management consultancies and law firms. I interviewed 120 decision makers and spent nine months observing the recruiting practices of one firm in particular. The professionals I spoke with, who were charged with reviewing applications and

873

conducting interviews, consistently underscored the importance of cultural fit in hiring. While résumés (and connections) influenced which applicants made it into the interview room, interviewers' perceptions of fit strongly shaped who walked out with job offers.

5   Crucially, though, for these gatekeepers, fit was not about a match with organizational values. It was about personal fit. In these time- and team-intensive jobs, professionals at all levels of seniority reported wanting to hire people with whom they enjoyed hanging out and could foresee developing close relationships with. Fit was different from the ability to get along with clients. Fundamentally, it was about interviewers' personal enjoyment and fun. Many, like one manager at a consulting firm, believed that "when it's done right, work is play."

To judge fit, interviewers commonly relied on chemistry. "The best way I could describe it," one member of a law firm's hiring committee told me, "is like if you were on a date. You kind of know when there's a match." Many used the "airport test." As a managing director at an investment bank put it, "Would I want to be stuck in an airport in Minneapolis in a snowstorm with them?"

Discovering shared experiences was one of the most powerful sources of chemistry, but interviewers were primarily interested in new hires whose hobbies, hometowns and biographies matched their own. Bonding over rowing college crew,* getting certified in scuba, sipping single-malt Scotches in the Highlands or dining at Michelin-starred restaurants* was evidence of fit; sharing a love of teamwork or a passion for pleasing clients was not. Some (former) athletes fit exclusively with other athletes; others fit only with those who played the same sport. At one hiring committee meeting I attended, I watched a partner who was an avid Red Sox fan argue for rejecting a Yankees supporter on the grounds of misfit.

Selecting new employees based on personal similarities is by no means unique to banking, consulting or law; it has become a common feature of American corporate culture. Employers routinely ask job applicants about their hobbies and what they like to do for fun, while a complementary self-help industry informs white-collar job seekers that chemistry, not qualifications, will win them an offer.

Although diversity in many industries has increased in recent decades, progress in the corporate realm has been slower than expected. Selection based on personal fit can keep demographic and cultural diversity low. In the elite firms I studied, the types of shared experiences associated with fit typically required large investments of time and money.

10   Class-biased definitions of fit are one reason investment banks, management consulting firms and law firms are dominated by people from the highest socioeconomic backgrounds. Also, whether the industry is finance, high-tech or fashion, a good fit in most American corporations still tends to

be stereotypically masculine. Consequently, fit can exclude high-performing candidates—female or male—who are more stereotypically feminine.

Some may wonder, "Don't similar people work better together?" Yes and no. For jobs involving complex decisions and creativity, more diverse teams outperform less diverse ones. Too much similarity can lead to teams that are overconfident, ignore vital information and make poor (or even unethical) decisions.

When it comes to creating a cohesive work force, managers often discount the power of shared experiences on the job, especially working interdependently on a high-stakes project. The more time we spend with co-workers, the more similar to them we tend to become. When hiring, do we really need an additional screen on whether people drink wine or whiskey or enjoy Nascar or Nabokov?[1]

Perhaps most important, it is easy to mistake rapport for skill. Just as they erroneously believe that they can accurately tell when someone is lying, people tend to be overly confident in their ability to spot talent. Unstructured interviews, which are the most popular hiring tools for American managers and the primary way they judge fit, are notoriously poor predictors of job performance.

Fit can work, but personal similarity is not the key. Organizations that use cultural fit for competitive advantage tend to favor concrete tools like surveys and structured interviews that systematically test behaviors associated with increased performance and employee retention. For managers who want to use cultural fit in a more productive way, I have several suggestions.

First, communicate a clear and consistent idea of what the organization's culture is (and is not) to potential employees. Second, make sure the definition of cultural fit is closely aligned with business goals. Ideally, fit should be based on data-driven analysis of what types of values, traits and behaviors actually predict on-the-job success. Third, create formal procedures like checklists for measuring fit, so that assessment is not left up to the eyes (and extracurriculars) of the beholder.

Finally, consider putting concrete limits on how much fit can sway hiring. Many organizations tell interviewers what to look for but provide little guidance about how to weigh these different qualities. Left to their own devices, interviewers often define merit in their own image.

Wanting to work with people like ourselves is not new. In the past, employers overtly restricted job opportunities based on sex, race and religion, which is now illegal. But cultural fit has become a new form of discrimination that keeps demographic and cultural diversity down, all in the name of employee enjoyment and fun.

(2015)

15

---

1   *Nascar or Nabokov*   Nascar is the National Association for Stock Car Auto Racing; Vladimir Nabokov was a Russian-American novelist (1899–1977).

Jonathan M. Metzl and Kenneth T. MacLeish

from Mental Illness, Mass Shootings, and the Politics of American Firearms

This academic article from the American Journal of Public Health *questions several assumptions often made about gun violence. The article focuses in particular on the links that are often presumed to exist between such violence and mental illness. The researchers conclude that "notions of mental illness that emerge in relation to mass shootings frequently reflect larger cultural stereotypes and anxieties about matters such as race/ethnicity, social class, and politics; these issues become obscured when mass shootings come to stand in for all gun crime, and when 'mentally ill' ceases to be a medical designation and becomes a sign of violent threat." Excerpted here is the first of four sections on particular assumptions discussed in the article.*

The Assumption That Mental Illness Causes Gun Violence

The focus on mental illness in the wake of recent mass shootings[1] reflects a decades-long history of more general debates in psychiatry and law about guns, gun violence, and "mental competence." Psychiatric articles in the 1960s deliberated ways to assess whether mental patients were "of sound mind enough" to possess firearms.[21] Following the 1999 mass shooting at Columbine High School,* Breggin decried the toxic combination of mental illness, guns,

---

1   *recent mass shootings*   This article was published online in February 2015. High-profile mass shootings in the United States in the immediately preceding years included incidents in Newtown, CT (2012, 27 dead); Washington, DC (2013, 12 dead); and Isla Vista, CA (2014, 6 dead).

   NB To distinguish notes added for this anthology from the authors' note numbers referring to their list of references at the end of the article, subscript numbers have been used here for the latter.

and psychotropic medications that contributed to the actions of shooter Eric Harris.[22] After the 2012 shooting at Newtown,* Torrey amplified his earlier warnings about dangerous "subgroups" of persons with mental illness who, he contended, were perpetrators of gun crimes. Speaking to a national television audience, Torrey, a psychiatrist, claimed that "about half of ... mass killings are being done by people with severe mental illness, mostly schizophrenia, and if they were being treated they would have been preventable."[23] Similar themes appear in legal dialogues as well. Even the US Supreme Court, which in 2008 strongly affirmed a broad right to bear arms,* endorsed prohibitions on gun ownership "by felons and the mentally ill" because of their special potential for violence.[24]

Yet surprisingly little population-level evidence supports the notion that individuals diagnosed with mental illness are more likely than anyone else to commit gun crimes. According to Appelbaum,[25] less than 3% to 5% of US crimes involve people with mental illness, and the percentages of crimes that involve guns are lower than the national average for persons not diagnosed with mental illness. Databases that track gun homicides, such as the National Center for Health Statistics, similarly show that fewer than 5% of the 120,000 gun-related killings in the United States between 2001 and 2010 were perpetrated by people diagnosed with mental illness.[26]

Meanwhile, a growing body of research suggests that mass shootings represent anecdotal distortions of, rather than representations of, the actions of "mentally ill" people as an aggregate group. By most estimates, there were fewer than 200 mass shootings reported in the United States—often defined as crimes in which four or more people are shot in an event, or related series of events—between 1982 and 2012.[27,28] Recent reports suggest that 160 of these events occurred after the year 2000[29] and that mass shootings rose particularly in 2013 and 2014.[28] As anthropologists and sociologists of medicine have noted, the time since the early 1980s also marked a consistent broadening of diagnostic categories and an expanding number of persons classifiable as "mentally ill."[30] Scholars who study violence prevention thus contend that mass shootings occur far too infrequently to allow for the statistical modeling and predictability—factors that lie at the heart of effective public health interventions. Swanson argues that mass shootings denote "rare acts of violence"[31] that have little predictive or preventive validity in relation to the bigger picture of the 32,000 fatalities and 74,000 injuries caused on average by gun violence and gun suicide each year in the United States.[32]

Links between mental illness and other types of violence are similarly contentious among researchers who study such trends. Several studies[33-35] suggest that subgroups of persons with severe or untreated mental illness might be at increased risk for violence in periods surrounding psychotic episodes or psychiatric hospitalizations. Writing in the *American Journal of Psychiatry*, Keers et al. found that the emergence of "persecutory delusions" partially explained associations between untreated schizophrenia and violence.[36] At the same time, a number of seminal studies asserting links between violence and mental illness—including a 1990 study by Swanson et al.[37] cited as fact by the *New York Times* in 2013[38]—have been critiqued for overstating connections between serious mental illness and violent acts.[39]

5   Media reports often assume a binary distinction between mild and severe mental illness, and connect the latter form to unpredictability and lack of self-control. However, this distinction, too, is called into question by mental health research. To be sure, a number of the most common psychiatric diagnoses, including depressive, anxiety, and attention-deficit disorders, have no correlation with violence whatsoever.[18] Community studies find that serious mental illness without substance abuse is also "statistically unrelated" to community violence.[40] At the aggregate level, the vast majority of people diagnosed with psychiatric disorders do not commit violent acts—only about 4% of violence in the United States can be attributed to people diagnosed with mental illness.[41,42]

A number of studies also suggest that stereotypes of "violent madmen" invert on-the-ground realities. Nestor theorizes that serious mental illnesses such as schizophrenia actually reduce the risk of violence over time, as the illnesses are in many cases marked by social isolation and withdrawal.[43] Brekke et al. illustrate that the risk is exponentially greater that individuals diagnosed with serious mental illness will be assaulted by others, rather than the other way around. Their extensive surveys of police incident reports demonstrate that, far from posing threats to others, people diagnosed with schizophrenia have victimization rates 65% to 130% higher than those of the general public.[44] Similarly, a meta-analysis by Choe et al. of published studies comparing perpetuation of violence with violent victimization by and against persons with mental illness concludes that "victimization is a greater public health concern than perpetration."[33(p153)] Media reports sound similar themes: a 2013 investigation by the *Portland Press Herald* found that "at least half" of persons shot and killed by police in Maine suffered from diagnosable mental illness.[45–48]

This is not to suggest that researchers know nothing about predictive factors for gun violence. However, credible studies suggest that a number of risk factors more strongly correlate with gun violence than mental illness alone. For instance, alcohol and drug use increase the risk of violent crime by as much as 7-fold, even among persons with no history of mental illness—a concerning statistic in the face of recent legislation that allows persons in certain US states to bring loaded handguns into bars and nightclubs.[49,50] According to Van Dorn et al., a history of childhood abuse, binge drinking, and male gender are all predictive risk factors for serious violence.[51]

A number of studies suggest that laws and policies that enable firearm access during emotionally charged moments also seem to correlate with gun violence more strongly than does mental illness alone. Belying Lott's argument that "more guns" lead to "less crime,"[52] Miller et al. found that homicide was more common in areas where household firearms ownership was higher.[53] Siegel et al. found that states with high rates of gun ownership had disproportionately high numbers of deaths from firearm-related homicides.[54] Webster's analysis uncovered that the repeal of Missouri's background check law led to an additional 49 to 68 murders per year,[55] and the rate of interpersonal conflicts resolved by fatal shootings jumped by 200% after Florida passed "stand your ground"[2] in 2005.[56] Availability of guns is also considered a more predictive factor than is psychiatric diagnosis in many of the 19,000 US completed gun suicides each year.[11,57,58] (By comparison, gun-related homicides and suicides fell precipitously, and mass-shootings dropped to zero, when the Australian government passed a series of gun-access restrictions in 1996.[59])

Contrary to the image of the marauding lone gunman, social relationships also predict gun violence. Regression analyses by Papachristos et al. demonstrate that up to 85% of shootings occur within social networks.[60] In other words, people are far more likely to be shot by relatives, friends, enemies, or acquaintances than they are by lone violent psychopaths. Meanwhile, a report by the police department of New York City found that, in 2013, a person was "more likely to die in a plane crash, drown in a bathtub or perish in an earthquake" than be murdered by a crazed stranger in that city.[61]

Again, certain persons with mental illness undoubtedly commit violent acts. Reports argue that mental illness might even be underdiagnosed in people who commit random school shootings.[62] Yet growing evidence suggests that mass shootings represent statistical aberrations that reveal more about particularly horrible instances than they do about population-level events. To use Swanson's phrasing, basing gun crime–prevention efforts on the mental health histories of mass shooters risks building "common evidence" from "uncommon things."[31] Such an approach thereby loses the opportunity to build common evidence from common things—such as the types of evidence that clinicians of many medical specialties might catalog, in alliance with communities, about substance abuse, domestic violence, availability of firearms, suicidality, social networks, economic stress, and other factors.

Gun crime narratives that attribute causality to mental illness also invert the material realities of serious mental illness in the United States. Commentators

10

---

2   *stand your ground* Colloquial way of referring to a law authorizing people to use deadly force if they believe it necessary for self-defence, with no duty to attempt to escape from rather than killing a potential attacker.

such as Coulter[3] blame "the mentally ill" for violence, and even psychiatric journals are more likely to publish articles about mentally ill aggression than about victimhood.[5] But, in the real world, these persons are far more likely to be assaulted by others or shot by the police than to commit violent crime themselves. In this sense, persons with mental illness might well have more to fear from "us" than we do from "them." And blaming persons with mental disorders for gun crime overlooks the threats posed to society by a much larger population—the sane....

(2015)

References

5. Kaplan T, Hakim D. New York lawmakers reach deal on new gun curbs. New York Times. January 14, 2013: NY/Region. Available at: http://www.nytimes.com/2013/01/15/ nyregion/new-york-legislators-hope-for-speedy-vote-on-gun-laws.html. Accessed July 23, 2014....

11. Martin A. Asperger's is accused but still not guilty. Huffington Post. June 6, 2014. Available at: http://www.huffingtonpost.com/areva-martin/aspergers-is-accused-but-_b_5434413.html. Accessed July 20, 2014....

18. Johns Hopkins Center for Gun Policy and Research. Guns, public health and mental illness: an evidence-based approach for state policy. Consortium for Risk-Based Firearm Policy. 2013. Available at: http://www.jhsph.edu/research/centers-and-institutes/johns-hopkins-center-for-gun-policy-and-research/publications/GPHMI-State.pdf. Accessed October 1, 2014....

21. Rotenberg LA, Sadoff RL. Who should have a gun? Some preliminary psychiatric thoughts. Am J Psychiatry. 1968;125(6):841–843.

22. Breggin P. Reclaiming Our Children: A Healing Plan for a Nation in Crisis. New York, NY: Basic Books; 2000.

23. Preview: imminent danger. *60 Minutes*. CBS. 2013. Available at: http://www.cbsnews.com/videos/preview-imminent-danger. Accessed July 23, 2014.

24. *District of Columbia v Heller*, 07–290 (DC Cir 2008).

25. Appelbaum PS. Violence and mental disorders: data and public policy. Am J Psychiatry. 2006;163(8):1319–1321.

26. Centers for Disease Control and Prevention Leading causes of death reports National and regional 1999–2010 February 19, 2013. Available at: http://webappa.cdc.gov/sasweb/ncipc/leadcaus10_us.html. Accessed July 23, 2014.

27. Follman M, Aronsen G, Pan D. A guide to mass shootings in America. Mother Jones. May 24, 2014. Available at: http://www.motherjones.com/politics/2012/07/mass-shootings-map?page=2. Accessed July 20, 2014.

28. Mass shooting tracker. Available at: http://shootingtracker.com/wiki/Main_Page. Accessed July 20, 2014.

29. US Department of Justice. A study of active shooter incidents in the United States between 2000 and 2013. Available at: http://www.fbi.gov/news/stories/2014/september/

---

3   *Coulter*   Ann Coulter (b. 1961), controversial conservative commentator.

fbi-releases-study-on-active-shooter-incidents/pdfs/a-study-of-active-shooter-incidents-in-the-u.s.-between-2000-and-2013. Accessed October 1, 2014.

30. Horwitz AV. Creating Mental Illness. Chicago, IL: University of Chicago Press; 2003.

31. Swanson JW. Explaining rare acts of violence: the limits of evidence from population research. Psychiatr Serv. 2011;62(11):1369–1371.

32. Firearm and Injury Center at Penn. Firearm injury in the U.S. 2009. Available at: http://www.uphs.upenn.edu/ficap/resourcebook/Final%20Resource%20Book%20Updated%202009%20Section%201.pdf. Accessed July 23, 2014.

33. Choe JY, Teplin LA, Abram KM. Perpetration of violence, violent victimization, and severe mental illness: balancing public health concerns. Psychiatr Serv. 2008;59(2):153–164.

34. McNiel DE, Weaver CM, Hall SE. Base rates of firearm possession by hospitalized psychiatric patients. Psychiatr Serv. 2007;58(4):551–553.

35. Large MM. Treatment of psychosis and risk assessment for violence. Am J Psychiatry. 2014;171(3):256–258.

36. Keers R, Ullrich S, DeStavola BL, Coid JW. Association of violence with emergence of persecutory delusions in untreated schizophrenia. Am J Psychiatry. 2014;171(3):332–339.

37. Swanson JW, Holzer CE, Ganju VK, Jono RT. Violence and psychiatric disorder in the community: evidence from the epidemiologic catchment area surveys. Psychiatr Serv. 1990;41(7):761–770.

38. Luo M, Mcintire M. When the right to bear arms includes the mentally ill. New York Times. December 21, 2013: US. Available at: http://www.nytimes.com/2013/12/22/us/when-the-right-to-bear-arms-includes-the-mentally-ill.html. Accessed July 23, 2014.

39. Grohol J. Violence and mental illness: simplifying complex data relationships. Psych Central. Available at: http://psychcentral.com/blog/archives/2007/05/02/violence-and-mental-illness-simplifying-complex-data-relationships. Accessed July 1, 2014.

40. Elbogen EB, Johnson SC. The intricate link between violence and mental disorder: results from the National Epidemiologic Survey on Alcohol and Related Conditions. Arch Gen Psychiatry. 2009;66(2):152–161.

41. Fazel S, Grann M. The population impact of severe mental illness on violent crime. Am J Psychiatry. 2006;163(8):1397–1403.

42. Friedman R. A misguided focus on mental illness in gun control debate. New York Times. December 17, 2012: Health. Available at: http://www.nytimes.com/2012/12/18/health/a-misguided-focus-on-mental-illness-in-gun-control-debate.html. Accessed July 23, 2014.

43. Nestor PG. Mental disorder and violence: personality dimensions and clinical features. Am J Psychiatry. 2002;159(12):1973–1978.

44. Brekke JS, Prindle C, Bae SW, Long JD. Risks for individuals with schizophrenia who are living in the community. Psychiatr Serv. 2001;52(10):1358–1366.

45. Deadly force. Police and the mentally ill. Portland Press Herald. Available at: http://www.pressherald.com/special/Maine_police_deadly_force_series_Day_1.html. Accessed March 23, 2014.

46. Steadman HJ, Mulvey EP, Monahan J. et al. Violence by people discharged from acute psychiatric inpatient facilities and by others in the same neighborhoods. Arch Gen Psychiatry. 1998;55(5):393–401.

47. Soliman AE, Reza H. Risk factors and correlates of violence among acutely ill adult psychiatric inpatients. Psychiatr Serv. 2001;52(1):75–80.

48. Rapoport A. Guns—not the mentally ill—kill people. Am Prospect. February 7, 2013. Available at: http://prospect.org/article/guns%E2%80%94not-mentally-ill%E2%80%94kill-people. Accessed July 23, 2014.

49. Brammer J. Kentucky Senate approves bill allowing concealed guns in bars if owner doesn't drink. February 20, 2014. Available at: http://www.kentucky.com/2014/02/20/3100119/kentucky-senate-approves-bill.html. Accessed July 23, 2014.

50. Monahan J, Steadman H, Silver E. Rethinking Risk Assessment: The MacArthur Study of Mental Disorder and Violence. New York, NY: Oxford University Press; 2001.

51. Van Dorn R, Volavka J, Johnson N. Mental disorder and violence: is there a relationship beyond substance use? Soc Psychiatry Psychiatr Epidemiol. 2012;47(3):487–503.

52. Lott JR. More Guns, Less Crime: Understanding Crime and Gun-Control Laws. Chicago, IL: The University of Chicago Press; 2010.

53. Miller M, Azrael D, Hemenway D. Rates of household firearm ownership and homicide across US regions and states, 1988–1997. Am J Public Health. 2002;92(12):1988–1993.

54. Siegel M, Ross CD, King C. The relationship between gun ownership and firearm homicide rates in the United States, 1981–2010. Am J Public Health. 2013;103(11):2098–2105.

55. Webster D, Crifasi CK, Vernick JS. Effects of the repeal of Missouri's handgun purchaser licensing law on homicides. J Urban Health. 2014;9(2):293–302.

56. The Editorial Board. Craven statehouse behavior. New York Times. March 14, 2014. Available at: http://www.nytimes.com/2014/03/15/opinion/craven-statehouse-behavior.html. Accessed July 23, 2014.

57. Lewiecki EM, Miller SA. Suicide, guns, and public policy. Am J Public Health. 2013;103(1):27–31.

58. Centers for Disease Control and Prevention. FASTSTATS - Suicide and self-inflicted injury. December 30, 2013. Available at: http://www.cdc.gov/nchs/fastats/suicide.htm. Accessed July 23, 2014.

59. Chapman S, Alpers P, Agho K, Jones M. Australia's 1996 gun law reforms: faster falls in firearm deaths, firearm suicides, and a decade without mass shootings. Inj Prev. 2006;12(6):365–372.

60. Papachristos AV, Braga AA, Hureau DM. Social networks and the risk of gunshot injury. J Urban Health. 2012;89(6):992–1003.

61. Hamilton B. Odds that you'll be killed by a stranger in NYC on the decline. New York Post. January 5, 2014. Available at: http://nypost.com/2014/01/05/odds-that-youll-be-killed-by-a-stranger-in-nyc-on-the-decline. Accessed July 23, 2014.

62. US Secret Service and US Department of Education. Final report and findings of the safe school initiative: implications for the prevention of school attacks in the United States. Available at: http://www2.ed.gov/admins/lead/safety/preventingattacksreport.pdf. Accessed July 20, 2014.

ATUL GAWANDE

from OVERKILL

*A surgeon, policy advisor, professor, and medical administrator as
well as a best-selling writer, Gawande is as much at home exploring
large social and public policy issues relating to medicine and health
as he is recounting "inside stories" of medical professionals at
work. In this essay, which first appeared in the 11 May 2015 issue of*
The New Yorker, *he suggests that Americans may be suffering from
too much medical care.*

I t was lunchtime before my afternoon surgery clinic, which meant that I was
at my desk, eating a ham-and-cheese sandwich and clicking through medical articles. Among those which caught my eye: a British case report on the
first 3-D-printed hip implanted in a human being, a Canadian analysis of the
rising volume of emergency-room visits by children who have ingested magnets, and a Colorado study finding that the percentage of fatal motor-vehicle
accidents involving marijuana had doubled since its commercial distribution
became legal. The one that got me thinking, however, was a study of more than
a million Medicare patients.* It suggested that a huge proportion had received
care that was simply a waste.

The researchers called it "low-value care." But, really, it was no-value care.
They studied how often people received one of twenty-six tests or treatments
that scientific and professional organizations have consistently determined to
have no benefit or to be outright harmful. Their list included doing an EEG for
an uncomplicated headache (EEGs are for diagnosing seizure disorders, not
headaches), or doing a CT or MRI scan for low-back pain in patients without
any signs of a neurological problem (studies consistently show that scanning
such patients adds nothing except cost), or putting a coronary-artery stent in
patients with stable cardiac disease (the likelihood of a heart attack or death
after five years is unaffected by the stent). In just a single year, the researchers
reported, twenty-five to forty-two per cent of Medicare patients received at
least one of the twenty-six useless tests and treatments.

Could pointless medical care really be that widespread? Six years ago,
I wrote an article for this magazine, titled "The Cost Conundrum," which

explored the problem of unnecessary care in McAllen, Texas, a community with some of the highest per-capita costs for Medicare in the nation. But was McAllen an anomaly or did it represent an emerging norm? In 2010, the Institute of Medicine issued a report stating that waste accounted for thirty per cent of health-care spending, or some seven hundred and fifty billion dollars a year, which was more than our nation's entire budget for K-12 education.* The report found that higher prices, administrative expenses, and fraud accounted for almost half of this waste. Bigger than any of those, however, was the amount spent on unnecessary health-care services. Now a far more detailed study confirmed that such waste was pervasive.

I decided to do a crude check. I am a general surgeon with a specialty in tumors of the thyroid and other endocrine organs. In my clinic that afternoon, I saw eight new patients with records complete enough that I could review their past medical history in detail. One saw me about a hernia, one about a fatty lump growing in her arm, one about a hormone-secreting mass in her chest, and five about thyroid cancer.

5   To my surprise, it appeared that seven of those eight had received unnecessary care. Two of the patients had been given high-cost diagnostic tests of no value. One was sent for an MRI after an ultrasound and a biopsy of a neck lump proved suspicious for thyroid cancer. (An MRI does not image thyroid cancer nearly as well as the ultrasound the patient had already had.) The other received a new, expensive, and, in her circumstances, irrelevant type of genetic testing. A third patient had undergone surgery for a lump that was bothering him, but whatever the surgeon removed it wasn't the lump—the patient still had it after the operation. Four patients had undergone inappropriate arthroscopic knee surgery for chronic joint damage. (Arthroscopy can repair certain types of acute tears to the cartilage of the knee. But years of research, including randomized trials, have shown that the operation is of no help for chronic arthritis- or age-related damage.)

Virtually every family in the country, the research indicates, has been subject to overtesting and overtreatment in one form or another. The costs appear to take thousands of dollars out of the paychecks of every household each year. Researchers have come to refer to financial as well as physical "toxicities" of inappropriate care—including reduced spending on food, clothing, education, and shelter. Millions of people are receiving drugs that aren't helping them, operations that aren't going to make them better, and scans and tests that do nothing beneficial for them, and often cause harm.

Why does this fact barely seem to register publicly? Well, as a doctor, I am far more concerned about doing too little than doing too much. It's the scan, the test, the operation that I should have done that sticks with me—sometimes for years. More than a decade ago, I saw a young woman in the emergency room who had severe pelvic pain. A standard X-ray showed nothing. I examined her and found signs of pelvic inflammatory disease, which is most often caused by sexually transmitted diseases. She insisted that she hadn't been sexually active, but I didn't listen. If I had, I might have ordered a pelvic CT scan or even recommended exploratory surgery to investigate further. We didn't do that until later, by which time the real source of her symptoms, a twisted loop of bowel in her pelvis, had turned gangrenous, requiring surgery. By contrast, I can't remember anyone I sent for an unnecessary CT scan or operated on for questionable reasons a decade ago. There's nothing less memorable.

It is different, however, when I think about my experience as a patient or a family member. I can readily recall a disturbing number of instances of unnecessary care. My mother once fainted in the Kroger's grocery store in our Ohio home town. Emergency workers transported her to a hospital eighty miles away, in Columbus, where doctors did an ultrasound of her carotid arteries and a cardiac catheterization, too, neither of which is recommended as part of the diagnostic workup for someone who's had a fainting episode, and neither of which revealed anything significant. Only then did someone sit down with her and take a proper history; it revealed that she'd had dizziness, likely from dehydration and lack of food, which caused her to pass out.

I began asking people if they or their family had been subject to what they thought was unnecessary testing or treatment. Almost everyone had a story to tell. Some were appalling.

My friend Bruce told me what happened when his eighty-two-year-old father developed fainting episodes. His doctors did a carotid ultrasound and a cardiac catheterization. The tests showed severe atherosclerotic blockages in three coronary arteries and both carotid arteries. The news didn't come as a shock. He had smoked two packs of cigarettes a day since the age of seventeen, and in his retirement years was paying the price, with chronic lung disease, an aortic-aneurysm repair at sixty-five, a pacemaker at seventy-four, and kidney failure at seventy-nine, requiring dialysis three days a week. The doctors recommended doing a three-vessel cardiac-bypass operation as soon as possible, followed, a week or two later, by surgery to open up one of his carotid arteries. The father deferred the decision-making to the son, who researched hospitals and found a team with a great reputation and lots of experience. The team told him that the combined procedures posed clear risks to his father—for instance, his chance of a stroke would be around fifteen per cent—but that the procedures had become very routine, and the doctors were confident that they were far more likely to be successful than not.

It didn't occur to Bruce until later to question what the doctors meant by "successful." The blockages weren't causing his father's fainting episodes or any other impairments to his life. The operation would not make him feel

10

better. Instead, "success" to the doctors meant reducing his future risk of a stroke. How long would it take for the future benefit to outweigh the immediate risk of surgery? The doctors didn't say, but carotid surgery in a patient like Bruce's father reduces stroke risk by about one percentage point per year. Therefore, it would take fifteen years before the benefit of the operation would exceed the fifteen-per-cent risk of the operation. And he had a life expectancy far shorter than that—very likely just two or three years. The potential benefits of the procedures were dwarfed by their risks.

Bruce's father had a stroke during the cardiac surgery. "For me, I'm kicking myself," Bruce now says. "Because I remember who he was before he went into the operating room, and I'm thinking, Why did I green-light an eighty-something-year-old, very diseased man to have a major operation like this? I'm looking in his eyes and they're like stones. There's no life in his eyes. There's no recognition. He's like the living dead."

A week later, Bruce's father recovered his ability to talk, although much of what he said didn't make sense. But he had at least survived. "We're going to put this one in the win column," Bruce recalls the surgeon saying.

"I said, 'Are you fucking kidding me?'"

15   His dad had to move into a nursing home. "He was only half there mentally," Bruce said. Nine months later, his father died. That is what low-value health care can be like.

• • •

… [Even when patients make informed choices, they are] up against long odds. One major problem is what economists call information asymmetry. In 1963, Kenneth Arrow, who went on to win the Nobel Prize in Economics, demonstrated the severe disadvantages that buyers have when they know less about a good than the seller does. His prime example was health care. Doctors generally know more about the value of a given medical treatment than patients, who have little ability to determine the quality of the advice they are getting. Doctors, therefore, are in a powerful position. We can recommend care of little or no value because it enhances our incomes, because it's our habit, or because we genuinely but incorrectly believe in it, and patients will tend to follow our recommendations.

Another powerful force toward unnecessary care emerged years after Arrow's paper: the phenomenon of overtesting, which is a by-product of all the new technologies we have for peering into the human body. It has been hard for patients and doctors to recognize that tests and scans can be harmful. Why not take a look and see if anything is abnormal? People are discovering why not. The United States is a country of three hundred million people who annually undergo around fifteen million nuclear medicine scans, a hundred million CT and MRI scans, and almost ten billion laboratory tests. Often, these are fishing expeditions, and since no one is perfectly normal you tend to find a lot of fish. If you look closely and often enough, almost everyone will have a little nodule that can't be completely explained, a lab result that is a bit off, a heart tracing that doesn't look quite right.

Excessive testing is a problem for a number of reasons. For one thing, some diagnostic studies are harmful in themselves—we're doing so many CT scans and other forms of imaging that rely on radiation that they are believed to be increasing the population's cancer rates. These direct risks are often greater than we account for.

What's more, the value of any test depends on how likely you are to be having a significant problem in the first place. If you have crushing chest pain and shortness of breath, you start with a high likelihood of having a serious heart condition, and an electrocardiogram has significant value. A heart tracing that doesn't look quite right usually means trouble. But, if you have no signs or symptoms of heart trouble, an electrocardiogram adds no useful information; a heart tracing that doesn't look quite right is mostly noise. Experts recommend against doing electrocardiograms on healthy people, but millions are done each year, anyway....

Overtesting has also created a new, unanticipated problem: overdiagnosis. 20
This isn't misdiagnosis—the erroneous diagnosis of a disease. This is the correct diagnosis of a disease that is never going to bother you in your lifetime. We've long assumed that if we screen a healthy population for diseases like cancer or coronary-artery disease, and catch those diseases early, we'll be able to treat them before they get dangerously advanced, and save lives in large numbers. But it hasn't turned out that way. For instance, cancer screening with mammography, ultrasound, and blood testing has dramatically increased the detection of breast, thyroid, and prostate cancer during the past quarter century. We're treating hundreds of thousands more people each year for these diseases than we ever have. Yet only a tiny reduction in death, if any, has resulted.

My last patient in clinic that day, Mrs. E., a woman in her fifties, had been found to have a thyroid lump. A surgeon removed it, and a biopsy was done. The lump was benign. But, under the microscope, the pathologist found a pinpoint "microcarcinoma" next to it, just five millimetres in size. Anything with the term "carcinoma" in it is bound to be alarming—"carcinoma" means cancer, however "micro" it might be. So when the surgeon told Mrs. E. that a cancer had been found in her thyroid, which was not exactly wrong, she believed he'd saved her life, which was not exactly right. More than a third of the population turns out to have these tiny cancers in their thyroid, but fewer than one in a hundred thousand people die from thyroid cancer a year. Only the rare microcarcinoma develops the capacity to behave like a dangerous, invasive cancer. (Indeed, some experts argue that we should stop calling them "cancers" at all.) That's why expert guidelines recommend no further treatment when microcarcinomas are found.

Nonetheless, it's difficult to do nothing. The patient's surgeon ordered a series of ultrasounds, every few months, to monitor the remainder of her thyroid. When the imaging revealed another five-millimeter nodule, he recommended removing the rest of her thyroid, out of an abundance of caution. The patient was seeing me only because the surgeon had to cancel her operation, owing to his own medical issues. She simply wanted me to fill in for the job—but it was a job, I advised her, that didn't need doing in the first place. The surgery posed a greater risk of causing harm than any microcarcinoma we might find, I explained. There was a risk of vocal-cord paralysis and life-threatening bleeding. Removing the thyroid would require that she take a daily hormone-replacement pill for the rest of her life. We were better off just checking her nodules in a year and acting only if there was significant enlargement.

H. Gilbert Welch, a Dartmouth Medical School professor, is an expert on overdiagnosis, and in his excellent new book, *Less Medicine, More Health*, he explains the phenomenon this way: we've assumed, he says, that cancers are all like rabbits that you want to catch before they escape the barnyard pen. But some are more like birds—the most aggressive cancers have already taken flight before you can discover them, which is why some people still die from cancer, despite early detection. And lots are more like turtles. They aren't going anywhere. Removing them won't make any difference.

We've learned these lessons the hard way. Over the past two decades, we've tripled the number of thyroid cancers we detect and remove in the United States, but we haven't reduced the death rate at all. In South Korea, widespread ultrasound screening has led to a fifteen-fold increase in detection of small thyroid cancers. Thyroid cancer is now the No. 1 cancer diagnosed and treated in that country. But, as Welch points out, the death rate hasn't dropped one iota there, either. (Meanwhile, the number of people with permanent complications from thyroid surgery has skyrocketed.) It's all over-diagnosis. We're just catching turtles.

25 Every cancer has a different ratio of rabbits, turtles, and birds, which makes the story enormously complicated. A recent review concludes that, depending on the organ involved, anywhere from fifteen to seventy-five per cent of cancers found are indolent tumors—turtles—that have stopped growing or are growing too slowly to be life-threatening. Cervical and colon cancers are rarely indolent; screening and early treatment have been associated with a notable reduction in deaths from those cancers. Prostate and breast cancers are more like thyroid cancers. Imaging tends to uncover a substantial reservoir of indolent disease and relatively few rabbit-like cancers that are life-threatening but treatable.

We now have a vast and costly health-care industry devoted to finding and responding to turtles. Our ever more sensitive technologies turn up more and more abnormalities—cancers, clogged arteries, damaged-looking knees and backs—that aren't actually causing problems and never will. And then we doctors try to fix them, even though the result is often more harm than good.

The forces that have led to a global epidemic of overtesting, overdiagnosis, and overtreatment are easy to grasp. Doctors get paid for doing more, not less. We're more afraid of doing too little than of doing too much. And patients often feel the same way. They're likely to be grateful for the extra test done in the name of "being thorough"—and then for the procedure to address what's found. Mrs. E. was such a patient.

Mrs. E. had a turtle. She would have been better off if we'd never monitored her thyroid in the first place. But, now that we'd found something abnormal, she couldn't imagine just keeping an eye on it. She wanted to take her chances with surgery.

The main way we've tried to stop unnecessary treatments has been through policing by insurers: they could refuse to pay for anything that looked like inappropriate care, whether it was an emergency-room visit, an MRI scan, or an operation. And it worked. During the nineteen-nineties, the "Mother, may I?" strategy flattened health-care costs. But it also provoked a backlash. Faceless corporate bureaucrats second-guessing medical decisions from afar created an infuriating amount of hassle for physicians and patients trying to orchestrate necessary care—and sometimes led to outrageous mistakes. Insurance executives were accused of killing people. Facing a public outcry, they backed off, and health-care costs resumed their climb. A decade and a half later, however, more interesting approaches have emerged.

Consider the case of Michael Taylor. A six-foot-tall, fifty-five-year-old optician from Ogden, Utah, Taylor threw his back out a year ago, while pulling weeds from his lawn. When he tried to straighten up, pain bolted from his lower back through his hips and down both thighs. He made his stooped way up his front-porch steps, into his house, and called his wife, Sandy, at work....

After four weeks with no improvement, he finally went to see the surgeon, who recommended fusing Taylor's spine where his disk was bulging. Taylor would lose some mobility—his days of spinning kicks were over—and success was not guaranteed, but the doctor thought that it was the best option.

"He said the surgery would be, like, a fifty-fifty thing," Taylor recalled. "Half of people would see great success. The other half would see little or no difference. And there'd be a few who find it makes the pain worse." There was also the matter of cost. The vision center he managed was in a Walmart superstore, and the co-payments and deductibles with the company insurance plan were substantial. His bills were likely to run past a thousand dollars.

30

But Taylor had heard about a program that Walmart had launched for employees undergoing spine, heart, or transplant procedures. Employees would have no out-of-pocket costs at all if they got the procedure at one of six chosen "centers of excellence": the Cleveland Clinic; the Mayo Clinic; Virginia Mason Medical Center, in Washington; Scott and White Memorial Hospital, in Texas; Geisinger Medical Center, in Pennsylvania; and Mercy Hospital Springfield, in Missouri. Taylor learned that the designated spine center for his region was Virginia Mason, in Seattle. He used to live in Washington, and the back surgery he'd had when he was younger was at the same hospital. He trusted the place, and it had a good reputation. He decided to proceed.

The program connected him to the hospital, and its staff took care of everything from there. They set up his appointments and arranged the travel for him and his wife. All expenses were covered, even their food and hotel costs.

35   "They flew us from Salt Lake City and picked us up at the airport in a town car," Taylor said. He said he felt like royalty.

Walmart wasn't providing this benefit out of the goodness of its corporate heart, of course. It was hoping that employees would get better surgical results, sure, but also that the company would save money. Spine, heart, and transplant procedures are among the most expensive in medicine, running from tens of thousands to hundreds of thousands of dollars. Nationwide, we spend more money on spinal fusions, for instance, than on any other operation—thirteen billion dollars in 2011. And if there are complications the costs of the procedure go up further. The medical and disability costs can be enormous, especially if an employee is left permanently unable to return to work. These six centers had notably low complication rates and provided Walmart a fixed, package price.

Two years into the program, an unexpected pattern is emerging: the biggest savings and improvements in care are coming from avoiding procedures that shouldn't be done in the first place. Before the participating hospitals operate, their doctors conduct their own evaluation. And, according to Sally Welborn, the senior vice-president for benefits at Walmart, those doctors are finding that around thirty per cent of the spinal procedures that employees were told they needed are inappropriate. Dr. Charles Nussbaum, until recently the head of neurosurgery at Virginia Mason Medical Center, confirmed that large numbers of the patients sent to his hospital for spine surgery do not meet its criteria.

Michael Taylor was one of those patients. Disk disease like the kind seen on his MRI is exceedingly common. Studies of adults with no back pain find that half or more have degenerative disk disease on imaging. Disk disease is a turtle—an abnormality that generally causes no harm. It's different when a diseased disk compresses the spinal cord or nerve root enough to cause specific symptoms, such as pain or weakness along the affected nerve's territory, typically the leg or the arm. In those situations, surgery is proved to be more effective than nonsurgical treatment. For someone without such symptoms, though, there is no evidence that surgery helps to reduce pain or to prevent problems. One study found that between 1997 and 2005 national health-care expenditures for back-pain patients increased by nearly two-thirds, yet population surveys revealed no improvement in the level of back pain reported by patients.

There are gray-zone cases, but Taylor's case was straightforward. Nussbaum said that Taylor's MRI showed no disk abnormality compressing his spinal cord or nerve root. He had no new leg or foot weakness. His pain went down both legs and not past the knee, which didn't fit with disk disease. The symptoms were consistent with muscle spasms or chronic nerve sensitivity resulting from his previous injuries. Fusing Taylor's spine—locking two vertebrae together with bolts and screws—wouldn't fix these problems. At best, it would stop him from bending where it hurt, but that was like wiring a person's jaw shut because his tooth hurts when he chews. Fusing the spine also increases the load on the disks above and below the level of fusion, making future back problems significantly more likely. And that's if things go well. Nussbaum recommended against the surgery.

This was not what Taylor's wife wanted to hear. Had they come all this way for nothing? "I got kind of angry," Sandy told me later. She wanted his back problem solved.

He did, too. But he was relieved to hear that he wouldn't have to undergo another back operation. Nussbaum's explanations made sense to him, and he had never liked the idea of having his spine fused. Moreover, unlike most places, the Virginia Mason spine center had him seen not only by a surgeon but also by a rehabilitation-medicine specialist, who suggested a nonsurgical approach: a spinal injection that afternoon, continued back exercises, and a medication specifically for neuropathic pain—chronic nerve sensitivity.

"Within a couple of weeks, I was literally pain free," Taylor said. It was six months after his visit to Seattle, and he could do things he hadn't been able to do in decades.

"I was just amazed," Sandy said. "The longer it's been, the better he is."

If an insurer had simply decreed Taylor's back surgery to be unnecessary, and denied coverage, the Taylors would have been outraged. But the worst part is that he would not have got better. It isn't enough to eliminate unnecessary care. It has to be replaced with necessary care. And that is the hidden harm: unnecessary care often crowds out necessary care, particularly when the necessary care is less remunerative. Walmart, of all places, is showing one way to take action against no-value care—rewarding the doctors and systems that do a better job and the patients who seek them out.

· · ·

45   ... I spoke to Carlos Hernandez, an internist and the president of WellMed. He explained that the medical group was founded twenty-five years ago, in San Antonio, by a geriatrician who believed that what the oldest and sickest most needed in our hyper-specialized medical system was slower, more dedicated primary care. "Our philosophy is that the primary-care physician and patient should become the hub of the entire health-care-delivery system," Hernandez said. He viewed the primary-care doctor as a kind of contractor for patients, reining in pointless testing, procedures, and emergency-room visits, coordinating treatment, and helping to find specialists who practice thoughtfully and effectively. Our technology- and specialty-intensive health system has resisted this kind of role, but countries that have higher proportions of general practitioners have better medical outcomes, better patient experiences, and, according to a European study, lower cost growth. WellMed found insurers who saw these advantages and were willing to pay for this model of care. Today, WellMed has more than a hundred clinics, fifteen hundred primary-care doctors, and around a quarter of a million patients across Texas and Florida.

There's a reason that WellMed focused on these two states. They are among the nation's most expensive states for Medicare and are less well-supplied with primary care. An independent 2011 analysis of the company's Texas clinics found that, although the patient population they drew from tended to be less healthy than the over-all Medicare population (being older and having higher rates of diabetes and chronic lung disease, for instance), their death rates were half of the Texas average.

This last part puzzled me. I had started to recognize how unnecessary care could crowd out necessary care—but enough that dedicated primary care could cut death rates in half? That seemed hard to believe. As I learned more about how Dr. Osio's[1] practice had changed, though, I began to grasp how it could happen.

He told me, for instance, about a new patient he'd seen, a sixty-five-year-old man with diabetes. His blood-sugar level was dangerously high, at a level that can signify a full-blown diabetic crisis, with severe dehydration, rising acid levels in the blood, and a risk of death. The man didn't look ill, though. His vital signs were normal. Osio ordered a urine test, which confirmed that the man was not in crisis. That was, in a way, a bad sign. It meant that his diabetes was so out of control that his body had developed a tolerance to big spikes in blood sugar. Unchecked, his diabetes would eventually cause something

---

1   *Dr. Osio*   Armando Osio, a family doctor in McAllen, Texas. An earlier portion of the article not included here describes Osio's arrangement with WellMed, in which he sees fewer patients and receives bonuses for improvements in quality of care.

terrible—kidney failure, a heart attack, blindness, or the kind of wound-healing problem that leads to amputation.

Previously, Osio would not have had the time or the resources to do much for the man. So he would have sent him to the hospital. The staff there would have done a battery of tests to confirm what Osio already knew—that his blood sugar was way too high. They would have admitted him, given him insulin, and brought his blood sugar down to normal. And that would have been about it. The thousands of dollars spent on the hospital admission would have masked a galling reality: no one was addressing the man's core medical problem, which was that he had a chronic and deadly disease that remained dangerously out of control.

But now WellMed gave Osio bonuses if his patients' diabetes was under   50
better control, and helped him to develop a system for achieving this. Osio spent three-quarters of an hour with the man, going over his pill bottles and getting him to explain what he understood about his condition and how to treat it. The man was a blue-collar worker with limited schooling, and Osio discovered that he had some critical misunderstandings. For instance, although he checked his blood-sugar level every day, he wrongly believed that if the level was normal he didn't need to take his medicine. No, Osio told him; his diabetes medication was like his blood-pressure medication—he should never skip a dose unless the home measurements were too low.

Osio explained what diabetes is, how dangerous it can be, how insulin works. Then he turned the man over to an office nurse who had taken classes to become certified as a diabetes educator. She spent another forty-five minutes having him practice how to draw up and take his insulin, and how to track his sugar levels in a logbook. She set a plan to call him every other day for a week and then, if necessary, bring him back for another review. This would continue until his disease was demonstrably under control. After that, she'd check on him once a month by phone, and Osio would see him every three to four months. The nurse gave him her direct phone number. If he had any problems or questions, she told him, "Llámame"—call me.

Step by deliberate step, Osio and his team were replacing unnecessary care with the care that people needed. Since 2009, in Hidalgo County, where McAllen is situated, WellMed has contracted with physicians taking care of around fourteen thousand Medicare patients. According to its data, the local WellMed practices have achieved the same results as WellMed has elsewhere: large reductions in overuse of care and better outcomes for patients....

The passage of the Affordable Care Act,* in 2010, created opportunities for physicians to practice this kind of dedicated care. The law allows any group of physicians with five thousand or more Medicare patients to contract directly with the government as an "accountable-care organization," and to receive up to sixty per cent of any savings they produce. In McAllen, two primary-care groups, with a total of nearly thirteen thousand patients, formed to take advantage of the deal. One, as it happens, was led by Jose Peña, the Doctors Hospital at Renaissance internist.[2] Two years later, Medicare reported that Peña's team had markedly improved control of its patients' diabetes; patients also had dramatically lower emergency-room visits and hospital admissions. And the two McAllen accountable-care organizations together managed to save Medicare a total of twenty-six million dollars....

McAllen, in large part because of changes led by primary-care doctors, has gone from a cautionary tale to something more hopeful. Nationwide, the picture is changing almost as fast. Just five years after the passage of health-care reform, twenty per cent of Medicare payments are being made to physicians who have enrolled in alternative-payment programs, whether through accountable-care organizations like those in McAllen or by accepting Walmart-like packaged-price care—known as bundled payment—for spine surgery, joint surgery, and other high-cost procedures....

55   Waste is not just consuming a third of health-care spending; it's costing people's lives. As long as a more thoughtful, more measured style of medicine keeps improving outcomes, change should be easy to cheer for. Still, when it's your turn to sit across from a doctor, in the white glare of a clinic, with your back aching, or your head throbbing, or a scan showing some small possible abnormality, what are you going to fear more—the prospect of doing too little or of doing too much?

Mrs. E., my patient with a five-millimeter thyroid nodule that I recommended leaving alone, feared doing too little. So one morning I took her to the operating room, opened her neck, and, in the course of an hour, removed her thyroid gland from its delicate nest of arteries and veins and critical nerves. Given that the surgery posed a greater likelihood of harm than of benefit, some people would argue that I shouldn't have done it. I took her thyroid out because the idea of tracking a cancer over time filled her with dread, as it does many people. A decade from now, that may change. The idea that we are overdiagnosing and overtreating many diseases, including cancer, will surely become less contentious. That will make it easier to calm people's worries. But the worries cannot be dismissed. Right now, even doctors are still coming to terms with the evidence....

Two hours after the surgery, Mrs. E.'s nurse called me urgently to see her in the recovery room. Her neck was swelling rapidly; she was bleeding. We rushed her back to the operating room and reopened her neck before accumulating

---

2   *Jose ... internist* An earlier portion of the article not excerpted here includes comments from Peña regarding overspending at the hospital.

blood cut off her airway. A small pumping artery had opened up in a thin band of muscle I'd cauterized. I tied the vessel off, washed the blood away, and took her back to the recovery room.

I saw her in my office a few weeks later, and was relieved to see she'd suffered no permanent harm. The black and blue of her neck was fading. Her voice was normal. And she hadn't needed the pain medication I'd prescribed. I arranged for a blood test to check the level of her thyroid hormone, which she now had to take by pill for the rest of her life. Then I showed her the pathology report. She did have a thyroid cancer, a microcarcinoma about the size of this "O," with no signs of unusual invasion or spread. I wished we had a better word for this than "cancer"—because what she had was not a danger to her life, and would almost certainly never have bothered her if it had not been caught on a scan.

All the same, she thanked me profusely for relieving her anxiety. I couldn't help reflect on how that anxiety had been created. The medical system had done what it so often does: performed tests, unnecessarily, to reveal problems that aren't quite problems to then be fixed, unnecessarily, at great expense and no little risk. Meanwhile, we avoid taking adequate care of the biggest problems that people face—problems like diabetes, high blood pressure, or any number of less technologically intensive conditions. An entire health-care system has been devoted to this game. Yet we're finally seeing evidence that the system can change—even in the most expensive places for health care in the country.

(2015)

NATHANAEL JOHNSON

IS THERE A MORAL CASE FOR MEAT?

This essay is by the food editor for Grist, *an online source of news and commentary, primarily on matters relating to the environment; Johnson is also the author of the 2013 book* All Natural: A Skeptic's Quest to Discover If the Natural Approach to Diet, Childbirth, Healing, and the Environment Really Keeps Us Healthier and Happier. *"Is There a Moral Case for Meat?" was published on the* Grist *site on 20 July 2015.*

Where are the philosophers arguing that eating meat is moral?

When I started researching this piece, I'd already read a lot of arguments against meat, but I hadn't seen a serious philosophical defense of carnivores. So I started asking around. I asked academics, meat industry representatives, and farmers: Who was the philosophical counterweight to Peter Singer?

In 1975, Singer wrote *Animal Liberation*, which launched the modern animal rights movement with its argument that causing animal suffering is immoral. There are plenty of other arguments against eating animals besides Singer's, going back to the ancient Greeks and Hindus. There are even arguments that Christianity contains a mandate for vegetarianism. Matthew Scully's *Dominion* argues against animal suffering; Scully rejects Singer's utilitarian assertion that humans and animals are equal but says that, since God gave people "dominion over the fish of the sea and the fowl of the air, and over the cattle, and over all the earth," so we have a responsibility to care for them and show them mercy.

The arguments against eating animals are pretty convincing. But surely, I thought, there were also intellectuals making convincing counterarguments. Right? Nope. Not really.

5   There is the Cartesian[1] idea that animals are unfeeling machines, incapable of suffering—but I just wasn't buying that. It's clear that animals have an aversive response to pain, and careful, well-respected scientists are saying that animals are probably capable of feeling and consciousness. Once we admit

---

1   *Cartesian*   Associated with the work of René Descartes (1596–1650), an influential French philosopher.

even the possibility that animals are sentient, the ethical game is on: It doesn't matter that an animal is *just an animal*; if you're against suffering and you agree animals can feel pain, it's pretty hard to justify eating them. (Of course, the further you get from humans the harder it is to judge—plants may be sentient in a totally alien way! Singer says we can stop caring somewhere between a shrimp and oyster.)

My enquiries didn't turn up any sophisticated defense of meat. Certainly there are a few people here and there making arguments around the edges, but nothing that looked to me like a serious challenge to Singer. In fact, the lack of philosophical work to justify meat eating is so extreme that people kept referring me not to scholarly publications, but to an essay contest that the *New York Times* held back in 2012. Ariel Kaminer organized that contest after noticing the same gaping hole in the philosophical literature that I'd stumbled upon. Vegetarians have claimed the ethical high ground with book after book and, Kaminer wrote:

> In response, those who love meat have had surprisingly little to say. They say, of course, that, well, they love meat or that meat is deeply ingrained in our habit or culture or cuisine or that it's nutritious or that it's just part of the natural order.... But few have tried to answer the fundamental ethical issue: Whether it is right to eat animals in the first place, at least when human survival is not at stake.

The winner of that contest, Jay Bost, didn't take it much farther than that, basically arguing that "meat is just part of the natural order," because animals are an integral part of the food web. That's a start, but I'd want a lot more than a 600-word essay to flesh out the idea and respond to the obvious criticisms—since almost all the animals we eat are far removed from natural food webs, it's still basically a prescription for veganism. Plus, where do you draw the line on what's natural?

I found several beginnings of arguments like this—no real philosophical shelter for a meat eater, but a few foundational observations that you might build something upon if you carefully thought through all the implications.

Animal welfare expert Temple Grandin offered one potential plank for building a defense of meat eating. "We've gotta give animals a life worth living," she told me. Later in the interview, she reminded me that most farm animals wouldn't have a life at all if no one ate meat. Combine these points and you could argue that it's better to have a life worth living than no life at all—even if it ends with slaughter and consumption.

When I bounced this argument off the ethicist Paul Thompson, he said, "That may be a defensible position, but a philosopher should also be prepared to apply it to humans."

10   Right. It's hard to limit the "a life worth living is better than no life at all" argument to farm animals. Using the same argument we might raise children for the purpose of producing organs: As long as they were well cared for, ignorant of their fate, and painlessly slaughtered, you could say they had a life worth living. The clone gets a (short) life, a dying girl get a new heart, everyone wins! It's rationally consistent, but certainly doesn't feel right to me.

Perhaps some brilliant philosopher will develop these points, but, since I am not one of those, I was left with the conclusion that the vegans were right. Oddly, however, that didn't make me think twice about laying sliced turkey on my sandwich the next day. I was convinced on a rational level, but not in an embodied, visceral way.

"*Animal Liberation* is one of those rare books that demand that you either defend the way you live or change it," Michael Pollan once wrote. I know what he means—when I first read it, I felt battered and stupefied by the horrors of animal suffering that Singer paraded before me. Nevertheless, despite my inability to muster a defense for my meat eating, I didn't change my way of life. Pollan didn't, either: His piece is set up as a stunt—he's reading *Animal Liberation* while eating rib-eye in a steakhouse. And, though Pollan finds himself agreeing with Singer, he has no problem finishing his steak.

I tend to think of rational argument as a powerful force, certainly more powerful than the trivial pleasure of eating meat. But it turns out that's backwards: Rational morality tugs at us with the slenderest of threads, while meat pulls with the thick-twined cords of culture, tradition, pleasure, the flow of the crowd, and physical yearning—and it pulls at us three times a day. Thousands, convinced by Singer and the like, become vegetarians for moral reasons. And then most of those thousands start eating meat again. Vaclav Smil notes: "Prevalence of all forms of 'vegetarianism' is no higher than 2-4 percent in any Western society and that long-term (at least a decade) or life-long adherence to solely plant-based diets is less than 1 percent." As the psychologist Hal Herzog told *Grist*'s Katie Herzog in this podcast, "It's the single biggest failure of the animal rights movement."

How do we deal with this? Some people just shrug and say, "Whatever, animals are different, it's OK to kill them." I can't quite bring myself to do that, because I value rational consistency. And yet, I don't feel immoral when I eat meat—I actually feel pretty good.

15   Whenever you have lots of people agreeing in principle to a goal that is impossible for most to achieve in practice, you have something resembling religion. Religions are all about setting standards that most people will never live up to. And Thompson thinks they have something to teach us on this issue.

Thompson's solution is to treat vegetarianism the way religious traditions treat virtues. Christians strive to love their neighbors, but they don't say that people who fail to reach Jesus-level self-sacrifice are immoral. Buddhists strive for detachment, but they don't flagellate themselves when they fail to achieve it.

Thompson suggests that we should strive to do better by animals, but that doesn't mean we should condemn ourselves for eating meat. There are lots of cases like this, he told me. "Some people are going to take these issues up in a way that other people would find really difficult," Thompson said. "For instance, we all respect Mother Theresa for taking on amazing burdens, but we don't say that you are evil for not doing it."

This makes sense to me. Louis CK* can make a pretty solid argument that people who have enough money to buy a nice car (or to spend time reading long essays about meat philosophy) should be donating 90 percent of their income to the poor.

And yet most of us don't give up our luxuries. By Thompson's reasoning, that doesn't make us immoral. In fact, he says, it's just wrong to condemn people who eat meat. When people rise out of extreme poverty, that is, when they start earning $2.60 a day, they almost invariably spend that newfound money on animal protein: milk, meat, or eggs. Now, you might roll your eyes and say that *of course* the desperate should be excused from the moral obligation—but wait. As Thompson writes in his book, *From Field to Fork: Food Ethics for Everyone*:

> [T]his response misses my point. Excuses apply in extenuating circumstances, but the logic of excuses implies that the action itself is still morally wrong. A poor person might be excused for stealing a loaf of bread. Theft might be excused when a poor person's situation takes a turn for the worse, but in the case at hand, their situation has taken a turn toward the better. Under modestly improved circumstances, the extremely poor add a little meat, milk, or eggs into their diet. My claim is that there is something curious with a moral system that reclassifies legally and traditionally sanctioned conduct of people at the utter margins of society as something that needs to be excused.

Is it morally wrong for a hungry child in India to eat an egg? This isn't just a thought experiment —it's a real controversy. It's not enough to wave it off by saying it's easy to provide vegan alternatives, because those alternatives just don't exist for many people. Often, the cheapest high-quality protein available to the poor comes from animals. Thompson's point is that allowing people to access that protein should be *moral*, not just an excusable lapse.

If we accept Thompson's formulation (and I'm inclined to), it lets us stop wringing our hands over our hypocrisy and strive to improve conditions for animals. That's what Temple Grandin does. She didn't have much patience for my philosophical questions. Instead, she is focused on the realistic changes

20

that will give animals better lives. And as I talked to her, she served up surprise after surprise. Many of the elements in confined animal feeding operations (CAFOs) that people find most abhorrent, she said, may be fine from the animal's perspective. For instance, consider egg-laying hens: What's better for them—an open barn or stacked cages? Small battery cages, with several hens packed inside each, are bad news, according to Grandin, but enriched cages are a really good alternative.

"There are objective ways to measure a hen's motivation to get something she wants—like a private nest box," Grandin told me. "How long is she willing to not eat to get it, or how heavy a door will she push to get it? How many times will she push a switch to get it? A private nest box is something she wants, because in the wild she has an instinct to hide in the bushes so that a fox doesn't get [her eggs]. Give her some pieces of plastic to hang down that she can hide behind. Give her a little piece of astroturf to lay [her eggs] on. Give her a perch, and a piece of plastic to scratch on, and at least enough cage height so she can walk normally. I'm gonna call that apartment living for chickens. Do they need natural elements? Being outside? Science can't answer that. I mean, there are people in New York that hardly go outside."

I pressed her: Can't you use those same objective measurement techniques to see how badly the hens want to go outside and scratch for bugs?

"Well you can," Grandin said, "and the motivation is pretty weak compared to something like the nest box, which is hardwired. Take dust bathing. For a hen dust bathing is nice to do, but it's kind of like, yes, it's nice to have a fancy hotel room, but the EconoLodge* will do too."

And in fact, the free-range system that I would instinctively choose for chickens may be worse than an enriched cage—because the birds get sick and injured a lot more. And laying hens, unlike meat chickens, are pretty nasty about setting up pecking orders. As Thompson observes in his book, "This is well and good in the flocks of 10 to 20 birds, as might be observed among wild jungle fowl, and it is probably tolerable in a flock of 40 to 60 birds that might have been seen on a typical farmstead in 1900.... But a cage-free/free-range commercial egg barn will have between 150,000 to 500,000 hens occupying the same space. If you are a hen at the bottom end of the pecking order in an environment like that, you are going to get pecked. A lot."

25 Even small farms with pastured hens that produce $9-a-dozen eggs often have hundreds of birds, which means the most submissive hens are going to get beat up. I certainly prefer Joel Salatin's 400-bird Eggmobile[2] on lush grass, because to my human eyes it's beautiful—and chicken cages look horrible. But I have real doubt as to what's better from the chicken's perspective.

---

2   *Eggmobile*   Portable henhouse.

There are a lot of counterintuitive things like this when it comes to animal farming.... So I asked Grandin how we should feel about animal agriculture in the United States as it's currently practiced: Do these animals really have a life worth living?

It varies greatly, she said, but some CAFOs really are good. "I think cattle done right have a decent life," she said. I couldn't get her to give a simple thumbs up or down to chicken or pork CAFOs.

Talking to Grandin didn't make me want to go stock up on corn-fed beef, but it did significantly soften my (negative) feelings about industrial animal production. And talking to Thompson made me realize that I was willing to compromise the needs of animals for the needs of humans if they come into direct conflict. In that way I'm a speciesist—I have an unshakeable favoritism for humans. Perhaps it's irrational, but I really want that little girl in India to get her egg, even if it means hens suffer, even if there's a good vegan alternative for a slightly higher cost.

Perhaps there's a philosophical argument to be made in defense of killing animals, but no one has spelled that out in a way that I found convincing. Does this mean that we should join the vegans?

I think the answer is yes, but in a very limited way—in the same way that 30 we all *should* take vows of poverty and stop thinking impure thoughts. Ending deaths and suffering is a worthy moral goal for those of us who have the wealth to make choices. But saying that it's wrong and immoral to eat meat is just too absolutist. I mean, even the Dalai Lama, who says vegetarianism is preferable, eats meat twice a week.

The binary, good-or-evil view of meat is pragmatically counterproductive—the black and white strategy hasn't gotten many people to become vegan. Instead, let's focus on giving farm animals a life worth living.

(2015)

MICHAEL POLLAN

WHY "NATURAL" DOESN'T MEAN ANYTHING ANYMORE

Pollan became famous with two bestselling books on food and the environment, The Omnivore's Dilemma *(2006) and* In Defense of Food *(2008). He has continued since then to publish both on those topics and on related issues—as in the essay included here, in which he explores belief systems around the nature, and assumed superiority, of "natural" states. The piece first appeared in the 28 April 2015 issue of* The New York Times Magazine. *The above title was assigned to the piece online; in print, it was entitled "Altered State."*

It isn't every day that the definition of a common English word that is ubiquitous in common parlance* is challenged in federal court, but that is precisely what has happened with the word "natural." During the past few years, some 200 class-action suits have been filed against food manufacturers, charging them with misuse of the adjective in marketing such edible oxymorons as "natural" Cheetos Puffs, "all-natural" Sun Chips, "all-natural" Naked Juice, "100 percent all-natural" Tyson chicken nuggets and so forth. The plaintiffs argue that many of these products contain ingredients—high-fructose corn syrup, artificial flavors and colorings, chemical preservatives and genetically modified organisms—that the typical consumer wouldn't think of as "natural."

Judges hearing these cases—many of them in the Northern District of California—have sought a standard definition of the adjective that they could cite to adjudicate these claims, only to discover that no such thing exists.

Something in the human mind, or heart, seems to need a word of praise for all that humanity hasn't contaminated, and for us that word now is "natural." Such an ideal can be put to all sorts of rhetorical uses. Among the antivaccination crowd,* for example, it's not uncommon to read about the superiority of something called "natural immunity," brought about by exposure to the pathogen in question rather than to the deactivated (and therefore harmless) version of it made by humans in laboratories. "When you inject a vaccine into the body," reads a post on an antivaxxer website, Campaign for Truth in Medicine, "you're actually performing an unnatural act." This, of course, is the very same term once used to decry homosexuality and, more recently, same-sex marriage, which the Family Research Council[1] has taken to comparing unfavorably to what it calls "natural marriage."

If nature offers a moral standard by which we measure ourselves, and a set of values to which we should aspire, exactly what sort of values are they?

So what are we really talking about when we talk about natural? It depends; the adjective is impressively slippery, its use steeped in dubious assumptions that are easy to overlook. Perhaps the most incoherent of these is the notion that nature consists of everything in the world except us and all that we have done or made. In our heart of hearts, it seems, we are all creationists.*

In the case of "natural immunity," the modifier implies the absence of human intervention, allowing for a process to unfold as it would if we did nothing, as in "letting nature take its course." In fact, most of medicine sets itself against nature's course, which is precisely what we like about it—at least when it's saving us from dying, an eventuality that is perhaps more natural than it is desirable.

Yet sometimes medicine's interventions are unwelcome or go overboard, and nature's way of doing things can serve as a useful corrective. This seems to be especially true at the beginning and end of life, where we've seen a backlash against humanity's technological ingenuity that has given us both "natural childbirth" and, more recently, "natural death."*

This last phrase, which I expect will soon be on many doctors' lips, indicates the enduring power of the adjective to improve just about anything you attach it to, from cereal bars all the way on up to dying. It seems that getting end-of-life patients and their families to endorse "do not resuscitate" orders has been challenging. To many ears, "D.N.R."[2] sounds a little too much like throwing Grandpa under the bus. But according to a paper in *The Journal of Medical Ethics*, when the orders are reworded to say "allow natural death," patients and family members and even medical professionals are much more likely to give their consent to what amounts to exactly the same protocols.

The word means something a little different when applied to human behavior rather than biology (let alone snack foods). When marriage or certain sexual practices are described as "natural," the word is being strategically deployed as a synonym for "normal" or "traditional," neither of which carries nearly as much rhetorical weight. "Normal" is by now too obviously soaked in moral bigotry; by comparison, "natural" seems to float high above human squabbling,

5

---

1   *Family Research Council*   Christian public policy ministry in Washington, D.C.
2   *D.N.R.*   Do Not Resuscitate.

offering a kind of secular version of what used to be called divine law.* Of course, that's exactly the role that "natural law" played for America's founding fathers, who invoked nature rather than God as the granter of rights and the arbiter of right and wrong.

10   "Traditional" marriage might be a more defensible term, but traditional is a much weaker modifier than natural. Tradition changes over time and from culture to culture, and so commands a fraction of the authority of nature, which we think of as timeless and universal, beyond the reach of messy, contested history.

    Implicit here is the idea that nature is a repository of abiding moral and ethical values—and that we can say with confidence exactly what those values are. Philosophers often call this the "naturalistic fallacy": the idea that whatever is (in nature) is what ought to be (in human behavior). But if nature offers a moral standard by which we can measure ourselves, and a set of values to which we should aspire, exactly what sort of values are they? Are they the brutally competitive values of "nature, red in tooth and claw," in which every individual is out for him- or herself? Or are they the values of cooperation on display in a beehive or ant colony, where the interests of the community trump* those of the individual? Opponents of same-sex marriage can find examples of monogamy in the animal kingdom, and yet to do so they need to look past equally compelling examples of animal polygamy as well as increasing evidence of apparent animal homosexuality. And let's not overlook the dismaying rates of what looks very much like rape in the animal kingdom, or infanticide, or the apparent sadism of your average house cat.

    The American Puritans* called nature "God's Second Book," and they read it for moral guidance, just as we do today. Yet in the same way we can rummage around in the Bible and find textual support for pretty much whatever we want to do or argue, we can ransack nature to justify just about anything. Like the maddening whiteness of Ahab's whale,[3] nature is an obligingly blank screen on which we can project what we want to see.

    So does this mean that, when it comes to saying what's natural, anything goes? I don't think so. In fact, I think there's some philosophical wisdom we can harvest from, of all places, the Food and Drug Administration.* When the federal judges couldn't find a definition of "natural" to apply to the class-action suits before them, three of them wrote to the F.D.A., ordering the agency to define the word. But the F.D.A. had considered the question several times before, and refused to attempt a definition. The only advice the F.D.A. was willing

---

3   *Ahab's whale* Reference to Herman Melville's classic novel *Moby Dick* (1851), in which Captain Ahab is obsessed with seeking revenge on the whale who destroyed his previous ship.

to offer the jurists was that a food labeled "natural" should have "nothing artificial or synthetic" in it "that would not normally be expected in the food." The F.D.A. states on its website that "it is difficult to define a food product as 'natural' because the food has probably been processed and is no longer the product of the earth," suggesting that the industry might not want to press the point too hard, lest it discover that nothing it sells is natural.

The F.D.A.'s philosopher-bureaucrats are probably right: At least at the margins, it's impossible to fix a definition of "natural." Yet somewhere between those margins there lies a broad expanse of common sense. "Natural" has a fairly sturdy antonym—artificial, or synthetic—and, at least on a scale of relative values, it's not hard to say which of two things is "more natural" than the other: cane sugar or high-fructose corn syrup? Chicken or chicken nuggets? G.M.O.s or heirloom seeds?* The most natural foods in the supermarket seldom bother with the word; any food product that feels compelled to tell you it's natural in all likelihood is not.

But it is probably unwise to venture beyond the shores of common sense, for it isn't long before you encounter either Scylla or Charybdis.[4] At one extreme end of the spectrum of possible meanings, there's nothing but nature. Our species is a result of the same process—natural selection—that created every other species, meaning that we and whatever we do are natural, too. So go ahead and call your nuggets natural: It's like saying they're made with matter, or molecules, which is to say, it's like saying nothing at all.

15

And yet at the opposite end of the spectrum of meaning, where humanity in some sense stands outside nature—as most of us still unthinkingly believe—what is left of the natural that we haven't altered in some way? We're mixed up with all of it now, from the chemical composition of the atmosphere to the genome of every plant or animal in the supermarket to the human body itself, which has long since evolved in response to cultural practices we invented, like agriculture and cooking. Nature, if you believe in human exceptionalism,[5] is over. We probably ought to search elsewhere for our values.

(2015)

---

4   *before you encounter Scylla or Charybdis*   I.e., before you have to choose between two evils. (The reference is to a story in Greek mythology.)

5   *human exceptionalism*   The belief that humans are different from (and superior to) all other animals.

LAILA LALAMI

MY LIFE AS A MUSLIM IN THE WEST'S "GRAY ZONE"

This essay discussing the position of Muslims in Western societies since 2001 was first published in the 20 November 2015 issue of The New York Times Magazine.

Some months ago, I gave a reading from my most recent novel in Scottsdale, Ariz. During the discussion that followed, a woman asked me to talk about my upbringing in Morocco. It's natural for readers to be curious about a writer they've come to hear, I told myself. I continued to tell myself this even after the conversation drifted to Islam, and then to ISIS. Eventually, another woman raised her hand and said that the only Muslims she saw when she turned on the television were extremists. "Why aren't we hearing more from people like you?" she asked me.

"You are," I said with a nervous laugh. "Right now." I wanted to tell her that there were plenty of ordinary Muslims in this country. We come in all races and ethnicities. Some of us are more visible by virtue of beards or head scarves. Others are less conspicuous, unless they give book talks and it becomes clear that they, too, identify as Muslims.

To be fair, I'm not a very good Muslim. I don't perform daily prayers anymore. I have never been on a pilgrimage to Mecca.[1] I partake of the forbidden drink.[2] I do give to charity whenever I can, but I imagine that this would not be enough to save me were I to have the misfortune, through an accident of birth or migration, to live in a place like Raqqa, Syria, where in the last two years, the group variously known as Daesh, ISIL or ISIS has established a caliphate: a successor to past Islamic empires. Life in Raqqa reportedly follows rules that range from the horrifying to the absurd: The heads of people who have been executed are posted on spikes in the town's main square; women must wear a

---

1   *pilgrimage to Mecca*   The Hajj is an annual journey to Saudi Arabia to visit the most holy city in Islam; making this pilgrimage at least once in an adult's lifetime is a religious requirement within most branches of Islam.

2   *forbidden drink*   Alcohol, which is forbidden in the Qu'ran.

906

niqab[3] and be accompanied by a male companion when they go out; smoking and swearing are not allowed; chemistry is no longer taught in schools and traffic police are not permitted to have whistles because ISIS considers them un-Islamic.

As part of its efforts to spread its message outside the territory it controls, ISIS puts out an English-language magazine, *Dabiq*, which can be found online. In February, *Dabiq* featured a 12-page article, complete with high-resolution photos and multiple footnotes, cheering the terrorist attacks of Sept. 11 and claiming that they made manifest for the world two camps: the camp of Islam under the caliphate and the camp of the West under the crusaders. The article ran under the title "The Extinction of the Grayzone." The gray zone is the space inhabited by any Muslim who has not joined the ranks of either ISIS or the crusaders. Throughout the article, these Muslims are called "the grayish," "the hypocrites" and, for variety, "the grayish hypocrites."

On Nov. 13, men who had sworn allegiance to ISIS struck the city of Paris, killing 130 people at different locations mostly in the 10th and 11th arrondissements, neighborhoods that are known for their multiculturalism. As soon as I heard about the attacks, I tried to reach a cousin of mine, who is studying in Paris. I couldn't. I spent the next two hours in a state of crushing fear until he posted on Facebook that he was safe. Relieved, I went back to scrolling through my feed, which is how I found out that my friend Najlae Benmbarek, a Moroccan journalist, lost her cousin. A recently married architect, Mohamed Amine Ibnolmobarak was eating dinner with his wife at the Carillon restaurant when an ISIS terrorist killed him.

It was probably not a coincidence that the Paris attacks were aimed at restaurants, a concert hall and a sports stadium, places of leisure and community, nor that the victims included Muslims. As Dabiq makes clear, ISIS wants to eliminate coexistence between religions and to create a response from the West that will force Muslims to choose sides: either they "apostatize and adopt" the infidel religion of the crusaders [4] or "they perform *hijrah*[5] to the Islamic State and thereby escape persecution from the crusader governments and citizens." For ISIS to win, the gray zone must be eliminated.

Whose lives are gray? Mine, certainly. I was born in one nation (Morocco) speaking Arabic, came to my love of literature through a second language (French) and now live in a third country (America), where I write books and teach classes in yet another language (English). I have made my home in

5

---

3   *niqab*   Cloth to cover the face.

4   *apostatize and ... crusaders*   I.e., relinquish Islam and adopt Christianity.

5   *hijrah*   Migration for religious purposes; "the Hijrah" typically refers to Muhammad's migration from Mecca to Medina to escape assassination.

between all these cultures, all these languages, all these countries. And I have found it a glorious place to be. My friends are atheists and Muslims, Jews and Christians, believers and doubters. Each one makes my life richer.

This gray life of mine is not unique. I share it with millions of people around the world. My brother in Dallas is a practicing Muslim—he prays, he fasts, he attends mosque—but he, too, would be considered to be in the gray zone, because he despises ISIS and everything it stands for.

Most of the time, gray lives go unnoticed in America. Other times, especially when people are scared, gray lives become targets. Hate crimes against Muslims spike after every major terrorist attack. But rather than stigmatize this hate, politicians and pundits often stoke it with fiery rhetoric, further diminishing the gray zone. Every time the gray zone recedes, ISIS gains ground.

10
The language that ISIS uses may be new, but the message is not. When President George W. Bush spoke to a joint session of Congress after the terrorist attacks of Sept. 11, he declared, "Either you are with us or you are with the terrorists." It was a decisive threat, and it worked well for him in those early, confusing days, so he returned to it. "Either you are with us," he said in 2002, "or you are with the enemy. There's no in between." This polarized thinking led to the United States invasion of Iraq, which led to the destabilization of the Middle East, which in turn led to the creation of ISIS.

Terrorist attacks affect all of us in the same way: We experience sorrow and anger at the loss of life. For Muslims, however, there is an additional layer of grief as we become subjects of suspicion. Muslims are called upon to condemn terrorism, but no matter how often or how loud or how clear the condemnations, the calls remain. Imagine if, after every mass shooting in a school or a movie theater in the United States, young white men in this country were told that they must publicly denounce gun violence. The reason this is not the case is that we presume each young white man to be solely responsible for his actions, whereas Muslims are held collectively responsible. To be a Muslim in the West is to be constantly on trial.

The attacks in Paris have generated the same polarization as all previous attacks have. Even though most of the suspects were French and Belgian nationals who could have gained entry to the United States on their passports, Republican governors in 30 states say that they will refuse to take in any refugees from Syria without even more stringent screening. Barely two days after the attacks, Jeb Bush* told CNN's Jake Tapper that the United States should focus its efforts only on helping Syrian refugees who are Christian.

Ted Cruz* went a step further, offering to draft legislation that would ban Muslim Syrian refugees from the United States. When he was asked by Dana Bash of CNN what would have happened to him if his father, a Cuban refugee who was fleeing communism, had been refused entry, he implied that it was a different situation because of the special risks associated with ISIS.

As it happens, I am married to a son of Cuban refugees. Like Cruz's father, they came to this country because America was a safe haven. What would have been their fate if an American legislator said that they could not be allowed in because the Soviet Union was trying to infiltrate the United States?

The other day, my daughter said to me, "I want to be president." She has been saying this a lot lately, usually the morning after a presidential debate, when our breakfast-table conversation veers toward the elections. My daughter is 12. She plays the violin and the guitar; she loves math and history; she's quick-witted and sharp-tongued and above all she's very kind to others. "I'd vote for you," I told her. And then I looked away, because I didn't have the heart to tell her that half the people in this country—in her country—say they would not vote for a Muslim presidential candidate.

I worry about her growing up in a place where some of the people who are seeking the highest office in the land cannot make a simple distinction between Islam and ISIS, between Muslim and terrorist. Ben Carson* has said he "would not advocate that we put a Muslim in charge of this nation."

Right now, my daughter still has the innocence and ambition that are the natural attributes of the young. But what will happen when she comes of age and starts to realize that her life, like mine, is constantly under question? How do you explain to a child that she is not wanted in her own country? I have not yet had the courage to do that. My daughter has never heard of the gray zone, though she has lived in it her entire life. Perhaps this is my attempt at keeping the world around all of us as gray as possible. It is a form of resistance, the only form of resistance I know.

(2015)

SARAH KURCHAK

AUTISTIC PEOPLE ARE NOT TRAGEDIES

This opinion piece was published online at the end of April 2015 on the website of The Guardian, *a British newspaper with a worldwide audience.*

T he existence of autistic people like me is not a "tragedy." Yet many autism awareness narratives[1] insist it is because they prioritize the feelings of neurotypicals (non-autistic people) and dismisses the rest of us as little more than zombies. And when people buy into this idea, it actively hurts autistic people.

When I was finally diagnosed with autism spectrum disorder six years ago, I wouldn't shut up about it. In part, this was because I, like many autistics, tend to perseverate[2] about the things that intensely fascinate me and, at that moment, there was nothing more fascinating to me than discovering that there was an explanation for all of my sensory sensitivities, social issues, repetitive behaviors and obsessive interests. I also believed in the importance of autism awareness.

But once I started participating in awareness campaigns I found the same overly simplistic and fear-mongering message over and over again: autism is a "crisis." According to the highly influential charity Autism Speaks (which doesn't have a single autistic person on its board), autistic people are "missing"—we leave our family members "depleted. Mentally. Physically. And especially emotionally." Defining our existences solely as a tragedy for non-autistic people is hurtful on a personal level. No one deserves to be told that they are nothing but a burden to the people who love them and everyone has the right to feel like their lives have value.

But it also has troubling implications for public policy.

---

1   *autism awareness narratives*   The piece appeared at the end of April, the month that has been put forward by Autism Speaks and many other autism organizations as World Autism Awareness Month.

2   *perseverate*   Continue to do or think about something after the reason for the original thought or action has passed.

If autism is only presented as an unequivocally terrible curse that must be   5
"cured" and eliminated, then charities that are primarily focused on finding a
cure—like Autism Speaks—will continue to receive the bulk of ASD[3]-related
funding and volunteer hours. Even if a cure is possible or preferable (both of
which are arguable) these wild stabs at hunting down genetic bogeymen in the
hopes of eliminating them in the future do nothing to improve the lives of the
autistic people and their caregivers who are struggling with a scarcity of both
resources and understanding right now.

This line of thought also eclipses more nuanced discussions that might
help to make life more manageable for the people who make up this so-called
autism epidemic. If you spend time following hashtags like #ActuallyAutistic
and the work of organizations like the Autistic Self Advocacy Network and the
Autism Women's Network, a cure is the last thing on any of our minds.

We want to talk about autism acceptance. We want people to understand
that everyone on the spectrum, verbal or otherwise,[4] has value and we want to
work so that everyone has a voice, be it verbal, written, assisted or otherwise.
We want to talk about which therapies and treatments are actually effective for
us and which ones are detrimental to our well-being. And we want to know
how we can create an environment in which autistic children are not at constant
risk of wildly disproportionate punishment due to misunderstanding and fear.
This is a particular concern with autistic children of color who face both ableism[5] and racism, like 12-year-old Kayleb Moon-Robinson, who was charged
with a felony after kicking a garbage can.

Genuine awareness of autistic people, of our lives, our needs and our value,
could greatly improve the lives of people both on and off the spectrum. Autistic
people and our allies just need the rest of the world to stop spreading "autism
awareness" long enough to actually listen and gain some.

(2015)

---

3   *ASD*   Autism spectrum disorder
4   *verbal or otherwise*   Verbal communication skills in people with ASD range from
excellent to completely absent. Augmentative communication devices and other strategies
may facilitate expressive communication for some who would otherwise be perceived as
cognitively disabled.
5   *ableism*   Discrimination against people with disabilities.

EMILY NUSSBAUM

THE PRICE IS RIGHT: WHAT
ADVERTISING DOES TO TV

Mad Men, a highly popular television show about the world of New York advertising firms in the 1950s and 1960s, ran from 2007 to 2015 on the American basic cable network AMC. In this essay, a television critic for The New Yorker *magazine is prompted by the conclusion of that program to consider the role advertising itself plays in shaping television and popular culture. The article was published in the 12 October 2015 issue of* The New Yorker.

E ver since the finale of "Mad Men," I've been meditating on its audacious last image. Don Draper,* sitting cross-legged and purring "Ommmm," is achieving inner peace at an Esalen[1]-like retreat. He's as handsome as ever, in khakis and a crisp white shirt. A bell rings, and a grin widens across his face. Then, as if cutting to a sponsor, we move to the iconic Coke ad from 1971—a green hillside covered with a racially diverse chorus of young people, trilling, in harmony, "I'd like to teach the world to sing." Don Draper, recently suicidal, has invented the world's greatest ad. He's back, baby.

The scene triggered a debate online. From one perspective, the image looked cynical: the viewer is tricked into thinking that Draper has achieved Nirvana,* only to be slapped with the source of his smile. It's the grin of an ad-man who has figured out how to use enlightenment to peddle sugar water, co-opting the counterculture as a brand. Yet, from another angle, the scene looked idealistic. Draper has indeed had a spiritual revelation, one that he's expressing in a beautiful way—through advertising, his great gift. The night the episode aired, it struck me as a dark joke. But, at a discussion a couple of days later, at the New York Public Library, Matthew Weiner, the show's creator, told the novelist A.M. Homes that viewers should see the hilltop ad as "very pure," the product of "an enlightened state." To regard it otherwise, he warned, was itself the symptom of a poisonous mind-set.

---

1   *Esalen*   New Age educational facility.

The question of how television fits together with advertising—and whether we should resist that relationship or embrace it—has haunted the medium since its origins. Advertising is TV's original sin. When people called TV shows garbage, which they did all the time, until recently, commercialism was at the heart of the complaint. Even great TV could never be good art, because it was tainted by definition. It was there to sell.

That was the argument made by George W.S. Trow in this magazine, in a feverish manifesto called "Within the Context of No Context." That essay, which ran in 1980, became a sensation, as coruscating denunciations of modernity so often do. In television, "the trivial is raised up to power," Trow wrote. "The powerful is lowered toward the trivial." Driven by "demography"—that is, by the corrupting force of money and ratings—television treats those who consume it like sales targets, encouraging them to view themselves that way. In one of several sections titled "Celebrities," he writes, "The most successful celebrities are products. Consider the real role in American life of Coca-Cola. Is any man as well-loved as this soft drink is?"

Much of Trow's essay, which runs to more than a hundred pages, makes little sense. It is written in the style of oracular[2] poetry, full of elegant repetitions, elegant repetitions that induce a hypnotic effect, elegant repetitions that suggest authority through their wonderful numbing rhythms, but which contain few facts. It's élitism in the guise of hipness. It is more nostalgic than *Mad Men* ever was for the era when Wasp* men in hats ran New York. It's a screed against TV written at the medium's low point—after the energy of the sitcoms of the seventies had faded but before the innovations of the nineties—and it paints TV fans as brainwashed dummies.

And yet there's something in Trow's manifesto that I find myself craving these days: that rude resistance to being sold to, the insistence that there is, after all, such a thing as selling out. Those of us who love TV have won the war. The best scripted shows are regarded as significant art—debated, revered, denounced. TV showrunners are embraced as heroes and role models, even philosophers. At the same time, television's business model is in chaos, splintered and re-forming itself, struggling with its own history. Making television has always meant bending to the money—and TV history has taught us to be cool with any compromise. But sometimes we're knowing about things that we don't know much about at all.

Once upon a time, TV made sense, economically and structurally: a few dominant network shows ran weekly, with ads breaking them up, like choruses between verses. Then came pay cable, the VCR, the DVD, the DVR, and the

5

---

2   *oracular*   Prophetic.

Internet. At this point, the model seems to morph every six months. Oceanic flat screens give way to palm-size iPhones. A cheap writer-dominated medium absorbs pricey Hollywood directors. You can steal TV; you can buy TV; you can get it free. Netflix, a distributor, becomes a producer. On Amazon, customers vote for which pilots will survive. Shows cancelled by NBC jump to Yahoo, which used to be a failing search engine. The two most ambitious and original début series this summer came not from HBO or AMC but from a pair of lightweight cable networks whose slogans might as well be "Please underestimate us": Lifetime, with *UnREAL*, and USA Network, with *Mr. Robot*. That there is a summer season at all is a new phenomenon. This fall, as the networks launch a bland slate of pilots, we know there are better options.

A couple of months ago, at a meeting of the Television Critics Association, the C.E.O. of FX,[3] John Landgraf, delivered a speech about "peak TV," in which he lamented the exponential rise in production: three hundred and seventy-one scripted shows last year, more than four hundred expected this year—a bubble, Landgraf said, that would surely deflate. He got some pushback: Why now, when the door had cracked open to more than white-guy anti-heroes, was it "too much" for viewers? But just as worrisome was the second part of Landgraf's speech, in which he wondered how the industry could fund so much TV. What was the model, now that the pie had been sliced into slivers? When Landgraf took his job, in 2005, ad buys made up more than fifty per cent of FX's revenue, he said. Now that figure was thirty-two per cent. When ratings drop, ad rates drop, too, and when people fast-forward producers look for new forms of access: through apps, through data mining, through deals that shape the shows we see, both visibly and invisibly. Some of this involves the ancient art of product integration, by which sponsors buy the right to be part of the story: these are the ads that can't be fast-forwarded.

This is both a new crisis and an old one. When television began, it was a live medium. Replicating radio, it was not merely supported by admen; it was run by them. In TV's early years, there were no showrunners: the person with ultimate authority was the product representative, the guy from Lysol or Lucky Strike.[4] Beneath that man (always a man) was a network exec. A layer down were writers, who were fungible, nameless figures, with the exception of people like Paddy Chayefsky, machers[5] who often retreated when they grew frustrated by the industry's censorious limits. The result was that TV writers developed a complex mix of pride and shame, a sense that they were hired

---

3   *FX*   Basic cable network known for the quality of its original programming.

4   *Lucky Strike*   Cigarette brand. Though Lucky Strike is a real company, Draper's firm advertises for it in *Mad Men*.

5   *machers*   People with influence, but lacking substance.

hands, not artists. It was a working-class model of creativity. The shows might be funny or beautiful, but their creators would never own them.

Advertisements shaped everything about early television programs, including their length and structure, with clear acts to provide logical inlets for ads to appear. Initially, there were rules governing how many ads could run: the industry standard was six minutes per hour. (Today, on network, it's about fourteen minutes.) But this didn't include the vast amounts of product integration that were folded into the scripts. (Product placement,* which involves props, was a given.) Viewers take for granted that this is native to the medium, but it's unique to the U.S.; in the United Kingdom, such deals were prohibited until 2011. Even then, they were barred from the BBC, banned for alcohol and junk food, and required to be visibly declared—a "P" must appear onscreen.

In *Brought to You By: Postwar Television Advertising and the American Dream*, Lawrence R. Samuel describes early shows like NBC's *Coke Time*, in which Eddie Fisher sipped the soda. On an episode of *I Love Lucy* called "The Diet," Lucy and Desi smoked Philip Morris cigarettes. On *The Flintstones*, the sponsor Alka-Seltzer ruled that no character get a stomach ache, and that there be no derogatory presentations of doctors, dentists, or druggists. On *My Little Margie*, Philip Morris reps struck the phrase "I'm real cool!," lest it be associated with their competitors Kool cigarettes. If you were a big name—like Jack Benny, whom Samuel calls "the king of integrated advertising"—"plugola"* was par for the course. (Benny once mentioned Schwinn bikes, then looked directly into the camera and deadpanned, "Send three.") There were only a few exceptions, including Sid Caesar, who refused to tout brands on *Your Show of Shows*.

Sponsors were a conservative force. They helped blacklist* writers suspected of being Communists, and, for decades, banned plots about homosexuality and "miscegenation."[6] In Jeff Kisseloff's oral history *The Box*, from 1995, Bob Lewine, of ABC, describes pitching Sammy Davis, Jr.,[7] in an all-black variety show: Young & Rubicam execs walked out, so the idea was dropped. This tight leash affected even that era's version of prestige TV. In *Brought to You By*, Samuel lists topics deemed off limits as "politics, sex, adultery, unemployment, poverty, successful criminality and alcohol"—now the basic food groups of cable. In one notorious incident, the American Gas Association sponsored CBS's anthology series *Playhouse 90*. When an episode called "Portrait of a Murderer" ended, it created an unfortunate juxtaposition: after the killer was executed, the show cut to an ad with the slogan "Nothing but gas does so many jobs so well." Spooked, American Gas took a closer

10

---

6   *miscegenation*   Conception of children by or marriage between people of different races.

7   *Sammy Davis, Jr.*   African American actor, dancer, and musician (1925–90).

look at an upcoming project, George Roy Hill's *Judgment at Nuremberg*. The company objected to any mention of the gas chambers—and though the writers resisted, the admen won.

This sponsor-down model held until the late fifties, around the time that the quiz-show scandals[8] traumatized viewers: producers, in their quest to please ad reps, had cheated. Both economic pressures and the public mood contributed to increased creative control by networks, as the old one-sponsor model dissolved. But the precedent had been established: when people talked about TV, ratings and quality were existentially linked, the business and the art covered by critics as one thing. Or, as Trow put it, "What is loved is a hit. What is a hit is loved."

Kenya Barris's original concept for the ABC series *Black-ish*, last year's smartest network-sitcom début, was about a black writer in a TV writers' room. But then he made the lead role a copywriter at an ad agency, which allowed the network to cut a deal with Buick, so that the show's hero, Dre, is seen brainstorming ads for its car. In *Automotive News*, Buick's marketing manager, Molly Peck, said that the company worked closely with Barris. "We get the benefit of being part of the program, so people are actually watching it as opposed to advertising where viewers often don't watch it."

15 Product integration is a small slice of the advertising budget, but it can take on outsized symbolic importance, as the watermark of a sponsor's power to alter the story—and it is often impossible to tell whether the mention is paid or not. *The Mindy Project* celebrates Tinder. An episode of *Modern Family* takes place on iPods and iPhones. On the ABC Family drama *The Fosters*, one of the main characters, a vice-principal, talks eagerly about the tablets her school is buying. "Wow, it's so light!" she says, calling the product by its full name, the "Kindle Paperwhite e-reader," and listing its useful features. On last year's most charming début drama, the CW's *Jane the Virgin*, characters make trips to Target, carry Target bags, and prominently display the logo.

Those are shows on channels that are explicitly commercialized. But similar deals ripple through cable television and the new streaming producers. FX cut a deal with MillerCoors, so that every character who drinks or discusses a beer is drinking its brands. (MillerCoors designs retro bottles for *The Americans*.) According to *Ad Age*, Anheuser-Busch struck a deal with *House of Cards*, trading supplies of booze for onscreen appearances; purportedly, Samsung struck another, to be the show's "tech of choice." Unilever's Choco Taco paid for integration on Comedy Central's *Workaholics*, aiming to

---

8 *quiz-show scandals* In the 1950s, the public discovered that several popular game shows were rigged.

be "the dessert for millennials." On NBC, Dan Harmon's avant-garde comedy, *Community*, featured an anti-corporate plot about Subway paid for by Subway. When the show jumped to Yahoo, the episode "Advanced Safety Features" was about Honda. "It's not there were just a couple of guys driving the car; it was the whole episode about Honda," Tom Peyton, an assistant V.P. of marketing at Honda, told *Ad Week*. "You hold your breath as an advertiser, and I'm sure they did too—did you go too far and commercialize the whole thing and take it away from it?—but I think the opposite happened.... Huge positives."

Whether that bothers you or impresses you may depend on whether you laughed and whether you noticed. There's a common notion that there's good and bad integration. The "bad" stuff is bumptious—unfunny and in your face. "Good" integration is either invisible or ironic, and it's done by people we trust, like Stephen Colbert or Tina Fey. But it brings out my inner George Trow. To my mind, the cleverer the integration, the more harmful it is. It's a sedative designed to make viewers feel that there's nothing to be angry about, to admire the ad inside the story, to train us to shrug off every compromise as necessary and normal.

Self-mocking integration used to seem modern to me—the irony of a post-*Simpsons* generation—until I realized that it was actually nostalgic: Jack Benny did sketches in which he playfully "resisted" sponsors like Lucky Strike and Lipton tea. Alfred Hitchcock, on *Alfred Hitchcock Presents*, made snide remarks about Bristol-Myers. The audience had no idea that those wisecracks were scripted by a copywriter who had submitted them to Bristol-Myers for approval.

A few weeks ago, Stephen Colbert began hosting CBS's *Late Show*. In his first show, he pointed to a "cursed" amulet. He was under the amulet's control, Colbert moaned, and thus had been forced to "make certain"—he paused— "regrettable compromises." Then he did a bit in which he slavered over Sabra hummus and Rold Gold pretzels. Some critics described the act as satire, but that's a distinction without a difference. Colbert embraced "sponsortunities" when he was on Comedy Central, too, behind the mask of an ironic persona; it's likely one factor that made him a desirable replacement for Letterman, the worst salesman on late-night TV.

During this summer of industry chaos, one TV show did make a pungent case against consumerism: *Mr. Robot*, on USA Network. A dystopian thriller with Occupy-inflected politics,[9] the series was refreshing, both for its melancholy beauty and for its unusually direct attack on corporate manipulation. *Mr. Robot* was the creation of a TV newcomer, Sam Esmail, who found himself

20

---

9   *Occupy-inflected politics*   Reference to the Occupy Wall Street movement against economic inequality.

in an odd position: his anti-branding show was itself rebranding an aggressively corporate network, known for its "blue sky"[10] procedurals—a division of NBCUniversal, a subsidiary of Comcast.

Mr. Robot tells the story of Elliott Alderson, corporate cog by day, hacker by night, a mentally unstable junkie who is part of an Anonymous-like[11] collective that conspires to delete global debt. In one scene, Elliott fantasizes about being conventional enough for a girlfriend: "I'll go see those stupid Marvel movies with her. I'll join a gym. I'll heart things on Instagram." He walks into his boss's office with a Starbucks vanilla latte, the most basic of beverages. This sort of straightforwardly hostile namecheck is generally taboo, both to avoid offending potential sponsors and to leave doors open for their competitors. Esmail says he fought to get real brands in the story, citing *Mad Men* as precedent, as his phone calls with the network's lawyers went from "weekly to daily."

Were any of these mentions paid for? Not in the first season—although Esmail says that he did pursue integrations with brands, some of which turned him down and some of which he turned down (including tech companies that demanded "awkward language" about their features). He's open to these deals in Season 2. "If the idea is to inspire an interesting debate over capitalism, I actually think (depending on how we use it) it can help provoke that conversation even more," he said. As long as such arrangements are "organic and not forced," they're fine with him—what's crucial is not the money but the verisimilitude that brands provide. Only one major conflict came up, Esmail said, in the finale, when Elliott's mysterious alter ego screams in the middle of Times Square, "I'm no less real than the fucking meat patty in your Big Mac." Esmail and USA agreed to bleep "Big Mac"—"to be sensitive to ad sales," Esmail told me—but they left it in for online airings. Esmail said he's confident that the network fought for him. "Maybe Comcast has a relationship with McDonald's?" he mused. (USA told me that the reason was "standards and practices.")

"Are you asking me how I feel about product integration?" Matt Weiner said. "I'm for it." Everything on TV is an ad for something, he pointed out, down to Jon Hamm's beautifully pomaded hair—and he argued that a paid integration is far less harmful than other propaganda embedded in television, such as how cop shows celebrate the virtues of the state. We all have our sponsors. Michelangelo painted for the Pope! What's dangerous about modern TV isn't advertisers, Weiner told me; it's creatives not getting enough of a cut of the proceeds.

Weiner used to work in network television, in a more restrictive creative environment, until he got his break, on *The Sopranos*. Stepping into HBO's

---

10   *blue sky*   Optimistic and pleasantly escapist.

11   *Anonymous-like*   Anonymous is an internet-based anarchic collective of activists.

subscription-only chamber meant being part of a prestige brand: no ads, that gorgeous hissing logo, critical bennies.[12] The move to AMC, then a minor cable station, was a challenge. Weiner longed for the most elegant model, with one sponsor—the approach of *Playhouse 90*. But getting ads took hustle, even in a show about them. Weiner's description of the experience of writing integrations is full of cognitive dissonance. On the one hand, he said, wistfully, he didn't realize at first that he could say no to integrations. Yet he was frustrated by the ones he couldn't get, like attaching Revlon to Peggy's "Basket of Kisses" plot about lipstick. Such deals were valuable—"money you don't leave on the floor"—but it was crucial that the audience not know about them, and that there be few.

The first integration on *Mad Men*, for Jack Daniel's,* was procured before Weiner got involved; writing it into the script made him feel "icky." (Draper wouldn't drink Jack Daniel's, Weiner told me.) Pond's cold cream was a more successful fit. But he tried to impose rules: the sponsor could see only the pages its brand was on; dialogue would mention competitors; and, most important, the company couldn't run ads the night its episode was on the air. Unilever cheated, Weiner claimed—and AMC allowed it. The company filmed ads mimicking the *Mad Men* aesthetic, making the tie with the show visible. If viewers knew that Pond's was integrated, they wouldn't lose themselves in the story, Weiner worried.

In the end, he says, he did only three—Heineken was the third (an integration procured after Michelob backed out). I naïvely remarked that Jaguar couldn't have paid: who would want to be the brand of sexual coercion? "You'd be surprised," he said. Jaguar didn't buy a plug, but the company loved the plot—and hired Christina Hendricks to flack the car,* wearing a bright-red pantsuit.

Weiner had spent the Television Critics Association convention talking up *Mr. Robot* and he told me that he was "stunned" by Esmail's show, which he called American TV's "first truly contemporary anti-corporate message." Then again, he said, "show business in general has been very good at co-opting the people that bite the hands that feed them." NBCUniversal was wise to buy into Esmail's radical themes, he said, because these are ideas that the audience is ready for—"even the Tea Party* knows we don't want to give the country over to corporations."

Weiner made clear that Coke hadn't paid for any integration; he mentioned it a few times. Finally, I asked, Why not? *Mad Men* ended in a way that both Coke and viewers could admire. Why not take the money? Two reasons, he

25

---

12 *critical bennies* Critical "buzz." ("Bennies" is a slang term for benzedrine, an amphetamine.)

said. First, Coca-Cola could "get excited and start making demands." But, really, he didn't want to "disturb the purity of treating that ad as what it was." Weiner is proud that *Mad Men* had a lasting legacy, influencing how viewers saw television's potential, how they thought about money and power, creativity and the nature of work. He didn't want them to think that Coke had bought his finale.

There is no art form that doesn't run a three-legged race with the sponsors that support its production, and the weaker an industry gets (journalism, this means you; music, too) the more ethical resistance flags. But readers would be grossed out to hear that Karl Ove Knausgaard[13] had accepted a bribe to put the Talking Heads into his childhood memories. They'd be angry if Stephen Sondheim[14] slipped a Dewar's jingle into *Company*. That's not priggishness or élitism. It's a belief that art is powerful, that storytelling is real, that when we immerse ourselves in that way it's a vulnerable act of trust. Why wouldn't this be true for television, too?

30   Viewers have little control over how any show gets made; TV writers and directors have only a bit more—their roles mingle creativity and management in a way that's designed to create confusion. Even the experts lack expertise, these days. But I wonder if there's a way for us to be less comfortable as consumers, to imagine ourselves as the partners not of the advertisers but of the artists—to crave purity, naïve as that may sound. I miss *Mad Men*, that nostalgic meditation on nostalgia. But embedded in its vision was the notion that television writing and copywriting are and should be mirrors, twins. Our comfort with being sold to may look like savvy, but it feels like innocence. There's something to be said for the emotions that Trow tapped into, disgust and outrage and betrayal—emotions that can be embarrassing but are useful when we're faced with something ugly.

     Perhaps this makes me sound like a drunken twenty-two-year-old waving a battered copy of Naomi Klein's *No Logo*.[15] But that's what happens when you love an art form. In my imagination, television would be capable of anything. It could offend anyone; it could violate any rule. For it to get there, we might have to expect of it what we expect of any art.

(2015)

---

13   *Karl Ove Knausgaard*   Author of *My Struggle*, a six-volume autobiography that has been much discussed in the literary world.

14   *Stephen Sondheim*   Songwriter known for acclaimed musicals such as *Company* and *West Side Story*.

15   *No Logo*   Influential 1999 book critiquing corporate branding.

Katy Waldman

from There Once Was a Girl:

Against the False Narratives of Anorexia

This personal essay was published 7 December 2015 in the online magazine Slate*; Waldman is a columnist for the magazine.*

My parents have a small framed photograph of E and me in their upstairs hall. We must be 6 or 7. We are smiling in someone's backyard, our heads damp from running through a sprinkler, and we wear matching checkered bathing suits—mine pink, hers blue. My sister is lissome. To my eye, critical even now, I'm a little chubby. We look nice together, like two parts of a whole, both grinning. We look like we know all each other's secrets.

A neighbor has painted a Princess Jasmine[1] diadem on my forehead—a brilliant band of turquoise with a fat yellow jewel in the center. I think I remember how excited I was, feeling the tickle of the brush and the colors spreading over my skin. E isn't wearing face paint in the picture. I think I remember that, too—my sister turning the offer down, on some level aware that she needed no embellishment.

As I grew up with that photograph, I started to see it differently. At first I loved my Jasmine crown, but eventually the bewitching strap of blue began to strike me as tacky. It had something in common with the gaudy excess of my stomach curving out beneath my swimsuit. I came to understand my nature. I was the girl who used every art supply in the box instead of picking the best few; I told circular, giddy stories; I flailed around the pool, the slowest swimmer on the team. I realized how elegant E had always been, how she eschewed splashy statements even in kindergarten. She had a native understanding of an aesthetic principle that I couldn't grasp. *Less is more.*

If you were to ask me when the spores of anorexia first crept into my heart, that's the moment I might point to, me standing in front of the picture in the hall and seeing it with fresh eyes. *There. Start there.*

---

1   *Princess Jasmine*   Character in the Walt Disney animated feature film *Aladdin* (1992).

5   Here is a story for you. My parents, D and J, are lovely and kind and interest-ing people. My twin sister (we're fraternal) is beautiful and accomplished. When we were 14, my sister developed anorexia, impelled by perfectionism, genes, whatever spectral lever it is that tilts the cosmic pinball board and then everything changes. When we were 17, *I* developed anorexia, impelled by some unpoetic cacophony of motivations: wanting to be close to her, wanting to compete with her, wanting to rescue her, wanting to cancel her out. E has a routine that's more or less stayed the same since eighth grade—it allows her to eat (not much) and exercise (a lot) without really asking why. My parents raged for a few years against the routine but at this point regard it as normal-ish. (Their habit of ignoring it and at times facilitating it indicates something between denial and acceptance.) Are they wrong? Who knows. As I write these words, my sister is an exceedingly thin, charismatic, disciplined woman who does brilliant work in her Ivy League Ph.D. program, and is unhappy.

I, meanwhile, tried for years to undo what I'd done to myself. I saw nutritionists (and refused to follow the menus they gave me). I tried medica-tion (taken sporadically). After college, I moved back to my parents' house in Washington, found a spectacular therapist, and achieved a measure of clarity. It helped, strange as it may sound, that I was a miserable anorexic, convinced that the disease was deeply *wrong for me* yet unable to shake its influence. Until I did. The sunlight of the real world began to disinfect my brain. I had friends, books, a job I loved. I moved out of my parents' home. I got better.

Even now I worry I'm telling the story wrong. *Is* E unhappy? Did my parents enable us in our sickness, or were they just powerless to reverse the tide? I can hardly conjure those years of my life in memory without thinking I've committed some grave narrative sin.

I'm not the most reliable narrator. (To be fair, you probably aren't, either.) I spin stories about people in order to understand them better, or to soothe or entertain myself. I sometimes balance my sanity on unstable materials—love objects that don't stay put where I've left them. It can be hard to accept that your "characters"—Mom, Dad, sister—don't belong to you, the tale-teller.

The narrative impulse is one entwined with anorexia itself. Being sick means constructing an alternate reality, strapping it in place with sturdy mantras, surrendering to the beguiling logic of an old fairy tale: *There once was a girl who ate very little. There once lived a witch in a deep, dark wood.* Anorexics are convinced that they are hideous, bad, and unlovable. At the same time, they are constantly soliloquizing about their sacrifice, their nobility, their ethereal powers.

10   "[A]norexia emerges less palpably as a humiliating physical and psycho-logical affliction than as an elevated state of mind, an intellectualized halluci-nation," wrote Ginia Bellafante in a review of *Going Hungry*, a collection of

essays on eating disorders. "To read *Going Hungry* is to suspect an effort has been made to convince us there is no such thing as a superficial anorexic, no creature whose radical self-regulation comes unaccompanied by an impressive imagination or intelligence." Was this—an overestimation of sensitivities, a be-atification—my particular problem? I'm not sure. In the depths of my disorder, I didn't regard myself as a fragile poet-fairy or believe I could paint with all the colors of the wind.* But perhaps the myths of beauty girdling anorexia fed into how I idealized my *sister*, how I assumed that she presided over aesthetic secrets I'd never understand. And I certainly permitted the voice of the disease to mingle confusingly with my parents', so that I ended up ascribing to them the hate I sometimes felt for myself. A kind of self-protective/self-destructive logic drove me to pin my family and me on a storyboard.

The anorexic impulse to lyricize one's illness is a prescription for estrange-ment, for controlling and muffling the messy truths about who we are. Despite its promise of expressiveness, it is the enemy of writing. It is certainly the enemy of living. We need to tackle the false narratives clustered around eating disorders in our culture—clichés that vex and complicate treatment, contribut-ing to low recovery rates and a frightening death toll. By looking harder at both the literature and the science of anorexia, we can expose where the plotlines conflict, where the self-deception and self-sabotage sneak in.

The most specific thing I can contribute is my story. I want to tell it as honestly and accurately as I can.

Anorexia is one of nature's bleaker illustrations of "monkey see, monkey do."* I learned how to torture my portion of dinner—to endlessly deconstruct and rebuild and microwave it—from my sister. I also learned from her how to sit up straight, even in front of the television, clenching my abs and jiggling my legs. Most of all, I learned to say no, over and over, regardless of rhyme or reason or incentive or penalty. *No*, I will not eat starch. *No*, I will not have another bite of chicken. *No*, I do not want dessert or breakfast or lunch; I am not hungry; I will not use my common sense; *no, no, no*. I am sure E picked up equally delightful tics from me. Her methods were openly antagonistic, mine more deceitful. I used to throw away food, hiding it in napkins or slipping it to the dog. ("K is Ziggy's *favorite*," Mom would tease as our flop-eared pit-bull mix trailed me around the kitchen. "I love you too, buddy!" I'd trill, while fixing him with a lethal stare: *Not. One. Fucking. Word.*)

The contagion also spreads through language. The charge that anorexia memoirs are "how-to manuals in disguise" is well-established by now: Writers from Emma Woolf (Virginia's* great-niece) to teens on eating disorder-related Internet forums have faced criticism for wreathing their anorexia stories in beckoning particulars: minutes on the treadmill, target weights attained, calories consumed. Thanks to the disease's competitive nature, these tidbits, ostensibly offered as warnings, can read as inspiring benchmarks or even veiled instructions. Recalling her student-sensei relationship with Marya Hornbacher's *Wasted*, "a cornerstone, a beloved, poetic contemporary classic" of eating disorder literature, the writer Kelsey Osgood reports that she "incorporated some of Hornbacher's tricks into my own weight loss repertoire."

15 　　More fundamentally, though, anorexia is an inveterate liar whose grand theme is your identity. Because the channels through which it flows and acts are so often linguistic, the disorder has inspired a perverse literary tradition, replete with patron saints (Catherine of Siena, herself a twin, who recorded the details of her miraculous asceticism in letters she sent to aspiring female mystics), glamorous elders (Emily Dickinson, Anne Sexton, Sylvia Plath), tropes (fairies, snow), and devices (paradox, irony, the unreliable narrator). "Anorexic literature" commits the inherently literary, self-mythologizing qualities of anorexia to paper. From the novels of Charles Dickens to the poetry of Louise Glück, it contains and reproduces something more amoebic, perhaps more dangerous, than dieting tips: a specific persona and sensibility.

　　Who is this gauntly bewitching character? Ask Persephone, the goddess undone by six pomegranate seeds,[2] or one of opera's frail, tubercular heroines. Ask Sia[3] singing scratchy-voiced about hurt and smallness, or even Tinker Bell,* wasp-waisted, gossamer-winged, sacrificing her body for love and literally a goner if we don't clap for her. I don't mean to be snide: The eating-disordered quest for an audience speaks more to profound self-alienation than to any diva tendencies. Anorexia is the mental health equivalent of the red shoes that make you dance until you die.[4] It is a performance—of femininity, of damage, of power—that turns into a prison. The choreography becomes so absorbing that you can no longer access your own will or desires. You may require an external party to confirm for you that you exist.

　　We've long linked pathological thinness to profundity or poetic sensitivity. The roots of the romance go back to Catherine, who felt closer to God when she stopped eating and later, unable to consume food in spite of herself, considered her affliction holy. If excess flesh on a woman implied gluttony (a sin) or pregnancy (a shame), emaciation helped demonstrate the soul's dominion over the body. Anorexia mirabilis—the saintly loss of appetite—signaled an

---

2　　*Persephone ... seeds*　In Greek mythology, Persephone was abducted to the underworld, where she was tricked into eating pomegranate seeds before being allowed to leave. Because she had eaten food in the underworld, she was obliged to return there every year; her absence from the world of the living causes winter.

3　　*Sia*　Australian singer-songwriter (b. 1975).

4　　*red shoes ... you die*　Element in the Hans Christian Andersen fairy tale "The Red Shoes."

embrace of Christ-like abnegation[5] and suffering, or else a spirituality too pure to incline toward earthly pleasures.

And guess what? The archetype of the fasting mystic had a daughter. Equally lovely, equally slender—in her the delicacy of spirit won out once more over the coarseness of tissue. She rebelled against her mother by applying her native rigor not to prayer, but to an artistic sort of femininity. Think Jane Eyre, "delicate and aerial," or Elizabeth Gaskell's Ruth, "little" and "beautiful lithe." Consider Dorothea Brooke from *Middlemarch*,[6] her "hand and wrist … so finely formed that she could wear sleeves not less bare of style than those in which the Blessed Virgin appeared to Italian painters." That Mary* reference is not coincidental—like her mom, the new anorexic was pure and asexual. Yet she was also a creator, driven and intense. As Florence Nightingale wrote in 1852: "If [a woman] has a knife and fork in her hands during three hours of the day, she cannot have a pencil or brush." The new anorexic's hands overflowed with pencils and brushes. When she suffered, her suffering became oil paintings, poetry....

In *Going Hungry*, young adult author Francesca Lia Block equates anorexia with "that perfect blend of angelic and demonic—the faerie. Ethereal, delicate, able to fly." She recalls her time under the sprite's spell in an outrageously irresponsible bout of lyricism: "I stared out the windows at the twisting, starving trees, the silvery, sorrowful sky. I wrote strange, surreal poetry. My father stopped at a Dairy Queen, and I ate a vanilla cone. It tasted fearsome and frightening. Like mortality."

It makes me wish there were a Bad Sex in Fiction award, but for thinspo.[7] And yet—who was one of my favorite authors as a preteen? I remember 1999, when I was 11 years old, my whole being magnetized to Block's waifish bohemians, her purple-haired witch babies and genie changelings. I remember the spicy explosions of jacaranda, the porch scents of tangerine and cinnamon, all the deferred deliciousness of imaginary pleasure. Block recounts "a kiss about apple pie a la mode with the vanilla creaminess melting in the pie heat. A kiss about chocolate, when you haven't eaten chocolate for a year." Why didn't it strike me as weird that she always used food metaphors to describe nonfoods? That her protagonists were unfailingly languid and small-boned and lean? Most of all, I remember the moment in *The Hanged Man* when the heroine declares: "I will be thin and pure like a glass cup." A glass cup! It seemed impossibly

20

---

5   *abnegation*   Self-sacrifice.

6   *Jane Eyre … Middlemarch*   Jane Eyre, Ruth, and Dorothea Brooke are all characters in nineteenth-century novels.

7   *thinspo*   Thinspiration, a source of motivation for someone with very low body weight goals.

poetic. This was years before Alice Gregory poked fun at Block in the *New Yorker* for composing "laughably elliptical passages that read like demented ads for diamonds or bottled water."

Though their effect is hard to quantify, "a lot of war stories and memoirs out there … glorify the specialness and suffering of anorexia," says Dr. Angela Guarda, director of the Johns Hopkins Eating Disorders Program. "Anecdotally, patients often acknowledge that these writings romanticize the disorder," and that "reading them can be triggering and worsen their ED."[8] While the actual disease is not glamorous at all, Guarda reiterates (do you remember the boring calorie records from Lena Dunham's *Not That Kind of Girl*? Imagine them as the script for your entire life), "the idea of anorexia often is." Doctors at Johns Hopkins generally discourage patients from reading most autobiographical accounts of eating disorders, including the not-inconsiderable portion written by authors who "describe themselves as recovered and appear to still be ill."

But what happened with me and Block felt like a slightly different thing. I wasn't anorexic (yet), she wasn't writing an anorexia memoir (explicitly), and I'm not sure how anyone could have known to intervene.

Sadness is "interesting," notes Leslie Jamison in her magisterial essay on female pain, "and sickness [is] its handmaiden, providing not only cause but also symptoms and metaphors: a wracking cough, a wan pallor, an emaciated body." Children want desperately to be interesting. Block's slender, graceful wraiths with their dark secrets appealed to my ambition and sense of drama, not to mention my kiddie narcissism. Here's one Blockian character indulging in a Petrarchan inventory[9] of her own gaunt figure: "My shoulders, my collarbone, my rib cage, my hip bones like part of an animal skull, my small thighs. In the mirror my face is pale and my eyes look bruised. My hair is pale and thin and the light comes through." *Bones, small, mirror, hair, pale, eyes, thin, light.* The single syllables stream by like stars, all of them smooth, bright, reflective, or feminine. The hair's thinness allows the light in. Projecting myself into that body, I think I loved the implication that someone might pay close enough attention to me to worry about my collarbone.

Was my collarbone interesting, though? Did it "unfurl like a bird's wing"? …

25   Maybe Louise Glück could teach me how to be beautiful.

That's what I thought in college, when I signed up for my first poetry class. The conscious hope was probably closer to *Maybe Louise Glück can teach me how to write beautifully*, but, in practice, they amounted to the same thing.

---

8   *ED*   Eating disorder.

9   *Petrarchan inventory*   The Italian writer Francesco Petrarca (1304–74) is best known for his sonnets, some of which describe the attributes of Laura, the object of his unrequited love.

If Block embodies the anorexic sensibility at its most childish and theatrical, then the poetry of Glück (another *Going Hungry* contributor) gives it a mature shape. Excising and refusing her way into loveliness, Glück distills in her first few books something of the anorexic mindset. She distrusts flourish, noise, and glitter. She sends critics scrambling for stern phrases like "lean intensity" and "exacting precision." Just as an anorexic returns again and again to the same menu ingredients, the same routines, Glück shuffles and reshuffles her ascetic hand of nouns: *pond, ice, hill, moon, stars.* These early poems read as meticulous renunciations, careful puncturings undertaken in order to pare back the many false things from the few true ones.

Depressed and isolated in my post-college eating disorder, I dwelt obsessively on a trio of lines from "Persephone the Wanderer": "Unlike the rest of us, she doesn't know/ what winter is, only that/ she is what causes it." For me, it gave anorexia the status of a season, dignifying it with myth.

During my eating disorder years, I dreaded the chaos I might unleash at any moment, my secret flaws irrupting in plain sight. Anorexia told me I was gross but promised me safety as soon as I attained some enchanted state of skinniness. My perfect body would be my charm against interior disaster, sheltering me from the storms of the Underworld, enfolding me in eternal summer.

I starved, in other words, to acquire that old classical capability: metamorphosis. We tell stories for the same reason—to transform, elevate, and save. 30

A fantasy of anorexia: total expressivity. See the anorexic's sadness, legible on her anatomy, her inner life and emotions immediately present to anyone who looks at her. In a reverse transubstantiation, flesh becomes word, becomes character. Only the most authentic artist could possibly live her art like that.

By definition, a sign *means* something. What does a body mean? Tell me in words free of romance. *Free of blossom and subterfuge.* Tell me what winter is.

Anorexic literature, Jamison says, is "nostalgic for the belief that starving could render angst articulate." Its valorizing metaphors—"bone as hieroglyph, clavicle as cry"—ascribe "eloquence to the starving body, a kind of lyric grace."

I have nothing pretty to say about my body when I get too thin. My skin dulls and develops scaly patches; my oversized noggin bobs on my pencil-neck like an idiot balloon. Eating disorder memoirists love to fetishize hipbones, but I am here to tell you that mine made zero aesthetic contributions to my stomach area. My hair! Stringy, limp, bad for the Jews.[10]

---

10 *bad for the Jews* Phrase used (often tongue-in-cheek) by Jewish people, with reference to those Jews who, through their behavior or appearance, are considered to embarrass Jews as a group.

35   But unloveliness aside, instrumentalizing my body—presenting it for others to read like a character in a text—proved a highly effective way of losing myself. I don't mean that simply in the theoretical sense. I mean that the act of starving yourself is one of the most alienating experiences you can possibly have. Have you ever tried to do *anything* on a profoundly empty stomach? Despite myths about increased concentration, intensity, or imagination, you feel like a trace of grime on a countertop. Sure, hunger energizes you at first—experts disagree over whether hyperactivity in anorexics is primarily the result of hormonal cues or the conscious. But then the fatigue sets in. You feel like a torn net through which the thoughts pass, hazily. You cannot speak or write or do. Starving doesn't transform your life into one glorious act of self-expression. Starving silences who you really are.

A more scientific explanation for this is that anorexia eats your brain. As Arielle Pardes writes in *Vice*, "When your body is in a period of starvation, it uses the fattiest tissue first—which, in the absence of body fat, is the brain. The brain is literally broken down, piece by piece, causing mental fogginess, lack of concentration, and an inability to focus." (Luckily, such volume loss is usually reversible with weight restoration.) Starvation also reduces cortical blood flow, further slowing the cognitive machinery and allowing anorexia's distortions to take root....

In 1873, the French doctor Charles Lasègue and the English physician Sir William Gull (who personally practiced on Queen Victoria) independently published papers defining *anorexia nervosa*, the nervous loss of appetite. For Lasègue, the anorexic was "a young girl, between fifteen and twenty years of age," who "suffers from some emotion which she avows or conceals." "Generally," he continued, the symptoms relate "to some real or imaginary marriage project, to a violence done to some sympathy, or to some more or less conscient[11] desire." In a cosmically apt coincidence, Lasègue also fathered the Waldman-friendly concept of folie à deux—"a delusion or mental illness shared by two people in close association."

Gull, for his part, prescribed "various remedies ... the preparation of cinchona, the bichloride of mercury, syrup of the phosphate of iron, citrate of quinine and iron." Alas, "no perceptible effect followed their administration."

So dawned a long history of people getting anorexia wrong. We still don't know exactly what causes it. In part this is because the type of controlled longitudinal study that would shed light on etiology is too vast and expensive for most researchers to undertake. (Anorexia afflicts only 1 percent of the population, so any experiment tracking a randomized group of people to see

---

11 *conscient* Conscious.

who falls ill would need thousands of participants to get significant results.) It's also because the U.S. underfunds eating disorder research: The National Institutes of Health allots only $1.20 in research dollars per affected ED patient, compared with, for instance, $159 per patient with schizophrenia (which also affects about 1 percent of the population). Mostly, though, it's because eating disorders are savagely complicated, the consummation of multiple interwoven genetic, environmental, and cultural factors. The history of anorexia is a history of simplistic explanations—of false narratives—that derive their staying power from the tiny grain of truth each one contains.

A Selection of Anorexia Narratives through History

Hysterical Women

As Julie Hepworth points out in her book *The Social Construction of Anorexia Nervosa*, the terms *anorexia* and *hysteria* were used interchangeably throughout the late 19th century. Lasègue proposed that hysteria disrupted the "gastric centre," prompting food aversion. Gull originally referred to anorexia as *hysteria apepsia*, on the theory that neurasthenic[12] women suffered from a pepsin imbalance that dulled their appetites. In his 1884 lecture series *On Visceral Neuroses*, physician T. Clifford Allbutt suggested that, like hysterics, fasting girls were responding histrionically—aka *overreacting*—to the day's gender imperatives. The "invincible distaste for food," he said, reflected a normal desire to tame "animal propensities" gone awry in "high-spirited" patients.

40

An Endocrine Disorder

In the early 1900s, doctors performed an autopsy on an anorexic woman and discovered a shrunken pituitary gland. Hypothesizing that the disease arose from low levels of pituitary hormone, they proposed a treatment in which eating-disordered patients were injected with pituitary extract. When that didn't work, the sufferers had their bloodstreams flooded with thyroid juices, insulin, and estrogen. It took until 1940 or so for lackluster results—apparently hormone shots *can* help treat an eating disorder, but only when they are accompanied by high-calorie foods—to discredit the notion of anorexia as a purely endocrinological illness.

---

12 *neurasthenic* Suffering from neurasthenia, a condition whose symptoms include lethargy, headache, and anxiety.

Fear of Pregnancy
In 1939, George H. Alexander, a Freudian analyst from Rhode Island, published a paper describing an anorexic teenager who started dieting after two of her classmates got pregnant and left school. Alexander theorized that his patient was in thrall to a paranoid fantasy in which "fat" equaled "expecting" and food symbolized an "impregnating agent." The suspicion that anorexic individuals starved themselves to quell an irrational terror of pregnancy took two decades to shake.

Controlling Moms, Indifferent Dads
With the rise of family systems therapy in the '60s and '70s, doctors tried to divine answers to the anorexia question in the entrails of household dynamics. Eating disorders were (and occasionally are still) viewed as veiled power struggles between compliant kids and pressuring mothers. [Anna Krugovoy] Silver, the author of *Victorian Literature and the Anorexic Body*, writes that anorexia "is, at least in part, a power stratagem in which a girl refuses to eat in order to gain influence and attention in her family." The typical family in this scenario is "controlling and non-confrontational," the girl "a goal-oriented perfectionist" who "often has a problematic, conflicted relationship with her mother."

The Patriarchy
In the '80s, feminism transformed our understanding of anorexia once more. Books like Susie Orbach's *Fat Is a Feminist Issue* and Naomi Wolf's *The Beauty Myth* raised awareness about the unrealistic representations of female bodies in media. Eating disorders became potent symbols of the way society expected women to turn themselves into broken ornaments, shrinking their identities and ambitions. "By the '90s," wrote *Going Hungry* editor Kate Taylor in *Slate* in 2005, "health-class presentations on eating disorders often involved rifling through magazines and discussing how unreasonably skinny the models were." If we could only change societal beauty standards and diet culture, we could defeat anorexia for good.

45   None of these narratives are entirely without merit. Hormones probably *do* play a role in eating disorders. Many women get sick on the threshold of puberty, which has led doctors to isolate estrogen as a possible precipitating factor. Both leptin (a satiety hormone synthesized in fat tissue) and ghrelin (a hunger hormone produced in the stomach and pancreas) are processed by the insula, an area of the brain that tends to malfunction in eating-disordered patients. Individuals with anorexia also demonstrate elevated cortisol levels, though their heightened stress could as easily be a corollary of starvation as a cause.

And it is true that some anorexia patients have overbearing mothers. It is equally true that watching your daughter starve and exercise herself to death tends to activate your inner control freak. One study found similarly chaotic and unhelpful parental behavior at family dinners involving anorexic children and those involving children with cystic fibrosis, a condition in which the patient is often too sick to eat.

And it's true that a desire to forestall growing up and all the adult milestones that entails—sex, marriage, pregnancy—might inspire a girl to start dieting. So could saturation in our thin-is-in culture. Any impetus that gets a teenage girl to begin restricting calories can trip the biological wire that detonates an eating disorder.

That's what these explanations leave out: *There is a biological wire.* Otherwise, why wouldn't we all have anorexia, inundated as we are in Photoshop, thigh gaps,* and ambient pressure to look like Cara Delevingne?[13] (As Guarda, of the Johns Hopkins Eating Disorders Program, told me: "The same rain falls on everyone, which points to some degree of individual vulnerability.")

Conversely, why would anorexia erupt in Ghana and among the Amish, where super-skinny frames aren't in vogue? And if eating disorders were truly "about" control and remastering the self—especially in the face of a domineering parent—then how should we parse all the girls with perfectly happy, healthy childhoods who nevertheless fall under anorexia's spell? I don't remember feeling lost or powerless when I started dieting at 17. I was simply terrified of gaining weight.

The facts are: You are seven to 11 times more likely to become anorexic if you have a first-degree relative with the disease, and identical twins run a 50 to 80 percent larger risk of developing anorexia than fraternal twins. Individuals who go on to develop anorexia also exhibit common personality traits, such as introversion, perfectionism, sensitivity to criticism, vigilance, competitiveness, obsessiveness, and risk-aversion.

Biology is the piece of the puzzle that most directly contradicts societal myths about anorexia, and it's the one that has the hardest time finding traction. Drawing instead on family systems theory, doctors with young anorexic patients often recommend what National Institute of Mental Health Director Tom Insel calls a "parentectomy": "exclusion of the parents or caregivers from … the treatment plan." But studies in both the U.S. and the U.K. show that "outcomes appear much better if parents are empowered and included." Likewise, many therapists treat eating disorders by attempting to crack some psychological code—to unearth the mysterious psychic forces driving the illness. They should be prioritizing nutrition and weight restoration: Regardless of what precipitated

50

---

13 *Cara Delevingne* English actor and fashion model (b. 1992).

the initial dieting behavior, a lion's share of anorexic symptoms—from erratic hunger cues to obsessive thinking—result from physical changes to the starving brain. In other words, much of what propels anorexia is simply anorexia....

Sometimes I start eating, and I can't stop.

This part is hard to write, but it is also part of the narrative. As I dipped in and out of recovery after college, my disorder started to morph, losing any illusory claim it could have made on wan, heroic reserve or glamorous pallor or what have you. I stored up my denials. Then I binged on whole boxes of cereal, cartons of cookie dough ice cream, vats of raisins stirred into Nutella or hot fudge. The beginnings of these episodes were glorious—radiant increments of permission in a fascistically regulated life, Bosch gardens[14] in which all the naked people were made of marzipan. But the middles and ends were crushing. The conviction, post binge, that you are the most disgusting, worthless, execrable creature on Earth is total, as consuming a psychic pain as I have ever experienced. I'd walk to work wondering why people weren't throwing things at me. If a colleague was kind, I'd feel so ashamed and undeserving my eyes would tear up. Time after time, the emotional fallout from bingeing proved so excruciating I would vow to never, *never*, do it again. And then—surprise!—I would.

This twist in the anorexia story often goes untold, because it doesn't harmonize with the martyr-romance of the eating disorder. But overeating is a common response to the physiological and psychological stresses of starvation: More than one-half of anorexics will flirt with bulimia or binge-eating disorder on their path to recovery. "Restricting makes food more rewarding," says Carrie Arnold, author of *Decoding Anorexia: How Breakthroughs in Science Offer Hope for Eating Disorders*. "After billions of years of evolution, our brains and bodies *really* don't want to starve." The chronically hungry contend with a primal drive not only to ease their immediate pangs but to counteract profound nutritional deficits. As Arnold explains, "a flashing neon sign in the eating disordered brain is saying GORGE NONSTOP." For the most part, people with anorexia prove adept at ignoring it—until they don't....

55   I used to flinch at that photograph of my sister and me in our bathing suits. Now I come back to it with questions in my hands. E was always perfectionistic and risk-averse—the anorexic profile. I spent so much time resenting her for

---

14 *Bosch gardens*   Refers to the Hieronymous Bosch painting *The Garden of Earthly Delights*, which depicts fantastical landscapes occupied by nude people and bizarre creatures.

"choosing" to act out her eating disorder. But looking at the image with more than a decade of hindsight, I feel like she never even had a chance.

I was the daughter who wasn't allowed to touch the coloring books because I just scribbled all over them. And yet I had done this—I had seen what E's anorexia had wrought, and I had decided: *me too*. I had skipped meals and counted calories and performed crunches until the illness reached through the mirror and grabbed me and it was too late. Were my parents right that (if I'm keeping score) I was the truly sick one? The girl without as potent a genetic predisposition who nevertheless called down the demon, mustered it through sheer force of will?

Then I look at the picture for a third time, and something else jumps out at me. E and I are both smiling hugely. We're *happy*. She's rigid, and I'm sloppy, but neither of us is sick.

Though it makes me sad, I love to imagine the alternate world in which the W twins never got anorexia, in which no circumstance held a match to our biological kindling and convulsed the lives we should have led. I love to imagine all the things we would have accomplished already, the relationships we would have nourished. I love to envision my mom and dad without the lines of worry on their faces from years of beseeching their daughters to eat, the relaxed holiday visits, the quirky interests we've all cultivated in so much time *not* spent squalling about food. I picture E and me standing next to each other, as adults, our bond unbroken, looking like two parts of a whole, two people who know each other's secrets.

Memory, though, has furnished me with the artifacts I have, and I can't help seeing them through the gauze of the old story. I kneel on the floorboards of this attic and look into a box, one containing knickknacks from a gentler past: my dad's sweaty, post-tennis bear hugs; the sound of my mom puttering around the kitchen in the morning as she brews coffee. Gingerly I take out and examine the delicate things. Each is light as an insect, its surface worn and luminous with use. I stare at the box, sadness opening in me like a flower. I am frozen, and on the stair I hear the footsteps of my life.

(2015)

Dawn Marie Dow

The Deadly Challenges of Raising African American Boys:

Navigating the Controlling Image of the "Thug"

The following article by sociologist Dawn Marie Dow appeared in the April 2016 issue of the academic journal Gender and Society; *it had been published online on the journal's website earlier that year.*

ABSTRACT

Through 60 in-depth interviews with African American middle- and upper-middle-class mothers, this article examines how the controlling image of the "thug"* influences the concerns these mothers have for their sons and how they parent their sons in light of those concerns. Participants were principally concerned with preventing their sons from being perceived as criminals, protecting their sons' physical safety, and ensuring they did not enact the "thug," a form of subordinate masculinity. Although this image is associated with strength and toughness, participants believed it made their sons vulnerable in various social contexts. They used four strategies to navigate the challenges they and their sons confronted related to the thug image. Two of these strategies—experience and environment management—were directed at managing characteristics of their sons' regular social interactions—and two—image and emotion management—were directed at managing their sons' appearance. By examining parenting practices, this research illuminates the strategies mothers use to prepare their sons to address gendered racism through managing the expression of their masculinity, racial identity, and class status.

I interviewed Karin, a married mother, in her apartment while she nursed her only child. Karin let out a deep sigh before describing how she felt when she learned the baby's gender:

> I was thrilled [the baby] wasn't a boy. I think it is hard to be a black girl and a black woman in America, but I think it is dangerous and

sometimes deadly to be a black boy and black man. Oscar Grant[1] and beyond, there are lots of dangerous interactions with police in urban areas for black men … so I was very nervous because we thought she was a boy.... I was relieved when she wasn't. It is terrible, but it is true.

Karin's relief upon learning her child was not a boy underscores how intersections of racial identity, class, and gender influence African American middle- and upper-middle-class mothers' parenting concerns. They are aware their children will likely confront racism, often start addressing racism during their children's infant and toddler years (Feagin and Sikes 1994; Staples and Johnson 1993; Tatum 1992, 2003), and attempt to protect their children from racially charged experiences (Uttal 1999). Responding to these potential experiences of racism, parents believe giving their children the skills to address racism is an essential parenting duty (Feagin and Sikes 1994; Hill 2001; Staples and Johnson 1993; Tatum 1992, 2003). Although the participants in this research were middle- and upper-middle-class, and thus had more resources than their lower-income counterparts, they felt limited in their abilities to protect their sons from the harsh realities of being African American boys and men in America.

Research demonstrates that race and gender influence how African Americans are treated by societal institutions, including schools (Eitle and Eitle 2004; Ferguson 2000; Holland 2012; Morris 2005; Pascoe 2007; Pringle, Lyons, and Booker 2010; Strayhorn 2010), law enforcement (Brunson and Miller 2006; Hagan, Shedd, and Payne 2005; Rios 2009), and employment (Bertrand and Mullainathan 2004; Grodsky and Pager 2001; Pager 2003; Wingfield 2009, 2011). African American children also experience gendered racism (Essed 1991). African American boys face harsher discipline in school and are labeled aggressive and violent more often than whites or African American girls (Eitle and Eitle 2004; Ferguson 2000; Morris 2005, 2007; Pascoe 2007). Although African American families engage in bias preparation with their children (McHale et al. 2006), the content of that preparation and how gender and class influence it is often not researched. Anecdotal evidence depicts African American parents as compelled to provide gender- and race-specific guidance to their sons about remaining safe in various social interactions, even within their own,

---

1   On New Year's Day 2010, Johannes Mehserle, a white Bay Area Rapid Transit police officer, fatally shot Oscar Grant, an African American teenager, in Oakland. During the incident, Grant was unarmed, lying face-down on the train platform, and had been subdued by several other officers. On July 8, 2010, Mehserle was found guilty of involuntary manslaughter, not the higher charges of second-degree murder or voluntary manslaughter (McLaughlin 2014). [author's note]

often middle-class, neighborhoods (Graham 2014; Martinez, Elam, and Henry 2015; Washington 2012).

5   This article examines how African American middle- and upper-middle-class mothers raising young children conceptualize the challenges their sons will face and how they parent them in light of these challenges. I focus on mothers because they are often primarily responsible for socializing young children (Hays 1996), and specifically on middle- and upper-middle-class African American mothers because they typically have more resources to address discrimination than do lower-income mothers. Indeed, one might assume that these mothers' resources would enable them to protect their sons from certain challenges. African American mothers are more likely to engage in the racial socialization of younger children and to prepare children to address experiences of racism than are African American fathers (McHale et al. 2006; Thornton et al. 1990). They are also more likely to be single and, thus, principally responsible for decisions related to their children's educational, social, and cultural resources and experiences. Although there has been substantial public discourse about African American mothers' ability to teach their sons to be men, there has been little systematic analysis of their involvement in these processes (Bush 1999, 2004). Also, cultural stereotypes of uninvolved African American fathers overshadow research demonstrating their more active involvement (Coles and Green 2010; Edin, Tach, and Mincy 2009; Salem, Zimmerman, and Notaro 1998).

     Although masculinity is associated with strength, participants' accounts of their parenting practices revealed their belief that the thug image made their sons vulnerable in many social interactions. Participants feared for their sons' physical safety and believed their sons would face harsher treatment and be criminalized* by teachers, police officers, and the public because of their racial identity and gender. Their accounts revealed four strategies used to navigate these challenges, which I term experience, environment, emotion, and image management.

RACED, CLASSED, AND GENDERED PARENTING CHALLENGES

Gendered Racism and Controlling Images

Scholars have examined how race, class, and gender influence African Americans' experiences in various settings (Ferguson 2000; Morris 2005, 2007; Wingfield 2007, 2009). African American boys and girls experience different levels of social integration within suburban schools (Holland 2012; Ispa-Landa 2013). Boys are viewed as "cool" and "athletic" by classmates and are provided more opportunities to participate in high-value institutional activities, while girls are viewed as aggressive and unfeminine, and are provided with fewer similar opportunities (Holland 2012; Ispa-Landa 2013). Despite having somewhat positive experiences with peers, boys' encounters with teachers and administrators are fraught, as educators often perceive them as aggressive, violent, and potential criminals (Ferguson 2000; Morris 2005; Pascoe 2007). Compared to whites and African American girls, African American boys are disciplined more severely in school (Welch and Payne 2010), and their in-school discipline is more likely to lead to criminal charges (Brunson and Miller 2006).

African American boys are also more likely to have encounters with law enforcement than are whites or African American girls, and these interactions are more likely to have negative outcomes (Brunson and Miller 2006; Quillian, Pager, and University of Wisconsin-Madison 2000) and become violent (Brunson and Miller 2006). The news provides numerous examples of fatal shootings of unarmed African American teenage boys, often by white police officers and private citizens (Alvarez and Buckley 2013; McKinley 2009; Severson 2013; Yee and Goodman 2013). Initiatives like the White House-sponsored "My Brother's Keeper" are responding to an expansive body of research that demonstrates African American boys face disproportionate challenges to their success from schools, their communities, law enforcement, the workplace, and beyond (Jarrett and Johnson 2014).

Collins (2009) theorizes how controlling images function as racialized and gendered stereotypes that justify the oppression of certain groups and naturalize existing power relations, while forcing oppressed populations to police their own behavior. Scholars studying controlling images examine how these inaccurate depictions of black sexuality, lawfulness, temperament, and financial well-being are used to justify policies that disempower women of color (Collins 2004, 2009; Gilliam 1999; Hancock 2003; Harris-Perry 2011) and impact African Americans' experiences in their workplaces, school settings, and other social contexts (Beauboeuf-Lafontant 2009; Dow 2015; Ong 2005; Wingfield 2007, 2009). These images depict African American men as hypermasculine:* revering them as superhuman or reviling them as threats to be contained (Ferber 2007; Noguera 2008). Scholars suggest that African American men enact the thug, a version of subordinate masculinity associated with violence, criminality, and toughness, because they are not permitted to attain hegemonic[2] masculinity (Schrock and Schwalbe 2009). Indeed, African American men who enact alternative versions of manhood that are associated with being educated or middle class confront challenges to their masculinity and racial authenticity (Ford 2011; Harper 2004; Harris III 2008; Noguera 2008; Young 2011).

---

2   *hegemonic* Socially and/or politically dominant.

10   Expanding on this scholarship, I examine how the thug image influences African American middle- and upper-middle-class mothers' parenting concerns and practices when raising sons. Building on Ford's view that "black manhood refers to imagined constructions of self that allow for more fluid interactions in Black and nonblack, public and private social spaces" (Ford 2011, 42), I argue that this fluidity is not just permitted but required to protect black male bodies and manage their vulnerability in different contexts. Black manhood and double consciousness (Du Bois [1903] 1994) are complementary concepts because each requires individuals to see themselves through the broader society's eyes. These concepts also illuminate how individuals who are associated with privileged identities, such as "man" or "American," confront obstacles that prevent them from benefiting from those identities' privileges.

Emotional Labor and Identity Work

Scholarship on emotional labor and identity work examines how African Americans navigate stereotypes. Hochschild (2003) argues that individuals who perform emotional labor induce or suppress the display of certain feelings to produce specific emotional states in others, thereby contributing to their subordinate position. Studying a predominately white law firm, Pierce (1995) uncovers how men, but not women, garner rewards for expressing a range of negative emotions. Summers-Effler (2002) examines how "feeling rules" become associated with particular positions in society and the members of groups generally occupying those positions. Building on Hochschild's (2003) theories, scholars demonstrate that, fearing they will affirm controlling images, African Americans believe there is a limited range of emotions they can display in the workplace without confronting negative stereotypes, and thus feel less entitled to express discontent or anger (Jackson and Wingfield 2013; Wingfield 2007, 2011, 2013).

Historically, interactions between whites and African Americans have been guided by unspoken rules of conduct that signaled different status positions and maintained and reproduced a social structure that subordinated African Americans through acts of deference (Doyle 1937). These acts included African Americans using formal greetings to signal respect to whites, while whites used less formal greetings to signal their superiority (Doyle 1937). Violations of these rules resulted in frustration, anger, and violence from whites and anxiety, fear, and submission among African Americans (Doyle 1937). Rollins's (1985) research reveals how African American women employed as domestics suppressed their emotions and physical presence in interactions with white female employers. Indeed, adhering to specific feeling rules maintains and reproduces racial, class, and gender hierarchies, even as individuals circumvent them.

As African Americans traverse different economic and social strata that are governed by different rules, scholars identify how they manage the expression of their racial identity and class through code-switching (Anderson 1990), shifting (Jones and Shorter-Gooden 2003), identity work (Carbado and Gulati 2013), and cultural flexibility[3] (Carter 2003, 2006). Carter's (2003, 2006) and Pugh's (2009) research demonstrates that African American children and families, respectively, often necessarily retain some fluency in "low-status" cultural capital,[4] even as they ascend economically. Lacy's (2007) research also suggests that some middle-class African Americans emphasize their racial identity, class identity, or racially infused class identities, depending on social context, to gain acceptance. Although these scholars examine how African American middle-class children and families negotiate race and class, gender is not central to their analysis. This article complicates their scholarship by analyzing how race, class, and gender affect how mothers encourage their sons to express their racial identity and masculinity. Schrock and Schwalbe argue, "learning how to signify a masculine self entails learning how to adjust to audiences and situations and learning how one's other identities bear on the acceptability of a performance" (Schrock and Schwalbe 2009, 282). Mothers play an important part in this gendered, classed, and racialized socialization process (Schrock and Schwalbe 2009).

METHODS

This article is based on data from a larger project that examined how African American middle- and upper-middle-class mothers approach work, family, parenting, and child care. Participants were recruited using modified snowball sampling[5] techniques. Study announcements were sent via email to African American and predominately white professional and women's organizations. Announcements were made at church services and in bulletins, and were posted at local businesses and on physical or Internet bulletin boards of community colleges, local unions, and sororities.* Announcements were also posted to list

---

3   *code-switching*   Switching between linguistic styles;   *shifting*   In their book *The Double Lives of Black Women in America*, Jones and Shorter-Gooden suggest that black women "shift" in a variety of ways—modifying speech and appearance, for example, as they "shift 'White' as they head to work in the morning and 'Black' as they come back home each night";   *identity work*   In their research, Devon W. Carbado and Mitu Gulati explore ways in which the performance of the identities assumed, for example, in the workplace, requires work;   *cultural flexibility*   I.e., the flexibility to act as a part of different cultural and social groups.

4   *cultural capital*   Assets that are social, not financial.

5   *snowball sampling*   Method of obtaining a study sample in which study participants recruit their own acquaintances to also participate in the study.

servers catering to parents, mothers, or African American mothers. Participants who were interviewed were asked to refer others. Through these methods, 60 participants[6] were recruited to the study, of which 40 were raising sons only or sons and daughters. Aside from the opening quote describing a mother's relief upon learning she was not having a son, this analysis focuses on participants raising sons.

15   Interviews were conducted in person in a location of each participant's choosing, including her home or office, cafés or restaurants, and local parks. Interviews lasted from one hour to two and a half hours, and were conducted between 2009 and 2011. I asked participants about the families in which they were raised, becoming mothers, and their parenting concerns and practices. Before each interview, participants completed a Demographic Information Sheet that included questions about their marital status, education, total family income, and family composition. Table 1 lists participants' pseudonyms and demographic information.

All participants lived in the San Francisco Bay Area and were middle- or upper-middle-class as determined by their education and total family income. Participants attended college for at least two years, and their total annual family incomes ranged from $50,000 to $300,000. Participants' total family incomes were as follows: (1) 27 percent were between $50,000 and 99,000;

Table 1. Names and Interviewee Characteristics ($N = 60$).

	Name	Age	Occupation	Degree	Marital Status	Spouse or Domestic Partner's Degree	Number of Kids
1	Netia	27	SAHM	SC	S	N/A	1
2	Jameela	26	Administrative assistant	SC	S	N/A	1
3	Calliope	28	Graduate Student / SAHM[7]	BA	S	N/A	1
4	Heather	35	Administrator and teacher / SAHM	BA	D	N/A	3
5	Elizabeth	40	Program manager	MA	M	BA	1
6	Riana	36	Analyst	MA	S	N/A	1
7	Rochelle	35	Clerical / SAHM	AS	M	AS	3
8	Tracy	35	Paralegal	BA	M	BA	5
9	Hana	37	Part-time consultant / SAHM	MA	M	BA	2
10	Nia	30	Teacher	MA	M	BA	2
11	Monique	28	Social worker	MA	M	BA	1
12	Jennifer	34	Dentist	DDS	D	N/A	1
13	Karin	27	Writer / SAHM	MA	M	MA	1
14	Sharon	44	Program manager	BA	M	BA	2
15	Trina	25	Part-time teacher	MA	M	MA	1
16	Nora	40	Educator	PhD	M	MA	2
17	Brandy	45	Project manager	BA	M	HS	2
18	Cara	48	Nurse weekends / SAHM during week	MA	D	N/A	2
19	Vera	45	Dentist	DDS	M	MA	2
20	Mary	44	Educator / SAHM	MA	M	SC	2
21	Kera	34	SAHM	MA	M	SC	2

(Continued)

6   Sixty-five mothers were interviewed. Five were excluded because they did not meet the income and educational criteria of the study. [author's note]

7   She raised her nephew during his teen years with her, now deceased, husband. [author's note]

TABLE 1 (continued)

	Name	Age	Occupation	Degree	Marital Status	Spouse or Domestic Partner's Degree	Number of Kids
22	Farah	32	Academic	PhD	M	SC	2
23	Maya	37	Professor	PhD	M	BA	4
24	Reagan	45	Senior manager	BA	D	N/A	1
25	Sarah	36	Graduate student / SAHM	BA	M	MA	1
26	Sydney	32	Public health administrator	MA	M	MA	1
27	Mera	32	SAHM	MA	M	MA	2
28	Tamika	41	Freelance administrator / SAHM	BA	M	BA	1
29	Robinne	40	Administrator	MA	M	BA	1
30	Ann	49	Teacher coach	MA	M	SC	2
31	Audra	37	Meeting planner	BA	M	BA	2
32	Teresa	30	Project coordinator	BA	M	BA	2
33	Ashley	44	Project manager	MA	M	SC	1
34	Asa	40	Development director	BA	M	PhD	1
35	Lakeisha	35	Marketing manager	MA	M	MA	1
36	Claudette	34	Freelance paraprofessional / merchandiser / gym teacher/ substitute teacher / SAHM	BA	M	SC	2
37	Jessica	42	Administrator	BA	D	N/A	1
38	Alana	40	Probation officer	BA	M	BA	2
39	Chandra	41	Program coordinator	MA	D	N/A	2
40	Cheryl	39	Pediatrician	MD	M	JD	1
41	Charlene	33	Attorney	JD	M	SC	1

(Continued)

TABLE 1 (continued)

	Name	Age	Occupation	Degree	Marital Status	Spouse or Domestic Partner's Degree	Number of Kids
42	Essence	37	Health educator / program manager	MA	M	SC	1
43	Christine	43	Acupuncturist	MA	S	MA	1
44	Kristen	42	Attorney	JD	M	BA	1
45	Jordana	40	Marketing program manager	MA	M	BA	2
46	Kellie	44	SAHM	AS	M	MA	4
47	Karlyn	35	Research compliance manager	MA	S	N/A	2
48	Rachel	36	Operations manager	MA	M	BA	2
49	Tammy	37	Team leader	AS	M	BA	3
50	Rebecca	40	Educator	MA	W	N/A	1
51	Charlotte	40	Self-Eeployed / SAHM	MA	M	MA	4
52	Remi	36	Nurse	MA	M	BA	6
53	Harper	37	Child psychologist	MD	M	MA	1
54	Samantha	35	Human resources director	MA	M	MA	2
55	Claire	36	SAHM	PhD	M	MA	1
56	Ava	42	Project manager	MA	M	SC	2
57	Emma	34	Public relations project manager	BA	M	BA	1
58	Grace	30	Admissions director	SC	S	N/A	1
59	Hannah	45	Training manager	BA	DP	BA	2
60	Sophia	38	Grant writer	MA	S	N/A	1

NOTE: All names are pseudonyms. Occupation: SAHM -= stay-at-home mother.[8] Degree: AS = associate's degree; BA = bachelor's degree; DDS = doctor of dental medicine; HS = high school; JD = juris doctorate; MA = master's degree; MD = doctor of medicine; PhD = doctorate; SC = some college. Marital status: S = single; M = married; D = divorced; DP = domestic partner; Sep. = separated; W = widowed.

---

8   Notably, almost half of the participants who identified as stay-at-home mothers were employed in part-time to full-time jobs. [author's note]

(2) 23 percent were between $100,000 and $149,000; (3) 23 percent were between $150,000 and $199,000; and (4) 27 percent were between $200,000 and $300,000. The upper end of this income range is high by national standards; however, in the San Francisco Bay Area between 2006 and 2010, the median owner-occupied home value was $637,000 (Bay Area Census 2010). Home-ownership is an important marker of middle-class status (Sullivan, Warren, and Westbrook 2000). Participants at the upper end of this income range were among the few who could easily attain that marker. Half of the participants were homeowners and half were renters. Participants' ages spanned from 25 to 49 years. The majority of participants (63 percent) earned advanced degrees such as MD, JD, PhD, or MA, with 27 percent earning college degrees and 10 percent attending some college. Three-fourths of the participants were married or in a domestic partnership, and one-fourth were divorced, never married, or widowed. All participants were raising at least one child who was 10 years old or younger, as this research focused on mothers who are raising young children. Participants' employment status included working full-time or part-time, or not working outside of the home (i.e., stay-at-home mothers).

Using grounded theory[9] (Glaser and Strauss 1967) and the procedures and techniques described by Strauss and Corbin (1998), I transcribed interviews and coded them to identify and differentiate recurring concepts and categories. A key concept that emerged was the controlling image of the "thug," a version of subordinate masculinity identified in masculinity and black feminist scholarship. Some participants used the term "thug" or "thuggish." Others used language that referred to components of the thug, such as criminality, violence, and toughness. Outliers[10] within the data were examined to determine how they challenged or could be reconciled with emerging themes. My focus here on the accounts of mothers precluded a direct analysis of fathers' views, but fathers were involved in these strategies. This focus also precluded an analysis of how African boys and teenagers navigated these challenges themselves.

As a middle-class African American mother, I shared traits with my participants. These characteristics, in some ways, positioned me as an insider with participants and facilitated building rapport and their willingness to share information about their lives. This status also required that I refrain from assuming I understood a participant's meanings. I balanced building rapport with

---

9   *grounded theory*   Before Glaser and Strauss's 1967 book *The Discovery of Grounded Theory*, sociological theory was often developed in the abstract—without any data having been collected and analyzed; only after theories had been developed would they be tested against empirical evidence. The Glaser and Strauss approach advocated linking data collection and analysis to theory development throughout the process—in other words, grounding theory in evidence even as the theory is being developed.

10   *Outliers*   Pieces of evidence that do not follow the pattern of the main body of data.

guarding against making assumptions by probing for additional clarification when a participant suggested I understood something based on our shared background.

PROTECTING SONS FROM BABY RACISM AND CRIMINALIZATION

Although participants described parenting concerns that transcended gender and related to fostering other aspects of their children's identity, this article examines their specific concerns about raising sons. Participants' concerns included ensuring the physical safety of their sons in interactions with police officers, educators, and the public, and preventing their sons from being criminalized by these same groups.

Gender, Racial Identity, and Parenting

Generally, middle-class children are thought to live in realms of safety, characterized by good schools, an abundance of educational resources, and protection from harsh treatment from police, teachers, and the public. However, numerous scholars have demonstrated that despite the expansion of the African American middle class, its members face economic, social, residential, and educational opportunities that are substantively different from those of middle-class whites (Feagin and Sikes 1994; Lacy 2007; Pattillo 1999). Middle-class African Americans continue to face discrimination in lending, housing (Massey and Denton 1993; Oliver and Shapiro 1995; Sharkey 2014), and employment (Pager 2003). African American middle-class children often attend schools that are poorly funded, lack adequate infrastructure, and are characterized by lower academic achievement than their white counterparts (Pattillo 1999, 2007). These children are also more likely to grow up in neighborhoods with higher levels of crime and inferior community services as compared to their white counterparts (Oliver and Shapiro 1995; Pattillo 1999). Although participants recognized that their middle-class status afforded them additional resources, they believed that their sons' access to middle-class realms of safety were destabilized and diminished because of their racial identity and gender.

Charlotte, a married mother of four sons, who lived in an elite and predominately white neighborhood, held back tears as she described her fears about how others would respond to them:

> I look at the president.* I see how he is treated and it scares me. I want people to look at my sons and see them for the beautiful, intelligent, gifted, wonderful creatures that they are and nothing else. I do not want them to look at my sons and say, "There goes that Black guy," or hold onto their purse.

20

Similarly, Nia, a married mother of two sons, who lived in an economically diverse, predominantly African American neighborhood, described interactions with other families at local children's activities that she called "baby racism":

> From the time our first son was a baby and we would go [to different children's activities]. Our son would go and hug a kid and a parent would grab their child and be like, "Oh, he's going to attack him!" And it was just, like, "Really? Are you serious?" He was actually going to hug him. You see, like little "baby racism." ... I have even written to local parents' listservs to ask, "Am I imagining this ... ?" And the response was interesting. Almost all the black mothers wrote in, "You're not imagining this, this is real. You're going to have to spend the rest of your life fighting for your child." And all the white mothers said, "You're imagining it. It's not like that. You're misinterpreting it." And it was like, okay, so I'm not imagining this.

Charlotte and Nia, like other participants, believed that when African American boys participated in activities that were engaged in by predominantly white and middle-class families, their behavior faced greater scrutiny. Race and gender trumped class;* poverty and crime were associated with being an African American boy. Participants believed the process of criminalizing their sons' behaviors began at an early age, and was not confined to educational settings but was pervasive. Although participants had no way of knowing how others were thinking about their sons, numerous studies support their belief that African American boys' actions are interpreted differently in a range of settings (Ferguson 2000; Morris 2005; Pascoe 2007).

Participants also saw teachers and educators as potential threats to their sons' development. Karlyn, a single mother of a son and daughter, described her son's experience of being harshly disciplined at school:

> A teacher was yelling at my son because some girls reported that he cheated in Four Square.[11] ... I had to let her know "don't ever pull my son out of class for a Four Square game again.... And don't ever yell at my child unless he has done something horrible." ... I told the principal, "You know, she may not think she is racist but what would make her yell at a little black boy over a stupid Four Square game?" ... He said, "Oh my God, I am just so glad that you have the amount of restraint that you did because I would have been really upset." I said, "As the mother of a black son, I am always concerned about how he is treated by people."

---

11 *Four Square*   Game played on school grounds.

Like Karlyn, others relayed stories of educators having disproportionately negative responses to their sons' behavior, describing them as aggressive or scary, when similar behavior in white boys was described as more benign. Karlyn, and others, continuously monitored their sons' schools to ensure they received fair treatment. Ferguson's (2000) and Noguera's (2008) research supports their assessment, identifying a tendency among educators to criminalize the behavior of African American boys. Participants' middle-class status did not protect their sons from these experiences.

Mary, a married mother of a son and daughter, also believed her son faced distinct challenges related to his racial identity, class, and gender and sought out an African American middle- and upper-middle-class mothers' group to get support from mothers who were negotiating similar challenges. Mary described a conversation that regularly occurred in her mothers' group, revealing her worries about adequately preparing her son to navigate interactions with teachers and police officers:

> With our sons, we talk about how can we prepare them or teach them about how to deal with a society, especially in a community like Oakland, where black men are held to a different standard than others, and not necessarily a better one.... When you are a black man and you get stopped by the policeman, you can't do the same things a white person would do because they might already have some preconceived notions, and that might get you into a heap more trouble.... We talk about our sons who are a little younger and starting kindergarten. What do we have to do to make sure teachers don't have preconceived ideas that stop our sons from learning because they believe little brown boys are rambunctious, or little brown boys are hitting more than Caucasian boys?

It is worth emphasizing that although these participants were middle- and upper-middle-class African American mothers with more resources than lower-income mothers, these resources did not protect their sons from gendered racism. Also, middle-class mothers are depicted as viewing educators as resources (Lareau 2011), but these participants viewed educators as potential threats. They believed their sons' racial identity marked them as poor, uneducated, violent, and criminal, and they would have to actively and continuously challenge that marking and assert their middle-class status in mainstream white society—a version of the politics of respectability (Collins 2004). Some participants attended workshops aimed at helping them teach their sons to safely engage with teachers, police officers, and the public. Like the parents described by Lareau and McNamara (1999), some used race-conscious strategies and others used color-blind strategies to address concerns about gendered racism.

25

Although most participants believed their sons faced challenges related to the thug, a few did not. These participants attributed their lack of concern to their sons' racially ambiguous appearance. Kera, a married mother of two sons, said, "The way they look, they're like me. They could be damn near anything depending on how they put their hair.... I don't think they'll have the full repercussions of being a black man like my brothers or my husband." Kera's comments echo research suggesting that skin color differences impact African Americans' experiences in employment, school, and relationships (Hunter 2007).

Participants also believed their sons faced pressure to perform specific versions of African American masculinity that conformed to existing raced, classed, and gendered hierarchies. Nora, a married mother of a son and daughter, said, "There is a lot of pressure for black boys to assume a more 'thuggish' identity. There aren't enough different identity spaces for black boys in schools ... and so I want my kids to have choices. And if that's the choice, I might cringe ... but I would want it to be among a menu of choices." Elements of the thug, such as criminality, aggression, and low academic performance, recurred in participants' accounts as something they and their sons navigated. Scholars (Ong 2005; Wingfield 2007) have identified how African American adults negotiate controlling images, but Nora's comments underscore that these negotiations begin at a young age.

Given these pressures to perform specific versions of African American masculinity associated with poverty and criminality, participants tried to protect their sons from early experiences of subtle and explicit racism because of the potential impact on their identity formation. Sharon, a married mother of a son and daughter, captured a sentiment shared by many participants when she stated,

> Each time a black boy has a racially charged interaction with a police officer, a teacher, or a shop owner, those experiences will gradually start to eat at his self-worth and damage his spirit. He might become so damaged that he starts to believe and enact the person he is expected to be, rather than who he truly is as a person.

Participants believed their sons were bombarded by negative messages about African American manhood from the broader white society and, at times, the African American community. Participants worried about the toll these messages might take on their sons' self-perception as they transitioned to manhood. They steered their sons away from enacting the thug, but also observed an absence of other viable expressions of racially authentic middle-class masculinity.

Strategies to Navigate the Thug

Legal scholar Krieger (1995) argues that the law has a flawed understanding of racial prejudice and that, rather than being an active and explicit set of beliefs, racism operates by shaping our perceptions of behaviors. A loud white boy is viewed as animated and outgoing; a loud black boy is viewed as aggressive and disruptive (Ferguson 2000). Similar to the interracial interactions in the South that Doyle (1937) describes, participants believed that whites expected African American boys to adjust their behavior depending on the racial identity of the person with whom they were interacting. Participants walked a tightrope between preparing their sons to overcome the gendered racism they might confront and ensuring they did not internalize these views or use them as excuses to fail. Christine, who was engaged to be married and the mother of a son, explained that in teaching her son what it means to be an African American man, she wanted to ensure that he did not grow up "with that black man chip on the shoulder. Feeling we are weak. Whites have done something to us and we can't do something because of white people." Christine wanted her son to understand how some viewed him, but she tried to foster a version of double consciousness that emphasized his agency and discouraged him from feeling bitter toward whites, disempowered, or constrained by others' views.

Next, I outline the strategies participants used to navigate the thug image and teach their sons how to modulate their expression of masculinity, race, and class. Participants often preferred one strategy but they may have used other strategies, or a combination of strategies, during different periods of their sons' lives.

Experience and Environment Management

Participants used two explicitly race-, class-, and gender-conscious strategies to manage their sons' regular social interactions: experience and environment management. Experience management focused on seeking out opportunities for sons to engage in activities to gain fluency in different experiences—both empowering and challenging—of being African American boys and men. Environment management focused on monitoring their sons' regular social environment, such as their school or neighborhood, with the aim of excluding sources of discrimination. These environments were often primarily middle-class but diverse in terms of racial identity, religion, and sexual orientation. Participants often used environment management when children were preschool age to avoid early experiences of discrimination. Despite having additional resources, participants navigated a landscape of institutionalized child care, which they believed included racially insensitive providers.

Participants using experience management tried to help their sons acquire what they viewed as an essential life skill: the ability to seamlessly shift from communities that differed by race, class, and gender. Experience management involved shuttling sons to activities, such as Little League baseball, basketball, or music lessons, in a variety of neighborhoods comprising African Americans from different economic backgrounds. Participants also exposed sons to African American culture and history and African American men, including fathers, uncles, cousins, coaches, or friends, whom they believed expressed healthy versions of masculinity. Karlyn said, "I worry about my son because he is not growing up with the kind of 'hood' mentality* that me and his father had, but he will have to interact with those people." Karlyn's son was not completely ensconced within the safety of a middle-class community. She believed as her son traveled through his day—to school, riding on buses, walking down the street, going in and out of stores, and interacting with police officers and the public—he would be perceived in a range of different and primarily negative ways. Karlyn believed her son would have to adjust the expression of his masculinity, racial identity, and class to successfully interact with people from that "hood mentality"—a version of subordinate masculinity and people from other racial and class backgrounds. She believed that lacking regular experiences in settings like the one she grew up in put her son at a disadvantage in these situations. Karlyn sought out experiences to help her son learn to navigate a world that she believed viewed him primarily as an African American boy and potential troublemaker, rather than a good middle-class kid. She ensured that her son had regular contact with his father and other African American men. She also regularly discussed examples of clashes between African American men and the police with her son.

Maya, a married mother of four, also used experience management. She described how she and her husband exposed their son to alternative and, in her view, more positive ideals of masculinity:

> With our son, we definitely have a heightened level of concern, especially around public schools, about what it means to be a black male in this society.... [My] husband does stuff with him that is very much male socializing stuff.... But, it is worrisome to think about sending him into the world where he is such a potential target.... I know how to make a kid that does well in school and can navigate academic environments. My husband knows how to help young people—black young people—understand their position, how the world sees them and how they might see themselves in a different and much more positive way.

Through these experiences, out of necessity, participants aimed to help their sons develop a double consciousness—"a sense of always looking at one's self through the eyes of others" (Du Bois [1903] 1994, 5). Maya and her husband did this by teaching their son how others might perceive him while rejecting prevailing images of African American masculinity and crafting alternatives.

Environment management involved managing sons' daily social interactions by excluding specific kinds of exposures. Rachel, a married mother of a son and daughter, said, "My son thinks he is street-smart but he is used to being in an environment in which he is known. No one thinks of my son as a black boy, they think of him as my son, but when he goes out into the real world people will make assumptions about him." Rachel lived in a predominately white neighborhood with few other African American families. She believed her neighbors did not view her family as "the African American family," but simply as a family, and this protected her son from challenges associated with being an African American male in the broader society where he might be assumed to be part of the urban underclass. Charlotte, mentioned earlier, described her efforts to find a neighborhood with the right kind of community:

35

> When we lived in [a different predominately white suburb], none of the mothers spoke to me. Maybe they would wave but I was really taken aback by how shunned I felt. We were the only black family in the school and no one spoke [to us].... Here [another predominately white area], over the summer, people knew my name and I didn't know their name.... There was a feeling of welcome and friendliness from the group.... You know, I just worry so much for them. I want them to be accepted, and not judged, and not looked at like a black kid. I want people to look at them as "that is a good young man or a good boy." ... Maybe if they know my sons and me and my husband, it won't be "Oh, there are the black kids"; it will be "There is us."

Charlotte wanted her sons to have access to better resources and schools, and that translated to living in primarily white neighborhoods. Nonetheless, revealing the diversity in white settings, she looked for white neighborhoods where she believed her sons would not face discrimination. Charlotte hoped to transform her sons from "anonymous" African American boys, assumed to be up to no good, to "the kid next door." Being African American was accompanied by assumptions about lower-class status and criminality that participants sought to overcome. Charlotte's experience underscores how intersections of race, gender, and class are used to value individuals and the challenges her sons confronted to be seen as both African American and "good middle-class kids."

Participants living in economically diverse predominantly African American communities with higher crime rates faced particular challenges when using environment management. Jameela, a single mother of a son, explained, "I live in Richmond because it is more affordable, but I don't see a lot of parents like me. I keep a tight leash on my son because of where we live. I don't want him to get involved with the wrong element." Jameela, and participants living in similar environments, often did not let their sons play with neighborhood children. Her experiences highlight class divisions within African American communities and the intensive peer group monitoring parents engaged in when their residential choices were limited. These children's regular environment did not include their immediate neighborhood but was confined to controlled spaces, including their school, church, or other settings that were diverse, free of racial discrimination, and often primarily middle class.

Experience and environment management both focus on social interactions but with different aims. Experience management aims to inform sons through regular controlled activities about the challenges they may face as African American boys and men and teach them how to modify the expression of their masculinity, class, and racial identity. Environment management aims to reduce or eliminate the challenges of being an African American male so they are not the defining features of their sons' lives. These mothers tried to find or create bias-free environments that would not limit their sons' expression of their masculinity but worried about their sons' treatment outside of these "safe havens."

Image and Emotion Management

Participants also used image and emotion management to reduce the vulnerability they believed their sons experienced related to the thug image and to prevent them from being associated with poor urban African Americans. These strategies were also explicitly race, gender, and class conscious and focused on their sons' emotional expressions and physical appearance. Sons were encouraged to restrain their expressions of anger, frustration, or excitement lest others view them as aggressive or violent. Participants also counseled their sons to strictly monitor their dress and appearance so they would be viewed not as criminals but as middle-class kids.

40   Karlyn engaged in something she called "prepping for life" with her son. She said, "I talk to [my son] constantly. We do scenarios and we talk about stuff. I'll pose a situation, like say, if you are ever kidnapped, what do you do? If the police ever pull you over, how do you need to react? So we do scenarios for all of that, it's just prepping for life." It would not be unreasonable for a parent to instruct their child to view police officers as sources of help. What is striking about Karlyn's examples is that she viewed child predators and police officers as equally dangerous to her son. She used emotion management with the hope

that preparing her son for these scenarios would give him some agency* in his response in the moment.

Some participants looked for places where their sons could safely express "normal boy" behaviors while gaining control over those behaviors. Heather, a divorced mother of a son and two daughters described her plan to help her son control his emotions at school: "I'm hoping to get [my son] into enough relaxation-type yoga classes so he is a little bit calmer when he does go to school. I want to make sure he lets it all out in the play yard and activities after school." Through activities like yoga, karate, and meditation, these participants hoped their sons would learn to restrain their emotions, and that this ability would translate to their interactions with teachers, police officers, peers, and the public. Participants emphasized that there were appropriate times to express feelings and advised their sons to refrain from responding to discrimination in the moment, instead taking their time to determine the best approach. This often meant reframing race-related grievances in nonracial terms so they would be better received by white teachers and administrators. Although masculinity is associated with strength, participants believed their sons were vulnerable and did not have the freedom to exhibit certain feelings or behaviors.

Participants also encouraged their sons to engage in image management to avoid being viewed as thugs. Rebecca, a widow with one son who also raised her nephew in his teenage years, recounted discussions during which she counseled her nephew about how people interpreted his clothing:

> Things like him wearing his hoodie and the assumption that he is up to no good. I tried to explain that to him because he didn't understand. He said, "I am just wearing my hoodie." "But baby, I understand what you are doing, and there is nothing wrong with that, but if you walk through the [poor, primarily African American and high-crime] neighborhood near my school, we see something different." You know, just having to protect him and trying to shelter him from unnecessary stress and trauma.... You know, the sagging pants and all the things that teenage boys do that don't necessarily mean they are doing anything wrong..... Is it fair? No. Is it reality? Yes.

Rebecca's comments illustrate a parenting paradox. Even as Rebecca challenged the double standards that she believed were used to evaluate her nephew's and son's behavior and appearance, as a practical matter, she felt compelled to educate them about these different standards. At times, she counseled them to adhere to those standards for their own safety. Given the recurring news stories of unarmed African American boys shot by police officers and private citizens, Rebecca's approach seems reasonable. Participants believed their sons might be labeled thugs because of their attire, thus leaving them vulnerable to attacks from others. Participants could not prevent these interactions from happening, but wanted their sons to survive them.

CONCLUSION

This research was bookended* by two shooting deaths of unarmed African American males. The first, Oscar Grant, was shot in the back by Officer Johannes Mehserle while lying face-down on a Bay Area Rapid Transit platform (McLaughlin 2014). The second, Trayvon Martin, was pursued, shot, and killed by George Zimmerman, a neighborhood watch coordinator, while walking home in his father's "safe," middle-class, gated community (Alvarez and Buckley 2013). Despite being a child from that community, it was not safe for Mr. Martin. He was not viewed as a good middle-class kid, but was instead interpreted as a threat. Since these incidents, African American parents are increasingly sharing the concerns they have for their sons' safety. Associated Press writer Jesse Washington (2012) wrote a heart-wrenching but matter-of-fact editorial describing how he advises his son to behave in affluent neighborhoods and in interactions with police and others. These instructions may have damaged his son's spirit but increased his chance of remaining alive. Incidents like these reminded participants that their sons have different experiences with the public than do white boys and men.

Initiatives like My Brother's Keeper focus on heightening African American male youths' agency in their lives, often paying less attention to the societal constraints they face. Some might suggest that recent videos of unarmed African American boys and men being shot by officers are shedding light on those constraints and are compelling the US government to take a closer look at law enforcement's interactions with African American boys and men. These incidents draw attention to contradictions between American ideals and practices, underscoring the fact that solving these challenges is not just a matter of changing behavior or increasing resources. These concerns about safety and vulnerability transcend class and are produced by societal forces.

45 Although the practices of fathers were not directly examined, it is clear from participants' statements that they helped to execute these strategies. Nonetheless, given that African American fathers' parenting practices at times differ from those of mothers (McHale et al. 2006), future research might directly examine their concerns and strategies. Researchers might also examine how different intersections of race, class, and gender produce different forms of vulnerability and protection.

Existing research suggests that having a male body and access to masculinity confers privileges and protections that serve as a symbolic asset in social interactions. However, my research demonstrates that depending on its racialization, the male body can be a "symbolic liability." The thug image derives its power and strength from intimidation and is used to justify attacks on African American boys' and men's bodies and minds. Participants' additional labor to protect their sons and its raced, classed, and gendered nature is largely invisible to the people it is meant to make more comfortable. Despite having additional resources, participants and their sons were not immune to a social system that required them to police their behaviors, emotions, and appearance to signal to others that they were respectable and safe middle-class African American males. Ironically, by feeling compelled to engage in strategies that encouraged their sons to conform to stricter standards and engage in acts of deference, participants contributed to reproducing a social structure that subordinates African Americans. Their accounts show a continuing need for African Americans to have a double consciousness through which they understand how society views them. Their actions also suggest a tension between individual strategies of survival and strategies that challenge and transform existing gendered, classed, and raced hierarchies.

(2016)

NOTES

Author's Note: I am greatly indebted and grateful to Raka Ray, Barrie Thorne, Evelyn Nakano Glenn, Katie Hasson, Jennifer Carlson, Katherine Mason, Oluwakemi Balogun, Kimberly Hoang, Sarah Anne Minkin, Nazanin Shahrokni, Abigail Andrews, Jordana Matlon, and the members of Raka Ray's Gender Working Group for their guidance, encouragement, and incisive suggestions on previous drafts of this manuscript. I would also like to thank David Minkus, Deborah Lustig and Christine Trost, who served as the program directors for the Graduate Fellows Program at the Institute for the Study of Societal Issues during my fellowship period, and my cohort of graduate fellows for their contributions to improving an early version of this manuscript. I am also thankful to Joya Misra, Adia Harvey Wingfield, and the anonymous reviewers at *Gender & Society* for their insightful feedback and comments on this manuscript. An earlier version of this paper was presented at the 2015 American Sociological Association Annual Meeting.

REFERENCES

Alvarez Lizzett, Buckley Cara. 2013. Zimmerman is acquitted in Trayvon Martin killing. *The New York Times*, 13 July.

Anderson Elijah. 1990. *Streetwise: Race, class, and change in an urban community*. Chicago: University of Chicago Press.

Bay Area Census. 2010. http://www.bayareacensus.ca.gov/counties/alamedacounty.htm.

Beauboeuf-Lafontant Tamara. 2009. Behind the mask of the strong black woman: Voice and the embodiment of a costly performance. Philadelphia: Temple University Press.

Bertrand Marianne, Mullainathan Sendhil. 2004. Are Emily and Greg more employable than Lakisha and Jamal? A field experiment on labor market discrimination. *American Economic Review* 94:991–1013.

Brunson Rod K., Miller Jody. 2006. Gender, race, and urban policing: The experience of African American youths. *Gender & Society* 20:531–52.

Bush Lawson. 1999. *Can black mothers raise our sons?* 1st ed. Chicago: African American Images.

Bush Lawson. 2004. How black mothers participate in the development of manhood and masculinity: What do we know about black mothers and their sons? *Journal of Negro Education* 73:381–91.

Carbado Devon W., Gulati Mitu. 2013. *Acting white? Rethinking race in post-racial America*. New York: Oxford University Press.

Carter Prudence L. 2003. "Black" cultural capital, status positioning, and schooling conflicts for low-income African American youth. *Social Problems* 50:136–55.

Carter Prudence L. 2006. Straddling boundaries: Identity, culture, and school. *Sociology of Education* 79:304–28.

Coles Roberta L., Green Charles. 2010. *The myth of the missing black father*. New York: Columbia University Press.

Collins Patricia Hill. 2004. *Black sexual politics: African Americans, gender, and the new racism*. New York: Routledge.

Collins Patricia Hill. 2009. *Black feminist thought: Knowledge, consciousness, and the politics of empowerment*, 2nd ed., Routledge classics. New York: Routledge.

Dow Dawn. 2015. Negotiating "The Welfare Queen" and "The Strong Black Woman": African American middle-class mothers' work and family perspectives. *Sociological Perspectives* 58:36–55.

Doyle Bertram Wilbur. 1937. *The etiquette of race relations in the South: A study in social control*. Chicago: University of Chicago Press.

Du Bois William Edward Burghardt. (1903) 1994. *The souls of black folks*. New York: Gramercy Books.

Edin Kathryn, Tach Laura, Mincy Ronald. 2009. Claiming fatherhood: Race and the dynamics of paternal involvement among unmarried men. *Annals of the American Academy of Political and Social Science* 621:149–77.

Eitle Tamela McNulty, Eitle David James. 2004. Inequality, segregation, and the overrepresentation of African Americans in school suspensions. *Sociological Perspectives* 47:269–87.

Essed Philomena. 1991. *Understanding everyday racism*. New York: Russell Sage.

Feagin Joseph R., Sikes Melvin P. 1994. *Living with racism: The black middle-class experience*. Boston: Beacon Press.

Ferber Abby L. 2007. The construction of black masculinity: White supremacy now and then. *Journal of Sport & Social Issues* 31:11–24.

Ferguson Ann Arnett. 2000. *Bad boys: Public schools in the making of black masculinity, law, meaning, and violence*. Ann Arbor: University of Michigan Press.

Ford Kristie A. 2011. Doing fake masculinity, being real men: Present and future constructions of self among black college men. *Symbolic Interaction* 34:38–62.

Gilliam Franklin D. Jr.. 1999. The "Welfare Queen" experiment. *Nieman Reports* 53:49–52.

Glaser Barney G., Strauss Anselm L. 1967. *The discovery of grounded theory: Strategies for qualitative research, observations*. Chicago: Aldine.

Graham Lawrence O. 2014. I taught my black kids that their elite upbringing would protect them from discrimination. I was wrong. *The Washington Post*, 6 November.

Grodsky Eric, Pager Devah. 2001. The structure of disadvantage: Individual and occupational determinants of the black-white wage gap. *American Sociological Review* 66:542–67.

Hagan John, Shedd Carla, Payne Monique R. 2005. Race, ethnicity, and youth perceptions of criminal injustice. *American Sociological Review* 70:381–407.

Hancock Ange-Marie. 2003. Contemporary welfare reform and the public identity of the "Welfare Queen." *Race, Gender & Class* 10:31–59.

Harper Shaun R. 2004. The measure of a man: Conceptualizations of masculinity among high-achieving African American male college students. *Berkeley Journal of Sociology* 48:89–107.

Harris Frank III. 2008. Deconstructing masculinity: A qualitative study of college men's masculine conceptualizations and gender performance. *NASPA Journal* 45:453–74.

Harris-Perry Melissa V. 2011. *Sister citizen: Shame, stereotypes, and black women in America*. New Haven, CT: Yale University Press.

Hays Sharon. 1996. *The cultural contradictions of motherhood*. New Haven, CT: Yale University Press.

Hill Shirley A. 2001. Class, race, and gender dimensions of child rearing in African American families. *Journal of Black Studies* 31:494–508.

Hochschild Arlie Russell. 2003. *The managed heart: Commercialization of human feeling, 20th anniversary ed.* Berkeley: University of California Press.

Holland Megan M. 2012. Only here for the day: The social integration of minority students at a majority white high school. *Sociology of Education* 85:101–20.

Hunter Margaret. 2007. The persistent problem of colorism: Skin tone, status, and inequality. *Sociology Compass* 1:237–54.

Ispa-Landa Simone. 2013. Gender, race, and justifications for group exclusion: Urban black students bused to affluent suburban schools. *Sociology of Education* 86:218–33.

Jackson Brandon A., Wingfield Adia Harvey. 2013. Getting angry to get ahead: Black college men, emotional performance, and encouraging respectable masculinity. *Symbolic Interaction* 36:275–92.

Jarrett Valeria, Johnson Broderick. 2014. My brother's keeper: A new White House initiative to empower boys and young men of color. The White House Blog, 27 Feburary. https://www.whitehouse.gov/blog/2014/02/27/my-brother-s-keeper-new-white-house-initiative-empower-boys-and-young-men-color.

Jones Charisse, Shorter-Gooden Kumea. 2003. *Shifting: The double lives of black women in America*. New York: HarperCollins.

Krieger Linda Hamilton. 1995. The content of our categories: A cognitive bias approach to discrimination and equal employment opportunity. *Stanford Law Review* 47:1161–1248.

Lacy Karyn R. 2007. *Blue-chip black: Race, class, and status in the new black middle class*. Berkeley: University of California Press.

Lareau Annette. 2011. *Unequal childhoods: Class, race, and family life*, 2nd ed. Berkeley: University of California Press.

Lareau Annette, McNamara Horvat Erin. 1999. Moments of social inclusion and exclusion: Race, class, and cultural capital in family-school relationships. *Sociology of Education* 72:37–53.

Martinez Michael, Elam Stephanie, Henry Eric. 2015. Within black families, hard truths told to sons amid Ferguson unrest. *CNN*, 5 February. http://www.cnn.com/2014/08/15/living/parenting-black-sons-ferguson-missouri.

Massey Douglas S., Denton Nancy A. 1993. *American apartheid: Segregation and the making of the underclass*. Cambridge, MA: Harvard University Press.

McHale Susan M., Crouter Ann C., Ji-Yeon Kim, Burton Linda M., Davis Kelly D., Dotterer Aryn M., Swanson Dena P. 2006. Mothers' and fathers' racial socialization in African American families: Implications for youth. *Child Development* 77:1387–1402.

McKinley Jesse. 2009. In California, protests after man dies at hands of transit police. *The New York Times*, 8 January.

McLaughlin Michael. 2014. Ex-transit officer who killed Oscar Grant, unarmed black man, wins lawsuit. *Huffington Post*, 1 February. http://www.huffingtonpost.com/2014/07/01/oscar-grant-lawsuit-bart-officer_n_5548719.html.

Morris Edward W. 2005. "Tuck in that shirt!": Race, class, gender, and discipline in an urban school. *Sociological Perspectives* 48:25–48.

Morris Edward W. 2007. "Ladies" or "loudies"?: Perceptions and experiences of black girls in classrooms. *Youth & Society* 38:490–515.

Noguera Pedro. 2008. *The trouble with black boys: And other reflections on race, equity, and the future of public education*. San Francisco: Jossey-Bass.

Oliver Melvin L., Shapiro Thomas M. 1995. *Black wealth/white wealth: A new perspective on racial inequality*. New York: Routledge.

Ong Maria. 2005. Body projects of young women of color in physics: Intersections of gender, race, and science. *Social Problems* 52:593–617.

Pager Devah. 2003. The mark of a criminal record. *American Journal of Sociology* 108:937–75.

Pascoe C. J. 2007. *Dude, you're a fag: Masculinity and sexuality in high school*. Berkeley: University of California Press.

Pattillo Mary E. 1999. *Black picket fences: Privilege and peril among the black middle class*. Chicago: University of Chicago Press.

Pattillo Mary E. 2007. *Black on the block: The politics of race and class in the city*. Chicago: University of Chicago Press.

Pierce Jennifer L. 1995. *Gender trials: Emotional lives in contemporary law firms*. Berkeley: University of California Press.

Pringle Beverley E., Lyons James E., Booker Keonya C. 2010. Perceptions of teacher expectations by African American high school students. *Journal of Negro Education* 79:33–40.

Pugh Allison J. 2009. *Longing and belonging: Parents, children, and consumer culture*. Berkeley: University of California Press.

Quillian Lincoln Grey, Pager Devah, University of Wisconsin-Madison. 2000. Black neighbors, higher crime? The role of racial stereotypes in evaluations of neighborhood crime. CDE working paper. Madison: Center for Demography and Ecology, University of Wisconsin-Madison.

Rios Victor M. 2009. The consequences of the criminal justice pipeline on black and Latino masculinity. *Annals of the American Academy of Political and Social Science* 623:150–62.

Rollins Judith. 1985. *Between women: Domestics and their employers, labor and social change*. Philadelphia: Temple University Press.

Salem Deborah A., Zimmerman Marc A., Notaro Paul C. 1998. Effects of family structure, family process, and father involvement on psychosocial outcomes among African

American adolescents. *Family Relations* 117:331–41.

Schrock Douglas, Schwalbe Michael. 2009. Men, masculinity, and manhood acts. *Annual Review of Sociology* 35:277–95.

Severson Kim. 2013. Asking for help, then killed by an officer's barrage. *The New York Times*, 16 September.

Sharkey Patrick. 2014. Spatial segmentation and the black middle class. *American Journal of Sociology* 119:903–54.

Staples Robert, Johnson Leanor Boulin. 1993. *Black families at the crossroads: Challenges and prospects*. San Francisco: Jossey-Bass.

Strauss Anselm L., Corbin Juliet M. 1998. *Basics of qualitative research: Techniques and procedures for developing grounded theory*. Thousand Oaks, CA: Sage.

Strayhorn Terrell L. 2010. When race and gender collide: Social and cultural capital's influence on the academic achievement of African American and Latino males. *Review of Higher Education* 33:307–32.

Sullivan Teresa A., Warren Elizabeth, Westbrook Jay Lawrence. 2000. *The fragile middle class: Americans in debt*. New Haven, CT: Yale University Press.

Summers-Effler Erika. 2002. The micro potential for social change: Emotion, consciousness, and social movement formation. *Sociological Theory* 20:41–60.

Tatum Beverly Daniel. 1992. *Assimilation blues: Black families in a white community*, 1st ed. Northampton, MA: Hazel-Maxwell.

Tatum Beverly Daniel. 2003. *"Why are all the black kids sitting together in the cafeteria?" And other conversations about race*. New York: Basic Books.

Thornton Michael C., Chatters Linda M., Taylor Robert Joseph, Allen Walter R. 1990. Sociodemographic and environmental correlates of racial socialization by black parents. *Child Development* 61:401–09.

Uttal Lynet. 1999. Using kin for child care: Embedment in the socioeconomic networks of extended families. *Journal of Marriage and the Family* 61:845–57.

Washington Jesse. 2012. Trayvon Martin, my son, and the "black male code." *Huffington Post*, 24 March. http://www.huffingtonpost.com/2012/03/24/trayvon-martin-my-son-and_1_n_1377003.html.

Welch Kelly, Payne Allison Ann. 2010. Racial threat and punitive school discipline. *Social Problems* 57:25–48.

Wingfield Adia Harvey. 2007. The modern mammy and the angry black man: African American professionals' experiences with gendered racism in the workplace. *Race, Gender & Class* 14:196–212.

Wingfield Adia Harvey. 2009. Racializing the glass escalator: Reconsidering men's experiences with women's work. *Gender & Society* 23:5–26.

Wingfield Adia Harvey. 2011. *Changing times for black professionals*, 1st edition, Framing 21st-century social issues. New York: Routledge.

Wingfield Adia Harvey. 2013. *No more invisible man: Race and gender in men's work*. Philadelphia: Temple University Press.

Yee Vivian, Goodman J. David. 2013. Teenager is shot and killed by officer on foot patrol in the Bronx. *The New York Times*, 4 August.

Young Alford A. Jr.. 2011. The black masculinities of Barack Obama: Some implications for African American men. *Daedalus* 140:206–14.

MARILYNNE ROBINSON

FEAR

Robinson, a Pulitzer Prize-winning novelist, is also an acclaimed essayist; her collection The Givenness of Things, *in which this essay is included, appeared in 2015. "Fear" was first published in the 24 September 2015 issue of* The New York Review of Books.

A merica is a Christian country. This is true in a number of senses. Most people, if asked, will identify themselves as Christian, which may mean only that they aren't something else. Non-Christians will say America is Christian, meaning that they feel somewhat apart from the majority culture. There are a large number of demographic Christians in North America because of our history of immigration from countries that are or were also Christian. We are identified in the world at large with this religion because some of us espouse it not only publicly but also vociferously.* As a consequence, we carry a considerable responsibility for its good name in the world, though we seem not much inclined to consider the implications of this fact. If we did, some of us might think a little longer about associating the precious Lord with ignorance, intolerance, and belligerent nationalism. These few simple precautions would also make it more attractive to the growing numbers among our people who have begun to reject it as ignorant, intolerant, and belligerently nationalistic, as they might reasonably conclude that it is, if they hear only the loudest voices.

There is something I have felt the need to say, that I have spoken about in various settings, extemporaneously,* because my thoughts on the subject have not been entirely formed, and because it is painful to me to have to express them. However, my thesis is always the same, and it is very simply stated, though it has two parts: first, contemporary America is full of fear. And second, fear is not a Christian habit of mind. As children we learn to say, "Yea, though I walk through the valley of the shadow of death, I will fear no evil, for Thou art with me."[1] We learn that, after his resurrection, Jesus told his disciples, "Lo, I am with you always, to the close of the age."[2] Christ is a gracious, abiding presence in all reality, and in him history will finally be resolved.

---

1   *Yea ... me*   See Psalm 23.4.
2   *Lo ... age*   Matthew 28.20.

These are larger, more embracing terms than contemporary Christianity is in the habit of using. But we are taught that Christ "was in the beginning with God; all things were made through him, and without him was not anything made that was made.... The light shines in the darkness, and the darkness has not overcome it."[3] The present tense here is to be noted. John's First Letter proclaims "the eternal life which was with the Father and was made manifest to us."[4] We as Christians cannot think of Christ as isolated in space or time if we really do accept the authority of our own texts. Nor can we imagine that this life on earth is our only life, our primary life. As Christians we are to believe that we are to fear not the death of our bodies but the loss of our souls.

We hear a great deal now about the drift of America away from a Christian identity. Whenever there is talk of decline—as in fact there always is—the one thing that seems to be lacking is a meaningful standard of change. How can we know where we are if we don't know where we were, in those days when things were as they ought to be? How can we know there has been decline, an invidious qualitative change,[5] if we cannot establish a *terminus a quo*?[6] I propose attention to the marked and oddly general fearfulness of our culture at present as one way of dealing with the problem. In the twenty-sixth chapter of Leviticus we find a description of the state the people of Israel* will find themselves in if they depart from their loyalty to God: "The sound of a driven leaf shall put them to flight, and they shall flee as one flees from the sword, and they shall fall when none pursues. They shall stumble over one another, as if to escape a sword, though none pursues."[7]

Now, of course, there are numbers among us who have weapons that would blast that leaf to atoms, and feel brave as they did it, confirmed in their alarm by the fact that there are so very many leaves. But the point is the same. Those who forget God, the single assurance of our safety however that word may be defined, can be recognized in the fact that they make irrational responses to irrational fears. The text specifies the very real threat that fear itself poses—"you shall have no power to stand before your enemies."[8] There are always real dangers in the world, sufficient to their day. Fearfulness obscures the distinction between real threat on one hand and on the other the terrors that beset those who see threat everywhere. It is clear enough, to an objective viewer at

5

---

3 *in the beginning ... overcome it* John 1.3–5.

4 *the eternal ... to us* 1 John 1.2.

5 *invidious qualitative change* Unjust or otherwise negative change in quality.

6 *terminus a quo* Latin: limit from which. The term literally refers to the earliest possible date of an era or period, and more generally to a point of origin.

7 *The sound ... pursues* Leviticus 26.36–37.

8 *you ... enemies* Leviticus 26.37.

least, with whom one would choose to share a crisis, whose judgment should be trusted when sound judgment is most needed.

Granting the perils of the world, it is potentially a very costly indulgence to fear indiscriminately, and to try to stimulate fear in others, just for the excitement of it, or because to do so channels anxiety or loneliness or prejudice or resentment into an emotion that can seem to those who indulge it like shrewdness or courage or patriotism. But no one seems to have an unkind word to say about fear these days, un-Christian as it surely is.

We who are students of Calvin's[9] tradition know that our ancestors in the tradition did not spare their lives or their fortunes. They were loyal to the will of God as they understood it at the most extreme cost to themselves—in worldly terms, that is. They also defended their faith militarily, with intelligence and great courage, but without ultimate success, except in the Low Countries.[10] Therefore the migration of Pilgrims and Puritans, and Huguenots[11] as well, and the great flourishing of Calvinist civilization in the New World. We might say that the oppressors meant it for evil, but God meant it for good, except this might lead us to forget a crucial thing, a factor not present in the story of Joseph and his brothers.[12] Those oppressors were motivated by fear of us. We were heretics by their lights, and therefore a threat to the church, to Christian civilization, to every soul who felt our influence. We filled more or less the same place in the European imagination that Islam does now, one difference being that the Christianity now assumed to be under threat on that most secular continent is merely sociological and cultural, in effect racial, and another difference being that there was no ideal of tolerance and little concept of due

---

9 *Calvin* John Calvin (1509–64), French Protestant theologian and a primary figure of the Protestant Reformation, in which new branches of Christianity formed in opposition to the Roman Catholic Church. Calvinism serves as the theological basis of many American churches.

10 *Low Countries* The Netherlands, Belgium, and also Luxembourg. These areas (named for their being geographically near sea level), adopted forms of Protestant religion early on; Robinson refers here to the Dutch Revolt (1566–1648), through which seven Protestant provinces in the Netherlands achieved independence from Catholic Spain.

11 *Pilgrims and Puritans* Groups of English Calvinists who settled in New England in the first half of the seventeenth century seeking freedom of religion; *Huguenots* French Calvinists who were persecuted by French Catholics during the 16th and 17th centuries; many Huguenots were forced to leave France.

12 *Joseph and his brothers* In Genesis 37 Joseph's brothers plot to have him trapped in a well and sold into Egyptian slavery, not out of fear of their brother but out of hatred and jealousy for their father Jacob's favoritism to Joseph.

process to mitigate the violence the presence of our ancestors inspired. Quite the opposite. To suppress our tradition however viciously was a pious act.

The terrible massacres of Protestants in France in the sixteenth century, whether official or popular in their origins, reflect the fear that is engendered by the thought that someone really might destroy one's soul, plunge one into eternal fire by corrupting true belief even inadvertently. If someone had asked a citizen of Lyon, on his way to help exterminate the Calvinists, to explain what he and his friends were doing, he would no doubt have said that he was taking back his city, taking back his culture, taking back his country, fighting for the soul of France. This kind of language was not invented in order to be used against Calvinists—Europe had been purging itself of heretics since the thirteenth century, so the pattern was already well established. These same terms had been used centuries before by the Roman emperor Julian, called the Apostate, when he tried to return Rome from its emerging Christianity to the old classical paganism. But it was applied to our case with notable rigor and persistence, and with great effect.

I spoke not long ago at a homiletics[13] conference in Wittenberg. There were people there from many distant parts of the world, and not a soul from France. I asked why there were no French people there, and was told that Catholics were not as focused on preaching as Protestants. I told them there are in fact Protestants in France. I told them how to find the Église Réformée[14] on the Internet, preaching and music and all. I am aware of them myself because no Christian population anywhere has ever defended its beliefs with more courage against more entrenched persecution than the Protestants of France. These cultural erasures are almost always more apparent than real, and still they matter, because they assert the unique legitimacy of one descriptor, narrowly defined—Roman, or French, or Aryan,[15] or Catholic, or Christian, or American.

It is difficult for any number of reasons to define a religion, to establish an essence and a circumference, and this is true not least because it always has its supernumeraries,[16] often legions of them. I saw a cinema spectacular when I was growing up, *Demetrius and the Gladiators*,[17] directed by Delmer Daves. Demetrius, who bore an uncanny resemblance to Victor Mature, was a

10

---

13   *homiletics*   Study of the art of preaching.

14   *Église Réformée*   Reformed Church of France. Originally Calvinist, in 2013 it united with the Lutheran Church of France and became the United Protestant Church of France.

15   *Aryan*   Term used in the early 20th century to refer to white people; it is associated with Nazism.

16   *supernumeraries*   I.e., people who are not true adherents of the religion but who support it in some way.

17   *Demetrius and the Gladiators*   1954 drama film and sequel to the 1953 biblical epic film *The Robe*.

Christian convert, obliged therefore to turn the other cheek when taunted by a bully. A gladiator acquaintance of his, an enormous Nubian[18] man, walloped the bully with a plated forearm, sending him sprawling, then growled after him, exultingly, "I am no Christian!" Needless to say, the theater audience erupted in cheers. There was popcorn all over the place. (Parenthetically: I watched this film and *The Robe*, directed by Henry Koster, to see if I had been fair to Koster and Daves, and I had not. Both represent the Christian community as gentle and serene, startlingly so by our standards. But then, in those early days Christians had only such emperors as Caligula[19] to worry about.)

Calvin had his supernumeraries, great French lords who were more than ready to take up arms in his cause, which was under severe persecution. He managed to restrain them while he lived, saying that the first drop of blood they shed would become a torrent that drowned France. And, after he died, Europe was indeed drenched in blood. So there is every reason to suppose that Calvin would have thought his movement had lost at least as much as it gained in these efforts to defend it, as he anticipated it would. Specifically, in some degree it lost its Christian character, as Christianity, or any branch of it, always does when its self-proclaimed supporters outnumber and outshout its actual adherents. What is true when there is warfare is just as true when the bonding around religious identity is militantly cultural or political.

At the core of all this is fear, real or pretended. What if these dissenters in our midst really are a threat to all we hold dear? Better to deal with the problem before their evil schemes are irreversible, before our country has lost its soul and the United Nations has invaded Texas. We might step back and say that there are hundreds of millions of people who love this nation's soul, who in fact are its soul, and patriotism should begin by acknowledging this fact. But there is not much fear to be enjoyed from this view of things. Why stockpile ammunition if the people over the horizon are no threat? If they would in fact grieve with your sorrows and help you through your troubles?

At a lunch recently Lord Jonathan Sacks,[20] then chief rabbi of the United Kingdom, said that the United States is the world's only covenant nation,[21]

---

18 *Nubian* Nubians are an ethnic group native to an area that is now part of Egypt and Sudan, but the word is also used to refer to people of past North African kingdoms (and more generally to black people of antiquity).

19 *Caligula* Third Emperor of Rome (31–41 CE), often presented as a tyrant. He was assassinated at the age of 28.

20 *Jonathan Sacks* Jonathan Sacks (b. 1948) was chief rabbi of the United Hebrew Congregations from 1991 to 2013, and is a member of the British House of Lords.

21 *covenant nation* I.e., a nation based on the forming of a covenant, or agreement, such as that made between God and his people in the Bible.

that the phrase "We the People"[22] has no equivalent in the political language of other nations, and that the State of the Union Address should be called the renewal of the covenant. I have read that Americans are now buying Kalashnikovs[23] in numbers sufficient to help subsidize Russian rearmament, to help their manufacturers achieve economies of scale. In the old days these famous weapons were made with the thought that they would be used in a land war between great powers, that is, that they would kill Americans. Now, since they are being brought into this country, the odds are great that they will indeed kill Americans. But only those scary ones who want to destroy all we hold dear. Or, more likely, assorted adolescents in a classroom or a movie theater.

I know there are any number of people who collect guns as sculpture, marvels of engineering. When we mount a cross on a wall, we don't do it with the thought that, in a pinch, we might crucify someone.* This seems to be a little different when the icon in question is a gun. A "civilian" Kalashnikov can easily be modified into a weapon that would blast a deer to smithereens. That's illegal, of course, and unsportsmanlike. I have heard the asymmetry rationalized thus: deer can't shoot back. Neither can adolescents in a movie theater, of course. Neither can anyone not prepared for mayhem to break loose anywhere, at any time. And, imagining an extremely improbable best case, it is very hard to threaten or deter someone who is suicidal, as most of these assailants are. Gun sales stimulate gun sales—a splendid business model, no doubt about that. Fear operates as an appetite or an addiction. You can never be safe enough.

I know that hunting is sacrosanct* in this country. This is beside the point, since hunting rifles are not the problem. And the conversation around this issue never stays long with hunting. It goes instead to the Second Amendment.[24] Any literalist reading would notice the founders' words "well-regulated" on one hand, and on the other the alarm that arises among the pro-gun people at the slightest mention of anything that resembles regulation, and their constant efforts to erode what little regulation there is. The supposed neglect or abuse of this revered document, and the supposed "defense of the Second Amendment," is leveraged on that other fear, the fear that those bland blue helmets[25] might be gathering even now, maybe in Canada, to commence their internationalist

15

---

22 *We the people* First words of the preamble of the American Constitution.

23 *Kalashnikovs* Automatic rifles first designed by Russian military engineer Mikhail Kalashnikov; the AK-47 assault rifle is a well-known example.

24 *Second Amendment* The 1791 Second Amendment to the U.S. Constitution, contained within the Bill of Rights, reads as follows: "A well regulated Militia, being necessary to the security of a free State, the right of the people to keep and bear Arms, shall not be infringed." (In different versions the punctuation varies.)

25 *blue helmets* Peacekeepers of the United Nations.

march into the heart of Texas. Will we wake to find ourselves betrayed by our own government!! Maybe nothing has deterred them to this point but those Kalashnikovs. How fortunate that the factory in Russia is up and running. And how hard those Russians must be laughing, all the way to the bank. And all those homicidal insurgents and oppressors in the turbulent parts of the world, how pleased they must be that we cheapen these marvelous weapons for them. Oh, I know there are all sorts of reliable gun manufacturers, in Austria, for example. Our appetite for weapons is one of those vacuums nature hates, that is to say, fills.

The Second Amendment argument is brilliant in its way, because the Constitution is central to everything American. The president takes an oath to preserve, protect, and defend the Constitution—nothing more, nothing other. I took a rather similar oath myself once, when I accepted a generous fellowship[26] of a kind established under President Eisenhower and continued under Presidents Kennedy and Johnson. But of course J. Edgar Hoover identified Dwight Eisenhower as a Communist sympathizer. I guess he would cite me as proof, since I did indeed study Shakespeare with the sponsorship of the federal government, on a National Defense Education Act fellowship. I flatter myself that we are no worse for it.

The government at that time felt that humanists also contributed to the well-being of the United States. How times change. I have in fact a number of credentials that would make me a driven leaf, as things are reckoned now. I have lived in Massachusetts and other foreign countries. My command of French is not absolutely minimal. I have degrees from elite institutions. I am a professor in a secular university. All in all I am a pretty good example of the sort who inspire fight-or-flight responses in certain segments of the population. I find myself musing over this from time to time.

Be that as it may. Our first loyalty in this country is to the Constitution, so if the case can be made that any part of the Bill of Rights,[27] for heaven's sake, is under threat, then the whole edifice is imperiled.* And what is a patriot to do in the face of such peril? Carry, as they say, just to assert the right. In the old movies a concealed weapon was the unfailing mark of a coward, but Clint Eastwood* came along to rescue us from our scruples about such

---

26 *oath ... fellowship* The National Defense Education Act, established by President Eisenhower in 1958, provided scholarship funding to universities for the sake of technological advancement during the Cold War arms race. Receiving the scholarship money required a statement of loyalty to the U.S. Government, a requirement which was repealed in 1962.

27 *Bill of Rights* Collective name for the first ten amendments to the American Constitution.

things. And besides, a visible weapon would not only spoil the lines of a business suit, it would also alarm and no doubt alienate anyone who watches the news.

By pure coincidence, as I was writing these thoughts, sitting on my back porch in my quiet, crime-free neighborhood, I heard one man loudly lecturing another on the inappropriateness of going armed into a grocery store, telling him that if he did he could expect the manager to call the police, and that when the police ordered him to leave he was indeed obliged to leave. Do I feel safer in my neighborhood because this unknown man is wandering around with a gun, licensed though it seems to be? No I don't. Since everything is economics these days, what would it cost a store in terms of trade if word got out that he frequented it, with his loyalty to the Second Amendment on display? Or possibly concealed? I'm betting he could put them out of business, because when people see weapons, they have every reason on earth to fear the worst. And what does it cost to police this sort of thing, in this time of budget cuts? If there is any argument for weapons from a public safety point of view, there is a much stronger argument for sparing the police the problem of dealing with such distractions, and for minimizing the risk of their killing or being killed by someone they must assume to be armed.

So, concealed carry. The gun lobby has made its product socially accept-   20
able by putting it out of sight, issues of cowardice notwithstanding.

The next thing to do is to stockpile weapons. Buy gold from that man on TV, maybe some of that dried food, too. Prowl around in the woods with people who share your views. Some pretty intense bonding goes on, swapping fears around a campfire, as any girl scout can testify. And keep an eye out for traitors, active or passive, intentional or not. Who can say, after all, that the Christians did not turn the gods against Rome, that the Cathars[28] did not kill souls, that witches did not cast spells, that Jews did not poison wells, that Gypsies did not steal infants, that a Republican president did not send English majors to graduate school as part of a scheme to soften the national resolve? It is notoriously impossible to prove a negative. I think the army of the United Nations is invoked in these cases as a small and rare concession to standards of plausibility. No one would imagine such a thing of the United States Army. Other plausibility issues arise, of course. To the best of my knowledge, the forces of the United Nations exist primarily to be ineffectual in hopeless situations. Never mind. They are an ominous threat. We might need to shoot at them.

---

28 *Cathars* Catharism was a Christian movement in late medieval France and Italy, denounced by the Catholic Church.

This is the point at which that supernumerary phenomenon I mentioned becomes a factor. There is a First Amendment,[29] too, and it is directed toward, among other things, forbidding an establishment of religion.* Yet among the self-declared Constitutionalists the word "Christian" has become the kind of test for electoral eligibility that the founders specifically meant to forbid. Is Mitt Romney[30] a Christian? Mormonism has a pretty exotic theology, after all. Is Barack Obama a Christian? He adopted Christianity as an adult, true, having been unaffiliated with institutional religion until then, but the whole history of the Spanish Inquisition[31] proves how hard some people find it to trust a convert. There was a time when we Calvinists felt the force of the terror and antagonism that can be raised against those who are not Christian in a sense other people are willing to accept. This doleful trait* is being played upon in our current politics. Supernumeraries who strike out against the free exercise of religion might say, "I am no Christian." With equal truth they might also say, "I am no American." And a pretty large part of the crowd would probably cheer.

I defer to no one in my love for America and for Christianity. I have devoted my life to the study of both of them. I have tried to live up to my association with them. And I take very seriously Jesus's teachings, in this case his saying that those who live by the sword will also die by the sword. Something called Christianity has become entangled in exactly the strain of nationalism that is militaristic, ready to spend away the lives of our young, and that can only understand dissent from its views as a threat or a defection, a heresy in the most alienating and stigmatizing sense of the word. We are not the first country where this has happened. The fact that it was the usual thing in Europe, and had been for many centuries, was one great reason for attempting to separate church and state here.

Jesus's aphorism* may be taken to mean simply that those who deal in violence are especially liable to suffer violence. True enough. But death is no simple thing when Jesus speaks of it. His thoughts are not our thoughts, the limits of our perceptions are not limits he shares. We must imagine him seeing the whole of our existence, our being beyond mortality, beyond time. There is that other death he can foresee, the one that really matters. When Christians abandon Christian standards of behavior in the defense of Christianity, when

---

29 *First Amendment* Amendment stating that "Congress shall make no law respecting an establishment of religion, or prohibiting the free exercise thereof...."

30 *Mitt Romney* Governor of Massachusetts and Republican nominee for the 2012 presidential election. Romney's Mormonism was a frequent talking point of the election.

31 *Spanish Inquisition* Established by Ferdinand II and Isabella I of Spain, the inquisition strove to impose Catholic orthodoxy; it is infamous for the punishments and tortures inflicted upon Jews, Muslims, and Protestant Christians (many of whom claimed to have converted to Catholicism).

Americans abandon American standards of conduct in the name of America, they inflict harm that would not be in the power of any enemy. As Christians they risk the kind of harm to themselves to which the Bible applies adjectives like "everlasting."

American exceptionalism* is more imperiled in these moments than in any others, and so is organized religion. Try to persuade a skeptic of the value of religion, and he or she will mention some horror of European history carried out under the sign of the cross. They are innumerable. I have mentioned St. Bartholomew's Day.[32] One hears of the secularization of Europe, often in the context of socialist economics, rarely in the context of a frankly terrifying history. We must be very careful not to defeat the safeguards our laws and traditions have put in place. Christian "establishment," the making of Christianity in effect the official religion, is the first thing its supernumeraries would try for, and the last thing its faithful should condone.

As for America, we have a way of plunging into wars we weary of and abandon after a few years and a few thousand casualties, having forgotten what our object was; these wars demonstrate an overwhelming power to destroy without any comparable regard to life and liberty, to the responsibilities of power, that would be consistent with maintaining our good name. We throw away our status in the world at the urging of those who think it has nothing to do with our laws and institutions, impressed by the zeal of those supernumeraries who are convinced that it all comes down to shock and awe and boots on the ground. This notion of glory explains, I suppose, some part of the fantasizing, the make-believe wars against make-believe enemies, and a great many of the very real Kalashnikovs.

(2015)

---

32 *St. Bartholomew's Day* Assassinations and mob violence which occurred in France on the 1572 eve of St. Bartholomew's feast. The massacre followed the wedding of Charles IX's sister Margaret to the Protestant King Henry III of Navarre and involved the targeted killing of thousands of Huguenots by Catholics over several weeks.

ALEX BOZIKOVIC

CHICAGO ARCHITECT AIMS TO REPAIR RELATIONS BETWEEN POLICE, RESIDENTS

Architect Jeanne Gang has received considerable attention worldwide for the striking appearance of many of the buildings she designs—and for her progressive ideas about architecture and society. The article included here, by the architecture critic for The Globe and Mail, *a Canadian national newspaper, was first published on 3 April 2016. The above title is that given to the piece online; in the print newspaper it bore the following title and subtitle: "Remaking Space to Remake a Culture: Architect Espouses Rounded Vision of What Design Is About—Beauty, But Also Prosperity and Justice."*

D esigning a building, or a block: This is an architect's job. But what about repairing the relationship between police departments and urban residents?

The Chicago architect Jeanne Gang is aiming for exactly that. By altering police stations from fortresses to community hubs, you can change the mindset of officers and of the community around them. "Spaces and environments are a huge influence on how we behave," Gang suggests. "It's a small example, but a police station could be welcoming. Why not make it a space where there's free WiFi and free computers? That way, it can serve a policing function and a community function at the same time.

"And if you can remake space, you can change a culture."

That sort of statement has been too rare; for a generation, architects have eschewed[1] such social ambition and the responsibility that comes with it. But Gang, an intellectual leader in the field, is trying to knit together the work of making beautiful buildings and the larger job of building a city that holds

---

1   *eschewed*   Avoided using.

together. It's a rounded vision of what design is about: beauty, but also prosperity and justice.

"It's what I call actionable idealism," says Gang, 52, who spoke earlier   5
this month at Carleton University. "We want to help our cities, and help in a physical sense."

Out of that comes Polis Station, a proposal from her office Studio Gang that was a highlight at the Chicago Architecture Biennial[2] last fall. Working in their home city, Gang's team of architects and urbanists looked at a typical [police] station on the troubled West Side. Their proposal reimagines the station house, placing the secure areas at the back and a variety of public services—a library, daycare, mental-health-care providers and a community room—all sharing a grand public entrance and adjacent to new park space.

"When you have a fire station in your neighborhood, people feel comfortable going there for help," Gang says. "People have a relationship with the workers. It's nice, and friendly. I was struck thinking about the architecture of police stations: People are scared to go inside."

Polis Station would change that. Although speculative, it is technically and economically feasible. It is also deeply relevant, a response to the Black Lives Matter movement,* the controversy in Chicago over the 2014 police shooting of Laquan McDonald, and to an increasing sense that urban police departments are detached, even after a long vogue for "community policing," from many of the people they serve. (Canadians shouldn't feel superior about any of this; urban police stations here are much the same. The best contemporary example I've seen, Toronto's 14 Division by architects Stantec, is essentially a handsome fortress.)

But it's a sign of the times that Studio Gang is even interested in such questions; Gang, who won a "genius grant" McArthur Fellowship in 2011, is a star in the field. She was recently named Architect of the Year in *Architectural Review*'s 2016 Women in Architecture Awards. She and her firm could focus on easier and far more profitable things. They recently won the plum job* to expand the American Museum of Natural History in New York, and a new American embassy in Brasilia.

Gang founded her practice in 1997 after school in Switzerland and at Harvard;   10
she spent several years at OMA, the Dutch office led by Rem Koolhaas that was, and remains, an intellectual hotbed.

She rose to prominence back in Chicago (she is from rural Illinois) with a mix of commercial and institutional projects. The former offered scale and revenue; the latter, creative freedom and the budgets to innovate. But her office has proved its ability to innovate on all types of projects.

---

2   *Biennial*   Exhibition held every two years.

With the 87-storey Aqua tower in Chicago, she found a way to turn the boxy residential tower into sculpture—by working with the balconies on its outside. Their curvy contours ripple down the surface of the high-rise. That move was brilliant and economical—just as beautiful in real life as in drawings—and it has been widely borrowed.

And yet, she argues, even that building is not merely an object. "It is closely connected to the city fabric," she argues. "There is a ripple in our work, that's getting bigger, from what was present there: a concern for cities in North America."

On a current project for a developer, the 500,000-square-foot City Hyde Park, Studio Gang designed a complex weave of balconies and sunshades that will allow residents to actually see and speak to their neighbors. "For us, residential buildings are about creating community," she says, "and that's true in a tower building as well. What does a balcony mean? What can it do in the city?"

15   Coming from Gang, that is not just lip service.* Buildings like that one share an ethic with the firm's civic work, such as the Polis Station proposal; planner Gia Biagi is the studio's senior director for urbanism and civic impact. Their work includes the master plan for the 91-acre Northerly Island Park in Chicago, now under construction.

The collective message of all this work, much of it now being realized, is a broader sense of architecture's role in society, one that captures the growing spirit of public service in the world of architecture. "It's an exciting time of engagement between the profession and the world," Gang says.

And yet, beauty matters, too. "Architecture doesn't work unless it gives you this element of wonder and joy," Gang adds, "and you want to be there and you want to go out of your way to see it. That's the thing that ties together the generation that created eye-popping structures with the one that is now looking more at cities.

"I think what's happening now is looking beyond the buildings themselves to make a city that's even stronger," Gang says. "A building can have a magnetic presence that changes the place it's in." Even a police station.

(2016)

TEJU COLE

A TOO-PERFECT PICTURE

Cole, well-known as a writer of fiction as well as an essayist, contributes a monthly column entitled "On Photography" to The New York Times Magazine. *This essay was published in that space in the 30 March 2016 issue of the magazine. The above title is given to the piece online; in the print version of the magazine it bore a much longer title: "How Can You Tell When a Picture Is Giving Us the Truth and Not Simply Trafficking in Fantasy?"*

You know a Steve McCurry picture when you see one. His portrait of an Afghan girl with vivid green eyes, printed on the cover of *National Geographic* in June 1985, is one of the iconic images of the 20th century. McCurry's work is stark and direct, with strong colors, a clear emotional appeal and crisp composition. His most recent volume of photographs, *India*, is a compendium of the pictures he took in that country between 1978 and 2014, and it also gives us the essential McCurry. There are Hindu festivals, men in turbans, women in saris, red-robed monks, long mustaches, large beards, preternaturally soulful children and people in rudimentary canoes against dramatic landscapes.

In McCurry's portraits, the subject looks directly at the camera, wide-eyed and usually marked by some peculiarity, like pale irises, face paint or a snake around the neck. And when he shoots a wider scene, the result feels like a certain ideal of photography: the rule of thirds,[1] a neat counterpoise of foreground and background and an obvious point of primary interest, placed just so. Here's an old-timer with a dyed beard. Here's a doe-eyed child in a head scarf. The pictures are staged or shot to look as if they were. They are astonishingly boring.

Boring, but also extremely popular: McCurry's photographs adorn calendars and books, and command vertiginous[2] prices at auction. He has more than

---

1   *rule of thirds*   Principle of visual composition according to which the elements of an image should be placed based on imagined lines dividing the picture into thirds horizontally and vertically.

2   *vertiginous*   So high as to cause vertigo.

a million followers on Instagram. This popularity does not come about merely because of the technical finesse of his pictures. The photographs in *India*, all taken in the last 40 years, are popular in part because they evoke an earlier time in Indian history, as well as old ideas of what photographs of Indians should look like, what the accouterments of their lives should be: umbrellas, looms, sewing machines; not laptops, wireless printers, escalators. In a single photograph, taken in Agra in 1983, the Taj Mahal is in the background, a steam train is in the foreground and two men ride in front of the engine, one of them crouched, white-bearded and wearing a white cap, the other in a loosefitting brown uniform and a red turban. The men are real, of course, but they have also been chosen for how well they work as types.

A defender of McCurry's work might suggest that he is interested in exploring vanishing cultures. After all, even in the 21st century, not all Indians go to malls or fly in planes. Should he not be celebrated for seeking out the picturesque and using it to show us quintessential India? What is wrong with showing a culture in its most authentic form? The problem is that the uniqueness of any given country is a mixture not only of its indigenous practices and borrowed customs but also of its past and its present. Any given photograph encloses only a section of the world within its borders. A sequence of photographs, taken over many years and carefully arranged, however, reveals a worldview. To consider a place largely from the perspective of a permanent anthropological past, to settle on a notion of authenticity that edits out the present day, is not simply to present an alternative truth: It is to indulge in fantasy.

5   What a relief it is to move from Steve McCurry's work to that of someone like Raghubir Singh. Singh worked from the late '60s until his untimely death in 1999, traveling all over India to create a series of powerful books about his homeland. His work shares formal content with McCurry's: the subcontinental terrain, the eye-popping color, the human presence. Within these shared parameters, however, Singh gives us photographs charged with life: not only beautiful experiences or painful scenes but also those in-between moments of drift that make up most of our days. Singh had a democratic eye, and he took pictures of everything: cities, towns, villages, shops, rivers, worshipers, workers, construction sites, motorbikes, statues, modern furniture, balconies, suits, dresses and, sure, turbans and saris.

The power of Singh's pictures lies in part in their capacious content. But it also lies in their composition, which rises well beyond mere competence, as he demonstrated in books like *River of Colour*, *The Ganges* and *Bombay: Gateway of India*. Singh has cited Edgar Degas[3] and the American photographer

---

3   *Edgar Degas*   French artist (1834–1917) best known for his paintings and sculptures of dancers.

Helen Levitt[4] as influences, and you can see what he has learned from their highly sophisticated approaches (Degas's casual grace, Levitt's sympathetic view of urban oddity and the way both of them let in messiness at the edges of their images—a messiness that reminds us of the life happening outside the frame as well as within it). A photograph like the one Singh made of a crowded intersection in Kolkata in 1987 draws a breathtaking coherence out of the chaos of the everyday. The image, of which the key elements are a green door, a distant statue, an arm and a bus, is slightly surreal. But everything is in its right place. It reads as a moment of truth snipped from the flow of life.

I love even more a photograph Singh made in Mumbai a couple of years later. Taken in a busy shopping district called Kemp's Corner, this photograph has less-obvious charms. The picture is divided into four vertical parts by the glass frontage of a leather-goods shop and its open glass door, and within this grid is a scatter of incident. The main figure, if we can call her that, is a woman past middle age who wears a red blouse and a dark floral skirt and carries a cloth bag on a string. She is seen in profile and looks tired. Beyond her and behind are various other walkers in the city, going about their serious business. An overpass cuts across the picture horizontally. The foreground, red with dust, is curiously open, a potential space for people not yet in the picture. The glass on the left is a display of handbags for sale, and the peculiar lighting of the bags indicates that Singh used flash in taking the shot. The image, unforgettable because it stretches compositional coherence nearly to its snapping point, reminds me of Degas's painting "Place de la Concorde," another picture in which easy, classically balanced composition is jettisoned for something more exciting and discomfiting and grounded.

How do we know when a photographer caters to life and not to some previous prejudice? One clue is when the picture evades compositional cliché. But there is also the question of what the photograph is for, what role it plays within the economic circulation of images. Some photographs, like Singh's, are freer of the censorship of the market. Others are taken only to elicit particular conventional responses—images that masquerade as art but fully inhabit the vocabulary of advertising. As Justice Potter Stewart said when pressed to define hard-core pornography in 1964, "I know it when I see it."

I saw "it" when I recently watched the video for Coldplay's "Hymn for the Weekend." The song is typical Coldplay, written for vague uplift but resistant to sense ("You said, 'Drink from me, drink from me'/When I was so thirsty/Poured on a symphony/Now I just can't get enough"). Filmed in India, with a cameo by Beyoncé, the video is a kind of exotification bingo,* and almost like

---

4   *Helen Levitt*   Levitt (1913–2009) is best known for her photographs taken on the streets of New York.

a live-action version of Steve McCurry's vision: peacocks, holy men, painted children, incense. Almost nothing in the video allows true contemporaneity to Indians. They seem to have been placed there as a colorful backdrop to the fantasies of Western visitors. A fantasy withers in the sunlight of realism. But as long as realism is held at bay, the fantasy can remain satisfying to an enormous audience. More than a hundred million people have watched the Coldplay video since it was posted at the end of January.

10   Are we then to cry "appropriation"[5] whenever a Westerner approaches a non-Western subject? Quite the contrary: Some of the most insightful stories about any place can be told by outsiders. I have, for instance, seen few documentary series as moving and humane as *Phantom India*, released in 1969 by the French auteur Louis Malle. Mary Ellen Mark, not Indian herself, did extraordinary work photographing prostitutes in Mumbai. Non-Indians have made images that capture aspects of the endlessly complicated Indian experience, just as have Indian photographers like Ketaki Sheth, Sooni Taraporevala, Raghu Rai and Richard Bartholomew.

Art is always difficult, but it is especially difficult when it comes to telling other people's stories. And it is ferociously difficult when those others are tangled up in your history and you are tangled up in theirs. What honors those we look at, those whose stories we try to tell, is work that acknowledges their complex sense of their own reality. Good photography, regardless of its style, is always emotionally generous in this way. For this reason, it outlives the moment that occasions it. Weaker photography delivers a quick message—sweetness, pathos, humor—and fails to do more. But more is what we are.

(2016)

---

5   *appropriation*   I.e., cultural appropriation, the adoption by one culture of an element of another culture. This is often viewed as ethically unacceptable, especially when a more privileged culture takes elements of a less privileged one.

MALIK JALAL

I'M ON THE KILL LIST.
THIS IS WHAT IT FEELS LIKE TO
BE HUNTED BY DRONES

In 2001 the CIA began using the remote-controlled Predator drone to carry out attacks on enemies in war zones and individuals suspected of terrorism. More than 400 drone strikes have been carried out in the tribal regions of Pakistan; though accurate records of the identities and numbers of the casualties of these attacks are not available, of the several thousand people killed, hundreds have been civilians rather than members of terrorist organizations. (The American government estimates that its drone strikes caused somewhere between 64 and 116 civilian deaths worldwide between 2009 and mid-2016, but many reputable organizations estimate 100 to 200 more than that.)

A tribal elder in Waziristan, a region in Pakistan near the border with Afghanistan, Malik Jalal claims to have narrowly avoided multiple drone strikes and believes that his name is on the US government's notoriously secret "kill list." (Jalal is a member of the North Waziristan Peace Committee, which he describes as an organization that negotiates with the Taliban to maintain peace; American and British intelligence view the organization as offering refuge to the Taliban.) In 2016 Jalal visited the United Kingdom to share his personal experience with a world audience. His essay "I'm on the Kill List" was published by the Independent, *a UK newspaper.*

I am in the strange position of knowing that I am on the "Kill List." I know this because I have been told, and I know because I have been targeted for death over and over again. Four times missiles have been fired at me. I am extraordinarily fortunate to be alive.

I don't want to end up a "Bugsplat"—the ugly word that is used for what remains of a human being after being blown up by a Hellfire missile[1] fired from a Predator drone. More importantly, I don't want my family to become victims, or even to live with the droning engines overhead, knowing that at any moment they could be vaporized.

I am in England this week because I decided that if Westerners wanted to kill me without bothering to come to speak with me first, perhaps I should come to speak to them instead. I'll tell my story so that you can judge for yourselves whether I am the kind of person you want to be murdered.

I am from Waziristan, the border area between Pakistan and Afghanistan. I am one of the leaders of the North Waziristan Peace Committee (NWPC), which is a body of local Maliks (or community leaders) that is devoted to trying to keep the peace in our region. We are sanctioned by the Pakistan government, and our main mission is to try to prevent violence between the local Taliban and the authorities.

5   In January 2010, I lent my vehicle to my nephew, Salimullah, to drive to Deegan for an oil change and to have one of the tires checked. Rumors had surfaced that drones were targeting particular vehicles, and tracking particular phone signals. The sky was clear and there were drones circling overhead.

As Salimullah conversed with the mechanic, a second vehicle pulled up next to mine. There were four men inside, just local chromite miners. A missile destroyed both vehicles, killed all four men, and seriously injured Salimullah, who spent the next 31 days in hospital.

Upon reflection, because the drones target the vehicles of people they want to kill in Waziristan, I was worried that they were aiming for me.

The next attack came on 3 September 2010. That day, I was driving a red Toyota Hilux Surf SUV to a "Jirga," a community meeting of elders. Another red vehicle, almost identical to mine, was some 40 meters behind. When we reached Khader Khel, a missile blew up the other vehicle, killing all four occupants. I sped away, with flames and debris in my rear view mirror.

Initially I thought the vehicle behind was perhaps being used by militants, and I just happened to be nearby. But I learned later the casualties were four local laborers from the Mada Khel tribe, none of whom had any ties to militant groups. Now it seemed more likely that I was the target.

10   The third drone strike came on 6 October 2010. My friend Salim Khan invited me to dinner. I used my phone to call Salim to announce my arrival, and just before I got there a missile struck, instantly killing three people, including

---

1   *Hellfire missile*   American-created missile fired at tanks and other targets on the ground from the air.

my cousin, Kaleem Ullah, a married man with children, and a mentally handicapped man. Again, none of the casualties were involved in extremism.

Now I knew for certain it was me they were after.

Five months later, on 27 March 2011, an American missile targeted a Jirga, where local Maliks—all friends and associates of mine—were working to resolve a local dispute and bring peace. Some 40 civilians died that day, all innocent, and some of them fellow members of the NWPC. I was early to the scene of this horror.

Like others that day, I said some things I regret.[2] I was angry, and I said we would get our revenge. But, in truth, how would we ever do such a thing? Our true frustration was that we—the elders of our villages—are now powerless to protect our people.

I have been warned that Americans and their allies had me and others from the Peace Committee on their Kill List. I cannot name my sources, as they would find themselves targeted for trying to save my life. But it leaves me in no doubt that I am one of the hunted.

I soon began to park any vehicle far from my destination, to avoid making it a target. My friends began to decline my invitations, afraid that dinner might be interrupted by a missile.

I took to the habit of sleeping under the trees, well above my home, to avoid acting as a magnet of death for my whole family. But one night my youngest son, Hilal (then aged six), followed me out to the mountainside. He said that he, too, feared the droning engines at night. I tried to comfort him. I said that drones wouldn't target children, but Hilal refused to believe me. He said that missiles had often killed children. It was then that I knew that I could not let them go on living like this.

I know the Americans think me an opponent of their drone wars. They are right; I am. Singling out people to assassinate, and killing nine of our innocent children for each person they target, is a crime of unspeakable proportions. Their policy is as foolish as it is criminal, as it radicalizes the very people we are trying to calm down.

I am aware that the Americans and their allies think the Peace Committee is a front, and that we are merely creating a safe space for the Pakistan Taliban. To this I say: you are wrong. You have never been to Waziristan, so how would you know?

The mantra that the West should not negotiate with "terrorists" is naive. There has hardly ever been a time when terrorists have been brought back into

15

---

2   *I said ... regret*   Jalal made a statement in support of "blood revenge" against the United States.

the fold of society without negotiation. Remember the IRA;[3] once they tried to blow up your prime minister, and now they are in parliament. It is always better to talk than to kill.

20   I have travelled half way across the world because I want to resolve this dispute the way you teach: by using the law and the courts, not guns and explosives.

Ask me any question you wish, but judge me fairly—and please stop terrorizing my wife and children. And take me off that Kill List.

(2016)

---

3   *IRA* Irish Republican Army, a paramilitary organization whose members sought to gain independence for Ireland through violent attacks on British targets. The conflict over Irish independence lasted for decades in the late twentieth century until negotiations involving the IRA resulted in the Good Friday Agreement (1998), which brought an almost complete end to the violence.

JACOB BROGAN

DON'T ANTHROPOMORPHIZE
INKY THE OCTOPUS!

Jacob Brogan's essay "Don't Anthropomorphize Inky the Octopus!" appeared in the online magazine Slate *in April 2016. That month, media outlets enthusiastically shared the story of the presumed escape of an octopus named Inky from New Zealand's National Aquarium. Startled aquarium employees had arrived one morning a few months earlier to find that Inky had gone missing, and a wet trail on the floor led from his tank to a pipe that drained into the ocean. Though he was not sighted again, Inky was presumed to have escaped to nearby Hawke's Bay, the evidence he left behind was carefully analyzed, and a daring tale of his escape was constructed.*

The story is familiar by now: Inky the octopus somehow escaped his tank at the New Zealand National Aquarium. Making his way across the floor, he compressed his body into a drainage pipe and made his way out to the ocean. Inky's bemused keepers attributed this sly exit to his desire for more. In a widely quoted remark, the aquarium's Rob Yarrell observed, "I don't think he was unhappy with us, or lonely, as octopus are solitary creatures. But he is such a curious boy. He would want to know what's happening on the outside. That's just his personality."

Others embraced and amplified this human account of Inky's actions after his escape (though it occurred months ago, it penetrated the international news on Tuesday). The *Washington Post* describes the story as a cephalopod version of the *Shawshank Redemption*[1] and cites a tweet from the Canadian organization Animal Justice celebrating Inky "for breaking out of aquarium jail." Other filmic references and cultural allusions proliferate in further coverage, with the

---

1   *cephalopod*   Mollusc belonging to a group of marine-dwelling invertebrates that includes the squid, octopus, nautilus, and cuttlefish;   *Shawshank Redemption*   1994 film depicting the incarceration of a pair of inmates with a long-term plan to escape the prison.

Guardian proposing that it is "reminiscent of *Finding Nemo*" and the *New York Times* comparing Inky to Houdini.[2]

A roundup of journalistic reactions from the site Muckrack points to an even more aggressive pattern of anthropomorphism. Particularly on social media, journalists seemed to find a personal hero in the octopus. "Je suis Inky,"[3] one cephalopod rights activist jokes, while another announces, "Today, we are all this octopus, who looked around at his life situation and said, 'F**k this.'" These responses are all in good fun, of course, but they speak to a familiar pattern, one that finds humans turning the most unusual creatures into simple metaphors for our own plights. Unable to domesticate the animals themselves, we tame their strangeness instead.

Anthropomorphism has long divided biologists and naturalists. In theory, at least, avoiding it helps us see animals as they are instead of turning them into distorted mirrors of our own experiences and expectations. And yet, as the primatologist Frans de Waal proposes in a recent *New York Times* article, an absolute prohibition against anthropomorphism may paradoxically affirm human exceptionalism.[4] Instead, when we recognize how *human* nonhuman species can be, de Waal suggests, we may be able to treat them a little more generously—and may come to understand ourselves a little more fully in the process. The journalist Katherine Harmon Courage points to a similar conclusion in her book *Octopus!*, quoting the filmmaker Jean Painlevé,[5] who claims "we couldn't appreciate anything around us" without anthropomorphism.

5   But when we speak of celebrity octopuses as if they were *just like us*, we may actually minimize how wonderfully strange they are. What's astonishing about Inky's story isn't *that* he escaped—in fact, octopus literature is full of such flights to freedom—but *how* he figured out that such a path to freedom might be feasible in the first place. By minimizing those details, we're effectively recontaining Inky and his ilk, trapping them in aquariums of a different sort, enclosures with walls made of misconceptions rather than glass.

---

2   *Finding Nemo*   2003 animated film about a clownfish father's journey through the ocean to reunite with his son, Nemo, who has been captured and placed in a dentist's aquarium;   *Houdini*   Harry Houdini (1874–1926), a magician who became famous in America and around the world for his ability to escape from a variety of confinements.

3   *Je suis Inky*   French: I am Inky. The phrase references "Je suis Charlie," an oft-repeated statement of support for free speech in solidarity with the victims of a 2015 shooting at the controversial satirical newspaper *Charlie Hebdo*.

4   *human exceptionalism*   Belief by humans that humans are vastly different from (and superior to) all other species.

5   *Jean Painlevé*   Documentary filmmaker (1902–89) who used underwater cameras to capture sea life in films including *The Love Life of the Octopus*.

And the octopus should be put in anything but. Alien as these creatures look on the outside, they are even more so within: The primary mass of their unusually large brains isn't located in the head, but is instead wrapped around the esophagus. Neural tissue also spreads throughout their eight arms, with "a ganglion[6] controlling every sucker," as octopus researcher Jennifer Mather explains, which allows them to perform thousands of independent gripping motions.

All that extra-cranial complexity doesn't exactly make octopuses "smart" by conventional human standards, but it helps reveal why they're such compelling subjects. Solitary hunters, theirs is an embodied intelligence altogether different from humans' socially focused forms of cognition. In her deeply moving book *Soul of an Octopus*, Sy Montgomery writes of her first encounter with a giant Pacific octopus named Athena. As Montgomery dips her hands into the water, Athena reaches out to meet them. "She is at once touching and tasting my skin, and possibly the muscle, bone, and blood beneath," Montgomery writes. Octopus researchers often speak of their subjects as curious creatures, and it's easy to see why: They explore and interrogate their world with their arms, which in the case of the octopus, means with their brains—a profoundly alien sensory apparatus, as Montgomery's description suggests.

Montgomery quickly comes to feel that Athena *understands* her, a conviction informed by her belief that this creature has attitudes and orientations all its own. Many cephalopod biologists seem to agree with some version of this stance, holding that octopuses have personalities. Courage, for example, writes that aquarium keepers tend to name individual octopuses in part because they "exhibit individual behavior patterns distinct enough that we humans could pick up on them," an anomalous trait among invertebrate marine animals.

Those identifiable eccentricities may allow us to distinguish them, but they actually make these cephalopods *harder* to understand as a species, contributing to their alienness instead of dispelling it. Even researchers who work with them regularly do not understand what whimsical tides convince these temperamental creatures to occasionally participate in research experiments—and occasionally decline, for reasons all their own.

Further complicating this difficulty, octopuses are largely solitary creatures, and their intelligence evolved in relation to their isolated form of existence. As Mather explains in a book[7] that she co-authored with Roland C. Anderson and James B. Wood, this makes it hard to apply conventional tests of consciousness to them. On the tendency of octopuses to eat others of their kind, they write,

10

---

6   *ganglion*   Tissue mass containing nerves.

7   *a book*   Published in 2010, Mather, Anderson, and Wood's text is entitled *Octopus: The Ocean's Intelligent Invertebrate*.

"The fact that octopuses will be cannibals if they can, suggests that octopuses don't have an octopus-recognition-template in the brain." In its own turn, this implies that they're not capable of recognizing themselves in a mirror, a capacity we often use as an index of supposedly higher forms of intelligence.

But even if octopuses presumably aren't conscious in the way that humans are, that doesn't mean these tool-using, playful creatures aren't intelligent. They are simply intelligent in a *qualitatively* different way than we are. Mather and her collaborators describe an experiment testing octopuses' ability to open a glass jar with a herring inside. Though the invertebrates were able to unscrew the lid, doing so took time. When a researcher smeared herring on the outside of the jar, however, the creatures learned to open it much more quickly. Part of the issue, the authors suggest, may have been that when the jar was caught up in the tangle of octopus arms the creatures literally lost sight of their goal, while the nonvisual sensory cue kept them focused on the task.

Try to understand an octopus solely in human terms, in other words, and you'll never get at what makes them fascinating. Even de Waal dwells on this truth, despite his cautious call for anthropomorphism. "It makes no sense to compare our cognition with one that is distributed over eight independently moving arms, each with its own neural supply," he writes. Montgomery, for her own part, quotes a famous maxim from Ludwig Wittgenstein's[8] *Philosophical Investigations*: "If a lion could talk, we could not understand him." Language, Wittgenstein held, is fundamentally embedded in the ways we move through and make sense of the world. If we could not comprehend a lion, how could we hope to approach something as *strange* as an octopus?

In context, however, that Wittgensteinian aphorism is surrounded by thornier reflections on the difficulty of understanding our fellow humans. That difficulty—the ostensibly essential unknowability of the other's interiority—doesn't preclude us from trying to understand them or acting as if we do. He writes, "If I see someone writhing in pain with evident cause I do not think: all the same, his feelings are hidden from me." Montgomery, likewise, lets the uniqueness of the creatures she studies draw her in, an experience not unlike reading a difficult poem whose beauty attracts even as its full import always eludes us. "As I stroke her with my fingertips, her skin goes white beneath my touch," she writes of meeting Athena. And white, she learns, "is the color of a relaxed octopus," the hue cuttlefish take on when they know that they're safe. If she attributes emotion to Athena here, she attempts to do so on Athena's terms, not her own.

8   *Ludwig Wittgenstein*   Austrian-British philosopher (1889–1951) whose work posed many questions about language and consciousness.

That may be why Montgomery saturates her descriptions of cephalopods with a vocabulary of suggestive uncertainty. "As if," "seems," and "like" are her watchwords. Because it is so hard to know the octopus, we want to. And because we want to, we are all but obliged to describe them by way of simile. These poetic gestures at once acknowledge their distance from us and attempt to cross that briny divide. This is how we honor our most radical others: not by holding them in place with our language as a biologist pins a specimen to a board, but by caressing them with our words, as an octopus does when it meets a stranger.

There's a lesson here for those celebrating Inky's unlikely escape, a re-   15
minder to celebrate his strangeness as well. An octopus' life in an aquarium might be boring, but it's not dull in the same way that a slow day at the office is. Perhaps instead of equating Inky's adventure with our own banal travails, we should stretch our imaginations to better understand his plight.

(2016)

Biographical Notes

Addams, Jane (1860–1935)
American reformer and founder in 1889 of Hull-House, a Chicago settlement-house. Through her activities there, she created a strong social reform movement and was instrumental in the passage of several child labor and education laws. Her written works include *Democracy and Social Ethics* (1902), *Twenty Years at Hull-House* (1910), and *A New Conscience and an Ancient Evil* (1912). In recognition of her reform efforts, Addams was awarded the 1931 Nobel Peace Prize.

Ai Weiwei (1957–)
A leading Chinese artist and activist, Ai Weiwei has received worldwide acclaim for his video art, installations, and photographs. Within China, however, Ai, who has strongly criticized the government over a variety of issues, has been subjected to government censorship measures including arrest, the shutdown of his popular blog, the demolition of his studio, and restrictions on his ability to travel. In 2008, Ai received a lifetime achievement award from the Chinese Contemporary Art Awards; in 2012, he was awarded the Václav Havel Prize for Creative Dissent.

Alexie, Sherman (1966–)
Sherman Alexie is an American writer. A member of the Spokane and Coeur d'Alene tribes, he confronts in his writing the systemic poverty that marked his childhood experience of rural reservation life. His works, which often hover on the border between fiction and non-fiction, include *Reservation Blues* (1996), *The Lone Ranger and Tonto Fistfight in Heaven* (1993), *The Absolutely True Diary of a Part-Time Indian* (2007), and *Ten Little Indians* (2009).

Baldwin, James (1924–87)
Born and raised in New York City, the African American writer James Baldwin left America for Paris at the age of 24, and remained an expatriate for most of the rest of his life. His 1955 collection of essays, *Notes of a Native Son* (now an established classic), was followed by numerous other collections of essays—notably *Nobody Knows My Name: More Notes of a Native Son* (1961) and *The Fire Next Time* (1963). His novels include *Go Tell It on the Mountain* (1953), *Giovanni's Room* (1956), and *Tell Me How Long the Train's Been Gone* (1968).

Barthes, Roland (1915–80)
Roland Barthes was a French social and literary critic known for his influential writings on semiotics and structuralism. His written works include *Mythologies* (1957), *Elements of Semiology* (1967), *The Empire of Signs* (1970), and *The Luminous Room* (1980).

Berger, John (1926–)
An English social commentator, visual arts critic, and writer, John Berger is the author of novels, plays, screenplays, volumes of poems, and over 30 non-fiction works. He received the Booker Prize for his novel *G.* (1972), but is perhaps best-known for his introduction to the study of artistic images, *Ways of Seeing* (1972).

Biss, Eula (?1977–)
An award-winning American essayist, Eula Biss has published her work in *Harper's* and *The New York Times Magazine*, among many others. Her books include a collection of prose poems, *The Balloonists* (2002); *Notes from No Man's Land* (2009), a collection of essays; and an examination of the anti-vaccination movement, *On Immunity: An Inoculation* (2014).

Borges, Jorge Luis (1899-1986)
A key figure in twentieth-century world literature, Borges was an essayist, translator, poet, and short story writer whose work was informed by his interests in theology, mythology, and mathematics. He is best known for the short story collection *Ficciones* (*Fictions*, first English translation 1962), in which he explores such subjects as time, infinity, and the relationship between fiction and reality; this and his other works were influential in the development of the genre now called magic realism.

Boudway, Ira (unknown)
Ira Boudway is a Bloomberg Businessweek reporter who focuses on the NBA.

Bozikovic, Alex (unknown)
Alex Bozikovic is a journalist who covers urbanism and architecture for *The Globe and Mail*. He has also written for *Azure*, *Dwell*, *Wallpaper*, *Architect*, *The Walrus*, and *The Literary Review of Canada*.

Brogan, Jacob (unknown)
Jacob Brogan is a writer for *The Washington Post*, *The Atlantic*, *Slate* magazine, and other publications.

Broyard, Anatole (1920–90)
An essayist and book reviewer for *The New York Times*, Broyard was also a writer of fiction. The essay collection *Intoxicated by My Illness and Other Writings on*

Life and Death (1992) was written mainly in the period between Broyard's 1989 diagnosis of metastatic prostate cancer and his death the following year. His other books include *Kafka Was the Rage: A Greenwich Village Memoir*, which was released posthumously in 1993.

Card, David (1956–)
Canadian-born economist David Card is a Professor at the University of California, Berkeley as well as Director of Labor Studies at the National Bureau of Economic Research. The author of close to 100 journal articles and book chapters, Card is the recipient of many honors in the discipline of Economics.

Carson, Anne (1950–)
Carson's many books include *Autobiography of Red: A Novel in Verse* (1998) and its sequel, *Red Doc>* (2013); *Men in the Off Hours* (2001), winner of the Griffin Poetry Prize; and *Eros the Bittersweet* (1986), her first book, which was listed by The Modern Library as one of the 100 best non-fiction books of all time. Poet-in-residence at New York University, Carson was for many years a professor of Classics; she is also renowned for her translations from ancient Greek, which include *Grief Lessons: Four Plays by Euripides* (2006) and *An Oresteia* (2009).

Coates, Ta-Nehisi (1975–)
An American born writer and journalist, Ta-Nehisi Coates is a national correspondent for *The Atlantic* magazine. He is also journalist-in-residence at the City University of New York, and previously was Martin Luther King visiting professor at the Massachusetts Institute of Technology. His *Between the World and Me* (2015), about black life in the United States, received the National Book Award and was a finalist for the Pulitzer Prize.

Cohen, Jeffrey Jerome (unknown)
A Professor of English at George Washington University, Jeffrey Jerome Cohen writes in a variety of media and genres on topics including monster theory, ecocriticism, and medieval studies. His books include *Monster Theory: Reading Culture* (1996) and *Stone: An Ecology of the Inhuman* (2015).

Cole, Teju (1975–)
Nigerian-American writer Teju Cole has lived in the United States since he was 17. Author of a regular photography column for *The New York Times Magazine*, Cole is also writer-in-residence at Bard College. His novel *Open City* (2011) received both the PEN/Hemingway Award and the New York City Book Award, and has been translated into ten languages.

Czap, Natalia V. (unknown)
Natalia Czap focuses on behavioral, consumer, and environmental economics and their intersections in human and organizational behavior. She co-authored the essay

"Empathy Nudging as a New Component of Conservation Programs" (2013) with colleagues at the University of Michigan-Dearborn (where she is an Associate Professor of Economics) and at the University of Nebraska-Lincoln.

Darwin, Charles (1809–82)

The son of an English doctor, Darwin attended medical school at the University of Edinburgh from 1825–27. During his later service as a naturalist aboard *HMS Beagle*, 1831–36, he observed similarities and differences among various species, and began to formulate his theory regarding evolution by means of natural selection. Darwin delayed publishing his theory for more than twenty years; *On the Origin of Species* was eventually published in 1859.

Didion, Joan (1934–)

American writer Joan Didion has published several works of fiction and many works of non-fiction. Her first collection, *Slouching Towards Bethlehem* (1968), remains her best-known book; it focuses on life in California in the 1960s. Her memoirs *The Year of Magical Thinking* (2005) and *Blue Nights* (2011) recount her experiences of grief after the respective deaths of her husband and daughter; both are regarded as important works on the subject of mourning.

Dillard, Annie (1945–)

Pennsylvania-born Annie Dillard has published more than a dozen books, including poetry, non-fiction narrative prose, novels, and memoirs. She has described her second (and best-known) work, *Pilgrim at Tinker Creek* (1974), as an attempt at "what Thoreau called 'a meteorological journal of the mind'"; the book was awarded the Pulitzer Prize for General Nonfiction. Other notable publications include *Holy the Firm* (1977), *Teaching a Stone to Talk* (1982), and *An American Childhood* (1987). Dillard, who taught in the English department at Wesleyan University for twenty-one years, published *The Abundance: Narrative Essays Old and New* in 2016.

Douglass, Frederick (1818–95)

Frederick Douglass, an escaped slave who became America's leading abolitionist, developed a reputation for inspiring oratory and powerful writing. He wrote several versions of his autobiography; *Narrative of the Life of Frederick Douglass, an American Slave* (1845) has become a classic American text.

Dow, Dawn Marie (unknown)

Dawn Marie Dow's research examines the intersections of class, gender, and race within institutions such as the family, workplace, and school. She is an assistant professor in the sociology department of the Maxwell School of Citizenship and Public Affairs at Syracuse University.

Du Bois, W.E.B. (1868–1963)

W.E.B. Du Bois was an African American educator and historian, a founder of the Niagara Movement and of the National Association for the Advancement of Colored People, and the editor of the NAACP journal *Crisis* from 1910 to 1934. His books include *The Philadelphia Negro* (1899) and *The Souls of Black Folk* (1903); the latter has long been recognized as a classic of American non-fiction.

Ehrenreich, Barbara (1941–)

Barbara Ehrenreich's 2001 memoir *Nickel and Dimed: On (Not) Getting by in America* has been as influential as it has been widely read. She has also written books on a variety of other topics, including women's health, politics, poverty, and American culture. Her journalism has often appeared in *The New York Times*.

Ferré, Rosario (1938–2016)

Rosario Ferré had a distinguished career not only as an essayist but also as a writer of short stories and as a poet; in all, she published more than 25 books. A Puerto Rican, she began to publish in the 1970s, writing in Spanish, as well as often translating her own work into English. In 2002 she began to write in English first.

Foer, Jonathan Safran (1977–)

American writer Jonathan Safran Foer is a distinguished writer-in-residence at New York University. His best-selling debut novel *Everything Is Illuminated* (2002) was named Book of the Year by *The Los Angeles Times* and his second novel, *Extremely Loud and Incredibly Close* (2005) was also widely acclaimed. Since the publication of *Eating Animals* (2009), Foer has continued to campaign for change in the way humans treat other animals.

Foucault, Michel (1926–84)

French philosopher and historian Michel Foucault was a leading figure in late twentieth-century poststructuralist thought. His histories of medical and social sciences—notable among them *L'Histoire de la sexualité* (*The History of Sexuality*, first English translation 1978–86) and *Surveiller et punir: Naissance de la prison* (*Discipline and Punish: The Birth of the Prison*, first English translation 1977)—study the relationship between power and knowledge, and explore how societies use power to "objectivize subjects."

Franklin, Ursula M. (1921–2016)

Ursula Franklin, an experimental physicist and University Professor Emerita at the University of Toronto, was the author of many scholarly articles and several books, including *The Real World of Technology* (1989). The recipient of more than twelve honorary degrees, she was inducted into the Canadian Science and Engineering Hall of Fame in 2012.

Frey, William H. (unknown)

A demographer of international renown, William H. Frey specializes in the study of migration, immigration, race, demographics, and aging in the U.S. He has written several books including *Investigating Change in American Society* (2003) and *America: A Social Atlas* (2007). His 2014 book *Diversity Explosion: How New Racial Demographics Are Remaking America*, explores the effects of increasing ethnic diversity in the U.S.

Galloway, Gloria (unknown)

Gloria Galloway has been a reporter for the Canadian newspaper *The Globe and Mail* since 2001.

Gates, Henry Louis, Jr. (1950–)

Author of close to twenty books, Henry Louis Gates Jr. is one of America's leading historians and public intellectuals. Director of the Center for African and African American Research at Harvard University, he is also the general editor of *The Norton Anthology of African American Literature*.

Gawande, Atul (1965–)

A practicing surgeon as well as a writer, Atul Gawande has published in the *New England Journal of Medicine* as well as *Slate* magazine and *The New Yorker*, where he focuses on public health and medicine. His books include *Complications* (2002), *Better: A Surgeon's Notes on Performance* (2007), *The Checklist Manifesto: How to Get Things Right* (2009), and *Being Mortal: Medicine and What Matters in the End* (2014). The latter was made into a documentary for *Frontline* on PBS in 2015.

Gay, Roxane (1974–)

Roxane Gay is Associate Professor of English at Purdue University, an editor, and a writer of essays, reviews, and short fiction. Her books include *Ayiti* (2011), the bestselling *Bad Feminist* (2014), and *Hunger* (2016), a memoir. She has also contributed to numerous newspapers and both online and print magazines, among them *McSweeney's*, *The New York Times*, *xoJane*, *Jezebel*, *The Nation*, and *Salon*.

Gladwell, Malcolm (1963–)

Malcolm Gladwell was born in England and raised in Canada; since 1996 he has been a staff writer for *The New Yorker* magazine. He is the bestselling author of *The Tipping Point* (2000), *Blink* (2005), *Outliers* (2008), and *What the Dog Saw* (2009). In 2013 he released *David and Goliath: Underdogs, Misfits, and the Art of Battling Giants*, a collection of journalism.

Gourevitch, Philip (1961–)

As a staff writer for *The New Yorker*, Philip Gourevitch was sent by that magazine to Rwanda in 1995 to study the aftermath of the 1994 genocide of the Tutsi minority.

He stayed nine months in Rwanda and in neighboring Congo; out of his experiences there came one of the most important non-fiction books of the 1990s, *We Wish to Inform You That Tomorrow We Will Be Killed with Our Families* (1998). Gourevitch's other works include *A Cold Case* (2001) and *The Ballad of Abu Ghraib* (2008).

Gopnik, Adam (1956–)

A contributor to *The New Yorker* since 1986, Adam Gopnik has received the National Magazine Award for Essay and Criticism as well as the George Polk Award for Magazine Reporting. He is also a regular broadcaster for the Canadian Broadcasting Corporation, and is the author of *Paris to the Moon* (2000) and *The Table Comes First: Family, France, and the Meaning of Food* (2012).

Greenblatt, Stephen (1943–)

American scholar Stephen Greenblatt, a literary critic and literary historian, played a leading role in the late twentieth-century emergence of the New Historicist approach to literature. Greenblatt has served as the general editor both of *The Norton Anthology of English Literature* and of *The Norton Shakespeare*. His own books include *Will in the World: How Shakespeare Became Shakespeare* (2005) and *The Swerve: How the World Became Modern* (2011), which won the Pulitzer Prize for General Nonfiction as well as the National Book Award for Nonfiction.

Hannah-Jones, Nikole (1976–)

Nikole Hannah-Jones is an American investigative journalist whose work has focused largely on racial injustice. Her work has appeared in *The Atlantic*, *Huffington Post*, *Essence Magazine*, *Grist*, and *Politico*. She became a staff writer for *The New York Times Magazine* in 2015.

hooks, bell (1952–)

An award-winning author and social activist, Gloria Jean Watkins—writing under the name bell hooks—has written over 30 books of feminist and critical theory, social commentary, and poetry. Her 1981 book *Ain't I a Woman?: Black Women and Feminism* has become an important touchstone in feminist thought. hooks, who became a professor of English in 1976, has also been active in media and film theory; her *Reel to Real* was published in 1996.

Hurka, Thomas (1952–)

Educated at the University of Toronto and Oxford University, Thomas Hurka is Chancellor N.R. Jackman Distinguished Professor of Philosophical Studies at the University of Toronto. He is the author of *Perfectionism* (1993), *Virtue, Vice and Value* (2001), *The Best Things in Life* (2010), and *British Ethical Theorists from Sidgwick to Ewing* (2014). He has been a frequent radio and television commentator and for some years contributed a regular column to the Toronto-based newspaper *The Globe and Mail*.

Hurston, Zora Neale (1891–1960)

African American novelist, playwright, and folklorist Zora Neale Hurston was a significant figure in the Harlem Renaissance of the 1920s. Her novel *Their Eyes Were Watching God* (1937) has come to be considered a twentieth-century classic—though it had been largely forgotten by 1975, when Alice Walker published her essay "In Search of Zora Neale Hurston"; Walker argued that Hurston deserved recognition as "the intellectual and spiritual foremother of a generation of black women writers." Hurston's other books include the novels *Jonah's Gourd Vine* (1934) and *Dust Tracks on a Road* (1942), and an anthropological study, *Mules and Men* (1935). She died in a welfare home in Florida and was buried in an unmarked grave.

Iyer, Pico (1957–)

Born in England to Indian parents and partly raised in California, Pico Iyer attended Oxford and Harvard universities. Best known for travel writing and essays on cross-cultural themes, Iyer is a regular columnist for *TIME* magazine. His books include *Video Night in Kathmandu* (1988), *Falling Off the Map: Some Lonely Places of the World* (1994), and *The Art of Stillness: Adventures in Going Nowhere* (2014).

Jalal, Malik (unknown)

Malik Jalal is a tribal elder in North Waziristan, Pakistan.

Johnson, Nathanael (unknown)

An award-winning journalist and Food writer for *Grist*, Nathanael Johnson has contributed to *Harper's*, *Outside*, *San Francisco*, and *New York* magazine. His books include *All Natural* (2013) and *Unseen City* (2016).

Keegan, Marina (1989–2012)

Marina Keegan graduated from Yale University magna cum laude in the spring of 2012, and was killed in a car crash less than a week afterwards. Her short story "Cold Pastoral" was published later that year by *The New Yorker*, where she had been about to start work as an editorial assistant when she died. A selection of her writing was published in the posthumous collection *The Opposite of Loneliness* (2014).

Kehoe, Alice Beck (1936–)

Alice Beck Kehoe, a professor of anthropology at Marquette University in Milwaukee, is the author of *The Ghost Dance: Ethnohistory and Revitalization* (1989), *North American Indians: A Comprehensive Account* (1992), and the 2016 textbook *Controversies in Archeology*.

Kincaid, Jamaica (1949–)
Jamaica Kincaid is an Antiguan-born American novelist and Professor of Literature at Claremont McKenna College. Her writings, which often explore issues of colonialism, include the novels *Annie John* (1985), *Lucy* (1990), and *See Now Then* (2013), and the essay collection *A Small Place* (1988).

King, Martin Luther, Jr. (1929–68)
A Baptist minister and the leading figure of the American civil-rights movement in the 1950s and 1960s, Martin Luther King Jr. received the 1964 Nobel Peace Prize in recognition of his work promoting both civil rights and nonviolence. King was a charismatic speaker and bestselling author; his books include *Stride Toward Freedom* (1958), *Why We Can't Wait* (1964), and *Where Do We Go From Here: Chaos or Community?* (1967). He was assassinated in Memphis, Tennessee.

Kolbert, Elizabeth (1961–)
An American journalist and staff writer for *The New Yorker*, Elizabeth Kolbert is best known for her writings on environmental issues. She is the author of *Field Notes from a Catastrophe: Man, Nature, and Climate Change* (2006) and was awarded the 2015 Pulitzer Prize for General Nonfiction for *The Sixth Extinction: An Unnatural History* (2014).

Kristof, Nicholas (1959–)
Seven times a finalist for the Pulitzer Prize, American-born journalist Nicholas Kristof has won that award twice (once together with this wife, Sheryl WuDunn). Kristof is best-known as a writer for *The New York Times* (where he has worked since 1984); he and WuDunn have also co-authored four best-selling books together, among them *Half the Sky: Turning Oppression into Opportunity for Women Worldwide* (2009).

Kross, Ethan (unknown)
Associate Professor of Social Psychology at the University of Michigan-Ann Arbor and Director of the University of Michigan Self-Control and Emotion Laboratory, Ethan Kross has been teaching and conducting research since 2005. His article on the psychological effects of Facebook use, co-authored with several of his students, was covered extensively in mainstream broadcast and print media.

Krueger, Alan B. (1960–)
A former chair of the Council of Economic Advisers and a former Chief Economist at the U.S. Treasury, Alan B. Krueger teaches Economics and Public Affairs at Princeton University. He has been the recipient of numerous awards since he and David Card broke new ground in contemporary economic theory with the article excerpted in this anthology and the book that followed, *Myth and Measurement: The New Economics of the Minimum Wage* (1995).

Kurchak, Sarah (unknown)
Sarah Kurchak is a writer and autistic self-advocate from Toronto, Canada. Her writing has focused on music, film, mixed martial arts, and autistic issues; she has been a contributor to *Vice*, *Huffington Post*, *The National Post*, and *Consequence of Sound*.

Lalami, Laila (1968–)
A Moroccan-American writer, Laila Lalami is best known for her novel *The Moor's Account* (2014), which was a finalist for the Pulitzer Prize and was long-listed for the Man Booker Prize. Lalami, who moved from Morocco to America in 1992 and began to publish her work shortly thereafter, is known for her literary and social criticism as well as her several works of fiction.

Lepore, Jill (1966–)
Jill Lepore's books include *New York Burning: Liberty, Slavery and Conspiracy in Eighteenth-Century Manhattan* (2005), which was a finalist for the Pulitzer Prize; *The Secret History of Wonder Woman* (2014); and *Joe Gould's Teeth* (2016). Lepore is a staff writer at *The New Yorker*, where she began contributing in 2005.

Lincoln, Abraham (1809–65)
Abraham Lincoln was the sixteenth president of the United States. Lincoln held the office of president from March 1861 until his assassination on 14 April 1865; at the time of his death he had just begun his second term.

Lorde, Audre (1934–92)
Poet, non-fiction writer, novelist, and educator, Audre Lorde was part of the Black Arts Movement, dedicated to exploring the cultural and political foundations of African American experience. She is known for her sensitive depictions of lesbian sexuality, as well as for her powerful attacks on racism, sexism, and other forms of social injustice. Her books include *The First Cities* (1968), *Cables to Rage* (1970), *From a Land Where Other People Live* (1973), *Coal* (1976), *The Cancer Journals* (1980), and *Sister Outsider* (1984).

MacLeish, Kenneth T. (1979–)
Assistant Professor of Medicine, Health, and Society and Anthropology at Vanderbilt College, Kenneth MacLeish studies the effects of war on those in military service and their families. His book, *Making War at Fort Hood: Life and Uncertainty in a Military Community*, was published in 2013.

Mandela, Nelson (1918–2013)
Nelson Mandela was a South African activist and politician. Initially committed to purely non-violent protest against apartheid, he eventually participated in the sabotage campaign that had been launched in reaction to the violent actions of the

white minority government. He was arrested in 1962 and served 27 years in prison, never faltering in his dedication to democracy, equality, and education. Together with F.W. de Klerk (with whom he negotiated the ground rules for a transition to majority rule), he was awarded the Nobel Peace Prize in 1993. Mandela served as the first democratically elected President of South Africa from 1994–1999.

Martin, Emily (1944–)

A socio-cultural anthropology professor at New York University, Emily Martin studies the effects of race, gender, and class on science and medicine in culture. Her books include *The Cult of the Dead in a Chinese Village* (1973), *The Anthropology of Taiwanese Society* (1981), and *Bipolar Expeditions: Mania and Depression in American Culture* (2007).

Martineau, Harriet (1802–76)

Harriet Martineau was one of the Victorian era's foremost writers on social and political issues. A professional writer at a time when that was a rare profession for women, Martineau became famous for her *Illustrations of Political Economy* (1834), a collection of narrative vignettes designed to educate readers on the principles of economic society. Her other works include *Society in America* (1837) and *A Retrospect of Western Travel* (1838), both of which combine travel writing with incisive social commentary; the novel *Life in the Sickroom* (1844); and her acclaimed *Autobiography* (1877).

Metzl, Jonathan M. (unknown)

Jonathan Metzl is Associate Professor of Psychiatry and Women's Studies at the University of Michigan, where he also practices psychiatry. He is the author of *Prozac on the Couch: Prescribing Gender in the Era of Wonder Drugs* (2003) and *The Protest Psychosis: How Schizophrenia Became a Black Disease* (2010).

Milgram, Stanley (1933–84)

Stanley Milgram's human obedience experiments at Yale University (1961–62) established him as one of the most famous—and most controversial—psychologists of the twentieth century. He is also noted for the small-world method, which became the inspiration for John Guare's *Six Degrees of Separation*, and for an experiment on the effects of televised antisocial behavior. His books include *Obedience to Authority: An Experimental View* (1983).

Montagu, Lady Mary Wortley (1689–1762)

English poet and essayist Lady Mary Wortley Montagu was a celebrated writer of her age. Her works include "Six Town Eclogues" (1715–16), a series of poems satirizing city life; the political periodical *The Nonsense of Common-Sense* (1737–38); and the posthumously published *Turkish Embassy Letters* (1763), a collection of letters written during her travels in the Ottoman Empire.

Montaigne, Michel Eyquem de (1533–92)
French thinker Michel Eyquem de Montaigne arguably did more than any other individual to establish the essay form—including giving it a name. His *Essais* were published in three volumes between 1580 and 1588. Montaigne also published a translation of Spanish theologian Raymond of Sebond's *Theologia Naturalis* (1569).

Munro, Alice (1931–)
Award-winning Canadian writer of short fiction Alice Munro has seen her reputation grow steadily over more than four decades. Her collections include *Dance of the Happy Shades* (1968), *Who Do You Think You Are?* (1978), *The Love of a Good Woman* (1998), *Runaway* (2004), *Too Much Happiness* (2009), *Hateship, Friendship, Courtship, Loveship, Marriage* (2011), and *Dear Life: Stories* (2012). She announced her retirement in 2013—the same year she was awarded the 2013 Nobel Prize in Literature for her work as "master of the contemporary short story."

Nelson, Maggie (1973–)
The author of a wide variety of non-fiction works, Maggie Nelson directs the MFA writing program at the California Institute of the Arts. Her 2015 book, *The Argonauts*, was a *New York Times* bestseller and winner of the National Book Critics Circle Award in Criticism. Nelson's other books of non-fiction include *The Art of Cruelty: A Reckoning* (2011) and *Bluets* (2009)—both excerpted here. *The Red Parts: Autobiography of a Trial* (2007) forms the second part of her memoir; the first part, a book of poetry entitled *Jane: A Murder*, was released in 2005.

Ngũgĩ wa Thiong'o (1938–)
Ngũgĩ wa Thiong'o, East Africa's leading novelist, social critic, and essayist, writes both in English and in Gĩkũyũ. His novels include *Weep Not, Child* (1964), *The River Between* (1965), and *Devil on the Cross* (1980). His non-fiction works include *Detained* (1982), *Decolonising the Mind: The Politics of Language in African Literature* (1986), *Dreams in a Time of War: A Childhood Memoir* (2010), and *In the House of the Interpreter: A Memoir* (2012). A collection of his essays, *Secure the Base: Making Africa Visible in the Globe*, was published in 2015.

Nussbaum, Emily (1966–)
Emily Nussbaum, the 2016 winner of the Pulitzer Prize for Criticism, has been the television critic for *The New Yorker* since 2011. She has also worked as a writer and editor for *New York* magazine and as Editor-in-Chief of *Nerve* (one of the first digital-only magazines). In 2014 her columns "Shark Week," "Difficult Women," and "Private Practice" together won her the National Magazine Award for columns and commentary.

Obama, Barack (1961–)
The first African American President of the United States, Barack Obama was inaugurated in 2009, and led America out of the 2008–09 recession; his signature legislative achievement was the passage of the 2009 Affordable Care Act. Obama is also known for his writing—notably his memoir *Dreams from My Father* (1995).

Orwell, George (1903–50)
Born Eric Blair to English parents in Motihari, India, and educated largely at English boarding schools, Blair published his writing under the pseudonym George Orwell. He served with the Indian Imperial Police in Burma, 1922–27, and fought with the Republicans in the Spanish Civil War (an experience he described in his 1938 *Homage to Catalonia*). During World War II he established a reputation as one of Britain's leading journalists—but he remains best-known for two novels, *Animal Farm* (1945) and *Nineteen Eighty-Four* (1949).

Ozick, Cynthia (1928–)
Cynthia Ozick is an award-winning American writer whose work explores politics, history, and Jewish American life. Her books include the novels *Heir to the Glimmering World* (2004), the short fiction collection *The Pagan Rabbi and Other Stories* (1971); and the collection of essays *Critics, Monsters, Fanatics, and Other Literary Essays* (2016).

Pollan, Michael (1955–)
An award-winning essayist and bestselling author, Michael Pollan is a professor at UC Berkeley's Graduate School of Journalism, and the director of the Knight Program in Science and Environmental Journalism; he has also been a contributing writer for *The New York Times Magazine* since 1987. He has written several bestselling books, among them *The Omnivore's Dilemma: A Natural History of Four Meals* (2006); *In Defense of Food: An Eater's Manifesto* (2008); *Food Rules: An Eater's Manual* (2010); and *Cooked: A Natural History of Transformation* (2013).

Proulx, Lawrence G. (unknown)
Lawrence Proulx is a copyeditor at the *International New York Times* in France.

Putnam, Robert D. (1941–)
A Professor of American politics, international relations, and public policy at Harvard, Putnam is the author of *Double-Edged Diplomacy: International Bargaining and Domestic Politics* (1993), *Making Democracy Work: Civic Traditions in Modern Italy* (1993), *Bowling Alone: America's Declining Social Capital* (1995), and *Our Kids: The American Dream in Crisis* (2015).

Rankine, Claudia (1963–)

Claudia Rankine was born in Kingston, Jamaica, and earned degrees from Williams College and Columbia University. Her published work, which straddles the boundary between poetry and non-fiction prose, includes *Nothing in Nature Is Private* (1995), *Don't Let Me Be Lonely: An American Lyric* (2004), and *Citizen: An American Lyric* (2014), which received a National Book Critics Circle Award.

Rich, Adrienne (1929–2012)

Adrienne Rich was a major poet, feminist critic, and activist. Over her long career, she published more than sixteen volumes of poetry and five volumes of critical prose. She was the 2006 recipient of the National Book Foundation's Medal for Distinguished Contribution to American Letters. Her poetry and essays have been widely translated and published internationally.

Rivera, Lauren A. (1978–)

Lauren Rivera is Associate Professor of Management and Organizations at Northwestern University's Kellogg School of Management. She has contributed to publications including the *Wall Street Journal*, *Forbes*, *New York Times*, *Huffington Post*, *New Yorker*, and *Fortune*. Her book *Pedigree: How Elite Students Get Elite Jobs* was published in 2015.

Robinson, Marilynne (1943–)

Marilynne Robinson's reputation rests very largely on the novels *Housekeeping* (1980), the Pulitzer Prize-winning *Gilead* (2004), *Home* (2008), and *Lila* (2014); the latter three are all set in the fictional Iowa town of Gilead. Robinson is also an acclaimed essayist and the author of several full-length works of non-fiction. Much of her writing is informed by her religious beliefs; she is a member of the Congregational United Church of Christ in Iowa City.

Rodriguez, Richard (1944–)

Eloquent and at times controversial, Richard Rodriguez has received critical acclaim since the publication of his first book, *Hunger of Memory: The Education of Richard Rodriguez* (1982). Notable among his other works is *Days of Obligation: An Argument with My Mexican Father* (1992), in which Rodriguez revealed that he was gay; the book was a finalist for the Pulitzer Prize.

Roosevelt, Franklin Delano (1882–1945)

As thirty-second president of the United States, Franklin Delano Roosevelt led America through the Great Depression and World War II; he held the office of president from March 1933 until his death in April 1945.

Ruiz, Judy (1944–)
Judy Ruiz's poetry has been published in a wide variety of journals, and collected in *Talking Razzmatazz: Poems* (1991). She is also a non-fiction writer.

Rushdie, Salman (1947–)
Born Ahmed Salman Rushdie to devout Muslim parents in Bombay, Salman Rushdie moved with his family to England when he was 14; he attended Rugby School and Cambridge University. His second novel, *Midnight's Children* (1981), won the Booker Prize and catapulted him to world-wide fame as a writer of postmodern fiction. His other novels include *Shame* (1983), *The Satanic Verses* (1988), *The Moor's Last Sigh* (1995), and *The Enchantress of Florence* (2008).

Ryka Aoki (unknown)
A transgender Japanese American writer and activist, Ryka Aoki is also a professor of English at Santa Monica College and teaches Queer Studies at Antioch University. She is best-known for her poetry collections *Seasonal Velocities* (2012) and *Why Dust Shall Never Settle Upon This Soul* (2015), as well as the novel *He Mele a Hilo* (2014).

Sedaris, David (1956–)
An American humorist, comedian, and writer, David Sedaris is known for his short stories and autobiographical essays, which he has published in best-selling collections such as *Me Talk Pretty One Day* (2000), *Dress Your Family in Corduroy and Denim* (2004), *When You Are Engulfed in Flames* (2008), and *Let's Explore Diabetes with Owls*. His work has appeared in *The Atlantic*, *Harper's*, *Rolling Stone*, and *The Daily Beast*, and he is contributing writer at *The New Yorker*.

Seneca, Lucius Annaeus (c. 4 BCE–65 CE)
Born in Córdoba, Spain, Lucius Annaeus Seneca was educated as a rhetorician in Rome, and pursued a career in law and politics. His literary output includes numerous dialogues, treatises, and letters in the Stoic tradition; he also wrote at least eight tragedies, which were in several respects regarded as models by Shakespeare and other early modern dramatists in England and France. Seneca was tutor and advisor to the emperor Nero, though he failed to curb Nero's increasing tyranny; Seneca was accused of conspiracy in 65 CE and forced to commit suicide.

Schalet, Amy (unknown)
American-born, Dutch-raised Professor of Sociology Amy Schalet was educated at Berkeley, Harvard, and the University of Rotterdam; she has been a professor at the University of Massachusetts, Amherst since 2006. *Not Under My Roof: Parents, Teens and the Culture of Sex* (2011) was the recipient of both an American Sociological Association Distinguished Scholarly Research Award and a Goode Book Award from the American Sociological Association.

Shields, David (1956–)

David Shields is an award-winning writer of fiction and non-fiction who has become known for blurring the line between the two genres. He is recognized for titles such as *Black Planet: Facing Race During an NBA Season* (1999), *The Thing About Life Is That One Day You'll Be Dead* (2008), *Reality Hunger* (2010), and *War Is Beautiful* (2015). His work has appeared in *The New York Times Magazine*, *Harper's*, *Esquire*, *McSweeney's*, *Village Voice*, *Salon*, and *Slate*.

Shore, Bill (1955–)

Bill Shore is founder and CEO of Share Our Strength, a nonprofit that is working to end child hunger in America. He has written several books on the subject of social change, among them *Revolution of the Heart* (1995), *The Cathedral Within* (1999), *The Light of Conscience* (2004), and *The Imaginations of Unreasonable Men* (2010).

Showalter, Elaine (1941–)

A professor in the English department of Princeton University, Elaine Showalter is one of the founders of contemporary feminist criticism. Her works include *A Literature of Their Own* (1977), *The Female Malady: Women, Madness, and English Culture 1830–1980* (1985), *Hystories: Historical Epidemics and Modern Culture* (1997), *Inventing Herself: Claiming a Feminist Intellectual Heritage* (2001), and *A Jury of Her Peers: American Women Writers from Anne Bradstreet to Annie Proulx* (2009).

Silko, Leslie Marmon (1948–)

Leslie Marmon Silko's poetry, essays, and novels are influenced by the Pueblo storytelling tradition she learned in childhood from her aunt, grandmother, and great-grandmother in New Mexico on the Laguna Pueblo Reservation. Her novel *Ceremony* was released in 1977 to critical acclaim. Among her other books are *Storyteller* (1981), a collection of poetry and short stories, and *Yellow Woman and a Beauty of the Spirit: Essays on Native American Life Today* (1997), a collection of short stories and essays.

Singer, Peter (1946–)

Peter Singer, often described as the world's most influential philosopher, is a professor both at Princeton University and at the University of Melbourne in his native Australia. In addition to his groundbreaking writings on human and non-human animals, he is known for taking a utilitarian approach to the ethical issues involved in genetic engineering, abortion, euthanasia, and embryo experimentation. Singer's books include *Animal Liberation* (1975), *Practical Ethics* (1979), *The Life You Can Save* (2009), and *The Most Good You Can Do: How Effective Altruism Is Changing Ideas About Living Ethically* (2016).

Smith, Zadie (1975–)
The daughter of a black Jamaican mother and a white English father, Zadie Smith was raised in North London, and began her writing career while a student at Cambridge University. The great success of her first book, *White Teeth* (2000), established her reputation as an important writer of fiction; her subsequent novels include *On Beauty* (2005), *NW* (2012), and *Swing Time* (2016). In 2010 Smith became a professor of Creative Writing at New York University.

Solnit, Rebecca (1961–)
An award-winning American writer and contributing editor at *Harper's* magazine, Rebecca Solnit has written on many topics, among them the arts, politics, and the environment. Her books include *Wanderlust: A History of Walking* (2001), *Hope in the Dark: Untold Histories, Wild Possibilities* (2004), *A Field Guide to Getting Lost* (2006), *The Faraway Nearby* (2014), and *Men Explain Things to Me* (2015).

Sontag, Susan (1933–2004)
Susan Sontag was for several decades a central figure in American intellectual life. Among her most important works of non-fiction are *Against Interpretation* (1966), *On Photography* (1977), and *Regarding the Pain of Others* (2003). She was also known for her several volumes of fiction and for her outspoken political views.

Stanton, Elizabeth Cady (1815–1902)
An anti-slavery activist, Elizabeth Cady Stanton was also a leader of the early American women's rights movement. As well as campaigning for women's suffrage, she addressed issues such as employment and income rights, parental and custody rights, birth control, and property rights for women.

Sunstein, Cass R. (1954–)
The Robert Walmsley University Professor at Harvard Law School, Cass Sunstein founded that school's Program on Behavioral Economics and Public Policy. His many books include *The Second Bill of Rights: FDR's Unfinished Revolution and Why We Need It More than Ever* (2004), and *Infotopia: How Many Minds Produce Knowledge* (2006). He also co-authored *Nudge: Improving Decisions about Health, Wealth, and Happiness* in 2008 with Richard Thaler.

Surowiecki, James (1967–)
James Surowiecki has written on a wide range of topics for magazines including *Fortune*, *Slate*, *Talk*, and *Wired*, as well as contributing to *The Washington Post* and *The Wall Street Journal*. His most influential book, *The Wisdom of Crowds: Why the Many Are Smarter than the Few and How Collective Wisdom Shapes Business, Economies, Societies, and Nations*, was published in 2004. Surowiecki has been a staff writer at *The New Yorker* since 2000.

Swift, Jonathan (1667–1745)

Jonathan Swift was an Irish poet, fiction writer, essayist, and political pamphleteer, best known for works of satire aimed at political hypocrisy, literary pretension, and the folly of human society. Among his best-known works are *Tale of a Tub* (1704) and *Gulliver's Travels* (1726).

Thaler, Richard H. (1945–)

Richard Thaler is a Professor of Behavioral Science and Economics at the University of Chicago Booth School of Business. His books include *Misbehaving: The Making of Behavioral Economics* (2015) and *Nudge: Improving Decisions about Health, Wealth, and Happiness* (2008), the latter co-authored with Cass R. Sunstein.

Thoreau, Henry David (1817–62)

Henry David Thoreau is the best-known of all American naturalist writers; he is the author of the classic *Walden; or, Life in the Woods* (1854). Thoreau's other books include *A Week on the Concord and Merrimack Rivers* (1849) and the posthumously published *Excursions* (1863), *Cape Cod* (1865), and *Faith in a Seed* (1993).

Toews, Miriam (1964–)

Miriam Toews's work is heavily influenced by her upbringing in Manitoba, Canada; her award-winning 2000 memoir, *Swing Low: A Life*, details her experiences growing up in a Mennonite town. Her bestselling novel *A Complicated Kindness* (2004), which won the Governor General's Award, is also set in a Manitoba Mennonite community. Her other novels include *The Flying Troutmans* (2008) and *All My Puny Sorrows* (2014).

Travis, Anthony S. (1943–)

Anthony Travis is Senior Research Fellow at the Leo Beck Institute in London, and Deputy Director of the Center for the History and Philosophy of Science at the Hebrew University of Jerusalem. Travis has published widely on the history of chemical technology; his books include *The Rainbow Makers: The Origins of the Synthetic Dyestuffs Industry in Western Europe* (1993) and *Heinrich Caro and the Creation of Modern Chemical Industry* (2000).

Twain, Mark (1835–1910)

Born Samuel Langhorne Clemens, Mark Twain grew up in Missouri, and at 22 became a Mississippi river pilot. Five years later he began writing for a living, and was soon publishing humorous tales and delivering public lectures. After he married and moved to Hartford in 1870, Twain began to write the works for which he is now most famous, including *The Adventures of Tom Sawyer* (1876), *Life on the Mississippi* (1883), and *Adventures of Huckleberry Finn* (1884).

Vasconcelos, José (1882–1959)

Mexican lawyer, revolutionary, and intellectual figure José Vasconcelos also served at one time as Mexico's Minister of Education. His books include *La Raza Cósmica* (The Cosmic Race), in which he presents a philosophical argument for mixing races; a multi-volume autobiography published in the 1930s; and *La flama* (1959), an important work of sociocultural theory.

Wainaina, Binyavanga (1971–)

A Kenyan satirist and short story writer, Wainaina Binyavanga won the Caine Prize for African Writing in 2002. He is the founding editor of the literary magazine *Kwani?*, and his work has appeared in *The New York Times*, *Granta*, *The Guardian*, and *National Geographic*. He is also an expert on African cuisines, and has collected more than 13,000 traditional and modern African recipes. His memoir about his youth in Kenya, *One Day I Will Write about This Place* (2011), was named a *New York Times* notable book.

Waldman, Katy (unknown)

A columnist at *Slate*, Katy Waldman is an American sociocultural critic. She graduated summa cum laude from Yale University, where she was the recipient of several awards.

Wallace, David Foster (1962–2008)

David Foster Wallace, an American writer of short stories, novels, and essays, is perhaps best-known for his ambitious novel *Infinite Jest* (1996). His essays, several of which have been widely anthologized, have become touchstones in discussions of alternative styles of contemporary essay writing. Wallace's unfinished draft of a novel, *The Pale King* (2011), was published after his death; it was a finalist for the 2012 Pulitzer Prize in fiction.

wallace, j (unknown)

j wallace is a writer and activist focused on LGBTQ issues in education, support, and policy direction.

Wilde, Oscar (1854–1900)

Born and raised in Ireland, Oscar Wilde attended Oxford University and then settled in London. His works include the novel *The Picture of Dorian Gray* (1890) and the plays *Lady Windermere's Fan*, *A Woman of No Importance*, *An Ideal Husband*, and *The Importance of Being Earnest* (all 1892–95). In 1895 he was tried, convicted, and imprisoned for having sexual relationships with men. After serving two years of hard labor, he left England for France, where he died a few years later.

Winterson, Jeanette (1959–)

An award-winning poet, essayist, and author, Jeanette Winterson is best known for the semi-autobiographical novel *Oranges Aren't the Only Fruit* (1985) and the memoir *Why Be Happy When You Can Be Normal?* (2013). In 2015 she released *The Gap in Time*, a retelling of Shakespeare's *The Winter's Tale*. Her journalism has been published in the *Daily Mail*, *The New York Times*, *The Times*, *The Guardian*, and *Vogue*. She lives, writes, and farms in the Cotswolds, UK, and is a Professor of New Writing at the University of Manchester.

Wollstonecraft, Mary (1759–97)

Mary Wollstonecraft, an English writer and political activist, was a trailblazing advocate of women's rights; she is best known for *A Vindication of the Rights of Woman* (1792), which has become a classic of political philosophy. Her other works include political writings such as *A Vindication of the Rights of Men* (1790), novels such as *Maria: or, the Wrongs of Woman* (posthumously published in 1798), and the travel narrative *Letters Written during a Short Residence in Sweden, Norway, and Denmark* (1796).

Woolf, Virginia (1882–1941)

Virginia Woolf was among the most innovative and influential English writers of the twentieth century. Her novels include *Mrs. Dalloway* (1925), *To the Lighthouse* (1927), and *The Waves* (1931). She was also an important literary critic and a strong voice for feminism, most notably in her books *A Room of One's Own* (1929) and *Three Guineas* (1938).

Wroe, Ann (unknown)

English writer Ann Wroe is co-author (with Keith Colquhoun, who preceded her as *Economist* Obituaries Editor) of *The Economist Book of Obituaries* (2008), and author of several other books of history and literary history.

Permissions Acknowledgments

Ai Weiwei. "Heartless" and "Let Us Forget," from *Ai Weiwei's Blog: Writings, Interviews, and Digital Rants, 2006–2009*, edited and translated by Lee Ambrozy; pages 201–203, 231. Copyright © 2011 Massachusetts Institute of Technology. Reprinted with the permission of The MIT Press.

Alexie, Sherman. "Indian Education," from *The Lone Ranger and Tonto Fistfight In Heaven*. Copyright © 1993, 2005 by Sherman Alexie. Used by permission of Grove/Atlantic, Inc. Any third party use of this material, outside of this publication, is prohibited.

Baldwin, James. "Stranger in the Village," from *Notes of a Native Son*. Copyright ©1955, 1984. Reprinted with the permission of Beacon Press via Copyright Clearance Center, Inc.

Barthes, Roland. "The World of Wrestling," from *Mythologies* by Roland Barthes, translated by Annette Lavers. Copyright © 1972 by Roland Barthes.

Berger, John. "Photographs of Agony" and "Turner and the Barber's Shop," from *About Looking*. Copyright © 1980 by John Berger. Used by permission of Pantheon Books, an imprint of the Knopf Doubleday Publishing Group, a division of Penguin Random House LLC. All rights reserved. Any third party use of this material, outside of this publication, is prohibited. Interested parties must apply directly to Penguin Random House LLC for permission.

Biss, Eula. Excerpt from "The Pain Scale," originally published in *Seneca Review*. Copyright © 2005 by Eula Biss. Reprinted with the permission of The Frances Goldin Literary Agency. "Time and Distance Overcome," from *Notes from No Man's Land: American Essays*. Copyright © 2009 by Eula Biss. Reprinted with the permission of The Permissions Company, Inc., on behalf of Graywolf Press, www.graywolfpress.org.

Borges, Jorge Luis. "Borges and I," from *Labyrinths*, translated by James E. Irby. Copyright © 1962, 1964 by New Directions Publishing Corp. Reprinted by permission of New Directions Publishing Corp.

Boudway, Ira. "NBA Refs Learned They Were Racist, and That Made Them Less Racist," from *Bloomberg.com*, February 7, 2014. Reprinted with the permission of The YGS Group.

Bozikovic, Alex. "Remaking Space to Remake a Culture," from *The Globe and Mail*, April 4, 2016. Copyright © The Globe and Mail, Inc. Reprinted with permission.

Brogan, Jacob. "Don't Anthropomorphize Inky the Octopus!" from *Slate*, April 14, 2016. Copyright © 2016 The Slate Group. All rights reserved. Used by permission and protected by the Copyright Laws of the United States. The printing, copying, redistribution, or retransmission of this Content without express written permission is prohibited.

Broyard, Anatole. "Intoxicated by My Illness," from *Intoxicated by My Illness: And Other Writings on Life and Death*. Copyright © 1992 by the Estate of Anatole Broyard. Used by permission of Clarkson Potter/Publishers, an imprint of the Crown Publishing Group, a division of Penguin Random House LLC. All rights reserved. Any third party use of this material, outside of this publication, is prohibited. Interested parties must apply directly to Penguin Random House LLC for permission.

Card, David, and Krueger, Alan B. Excerpt from "Minimum Wages and Employment: A Case Study of the Fast Food Industry in New Jersey and Pennsylvania," from *American Economic Review*, Vol. 84, No. 4, pp. 772–793, September 1994. Reprinted with the permission of David Card and the American Economic Association.

Carson, Anne. Excerpts from "Introduction," "On Parmenides," "On Sleep Stones," "On Walking Backwards," "On the Total Collection," and "On Sunday Dinner with Father," from *Plainwater: Essays and Poetry*. Copyright © 1995 by Anne Carson. Used by permission of Alfred A. Knopf, an imprint of the Knopf Doubleday Publishing Group, a division of Penguin Random House LLC. All rights reserved. Any third party use of this material, outside of this publication, is prohibited. Interested parties must apply directly to Penguin Random House LLC for permission.

Coates, Ta-Nehisi. "The Case for Reparations," from *The Atlantic*, June 2014. Copyright © 2014 The Atlantic Media Co., as first published in *The Atlantic Magazine*. All rights reserved. Distributed by Tribune Content Agency.

Cohen, Jeffrey Jerome. "Monster Culture (Seven Theses)," from *Monster Theory: Reading Culture*. University of Minnesota Press, 1996. Copyright © 1996 by the Regents of the University of Minnesota. Reprinted with permission.

Cole, Teju. "How Can You Tell When a Picture Is Giving Us the Truth and Not Simply Trafficking in Fantasy?" from *The New York Times Magazine*, March 30, 2016. Copyright © 2016 The New York Times. All rights reserved. Used by permission and protected by the Copyright Laws of the United States. The printing, copying, redistribution, or retransmission of the Content without express written permission is prohibited.

Czap, Natalia V., Hans J. Czap, Gary D. Lynnec, and Mark E. Burbach. "Empathy Nudging as a New Component of Conservation Programs," 2013. *Cornhusker Economics*, September 4, 2013. Published by University of Nebraska–Lincoln

Extension, Institute of Agriculture & Natural Resources, Department of Agricultural Economics. Copyright © 2013 Board of Regents, University of Nebraska. Reprinted with the permission of the University of Nebraska–Lincoln.

de Montaigne, Michel. Excerpts from *On Cannibals*, translated by Ian Johnston. Reprinted with the permission of Ian Johnston.

Didion, Joan. "On Going Home" and "On Morality," from *Slouching Towards Bethlehem*. Copyright © 1966, 1968, renewed 1996 by Joan Didion. Farrar, Straus & Giroux, 1968.

Dillard, Annie. "On Foot in Virginia's Roanoke Valley," from *The Abundance: Narrative Essays Old and New*. Copyright © 2016 by Geoff Dyer. Reprinted by permission of HarperCollins Publishers. Excerpt from "Sand," from *For the Time Being*. Copyright © 1999 by Annie Dillard. Used by permission of Alfred A. Knopf, an imprint of the Knopf Doubleday Publishing Group, a division of Penguin Random House LLC. All rights reserved. Any third party use of this material, outside of this publication, is prohibited. Interested parties must apply directly to Penguin Random House LLC for permission.

Dow, Dawn Marie. "The Deadly Challenge of Raising African American Boys," from *Gender and Society*, April 2016, volume 20, number 2, p 161–188. Copyright © 2016, © Sage Publications. Reprinted by Permission of Sage Publications, Inc.

The Economist. "Facebook Is Bad for You—Get a Life!" Copyright © *The Economist Newspaper* Limited, London, August 17, 2013. "Chester Nez," copyright © *The Economist Newspaper* Limited, London, June 21, 2014. "Hate and Love," copyright © *The Economist Newspaper* Limited, London, July 2, 2016. "Keeping Control," copyright © *The Economist Newspaper* Limited, London, March 12, 2016.

Ehrenreich, Barbara. "Serving in Florida," from *Nickel and Dimed*. Copyright © 2011 by Barbara Ehrenreich. Metropolitan Books/Picador, 2011.

Ferré, Rosario. "On Destiny, Language, and Translation; or, Ophelia Adrift in the C. & O. Canal," from *The Youngest Doll*, University of Nebraska Press, 1991. Translation © 1991 by the University of Nebraska Press. Originally published as *Papdes de Pandora*, copyright © 1976 by Editorial Joaquin Mortiz, S. A., Mexico City.

Foer, Jonathan Safran. "The Last Thanksgiving of My Childhood," from *Eating Animals*. Copyright © 2009 by Jonathan Safran Foer. Hachette Book Group, 2009.

Foucault, Michel. "The Perverse Implantation," from *The History of Sexuality*. Originally published in French as *La Volonté du Savoir*. Copyright © 1976 by Editions Gallimard. Reprinted by permission of Georges Borchardt, Inc., for Editions Gallimard.

Franklin, Ursula. "Silence and the Notion of the Commons," presented as a lecture at the First International Conference on Acoustic Ecology, Banff, Alberta, 1993. Subsequently published in *The Ursula Franklin Reader: Pacifism as a Map*. Toronto: Between the Lines, 2006. Reprinted with the permission of Ursula Franklin.

Frey, William H. "Census Shows Modest Declines in Black-white Segregation," from The Brookings Institution blog, December 8, 2015. Reprinted with the permission of William H. Frey.

Galloway, Gloria. "Climate-change Emphasis Is Misguided, Professor Says," from *The Globe and Mail*, June 12, 2015. Copyright © The Globe and Mail, Inc. Reprinted with permission.

Gates, Henry Louis, Jr. Excerpt from "The Passing of Anatole Broyard," from *Thirteen Ways of Looking at a Black Man*. Copyright © 1997 by Henry Louis Gates, Jr. Used by permission of Random House, an imprint and division of Penguin Random House LLC. All rights reserved. Any third party use of this material, outside of this publication, is prohibited. Interested parties must apply directly to Penguin Random House LLC for permission.

Gawande, Atul. Excerpt from "Overkill," from *The New Yorker*, May 11, 2015. Copyright © 2015 by Atul Gawande.

Gay, Roxane. "Bad Feminist: Take One," from *Bad Feminist*. Copyright © 2014 by Roxane Gay. Reprinted by permission of HarperCollins Publishers.

Gladwell, Malcolm, "None of the Above: What I.Q. Doesn't Tell You About Race," from *The New Yorker,* December 17, 2007. Copyright © 2007 by Malcolm Gladwell.

Gopnik, Adam. "The Corrections," first published in *The New Yorker*. Copyright © 2007 by Adam Gopnik. Used by permission of The Wylie Agency LLC.

Gourevitch, Philip. Excerpt (Chapter 1) from *We Wish to Inform You that Tomorrow We Will Be Killed with Our Families*. Copyright © 1998 by Philip Gourevitch. Picador/Farrar, Straus & Giroux, 1998.

Greenblatt, Stephen. "The Answer Man," from *The New Yorker*, August 9, 2011. Copyright © 2011 by Stephen Greenblatt.

Hannah-Jones, Nikole. "School Segregation: The Continuing Tragedy of Ferguson," from *ProPublica*, December 19, 2014. Reprinted with the permission of ProPublica, https://www.propublica.org/

hooks, bell. "In Our Glory," from *Art on My Mind*. Copyright © 1995 by bell hooks. Reprinted with the permission of The New Press, www.thenewpress.com

Hurka, Thomas. "Philosophy, Morality, and *The English Patient*," from *Queen's Quarterly* 104:1, Spring 1997. Copyright © 1997 by Thomas Hurka.

Hurston, Zora Neale. "How It Feels to Be Colored Me," copyright © 1928 by Zora Neale Hurston.

Iyer, Pico. "The Terminal Check," copyright © 2011 by Pico Iyer. Originally published in *Granta*. Reprinted with the permission of the author.

Jalal, Malik. "I'm on the Kill List. This Is What It Feels Like to Be Hunted by Drones," from *The Independent*, April 12, 2016. Reprinted with the permission of Independent Print Limited.

Johnson, Nathanael. "Is There a Moral Case for Eating Meat?" *Grist*, Issue 50, July 20, 2015. Copyright © 2015 Nathanael Johnson. Reprinted with the permission of Grist, https://grist.org/

Keegan, Marina. "Why We Care about Whales," from *The Opposite of Loneliness: Essays and Stories*. Copyright © 2014 by Tracy and Kevin Keegan. Scribner, 2014.

Kehoe, Alice Beck. "Transcribing Insima, A Blackfoot 'Old Lady,'" from *Reading Beyond Words*. University of Toronto Press, 2003. Reprinted with the permission of Alice Beck Kehoe.

Kincaid, Jamaica. "On Seeing England for the First Time," originally published in *Harper's Magazine*, August 1991. Copyright © 1991 by Jamaica Kincaid. Used by permission of The Wylie Agency LLC.

King, Martin Luther, Jr. "Letter from Birmingham Jail," from *Why We Can't Wait*. New York: Harper & Row, 1964. Copyright © 1963 by Dr. Martin Luther King, Jr. Copyright renewed 1991 Coretta Scott King.

Kolbert, Elizabeth. "The Sixth Extinction?" from *The New Yorker*, May 25, 2009. Reprinted with the permission of Elizabeth Kolbert.

Kristof, Nicholas. "When Whites Just Don't Get It," from *The New York Times*, August 30, 2014. Copyright © 2014 The New York Times. All rights reserved. Used by permission and protected by the Copyright Laws of the United States. The printing, copying, redistribution, or retransmission of the Content without express written permission is prohibited. "When Whites Just Don't Get It, Part 6," from *The New York Times*, April 2, 2016. Copyright © 2016 The New York Times. All rights reserved. Used by permission and protected by the Copyright Laws of the United States. The printing, copying, redistribution, or retransmission of the Content without express written permission is prohibited.

Kross E., Verduyn P., Demiralp E., Park J., Lee D.S., Lin N., et al. "Facebook Use Predicts Declines in Subjective Well-Being in Young Adults." Copyright © Kross et al. *PLoS ONE* 8(8): e69841. doi:10.1371/journal.pone.0069841

Kurchak, Sarah. "Autistic People Are Not Tragedies," from *The Guardian*, April 20, 2015. Copyright © Guardian News & Media Ltd 2016. Reprinted with permission.

Lalami, Laila. "My Life as a Muslim in the West's 'Gray Zone,'" from *The New York Times Magazine*, November 20, 2015. Copyright © 2015 The New York Times. All rights reserved. Used by permission and protected by the Copyright Laws of the United States. The printing, copying, redistribution, or retransmission of the Content without express written permission is prohibited.

Lepore, Jill. Excerpt from "Richer and Poorer: Accounting for Inequality," from *The New Yorker*, March 16, 2015. Copyright © 2015 by Jill Lepore.

London, Scott. Excerpt from "Crossing Borders," an interview with Richard Rodriguez. *The Sun Magazine*, Issue 260, August 1997. Reprinted with the permission of Scott London.

Lorde, Audre. "Poetry Is Not a Luxury" and "The Uses of Anger," from *Sister Outsider*. Copyright © 1984, 2007 by Audre Lorde. Published by Crossing Press. Reprinted with the permission of the Charlotte Sheedy Literary Agency.

Mandela, Nelson. "An Ideal for Which I Am Prepared To Die," excerpted from the Speech From the Dock, April 20, 1964. Reprinted with permission.

Martin, Emily. "The Egg and the Sperm: How Science Has Constructed a Romance Based on Stereotypical Male-Female Roles," from *Signs: Journal of Women in Culture and Society*, Vol. 16, No. 3, Spring 1991. Copyright © 1991 by The University of Chicago. Reprinted with the permission of The University of Chicago Press.

Metzl, Jonathan M., and Kenneth T. MacLeish. Excerpt from "Mental Illness, Mass Shootings, and the Politics of American Firearms," from *American Journal of Public Health*, Feburary 2015, Volume 105, Number 2, pp 240–249. Reprinted with the permission of The Sheridan Press on behalf of The American Public Health Association.

Milgram, Stanley. "Behavioral Study of Obedience," from *Journal of Abnormal and Social Psychology*, Volume 67, Issue 4, October 1963. Copyright © by The Estate of Stanley Milgram.

Munro, Alice. "What Is Real?" from *Making It New: Contemporary Canadian Stories*. Copyright © 1982 by Alice Munro. Methuen, 1982

Nelson, Maggie. Excerpt from *The Art of Cruelty*. Copyright © 2011 by Maggie Nelson. Used by permission of W.W. Norton & Company, Inc. Excerpt from *Bluets*. Wave Press, 2009. Reprinted with the permission of Wave Books.

Ngũgĩ wa Thiong'o. "Decolonizing the Mind," from *Decolonizing the Mind: The Politics of Language in African Literature* by Ngũgĩ wa Thiong'o. Copyright © 1981, 1982, 1984, and 1986 by Ngũgĩ wa Thiong'o.

Nussbaum, Emily. "The Price Is Right," from *The New Yorker*, October 12, 2015. Reprinted with permission.

Orwell, George. "Shooting an Elephant" and "Politics and the English Language," from *A Collection of Essays*. Copyright © 1946 by Sonia Brownell Orwell. Copyright © renewed 1974 by Sonia Orwell. Reprinted by permission of Houghton Mifflin Harcourt Publishing Company. All rights reserved.

Ozick, Cynthia. "Highbrow Blues," from *The Din in the Head: Essays*. Copyright © 2006 by Cynthia Ozick. Reprinted with the permission of Houghton Mifflin Harcourt Publishing Company. All rights reserved.

Pollan, Michael. "Why Natural Doesn't Mean Anything Anymore," from *The New York Times Magazine*, April 28, 2015. Used by permission. All rights reserved.

Proulx, Lawrence. "A Group You Can Safely Attack," from *The Providence Journal*, September 2, 2015. Copyright © 2015 by Lawrence Proulx.

Putnam, Robert D. Excerpt from *Our Kids: The American Dream in Crisis*. Copyright © 2015 by Robert D. Putnam. Simon & Schuster, 2015.

Rankine, Claudia. Excerpt (pp 23–36) from Part II of *Citizen: An American Lyric*. Copyright © 2014 by Claudia Rankine. Reprinted with the permission of the Permissions Company, Inc., on behalf of Graywolf Press, www.graywolfpress.org. "The Condition of Black Life Is One of Mourning," from *The New York Times Magazine*, June 22, 2015. Copyright © 2015 The New York Times. All rights reserved. Used by permission and protected by the Copyright Laws of the United States. The printing, copying, redistribution, or retransmission of the Content without express written permission is prohibited.

Rich, Adrienne. "Claiming An Education," from *On Lies, Secrets, and Silence: Selected Prose 1966–1978*. W.W. Norton, 1979. Copyright © 1979 by W.W. Norton & Company, Inc. "Compulsory Heterosexuality and Lesbian Existence," from *Blood, Bread, and Poetry: Selected Prose*. W.W. Norton, 1994. Copyright © 1986 by Adrienne Rich.

Rivera, Lauren A. "Guess Who Doesn't Fit in at Work?" from *The New York Times*, May 30, 2015. Copyright © 2015 The New York Times. All rights reserved. Used by permission and protected by the Copyright Laws of the United States. The printing, copying, redistribution, or retransmission of the Content without express written permission is prohibited.

Robinson, Marilynne. "Fear," from *The Givenness of Things*. Copyright © 2015 by Marilynne Robinson. Farrar, Straus & Giroux, 2015.

Rodriguez, Richard. Excerpt from *Darling: A Spiritual Autobiography*. Copyright © 2013 by Richard Rodriguez. Used by permission of Viking Books, an imprint of Penguin Publishing Group, a division of Penguin Random House LLC.

Ruiz, Judy. "Oranges and Sweet Sister Boy," copyright © 1988 by Judy Ruiz. Originally published in *Iowa Woman*; reprinted in *Best American Essays*, Ticknor

& Fields, 1989. Subsequently reprinted in *Occasions for Writing*, edited by Robert DiYanni and Pat C. Hoy II.

Rushdie, Salman. "Is Nothing Sacred?" from *Imaginary Homelands: Essays and Criticism 1981–1991*. Copyright © 1990 by Salman Rushdie. Used by permission of Viking Books, an imprint of Penguin Publishing Group, a division of Penguin Random House LLC.

Ryka Aoki. "On Living Well and Coming Free," from *Gender Outlaws: The Next Generation*, edited by Kate Bornstein and S. Bear Bergman. Seal Press, 2010. Reprinted with the permission of Ryka Aoki.

Schalet, Amy. Excerpt from "Raging Hormones, Regulated Love," Chapter 1 of Not Under My Roof: Parents, Teens, and the Culture of Sex. Copyright © 2011 by The University of Chicago. Reprinted with permission. "The Sleepover Question," from *The New York Times*, July 23, 2011. Copyright © 2011 The New York Times. All rights reserved. Used by permission and protected by the Copyright Laws of the United States. The printing, copying, redistribution, or retransmission of the Content without express written permission is prohibited.

Sedaris, David. "Guy Walks Into A Bar Car," from *Let's Explore Diabetes with Owls*. Copyright © 2013 by David Sedaris. Little, Brown and Company, 2013.

Seneca, Lucius Anneus. "Epistle 47" from *Moral Letters to Lucilius*, translated by Ian Johnston. Reprinted with the permission of Ian Johnston.

Shields, David. "I Can't Stop Thinking through What Other People Are Thinking," from *The White Review*. Copyright © 2013 by David Shields. Reprinted by permission of The Frances Goldin Literary Agency.

Shore, Bill. "Stolen Future," from *Stanford Social Innovation Review*, Summer 2015. Reprinted with permission.

Showalter, Elaine. "Representing Ophelia: Women, Madness, and the Responsibilities of Feminist Criticism," from *Shakespeare and the Question of Theory*, edited by Patricia Parker and Geoffrey Hartman. Copyright © 1985 by Methuen & Co.

Silko, Leslie Marmon. "Language and Literature from a Pueblo Indian Perspective," from *English Literature: Opening Up the Canon*, edited by Fiedler and Baker. Copyright © 1979 by Leslie Marmon Silko. The Johns Hopkins University Press, 1981.

Singer, Peter. "Speciesism and the Equality of Animals," from *Animal Liberation*. Avon Books, 1977. Reprinted with the permission of Peter Singer.

Smith, Zadie. "Generation Why," from *The New York Review of Books*, published November 25, 2010. Copyright © Zadie Smith. Reproduced with the permission of the author, c/o Rogers, Coleridge & White Ltd., 20 Powis Mews, London W11 1JN.

Solnit, Rebecca. "The Mother of All Questions," copyright © 2015 *Harper's Magazine*. All rights reserved. Reprinted from the October issue by special permission. "Climate Change Is Violence," from *The Encyclopedia of Trouble and Spaciousness*, Trinity University Press, 2015. Copyright © 2014 by Rebecca Solnit.

Sontag, Susan. Excerpt from "Freak Show," from *On Photography*. Copyright © 1973, 1974, 1977 by Susan Sontag. New York: Picador, 2001. Excerpt from "Regarding the Pain of Others," copyright © 2003 by Susan Sontag.

Surowiecki, James. "A Fair Day's Wage," from *The New Yorker*, February 9, 2015. Reprinted with permission.

Thaler, Richard H., and Cass R. Sunstein. Excerpts from *Nudge: Improving Decisions about Health, Wealth, and Hapiness*. Yale University Press, 2008. Copyright © 2008 by Richard H. Thaler and Cass R. Sunstein. All rights reserved. Reprinted with the permission of Yale University Press.

Toews, Miriam. "A Father's Faith," first published in *Saturday Night Magazine*. Copyright © 1999 by Miriam Toews. Used by permission of The Wylie Agency LLC.

Travis, Anthony S. "The Accidental Discovery of Mauve," from *The Victorian Review*, Volume 40, Number 2, Fall 2014. Reprinted with permission.

Vasconcelos, José. "Books I Read Sitting and Books I Read Standing," 1919. Translated from the Spanish by H.W. Hilborn in *The Modern Mexican Essay*, University of Toronto Press, 1965.

Wainaina, Binyavanga. "How to Write About Africa," first published in *Granta 92: The View from Africa*. Copyright © 2006 by Binyavanga Wainaina. Used by permission of The Wylie Agency LLC.

Waldman, Katy. Excerpt from "There Once Was a Girl," from *Slate*, December 7, 2015. Copyright © 2015 The Slate Group. All rights reserved. Used by permission and protected by the Copyright Laws of the United States. The printing, copying, redistribution, or retransmission of this Content without express written permission is prohibited.

Wallace, David Foster. "Consider the Lobster," copyright © 2005, David Foster Wallace. Reprinted with the permission of the David Foster Wallace Literary Trust.

wallace, j. "The Manly Art of Pregnancy," from *Gender Outlaws: The Next Generation*, edited by Kate Bornstein and S. Bear Bergman. Copyright © 2010 by j. wallace. Seal Press/Perseus Books Group, 2010.

Winterson, Jeanette. "The Wrong Crib," from *Why Be Happy When You Could Be Normal?* Copyright © 2011 by Jeanette Winterson. Used by permission of Grove/Atlantic, Inc. Any third party use of this material, outside of this publication, is prohibited.

Woolf, Virginia. Excerpts from "Three Guineas," by Virginia Woolf. Copyright © 1938 by Houghton Mifflin Harcourt Publishing Company. Copyright renewed 1966 by Leonard Woolf. Reprinted with the permission of Houghton Mifflin Harcourt Publishing Company. All rights reserved. "The Death of the Moth," from *The Death of the Moth and Other Essays*. Copyright © 1942 by Houghton Mifflin Harcourt Publishing Company and renewed 1970 by Marjorie T. Parsons, Executrix. Reprinted with the permission of Houghton Mifflin Harcourt Publishing Company. All rights reserved.

Color Insert

Bacon, Francis. Study after Velázquez's *Portrait of Pope Innocent X* (1953). Copyright © The Estate of Francis Bacon / SODRAC (2016).

Capa, Robert. After an Italo-German Air Raid, Winter 1936–1937. Robert Capa/ Magnum Photos.

Curtis, Whitney. Rashaad Davis, 23, backs away slowly as St. Louis County police officers approach him with guns drawn and eventually arrest him on Monday, Aug. 11, 2014, at the corner of Canfield Drive and West Florissant Avenue in Ferguson, Missouri. Copyright © Whitney Curtis, 2014.

McCullin, Don. Vietnamese father and daughter wounded when U.S. Marines dropped hand grenades into their bunker, Têt offensive, Battle of Hué, Vietnam, February 1968. Copyright © Don McCullin/Contact Press Images.

McCurry, Steve. Holi festival, Rajasthan, 1966. Steve McCurry/Magnum Photos. HSBC Assignment, Jodhpur, India, 2007. Steve McCurry/Magnum Photos.

Mercy for Animals. Overcrowding of turkeys found during an undercover investigation at a factory farm in North Carolina owned by Butterball. https://www.flickr.com/photos/40420442@N06/6556759163

Singh, Raghubir. Below the Howrah Bridge, 1968. Copyright © 2015 Succession Raghubir Singh. Pedestrians, Kemp's Corner, Mumbai, 1989. Copyright © Succession Raghubir Singh.

INDEX

From the Publisher

A name never says it all, but the word "Broadview" expresses a good deal of the philosophy behind our company. We are open to a broad range of academic approaches and political viewpoints. We pay attention to the broad impact book publishing and book printing has in the wider world; we began using recycled stock more than a decade ago, and for some years now we have used 100% recycled paper for most titles. Our publishing program is internationally oriented and broad-ranging. Our individual titles often appeal to a broad readership too; many are of interest as much to general readers as to academics and students.

Founded in 1985, Broadview remains a fully independent company owned by its shareholders—not an imprint or subsidiary of a larger multinational.

For the most accurate information on our books (including information on pricing, editions, and formats) please visit our website at www.broadviewpress. com. Our print books and ebooks are also available for sale on our site.

On the Broadview website we also offer several goods that are not books— among them the Broadview coffee mug, the Broadview beer stein (inscribed with a line from Geoffrey Chaucer's *Canterbury Tales*), the Broadview fridge magnets (your choice of philosophical or literary), and a range of T-shirts (made from combinations of hemp, bamboo, and/or high-quality pima cotton, with no child labor, sweatshop labor, or environmental degradation involved in their manufacture).

All these goods are available through the "merchandise" section of the Broadview website. When you buy Broadview goods you can support other goods too.

broadview press
www.broadviewpress.com